## standard catalog of

# FIREARMS

### by
### Dan E. Brdlik

First Edition


Published by:

 krause
publications

**700 E. State St., Iola, WI 54990**
**Telephone: (715) 445-2214**


Library of Congress Catalog Number: 90-62405


ISBN: 0-87341-156-0


Printed in the United States of America

## DEDICATION

This book is dedicated to my wife, Rosemarie. She encouraged and motivated me and took total charge of the word processor. Without her, this book wouldn't be.

## ACKNOWLEDGEMENTS

I would like to thank all of the gun collectors and dealers who were considerate enough to share their time and knowledge with me during the past year, Al Novak and Tim Olson, who allowed me unlimited access to their extensive firearms libraries, and all of the gun companies and collectors who opened their archives to furnish the photos used in this book.

# INTRODUCTION

Firearms have been collected since they were first invented. There are a number of reasons why this is so. The first collectors were primarily concerned with the practical value and application of their acquisitions, as times were different and the environment more openly hostile. Later on, firearms became appreciated as an art form. Engravers, carvers, and metalsmiths used them as canvases on which to display their finest work. As civilization advanced, the historical significance of certain firearms made them desirable to those of us interested in maintaining a link with our past heritage. In more recent times, some have collected firearms for their investment potential and their ability to hedge against the inflation that sometimes erodes more conventional investments.

Regardless of the particular reason, there are a large number of us who share a common interest in the acquisition of firearms. It is for these individuals that this book has been created. No matter what an individual's reason to collect, one wants to receive a fair value for the money one spends. This publication can help achieve that goal.

We have attempted to list and evaluate the products of nearly 1,100 gunmakers, spanning a period from 1836 to the present. We have supplied as much information on the individual models as possible within the boundaries our space would allow and have furnished a photo if available.

The subject of grading systems deserves some discussion at this time. Recently the percent-of-finish method of grading firearms has come into vogue. I was instrumental in developing this system twelve years ago when I ran the investment firearms division for Investment Rarities, Inc., of Minneapolis, Minnesota. At the time, it seemed like an excellent grading system. Since then I have observed many flaws in the concept and see a need for change. The predominant problem is grading the older historically significant collectible firearms. I have seen far too many fine examples in excellent original mechanical condition, but without much finish remaining, be grossly undervalued by the percent-of-finish system. I am convinced at this time that the only way to properly grade is to use the tried-and-proven overall grading method that we have chosen for this book. Our grading system is as follows:

# Grading System

**NIB--New in Box**
This category is simply what it says--brand new in the original factory box with all supplied materials and papers.

**Excellent**
Firearms in this category must be 100 percent factory original in as-new working order. Modern firearms must retain a minimum of 95 percent original finish overall; and antique examples, at least 80 percent finish. The bore must be sharp and clean, and there can be no evidence of tampering or repair.

**Very Good**
Firearms in this category must be in fine working order. Modern firearms must retain between 85 percent and 95 percent original finish. Antiques must retain over 25 percent finish. There can be no evidence of repair, and the bore must be in good shape.

**Good**
Firearms in this category must be in good working order. Modern firearms must retain between 60 percent and 85 percent original finish. Antique guns in this category can be refinished or cleaned. Modern bores must be moderately clean. Antique bores are not regarded as important.

**Fair**
Firearms in this category must work fairly well but can show evidence of repair. Refinished firearms done well will fit into this slot. Modern firearms in this category should retain between 25 percent and 60 percent of original finish. Stocks, grips, and some original parts can be replaced and be accepted in this category. Modern bores should be shootable. Antique bores are unimportant.

**Poor**
Firearms in this category are marginal as to collectibility. Some extremely rare antiques may be desirable even if in poor condition. Some poor guns are inoperable. Some may be unsafe to fire and should be treated as such. Original modern firearms would have 0 percent to 25 percent finish. Some show bad refinishing; others may be candidates for reblueing. Modern bores would be rough and dark; antique bores, nonexistent. This is generally a category that the serious collector avoids in all but the rarest of antique firearms.

We feel that if the preceding system is learned and utilized properly, it is a very accurate method of grading condition.

### Sample of pricing array

| NIB | Exc. | V.G. | Good | Fair | Poor |
|-----|------|------|------|------|------|
| 475 | 400 | 325 | 300 | 250 | 200 |

# Pricing

This book is intended as a reference and identification guide, as well as a price guide; and we have labored to make the descriptions as detailed and informative as possible. The price guide aspect of the book is also the product of a good deal of research. Our prices are derived from a number of sources: gun shows attended throughout the year, discussion with numerous dealers, and observation of actual sales. It is important to note that there are geographic differences regarding pricing of certain models, and we have averaged in some cases for the sake of general accuracy. Another source that we utilized was the prices found in the Gun List. By researching and recording prices over a period of time, an average price was arrived at which we feel is reasonably accurate.

The prices published in this book reflect retail values; and it is important to note that when one chooses to sell to a gunshop or a gunshow dealer, one must expect the offer to be considerably less than retail--depending on the markup with which the particular dealer chooses to work. Some complain about the difference between dealer cost and retail, but remember that the cost of doing business today is considerable and no one is forcing you to sell wholesale. It is quite a bit easier, and as such it can be expensive.

Do not lose sight of the fact that this book, as well as any other price guide, can only give a general reference point. The actual deal must be negotiated between the buyer and seller, and both must be satisfied for it to be a successful transaction. If we can assist in the realization of this goal, we have been successful.

# Other Factors

When using this guide, it is important to note that the pricing furnished is for the specifically listed model only and does not and cannot take special circumstances into consideration. There are a number of factors that can have a profoundly elevating effect on standard pricing and when encountered definitely warrant individual appraisal. They are as follows:

**Cased Sets**
Certain firearms companies made a practice of presenting examples of their products to certain dignitaries who could perhaps help their sales. Colonel Colt was said to have been the originator of this practice. Likewise, private individuals also ordered these firearms as gifts for others. When encountered, they will be worth a sizeable premium over the firearm alone and should definitely be individually appraised.

## Historical Significance

Certain firearms can be accurately associated with famous or perhaps notorious historic personages. Those examples then must be regarded entirely different than the normally encountered examples. Depending on who the former owner was, values can rise astronomically. When attempting to collect this type of firearm, it is important to be extremely wary of fraudulent examples and enlist qualified assistance to authenticate documentation.

## Engraving, Ornamentation

Certain specimens encountered will be ornamentally embellished by engraving, etching, carving and/or plating. This does not always increase value. This, perhaps more than any other factor, makes general evaluation difficult. High quality contemporary ornamentation, as a rule, increases value on an early firearm. Modern or poor-quality embellishment may decrease value. It is quite important to have these special firearms individually appraised. Likewise, the addition of special grips and stocks can have a profound effect on value--carved ivory, pearl, or the silver Tiffany grips found on early Colts can seriously add to firearm value and should be appraised.

## Bores

The condition of the bore can also add or detract from the value of a collectible firearm, as well as of a shooter; and it is a good idea to acquire a borelight and learn to look on any potential acquisition.

## Serial Numbers

Certain collectors among us will pay a premium (or charge one) for low or unique serial numbers. This is not always true and is entirely up to the discretion of the dealing parties.

## "Assault and Paramilitary Weapons"

Throughout this book, the reader will notice the absences of prices on the paramilitary-type firearms. We do not wish this to be construed as an indictment of this type of firearm. Indeed, we have always had a fondness for them and have collected more than a few over the years. It is simply that the price situation that has been created by certain dealers across the Country has simply produced a market that is too diverse and volatile to accurately predict. Price gougers in some of the more metropolitan areas are asking as much as three times the going prices in the Upper Midwest, for example. When one adds this to the illegality of their ownership on the West Coast and the ongoing litigation concerning ownership and importation, we felt that to give pricing estimates would have been irresponsible and also inaccurate. If you care to deal in this type of firearm, survey your local market and act accordingly. Hopefully this situation will change for the better, and we will add values in a subsequent edition.

In summation, we would like to emphasize what we feel is the most important aspect of firearms collecting--"Knowledge is Power." Acquiring an education in this hobby can be extremely expensive if left to the trial-and-error method. The astute individual will acquire at least a basic library covering his field of interest and test the waters by attending gun shows and asking questions. It is also a good idea to subscribe to a firearms periodical such as **Gun List** to study prices. A firearms hobbyist should definitely belong to the National Rifle Association and to a local collectors club if one is available.

If all of these guidelines are followed and this book is utilized as intended, firearms collecting can be a pleasurable and potentially profitable pastime.

Edward Weatherby, of the Weatherby firearms manufacturer, presents a Weatherby shotgun to President George Bush.

# A.A.
## Azanza & Arrizabalaga
## Eibar, Spain

This company operated prior to WWI. They manufactured the usual Eibar pattern auto pistols. The quality of these weapons is not very high and collector interest almost non existent.

## A.A.
A rather large 7.65 mm, 9-shot magazine pistol of blow back design. The slide is marked "Modelo 1916 Eibar (Espana)." The trademark "AA" appears on the left rear of the frame.

| Exc. | V.G. | Good | Fair | Poor |
|------|------|------|------|------|
| 125  | 100  | 75   | 50   | 25   |

### Reims
This model was made in 7.65 mm and 6.35 mm. They are copies of the 1906 Browning--marked "1914 Model Automatic Pistol Reims Patent." The trademark "AA" also appears on the frame.

| Exc. | V.G. | Good | Fair | Poor |
|------|------|------|------|------|
| 110  | 90   | 65   | 45   | 25   |

## A.A.A.
## Aldazabal
## Eibar, Spain

### Modelo 1919
Another typical, poor quality, Eibar, 7.65mm blowback pistol.

| Exc. | V.G. | Good | Fair | Poor |
|------|------|------|------|------|
| 100  | 80   | 60   | 40   | 25   |

## A & R SALES SOUTH
## El Monte, California

### 45 Auto
A lighter-weight, alloy-frame version of the 1911 Colt Auto pistol. It was made in .45 ACP cal. only.

| NIB | Exc. | V.G. | Good | Fair | Poor |
|-----|------|------|------|------|------|
| 275 | 240  | 200  | 175  | 125  | 100  |

### Mark IV Sporter
A semi-automatic copy of the M-14 military rifle. Manufactured in .308 cal. (7.65mm Nato) only.

| NIB | Exc. | V.G | Good | Fair | Poor |
|-----|------|-----|------|------|------|
| 350 | 300  | 260 | 225  | 175  | 150  |

## AFC
## Auguste Francotte
## Liege, Belgium

This was one of the most prolific makers of revolvers in Liege during the last half of the 19th century. It is estimated that over 150 different revolvers were made and marketed by them before they were forced out of business by the German occupation of 1914. Francotte produced many variations from Tranter copies to pinfires, early Smith & Wesson designs to the 11mm M1871 Swedish troopers revolver. They made break-open revolvers and produced only one semi-auto, a 6.35mm blowback design. A good portion of their pistols were produced for the wholesale market and were sold under other names. These particular revolvers will bear the letters "AF" stamped somewhere on the frame. Because of the vast number and variety of pistols produced by this company, cataloging and pricing is beyond the scope of this or any general reference book. It is suggested that any examples encountered be researched on an individual basis. The lone semi-auto, produced in 1912, can be priced rather easily since it is the only one the company ever manufactured.

### Semi-Auto
A 6.35mm, 6-shot detachable magazine pocket pistol with blue finish. This model was marked "Francotte Liege."

| Exc. | V.G. | Good | Fair | Poor |
|------|------|------|------|------|
| 285  | 250  | 200  | 165  | 100  |

## A. J. ORDNANCE
## Thomas

This is a delayed blowback action that is unique in that every shot was double action. This pistol was chambered for the .45 ACP cartridge and had a 3.5" stainless steel barrel with fixed sights and plastic grips. The detachable magazine held 6 shots, and the standard finish was matte blue. Chrome plating was available and would add approximately 15 percent to the values given.

| NIB | Exc. | V.G. | Good | Fair | Poor |
|-----|------|------|------|------|------|
| 500 | 475  | 425  | 350  | 275  | 200  |

## AMAC
## American Military Arms Corporation
## formerly
## Iver Johnson
## Jacksonville, Arkansas

The Iver Johnson Arms Co. was founded in 1871 in Fitchsburg, Massachusetts. It was one of the oldest and most successful of the old-line arms companies on which our modern era has taken its toll. In 1984 the company moved to Jacksonville, Arkansas; and in 1987 it was purchased by the American Military Arms Corporation. This company has released some of the older designs as well as some new models. The original Iver Johnson line will be listed under its own heading later in this text.

### U.S.Carbine .22
This is a semi-automatic, military-style carbine that is patterned after the M1 of WWII fame. It is chambered for the .22 l.r. cartridge, has an 18.5" barrel and features military-style peep sights and a 15-shot detachable magazine.

| NIB | Exc. | V.G. | Good | Fair | Poor |
|-----|------|------|------|------|------|
| 166 | 150  | 120  | 100  | 75   | 50   |

### Wagonmaster Lever Action Rifle
This model is chambered for the .22 rimfire cartridge, has an 18.5" barrel and is styled after the Win. 94. The stock has a straight grip; and the forend, a barrel band. There are adjustable sights and a tube magazine that holds 15 l.r. cartridges.

| NIB | Exc. | V.G. | Good | Fair | Poor |
|-----|------|------|------|------|------|
| 166 | 150  | 120  | 100  | 75   | 50   |

### Wagonmaster .22 Magnum
This model is the same as the Wagonmaster except that it is chambered for the .22 rimfire magnum.

| NIB | Exc. | V.G. | Good | Fair | Poor |
|-----|------|------|------|------|------|
| 187 | 160  | 130  | 110  | 75   | 50   |

### Targetmaster Pump Action Rifle
This model is a slide- or pump-action that is chambered for the .22 rimfire cartridges. It has an 18.5" barrel with adjustable sights and a straight-grip stock. It holds 12 l.r. cartridges.

| NIB | Exc. | V.G. | Good | Fair | Poor |
|-----|------|------|------|------|------|
| 166 | 150  | 120  | 100  | 75   | 50   |

### Li'L Champ Bolt Action Rifle

This model is a scaled-down single shot that is chambered for the .22 rimfire cartridges. It has a 16.25" barrel, adjustable sights, a molded stock, and nickel plated bolt. This model is 33" overall and is designed to be the ideal first rifle for a young shooter.

| NIB | Exc. | V.G. | Good | Fair | Poor |
|-----|------|------|------|------|------|
| 91 | 75 | 60 | 45 | 35 | 20 |

### M1 .30 Cal. Carbine

A military-style carbine styled after the M1 of WWII fame. It is chambered for the .30 Carbine cartridge and has an 18" barrel with military-style sights and hardwood stock. There are detachable 5-, 15-, and 30-round magazines available.

| NIB | Exc. | V.G. | Good | Fair | Poor |
|-----|------|------|------|------|------|
| 265 | 245 | 200 | 175 | 140 | 90 |

### Paratrooper .30 Carbine

This model is similar to the M1 model with a folding stock.

| NIB | Exc. | V.G. | Good | Fair | Poor |
|-----|------|------|------|------|------|
| 291 | 265 | 225 | 200 | 165 | 125 |

### Enforcer .30 Carbine

This is a 9.5" pistol version of the M1 Carbine. It has no buttstock.

| NIB | Exc. | V.G. | Good | Fair | Poor |
|-----|------|------|------|------|------|
| 333 | 300 | 265 | 225 | 185 | 140 |

### Long Range Rifle System

This is a specialized long-range, bolt-action rifle chambered for the .50 Cal. Browning Machinegun cartridge. It has a 33" barrel and a special muzzle brake system. A custom-order version in the .338/416 caliber is also available.

| NIB | Exc. | V.G. | Good | Fair | Poor |
|-----|------|------|------|------|------|
| 8500 | 7000 | 5000 | 3500 | 2500 | 2000 |

### TP-22 and TP-25

This model is a compact, double-action, pocket automatic that was styled after the the Walther TP series. Chambered for either the .22 rimfire or the .25 centerfire cartridges, it has a 2.75" barrel, fixed sights and black plastic grips. The detachable magazine holds 7 shots and the finish is either blue or nickel-plated. The nickel-plated version is worth 10 percent more than the blue (shown).

| NIB | Exc. | V.G. | Good | Fair | Poor |
|-----|------|------|------|------|------|
| 191 | 175 | 145 | 110 | 85 | 50 |

### AMAC -22 Compact or 25 Compact

This is a compact, single-action, semi-automatic pocket pistol that is chambered for the .22 rimfire or the .25 ACP cartridge. It has a 2" barrel, 5-shot magazine, plastic grips, and blue or nickel finish. The nickel finish is 10 percent higher in cost than the blue (shown).

| NIB | Exc. | V.G. | Good | Fair | Poor |
|-----|------|------|------|------|------|
| 157 | 125 | 100 | 80 | 55 | 35 |

## AMT
### Arcadia Machine and Tool
### Irwindale, California

### Lightning

This is a single-action, semi-automatic, blowback pistol chambered for the .22 l.r. cartridge. It was made of stainless steel and offered with barrel lengths of 5" (Bull only), 6.5", 8.5", 10.5" and 12.5" (either Bull or tapered). The sights, as well as the trigger, were adjustable. The grips were checkered black rubber. This pistol resembled and was based on the Ruger semi-automatic pistol. It was manufactured between 1984 and 1987.

| Exc. | V.G. | Good | Fair | Poor |
|------|------|------|------|------|
| 250 | 210 | 175 | 125 | 100 |

### Bull's Eye Regulation Target

This was similar to the Lightning, with a 6.5" vent-rib bull barrel, wooden target grips, and an extended rear sight. Manufactured in 1986 only.

| Exc. | V.G. | Good | Fair | Poor |
|------|------|------|------|------|
| 350 | 300 | 250 | 200 | 150 |

### Baby Automag

This model was similar in appearance to the Lightning, with an 8.5" vent-rib barrel, chambered for the .22 l.r. It had Millett adjustable sights and smooth walnut grips. There were 1,000 manufactured.

| Exc. | V.G. | Good | Fair | Poor |
|------|------|------|------|------|
| 400 | 350 | 285 | 225 | 175 |

### Automag II

This is a stainless-steel, semi-automatic single action chambered for the .22 Magnum cartridge. It is offered with barrel lengths of 3.5", 4.5", and 6" and has Millett adjustable sights and black, grooved, plastic grips. It was introduced in 1987.

| NIB | Exc. | V.G. | Good | Fair | Poor |
|-----|------|------|------|------|------|
| 330 | 275 | 225 | 175 | 135 | 100 |

### Automag III

This model is similar to the Automag II except that it is chambered for the .30 carbine cartridge.

| NIB | Exc. | V.G. | Good | Fair | Poor |
|-----|------|------|------|------|------|
| 450 | 400 | 350 | 275 | 200 | 150 |

### Back Up Pistol

This model is a semi-automatic, blowback pocket pistol that is chambered for the .22 rimfire or the .380 ACP cartridges. It has a 2.5" barrel and fixed sights and is constructed of stainless steel. The grips are black lexan on later models and walnut on the earlier ones. The detachable magazine holds 5 shots in .380 and 8 shots in .22 rimfire. This pistol was formerly manufactured by TDE and is currently made by Irwindale Arms Inc.

| NIB | Exc. | V.G. | Good | Fair | Poor |
|-----|------|------|------|------|------|
| 245 | 200 | 175 | 150 | 125 | 100 |

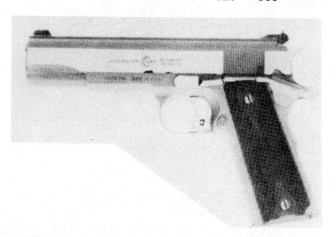

### Hard Baller

This model was the first of the stainless steel .45 automatics. It is similar in appearance to a Colt Gold Cup with Millett adjustable sights and a serrated rib on top of the slide. It has a 5" barrel and is chambered for the .45 ACP cartridge. The trigger is adjustable, and the grips are wraparound black checkered rubber.

| NIB | Exc. | V.G. | Good | Fair | Poor |
|-----|------|------|------|------|------|
| 450 | 400 | 350 | 300 | 250 | 200 |

## Hard Baller Longslide

This model is similar to the Hard Baller with a 7" barrel and long slide assembly to accommodate it.

| NIB | Exc. | V.G. | Good | Fair | Poor |
|-----|------|------|------|------|------|
| 525 | 475 | 400 | 325 | 275 | 225 |

## Government Model

This Model is AMT's stainless-steel version of the Colt Government Model with fixed sights and wraparound grips.

| NIB | Exc. | V.G. | Good | Fair | Poor |
|-----|------|------|------|------|------|
| 450 | 400 | 350 | 300 | 250 | 200 |

## Skipper

This model was the same as the Hard Baller with a 1" shorter barrel and slide. It was discontinued in 1984.

| Exc. | V.G. | Good | Fair | Poor |
|------|------|------|------|------|
| 375 | 325 | 275 | 225 | 200 |

## Combat Skipper

This is a fixed-sight version of the stainless-steel Skipper. It is similar to a Colt Commander and was dropped from the line in 1984.

| Exc. | V.G. | Good | Fair | Poor |
|------|------|------|------|------|
| 350 | 300 | 250 | 200 | 175 |

## Lightning Rifle

This semi-automatic, stainless-steel rifle is based on the Ruger 10/22. It is chambered for the .22 l.r. and has a 22" barrel and a 25-round, detachable magazine. The stock is a folding synthetic type. It was introduced in 1986.

| NIB | Exc. | V.G. | Good | Fair | Poor |
|-----|------|------|------|------|------|
| 275 | 225 | 175 | 150 | 125 | 100 |

## Small Game Hunter

This model is similar to the Lightning but has a full-length, black synthetic stock and 10-round magazine. It is furnished with a 4X scope. This model was also introduced in 1986.

| NIB | Exc. | V.G. | Good | Fair | Poor |
|-----|------|------|------|------|------|
| 275 | 225 | 175 | 150 | 125 | 100 |

# A-SQUARE
### Madison, Indiana

This company offers high-quality, bolt action rifles based on the P-17 Enfield or the Remington Model 700 actions. They are offered in two basic grades but at extra cost can be supplied with other options such as select wood and engraving.

## Hannibal Grade

This model is based on the P-17 Enfield action, has a 22" to 26" barrel, and is chambered for various calibers from .270 up to and including the .458 Magnum. The Weatherby calibers, as well as A-Square's own calibers, are chambered as well. The pistol-grip stock is made of select walnut. This rifle was introduced in 1986.

| NIB | Exc. | V.G. | Good | Fair | Poor |
|-----|------|------|------|------|------|
| 1600 | 1400 | 1000 | 850 | 750 | 500 |

## Caesar Grade

This model is based on the Remington 700 action and is available in the same calibers as the Hannibal Grade, except the A-Square Calibers are not chambered. This model is also available in a left-hand version which also was introduced in 1986.

| NIB | Exc. | V.G. | Good | Fair | Poor |
|-----|------|------|------|------|------|
| 1650 | 1450 | 1050 | 900 | 800 | 500 |

# ATCSA
### Armas De Tiro Y Casa
### Eibar, Spain

## Colt Police Positive Copy

This is a typical early Spanish effort, chambered for the .38 cartridge. It held six shots and resembled the Colt pistol in appearance but not in quality. There is no collector interest in this type of revolver.

| Exc. | V.G. | Good | Fair | Poor |
|------|------|------|------|------|
| 150 | 125 | 100 | 60 | 40 |

## Target Pistol

This model was a .22 caliber, target single shot that was built on the revolver frame.

| Exc. | V.G. | Good | Fair | Poor |
|------|------|------|------|------|
| 200 | 175 | 140 | 100 | 65 |

# AGUIRRE Y ARANZABAL (AYA)
### Eibar, Spain

The shotguns manufactured by this company ran the gamut from mediocre to fine. As of 1988, they are no longer exported from Spain. Their manufacture has been cut to a minimum, and new guns will be very hard to obtain in the U.S.A.

### Side X Side Shotguns
## Matador Side X Side

This was one of AYA's most popular models. It was available in 12, 16, 20, and 28 gauge and .410 with 26", 28" and 30" barrels and various different choke combinations. The action was the Anson and Deeley boxlock with a single-selective trigger and automatic ejectors. The checkered walnut buttstock had a pistol grip, and the forearm was the beavertail type. This model was manufactured between 1955 and 1963. 28 gauge and .410--Add 20 Percent

| Exc. | V.G. | Good | Fair | Poor |
|------|------|------|------|------|
| 475 | 450 | 375 | 300 | 250 |

## Matador II Side X Side

This model was similar in appearance and features to the Matador except that it had a ventilated rib and was chambered for the 12 and 20 gauge only.

| Exc. | V.G. | Good | Fair | Poor |
|------|------|------|------|------|
| 500 | 460 | 390 | 300 | 250 |

## Matador III Side X Side

This model had all the features of the Matador II with the addition of 3" chambers. It was manufactured until 1985.

| NIB | Exc. | V.G. | Good | Fair | Poor |
|-----|------|------|------|------|------|
| 1235 | 950 | 800 | 700 | 550 | 400 |

## Bolero Side X Side

This model was essentially similar to the Matador except that it featured a non-selective, single trigger and extractors instead of the automatic ejectors. It was manufactured until 1984.

| Exc. | V.G. | Good | Fair | Poor |
|------|------|------|------|------|
| 450 | 380 | 300 | 250 | 200 |

## Iberia Side X Side

This was an economy model that was chambered for 12 and 20 gauge with 3" chambers. It was a boxlock with double triggers and extractors. The barrel lengths available were 26", 28", and 30"; and the walnut stock was plain. This model was manufactured until 1984.

| Exc. | V.G. | Good | Fair | Poor |
|------|------|------|------|------|
| 575 | 480 | 375 | 285 | 225 |

### Side X Sides
## Iberia II Side X Side

This model was chambered for 12 and 16 gauge and featured 28" barrels with various chokes. The chambers were 2-3/4", and the gun had double triggers and a plain walnut stock. It was manufactured in 1984 and 1985 only.

| NIB | Exc. | V.G. | Good | Fair | Poor |
|-----|------|------|------|------|------|
| 575 | 500 | 425 | 335 | 250 | 200 |

## Model 106 Side X Side

This Model was chambered for 12, 16 and 20 gauge. It had a boxlock action, double triggers and extractors. The barrels were 28", and the walnut stock had a pistol grip. This model was manufactured until 1985.

| NIB | Exc. | V.G. | Good | Fair | Poor |
|-----|------|------|------|------|------|
| 585 | 525 | 450 | 350 | 300 | 225 |

### Model 107-LI Side X Side

This Model was chambered for 12 and 16 gauge and featured a boxlock action with light English scroll engraving and an English-style straight grip stock. It had double triggers and was manufactured until 1985.

| NIB | Exc. | V.G. | Good | Fair | Poor |
|-----|------|------|------|------|------|
| 750 | 675 | 525 | 465 | 375 | 275 |

### Model 116 Side X Side

This was a more deluxe gun with hand-detachable H&H-style sidelocks. It was chambered for 12, 16, and 20 gauge, with barrels from 27" through 30" in length. This gun featured double triggers, a select walnut, hand-checkered pistolgrip stock, and an engraved receiver. It was manufactured until 1985.

| NIB | Exc. | V.G. | Good | Fair | Poor |
|-----|------|------|------|------|------|
| 1125 | 1000 | 800 | 675 | 600 | 475 |

### Model 117 Side X Side

This Model was similar to the Model 116 with 3" magnum chambers and slightly less embellishment. It was manufactured until 1986.

| NIB | Exc. | V.G. | Good | Fair | Poor |
|-----|------|------|------|------|------|
| 1075 | 875 | 725 | 625 | 550 | 475 |

### Side X Side

### Model 117 "Quail Unlimited" Side X Side

This Model was chambered for 12 gauge, 3" only. It had 26" modified-and-improved-cylinder barrels and a gold-plated single trigger. The stock was a higher grade of walnut than the standard Model 117, and the receiver was engraved specially for "Quail Unlimited of North America" by Baron Industries. The checkering was finer, and the finish was a higher gloss. There were only 42 manufactured.

| Exc. | V.G. | Good | Fair | Poor |
|------|------|------|------|------|
| 1500 | 1200 | 875 | 750 | 625 |

### Model 210 Side X Side

This Model was chambered for 12 and 16 gauge, with 26" to 28" barrels. It was a boxlock with exposed hammers and double triggers. It featured a plain walnut stock and was lightly engraved. The Model 210 was manufactured until 1985.

| Exc. | V.G. | Good | Fair | Poor |
|------|------|------|------|------|
| 800 | 575 | 485 | 395 | 325 |

### Model 711 Boxlock Side X Side

This Model was chambered for 12 gauge only and had 28" or 30" barrels with a ventilated rib. There was a single-selective trigger and automatic ejectors. It was manufactured until 1984.

| Exc. | V.G. | Good | Fair | Poor |
|------|------|------|------|------|
| 900 | 800 | 700 | 550 | 450 |

### Model 711 Sidelock Side X Side

This was a higher-grade version of the Model 711 with a functional sidelock action. It was manufactured in 1985 only.

| Exc. | V.G. | Good | Fair | Poor |
|------|------|------|------|------|
| 1000 | 900 | 765 | 625 | 500 |

### Model 53-E Side X Side

This was a made-to-order gun with engraved sidelocks and side clips. It was chambered for 12, 16, and 20 gauge with automatic ejectors and customer's choice of barrel lengths, trigger and stock style, and dimensions. The action was engraved. This Model was manufactured until 1986.
Single-selective trigger--Add $100.00.

| Exc. | V.G. | Good | Fair | Poor |
|------|------|------|------|------|
| 1500 | 1250 | 950 | 700 | 600 |

### Model 56 Side X Side

This was a high-grade gun, chambered for 12, 16, and 20 gauge. It had a highly engraved sidelock action, automatic ejectors, single-selective trigger and high-grade, hand-checkered walnut stock. It was manufactured until 1985.

| Exc. | V.G. | Good | Fair | Poor |
|------|------|------|------|------|
| 4750 | 3900 | 3100 | 2500 | 2000 |

### Model XXV BL Side X Side

This was a boxlock chambered for 12 and 20 gauge with 25" barrels and a Churchill-style rib. It featured automatic ejectors and a stock forearm and triggers made to the customer's order. This Model was manufactured until 1986.
Single Selective Trigger--Add $100.00.

| Exc. | V.G. | Good | Fair | Poor |
|------|------|------|------|------|
| 1000 | 900 | 775 | 685 | 600 |

### Model XXV SL Side X Side

This Model was a sidelock chambered for 12, 16, 20, or 28 gauge and .410. It had 25" barrels with the Churchill-style rib. It featured automatic ejectors and was stocked and triggered to the customer's specifications. This Model was manufactured until 1986.
Single Selective Trigger--Add 100.00.
28 Gauge and .410 add 10%.

| Exc. | V.G. | Good | Fair | Poor |
|------|------|------|------|------|
| 1750 | 1300 | 950 | 725 | 625 |

### Model No. 1 Side X Side

This was a high quality gun chambered for 12, 20, or 28 gauge and .410 with 26" or 28" barrels. It had an elaborately engraved, full sidelock action with a third lever opener, automatic ejectors, and a straight grip, checkered walnut stock. The triggers were made to the customer's specifications. This Model was manufactured until 1987.
Single Selective Trigger--Add $150.00.
28 gauge and .410--Add 10 Percent.

| Exc. | V.G. | Good | Fair | Poor |
|------|------|------|------|------|
| 2500 | 2250 | 1750 | 1200 | 850 |

### Model No. 2 Side X Side

This was a less elaborate model chambered for 12, 16, 20, or 28 gauge and .410. It had 26" or 28" barrels with 3" chambers. It featured a full sidelock, automatic ejectors, cocking indicators, double triggers, and a third lever fastener. It was manufactured until 1987.
28 Gauge and .410--Add 10 Percent.

| Exc. | V.G. | Good | Fair | Poor |
|------|------|------|------|------|
| 1150 | 1000 | 800 | 575 | 450 |

### Model No.3-A Side X Side

This gun was a boxlock chambered for 12, 16, 20, 28 gauge and .410. It had extractors and double triggers and was a more utilitarian-grade gun. It was manufactured until 1985.

| Exc. | V.G. | Good | Fair | Poor |
|------|------|------|------|------|
| 650 | 550 | 450 | 375 | 300 |

### Model No. 4-A Side X Side

This Model was similar to the Model No.3-A, with 3" chambers and an English-style, straight grip stock. It was manufactured until 1987.

| Exc. | V.G. | Good | Fair | Poor |
|------|------|------|------|------|
| 625 | 525 | 475 | 380 | 310 |

### Model No 4-A Deluxe Side X Side

This was a higher-grade version with automatic ejectors and made-to-order trigger and stock work. It was manufactured until 1985.
28 gauge and .410--Add 10 Percent.

| Exc. | V.G. | Good | Fair | Poor |
|------|------|------|------|------|
| 1800 | 1450 | 1000 | 675 | 550 |

### Senior Side X Side

This was the highest-grade gun that AYA offered. It was made in 12 gauge only with an elaborately engraved and inlaid, self opening, full sidelock action. This gun was strictly made to the customer's specifications and utilized the best walnut and finest checkering the company had available. Barrel lengths, triggers, etc., were optional. An upland game version was also available in a lighter weight. This model was manufactured until 1987.

| Exc. | V.G. | Good | Fair | Poor |
|------|------|------|------|------|
| 15000 | 12500 | 9000 | 7000 | 4750 |

**Over/Unders**

**Model 79 "A" O/U**

This was a 12-gauge boxlock with 26", 28", or 30" barrels. It featured a single-selective trigger, automatic ejectors, double locking lugs, and a pistolgrip walnut stock. It was manufactured until 1985.

| Exc. | V.G. | Good | Fair | Poor |
|------|------|------|------|------|
| 1250 | 1050 | 925 | 750 | 650 |

**Model 79 "B" O/U**

This Model is similar to the 79"A" with a higher degree of engraving. It was manufactured until 1985.

| Exc. | V.G. | Good | Fair | Poor |
|------|------|------|------|------|
| 1350 | 1150 | 950 | 800 | 675 |

**Model 79 "C" O/U**

This is an even more elaborately engraved version of the Model 79. It was manufactured until 1985.

| Exc. | V.G. | Good | Fair | Poor |
|------|------|------|------|------|
| 2000 | 1800 | 1500 | 1150 | 975 |

**Model 77 O/U**

This Model was a high-grade gun that was patterned after the very distinctive Merkel, boxlock, O/U gun. It featured a Greener cross bolt and elaborate engraving. The wood was first-class with deluxe checkering. The other basics were variable with the customer's specifications. This Model was manufactured until 1985.

| Exc. | V.G. | Good | Fair | Poor |
|------|------|------|------|------|
| 3000 | 2700 | 2150 | 1750 | 1500 |

**Coral "A" O/U**

This model was chambered for 12 and 16 gauge and had 26" and 28" ventilated rib barrels. It featured the "Kersten" cross bolt, boxlock action, automatic ejectors, and double triggers. It was manufactured until 1985.

| Exc. | V.G. | Good | Fair | Poor |
|------|------|------|------|------|
| 1250 | 900 | 725 | 600 | 500 |

**Coral "B" O/U**

This model was similar to the Model "A" with an engraved, coin-finished receiver. It was manufactured until 1985.

| Exc. | V.G. | Good | Fair | Poor |
|------|------|------|------|------|
| 1400 | 1150 | 800 | 675 | 550 |

**Model 37 Super O/U**

This Model is a high-grade, Merkel-style sidelock that was chambered for 12, 16, and 20 gauge. It was available in various barrel lengths and chokes with a ventilated rib, automatic ejectors, and customer's choice of triggers. The wood was high grade; and the action, profusely engraved. This Model was made until 1985.

| Exc. | V.G. | Good | Fair | Poor |
|------|------|------|------|------|
| 2500 | 2200 | 1900 | 1500 | 1225 |

**Model 37 Super "A" O/U**

This Model was similar to the Model 37 Super with an engraved game scene and a hand-detachable sidelock.

| Exc. | V.G. | Good | Fair | Poor |
|------|------|------|------|------|
| 5000 | 4500 | 3800 | 2700 | 2000 |

**Model 37 Super "B" O/U**

This Model is a more elaborately engraved version of the Super "A."

| Exc. | V.G. | Good | Fair | Poor |
|------|------|------|------|------|
| 5200 | 4750 | 4000 | 2950 | 2250 |

**Augusta O/U**

This was the top of the AYA Over/Under line. It was chambered for 12 gauge only. It was a full sidelock that was essentially built to the customer's specifications. The walnut used was select, and the deep relief engraving was elaborate. This model was manufactured until 1985.

| Exc. | V.G. | Good | Fair | Poor |
|------|------|------|------|------|
| 8000 | 7000 | 5500 | 3800 | 3000 |

# ABADIE
## Liege, Belgium

Abadie was a Belgian gunsmith who developed the loading-gate safety system found on European service revolvers made between 1878 and 1900. This invention was quite commonly used, but Abadie's name was used on only these two Portuguese service revolvers:

**System Abadie Model 1878**

A 6-shot, double-action, 9.1mm revolver. It has a solid frame with a permanently aligned ejector rod and an octagonal barrel. The Model 1878 was issued as an officer's sidearm.

| Exc. | V.G. | Good | Fair | Poor |
|------|------|------|------|------|
| 250 | 225 | 175 | 125 | 90 |

**System Abadie Model 1886**

The Model 1886 was a larger, heavier version of the Model 1878. It was issued to enlisted troopers.

| Exc. | V.G. | Good | Fair | Poor |
|------|------|------|------|------|
| 225 | 200 | 150 | 110 | 75 |

# ABBEY, F. J. & CO.
## Chicago, Illinois

This Company was in business between 1858 and 1878. They manufactured percussion rifles and shotguns. There is little known about the Company, and it is extremely difficult to research their products. The general value for a marked example of an F. J. Abbey percussion rifle or shotgun is as follows:

**Rifle**

| Exc. | V.G. | Good | Fair | Poor |
|------|------|------|------|------|
| 650 | 525 | 375 | 200 | 125 |

**Shotgun**

| Exc. | V.G. | Good | Fair | Poor |
|------|------|------|------|------|
| 775 | 650 | 425 | 275 | 150 |

# ABBEY, GEORGE T.
## Utica, New York, and Chicago, Illinois

This company was in business between 1845 and 1852 in Utica, New York. They moved to Chicago, Illinois, in 1852 and operated there until 1874, when they ceased production of firearms. Little is known about the company or its products, and research is very difficult. They manufactured single-barrel and double-barrel percussion rifles, and the general values are as follows:

**Single Barrel .44 Cal.**

| Exc. | V.G. | Good | Fair | Poor |
|------|------|------|------|------|
| 700 | 575 | 450 | 335 | 225 |

**Side X Side Double Barrel**

| Exc. | V.G. | Good | Fair | Poor |
|------|------|------|------|------|
| 1250 | 1000 | 800 | 525 | 375 |

**Over/Under Double Barrel**

| Exc. | V.G. | Good | Fair | Poor |
|------|------|------|------|------|
| 1500 | 1285 | 900 | 700 | 450 |

# ACHA
## Vizcaya, Spain

**Domingo Acha**

The Acha company was another producer of typically low quality, Eibar-type pistols. They conducted business during the period between WWI and the Spanish Civil War.

**Acha Model 1916**

A 7.65mm, semi-auto, blowback pistol with internal hammer. It will usually be found with the markings "F de Acha Hrs C 7.65."

| Exc. | V.G. | Good | Fair | Poor |
|------|------|------|------|------|
| 200 | 160 | 125 | 90 | 65 |

**Atlas**

A copy of the 1906 Browning, chambered for the 6.35mm round. It will be found marked either "Domingo Acha y Cia" or "Pistolet automatique 6.35 Atlas."

| Exc. | V.G. | Good | Fair | Poor |
|------|------|------|------|------|
| 150 | 110 | 85 | 60 | 40 |

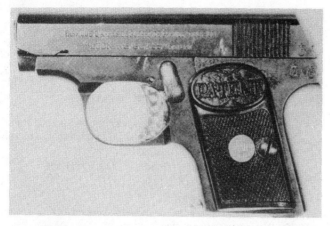

## Looking Glass

This is simply another copy of the 1906 Browning. It is also a 6.35mm. The slide and grips are marked "Looking Glass." This very common pistol has been noted with a number of different barrel lengths. The finish and the markings also vary.

| Exc. | V.G. | Good | Fair | Poor |
|------|------|------|------|------|
| 200 | 160 | 125 | 90 | 65 |

## ACME

SEE--Davenport Arms Co., Maltby Henley & Co., and Merwin & Hulbert & Co.

## ACME ARMS
### New York, New York

Acme Arms was the trade name used by the Cornwall Hardware Co. for the firearms that they marketed. They were manufactured in the 1890's.

### .22 Revolver

This was a single-action revolver that was chambered for the .22 short rimfire. The cylinder held 7 rounds.

| Exc. | V.G. | Good | Fair | Poor |
|------|------|------|------|------|
| 250 | 210 | 175 | 125 | 100 |

### .32 Revolver

This was a single-action revolver that was chambered for the .32 short rimfire. The cylinder held 5 rounds.

| Exc. | V.G. | Good | Fair | Poor |
|------|------|------|------|------|
| 260 | 225 | 200 | 150 | 110 |

### Shotgun

This was a Side X Side, 12 gauge, Damascus-barreled shotgun with exposed hammers.

| Exc. | V.G. | Good | Fair | Poor |
|------|------|------|------|------|
| 250 | 210 | 175 | 125 | 100 |

## ACME HAMMERLESS
### Norwich, Connecticut
### Made by Hopkins & Allen

The Acme Hammerless revolver was manufactured in 1893 by the firm of Hopkins & Allen of Norwich, Connecticut. This revolver was also known as the "Forehand 1891."

### Acme Hammerless

This was a 5 shot, solid-frame revolver chambered for the .32 or .38 centerfire cartridges. It utilized a loading gate and had no ejector except the centerpin. This was a cheaply made revolver that was found in both hammerless and exposed hammer versions. The collector interest in these revolvers is low, and consequently the value is likewise.

| Exc. | V.G. | Good | Fair | Poor |
|------|------|------|------|------|
| 135 | 110 | 90 | 60 | 35 |

## ACTION
### Eibar, Spain
### Maker-- Modesto Santos

This was another small Spanish company formed to take advantage of the French contract to supply handguns for WWI. They manufactured the usual low-quality "Eibar" type semi- automat-ics in 7.65mm. After the end of the War, they continued to produce Browning 1906 copies in 7.65mm and 6.35mm until they ceased business at the onset of the Spanish Civil War.

### Action

This pistol was originally made for France in WWI. After the War, it was continued on a commercial basis. It is an "Eibar"-type 1906 Browning copy chambered for the 7.65 and the 6.35mm. It is a blowback semi-automatic with a blued finish and checkered, molded plastic grips that bear the markings "MS." The slide is marked "Pistolet Automatique Modele 1920." This pistol was also marketed under the trade name "Corrientes" or simply the "MS."

| Exc. | V.G. | Good | Fair | Poor |
|------|------|------|------|------|
| 175 | 150 | 120 | 90 | 60 |

## ACTION ARMS LTD.
### Philadelphia, Pennsylvania
### Importers of the Uzi and Galil
### for Israeli Military Industries.

## AT-84, AT-88

This is a locked breech, semi-automatic, double action weapon with an inertia firing pin. It is a Swiss-made copy of the CZ-75 which many believe to be the finest combat handgun in the world today. The AT-84 was the original designation, and the pistol is now known as the AT-88S. It has a 4.75" barrel and is chambered for the 9mm Parabellum or the new .41 Action Express cartridges. The sights are fixed, and the double-stacked magazine holds 15 shots in 9mm and 10 in .41 Action Express. There is a thumb safety; and this weapon can be carried cocked and locked, as well as double-action. The finish is blued or matte chrome-plated with checkered walnut grips. It was introduced in 1987.

| NIB | Exc. | V.G. | Good | Fair | Poor |
|-----|------|------|------|------|------|
| 600 | 500 | 425 | 350 | 300 | 275 |

### AT-84P, AT-88P

This is a compact version of the AT-84, A88 with a 3.7" barrel and a 13-shot, 9mm magazine--8 shot in .41 Action Express. It was introduced in 1987.

| NIB | Exc. | V.G. | Good | Fair | Poor |
|-----|------|------|------|------|------|
| 700 | 600 | 525 | 450 | 400 | 350 |

### AT-88H

This model is an even more compact version with a 3.4" barrel and a 10-shot magazine in 9mm. It is also chambered for the .41 Action Express. It was introduced in 1989.

| NIB | Exc. | V.G. | Good | Fair | Poor |
|-----|------|------|------|------|------|
| 600 | 500 | 425 | 350 | 300 | 275 |

### Timberwolf Carbine

This is a slide-action carbine with an 18.5" barrel chambered for the .357 Magnum cartridge. It features a straight-grip stock, open sights, and an integral scope-mounting system. It was introduced in 1989.

| NIB | Exc. | V.G. | Good | Fair | Poor |
|-----|------|------|------|------|------|
| 475 | 400  | 350  | 300  | 250  | 225  |

### Galil Model AR

This is a gas-operated, rotary-bolt, semi-automatic version of the Israeli assault weapon. It is chambered for either the 5.56mm (.223) or the .308 cartridges. The barrel length in .223 is 16.1"; and in .308, 19". It has adjustable, flip-up Tritium night sights. The finish is parkerized, and the rear stock folds. This is a fine weapon and has a well-deserved reputation for dependability and accuracy. But unfortunately, there are those who wish to blame an inanimate object for the actions of those who use it. This weapon is one that mass hysteria has affected, and the values have fluctuated wildly in the past few years. Different parts of the country list great variances in price. We will, for reference purposes only, list these weapons. We recommend individual appraisal. This rifle was formerly imported by Magnum Research, Minneapolis, Minnesota.

### Galil Model ARM

This Model is similar to the Model AR, with a folding metal bipod and a wooden handguard. It is furnished with a carrying handle.

### Hadar II

Introduced in 1989, this is essentially the same rugged action as found on the Models AR and Arm except it is in a hunting rifle, walnut, thumbhole pistolgrip stock. It is chambered for the .308 cartridge only and has an adjustable sight and a recoil pad.

### Sniper Rifle

This model is a specially built rifle that holds exacting tolerances needed for pinpoint accuracy. It is produced on a limited basis. It has a 20" heavy barrel chambered for the .308 cartridge, an adjustable cheekpiece and walnut folding stock and forend. It features Tritium night sights and is furnished with a 6-power Nimrod scope, a bipod, and carrying case. This model was first imported in 1989.

### Uzi Carbine Model B

This is a closed breech, blowback, semi-automatic, carbine with a 16.1" operational barrel. It is also supplied with a dummy, solid, short barrel which can be installed for looks but will not chamber a round. This model is chambered for 9mm Parabellum, .41 Action Express, and .45 ACP. It has a folding metal stock and adjustable sights and is finished in black. Caliber conversion kits are available.

### Uzi Model A

This model is the earlier version and is quite similar in appearance to the Model B. The designation is marked on the rear of the receiver. The differences are internal, and the Model A will bring a premium from some buyers.

### Uzi Mini Carbine

This is a scaled-down version of the carbine with a 19.75" barrel. It is chambered for the 9mm or the .45 ACP cartridges and features a swing-away styled folding stock. It was introduced in 1987.

### Uzi Pistol

This is a miniaturized version of the Uzi with a 4.5" barrel and no provisions for a stock. It is chambered for the 9mm and .45 ACP cartridges.

# ADAMS
### Deane, Adams & Deane
### London, England
### London Armory Co. (After 1856)

In 1851 Colt displayed their new percussion revolvers at the Great Exhibition, held at the Crystal Palace in London's Hyde Park. A London gunmaker named Robert Adams also exhibited a percussion revolver which was accepted and put into large-scale production. It was regarded by many to be a viable rival for the Colt and indeed the Adams revolver, along with its improvements and conversions, did successfully compete, at least in Europe, with the Colt until 1880, when the more modern Enfield replaced it as a service revolver.

### Adams Model 1851 Self-Cocking Revolver

This is a very large, Dragoon-style revolver. It has a 7.5" octagonal barrel and weighs 45 ounces. This double-action-only weapon has a 5-shot cylinder and is chambered for a 12.4mm round. The top of the barrel is marked "Deane, Adams and Deane (Maker to HRH Prince Albert) 30 King William St. London Bridge." It is an extremely strong and well made firearm, although too large to be used as anything but a cavalry or horse pistol.

| Exc. | V.G. | Good | Fair | Poor |
|------|------|------|------|------|
| 1300 | 1050 | 850  | 625  | 400  |

### Adams Pocket Revolver

This smaller revolver was designed as a personal or pocket weapon. It weighs 20 ounces, has a 4.5" barrel, and is chambered for 8.1mm. It is also double-action only, but this is not a handicap in a close quarter pocket pistol.

| Exc. | V.G. | Good | Fair | Poor |
|------|------|------|------|------|
| 950  | 800  | 575  | 400  | 300  |

### Beaumont-Adams Revolver

An improved version of the original Adams, this revolver features a single action as well as double action lock work and an integral rammer for a tighter bullet seal. These features would definitely have had a positive effect on accuracy. The basic specifications are quite similar, but the grip features a more modern, raked design.

| Exc. | V.G. | Good | Fair | Poor |
|------|------|------|------|------|
| 1300 | 1050 | 850 | 625 | 400 |

## ADAMY GEBRUDER
### Suhl, Germany

### Over/Under Shotgun

This was a high grade, O/U shotgun that was produced in the 1920's. It was a boxlock with barrel lengths from 26" to 30" and was chambered for the 12 and 16 gauges. It featured the deep relief engraving common to German guns of that era and had double triggers. It had a select walnut pistolgrip stock with hand-cut checkering and was furnished in a fitted leather carrying case.

| Exc. | V.G. | Good | Fair | Poor |
|------|------|------|------|------|
| 1850 | 1600 | 1275 | 875 | 700 |

## ADIRONDACK ARMS CO.
### Plattsburgh, New York
### or
### A.S. Babbitt Co.

### Orvil M. Robinson Patent Rifle

The Robinson tube-fed repeating rifle was made in New York between 1870 and 1874. The early models, 1870-1872, are marked "A.S. Babbitt"; the later models, 1872-1874, "Adirondack Arms Co." It is believed that all were manufactured by Babbitt and that Adirondack was a holding company set up purely for economic reasons. The Company was sold to Winchester in 1874, but they never produced the Robinson after that date. The rifle has been found in two major variations. The first has small fingers on the hammer to cock and cycle the mechanism. The second has buttons on the receiver to retract the bolt and cock the hammer. The rifle was made in .44 cal. with an octagonal barrel usually found in 26" or 28" length. The frames were predominantly brass; but some iron frames have been noted, and they will bring a premium of approximately 25 percent. The barrel and magazine tube have a blued finish.

**First Model**

| Exc. | V.G. | Good | Fair | Poor |
|------|------|------|------|------|
| 2400 | 2050 | 1450 | 775 | 600 |

**Second Model**

| Exc. | V.G. | Good | Fair | Poor |
|------|------|------|------|------|
| 2150 | 1700 | 1100 | 650 | 500 |

## ADLER
### Engelbrecht & Wolff
### Blasii, Germany

The Adler was a very confusing and complex pistol. It was quite awkward in its design. Coupled with this was the cartridge, which was chambered for 7.2mm Adler. This was a special bottleneck cartridge that was never adopted by another gunmaker. These factors made the Adler quite non-competitive in its market. It was only made between 1905 and 1907. Very few exist today.

| Exc. | V.G. | Good | Fair | Poor |
|------|------|------|------|------|
| 2000 | 1650 | 1100 | 750 | 400 |

## ADVANTAGE ARMS U.S.A., INC.
### St Paul, Minnesota
### Distributed by Wildfire Sports

### Model 422

This is a four-barreled, double-action derringer chambered for the .22 rimfire and .22 rimfire magnum cartridges. It had 2.5" barrels and rotating firing pins to fire the four barrels one at a time, with each pull of the trigger. The entire gun receiver and barrels were made of aluminum alloy, and it weighed only 15 oz. The available finishes were blue, nickel-plated, and a heat-applied finish that appeared as blue but was known as "QPQ." This pistol was only manufactured in 1986 and 1987.

| NIB | Exc. | V.G. | Good | Fair | Poor |
|-----|------|------|------|------|------|
| 165 | 150 | 125 | 100 | 85 | 70 |

## AETNA ARMS CO.
### New York

This Company began copying Smith & Wesson firearms as soon as the Rollin White patent expired. They made brass framed, 7-shot, .22 rimfire revolvers. The finish was either blued or nickel with birdshead grips. The octagonal barrel was marked "Aetna Arms Co. New York." Roughly 6,000 were manufactured between 1869 and 1890.

| Exc. | V.G. | Good | Fair | Poor |
|------|------|------|------|------|
| 250 | 225 | 185 | 135 | 100 |

## AFFERBACH, W. A.
### Philadelphia, Pennsylvania

This .41 cal. percussion pistol is a very close copy of the one manufactured by Henry Deringer in the 1850's. The barrel was marked "W. Afferbach Phila." These guns are very rare in today's market.

| Exc. | V.G. | Good | Fair | Poor |
|------|------|------|------|------|
| 775 | 700 | 500 | 375 | 250 |

## AGNER (SAXHOJ PRODUCTS INC.)
### Copenhagen, Denmark
### Importer: Beeman Arms
### Santa Rosa, California

### Model M 80

This was a high-grade target pistol that was chambered for the .22 l.r. cartridge. It was constructed of stainless steel and featured a key-locked security system that rendered it unfireable when locked. It had a 5.9" barrel, adjustable sights, and French walnut grips. It also featured a dry-fire mechanism for practicing without damaging the firing pin or the edge of the chamber. There was a limited production left-hand model available, but this would not really bring a premium unless the buyer was left-handed. This is not a collector's item as such but would be used by most potential purchasers. It was imported between 1981 and 1986.

| Exc. | V.G. | Good | Fair | Poor |
|------|------|------|------|------|
| 1200 | 1050 | 900 | 700 | 500 |

## AGUIRRE
### Eibar, Spain

### Basculant

Another poor-quality Eibar semi-auto. A 6.35mm copy of Browning's 1906 blowback design.

| Exc. | V.G. | Good | Fair | Poor |
|------|------|------|------|------|
| 150 | 125 | 100 | 75 | 45 |

## LeDragon

The same pistol as the Basculant with the slide marked "Cal. 6.35 Automatic Pistol LeDragon" and a stylized dragon molded into the grips.

| Exc. | V.G. | Good | Fair | Poor |
|------|------|------|------|------|
| 150 | 125 | 100 | 75 | 45 |

## AIR MATCH
### Importer: Kendall International
### Paris, Kentucky

**Air Match 500**

This was a high-quality, single-shot target pistol that was chambered for the .22 rimfire cartridges. It featured adjustable target sights and a 10.5" barrel, with an adjustable counterweight on the front. The finish was blued and it had walnut target grips. This pistol was imported between 1984 and 1986.

| Exc. | V.G. | Good | Fair | Poor |
|------|------|------|------|------|
| 700 | 575 | 475 | 400 | 300 |

## AJAX ARMY
### Unknown

**Single Action**

This was a spur-trigger, single-action, solid-frame revolver that was chambered for the .44 rimfire cartridge. It had a 7" barrel and was blued with walnut grips. It was manufactured in the 1880's.

| Exc. | V.G. | Good | Fair | Poor |
|------|------|------|------|------|
| 575 | 500 | 425 | 310 | 175 |

## ALAMO RANGER
### Spain

**Alamo Ranger**

This is a typical low-quality, early Spanish copy of the Colt Police Positive. It was chambered for the .38 cal. centerfire, and the cylinder held 6 shots. The finish was blued, and the grips were checkered hard rubber. The maker of this pistol is unknown.

| Exc. | V.G. | Good | Fair | Poor |
|------|------|------|------|------|
| 150 | 125 | 100 | 75 | 45 |

## ALASKA
### SEE--Hood Firearms Co.
### Norwich, Connecticut

## ALDAZABAL
### Eibar, Spain
### Aldazabal, Leturiondo & CIA.

**Aldazabal**

This was another typical low-quality, "Eibar"-type semi-automatic. It was a Browning blowback copy, chambered for the 7.65mm cartridge. It had a 7-shot detachable magazine and blued finish with checkered wood grips. This company ceased production before the Spanish Civil War.

| Exc. | V.G. | Good | Fair | Poor |
|------|------|------|------|------|
| 175 | 135 | 95 | 65 | 40 |

## ALERT
### SEE--Hood Firearms Co.
### Norwich, Connecticut

## ALEXIA
### SEE--Hopkins & Allen
### Norwich, Connecticut

## ALFA
### SEE--Armero Especialistas Reunides
### Eibar, Spain

## ALKARTASUNA FABRICA DE ARMAS
### Guernica, Spain

This company began production during the First World War to help Gabilondo y Urresti supply sidearms to the French. After the hostilities ceased, they continued to produce firearms under their own name. They manufactured the typical poor-quality, unimaginative weapons usually associated with Spain during this era. They produced a number of variations in both 6.35mm and 7.65mm marked "Alkar." Collector interest is very thin. The factory burned down in 1920, and by 1922 business had totally ceased.

| Exc. | V.G. | Good | Fair | Poor |
|------|------|------|------|------|
| 200 | 175 | 135 | 95 | 50 |

## ALLEN, ETHAN
### Grafton, Massachusetts

The company was founded by Ethan Allen in the early 1800's. It became a prolific gunmaking firm that evolved from Ethan Allen to Allen & Thurber, as well as the Allen & Wheelock Company. It was located in Norwich, Connecticut, and Worchester, Massachusetts, as well as Grafton. It eventually became the Forehand & Wadsworth Company in 1871 after the death of Ethan Allen. There were many and varied firearms produced under all of the headings described above. If one desires to collect Ethan Allen firearms, it would be advisable to educate oneself, as there are a number of fine publications available on the subject. The basic models and their values are as follows:

**First Model Pocket Rifle**

This firearm was manufactured by Ethan Allen in Grafton, Massachusetts. It was a bootleg-type, under-hammer, single-shot pistol chambered for .31 percussion. Larger-caliber versions have also been noted. It had barrel lengths from 5" to 9" that were part-octagon in configuration. It had iron mountings and was blued with walnut grips. The barrel was marked, "E. Allen/Grafton/Mass." as well as "Pocket Rifle/Cast Steel/ Warranted." There were approximately 2,000 manufactured from 1831 to 1842.

| Exc. | V.G. | Good | Fair | Poor |
|------|------|------|------|------|
| 500 | 375 | 275 | 200 | 175 |

**Second Model Pocket Rifle**

This is simply a rounded-frame, round-grip version of the First Model.

| Exc. | V.G. | Good | Fair | Poor |
|------|------|------|------|------|
| 750 | 575 | 375 | 275 | 225 |

**Bar Hammer Pistol**

This was a double-action pistol with a top-mounted bar hammer. It was chambered for .28 to .36 caliber percussion. The half-octagon barrels were from 2" to 10" in length. They screwed out of the frame so it was possible to breech load them. The finish was blued with rounded walnut grips. They were marked, "Allen & Thurber/Grafton Mass." There were approximately 2,000 manufactured between the early 1830's and 1860.

| Exc. | V.G. | Good | Fair | Poor |
|------|------|------|------|------|
| 900  | 750  | 550  | 425  | 350  |

**Tube Hammer Pistol**

This version was similar to the Bar Hammer with a curved hammer without a spur. There were only a few hundred manufactured between the early 1830's and the early 1840's.

| Exc. | V.G. | Good | Fair | Poor |
|------|------|------|------|------|
| 1000 | 850  | 675  | 525  | 400  |

**Side Hammer Pistol**

This was a single-shot, target-type pistol that was chambered for .34, .41, and .45 caliber percussion. It had a part-octagon barrel that was from 6" to 10" in length. There was a wooden ramrod mounted under the barrel. This model had a good-quality rear sight that was adjustable. The ornate triggerguard had a graceful spur at its rear. The finish was blued with a rounded walnut grip. The barrel was marked, "Allen & Thurber, Worchester." There were approximately 300 manufactured in the late 1840's and early 1850's.

| Exc. | V.G. | Good | Fair | Poor |
|------|------|------|------|------|
| 500  | 375  | 300  | 225  | 175  |

**Center Hammer Pistol**

This model was a single action chambered for .34, .36, or .44 percussion. It had a half-octagon barrel from 4" to 12" in length. It had a centrally mounted hammer that was offset to the right side to allow for sighting the pistol. The finish was blued with walnut grips. It was marked, "Allen & Thurber, Allen Thurber & Company." Some specimens are marked, "Allen & Wheelock." There were several thousand manufactured between the late 1840's and 1860.

| Exc. | V.G. | Good | Fair | Poor |
|------|------|------|------|------|
| 350  | 250  | 200  | 150  | 125  |

**Double Barrel Pistol**

This was a SxS, double-barrel pistol with a single trigger. It was chambered for .36 caliber percussion with 3" to 6" round barrels. The finish was blued with walnut grips. Examples with a ramrod mounted under the barrel have been noted. The flute between the barrels was marked, "Allen & Thurber," "Allen Thurber & Company," or "Allen & Wheelock." There were approximately 1,000 manufactured in the 1850's.

| Exc. | V.G. | Good | Fair | Poor |
|------|------|------|------|------|
| 375  | 275  | 225  | 175  | 135  |

**Allen & Wheelock Center Hammer Pistol**

This was a single-action pocket pistol chambered for .31 to .38 caliber percussion. It had octagon barrels from 3" to 6" in length. The finish was blued with square-butt walnut grips. The barrel was marked, "Allen & Wheelock." There were approximately 500 manufactured between 1858 and 1865.

| Exc. | V.G. | Good | Fair | Poor |
|------|------|------|------|------|
| 350  | 300  | 250  | 185  | 145  |

**Allen Thurber & Company Target Pistol**

This was a deluxe, single-action target pistol that was chambered for .31 or .36 caliber percussion. It had a heavy, octagon barrel that was from 11" to 16" in length. There was a wooden ramrod mounted underneath the barrel. The mountings were of German silver, and there was a detachable walnut stock with a deluxe, engraved patchbox. This weapon was engraved, and the barrel was marked, "Allen Thurber & Co/Worchester/Cast Steel." This firearm was furnished in a fitted case with the stock, false muzzle, and various accessories. It was considered to be a very high grade target pistol in its era. The values shown are for a complete-cased outfit. There were very few manufactured in the 1850's.

| Exc. | V.G. | Good | Fair | Poor |
|------|------|------|------|------|
| 4000 | 3450 | 2800 | 1850 | 900  |

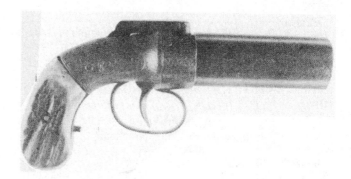

**Ethan Allen Pepperboxes**

During the period from the early 1830's to the 1860's, this company manufactured over 50 different variations of the revolving, pepperbox-type pistol. They were commercially quite successful and actually competed successfully with the Colt revolving handguns for more than a decade. They were widely used throughout the United States, as well as in Mexico, and during our Civil War. They are widely collectible because of the number of variations that exist. The potential collector should avail himself of the information available on the subject. These pepperboxes can be divided into three categories.

No. 1--Manufactured from the 1830's until 1842, at Grafton, Massachusetts.

No. 2--Manufactured from 1842 to 1847, at Norwich, Connecticut.

No. 3--Manufactured from 1847 to 1865, at Worchester, Massachusetts.

There are a number of subdivisions among these three basic groups that would pertain to trigger type, size, barrel length etc. It would be impossible to cover all 50 of these variations in a text of this type. We strongly suggest that qualified, individual appraisal be secured if contemplating a transaction. The values of these pepperbox pistols in excellent condition would be between $500 and $2,800.

**Large Frame Pocket Revolver**

This was a double-action pocket revolver that was chambered for .34 caliber percussion. It had an octagon barrel from 3" to 5" in length. There were no sights. The 5-shot, unfluted cylinder was game scene-engraved. The finish was blued with rounded walnut grips. It had a bar-type hammer. This was the first conventional revolver manufactured by this company, and it was directly influenced by the pepperbox pistol for which Ethan Allen had become famous. It was marked, "Allen & Wheelock" as well as "Patented April 16, 1845." There were approximately 1,500 manufactured between 1857 and 1860.

| Exc. | V.G. | Good | Fair | Poor |
|------|------|------|------|------|
| 500  | 425  | 285  | 210  | 165  |

**Small Frame Pocket Revolver**

This version was similar to the Large Frame Pocket Revolver except chambered for .31 caliber percussion, with a 2" to 3.5" octagon barrel. It was slightly smaller in size, finished and marked the same. There were approximately 1,000 made between 1858 and 1860.

| Exc. | V.G. | Good | Fair | Poor |
|------|------|------|------|------|
| 400  | 325  | 195  | 150  | 110  |

**Side Hammer Belt Revolver**

This was a single-action revolver chambered for .34 caliber percussion. It had an octagon barrel from 3" to 7.5" in length. It featured a hammer that was mounted on the right side of the frame and a 5-shot, engraved, unfluted cylinder. The cylinder access pin is inserted from the rear of the weapon. The finish is blued with a case-colored hammer and triggerguard and flared-butt walnut grips. It is marked, "Allen & Wheelock." There were two basic types. Values for the early model, of which 100 were manufactured between 1858 and 1861, are as follows:

| Exc. | V.G. | Good | Fair | Poor |
|------|------|------|------|------|
| 800 | 700 | 575 | 400 | 285 |

## Standard Model

The second type was the Standard Model, with a spring-loaded catch on the triggerguard as opposed to a friction catch on the early model. There were approximately 1,000 manufactured between 1858 and 1861.

| Exc. | V.G. | Good | Fair | Poor |
|------|------|------|------|------|
| 550 | 475 | 400 | 325 | 200 |

## Sidehammer Pocket Revolver

This version was chambered for .28 caliber percussion and had a 2" to 5" octagon barrel. The frame was slightly smaller than the belt model.

### Early Production, 100 Manufactured

| Exc. | V.G. | Good | Fair | Poor |
|------|------|------|------|------|
| 700 | 525 | 450 | 375 | 225 |

### Standard Production, 1,000 Manufactured

| Exc. | V.G. | Good | Fair | Poor |
|------|------|------|------|------|
| 500 | 400 | 300 | 225 | 190 |

## Sidehammer Navy Revolver

This was a large-frame, military-type revolver that was similar to the Sidehammer Belt Model, chambered for .36 caliber percussion. It features an octagon, 5.5" to 8" barrel with a 6-shot, engraved cylinder. There was an early-production type with a friction catch on the triggerguard. There were approximately 100 manufactured between 1858 and 1861.

| Exc. | V.G. | Good | Fair | Poor |
|------|------|------|------|------|
| 1250 | 1000 | 800 | 500 | 350 |

### Standard Model, 1,000 Manufactured

| Exc. | V.G. | Good | Fair | Poor |
|------|------|------|------|------|
| 1000 | 850 | 600 | 325 | 250 |

## Center Hammer Army Revolver

This was a large, military-type, single-action revolver that was chambered for .44 caliber percussion. It had a 7.5", half-octagon barrel and a 6-shot, unfluted cylinder. The hammer was mounted in the center of the frame. The finish was blued with a case-colored hammer and triggerguard and walnut grips. The barrel was marked, "Allen & Wheelock. Worchester, Mass. U.S./Allen's Pt's. Jan. 13, 1857. Dec. 15, 1857, Sept. 7, 1858." There were approximately 700 manufactured between 1861 and 1862.

| Exc. | V.G. | Good | Fair | Poor |
|------|------|------|------|------|
| 1000 | 800 | 650 | 425 | 300 |

## Center Hammer Navy Revolver

This model was similar to the Army Revolver except chambered for .36 caliber percussion with a 7.5", full-octagon barrel. Examples have been noted with 5", 6", or 8" barrels. Otherwise, it was similar to the Army model.

| Exc. | V.G. | Good | Fair | Poor |
|------|------|------|------|------|
| 1100 | 900 | 750 | 525 | 425 |

## Center Hammer Percussion Revolver

This was a single-action revolver chambered for .36 caliber percussion. It had an octagonal, 3" or 4" barrel with a 6-shot, unfluted cylinder. The finish was blued with walnut grips. This model supposedly was made for the Providence, Rhode Island, Police Department and has become commonly referred to as the "Providence Police Model." There were approximately 700 manufactured between 1858 and 1862.

| Exc. | V.G. | Good | Fair | Poor |
|------|------|------|------|------|
| 600 | 500 | 400 | 300 | 200 |

## Lipfire Army Revolver

This was a large, military-type, single-action revolver that was chambered for the .44 lipfire cartridge. It had a 7.5", half-octagon barrel with a 6-shot, unfluted cylinder that had notches at its rear for the cartridge lips. The finish was blued with a case-colored hammer and triggerguard and square-butt walnut grips. The barrel was marked, "Allen & Wheelock, Worchester,

Mass." It resembled the Center Hammer Percussion Army Revolver. There were two basic variations, with a total of 250 manufactured in the early 1860's.

### Early Model Top Hinged Loading Gate

| Exc. | V.G. | Good | Fair | Poor |
|------|------|------|------|------|
| 900 | 800 | 625 | 500 | 350 |

### Late Model Bottom Hinged Loading Gate

| Exc. | V.G. | Good | Fair | Poor |
|------|------|------|------|------|
| 825 | 700 | 575 | 450 | 300 |

## Lipfire Navy Revolver

This version was similar to the Army model, except chambered for the .36 lipfire cartridge, with an octagonal, 4", 5", 6", 7.5", or 8" barrel. There were approximately 500 manufactured in the 1860's.

| Exc. | V.G. | Good | Fair | Poor |
|------|------|------|------|------|
| 900 | 800 | 675 | 450 | 350 |

## Lipfire Pocket Revolver

This was a smaller version chambered for the .32 lipfire cartridge, with an octagonal, 4", 5", or 6" barrel. There were approximately 200 manufactured in the early 1860's.

| Exc. | V.G. | Good | Fair | Poor |
|------|------|------|------|------|
| 750 | 625 | 500 | 400 | 300 |

*Allen & Wheelock .32 Pocket Model*

## .32 Sidehammer Rimfire Revolver

This was a single-action, spur-trigger, pocket revolver chambered for the .32-caliber rimfire cartridge. It had octagonal barrels from 3" to 5" in length. The finish was blued with flared-butt, walnut grips. It was marked, "Allen & Wheelock Worchester, Mass." There were three variations with a total of approximately 1,000 manufactured between 1859 and 1862.

### First Model--Rounded Top Strap

| Exc. | V.G. | Good | Fair | Poor |
|------|------|------|------|------|
| 500 | 425 | 350 | 265 | 200 |

### Second Model--July 3, 1860 Marked on Frame

| Exc. | V.G. | Good | Fair | Poor |
|------|------|------|------|------|
| 450 | 375 | 300 | 225 | 185 |

### Third Model--1858 and 1861 Patent Dates

| Exc. | V.G. | Good | Fair | Poor |
|------|------|------|------|------|
| 350 | 300 | 225 | 150 | 110 |

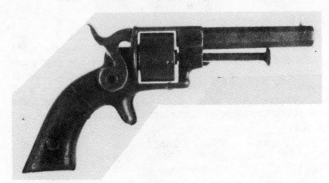

## .22 Sidehammer Rimfire Revolver

This is a smaller version of the .32 revolver, chambered for the

.22 rimfire cartridge. It has octagonal barrels from 2.25" to 4" in length. It has a 7-shot, unfluted cylinder. There were approximately 1,500 manufactured between 1858 and 1862. There were many variations.

### Early Model First Issue--Access Pin Enters from Rear

| Exc. | V.G. | Good | Fair | Poor |
|------|------|------|------|------|
| 450 | 375 | 300 | 200 | 125 |

### Second Issue--Access Pin Enters from Front

| Exc. | V.G. | Good | Fair | Poor |
|------|------|------|------|------|
| 475 | 400 | 325 | 225 | 150 |

### Third Issue--Separate Rear Sight

| Exc. | V.G. | Good | Fair | Poor |
|------|------|------|------|------|
| 650 | 525 | 425 | 300 | 200 |

### Fourth to Eighth Issue--Very Similar, Values the Same

| Exc. | V.G. | Good | Fair | Poor |
|------|------|------|------|------|
| 350 | 300 | 250 | 175 | 100 |

### Single Shot Center Hammer

This was a single-shot derringer-type pistol that was chambered for the .22-caliber rimfire cartridge. It had part-octagon barrels from 2" to 5.5" in length that swung to the right side for loading. Some had automatic ejectors; others did not. The frame was either brass or iron with birdshead or squared-butt walnut grips. It was marked, "Allen & Wheelock" or "E. Allen & Co." There were very few manufactured in the early 1860's.

### Early Issue

This has a full-length, octagon barrel and a round, iron frame. It is rarely encountered.

| Exc. | V.G. | Good | Fair | Poor |
|------|------|------|------|------|
| 425 | 375 | 300 | 225 | 150 |

### Standard Issue--Squared Butt or Birdshead

| Exc. | V.G. | Good | Fair | Poor |
|------|------|------|------|------|
| 375 | 300 | 250 | 200 | 125 |

### .32 Single Shot Center Hammer

This is a larger-frame pocket pistol chambered for the .32 rimfire cartridge. It has a part-octagon or full-octagon barrel of 4" or 5" in length. It swung to the right side for loading. Otherwise, this model was similar to the .22-caliber version.

| Exc. | V.G. | Good | Fair | Poor |
|------|------|------|------|------|
| 400 | 325 | 275 | 200 | 150 |

### Vest Pocket Derringer

This was a small pocket pistol chambered for the .22 rimfire cartridge. It had a 2", part-octagon barrel that swung to the righthand side for loading. The cartridges were manually extracted. It featured a brass frame with a blued or plated barrel and walnut, birdshead grips. The barrel was marked, "Allen & Co. Makers." This was an extremely small firearm, and there were approximately 200 manufactured between 1869 and 1871.

| Exc. | V.G. | Good | Fair | Poor |
|------|------|------|------|------|
| 350 | 300 | 250 | 200 | 150 |

### .32 Derringer

This model was similar to the Vest Pocket Version, larger in size, and chambered for the .32 rimfire cartridge. It had a part-octagon barrel from 2" to 4" in length that swung to the right for

loading. This version featured an automatic extractor. The barrel was marked, "E. Allen & Co Worchester Mass." This was a very rare firearm, made between 1865 and 1871.

| Exc. | V.G. | Good | Fair | Poor |
|------|------|------|------|------|
| 800 | 725 | 600 | 450 | 350 |

### .41 Derringer

This version was the same size and configuration as the .32-caliber model except it was chambered for the .41 rimfire cartridge with barrel lengths of 2.5" to 2.75" in length. The markings were the same. There were approximately 100 manufactured between 1865 and 1871.

| Exc. | V.G. | Good | Fair | Poor |
|------|------|------|------|------|
| 600 | 525 | 400 | 325 | 250 |

### Center Hammer Muzzle-loading Rifle

This was a single-shot rifle chambered for .44 caliber percussion. It had a 36" round barrel with an octagonal breech. It had a center-mounted hammer that was offset to the right for sighting. It had iron mountings. The finish was browned with a case-colored lock. There was a ramrod mounted under the barrel. It had a walnut buttstock with a crescent buttplate and no forearm. There were approximately 100 manufactured in the 1850's.

| Exc. | V.G. | Good | Fair | Poor |
|------|------|------|------|------|
| 800 | 725 | 600 | 375 | 300 |

### Sidehammer Muzzle-loading Rifle

This rifle is similar to the Center Hammer model, with the hammer mounted on the right side of the lock. It was chambered for .38 caliber percussion, with an octagon barrel from 28" to 32" in length. It is occasionally found with a patchbox. The barrel is browned with a case-colored lock and a walnut stock with crescent buttplate. There were several hundred manufactured from the early 1840's to the 1860's.

| Exc. | V.G. | Good | Fair | Poor |
|------|------|------|------|------|
| 950 | 875 | 750 | 500 | 350 |

### Combination Gun

This was either an Over/Under or SxS rifle chambered for 12 gauge and .38 caliber percussion. The barrels were from 28" to 34" in length. It had two hammers and double triggers with a ramrod mounted either beneath or on the right side of the barrels. The finish was browned with a walnut stock. Examples with a patchbox have been noted. Production was very limited, with the Over/Under versions worth approximately 10 percent more than the SxS values given. They were manufactured between the 1840's and the 1860's.

| Exc. | V.G. | Good | Fair | Poor |
|------|------|------|------|------|
| 1500 | 1350 | 1000 | 750 | 600 |

### Sidehammer Breech-loading Rifle

This was a unique rifle chambered for .36 to .50 caliber percussion. It was offered with various-length, part-octagon barrels. It had an unusual breech mechanism that was activated by a rotating lever which resembled a water faucet. The barrel was browned with a case-colored lock and a walnut stock. It was marked, "Allen & Wheelock/ Allen's Patent July 3, 1855." There were approximately 500 manufactured between 1855 and 1860.

| Exc. | V.G. | Good | Fair | Poor |
|------|------|------|------|------|
| 900 | 775 | 600 | 375 | 300 |

### Drop Breech Rifle

This single-shot rifle was chambered for the .22 through the .44 rimfire cartridges. It had a part-octagon barrel from 23" to 28" in length. The breech was activated by the combination triggerguard action lever. Opening the breech automatically ejected the empty cartridge. The external hammer was manually cocked, and it featured an adjustable sight. The barrel was blued with a case-colored frame and a walnut stock. It was marked, "Allen & Wheelock/ Allen's Pat. Sept. 18, 1860." There were approximately 2,000 manufactured between 1860 and 1871.

| Exc. | V.G. | Good | Fair | Poor |
|---|---|---|---|---|
| 400 | 325 | 250 | 175 | 135 |

### Lipfire Revolving Rifle
This was a six-shot, cylinder-type rifle chambered for the .44-caliber lipfire cartridge. It had an unfluted cylinder with slots at its rear to allow for the cartridge lips. The round barrels were 26" to 28" in length with an octagon breech. The finish was blued with a case-colored frame and a walnut buttstock. This model was not marked with the maker's name. There were approximately 100 manufactured between 1861 and 1863.

| Exc. | V.G. | Good | Fair | Poor |
|---|---|---|---|---|
| 9500 | 8750 | 7000 | 5000 | 3250 |

### Double Barrel Shotgun
This was a SxS gun chambered for 10 or 12 gauge. The barrel length was 28". It was loaded by means of a trapdoor-type breech that had a lever handle. The finish was blued with checkered walnut stock. There were a few hundred manufactured between 1865 and 1871.

| Exc. | V.G. | Good | Fair | Poor |
|---|---|---|---|---|
| 650 | 575 | 450 | 300 | 225 |

## ALLEN & THURBER
### SEE--Ethan Allen

## ALLEN & WHEELOCK
### SEE--Ethan Allen

## ALLEN FIREARMS
### Santa Fe, New Mexico
### SEE--Aldo Uberti

## ALL RIGHT F. A. CO.
### Lawrence, Massachusetts

### Little All Right Palm Pistol
This squeezer-type pocket pistol was invented by E. Boardman and A. Peavy in 1876. It was made in .22 cal. and had a 5-shot cylinder with a 1-5/8" or 2-3/8" barrel. The barrel is octagonal with a tube on top of it which houses the sliding trigger. The finish is nickel. The black hard rubber grips have "Little All Right" & "All Right Firearms Co., Manufacturers Lawrence, Mass. U.S.A." molded into them. There were several hundred produced in the late 1870's.

| Exc. | V.G. | Good | Fair | Poor |
|---|---|---|---|---|
| 900 | 800 | 650 | 500 | 400 |

## ALPHA ARMS CO.
### Flower Mound, Texas
This company produced high-grade bolt-action rifles on a semi-custom basis. They manufactured a number of standard models but offered many options at additional cost. Some of these options were custom sights and finishes and an octagonal barrel. These extra features would add to the value of the models listed. This company operated from 1983 until 1987.

### Alpha Jaguar Grade I
This model was built on a Mauser-type action with barrel lengths from 20" to 24". It was chambered for most calibers between .222 Rem. and .338 Win. Mag. The stock was made from a synthetic laminated material that the company called Alphawood. This model was introduced in 1987 and only produced that year.

| Exc. | V.G. | Good | Fair | Poor |
|---|---|---|---|---|
| 900 | 750 | 550 | 425 | 325 |

### Jaguar Grade II
This model is similar to the Grade I with a Douglas Premium barrel.

| Exc. | V.G. | Good | Fair | Poor |
|---|---|---|---|---|
| 1000 | 850 | 650 | 525 | 400 |

### Jaguar Grade III
This model has the Douglas barrel plus a hand-honed trigger and action and a three-position safety like the Winchester Model 70.

| Exc. | V.G. | Good | Fair | Poor |
|---|---|---|---|---|
| 1200 | 1000 | 850 | 700 | 500 |

### Jaguar Grade IV
This model has all the features of the Grade III with a specially lightened action and sling-swivel studs.

| Exc. | V.G. | Good | Fair | Poor |
|---|---|---|---|---|
| 1300 | 1100 | 950 | 800 | 600 |

### Alpha Grand Slam
This model features the same high quality as the Jaguar models and is available in a lefthand model. It has a fluted bolt, laminated stock, and a matte blue finish.

| Exc. | V.G. | Good | Fair | Poor |
|---|---|---|---|---|
| 1200 | 1000 | 850 | 700 | 500 |

### Alpha Custom
This model is similar to the Grand Slam with a select grade stock.

| Exc. | V.G. | Good | Fair | Poor |
|---|---|---|---|---|
| 1500 | 1275 | 1000 | 750 | 500 |

### Alpha Alaskan
This model is similar to the Grand Slam but chambered for the .308 Win., .350 Rem.Mag., .358 Win. and the .458 Win. Mag. It features all stainless steel construction.

| Exc. | V.G. | Good | Fair | Poor |
|---|---|---|---|---|
| 1500 | 1275 | 1000 | 750 | 500 |

### Alpha Big - Five
This model is similar to the Jaguar Grade IV chambered for the .300 Win Mag., .375 H&H Mag. and the .458 Win. Mag. It had a reinforced through-bolt stock to accommodate the recoil of the larger caliber cartridges for which it was chambered. It also had a decelerator recoil pad. This model was manufactured in 1987 only.

| Exc. | V.G. | Good | Fair | Poor |
|---|---|---|---|---|
| 1600 | 1375 | 1100 | 850 | 600 |

## ALSOP, C.R.
### Middletown, Connecticut
The Alsop Company manufactured revolvers during 1862 and 1863. They made two basic models, the Navy and the Pocket model. Some collectors consider the Alsop to be a secondary U.S. martial handgun, but no verifying government contracts are known to exist.

### First Model Navy Revolver
A .36 cal. revolver with a 3.5", 4.5", 5.5", or 6.5" barrel length and a 5-shot cylinder. It has a blued finish, wood grips, and a peculiar hump in its backstrap. The first model has a safety device which blocks the spur trigger. This device is found on serial numbers 1-100. Markings are as follows: "C.R. Alsop Middletown, Conn. 1860 & 1861" on the barrel. The cylinder is marked "C.R. Alsop" & Nov.26th, 1861"; the sideplate, "Patented Jan. 21st,1862."

| Exc. | V.G. | Good | Fair | Poor |
|---|---|---|---|---|
| 1750 | 1575 | 1300 | 1000 | 800 |

### Standard Model Navy Revolver
Exactly the same as the First Model without the safety device. They are serial numbered 101 to 300.

| Exc. | V.G. | Good | Fair | Poor |
|---|---|---|---|---|
| 1500 | 1375 | 1100 | 800 | 600 |

**Pocket Model Revolver**
A .31 cal. 5-shot revolver with spur trigger, 4" round barrel, blued finish, and wood grips. It is very similar in appearance to the Navy model but smaller in size. It is marked "C.R. Alsop Middletown, Conn. 1860 & 1861" on the barrel. The cylinder is marked "C.R. Alsop Nov. 26th, 1861." They are serial numbered 1-300.

| Exc. | V.G. | Good | Fair | Poor |
|------|------|------|------|------|
| 850 | 725 | 600 | 450 | 350 |

## AMERICAN ARMS
### Garden Grove, California

**Eagle .380**
This pistol was a stainless-steel copy of the Walther PPKS. It was a semi-auto blowback that was chambered for the .380 ACP. It was double-action and had a 3.25" barrel and a 6-shot detachable magazine. An optional feature was a black teflon finish that would increase the value by 10 percent. This company ceased production in 1985.

| Exc. | V.G. | Good | Fair | Poor |
|------|------|------|------|------|
| 275 | 225 | 195 | 150 | 125 |

## AMERICAN ARMS CO.
### Boston, Massachusetts

This company manufactured a rather unique two-barrel derringer-style pocket pistol. The barrels were manually rotated to load and fire the weapon. The pistol had a nickel-plated brass frame, blued barrels, and walnut grips. The markings were as follows: "American Arms Co. Boston, Mass." on one barrel and "Pat. Oct. 31,1865" on the other barrel. There were approximately 2,000-3,000 produced between 1866 and 1878.

**Combination .22 cal. R.F. and .32 cal. R.F.**
A two-caliber combination with 3" barrel, square butt only. The most common variation.

| Exc. | V.G. | Good | Fair | Poor |
|------|------|------|------|------|
| 500 | 425 | 325 | 265 | 200 |

**.32 cal. R.F., both barrels**
3" barrel with square butt.

| Exc. | V.G. | Good | Fair | Poor |
|------|------|------|------|------|
| 600 | 525 | 425 | 350 | 265 |

**.32 cal. R.F. both barrels**
2-5/8" barrel with birdshead grips.

| Exc. | V.G. | Good | Fair | Poor |
|------|------|------|------|------|
| 625 | 550 | 450 | 375 | 295 |

**.38 cal. R.F. both barrels**
2-5/8" barrel with birdshead grips. A very rare variation.

| Exc. | V.G. | Good | Fair | Poor |
|------|------|------|------|------|
| 750 | 675 | 525 | 450 | 325 |

**.41 cal. R.F. both barrels**
2-5/8" barrel with square butt only.

| Exc. | V.G. | Good | Fair | Poor |
|------|------|------|------|------|
| 800 | 700 | 600 | 500 | 400 |

## AMERICAN ARMS CO.
### Boston, Massachusetts

This company manufactured top break revolvers during the late 1800's and early 1900's.

**Spur Trigger - Single Action Revolver**
These revolvers were made in .38 cal. only. They were nickel plated with hard rubber grips and were marked "American Arms Company Boston, Mass."

| Exc. | V.G. | Good | Fair | Poor |
|------|------|------|------|------|
| 200 | 175 | 125 | 65 | 45 |

**Standard Trigger - Double Action Revolver**
The same as above model except with standard trigger and triggerguard--available in .32 cal. as well as .38 cal.

| Exc. | V.G. | Good | Fair | Poor |
|------|------|------|------|------|
| 200 | 175 | 125 | 65 | 45 |

**Concealed Hammer 1886 Model**
A unique design, this .32 cal. centerfire revolver has a 3.25" ribbed barrel, fluted cylinder, nickel finish, and hard rubber grips with logo. It has an adjustable single or double stage trigger pull and several odd safety devices. It is marked "American Arms Co. Boston/Pat. May 25, 1886." The top strap is marked "Pat. Pending."

| Exc. | V.G. | Good | Fair | Poor |
|------|------|------|------|------|
| 225 | 200 | 150 | 110 | 75 |

## AMERICAN ARMS, INC.
### No. Kansas City, Missouri

This company is basically an importer of firearms: shotguns from Spain, rifles from Yugoslavia, and handguns from Germany and Yugoslavia. They also manufacture in the U.S.A. There are certain rifles that they are no longer allowed to import because of the Bush administration's ban on foreign semi-automatic rifles. These weapons are listed for reference but are not priced due to the extreme fluctuations in values as this is written.

**Shotguns Side X Side**
**Gentry - York**
These two designations cover the same model. Prior to 1988 this model was called the York. In 1988 the receiver was case-colored and the designation was changed to the Gentry. This model was chambered for 12, 20, and 28 gauge and .410. It had chrome-lined barrels from 26" -30" in length, double triggers, 3" chambers, and automatic ejectors. The boxlock action featured scroll engraving, and the walnut stock was hand-checkered. It was introduced in 1986.

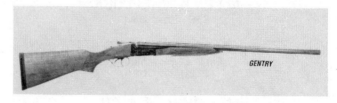

| NIB | Exc. | V.G. | Good | Fair | Poor |
|-----|------|------|------|------|------|
| 469 | 425 | 375 | 300 | 210 | 165 |

**Shogun**
This was a 10 gauge with 3.5" chambers and 32" barrels. It featured a scroll-engraved, chromed boxlock action and double triggers. It was imported from Spain in 1986 only.

| Exc. | V.G. | Good | Fair | Poor |
|------|------|------|------|------|
| 450 | 375 | 285 | 200 | 150 |

**Brittany**
This model was chambered for 12 and 20 gauge with 27" or 25" barrels with screw-in choke tubes. It had a solid matted rib and a case-colored, engraved boxlock action. Automatic ejectors and a single selective trigger were standard on this model as was a hand-checkered, walnut, straight-grip stock with semi-beavertail forend. This model was introduced in 1989.

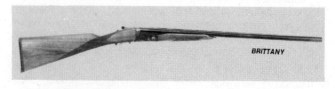

| NIB | Exc. | V.G. | Good | Fair | Poor |
|-----|------|------|------|------|------|
| 650 | 600 | 525 | 450 | 375 | 275 |

**Turkey Special**
This is a utilitarian model designed to be an effective turkey hunting tool. It is chambered for the Magnum 10 and 12 gauges and has 26" barrels. The finish is parkerized, and the

stock is also finished in a non-glare matte. Sling- swivel studs and a recoil pad are standard. This model was introduced in 1987.

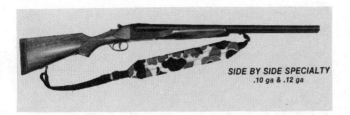

SIDE BY SIDE SPECIALTY
.10 ga & .12 ga

| NIB | Exc. | V.G. | Good | Fair | Poor |
| --- | --- | --- | --- | --- | --- |
| 560 | 500 | 425 | 350 | 275 | 200 |

**Waterfowl Special**

This model is similar to the Turkey Special but chambered for the 10 gauge only. It is furnished with a camouflaged sling. It was introduced in 1987.

| NIB | Exc. | V.G. | Good | Fair | Poor |
| --- | --- | --- | --- | --- | --- |
| 610 | 575 | 450 | 375 | 275 | 200 |

**Derby**

This model is chambered for the 12, 20, and 28 gauge and the .410. It has 26" or 28" barrels with 3" chambers and automatic ejectors. Either double or single-selective triggers are offered, and the sidelock action is scroll engraved and chromed. The checkered straight-grip stock and forearm are oil-finished. This model was introduced in 1986.

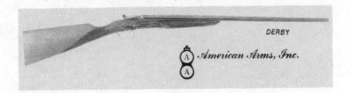

DERBY
American Arms, Inc.

| NIB | Exc. | V.G. | Good | Fair | Poor |
| --- | --- | --- | --- | --- | --- |
| 790 | 700 | 625 | 500 | 375 | 300 |

**Grulla #2**

This is the top-of-the-line model chambered for 12, 20 and 28 gauge and .410. The barrels are 26" or 28" with a concave rib. The hand-fitted full sidelock action is extensively engraved and case-colored. There are various chokes, double triggers, and automatic ejectors. The select walnut, straight-grip stock and splinter forend is hand-checkered and has a hand-rubbed oil finish. This model was introduced in 1989.

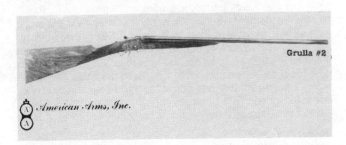

Grulla #2
American Arms, Inc.

| NIB | Exc. | V.G. | Good | Fair | Poor |
| --- | --- | --- | --- | --- | --- |
| 2100 | 1850 | 1650 | 1400 | 1000 | 750 |

**Shotguns Over/Under**

**F.S. 200**

This was a trap or skeet model that was chambered for 12 gauge only. It had 26" Skeet & Skeet barrels or 32" full choke barrels on the trap model. The barrels were separated and had a vent rib. The boxlock action had a Greener crossbolt and was either black or matte chrome-plated. It featured a single-selective trigger, automatic ejectors, and a checkered walnut

pistolgrip stock. The F.S. 200 was imported in 1986 and 1987 only.

| Exc. | V.G. | Good | Fair | Poor |
| --- | --- | --- | --- | --- |
| 675 | 575 | 465 | 350 | 275 |

**F.S. 300**

This model is similar to the F.S. 200 with lightly engraved side plates and a 30" barrel offered in the trap grade. It was imported in 1986 only.

| Exc. | V.G. | Good | Fair | Poor |
| --- | --- | --- | --- | --- |
| 800 | 675 | 565 | 450 | 400 |

**F.S. 400**

This model is similar to the F.S. 300 with an engraved, matte chrome-plated receiver. It was imported in 1986 only.

| Exc. | V.G. | Good | Fair | Poor |
| --- | --- | --- | --- | --- |
| 1100 | 950 | 800 | 650 | 475 |

**F.S. 500**

This model is similar to the F.S. 400 with the same general specifications. It was not imported after 1985.

| Exc. | V.G. | Good | Fair | Poor |
| --- | --- | --- | --- | --- |
| 1150 | 1000 | 850 | 700 | 500 |

**Waterfowl Special**

This model is chambered for the 12 gauge Magnum with 3.5" chambers. It has 28" barrels with screw-in choke tubes. There are automatic ejectors and a single-selective trigger. The finish is parkerized with a matte finished stock, sling swivels, and camouflaged sling and a recoil pad. It was introduced in 1987.

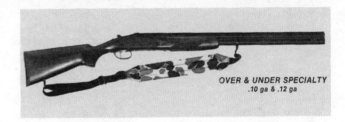

OVER & UNDER SPECIALTY
.10 ga & .12 ga

| NIB | Exc. | V.G. | Good | Fair | Poor |
| --- | --- | --- | --- | --- | --- |
| 610 | 575 | 500 | 425 | 350 | 275 |

**Waterfowl 10 Gauge**

This model is the same as the Waterfowl Special but is chambered for the 10 gauge Magnum with double triggers.

| NIB | Exc. | V.G. | Good | Fair | Poor |
| --- | --- | --- | --- | --- | --- |
| 830 | 775 | 700 | 625 | 550 | 450 |

**Turkey Special**

This model is similar to the Waterfowl Special 10 gauge with a 26" barrel with screw-in choke tubes.

| NIB | Exc. | V.G. | Good | Fair | Poor |
| --- | --- | --- | --- | --- | --- |
| 875 | 800 | 725 | 650 | 575 | 475 |

**Lince**

This model was chambered for the 12 and 20 gauge and had 26" or 28" barrels with 3" chambers and various chokes. The boxlock action had a Greener crossbolt and was either blued or polished and chrome-plated. The barrels were blued with a ventilated rib. It had a single-selective trigger and automatic ejectors. The Lince was imported in 1986 only.

| Exc. | V.G. | Good | Fair | Poor |
| --- | --- | --- | --- | --- |
| 500 | 425 | 350 | 300 | 225 |

**Silver Model**

This model was similar to the Lince with a plain, unengraved, brushed-chrome-finished receiver. It was imported in 1986 and 1987.

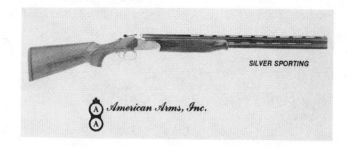

SILVER SPORTING

American Arms, Inc.

| Exc. | V.G. | Good | Fair | Poor |
|------|------|------|------|------|
| 500 | 425 | 350 | 300 | 225 |

**Silver I**

This model is similar to the Silver but is available in 28 gauge and .410, as well as 12 and 20 gauge. It also has a single-selective trigger, fixed chokes, extractors, and a recoil pad. It was introduced in 1987.

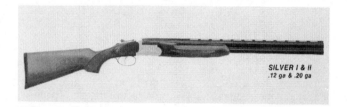

SILVER I & II
.12 ga & .20 ga

| NIB | Exc. | V.G. | Good | Fair | Poor |
|-----|------|------|------|------|------|
| 440 | 400 | 325 | 275 | 210 | 175 |

**Silver II**

This model is similar to the Silver II with screw-in choke tubes, automatic ejectors, and select walnut. It was introduced in 1987.

| NIB | Exc. | V.G. | Good | Fair | Poor |
|-----|------|------|------|------|------|
| 580 | 525 | 450 | 375 | 300 | 250 |

**Bristol**

This model is chambered for 12 and 20 gauge. It has various barrel lengths with a vent rib and screw-in choke tubes. The chambers are 3", and the chrome-finished action is a boxlock with Greener crossbolt and gamescene-engraved side plates. There are automatic ejectors and a single-selective trigger. It was introduced in 1986, and in 1989 the designation was changed to the Sterling.

| NIB | Exc. | V.G. | Good | Fair | Poor |
|-----|------|------|------|------|------|
| 825 | 750 | 675 | 500 | 400 | 300 |

**Sir**

This model was chambered for the 12 and 20 gauge with 3" chambers, various barrel lengths and chokings and a ventilated rib. The chrome-finished sidelock action has a Greener crossbolt and is engraved with a gamescene. There are automatic ejectors and a single-selective trigger. This model was imported in 1986.

| Exc. | V.G. | Good | Fair | Poor |
|------|------|------|------|------|
| 875 | 750 | 625 | 500 | 400 |

**Royal**

This model is chambered for the 12 and 20 gauge. It is manufactured in various barrel lengths and chokes with a vent rib and 3" chambers. The chrome-finished sidelock action has a Greener crossbolt and is profusely scroll-engraved. It has automatic ejectors and a single-selective trigger. The select pistolgrip walnut stock is hand-checkered and oil-finished. This model was imported in 1986 and 1987.

| Exc. | V.G. | Good | Fair | Poor |
|------|------|------|------|------|
| 1500 | 1275 | 1000 | 800 | 625 |

**Excelsior**

This model is similar to the Royal with extensive deep relief engraving and gold inlays. This model was imported in 1986 and 1987.

| Exc. | V.G. | Good | Fair | Poor |
|------|------|------|------|------|
| 1750 | 1500 | 1200 | 875 | 725 |

**Single Barrel Shotguns**
**AASB**

This is the standard single-barrel, break-open, hammerless shotgun. It is chambered for 12 and 20 gauge and .410. It has a 26" barrel with various chokes and 3" chambers. It has a pistol grip stock and a matte finish. It was introduced in 1988.

| NIB | Exc. | V.G. | Good | Fair | Poor |
|-----|------|------|------|------|------|
| 100 | 85 | 75 | 60 | 45 | 25 |

**Campers Special**

This model is similar to the standard model with a 21" barrel and a folding stock. It was introduced in 1988.

| NIB | Exc. | V.G. | Good | Fair | Poor |
|-----|------|------|------|------|------|
| 107 | 95 | 85 | 70 | 50 | 35 |

**Single Barrel Shotguns**
**Youth Model**

This Model is chambered for the 20 gauge and .410 and has a 12.5" stock with a recoil pad. It was introduced in 1989.

| NIB | Exc. | V.G. | Good | Fair | Poor |
|-----|------|------|------|------|------|
| 115 | 100 | 80 | 65 | 50 | 35 |

**Slugger**

This version has a 24" barrel with rifle sights. It is chambered for the 12 and 20 gauge and has a recoil pad.

| NIB | Exc. | V.G. | Good | Fair | Poor |
|-----|------|------|------|------|------|
| 115 | 100 | 80 | 65 | 50 | 35 |

**10 Gauge Model**

This Model is chambered for the 10 gauge 3.5" Magnum. It has a 32" full choke barrel and a recoil pad. This model was introduced in 1988.

| NIB | Exc. | V.G. | Good | Fair | Poor |
|-----|------|------|------|------|------|
| 150 | 135 | 100 | 85 | 60 | 45 |

**Combo Model**

This Model is similar in appearance to the other single-barrel models but is offered in an interchangeable-barreled rifle/shotgun combination--the 28" barreled .22 Hornet and the 12 Gauge, or the 26" barreled .22 l.r. and 20 Gauge. This Model was furnished with a fitted hard case to hold the interchangeable barrels. It was introduced in 1989.

| NIB | Exc. | V.G. | Good | Fair | Poor |
|-----|------|------|------|------|------|
| 235 | 200 | 175 | 145 | 110 | 75 |

**Rifles**
**Model ZCY .223**

This is a gas-operated, semi-automatic rifle that is chambered for the .223. It is the civilian version of the Yugoslavian Military rifle and was never actually imported --only advertised. This is another model that would have wildly fluctuating values; and if one were to be located for sale, it would be a market-will-bear situation. It is important to note that these inflated figures that have been attached to these "Assault" rifles are not true values and could cause serious grief to those who pay them should the market stabilize or ultimate sale of them be banned. These rifles are listed for reference purposes only. An independent appraisal should be secured if a transaction is contemplated.

**Model ZCY .308**

This is essentially the same rifle as the ZCY .223-- only it is chambered for the .308 cartridge. This Model was imported in 1988 only.

**AKY 39**

This is the semi-automatic version of the Soviet AK-47 as it is manufactured by Yugoslavia. It is offered with folding Tritium night sights and a wooden fixed stock. It was imported in 1988 and is now banned from further importation.

**AKF 39**

This is the same rifle as the AKY 39 with a metal folding stock.

## AKC 47
This is basically the same rifle as the AKY 39 without the Tritium night sights. Importation is no longer allowed.

## AKF 47
This is the same rifle as the AKC 47 with a metal folding stock.

## EXP-64 Survival Rifle
This model is a .22 caliber, semi-automatic takedown rifle. It is self-storing in a floating, oversized plastic stock. The rifle has a 21" barrel with open sights and a crossbolt safety. There is a 10 shot detachable magazine. Importation by American Arms began in 1989.

| NIB | Exc. | V.G. | Good | Fair | Poor |
|-----|------|------|------|------|------|
| 165 | 150  | 125  | 95   | 75   | 50   |

## SM-64 TD Sporter
This is a .22 l.r. semi-automatic with a takedown 21" barrel. It has adjustable sights and a checkered hardwood stock and forend. Importation commenced in 1989.

| NIB | Exc. | V.G. | Good | Fair | Poor |
|-----|------|------|------|------|------|
| 150 | 135  | 110  | 85   | 65   | 45   |

## Handguns

## Model TT Tokarev
This is the Yugoslavian version of the Soviet Tokarev chambered for 9mm Parabellum and with a safety added to make importation legal. It has a 4.5" barrel, 9-shot magazine and a blued finish with checkered plastic grips. Importation began in 1988.

| NIB | Exc. | V.G. | Good | Fair | Poor |
|-----|------|------|------|------|------|
| 290 | 265  | 225  | 175  | 140  | 100  |

## Model ZC-.380
This is a scaled-down version of the Tokarev that is chambered for the .380 ACP. It has a 3.5" barrel and holds 8 shots. The finish and grips are the same as on the full-sized version. Importation from Yugoslavia began in 1988.

| NIB | Exc. | V.G. | Good | Fair | Poor |
|-----|------|------|------|------|------|
| 290 | 265  | 225  | 175  | 140  | 100  |

## Model EP-.380
This model is a high-quality, stainless-steel pocket pistol that is chambered for the .380 ACP cartridge. It is a double-action semi-automatic that holds 7 shots and has a 3.5" barrel. The grips are checkered walnut. This pistol has been imported from West Germany since 1988.

| NIB | Exc. | V.G. | Good | Fair | Poor |
|-----|------|------|------|------|------|
| 450 | 400  | 350  | 275  | 225  | 175  |

## Model PK-22
This is a domestic semi-automatic that is chambered for the .22 l.r. It is a double action with a 3.5" barrel and an 8-shot finger extension magazine. It is made of stainless steel and has black plastic grips. This model is manufactured in the U.S.A. by American Arms.

| NIB | Exc. | V.G. | Good | Fair | Poor |
|-----|------|------|------|------|------|
| 200 | 175  | 150  | 125  | 100  | 75   |

## Model PX-22
This is a compact version of the PK-22 with a 2.75" barrel and a 7-shot magazine. Manufacture commenced in 1989.

| NIB | Exc. | V.G. | Good | Fair | Poor |
|-----|------|------|------|------|------|
| 190 | 175  | 150  | 130  | 110  | 75   |

# AMERICAN BARLOCK WONDER
### Norwich, Connecticut Crescent Arms Co.
American Barlock Wonder was the tradename for a side-by-side and a single-barrel shotgun made by Crescent Arms Co. between 1888 and 1893 to be marketed by Sears Roebuck & Co.

## Single Shot
This gun was made in 12, 16, 20, and 28 gauge and .410. Barrel lengths were 26", 28", 30" and 32", with various chokes. It had an exposed hammer, fluid steel barrel, and walnut pistol grip stock.

| Exc. | V.G. | Good | Fair | Poor |
|------|------|------|------|------|
| 150  | 125  | 100  | 75   | 50   |

## Side X Side
This model was available in the same gauges, barrel lengths, and chokes as the single barrel. It was offered with hammers or hammerless, and the barrels were either fluid steel or Damascus.
Steel Barrels--Add 20 Percent.
28 Gauge and .410--Add 20 Percent.

| Exc. | V.G. | Good | Fair | Poor |
|------|------|------|------|------|
| 275  | 240  | 200  | 160  | 125  |

# AMERICAN DERRINGER CORP.
### Waco, Texas
## Model 1 Derringer
This is a high quality, stainless-steel derringer that is similar in appearance to the old Remington double derringer made famous by the frontier gamblers. This Model is made with space-age materials and technology to handle some very powerful cartridges. It is available up to and including the .44 Magnum, .45-70, and the .30-30 Winchester. The Model 1 has 3" O/U double barrels that pivot upward for loading. It weighs approximately 15 ounces and is a single action with automatic barrel selection. There is a manually operated crossbolt safety. They are furnished in either high polished or satin finish with exotic hardwood grips standard. They are also furnished with a French fitted leatherette case. The prices of these pistols are determined in part by the caliber for which they are chambered.

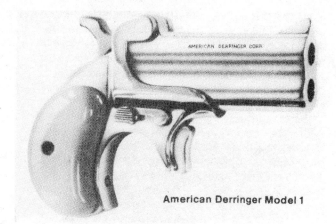

American Derringer Model 1

### Calibers .22 L.R. up to .357 Magnum and .45 ACP

| NIB | Exc. | V.G. | Good | Fair | Poor |
|-----|------|------|------|------|------|
| 200 | 180 | 160 | 130 | 100 | 75 |

### Calibers .41 Magnum, .44-40, .44 Special, .44 Magnum, .45 Colt and .410

| NIB | Exc. | V.G. | Good | Fair | Poor |
|-----|------|------|------|------|------|
| 295 | 275 | 225 | 175 | 150 | 110 |

### Calibers .22 Hornet, .223 Remington, .30-30 and .45-70

| NIB | Exc. | V.G. | Good | Fair | Poor |
|-----|------|------|------|------|------|
| 365 | 340 | 300 | 265 | 225 | 165 |

### Model 1 Texas Commemorative Derringer

This Model is similar in appearance to the Model 1 with a frame of solid brass, stainless steel, 3" barrels, and stag grips when chambered for the .44-40 or .45 Colt and rosewood when chambered for the .32 Magnum or .38 Special. The barrels are marked "Made in the 150th Year of Texas Freedom."

#### .32 Magnum and .38 Special

| NIB | Exc. | V.G. | Good | Fair | Poor |
|-----|------|------|------|------|------|
| 188 | 175 | 145 | 125 | 100 | 85 |

#### .44-40 and .45 Colt

| NIB | Exc. | V.G. | Good | Fair | Poor |
|-----|------|------|------|------|------|
| 285 | 265 | 225 | 175 | 145 | 110 |

### Model 3 Single Shot Derringer

This Model has one 2.5" barrel that pivots downward for loading. It weighs 8.5 ounces and features a manual hammer-block safety. It is made of stainless steel and has rosewood grips. It is chambered for .38 Special only.

| NIB | Exc. | V.G. | Good | Fair | Poor |
|-----|------|------|------|------|------|
| 115 | 100 | 90 | 75 | 50 | 40 |

### Model 4 Derringer

This is a specialized firearm. It has 4.1" barrels and is similar in appearance to the Model 1, only longer. Both barrels are chambered to fire either the .45 Colt or the 3" .410 shotgun shell. This Model was intended to be useful protection in snake country. It is stainless steel with rosewood grips standard. Stag grips are available for $25 extra. This longer-barreled gun is also available chambered for the .357 Magnum. .357 Maximum, .44 Special and .45 ACP. A special single-barreled version is available, chambered for .50-70 and the .50 Saunders.

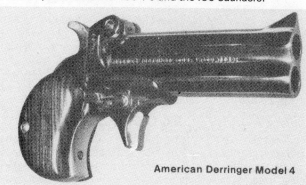

American Derringer Model 4

| NIB | Exc. | V.G. | Good | Fair | Poor |
|-----|------|------|------|------|------|
| 338 | 310 | 275 | 235 | 185 | 145 |

### Model 4 Alaskan Survival Derringer

This Model is the same configuration as the Model 4 except the upper barrel is chambered for the .45-70.

| NIB | Exc. | V.G. | Good | Fair | Poor |
|-----|------|------|------|------|------|
| 370 | 350 | 300 | 265 | 225 | 175 |

### Model 6 Derringer

This Model is similar in appearance and identical in function to the Model 4, with barrels 6" long. Extended rosewood finger-groove grips are an option at an extra $25. This Model is chambered for the .45 Colt/.410 3" standard and available also in .45 ACP and .357 Magnum. The three available finishes to the stainless steel are high polish, satin, and a grey matte.

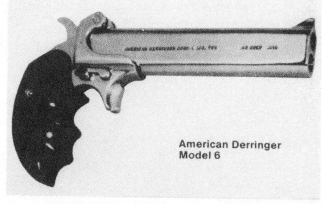

American Derringer Model 6

| NIB | Exc. | V.G. | Good | Fair | Poor |
|-----|------|------|------|------|------|
| 338 | 310 | 275 | 235 | 185 | 145 |

### Model 7 Derringer

This Model is manufactured as a backup gun for police officers. The frame and barrels are made of aircraft aluminum alloy; the other parts are stainless steel. This gun weighs 7.5 ounces. Its appearance and function are similar to the Model 1. The finish is a grey matte with thin, matte-finished grips of rosewood or bacote. This Model is chambered for and priced as follows:

#### .32 S&W Long/.32 Magnum

| NIB | Exc. | V.G. | Good | Fair | Poor |
|-----|------|------|------|------|------|
| 158 | 140 | 120 | 100 | 80 | 50 |

#### .38 S&W and .380 ACP

| NIB | Exc. | V.G. | Good | Fair | Poor |
|-----|------|------|------|------|------|
| 158 | 140 | 120 | 100 | 80 | 50 |

#### .22 L.R. and .38 Special

| NIB | Exc. | V.G. | Good | Fair | Poor |
|-----|------|------|------|------|------|
| 188 | 170 | 150 | 130 | 110 | 75 |

#### .44 Special

| NIB | Exc. | V.G. | Good | Fair | Poor |
|-----|------|------|------|------|------|
| 500 | 450 | 400 | 325 | 265 | 200 |

### Model 10 Derringer

This Model is similar to the Model 1 with a frame of aluminum alloy and all other parts, including the barrels, stainless steel. It has a grey matte finish and thin grips of rosewood or bacote. It weighs 10 ounces and is chambered for the .45 ACP or the .45 Colt.
.45 Colt--Add 10 Percent.

| NIB | Exc. | V.G. | Good | Fair | Poor |
|-----|------|------|------|------|------|
| 218 | 195 | 175 | 140 | 110 | 80 |

### Model 11 Derringer

This Model has an aluminum barrel and all other parts stainless steel. It weighs 11 ounces and is chambered for the .38 Special. The grips and finish are the same as on the Model 10.

| NIB | Exc. | V.G. | Good | Fair | Poor |
|-----|------|------|------|------|------|
| 180 | 165 | 135 | 110 | 85 | 60 |

## Semmerling LM-4

This unique gun has been in production for approximately 10 years, built by various companies. This latest offering by American Derringer may, with the right marketing and manufacturing approach, be the one that makes a commercial success of this fine firearm concept. The LM-4 was designed as the ultimate police backup/defense weapon. It is a manually operated, 5-shot repeater only 5.2" long, 3.7" high, and 1" wide. It is chambered for the .45 ACP and is undoubtedly the smallest 5-shot .45 ever produced. The LM-4 is made of a special tool steel and is either blued or, at extra cost, hard chrome-plated. A stainless-steel version is also available. The LM-4 is not a semi-automatic, although it physically resembles one. The slide is flicked forward and back after each double-action squeeze of the trigger. This weapon is virtually hand-built and features high visibility sights and a smooth trigger. It is an extremely limited-production item, and the company produces only two per week. The price and availability may fluctuate, so the company should be contacted for accurate figures. The values for the guns produced before American Derringer's involvement will be found in the section dealing with the Semmerling. These values are for the latest production by American Derringer. There is a 12- to 14- month waiting period for delivery, and the manufacturer's suggested list price is $1,250. Prices listed below reflect supply and demand.

American Derringer
Semmerling LM-4

Hard Chrome--Add $200.00.
Stainless Steel--Add 35 Percent.

| NIB | Exc. | V.G. | Good | Fair | Poor |
|------|------|------|------|------|------|
| 3250 | 3000 | 2700 | 2250 | 1600 | 1250 |

## AMERICAN F.A. MFG. CO., INC.
### San Antonio, Texas

This Company operated between 1972 and 1974. They produced a .25 ACP pocket pistol and a stainless-steel .38 Special derringer. A .380 auto was produced on an extremely limited basis.

### American .25 Automatic

This was a small, blowback, semi-automatic pocket pistol that was chambered for the .25 ACP cartridge. It had a 2" barrel and was made of either stainless steel or blued carbon steel. The grips were of plain uncheckered walnut, and the detachable magazine held 7 shots. It was manufactured until 1974.
Stainless Steel--Add 20 Percent.

| Exc. | V.G. | Good | Fair | Poor |
|------|------|------|------|------|
| 175 | 150 | 125 | 100 | 75 |

### American .380 Automatic

This model was similar to the .25 except larger. The barrel was 3.5", and the gun was made in stainless steel only. The grips were of smooth walnut, and it held 8 shots. There were only 10 of these .380's manufactured between 1972 and 1974. They are extremely rare, but there is little collector base for this company's products, and the value is very difficult to estimate.

| Exc. | V.G. | Good | Fair | Poor |
|------|------|------|------|------|
| 600 | 550 | 475 | 375 | 300 |

### American .38 Special Derringer

This model was a well-made, stainless-steel O/U derringer that was similar in appearance and function to the old Remington O/U. It had 3" barrels, that pivoted upward for loading. This gun was a single action that had an automatic selector and a spur trigger. The smooth grips were of walnut. There were approximately 3,500 manufactured between 1972 and 1974.

| Exc. | V.G. | Good | Fair | Poor |
|------|------|------|------|------|
| 200 | 180 | 150 | 125 | 90 |

## AMERICAN GUN CO.
### Norwich, Connecticut
### Crescent Firearms Co.--Maker
### H. & D. Folsom Co.--Distributor

### Revolver

This model was a typical S&W copy made by Crescent in Norwich, Connecticut. It was a top-break, double action, that was found either blued or nickel-plated with checkered, black hard rubber grips. The cylinder held 5 shots and was chambered for the .32 S&W cartridge.

| Exc. | V.G. | Good | Fair | Poor |
|------|------|------|------|------|
| 175 | 150 | 125 | 85 | 40 |

### Side X Side Shotgun

This was a typical trade gun made around the turn of the century by the Crescent Firearms Co. to be distributed by H. & D. Folsom. These are sometimes known as "Hardware Store Guns," as that is where many were sold. This particular gun was chambered for 12, 16, and 20 gauges and was produced with or without external hammers. The length of the barrels varied, as did the chokes. Some were produced with Damascus barrels; some, with fluid steel. The latter are worth approximately 20 percent more.

| Exc. | V.G. | Good | Fair | Poor |
|------|------|------|------|------|
| 250 | 225 | 175 | 125 | 90 |

## AMERICA HISTORICAL FOUNDATION
### Richmond, Virginia

This is a private commercial organization that commissions the manufacture of commemorative, limited-production firearms. They have produced a diverse array to date that runs the gamut from a Single Action Army to a Vietnam Commemorative AR-15. Their products are highly ornamented and well executed. The collector base for these instant collectibles is somewhat thin, but there are many individuals out there who desire to purchase weapons of this nature for their aesthetic value alone. It is important to note that these firearms, as with all commemoratives, will only be of interest to collectors if they are new, uncocked and unfired in the original packaging they were shipped in. Used commemoratives are nearly impossible to sell for any premium over a like model shooter. Many buyers would rather have the original, regardless of the condition.

### M1 Garand Rifle

This reproduction of the WWII battle rifle was manufactured by Springfield Armory of Geneseo, Illinois. It was chambered for the .30-06 cartridge and featured a high- gloss blue finish with contrasting 24 kt. plated parts. The walnut stock was a special select grade, and it was furnished in a walnut display case. The special serial-number range was WW0001-WW2500. This rifle was manufactured in 1984.

| NIB | Exc. | V.G. | Good | Fair | Poor |
|------|------|------|------|------|------|
| 1695 | 1100 | 800 | 600 | 400 | 350 |

### Korean War Thompson Rifle

This model was manufactured by Auto-Ordnance and was a semi-automatic, 16" barreled version of the Thompson Submachinegun. There was a fully automatic version available to Class III buyers only. This firearm was highly polished and blued with contrasting 24 kt. gold-plated parts. The stock, pistol grip and forearm were of specially selected walnut, and a walnut display case was furnished. The serial range was KW0001-KW1500. There were only 1,500 manufactured in 1985. There were 50 of these produced with full coverage engraving, and these would be worth approximately 80 percent more than the standard model listed.

| NIB | Exc. | V.G. | Good | Fair | Poor |
|---|---|---|---|---|---|
| 1200 | 850 | 600 | 450 | 350 | 300 |

**Vietnam M14 Rifle**

Produced by Springfield Armory, this is an M1-A, high-polished and blued with contrasting gold-plated parts. The stock was select-grade walnut, and there were two versions--a Marine Corps commemorative and one for the Army. There were 1,500 of each, and they were all chambered for the .308 and manufactured in 1987.

| NIB | Exc. | V.G. | Good | Fair | Poor |
|---|---|---|---|---|---|
| 1600 | 1200 | 800 | 650 | 550 | 500 |

**200th Constitution Revolver**

This model is a Dan Wesson .44 Magnum with a 10" barrel. It is gold plated with etchings and ivory grips. There were 950 manufactured in 1987.

| NIB | Exc. | V.G. | Good | Fair | Poor |
|---|---|---|---|---|---|
| 995 | 750 | 650 | 450 | 375 | 300 |

**General Patton SAA Commemorative**

This revolver was produced by Aldo Uberti of Italy. It is patterned after the extensively engraved and silver-plated with Ajax simulated ivory grips. It has a lanyard ring on the butt. There were 2,500 manufactured, serial numbered P0001-P2500.

| NIB | Exc. | V.G. | Good | Fair | Poor |
|---|---|---|---|---|---|
| 1500 | 1250 | 1000 | 750 | 500 | 350 |

**M16 Vietnam Commemorative**

This is a semi-automatic AR-15 that was produced by Colt. It is extensively engraved with black and 24 kt. gold contrasting parts. There are bipod and commemorative medallions inlayed in the stock. There were 1,500 produced in 1988, serial numbered V0001-V1500.

| NIB | Exc. | V.G. | Good | Fair | Poor |
|---|---|---|---|---|---|
| 2000 | 1400 | 1200 | 900 | 600 | 400 |

**Second Amendment Commemorative**

This is a 10" barrel Dan Wesson revolver that is fully engraved and blued with contrasting 24 kt. parts. It has walnut grips with inlayed medallions. There were 1,500 manufactured in 1989, serial numbered 2AC0001-2AC1500. This was known as the Collector's Edition.

The Deluxe Museum Edition was similar except that it was completely 24 kt. gold-plated. There were only 750 produced, serial numbered 2AD001-2AD750.

**Deluxe Museum Edition - Add 25%**

| NIB | Exc. | V.G. | Good | Fair | Poor |
|---|---|---|---|---|---|
| 1495 | 1200 | 1000 | 750 | 500 | 350 |

**American Armed Forces Uzi**

This model, produced by Iaeli Military Industries, was a 9mm semi-automitic Uzi pistol. It was black and had many gold inlays with contrasting 24 kt. gold-plated parts. It was furnished with a detachable wooden stock with an optional $200 walnut display case. There were 1,500 manufactured, serial numbered UZI001-UZI1500. They were released in 1989.

| NIB | Exc. | V.G. | Good | Fair | Poor |
|---|---|---|---|---|---|
| 2200 | 1800 | 1500 | 1100 | 750 | 500 |

**Vietnam War Combat Shotgun**

This is a 12-gauge slide action produced by Savage. It was hand engraved and blued with contrasting 24 kt. gold-plated parts. The stock and forearm are select walnut. There were

750 produced in 1989, serial numbered VN 001-VN 750. A walnut display case was available for an additional $250.

| NIB | Exc. | V.G. | Good | Fair | Poor |
|---|---|---|---|---|---|
| 1600 | 1150 | 900 | 650 | 500 | 350 |

# AMERICAN INDUSTRIES
## Cleveland, Ohio

**Calico M-100**

This is a semi-automatic carbine that has a 16.1" barrel with a flash suppressor. It is chambered for the .22 l.r. and features a folding stock, full shrouding hand-guards, a 100-round capacity, helical feed, and detachable magazine. It features an ambidextrous safety, pistol grip storage compartment, and a black finished alloy frame and adjustable sights. This model was introduced in 1986.

| NIB | Exc. | V.G. | Good | Fair | Poor |
|---|---|---|---|---|---|
| 300 | 275 | 250 | 210 | 175 | 140 |

**Calico M-100S Sporter**

This model is similar to the Model 100 with a futuristically styled walnut buttstock and forearm. This model is also known as the M-105.

| NIB | Exc. | V.G. | Good | Fair | Poor |
|---|---|---|---|---|---|
| 319 | 290 | 265 | 225 | 185 | 150 |

**Calico M-900**

This is a black polymer-stocked rifle that is similar to the M-100S, chambered for the 9mm Parabellum. It has a delayed blowback action and features a stainless-steel bolt and alloy receiver. The cocking handle is non-reciprocating, and the rear sight is fixed with an adjustable front. There is a 50-round magazine standard and a 100-round capacity model optional. This model was introduced in 1989.

| NIB | Exc. | V.G. | Good | Fair | Poor |
|---|---|---|---|---|---|
| 460 | 410 | 365 | 300 | 265 | 240 |

**Calico M-950 Pistol**

This model is similar to the Model 900 rifle with a 6" barrel and no shoulder stock.

| NIB | Exc. | V.G. | Good | Fair | Poor |
|---|---|---|---|---|---|
| 443 | 400 | 345 | 285 | 250 | 200 |

**Calico M-100P**

This model is similar to the M-100 .22 rimfire with a 6" barrel with muzzle brake and no shoulder stock. This is also known as the M-110.

| NIB | Exc. | V.G. | Good | Fair | Poor |
|---|---|---|---|---|---|
| 250 | 225 | 195 | 150 | 125 | 100 |

# AMERICAN INTERNATIONAL
## Salt Lake City, Utah
### A/K/A American Research & Development

**American 180 Carbine**

This firearm was imported from Austria. It is a semi-automatic, 16.5"-barreled carbine chambered for the .22 l.r. The sights are adjustable, and the stock is made of high-impact plastic. The unique drum magazine holds 177 rounds and is affixed to the top of the receiver. There is a select-fire version available for law enforcement agencies only and an optional laser lock sight system. This firearm was discontinued and recently has become available again from Feather Industries in Boulder, Colorado. It is now known as the SAR-180.

| Exc. | V.G. | Good | Fair | Poor |
|---|---|---|---|---|
| 675 | 600 | 525 | 400 | 275 |

# AMES SWORD CO.
## Chicopee Falls, Massachusetts

**Turbiaux Le Protector**

Ames Sword Co. became one of three U.S. companies that produced this unique, French palm-sqeezer pistol. The design consists of a round disk with a protruding barrel on one side and a lever on the other. The disk contains the cylinder that holds either seven 8mm rimfire or ten 6mm rimfire cartridges. The barrel protrudes between the fingers, and the lever trigger is squeezed to fire the weapon. The design was patented in 1883. It sold successfully in France into the 1890's. In 1892 Peter Finnegan bought the patents and brought them to Ames Sword. He contracted them to produce 25,000 pistols. Ames was only able to deliver 1,500 in the allotted time period, so Finnegan sued. Ames countersued, and the bottom line was that somehow Ames wound up owning the patent rights to a pistol that they did not want to manufacture. Production ceased shortly thereafter.

**(See Chicago Firearms Co. and Minneapolis Firearms Co.)**

| Exc. | V.G. | Good | Fair | Poor |
| --- | --- | --- | --- | --- |
| 600 | 525 | 450 | 350 | 265 |

## ANCION MARX
### Liege, Belgium

This company began production in the 1860's with a variety of cheaply made pinfire revolvers. They later switched to solid-frame, centerfire, "Velo-Dog" type revolvers chambered for 5.5mm or 6.35mm. They were marketed in various countries under many different trade names. Some of the names that they will be found under are Cobalt, Extracteur, LeNovo, Lincoln, and Milady. The quality of these revolvers is quite poor; and collector interest, almost non-existent. Values do not usually vary because of trade names.

| Exc. | V.G. | Good | Fair | Poor |
| --- | --- | --- | --- | --- |
| 150 | 125 | 100 | 65 | 45 |

## ANDERSON
### Anderson, Texas
**Anderson Underhammer Pistol**

This was an unmarked, underhammer percussion pistol that was chambered for .45 caliber. It had a 5" part-round/part-octagonal barrel with an all steel, saw-handle-shaped frame. There was a flared butt with walnut grips. The finish was blued. There is very little information on this pistol, and its origin is merely strongly suspected but not confirmed.

| Exc. | V.G. | Good | Fair | Poor |
| --- | --- | --- | --- | --- |
| 425 | 375 | 325 | 250 | 200 |

## ANDRUS & OSBORN
### Stafford, Connecticut
**Andrus & Osborn Underhammer Pistol**

This pistol is of the percussion type and chambered for .25 caliber. The part-round/part-octagonal barrel is 6" long and features small silver star inlays along its length. The barrel is marked "Andrus & Osborn/Canton Conn." with an eagle stamped beside it. It is marked "Cast Steel" near the breech. The grips are of walnut, and the finish is browned.

| Exc. | V.G. | Good | Fair | Poor |
| --- | --- | --- | --- | --- |
| 425 | 375 | 300 | 225 | 160 |

## ANSCHUTZ
### Ulm, Germany
### Importer--Precision Sales
### International, Westfield, Massachusetts
**Mark 10 Target Rifle**

This is a single-shot, bolt-action rifle that is chambered for the .22 l.r. cartridge. It has a 26" heavy barrel with adjustable target-type sights. The finish was blued, and the walnut target stock had an adjustable palm rest. It was manufactured between 1963 and 1981.

| Exc. | V.G. | Good | Fair | Poor |
| --- | --- | --- | --- | --- |
| 350 | 300 | 250 | 210 | 150 |

**Model 1407**

This version is similar to the Mark 10 but is furnished without sights. It was known as the "I.S.U." model. It is discontinued in 1981.

| Exc. | V.G. | Good | Fair | Poor |
| --- | --- | --- | --- | --- |
| 375 | 325 | 275 | 235 | 175 |

**Model 1408**

This is a heavier-barrelled version of the Model 1407.

| Exc. | V.G. | Good | Fair | Poor |
| --- | --- | --- | --- | --- |
| 375 | 325 | 275 | 235 | 175 |

**Model 1411**

This version was designed specifically to be fired from the prone position.

| Exc. | V.G. | Good | Fair | Poor |
| --- | --- | --- | --- | --- |
| 350 | 300 | 250 | 210 | 150 |

**Model 1413 Match**

This is a high-grade, competition version with a heavy target barrel that is furnished without sights. The walnut stock has an adjustable cheekpiece.

| Exc. | V.G. | Good | Fair | Poor |
| --- | --- | --- | --- | --- |
| 550 | 500 | 450 | 400 | 275 |

**Model 1418 Mannlicher**

This is a hunting rifle with a full-length, Mannlicher-type stock made with hand-checkered walnut.

| Exc. | V.G. | Good | Fair | Poor |
| --- | --- | --- | --- | --- |
| 625 | 575 | 500 | 450 | 325 |

**Model 1418/19**

This is a lower-priced sporter model that was formerly imported by Savage Arms.

| Exc. | V.G. | Good | Fair | Poor |
| --- | --- | --- | --- | --- |
| 300 | 250 | 200 | 150 | 125 |

**Model 184**

This is a high-grade, bolt-action sporting rifle chambered for the .22 l.r. cartridge. It has a 21.5" barrel with a folding-leaf sight. The finish is blued with a checkered walnut, Monte Carlo stock with a Schnabel forend. It was manufactured between 1963 and 1981.

| Exc. | V.G. | Good | Fair | Poor |
| --- | --- | --- | --- | --- |
| 375 | 335 | 280 | 220 | 150 |

**Model 54 Sporter**

This is a high-grade, bolt-action sporting rifle chambered for the .22 l.r. cartridge. It has a 24", tapered round barrel and a 5-shot detachable magazine. It features a folding leaf-type rear sight. The finish is blued with a checkered walnut, Monte Carlo stock. It was manufactured between 1963 and 1981.

| Exc. | V.G. | Good | Fair | Poor |
| --- | --- | --- | --- | --- |
| 650 | 575 | 500 | 350 | 250 |

**Model 54M**

This version is chambered for the .22 rimfire Magnum cartridge.

| Exc. | V.G. | Good | Fair | Poor |
| --- | --- | --- | --- | --- |
| 700 | 600 | 525 | 375 | 275 |

**Model 141**

This is a bolt-action sporter chambered for the .22 l.r. cartridge. It has a 23" round barrel with a blued finish and walnut, Monte Carlo stock. It was manufactured between 1963 and 1981.

| Exc. | V.G. | Good | Fair | Poor |
| --- | --- | --- | --- | --- |
| 350 | 300 | 250 | 200 | 150 |

**Model 141M**

This version is chambered for the .22 rimfire Magnum cartridge.

| Exc. | V.G. | Good | Fair | Poor |
| --- | --- | --- | --- | --- |
| 375 | 325 | 275 | 225 | 175 |

**Model 153**

This is a bolt-action sporting rifle chambered for the .222 Remington cartridge. It has a 24" barrel with folding-leaf rear sight. The finish is blued with a checkered, French walnut stock featuring a rosewood forend tip and pistol grip cap. It was manufactured between 1963 and 1981.

| Exc. | V.G. | Good | Fair | Poor |
| --- | --- | --- | --- | --- |
| 575 | 500 | 385 | 300 | 240 |

## Model 153-S
This version was offered with double-set triggers.

| Exc. | V.G. | Good | Fair | Poor |
|------|------|------|------|------|
| 625 | 550 | 435 | 350 | 275 |

## Model 64
This is a single-shot, bolt-action rifle that is chambered for the .22 l.r. cartridge. It has a 26" round barrel and is furnished without sights. The finish is blued, and the walnut, target-type stock featured a beaver-tail forearm and adjustable buttplate. It was manufactured between 1963 and 1981.

| Exc. | V.G. | Good | Fair | Poor |
|------|------|------|------|------|
| 350 | 300 | 250 | 200 | 150 |

## Model 64MS
This version was designed for silhouette shooting and has a 21.25" barrel, blued finish, and a target-type, walnut stock with a stippled pistol grip.

| Exc. | V.G. | Good | Fair | Poor |
|------|------|------|------|------|
| 650 | 600 | 525 | 400 | 300 |

## Model 54.18MS
This is a high-grade silhouette rifle chambered for the .22 l.r. cartridge. It has a 22" barrel and a match-grade action with fully adjustable trigger. It is furnished without sights. The finish is blued with a target-type, walnut stock.

| NIB | Exc. | V.G. | Good | Fair | Poor |
|-----|------|------|------|------|------|
| 1212 | 1100 | 950 | 750 | 475 | 375 |

## Model 54.MS REP
This version is a repeating rifle with a 5-shot, detachable magazine with a thumbhole stock with vented forearm.

| NIB | Exc. | V.G. | Good | Fair | Poor |
|-----|------|------|------|------|------|
| 1650 | 1450 | 1150 | 900 | 675 | 450 |

## Model 2000 MK
This is a single-shot rifle chambered for the .22 l.r. cartridge. It has a 26", round barrel with target-type sights. The finish was blued with a checkered walnut stock. It was not imported after 1988.

| Exc. | V.G. | Good | Fair | Poor |
|------|------|------|------|------|
| 350 | 300 | 250 | 200 | 140 |

## Model 1403D
This is a single-shot target rifle chambered for the .22 l.r. cartridge. It has a 26" barrel and is furnished without sights. It has a fully adjustable trigger and a blued finish with a walnut, target-type stock.

| NIB | Exc. | V.G. | Good | Fair | Poor |
|-----|------|------|------|------|------|
| 700 | 650 | 575 | 500 | 375 | 250 |

## Model 1803D
This is a high-grade target rifle that is chambered for the .22 l.r. cartridge. It has a 25.5" heavy barrel with adjustable target sights. It features an adjustable trigger. The finish is blued with a light-colored wood stock with dark stippling on the pistol grip and forearm. The stock features an adjustable cheekpiece and buttplate. It was introduced in 1987.

| NIB | Exc. | V.G. | Good | Fair | Poor |
|-----|------|------|------|------|------|
| 810 | 750 | 675 | 600 | 475 | 350 |

## Model 1808ED Super
This is a single-shot, running bore-type rifle that is chambered for the .22 l.r. cartridge. It has a 32.5" barrel furnished without sights. The finish is blued with a heavy, target-type walnut stock. It is furnished with barrel weights.

| NIB | Exc. | V.G. | Good | Fair | Poor |
|-----|------|------|------|------|------|
| 1300 | 1200 | 1050 | 900 | 625 | 500 |

## Model 1910 Super Match II
This is a very high-grade, single-shot target rifle chambered for the .22 l.r. cartridge. It has a 27.25" barrel and is furnished with diopter-type target sights. The finish is blued with a walnut, thumbhole stock with adjustable cheekpiece and buttplate.

| NIB | Exc. | V.G. | Good | Fair | Poor |
|-----|------|------|------|------|------|
| 2000 | 1800 | 1550 | 1400 | 1000 | 700 |

## Model 1911 Prone Match
This version has a stock designed specifically for firing from the prone position.

| NIB | Exc. | V.G. | Good | Fair | Poor |
|-----|------|------|------|------|------|
| 1600 | 1450 | 1050 | 800 | 550 | 450 |

## Model 1913 Super Match
This is a virtually hand-built, match target rifle. It is chambered for the .22 l.r. cartridge and features a single-shot action. It has adjustable, diopter-type sights on a 27.25" heavy barrel. This is a custom-made gun that features every target option conceivable. The finish is blued with a fully adjustable walnut stock.

| NIB | Exc. | V.G. | Good | Fair | Poor |
|-----|------|------|------|------|------|
| 2200 | 2000 | 1400 | 1000 | 700 | 600 |

## Model 1827B Biathlon
This is a repeating, bolt-action target rifle chambered for the .22 l.r. cartridge. It is specially designed for the biathlon competition. Production is quite limited and on a custom basis.

| NIB | Exc. | V.G. | Good | Fair | Poor |
|-----|------|------|------|------|------|
| 1750 | 1500 | 1050 | 800 | 550 | 475 |

## Model 1433D
This is a centerfire version of the Model 54 target rifle chambered for the .22 Hornet. It is a special-order item and features a set trigger and a 4-round, detachable magazine. The finish was blued with a full-length, Mannlicher stock. It was discontinued in 1986.

| Exc. | V.G. | Good | Fair | Poor |
|------|------|------|------|------|
| 1000 | 850 | 750 | 550 | 375 |

## Bavarian 1700
This classic-style sporting rifle was chambered for the .22 l.r., .22 rimfire Magnum., .22 Hornet, and the .222 Remington cartridges. It features a 24" barrel with adjustable sights. It has a detachable magazine and a blued finish with a checkered, walnut, European-style stock. It was introduced in 1988.

| NIB | Exc. | V.G. | Good | Fair | Poor |
|-----|------|------|------|------|------|
| 2000 | 850 | 725 | 525 | 450 | 335 |

## Model 520/61
This is a blowback-operated, semi-automatic rifle that is chambered for the .22 l.r. cartridge. It has a 24" barrel and a 10-round, detachable magazine. The finish is blued with a checkered walnut stock. It was discontinued in 1983.

| Exc. | V.G. | Good | Fair | Poor |
|------|------|------|------|------|
| 275 | 200 | 155 | 130 | 100 |

## Model 525 Sporter
This is a semi-automatic rifle chambered for the .22 l.r. cartridge. It has a 24" barrel with adjustable sights and a 10-round, detachable magazine. The finish is blued with a checkered, Monte Carlo-type stock. It was introduced in 1984. A carbine version with a 20" barrel was originally offered but was

discontinued in 1986.

| NIB | Exc. | V.G. | Good | Fair | Poor |
|-----|------|------|------|------|------|
| 435 | 400 | 350 | 300 | 195 | 145 |

### Exemplar

This is a bolt-action pistol that is built on the Model 64 Match Action. It is chambered for the .22 l.r. cartridge and has a 10" barrel with adjustable sights and a 5-shot, detachable magazine. It features an adjustable, two-stage trigger with the receiver grooved for attaching a scope. The walnut stock and forend are stippled. It was introduced in 1987.

| NIB | Exc. | V.G. | Good | Fair | Poor |
|-----|------|------|------|------|------|
| 400 | 365 | 275 | 210 | 185 | 150 |

### Exemplar XIV

This version is similar to the standard Exemplar with a 14" barrel. It was introduced in 1988.

| NIB | Exc. | V.G. | Good | Fair | Poor |
|-----|------|------|------|------|------|
| 405 | 370 | 280 | 215 | 190 | 150 |

### Exemplar Hornet

This version is chambered for the .22 Hornet cartridge. It was introduced in 1988.

| NIB | Exc. | V.G. | Good | Fair | Poor |
|-----|------|------|------|------|------|
| 750 | 675 | 580 | 500 | 400 | 275 |

# APACHE
### Eibar, Spain
### SEE--Ojanguren Y Vidosa

# APALOZO HERMANOS
### Zumorraga, Spain

This is yet another Spanish gunmaker who was in business from the 1920's until the advent of the Spanish Civil War. The quality of the firearms they manufactured was typically poor, and the company never put its name on any of them. The company trademark, a dove-like bird, was impressed into the grips. This was the sole identifying feature.

### Apaloza

A poor-quality copy of the Colt Police Positive revolver.

| Exc. | V.G. | Good | Fair | Poor |
|------|------|------|------|------|
| 150 | 125 | 100 | 65 | 45 |

### Paramount

This is a copy of the 1906 Browning chambered for the 6.35mm. The slide is marked "Paramount Cal. .25." The grips have the bird trademark and "Cal. .25."

| Exc. | V.G. | Good | Fair | Poor |
|------|------|------|------|------|
| 150 | 125 | 100 | 65 | 45 |

### Triomphe

This model is identical to the Paramount except that the slide inscription reads " Pistolet Automatique Triomphe Acier Comprime."

| Exc. | V.G. | Good | Fair | Poor |
|------|------|------|------|------|
| 150 | 125 | 100 | 65 | 45 |

# ARIZAGA, G.
### Eibar, Spain

This company produced poor-quality semi-automatic handguns. They are of little interest to collectors. The company went out of business at the beginning of the Spanish Civil War.

### Arizaga

A typical Eibar-type 7.65mm semi-auto.

| Exc. | V.G. | Good | Fair | Poor |
|------|------|------|------|------|
| 150 | 125 | 100 | 65 | 45 |

### Mondial

This pistol is rather unique for an Eibar creation. Externally it resembles a Savage semi-auto design. Sadly, on the inside it is the same old Browning Blowback copy normally found on the firearms. The mondial is striker fired, is chambered for 6.35mm, and has been noted with or without a grip safety. The grip features the owl in a circle trademark and the word "Mondial."

| Exc. | V.G. | Good | Fair | Poor |
|------|------|------|------|------|
| 175 | 140 | 110 | 75 | 50 |

### Pinkerton

The Pinkerton is Arizaga's most common model. It is chambered for the 6.35mm. Two separate types have been noted. One has holes in the right grip so that it acts as a cartridge counter window. The second type has course serrations on the slide, as does the Mondial. The Arizaga owl trademark is not found on either variation, and both have slide markings "Pinkerton Automatic 6.35."

| Exc. | V.G. | Good | Fair | Poor |
|------|------|------|------|------|
| 135 | 110 | 80 | 55 | 35 |

### Warwinck

The Warwinck is a larger version of the Mondial chambered for 7.65mm. The top of the slide is marked "Automatic Pistol 7.65 Warwinck." The grips have the circled owl trademark.

| Exc. | V.G. | Good | Fair | Poor |
|------|------|------|------|------|
| 175 | 140 | 110 | 75 | 50 |

# ARIZMENDI
### Eibar, Spain

Arizmendi began business in the 1890's, producing "Velo- Dog" type revolvers. In 1914 the company was reorganized and began developing a line of semi-automatic pistols. They were distinguishable because of a patented loaded chamber indicator that the other Eibar-type pistols did not have. This company, like most of the other Spanish gun companies, ceased trading with the advent of the Spanish Civil War.

### Singer

The Singer was chambered for both the 6.35mm and the 7.65mm. It was made from 1913 until the company's demise. The markings are as follows: "Pistola Automatica" along with the company trademark "AG" with crown and crescent stamped on the slide and the frame.

| Exc. | V.G. | Good | Fair | Poor |
|------|------|------|------|------|
| 150 | 125 | 100 | 65 | 45 |

### Teuf - Teuf

Another cheaply made 7.65mm Eibar-type semi-auto, this model was made in 1912. The slide is marked "Automatic Teuf-Teuf pistol 7.65mm" along with the Arizmendi trademark.

| Exc. | V.G. | Good | Fair | Poor |
|------|------|------|------|------|
| 150 | 125 | 100 | 65 | 45 |

### Walman

The Walman is the most common of the Arizmendi pistols. It was produced in 7.65mm and 6.35mm. It has been noted, although rarely, in 9mm/.380. The slide is usually marked "American Automatic Pistol Walman Patent." The grips are marked "Walman." This pistol was made into the late 1920's.

| Exc. | V.G. | Good | Fair | Poor |
|------|------|------|------|------|
| 150 | 125 | 100 | 65 | 45 |

### Arizmendi

This is a solid-frame, folding-trigger revolver. It is chambered for 7.65mm or .32 cal. revolver. It is marked with the "FA" trademark and circled five point star.

| Exc. | V.G. | Good | Fair | Poor |
|------|------|------|------|------|
| 140 | 110 | 90 | 50 | 25 |

### Boltun

This model was also produced in two calibers. The 6.35mm is marked "Automatic Pistol Boltun Patent"; the 7.65mm, "Automatic Pistol Boltun Patent Marca Registrada 7375 Cal. 7.65."

| Exc. | V.G. | Good | Fair | Poor |
|------|------|------|------|------|
| 150 | 125 | 100 | 65 | 45 |

### Puppy

A 5.5mm solid-frame, folding-trigger, "Velo-Dog" revolver, the barrel is stamped "Puppy"; the frame, stamped with the "FA" trademark.

| Exc. | V.G. | Good | Fair | Poor |
|------|------|------|------|------|
| 140 | 110 | 80 | 50 | 35 |

### Pistolet Automatique
This is a 6.35mm blowback which bears the "FA" trademark.

| Exc. | V.G. | Good | Fair | Poor |
|------|------|------|------|------|
| 150 | 125 | 100 | 65 | 45 |

### Kaba Spezial
The Spanish gun companies of this period had few qualms regarding copying successful designs, names, or trademarks. This model bears no resemblance to the Kaba Spezial made in Germany by Menz. The Spanish version is a poor-quality gun made in 6.35mm and 7.65mm. The slide is marked "Pistol Automatique Kaba Spezial." The word "Kaba" is molded into the grips.

| Exc. | V.G. | Good | Fair | Poor |
|------|------|------|------|------|
| 150 | 125 | 100 | 65 | 45 |

### Roland
An ordinary "Eibar"-type semi-automatic pistol chambered in both 6.35mm and 7.65mm, this model was made in the 1920's and was stamped with the circled star and crescent trademark.

| Exc. | V.G. | Good | Fair | Poor |
|------|------|------|------|------|
| 150 | 125 | 100 | 65 | 45 |

### Ydeal
Another 1906 Browning copy chambered in 6.35mm or 7.65mm, this model is stamped "Pistolet Automatique Ydeal" on the slide. "Ydeal" is molded into the grips.

| Exc. | V.G. | Good | Fair | Poor |
|------|------|------|------|------|
| 150 | 125 | 100 | 65 | 45 |

## ARIZMENDI ZULAICA
### Eibar, Spain
Another Spanish manufacturer of poor-quality pistols, they went out of business at the start of the Spanish Civil War.

### Cebra
An "Eibar"-type 7.65mm semi-auto with the slide stamped "Pistolet Automatique Cebra Zulaica Eibar." The letters "AZ" are stamped in an oval on the frame.

| Exc. | V.G. | Good | Fair | Poor |
|------|------|------|------|------|
| 150 | 125 | 100 | 65 | 40 |

### Cebra Revolver
A Colt Police Positive copy chambered for .38 Colt, it is marked simply "Made in Spain" with the word "Cebra" molded into the grips.

| Exc. | V.G. | Good | Fair | Poor |
|------|------|------|------|------|
| 140 | 110 | 80 | 50 | 25 |

## ARMALITE, INC.
### Costa Mesa, California
### AR-17 Shotgun
This was a gas-operated semi-automatic shotgun chambered for 12 gauge. It had a 24" barrel and interchangeable choke tubes. The receiver and the barrel were made of an aluminum alloy anodized either black or gold. The stock and forearm were plastic. There were approximately 2,000 manufactured in 1964 and 1965.

| Exc. | V.G. | Good | Fair | Poor |
|------|------|------|------|------|
| 550 | 475 | 400 | 300 | 225 |

### AR-7 Explorer Rifle
This is a 16"-barreled .22 l.r. semi-auto carbine. It has an alloy receiver and a steel-lined alloy barrel. The gun comes apart quickly and can be stored in the compartmented floating plastic stock. The rear sight is a peep type with a blade front. This rifle was manufactured between 1959 and 1973. After it was discontinued, production was resumed by Charter Arms.

| Exc. | V.G. | Good | Fair | Poor |
|------|------|------|------|------|
| 100 | 85 | 70 | 60 | 45 |

### AR-7 Custom
This version was similar to the Explorer with a walnut cheekpiece stock. It was manufactured between 1964 and 1970.

| Exc. | V.G. | Good | Fair | Poor |
|------|------|------|------|------|
| 160 | 135 | 100 | 80 | 60 |

## ARMAS DE FUEGO
### Guernica, Spain
This is a little-known manufacturer of poor-quality "Eibar"-type Spanish pistols. They remained in business only four years, from 1920 through 1924. Collector interest is nearly non-existent.

### Alkar
This company's Alkar is a 6.35mm copy of the 1906 Browning blowback. It is distinguishable by having eight slots cut into the left side of the grip which enables the contents of the magazine to be checked.

| Exc. | V.G. | Good | Fair | Poor |
|------|------|------|------|------|
| 175 | 145 | 100 | 75 | 50 |

## ARMERO ESPECIALISTAS
### Eibar, Spain
This company consisted of a group of workmen from the Eibar gun trade who set themselves up to produce their own product. They remained in business until the Spanish Civil War. The quality of their firearms was noticeably better than most Spanish guns of this era.

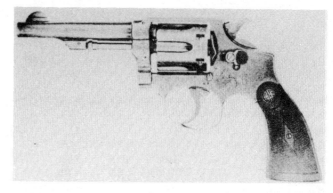

### Alfa
The company manufactured many different revolvers under this trademark. Smith & Wesson, as well as Colt, designs were copied in .22, .32, .38, and .44 calibers. All bore the tradename "Alfa."

| Exc. | V.G. | Good | Fair | Poor |
|------|------|------|------|------|
| 175 | 145 | 110 | 75 | 50 |

### Omega
Another "Eibar"-type semi-auto pistol that is chambered in both 6.35mm and 7.65mm. They are marked "Omega" on the slide and the grips.

| Exc. | V.G. | Good | Fair | Poor |
|------|------|------|------|------|
| 175 | 145 | 110 | 75 | 50 |

## ARMES DE CHASSE
### Chadds Ford, Pennsylvania
This company imports firearms manufactured by F. Beretta, as well as a line of guns manufactured in Suhl, Germany.

### Model EJ
This is an Over/Under shotgun chambered for 12 gauge. It features various-length barrels and choke combinations. It has an Anson & Deeley action with double triggers and automatic ejectors. The receiver is moderately engraved and coin-finished. The remainder is blued with a checkered walnut stock. It is manufactured in Germany and was introduced in 1989.

| NIB | Exc. | V.G. | Good | Fair | Poor |
|-----|------|------|------|------|------|
| 1000 | 950 | 800 | 650 | 500 | 425 |

## Model EU
This version features a ventilated-rib barrel and a non-selective single trigger. It was introduced in 1989.

| NIB | Exc. | V.G. | Good | Fair | Poor |
|-----|------|------|------|------|------|
| 1200 | 1150 | 1000 | 850 | 600 | 475 |

## Highlander
This is a SxS double barrel chambered for 20 gauge. It has a boxlock action and various barrel lengths and choke combinations. It has double triggers and manual extractors and is blued with a checkered walnut stock. It is manufactured in Italy and was introduced in 1989.

| NIB | Exc. | V.G. | Good | Fair | Poor |
|-----|------|------|------|------|------|
| 675 | 625 | 500 | 375 | 300 | 225 |

## Chesapeake
This model is similar to the Highlander but chambered for the 3.5", 12-gauge shell. It has chrome-lined bores and was designed to fire steel shot. It has automatic ejectors and double triggers. It is manufactured in Italy and was introduced in 1989.

| NIB | Exc. | V.G. | Good | Fair | Poor |
|-----|------|------|------|------|------|
| 775 | 725 | 600 | 475 | 400 | 300 |

## Balmoral
This version is chambered for 12, 16, or 20 gauge and has various lengths and choke combinations. It has a boxlock action with false sideplates. It has a single trigger and automatic ejectors. The receiver is case-colored with blued barrels and a checkered, English-style, straight-grip walnut stock. It is manufactured in Italy and was introduced in 1989.

| NIB | Exc. | V.G. | Good | Fair | Poor |
|-----|------|------|------|------|------|
| 800 | 725 | 625 | 500 | 425 | 325 |

## Model 70E
This is a SxS, double-barrel shotgun chambered for 12, 16, or 20 gauge, with 27" or 28", solid-ribbed barrels. It was offered with various choke combinations. It features an Anson & Deeley action with a Greener crossbolt. It has double triggers and automatic ejectors. The engraved frame is case-colored with blued barrels and a checkered walnut stock. It is manufactured in Germany and was introduced in 1989.

| NIB | Exc. | V.G. | Good | Fair | Poor |
|-----|------|------|------|------|------|
| 815 | 775 | 625 | 500 | 425 | 350 |

## Model 74E
This version has game scene engraving and higher-grade walnut. It was introduced in 1989.

| NIB | Exc. | V.G. | Good | Fair | Poor |
|-----|------|------|------|------|------|
| 1000 | 925 | 775 | 625 | 500 | 400 |

## Model 76E
This version has heavily engraved, false sideplates with hunting scenes and a high-grade, checkered walnut stock. It was introduced in 1989.

| NIB | Exc. | V.G. | Good | Fair | Poor |
|-----|------|------|------|------|------|
| 1500 | 1450 | 1075 | 900 | 750 | 500 |

# ARMINEX LTD.
## Scottsdale, Arizona

### Tri-Fire
This is a single-action, semi-automatic pistol that is chambered for 9mm, .45 ACP and .38 Super cartridges. It is convertible, and the conversion units add approximately $130 to the value of an excellent specimen. The stainless-steel barrels were offered in lengths of 5", 6", or 7". The frame is steel, and there is an ambidextrous safety on the target model. The grips are of smooth walnut, and there was a presentation case available for an additional $48. There were only 250 manufactured between 1981 and 1985.

| Exc. | V.G. | Good | Fair | Poor |
|------|------|------|------|------|
| 400 | 350 | 275 | 225 | 175 |

## Target Model
This model is similar to the standard model with a 6" or 7" barrel and ambidextrous safety.

| Exc. | V.G. | Good | Fair | Poor |
|------|------|------|------|------|
| 450 | 400 | 325 | 275 | 200 |

# ARMINIUS
SEE--Freidrich Pickert
Zella-Mehlis, Germany
Hermann Weirauch
Melrichstadt, Germany
F.I.E.
Hialeah, Florida

# ARMITAGE INTERNATIONAL, LTD.
## Seneca, South Carolina

### Scarab Skorpion
This is a blowback-operated, semi-automatic, assault-type pistol that was patterned after the Czechoslovakian Scorpion submachine gun. It is chambered for the 9mm parabellum cartridge and has a 4.6" barrel with military-type protected sights. It utilizes a 32-round, detachable box magazine and has a matte-black finish with synthetic grips.

| NIB | Exc. | V.G. | Good | Fair | Poor |
|-----|------|------|------|------|------|
| 285 | 250 | 200 | 150 | 125 | 95 |

# ARMS CORPORATION OF THE PHILIPPINES
## Armscor Precision
## Foster City, California

This company manufactures firearms in the Philippines. They are relatively inexpensive, serviceable firearms. There is little or no collector interest in these weapons. They are most recently imported by Armscor Precision in California.

## Shotguns
### Model 30 D
This is a slide action 12 gauge with a 28"or 30" plain barrel with various chokes. It is constructed of steel and blued with a checkered mahogany stock and forearm. It holds 6 shots and was introduced in 1986.

| NIB | Exc. | V.G. | Good | Fair | Poor |
|-----|------|------|------|------|------|
| 225 | 200 | 165 | 135 | 100 | 75 |

### Model 30 DG
This Model is the 20" law enforcement version of the Model 30 D. It is similar except that it has rifle sights and is available with an 8-shot magazine.

| NIB | Exc. | V.G. | Good | Fair | Poor |
|-----|------|------|------|------|------|
| 225 | 200 | 165 | 135 | 100 | 75 |

### Model 30 R
This Model is the same as the Model 30 DG with a shotgun bead instead of the sights.

| NIB | Exc. | V.G. | Good | Fair | Poor |
|-----|------|------|------|------|------|
| 225 | 200 | 165 | 135 | 100 | 75 |

### Model 30 RP
This is similar to the Model 30 R with an interchangeable, black synthetic pistolgrip furnished along with the regular stock. It has an 18.5" barrel.

| NIB | Exc. | V.G. | Good | Fair | Poor |
|-----|------|------|------|------|------|
| 225 | 200 | 165 | 135 | 100 | 75 |

## Rifles
### Model M14P
Introduced in 1986, this is a 23"-barreled, bolt-action rifle chambered for the .22 l.r. cartridge. It has open sights, a 5-shot detachable magazine, and a mahogany stock.

| NIB | Exc. | V.G. | Good | Fair | Poor |
|-----|------|------|------|------|------|
| 110 | 95 | 75 | 50 | 35 | 25 |

### Model M14D
This is basically the same rifle as the Model 14P with an adjustable rear sight and checkered stock. It was manufactured in 1987 only.

| NIB | Exc. | V.G. | Good | Fair | Poor |
|-----|------|------|------|------|------|
| 120 | 100 | 85 | 65 | 45 | 25 |

### Model M1500
This is a 21.5"-barrelled bolt action that is chambered for the .22 rimfire magnum cartridge. It holds 5 shots and has open sights and a checkered mahogany stock. It was introduced in 1986.

| NIB | Exc. | V.G. | Good | Fair | Poor |
|-----|------|------|------|------|------|
| 145 | 120 | 100 | 80 | 60 | 35 |

### Model M1600
This is a semi-automatic, .22 l.r. copy of the M16. It has an ebony stock, 18" barrel, and a detachable 15-round magazine. It was introduced in 1986.

| NIB | Exc. | V.G. | Good | Fair | Poor |
|-----|------|------|------|------|------|
| 125 | 100 | 80 | 60 | 40 | 25 |

### Model M1600R
This is essentially the M1600 with a stainless-steel retractable stock and vented barrel shroud. It was introduced in 1986.

| NIB | Exc. | V.G. | Good | Fair | Poor |
|-----|------|------|------|------|------|
| 135 | 110 | 90 | 70 | 50 | 35 |

### Model M1600C
This model is similar to the M1600 with a 20" shrouded barrel and a fiberglas stock.

| NIB | Exc. | V.G. | Good | Fair | Poor |
|-----|------|------|------|------|------|
| 135 | 110 | 90 | 70 | 50 | 35 |

### Model M1600W
This model is similar to the M1600C with a mahogany stock. It was manufactured in 1986 only.

| NIB | Exc. | V.G. | Good | Fair | Poor |
|-----|------|------|------|------|------|
| 135 | 110 | 90 | 70 | 50 | 35 |

### Model M1800
This was a 23"-barreled bolt action chambered for the .22 Hornet cartridge. It had a 5-shot magazine and a checkered, mahogany, Monte Carlo stock. It was manufactured in 1986 only.

| Exc. | V.G. | Good | Fair | Poor |
|------|------|------|------|------|
| 150 | 125 | 100 | 75 | 50 |

### Model M20P
This Model is a 15-shot semi-automatic chambered for the .22 l.r. It has a 20.75" barrel, open sights, and a plain mahogany stock. It was introduced in 1986.

| NIB | Exc. | V.G. | Good | Fair | Poor |
|-----|------|------|------|------|------|
| 95 | 80 | 65 | 50 | 35 | 25 |

### Model M2000
This Model was similar to the M20P with adjustable sights and a checkered mahogany stock. It was manufactured in 1986 only.

| Exc. | V.G. | Good | Fair | Poor |
|------|------|------|------|------|
| 80 | 60 | 50 | 35 | 25 |

### Model MAK22S
This Model is a .22 rimfire semi-automatic that was designed to resemble the Russian AK-47 rifle. It has an 18.5" barrel and a mahogany stock. The detachable magazine holds 15 rounds.

| NIB | Exc. | V.G. | Good | Fair | Poor |
|-----|------|------|------|------|------|
| 175 | 150 | 125 | 100 | 75 | 50 |

### Model MAK22F
Introduced in 1989, this version is similar to the MAK22S with a folding stock.

| NIB | Exc. | V.G. | Good | Fair | Poor |
|-----|------|------|------|------|------|
| 200 | 175 | 145 | 110 | 85 | 65 |

### Handguns
### Model M100
This was a double-action, swingout-cylinder revolver that was chambered for the .22 l.r., .22 Magnum, and the .38 Special cartridges. It had a 4" vent-rib barrel, a 6-shot cylinder, and adjustable sights. The finish was blued with checkered mahogany grips. This Model was introduced in 1985.

| NIB | Exc. | V.G. | Good | Fair | Poor |
|-----|------|------|------|------|------|
| 200 | 175 | 150 | 110 | 80 | 50 |

# ARMSCORP OF AMERICA
## Baltimore, Maryland
This company both imports and manufactures firearms. They built a reputation for being a prime source for assault and combat-style weapons. The hysteria that has recently swept our country has had a profound effect on a number of companies-- this is one of them. We will list their products for reference purposes and will provide values for the ones that exhibit stability, but for the assault type rifles we are unable to provide this data at this time.

### Rifles
### M-14R
This model is a recently manufactured rifle which utilizes a new receiver and original surplus parts. It is chambered for the .308 and has a 22" barrel and a detachable 20-round magazine. The fiberglas stock is used government surplus. This model was introduced in 1986.

### M-14 National Match
This is similar to the M-14R but built to A.M.T.U. MIL specifications. It is a high-grade target version that utilizes National Match parts. This model was introduced in 1987.

### FAL
This rifle is constructed with a newly manufactured receiver forged by Armscor and Argentine surplus parts. The barrel is 21" and is chambered for the .308 cartridge. The sights are adjustable, and the stock is a black synthetic. The rifle is furnished with a 20-round magazine. It was introduced in 1987.

### M36 Israeli Sniper Rifle
This is a specialized weapon built around the Armscor M-14 receiver. It is a gas-operated, semi-automatic in the Bullpup style. It has a 22" barrel that has been free floated for accuracy and is chambered for the .308 cartridge. There is an integral flash suppressor and a bipod. It is furnished with a 20-shot detachable magazine. This civilian version was first offered for sale in 1989.

### Expert Model
This is a semi-automatic rifle that is chambered for the .22 l.r. It has a 21" barrel and open sights with a receiver that is grooved for scope mounting. There is a 10-shot magazine and a hardwood stock. This Model was introduced in 1989.

| NIB | Exc. | V.G. | Good | Fair | Poor |
|-----|------|------|------|------|------|
| 225 | 200 | 175 | 145 | 100 | 80 |

### Handguns
### Hi-Power
This is an Argentine-manufactured version of the Browning semi-automatic pistol. It is chambered for the 9mm Parabellum, has a 4.75" barrel, and is matte finished in the military manner. It features fixed sights and a spur-type hammer. The grips are a checkered synthetic. This model was introduced in 1989.

| NIB | Exc. | V.G. | Good | Fair | Poor |
|-----|------|------|------|------|------|
| 425 | 385 | 325 | 280 | 245 | 200 |

### Detective HP - Compact
This is a 3.5"-barrelled compact version of the Hi-Power. It was introduced in 1989.

| NIB | Exc. | V.G. | Good | Fair | Poor |
|-----|------|------|------|------|------|
| 475 | 425 | 350 | 310 | 275 | 225 |

## SD 9

This Israeli-manufactured compact pistol features a blowback-operated double action. It is chambered for the 9mm Parabellum and has a 3" barrel. The pistol is constructed of sheet metal stampings, an effective and cost-efficient method. It has a 6-round magazine and a loaded chamber indicator. It is also called the Sirkus, SD 9 and is manufactured by Sirkus Industries in Israel. This pistol was introduced in 1989.

| NIB | Exc. | V.G. | Good | Fair | Poor |
|-----|------|------|------|------|------|
| 350 | 300  | 260  | 210  | 165  | 120  |

## P 22

This is a blowback-operated, semi-automatic pistol that was copied from the Colt Woodsman. It is chambered for the .22 l.r. and is offered with a 4" or 6" barrel with fixed sights and a 10-round detachable magazine. The finish is blued with checkered hardwood grips. This model was introduced in 1989.

| NIB | Exc. | V.G. | Good | Fair | Poor |
|-----|------|------|------|------|------|
| 200 | 175  | 135  | 100  | 75   | 50   |

# AROSTEGUI
### Eibar, Spain

This was a small company that operated from the early 1920's until the Spanish Civil War.

## Azul, Royal

This is a rarity among Eibar guns, an extremely collectible model. The Royal Azul is a very close copy of the German C96 "Broomhandle" Mauser. It is regarded as one of the better quality copies. If one examines the amount and complexity of the machining on this firearm, one realizes that duplicating was not an easy task, especially with the equipment available at the time.

| Exc. | V.G. | Good | Fair | Poor |
|------|------|------|------|------|
| 1100 | 950  | 800  | 675  | 500  |

## E.A.

Another 1906 Browning copy chambered in 6.35mm. The frame is stamped "EA" in a circle. A retrieving dog is molded into the grips.

| Exc. | V.G. | Good | Fair | Poor |
|------|------|------|------|------|
| 175  | 150  | 100  | 75   | 50   |

## Velo-Dog

A typical, solid-frame, folding-trigger "Velo-Dog" revolver, this one was chambered for 5.5mm or 6.35mm and bore the circled "EA" trademark.

| Exc. | V.G. | Good | Fair | Poor |
|------|------|------|------|------|
| 125  | 100  | 75   | 50   | 30   |

# ARRIETA S.L.ELGOIBAR
### Spain
### Importer--Morton's Ltd.
### Lexington, Kentucky

This company manufactures SxS, double-barrelled shotguns chambered for 12, 16, 20 and 28 gauge, as well as .410. They are produced with various barrel lengths and choke combinations. The versions produced run the gamut in values from $450 to nearly $14,000. The smaller-bore guns have scaled-down frames. They are available with single triggers, double triggers, and extractors, as well as automatic ejectors. There is a wide variety of ornamentation, as well as a variety of quality in the materials used. We will list the models and their estimated values but recommend qualified appraisal on the higher-grade models.

## 490 Eder

This is a boxlock gun with double triggers and extractors. It was discontinued in 1986.

| Exc. | V.G. | Good | Fair | Poor |
|------|------|------|------|------|
| 460  | 420  | 335  | 275  | 200  |

## 500 Titan

This model features a H&H-type sidelock action. The receiver is engraved and coin-finished. It has double triggers and extractors. It was not imported after 1986.

| Exc. | V.G. | Good | Fair | Poor |
|------|------|------|------|------|
| 560  | 520  | 435  | 375  | 300  |

## 501 Palomara

This is a more-deluxe version of the 500 Titan. It was discontinued in 1986.

| Exc. | V.G. | Good | Fair | Poor |
|------|------|------|------|------|
| 700  | 625  | 550  | 425  | 350  |

## 505 Alaska

This is a heavily engraved version of the 501 Palomara. It was not imported after 1986.

| Exc. | V.G. | Good | Fair | Poor |
|------|------|------|------|------|
| 800  | 775  | 625  | 500  | 400  |

## 510 Montana

This model had H&H-type sidelocks and featured gold-plated internal parts.

| NIB  | Exc. | V.G. | Good | Fair | Poor |
|------|------|------|------|------|------|
| 2200 | 2000 | 1750 | 1250 | 900  | 600  |

## 550 Field

This version is similar to the 510 Montana without the gold plating. The action is hand-honed.

| NIB  | Exc. | V.G. | Good | Fair | Poor |
|------|------|------|------|------|------|
| 2200 | 2000 | 1750 | 1250 | 900  | 600  |

## 557 Standard

This is a more-deluxe version of the 550 Field.

| NIB  | Exc. | V.G. | Good | Fair | Poor |
|------|------|------|------|------|------|
| 2600 | 2400 | 2000 | 1500 | 1100 | 675  |

## 558 Patria

This is a more-deluxe version of the previous models.

| NIB  | Exc. | V.G. | Good | Fair | Poor |
|------|------|------|------|------|------|
| 2650 | 2450 | 2050 | 1550 | 1150 | 700  |

## 560 Cumbre

This model features still more ornamentation.

| NIB  | Exc. | V.G. | Good | Fair | Poor |
|------|------|------|------|------|------|
| 2800 | 2600 | 2200 | 1700 | 1200 | 800  |

## 570 Lieja

| NIB  | Exc. | V.G. | Good | Fair | Poor |
|------|------|------|------|------|------|
| 3000 | 2800 | 2400 | 1800 | 1300 | 850  |

## 575 Sport

| NIB  | Exc. | V.G. | Good | Fair | Poor |
|------|------|------|------|------|------|
| 3000 | 2800 | 2400 | 1800 | 1300 | 850  |

## 578 Victoria

This model features English-style engraving.

| NIB  | Exc. | V.G. | Good | Fair | Poor |
|------|------|------|------|------|------|
| 3300 | 3000 | 2500 | 1900 | 1375 | 900  |

## 585 Liria

This is a more-deluxe version of the 578 Victoria.

| NIB  | Exc. | V.G. | Good | Fair | Poor |
|------|------|------|------|------|------|
| 3800 | 3500 | 3000 | 2400 | 1600 | 1100 |

## 588 Cima

| NIB  | Exc. | V.G. | Good | Fair | Poor |
|------|------|------|------|------|------|
| 3800 | 3500 | 3000 | 2400 | 1600 | 1100 |

## 590 Regina

| NIB  | Exc. | V.G. | Good | Fair | Poor |
|------|------|------|------|------|------|
| 4000 | 3500 | 3000 | 2500 | 1750 | 1100 |

## 595 Principe

This version has deep relief-engraved gamescenes.

| NIB  | Exc. | V.G. | Good | Fair | Poor |
|------|------|------|------|------|------|
| 6000 | 5500 | 4500 | 3750 | 2500 | 1750 |

### 600 Imperial
This version features a self-opening action.

| NIB | Exc. | V.G. | Good | Fair | Poor |
|------|------|------|------|------|------|
| 5300 | 4750 | 4000 | 3250 | 2000 | 1500 |

### 601 Tiro
This version has a nickle-plated, self-opening action.

| NIB | Exc. | V.G. | Good | Fair | Poor |
|------|------|------|------|------|------|
| 6500 | 6000 | 5000 | 3950 | 2750 | 1950 |

### 801
This version features a self-opening action with detachable side-locks and the highest-grade, English-style engraving in the Churchill fashion.

| NIB | Exc. | V.G. | Good | Fair | Poor |
|------|------|------|------|------|------|
| 9000 | 8000 | 7200 | 5000 | 3250 | 2400 |

### 802
This version features Holland and Holland-type engraving.

| NIB | Exc. | V.G. | Good | Fair | Poor |
|------|------|------|------|------|------|
| 9000 | 8000 | 7200 | 5000 | 3250 | 2400 |

### 803
This version features Purdey-type engraving.

| NIB | Exc. | V.G. | Good | Fair | Poor |
|------|------|------|------|------|------|
| 6000 | 5500 | 4500 | 3750 | 2500 | 1750 |

### 875
This is the best-grade Arrieta gun. It is completely hand-built to the customer's specifications and features elaborate ornamentation, including gold inlays.

| NIB | Exc. | V.G. | Good | Fair | Poor |
|-------|-------|------|------|------|------|
| 14000 | 12000 | 8500 | 6750 | 5500 | 4500 |

## ARRIZABALAGA
### Eibar, Spain
This Spanish company engaged in the manufacture of pistols from WWI until the Spanish Civil War.

### Arrizabalaga
A typical Eibar blowback, semi-automatic pistol chambered for 7.65mm, this model has a 9-shot magazine and a lanyard ring on the butt. The slide is stamped with the company name.

| Exc. | V.G. | Good | Fair | Poor |
|------|------|------|------|------|
| 150 | 125 | 100 | 65 | 40 |

### Campeon
This model was chambered for 7.65mm or 6.35mm. The slide is stamped "Campeon Patent 1919," and the grips have "Campeon" molded into them.

| Exc. | V.G. | Good | Fair | Poor |
|------|------|------|------|------|
| 150 | 125 | 100 | 65 | 40 |

### Sharpshooter - JoLoAr
These two models are nearly identical, and they are a radical departure from the usual "Eibar" pistols. Most of them are fitted with a lever that, when squeezed, would cock the weapon. Rotating the safety completely to the rear would enable the barrel to be pivoted upward for cleaning or single-shot loading. The "Sharpshooter" was chambered for 6.35mm, 7.65mm, and 9mm Corto (short). The "JoLoAr" has the same calibers plus 9mm Bergman Bayard and a very limited number in .45ACP. This model is a rarity in that it is a Spanish gun of this era that does have quite a bit of collector appeal.

(The .45ACP would bring a 40 percent premium.)

| Exc. | V.G. | Good | Fair | Poor |
|------|------|------|------|------|
| 300 | 275 | 200 | 160 | 125 |

## ASCASO
### Cataluna, Spain
This pistol is a copy of the Astra 400. The quality is reasonably good, but the finish is not as fine as the original. This pistol is somewhat mysterious in that it was named after Francisco Ascaso, a Spanish revolutionary who was killed three days after the outbreak of hostilities in July of 1936. There does not appear to be any connection between the man and the firearms business. The forward portion of the barrel is stamped "F. Ascaso Tarrassa" inside an oval.

| Exc. | V.G. | Good | Fair | Poor |
|------|------|------|------|------|
| 1000 | 900 | 700 | 500 | 375 |

## ASHEVILLE ARMORY
### Asheville, North Carolina
**Enfield Type Rifle**
This weapon was made for use by the Confederate Army during the Civil War. It was a crude copy of the Short Pattern British Enfield Rifle. Chambered in .58 caliber, it was a muzzleloader that utilized the percussion ignition system. The barrel was 32.5" long and was held in place by two iron barrel bands. It had an iron ramrod and a lug to mount a sabre bayonet; all other metal parts were brass. The lock was marked "Asheville, N.C." There were approximately 300 manufactured in 1862 and 1863; and, as with all Confederate arms, this weapon is quite rare and desirable from a collector's viewpoint.

| Exc. | V.G. | Good | Fair | Poor |
|------|------|------|------|------|
| 6500 | 5000 | 3500 | 2000 | 1500 |

## PETER & WILLIAM ASHTON
### Middletown, Connecticut
**Ashton Underhammer Pistol**
This underhammer, or boot pistol as they were sometimes called, was chambered for the .28 through .38 caliber and utilized the percussion ignition system. They featured a 4" or 5" part-round/part-octagonal barrel, which was blued or browned. The large walnut grip panels were held in place by a larger than normal screw, a distinctive feature of these pistols that had their barrels marked, "W. Ashton" or "P. H. Ashton."

| Exc. | V.G. | Good | Fair | Poor |
|------|------|------|------|------|
| 550 | 450 | 375 | 275 | 200 |

## ASTRA
### SEE--Unceta

## AUER, B.
### Louisville, Kentucky
**Auer Pocket Pistol**
Most of these derringer-styled pistols were chambered for .60 caliber with a 4" octagonal barrel. They utilized the percussion ignition system. A prime identifying feature is a long iron tang that extends back approximately 75 percent of the handle. The stock was checkered walnut; the sideplate and other mountings were of German silver. The triggerguard was engraved and made of iron, and the forend tip was pewter. The lock was engraved by hand "B. Auer." This rare weapon that was produced on a limited basis in the 1850's.

| Exc. | V.G. | Good | Fair | Poor |
|------|------|------|------|------|
| 1000 | 800 | 700 | 500 | 450 |

## AUGUSTA MACHINE WORKS
### Augusta, Georgia
### 1851 Colt Navy Copy
This revolver was a well-made Confederate copy of the Navy Colt. It was produced in Georgia for use in the Civil War. It was chambered for .36 caliber with an 8" barrel and 6-shot cylinder. It utilized the percussion ignition system, and specimens have been noted with either 6- or 12- cylinder stop slots. The finish was browned with brass grip straps and walnut grip panels. This revolver was serial- numbered but bore no other identifying marks. It is an extremely rare and desirable piece of Americana as it is believed that there were only 100 manufactured. One should be cautious when considering acquisition.

| Exc. | V.G. | Good | Fair | Poor |
|------|------|------|------|------|
| 7500 | 6500 | 4500 | 3250 | 2000 |

## AUSTRALIAN AUTOMATIC ARMS LTD.
### Tasmania, Australia
### Importer--North American Sales International, Inc.
### Midland, Texas
The firearms made by this company fall into the category commonly known as assault weapons, whatever that may mean. As such they are extremely difficult to accurately evaluate in today's economy. The prices of these firearms have been fluctuating wildly and vary tremendously from one part of the Country to another. They are not even legal to possess in some municipalities. We are listing them for reference only and urge the potential buyer to individually research market conditions if a purchase is planned.

### SAR
This is a semi-automatic, assault-type rifle that is chambered for the .223 cartridge. It has either a 16.25" or 20" barrel and a black synthetic stock and forend. It is furnished with a 5- or 20-round AR-15-type magazine. This model was imported between 1986 and 1989.

### SAP
This is a 10.5"-barrelled, semi-automatic pistol version of the SAR. It was also imported from 1986-1989.

### SP
This rifle is a sporting version of the SAR with a wood stock and forend and 5-shot magazine. It was introduced in 1989.

## AUTO MAG
### Various Manufacturers
This very formidable stainless-steel pistol was developed in the 1960's by Sanford Arms Co. of Pasadena, California. It was originally built around a wildcat cartridge called the .44AMP made from a cutdown and trimmed .308 Winchester case and a 240- grain .44 caliber bullet. The gun's release was announced for early 1970. It actually first saw the light of day in October of 1970; but by that time, manufacture had been taken over by the Auto Mag Corp. of Pasadena, California. This was merely the beginning of its roller coaster ride through firearms history.

In all, the Auto Mag was produced by six different companies and two custom makers, even though fewer than 10,000 total were produced--the reason being, for the most part, the extreme difficulty and high cost in the production of this rather amazing firearm. It was simply too expensive an item to market successfully at that time. The "Dirty Harry" movie Sudden Impact caused prices and demand to rise sharply for a time, but this trend has subsided.

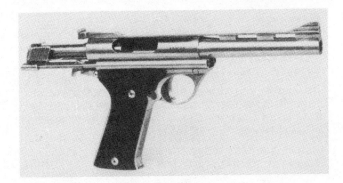

### AUTO-MAG CORP.
### Pasadena, California
Serial number range A0000 through A3300, made with a 6.5" vent-rib barrel, chambered in .44AMP only.

| NIB | Exc. | V.G. | Good | Fair | Poor |
|-----|------|------|------|------|------|
| 2000 | 1850 | 1500 | 1250 | 1000 | 800 |

### TDE CORP.
### North Hollywood, California
Serial number range A3400 through AO5015, made with a 6.5" vent-rib barrel, chambered in .44AMP and .357AMP.

#### .44AMP
| NIB | Exc. | V.G. | Good | Fair | Poor |
|-----|------|------|------|------|------|
| 2000 | 1850 | 1500 | 1250 | 1000 | 800 |

#### .357AMP
| NIB | Exc. | V.G. | Good | Fair | Poor |
|-----|------|------|------|------|------|
| 2050 | 1900 | 1550 | 130C | 1050 | 850 |

### TDE CORP.
### El Monte, California
Serial number range AO5016 thruogh AO8300, 6.5" vent- rib barrel standard. Also available in 8" and 10" barrel lengths chambered for .44AMP and .357AMP.

#### .44AMP
| NIB | Exc. | V.G. | Good | Fair | Poor |
|-----|------|------|------|------|------|
| 1800 | 1650 | 1300 | 1050 | 800 | 650 |

#### .357AMP
| NIB | Exc. | V.G. | Good | Fair | Poor |
|-----|------|------|------|------|------|
| 1600 | 1450 | 1100 | 850 | 650 | 500 |

### HIGH STANDARD
### New Haven, Connecticut
High Standard made 132 guns, all with "H" prefix serial numbers.

| NIB | Exc. | V.G. | Good | Fair | Poor |
|-----|------|------|------|------|------|
| 2300 | 2000 | 1750 | 1300 | 1000 | 850 |

### TDE-OMC
This is known as the solid-bolt or "B" series. The serial-number range is B00001 through B00370. Either 6.5" vent-rib or 10" tapered barrels are available.

| NIB | Exc. | V.G. | Good | Fair | Poor |
|-----|------|------|------|------|------|
| 2000 | 1850 | 1500 | 1250 | 1000 | 800 |

### AMT "C" SERIES
There were 100 guns produced in this Series. The first 50 were serial-numbered with a "C" prefix. The second 50 were serial-numbered "LAST 1" through "LAST 50." They were available with a 6.5" vent-rib or 10" tapered barrel.

| NIB | Exc. | V.G. | Good | Fair | Poor |
|-----|------|------|------|------|------|
| 2100 | 1950 | 1600 | 1350 | 1100 | 900 |

### L. E. JURRAS CUSTOM
In 1977 Lee Jurras of Super Vel fame became involved in the production of the Auto Mag pistol. He turned out versions with custom barrels, grips, and cases. These guns will usually command a 35 percent to 50 percent premium over standard variations on the collector market.

### KENT LOMONT

These variations, made by Mr. LoMont, are non-factory proto-types produced in wildcat calibers, notably .22AMP and .25AMP. They also feature non-standard barrel lengths. They must be individually appraised.

The AutoMag was originally furnished with a hard plastic, foam-lined, attache-style carrying case. There were also basic tools, an oil bottle, and owner's manual. Collectors will demand that all this be intact to bring top value.

Original Auto Mag factory ammunition was manufactured in Mexico and is currently worth $50-$60 per box.

# AUTO ORDNANCE CORP.
## West Hurley, New York

### 1911 A1

This pistol is a faithful copy of the Colt 1911 A1. It is chambered for the 9mm, .38 Super and the .45 ACP. The finish is blued and the grips are checkered plastic.

| NIB | Exc. | V.G. | Good | Fair | Poor |
|-----|------|------|------|------|------|
| 350 | 325  | 275  | 225  | 175  | 135  |

### ZG-51 "Pit Bull"

This model is a compact, 3.5"-barrelled version of the 1911 A1. It is chambered for the .45 ACP and was introduced in 1988.

| NIB | Exc. | V.G. | Good | Fair | Poor |
|-----|------|------|------|------|------|
| 385 | 350  | 300  | 250  | 200  | 175  |

### 1927 A1 Standard

This is a semi-automatic version of the Thompson Submachinegun. It is chambered for the .45 ACP cartridge and has a 16" barrel. This model is constructed of steel and blued. It has military-type sights and a walnut stock with vertical handguard. This model was manufactured until 1986.

| Exc. | V.G. | Good | Fair | Poor |
|------|------|------|------|------|
| 575  | 500  | 425  | 300  | 275  |

### 1927 A1 Deluxe

This model is similar to the standard except that it has a finned barrel, adjustable sights, and the pistol grip forearm. A 50 round-drum magazine is available for an additional $140. The violin-shaped hard case adds $115.

| NIB | Exc. | V.G. | Good | Fair | Poor |
|-----|------|------|------|------|------|
| 725 | 650  | 575  | 500  | 350  | 300  |

### 1927 A1C

This is a lightweight version with an aluminum alloy receiver. It is similar to the 1927 Deluxe in all other respects. This model was introduced in 1984.

| NIB | Exc. | V.G. | Good | Fair | Poor |
|-----|------|------|------|------|------|
| 635 | 600  | 525  | 400  | 325  | 275  |

### 1927 A5

This version has a 13" finned barrel and no provision for a shoulder stock. The receiver is aluminum alloy.

| NIB | Exc. | V.G. | Good | Fair | Poor |
|-----|------|------|------|------|------|
| 625 | 575  | 500  | 375  | 300  | 250  |

### 1927 A3

This is an alloy-framed, deluxe model with 16" barrel chambered for the .22 l.r. cartridge.

| NIB | Exc. | V.G. | Good | Fair | Poor |
|-----|------|------|------|------|------|
| 485 | 450  | 400  | 350  | 275  | 225  |

# AUTO POINTER
## Yamamoto Co.
## Tokyo, Japan

### Auto - Pointer Shotgun

This was a gas-operated, semi-automatic shotgun, that was chambered for 12 and 20 gauge. It was offered in barrel lengths of 26", 28", and 30", with various chokes. The receiver was aluminum alloy with a blued finish and a checkered walnut stock and forearm. It was imported by Sloans and is no longer available.

| Exc. | V.G. | Good | Fair | Poor |
|------|------|------|------|------|
| 325  | 275  | 225  | 175  | 125  |

## AZPIRI
### Eibar, Spain

This obscure company remained in business only four years, 1914-1918.

### Avion

This model is a rarity among "Eibar" pistols. It is actually quite well made. It ia chambered for 6.35mm and is the usual copy of the 1906 Browning blowback design. It is marked "Pistolet Automatique Avion Brevete."

| Exc. | V.G. | Good | Fair | Poor |
|------|------|------|------|------|
| 200 | 175 | 125 | 95 | 65 |

### Colon

The Colon is also chambered for the 6.35mm. It is marked "Automatic Pistol Colon" and is of the usual poor "Eibar" quality.

| Exc. | V.G. | Good | Fair | Poor |
|------|------|------|------|------|
| 150 | 125 | 100 | 75 | 50 |

## BSA GUNS LTD.
### Birmingham, England
### Birmingham Small Arms

This is an old British firearms company. They began manufacturing guns in 1861 and were a fixture in England until recently when they began a move to Karachi, Pakistan. Up until 1985 they were imported by Precision Sports of Ithaca, New York; then in 1986, by BSA Guns Ltd. of Grand Prairie, Texas. They are now imported by Samco Global Arms of Miami, Florida.

BSA has marketed a series of single-shot rifles that were based on the Martini Cadet action. This smaller version of the Peabody-Martini was infinitely suited for building smaller caliber target and sporting rifles. It is estimated that there were some 80,000 of these produced by BSA before WWI. The characteristics of the Martini Cadet action is as follows: it is a single-shot, swinging breech block action that is actuated by a finger lever at the bottom. It is machined from steel and blued. It has an internal striker powered by a coil spring. The trigger is non adjustable, and there is no external safety. The rifles made from this action and their values are as follows:

### No. 12 Cadet Martini

This rifle was originally chambered for the .310 cartridge. It has a 29" barrel, target sights, and a straight grip stock. The finish is blued. Approximately 80,000 were manufactured between 1911 and 1913. They were introduced to America by a surplus arms dealer in 1955, and they became the basis for many custom single-shot rifles.

| Exc. | V.G. | Good | Fair | Poor |
|------|------|------|------|------|
| 350 | 300 | 250 | 175 | 125 |

### Centurian Match Rifle

This is a deluxe version of the No. 12. It is chambered for .22 rimfire, has a pistol grip stock and better-grade target sights. The barrel is 24" long. It was furnished with a guarantee to group in 1.5" at 100 yards.

| Exc. | V.G. | Good | Fair | Poor |
|------|------|------|------|------|
| 450 | 400 | 350 | 275 | 200 |

### Model 13 Sporter

This rifle is similar to the Model 12 with hunting sights and chambered for the .22 Hornet.

| Exc. | V.G. | Good | Fair | Poor |
|------|------|------|------|------|
| 400 | 350 | 300 | 225 | 150 |

### Martini International Match

This is a heavy-barreled target variation of the Martini Cadet. It is chambered for .22 rimfire and features international-style target sights. It was manufactured between 1950 and 1953.

| Exc. | V.G. | Good | Fair | Poor |
|------|------|------|------|------|
| 425 | 375 | 325 | 250 | 175 |

### Martini International Light

This model is similar to the International with a lighter-weight 26" barrel.

| Exc. | V.G. | Good | Fair | Poor |
|------|------|------|------|------|
| 425 | 375 | 325 | 250 | 175 |

### Martini International ISU

This 28"-barrelled version of the International was built to meet ISU specifications. It was manufactured between 1968 and 1976.

| Exc. | V.G. | Good | Fair | Poor |
|------|------|------|------|------|
| 500 | 450 | 400 | 325 | 250 |

### Bolt Actions
### Royal

In 1954 BSA imported its first bolt-action rifle into the U.S.A. It was marketed through Freelands in Rock Island, Illinois, and was known as the "Royal." It is basically a short-action "Varmint" rifle chambered for either .22 Hornet or .222 Remington. The action is a modified Mauser type of substantial size and weight. It has a dovetail milled into it to mount Parker Hale clamp on scope rings, a definite drawback. There are no gas escape holes in the bolt or receiver. It has a 24", tapered round barrel and a well-made French walnut stock. In 1956 this rifle was introduced with a medium-length action. It is chambered for the .257 Roberts, 7X57, .300 Savage, and .308 Winchester and features a three-leaf, open rear sight. One year later, in 1957, the long action was introduced, completing the "Royal Line" as it was called. This model is chambered for the .30-06 in its standard weight. A featherweight version was offered in .270 and .30-06, as well as an 8.5 lb. rifle chambered for the .458 Winchester Magnum. The entire "Royal Line" was discontinued in 1959.

| Exc. | V.G. | Good | Fair | Poor |
|------|------|------|------|------|
| 350 | 300 | 250 | 200 | 150 |

### Majestic Deluxe

In 1959 BSA introduced the improved "Majestic Line," which was imported by Galef. The improvements were chiefly to the bolt face, ejector, and extractor; and in other respects the action was similar to the Royal. It has a 22" barrel with folding rear sight and a European-style walnut stock with a Schnabel forearm. It is chambered for the .22 Hornet, .222, .243, 7X57, .308, and .30-06. This model was imported between 1959 and 1965.

| Exc. | V.G. | Good | Fair | Poor |
|------|------|------|------|------|
| 350 | 300 | 250 | 200 | 150 |

### Majestic Deluxe Featherweight

This model is similar to the standard-weight model with a thinner barrel and the addition of the .270 and .458 Magnum chamberings.

| Exc. | V.G. | Good | Fair | Poor |
|------|------|------|------|------|
| 350 | 300 | 250 | 200 | 150 |

### Monarch Deluxe

This is still another improvement to the BSA line. The dovetailed scope-mounting provisions were removed; and the actions were drilled, tapped, and designated the Monarch. It is essentially very similar to the Majestic rifle with an American-styled stock. A heavy-barreled Varmint model was also available chambered for .222 and .243. This model was imported from 1966 until 1974.

| Exc. | V.G. | Good | Fair | Poor |
|------|------|------|------|------|
| 375 | 325 | 275 | 225 | 175 |

### Herters U9

In 1965 Herters Inc., formerly of Waseca, Minnesota, began to import the BSA action. They were never advertised as being from BSA, and the stamping "Made in England" was very shallow and in small letters. British proof marks were evident. This action was not finished as well as the BSA- manufactured product, and they were sold quite reasonably priced. These were used as the basis for many hand-built rifles, and each would have to be individually appraised for value.

## Martini ISU Match Rifle

This is a heavy-barrelled target rifle that is chambered for the .22 rimfire cartridge. It is a single-shot, bolt action with target sights. It was imported until 1985.

| Exc. | V.G. | Good | Fair | Poor |
|------|------|------|------|------|
| 800 | 725 | 600 | 500 | 375 |

In 1986 BSA introduced another line of rifles based on what they call the CF-2 action. It was manufactured in various configurations for a period of approximately two years and, as mentioned in the introduction to this chapter, is now in the process of being produced in Pakistan. There are very few English made-units still available. These rifles are chambered for .222 Remington through .300 Winchester Magnum in most popular calibers. Barrel lengths offered were 23"-26," and options included double-set triggers at $70 extra.

## Sporter/Classic

This is the basic hunter's rifle with a checkered walnut stock, available in all the standard calibers. It was introduced in 1986.

| Exc. | V.G. | Good | Fair | Poor |
|------|------|------|------|------|
| 350 | 325 | 275 | 200 | 150 |

## Varminter

This is a heavy-barrelled, matte-finished rifle chambered for .222, .22-250, and .243. It has no sights and is furnished with sling swivels. It was introduced in 1986.

| Exc. | V.G. | Good | Fair | Poor |
|------|------|------|------|------|
| 325 | 275 | 225 | 175 | 135 |

## Stutzen Rifle

This version features a full-length, Mannlicher-style stock with a large Schnabel tip. It has a 20.5" barrel and was introduced in 1986.

| Exc. | V.G. | Good | Fair | Poor |
|------|------|------|------|------|
| 375 | 350 | 300 | 225 | 175 |

## Regal Custom

This is a deluxe version with a select walnut stock, finer checkering, and an ebony forend tip. The receiver is engraved. This model was only imported in 1986.

| Exc. | V.G. | Good | Fair | Poor |
|------|------|------|------|------|
| 850 | 800 | 700 | 550 | 400 |

## CFT Target Rifle

This is a heavy-barrelled, single-shot, bolt-action target rifle that is chambered for the .308 cartridge. The barrel is 26.5" long and features target open sights. The rifle weighs 11 lbs. and was only available until 1987.

| Exc. | V.G. | Good | Fair | Poor |
|------|------|------|------|------|
| 650 | 600 | 550 | 400 | 300 |

# BABCOCK, MOSES
### Charlestown, Massachusetts

## Babcock Underhammer Cane Gun

This is a specialized concealment weapon that is chambered for .52 caliber and utilizes the percussion ignition system. It features a 27"-long round barrel with an overall length of approximately 33". The wood handle is similar to that of a walking stick, and the trigger is hidden and does not snap open until the underhammer is cocked. The entire weapon is painted to represent woodgrain to further enhance the concealability. The hammer is stamped with the maker's name and town of origin.

| Exc. | V.G. | Good | Fair | Poor |
|------|------|------|------|------|
| 400 | 350 | 300 | 250 | 200 |

# BABBIT, A. S.
### Plattsburgh, New York
### SEE--Adirondack Arms

# BACON ARMS CO.
### Norwich, Connecticut

Bacon Arms operated from 1862 until 1891. They have become known primarily for the production of cheaply made, solid-frame, rim-fire revolvers known as "Suicide Specials." Bacon manufactured and sold under a number of different trademarks. They were: Bacon, Bonanza, Conqueror, Express, Gem, Governor, Guardian, and Little Giant. Collector interest is low, and values for all trademarks are quite similar.

| Exc. | V.G. | Good | Fair | Poor |
|------|------|------|------|------|
| 150 | 125 | 90 | 65 | 35 |

# BAFORD ARMS, INC.
### Bristol, Tennessee
### C. L. Reedy & Assoc.--Distributors
### Melbourne, Florida

## Thunder Derringer

This is an interchangeable-barrelled, single-shot derringer that comes standard chambered for the .44 Special and .410 shotshell. It has 3" barrels and tips to the side for loading. It has a spur trigger, and the finish is blued with a wood grip. The interchangeable barrels are available chambered from .22 short up to 9mm and are available for mounting a scope. The cost of the interchangeable barrels are $90. This pistol was introduced in 1988.

| NIB | Exc. | V.G. | Good | Fair | Poor |
|-----|------|------|------|------|------|
| 130 | 115 | 100 | 80 | 65 | 45 |

## Fire Power Model 35

This is a stainless-steel copy of the Browning Hi-Power with a removable barrel bushing. It is chambered for the 9mm Parabellum and has a 4.75" barrel and Millett adjustable sights. This pistol is furnished with a 14-round detachable magazine, combat safety and hammer, and Pachmayr rubber grips. It was introduced in 1988.

| NIB | Exc. | V.G. | Good | Fair | Poor |
|-----|------|------|------|------|------|
| 495 | 450 | 375 | 300 | 250 | 175 |

# BAIKAL
### U.S.S.R.
### Commercial Trading Imports
### Bloomington, Minnesota

This line of sporting shotguns cannot currently be imported into the U.S.A. Approximately ten years ago this was not so, as Commercial Trading Imports, at that time a division of Control Data Corp., imported a large number as part of a trade agreement with the Soviets. This venture was less than successful from a commercial standpoint, and the guns were not competitive from a quality or a price standpoint. Repair was, and still is, a serious problem as most gunsmiths have no way to secure parts. There is little or no collector interest, and the guns are hardly the choice of a serious shooter. The values we will illustrate will be what Commercial Trading established as a manufacturer's suggested retail when they were last offered. The current values would not equal these prices and, with the limited demand, would have to be individually appraised.

## Baikal IJ-27E1C

This is the low end Over/Under shotgun chambered for 12 gauge and 20 gauge 3" Magnum. The barrels offered were 26" Skeet/Skeet and 28" Modified/Full. There was a vent rib, chrome-lined bores, single-selective trigger, extractors, and a checkered walnut stock with vented forearm. The standard finish was blued with silver inlays available for an additional $130.

**Mfg. Last Price**
$449.95

## Baikal TOZ - 34

This model is available chambered for 12 and 28 gauge with 26" or 28" barrels with various chokes. It has double triggers, cocking indicators, and chrome-lined bores. It features a checkered walnut stock and a permanently mounted forend. The standard finish is blued with an engraved, silver-plated version available for an additional $175.

**Mfg. Last Price**
$465.95

**Model MC-8-0**
This is a trap and skeet model chambered for the 12 gauge with either 26" Skeet/Skeet or 28" Full/Modified barrels. It has all the previously mentioned features plus a hand-fitted action and a heavily engraved receiver. It is furnished with a fitted case.

**Mfg. Last Price**
$2,295.00

**Model MC-5-105**
This was a higher-grade version with all the standard features of the TOZ-34 and a fully engraved receiver.

**Mfg. Last Price**
$1,325.00

**Model MC-7**
This model has all the standard features of the MC-5- 105 with a deep relief- engraved receiver.

**Mfg. Last Price**
$2,695.00

**Model MC -109**
This is the top of the line Over/Under shotgun. It has hand-detachable sidelocks and is virtually handmade.

**Mfg. Last Price**
$3,695.00

## BAILONS GUNMAKERS, LTD.
### Birmingham, England
This company manufactures boxlock and sidelock shotguns on a special-order, made-to-order basis only. The importation has been extremely limited on these firearms; and if one is contemplating a transaction, a qualified appraisal should be secured. The options that are offered on these firearms, as well as the degree of ornamentation, precludes accurate pricing in a publication of this nature.

**Hunting Rifle**
This is a Mauser-type, bolt-action rifle that is chambered for various popular American and European calibers. It has a 24" barrel with open sights and features a 3- or 4-round magazine and double-set triggers. The finish is blued with a select, checkered walnut stock. There are a number of options available, including degrees of ornamentation. The prices we are furnishing are for a standard-model rifle. This model was introduced in 1986.

| NIB | Exc. | V.G. | Good | Fair | Poor |
|-----|------|------|------|------|------|
| 1850 | 1700 | 1450 | 1100 | 900 | 700 |

## BAKER GAS SEAL
### London, England
This is a unique, heavy, service-type weapon that is chambered for the .577 caliber and utilizes the percussion ignition system. The octagonal barrel is 6.5" long, and the cylinder holds 6 shots. The percussion nipples are somewhat different than on most revolvers of this era; they are at right angles to the barrel. The hammer is single action only and employs a long spur at the rear to cock it. The cylinder on this pistol moves forward into the barrel when cocked, to create the "Gas Seal," a feature not uncommon at the time. This revolver has a blued barrel, case-colored cylinder, and a frame made of German silver. The grips are of a black rubberlike composite. This revolver was patented on the 24th of April in 1852 by T. K. Baker.

| Exc. | V.G. | Good | Fair | Poor |
|------|------|------|------|------|
| 750 | 675 | 600 | 475 | 400 |

## BAKER GUN & FORGING CO.
### Batavia, New York
The Baker Gun & Forging Co. was one of the foremost makers of American, side-by-side, double-barrelled shotguns. Their products were on par with L. C. Smith, Ainsley Fox, and Ithaca.

They were in the firearms business from 1889, when they manufactured high-grade, Damascus-barrelled guns, until 1933 when they were forced to close their doors, another casualty of the great depression. Their products are very collectible today, especially the better-conditioned specimens.

**Note:**
Values listed are for fluid steel-barrelled examples unless otherwise indicated. Damascus barrelled guns are generally worth approximately 60 percent to 75 percent of these figures. On the higher-grade guns where it was available, a single trigger would add approximately $200 to $250.

**Batavia Special**
This is Baker's basic model. It was offered with 26", 28", 30", and 32" barrels in various choke combinations. It is chambered for 12, 16, and 20 gauge and featured sidelocks with extractors and double triggers. The walnut pistolgrip stock is checkered.

| Exc. | V.G. | Good | Fair | Poor |
|------|------|------|------|------|
| 400 | 325 | 275 | 225 | 175 |

**Batavia Leader**
This model is similar to the Batavia Special with a higher degree of finish. Other specifications are the same.

| Exc. | V.G. | Good | Fair | Poor |
|------|------|------|------|------|
| 500 | 425 | 375 | 325 | 275 |

**Black Beauty Special**
This model is similar to the Batavia Leader with an engraved receiver and select walnut for the stock. It is also available with automatic ejectors which would be worth approximately 15 percent additional.

| Exc. | V.G. | Good | Fair | Poor |
|------|------|------|------|------|
| 850 | 750 | 675 | 500 | 375 |

**Batavia Ejector**
This is a deluxe version of the Batavia Leader with all the same specifications and a finer finish.

| Exc. | V.G. | Good | Fair | Poor |
|------|------|------|------|------|
| 900 | 800 | 725 | 550 | 425 |

**Baker S Grade**
This is a still higher-grade version of the Leader with higher-grade walnut and degree of finish.

| Exc. | V.G. | Good | Fair | Poor |
|------|------|------|------|------|
| 1050 | 975 | 875 | 650 | 525 |

**Baker R Grade**
This model is similar to the Baker S Grade with extensive engraving and Krupp steel barrels.

| Exc. | V.G. | Good | Fair | Poor |
|------|------|------|------|------|
| 1300 | 1175 | 1050 | 800 | 650 |

**Paragon Grade**
One of the highest-grade guns that Baker produced, the Paragon was built on a custom-order basis. The automatic ejector model will bring an additional 15 percent.

| Exc. | V.G. | Good | Fair | Poor |
|------|------|------|------|------|
| 1800 | 1675 | 1500 | 1250 | 975 |

**Expert Grade**
This model has standard automatic ejectors and was more profusely engraved.

| Exc. | V.G. | Good | Fair | Poor |
|------|------|------|------|------|
| 2500 | 2200 | 1900 | 1600 | 1000 |

**Deluxe Grade**
This is the top-of-the-line gun. Essentially the same as the Paragon, it has a generally higher-grade finish with more engraving and better-quality wood.

| Exc. | V.G. | Good | Fair | Poor |
|------|------|------|------|------|
| 4000 | 3400 | 2950 | 2100 | 1500 |

## BAKER, M. A.
### Fayetteville, North Carolina

**Percussion Rifle**

This was a single-shot, muzzle-loading rifle that was chambered for .52 caliber percussion. It was converted by Baker on a contract from the state of North Carolina from the U.S. Model 1817 Rifled Musket. It had a 36" round barrel and a full-length walnut stock held on by three barrel bands. The finish was white, and the lockplate was marked, "M. A. Baker/Fayetteville, N.C." The breech was marked, "N. Carolina." This was a very limited-production item that was used by Confederate forces during the Civil War. We recommend competent, individual appraisal on this, as well as on any other Confederate Civil War weapon.

| Exc. | V.G. | Good | Fair | Poor |
|------|------|------|------|------|
| 4500 | 3800 | 3250 | 2500 | 1750 |

## BALL REPEATING CARBINE
### Lamson & Co.
### Windsor, Vermont

**Ball Repeating Carbine**

This unique weapon has a 7-shot repeater with its action activated by a lever that looks like the triggerguard. It is chambered for the .50 caliber rimfire and has a 20.5" round barrel. The walnut stock is two-piece with a straight grip, and the forearm is held on by one barrel band. The receiver is stamped, "E. G.Lamson & Co./Windsor, Vt./U.S./Ball's Patent/June 23, 1863/Mar 15, 1864." There is an inspector's cartouche on the stock at the top of the wrist. There is no evidence that this weapon was actually used in the Civil War, but it is still sought by collectors of Civil War rifles. There were approximately 1,000 manufactured.

| Exc. | V.G. | Good | Fair | Poor |
|------|------|------|------|------|
| 1250 | 1050 | 900 | 750 | 500 |

## BALLARD
### SEE--Marlin Firearms Co.

## BALLARD, C. H.
### Worcester, Massachusetts

**Single Shot Derringer**

This was a small, concealable pistol chambered for .41 caliber rimfire. It has a 2.75" barrel that pivots downward for loading. The barrel is part round and part octagonal. Most examples had silver-plated brass frames, with a few iron-framed models noted. Barrels were either blued or silver-plated, and the birdshead grips were made of walnut. The top of the barrel was stamped "Ballard's." There were only a few thousand manufactured in the 1870's.

**Iron Frame Model--Add 25 Percent.**

| Exc. | V.G. | Good | Fair | Poor |
|------|------|------|------|------|
| 375 | 325 | 250 | 200 | 165 |

## BALLESTER-MOLINA
### SEE--Hafdasa

## BARRET F. A. MFG. CO.
### Murfreesboro, Tenessee

This company manufactures a highly specialized firearm. It has the power and accuarcy to be effective at a range of over a mile. This is basically a military-type weapon, but recently long-range shooting matches have shown the greater potential of this weapon.

**Model 82 Rifle**

This Model is chambered for the .50-caliber Browning machinegun cartridge and has a 37" barrel. It is a recoil-operated, semi-automatic that features an 11-round detachable magazine. It has an integral muzzle brake, is scope-sighted, and weighs approximately 35 lbs. The finish was parkerized. This firearm was manufactured between 1985 and 1987.

| Exc. | V.G. | Good | Fair | Poor |
|------|------|------|------|------|
| 3900 | 3500 | 2900 | 2250 | 1750 |

**Model 82A1**

This Model, also known as the "Barret Light 50," is the only model available to the civilian market. It is an improved version of the Model 82, with a 33" barrel, Luepold M3 10X scope, and backup iron sights. The gun is furnished with a fitted hard case and two 11-round magazines.

| Exc. | V.G. | Good | Fair | Poor |
|------|------|------|------|------|
| 5800 | 5000 | 4000 | 2950 | 2100 |

## BARRET, J. B.
### Wytheville, Virginia

**Barret Rifle**

This weapon is quite an oddity as it was one of very few started out as a breechloader and converted back to a muzzleloader. This was a Confederate weapon that was constructed from Hall rifle and carbine parts captured at the Harpers Ferry Armory. They are chambered for .54 caliber and utilize the percussion ignition system. They have 32.5" barrels that were converted by adding a bronze unit at the breech, which had an inline nipple and flash shield. The full-length stocks appear identical to those of the Hall rifle, but it is obvious that they were made specifically for the Barret as the inletting around the bronze breech unit has not been altered. There are three barrel bands. This is a very rare weapon with limited manufacture in 1862 and 1863.

| Exc. | V.G. | Good | Fair | Poor |
|------|------|------|------|------|
| 4500 | 3750 | 3000 | 2000 | 1500 |

**Barret Carbine**

This is basically the same as the Rifle with a 26" barrel and half stock fastened by two barrel bands. Both weapons were made for use by Confederate troops and are eagerly sought by Civil War collectors.

| Exc. | V.G. | Good | Fair | Poor |
|------|------|------|------|------|
| 5000 | 4250 | 3500 | 2500 | 2000 |

## BAR-STO PRECISION MACHINE
### Burbank, California

**Bar-Sto 25**

This is a blowback, semi-automatic pocket pistol that was patterned after the "Baby Browning." It is chambered for the .25 ACP and constructed of stainless steel with a brushed non-glare finish and walnut grip panels. There were approximately 250 manufactured by this firm, which is known primarily as a producer of fine after-market stainless-steel barrels for the Colt Government Model. They were produced in 1974.

| Exc. | V.G. | Good | Fair | Poor |
|------|------|------|------|------|
| 200 | 175 | 150 | 125 | 100 |

## BASCARAN
### Eibar, Spain

Bascaran's products were quite a rarity in Spain during the early part of this century. This company actually brought out a new design instead of simply copying an existing pattern. Bascaran's pistols were also reasonably well made and nicely finished.

**Martian**

This model has a squared-off barrel and hinged triggerguard. The slide is stamped, "Automatic Pistol Martian." It is a blowback action chambered for 6.35mm and 7.65mm. The grips have "MAB" molded into them.

| Exc. | V.G. | Good | Fair | Poor |
|------|------|------|------|------|
| 225 | 175 | 135 | 100 | 75 |

**Thunder**

This model is a better-quality version of the Martian. It is chambered for the 6.35mm only. The slide is not marked, and "Thunder" appears on the grips.

| Exc. | V.G. | Good | Fair | Poor |
|------|------|------|------|------|
| 250 | 200 | 165 | 125 | 90 |

# BAUER F. A. CORP.
### Fraser, Michigan

**Bauer 25 Automatic**

This is a very small pocket pistol that was identical to the "Baby Browning" except that it was constructed of stainless steel. It is chambered for the .25 ACP and has a 2.5" barrel, rudimentary fixed sights, and a detachable 6- shot magazine. The grips are either checkered walnut or white imitation pearl. This pistol was manufactured between 1972 and 1984.

| Exc. | V.G. | Good | Fair | Poor |
|------|------|------|------|------|
| 200 | 175 | 150 | 110 | 80 |

**The Rabbit**

This is a combination Over/Under gun chambered for the .22 rimfire and the .410. It is made of all alloy with steel barrel liners and has a skeleton metal stock. It was manufactured between 1982 and 1984.

| Exc. | V.G. | Good | Fair | Poor |
|------|------|------|------|------|
| 135 | 110 | 100 | 75 | 50 |

# BAYARD
### SEE--Pieper, H. & N.
### Herstal, Belgium

# BAYONNE, MANUFACTURE D'ARMES
### Bayonne, France
### A/K/A MAB

This company began firearms manufacture in 1921 and is still in business today. They were taken over by the Germans during the occupation, and pistols produced during the years 1940--1944 will bear the German military acceptance marks. After the end of WWII there commercial production was resumed.

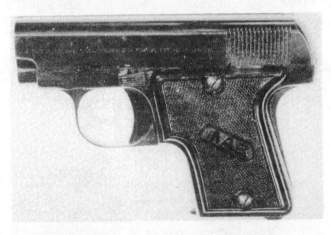

**MAB Modele A**

This is the first pistol produced by this company, and it is still produced. It is a pocket pistol chambered for the 6.35mm. It has a blowback action patterned after the Browning 1906. It features a 2" barrel, a grip safety as well as a manual, and a magazine safety. The finish is blued, and the grips are checkered molded plastic with "MAB" molded into them. This model was first manufactured in 1921 and is currently produced.

| Exc. | V.G. | Good | Fair | Poor |
|------|------|------|------|------|
| 175 | 150 | 125 | 100 | 75 |

**MAB Modele B**

This is another pocket pistol patterned after the early Walther designs. It is chambered for the 6.35mm and features a fixed barrel. The slide is marked "Pistolet Automatique MAB Brevete." This marking became standard and appeared on all MAB pistols after this date. This model was manufactured between 1932 and 1949.

| Exc. | V.G. | Good | Fair | Poor |
|------|------|------|------|------|
| 250 | 225 | 200 | 150 | 110 |

**MAB Modele C**

This model is patterned after the 1910 Browning and has the recoil spring around the barrel. It is chambered for the 7.65mm or the .380 ACP. It features the MAB markings and was manufactured after 1933.

| Exc. | V.G. | Good | Fair | Poor |
|------|------|------|------|------|
| 235 | 210 | 175 | 135 | 110 |

**MAB Modele D**

This model is similar to the Modele C but longer, with a 4" barrel. It was introduced in 1933 and is still manufactured.

| Exc. | V.G. | Good | Fair | Poor |
|------|------|------|------|------|
| 175 | 150 | 125 | 100 | 75 |

**MAB Modele E**

This model, manufactured after WWII, is chambered for the 6.35mm and patterned after the Modele D--but was actually larger than the 7.65 pistol. It was introduced in 1949.

| Exc. | V.G. | Good | Fair | Poor |
|------|------|------|------|------|
| 235 | 210 | 175 | 135 | 100 |

**MAB Modele F**

This unusual pistol is similar to the Modele B, but the barrels could be interchanged in lengths from 2.65" to 7.25". It is chambered for the .22 rimfire and was offered with target sights. This is a very good target pistol when fitted with a longer barrel and is a good value for the money.

| Exc. | V.G. | Good | Fair | Poor |
|------|------|------|------|------|
| 210 | 185 | 150 | 110 | 85 |

**MAB Modele GZ**

This model was not made by Bayonne but was contracted to Arizmendi of Eibar, Spain. It is chambered for 7.65mm and resembles the Modele C. The slide was marked, "Echasa Eibar(Espana) Cal..32 Modelo GZ-MAB Espanola."

| Exc. | V.G. | Good | Fair | Poor |
|------|------|------|------|------|
| 210  | 185  | 150  | 110  | 85   |

## MAB Modele R
This model is similar to the Modele D with an external hammer. It is chambered for 7.65mm and 7.65mm long.

| Exc. | V.G. | Good | Fair | Poor |
|------|------|------|------|------|
| 285  | 250  | 200  | 150  | 110  |

## MAB Modele R Para
This model is a larger version of the Modele R, that is chambered for the 9mm Parabellum. It features a locked breech activated by a rotating barrel to accommodate the increased power of the cartridge. This model is quite scarce and is rarely encountered on todays market.

| Exc. | V.G. | Good | Fair | Poor |
|------|------|------|------|------|
| 400  | 350  | 300  | 225  | 150  |

## MAB Modele PA-15
This is the military version of the Modele R Para. It is similar except that the butt accommodates a 15-round magazine. This was the French service pistol.

| Exc. | V.G. | Good | Fair | Poor |
|------|------|------|------|------|
| 400  | 350  | 300  | 225  | 150  |

## Modele "Le Chasseur"
This is essentially the Modele F with an external hammer chambered for .22 rimfire. It was offered with a number of barrel lengths and types of sights. It was introduced in 1953.

| Exc. | V.G. | Good | Fair | Poor |
|------|------|------|------|------|
| 225  | 200  | 175  | 145  | 100  |

### Note:
MAB pistols that were sold in the U.S.A. were sold by the Winfield Arms Company of Los Angeles, California, and were marked "Made in France for WAC." This would not effect values to any appreciable degree.

## BEATTIE, J.
### London, England

### Beattie Gas Seal Revolver
This is a large, service-type revolver that features the gas seal cylinder that moves forward into the barrel when the pistol is cocked. This revolver has a 6.25" octagonal barrel and is chambered for .42 caliber. It utilizes the percussion ignition system. The cylinder, with its nipples at right angles to the barrel, holds 6 shots. The hammer was a single action only; and there was no rammer, so the bullets could not be tight in the cylinder--a defect that caused chain fires on revolvers. The gas seal feature prevented this and was the basis for the gun's popularity during this era. This revolver has a blued barrel and a case-colored and engraved frame. The cylinder is case colored as well. The grip is of a checkered, hard rubberlike material with a metal end cap. This revolver was manufactured in the mid 1850's.

| Exc.  | V.G.  | Good  | Fair  | Poor  |
|-------|-------|-------|-------|-------|
| 4250  | 3950  | 3250  | 2700  | 2200  |

## BEAUMONT
### Maastrict, Netherlands

### 1873 Dutch Service Revolver, Old Model
This is a solid-frame, gate-loading revolver. It weighs 2 lbs. 12 ounces and is chambered for the 9.4mm Dutch service cartridge. The ejector rod is carried separately from the weapon, and the lockwork is double action only.

| Exc. | V.G. | Good | Fair | Poor |
|------|------|------|------|------|
| 250  | 225  | 185  | 145  | 100  |

### 1873 Dutch Service Revolver, New Model
This variation is identical to the Old Model in every aspect except that it has a round barrel and is slightly lighter in weight.

| Exc. | V.G. | Good | Fair | Poor |
|------|------|------|------|------|
| 250  | 225  | 185  | 145  | 100  |

### 1873 KIM, Small Model
The KIM is chambered in the same caliber as the Service Models, but the cylinder carries only 5 shots instead of 6. This enabled the octagonal barrelled KIM to be smaller and lighter in all respects.

| Exc. | V.G. | Good | Fair | Poor |
|------|------|------|------|------|
| 265  | 240  | 200  | 150  | 110  |

## BEAUMONT, ADAMS
### SEE--Adams

## BEAUMONT-VITALI
### Holland

### Beaumont-Vitali
This is a bolt-action military rifle that is chambered for the 11mm cartridge. It is basically a modification of the original M 1871 Single-Shot Rifle, that was modified to accept the Italian Vitali box magazine. The barrel is 30" in length with military-type sights. The finish is blued with a full-length walnut stock held on by two barrel bands. This rifle is not as common as other contemporary military models.

| Exc. | V.G. | Good | Fair | Poor |
|------|------|------|------|------|
| 200  | 175  | 125  | 90   | 65   |

## BECKER AND HOLLANDER
### Suhl, Germany

### Beholla
This company was very well respected in pre-WWI Germany. With the War on the horizon, they developed the Beholla, a well-made, simple and strong 7.65mm semi- automatic pistol. The entire production was manufactured for the German war

department. They were never intended as a commercial endeavor. The left side of the slide is stamped "Selbstlade Pistol Beholla Cal. 7.65"; "Becker U Hollander Waffenbau Suhl" is marked on the right. Toward the latter part of the War, manufacture of the Beholla was licensed to other German gun companies.

| Exc. | V.G. | Good | Fair | Poor |
|---|---|---|---|---|
| 300 | 275 | 225 | 175 | 125 |

# BEEMAN PRECISION ARMS, INC.
## Santa Rosa, California

Beeman is a large company engaged in the importation of high-quality firearms and air guns. They are perhaps best known for their air rifles, but the following weapons are manufactured expressly for them to their specifications and bear their name so they have been listed here. Other Beeman imports will be found in their own respective sections under the manufacturer's heading.

### MP-08
This is a toggle-action semi-automatic similar in function to the German luger. It is chambered for the .380 ACP and has a 3.5" barrel and a 6-shot detachable magazine. The finish is blue. This model was introduced in 1968 and is still being manufactured.

| NIB | Exc. | V.G. | Good | Fair | Poor |
|---|---|---|---|---|---|
| 390 | 350 | 300 | 210 | 175 | 110 |

### P-08
This model is similar in appearance to the MP-08 but is chambered for the .22 rimfire, with an 8-shot magazine and checkered walnut grips. It was introduced in 1969.

| NIB | Exc. | V.G. | Good | Fair | Poor |
|---|---|---|---|---|---|
| 390 | 350 | 300 | 210 | 175 | 110 |

### SP Standard
This is a German-made, single-shot target pistol with barrel lengths from 8" to 15". It has a side-mounted opening lever and is chambered for the .22 rimfire. It has adjustable sights and walnut grips. It was imported in 1985 and 1986 only.

| NIB | Exc. | V.G. | Good | Fair | Poor |
|---|---|---|---|---|---|
| 225 | 200 | 175 | 150 | 125 | 100 |

### SP Deluxe
This model is similar to the SP Standard except that it has a walnut forearm.

| Exc. | V.G. | Good | Fair | Poor |
|---|---|---|---|---|
| 250 | 225 | 200 | 175 | 125 |

# BEERSTECHER, FREDERICK
## Philadelphia, Pennsylvania
### Superposed Load Pocket Pistol
This is a rather unique pistol as it has one barrel but is capable of firing two successive shots. The two separate loads are placed one on top of the other in the barrel, and there are two nipples on the double bolster. The hammer has a large double strike that is hinged to fire the top charge and then the second charge. This pistol was offered with various barrel lengths, with 3" being the average. It was chambered for .41 caliber, with the percussion ignition system used. The walnut stock has a birdshead butt without a cap, and the pistol is available in belt or large derringer size. It is marked "F. Beerstecher's/Patent 1855" on the lock. There is the possibility that this gun was made by other manufacturers for Beerstecher. It is a very rare firearm with limited production in the 1850's.

| Exc. | V.G. | Good | Fair | Poor |
|---|---|---|---|---|
| 5000 | 4500 | 4000 | 3000 | 2500 |

# BEHOLLA
## SEE--Becher and Hollander

# BEISTEGUI, HERMANOS
## Eibar, Spain
### Beistegui "RUBY"
This model appears to be the first contract copy of the Ruby-style Eibar pistol. It was initially manufactured in 1914 and marked "1914 Model Automatic Pistol Beistegui Hermanos Eibar [Espana]." It is a rather large-sized pistol chambered for 7.65mm. There is a lanyard ring on the butt.

| Exc. | V.G. | Good | Fair | Poor |
|---|---|---|---|---|
| 200 | 150 | 125 | 80 | 50 |

### Bulwark #1
The Bulwark is a fixed-barrel, external-hammer, blowback semi-automatic chambered for the 7.65mm cartridge. It bears no external markings except the monogram "B&H" molded into the grips.

| Exc. | V.G. | Good | Fair | Poor |
|---|---|---|---|---|
| 150 | 125 | 100 | 75 | 50 |

### Bulwark #2
This pistol is totally different from the #1 model. It is a faithful but poor-quality copy of the "Baby Browning" chambered for 6.35mm. It is marked "Fabrique de Armes de Guerre de Grand Precision Bulwark Patent Depose No. 67259."

| Exc. | V.G. | Good | Fair | Poor |
|---|---|---|---|---|
| 150 | 125 | 100 | 75 | 50 |

### Libia
This model is identical to the Bulwark #2 but bears the marking "Libia", obviously indicating export production.

| Exc. | V.G. | Good | Fair | Poor |
|---|---|---|---|---|
| 150 | 125 | 100 | 75 | 50 |

# BENELLI
## Italy
## Importer--Heckler & Koch
## Chantilly, Virginia
### Shotguns
### Model SL-121 V
This is a semi-automatic 12 gauge with 3" chambers and various barrel lengths and chokes. It has a black anodized alloy receiver and was discontinued in 1985.

| Exc. | V.G. | Good | Fair | Poor |
|---|---|---|---|---|
| 350 | 300 | 250 | 200 | 150 |

### Model SL 121 Slug
This model is similar to the SL-121 V with a 21" cylinder-bore barrel and rifle sights. It too was discontinued in 1985.

| Exc. | V.G. | Good | Fair | Poor |
|---|---|---|---|---|
| 375 | 325 | 275 | 225 | 175 |

### Model SL-123 V
This model has the improved, fast, third-generation action. Otherwise it resembles the earlier SL-121.

| Exc. | V.G. | Good | Fair | Poor |
|---|---|---|---|---|
| 400 | 350 | 300 | 250 | 200 |

### Model SL201
This is a 20 gauge with a 26", improved cylinder barrel. It is similar in appearance to the SL-123.

| Exc. | V.G. | Good | Fair | Poor |
|---|---|---|---|---|
| 350 | 300 | 250 | 200 | 175 |

### M1 Super 90
This is an improved version of the Benelli semi-automatic action. It has a rotating bolt system and is chambered for 12 gauge, with a 3" chamber. This model has a 19.75" barrel with cylinder bore and rifle sights. It has a matte black finish and a black fiberglas stock and forearm. This model was introduced in 1986.

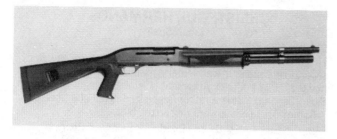

| NIB | Exc. | V.G. | Good | Fair | Poor |
|-----|------|------|------|------|------|
| 610 | 550 | 450 | 350 | 275 | 225 |

**M1 Super 90 Field**

This model is similar to the Super 90 above with a 26" or 28" barrel with screw-in choke tubes.

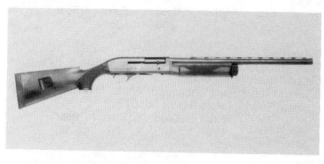

| NIB | Exc. | V.G. | Good | Fair | Poor |
|-----|------|------|------|------|------|
| 650 | 600 | 500 | 400 | 325 | 250 |

**Montefeltro Super 90 Hunter**

Introduced in 1988, this model is similar to the Super 90 Field with a checkered walnut stock and forearm in choice of gloss or matte finish.

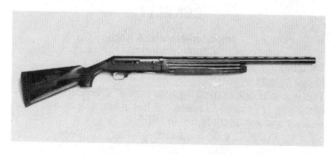

| NIB | Exc. | V.G. | Good | Fair | Poor |
|-----|------|------|------|------|------|
| 675 | 625 | 525 | 425 | 350 | 275 |

**Black Eagle**

This model is similar to the Montefeltro Super 90 Hunter with a black fiberglas stock and forearm. It is offered with a 21", 24", or 26" vent rib-barrel with screw-in choke tubes. It was introduced in 1989.

| NIB | Exc. | V.G. | Good | Fair | Poor |
|-----|------|------|------|------|------|
| 800 | 725 | 600 | 500 | 425 | 325 |

**M3 Super 90**

This is a convertible pump to semi-automatic action in a paramilitary configuration. It is chambered for 12 gauge and has a 19.75" cylinder-bore barrel with rifle sights and a pistolgrip polymer stock. It was introduced in 1989.

| NIB | Exc. | V.G. | Good | Fair | Poor |
|-----|------|------|------|------|------|
| 800 | 725 | 600 | 500 | 425 | 325 |

**Handguns**

**Model B-76**

This is an all-steel, double-action semi-automatic chambered for the 9mm Parabellum. It has a 4.25" barrel, fixed sights, and an 8-round detachable magazine.

| NIB | Exc. | V.G. | Good | Fair | Poor |
|-----|------|------|------|------|------|
| 425 | 400 | 350 | 290 | 225 | 175 |

**Model B-76S**

This is the target version of the B-76. It has a 5.5" barrel, adjustable sights, and target grips.

| NIB | Exc. | V.G. | Good | Fair | Poor |
|-----|------|------|------|------|------|
| 595 | 525 | 450 | 350 | 300 | 225 |

**Model B-77**

This Model is similar to the B-76 except that it is chambered for the .32 ACP.

| NIB | Exc. | V.G. | Good | Fair | Poor |
|-----|------|------|------|------|------|
| 400 | 375 | 325 | 275 | 200 | 150 |

**Model B-80**

This is another model similar to the B-76 except that it is chambered for the .30 Luger cartridge.

| NIB | Exc. | V.G. | Good | Fair | Poor |
|-----|------|------|------|------|------|
| 385 | 350 | 300 | 250 | 175 | 125 |

**Model B-80S**

This is the target version of the B-80 with a 5.5" barrel and adjustable sights. It also features target grips.

| NIB | Exc. | V.G. | Good | Fair | Poor |
|-----|------|------|------|------|------|
| 575 | 500 | 425 | 325 | 250 | 200 |

## BENSON FIREARMS
### Seattle, Washington
### SEE--Aldo Uberti

This was formerly the importer of the fine Italian Uberti firearms. Their arrangement ended in 1989, and these guns are now imported by Uberti U.S.A., Inc. Benson-imported guns would be so marked on the barrel, and this would have no effect on the value of the firearm. Uberti firearms will be found listed under their own section.

## BENTLEY, JOSEPH
### Birmingham, England

**Bentley Revolver**

This large revolver, chambered for .44 caliber, utilizes the percussion ignition system. This revolver is unique in that the frame and grip straps were forged from one piece and the 7" barrel is hexagonal. This is a double-action revolver that holds 5 shots. The quality of this revolver is mediocre, and the finish is browned. Bentley worked very closely with Webly, and the mutual influence is apparent. This revolver was manufactured in the mid-1850's, and the only identifying marks were "J. Parkinson, Macclesfield," who was probably the seller.

| Exc. | V.G. | Good | Fair | Poor |
|------|------|------|------|------|
| 3500 | 3000 | 2500 | 1850 | 1200 |

## BERETTA, DR. F.
### Brescia, Italy
### Importer--Double M Shooting Sports
### Guilford, Connecticut

**Black Diamond Field Grade**

This is an Over/Under shotgun chambered for all gauges with various barrel lengths and choke combinations. It features a single trigger, automatic ejectors, and a coin-finished boxlock action. The barrels are blued with a checkered walnut stock.

| NIB | Exc. | V.G. | Good | Fair | Poor |
|-----|------|------|------|------|------|
| 975 | 850 | 700 | 575 | 450 | 375 |

There are four other Black Diamond models that are similar to the Field model but differ in the amount of engraving and the quality of materials and workmanship utilized in their construction. Otherwise, they are similar.

### Grade One

| NIB | Exc. | V.G. | Good | Fair | Poor |
|---|---|---|---|---|---|
| 1450 | 1300 | 1000 | 850 | 600 | 500 |

### Grade Two

| NIB | Exc. | V.G. | Good | Fair | Poor |
|---|---|---|---|---|---|
| 2100 | 1850 | 1600 | 1250 | 1000 | 800 |

### Grade Three

| NIB | Exc. | V.G. | Good | Fair | Poor |
|---|---|---|---|---|---|
| 3000 | 2750 | 2200 | 1850 | 1500 | 1150 |

### Grade Four

| NIB | Exc. | V.G. | Good | Fair | Poor |
|---|---|---|---|---|---|
| 4000 | 3750 | 3200 | 2850 | 2500 | 2150 |

### Gamma Standard

This Over/Under shotgun was chambered for 12, 16, or 20 gauge. It was offered with 26" or 28" barrels with various choke combinations. It featured a boxlock action that was engraved and coin-finished. It had a single trigger and automatic ejectors. The barrels were blued with a walnut stock. It was imported between 1984 and 1988.

| Exc. | V.G. | Good | Fair | Poor |
|---|---|---|---|---|
| 400 | 375 | 300 | 225 | 150 |

### Gamma Deluxe

This was a more-deluxe version of the Gamma Standard.

| Exc. | V.G. | Good | Fair | Poor |
|---|---|---|---|---|
| 600 | 575 | 500 | 400 | 250 |

### Gamma Target

This was a trap or skeet competition version of the Gamma Standard. It was imported between 1986 and 1988.

| Exc. | V.G. | Good | Fair | Poor |
|---|---|---|---|---|
| 550 | 500 | 450 | 375 | 300 |

### America Standard

This Over/Under shotgun was chambered for .410 only. It was offered with 26" or 28" barrels with various choke combinations. It had an engraved, coin-finished, boxlock action, blued barrels, and a checkered walnut stock. It was imported between 1984 and 1988.

| Exc. | V.G. | Good | Fair | Poor |
|---|---|---|---|---|
| 300 | 275 | 225 | 185 | 150 |

### America Deluxe

This was a slightly better-grade version of the America Standard.

| Exc. | V.G. | Good | Fair | Poor |
|---|---|---|---|---|
| 375 | 325 | 275 | 220 | 175 |

### Black Eagle

This model is similar to the Montefeltro Super 90 Hunter with a black fiberglas stock and forearm. It is offered with a 21", 24", or 26" vent rib-barrel with screw-in choke tubes. It was introduced in 1989.

| NIB | Exc. | V.G. | Good | Fair | Poor |
|---|---|---|---|---|---|
| 800 | 725 | 600 | 500 | 425 | 325 |

### M3 Super 90

This is a convertible pump to semi-automatic action in a paramilitary configuration. It is chambered for 12 gauge and has a 19.75" cylinder-bore barrel with rifle sights and a pistolgrip polymer stock. It was introduced in 1989.

| NIB | Exc. | V.G. | Good | Fair | Poor |
|---|---|---|---|---|---|
| 800 | 725 | 600 | 500 | 425 | 325 |

### Handguns
### Model B-76

This is an all-steel, double-action semi-automatic chambered for the 9mm Parabellum. It has a 4.25" barrel, fixed sights, and an 8-round detachable magazine.

| NIB | Exc. | V.G. | Good | Fair | Poor |
|---|---|---|---|---|---|
| 425 | 400 | 350 | 290 | 225 | 175 |

### Model B-76S

This is the target version of the B-76. It has a 5.5" barrel, adjustable sights, and target grips.

| NIB | Exc. | V.G. | Good | Fair | Poor |
|---|---|---|---|---|---|
| 595 | 525 | 450 | 350 | 300 | 225 |

### Europa

This model was also chambered for .410 and offered with 26" barrels with various choke combinations. It had a coin-finished, engraved, boxlock action with a checkered walnut stock. It was imported between 1984 and 1988.

| Exc. | V.G. | Good | Fair | Poor |
|---|---|---|---|---|
| 275 | 250 | 185 | 150 | 125 |

### Europa Deluxe

This was a slightly better-grade version of the Europa standard.

| Exc. | V.G. | Good | Fair | Poor |
|---|---|---|---|---|
| 375 | 350 | 285 | 250 | 225 |

### Francia Standard

This was a SxS, double-barrel shotgun chambered for .410. It had a boxlock action, double triggers, and manual extractors. The finish was blued with a checkered walnut stock. It was imported between 1986 and 1988.

| Exc. | V.G. | Good | Fair | Poor |
|---|---|---|---|---|
| 240 | 210 | 185 | 150 | 125 |

### Alpha Three

This was a SxS, double-barrel shotgun chambered for 12, 16, or 20 gauge. It was offered with 26" or 28" barrels with various choke combinations. It had a heavily engraved, coin-finished, boxlock receiver with a single trigger and automatic ejectors. The barrels were blued with a checkered walnut stock. It was imported between 1984 and 1988.

| Exc. | V.G. | Good | Fair | Poor |
|---|---|---|---|---|
| 400 | 350 | 300 | 225 | 150 |

### Beta Three

This was a single-barrel, break-open, field-grade gun that was chambered for all gauges. It was offered with a vent-rib barrel from 24" to 32" in length. The receiver was chrome-plated, and the stock was walnut. It was imported between 1985 and 1988.

| Exc. | V.G. | Good | Fair | Poor |
|---|---|---|---|---|
| 150 | 135 | 110 | 75 | 50 |

## BERETTA, PIETRO
### Brescia, Italy
### Beretta U.S.A.
### Accokeek, Maryland

This is an old-line firearms company that has been producing high-grade weapons since the seventeenth century. They have a history of producing sporting rifles and shotguns as well as military longarms and handguns. As of January 15, 1985, they have been awarded the contract to produce the new 9mm double-action U.S. service pistol. This gun is currently being manufactured in the United States at Beretta's plant in Accokeek, Maryland.

### Model 1910

This is a blowback-operated, single-action, semi-automatic pocket pistol chambered for the 6.35mm cartridge. It has a 2" barrel with fixed sights and a 7-round, detachable magazine. The finish is blued with wood grips. It was manufactured between 1910 and 1934.

| Exc. | V.G. | Good | Fair | Poor |
|---|---|---|---|---|
| 300 | 275 | 200 | 150 | 100 |

### Model 1915

This was a WWI production item. It is a blowback-operated, single-action, semi-automatic pistol chambered for the 7.65mm cartridge. It has a 3.5" barrel with an open-top slide. It has fixed sights and an 8-shot, detachable magazine. The finish is blued with wood grips. The slide is marked, "Pietro Beretta Brescia Casa Fondata nel 1680 Cal. 7.65mm Brevetto

1915." It was manufactured between 1915 and 1919.

| Exc. | V.G. | Good | Fair | Poor |
|------|------|------|------|------|
| 295 | 270 | 200 | 150 | 100 |

## Model 1915 2nd Variation

This is a slightly larger version chambered for the 9mm Glisenti cartridge. This model is slightly larger than the original Model 1915 and features a stronger recoil spring with a recoil-softening buffer spring. It is less commonly encountered.

| Exc. | V.G. | Good | Fair | Poor |
|------|------|------|------|------|
| 375 | 325 | 250 | 200 | 125 |

## Model 1915/1919

This is an improved version that incorporated a new barrel-mounting method and a longer cutout in the top of the slide. Otherwise, it is similar to the Model 1915.

| Exc. | V.G. | Good | Fair | Poor |
|------|------|------|------|------|
| 300 | 275 | 200 | 150 | 100 |

## Model 1919

This was Beretta's initial commercial pistol. It is chambered for the 6.35mm and has a grip safety on the backstrap. Otherwise, it's similar in configuration to the Model 1915/1919. It was manufactured between 1920 and 1939.

| Exc. | V.G. | Good | Fair | Poor |
|------|------|------|------|------|
| 300 | 275 | 200 | 150 | 100 |

## Model 1923

This is a blowback-operated, semi-automatic pistol chambered for the 9mm Glisenti cartridge. It differs from its predecessors basically by the use of an external hammer. This model was originally a military pistol that was later sold commercially. It has a 4" barrel with an 8-shot magazine. The finish is blued with steel grips. The slide is marked, "Brev 1915-1919 Mlo 1923." This Model was manufactured between 1923 and 1935.

| Exc. | V.G. | Good | Fair | Poor |
|------|------|------|------|------|
| 450 | 400 | 325 | 225 | 150 |

## Model 1931

This is a blowback-operated, semi-automatic pistol that is chambered for the 7.65mm cartridge. It has a 3.5" barrel and an open-top slide. It fires by means of an external hammer. The majority of these pistols were issued to the Italian navy and were blued with wooden grips bearing a naval medallion marked, "RM" separated by an anchor.

| Exc. | V.G. | Good | Fair | Poor |
|------|------|------|------|------|
| 350 | 325 | 250 | 200 | 150 |

## Model 1934

This is the most commonly encountered Beretta. It was the standard Italian service pistol in WWII. It is very similar to the Model 1931 except that it is chambered for the 9mm short cartridge. The slide is marked, "P. Beretta Cal. 9 Corto-Mo 1934 Brevet Gardone VT." This inscription is followed by the date of

manufacture that was given numerically, followed by a Roman numeral that denoted the year of manufacture on the Fascist calendar which began in 1922. Examples are marked, "RM" (Navy), "RE" (Army), "RA" (Air Force), and "PS" (Police). It was manufactured between 1934 and 1959. Later post-war commercial versions have a better finish.

| Exc. | V.G. | Good | Fair | Poor |
|------|------|------|------|------|
| 300 | 275 | 200 | 150 | 100 |

## Model 1935

This pistol is similar to the Model 1934 except that it is chambered for the 7.65mm cartridge. After the War, it became known commercially as the Model 935. It was manufactured between 1935 and 1959.

| Exc. | V.G. | Good | Fair | Poor |
|------|------|------|------|------|
| 275 | 250 | 200 | 150 | 100 |

## Model 318

This is an improved version of the old Model 1919. The butt is re-shaped to afford a better grip. It is chambered for the .25 ACP cartridge and has a 2.5" barrel. It is finished in a number of ways and has plastic grips. In the United States it is known as the "Panther." It was manufactured between 1935 and 1946.

| Exc. | V.G. | Good | Fair | Poor |
|------|------|------|------|------|
| 275 | 250 | 200 | 150 | 100 |

## Model 418

This is an improved version of the Model 318 with a rounded grip and a cocking indicator. It is known as the "Bantam" in the U.S. It was introduced in 1947.

| Exc. | V.G. | Good | Fair | Poor |
|------|------|------|------|------|
| 225 | 200 | 175 | 135 | 90 |

## Model 420

This is an engraved and chrome-plated Model 418.

| Exc. | V.G. | Good | Fair | Poor |
|------|------|------|------|------|
| 325 | 300 | 275 | 200 | 150 |

## Model 421

This is an engraved, gold-plated Model 418 with tortoise-shell grips.

| Exc. | V.G. | Good | Fair | Poor |
|------|------|------|------|------|
| 475 | 425 | 325 | 250 | 185 |

## Model 948

This is a .22 l.r. version of the Model 1934. It has either a 3.5" or 6" barrel.

| Exc. | V.G. | Good | Fair | Poor |
|------|------|------|------|------|
| 190 | 165 | 135 | 100 | 75 |

## Model 949 Olympic Target

This is a semi-automatic target pistol that was designed to be competitive in the Olympics. It is chambered for either the .22 short or .22 l.r. cartridge. It has an open-top slide with an 8.75" barrel. It features adjustable sights, barrel weights, and a muzzle break. The finish is blued with checkered, walnut, thumbrest grips. It was manufactured between 1959 and 1964.

| Exc. | V.G. | Good | Fair | Poor |
|------|------|------|------|------|
| 700 | 650 | 550 | 400 | 250 |

### Model 950

This is a blowback-operated, semi-automatic pocket pistol that is chambered for the .22 short cartridge. It has a 2.25" barrel that is hinged at the front and could be pivoted forward for cleaning or loading, making this either a semi-auto or single-shot pistol. It has an open-top slide and a blued finish with plastic grips. It was introduced in 1955. There is a 4"-barrel version also available. In the U.S. this model is known as the "Minx."

| Exc. | V.G. | Good | Fair | Poor |
|------|------|------|------|------|
| 150 | 135 | 110 | 85 | 50 |

### Model 950B

This is a .25 ACP version of the "Minx." It is known as the "Jetfire" in the United States.

| Exc. | V.G. | Good | Fair | Poor |
|------|------|------|------|------|
| 150 | 135 | 110 | 85 | 50 |

### Model 951

This is Beretta's first locked-breech pistol. It is chambered for the 9mm Parabellum cartridge and has a 4.5" barrel. It uses a detachable magazine and has fixed sights. The finish is blued with plastic grips. This model was the standard service pistol in Italy as well as in Egypt. It was used extensively in Israel, as well. It is also known as the "Brigadier." It was introduced in 1952 and is still being produced today.

| Exc. | V.G. | Good | Fair | Poor |
|------|------|------|------|------|
| 250 | 225 | 200 | 175 | 125 |

### Model 70

This is a streamline version of the Model 948. It has a cross-bolt safety, hold-open device, and a push-button magazine release. There are a number of sub-variations available chambered for the .22 l.r., .32 ACP, and the .380 ACP cartridges. It is available with a 3.5" or 6" barrel and has a detachable magazine. It is also known as the "Puma" or the "Cougar." It was introduced in 1958 and discontinued in 1985.

| Exc. | V.G. | Good | Fair | Poor |
|------|------|------|------|------|
| 200 | 175 | 150 | 110 | 75 |

### Model 101

This is simply another name for the Model 70T pistol.

| Exc. | V.G. | Good | Fair | Poor |
|------|------|------|------|------|
| 250 | 225 | 175 | 150 | 100 |

### Model 20

This represents Beretta's first double-action, semi-automatic pistol. It is chambered for .25 ACP and has a 2.5" barrel with a 9-shot magazine. It has an alloy frame and is blued with either walnut or plastic grips. It was discontinued in 1985.

| Exc. | V.G. | Good | Fair | Poor |
|------|------|------|------|------|
| 175 | 150 | 125 | 90 | 75 |

### Model 71 (Jaguar)

This is an alloy-framed version of the Model 70 chambered for the .22 l.r. cartridge. It has a 3.5" barrel, as well as a 6" barrel when known as the Model 72. It was discontinued in 1985.

| Exc. | V.G. | Good | Fair | Poor |
|------|------|------|------|------|
| 225 | 200 | 175 | 125 | 100 |

### Model 90

This is a double-action, blowback-operated, semi-automatic pocket pistol with a streamlined shape and an enclosed 3.5" barrel. It has an 8-round magazine with an external hammer and loaded-chamber indicator. It was manufactured between 1969 and 1983.

| Exc. | V.G. | Good | Fair | Poor |
|------|------|------|------|------|
| 275 | 250 | 200 | 150 | 125 |

### Model 92

This is a double-action, semi-automatic pistol that is chambered for the 9mm Parabellum cartridge. It features a 5" barrel with fixed sights and a 16-round, double-stack magazine. The frame is aluminum alloy with a blued finish and plastic grips. It was introduced in 1976 and is now discontinued.

| Exc. | V.G. | Good | Fair | Poor |
|------|------|------|------|------|
| 400 | 375 | 300 | 250 | 200 |

### Model 92SB-P

This is an improved, polished version that was manufactured between 1980 and 1985.

| Exc. | V.G. | Good | Fair | Poor |
|------|------|------|------|------|
| 450 | 425 | 350 | 300 | 225 |

### Model 92SB Compact

This is a smaller version of the Model 92SB with a 4.3" barrel and a shortened grip frame that holds a 14-shot magazine. It is either blued or nickle-plated with wood or plastic grips. The nickle version would be worth an additional 15 percent. The wood grips would add $20 to the value. This Model was introduced in 1980 and discontinued in 1985.

| Exc. | V.G. | Good | Fair | Poor |
|------|------|------|------|------|
| 475 | 450 | 400 | 350 | 275 |

### Model 84

This is a double-action, semi-automatic pistol chambered for the .380 ACP cartridge. It has a 3.8" barrel with an alloy frame and a 14-round, detachable magazine. It is available either blued or nickle-plated, with wood or plastic grips. The nickle version would increase the value approximately 15 percent. The wood grips are worth an additional $25.

| NIB | Exc. | V.G. | Good | Fair | Poor |
|-----|------|------|------|------|------|
| 470 | 425 | 375 | 300 | 225 | 150 |

### Model 87

This is a double-action, semi-automatic target pistol chambered for the .22 l.r. cartridge. It is offered with a 3.8" or 6" barrel with adjustable sights and a barrel weight. It has a 7-round magazine and is blued with checkered walnut grips. It was introduced in 1986.

| NIB | Exc. | V.G. | Good | Fair | Poor |
|-----|------|------|------|------|------|
| 450 | 400 | 350 | 300 | 225 | 150 |

### Model 89

This is a single-action, semi-automatic target pistol chambered for the .22 l.r. cartridge. It has adjustable sights, a 10-round, detachable magazine, and a matte-black finish with hand-fitting walnut grips. It was introduced in 1988.

| NIB | Exc. | V.G. | Good | Fair | Poor |
|-----|------|------|------|------|------|
| 625 | 575 | 500 | 400 | 275 | 200 |

### Model 950 BS

This is a blowback-operated, semi-automatic pocket pistol chambered for the .22 short or the .25 ACP cartridges. It features a pivoting, 2.5" or 4" barrel that tips upward for cleaning or loading. It has either a 6-round or 8-round magazine and is offered in either blued or nickle-plate with black plastic grips. The nickle-plated version is worth an extra 15 percent.

| NIB | Exc. | V.G. | Good | Fair | Poor |
|-----|------|------|------|------|------|
| 150 | 125 | 100 | 75 | 60 | 45 |

### Model 92F

This is the current U.S. military service pistol. It is chambered for the 9mm Parabellum cartridge and has a 4.9" barrel, with fixed sights and an alloy frame. It has a 15-round, double-stack magazine with an extended base. It has a loaded chamber indicator and a non-glare, matte-blued finish. It is available with either walnut or plastic grips. It was introduced in 1984.

| NIB | Exc. | V.G. | Good | Fair | Poor |
|-----|------|------|------|------|------|
| 600 | 585 | 500 | 400 | 325 | 250 |

### Model 92F Compact

This is a smaller, compact version of the Model 92F with a 4.3" barrel and a 13-round magazine.

| NIB | Exc. | V.G. | Good | Fair | Poor |
|-----|------|------|------|------|------|
| 625 | 600 | 525 | 425 | 350 | 275 |

### AR-70

This is a high quality, semi-automatic, assault-type rifle that is chambered for the .222 or .223 cartridges. It is offered with a 17.7" barrel and either a 5-, 8-, or 30-round detachable magazine. It has adjustable diopter sights and a black epoxy finish. The stock is synthetic. Due to the current problems we are experiencing in this country regarding the importation of paramilitary, semi-automatic weapons, it is impossible to accurately appraise this rifle. We recommend qualified, local appraisal if a transaction is contemplated.

### Model 500 Custom

This is a high quality, bolt-action sporting rifle chambered for various popular calibers. It has a 24" barrel with open sights and was offered in three action lengths. It has either a 3- or 4-shot magazine and a blued finish with a checkered walnut stock with recoil pad.

| Exc. | V.G. | Good | Fair | Poor |
|------|------|------|------|------|
| 600 | 525 | 400 | 325 | 275 |

There were five other variations of this basic model that differed in the quality of materials and workmanship, as well as the degree of ornamentation. Otherwise, they were similar to the Model 500 Custom.

### Model 500S

| Exc. | V.G. | Good | Fair | Poor |
|------|------|------|------|------|
| 625 | 550 | 425 | 350 | 300 |

### Model 500DL

| Exc. | V.G. | Good | Fair | Poor |
|------|------|------|------|------|
| 1400 | 1250 | 1000 | 775 | 650 |

### Model 500EELL

| Exc. | V.G. | Good | Fair | Poor |
|------|------|------|------|------|
| 1600 | 1450 | 1200 | 975 | 800 |

### Model 500EELLS

| Exc. | V.G. | Good | Fair | Poor |
|------|------|------|------|------|
| 1625 | 1475 | 1225 | 1000 | 825 |

## Model 501

This is a medium-action rifle chambered for the .243 or .308 cartridges. It has a 23" barrel and is furnished without sights. It has a 6-shot magazine with a blued finish and a checkered walnut stock. It was discontinued in 1986. It was offered in the same variations as the Model 500 series--501S, 501DL, 501DLS, 501EELL, and 501EELLS. The values for this series are the same as for the 500 series rifles.

## Model 502

This is a long-action sporting rifle chambered for .270, 7mm Remington Magnum, and the .30-06 cartridges. It has a 24" barrel that is furnished without sights. It has a 5-round magazine, a blued finish, and a checkered walnut stock. It was discontinued in 1986. It is also available in the same variations as the Model 500 and the Model 501 but is valued at approximately 10 percent higher in each variation.

## Model S689

This is an Over/Under, double-barrelled rifle that is chambered for the 9.3x74R or the .30-06 cartridges. It features a boxlock action that is either case-colored or nickle-plated. It has 23" ribbed barrels with express-type sights. It features double triggers and automatic ejectors. The barrels were blued with a checkered, select walnut stock.

| NIB | Exc. | V.G. | Good | Fair | Poor |
|-----|------|------|------|------|------|
| 4950 | 3750 | 2750 | 1800 | 1250 | 1000 |

## SSO Express

This is a high-grade, Over/Under, double-barrelled rifle chambered for the .375 Holland & Holland and the .458 Winchester Magnum cartridges. It features a full, sidelock action with a case-colored receiver. It has 23" barrels with folding express sights, double triggers, and automatic ejectors. It is furnished with a fitted case. This firearm is available on a custom-order basis and should be individually appraised.

| NIB | Exc. | V.G. | Good | Fair | Poor |
|-----|------|------|------|------|------|
| 18000 | 13000 | 9500 | 6500 | 5000 | 4000 |

## SSO5 Express

This is a more deluxe, heavily engraved version of the SSO Express rifle. It should also be individually appraised.

| NIB | Exc. | V.G. | Good | Fair | Poor |
|-----|------|------|------|------|------|
| 20000 | 15000 | 11000 | 8500 | 7000 | 5500 |

The BL series of Over/Under shotguns were manufactured between 1968 and 1973. They are chambered for 12 or 20 gauge and were offered with 26", 28", or 30" vent-ribbed barrels with various choke combinations. They feature boxlock actions and were offered with either single or double triggers, and manual extractors or automatic ejectors. The finishes are blued with checkered walnut stocks. The configurations differ basically in the quality of materials and workmanship and the degree of ornamentation.

## BL-1

| Exc. | V.G. | Good | Fair | Poor |
|------|------|------|------|------|
| 400 | 350 | 275 | 225 | 175 |

## BL-2

| Exc. | V.G. | Good | Fair | Poor |
|------|------|------|------|------|
| 425 | 375 | 300 | 250 | 200 |

## BL-2/S (Speed Trigger)

| Exc. | V.G. | Good | Fair | Poor |
|------|------|------|------|------|
| 450 | 400 | 325 | 275 | 225 |

## BL-2 Stakeout (18" Barrel)

| Exc. | V.G. | Good | Fair | Poor |
|------|------|------|------|------|
| 400 | 350 | 275 | 225 | 175 |

## BL-3

| Exc. | V.G. | Good | Fair | Poor |
|------|------|------|------|------|
| 600 | 550 | 475 | 425 | 350 |

## BL-3 Competition

| Exc. | V.G. | Good | Fair | Poor |
|------|------|------|------|------|
| 650 | 600 | 525 | 475 | 400 |

## BL-4

| Exc. | V.G. | Good | Fair | Poor |
|------|------|------|------|------|
| 700 | 650 | 575 | 525 | 425 |

## BL-4 Competition

| Exc. | V.G. | Good | Fair | Poor |
|------|------|------|------|------|
| 750 | 700 | 625 | 575 | 450 |

## BL-5

| Exc. | V.G. | Good | Fair | Poor |
|------|------|------|------|------|
| 900 | 850 | 725 | 575 | 450 |

## BL-5 Competition

| Exc. | V.G. | Good | Fair | Poor |
|------|------|------|------|------|
| 950 | 900 | 775 | 600 | 475 |

## BL-6 (Sidelock)

| Exc. | V.G. | Good | Fair | Poor |
|------|------|------|------|------|
| 1250 | 1150 | 1000 | 850 | 675 |

## BL-6 Competition

| Exc. | V.G. | Good | Fair | Poor |
|------|------|------|------|------|
| 1300 | 1200 | 1050 | 900 | 725 |

## Model S55B

This is an Over/Under shotgun chambered for 12 or 20 gauge. It was offered with 26", 28", or 30" vent-ribbed barrels with various choke combinations. It features a boxlock action with a single-selective trigger and extractors. The finish is blued with a checkered walnut stock.

| Exc. | V.G. | Good | Fair | Poor |
|------|------|------|------|------|
| 550 | 500 | 400 | 325 | 275 |

## Model S56 E

This is a higher-grade, engraved version with automatic ejectors.

| Exc. | V.G. | Good | Fair | Poor |
|------|------|------|------|------|
| 600 | 550 | 450 | 375 | 325 |

## Model S58 Competition

This is the trapper-skeet configuration with either 26" or 30" barrels. It features wide vent ribs and competition-type stocks.

| Exc. | V.G. | Good | Fair | Poor |
|------|------|------|------|------|
| 700 | 650 | 550 | 475 | 400 |

## Silver Snipe

This is an Over/Under shotgun chambered for 12 or 20 gauge and offered with 26", 28", or 30" barrels. It features a boxlock action with a double trigger and extractors. The finish is blued with a checkered walnut stock. It was manufactured from 1955 through 1967. A single-selective-trigger version with ventilated rib and automatic ejectors would be worth approximately 50 percent additional.

| Exc. | V.G. | Good | Fair | Poor |
|------|------|------|------|------|
| 400 | 375 | 325 | 275 | 200 |

## Golden Snipe

This model was offered standard with a ventilated rib and automatic ejectors. Otherwise, it is similar to the Silver Snipe. If it has a single-selective trigger, add 10 percent.

| Exc. | V.G. | Good | Fair | Poor |
|------|------|------|------|------|
| 675 | 600 | 500 | 350 | 275 |

## Model 57 E

This is a more deluxe version of the Golden Snipe. It was manufactured between 1955 and 1967.

| Exc. | V.G. | Good | Fair | Poor |
|------|------|------|------|------|
| 825 | 775 | 600 | 475 | 350 |

## Asel Model

This Over/Under shotgun is chambered for 12 or 20 gauge and has a 26", 28", or 30" vent-rib barrel with various choke combinations. It features a single-selective trigger and automatic ejectors. The finish is blued with a checkered pistolgrip stock. It was manufactured between 1947 and 1964.

| Exc. | V.G. | Good | Fair | Poor |
|------|------|------|------|------|
| 1350 | 1150 | 850 | 575 | 450 |

### Model 409 PB

This is a SxS, double-barrel shotgun chambered for 12, 16, 20, and 28 gauge. It was offered with 27", 28", or 30" barrels with various choke combinations. It features a boxlock action with double triggers and extractors. The finish is blued with a checkered walnut stock. It was manufactured between 1934 and 1964.

| Exc. | V.G. | Good | Fair | Poor |
|------|------|------|------|------|
| 775 | 700 | 625 | 500 | 375 |

### Model 410 E

This is a more deluxe version of the Model 409 with automatic ejectors standard.

| Exc. | V.G. | Good | Fair | Poor |
|------|------|------|------|------|
| 900 | 825 | 650 | 500 | 425 |

### Model 410

This is a larger, heavier-duty version chambered for 10-gauge Magnum. It has 32" full-choke barrels. The finish is blued with a checkered walnut stock. It was introduced in 1934.

| Exc. | V.G. | Good | Fair | Poor |
|------|------|------|------|------|
| 1000 | 925 | 750 | 600 | 525 |

### Model 411 E

This version has false sideplates and is more heavily engraved. It was manufactured between 1934 and 1964.

| Exc. | V.G. | Good | Fair | Poor |
|------|------|------|------|------|
| 1200 | 1125 | 950 | 800 | 725 |

### Model 424

This version is chambered for 12 and 20 gauge and was offered with 26" or 28" barrels with various choke combinations. It has an engraved boxlock action with double triggers and extractors. The finish is blued with a checkered walnut stock. In 20 gauge it is designated the Model 426 and would be worth an additional $100.

| Exc. | V.G. | Good | Fair | Poor |
|------|------|------|------|------|
| 950 | 875 | 675 | 500 | 425 |

### Model 426 E

This is a higher-grade version with silver inlays and heavier engraving. It features a single-selective trigger and automatic ejectors. It was not imported after 1983.

| Exc. | V.G. | Good | Fair | Poor |
|------|------|------|------|------|
| 1150 | 1075 | 875 | 700 | 600 |

### Model 625

This is another SxS double, chambered for 12 or 20 gauge. It was offered with 26", 28", or 30" barrels with various choke combinations. It features a boxlock action with double triggers and extractors. It was moderately engraved and blued with a checkered, straight-grip, walnut stock. It was imported between 1984 and 1986.

| Exc. | V.G. | Good | Fair | Poor |
|------|------|------|------|------|
| 800 | 750 | 600 | 500 | 400 |

### Silver Hawk

This is a SxS, double-barrel shotgun chambered for 10 or 12 gauge Magnum. It has 30" barrels with a boxlock action, double triggers, and extractors. The barrels are blued with a silver-finished receiver and a checkered walnut stock. The 10-gauge version would be worth an additional 20 percent. It was discontinued in 1967.

| Exc. | V.G. | Good | Fair | Poor |
|------|------|------|------|------|
| 500 | 450 | 375 | 250 | 200 |

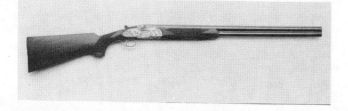

### SO-6

This is a high-grade, sidelock, SxS, double-barrel shotgun that is chambered for 12 gauge. It was available on a custom-order basis and offered with various barrel lengths and choke combinations. It features a great deal of engraving and high-grade walnut in the stock. It has a single-selective trigger and automatic ejectors. This model should be individually appraised. It was manufactured between 1948 and 1982.

| Exc. | V.G. | Good | Fair | Poor |
|------|------|------|------|------|
| 6000 | 5500 | 4850 | 4000 | 3250 |

### SO-7

This is Beretta's best-grade, sidelock, SxS gun. It is elaborately engraved and has the highest-grade walnut in the stock. It was basically a custom-order gun and should be individually appraised.

| Exc. | V.G. | Good | Fair | Poor |
|------|------|------|------|------|
| 8500 | 7850 | 6750 | 5500 | 4500 |

### SO-2 O/U

This is an Over/Under chambered for 12 gauge. It was offered with 26", 28", or 30" vent-rib barrels and features a sidelock action. It is furnished with various choke combinations. It has a single-selective trigger and automatic ejectors. It was offered with a number of options and should be individually appraised. It was introduced in 1948.

| Exc. | V.G. | Good | Fair | Poor |
|------|------|------|------|------|
| 5000 | 4500 | 3850 | 3000 | 2250 |

There were eight other versions in the "SO" series. They vary in the amount of engraving and the general quality of the materials and workmanship utilized in their construction. Otherwise, they are similar. They are as follows:

### SO-3

| Exc. | V.G. | Good | Fair | Poor |
|------|------|------|------|------|
| 7800 | 7000 | 5900 | 4250 | 3000 |

### SO-3 EL

| Exc. | V.G. | Good | Fair | Poor |
|------|------|------|------|------|
| 8200 | 7400 | 6300 | 4550 | 3200 |

### SO-3 EELL

| Exc. | V.G. | Good | Fair | Poor |
|------|------|------|------|------|
| 9000 | 8400 | 7200 | 5250 | 4000 |

### SO-4

| Exc. | V.G. | Good | Fair | Poor |
|------|------|------|------|------|
| 8300 | 7500 | 6400 | 4650 | 3300 |

### SO-5

| Exc. | V.G. | Good | Fair | Poor |
|------|------|------|------|------|
| 13750 | 10500 | 8500 | 6000 | 4750 |

### SO-5 EELL

| Exc. | V.G. | Good | Fair | Poor |
|------|------|------|------|------|
| 16000 | 12500 | 10500 | 8000 | 6000 |

### SO-6

| Exc. | V.G. | Good | Fair | Poor |
|------|------|------|------|------|
| 15500 | 12000 | 10000 | 7500 | 5500 |

### SO-6 EELL

| Exc. | V.G. | Good | Fair | Poor |
|------|------|------|------|------|
| 25000 | 18500 | 12000 | 8500 | 6000 |

## Model 682

This is a recent-production series, Over/Under shotgun that is chambered for 12, 20, or 28 gauge, as well as .410. It is offered with 26" or 28" vent-rib barrels with various choke combinations. It features a boxlock action with a single trigger and automatic ejectors. The receiver is engraved and silver-finished with a high-grade, checkered walnut stock. This series was introduced in 1984. There are nine versions that differ in the degree of ornamentation and the quality of workmanship and materials utilized in their construction. Current models have screw-in chokes available for an additional $70.

### 682 Sporting

| NIB | Exc. | V.G. | Good | Fair | Poor |
|-----|------|------|------|------|------|
| 2150 | 2000 | 1750 | 1200 | 1000 | 800 |

### 682 Deluxe

| NIB | Exc. | V.G. | Good | Fair | Poor |
|-----|------|------|------|------|------|
| 2650 | 2400 | 2000 | 1400 | 1200 | 1000 |

### 682 Skeet

| NIB | Exc. | V.G. | Good | Fair | Poor |
|-----|------|------|------|------|------|
| 2100 | 1950 | 1700 | 1100 | 950 | 750 |

### 682 4-Gauge Skeet Set

| NIB | Exc. | V.G. | Good | Fair | Poor |
|-----|------|------|------|------|------|
| 4900 | 4250 | 3500 | 2650 | 2150 | 1750 |

### 682 Trap

| NIB | Exc. | V.G. | Good | Fair | Poor |
|-----|------|------|------|------|------|
| 2100 | 1950 | 1700 | 1100 | 950 | 750 |

### 682 Mono (Single Barrel)

| NIB | Exc. | V.G. | Good | Fair | Poor |
|-----|------|------|------|------|------|
| 1550 | 1400 | 1200 | 950 | 750 | 500 |

### 682 Combo (Single and Over/Under Set)

| NIB | Exc. | V.G. | Good | Fair | Poor |
|-----|------|------|------|------|------|
| 2850 | 2600 | 2200 | 1600 | 1400 | 1200 |

### Super Sport

This version is similar to the 682 Sporting but is standard with screw-in chokes. It was introduced in 1989.

| NIB | Exc. | V.G. | Good | Fair | Poor |
|-----|------|------|------|------|------|
| 2300 | 2150 | 1900 | 1300 | 1150 | 900 |

## Model 685

This is a lower-priced Over/Under chambered for 12 or 20 gauge with 3" chambers. It features a satin-chromed boxlock action with a single trigger and extractors. It was offered with various barrel lengths and choke combinations. It was not imported after 1986.

| Exc. | V.G. | Good | Fair | Poor |
|------|------|------|------|------|
| 650 | 600 | 500 | 375 | 275 |

## Model 686 Field

This version features screw-in chokes, a single trigger, and automatic ejectors. The receiver is moderately engraved.

| NIB | Exc. | V.G. | Good | Fair | Poor |
|-----|------|------|------|------|------|
| 1150 | 1000 | 800 | 525 | 475 | 375 |

## Model 687 L

This version has an engraved, nickle-plated receiver and is furnished with a fitted case. It features screw-in chokes.

| NIB | Exc. | V.G. | Good | Fair | Poor |
|-----|------|------|------|------|------|
| 1575 | 1300 | 1000 | 825 | 600 | 475 |

## Model 687 Sporting Clays

This is a more deluxe version that is designed for sporting-clay competition. It was introduced in 1987.

| NIB | Exc. | V.G. | Good | Fair | Poor |
|-----|------|------|------|------|------|
| 2175 | 2000 | 1750 | 1200 | 975 | 800 |

The Model 687 is also available in the EL and EELL grades. They differ in the degree of ornamentation and the quality of materials and workmanship utilized in their construction. Otherwise, they are of similar configuration to the standard Model 687.

## Model 687 EL

| NIB | Exc. | V.G. | Good | Fair | Poor |
|-----|------|------|------|------|------|
| 2600 | 2450 | 2200 | 1600 | 1400 | 1100 |

## Model 687 EELL

| NIB | Exc. | V.G. | Good | Fair | Poor |
|-----|------|------|------|------|------|
| 3775 | 3250 | 2750 | 2100 | 1600 | 1200 |

## Model 626 Field Grade

This is a SxS, double-barrel shotgun chambered for 12 or 20 gauge. It has a 26" or 28" barrel with various choke combinations. It features an engraved, boxlock action with a single trigger and automatic ejectors. The finish was blued with a checkered walnut stock. It was imported between 1984 and 1988.

| Exc. | V.G. | Good | Fair | Poor |
|------|------|------|------|------|
| 900 | 825 | 700 | 575 | 475 |

## Model 626 Onyx

This is a SxS shotgun chambered for 12 or 20 gauge. It has 3" chambers. It is offered with 26" vent-rib barrels with screw-in chokes. It has a single-selective trigger and automatic ejectors. It has a matte-blued finish with a checkered, select walnut stock. It was introduced in 1988.

| NIB | Exc. | V.G. | Good | Fair | Poor |
|-----|------|------|------|------|------|
| 1535 | 1250 | 950 | 775 | 600 | 525 |

## Model 627 EL

This is a SxS, double-barrel shotgun chambered for 12 or 20 gauge. It is offered with 26" or 28" barrels with various choke combinations. It has a heavily engraved, boxlock action with a single-selective trigger and automatic ejectors. The finish is blued with a high-grade, checkered walnut stock. It was introduced in 1985, and screw-in chokes are available and worth an additional $50.

| NIB | Exc. | V.G. | Good | Fair | Poor |
|-----|------|------|------|------|------|
| 2600 | 2300 | 1950 | 1500 | 1200 | 950 |

## Model 627 EELL

This is a deluxe version of the Model 627 EL. Screw-in chokes are not available on this gun.

| NIB | Exc. | V.G. | Good | Fair | Poor |
|-----|------|------|------|------|------|
| 4500 | 3900 | 3250 | 2600 | 2250 | 1650 |

## Model 451 Series

This is an extremely high quality, full-sidelock, SxS, double-barrel shotgun. It is completely handmade on an individual-order basis. It is available in four grades that differ in the degree of ornamentation and the quality of materials and workmanship utilized in their construction. The lowest-priced version would be worth approximately $6,000 in excellent condition; and the top-of-the-line model, approximately $25,000. We strongly urge that anyone contemplating a transaction secures a qualified, individual appraisal. The variables affecting values on this series preclude accurate pricing in this, or any other, publication.

## Model FS-1

This is a single-barrel, break-open shotgun that was offered in all gauges with a 26" or 28", full-choke barrel. It was activated by an under lever and featured a folding action. The finish was blued with a checkered walnut stock. This Model was also known as the "Companion."

| Exc. | V.G. | Good | Fair | Poor |
|------|------|------|------|------|
| 250 | 225 | 175 | 125 | 90 |

### TR-1 Trap

This is a single-barrel trap gun chambered for 12 gauge with a 32", vent-rib, full-choke barrel. It was activated by an under lever. The finish was blued with a checkered, Monte Carlo stock. It was manufactured between 1968 and 1971.

| Exc. | V.G. | Good | Fair | Poor |
|------|------|------|------|------|
| 275  | 250  | 200  | 150  | 100  |

### TR-2 Trap

This version has a high, competition-type vent rib. It was manufactured between 1969 and 1973.

| Exc. | V.G. | Good | Fair | Poor |
|------|------|------|------|------|
| 300  | 275  | 225  | 175  | 125  |

### Mark II Trap

This is a high-grade, single-barrel trap gun that is chambered for 12 gauge and offered with a 32" or 34", full- choke barrel with a wide, competition-type rib. It had a boxlock action with an automatic ejector. The finish is blued with a checkered, Monte Carlo-type, walnut stock. It was manufactured between 1972 and 1976.

| Exc. | V.G. | Good | Fair | Poor |
|------|------|------|------|------|
| 700  | 625  | 525  | 450  | 375  |

### Model SL-2

This is a slide-action shotgun chambered for 12 gauge. It was offered with 26", 28", or 30", vent-rib barrels with various chokes. The finish is blued with a checkered walnut stock. It was manufactured between 1968 and 1971.

| Exc. | V.G. | Good | Fair | Poor |
|------|------|------|------|------|
| 350  | 300  | 250  | 200  | 150  |

### Pigeon Series

There are three grades in this series of slide-action shotguns. The specifications are basically as the SL-2; and the models differ in the amount of engraving offered, as well as the quality of walnut used in the stock.

### Silver Pigeon

| Exc. | V.G. | Good | Fair | Poor |
|------|------|------|------|------|
| 300  | 250  | 200  | 150  | 110  |

### Gold Pigeon

| Exc. | V.G. | Good | Fair | Poor |
|------|------|------|------|------|
| 450  | 400  | 300  | 250  | 200  |

### Ruby Pigeon

| Exc. | V.G. | Good | Fair | Poor |
|------|------|------|------|------|
| 600  | 550  | 450  | 375  | 275  |

### AL Series

These guns are gas-operated semi-automatics that are chambered for 12 or 20 gauge. They were offered with 26", 28", or 30" barrels with various choke combinations. The finish is blued with a checkered walnut stock. They were manufactured between 1969 and 1976. The models vary slightly in configuration and quality of materials and workmanship used in their construction.

### AL-1

| Exc. | V.G. | Good | Fair | Poor |
|------|------|------|------|------|
| 400  | 375  | 300  | 225  | 150  |

### AL-2

| Exc. | V.G. | Good | Fair | Poor |
|------|------|------|------|------|
| 350  | 300  | 250  | 175  | 125  |

### AL-2 Competition

| Exc. | V.G. | Good | Fair | Poor |
|------|------|------|------|------|
| 400  | 350  | 300  | 225  | 175  |

### AL-2 Magnum

| Exc. | V.G. | Good | Fair | Poor |
|------|------|------|------|------|
| 425  | 375  | 325  | 250  | 200  |

### AL-3

| Exc. | V.G. | Good | Fair | Poor |
|------|------|------|------|------|
| 400  | 350  | 300  | 225  | 175  |

### AL-3 Deluxe Trap

| Exc. | V.G. | Good | Fair | Poor |
|------|------|------|------|------|
| 775  | 700  | 600  | 500  | 425  |

### Model 301

This is an improved version of the AL Series that was manufactured between 1977 and 1982. It is also available as a slug gun with a 22" barrel with rifle sights.

| Exc. | V.G. | Good | Fair | Poor |
|------|------|------|------|------|
| 400  | 350  | 300  | 225  | 175  |

### Model 1200 Field Grade

This is a recoil-operated, semi-automatic shotgun chambered for 12 gauge. It has a 28" vent-rib barrel with screw-in choke tubes. It has a 4-round, tubular magazine. The finish is matte-blued with either a checkered walnut or black synthetic stock. It was introduced in 1984.

| NIB | Exc. | V.G. | Good | Fair | Poor |
|-----|------|------|------|------|------|
| 585 | 525  | 425  | 325  | 250  | 200  |

### Model 1200 Magnum (3" Chamber)

| NIB | Exc. | V.G. | Good | Fair | Poor |
|-----|------|------|------|------|------|
| 585 | 525  | 425  | 325  | 250  | 200  |

### Model 1200 Riot (20" Cyl. Bore Barrel)

| NIB | Exc. | V.G. | Good | Fair | Poor |
|-----|------|------|------|------|------|
| 585 | 525  | 425  | 325  | 250  | 200  |

### Model 302

This is a self-compensating, gas-operated, semi- automatic shotgun that is chambered for 12 or 20 gauge and would fire 2.75" or 3" shells interchangeably. It was offered with various barrel lengths and screw-in choke tubes. The finish is blued with a checkered walnut stock. It was manufactured between 1982 and 1987.

| Exc. | V.G. | Good | Fair | Poor |
|------|------|------|------|------|
| 400  | 350  | 275  | 200  | 150  |

### Model 302 Super Lusso

This is a very high-grade version of the Model 302 with a heavily engraved receiver and gold-plated, contrasting parts. Presentation-grade walnut was used for the hand- checkered stock. It was discontinued in 1986.

| Exc. | V.G.  | Good | Fair | Poor |
|------|-------|------|------|------|
| 2150 | 2000  | 1600 | 1050 | 850  |

### A-303 Series

This is the current semi-automatic shotgun that is offered by the Beretta company. It is chambered for 12 and 20 gauge and features the same self-compensating gas operation of the Model 302. It is offered with 26", 28", 30", or 32" vent-rib barrels with screw-in choke tubes. It has an alloy receiver that is anodized blue and features a select, checkered walnut stock. It was introduced in 1987. The various models offered differ slightly in configuration and/or quality of materials.

## Model A-303

| NIB | Exc. | V.G. | Good | Fair | Poor |
|-----|------|------|------|------|------|
| 650 | 600 | 475 | 375 | 300 | 250 |

## Model A-303 Upland (24" Barrel)

| NIB | Exc. | V.G. | Good | Fair | Poor |
|-----|------|------|------|------|------|
| 680 | 650 | 525 | 425 | 350 | 300 |

## Model A-303 Sporting Clays

| NIB | Exc. | V.G. | Good | Fair | Poor |
|-----|------|------|------|------|------|
| 735 | 700 | 575 | 475 | 400 | 350 |

## Model A-303 Competition (Trap or Skeet)

| NIB | Exc. | V.G. | Good | Fair | Poor |
|-----|------|------|------|------|------|
| 675 | 650 | 530 | 425 | 350 | 300 |

## Model A-303 Slug Gun (22" Barrel with Sights)

| NIB | Exc. | V.G. | Good | Fair | Poor |
|-----|------|------|------|------|------|
| 680 | 650 | 525 | 425 | 350 | 300 |

## Model A-303 Ducks Unlimited

This is a commemorative version of the Model 303. It is chambered for 12 or 20 gauge. There were 5,500 manufactured in 12 gauge in 1986 and 1987. There were 3,500 manufactured in 20 gauge in 1987 and 1988. These are commemorative firearms and are collectible when NIB with all furnished materials.

## 12 Gauge

| NIB | Exc. | V.G. | Good | Fair | Poor |
|-----|------|------|------|------|------|
| 575 | 500 | 425 | 325 | 275 | 225 |

## 20 Gauge

| NIB | Exc. | V.G. | Good | Fair | Poor |
|-----|------|------|------|------|------|
| 675 | 600 | 525 | 425 | 375 | 325 |

# BERGMAN, THEODOR WAFFENFABRIK
### Suhl, Germany

## Model 1894--Bergman Schmeisser

This is an extremely rare, early semi-automatic pistol that was chambered for the 5mm or the 8mm cartridges. This model was never commercially sold and is rarely encountered on today's market. It's a very compact pistol that features a folding trigger. The 5mm version would be worth approximately 50 percent additional.

| Exc. | V.G. | Good | Fair | Poor |
|------|------|------|------|------|
| 4000 | 3600 | 2500 | 1600 | 900 |

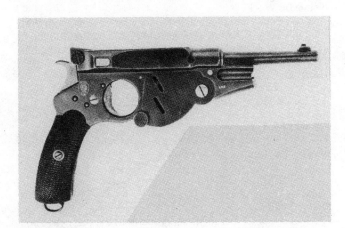

## Model 1896

This version is very similar to the Model 1894 with the recoil spring located inside the butt instead of beneath the barrel. The magazine has two slots machined in its cover and holds five rounds. It is chambered for the 5mm and 6.5mm cartridges. The early models, called the "No. 2," retain the folding trigger found on the Model 1894.

| Exc. | V.G. | Good | Fair | Poor |
|------|------|------|------|------|
| 2000 | 1750 | 1250 | 950 | 500 |

## Model 1896 No. 3

This version was produced without the folding trigger and with the addition of an extractor.

| Exc. | V.G. | Good | Fair | Poor |
|------|------|------|------|------|
| 2000 | 1750 | 1250 | 950 | 500 |

## Model 1896 No. 4

This pistol is similar to the No. 3 but is chambered for a tapered 8mm cartridge. There were approximately 200 manufactured.

| Exc. | V.G. | Good | Fair | Poor |
|------|------|------|------|------|
| 2200 | 1950 | 1400 | 1100 | 750 |

## Model 1897 No. 5

This is a locked-breech, semi-automatic pistol that is chambered for the 7.8mm Bergman cartridge. This version has a box magazine that is located in front of the triggerguard similar to that found on a C/96 Mauser. It is detachable but could be loaded with a stripper clip.

| Exc. | V.G. | Good | Fair | Poor |
|------|------|------|------|------|
| 2500 | 2250 | 1600 | 1300 | 850 |

## Model 1899 No. 6

This version is similar to the No. 5 with the early, side-loaded magazine. It was chambered for the 8mm cartridge and later chambered for 7.5mm. This is a poorly designed pistol that was not militarily or commercially successful.

| Exc. | V.G. | Good | Fair | Poor |
|------|------|------|------|------|
| 2500 | 2250 | 1600 | 1300 | 850 |

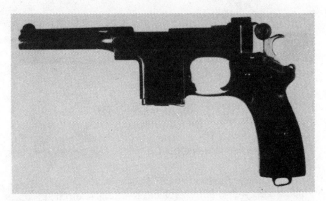

## Mars

This was Bergman's first successful semi-automatic pistol. It is chambered for the 9mm Bergman cartridge that was also known as the 9mm Largo in Spain. This was a powerful pistol that was accepted by the Spanish army as their service pistol in 1905. Bergman had contracted the manufacture of this model to the firm of Schilling & Company. In 1904 Heinrich Krieghoff took over the Schilling Company and cancelled the Bergman contract. This left Bergman with the Spanish contract and no manufacturing facility. He attempted to manufacture this model in his own factory but failed. He elected to abandon the pistol business. The Mars was licensed to the firm of Piper in Liege, Belgium; and the Spanish order was completed.

| Exc. | V.G. | Good | Fair | Poor |
|------|------|------|------|------|
| 3250 | 3000 | 2500 | 1850 | 1500 |

In 1921 Bergman died and Schmeisser left the company. They had been producing machine guns and other military weapons until this point. The firm was sold to a group headed by the firm of Lignose, and they began manufacture of the Lignose one-handed pistol that is covered in its own section of this text.

### Model 2
This is a blowback-operated pocket pistol that was based on the 1906 Browning design. It is chambered for 6.35mm and has a 2.5" barrel. The finish is blued with plastic grips.

| Exc. | V.G. | Good | Fair | Poor |
|------|------|------|------|------|
| 300 | 250 | 175 | 110 | 80 |

### No. 3
This is a larger version of the No. 2 with a 9-round, detachable magazine.

| Exc. | V.G. | Good | Fair | Poor |
|------|------|------|------|------|
| 300 | 250 | 175 | 110 | 80 |

### Bergman-Erben
This is a 7.65mm, blowback-operated, semi-automatic pistol with a 3.5" barrel. It has double-action lockwork, and the design was part of the acquisition of the Menz Company of Suhl. The finish is blued with plastic grips. It was manufactured between 1937 and 1939.

| Exc. | V.G. | Good | Fair | Poor |
|------|------|------|------|------|
| 350 | 300 | 225 | 150 | 110 |

### Bergman-Erben Model 2
This is a smaller version that is chambered for the 6.35mm cartridge. It was manufactured between 1937 and 1939.

| Exc. | V.G. | Good | Fair | Poor |
|------|------|------|------|------|
| 350 | 300 | 225 | 150 | 110 |

# BERN, WAFFENFABRIK
### Bern, Switzerland
This is actually the Swiss Government Arsenal and has manufactured Swiss service weapons, predominately machine guns, for many years.

### Swiss Ordnance Revolver M 1878
This large, well-made revolver is often referred to as a "Schmidt," after its designer. It is chambered for the 10.4mm centerfire cartridge. The lockwork is double action only. The barrel is octagonal, and the cylinder holds six shots. There is a loading gate and an integral ejector rod. The side plate is hinged and will swing forward, exposing the lockwork. The grips have the distinctive Swiss Cross molded into them.

| Exc. | V.G. | Good | Fair | Poor |
|------|------|------|------|------|
| 800 | 700 | 575 | 450 | 375 |

### M1872/78
This model is simply the Chamelot-Delvigne [see listing] that was initially chambered for 10.4mm rimfire converted by Waffenfabrik Bern to what was then the new 10.4mm centerfire.

| Exc. | V.G. | Good | Fair | Poor |
|------|------|------|------|------|
| 500 | 450 | 375 | 300 | 250 |

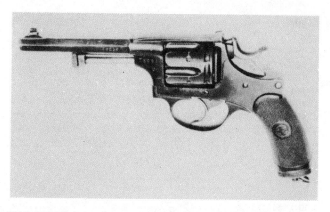

### Model 1882
This was the first of the small-bore, high-velocity, military service revolvers. It is chambered for the 7.5mm centerfire cartridge. The appearance is very similar to the Model 1878, but it featured a loading-gate safety lock.

| Exc. | V.G. | Good | Fair | Poor |
|------|------|------|------|------|
| 300 | 250 | 200 | 150 | 125 |

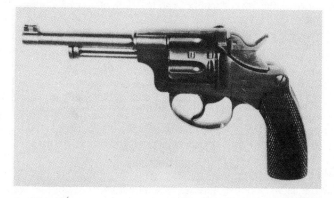

### Model 1889
This is basically the same pistol as the Model 1882 with a different angle to the butt and an improved lock on the hinged sideplate.

| Exc. | V.G. | Good | Fair | Poor |
|------|------|------|------|------|
| 300 | 250 | 200 | 150 | 125 |

### Pistole 06 W+F
This was Bern's first production Parabellum. It is marked "Waffenfabrik Bern." There is a Swiss Cross stamped on the top of the chamber. Except for these two markings the pistol is identical in appearance to the German-manufactured Model 1900/06.

| Exc. | V.G. | Good | Fair | Poor |
|------|------|------|------|------|
| 2100 | 1800 | 1500 | 1000 | 600 |

### Pistole 06/24
The 06/24 is very similar to the 06. The most notable difference is plastic grips instead of wood.

| Exc. | V.G. | Good | Fair | Poor |
|------|------|------|------|------|
| 2000 | 1750 | 1400 | 950 | 550 |

### Pistole 1929
The Model 06/29 is a slight departure from the distinctive and readily recognizable Parabellum appearance. The toggle knobs are smooth instead of checkered; the grip frame is uncurved; the safety lever is flat, and the grip safety is about twice as large as usual. The general appearance is quite disconcerting to one familiar with the Parabellum, almost as though the manufacturer made a mistake and did not quite finish the pistol. Production began in 1933, and the only identifying mark is the distinctive Swiss Cross.

| Exc. | V.G. | Good | Fair | Poor |
|------|------|------|------|------|
| 1750 | 1500 | 1250 | 850 | 500 |

Waffenfabrik Bern produced a total of 47,732 Parabellum pistols. They were issued to the Swiss military and police forces. All were chambered for 7.65mm Parabellum cartridge with the exception of 10 prototypes in 9mm (of which only one is reported to exist) and another 200 1929 models that were rebarrelled to 9mm and issued to selected units for testing. These barrels were proofmarked but not serial-numbered to the pistols. If such an example were authenticated, it would bring an approximate 50 percent premium.

The 1929 model was produced for commercial as well as military sales. The commercial pistol serial numbers were preceded by the letter "P."

After WWII Switzerland adopted the SIG as its service pistol, and Waffenfabrik Bern ceased production of all weapons other than full automatics.

# BERNARDELLI, VINCENZO
## Brescia, Italy
### Importer--Magnum Research, Inc., Minneapolis, Minnesota
### Aspen Outfitting Co., Aspen, Colorado

Vincenzo Bernardelli entered business as a gunbarrel maker in 1865. With the help of his son, he began manufacturing complete weapons shortly thereafter. The company produced sporting shotguns and entered into the pistol market in 1928 with the manufacture of the 10.4mm Italian service revolver known as the Bodeo M89. This revolver is found in its own section of this text.

## Vest Pocket Model
This is a very small, blowback-operated, semi-automatic pocket pistol that is patterned after the Walther Model 9. It is chambered for the 6.35mm cartridge and has a 2.25" barrel. It has a 5-round magazine, but an extended 8-round version was also available. The finish is blued with plastic grips. The 8-shot magazine has the last half inch covered with plastic to extend the grip. This model was manufactured between 1945 and 1948.

| Exc. | V.G. | Good | Fair | Poor |
|------|------|------|------|------|
| 275 | 225 | 155 | 100 | 75 |

## Pocket Model
This is a larger version of the VP, or Vest Pocket, Model, chambered for the 7.65mm cartridge. This model was also offered with extended barrels that protruded beyond the end of the slide. It was introduced in 1947.

| Exc. | V.G. | Good | Fair | Poor |
|------|------|------|------|------|
| 275 | 200 | 150 | 100 | 75 |

## Baby Model
This version is simply the VP Model chambered for either the .22 short or .22 long cartridges. It was manufactured between 1949 and 1968.

| Exc. | V.G. | Good | Fair | Poor |
|------|------|------|------|------|
| 275 | 200 | 150 | 100 | 75 |

## Sporter Model
This pistol is also known as the Standard Model and is basically similar to the Pocket Model, chambered for the .22 l.r. cartridge. It has a 6", 8", or 10" barrel with adjustable sights. The finish is blued with walnut grips. It was manufactured between 1949 and 1968.

| Exc. | V.G. | Good | Fair | Poor |
|------|------|------|------|------|
| 300 | 225 | 175 | 125 | 100 |

## Revolvers
Bernardelli produced a series of solid-frame, swing-out cylinder, double-action revolvers that were basically copies of the Smith & Wesson design. They were chambered for the .22 rimfire and the .32 centerfire cartridges. They had barrel lengths of 1.5", 2", or 5". A 7"-barrelled version with adjustable sights was also available in the .22 caliber chambering only. These revolvers

were manufactured between 1950 and 1962. Their values are similar.

| Exc. | V.G. | Good | Fair | Poor |
|------|------|------|------|------|
| 200 | 150 | 125 | 100 | 75 |

## Model 60
This is a blowback-operated, semi-automatic pistol that is chambered for the .22 l.r., .32 ACP, and the .380 ACP cartridges. It has a 3.5" barrel with fixed sights. The finish is blued with plastic grips. It has been manufactured since 1959.

| Exc. | V.G. | Good | Fair | Poor |
|------|------|------|------|------|
| 225 | 175 | 150 | 125 | 90 |

## Model 68
This is a very small, blowback-operated pocket pistol chambered for the .22 rimfire cartridge. It has a 2" barrel and a 6-round, detachable magazine. The finish is blued with plastic grips.

| Exc. | V.G. | Good | Fair | Poor |
|------|------|------|------|------|
| 150 | 125 | 100 | 75 | 50 |

## Model 80
This is a blowback-operated, semi-automatic pistol chambered for either the .22 l.r. or the .380 ACP cartridges. It has a 3.5" barrel with adjustable sights. The finish is blued with plastic, thumbrest grips. It was imported between 1968 and 1988.

| Exc. | V.G. | Good | Fair | Poor |
|------|------|------|------|------|
| 190 | 165 | 125 | 100 | 80 |

## Model USA
This is a single-action, blowback-operated, semi- automatic pistol chambered for the .22 l.r., .32 ACP, and the .380 ACP cartridges. It has a 3.5" barrel with adjustable sights and a steel frame with a loaded-chamber indicator. The finish is blued with plastic grips.

| NIB | Exc. | V.G. | Good | Fair | Poor |
|-----|------|------|------|------|------|
| 290 | 250 | 200 | 150 | 110 | 90 |

### Model AMR
This version is similar to the USA except that it has a 6" barrel.

| NIB | Exc. | V.G. | Good | Fair | Poor |
|-----|------|------|------|------|------|
| 310 | 275  | 225  | 150  | 110  | 90   |

### Model 69
This is a semi-automatic target pistol that is chambered for the .22 l.r. cartridge. It has single-action lockwork and a 6" heavy barrel. It has a 10-round, detachable magazine. The finish is blued with checkered walnut grips.

| NIB | Exc. | V.G. | Good | Fair | Poor |
|-----|------|------|------|------|------|
| 460 | 400  | 325  | 225  | 175  | 125  |

### Model PO10
This is a single-action, semi-automatic target pistol chambered for the .22 l.r. cartridge. It has a 6" barrel with target sights and an adjustable trigger. It has a matte-black finish with stippled walnut grips designed to fit the hand. This model was introduced in 1989.

| NIB | Exc. | V.G. | Good | Fair | Poor |
|-----|------|------|------|------|------|
| 525 | 475  | 400  | 300  | 225  | 150  |

### Model PO18
This is a double-action, semi-automatic pistol chambered for 7.65mm or the 9mm Parabellum cartridge. It has a 4.75" barrel and a 16-round, double-stack, detachable magazine. It features all-steel construction and a blued finish with plastic grips. Walnut grips are available for an additional $40. This model was introduced in 1985.

P 018 Wood Grip

P 018 Plastic Grip

| NIB | Exc. | V.G. | Good | Fair | Poor |
|-----|------|------|------|------|------|
| 500 | 450  | 375  | 275  | 200  | 150  |

## Model PO18 Compact

This is a smaller version with a 4" barrel and a shorter grip frame that holds a 14-round, double-stack magazine. It was introduced in 1989.

**P 018 Compact**

| NIB | Exc. | V.G. | Good | Fair | Poor |
|-----|------|------|------|------|------|
| 525 | 475  | 400  | 300  | 225  | 175  |

## Model 115 Series

These are high-quality, Over/Under, double-barrel shotguns chambered for 12 gauge. They feature boxlock actions with various length barrels and choke combinations. They have single triggers and automatic ejectors and differ by the degree of engraving and quality of workmanship and materials utilized in their construction.

### Model 115

| NIB  | Exc. | V.G. | Good | Fair | Poor |
|------|------|------|------|------|------|
| 1925 | 1750 | 1250 | 900  | 750  | 600  |

### Model 115S

| NIB  | Exc. | V.G. | Good | Fair | Poor |
|------|------|------|------|------|------|
| 2500 | 2250 | 1500 | 1200 | 900  | 700  |

### Model 115L

| NIB  | Exc. | V.G. | Good | Fair | Poor |
|------|------|------|------|------|------|
| 3200 | 2950 | 2200 | 1900 | 1500 | 1100 |

### Model 115E

| NIB  | Exc. | V.G. | Good | Fair | Poor |
|------|------|------|------|------|------|
| 5200 | 4800 | 4200 | 3500 | 2500 | 1850 |

### Model 115 Trap

| NIB  | Exc. | V.G. | Good | Fair | Poor |
|------|------|------|------|------|------|
| 2200 | 1950 | 1400 | 950  | 750  | 600  |

### Model 115S Trap

| NIB  | Exc. | V.G. | Good | Fair | Poor |
|------|------|------|------|------|------|
| 2700 | 2450 | 1900 | 1450 | 1150 | 900  |

### Model 115E Trap

| NIB  | Exc. | V.G. | Good | Fair | Poor |
|------|------|------|------|------|------|
| 5250 | 4800 | 4200 | 3500 | 2500 | 1850 |

## Model 190 Series

This is an Over/Under, chambered for 12 gauge, offered with various length barrels and choke combinations. It has a single-selective trigger and automatic ejectors. The receiver is engraved and silver-finished with a select, checkered walnut stock. It was introduced in 1986. The various versions differ in the degree of ornamentation and quality of materials utilized in construction.

### Model 190

| NIB  | Exc. | V.G. | Good | Fair | Poor |
|------|------|------|------|------|------|
| 1050 | 950  | 750  | 600  | 475  | 400  |

### Model 190MC

| NIB  | Exc. | V.G. | Good | Fair | Poor |
|------|------|------|------|------|------|
| 1150 | 1050 | 850  | 700  | 575  | 500  |

### Model 190 Special

| NIB  | Exc. | V.G. | Good | Fair | Poor |
|------|------|------|------|------|------|
| 1350 | 1150 | 950  | 800  | 675  | 600  |

### Model 190 Combo Gun

This version is an Over/Under combination gun chambered for 12, 16, or 20 gauge with a .243, .308, or .30-06 barrel on top. It featured a boxlock action with double triggers and automatic ejectors. The finish is blued with a checkered walnut stock. It was introduced in 1989.

| NIB  | Exc. | V.G. | Good | Fair | Poor |
|------|------|------|------|------|------|
| 1325 | 1125 | 925  | 775  | 650  | 575  |

## Orione Series

These are high-grade, Over/Under shotguns chambered for 12 gauge with various length barrels and choke combinations. They feature a boxlock action with double Purdey locks. The finishes and triggers were optional, as were extractors or automatic ejectors. The difference between the models is basically the degree of ornamentation, options, and quality of material and workmanship utilized in their construction.

### Orione

| NIB  | Exc. | V.G. | Good | Fair | Poor |
|------|------|------|------|------|------|
| 1400 | 1200 | 1000 | 800  | 700  | 625  |

### Orione S

| NIB  | Exc. | V.G. | Good | Fair | Poor |
|------|------|------|------|------|------|
| 1425 | 1225 | 1025 | 825  | 725  | 650  |

### Orione L

| NIB  | Exc. | V.G. | Good | Fair | Poor |
|------|------|------|------|------|------|
| 1550 | 1350 | 1200 | 900  | 800  | 700  |

### Orione E

| NIB  | Exc. | V.G. | Good | Fair | Poor |
|------|------|------|------|------|------|
| 1650 | 1450 | 1300 | 1000 | 900  | 800  |

## S. Uberto 1 Gamecock

This is a SxS, double-barrel shotgun chambered for 12, 16, 20, or 28 gauge. It has either 25.75" or 27.5" barrels with various chokes. It features a boxlock action with double triggers and extractors. Automatic ejectors were available and would be worth a 20 percent premium. The finish is blued with a checkered, straight-grip stock.

| Exc. | V.G. | Good | Fair | Poor |
|------|------|------|------|------|
| 1200 | 1050 | 900  | 700  | 500  |

## Brescia

This is a SxS, double-barrel shotgun with exposed hammers. It is chambered for 12, 16, or 20 gauge with various barrel lengths and choke combinations. It has a sidelock action, double triggers, and manual extractors. The finish is blued with an English-style, checkered walnut stock.

**Brescia**

| NIB  | Exc. | V.G. | Good | Fair | Poor |
|------|------|------|------|------|------|
| 1840 | 700  | 550  | 450  | 375  | 325  |

## Italia

This is a higher-grade version of the Brescia.

| NIB  | Exc. | V.G. | Good | Fair | Poor |
|------|------|------|------|------|------|
| 2050 | 950  | 700  | 600  | 475  | 425  |

### Italia Extra
This is the highest grade hammer gun that Bernardelli produces.

| NIB | Exc. | V.G. | Good | Fair | Poor |
|---|---|---|---|---|---|
| 4900 | 2800 | 2250 | 1750 | 1000 | 750 |

### Uberto Series
These guns are high-grade, SxS, double-barrel shotguns chambered for 12, 16, 20, and 28 gauge. They feature Anson & Deeley boxlock actions. They are offered in various barrel lengths and choke combinations. The increased value of the various models is dependent on the degree of engraving, options, and quality of materials and workmanship utilized in their construction.

### S. Uberto 1
| NIB | Exc. | V.G. | Good | Fair | Poor |
|---|---|---|---|---|---|
| 1200 | 1000 | 850 | 675 | 550 | 475 |

### S. Uberto 1E
| NIB | Exc. | V.G. | Good | Fair | Poor |
|---|---|---|---|---|---|
| 1635 | 1400 | 1250 | 1000 | 850 | 600 |

### S. Uberto 2
| NIB | Exc. | V.G. | Good | Fair | Poor |
|---|---|---|---|---|---|
| 1600 | 1350 | 1200 | 950 | 800 | 550 |

### S. Uberto 2E
| NIB | Exc. | V.G. | Good | Fair | Poor |
|---|---|---|---|---|---|
| 1675 | 1400 | 1250 | 1000 | 850 | 600 |

### S. Uberto F.S.
| NIB | Exc. | V.G. | Good | Fair | Poor |
|---|---|---|---|---|---|
| 1750 | 1500 | 1300 | 1100 | 850 | 625 |

### S. Uberto F.S.E.
| NIB | Exc. | V.G. | Good | Fair | Poor |
|---|---|---|---|---|---|
| 1835 | 1600 | 1450 | 1200 | 1000 | 800 |

### Roma Series
This model is similar to the S. Uberto Series with false sideplates. The values of the respective variations result from the degree of ornamentation and quality of materials and workmanship utilized in their construction.

Roma 6

### Roma 3
| NIB | Exc. | V.G. | Good | Fair | Poor |
|---|---|---|---|---|---|
| 1625 | 1375 | 1225 | 950 | 800 | 550 |

### Roma 3E
| NIB | Exc. | V.G. | Good | Fair | Poor |
|---|---|---|---|---|---|
| 1700 | 1400 | 1250 | 1000 | 850 | 575 |

### Roma 4
| NIB | Exc. | V.G. | Good | Fair | Poor |
|---|---|---|---|---|---|
| 1775 | 1450 | 1300 | 1150 | 900 | 600 |

### Roma 4E
| NIB | Exc. | V.G. | Good | Fair | Poor |
|---|---|---|---|---|---|
| 1850 | 1550 | 1375 | 1050 | 900 | 650 |

### Roma 6
| NIB | Exc. | V.G. | Good | Fair | Poor |
|---|---|---|---|---|---|
| 1995 | 1650 | 1475 | 1100 | 1000 | 750 |

### Roma 6E
| NIB | Exc. | V.G. | Good | Fair | Poor |
|---|---|---|---|---|---|
| 2075 | 1725 | 1525 | 1225 | 1050 | 825 |

### Elio
This is a SxS, double-barrel shotgun chambered for 12 gauge with various barrel lengths and choke combinations. It features a lightweight frame with double triggers and extractors. The silver finished receiver is scroll-engraved with blued barrels and a select, checkered walnut stock.

| NIB | Exc. | V.G. | Good | Fair | Poor |
|---|---|---|---|---|---|
| 1600 | 1400 | 1250 | 1000 | 850 | 600 |

### Elio E
This version has automatic ejectors.

| NIB | Exc. | V.G. | Good | Fair | Poor |
|---|---|---|---|---|---|
| 1700 | 1500 | 1350 | 1100 | 950 | 675 |

### Hemingway
This version has a coin-finished receiver with engraved game-scenes. It is offered with 23.5" barrels with double triggers and a select, checkered walnut stock.

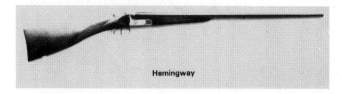

Hemingway

| NIB | Exc. | V.G. | Good | Fair | Poor |
|---|---|---|---|---|---|
| 1850 | 1600 | 1450 | 1200 | 1000 | 725 |

### Las Palomas Pigeon
This 12-gauge, SxS double is designed for live pigeon shooting.

| NIB | Exc. | V.G. | Good | Fair | Poor |
|---|---|---|---|---|---|
| 3800 | 3200 | 2650 | 2100 | 1650 | 1450 |

### Holland V.B. Series
This series of SxS guns features various barrel lengths and is chambered for 12 or 20 gauge. It has detachable, Holland & Holland-type sidelocks, single triggers, and automatic ejectors. The different models are valued according to the degree of ornamentation and the quality of the workmanship and materials utilized in their construction. These are extremely high-grade guns, and the values fluctuate greatly. We strongly recommend securing a qualified, individual appraisal if a transaction is contemplated.

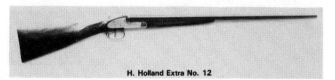

H. Holland Extra No. 12

### Holland V.B. Liscio
| NIB | Exc. | V.G. | Good | Fair | Poor |
|---|---|---|---|---|---|
| 6000 | 5500 | 4250 | 3650 | 3000 | 2450 |

### Holland V.B. Inciso
| NIB | Exc. | V.G. | Good | Fair | Poor |
|---|---|---|---|---|---|
| 7000 | 6500 | 5250 | 4650 | 4000 | 3450 |

### Holland V.B. Lusso
| NIB | Exc. | V.G. | Good | Fair | Poor |
|---|---|---|---|---|---|
| 8750 | 8200 | 7000 | 5650 | 4500 | 3750 |

### Holland V.B. Extra
| NIB | Exc. | V.G. | Good | Fair | Poor |
|---|---|---|---|---|---|
| 15000 | 13000 | 10500 | 7500 | 5250 | 4400 |

### Holland V.B. Gold
| NIB | Exc. | V.G. | Good | Fair | Poor |
|---|---|---|---|---|---|
| 35000 | 30000 | 22500 | 15000 | 12500 | 10000 |

## BERNARDON MARTIN
### St. Etienne, France

### 1907/8 Model
This is a rather large, 7.65mm, blowback semi-automatic pistol. The barrel is exposed at the top of the slide, and a spring catch on the triggerguard holds the slide to the rear. The left

side of the slide is marked "Cal. 7.65mm St. Etienne." The trademark "BM" is molded into the grips.

| Exc. | V.G. | Good | Fair | Poor |
|------|------|------|------|------|
| 325 | 295 | 225 | 185 | 150 |

### 1908/9 Model
Excepting the addition of a grip safety, this model is identical to the Model 1907/8.

| Exc. | V.G. | Good | Fair | Poor |
|------|------|------|------|------|
| 325 | 295 | 225 | 185 | 150 |

Occasionally the Bernardon Martin pistol will be noted with the word "Hermetic" stamped on the slide in letters that do not match the other markings on the weapon.

## BERNEDO, VINCENZO
### Eibar, Spain

### BC
This pistol is quite a rarity among the gunmakers of Eibar, a totally original design. This is a 6.35mm blowback with a completely exposed barrel held to the frame by a spring-loaded pin. The barrel could be easily removed for cleaning. The slide, which extended half the length of the frame, remained in position. The pistol was marked "Pistolet Automatique Bernedo Patent No. 69952."

| Exc. | V.G. | Good | Fair | Poor |
|------|------|------|------|------|
| 250 | 225 | 175 | 125 | 75 |

## BERSA
### Importer--Eagle Imports, Inc.
### Ocean, New Jersey
The Bersa is a good quality, inexpensive handgun manufactured in Italy. Prior to 1988 it was imported by Rock Island Armory in Geneseo, Illinois, and Outdoor Sports Inc. in Dayton, Ohio.

### Model 23
This Model is a double-action, semi-automatic chambered for the .22 rimfire cartridge. It has a 3.5" barrel and a 10-shot detachable magazine. The finish is either blued or satin nickel-plated with checkered walnut grips.

| NIB | Exc. | V.G. | Good | Fair | Poor |
|-----|------|------|------|------|------|
| 265 | 240 | 200 | 150 | 110 | 75 |

### Model 223
This model is similar to the Model 23 with a squared trigger guard and nylon grips. It was not imported after 1988.

| Exc. | V.G. | Good | Fair | Poor |
|------|------|------|------|------|
| 225 | 185 | 135 | 100 | 75 |

### Model 224
This is basically the same as the Model 223 with a 4" barrel. It was not imported after 1988.

| Exc. | V.G. | Good | Fair | Poor |
|------|------|------|------|------|
| 225 | 185 | 135 | 100 | 75 |

### Model 225
This is a 5"-barrelled version of the Model 223. It was discontinued in 1986.

| Exc. | V.G. | Good | Fair | Poor |
|------|------|------|------|------|
| 225 | 185 | 135 | 100 | 75 |

### Model 226
This version has a 6" barrel and was discontinued in 1988.

| Exc. | V.G. | Good | Fair | Poor |
|------|------|------|------|------|
| 225 | 185 | 135 | 100 | 75 |

### Model 323
This Model is a single-action semi-automatic chambered for the .32 ACP cartridge. It has a 3.5" barrel, fixed sights and a 7-shot detachable magazine. The finish is blued and the grips are molded plastic with a thumbrest. This Model was not imported after 1986.

| Exc. | V.G. | Good | Fair | Poor |
|------|------|------|------|------|
| 150 | 125 | 100 | 75 | 50 |

### Model 383
This is a similar pistol to the Model 323 chambered for the .380 ACP cartridge. It was also discontinued in 1988.

| Exc. | V.G. | Good | Fair | Poor |
|------|------|------|------|------|
| 175 | 150 | 125 | 90 | 75 |

### Model 383 DA
This is a double-action semi-automatic chambered for the .380 ACP cartridge. It has a 3.5" barrel, 7-shot magazine and a blued finish. The grips are checkered walnut. This Model was not imported after 1988.

| Exc. | V.G. | Good | Fair | Poor |
|------|------|------|------|------|
| 225 | 185 | 150 | 110 | 85 |

### Model 83
This is the new designation for the Model 383. It is quite similar and was introduced in 1988.

| NIB | Exc. | V.G. | Good | Fair | Poor |
|-----|------|------|------|------|------|
| 265 | 225 | 185 | 135 | 100 | 75 |

### Model 85
This Model is basically the same as the Model 83 except that it has a double-stacked 13-shot magazine. It was also introduced in 1988,

| NIB | Exc. | V.G. | Good | Fair | Poor |
|-----|------|------|------|------|------|
| 350 | 300 | 265 | 200 | 150 | 110 |

## BERTHIER
### French State
This is a series of military, bolt-action rifles and carbines that were adopted by the French military in 1890. Up to that point they had been using the Lebel system, but the development of the German Mauser Gewehr 88 and the Austrian Mannlicher made the French realize the obsolescence of their old rifle and led to the development of the Berthier system. This rifle is chambered for the 8mm cartridge and had a 3-shot magazine which was changed to a 5-shot after WWI proved a low capacity magazine inferior to the Mauser's 5-shot magazine. The carbine has a 17.5" barrel; and the rifle, a 31.5" barrel. This rifle continued in service until 1934 when it was replaced by one chambered for the 7.5mm cartridge. This new rifle was essentially still a Berthier design but chambered for a more efficient cartridge.

**Berthier Carbine**

| Exc. | V.G. | Good | Fair | Poor |
|------|------|------|------|------|
| 275 | 250 | 175 | 125 | 75 |

**Berthier Rifle**

| Exc. | V.G. | Good | Fair | Poor |
|------|------|------|------|------|
| 250 | 225 | 150 | 100 | 50 |

## BERTRAND, JULES
### Liege, Belgium

**Le Novo**

This is a poor quality, 6.35mm, solid frame, Velo-Dog type revolver. It was manufactured in the 1890's, and the only identifying markings are the "JB" trademark on the grips.

| Exc. | V.G. | Good | Fair | Poor |
|------|------|------|------|------|
| 100 | 75 | 50 | 35 | 20 |

**Lincoln**

This model is nearly identical to the Le Novo except that it is slightly larger and is chambered for 7.65mm cartridge.

| Exc. | V.G. | Good | Fair | Poor |
|------|------|------|------|------|
| 100 | 75 | 50 | 35 | 20 |

**LeRapide**

A simple, 6.35mm, blowback pocket pistol marked "Man Gr/d'Armes et Munitions Cal. Browning 6.35 LeRapide." The grips are marked "LeRapide" and "JB."

| Exc. | V.G. | Good | Fair | Poor |
|------|------|------|------|------|
| 125 | 100 | 75 | 50 | 25 |

## BERTUZZI
### Brescia, Italy
### Importer-- New England Arms
### Kittery Point, Maine

**Shotguns Over/Under**

**Zeus**

This model is a true sidelock 12 gauge with automatic ejectors, single-selective trigger, and deluxe checkered walnut stock. It is a special-order-only proposition that is heavily engraved and can be furnished to order in various barrel lengths and chokes. It is a very high grade O/U and is rarely seen on the used gun market.

| NIB | Exc. | V.G. | Good | Fair | Poor |
|-----|------|------|------|------|------|
| 10000 | 8500 | 6500 | 4500 | 3500 | 2500 |

**Zeus Extra Lusso**

This is simply a fancier version of the Zeus. Available on special order only.

| NIB | Exc. | V.G. | Good | Fair | Poor |
|-----|------|------|------|------|------|
| 15000 | 12000 | 8500 | 6000 | 4500 | 3500 |

**Shotguns SXS**

**Orione**

This is a 12-gauge boxlock with Anson & Deeley through bolt. It is available in various barrel lengths and chokes. It features a single-selective trigger and automatic ejectors. It has a hand-checkered, select walnut stock with a semi-beavertail forearm.

| NIB | Exc. | V.G. | Good | Fair | Poor |
|-----|------|------|------|------|------|
| 2500 | 3000 | 2500 | 1850 | 1500 | 1000 |

**Best Quality Side Lock**

This is a high grade custom-order shotgun. It is available in various gauges with barrel lengths and chokes to suit the customer. It features a true sidelock action with extensive engraving and a high grade walnut stock.

| NIB | Exc. | V.G. | Good | Fair | Poor |
|-----|------|------|------|------|------|
| 7500 | 7000 | 6000 | 4500 | 3500 | 2500 |

## BIGHORN ARMS CO.
### Watertown, South Dakota

**Target Pistol**

This is a unique-appearing, single-shot pistol that is chambered for the .22 short cartridge. Its configuration resembles a semi-automatic. It has a 6", vent-rib barrel. The futuristic-appearing stock is molded of plastic with oak leaves on the forearm. The finish is blued.

| Exc. | V.G. | Good | Fair | Poor |
|------|------|------|------|------|
| 150 | 125 | 100 | 85 | 65 |

**Shotgun**

This is a single-shot shotgun chambered for 12 gauge. It has a 26" barrel and is blued with a plastic stock.

| Exc. | V.G. | Good | Fair | Poor |
|------|------|------|------|------|
| 100 | 85 | 65 | 50 | 30 |

## BIGHORN RIFLE CO.
### Orem, Utah

**Bighorn Rifle**

This is a high-grade rifle manufactured for one year only, 1984. It was available on a custom made-to-order basis with interchangeable barrels that could be ordered in virtually any calibers desired. The barrel lengths were optional as was the finish. It was furnished with an adjustable trigger, two barrels, a select walnut stock, and a fitted case.

| Exc. | V.G. | Good | Fair | Poor |
|------|------|------|------|------|
| 2000 | 1750 | 1500 | 1250 | 950 |

## BILLINGHORST, WILLIAM
### Rochester, New York

**W. Billinghorst Underhammer Pistol**

This pistol is somewhat different than most of the underhammers encountered. The barrels are 12" to 18" in length and of a heavy octagonal construction. They are chambered from .30 to .38 caliber and utilize the percussion ignition system. Higher grade versions feature a part-round barrel, and it is important to note that no two pistols are alike. These pistols were furnished with detachable shoulder stocks, and a good many were cased with telescopic sights and false muzzles. This is a very high quality weapon; and if encounterd with the optional accessories, it would definitely warrant an individual appraisal. This firearm was manufactured in the 1850's. Shoulder Stock--Add 50 Percent to 75 Percent.

| Exc. | V.G. | Good | Fair | Poor |
|------|------|------|------|------|
| 1450 | 1200 | 850 | 650 | 500 |

## BILLINGS
### Location Unknown

**Billings Pocket Pistol**

This rarely encountered pistol has a 2.5" round barrel and an unusually large grip. It is chambered for the .32 caliber rimfire cartridge and features a single-shot, rolling-block-type action. The barrel is stamped "Billings Vest Pocket Pistol Pat. April 24, 1866." The finish is blued with walnut grips. The amount manufactured between 1865 and 1868 is not known.

| Exc. | V.G. | Good | Fair | Poor |
|------|------|------|------|------|
| 750 | 675 | 525 | 400 | 275 |

## BINGHAM LTD.
### Norcross, Georgia

**PPS 50**

This is a semi-automatic, blowback carbine that is patterned after the Soviet PPSH submachine gun. It is chambered for the

.22 rimfire cartridge, has a 16" barrel, and was furnished with a 50-round drum magazine. The stock is walnut or beech with a vented handguard. The finish is blued. This model was manufactured between 1976 and 1985.

| Exc. | V.G. | Good | Fair | Poor |
|------|------|------|------|------|
| 250  | 210  | 175  | 125  | 85   |

### AK-22
This blowback-operated semi-automatic was pattened after the Soviet AK-47. It is chambered for the .22 rimfire cartridge and was furnished with either a 15-or 29-shot magazine. The stock is walnut or beech. This model was manufactured between 1976 and 1985.

| Exc. | V.G. | Good | Fair | Poor |
|------|------|------|------|------|
| 200  | 165  | 135  | 100  | 75   |

### Bantam
This is a bolt-action single shot with an 18.5" barrel. It is chambered for the .22 rimfire cartridge and was designed as a youth model rifle. A .22 rimfire magnum version was also available. This model was manufactured between 1976 and 1985.

| Exc. | V.G. | Good | Fair | Poor |
|------|------|------|------|------|
| 100  | 85   | 70   | 50   | 35   |

## BISMARCK
### Location Unknown

**Bismarck Pocket Revolver**
This is a rarely encountered pocket revolver that is chambered for the .22 caliber rimfire cartridge. It has a 3" round ribbed barrel and a 7-shot, unfluted cylinder. It was an obvious Rollin White patent infringement as it was a faithful copy of the S&W Model 1. The frame is brass, and the remainder was plated. The birdshead grips are of rosewood. It has a spur trigger, and the barrel is marked "Bismarck." It was manufactured sometime in the 1870's, but the maker is not known.

| Exc. | V.G. | Good | Fair | Poor |
|------|------|------|------|------|
| 325  | 250  | 200  | 150  | 90   |

## BITTERLICH, FRANK J.
### Nashville, Tennessee

This maker produced derringer-styled pocket pistols. These pistols utilize the percussion ignition system and are chambered for .41 caliber. The barrel lengths varied but are always octagonal; the mountings are made of German silver, and the stock is walnut. There are two styles of stock--a birdshead grip and a square butt that is rarely encountered. The barrel and locks are marked "Fr.J. Bitterlich/Nashville, Tenn." There were also pistols manufactured for Glassick & Co., Nashville; and they are actually more common than the ones Bitterlich made under his own trademark. These pistols were produced between 1854 and 1862.

| Exc. | V.G. | Good | Fair | Poor |
|------|------|------|------|------|
| 1150 | 1000 | 875  | 700  | 550  |

## BITTNER, GUSTAV
### Wieport, Bohemia

**Bittner**
The Bittner is a true firearms oddity. It is somewhat of a cross between a semi-automatic and a revolver. It is striker-fired and has a reciprocating bolt operated by the ring triggerguard. The pistol is 10.5" overall with a 4.5" barrel. The weight is 29 ounces, and it is chambered for the 7.7mm Bittner cartridge. A 6-round magazine is removed for loading. The Bittner was introduced in 1893, has no external markings, and was not a commercial success. Approximately 1,000 were produced.

| Exc. | V.G. | Good | Fair | Poor |
|------|------|------|------|------|
| 3000 | 2500 | 1950 | 1400 | 950  |

## BLAKE, J. H.
### New York, New York

**Blake Bolt Action Rifle**
This extremely rare rifle was manufactured in limited quantities. It is chambered for the .30-40 Krag cartridge and has a 7-shot

rotary magazine that is fed from the underside of the rifle. The barrel is 30" long with a full-length walnut stock with a checkered pistolgrip. The stock is secured by three barrel bands, and there is an upper handguard that extends to the breech. The finish is blued. This rifle was produced for the U.S. Trials of 1893 when the Krag rifle was adopted. It is a well-made rifle, and its fade into oblivion may have been politically motivated. It was manufactured between 1892 and 1910.

| Exc. | V.G. | Good | Fair | Poor |
|------|------|------|------|------|
| 750  | 675  | 500  | 375  | 275  |

## BLANCH, JOHN
### London, England

**Blanch Percussion Pistol**
This is a streamlined, single-shot, percussion pistol chambered for .69 caliber. It is a service-type pistol with good sights and sufficient power for defensive capabilities. The gun is very well made and has a 5" Damascus barrel with an engraved frame and hammer. The grip is finely checkered walnut and has a grip cap with a compartment for cap storage. There is a hinged ramrod under the barrel. This pistol was manufactured in the 1830's.

| Exc. | V.G. | Good | Fair | Poor |
|------|------|------|------|------|
| 2650 | 2450 | 2025 | 1850 | 1550 |

## BLAND, THOMAS & SONS
### London, England

The Bland company began business in 1876 and produced, for the most part, heavy caliber, military service revolvers under license for others. In 1887 they manufactured a 4-barrelled, break-open pistol similar to the Lancaster. It is chambered for .455 caliber and has a rotating firing pin and a double-action hammer. It was not a commercial success, and very few were manufactured.

| Exc. | V.G. | Good | Fair | Poor |
|------|------|------|------|------|
| 2450 | 2000 | 1750 | 1250 | 900  |

## BLASER JAGDWAFFEN
### West Germany
### Importer--Autumn Sales Inc.
### Fort Worth, Texas

This company manufactures a line of high quality bolt-action rifles, available on a custom-order basis. They are virtually handmade and are not encountered very often in the used firearms market.

**Model K77**
This is a high quality, single-shot, break-open rifle. It is chambered for 11 different calibers between .22-250 and .300 Weatherby Magnum. The barrel length is 24", and the receiver is engraved and silver-plated. The stock is select walnut. This Model was introduced in 1988.
Extra Barrels--Add $750 Per Barrel.

| NIB  | Exc. | V.G. | Good | Fair | Poor |
|------|------|------|------|------|------|
| 2300 | 2050 | 1575 | 1300 | 950  | 750  |

**Model R-84**
This is a short-stroke bolt action with a 60-degree handle rotation. It is chambered for the .22-250 through and including the

.375 Holland & Holland Magnum and features either a 23" or 24" barrel. The barrels are inter-changeable, and extras are available at approximately $550. The select walnut stock and forend is hand-checkered. This Model was first imported in 1988.

| NIB | Exc. | V.G. | Good | Fair | Poor |
|------|------|------|------|------|------|
| 1600 | 1475 | 1100 | 850 | 750 | 600 |

### Ultimate Bolt Action

This model has a similar action to the Model R-84 and is available in the same calibers. This model has a single-set trigger and a lightly engraved silver-plated receiver. Extra barrels are available at $550. It has been imported since 1985.

| NIB | Exc. | V.G. | Good | Fair | Poor |
|------|------|------|------|------|------|
| 1500 | 1300 | 1050 | 825 | 700 | 575 |

### Special Order Ultimate

The Ultimate model is available with various degrees of embellishments. The model designations and prices are as follows:

### Ultimate Deluxe

| NIB | Exc. | V.G. | Good | Fair | Poor |
|------|------|------|------|------|------|
| 1600 | 1400 | 1150 | 925 | 800 | 675 |

### Ultimate Super Deluxe

| NIB | Exc. | V.G. | Good | Fair | Poor |
|------|------|------|------|------|------|
| 4050 | 3750 | 3250 | 2500 | 2000 | 1750 |

### Ultimate Exclusive

| NIB | Exc. | V.G. | Good | Fair | Poor |
|------|------|------|------|------|------|
| 5700 | 5250 | 4500 | 3750 | 2600 | 2000 |

### Ultimate Super Exclusive

| NIB | Exc. | V.G. | Good | Fair | Poor |
|------|------|------|------|------|------|
| 8900 | 8250 | 7100 | 5000 | 4250 | 3700 |

### Ultimate Royal

| NIB | Exc. | V.G. | Good | Fair | Poor |
|-------|-------|------|------|------|------|
| 11500 | 10000 | 7500 | 6000 | 5200 | 4500 |

Note; Extra interchangeable-caliber barrels for the above rifles are available at $700 to $1,200 per barrel depending on the grade.

# BLISS, F. D.
## New Haven, Connecticut

### Bliss Pocket Revolver

This is a 6-shot revolver chambered for the .25 caliber rimfire cartridge. It has a 3.25" octagon barrel, spur trigger, and a square butt. The finish is blued, and the grips are either hard rubber or wood. The barrel is stamped 'F.D.Bliss New Haven Ct." There was an all brass framed version made very early in the production, and this model would be worth approximately 50 percent more than the values listed here for the standard model. There were approximately 3,000 manufactured in 1863 and 1864.

| Exc. | V.G. | Good | Fair | Poor |
|------|------|------|------|------|
| 350 | 300 | 250 | 175 | 125 |

# BLISS & GOODYEAR
## New Haven, Connecticut

### Pocket Model Revolver

This is a 6-shot, 3" octagonal barrelled revolver chambered for .28 caliber. It utilizes the percussion ignition system. It has an unfluted cylinder, spur trigger, and a solid frame with a removable sideplate. It also features an attached hinged rammer for loading. The frame is brass and the remainder blued with walnut grips. There were approximately 3,000 manufactured in 1860.

| Exc. | V.G. | Good | Fair | Poor |
|------|------|------|------|------|
| 475 | 425 | 350 | 275 | 175 |

# BLUNT & SYMS
## New York, New York

This company made up of Orison Blunt and John G. Syms was in the firearms business from the late 1830's until the 1850's.

### Underhammer Pepperbox

This is an unusual firearm that is fired by means of a ring trigger with a hidden hammer. These weapons are chambered for .25 through .38 caliber and utilize the percussion ignition system. The revolving barrel unit holds 6 shots and is found with barrel lengths from 1.75" to 6". They are double-action, and the standard finish is blued with some engraving. The grips are walnut. There are two basic handle typed--the saw handle and the round handle. Each handle type was found in small, medium, and "Dragoon" or large size. Most were unmarked except for the letters "R-C" on the muzzle. Those that were marked "Blunt & Syms New York" are quite rare and worth approximately 50 percent more than the values listed. There were only a few thousand of these pistols manufactured between 1838 and 1852.

### Small Frame Round Handle .25--.28 Caliber

| Exc. | V.G. | Good | Fair | Poor |
|------|------|------|------|------|
| 450 | 400 | 350 | 275 | 175 |

### Medium Frame Round Handle .31 Caliber

| Exc. | V.G. | Good | Fair | Poor |
|------|------|------|------|------|
| 400 | 350 | 300 | 225 | 150 |

### Round Handle Dragoon .36 Caliber

| Exc. | V.G. | Good | Fair | Poor |
|------|------|------|------|------|
| 750 | 650 | 550 | 400 | 300 |

### Medium Frame Saw Handle .31 Caliber

| Exc. | V.G. | Good | Fair | Poor |
|------|------|------|------|------|
| 500 | 450 | 400 | 325 | 250 |

### Saw Handle Dragoon .36 Caliber

| Exc. | V.G. | Good | Fair | Poor |
|------|------|------|------|------|
| 800 | 700 | 600 | 425 | 350 |

### Dueling Pistol

This single-shot percussion pistol is chambered for .52 caliber. It was offered with various-length octagonal barrels; 9" was the most common. There is a ramrod mounted under the barrel, and the stock is walnut. The barrel is stamped "B & S New York" and "Cast Steel." They were manufactured between 1845 and 1855.

| Exc. | V.G. | Good | Fair | Poor |
|------|------|------|------|------|
| 800 | 700 | 600 | 425 | 350 |

### Bar Hammer Pistol

This is a large, double-action percussion pistol with a bar-type hammer and a 6" part-round/part-octagon barrel. It is chambered for .36 caliber and has a conventional trigger with a large guard. The handle is of the rounded configuration with walnut grips. It is marked in the usual B & S manner and was manufactured between 1845 and 1855.

| Exc. | V.G. | Good | Fair | Poor |
|------|------|------|------|------|
| 400 | 325 | 275 | 200 | 150 |

### Side Hammer Pocket Pistol

This is a single-shot pocket pistol chambered for .31 to .36 caliber percussion. It has octagonal barrels from 2.5" to 6" in length with a scroll-engraved iron frame and walnut grips. This is a single-action pistol with the usual B & S markings. This model was manufactured in the 1840's and 1850's.

| Exc. | V.G. | Good | Fair | Poor |
|------|------|------|------|------|
| 425 | 350 | 300 | 225 | 175 |

### Side Hammer Belt Pistol

This is simply a larger version of the side hammer pocket pistol chambered for .36 --.44 caliber with a 4" or 6" barrel. Its specifications and appearance are similar.

| Exc. | V.G. | Good | Fair | Poor |
|------|------|------|------|------|
| 500 | 425 | 375 | 300 | 250 |

### Ring Trigger Pistol

This model has a conventional hammer and a ring trigger. It is single-action and is chambered for .36--.38 caliber percussion. It has a part-round/part-octagon barrel between 3" and 5" in length. The iron frame is engraved and blued, and the round handle has walnut grips. Its markings are standard, and they were manufactured in the 1840's and 1850's.

| Exc. | V.G. | Good | Fair | Poor |
|------|------|------|------|------|
| 450  | 375  | 325  | 250  | 200  |

## Double Barrel Pistol

This model has two side by side 7.5" barrels with side-mounted hammers. It is chambered for .36 --.44 caliber percussion and has a ramrod mounted under the barrels. The frame is iron, and the grips are walnut. There is a ring-trigger version that is quite rare and worth approximately 25 percent more than the standard-trigger model listed.

| Exc. | V.G. | Good | Fair | Poor |
|------|------|------|------|------|
| 475  | 400  | 350  | 275  | 225  |

## Double Barrel Underhammer Pistol

This model has side-by-side octagonal barrels that are fired simultaneously by two underhammers released by one ring trigger. It is chambered for .34 caliber percussion. The barrels are 4" in length. The barrel markings are standard, and the grips are walnut.

| Exc. | V.G. | Good | Fair | Poor |
|------|------|------|------|------|
| 500  | 425  | 375  | 300  | 250  |

## Deringer Style Pistol

This pistol was patterned after the Henry Deringer Philadelphia-type pistol and is chambered for .50 caliber percussion. It has a 3" round barrel with a flat along the top. The frame, forend, and the gripstraps were cast in one piece out of German silver with small, walnut grip panels. The pistol is scroll-engraved and is of fine craftsmanship throughout. It is marked "Blunt & Syms/New York" in an arch and was manufactured in the 1850's.

| Exc. | V.G. | Good | Fair | Poor |
|------|------|------|------|------|
| 900  | 750  | 600  | 475  | 350  |

# BODEO
## Italian Service Revolver

### System Bodeo Modello 1889 [Enlisted Model]

This revolver was adopted as the Italian Service Revolver in 1889 and was replaced by the Glisenti in 1910. It was manufactured by various Italian Arms companies and actually saw service into WWII. It is 10.5" overall with a 4.5" octagon barrel. The 10.4mm cartridge is utilized. The total weight is 32 ounces. The cylinder has a 6-shot capacity. The pistol loads through a gate and has a folding trigger with no triggerguard.

| Exc. | V.G. | Good | Fair | Poor |
|------|------|------|------|------|
| 200  | 175  | 150  | 100  | 75   |

### Modello 1889 [Officers Model]

Essentially the same as the enlisted man's model with a round barrel, non-folding trigger, and conventional triggerguard.

| Exc. | V.G. | Good | Fair | Poor |
|------|------|------|------|------|
| 200  | 175  | 150  | 100  | 75   |

# BOLUMBURO, G.
## Eibar, Spain

This was another Eibar company that began production in 1906 copying Browning's designs. They operated until the Spanish Civil War manufacturing typical poor-quality, 6.35mm and 7.65mm semi-automatics under the trade names: Bristol, Giralda, Gloria, Marina, Regent, and Rex. The values on these would be quite similar, and they may be regarded the same.

| Exc. | V.G. | Good | Fair | Poor |
|------|------|------|------|------|
| 150  | 110  | 85   | 65   | 35   |

# BOOM
## SEE--Shattuck, C.S.
## Hatfield, Massachusetts

# BORCHARDT
## Berlin, Germany
## Waffenfabrik Lowe
## DWM

The Borchardt pistol was designed by Hugo Borchardt in the early 1890's. It appeared on the market in 1894, manufactured by the firm of Ludwig Lowe of Berlin, where Borchardt was employed. Borchardt was born in Germany but migrated to America, where he became a citizen and worked for Sharps. In the late 1880's he returned to Germany and went to work for Lowe. His pistol was not a great success from a commercial standpoint. It is very large and cumbersome and almost impossible to fire with one hand. A detachable shoulder stock was available with the pistol, and some looked upon it as more of a light carbine than a handgun. This pistol is chambered for the 7.65mm cartridge and has a 6.5" barrel and an 8-round magazine. The weapon is extremely difficult to strip, and even those of us who are comfortable with the mechanics of firearms avoid dismantling this one. The firm of Ludwig Lowe manufactured the pistol until the end of 1896, when a merger took place that created the firm of DWM. After January 1, 1897 the toggle link was marked "DWM" as on later Lugers of their manufacture. The Ludwig Lowe guns were serial numbered from 1-1104; and the DWM guns, 1105-3000. The Borchardt was the immediate forerunner of the Luger; George Luger was a fellow employee of Borchardts at Lowe's and DWM. This firearm was furnished cased with a shoulder stock and accessories. The values given should be increased by approximately 50 percent if the entire rig is complete. The Borchardt pistol is very rare and desirable from a collector standpoint. The originality should be authenticated by appraisal.

Lowe Manufacture--Add 15 Percent.

| Exc. | V.G. | Good | Fair | Poor |
|------|------|------|------|------|
| 9000 | 8500 | 7000 | 5000 | 3500 |

# BORSIG
## East Germany

The Borsig is the East German version of the Soviet Makarov pistol. It is a double action, chambered for the Soviet 9X18mm cartridge. Its appearance is nearly identical to the Makarov. It is very rarely encountered outside of the Soviet Bloc.

| Exc. | V.G. | Good | Fair | Poor |
|------|------|------|------|------|
| 1250 | 1000 | 750  | 550  | 450  |

# BOSS & CO.
## London, England

The firm of Boss & Co. has been in the firearms business since 1832 and enjoys a reputation for producing some of the finest shotguns in the world. The prices of these guns are quite high, and setting a value in a publication of this nature is nearly impossible. There are not enough bought and sold to give an accurate market value. There were less than 10,000 manufactured ever, and anyone contemplating purchase should secure an individual and expert appraisal. For reference purposes we list the basic models and their prices.

### Side By Side

This is a custom-order shotgun available in any gauge with barrel lengths and chokes to the customer's specifications. It has automatic ejectors and either a single or double trigger. The stock is made of the best-grade walnut and made to order with or without a pistolgrip. The small-gauge guns would bring a sizeable premium as few were made.

| Exc. | V.G. | Good | Fair | Poor |
|------|------|------|------|------|
| 15000 | 13500 | 10000 | 8000 | 5500 |

### Over/Under

The O/U was built to order and is similar in quality to the Side By Side.

| Exc. | V.G. | Good | Fair | Poor |
|------|------|------|------|------|
| 20000 | 17500 | 15000 | 10000 | 7500 |

The following is applicable to both models:
20 Gauge--Add 25 Percent.
28 Gauge--Add 40 Percent.
.410--Add 50 Percent.
Cased with Accessories--Add $1000.

# BOSWELL, CHARLES
### London, England

The firm of Charles Boswell is an old line maker of shotguns and double rifles in the best English tradition. Their products are of the highest quality and are essentially made-to-order items. Their early firearms were marked "Malin and Bosworth"; and the later ones, "Malin." In 1988 the firm was purchased by a group of U.S. investors. Cape Horn Outfitters of Charlotte, North Carolina, was appointed sole agent and given the rights to not only sell but also manufacture these firearms. They were formerly imported by Saxon Arms, Ltd., in Clearwater, Florida.

### Double Rifle, Boxlock

This model is a side-by-side that was custom-made to the customer's individual specifications. It was available chambered for .300 Express, .375 H&H, and .458 Winchester Magnum. The .600 Nitro Express was available as an extra cost option. The action was an Anson and Deeley boxlock with double triggers. The engraving was the buyer's choice, and the walnut used was of the highest grade possible. The gun and accessories were furnished in a fitted leather case.
.600 Nitro Express--Add 25 Percent.

| Exc. | V.G. | Good | Fair | Poor |
|------|------|------|------|------|
| 40000 | 32500 | 25000 | 17500 | 12500 |

### Double Rifle, Sidelock

This model is similar to the boxlock with a Holland-and-Holland-type sidelock action. All other options offered were the same.
.600 Nitro Express--Add 25 Percent.

| Exc. | V.G. | Good | Fair | Poor |
|------|------|------|------|------|
| 55000 | 40000 | 30000 | 20000 | 17500 |

### Shotgun, Boxlock

This model is a side-by-side with an Anson and Deeley boxlock action. It was available in any gauge and choke. All other options were, as with the double rifles, to the customer's order. The gun was offered cased. When evaluating, one should remember that small gauge guns of this quality always bring a premium as there were fewer manufactured.
.28 Gauge and .410--Add 20 Percent.

| Exc. | V.G. | Good | Fair | Poor |
|------|------|------|------|------|
| 8500 | 7000 | 5500 | 4000 | 3000 |

### Shotgun, Sidelock

This model is essentially similar to the boxlock with a Holland-and-Holland-type sidelock action. All other options were the same.
.28 Gauge and .410--Add 20 Percent.

| Exc. | V.G. | Good | Fair | Poor |
|------|------|------|------|------|
| 9500 | 8000 | 6500 | 5000 | 3750 |

# BOSWORTH, B. M.
### Warren, Pennsylvania

### Bosworth Underhammer Pistol

This is a .38-caliber percussion pistol with a 6" part- round/part- octagon barrel. The frame and handle are cast in one piece of brass, and the handle is hinged to create a storage compartment. The frame is marked "B.M. Bosworth" with a sunburst stamped under the name. The number produced is unknown, as is the exact period of time in which they were manufactured. It is safe to assume that they were made in the 1850-1860 era.

| Exc. | V.G. | Good | Fair | Poor |
|------|------|------|------|------|
| 500 | 425 | 350 | 275 | 200 |

# BRAENDLIN ARMOURY
### London, England

Braendlin Armoury manufactured an 8-barrelled, Mitrailleuse-type pistol. It is chambered for .450 caliber ammunition and breaks open for loading. The cartridges were affixed to a plate so that all 8 could be loaded at the same time. With each pull of the trigger, a cam would move the firing pin and a successive barrel would fire. The pistol was manufactured from 1880 through 1888 but was not a commercial success. Examples are very rarely encountered in today's market.

| Exc. | V.G. | Good | Fair | Poor |
|------|------|------|------|------|
| 5000 | 4500 | 3500 | 2750 | 2000 |

# BRAND
### E. Robinson, Maker
### New York

### Brand Breech Loading Carbine

This is a single-shot breech loader chambered for the .50-caliber rimfire cartridge. It has a 22" round barrel fastened by one band and a saddle ring and bar on the left side of the frame. They are marked "Brand's Patent July 29,1862/E. Robinson Manfr/New York." This is not a well known firearm, and it was not widely used in the Civil War. The patent holder, C. Brand of Norwich, Connecticut, was better known for his percussion Whaling lance gun made during the 1850's. This carbine was manufactured between 1863 and 1865.

| Exc. | V.G. | Good | Fair | Poor |
|------|------|------|------|------|
| 2000 | 1750 | 1500 | 1150 | 800 |

# BREDA, ERNESTO
### Milan, Italy
### Importer--Diana Imports Co.
### San Francisco, California

### Andromeda Special

This model is a side-by-side that was chambered for 12 gauge only. It was offered with various barrel lengths and chokes. It features single-selective triggers and automatic ejectors, and the satin-finished action is extensively engraved. The pistolgrip stock is of select hand-checkered walnut.

| Exc. | V.G. | Good | Fair | Poor |
|------|------|------|------|------|
| 700 | 650 | 550 | 425 | 300 |

### Vega Special

This is a boxlock Over/Under chambered for 12 gauge only. It was offered with 26" or 28" barrels with various choke combinations. It has a single-selective trigger and automatic ejectors. The finish is engraved and blued with a select checkered walnut stock.

| Exc. | V.G | Good | Fair | Poor |
|------|------|------|------|------|
| 650 | 600 | 500 | 375 | 275 |

### Vega Special Trap

This model is similar to the Vega Special with a competition-styled stock and 30" or 32" barrels with full chokes.

| Exc. | V.G. | Good | Fair | Poor |
|------|------|------|------|------|
| 1150 | 900 | 750 | 500 | 350 |

### Sirio Standard

This model is similar to the Vega with extensive engraving and a generally higher degree of finishing. There is a 28"-barrelled Skeet version available in this model.

| Exc. | V.G. | Good | Fair | Poor |
|------|------|------|------|------|
| 2250 | 2000 | 1750 | 1250 | 1000 |

### Standard Semi-Automatic

This model is a recoil-operated semi-automatic chambered for

12 gauge only. It has 25" or 27" vent-rib barrels with screw-in choke tubes, an engraved receiver, and checkered walnut stock.

| Exc. | V.G. | Good | Fair | Poor |
|---|---|---|---|---|
| 325 | 275 | 225 | 175 | 125 |

**Grade I**
This model is similar to the Standard with more engraving and better wood.

| Exc. | V.G. | Good | Fair | Poor |
|---|---|---|---|---|
| 550 | 475 | 325 | 225 | 175 |

**Grade II**
A more elaborately engraved version of the Grade I.

| Exc. | V.G. | Good | Fair | Poor |
|---|---|---|---|---|
| 675 | 600 | 450 | 375 | 250 |

**Grade III**
This is the most deluxe version in this line with select walnut and extensive engraving.

| Exc. | V.G. | Good | Fair | Poor |
|---|---|---|---|---|
| 875 | 800 | 650 | 575 | 450 |

**Magnum Model**
This Model is the same as the standard, only chambered for the 3" magnum 12 gauge.

| Exc. | V.G. | Good | Fair | Poor |
|---|---|---|---|---|
| 475 | 400 | 350 | 275 | 200 |

**Gold Series Antares Standard**
This model is a gas-operated semi-automatic chambered for the 12 gauge 2.75" shell only. It has a 25" or 27" vent-rib barrel with screw-in choke tubes. The receiver is all steel with a blued finish and a checkered walnut stock.

| Exc. | V.G. | Good | Fair | Poor |
|---|---|---|---|---|
| 500 | 400 | 350 | 275 | 225 |

**Gold Series Argus**
This model is an alloy-framed lightweight version of the Antares.

| Exc. | V.G. | Good | Fair | Poor |
|---|---|---|---|---|
| 525 | 425 | 375 | 300 | 250 |

**Gold Series Aries**
The Aries is similar to the Antares except that it is chambered for the 3" magnum 12-gauge shell.

| Exc. | V.G. | Good | Fair | Poor |
|---|---|---|---|---|
| 550 | 450 | 400 | 325 | 275 |

# BREN 10
**Dornaus & Dixon Inc.**
**Huntington Beach, California**

This is a very controversial pistol that was in production from 1983 until 1986. It was supposedly inspired by a gun writer who felt the need for another defensive cartridge. This pistol was touted and written about for a long time before it was actually produced. It appeared on "Miami Vice" on a weekly basis long before those who had ordered and paid for one ever saw one. The pistols were then supposedly delivered without magazines and were virtually useless as semi-autos. Magazines are reportedly selling for as much as $175. Anyway the manufacture of this pistol was discontinued in 1986 with the help of the Government, and there are those in the gun-buying fraternity who are willing to pay large amounts for that which is collectible only because Hollywood or Television chooses to use the product. This model is definitely a case of temporary inflation, and those purchasing for investment purposes should be aware of this.

**Standard Bren 10**
This model is a double-action semi-automatic with a stainless frame and satin-blued slide. It is chambered for the 10mm cartridge and has a 5" barrel. The magazine holds 11 rounds. It was manufactured between 1983 and 1986.

| NIB | Exc. | V.G. |
|---|---|---|
| 1250 | 1100 | 800 |

**M & P Model**
The same as the Standard with a matte black finish.

| NIB | Exc. | V.G. |
|---|---|---|
| 1350 | 1200 | 900 |

**Pocket Model**
This Model is smaller and more compact than the Standard model, with a 4" barrel. It holds 9 shots.

| NIB | Exc. | V.G. |
|---|---|---|
| 1300 | 1150 | 850 |

**Dual-Master Presentation Model**
This model is furnished with an extra barrel and slide that is chambered for the .45 ACP. It has a finer finish and is supplied in a fitted walnut case.

| NIB | Exc. | V.G. |
|---|---|---|
| 1750 | 1500 | 1050 |

**Marksman Model**
There were 250 manufactured for the "Marksman Shop" in Chicago, Illinois. This model is similar to the Standard model but is chambered for .45 ACP and is so marked.

| NIB | Exc. | V.G. |
|---|---|---|
| 1150 | 1000 | 750 |

**Initial Commemorative**
There were supposed to be 2,000 of these manufactured in 1986, but no one knows how many were actually produced. They are chambered for the 10mm and have a high-gloss blue finish with 22 kt. gold-plated details. The grips are laser engraved, and the whole affair is furnished in a walnut display case.

| NIB | Exc. | V.G. |
|---|---|---|
| 3000 | 2500 | 2000 |

# BRETTON
**Ste. Etienne, France**
**Importers--Quality Arms, Inc.**
**Houston, Texas**
**Mandall Shooting Supplies**
**Scottsdale, Arizona**

This is a unique shotgun with what is known as a sliding breech. The barrels slide straight forward for loading. This design enables the maker to create a very lightweight and fast-handling shotgun with a great degree of strength in the action lockup.

**Baby Standard**
This model is available from Mandall only and is an Over/Under chambered for 12 and 20 gauge. The barrel lengths and choke combinations are various, and the gun has double triggers. The finish is blued, and the stock is checkered walnut.

| NIB | Exc. | V.G. | Good | Fair | Poor |
|---|---|---|---|---|---|
| 800 | 725 | 625 | 500 | 425 | 375 |

**Deluxe Grade**
This model is imported by Quality Arms and is a more deluxe version of the Baby. It is available in 12, 16, and 20 gauge with an engraved, coin-finished receiver. The walnut is a select grade.

| NIB | Exc. | V.G. | Good | Fair | Poor |
|---|---|---|---|---|---|
| 1000 | 900 | 750 | 600 | 500 | 425 |

# BRIGGS, H. A.
**Norwich, Connecticut**

**Briggs Single Shot Pistol**
This pistol is chambered for the .22 rimfire and has a 4" part-round/part-octagonal barrel with a downward rotating breech block. It has a square butt that is flared at the bottom with walnut grips. The finish is blued, and the frame is marked "H.A. Briggs/Norwich, Ct." This pistol was manufactured in the 1850's. The quantity produced is not known.

| Exc. | V.G. | Good | Fair | Poor |
|---|---|---|---|---|
| 750 | 600 | 525 | 400 | 275 |

## BRIXIA
### Brescia, Italy

### Model 12
This pistol appears to have been an attempt to improve the 1910 Glisenti Italian service pistol. It is chambered for the 9mm and has no markings except for "MBT" molded into the grips. The Italian army put a limited quantity of them into use but did not accept them for duty. At the outbreak of WWI manufacture ceased.

| Exc. | V.G. | Good | Fair | Poor |
|------|------|------|------|------|
| 375 | 325 | 275 | 200 | 150 |

## BRNO ARMS
### Brno, Czechoslovakia
### Importer--T. D. Arms
### New Baltimore, Michigan

### ZH-Series
This series of Over/Under shotguns features interchangeable barrels--both of shotgun and rifle configuration. They feature various barrel lengths and choke combinations with double triggers and automatic ejectors. The boxlock action is engraved and blued with a checkered, select walnut stock. There are a number of options available, and the basic difference between the various models is in the calibers or gauges chambered and the options included. They are as follows:

### ZH-300
| NIB | Exc. | V.G. | Good | Fair | Poor |
|-----|------|------|------|------|------|
| 600 | 525 | 450 | 350 | 300 | 225 |

### ZH-301
| Exc. | V.G. | Good | Fair | Poor |
|------|------|------|------|------|
| 575 | 500 | 400 | 350 | 275 |

### ZH-302
| Exc. | V.G. | Good | Fair | Poor |
|------|------|------|------|------|
| 575 | 500 | 400 | 350 | 275 |

### ZH-303
| Exc. | V.G. | Good | Fair | Poor |
|------|------|------|------|------|
| 575 | 500 | 400 | 350 | 275 |

### ZH-304
| Exc. | V.G. | Good | Fair | Poor |
|------|------|------|------|------|
| 650 | 575 | 475 | 400 | 350 |

### ZH-305
| Exc. | V.G. | Good | Fair | Poor |
|------|------|------|------|------|
| 675 | 600 | 500 | 425 | 375 |

### ZH-306
| Exc. | V.G. | Good | Fair | Poor |
|------|------|------|------|------|
| 675 | 600 | 500 | 425 | 375 |

### ZH-321
| Exc. | V.G. | Good | Fair | Poor |
|------|------|------|------|------|
| 575 | 500 | 400 | 350 | 275 |

### ZH-324
| Exc. | V.G. | Good | Fair | Poor |
|------|------|------|------|------|
| 650 | 575 | 475 | 400 | 350 |

### Model 300 Combo
This is basically a Model ZH-300 furnished with all eight interchangeable-barrel sets. It is furnished in a fitted case and was introduced in 1986.

| NIB | Exc. | V.G. | Good | Fair | Poor |
|-----|------|------|------|------|------|
| 3500 | 3000 | 2500 | 2000 | 1500 | 1150 |

### Model 500
This version features deluxe acid etching and is chambered for 12 gauge only. It features automatic ejectors and was introduced in 1986.

| NIB | Exc. | V.G. | Good | Fair | Poor |
|-----|------|------|------|------|------|
| 625 | 550 | 450 | 375 | 300 | 250 |

### CZ-581
This is an Over/Under shotgun chambered for 12 gauge only. It has 28", vent-rib barrels with various choke combinations. It features a boxlock action with a Greener crossbolt. It has a single trigger and automatic ejectors. The finish is blued with a checkered walnut stock with sling swivels.

| NIB | Exc. | V.G. | Good | Fair | Poor |
|-----|------|------|------|------|------|
| 650 | 575 | 500 | 425 | 375 | 300 |

### CZ-584
This is an Over/Under combination gun chambered for 12 gauge over 7x57R, .222, or .308. It featured a boxlock action with 24.5", vent-rib barrels. It had a single trigger and automatic ejectors. The finish is blued with a checkered walnut stock. This model was discontinued in 1986.

| Exc. | V.G. | Good | Fair | Poor |
|------|------|------|------|------|
| 925 | 850 | 750 | 600 | 500 |

### ZP-49
This is a SxS, double-barrel shotgun chambered for 12 gauge only. It has various barrel lengths and choke combinations and features a true sidelock action. It has double triggers, cocking indicators, and automatic ejectors. The finish is blued with a checkered walnut stock. It is lightly engraved and was imported in 1986 only.

| Exc. | V.G. | Good | Fair | Poor |
|------|------|------|------|------|
| 600 | 525 | 450 | 350 | 275 |

### ZP-149
This model replaced the ZP-49 and is similar without the engraving. It was introduced in 1986.

| NIB | Exc. | V.G. | Good | Fair | Poor |
|-----|------|------|------|------|------|
| 590 | 525 | 450 | 350 | 275 | 225 |

### ZP-349
This version is similar to the ZP-49 but features a cheekpiece stock and a beavertail forearm. It was imported in 1986 only.

| Exc. | V.G. | Good | Fair | Poor |
|------|------|------|------|------|
| 450 | 375 | 300 | 250 | 200 |

### Hornet Sporter
This was a bolt-action sporting rifle built on a miniature Mauser action. It is chambered for the .22 Hornet cartridge and has a 23" barrel with a three-leaf, folding express sight. It is furnished with double-set triggers. The finish is blued with a checkered, select walnut stock. This model is sometimes referred to as the ZB Mauser.

| Exc. | V.G. | Good | Fair | Poor |
|------|------|------|------|------|
| 900 | 825 | 725 | 600 | 500 |

### Model 21H
This is a Mauser bolt-action sporting rifle chambered for 6.5x57, 7x57, and the 8x57 cartridges. It features a 20.5" barrel with a folding express sight and double-set triggers. The finish is blued with a checkered, select walnut stock.

| Exc. | V.G. | Good | Fair | Poor |
|------|------|------|------|------|
| 875 | 800 | 700 | 575 | 450 |

### Model 22F
This version is similar to the 21H, with a full-length, Mannlicher-type stock.

| Exc. | V.G. | Good | Fair | Poor |
|------|------|------|------|------|
| 1000 | 900 | 775 | 625 | 500 |

## Model I
This is a bolt-action sporting rifle chambered for the .22 l.r. cartridge. It has a 22.75" barrel with a three-leaf folding sight. The finish is blued with a walnut stock.

| Exc. | V.G. | Good | Fair | Poor |
|------|------|------|------|------|
| 575 | 500 | 400 | 325 | 250 |

## Model II
This version features a select checkered walnut stock.

| Exc. | V.G. | Good | Fair | Poor |
|------|------|------|------|------|
| 650 | 550 | 450 | 375 | 300 |

## ZKM-452
This is a bolt-action rifle chambered for the .22 l.r. cartridge. It has a 25" barrel and is furnished with either a 5-or 10-round detachable magazine. The finish is blued with a beechwood stock. It was discontinued in 1986.

| Exc. | V.G. | Good | Fair | Poor |
|------|------|------|------|------|
| 200 | 175 | 150 | 100 | 75 |

## ZKM-452D
This version is similar to the ZKM-452 but features a walnut, Monte Carlo-type stock.

| Exc. | V.G. | Good | Fair | Poor |
|------|------|------|------|------|
| 350 | 300 | 225 | 150 | 120 |

## ZKB 680
This is a bolt-action sporting rifle chambered for the .22 Hornet or .222 cartridges. It has a 23.5" barrel, double-set triggers, and a 5-round magazine. The finish is blued with a walnut stock.

| NIB | Exc. | V.G. | Good | Fair | Poor |
|-----|------|------|------|------|------|
| 500 | 425 | 350 | 300 | 225 | 150 |

## ZKK 600
This is a Mauser bolt-action rifle chambered for 7x57, 7x64, .270, and the .30-.06 cartridges. It has a 23.5" barrel and a 4-round magazine. The finish is blued with a select checkered, Monte Carlo-type walnut stock.

| NIB | Exc. | V.G. | Good | Fair | Poor |
|-----|------|------|------|------|------|
| 600 | 525 | 450 | 400 | 325 | 250 |

## ZKK 601
This model is similar to the ZKK 600 except that it is chambered for .243 and the .308 cartridges.

| NIB | Exc. | V.G. | Good | Fair | Poor |
|-----|------|------|------|------|------|
| 600 | 525 | 450 | 400 | 325 | 250 |

## ZKK 602
This version is chambered for the large, African game cartridges. It features a larger, more robust construction.

| NIB | Exc. | V.G. | Good | Fair | Poor |
|-----|------|------|------|------|------|
| 700 | 625 | 550 | 500 | 425 | 325 |

## CZ-511
This is a blowback-operated, semi-automatic rifle chambered for the .22 l.r. cartridge. It has adjustable sights and a blued finish. The stock is select walnut. It was discontinued in 1986.

| Exc. | V.G. | Good | Fair | Poor |
|------|------|------|------|------|
| 275 | 225 | 175 | 125 | 90 |

## Model 581
This is a high-grade, semi-automatic rifle chambered for the .22 l.r. cartridge. It has adjustable sights and a 5-round, detachable magazine. The finish is blued with a checkered, select walnut stock.

| Exc. | V.G. | Good | Fair | Poor |
|------|------|------|------|------|
| 600 | 525 | 450 | 400 | 325 |

## Super Express Rifle
This is an Over/Under express rifle chambered for various cartridges. It features a sidelock action with Kersten crossbolt. It has 23.5" barrels, double triggers, and automatic ejectors. The action is engraved; the finish, blued with a checkered walnut stock. There are six grades of this rifle other than the standard model. They differ in the amount of engraving and the general quality of the materials and workmanship utilized.

### Standard Model
| NIB | Exc. | V.G. | Good | Fair | Poor |
|-----|------|------|------|------|------|
| 3950 | 3250 | 2650 | 2250 | 1600 | 1250 |

### Grade I
| NIB | Exc. | V.G. | Good | Fair | Poor |
|-----|------|------|------|------|------|
| 6000 | 5250 | 4650 | 4250 | 3600 | 3250 |

### Grade II
| NIB | Exc. | V.G. | Good | Fair | Poor |
|-----|------|------|------|------|------|
| 4975 | 4250 | 3650 | 3250 | 2600 | 2250 |

### Grade III
| NIB | Exc. | V.G. | Good | Fair | Poor |
|-----|------|------|------|------|------|
| 5500 | 4750 | 4150 | 3750 | 3000 | 2750 |

### Grade IV
| NIB | Exc. | V.G. | Good | Fair | Poor |
|-----|------|------|------|------|------|
| 4975 | 4250 | 3650 | 3250 | 2600 | 2250 |

### Grade V
| NIB | Exc. | V.G. | Good | Fair | Poor |
|-----|------|------|------|------|------|
| 4500 | 3850 | 3000 | 2600 | 2000 | 1600 |

### Grade VI
| NIB | Exc. | V.G. | Good | Fair | Poor |
|-----|------|------|------|------|------|
| 4600 | 3950 | 3100 | 2750 | 2100 | 1750 |

## Drulov 70
This is a single-shot sporting pistol chambered for the .22 rimfire cartridge. It has a 6" barrel with adjustable sights. A set trigger was available. The finish is blued, with a walnut grip. It was discontinued in 1986.

| Exc. | V.G. | Good | Fair | Poor |
|------|------|------|------|------|
| 125 | 110 | 95 | 65 | 45 |

## Drulov 75
This version is a target model that was furnished standard with set triggers and micrometer-adjustable sights.

| Exc. | V.G. | Good | Fair | Poor |
|------|------|------|------|------|
| 300 | 250 | 200 | 150 | 100 |

## PAV
This is a single-shot sporting pistol chambered for the .22 l.r. cartridge. It has a 9.75" barrel with adjustable sights. The finish is blued with a walnut grip. It was imported in 1986 only.

| Exc. | V.G. | Good | Fair | Poor |
|------|------|------|------|------|
| 100 | 90 | 65 | 50 | 35 |

## CZ-70
This is a double-action, blowback-operated, semi-automatic pistol similar in configuration to the Walther Model PP. It is chambered for the 7.65mm cartridge. It has an 8-round, detachable magazine and is blued with checkered grips. This model is rarely encountered on today's market.

| Exc. | V.G. | Good | Fair | Poor |
|------|------|------|------|------|
| 1000 | 825 | 675 | 475 | 350 |

## CZ-75
This is a double-action, semi-automatic pistol chambered for the 9mm Parabellum cartridge. It has a 4.75" barrel and a 15-round, double-stack magazine. It has fixed sights and is finished in either high-polish blue, matte-blue, or baked black enamel. The grips are black plastic with a CZ logo molded into them. This pistol has been rated by some experts as the No. 1 defensive handgun currently available. They are currently difficult to locate.

| NIB | Exc. | V.G. | Good | Fair | Poor |
|-----|------|------|------|------|------|
| 700 | 550 | 450 | 375 | 275 | 225 |

## CZ-83
This double-action, semi-automatic pistol features a streamline design. It is chambered for the 7.65mm or the .380 ACP cartridges. It has a 3.5" barrel and a 15-round, double-stack magazine. Limited importation began in 1985.

| NIB | Exc. | V.G. | Good | Fair | Poor |
|-----|------|------|------|------|------|
| 600 | 500 | 400 | 325 | 250 | 200 |

## BRONCO
SEE--Arizmendi
Eibar, Spain

## BROOKLYN F. A. CO.
### Brooklyn, New York
**Slocum Pocket Revolver**

This revolver was an attempt to produce a cartridge arm without violating the Rollin White patent. The cylinder is a series of five individual tubes that slide forward to open for loading and then for ejecting the spent cartridges. It is chambered for the .32 rimfire cartridge and has a 3" round barrel. There is a spur trigger and a round handle with walnut grips. The frame is silver-plated brass; the remainder is either blued or plated. The frame is scroll-engraved. The barrel is marked "B.A. Co. Patented April 14, 1863." There were approximately 10,000 manufactured in 1863 and 1864.

| Exc. | V.G. | Good | Fair | Poor |
|------|------|------|------|------|
| 350 | 300 | 225 | 150 | 100 |

**Slocum Unfluted Cylinder Pocket Revolver**

This model is similar to the fluted-cylinder model described above with an unfluted cylinder and a flared, more conventional-appearing butt. It is also chambered for .22 rimfire in a 7-shot version, as well as the 5-shot .32. There were approximately 250 manufactured in .32 rimfire and 100 in .22 rimfire.
.22 Caliber--Add 25 Percent.

| Exc. | V.G. | Good | Fair | Poor |
|------|------|------|------|------|
| 450 | 400 | 325 | 250 | 200 |

## BROWN MANUFACTURING CO.
### Newburyport, Massachusetts
**Southerner Deringer**

This is a single-shot pocket pistol chambered for the .41 rimfire cartridge. It has a 2.5" or 4" octagonal barrel that pivoted to the side for loading. The frame is made of silver-plated brass or iron. The barrel is either plated or blued. The short-barrelled model has a squared butt; and the 4" barrelled model, a round butt. This Deringer was also made by Merrimack Arms Co. between 1867 and 1869, and they are so marked. Brown manufactured the Southerner from 1869 to 1873. Both models are marked "Southerner" on top of the barrel. There were approximately 2,000 made totally.

**Brass Framed 2.5" Barrel**

| Exc. | V.G. | Good | Fair | Poor |
|------|------|------|------|------|
| 350 | 300 | 225 | 175 | 125 |

**Iron Frame 2.5" Barrel (Brown Mfg. Only)**

| Exc. | V.G. | Good | Fair | Poor |
|------|------|------|------|------|
| 375 | 325 | 250 | 200 | 150 |

**Brass Frame 4" Barrel**

| Exc. | V.G. | Good | Fair | Poor |
|------|------|------|------|------|
| 750 | 650 | 550 | 425 | 300 |

## BROWN PRECISION, INC.
### Los Molinos, California

Brown Precision is primarily known as a manufacturer of high quality synthetic rifle stocks made of kevlar and graphite. They also produce highly accurate and specialized rifles utilizing barrelled actions supplied by Remington, Winchester, and Camex Blaser.

**High Country Standard**

This model utilizes a Remington action and is chambered for .243 through .30-06. It has a 22" barrel without sights and a kevlar stock. It is furnished with a recoil pad and sling swivels. Gray Camo Stock, Stainless Barrel and Leupold 2.5 x 10 Scope--Add $650.

| NIB | Exc. | V.G. | Good | Fair | Poor |
|-----|------|------|------|------|------|
| 985 | 925 | 775 | 575 | 450 | 375 |

**Open Country Varmint Rifle**

Available in standard varmint calibers, it has a heavy barrel and is precision-tuned for long-range pin-point accuracy. It was introduced in 1989.

| NIB | Exc. | V.G. | Good | Fair | Poor |
|-----|------|------|------|------|------|
| 1100 | 1000 | 850 | 650 | 500 | 400 |

**Law Enforcement Model**

This is a Remington Varmint action chambered for .308 with a 20" barrel and a Zeiss scope in Conetrol rings. The kevlar stock is green camo.

| NIB | Exc. | V.G. | Good | Fair | Poor |
|-----|------|------|------|------|------|
| 1050 | 950 | 800 | 600 | 450 | 375 |

**Pro-Hunter**

This model was designed for hunting big game and is chambered for .375 Holland & Holland and .458 Winchester Magnum. It is built on a Remington action converted to use a full-claw extractor for reliability in function. The finish is either matte electroless nickel plate, blued, or teflon-coated. It features folding express sights and a kevlar stock in choice of colors.

| NIB | Exc. | V.G. | Good | Fair | Poor |
|-----|------|------|------|------|------|
| 1800 | 1700 | 1450 | 1250 | 1000 | 750 |

**Custom Winchester Model 70**

This model is a Winchester-barrelled action stocked in a choice of colored kevlar stocks. It is chambered for .270 or .30-06 and has a 22" featherweight barrel and a recoil pad.

| NIB | Exc. | V.G. | Good | Fair | Poor |
|-----|------|------|------|------|------|
| 600 | 525 | 450 | 350 | 300 | 250 |

**Blaser Rifle**

This model is built on the Camex-Blaser action and is chambered for their own calibers. It features a Brown Precision stock.

| NIB | Exc. | V.G. | Good | Fair | Poor |
|-----|------|------|------|------|------|
| 1400 | 1250 | 1000 | 750 | 650 | 500 |

## BROWNING ARMS CO.
### Ogden, Utah

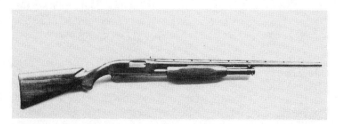

Contrary to popular belief, the firm of Browning Arms has actually manufactured only one gun in its long and colorful history. This was the Model 1878 single-shot rifle, which was actually the first gun that the prolific inventor John M. Browning patented. This firm was founded in 1880 as J. M. Browning & Bro. in Ogden, Utah. John Browning is considered by many to be the greatest firearms genius of all time. He created 80 firearms designs and held 128 individual patents. He sold designs to Winchester, Stevens, Remington, and Colt, as well as to the Belgian firm of Fabrique Nationale (FN). He was directly responsible for designing many of the firearms with which we have come to be familiar, including the 1911 Colt Government Model, the 1885 Winchester Single Shot (evolved from the Model 1878 that was actually Browning-manufactured), the Models 1886, 1892, 1894, and 1895 Lever Action Rifles, as well as the Model 1897 Shotgun. He was also directly responsible for producing the Model 1935 Hi-Power which achieved worldwide service pistol acceptance. In the 1890's Browning had difficulty dealing with the American arms corporations, so he went to Europe and established a lasting relationship with the firm of Fabrique Nationale in Herstal, Belgium. This agreement has lasted to this day, and many of the firearms sold under the Browning banner are still produced at FN. In the early 1970's, the Browning corporation contracted with the firm of B. C. Miroku in Japan and has since marketed guns produced by them. One should be cognizant of the fact that in the opinion of many experts Miroku-produced Browning firearms are as high in quality as any other produced; collector interest dictates greater values on the Belgian-manufactured versions.

### Early Semi-Automatic Pistols

In the period between 1900 and the development of the Model 1935 Hi-Power Pistol, Browning had a number of semi-automatic pistols manufactured by Fabrique Nationale of Herstal, Belgium. They were the Models 1900, 1903, 1905, 1910, 1922, the Baby, and the 1935 Model Hi-Power. These firearms will be listed in more detail with their respective values in the Fabrique Nationale section of this text.

### Hi-Power Modern Production

This version of the FN Model 1935 is quite similar in appearance to the original described in the FN section. It is chambered for the 9mm Parabellum cartridge and has a 4.75" barrel. It has a double column, 35-round, detachable box magazine and is blued with checkered walnut grips. It has fixed sights and has been produced in its present configuration since 1954. An adjustable-sight version is also available and would be valued at approximately 10 percent higher. A matte-nickel version is also available and would be worth approximately 5 percent additional.

| NIB | Exc. | V.G. | Good | Fair | Poor |
|-----|------|------|------|------|------|
| 475 | 400 | 350 | 300 | 275 | 200 |

### Hi-Power--.30 Luger

This version is similar to the standard Hi-Power except that it is chambered for the .30 Luger cartridge. There were approximately 1,500 imported between 1986 and 1989. The slide is marked "FN." The Browning-marked versions are quite rare and worth approximately 10 percent additional.

| Exc. | V.G. | Good | Fair | Poor |
|------|------|------|------|------|
| 425 | 375 | 300 | 225 | 175 |

### Tangent Sight Model

This version is similar to the standard Hi-Power with the addition of an adjustable rear sight calibrated to 500 meters. There were approximately 7,000 imported between 1965 and 1978. If the grip frame is slotted to accept a detachable shoulder stock, add approximately 20 percent to the value; but be wary of fakes.

| Exc. | V.G. | Good | Fair | Poor |
|------|------|------|------|------|
| 750 | 675 | 500 | 400 | 300 |

### Renaissance Hi-Power

This is a heavily engraved version with a matte-silver finish. It features synthetic-pearl grips and a gold-plated trigger. The adjustable-sight version would be worth approximately 5 percent additional. Import on this model ended in 1980.

| NIB | Exc. | V.G. | Good | Fair | Poor |
|-----|------|------|------|------|------|
| 1200 | 1050 | 800 | 600 | 500 | 400 |

### Cased Renaissance Set

This features one example of a fully engraved and silver-finished .25 ACP "Baby," one .380 ACP Pistol, and one Hi-Power. The set is furnished in a fitted walnut case and was imported between 1955 and 1969.

| NIB | Exc. | V.G. | Good | Fair | Poor |
|-----|------|------|------|------|------|
| 3500 | 3000 | 2500 | 2150 | 1750 | 1250 |

### Louis XVI Model

This is a heavily engraved Hi-Power pistol that features a leaf-and-scroll pattern. It is satin-finished and features checkered walnut grips. It is furnished in a fitted walnut case. To realize its true potential, this pistol must be NIB. It was not imported after 1984.

| NIB | Exc. | V.G. | Good | Fair | Poor |
|-----|------|------|------|------|------|
| 1000 | 875 | 750 | 600 | 500 | 400 |

### Hi-Power Centennial Model

This version is similar to the standard fixed-sight Hi-Power but is chrome-plated with the inscription, "Browning Centennial / 1878-1978" engraved on the slide. It is furnished with a fitted case. There were 3,500 manufactured in 1978. As with all commemorative pistols, in order to realize its collector potential, this model should be NIB with all supplied material.

| NIB | Exc. | V.G. | Good | Fair | Poor |
|-----|------|------|------|------|------|
| 600 | 525 | 450 | 400 | 350 | 275 |

### BDA-380

This is a double-action, semi-automatic pistol chambered for the .380 ACP cartridge. It features a 3.75" barrel with a 14-round, double-stack, detachable magazine. The finish is either blued or nickle-plated with smooth walnut grips. This pistol was manufactured in Italy by Beretta and introduced in 1982.

**Add 5 Percent for Nickle Finish.**

| NIB | Exc. | V.G. | Good | Fair | Poor |
|-----|------|------|------|------|------|
| 450 | 375 | 325 | 275 | 200 | 150 |

### Model BDA

This is a double-action, semi-automatic pistol manufactured for Browning by Sig-Sauer of Germany. It is identical to the Sig-Sauer Model 220. It is chambered for 9mm Parabellum, .38 Super, and the .45 ACP cartridges. The .38 Super would be worth approximately 30 percent additional.

| Exc. | V.G. | Good | Fair | Poor |
|------|------|------|------|------|
| 500 | 425 | 375 | 300 | 235 |

### Nomad

This is a blowback-operated, semi-automatic pistol chambered for the .22 l.r. cartridge. It was offered with a 4.5" or 6.75" barrel. It has a 10-round, detachable magazine with adjustable sights and all steel construction. The finish is blued with black plastic grips. It was manufactured between 1962 and 1974 by FN.

| Exc. | V.G. | Good | Fair | Poor |
|------|------|------|------|------|
| 300 | 250 | 200 | 150 | 100 |

### Challenger

This is a more deluxe target pistol chambered for the .22 l.r. cartridge. It was offered with a 4.5" or 6.75" barrel and has a 10-round magazine. It is constructed entirely of steel and has adjustable sights. The finish is blued with a gold-plated trigger and checkered, wrap-around, walnut grips. It was manufactured between 1962 and 1975 by FN.

| Exc. | V.G. | Good | Fair | Poor |
|------|------|------|------|------|
| 375 | 300 | 250 | 200 | 140 |

### Renaissance Challenger

This version is fully engraved with a satin-nickle finish and a fitted walnut case.

| NIB | Exc. | V.G. | Good | Fair | Poor |
|-----|------|------|------|------|------|
| 1000 | 850 | 600 | 500 | 350 | 275 |

### Gold Line Challenger

This version is blued and has a gold-inlaid line around the outer edges of the pistol. It was cased.

| NIB | Exc. | V.G. | Good | Fair | Poor |
|-----|------|------|------|------|------|
| 1400 | 1250 | 1000 | 750 | 500 | 350 |

### Challenger II

This is a blowback-operated, semi-automatic pistol chambered for the .22 l.r. cartridge. It has a 6.75" barrel with an alloy frame. The finish is blued with phenolic-impregnated hardwood grips. This pistol was manufactured between 1975 and 1982 in Salt Lake City, Utah.

| Exc. | V.G. | Good | Fair | Poor |
|------|------|------|------|------|
| 250 | 225 | 175 | 140 | 100 |

### Challenger III

This version features a 5.5" bull barrel with adjustable sights. It was manufactured between 1982 and 1985 in Salt Lake City, Utah. A 6.75", tapered-barrel version was also available and known as the Sporter.

| Exc. | V.G. | Good | Fair | Poor |
|------|------|------|------|------|
| 225 | 200 | 150 | 125 | 90 |

### Medalist

This is a high-grade, semi-automatic target pistol chambered for the .22 l.r. cartridge. It has a 6.75", vent-rib barrel with adjustable target sights. It was supplied with three barrel weights and a dry-fire-practice mechanism. The finish is blued with target-type, thumbrest, walnut grips. It was manufactured between 1962 and 1975 by FN. There were four additional high-grade versions of this pistol that differed in the degree of ornamentation.

| Exc. | V.G. | Good | Fair | Poor |
|------|------|------|------|------|
| 600 | 525 | 450 | 350 | 275 |

### Gold Line Medalist--407 Produced in 1963

| NIB | Exc. | V.G. | Good | Fair | Poor |
|-----|------|------|------|------|------|
| 1750 | 1600 | 1250 | 1000 | 750 | 500 |

### Renaissance Medalist

| NIB | Exc. | V.G. | Good | Fair | Poor |
|-----|------|------|------|------|------|
| 2200 | 2150 | 1800 | 1500 | 1200 | 950 |

### Browning Collector's Edition--Non-Engraved, 38 Manufactured

| NIB | Exc. | V.G. | Good | Fair | Poor |
|-----|------|------|------|------|------|
| 1500 | 1250 | 1000 | 750 | 500 | 400 |

### Browning Collector's Edition--Engraved, 22 Manufactured

| NIB | Exc. | V.G. | Good | Fair | Poor |
|-----|------|------|------|------|------|
| 2500 | 2250 | 2000 | 1750 | 1400 | 1100 |

### Buck Mark

This is a blowback-operated, semi-automatic pistol chambered for the .22 l.r. cartridge. It has a 5.5" bull barrel with adjustable sights. It has an 11-round, detachable magazine and is matte-blued with skip-line checkered synthetic grips. It was introduced in 1985.

| NIB | Exc. | V.G. | Good | Fair | Poor |
|-----|------|------|------|------|------|
| 210 | 175 | 150 | 135 | 110 | 85 |

### Buck Mark Plus

This version is similar to the standard with plain wood grips. It was introduced in 1987.

| NIB | Exc. | V.G. | Good | Fair | Poor |
|-----|------|------|------|------|------|
| 250 | 210 | 185 | 150 | 120 | 100 |

## Buck Mark Varmint
This version has a 9.75" bull barrel with a full-length ramp to allow scope mounting. It has no sights. It was introduced in 1987.

| NIB | Exc. | V.G. | Good | Fair | Poor |
|---|---|---|---|---|---|
| 320 | 285 | 250 | 200 | 175 | 125 |

## Buck Mark Silhouette
This version features a 9.75" bull barrel with adjustable sights.

| NIB | Exc. | V.G. | Good | Fair | Poor |
|---|---|---|---|---|---|
| 350 | 325 | 285 | 220 | 185 | 140 |

Certain Browning long guns used wood that was salt-cured, causing a rusting problem to the underside of barrels and actions. This should be carefully checked before purchase.

## Superposed Shotgun
This series of Over/Under, double-barrel shotguns is chambered for all gauges and is offered with vent-rib barrels from 26.5" to 32" in length. It features various choke combinations. This shotgun is built on a boxlock action and features either double or single-selective triggers and automatic ejectors. There were a number of versions offered that differ in the amount of ornamentation and the quality of the materials and workmanship utilized in manufacture. Values for small-bore models are generally higher. This series was introduced in 1931 and is manufactured by FN.
20 Gauge--Add 20 Percent.
28 Gauge--Add 30 Percent.
.410--Add 40 Percent.

### Grade I
| Exc. | V.G. | Good | Fair | Poor |
|---|---|---|---|---|
| 1250 | 1000 | 800 | 650 | 475 |

### Grade I Lightning
| Exc. | V.G. | Good | Fair | Poor |
|---|---|---|---|---|
| 1350 | 1100 | 900 | 750 | 525 |

### Grade I Magnum
| Exc. | V.G. | Good | Fair | Poor |
|---|---|---|---|---|
| 1500 | 1250 | 1050 | 900 | 700 |

### Pigeon Grade
| Exc. | V.G. | Good | Fair | Poor |
|---|---|---|---|---|
| 2250 | 2000 | 1750 | 1500 | 1200 |

### Grade III
| Exc. | V.G. | Good | Fair | Poor |
|---|---|---|---|---|
| 2500 | 2250 | 2000 | 1600 | 1300 |

### Pointer Grade
| Exc. | V.G. | Good | Fair | Poor |
|---|---|---|---|---|
| 2800 | 2500 | 2250 | 1800 | 1500 |

### Grade IV
| Exc. | V.G. | Good | Fair | Poor |
|---|---|---|---|---|
| 3200 | 2850 | 2500 | 2000 | 1750 |

### Diana Grade
| Exc. | V.G. | Good | Fair | Poor |
|---|---|---|---|---|
| 3300 | 3000 | 2750 | 2200 | 1850 |

### Midas Grade
| Exc. | V.G. | Good | Fair | Poor |
|---|---|---|---|---|
| 4500 | 4000 | 3500 | 2950 | 2300 |

### Grade VI
| Exc. | V.G. | Good | Fair | Poor |
|---|---|---|---|---|
| 5500 | 4750 | 4250 | 3500 | 2750 |

### 1981 Mallard Issue
| NIB | Exc. | V.G. | Good | Fair | Poor |
|---|---|---|---|---|---|
| 4500 | 3950 | 3500 | 3000 | 2500 | 2250 |

### 1982 Pintail Issue
| NIB | Exc. | V.G. | Good | Fair | Poor |
|---|---|---|---|---|---|
| 9000 | 6500 | 5500 | 4000 | 3000 | 2500 |

### 1983 Black Duck Issue
| NIB | Exc. | V.G. | Good | Fair | Poor |
|---|---|---|---|---|---|
| 9000 | 6500 | 5500 | 4000 | 3000 | 2500 |

## Superlight
This version was offered chambered for 12 and 20 gauge with a 26.5", ribbed barrel. It has a slimmer profile and is featured with a straight, English-style stock. It was produced from 1967 to 1976 by FN.

| Exc. | V.G. | Good | Fair | Poor |
|---|---|---|---|---|
| 1800 | 1500 | 1350 | 1000 | 800 |

The following superposed shotguns were manufactured between 1983 and 1986 by FN in Belgium. The following models differ in the amount of ornamentation and the quality of materials and workmanship utilized in construction. Additional values for small-bore chamberings are similar to the early superposed models listed previously. This series was also available in a superlight configuration. The following values would be increased approximately 25 percent for this lightweight variation.

### Presentation 1
| Exc. | V.G. | Good | Fair | Poor |
|---|---|---|---|---|
| 2600 | 2250 | 1750 | 1250 | 1000 |

### Presentation 1 Gold-Inlaid
| Exc. | V.G. | Good | Fair | Poor |
|---|---|---|---|---|
| 3000 | 2650 | 2150 | 1500 | 1250 |

### Presentation 2
| Exc. | V.G. | Good | Fair | Poor |
|---|---|---|---|---|
| 2950 | 2600 | 2100 | 1450 | 1275 |

### Presentation 2 Gold-Inlaid
| Exc. | V.G. | Good | Fair | Poor |
|---|---|---|---|---|
| 3500 | 3250 | 2750 | 2000 | 1500 |

### Presentation 3
| Exc. | V.G. | Good | Fair | Poor |
|---|---|---|---|---|
| 5000 | 4500 | 3800 | 2750 | 2000 |

### Presentation 4
| Exc. | V.G. | Good | Fair | Poor |
|---|---|---|---|---|
| 5500 | 4750 | 4000 | 3250 | 2750 |

### Late Manufacture High-Grade Superposed Guns
#### Pigeon Grade
| NIB | Exc. | V.G. | Good | Fair | Poor |
|---|---|---|---|---|---|
| 3850 | 3000 | 2500 | 2000 | 1550 | 1250 |

#### Pointer Grade
| NIB | Exc. | V.G. | Good | Fair | Poor |
|---|---|---|---|---|---|
| 4750 | 3500 | 3000 | 2500 | 1900 | 1400 |

#### Diana Grade
| NIB | Exc. | V.G. | Good | Fair | Poor |
|---|---|---|---|---|---|
| 5650 | 4500 | 4000 | 3500 | 2750 | 2000 |

#### Midas Grade
| NIB | Exc. | V.G. | Good | Fair | Poor |
|---|---|---|---|---|---|
| 7000 | 5750 | 5000 | 4500 | 3500 | 2750 |

## Liege
This is an Over/Under shotgun chambered for 12 gauge. It was offered with 26.5", 28", or 30" vent-rib barrels with various choke combinations. It features a boxlock action with a non-selective single trigger and automatic ejectors. The finish is blued with a checkered walnut stock. There were approximately 10,000 manufactured between 1973 and 1975.

| Exc. | V.G. | Good | Fair | Poor |
|---|---|---|---|---|
| 750 | 650 | 500 | 425 | 350 |

## B 27

This modified version of the Liege was imported into the U.S. without the Browning Arms Company markings. It was offered in a number of variations that differed in the amount of ornamentation and quality of materials and workmanship utilized. It features the same action as the Liege Over/Under gun.

### Standard

| Exc. | V.G. | Good | Fair | Poor |
|------|------|------|------|------|
| 750 | 675 | 550 | 450 | 375 |

### Grade II Deluxe

| Exc. | V.G. | Good | Fair | Poor |
|------|------|------|------|------|
| 875 | 750 | 575 | 475 | 400 |

### Grand Deluxe

| Exc. | V.G. | Good | Fair | Poor |
|------|------|------|------|------|
| 1100 | 900 | 700 | 600 | 500 |

### Deluxe Trap

| Exc. | V.G. | Good | Fair | Poor |
|------|------|------|------|------|
| 750 | 650 | 475 | 400 | 375 |

### Deluxe Skeet

| Exc. | V.G. | Good | Fair | Poor |
|------|------|------|------|------|
| 850 | 750 | 550 | 450 | 375 |

### City of Liege Commemorative--250 Manufactured

| NIB | Exc. | V.G. | Good | Fair | Poor |
|-----|------|------|------|------|------|
| 1150 | 1000 | 850 | 750 | 650 | 550 |

## ST-100

This is an Over/Under trap gun that features separated barrels with an adjustable point of impact. It is chambered for 12 gauge and has a 30" or 32" barrel with full choke and a floating ventilated rib. It features a single trigger and automatic ejectors. The finish is blued with a checkered walnut stock. It was manufactured by FN between 1979 and 1983. It was not marked "Browning."

| Exc. | V.G. | Good | Fair | Poor |
|------|------|------|------|------|
| 2200 | 2000 | 1750 | 1400 | 1000 |

## Citori Series

This is an Over/Under, double-barrel shotgun chambered for all gauges and offered with vent-rib barrels of 26" through 30" in length. It has a boxlock action with a single-selective trigger and automatic ejectors. The various grades differ in the amount of ornamentation and the quality of materials and workmanship utilized in construction. This Series is manufactured in Japan by B. C. Miroku and was introduced in 1973.

### Grade I

| NIB | Exc. | V.G. | Good | Fair | Poor |
|-----|------|------|------|------|------|
| 985 | 850 | 725 | 550 | 425 | 350 |

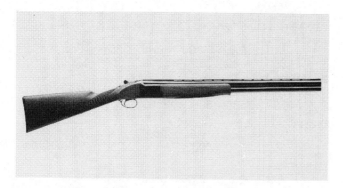

### Upland Special--Straight Stock, Choke Tubes

| NIB | Exc. | V.G. | Good | Fair | Poor |
|-----|------|------|------|------|------|
| 1000 | 850 | 700 | 575 | 450 | 375 |

### Grade II--Discontinued 1983

| Exc. | V.G. | Good | Fair | Poor |
|------|------|------|------|------|
| 950 | 800 | 675 | 550 | 475 |

### Grade III--Choke Tubes

| NIB | Exc. | V.G. | Good | Fair | Poor |
|-----|------|------|------|------|------|
| 1400 | 1250 | 950 | 775 | 650 | 550 |

### Grade V--Discontinued 1984

| Exc. | V.G. | Good | Fair | Poor |
|------|------|------|------|------|
| 1400 | 1250 | 950 | 775 | 600 |

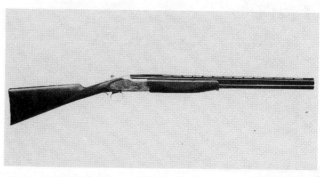

### Grade VI--Choke Tubes

| NIB | Exc. | V.G. | Good | Fair | Poor |
|-----|------|------|------|------|------|
| 2000 | 1700 | 1400 | 1000 | 750 | 550 |

## Citori Lightning

This is a lightweight version that features a slimmer profile and has a checkered, round-knob, pistolgrip stock. It is offered in all gauges and in the same barrel lengths as the standard Citori. It features screw-in choke tubes known as invectors. It was introduced in 1988. The models differ in the amount of ornamentation and quality of materials and workmanship utilized.

### Grade I

| NIB | Exc. | V.G. | Good | Fair | Poor |
|-----|------|------|------|------|------|
| 995 | 850 | 700 | 575 | 450 | 375 |

### Grade III

| NIB | Exc. | V.G. | Good | Fair | Poor |
|-----|------|------|------|------|------|
| 1400 | 1250 | 950 | 775 | 650 | 550 |

### Grade VI

| NIB | Exc. | V.G. | Good | Fair | Poor |
|-----|------|------|------|------|------|
| 2000 | 1850 | 1500 | 1150 | 950 | 800 |

## Citori Superlight

This is a lighter-weight version of the Citori chambered for all gauges and offered with the same features as the Lightning Series. The grades differ in the amount of ornamentation and quality of materials and workmanship utilized. This series was introduced in 1983.

### Grade I

| NIB | Exc. | V.G. | Good | Fair | Poor |
|-----|------|------|------|------|------|
| 1000 | 900 | 750 | 500 | 425 | 350 |

### Grade III

| NIB | Exc. | V.G. | Good | Fair | Poor |
|-----|------|------|------|------|------|
| 1400 | 1300 | 1050 | 750 | 550 | 450 |

### Grade V--Discontinued 1984

| Exc. | V.G. | Good | Fair | Poor |
|------|------|------|------|------|
| 1450 | 1350 | 1100 | 800 | 600 |

### Grade VI

| NIB | Exc. | V.G. | Good | Fair | Poor |
|-----|------|------|------|------|------|
| 2100 | 1850 | 1600 | 1400 | 1000 | 750 |

## Citori Skeet

This series of guns was chambered for all gauges and was designed for competition skeet shooting. It is similar to the standard Citori with a high-post target rib and 26" or 28" barrels. The versions differ in the amount of engraving and the quality of materials and workmanship utilized.

### Grade I

| NIB | Exc. | V.G. | Good | Fair | Poor |
|-----|------|------|------|------|------|
| 1050 | 925 | 750 | 550 | 425 | 350 |

### Grade II--Discontinued 1983

| Exc. | V.G. | Good | Fair | Poor |
|------|------|------|------|------|
| 1000 | 850 | 675 | 450 | 350 |

### Grade III

| NIB | Exc. | V.G. | Good | Fair | Poor |
|-----|------|------|------|------|------|
| 1500 | 1350 | 1000 | 750 | 600 | 500 |

**Grade V--Discontinued 1984**

| Exc. | V.G. | Good | Fair | Poor |
|---|---|---|---|---|
| 1400 | 1250 | 900 | 650 | 450 |

**Grade VI**

| NIB | Exc. | V.G. | Good | Fair | Poor |
|---|---|---|---|---|---|
| 2100 | 1800 | 1550 | 1250 | 1000 | 800 |

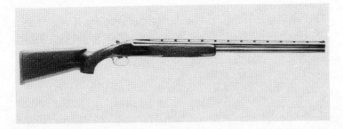

**Citori Trap**

This version is similar to the standard Citori, offered in 12 gauge only with 30" or 32" barrels. It features a high rib and a Monte Carlo-type stock with recoil pad. The versions differ as to the amount of ornamentation and the quality of materials and workmanship utilized.

**Grade I**

| NIB | Exc. | V.G. | Good | Fair | Poor |
|---|---|---|---|---|---|
| 1100 | 950 | 775 | 550 | 450 | 375 |

**Plus Trap--Adjustable Rib and Stock**

| NIB | Exc. | V.G. | Good | Fair | Poor |
|---|---|---|---|---|---|
| 1500 | 1350 | 1000 | 750 | 600 | 500 |

**Grade II--Discontinued 1983**

| Exc. | V.G. | Good | Fair | Poor |
|---|---|---|---|---|
| 1000 | 850 | 675 | 450 | 350 |

**Grade III**

| NIB | Exc. | V.G. | Good | Fair | Poor |
|---|---|---|---|---|---|
| 1500 | 1350 | 1000 | 750 | 600 | 500 |

**Grade V--Discontinued 1984**

| Exc. | V.G. | Good | Fair | Poor |
|---|---|---|---|---|
| 1400 | 1250 | 900 | 650 | 450 |

**Grade VI**

| NIB | Exc. | V.G. | Good | Fair | Poor |
|---|---|---|---|---|---|
| 2100 | 1800 | 1550 | 1250 | 1000 | 800 |

**Trap Combination Set**

This version is offered in Grade I only and features a 34" single barrel and a 32" set of Over/Under barrels. It is furnished in a fitted case and has been discontinued.

| Exc. | V.G. | Good | Fair | Poor |
|---|---|---|---|---|
| 1200 | 1050 | 950 | 800 | 700 |

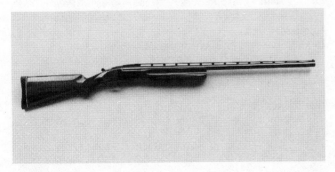

**BT-99**

This is a break-open, single-barrel trap gun chambered for 12 gauge only. It is offered with a 32" or 34", vent-rib barrel with screw-in choke tubes. It features a boxlock action with automatic ejectors. The finish is blued with a checkered walnut stock and beavertail forearm. It was introduced in 1971 by B. C. Miroku.

| NIB | Exc. | V.G. | Good | Fair | Poor |
|---|---|---|---|---|---|
| 1000 | 850 | 675 | 500 | 400 | 350 |

**BT-99 Plus**

This version features an adjustable vent rib and a recoil-reduction system. It has an adjustable stock and recoil pad, as well as a backboard barrel. It was introduced in 1989.

| NIB | Exc. | V.G. | Good | Fair | Poor |
|---|---|---|---|---|---|
| 1500 | 1350 | 1175 | 900 | 750 | 500 |

**BT-99 Pigeon Grade**

This is a heavily engraved version with a coin-finished receiver. It was discontinued in 1984.

| NIB | Exc. | V.G. | Good | Fair | Poor |
|---|---|---|---|---|---|
| 1200 | 1050 | 950 | 800 | 700 | |

**BSS**

This is an SxS, double-barrel shotgun chambered for 12 or 20 gauge. It was offered with a 26", 28", or 30" barrel with various choke combinations. It features a boxlock action and automatic ejectors. Early guns had a non-selective single trigger; late production, a selective trigger. The finish is blued with a checkered walnut stock and beavertail forearm. It was manufactured between 1971 and 1988 by B. C. Miroku
Single-Selective Trigger--Add 20 Percent.
20 Gauge--Add 10 Percent.

| Exc. | V.G. | Good | Fair | Poor |
|---|---|---|---|---|
| 500 | 450 | 375 | 300 | 250 |

**BSS Sporter**

This version features an English-style, straight-grip stock and a splinter forearm. The stock was oil-finished. It was offered with a 26" or 28" barrel.

| Exc. | V.G. | Good | Fair | Poor |
|---|---|---|---|---|
| 600 | 525 | 475 | 400 | 300 |

**BSS Grade II**

This version features gamescene engraving and a satin, coin-finished receiver. It was discontinued in 1983.

| Exc. | V.G. | Good | Fair | Poor |
|---|---|---|---|---|
| 1000 | 900 | 800 | 600 | 450 |

**BSS Sidelock**

This version features an engraved sidelock action and was offered in 12 or 20 gauge. It was offered with a 26" or 28" barrel and has a straight-grip stock and splintered forearm. It was manufactured in Korea between 1983 and 1988.

| Exc. | V.G. | Good | Fair | Poor |
|---|---|---|---|---|
| 1750 | 1350 | 1000 | 750 | 600 |

**Early Production Auto-5**

This series of recoil-operated, semi-automatic shotguns was designed by John M. Browning and was offered in 12 or 16 gauge. The barrel lengths were 26", 28", 30", or 32" with various chokes and ribs. It has a unique, square-back action that has become instantly recognizable. The finish is blued with a checkered walnut, round-knob stock. The various versions differ in the amount of ornamentation, type of rib, and quality of materials and workmanship utilized in construction. This series was manufactured in Belgium by FN between 1903 and 1939. The first example appeared in the United States in 1923. Pre-WWII 16-gauge guns had 2-9/16" chambers; early models should be inspected by a qualified gunsmith before firing.

**Grade I--Plain Barrel**

| Exc. | V.G. | Good | Fair | Poor |
|---|---|---|---|---|
| 450 | 400 | 300 | 250 | 150 |

**Grade I--Matte Rib**

| Exc. | V.G. | Good | Fair | Poor |
|---|---|---|---|---|
| 550 | 500 | 375 | 300 | 175 |

**Grade I--Vent Rib**

| Exc. | V.G. | Good | Fair | Poor |
|---|---|---|---|---|
| 650 | 600 | 475 | 375 | 200 |

**Grade II--Plain Barrel**

| Exc. | V.G. | Good | Fair | Poor |
|---|---|---|---|---|
| 1050 | 975 | 750 | 550 | 425 |

**Grade II--Matte Rib**

| Exc. | V.G. | Good | Fair | Poor |
|---|---|---|---|---|
| 1300 | 1175 | 850 | 650 | 500 |

### Grade II--Vent Rib

| Exc. | V.G. | Good | Fair | Poor |
|------|------|------|------|------|
| 1600 | 1450 | 1200 | 950 | 750 |

### Grade III--Plain Barrel

| Exc. | V.G. | Good | Fair | Poor |
|------|------|------|------|------|
| 2500 | 2250 | 1850 | 1450 | 1000 |

### Grade III--Matte Rib

| Exc. | V.G. | Good | Fair | Poor |
|------|------|------|------|------|
| 2750 | 2500 | 2000 | 1600 | 1250 |

### Grade III--Vent Rib

| Exc. | V.G. | Good | Fair | Poor |
|------|------|------|------|------|
| 3000 | 2750 | 2250 | 1800 | 1500 |

### Grade IV--Plain Barrel

| Exc. | V.G. | Good | Fair | Poor |
|------|------|------|------|------|
| 4000 | 3750 | 3250 | 2750 | 2400 |

### Grade IV--Matte Rib

| Exc. | V.G. | Good | Fair | Poor |
|------|------|------|------|------|
| 4200 | 3950 | 3450 | 3000 | 2600 |

### Grade IV--Vent Rib

| Exc. | V.G. | Good | Fair | Poor |
|------|------|------|------|------|
| 4400 | 4100 | 3750 | 3200 | 2750 |

## American Browning Auto-5

This recoil-operated, semi-automatic shotgun was another variation of the early-production Auto-5. It was chambered for 12, 16, or 20 gauge and was manufactured by the Remington Company for Browning. It is quite similar to Remington's Model 11 shotgun but features the Browning logo and a different type of engraving. There were approximately 45,000 manufactured between 1940 and 1942.

Vent Rib--Add 10 Percent.
20 Gauge--Add 10 Percent.

| Exc. | V.G. | Good | Fair | Poor |
|------|------|------|------|------|
| 400 | 350 | 300 | 200 | 170 |

## Mid-Production Auto-5--FN Manufacture

### Standard Weight

This version of the recoil-operated, semi-automatic Auto-5 shotgun was manufactured by FN in Belgium between 1952 and 1976. It was offered in 12 or 16 gauge with 26" through 32" barrels with various chokes. The finish is blued with a checkered walnut stock and a black buttplate that was marked "Browning." Some will be found with round-knob pistol grips. The flat-bottom variation was introduced in 1967.

### Plain Barrel

| Exc. | V.G. | Good | Fair | Poor |
|------|------|------|------|------|
| 425 | 375 | 300 | 250 | 175 |

### Matte Rib

| Exc. | V.G. | Good | Fair | Poor |
|------|------|------|------|------|
| 450 | 400 | 325 | 275 | 200 |

### Vent Rib

| Exc. | V.G. | Good | Fair | Poor |
|------|------|------|------|------|
| 500 | 450 | 350 | 300 | 250 |

## Auto-5 Lightweight

This version was chambered for 12 or 20 gauge and featured a lighter-weight, scroll-engraved receiver. It was manufactured between 1952 and 1976 by FN.

Vent Rib--Add 20 Percent.

| Exc. | V.G. | Good | Fair | Poor |
|------|------|------|------|------|
| 450 | 400 | 325 | 275 | 200 |

## Auto-5 Magnum

This version featured 3" chambers and was offered with 26" through 32", full-choke barrels. It was manufactured between 1958 and 1976 by FN.

Vent Rib--Add 20 Percent.

| Exc. | V.G. | Good | Fair | Poor |
|------|------|------|------|------|
| 550 | 500 | 425 | 325 | 250 |

## Auto-5 Skeet

This version is similar to the lightweight model, chambered for 12 or 20 gauge with a 26" or 28", vent-rib, skeet-choked barrel.

| Exc. | V.G. | Good | Fair | Poor |
|------|------|------|------|------|
| 550 | 500 | 425 | 325 | 250 |

## Auto-5 Trap Model

This version is similar to the standard-weight model except chambered for 12 gauge only, with a 30", vent-rib, full-choke barrel. It was manufactured by FN until 1971.

| Exc. | V.G. | Good | Fair | Poor |
|------|------|------|------|------|
| 525 | 475 | 400 | 300 | 225 |

## Sweet Sixteen

This version is similar to the standard-weight and is chambered for 16 gauge only. It has a gold-plated trigger and was manufactured by FN between 1953 and 1976.

Matte Rib--Add 25 Percent.
Vent Rib-- Add 50 Percent.

| Exc. | V.G. | Good | Fair | Poor |
|------|------|------|------|------|
| 500 | 450 | 375 | 275 | 200 |

## Buck Special

This version features a 24", cylinder-bore barrel with adjustable rifle sights. It was manufactured by FN between 1958 and 1976.

| Exc. | V.G. | Good | Fair | Poor |
|------|------|------|------|------|
| 550 | 500 | 425 | 325 | 250 |

## Two Millionth Commemorative

This version commemorated the two millionth Auto-5 shotgun produced by FN. It was engraved with a special high-polish blue finish and high-grade, checkered walnut in the stock. It was furnished in a fitted case along with a book on the Browning Company. There were 2,500 manufactured between 1971 and 1974. As with all commemoratives, it must be NIB to realize its top potential.

| NIB | V.G. | Good | Fair | Poor |
|------|------|------|------|------|
| 1200 | 800 | 500 | 350 | 250 |

## Late Production Auto-5--B. C. Miroku Manufacture

In 1976 production of the Auto-5 shotgun was begun by B. C. Miroku in Japan. This move was accomplished after approximately 2,750,000 Auto-5 shotguns were manufactured by FN in Belgium between 1903 and 1976. The Japanese-manufactured guns in the opinion of many knowledgeable people show no less quality or functionality but are simply not as desirable from a collector's standpoint. The variations and their values are as follows:

### Auto-5 Light 12

This version is chambered for 12 gauge only and is offered with a lightweight receiver. The barrel has a vent rib and choke tubes. It was introduced in 1986.

| NIB | Exc. | V.G. | Good | Fair | Poor |
|------|------|------|------|------|------|
| 685 | 600 | 500 | 400 | 300 | 225 |

### Auto-5 Light 20

This version is similar to the Light 12 except chambered for 20 gauge only.

| NIB | Exc. | V.G. | Good | Fair | Poor |
|------|------|------|------|------|------|
| 685 | 600 | 500 | 400 | 300 | 225 |

### Auto-5 Magnum

This version features 3" chambers and is offered with 26", 28", 30", or 32" barrels. It was introduced in 1976 by Miroku.

| NIB | Exc. | V.G. | Good | Fair | Poor |
|------|------|------|------|------|------|
| 700 | 600 | 500 | 400 | 300 | 225 |

### Auto-5 Buck Special

This version has a 24" barrel cylinder-bored with adjustable sights. It was introduced by Miroku in 1976.

| NIB | Exc. | V.G. | Good | Fair | Poor |
|------|------|------|------|------|------|
| 685 | 600 | 500 | 400 | 300 | 225 |

### Auto-5 Skeet

This is a competition model that features 26" or 28", skeet-bored barrels with a vent rib. It was manufactured between 1976 and 1983 by Miroku.

| Exc. | V.G. | Good | Fair | Poor |
|------|------|------|------|------|
| 450 | 400 | 350 | 250 | 200 |

### Sweet Sixteen

This version is similar to the Belgian-produced Sweet Sixteen but is offered standard with a vent rib and screw-in invector choke tubes. It was introduced in 1987 by Miroku.

| NIB | Exc. | V.G. | Good | Fair | Poor |
|-----|------|------|------|------|------|
| 685 | 600 | 500 | 400 | 300 | 225 |

### A-5 DU 50th Anniversary

This was a high-grade version of the Auto-5 produced to commemorate the fiftieth anniversary of Ducks Unlimited. It is highly engraved and features high-gloss bluing and a fancy checkered walnut stock. There were approximately 5,500 manufactured by Miroku in 1987. They were auctioned by the Ducks Unlimited chapters to raise money for the organization; and because of this fact, it is difficult to furnish an accurate value. This is a commemorative firearm and, as such, must be NIB with all furnished materials to command premium collector value. We furnish what we feel is a general value.

| NIB | Exc. | V.G. | Good | Fair | Poor |
|-----|------|------|------|------|------|
| 1750 | 1250 | 850 | 600 | 400 | 300 |

### A-5 DU Sweet Sixteen

This was a special version of the Miroku-manufactured Sweet Sixteen that was auctioned by the Ducks Unlimited chapters in 1988. There were 5,500 produced. All specifications and cautions that were furnished for the 50th Anniversary gun also apply here.

| NIB | Exc. | V.G. | Good | Fair | Poor |
|-----|------|------|------|------|------|
| 1500 | 1000 | 750 | 500 | 350 | 275 |

### Double Automatic Shotgun

This is a short recoil-operated, semi-automatic shotgun chambered for 12 gauge only. It was offered with a 26", 28", or 30" barrel that was either plain or vent-ribbed. It has various chokes. The receiver is steel, and the finish is blued with a checkered walnut stock. The tubular magazine holds only two shots--hence its name. It was manufactured between 1952 and 1971.

Vent Rib--Add 25 Percent.

| Exc. | V.G. | Good | Fair | Poor |
|------|------|------|------|------|
| 450 | 400 | 325 | 250 | 200 |

### Twelvette Double Auto

This version is similar to the Double Automatic except that it has an aircraft aluminum alloy frame color-anodized in either blue, silver, green, brown, or black. Red-, gold-, or royal blue-colored receivers were the rarest colors and would command approximately a 15 percent premium. It was offered with either a plain or vent-rib barrel. There were approximately 65,000 produced between 1952 and 1971.

Vent Rib--Add 25 Percent.

| Exc. | V.G. | Good | Fair | Poor |
|------|------|------|------|------|
| 475 | 425 | 350 | 275 | 225 |

### Twentyweight Double Auto

This version is similar in all respects to the Twelvette except that it is three-quarters of a pound lighter and was offered with a 26.5" barrel. It was manufactured between 1952 and 1971.

Vent Rib--Add 25 Percent.

| Exc. | V.G. | Good | Fair | Poor |
|------|------|------|------|------|
| 485 | 435 | 375 | 300 | 250 |

### B-2000

This is a gas-operated, semi-automatic shotgun chambered for 12 or 20 gauge and offered with a 26", 28", or 30", vent-rib barrel with various chokes. The finish is blued with a checkered walnut stock. This shotgun was assembled in Portugal from parts that were manufactured by FN in Belgium. There were approximately 115,000 imported between 1974 and 1983.

| Exc. | V.G. | Good | Fair | Poor |
|------|------|------|------|------|
| 385 | 325 | 300 | 250 | 150 |

### B-2000 Magnum

This version features 3" chambers and was offered standard with a recoil pad.

| Exc. | V.G. | Good | Fair | Poor |
|------|------|------|------|------|
| 425 | 350 | 325 | 275 | 175 |

### B-2000 Buck Special

This version has a 24", cylinder-bored barrel with rifle sights.

| Exc. | V.G. | Good | Fair | Poor |
|------|------|------|------|------|
| 400 | 340 | 300 | 250 | 175 |

### B-2000 Trap

This version has a 30", full-choke barrel with a floating rib and a Monte Carlo-type trap stock.

| Exc. | V.G. | Good | Fair | Poor |
|------|------|------|------|------|
| 400 | 340 | 300 | 250 | 175 |

### B-2000 Skeet

This version features a 26", skeet-bored barrel with a floating vent rib and a skeet-type stock.

| Exc. | V.G. | Good | Fair | Poor |
|------|------|------|------|------|
| 400 | 340 | 300 | 250 | 175 |

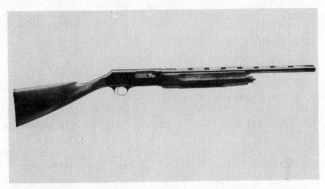

### Model B-80

This is a gas-operated, semi-automatic shotgun chambered for 12 or 20 gauge. It features 3" Magnum potential by simply exchanging the barrel. It features various-length barrels and was offered with screw-in Invector chokes as of 1985. The receiver is either steel or lightweight aluminum alloy. The finish is blued with a checkered walnut stock. This gun was assembled in Portugal from parts manufactured by Beretta in Italy. It was manufactured between 1981 and 1988.

| Exc. | V.G. | Good | Fair | Poor |
|------|------|------|------|------|
| 450 | 400 | 350 | 300 | 200 |

### Model B-80 Buck Special

This version features a 24", cylinder-bored barrel with rifle sights. It was discontinued in 1984.

| Exc. | V.G. | Good | Fair | Poor |
|------|------|------|------|------|
| 450 | 400 | 350 | 300 | 200 |

### Model B-80 DU Commemorative

This version was produced to be auctioned by American Ducks Unlimited chapters. In order to realize the collector potential, it must be NIB with all supplied materials. Values supplied are general.

| NIB | Exc. | V.G. | Good | Fair | Poor |
|-----|------|------|------|------|------|
| 900 | 700 | 500 | 375 | 300 | 250 |

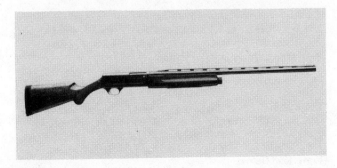

### A-500

This is a self-adjusting, gas-operated, semi-automatic shotgun chambered for 12 gauge only. It is offered with 26", 28", or 30" barrels with a vent rib and screw-in Invector choke tubes. It has 3" chambers and can fire any load interchangeably. The finish is blued with a checkered walnut stock and recoil pad. It features light engraving. It was introduced in 1987.

| NIB | Exc. | V.G. | Good | Fair | Poor |
|-----|------|------|------|------|------|
| 560 | 490 | 425 | 350 | 275 | 225 |

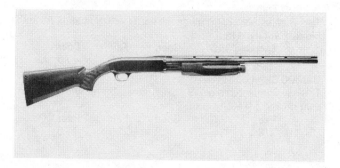

## BPS Model

This is a slide-action shotgun chambered for 10, 12, or 20 gauge. It is offered with various-length, vent-rib barrels with screw-in invector chokes. It features 3" Magnum chambers and a bottom-ejection system that effectively makes it ambidextrous. It has double slide bars and a 5-shot tubular magazine. It is constructed of all steel. It was introduced by B. C. Miroku in 1977.

**Field Grade**

| NIB | Exc. | V.G. | Good | Fair | Poor |
|-----|------|------|------|------|------|
| 435 | 390 | 325 | 275 | 200 | 150 |

**Magnum Model--10 or 12 Gauge, 3.5" Chambers**

| NIB | Exc. | V.G. | Good | Fair | Poor |
|-----|------|------|------|------|------|
| 510 | 450 | 375 | 325 | 250 | 200 |

**Upland Special--22" Barrel, Straight Stock**

| NIB | Exc. | V.G. | Good | Fair | Poor |
|-----|------|------|------|------|------|
| 435 | 390 | 325 | 275 | 200 | 150 |

**Stalker Model--Matte Finish, Black Stock**

| NIB | Exc. | V.G. | Good | Fair | Poor |
|-----|------|------|------|------|------|
| 435 | 390 | 325 | 275 | 200 | 150 |

**Buck Special--24" Barrel With Sights**

| NIB | Exc. | V.G. | Good | Fair | Poor |
|-----|------|------|------|------|------|
| 450 | 400 | 350 | 300 | 225 | 175 |

**Trap Model--Discontinued 1984**

| Exc. | V.G. | Good | Fair | Poor |
|------|------|------|------|------|
| 375 | 325 | 275 | 200 | 150 |

**Youth Model--Short Stock, 22" Barrel**

| NIB | Exc. | V.G. | Good | Fair | Poor |
|-----|------|------|------|------|------|
| 435 | 390 | 325 | 275 | 200 | 150 |

## Waterfowl Deluxe

This version is chambered for 12 gauge with a 3" chamber and features an etched receiver with a gold-plated trigger. Otherwise, it is similar to the standard BPS.

| Exc. | V.G. | Good | Fair | Poor |
|------|------|------|------|------|
| 600 | 525 | 425 | 325 | 250 |

## Ducks Unlimited Versions

These were limited-edition guns produced to be auctioned by Ducks Unlimited. They were furnished with a case and must be NIB with furnished materials to realize their collector potential.

| NIB | Exc. | V.G. | Good | Fair | Poor |
|-----|------|------|------|------|------|
| 650 | 525 | 425 | 325 | 250 | 175 |

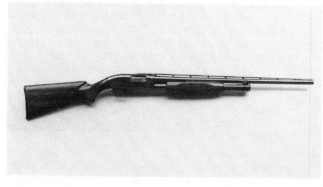

## Model 12--Grade I

This is a slide-action shotgun chambered for 20 gauge with a 26", modified-choke, vent-rib barrel. It is a reproduction of the Winchester Model 12 shotgun. It has a 5-round, tubular magazine with a floating, high-post rib. It has a take-down feature and is blued with a walnut stock. Introduced in 1988, total production will be limited to 8,500 guns.

| NIB | Exc. | V.G. | Good | Fair | Poor |
|-----|------|------|------|------|------|
| 725 | 650 | 575 | 475 | 400 | 300 |

## Model 12--Grade V

This is an extensively engraved version of the Grade I Model 12. It features a select walnut stock with deluxe checkering and a high-gloss finish. There are gold inlays. It was introduced in 1988, and production will be limited to 4,000 guns.

| NIB | Exc. | V.G. | Good | Fair | Poor |
|------|------|------|------|------|------|
| 1200 | 1050 | 900 | 750 | 500 | 350 |

## High-Power Bolt Action Rifle

This was a high-grade, bolt-action sporting rifle manufactured by FN in Belgium. It was built on either a Mauser or a Sako action and chambered for a number of popular calibers from the .222 Remington up to the .458 Winchester Magnum. There were three basic grades that differed in the amount of ornamentation and the quality of materials and workmanship utilized. Certain calibers are considered to be rare and will bring a premium from collectors of this firearm. We recommend securing a qualified appraisal on these rifles if a transaction is contemplated. We furnish general values only.

**Safari Grade--Standard Model, Standard Calibers**

| Exc. | V.G. | Good | Fair | Poor |
|------|------|------|------|------|
| 800 | 675 | 525 | 400 | 300 |

**Medallion Grade--Scroll Engraved**

| Exc. | V.G. | Good | Fair | Poor |
|------|------|------|------|------|
| 1500 | 1250 | 1000 | 750 | 500 |

**Olympian Grade--Extensive Engraving**

| Exc. | V.G. | Good | Fair | Poor |
|------|------|------|------|------|
| 2250 | 2000 | 1750 | 1450 | 1000 |

## Model BBR

This is a bolt-action sporting rifle chambered for various popular calibers. It has a 24" barrel with an adjustable trigger and fluted bolt. It features a detachable magazine under the floorplate and was furnished without sights. The finish is blued with a checkered walnut, Monte Carlo stock. It was manufactured between 1978 and 1984 by Miroku.

| Exc. | V.G. | Good | Fair | Poor |
|---|---|---|---|---|
| 475 | 400 | 350 | 275 | 200 |

## A-Bolt Hunter

This is the current bolt-action rifle manufactured by B. C. Miroku. It is chambered for various popular calibers and offered with a 22", 24", or 26" barrel. It has either a short or long action, an adjustable trigger, and a detachable box magazine that is mounted under the floorplate. It is furnished without sights and is blued with a checkered walnut stock. It was introduced in 1985.

| NIB | Exc. | V.G. | Good | Fair | Poor |
|---|---|---|---|---|---|
| 450 | 400 | 350 | 300 | 250 | 200 |

## Stainless Stalker

This version is chambered for the .270, .30-06, and the 7mm Remington Magnum cartridges. It is constructed of stainless steel and has a black, painted wood stock. It was introduced in 1987.

| NIB | Exc. | V.G. | Good | Fair | Poor |
|---|---|---|---|---|---|
| 580 | 525 | 450 | 350 | 300 | 250 |

## Medallion Model

This is a deluxe version of the A-Bolt Hunter with a high-polish blue finish and a select walnut stock with rosewood pistolgrip cap and forend tip.

| NIB | Exc. | V.G. | Good | Fair | Poor |
|---|---|---|---|---|---|
| 525 | 475 | 400 | 350 | 300 | 250 |

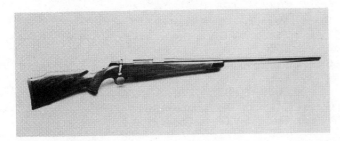

## Gold Medallion

This version has a fancy-grade walnut stock with a cheekpiece. It is lightly engraved and has gold-inlaid letters. It was introduced in 1988.

| NIB | Exc. | V.G. | Good | Fair | Poor |
|---|---|---|---|---|---|
| 690 | 625 | 550 | 450 | 400 | 325 |

## Big Horn Sheep Issue

This is a high-grade version of the A-Bolt chambered for the .270 cartridge. It features a deluxe skip-line checkered walnut stock with a heavily engraved receiver and floorplate. It has two gold sheep inlays. There were 600 manufactured in 1986 and 1987.

| NIB | Exc. | V.G. | Good | Fair | Poor |
|---|---|---|---|---|---|
| 1050 | 800 | 600 | 450 | 400 | 325 |

## Pronghorn Issue

This is a deluxe version of the A-Bolt chambered for the .243 cartridge. It is heavily engraved and gold inlaid and features a presentation-grade walnut stock with skip-line checkering and pearl-inlaid borders. There were 500 manufactured in 1987.

| NIB | Exc. | V.G. | Good | Fair | Poor |
|---|---|---|---|---|---|
| 1300 | 1000 | 750 | 500 | 400 | 325 |

## Micro-Medallion Model

This is a smaller version of the A-Bolt Hunter chambered for popular cartridges that fit a short action. It has a 20" barrel without sights and a 3-round magazine. It was introduced in 1988.

| NIB | Exc. | V.G. | Good | Fair | Poor |
|---|---|---|---|---|---|
| 525 | 475 | 400 | 350 | 300 | 250 |

## Grade I A-Bolt .22

This is a bolt-action sporting rifle chambered for the .22 l.r. or .22 Magnum cartridges. It features a 60-degree bolt and a 22" barrel available either with or without open sights. It has a 5-round, detachable magazine and an adjustable trigger. The finish is blued with a checkered walnut stock. It was introduced in 1986.

.22 Magnum--Add 15 Percent.

| NIB | Exc. | V.G. | Good | Fair | Poor |
|---|---|---|---|---|---|
| 340 | 275 | 210 | 150 | 125 | 100 |

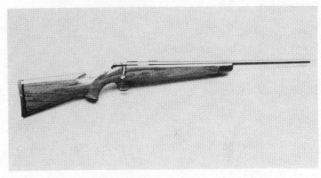

## Gold Medallion A-Bolt .22

This deluxe, high-grade version features a select stock with rose-wood pistolgrip cap and forend tip. It is lightly engraved and has gold-filled letters. It was introduced in 1988.

| NIB | Exc. | V.G. | Good | Fair | Poor |
|---|---|---|---|---|---|
| 450 | 400 | 350 | 300 | 225 | 175 |

## T-Bolt Model T-1

This is a unique, straight-pull, bolt-action sporting rifle chambered for the .22 l.r. cartridge. It has a 22" barrel with open sights and a 5-round magazine. The finish is blued with a plain walnut stock. It was manufactured between 1965 and 1974 by FN.

| Exc. | V.G. | Good | Fair | Poor |
|---|---|---|---|---|
| 300 | 275 | 225 | 150 | 100 |

## T-Bolt Model T-2

This version is similar to the T-1 with a select, checkered walnut stock and a 24" barrel.

| Exc. | V.G. | Good | Fair | Poor |
|---|---|---|---|---|
| 400 | 325 | 250 | 200 | 150 |

## Trombone Model

This is a slide-action rifle chambered for the .22 l.r. cartridge. It has a 24" barrel with open sights and a take-down design. It has a tubular magazine and a hammerless action. There were approximately 150,000 manufactured by FN between 1922 and 1974. Approximately 3,200 were imported by Browning in the 1960's. They are marked with either the FN barrel address or the Browning Arms address. The Browning-marked guns are worth approximately 20 percent additional. The values given are for FN-marked guns.

| Exc. | V.G. | Good | Fair | Poor |
|------|------|------|------|------|
| 550 | 500 | 450 | 375 | 275 |

### BPR-22

This is a short-stroke, slide-action rifle chambered for the .22 Magnum cartridge. It has a 20.25" barrel with open sights and an 11-round, tubular magazine. The finish is blued with a checkered walnut stock. It was manufactured between 1977 and 1982.

| Exc. | V.G. | Good | Fair | Poor |
|------|------|------|------|------|
| 275 | 200 | 150 | 125 | 95 |

### BPR-22 Grade II

This version is engraved and has a select walnut stock.

| Exc. | V.G. | Good | Fair | Poor |
|------|------|------|------|------|
| 375 | 300 | 250 | 200 | 125 |

### .22 Semi-Auto

This is a blowback-operated, semi-automatic rifle chambered for the .22 rimfire cartridge. It features a take-down barrel design with a 19.25" barrel and an 11-round, tubular magazine inside the buttstock. It is loaded through a hole in the middle of the buttstock. The finish is blued with a checkered walnut stock and beavertail forearm. This lightweight, compact firearm was manufactured by FN between 1914 and 1976. There are a number of versions that differ in the amount of ornamentation and the quality of materials and workmanship utilized.
.22 Short Only--Add 15 Percent.
Early Wheel Sight--Add 15 Percent.

#### Grade I

| Exc. | V.G. | Good | Fair | Poor |
|------|------|------|------|------|
| 400 | 375 | 300 | 200 | 125 |

#### Grade II--Satin Chromed Receiver

| Exc. | V.G. | Good | Fair | Poor |
|------|------|------|------|------|
| 700 | 600 | 425 | 300 | 225 |

#### Grade III--Coin Finished

| Exc. | V.G. | Good | Fair | Poor |
|------|------|------|------|------|
| 1250 | 1050 | 800 | 700 | 550 |

### .22 Semi-Auto (Miroku Mfg.)

This model is similar to the Belgian FN except that it was produced as of 1976 by B. C. Miroku in Japan. Collector interest is not as high as in the FN version.

#### Grade I

| NIB | Exc. | V.G. | Good | Fair | Poor |
|-----|------|------|------|------|------|
| 330 | 280 | 200 | 175 | 125 | 100 |

#### Grade II--Discontinued 1984

| Exc. | V.G. | Good | Fair | Poor |
|------|------|------|------|------|
| 425 | 375 | 300 | 225 | 150 |

#### Grade III--Discontinued 1983

| Exc. | V.G. | Good | Fair | Poor |
|------|------|------|------|------|
| 700 | 625 | 500 | 400 | 250 |

#### Grade VI--Gold Inlaid

| NIB | Exc. | V.G. | Good | Fair | Poor |
|-----|------|------|------|------|------|
| 675 | 600 | 500 | 425 | 325 | 275 |

### BAR-22

This is a blowback-operated, semi-automatic rifle chambered for the .22 l.r. cartridge. It has a 20.25" barrel with open sights and a 15-round, tubular magazine. It features a polished, lightweight alloy receiver. It was finished in blue with a checkered walnut stock. It is manufactured between 1977 and 1985 by Miroku.

| Exc. | V.G. | Good | Fair | Poor |
|------|------|------|------|------|
| 225 | 175 | 150 | 125 | 90 |

### BAR-22 Grade II

This is a deluxe version with an engraved, silver-finished receiver. It has a select walnut stock. It was discontinued in 1985.

| Exc. | V.G. | Good | Fair | Poor |
|------|------|------|------|------|
| 300 | 250 | 200 | 150 | 120 |

### Patent 1900 High Power

This is a semi-automatic sporting rifle chambered for the .35 Remington cartridge. It is similar in configuration to the Remington Model 8 rifle. It has a 22" barrel with open sights and a 5-round, integral magazine. The finish is blued with a plain walnut stock. There were approximately 5,000 manufactured between 1910 and 1931. A deluxe model with a ribbed barrel and checkered walnut stock was also available and would be worth approximately 15 percent additional.

| Exc. | V.G. | Good | Fair | Poor |
|------|------|------|------|------|
| 675 | 600 | 500 | 375 | 300 |

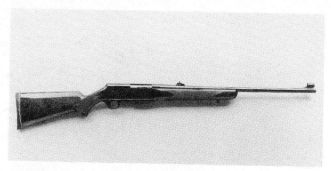

### BAR High Power Rifle

This is a gas-operated, semi-automatic sporting rifle chambered for various popular calibers from the .243 up to the .338 Magnum cartridges. It was offered with either a 22" or 24" barrel with folding leaf sight. The finish is blued with a checkered walnut stock. The various grades offered differed in the amount of ornamentation and the quality of materials and workmanship utilized. Earlier models were manufactured in Belgium by FN; these guns would be worth approximately 15 percent additional over the current guns that are assembled in Portugal from parts manufactured by FN. The .338 Magnum model is rarely encountered and would be worth approximately 25 percent additional. The values furnished are for current-production, Portuguese-assembled guns. This model was introduced in 1967.

#### Grade I

| NIB | Exc. | V.G. | Good | Fair | Poor |
|-----|------|------|------|------|------|
| 600 | 525 | 450 | 350 | 300 | 225 |

#### Grade I Magnum

| NIB | Exc. | V.G. | Good | Fair | Poor |
|-----|------|------|------|------|------|
| 650 | 575 | 500 | 400 | 350 | 250 |

#### Grade II--Discontinued 1974

| Exc. | V.G. | Good | Fair | Poor |
|------|------|------|------|------|
| 700 | 625 | 550 | 425 | 325 |

#### Grade II Magnum--Discontinued 1974

| Exc. | V.G. | Good | Fair | Poor |
|------|------|------|------|------|
| 775 | 700 | 625 | 500 | 400 |

#### Grade III--Discontinued 1984

| Exc. | V.G. | Good | Fair | Poor |
|------|------|------|------|------|
| 900 | 825 | 700 | 600 | 500 |

#### Grade III Magnum--Discontinued 1984

| Exc. | V.G. | Good | Fair | Poor |
|------|------|------|------|------|
| 950 | 875 | 750 | 650 | 550 |

#### Grade IV--Gamescene Engraved

| Exc. | V.G. | Good | Fair | Poor |
|------|------|------|------|------|
| 1250 | 1050 | 900 | 800 | 650 |

#### Grade IV Magnum--Discontinued 1984

| Exc. | V.G. | Good | Fair | Poor |
|------|------|------|------|------|
| 1375 | 1175 | 1000 | 900 | 700 |

#### Grade V--Gold Inlaid, Discontinued 1974

| Exc. | V.G. | Good | Fair | Poor |
|------|------|------|------|------|
| 3200 | 2850 | 2500 | 1600 | 1200 |

#### Grade V Magnum--Discontinued 1974

| Exc. | V.G. | Good | Fair | Poor |
|------|------|------|------|------|
| 3500 | 3000 | 2750 | 1850 | 1500 |

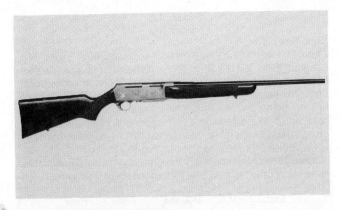

### North American Deer Rifle Issue

This is a deluxe version of the BAR chambered for .30-06 only. It features an engraved, silver-finished receiver and a deluxe, checkered walnut stock. There were 600 produced and furnished with a walnut case and accessories. This model was discontinued in 1983. As with all commemoratives, it must be NIB to command premium values.

| NIB | Exc. | V.G. | Good | Fair | Poor |
|---|---|---|---|---|---|
| 3600 | 2750 | 2000 | 1500 | 1200 | 800 |

### BL-22 Grade I

This is a lever-action rifle chambered for the .22 rimfire cartridge. It has an 18" barrel with a tubular magazine and a folding leaf rear sight. It is a Western-style firearm that features an exposed hammer. The finish is blued with a walnut stock. It was introduced in 1970 by Miroku.

| NIB | Exc. | V.G. | Good | Fair | Poor |
|---|---|---|---|---|---|
| 285 | 225 | 200 | 150 | 125 | 100 |

### BL-22 Grade II

This version is similar with a scroll-engraved receiver and a checkered, select walnut stock.

| NIB | Exc. | V.G. | Good | Fair | Poor |
|---|---|---|---|---|---|
| 325 | 250 | 225 | 175 | 150 | 125 |

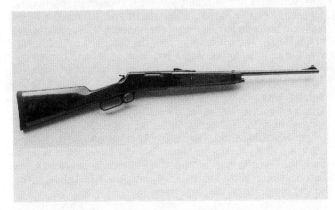

### Model 81 BLR

This is a contemporarily designed, lever-action sporting rifle chambered for various popular calibers from .22-250 up to .358 Winchester. It has a 20" barrel with adjustable sights. It features a 4-round, detachable magazine and a rotary locking bolt. The finish is blued with a checkered walnut stock and recoil pad. It was introduced in 1971 and manufactured that year in Belgium. In 1972 manufacture moved to Miroku in Japan. The Belgian-manufactured version is worth approximately 20 percent additional.

| NIB | Exc. | V.G. | Good | Fair | Poor |
|---|---|---|---|---|---|
| 475 | 400 | 325 | 275 | 200 | 150 |

### Model 65 Grade I

This was a limited-edition, lever-action rifle chambered for the .218 Bee cartridge. It has a tapered, round, 24" barrel with open sights. It was patterned after the Winchester Model 65 rifle. It has a 7-round, tubular magazine. The finish is blued with a plain walnut stock and metal buttplate. There were 3,500 manufactured in 1989.

| NIB | Exc. | V.G. | Good | Fair | Poor |
|---|---|---|---|---|---|
| 550 | 475 | 400 | 325 | 250 | 175 |

### Model 65 High Grade

This is a deluxe version that features a silver finished, scroll-engraved receiver with gold animal inlays and a gold-plated trigger. It features a select, checkered walnut stock. There were 1,500 manufactured in 1989.

| NIB | Exc. | V.G. | Good | Fair | Poor |
|---|---|---|---|---|---|
| 850 | 750 | 600 | 500 | 400 | 275 |

### Model 71 Grade I

This was a reproduction of the Winchester Model 71, chambered for the .348 cartridge. It has either a 20" or 24" barrel with open sights and a 4-round, tubular magazine. The finish is blued with a plain walnut stock. There were 4,000 twenty-inch carbines and 3,000 twenty-four-inch rifles manufactured in 1986 and 1987.

| Exc. | V.G. | Good | Fair | Poor |
|---|---|---|---|---|
| 595 | 500 | 400 | 300 | 225 |

### Model 71 High Grade

This version was similar to the Grade I except that it had a scroll-engraved, grayed receiver with a gold-plated trigger and gold inlays. There were 3,000 rifles and 3,000 carbines manufactured in 1986 and 1987.

| Exc. | V.G. | Good | Fair | Poor |
|---|---|---|---|---|
| 900 | 750 | 600 | 500 | 400 |

### Model 1886 Grade I

This was a lever-action sporting rifle patterned after the Model 1886 Winchester rifle. It was chambered for the .45-70 cartridge and has a 26", octagonal barrel with a full-length, tubular magazine. The finish is blued with a walnut stock and crescent buttplate. There were 7,000 manufactured in 1986.

| Exc. | V.G. | Good | Fair | Poor |
|---|---|---|---|---|
| 750 | 675 | 550 | 425 | 300 |

### Model 1886 High Grade

This deluxe version of the Model 1886 features gamescene engraving with gold accents and a checkered, select walnut stock. "1 of 3,000" is engraved on the top of the barrel. There were 3,000 manufactured in 1986.

| NIB | Exc. | V.G. | Good | Fair | Poor |
|---|---|---|---|---|---|
| 1000 | 900 | 800 | 650 | 500 | 425 |

### Model 1886 Montana Centennial

This version is similar to the High Grade with a different engraving pattern designed to commemorate the centennial of the state of Montana. There were 2,000 manufactured in 1986. As with all commemoratives, it must be NIB with all supplied materials to command collector interest.

| NIB | Exc. | V.G. | Good | Fair | Poor |
|---|---|---|---|---|---|
| 950 | 850 | 750 | 600 | 450 | 375 |

### 92 Carbine

This is a lever-action sporting rifle patterned after the Winchester Model 92. It was chambered for the .357 Mag. and the .44 Mag. cartridges. It has a 20" barrel with an 11-round, tubular magazine. The finish is blued with a walnut stock. It was discontinued in 1986.

| Exc. | V.G. | Good | Fair | Poor |
|---|---|---|---|---|
| 275 | 225 | 195 | 150 | 120 |

### Model 1895 Grade I

This is a lever-action sporting rifle chambered in .30-40 Krag and the .30-06 cartridge. It was patterned after the Model 1895 Winchester rifle. It has a 24" barrel and a 4-round, integral box magazine. It has a buckhorn rear sight and a blade front. The finish is blued with a walnut stock. There were 6,000 manufactured in .30-06 and 2,000 chambered for the .30-40 Krag. It was manufactured in 1984.

| Exc. | V.G. | Good | Fair | Poor |
|---|---|---|---|---|
| 600 | 525 | 450 | 375 | 275 |

**Model 1895 High Grade**

This is the deluxe engraved version of the Model 1895. It has gold-inlaid gamescenes and a gold-plated trigger and features a checkered select walnut stock. There were 2,000 produced in 1984--1,000 in each caliber.

| Exc. | V.G. | Good | Fair | Poor |
|------|------|------|------|------|
| 1000 | 900 | 700 | 575 | 400 |

**Express Rifle**

This is an Over/Under, superposed rifle chambered for the .270 Winchester or the .30-06 cartridges. It has 24" barrels with folding express sights and automatic ejectors. It features a single trigger. The receiver is engraved and is finished in blue with a deluxe checkered walnut stock. It was discontinued in 1986.

| Exc. | V.G. | Good | Fair | Poor |
|------|------|------|------|------|
| 2000 | 1800 | 1500 | 1100 | 800 |

**Continental Set**

This consists of an Express Rifle chambered for the .30-06 cartridge and furnished with an extra set of 20-gauge, Over/Under barrels. The shotgun barrels are 26.5" in length. There is a single trigger, automatic ejectors, and a heavily engraved receiver. The select walnut stock is hand-checkered and oil-finished. It was furnished with a fitted case. There were 500 manufactured in 1986.

| Exc. | V.G. | Good | Fair | Poor |
|------|------|------|------|------|
| 3000 | 2750 | 2200 | 1750 | 1000 |

# BRUCE & DAVIS
## Webster, Massachusetts

**Double Barrelled Pistol**

This pistol is a side by side percussion ignition affair with two hammers fired by a single trigger. It is chambered for .36 caliber with 3" to 6" round barrels. The pistol is scroll engraved and blued with walnut grips. The rib between the barrels is marked "Bruce & Davis." This company was known to be sales agents and not makers; and this pistol is thought to have been made by Allen & Thurber, but there is no proof to this effect. It was manufactured in the 1850's.

| Exc. | V.G. | Good | Fair | Poor |
|------|------|------|------|------|
| 450 | 375 | 300 | 200 | 150 |

# BRUCHET
## Ste. Etienne, France

**Model A Shotgun**

This side-by-side shotgun features the unique sliding action made famous by the Darne. Paul Bruchet was a foreman at Darne until they ceased operations in 1979, and he then started to produce his own guns. The Model A is chambered for 12 gauge through .410. The barrel lengths and chokes are to customer specifications. It has automatic ejectors and double triggers and is offered with four grades of embellishments. They have been produced on a limited basis (50 per year) since 1982.

Base Price as Follows; Add 25 Percent Per Grade.

| NIB | Exc. | V.G. | Good | Fair | Poor |
|-----|------|------|------|------|------|
| 1995 | 1800 | 1550 | 1250 | 1000 | 750 |

**Model B**

This model has an assisted-opening action and is more elaborately embellished. The walnut is more select; and the engraving, more profuse. It has been imported since 1982.

| NIB | Exc. | V.G. | Good | Fair | Poor |
|-----|------|------|------|------|------|
| 5800 | 5000 | 4250 | 3250 | 2500 | 1850 |

# BRUFF, R.P.
## New York, New York

**Bruff Pocket Pistol**

This deringer-styled pocket pistol is chambered for .41 caliber and utilizes the percussion ignition system. The round barrel is from 2.5" to 3" in length although longer barrels have been noted. The pistol is marked "R.P.Bruff NY" in an arch and "Cast Steel." The mountings are German silver with a checkered walnut stock. It was manufactured between 1855 and 1865.

| Exc. | V.G. | Good | Fair | Poor |
|------|------|------|------|------|
| 750 | 675 | 500 | 400 | 300 |

# BUCO
## Germany

**Buco Gas Pistol**

This odd firearm looks more like a telescope than a pistol. It is chambered for a 10.55mm gas cartridge and is a single shot. Overall it is approximately 5.5" long in its open or cocked position. The barrel is smooth bore and 3.75" in length. This pistol has no sights and no safety--one simply pulls the inner tube back much like extending a telescope, unscrews the end cap, inserts the round, and screws the cap back into place. When it is needed, a thumbnail is used to depress the sear and fire the pistol. They are marked on the end cap "Buco DRGM." No more information is available as to quantity or year of manufacture.

| Exc. | V.G. | Good | Fair | Poor |
|------|------|------|------|------|
| 300 | 250 | 200 | 150 | 100 |

# BUDISCHOWSKY
## Mt. Clemens, Michigan

**TP-70**

This is a double-action, semi-automatic, pocket pistol with a 2.5" barrel and fixed sights. It is constructed of stainless steel and has plastic grips. It is chambered for the .22 rimfire and the .25 ACP cartridges and has a detachable 6-shot magazine. It was manufactured between 1973 and 1977.

**.22 Rimfire Caliber**

| NIB | Exc. | V.G. | Good | Fair | Poor |
|-----|------|------|------|------|------|
| 475 | 425 | 350 | 300 | 225 | 150 |

**.25 ACP Caliber**

| NIB | Exc. | V.G. | Good | Fair | Poor |
|-----|------|------|------|------|------|
| 400 | 325 | 250 | 200 | 175 | 125 |

Note:

After 1977 Norton Arms produced this pistol; values are approximately 40 percent less than those made by Budischowsky.

# BULLARD REPEATING ARMS CO.
## Springfield, Massachusetts

This rifle was designed by James H. Bullard in the 1880's. Bullard worked as one of Smith & Wesson's foremost machinists. The action he developed was unique in that it allowed a single round to be loaded while the magazine was full. The rifles were of fine design and construction, but the Company could not survive the competition of Marlin and Winchester and ceased operation after approximately 12,000 were produced between 1886 and 1890.

**Small Frame**

This rifle is chambered for the .32-40 and the .38-45 cartridges. It has a 26" octagonal barrel and either a half-or full-length magazine tube. The finish is either all blued or case-colored frame with the remainder blued. The stock is walnut, and the receiver is stamped "Bullard Repeating Arms Company/Springfield, Mass.U.S.A.Pat. Aug.16, 1881." The caliber is marked on top of the frame.

| Exc. | V.G. | Good | Fair | Poor |
|------|------|------|------|------|
| 1000 | 900 | 750 | 600 | 475 |

**Large Frame**

This model is chambered for the .40-75 through the .45-85 and on custom order in .50-95 and .50-115. The frame is larger to accommodate the more potent and larger cartridges. The octagonal barrel is 28" in length. All other features and markings are similar to the Small Frame.

| Exc. | V.G. | Good | Fair | Poor |
|------|------|------|------|------|
| 1200 | 1050 | 950 | 800 | 650 |

**Carbine**

This model is chambered for the .45-70 only with a 22" round barrel and a sliding dust cover on the receiver. Markings and finishes are similar to the small and large Frame rifles.

| Exc. | V.G. | Good | Fair | Poor |
|------|------|------|------|------|
| 3500 | 3250 | 2750 | 2000 | 1500 |

**Musket**

This model is chambered for the .45-70 cartridge only and has a 30" round barrel with a full-length stock secured by two barrel bands. There is a rod under the barrel, military sights, and the same sliding cover on the receiver as found on the Carbine. There have been examples noted without the manufacturer's markings.

| Exc. | V.G. | Good | Fair | Poor |
|------|------|------|------|------|
| 3500 | 3250 | 2750 | 2000 | 1500 |

## BULLDOG SINGLE SHOT PISTOL
### Connecticut Arms & Manufacturing Co.
### Naubuc, Connecticut

**Bulldog**
This pistol has a 4" or 6" barrel chambered for the .44 or .50 caliber rimfire cartridge. It has a case-colored iron frame with a pivoting breechblock that moves to the left for loading. The barrel is blued and stamped "Connecticut Arms & Manf. Co. Naubuc Conn. Patented Oct 25, 1864." There were only a few hundred manufactured, and the .50-caliber, 6"-barrelled versions would be worth an additional 40 percent. They were produced between 1866 and 1868.

| Exc. | V.G. | Good | Fair | Poor |
|------|------|------|------|------|
| 400 | 325 | 275 | 200 | 150 |

## BURGESS GUN CO.
### Buffalo, New York
### ALSO SEE--Colt and Whitney

Andrew Burgess, the noted firearms designer who was responsible for the Colt lever and slide-action guns that bore his name and the Whitney lever-action rifles, formed this Company in 1892 for the purpose of manufacturing this unique firearm. The action of this repeater was activated by sliding an iron sleeve located at the wrist of the stock to the rear. Most of the firearms produced by this Company were shotguns, with rifles rarely seen. Although the general quality of Burgess products was high, it was impossible for them to compete with the likes of Marlin and Winchester; and in 1899 they were purchased by Winchester, and the entire line was discontinued. Winchester never used the patent rights or produced another Burgess arm.

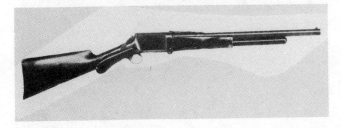

**12 Gauge Slide Action Shotgun**
This gun features the iron sleeve to activate the action that was discussed. It is chambered for 12 gauge only with 28" or 30" barrels with various chokes. There is a tubular magazine and a checkered walnut stock.

| Exc. | V.G. | Good | Fair | Poor |
|------|------|------|------|------|
| 500 | 425 | 350 | 250 | 175 |

**Folding Shotgun**
This 12 gauge has a 19.5" barrel and is hinged at the bottom, so that when the lever at the top of the receiver is released it would fold in half. This feature was advertised for concealment, and it was intended for sale to law enforcement agencies.

| Exc. | V.G. | Good | Fair | Poor |
|------|------|------|------|------|
| 850 | 725 | 600 | 400 | 300 |

**Slide Action Rifle**
This model is extremely scarce. It is chambered for the .30-30 and the .45-70 with a 26" round barrel and full-length magazine tube covered by the forend. The action is the same as that described for the Shotgun.

| Exc. | V.G. | Good | Fair | Poor |
|------|------|------|------|------|
| 2000 | 1800 | 1500 | 1250 | 900 |

## BURGSMULLER, K.
### Kreiensen, Germany

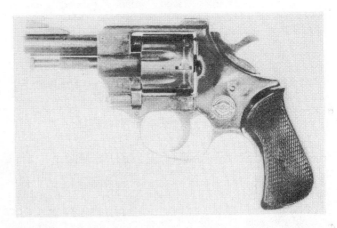

**Burgo**
The Burgo is simply the Rohm RG10 under another name. It is a poor-quality, inexpensive, .38-caliber revolver. The examples marketed by Burgsmuller are so marked.

| Exc. | V.G. | Good | Fair | Poor |
|------|------|------|------|------|
| 125 | 100 | 75 | 50 | 25 |

**Regent**
The Regent is a .22 caliber revolver that resembles the Colt Police Positive in appearance. It is of a higher quality than the Burgo. The manufacturer is not known.

| Exc. | V.G. | Good | Fair | Poor |
|------|------|------|------|------|
| 150 | 125 | 100 | 75 | 50 |

## BURNSIDE RIFLE CO.
### Providence, Rhode Island
### Bristol Firearms Co.
### Bristol, Rhode Island

This is a very historically desirable firearm for Civil War collectors as the designer, Ambrose E. Burnside was to become a well known Union general. The rifle, of which there were four distinct models, was used quite extensively in the Civil War. This carbine was manufactured first by the Bristol Firearms Co., which made the entire production of the first model and also some of the second model. In 1862 the Burnside Firearms Co. was formed, and they produced the remainder of the second models and all of the third and fourth models. Production ceased entirely in 1865.

**Burnside Carbine 1st Model**
This model was produced by Bristol and was chambered for the .54 caliber. It is a breechloader that uses the percussion ignition system but features a cartidge of sorts made of copper, and a tape priming device that was located inside the frame. It has a 22" round barrel with no forend and a walnut stock with inspector's cartouche. The finish is blued and case-colored, and the frame is stamped "Burnside's/Patent/March 25th/1856." There were approximately 250 1st Models manufactured.

| Exc. | V.G. | Good | Fair | Poor |
|------|------|------|------|------|
| 4000 | 3500 | 3000 | 2000 | 1200 |

**2nd Model**
The 2nd Model features an improved breech-block opening mechanism located inside the triggerguard. The barrel is 21" long, and the other features are similar to the 1st Model. They are marked either "Bristol Firearm Co." or "Burnside Rifle Co./Providence-R.I." The barrel is marked "Cast Steel 1861," and some of the breech-block devices are marked "G.P.Foster Pat./April 10th 1860." There were approximately 1,500 2nd Models manufactured in 1861 and 1862.

| Exc. | V.G. | Good | Fair | Poor |
|------|------|------|------|------|
| 2500 | 2000 | 1500 | 1000 | 650 |

**3rd Model**
This model differs from the 2nd Model in that it has a forend with a barrel band and a slightly modified hammer. The mark-

ings are the same as the Burnside-manufactured 2nd Models. There were approximately 2,000 produced in 1862.

| Exc. | V.G. | Good | Fair | Poor |
|------|------|------|------|------|
| 1250 | 1000 | 800 | 600 | 450 |

**4th Model**

This model differs from the others in that it features a hinged breech that permits simpler loading of the odd-shaped Burnside percussion cartridge. The frame is marked "Burnside's Patent/Model of 1864." The other features are similar to the 3rd Model. There were approximately 50,000 manufactured between 1862 and 1865.

| Exc. | V.G. | Good | Fair | Poor |
|------|------|------|------|------|
| 1200 | 950 | 750 | 550 | 400 |

# BUSHMASTER FIREARMS INC.
### North Windham, Maine

These firearms are currently involved in the assault weapon hysteria, and trends in our land make evaluating them accurately an impossibility. We list them for reference purposes but urge individual appraisal if purchase is contemplated as values can fluctuate wildly in different areas of the country.

**Bushmaster Pistol**

This is an 11.5"-barrelled semi-automatic pistol chambered for the .223 cartridge. Early models had alloy frames; later models, steel. The finish is parkerized, and the stock is wood. The magazine holds 30 shots and is the same as used on the M16-AR-15 rifle. This model has been manufactured since 1974.

**Bushmaster Rifle**

This model is similar in appearance to the pistol with an 18.5" barrel and either a wood stock or a folding metal one.

# BUTLER, WM. S.
### Rocky Hill, Connecticut

**Butler Single Shot Pistol**

This is a 2.5" round-barrelled pistol chambered for .36 caliber, utilizing the percussion ignition system. The frame and handle were cast in one piece, with no separate grip panels. The hammer was centrally located, and the frame was marked in the casting "Wm. S. Butler's Patent/Patented Feb.3,1857." There are no production figures available on this pistol.

| Exc. | V.G. | Good | Fair | Poor |
|------|------|------|------|------|
| 400 | 325 | 250 | 200 | 150 |

# BUTTERFIELD, JESSE
### Philadelphia, Pennsylvania

**Butterfield Army Revolver**

This is a large military pistol with a 7" octagonal barrel and an unfluted 5-shot cylinder. It is chambered for .41 caliber percussion and features a special priming device, a disk which was loaded in front of the triggerguard. The frame is of brass; the remainder is blued with walnut grips. The hammer is centered in the frame and there is a hinged ramrod under the barrel. The frame is stamped "Butterfield's Patent Dec.11,1855/Philada." There were approximately 650 manufactured in 1861 and 1862 before the initial order for 1,300 pistols was cancelled.

| Exc. | V.G. | Good | Fair | Poor |
|------|------|------|------|------|
| 2000 | 1800 | 1500 | 1250 | 900 |

**Butterfield Pocket Pistol**

This pistol has a 2" to 3.5" barrel and is chambered for the .41 caliber percussion. It was made in the classic Philadelphia derringer style and featured a patented priming device located in front of the triggerguard. The mountings are German silver; and the stock, walnut. There is a good deal of scroll engraving on the frame and mountings. The lock is marked "Butterfield's / Patent Dec 11,1855." These derringers are extremely rare and sought after. They were manufactured in the 1850's.

| Exc. | V.G. | Good | Fair | Poor |
|------|------|------|------|------|
| 5000 | 4650 | 4000 | 3000 | 2500 |

# CZ
### Pilsen, Czechoslovakia
### Ceska Zbrojovka
### ALSO SEE--Brno

This firm was founded in 1919 by Karel Bubla. Alois Tomiska, a noted gunsmith and firearms designer, became the plant manager. It was located in Pilsen. In 1921 the factory was moved to Strakonitz. Tomiska became a designer, and an engineer named Bartsch became the manager. They later merged with the Hubertus Engineering Company and began producing military pistols for the Czech army. In 1949 the company, under Communist control, became the Czech firearms state factory. Modern-production CZ pistols will be found in the Brno section.

**Fox**

This was the first CZ pistol manufactured. It is a blowback-operated semi-automatic chambered for the 6.35mm cartridge. It has a 2.5" barrel with a tubular slide and a folding trigger. There is no triggerguard. The finish is blued with plastic grips. This model was manufactured between 1919 and 1926.

| Exc. | V.G. | Good | Fair | Poor |
|------|------|------|------|------|
| 325 | 250 | 200 | 125 | 90 |

**CZ 1922**

This is an improved version of the Fox with a conventional trigger and guard. It is blued with checkered plastic grips and was manufactured between 1926 and 1936. A great number of these pistols were manufactured and exported.

| Exc. | V.G. | Good | Fair | Poor |
|------|------|------|------|------|
| 425 | 375 | 300 | 200 | 125 |

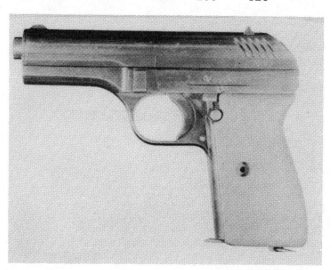

**CZ 1924**

This was the first military pistol produced by CZ. It is a locked-breech pistol with a rotating barrel chambered for the 9mm short cartridge. It has a 3.5" barrel with an external hammer and a magazine safety. It features a rounded slide and is blued with a wrap-around walnut grip. The slide is marked, "Ceska Zbrojovka A.S. v Praze." This was a very well-finished pistol.

| Exc. | V.G. | Good | Fair | Poor |
|------|------|------|------|------|
| 400 | 350 | 275 | 175 | 100 |

A limited number of pistols have been noted marked, "CZ 1925" and "CZ 1926." There are various minor design changes on each model, and it is conjectured that they were prototypes that were manufactured on the road to the production of the less-complicated, blowback-operated CZ 1927 pistol. There are too few to establish an average value; they should be individually appraised.

## CZ 1927

This is a blowback-operated, semi-automatic pistol chambered for the 7.65mm cartridge. It is marked the same as the CZ 1924, but the cocking grooves on the slide are cut vertically instead of sloped as on the earlier model. This model was blued with checkered, wrap-around, plastic grips. This version remained in production during the German occupation of Czechoslovakia between 1939 and 1945. Occupation pistols are marked, "Bohmische Waffenfabrik AG in Prag." After the War, these pistols continued in production until 1951. There were over 500,000 manufactured.

Nazi-Proofed--Add 50 Percent.

| Exc. | V.G. | Good | Fair | Poor |
|------|------|------|------|------|
| 250  | 225  | 175  | 100  | 75   |

## CZ 1936

This was a commercial pistol that was a blowback-operated semi-automatic chambered for the 6.35mm cartridge. It featured double-action-only lockwork but otherwise was loosely based on a Browning design. It has a 2.5" barrel and was designed by F. Myska. It was discontinued in 1940 because of wartime production.

| Exc. | V.G. | Good | Fair | Poor |
|------|------|------|------|------|
| 250  | 225  | 175  | 100  | 75   |

## CZ 1938

This very odd pistol has been rated as one of the worst military-service pistols ever manufactured. It is chambered for the 9mm short cartridge and has a 4.65" barrel. Except for a few examples with a conventional sear and exposed hammer, it is double-action only and very difficult to fire accurately. It utilizes an 8-round, detachable box magazine; and the slide is hinged at the muzzle to pivot upward for ease of cleaning and disassembly. It is well made and well finished but is as large in size as most 9mm Parabellum pistols. Production began in 1938, and the Germans adopted it as the "Pistole Mod 39" on paper; but it is doubtful that any were actually used by the German army.

| Exc. | V.G. | Good | Fair | Poor |
|------|------|------|------|------|
| 400  | 350  | 300  | 225  | 150  |

## CZ 1945

This was simply the CZ 1936 model revived after the close of WWII. This model has no safety catch.

| Exc. | V.G. | Good | Fair | Poor |
|------|------|------|------|------|
| 250  | 200  | 150  | 100  | 75   |

## CZ 1950

This is a blowback-operated, semi-automatic, double-action pistol chambered for the 7.65mm cartridge. It is patterned after the Walther Model PP with a few differences. The safety catch is located on the frame instead of the slide; and the triggerguard is not hinged, as on the Walther. It is dismantled by means of a catch on the side of the frame. Although intended to be a military pistol designed by the Kratochvil brothers, it proved to be under-powered and was adopted by the police. There were very few released on the commercial market.

| Exc. | V.G. | Good | Fair | Poor |
|------|------|------|------|------|
| 900  | 750  | 500  | 350  | 250  |

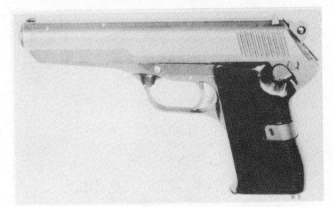

## CZ 1952

Since the Czechoslovakian army was not happy with the under-powered CZ 1950 pistol, they began using Soviet weapons until 1952, when this model was designed. It was designed for a new cartridge known as the 7.62mm M48. It was similar to the Soviet cartridge but loaded to a higher velocity. This is a double-action, semi-automatic pistol with a 4.5" barrel. It has a locked breech that utilizes two roller cams. This was an excellent pistol that has been replaced by the Soviet Makarov, a pistol that is decidedly inferior to it.

| Exc. | V.G. | Good | Fair | Poor |
|------|------|------|------|------|
| 1500 | 1250 | 1000 | 750  | 500  |

# CABANAS, INDUSTRIAS S.A.
### Aguilas, Mexico

This company manufactures rifles that shoot .177 pellets or BB's using .22 caliber blanks for propulsion. They produce seven different models, all capable of 1,150 fps velocities. They are single-shot bolt actions with open sights. The differences between the models are size, barrel length, and stock configuration. They are as follows:

**Mini-82 Youth**

| NIB | Exc. | V.G. | Good | Fair | Poor |
|-----|------|------|------|------|------|
| 75 | 65 | 50 | 40 | 30 | 20 |

**R-83 Larger Youth**

| NIB | Exc. | V.G. | Good | Fair | Poor |
|-----|------|------|------|------|------|
| 85 | 75 | 60 | 50 | 40 | 30 |

**Safari**

| NIB | Exc. | V.G. | Good | Fair | Poor |
|-----|------|------|------|------|------|
| 100 | 90 | 75 | 50 | 40 | 30 |

**Varmint**

| NIB | Exc. | V.G. | Good | Fair | Poor |
|-----|------|------|------|------|------|
| 125 | 110 | 90 | 75 | 50 | 35 |

**Espronceda IV**

| NIB | Exc. | V.G. | Good | Fair | Poor |
|-----|------|------|------|------|------|
| 125 | 110 | 90 | 75 | 50 | 35 |

**Leyre**

| NIB | Exc. | V.G. | Good | Fair | Poor |
|-----|------|------|------|------|------|
| 140 | 125 | 100 | 85 | 65 | 50 |

**Master**

| NIB | Exc. | V.G. | Good | Fair | Poor |
|-----|------|------|------|------|------|
| 150 | 130 | 110 | 100 | 75 | 60 |

# CABELAS, INC.
### Sidney, Nebraska

Cabelas is a mail-order dealer in quality sporting goods. Recently they have begun to offer high-grade shotguns that are manufactured by V. Berbardelli in Italy. They also offered a gun produced in Spain by AYA, but this model is now discontinued.

**AYA Grade II Custom**

This model is a side-by-side chambered for 12, 16, and 20 gauge. It features various barrel lengths and chokes, a single-selective trigger, and automatic ejectors. It is engraved with a hand-checkered walnut stock. This model is no longer available.

| Exc. | V.G. | Good | Fair | Poor |
|------|------|------|------|------|
| 1250 | 1175 | 950 | 700 | 575 |

**Hemingway Model**

This is a side-by-side chambered for 12 or 20 gauge with 28" barrels and various chokes. It features a single-selective trigger and automatic ejectors. It is lightly engraved and has a select, hand-checkered walnut stock. It is manufactured in Italy by V. Bernardelli.

| NIB | Exc. | V.G. | Good | Fair | Poor |
|-----|------|------|------|------|------|
| 975 | 900 | 750 | 600 | 525 | 450 |

# CALICO
### SEE--American Industries, Inc.
### Cleveland, Ohio

# CAMEX-BLASER USA, INC.
### SEE--Blaser Jagwaffen
### Ft. Worth, Texas

# CAMPO GIRO
### Eibar, Spain

**Esperanza y Unceta**
**Model 1904**

Lt. Col. Venancio Aguirre designed this rather interesting pistol. It was released in strictly prototype form as a locked-breech, magazine-fed weapon chambered for the 9mm Campo Giro cartridge. It features an external hammer and is very rare.

| Exc. | V.G. | Good | Fair | Poor |
|------|------|------|------|------|
| 1250 | 1000 | 800 | 600 | 450 |

**Model 1910**

One thousand Model 1910's were manufactured and tested by the Spanish army. The grip angle was slightly altered, and the caliber was changed to 9mm Largo.

| Exc. | V.G. | Good | Fair | Poor |
|------|------|------|------|------|
| 1000 | 800 | 650 | 500 | 450 |

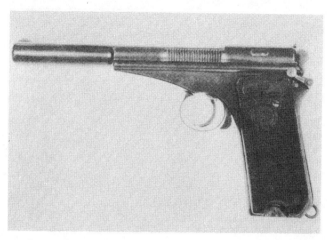

**Model 1913**

This model encompassed the most major modifications to date. The action was changed from a locked breech to a blowback design. An extremely strong recoil spring and shock-absorber system were utilized to handle the pounding recoil of this powerful cartridge. In 1914 this Model was accepted for duty as the Spanish service pistol. There were 1,000 made.

| Exc. | V.G. | Good | Fair | Poor |
|------|------|------|------|------|
| 900 | 750 | 650 | 500 | 450 |

**Model 1913/16**

This model featured an improved magazine release. There were 13,000 manufactured before production ceased.

| Exc. | V.G. | Good | Fair | Poor |
|------|------|------|------|------|
| 500 | 450 | 375 | 300 | 200 |

# CARCANO
### Turin, Italy

The Italian service rifle known as the Carcano was developed at the state arsenal in Turin in 1890. It was adopted in March of 1892. This rifle was more correctly identified as the "Fucile Modello 91." The name Carcano comes from Salvator Carcano, who was a technician at the arsenal and was instrumental in the rifle's development. This design was retained and improved upon for many years and was still in use as the Modello 38 in WWII.

**Fucile Modello 91**

This was the original model. It is chambered for the 6.5mm cartridge and has a 31" barrel and a 6-round integral box magazine. It features a full-length stock, split bridge receiver, and a tangent rear sight. There is a wooden handguard with barrel bands retaining the stock.

| Exc. | V.G. | Good | Fair | Poor |
|------|------|------|------|------|
| 100 | 80 | 65 | 40 | 20 |

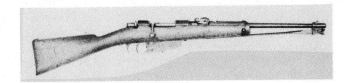

## Cavalry Carbine

This is simply a shorter-barrelled, half-stocked version with a folding bayonet.

| Exc. | V.G. | Good | Fair | Poor |
|------|------|------|------|------|
| 100 | 80 | 65 | 40 | 20 |

## Fucile Modello 38

This was the 1938 version that was chambered for the 7.35mm cartridge. Experience had taught the Italians that their 6.5mm round was not effective, so this rifle/cartridge combination was their answer. The only other difference between this model and the 1891 model was the 300-meter rear sight.

| Exc. | V.G. | Good | Fair | Poor |
|------|------|------|------|------|
| 100 | 80 | 65 | 40 | 20 |

## Cavalry Carbine

This was a shortened version with a folding bayonet and a fixed rear sight.

| Exc. | V.G. | Good | Fair | Poor |
|------|------|------|------|------|
| 125 | 100 | 80 | 60 | 40 |

# CARD, S. W.
### Unknown

## Underhammer Pistol

This pistol has a 7.75" part-round/part-octagonal barrel chambered for .34 caliber percussion. The frame is iron with rounded handle and walnut grips. The barrel is stamped "S.W.Card" and also "Cast Steel." Little is known about this pistol regarding origin and number produced.

| Exc. | V.G. | Good | Fair | Poor |
|------|------|------|------|------|
| 400 | 325 | 275 | 200 | 125 |

# CARLTON, M.
### Haverhill, New Hampshire

## Underhammer Pistol

This unique underhammer pistol has a patented hammer design that cocks in the opposite direction of the usual underhammer. The hammer is pulled toward the trigger in a vertical fashion using the triggerguard as a mainspring. The barrel length is 3.5" to 7.75" and is chambered for .34 caliber percussion. The frame is iron; and the grips, round with walnut panels. The barrel is stamped "M.Carleton & Co."

| Exc. | V.G. | Good | Fair | Poor |
|------|------|------|------|------|
| 500 | 425 | 350 | 250 | 175 |

# CASARTELLI, CARLO
### Brescia, Italy
### Importer--New England Arms Co.
### Kittery Point, Maine

These are high-grade firearms that are available on a special custom-order basis. Details would be available from the importer.

## Sidelock Shotgun

This model is a side-by-side, full side-lock gun that is available virtually to the customer's order in any gauge, barrel length, and choke. Automatic ejectors and single-selective trigger and choice of engraving style is available. There are very few of these made.

| NIB | Exc. | V.G. | Good | Fair | Poor |
|-----|------|------|------|------|------|
| 15000 | 13500 | 10000 | 8250 | 6000 | 4000 |

## Kenya Double Rifle

This is a made-to-order, full side-lock rifle that is available in all standard and magnum calibers. The customer may literally design this firearm if one desires and if one can afford it.

| NIB | Exc. | V.G. | Good | Fair | Poor |
|-----|------|------|------|------|------|
| 30000 | 27000 | 22500 | 18000 | 13000 | 9000 |

## Africa Model

This is a bolt-action rifle built on a square-bridge magnum Mauser action. It is chambered for the heavy magnum calibers and can be taken down for transport. The other features are on a custom-order basis.

| NIB | Exc. | V.G. | Good | Fair | Poor |
|-----|------|------|------|------|------|
| 8750 | 8000 | 7000 | 5750 | 4750 | 3750 |

## Safari Model

This Model is built on a standard Mauser bolt action and is chambered for the non-magnum calibers.

| NIB | Exc. | V.G. | Good | Fair | Poor |
|-----|------|------|------|------|------|
| 7000 | 6500 | 5500 | 4500 | 3250 | 2500 |

# CASE WILLARD & CO.
### New Hartford, Connecticut

## Underhammer Pistol

This pistol is chambered for .31 caliber, utilizes the percussion ignition system, and has a 3", part-round/part- octagonal barrel. The frame was brass, the barrel browned, and the one-piece grip was of maple. The markings are "Case Willard & Co./New Hartford Conn." The number produced is unknown.

| Exc. | V.G. | Good | Fair | Poor |
|------|------|------|------|------|
| 450 | 375 | 300 | 225 | 150 |

# CASPIAN ARMS, LTD.
### Hardwick, Vermont

## Government Model

This is a high quality version of the Colt 1911. It is produced in carbon steel or stainless steel and is chambered for .45 ACP with interchangeable slides for 9mm and .38 super available. This model features high profile sights, an adjustable trigger, and walnut grips. It has been manufactured since 1986.

| NIB | Exc. | V.G. | Good | Fair | Poor |
|-----|------|------|------|------|------|
| 550 | 475 | 425 | 375 | 300 | 225 |

## Model 110

This is a stainless-steel, fully customized version of the Colt 1911. It features a match-grade, stainless-steel barrel chambered for .45 ACP or .38 Super and has all the custom features one could cram on the Government Model. It has been manufactured since 1988.

| NIB | Exc. | V.G. | Good | Fair | Poor |
|-----|------|------|------|------|------|
| 900 | 825 | 700 | 600 | 475 | 400 |

## Vietnam Commemorative

This is basically a government model engraved by J.J. Adams and nickel-plated. The walnut grips have a branch service medallion inlaid, and gold plating was available for an additional $350. There were 1,000 manufactured in 1986.

| NIB | Exc. | V.G. | Good | Fair | Poor |
|-----|------|------|------|------|------|
| 1200 | 1000 | 800 | 600 | 475 | 400 |

# CENTURY GUN CO.
### Greenfield, Indiana

This was formerly a handmade revolver produced in Evansville, Indiana, and chambered for the .45-70 cartridge. This model was discontinued after only 524 were manufactured. They are now back in production as of 1986. The original guns are valued separately from the new production version.

## Model 100 Revolver

This is a very large revolver chambered for the .30-30, .375 Winchester, .444 Marlin, .45-70, and the .50-70 cartridges. It has a 6-shot steel cylinder and a manganese bronze alloyed frame. The barrel is available in lengths from 6.5" to 15". There is a crossbolt safety, adjustable sights, and walnut grips. This is a limited-production item, with only 600 produced since 1976. The .45-70 is considered the standard caliber, and all other calibers are custom-order only.

## .45-70 Caliber

| NIB | Exc. | V.G. | Good | Fair | Poor |
|-----|------|------|------|------|------|
| 750 | 700 | 600 | 500 | 400 | 325 |

**All Other Calibers**

| NIB | Exc. | V.G. | Good | Fair | Poor |
|---|---|---|---|---|---|
| 1600 | 1400 | 1200 | 1000 | 800 | 600 |

**Original Evansville Model 100**

| NIB | Exc. | V.G. | Good | Fair | Poor |
|---|---|---|---|---|---|
| 2500 | 2250 | 2000 | 1600 | 1250 | 950 |

## CENTURY INT. ARMS CO.
### St. Albans, Vermont

Century is one of the foremost importers of military surplus weapons of both foreign and U.S. manufacture. They offer firearms in various degrees of condition, and most of the weapons they sell are excellent values if one is seeking a shooter. It is important to note that Federal law demands that the importer stamp his name on the weapon and that this stamp destroys the collectibility of these firearms. The firearms imported are listed in their own sections; and before one purchases, it would be advisable to check the current market value in your area.

## CETME
### Madrid, Spain

**Cetme Autoloading Rifle**

This rifle was a direct descendant of the German WWII StG45 made by Mauser. After the end of the War, the German engineers migrated to Spain and built the Cetme. Eventually they returned to their homeland, and this design evolved into the H. & K. Model 91. This rifle has a 17.75" barrel and is a delayed, blowback-operated action with protruding roller cams that provide the delay. The rifle is chambered for the .308 cartridge, and the chamber is fluted to prevent the cartridge sticking to its walls during extraction. The finish is black with a military-style wood stock and an aperture rear sight. There is a 20-round detachable magazine. This is another of the assault-type rifles that we cannot accurately evaluate due to the unstable market. We urge that one secure individual appraisal when contemplating purchase or sale.

## CHAMELOT-DELVIGNE
### Liege, Belgium

**Pirlot Brothers**

The designation Chamelot-Delvigne is actually a catch-all name given to a number of heavy-caliber service revolvers made and used by several different countries. The common denominator among these revolvers is that they all utilize a locking system invented and patented by the Brothers Pirlot circa 1870. The revolvers commonly referred to as Chamelot-Delvigne are as follows:

**Model 1871 Belgian Troopers Revolver**

A large, solid-frame weapon chambered for the 11mm centerfire cartridge.

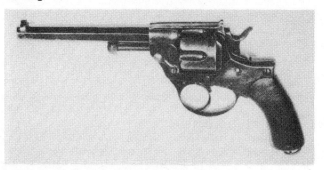

| Exc. | V.G. | Good | Fair | Poor |
|---|---|---|---|---|
| 400 | 325 | 250 | 175 | 125 |

**Model 1872 Swiss**

This model, also known as the "Schmidt," had some modifications in the lockwork. It was chambered for the 12mm rimfire, 9mm rimfire, and the 10.4mm rimfire for the Swiss. The Italian army used it chambered for the 10.4 centerfire cartridge.

| Exc. | V.G. | Good | Fair | Poor |
|---|---|---|---|---|
| 800 | 625 | 550 | 400 | 300 |

**Model 1873**

The Netherlands used the model 1873, chambered for the 9.4mm centerfire, as an officer's revolver. The French had it chambered in 11mm centerfire for the enlisted troopers.

| Exc. | V.G. | Good | Fair | Poor |
|---|---|---|---|---|
| 275 | 250 | 200 | 150 | 100 |

**Model 1874**

The model 1874 was used by French officers and was chambered for 11mm centerfire.

| Exc. | V.G. | Good | Fair | Poor |
|---|---|---|---|---|
| 300 | 275 | 225 | 175 | 125 |

**Model 1872/78 Swiss**

This model designation signifies a recall of the Swiss Schmidt version. The 10.4mm centerfire caliber was standardized, and all Model 1872 revolvers still in service were converted and re-marked.

| Exc. | V.G. | Good | Fair | Poor |
|---|---|---|---|---|
| 475 | 425 | 350 | 275 | 225 |

**Model 1879 Italian**

The Italian army used the model 1879 chambered for the 10.4mm centerfire as its officers' revolver.

| Exc. | V.G. | Good | Fair | Poor |
|---|---|---|---|---|
| 225 | 175 | 150 | 110 | 80 |

## CHAMPLIN FIREARMS
### Enid, Oklahoma

This was a maker of very high-grade bolt-action rifles. They were produced for the discriminating buyer with many custom order features. Production began in 1966 and has since been discontinued.

**Bolt Action Rifle**

This rifle was made in all calibers with either a round or octagon barrel of various lengths. It features an adjustable trigger, rib with express sights, and a deluxe-grade, hand-checkered walnut stock.

| NIB | Exc. | V.G. | Good | Fair | Poor |
|---|---|---|---|---|---|
| 5500 | 4500 | 3500 | 2900 | 2200 | 1500 |

## CHAPMAN, C.
### Unknown

**Chapman Rifle**

This very rare Confederate weapon was patterned after the U.S. Model 1841. It is chambered for .58 caliber and utilizes the percussion ignition system. The round barrel is 33" long, with a full-length stock and two barrel bands. The mountings are brass, and the stock is walnut. "C.Chapman" was stamped on the lock. This weapon was manufactured somewhere in the Confederate States of America during the Civil War, but little else is known.

| Exc. | V.G. | Good | Fair | Poor |
|---|---|---|---|---|
| 6000 | 5000 | 4000 | 2500 | 1750 |

## CHAPMAN, G. & J.
### Philadelphia, Pennsylvania

**Chapman Pocket Revolver**

This rare specimen is chambered for the .32-caliber rimfire cartridge. It has a 7-shot unfluted cylinder and a 4" round barrel. The frame is made of brass, and the barrel and cylinder were blued. The butt is flared with walnut grips, and the pistol is marked "G.& J. Chapman/Philada/ Patent Applied For/1861."

The number manufactured is unknown, and they were produced in the early 1860's.

| Exc. | V.G. | Good | Fair | Poor |
|------|------|------|------|------|
| 600 | 525 | 450 | 325 | 250 |

# CHAPUIS
### France
### Importer--Armes De Chasse
### Chadds Ford, Pennsylvania

This is a manufacturer of high-grade, custom-order shotguns and double rifles. They are rarely seen in the used gun market.

## RG Progress

A high-grade double-barrelled shotgun available chambered for 12, 16, or 20 gauge. Most options are available on order.

Chapuis Progress RG

| NIB | Exc. | V.G. | Good | Fair | Poor |
|-----|------|------|------|------|------|
| 2500 | 2250 | 2000 | 1800 | 1250 | 900 |

## RG Express Model 89

This is a full sidelock, double-barrelled rifle chambered for the 7 X 65R, 8 X 57 JRS, 9.3 X 74R, and .375 H&H. The other features are at the customer's order.

| NIB | Exc. | V.G. | Good | Fair | Poor |
|-----|------|------|------|------|------|
| 6500 | 5750 | 4800 | 4000 | 3250 | 2500 |

# CHARTER ARMS, CORP.
### Stratford, Connecticut

In 1964 Douglas McClenahan started the Charter Arms, Corp. He was an engineer who had worked with Colt, Ruger, and High Standard. He felt that there was a market for a short-barrelled pocket revolver and founded the company to produce it. His gamble paid off, as Charter Arms has survived to become one of the more stable of the American gun companies.

## Undercover

This was the first offering from Charter Arms. It is a 5-shot, swingout-cylinder revolver that was initially chambered for .38 Special. Later the .22 rimfire, .22 rimfire magnum, and the .32 S&W long was offered with 6- shot cylinders. The barrel length is 2" or 3". The frame is steel with an alloy butt and trigger guard. The firing pin is made of unbreakable beryllium. This model has very serviceable fixed sights and a blued finish with walnut grips.

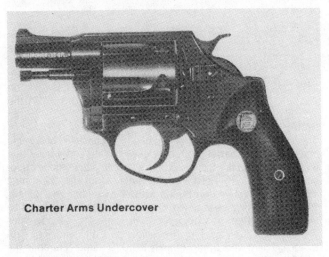

**Charter Arms Undercover**

| NIB | Exc. | V.G. | Good | Fair | Poor |
|-----|------|------|------|------|------|
| 220 | 195 | 175 | 150 | 100 | 75 |

## Undercover Stainless Steel

This model is similar to the undercover except that it is constructed of stainless steel.

| NIB | Exc. | V.G. | Good | Fair | Poor |
|-----|------|------|------|------|------|
| 275 | 250 | 225 | 175 | 125 | 100 |

## Undercoverette

This is a slimmer gripped version of the undercover chambered for .32 S&W long. It was designed with female shooters in mind.

| Exc. | V.G. | Good | Fair | Poor |
|------|------|------|------|------|
| 175 | 150 | 125 | 100 | 75 |

## Pathfinder

This revolver is similar to the undercover except that it is chambered for .22 l.r. or .22 W.M.R. It holds 6 shots and is offered with a 2", 3", or 6" barrel. It has adjustable sights and is intended to be used as a plinker and utility-type gun. There is a square-butt version available.

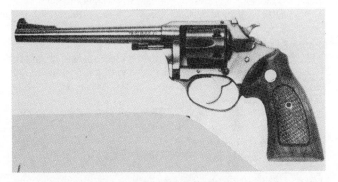

| NIB | Exc. | V.G. | Good | Fair | Poor |
|-----|------|------|------|------|------|
| 225 | 200 | 175 | 150 | 100 | 75 |

## Pathfinder Stainless Steel

This is similar to the standard model except that it is constructed of stainless steel.

| NIB | Exc. | V.G. | Good | Fair | Poor |
|-----|------|------|------|------|------|
| 290 | 275 | 200 | 175 | 125 | 100 |

## Bulldog

This model is a slightly larger version of the undercover, that has a 5-shot cylinder and is chambered for the .44 Special cartridge. It has a 2.5" or 3" barrel and oversized grips.

| NIB | Exc. | V.G. | Good | Fair | Poor |
|-----|------|------|------|------|------|
| 235 | 200 | 175 | 150 | 125 | 100 |

## Stainless Steel Bulldog

This model is the same as the standard Bulldog except that it is constructed of stainless steel.

| NIB | Exc. | V.G. | Good | Fair | Poor |
|-----|------|------|------|------|------|
| 285 | 250 | 225 | 175 | 150 | 110 |

## Target Bulldog

**Charter Arms Target Bulldog**

This model is chambered for .357 Magnum or .44 Special and holds 5 shots. The shrouded barrel is 4" in length, and there is an adjustable rear sight and a square butt. This model was available in blue only. It was manufactured between 1986 and 1988.

| NIB | Exc. | V.G. | Good | Fair | Poor |
|-----|------|------|------|------|------|
| 200 | 185  | 160  | 145  | 110  | 80   |

## Bulldog Pug

This is a 2.5" shrouded-barrel version of the .44 special Bulldog.

| NIB | Exc. | V.G. | Good | Fair | Poor |
|-----|------|------|------|------|------|
| 250 | 210  | 175  | 150  | 120  | 100  |

## Stainless Steel Bulldog Pug

This is the Pug constructed of stainless steel.

| NIB | Exc. | V.G. | Good | Fair | Poor |
|-----|------|------|------|------|------|
| 300 | 250  | 225  | 175  | 150  | 125  |

## Bulldog Tracker

This is a target version with adjustable sights and offered with a 2.5", 4", or 6" barrel. There is a square butt on the longer-barrelled models. It is chambered for .357 Magnum only.

| NIB | Exc. | V.G. | Good | Fair | Poor |
|-----|------|------|------|------|------|
| 250 | 225  | 200  | 165  | 140  | 110  |

## Police Bulldog

This is a fixed-sight version chambered for .32 H&R Magnum, .38 Special, or .44 Special. It is offered with a 3.5" or 4" barrel and holds 6 shots in all calibers except .44 Special, which holds 5 and has a square butt.

| NIB | Exc. | V.G. | Good | Fair | Poor |
|-----|------|------|------|------|------|
| 235 | 200  | 175  | 150  | 125  | 100  |

## Stainless Steel Police Bulldog

This model is similar to the standard model except that it is constructed of stainless steel and the .357 Magnum is also offered. A heavier bull barrel is optional.

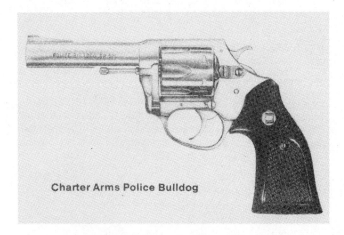

Charter Arms Police Bulldog

| NIB | Exc. | V.G. | Good | Fair | Poor |
|-----|------|------|------|------|------|
| 285 | 250  | 210  | 175  | 145  | 110  |

## Off Duty

This model is a 5-shot .38 Special that has a 2" barrel, fixed sights, and a matte black finish.

| NIB | Exc. | V.G. | Good | Fair | Poor |
|-----|------|------|------|------|------|
| 185 | 165  | 140  | 110  | 95   | 75   |

## Pit Bull

This model is chambered for the 9mm Federal, .38 Special, or .357 Magnum. It is offered with a 2.5", 3.5", or 4" shrouded barrel and rubber grips. It was introduced in 1989.

| NIB | Exc. | V.G. | Good | Fair | Poor |
|-----|------|------|------|------|------|
| 285 | 250  | 200  | 175  | 125  | 90   |

## Explorer II Pistol

This is a semi-automatic, survival-styled pistol chambered for the .22 rimfire cartridge. The barrel is removable and offered in 6", 8", or 10" lengths. The finish is either gold, silver, black, or camo; and the grips are wood-grained plastic. This model was discontinued in 1986.

| NIB | Exc. | V.G. | Good | Fair | Poor |
|-----|------|------|------|------|------|
| 110 | 95   | 75   | 65   | 45   | 25   |

## Model 40

This is a double-action, semi-automatic pistol chambered for the .22 rimfire cartridge. It is stainless steel and has a 3.5" barrel, fixed sights, and an 8-shot detachable magazine. It was manufactured between 1984 and 1986.

| Exc. | V.G. | Good | Fair | Poor |
|------|------|------|------|------|
| 250  | 225  | 200  | 150  | 100  |

## Model 79K

This is a double-action semi-automatic chambered for .32 or .380 ACP. It is stainless steel with a 3.5" barrel, fixed sights, and a 7-shot detachable magazine. It was manufactured between 1986 and 1988.

| Exc. | V.G. | Good | Fair | Poor |
|------|------|------|------|------|
| 325  | 300  | 250  | 180  | 125  |

## Model 42T

This Model is a single-action, semi-automatic target pistol chambered for the .22 l.r. cartridge. It has a 6" barrel and adjustable sights. It is blued with checkered walnut grips. This Model was manufactured in 1984 and 1985.

| NIB | Exc. | V.G. | Good | Fair | Poor |
|-----|------|------|------|------|------|
| 500 | 450  | 400  | 325  | 275  | 200  |

## AR - 7 Explorer Rifle

This is a semi-automatic takedown rifle chambered for the .22 l.r. cartridge. It has a 16" barrel, 8-shot detachable magazine, and a large, hollow cycolac stock which houses the barrelled action for storage. This stock is said to be waterproof, and the rifle is supposed to float. It is available in black, silver, and camo finish.

| NIB | Exc. | V.G. | Good | Fair | Poor |
|-----|------|------|------|------|------|
| 150 | 125  | 100  | 80   | 60   | 40   |

# CHASSEPOT
### French Military

**MLE 1866**

This was a French service rifle chambered for the 11mm paper cartridge. It has a 32" barrel with a full-length walnut stock held on by two barrel bands. There is a cleaning rod mounted under the barrel and a bayonet lug that allows the attaching of a brass-handled, saber-type bayonet. This rifle was a refinement of the German Dreyse needle gun. It features a rubber gas seal and is in a smaller caliber and has nearly twice the range of the Dreyse. The finish is white with a walnut stock.

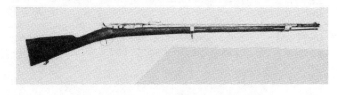

| Exc. | V.G. | Good | Fair | Poor |
|------|------|------|------|------|
| 275  | 225  | 175  | 125  | 100  |

# CHICAGO F. A. CO.
### Chicago, Illinois

**Protector Palm Pistol**

This unique design was French in origin. It consisted of a round chamber with a barrel protruding out one side and a lever that was squeezed to fire the weapon in a double-action mode opposite the barrel. This pistol was chambered for the .32 rimfire cartridge and was nickel plated with black rubber grip panels. Blue models have been noted; but they were rare and would be worth a premium, as would pearl grip panels. The sideplates were marked "Chicago Firearms Co.,Chicago,Ill." and "The Protector." There were approximately 20,000 manufactured in the 1890's. They are all considered antiques and not subject to the Gun Control Act of 1968.

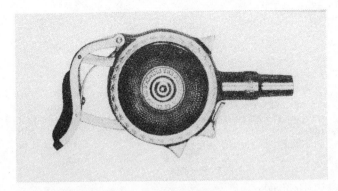

**Standard Model Nickle Plated/Black Grips**

| Exc. | V.G. | Good | Fair | Poor |
|---|---|---|---|---|
| 800 | 600 | 450 | 350 | 250 |

Blued Finish--Add 30 Percent.
Pearl Grips --Add 15 Percent.

# CHIPMUNK, INC.
## Medford, Oregon

### Chipmunk Single Shot Rifle
This is a very small, youth-model, bolt-action rifle. It is chambered for either the .22 l.r. or the .22 rimfire magnum cartridge. It must be manually cocked to fire and has a 16.25" barrel. It has open sights and is only 30" overall, weighing 2.5 lbs.

| NIB | Exc. | V.G. | Good | Fair | Poor |
|---|---|---|---|---|---|
| 130 | 110 | 100 | 80 | 60 | 40 |

### Deluxe Chipmunk
This is the same rifle with a hand-checkered walnut stock.

| NIB | Exc. | V.G. | Good | Fair | Poor |
|---|---|---|---|---|---|
| 180 | 160 | 135 | 100 | 80 | 50 |

### Silhouette Pistol
This is a 14.5"-barrelled, bolt-action, single-shot pistol with open sights and rear pistolgrip walnut stock.

| NIB | Exc. | V.G. | Good | Fair | Poor |
|---|---|---|---|---|---|
| 150 | 125 | 100 | 80 | 60 | 40 |

# CHURCHILL
## Importer--Ellet Bros.
## Chapin, South Carolina

### Windsor I
This is a side-by-side shotgun chambered for 10, 12, 16, 20, 28 gauge, and .410. It is offered with barrel lengths from 23" through 32" and various choke combinations. It features a scroll-engraved, silver-finished, Anson & Deeley boxlock action, double triggers and extractors. The stock is walnut with a checkered pistol grip and forend.

Churchill Windsor S/S

| NIB | Exc. | V.G. | Good | Fair | Poor |
|---|---|---|---|---|---|
| 650 | 600 | 500 | 400 | 300 | 200 |

### Windsor II
This model is similar to the Windsor I except that it is chambered for 10, 12, and 20 gauge only and features automatic ejectors. It was not imported after 1987.

| Exc. | V.G. | Good | Fair | Poor |
|---|---|---|---|---|
| 600 | 550 | 450 | 350 | 250 |

### Windsor VI
This is the deluxe sidelock version in the Windsor series. It is chambered for 12 and 20 gauge only and features automatic ejectors. It was not imported after 1987.

| Exc. | V.G. | Good | Fair | Poor |
|---|---|---|---|---|
| 800 | 750 | 650 | 500 | 350 |

### Royal
This side-by-side is chambered for 12, 20, 28 gauge, and .410. It is offered with various barrel lengths and chokes and has double triggers and extractors and a case-colored receiver. The pistol grip stock is of checkered walnut. This model was introduced in 1988.

| NIB | Exc. | V.G. | Good | Fair | Poor |
|---|---|---|---|---|---|
| 550 | 500 | 425 | 350 | 275 | 200 |

## Over/Unders
### Monarch
This is an Over/Under chambered for 12, 20, 28 gauge, or .410. It has a boxlock action and is offered with 25", 26", or 28" vent-rib barrels. It features either double or a single-selective trigger, extractors, and a checkered walnut stock.

Churchill Monarch

| NIB | Exc. | V.G. | Good | Fair | Poor |
|---|---|---|---|---|---|
| 530 | 475 | 425 | 375 | 300 | 225 |

### Windsor III
This model is a scroll-engraved, silver-finished boxlock chambered for 12 and 20 gauge and .410. It is offered with 27" or 30" vent-rib barrels, extractors, a single-selective trigger, and a checkered walnut stock.

| NIB | Exc. | V.G. | Good | Fair | Poor |
|---|---|---|---|---|---|
| 625 | 575 | 525 | 475 | 400 | 325 |

### Windsor IV
This Over/Under is a more deluxe-finished version of the Windsor III with screw-in choke tubes standard. It was introduced in 1989.

| NIB | Exc. | V.G. | Good | Fair | Poor |
|---|---|---|---|---|---|
| 850 | 775 | 650 | 500 | 425 | 325 |

### Regent
This Over/Under is chambered for 12 and 20 guage with 27" vent-rib barrels and screw-in choke tubes. The action is a boxlock with scroll-engraved false sideplates and a coin finish. This model features automatic ejectors, a single-selective trigger, and a checkered walnut stock. It was not imported after 1986.

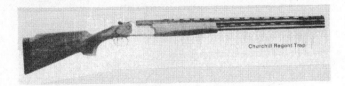

Churchill Regent Trap

| Exc. | V.G. | Good | Fair | Poor |
|---|---|---|---|---|
| 750 | 650 | 550 | 450 | 350 |

### Regent II
This is a more deluxe version of the Regent with finer overall finishing.

| NIB | Exc. | V.G. | Good | Fair | Poor |
|---|---|---|---|---|---|
| 1100 | 1000 | 850 | 750 | 500 | 375 |

### Regent Shotgun Rifle Combination
This is an Over/Under with a 25" vent rib and 12-gauge barrel over a rifle barrel chambered for .222, .223, .243, .270, .308, or .30-06. The action is a silver-finished, scroll-engraved boxlock with automatic ejectors and a single-selective trigger. The stock is of checkered walnut.

| NIB | Exc. | V.G. | Good | Fair | Poor |
|---|---|---|---|---|---|
| 925 | 825 | 725 | 600 | 450 | 400 |

### Windsor Grade Semi-Automatic
This is a gas-operated, semi-automatic shotgun chambered for 12 gauge only. It features 26", 28", or 30" vent-rib barrels with

screw-in choke tubes. It has an etched and anodized alloy receiver and a checkered walnut stock.

| NIB | Exc. | V.G. | Good | Fair | Poor |
|-----|------|------|------|------|------|
| 425 | 375 | 325 | 275 | 225 | 175 |

### Windsor Grade Slide Action

This is a slide-action shotgun chambered for 12 gauge with a 26" through 30" vent-rib barrel . It features various chokes, double slide rails, and an anodized alloy receiver. The stock is checkered walnut. This model was discontinued in 1986.

| Exc. | V.G. | Good | Fair | Poor |
|------|------|------|------|------|
| 400 | 375 | 300 | 250 | 175 |

### Rifles
### Highlander

This is a bolt-action rifle chambered for .25-06 through .300 Winchester Magnum. It has a 22" barrel with or without sights, a 3-shot magazine, and a checkered walnut stock.

| NIB | Exc. | V.G. | Good | Fair | Poor |
|-----|------|------|------|------|------|
| 460 | 420 | 375 | 300 | 250 | 200 |

### Regent

This is a similar rifle to the Highlander with a fancier grade walnut stock with Monte Carlo-style comb and cheekpiece. It was discontinued in 1988.

| Exc. | V.G. | Good | Fair | Poor |
|------|------|------|------|------|
| 550 | 500 | 425 | 350 | 275 |

# CHURCHILL, E. J. LTD.
## London, England

Churchill guns are known as some of the highest quality firearms in the world. They were made in London and imported into the U.S.A. until 1981, when the plant was relocated to Surrey, England, where limited production continues--although they are no longer imported into the U.S.A. If one contemplates sale or purchase of a high-grade gun of this nature, individual appraisal should be secured. We give the basic values for purposes of reference but feel that the options and variables involved in this type of firearm precludes any accurate pricing.

### One of One Thousand Rifle

This is a custom-built, bolt-action rifle based on a commercial Mauser-type action. It is chambered for the popular medium to big game cartridges from .270 to .458 Magnum. It has a 24" barrel and a select French walnut stock with a trap pistolgrip cap and recoil pad. There were only 100 produced for the 20th anniversary of Interarms in 1973.

| Exc. | V.G. | Good | Fair | Poor |
|------|------|------|------|------|
| 1500 | 1250 | 1000 | 700 | 550 |

### Premier Over/Under Shotgun

This gun was available chambered for 12, 16, and 20 gauge, with barrel lengths from 25" through 32" and any choke combinations desired. It is a fully engraved side-lock with automatic ejectors and a single-selective trigger. The stock is of the highest grade walnut available, either straight or in the pistolgrip configuration.

| Exc. | V.G. | Good | Fair | Poor |
|------|------|------|------|------|
| 17500 | 15000 | 12500 | 8000 | 5000 |

### Premier Side By Side

This is a similar model to the Over/Under Premier--only in the side-by-side configuration. It was available in all gauges and as a double rifle in most popular calibers at a higher cost.
Double Rifle--Add 40 Percent.

| Exc. | V.G. | Good | Fair | Poor |
|------|------|------|------|------|
| 17500 | 15000 | 12500 | 8000 | 5000 |

### Imperial

This is the second quality side by side made by this company; and it is a made-to-order gun available in all gauges, barrel lengths, and chokes. It was also made as a double rifle in most calibers at extra cost.
Double Rifle--Add 40 Percent.

| Exc. | V.G. | Good | Fair | Poor |
|------|------|------|------|------|
| 13000 | 11000 | 9000 | 6500 | 4000 |

### Field Model

This is the third quality sidelock, side-by-side shotgun available in 12 gauge only, with all other features available on order.

| Exc. | V.G. | Good | Fair | Poor |
|------|------|------|------|------|
| 9000 | 8000 | 6000 | 4500 | 3000 |

### Hercules

This was the best quality boxlock side by side. It was available in any gauge and barrel length. All other options were available on request. There were some produced as small-caliber double rifles.
Double Rifle--Add 40 Percent.

| Exc. | V.G. | Good | Fair | Poor |
|------|------|------|------|------|
| 9000 | 8000 | 6000 | 4500 | 3000 |

### Utility Model

This is the 2nd quality boxlock--available with custom features similar to the Hercules.

| Exc. | V.G. | Good | Fair | Poor |
|------|------|------|------|------|
| 6000 | 5000 | 3500 | 2500 | 2000 |

### Crown

This is the third quality boxlock and was available with many custom features.

| Exc. | V.G. | Good | Fair | Poor |
|------|------|------|------|------|
| 4000 | 3000 | 2500 | 1750 | 1200 |

We must again emphasize that guns of this nature must be appraised. There are too many variables for a book of this type to accurately cover. There are so many factors that would have a serious effect on the values that we intend our pricing as a reference guide only.

# CHYLEWSKI, WITOLD
## Austria

Chylewski has the distinction of being the one man who was successful in producing a one-hand operating semi-automatic pistol. The major drawback to the semi-auto design is that it takes two hands to cock the pistol and chamber a round. Chylewski overcame this problem by utilizing a small 6.35mm pistol with short slide travel and a weak recoil spring. He modified the triggerguard so that it contacted the slide and would bring it back to the cocking position. When the triggerguard was released, the slide would move forward to chamber a round, return to battery, and be ready to fire. The Swiss firm of Neuhausen made approximately 1,000 of these pistols between 1910 and 1918. They are marked "Brevete Chylewski" and bear the name Neuhausen on the left side of the pistol. Later versions of the Chylewski have the cocking devise disabled, and one can only guess at the reason for this--possibly a patent infringement. The design was later successfully developed by Bergman.

| Exc. | V.G. | Good | Fair | Poor |
|------|------|------|------|------|
| 850 | 750 | 675 | 500 | 375 |

# CIMARRON F. A. MFG. CO.
## Houston, Texas
### SEE--Aldo Uberti

Cimarron is in the business of importing and distributing the fine line of Aldo Uberti Replica Arms manufactured in Italy. Uberti Arms imported by Cimarron have their barrels stamped "Cimarron F.A. Mfg. Co. Houston, Tx. U.S.A." These firearms are listed under Uberti.

# CLARK, F. H.
## Memphis, Tennessee

### Pocket Pistol

This pistol was patterned in the classic derringer style. It was chambered for .41 caliber percussion with a 3.5" to 5" long round barrel. The mountings are of German silver and are not engraved. There is a German silver end cap, and the barrel is stamped "F.H.Clark & Co./Memphis." This pistol was manufactured in the 1850's.

| Exc. | V.G. | Good | Fair | Poor |
|------|------|------|------|------|
| 1250 | 1100 | 950 | 750 | 500 |

# CLASSIC DOUBLES
### Tochigi City, Japan
### Importer--Classic Doubles International
### St. Louis, Missouri

This company is in the business of importing the Japanese shotgun formerly imported by Winchester as the Model 101 and Model 23. These Models were discontinued by Winchester in 1987 and at this time are no longer being made. There are enough already in the country to insure availability for a while.

## Model 201 Classic
This is a side-by-side double chambered for 12 or 20 gauge. It has 26" barrels with a vent rib and screw-in choke tubes. There are 3" chambers, a single-selective trigger, and automatic ejectors. The finish is a high polished blue with a select, hand-checkered walnut stock and beavertail forearm.

| NIB | Exc. | V.G. | Good | Fair | Poor |
|-----|------|------|------|------|------|
| 2200 | 1950 | 1700 | 1500 | 1250 | 900 |

## Model 201 Small Bore Set
This is the same as the Model 201 with a smaller receiver and two sets of barrels chambered for 28 gauge and .410. The barrels are 28" in length.

| NIB | Exc. | V.G. | Good | Fair | Poor |
|-----|------|------|------|------|------|
| 3650 | 3200 | 2750 | 2250 | 1750 | 1250 |

## Model 101 Classic Field Grade I
This is an Over/Under double with 25.5" or 28" vent-rib barrels chambered for 12 and 20 gauge. There are 3" chambers and screw-in choke tubes. Automatic ejectors and a single-selective trigger are standard, and the lightly engraved receiver is blued. The stock is of select hand-checkered walnut.

| NIB | Exc. | V.G. | Good | Fair | Poor |
|-----|------|------|------|------|------|
| 1900 | 1750 | 1500 | 1250 | 1000 | 700 |

## Classic Field Grade II
This model is similar to the Grade I but is available in 28 gauge and .410, highly engraved with a coin-finished receiver and a deluxe walnut stock with a round-knob pistol-grip and fleur-de-lis checkering.

| NIB | Exc. | V.G. | Good | Fair | Poor |
|-----|------|------|------|------|------|
| 2200 | 2000 | 1750 | 1500 | 1250 | 900 |

## Classic Sporter
This model is chambered for 12 gauge only and has either 28" or 30" barrels with vent rib and screw-in choke tubes. The frame is coin-finished with light engraving and a matted upper surface to reduce glare. The stock is select walnut. This model was designed for "Sporting Clays."

| NIB | Exc. | V.G. | Good | Fair | Poor |
|-----|------|------|------|------|------|
| 2000 | 1800 | 1500 | 1250 | 1000 | 700 |

## Waterfowl Model
This model has 30" barrels with 3" chambers, vent rib, and screw-in choke tubes. The overall finish is a subdued matte with light engraving.

| NIB | Exc. | V.G. | Good | Fair | Poor |
|-----|------|------|------|------|------|
| 1500 | 1350 | 1000 | 850 | 650 | 500 |

## Classic Trap Over/Under
This model is designed for competition trap shooting. It has 30" or 32" barrels with ventilated center and top rib. There are automatic ejectors, screw-in choke tubes, and a single trigger. It is blued with light engraving and a walnut stock in straight or Monte Carlo style.

| NIB | Exc. | V.G. | Good | Fair | Poor |
|-----|------|------|------|------|------|
| 1900 | 1750 | 1500 | 1250 | 1000 | 700 |

## Classic Trap Single
This model is similar to the Trap Over/Under except that it has a single 32" or 34" barrel.

| NIB | Exc. | V.G. | Good | Fair | Poor |
|-----|------|------|------|------|------|
| 2000 | 1800 | 1500 | 1250 | 1000 | 700 |

## Classic Trap Combo
This set features a single barrel and a set of Over/Under barrels.

| NIB | Exc. | V.G. | Good | Fair | Poor |
|-----|------|------|------|------|------|
| 2800 | 2500 | 2000 | 1750 | 1250 | 1000 |

## Classic Skeet
This model is similar to the Classic Trap with 27.5" barrels.

| NIB | Exc. | V.G. | Good | Fair | Poor |
|-----|------|------|------|------|------|
| 1900 | 1750 | 1500 | 1250 | 1000 | 700 |

## Classic Skeet 4 Gauge Set
This model is the Skeet model furnished with four sets of barrels chambered for 12, 20, 28 gauge, and .410.

| NIB | Exc. | V.G. | Good | Fair | Poor |
|-----|------|------|------|------|------|
| 3700 | 3000 | 2500 | 2250 | 1850 | 1500 |

# CLEMENT, CHAS.
### Liege, Belgium

## Model 1903
This is an original design unlike anything previously encountered. The left side of the frame has a pillar machined onto it; and a fixed housing, which held the barrel in place, was screwed to it. The pistol is chambered for the 5.5mm Clement.

| Exc. | V.G. | Good | Fair | Poor |
|------|------|------|------|------|
| 600 | 500 | 450 | 375 | 300 |

## Model 1907
A model that is externally very similar to the 1903 but strenghtened somewhat. The 1907 is chambered for the 6.35mm amd 7.65mm cartridges.

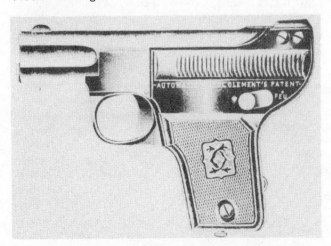

| Exc. | V.G. | Good | Fair | Poor |
|------|------|------|------|------|
| 350 | 300 | 250 | 200 | 150 |

## Model 1908
Another version of the Model 1903. The Model 1908 featured a modified, more comfortable grip frame and a repositioned magazine release.

| Exc. | V.G. | Good | Fair | Poor |
|------|------|------|------|------|
| 450 | 400 | 350 | 300 | 250 |

## Model 1910

The Model 1910 is a totally redesigned pistol. The barrel and housing are all one piece. This unit is held in position by the triggerguard.

| Exc. | V.G. | Good | Fair | Poor |
|------|------|------|------|------|
| 450 | 400 | 350 | 300 | 250 |

## Model 1912

A total departure from the other complex and novel Clement designs, the Model 1912 is simply a 6.35mm blowback very similar to the much-copied 1906 Browning but without the grip safety. Some are marked "Clement's Patent"; others, "Model 1912 Brevet 243839."

| Exc. | V.G. | Good | Fair | Poor |
|------|------|------|------|------|
| 750 | 650 | 550 | 400 | 325 |

Clement also produced a revolver circa 1912. It bore the Clement name and trademark and was a copy of the Colt Police Positive. It was chambered for .38 caliber.

| Exc. | V.G. | Good | Fair | Poor |
|------|------|------|------|------|
| 275 | 250 | 200 | 125 | 90 |

# CLERKE PRODS.
## Santa Monica, California

## Hi-Wall

This is a replica of the falling-block Winchester Model 1885 High Wall rifle. The action is activated by a lever, and the receiver is case-colored. This rifle is chambered for almost all of the modern calibers and features a 26" barrel and a walnut stock with a pistol grip and a Schnabel forend. It was manufactured between 1972 and 1974.

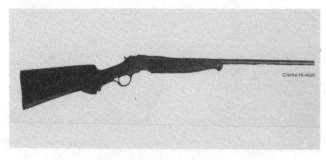

Clerke Hi-Wall

| Exc. | V.G. | Good | Fair | Poor |
|------|------|------|------|------|
| 275 | 250 | 200 | 150 | 100 |

## Deluxe Hi-Wall

This model is similar to the standard with a half-round/half-octagonal barrel, select walnut stock, and a recoil pad. It was manufactured between 1972 and 1974.

| Exc. | V.G. | Good | Fair | Poor |
|------|------|------|------|------|
| 325 | 300 | 250 | 200 | 150 |

# CLIFTON ARMS
## Grand Prairie, Texas

This company manufactures composite, laminated rifle stocks of high quality and, upon request, will build custom made-to-order rifles. The pricing of this rifle depends on the features desired. There are not enough on the used market to establish values.

# COBRAY INDUSTRIES
## Atlanta, Georgia
## S.W.D., Inc.

## M 11 Pistol

This is a blowback-operated semi-automatic chambered for the 9mm cartridge. It fires from the closed bolt and is made of steel stampings with a parkerized finish. It is patterned after, though a good deal smaller than, the Ingram Mac 10. This is another assault-type firearm that has been affected by the legislation-produced hysteria sweeping our Country. It is currently out of production and impossible to accurately price. If purchase or sale is contemplated, please check local values.

## M 11 Carbine

This model is similar in appearance to the M 11 pistol with a 16.25" shrouded barrel and a telescoping metal shoulder stock.

## Terminator Shotgun

This is a single-shot 12-or 20-gauge shotgun that is unique in that it fires from an open-bolt position. The cocked bolt is released to slam home on the shell when the trigger is pulled. The 18" barrel is cylinder-bored. There is a telescoping wire stock and the finish is parkerized.

| Exc. | V.G. | Good | Fair | Poor |
|------|------|------|------|------|
| 125 | 100 | 80 | 60 | 40 |

# COCHRAN TURRET
## C. B. Allen
## Springfield, Massachusetts

## Underhammer Turret Rifle

This was a true oddity in the firearms field--a cylinder that was laid on its side like a turret. It was not a practical method as a chain fire could have proved fatal. There were three basic models, as well as a carbine.

## 1st Type

This variation has a circular top strap that holds the turret in place with two screws, making the turret difficult to remove for loading. The underhammer doubles as a triggerguard. There were approximately 30 of these manufactured, and they are so numbered 1--30.

| Exc. | V.G. | Good | Fair | Poor |
|------|------|------|------|------|
| 6500 | 5750 | 5000 | 3750 | 2500 |

## 2nd Type

This is similar in appearance to the 1st Type, with an improved, rectangular-shaped top strap hinged in front, with a catch in the rear that acts as a rear sight. This makes the turret easier to remove for loading. There were 125 of the 2nd Type produced, and they were numbered 31--155.

| Exc. | V.G. | Good | Fair | Poor |
|------|------|------|------|------|
| 6000 | 5250 | 4500 | 3250 | 2000 |

## 3rd Type

The 3rd Type has a smaller hammer in front of the trigger and a less elaborate triggerguard. There were approximately 50 manufactured in the number 155 to 200 range.

| Exc. | V.G. | Good | Fair | Poor |
|------|------|------|------|------|
| 6000 | 5250 | 4500 | 3250 | 2000 |

## Carbine

This model is similar to the 3rd Type, with a 27" round barrel.

| Exc. | V.G. | Good | Fair | Poor |
|------|------|------|------|------|
| 7500 | 6750 | 6000 | 4500 | 3500 |

The standard Cochran Turret Rifles were chambered for .36 or .40 caliber and used the percussion ignition system. The barrels are 31" or 32" and are octagonal. The frames and turret are case-colored, with the remainder browned. The stocks are walnut. They are marked "Cochrans/Many/Chambered/&/Non Recoil/Rifle." The top strap is also marked "C.B. Allen / Springfield." These weapons were manufactured between 1835 and 1840.

## Cochran Turret Revolver
This was a 7-shot, handgun version of the Cochran system. It has a 5", part-round/part-octagonal barrel and is chambered for .36 caliber percussion. The action is similar to the 3rd Type rifle; and the frame is of the saw type with a round, one-piece walnut handle. The finish is case-colored and browned, and the top strap is stamped "Cochran's Patent/C.B. Allen/Springfield, Mass." There were approximately 150 manufactured between 1835 and 1840.

| Exc. | V.G. | Good | Fair | Poor |
|------|------|------|------|------|
| 5000 | 4500 | 3750 | 2750 | 1800 |

# COFER, T. W.
## Portsmouth, Virginia

### Cofer Navy Revolver
This was a Civil War era, Confederate-manufactured revolver patterned after the Whitney Navy revolver. It is chambered for .36 caliber percussion and has a 6-shot, unfluted cylinder. The frame is polished brass, and the remainder is blued. The octagonal barrel is 7.5" in length, and it has a spur-type trigger. The grips are walnut, and the top strap is crudely stamped "T.W. Cofer's/Patent." The barrel is similarly marked "Portsmouth, Va." There were approximately 100 estimated manufactured--with only 10 known to survive. This pistol was one of the privately produced weapons that was not backed by the Confederacy. The extreme rarity of these weapons makes evaluation only estimation as there are not enough sold to accurately average a price. On the rare occurrence of encountering such a firearm for sale, it is obvious that qualified individual appraisal should be secured.

| Exc. | V.G. | Good | Fair | Poor |
|------|------|------|------|------|
| 30000 | 27500 | 20000 | 15000 | 10000 |

# COGSWELL
## London, England

### Cogswell Pepperbox Pistol
This is a well-made, 6-shot, revolving-barrelled pepperbox chambered for .47 caliber percussion. It has an engraved German silver frame and grip straps marked "B. Cogswell, 224 Strand, London." On the reverse side is stamped "Improved Revolving Pistol." The round grips are walnut. This is a smooth-bore weapon, without sights of any kind. This pistol was manufactured in the 1850's.

| Exc. | V.G. | Good | Fair | Poor |
|------|------|------|------|------|
| 2500 | 2000 | 1750 | 1250 | 750 |

# COGSWELL & HARRISON, LTD.
## London, England

This company has been in the firearms business since 1770 and is noted for their high-quality, double-barrelled shotguns.

### Markor
This is a side-by-side chambered for 12, 16, or 20 gauge, with 27" or 30" barrels with various chokes. It is a boxlock available with automatic ejectors at extra cost and double triggers. The English-style straight stock is select walnut. This model is no longer manufactured.
Auto Ejectors--Add 20 Percent.

| Exc. | V.G. | Good | Fair | Poor |
|------|------|------|------|------|
| 1500 | 1400 | 1200 | 950 | 700 |

### Huntic
This is a higher-grade version of the Markor, that is offered standard with ejectors. A single-selective trigger was optional at an additional 10 percent. A 25" barrel was offered. It has also been discontinued.

| Exc. | V.G. | Good | Fair | Poor |
|------|------|------|------|------|
| 3600 | 3400 | 3000 | 2500 | 2000 |

### Regency Model
This side-by-side is chambered for 12, 16, or 20 gauge, with barrels of 26", 28", or 30" and various chokes. It features an Anson and Deeley boxlock with the throughbolt. It has double triggers, automatic ejectors, and an English style stock. This model has been manufactured since 1970.

| Exc. | V.G. | Good | Fair | Poor |
|------|------|------|------|------|
| 3250 | 2850 | 2400 | 1750 | 1400 |

### Ambassador Model
This Model is similar to the Regency, with false sideplates and a higher degree of engraving.

| Exc. | V.G. | Good | Fair | Poor |
|------|------|------|------|------|
| 4000 | 3500 | 3000 | 2500 | 2000 |

### Rex
This side-by-side is chambered for 12, 16, or 20 gauge. It has 25", 27.5", or 30" barrels. It is a boxlock with automatic ejectors, double triggers, and an English-style stock. It is no longer made.

| Exc. | V.G. | Good | Fair | Poor |
|------|------|------|------|------|
| 1750 | 1500 | 1250 | 1000 | 750 |

### Sandhurst
This is a more deluxe version of the Rex with false sideplates and more engraving.

| Exc. | V.G. | Good | Fair | Poor |
|------|------|------|------|------|
| 2500 | 2250 | 2000 | 1500 | 1000 |

### Konor
This is the top gun in this series and is similar to the Sandhurst with more elaborate engraving and a fancier grade stock. Single-selective triggers are available for an additional 15 percent.

| Exc. | V.G. | Good | Fair | Poor |
|------|------|------|------|------|
| 2900 | 2600 | 2250 | 1850 | 1500 |

### Primic
This model was the top of the line until it was discontinued. It is chambered for 12, 16, and 20 gauge with various barrel lengths and chokes. It has hand-detachable full sidelocks, automatic ejectors, and double triggers. A single-selective trigger was available for an additional charge. The select walnut stock is in the straight English style.

| Exc. | V.G. | Good | Fair | Poor |
|------|------|------|------|------|
| 6000 | 5000 | 3750 | 2500 | 2000 |

### Victor
This is the current "Best Quality" gun in the line and differs from the Primic in the amount of engraving and grade of wood used.

| Exc. | V.G. | Good | Fair | Poor |
|------|------|------|------|------|
| 10000 | 8750 | 6250 | 4500 | 2750 |

---

**An explanation of the Grading System is located in the introduction found at the front of the book.**

---

## COLTS PATENT F.A. MFG. CO.
### Hartford, Connecticut

Colt firearms have inspired more individuals to enter the area of gun collecting than any other. They supplied significant quantities of a great many different models. This is extremely important when a significant number of collectors are actively seeking the same prize. Colt has also been present at the right times in the history of our nation so that their products, perhaps more than any others in their field, have become associated with the evolution of our society.

As history has it, in 1831 Samuel Colt carved the first practical repeating revolver out of wood. He was sixteen years old and working at sea. The action of the ship's wheel gave him his inspiration. Upon his return Christopher Colt, his father, and H. L. Ellsworth, a family friend who was commissioner of the U.S. Patent Office, looked at his invention and were favorably impressed. They advised him to file an "Intent to Patent" and then to perfect a prototype before attempting to manufacture. Colt followed this advice and spent the next four years perfecting his design, raising funds, and having working prototypes made by qualified gunsmiths of the era. In 1835 he set out for England and France, where he obtained patents on his designs.

On February 25, 1836, the first U.S. Patent was issued for a Colt revolver. That year, with $300,000 in operating capital raised through the contacts his wealthy family and friends provided, Colt started the "Patent Arms Manufacturing Company" in Paterson, New Jersey. Sadly this company was doomed from the start; and up until 1842, when bankruptcy was declared and the assets were seized by John Ehlers, the company treasurer and major stockholder, there were 2,850 handguns and 1,912 long guns manufactured.

It was 1846 before the U.S. entry into the Mexican War gave Colt a sufficient reason to re-enter the repeating arms field. He began business in Hartford, Connecticut, with the manufacture of the Walkers and Dragoons. Of course, this time he met with success--and the rest is history.

Samuel Colt died prematurely at the age of 47 in 1862. Sadly, he did not live to see the great success his brainchild achieved during and after the Civil War.

When one considers the collecting of Colts, it is essential to be cognizant of a few very important points. Colts, perhaps more so than other firearms, have been very susceptible to the fraudulent practices of those who wish to take advantage of the uneducated. The extreme variation in values among some models that appear similar is undoubtedly the reason for this. It would definitely behoove anyone interested in acquiring Colt firearms to educate oneself and to deal with only reputable individuals. The good news is that there are a great many fine volumes written on Colt firearms; and if one is willing to spend the time and money, it is possible to learn a great deal.

It is also gratifying to note that on many of their models, Colt has extensive factory records available; and one can secure this information for what we consider a modest fee.

We are listing the Colt firearms in chronological order, supplying values for the standard models and some of the major variations. Colt manufactured so many different firearms that it would be physically impossible for us to list them all. We do repeatedly counsel to secure competent appraisal on any models that show variation from the norm. Colt also furnished firearms in different finishes and degrees of embellishment. They employed the finest engravers of the day to ply their craft on Colt's products. Ivory and pearl, silver and gold were all utilized to enhance the appearance of Colt's firearms. Some were cased in exotic hardwoods and supplied with fine accessories. This all adds considerably to the value of these fine weapons.

The historical significance of some of these firearms can also have a great influence on the value. The era in our Country's history, coupled with the quality of Colt's products, made them very sought after by personages both famous and infamous, who had a profound need for such devices. This creates another subdivision of collecting that can be very gratifying but can also be hazardous to one's financial health if care is not taken to educate oneself before acting.

## COLT PATERSON MODELS
### Paterson, New Jersey

### Pocket or Baby Paterson Model 1
The Paterson was the first production revolver manufactured by Colt. It was first made in 1837. The Model 1 or Pocket Model is the most diminutive of the Paterson line. It was designed to be carried as an undercover or hideout gun and was as concealable as the single-shot handguns of its day. The revolver is serial numbered in its own range, #1 through #500. The numbers are not visible without dismantling the revolver. The barrel lengths run from 1.75" to 4.75". The standard model has no attached loading lever. The chambering is .28 caliber percussion and it holds five shots. The finish is all blued, and the grips are varnished walnut. It has a roll-engraved cylinder scene, and the barrel is stamped "Patent Arms M'g Co. Paterson N.J.-Colt's Pt."

| Exc. | V.G. | Good | Fair | Poor |
|------|------|------|------|------|
| 12500 | 10000 | 7000 | 4000 | 2750 |

### Belt Model Paterson 2
The Belt Model Paterson is a larger revolver with a straight-grip and an octagonal barrel that is 2.5" to 5.5" in length. It is chambered for .31-caliber percussion and holds five shots. The finish is all blued, with varnished walnut grips and no attached loading lever. It has a roll-engraved cylinder scene, and the barrel is stamped "Patent Arms M'g Co. Paterson N.J. Colt's Pt." The serial number range is 1-850 and is shared with the 3 Belt Model. It was made from 1837-1840.

| Exc. | V.G. | Good | Fair | Poor |
|------|------|------|------|------|
| 12500 | 10000 | 7000 | 4000 | 2750 |

### Belt Model Paterson 3
This revolver is quite similar to the Model 2 except that the grips are curved outward at the bottom to form a more hand-filling configuration. They are serial numbered in the same 1-850 range. Some attached loading levers have been noted on this Model, but they are extremely rare and would add approximately 35 percent to the value.

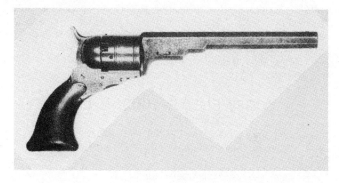

| Exc. | V.G. | Good | Fair | Poor |
|------|------|------|------|------|
| 11500 | 9500 | 6500 | 3500 | 2500 |

### Ehlers Model Pocket Paterson
John Ehlers was a major stockholder and treasurer of the Patent Arms Mfg. Co. when it went bankrupt. He seized the assets and inventory. These revolvers were Pocket model Patersons that were not finished at the time. Ehlers had them finished and marketed them. They had an attached loading lever, and the abbreviation "M'g Co." was deleted from the barrel stamping. There were 500 revolvers involved in the Ehlers variation totally, and they were produced from 1840-1843.

| Exc. | V.G. | Good | Fair | Poor |
|------|------|------|------|------|
| 13500 | 11000 | 8000 | 5000 | 3500 |

### Ehlers Belt Model Paterson
The same specifications apply to this larger revolver as they do to the Ehlers Pocket Model. It falls within the same 500 revolver involvement and is very rare.

| Exc. | V.G. | Good | Fair | Poor |
|------|------|------|------|------|
| 12500 | 10000 | 7000 | 4000 | 2750 |

### Texas Paterson Model 5
This is the largest and most sought after of the Paterson models. It is also known as the Holster model. It has been verified as actually seeing use by both the military and civilians on the American frontier. It is chambered for .36 caliber percussion, holds five shots, and has an octagonal barrel that ranges from 4" to 12" in length. It has been observed with and without the attached loading lever, but those with it are rare. The finish is blued, with a case-colored hammer. The grips are varnished walnut. The cylinder is roll- engraved; and the barrel is stamped "Patent Arms M'g. Co. Paterson, N.J. Colts Pt." Most Texas Patersons are well used and have a very worn appearance. One in Excellent or V.G. condition would be highly prized. A verified military model would be worth a great deal more than standard, so qualifed appraisal would be essential. The serial number range is 1-1,000, and they were manufactured from 1838-1840. The attached loading lever brings approximately a 25 percent premium.

| Exc. | V.G. | Good | Fair | Poor |
|------|------|------|------|------|
| 28500 | 22500 | 15000 | 8500 | 7500 |

## COLT REVOLVING LONG GUNS 1837-1847
### First Model Ring Lever Rifle
This was actually the first firearm manufactured by Colt; the first Paterson appeared a short time later. There were 200 of the First Models made in 1837 and 1838. The octagonal barrel of the First Model is 32" long and browned, while the rest of the finish is blued. The stock is varnished walnut with a cheekpiece inlaid with Colt's trademark. The ring lever located in front of the frame is pulled to rotate the 8-shot cylinder and cock the hammer. The rifle is chambered for .34, .36, .38, .40, and .44 caliber percussion. The cylinder is roll-engraved, and the barrel is stamped "Colt's Patent/Patent Arms Man'g Co., Paterson, N.Jersey." This Model has a top strap over the cylinder. They were made both with and without an attached loading lever. The latter is worth approximately 10 percent more.

| Exc. | V.G. | Good | Fair | Poor |
|------|------|------|------|------|
| 11000 | 8000 | 6500 | 5000 | 3500 |

### Second Model Ring Lever Rifle
This Model is quite similar in appearance to the First Model. Its function is identical. The major difference is the absence of the top strap over the cylinder. It had no trademark stamped on the cheekpiece. The Second Model is offered with a 28" and a 32" octagonal barrel and is chambered for .44 caliber percussion, holding 8 shots. There were approximately 500 produced from 1838-1841. The presence of an attached cheekpiece would add approximately 10 percent to the value.

| Exc. | V.G. | Good | Fair | Poor |
|------|------|------|------|------|
| 11000 | 8000 | 6500 | 5000 | 3500 |

### Model 1839 Carbine
This Model has no ring but features an exposed hammer for cocking and rotating the 6-shot cylinder. It is chambered for .525 smoothbore and comes standard with a 24" round barrel. Other barrel lengths have been noted. The finish is blued, with a browned barrel and a varnished walnut stock. The cylinder is roll- engraved, and the barrel is stamped "Patent Arms M'g. Co. Paterson, N.J.-Colt's Pt." There were 950 manufactured from 1838-1841. Later variations of this Model are found with the attached loading lever standard, and earlier models without one would bring approximately 25 percent additional. There were 360 purchased by the military and stamped "WAT" on the stock. These would be worth twice what a standard model

would bring. Anyone considering the purchase of one would be well advised to proceed with extreme caution.

| Exc. | V.G. | Good | Fair | Poor |
|------|------|------|------|------|
| 8500 | 7000 | 5000 | 4000 | 3250 |

### Model 1839 Shotgun
This Model is quite similar in appearance to the 1839 Carbine. It is chambered for 16 gauge and holds six shots. It has a damascus pattern barrel, and the most notable difference is a 3.5" (instead of a 2.5") long cylinder. There were only 225 of these made from 1839-1841. The markings are the same as on the Carbine.

| Exc. | V.G. | Good | Fair | Poor |
|------|------|------|------|------|
| 7500 | 6000 | 4500 | 3500 | 2750 |

## WALKER-DRAGOON MODELS
### Hartford, Connecticut
### Walker Model Revolver
The Walker is a massive revolver. It weighs 4 pounds 9 ounces and has a 9" part-round/part-octagonal barrel. The cylinder holds six shots and is chambered for .44 caliber percussion. There were 1,000 Walker Colts manufactured in 1847, and nearly all of them saw extremely hard use. Originally this Model had a roll-engraved cylinder, military inspection marks, and barrel stamping that read "Address Saml. Colt-New York City." Practically all examples noted have had these markings worn or rusted beyond recognition. Because the Walker is perhaps the most desirable and sought-after Colt from a collector's standpoint and because of the extremely high value of a Walker in any condition, qualified appraisal is definitely recommended.

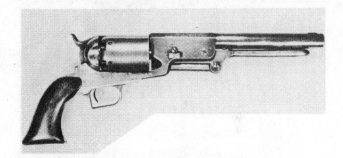

| Exc. | V.G. | Good | Fair | Poor |
|------|------|------|------|------|
| 50000 | 40000 | 30000 | 22500 | 20000 |

### Civilian Walker Revolver
This model is identical to the military model but has no martial markings. They are found serial numbered 1,001 through 1,100.

| Exc. | V.G. | Good | Fair | Poor |
|------|------|------|------|------|
| 45000 | 35000 | 27500 | 20000 | 18500 |

### Whitneyville Hartford Dragoon
This is a large, 6-shot, .44-caliber percussion revolver. It has a 7.5" part-round/part-octagonal barrel. The frame, hammer, and loading lever are case-colored. The remainder is blued, with a brass trigger guard and varnished walnut grips. There were only 240 made in late 1847. The serial numbers run from 1,100-1,340. This model is often referred to as a Transitional Walker. Some of the parts used in its manufacture were left over from the Walker production run. This model has a roll-engraved cylinder scene, and the barrel is stamped "Address Saml. Colt New York-City." This is an extremely rare model, and much care should be taken to authenticate any contemplated acquisitions.

| Exc. | V.G. | Good | Fair | Poor |
|------|------|------|------|------|
| 45000 | 35000 | 27500 | 20000 | 18500 |

### Walker Replacement Dragoon
This extremely rare Colt (300 produced) is sometimes referred to as the "Fluck" in memory of the gentleman who first identified it as a distinct and separate model. They were produced by Colt as replacements to the military for Walkers that were no longer

fit for service due to mechanical failures. They were large, 6-shot, .44-caliber percussion revolvers with 7.5" part-round/part-octagonal barrels. Serial numbers ran from 2,216 to 2,515. The frame, hammer, and loading lever are case-colored; the remainder, blued. The grips, which are longer than other Dragoons and similar to the Walker's, are of varnished walnut and bear the inspector's mark "WAT" inside an oval cartouche on one side and the letters "JH" on the other. The frame is stamped "Colt's/Patent/U.S." The letter "P" appears on various parts of the gun. This is another model that should definitely be authenticated before any acquisition is made.

| Exc. | V.G. | Good | Fair | Poor |
|------|------|------|------|------|
| 10000 | 7500 | 6000 | 4000 | 2500 |

### First Model Dragoon

Another large, 6-shot, .44-caliber percussion revolver. It has a 7.5" part-round/part-octagonal barrel. The frame, hammer, and loading lever are case-colored; the remainder, blued with a brass grip frame and square backed triggerguard. The triggerguard is silver-plated on the Civilian Model only. Another distinguishing feature on the First Model is the oval cylinder stop notches. The serial number range is 1,341-8,000. There were approximately 5,000 made. The cylinder is roll-engraved; and the barrel stampings read "Address Saml. Colt, New York City." "Colt's Patent" appears on the frame. On Military Models the letters "U.S." also appear on the frame.

**Military Model**

| Exc. | V.G. | Good | Fair | Poor |
|------|------|------|------|------|
| 10000 | 7500 | 6000 | 3500 | 1500 |

**Civilian Model**

| Exc. | V.G. | Good | Fair | Poor |
|------|------|------|------|------|
| 8000 | 6000 | 4000 | 2000 | 1000 |

### Second Model Dragoon

Most of the improvements that distinguish this Model from the First Model are internal and not readily apparent. The most obvious external change is the rectangular cylinder-stop notches. This Model is serial numbered from 8,000-10,700, for a total production of approximately 2,700 revolvers manufactured in 1850 and 1851. There is a Civilian Model, a Military Model, and an extremely rare variation that was issued to the militias of New Hampshire and Massachusets (marked "MS."). Once again, caution is advised in acquisition.

**Civilian Model**

| Exc. | V.G. | Good | Fair | Poor |
|------|------|------|------|------|
| 7000 | 5000 | 3250 | 2000 | 1200 |

**Military Model**

| Exc. | V.G. | Good | Fair | Poor |
|------|------|------|------|------|
| 8500 | 6500 | 4500 | 2500 | 1500 |

**Militia Model**

| Exc. | V.G. | Good | Fair | Poor |
|------|------|------|------|------|
| 8500 | 6500 | 4500 | 2500 | 1500 |

### Third Model Dragoon

This is the most common of all the large Colt percussion revolvers. Approximately 10,500 were manufactured from 1851 through 1861. It is quite similar in appearance to the Second Model, and the most obvious external difference is the round triggerguard. The Third Model Dragoon was the first Colt revolver available with a detachable shoulder stock. There are three basic types of stocks, and all are quite rare as only 1,250 were produced. There are two other major variations we will note--the "C.L." Dragoon, which was a militia-issued model and is very rare, and the late-issue model with 8" barrel. These are found over serial number 18,000, and only 50 were produced. Qualified appraisal should be secured before acquisition as many fakes abound.

**Civilian Model**

| Exc. | V.G. | Good | Fair | Poor |
|------|------|------|------|------|
| 4500 | 3750 | 2750 | 2000 | 1500 |

**Military Model**

| Exc. | V.G. | Good | Fair | Poor |
|------|------|------|------|------|
| 5000 | 4000 | 3000 | 2500 | 2000 |

**Shoulder Stock Cut Revolvers**

| Exc. | V.G. | Good | Fair | Poor |
|------|------|------|------|------|
| 9000 | 7500 | 6000 | 4250 | 3500 |

**Shoulder Stocks**

| Exc. | V.G. | Good | Fair | Poor |
|------|------|------|------|------|
| 3000 | 2500 | 2000 | 1500 | 1000 |

**C.L. Dragoon (Hand Engraved, Not Stamped)**

| Exc. | V.G. | Good | Fair | Poor |
|------|------|------|------|------|
| 7000 | 5500 | 4000 | 3250 | 2500 |

**8" Barrel Late Issue**

| Exc. | V.G. | Good | Fair | Poor |
|------|------|------|------|------|
| 9000 | 7500 | 6000 | 4250 | 3500 |

### Hartford English Dragoon

This is a variation of the Third Model Dragoon. The only notable differences are the British proofmarks and the distinct 1-700 serial-number range. Other than these two features, the description given for the Third Model would apply. These revolvers were manufactured in Hartford but were finished at Colt's London factory from 1853-1857. Some bear the hand-engraved barrel marking "Coln. Colt London." Many of the English Dragoons were elaborately engraved, and individual appraisal would be a must. Two hundred revolvers came back to America in 1861 to be used in the Civil War. As with all the early Colts, caution is advised in acquisition.

| Exc. | V.G. | Good | Fair | Poor |
|------|------|------|------|------|
| 5000 | 4500 | 3500 | 2250 | 1400 |

### Model 1848 Baby Dragoon

This is a small, 5-shot, .31-caliber percussion revolver. It has an octagonal barrel in lengths of 3", 4", 5", and 6". Most were made without an attached loading lever, although some with loading levers have been noted. The frame, hammer, and loading lever (when present) are case-colored; the barrel and cylinder, blued. The grip frame and triggerguard are silverplated brass. There were approximately 15,500 manufactured between 1847 and 1850. The serial range is between #1-5,500. The barrels are stamped "Address Saml. Colt/New York City." Some have been noted with the barrel address inside brackets. The frame is marked "Colt's/Patent." The first 10,000 revolvers have the Texas Ranger/Indian roll-engraved cylinder scene; the later guns the Stagecoach Holdup scene. This is a very popular Model, and many fakes have been noted.
Attached Loading Lever--Add 15 Percent.

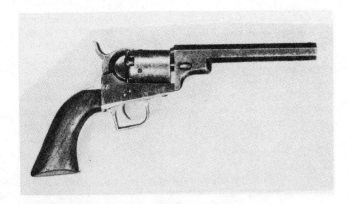

**Texas Ranger/Indian Scene**

| Exc. | V.G. | Good | Fair | Poor |
|------|------|------|------|------|
| 2500 | 2000 | 1500 | 1000 | 750 |

**Stagecoach Holdup Scene**

| Exc. | V.G. | Good | Fair | Poor |
|------|------|------|------|------|
| 3000 | 2500 | 1750 | 1250 | 1000 |

## Model 1849 Pocket Revolver

This is a small, either 5- or 6-shot, .31-caliber percussion revolver. It has an octagonal barrel 3", 4", 5", or 6" in length. Most had loading gates, but some did not. The frame, hammer, and loading lever are case-colored; the cylinder and barrel are blued. The grip frame and round triggerguard are made of brass and silver-plated. There are both large and small triggerguard variations noted. This is the most plentiful of all the Colt percussion revolvers, with approximately 325,000 manufactured over a 23-year period, 1850-1873. There are over 200 variations of this Model, and one should consult an expert for individual appraisals. There are many fine publications specializing in the field of Colt percussion revolvers that would be helpful in the identification of the variations. The values represented here are for the standard model.

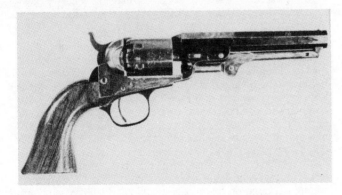

| Exc. | V.G. | Good | Fair | Poor |
|------|------|------|------|------|
| 2000 | 1750 | 1250 | 850 | 600 |

## London Model 1849 Pocket Revolver

Identical in configuration to the standard 1849 Pocket Revolver, the London-made models have a higher quality finish and their own serial number range, 1-11,000. They were manufactured from 1853 through 1857. They feature a roll-engraved cylinder scene, and the barrels are stamped "Address Col. Colt/London." The first 265 revolvers, known as early models, have brass grip frames and small round triggerguards. They are quite rare and worth approximately 50 percent more than the standard model which has a steel grip frame and large oval triggerguard.

| Exc. | V.G. | Good | Fair | Poor |
|------|------|------|------|------|
| 2250 | 1850 | 1450 | 1000 | 800 |

## Model 1851 Navy Revolver

This is undoubtedly the most popular revolver Colt produced in the medium size and power range. It is a 6-shot, .36-caliber percussion revolver with a 7.5" octagonal barrel. It has an at-tached loading lever. The basic model has a case-colored frame, hammer, and loading lever, with silver-plated brass grip frame and triggerguard. The grips are varnished walnut. Colt manufactured approximately 215,000 of these fine revolvers between 1850 and 1873. The basic Navy features a roll-engraved cylinder scene of a battle between the navies of Texas and Mexico. There are three distinct barrel stampings--serial number 1-74,000, "Address Saml. Colt New-York City"; serial number 74,001-101,000 "Address Saml. Colt. Hartford, Ct."; and serial number 101,001-215,000 "Address Saml. Colt New York U.S. America."

The left side of the frame is stamped "Colt's/Patent" on all variations. This Model is also available with a detached shoulder stock, and values for the stocks today are nearly as high as for the revolver itself. Careful appraisal should be secured before purchase. The number of variations within the 1851 Navy model designation makes it neccessary to read specialized text available on the subject. We furnish values for the major variations but again caution potential purchasers to acquire appraisals.

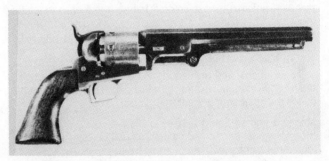

**Square Back Trigger Guard Serial #1-4,200**

| Exc. | V.G. | Good | Fair | Poor |
|------|------|------|------|------|
| 7500 | 6000 | 4000 | 2500 | 1500 |

**Small Round Trigger Guard Serial #4,201-85,000**

| Exc. | V.G. | Good | Fair | Poor |
|------|------|------|------|------|
| 3000 | 2500 | 2000 | 1500 | 850 |

**Large Round Trigger Guard Serial #85,001-215,000**

| Exc. | V.G. | Good | Fair | Poor |
|------|------|------|------|------|
| 2500 | 2000 | 1750 | 1250 | 750 |

**Martial Model**
"U.S." stamped on the left side of frame; inspector's marks and cartouche on the grips.

| Exc. | V.G. | Good | Fair | Poor |
|------|------|------|------|------|
| 3500 | 2750 | 2250 | 1750 | 1000 |

**Shoulder Stock Variations**
1st and 2nd Model Revolver Cut for Stock Only

| Exc. | V.G. | Good | Fair | Poor |
|------|------|------|------|------|
| 5000 | 4000 | 3000 | 2250 | 1750 |

**Stock Only**

| Exc. | V.G. | Good | Fair | Poor |
|------|------|------|------|------|
| 3500 | 2500 | 2000 | 1750 | 1250 |

**3rd Model**
Revolver Only

| Exc. | V.G. | Good | Fair | Poor |
|------|------|------|------|------|
| 4500 | 3250 | 2750 | 2000 | 1400 |

**Stock**

| Exc. | V.G. | Good | Fair | Poor |
|------|------|------|------|------|
| 2500 | 2000 | 1750 | 1250 | 850 |

## London Model 1851 Navy Revolver

These revolvers are physically similar to the U.S.-made model with the exception of the barrel address, which reads "Address Col. Colt. London." There are also British proofmarks stamped on the barrel and cylinder. There were 42,000 made between

1853 and 1857. They have their own serial-number range, 1-42,000. There are two major variations of the London Navy, and again a serious purchaser would be well advised to seek qualified appraisal as fakes have been noted.

### 1st Model
Serial 1-2,000 with a small round brass triggerguard and grip frame. Squareback guard worth a 40 percent premium.

| Exc. | V.G. | Good | Fair | Poor |
|------|------|------|------|------|
| 3500 | 2750 | 2000 | 1500 | 750 |

### 2nd Model
Serial 2,001-42,000, steel grip frame, and large round triggerguard.

| Exc. | V.G. | Good | Fair | Poor |
|------|------|------|------|------|
| 2250 | 1800 | 1250 | 800 | 600 |

## SIDEHAMMER MODELS

### Model 1855 Sidehammer "Root" Pocket Revolver
The "Root", as it is popularly known, was the only solid-frame revolver Colt ever made. It has a spur trigger and walnut grips, and the hammer is mounted on the right side of the frame. The standard finish is a case-colored frame, hammer, and loading lever, with the barrel and cylinder blued. It is chambered for both .28 caliber and .31 caliber percussion. Each caliber has its own serial number range--#1-30,000 for the .28 caliber and #1-14,000 for the .31 caliber. The Model consists of seven basic variations, and the serious student should avail oneself of the fine publications dealing with this model in depth. Colt produced the Sidehammer Root from 1855-1870.

### Models 1 and 1A Serial 1-384
3.5" octagonal barrel, .28 caliber, roll-engraved cylinder, Hartford barrel address without pointing hand.

| Exc. | V.G. | Good | Fair | Poor |
|------|------|------|------|------|
| 3000 | 2500 | 1750 | 1250 | 800 |

### Model 2 Serial #476-25,000
Same as Model 1 with pointing hand barrel address.

| Exc. | V.G. | Good | Fair | Poor |
|------|------|------|------|------|
| 1750 | 1400 | 1100 | 850 | 650 |

### Model 3 Serial 25,001-30,000
Same as the Model 2 with a full fluted cylinder.

| Exc. | V.G. | Good | Fair | Poor |
|------|------|------|------|------|
| 1750 | 1400 | 1100 | 850 | 650 |

### Model 3A and 4 Serial #1-2400
.31 caliber, 3.5" barrel, Hartford address, full fluted cylinder.

| Exc. | V.G. | Good | Fair | Poor |
|------|------|------|------|------|
| 2000 | 1750 | 1250 | 1000 | 750 |

### Model 5 Serial #2,401-8,000
.31 caliber, 3.5" round barrel, address "Col. Colt New York."

| Exc. | V.G. | Good | Fair | Poor |
|------|------|------|------|------|
| 1750 | 1400 | 1100 | 850 | 650 |

### Model 5A Serial #2,401-8,000
Same as Model 5 with a 4.5" barrel.

| Exc. | V.G. | Good | Fair | Poor |
|------|------|------|------|------|
| 1850 | 1500 | 1200 | 950 | 750 |

### Models 6 and 6A Serial #8,001-11,074
Same as Model 5 and 5A with roll-engraved cylinder scene.

| Exc. | V.G. | Good | Fair | Poor |
|------|------|------|------|------|
| 1750 | 1400 | 1100 | 850 | 650 |

### Models 7 and 7A Serial #11,075-14,000
Same as Models 6 and 6A with a screw holding in the cylinder pin.

| Exc. | V.G. | Good | Fair | Poor |
|------|------|------|------|------|
| 2250 | 2000 | 1600 | 1250 | 1000 |

## SIDEHAMMER LONG GUNS

### 1855 Sporting Rifle, 1st Model
This is a 6-shot revolving rifle chambered for .36 caliber percussion. It comes with a 21", 24", 27", or 30" round barrel that is part octagonal where it joins the frame. The stock is walnut with either an oil or a varnish finish. The frame, hammer, and loading lever are case-colored; the rest of the metal, blued. The hammer is on the right side of the frame. The 1st Model has no forend, and an oiling devise is attached to the barrel underlug. The triggerguard has two spurlike projections in front and in back of the bow. The roll-engraved cylinder scene depicts a hunter shooting at five deer and is found only on this Model. The standard stampings are "Colt's Pt./1856" and "Address S. Colt Hartford,Ct. U.S.A."

### Early Model
Low serial numbers with a hand-engraved barrel marking "Address S. Colt Hartford,U.S.A."

| Exc. | V.G. | Good | Fair | Poor |
|------|------|------|------|------|
| 6000 | 4750 | 3750 | 2500 | 1750 |

### Production Model

| Exc. | V.G. | Good | Fair | Poor |
|------|------|------|------|------|
| 4500 | 3500 | 2750 | 2000 | 1500 |

### 1855 1st Model Carbine
Identical to the 1st Model Rifle but offered with a 15" and 18" barrel.

| Exc. | V.G. | Good | Fair | Poor |
|------|------|------|------|------|
| 6500 | 5000 | 4000 | 2750 | 2000 |

### 1855 Half Stock Sporting Rifle
Although this Rifle is quite similar in appearance and finish to the 1st Model, there are some notable differences. It features a walnut forend that protrudes half way down the barrel. There are two types of triggerguards--a short projectionless one or a long model with a graceful scroll. There is a 6-shot model chambered for .36 or .44 caliber or a 5-shot model chambered for .56 caliber. The cylinder is fully fluted. The markings are "Colt's Pt/1856" and "Address Col. Colt/Hartford Ct.U.S.A." There were approximately 1,500 manufactured between 1857 and 1864.

| Exc. | V.G. | Good | Fair | Poor |
|------|------|------|------|------|
| 3200 | 2750 | 2000 | 1500 | 1250 |

### 1855 Full Stock Military Rifle
This model holds 6 shots in its .44-caliber chambering and 5 shots when chambered for .56 caliber. It is another sidehammer revolving rifle that resembles the Half Stock model. The barrels are round and part-octagonal where they join the frame. They come in lengths of 21", 24", 27", 31", and 37". The hammer and loading lever are case-colored; the rest of the metal parts, blued. The walnut butt stock and full-length forend are oil finished, and this model has sling swivels. The cylinder is fully fluted. Military models have provisions for affixing a bayonet and military-style sights and bear the "U.S." martial mark on examples that were actually issued to the military. The standard stampings found on this model are "Colt's Pt/1856" and "Address Col. Colt Hartford, Ct. U.S.A." There were an estimated 9,300 manufactured between 1856 and 1864.

### Martially Marked Models

| Exc. | V.G. | Good | Fair | Poor |
|------|------|------|------|------|
| 6000 | 4750 | 3750 | 2500 | 1750 |

### Without Martial Markings

| Exc. | V.G. | Good | Fair | Poor |
|------|------|------|------|------|
| 4500 | 3500 | 2750 | 2000 | 1500 |

### 1855 Full Stock Sporting Rifle
This model is very similar in appearance to the Military model, with these notable exceptions. There is no provision for attaching a bayonet; there are no sling swivels, and it has sporting-style sights. The buttplate is crescent shaped. This model has been noted chambered for .56 caliber in a 5-shot version and chambered for .36, .40, .44, and .50 caliber in the 6-shot variation. They are quite scarce in .40 and .50 caliber and will bring a 10 percent premium. The standard markings are "Colt's Pt/1856" and "Address Col.Colt/Hartford Ct. U.S.A." Produc-

tion on this model was quite limited (several hundred at most) between the years 1856 and 1864.

| Exc. | V.G. | Good | Fair | Poor |
|------|------|------|------|------|
| 4000 | 3000 | 2250 | 1750 | 1250 |

## Model 1855 Revolving Carbine

This Model is very similar in appearance to the 1855 Military Rifle. The barrel lengths of 15", 18" and 21" plus the absence of a forend make the standard Carbine Model readily identifiable. The markings are the same. Approximately 4,400 were manufactured between 1856 and 1864.

| Exc. | V.G. | Good | Fair | Poor |
|------|------|------|------|------|
| 6500 | 5500 | 4000 | 2750 | 1500 |

## Model 1855 Artillery Carbine

Identical to the standard Carbine but chambered for .56 caliber only, it has a 24" barrel, full-length walnut forend, and a bayonet lug.

| Exc. | V.G. | Good | Fair | Poor |
|------|------|------|------|------|
| 7250 | 6500 | 4750 | 3500 | 2250 |

## Model 1855 British Carbine

This is a British-proofed version with barrel lengths of up to 30". It has a brass triggerguard and buttplate and is chambered for .56 caliber only. This variation is usually found in the 10,000-12,000 serial-number range.

| Exc. | V.G. | Good | Fair | Poor |
|------|------|------|------|------|
| 6000 | 5000 | 3500 | 2250 | 1150 |

## Model 1855 Revolving Shotgun

This model very much resembles the Half Stock Sporting Rifle but was made with a 27", 30", 33" and 36" smoothbore barrel. It has a 5-shot cylinder chambered for .60 or .75 caliber (20 or 10 gauge). This Model has a case-colored hammer and loading lever; the rest of the metal is blued, with an occasional browned barrel noted. The buttstock and forend are of walnut, either oil- or varnish-finished. This Model has no rear sight and a small triggerguard with the caliber stamped on it. Some have been noted with the large scroll triggerguard; these would add 10 percent to the value. The rarest shotgun variation would be a full-stocked version in either gauge, and qualified appraisal would be highly recommended. This Model is serial numbered in its own range, #1-1,100. They were manufactured from 1860-1863.

### .60 Caliber (20 gauge)

| Exc. | V.G. | Good | Fair | Poor |
|------|------|------|------|------|
| 4250 | 3500 | 2750 | 2000 | 1200 |

### .75 Caliber (10 gauge)

| Exc. | V.G. | Good | Fair | Poor |
|------|------|------|------|------|
| 4000 | 3250 | 2500 | 1750 | 1500 |

## Model 1861 Single shot Rifled Musket

With the advent of the Civil War, the army of the Union seriously needed military arms. Colt was given a contract to supply 112,500 1861-pattern percussion single-shot muskets. Between 1861 and 1865, 75,000 were delivered. They have 40" rifled barrels chambered for .58 caliber. The musket is equipped with military sights, sling swivels, and a bayonet lug. The metal finish is bright steel, and the stock is oil-finished walnut. Military inspector's marks are found on all major parts. "VP" over an eagle is stamped on the breech along with a date. The Colt address and a date are stamped on the lockplate. Not very many of these muskets survived as after the war 50,000 were purchased surplus by Bannerman's, converted to flintlock, and sent to Africa. Several thousand more were converted to the Snider Pivoting Breech Cartridge system in 1867 and sent to Egypt.

### Production Model

| Exc. | V.G. | Good | Fair | Poor |
|------|------|------|------|------|
| 1500 | 1250 | 1000 | 750 | 450 |

## Model 1860 Army Revolver

This Model was the third most produced of the Colt percussion handguns. It was the primary revolver used by the Union Army during the Civil War. Colt delivered 127,156 of these revolvers to be used during those hostilities. This is a 6-shot .44-caliber percussion revolver. It has either a 7.5" or 8" round barrel with an attached loading lever. The frame, hammer, and loading lever are case-colored; the barrel and cylinder are blued. The triggerguard and front strap are brass, and the backstrap is blued steel. The grips are one-piece walnut. The early models have the barrels stamped "Address Saml. Colt Hartford Ct." Later models are stamped "Address Col. Saml. Colt New-York U.S. America." "Colt's/Patent" is stamped on the left side of the frame; ".44 Cal.," on the triggerguard. The cylinder is roll-engraved with the naval battle scene. There were a total of 200,500 1860 Army Revolvers manufactured between 1860 and 1873.

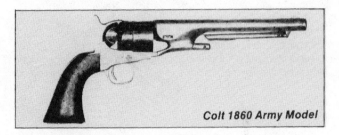

*Colt 1860 Army Model*

### Production Model

| Exc. | V.G. | Good | Fair | Poor |
|------|------|------|------|------|
| 4000 | 3500 | 2750 | 2000 | 1500 |

### Civilian Model

The difference between this variation and the standard Army is the three-screw instead of four-screw frame and the absence of shoulder stock attaching cuts. Civilian models are usually better finished.

| Exc. | V.G. | Good | Fair | Poor |
|------|------|------|------|------|
| 4500 | 4000 | 3250 | 2500 | 1750 |

### Fluted Cylinder Model

Approximately 4,000 Armies were made with full fluted cylinders. They appear in the first 8,000 serial numbers.

| Exc. | V.G. | Good | Fair | Poor |
|------|------|------|------|------|
| 5000 | 4500 | 3500 | 2750 | 2000 |

### Shoulder Stock 2nd Type (Fluted Cylinder Model)

| Exc. | V.G. | Good | Fair | Poor |
|------|------|------|------|------|
| 3500 | 3000 | 2000 | 1500 | 1250 |

### Shoulder Stock 3rd Type (Standard Model)

| Exc. | V.G. | Good | Fair | Poor |
|------|------|------|------|------|
| 2500 | 2000 | 1500 | 1000 | 750 |

## Model 1861 Navy Revolver

This Model is a 6-shot, 7.5" round-barrelled, .36-caliber percussion revolver. The frame, hammer, and attached loading lever are case-colored. The barrel and cylinder are blued. The gripframe and triggerguard are silver-plated brass. The grips are of one-piece walnut. The cylinder has the roll-engraved naval battle scene, and the barrel stamping is "Address Col. Saml. Colt New-York U.S.America." The frame is stamped "Colts/Patent" with "36 Cal." on the triggerguard. There are not many variations within the 1861 Navy model designation, as less than 39,000 were made between 1861 and 1873.

### Production Model

| Exc. | V.G. | Good | Fair | Poor |
|------|------|------|------|------|
| 3500 | 3000 | 2000 | 1250 | 750 |

### Military Model

Marked "U.S." on frame, inspector's cartouche on grip. 650 were marked "U.S.N." on the butt.

| Exc. | V.G. | Good | Fair | Poor |
|------|------|------|------|------|
| 5000 | 4500 | 3500 | 2750 | 2000 |

## Shoulder Stock Model

Only 100 3rd-type stocks were made. They appear between serial #11,000-14,000.

### Revolver

| Exc. | V.G. | Good | Fair | Poor |
|---|---|---|---|---|
| 5500 | 5000 | 4000 | 3250 | 2250 |

### Stock

| Exc. | V.G. | Good | Fair | Poor |
|---|---|---|---|---|
| 3000 | 2500 | 2000 | 1500 | 1250 |

### Fluted Cylinder Model

Approximately the first 100 were made with full fluted cylinders.

| Exc. | V.G. | Good | Fair | Poor |
|---|---|---|---|---|
| 10000 | 8000 | 5500 | 3000 | 2250 |

## Model 1862 Pocket Navy Revolver

This is a smaller, 5-shot, .36-caliber percussion revolver that resembles the configuration of the 1851 Navy. It has a 4.5", 5.5", or 6.5" octagonal barrel with an attached loading lever. The frame, hammer, and loading lever are case-colored; the barrel and cylinder, blued. The grip frame and triggerguard are silver-plated brass; and the one-piece grips, of varnished walnut. The stagecoach holdup scene is roll-engraved on the cylinder. The frame is stamped "Colt's/Patent"; and the barrel, "Address Col. Saml. Colt New-York U.S. America." There were approximately 19,000 manufactured between 1861 and 1873. They are serial numbered in the same range as the Model 1862 Police. Because a great many were used for metallic cartridge conversions, they are quite scarce today.

The London Address Model with blued steel gripframe would be worth approximately twice the value of the standard model.

### Production Model

| Exc. | V.G. | Good | Fair | Poor |
|---|---|---|---|---|
| 3000 | 2500 | 1750 | 1250 | 750 |

## Model 1862 Police Revolver

This is a very slim, attractively designed revolver that some consider to be the most aesthetically pleasing of all the Colt percussion designs. It has a 5-shot, half-fluted cylinder chambered for .36 caliber. It is offered with a 3.5", 4.5", 5.5", or 6.5" round barrel. The frame, hammer, and loading lever are case-colored; the barrel and cylinder, blued. The grip frame is silver-plated brass; and the one-piece grips, varnished walnut. The barrel is stamped "Address Col. Saml Colt New-York U.S. America"; the frame has "Colt's/Patent" on the left side. One of the cylinder flutes is marked "Pat Sept 10th 1850." There were approximately 28,000 of these manufactured between 1861 and 1873. Many were converted to metallic cartridge use, so they are quite scarce on today's market.

The London Model would be worth approximately twice the value of the standard model.

### Production Model

| Exc. | V.G. | Good | Fair | Poor |
|---|---|---|---|---|
| 3000 | 2500 | 1750 | 1250 | 750 |

# METALLIC CARTRIDGE CONVERSIONS

## Thuer Conversion Revolver

Although quite simplistic and not commercially successful, the Thuer Conversion was the first attempt by Colt to convert the percussion revolvers to the new metallic cartridge system. This conversion was designed around the tapered Thuer cartridge and consists of a ring that replaced the back part of the cylinder, which had been milled off. This ring is stamped "Pat.Sep./15.1868." The ejection position is marked with the letter "E." These conversions have rebounding firing pins and are milled to allow loading from the front of the revolver. This conversion was undertaken on the six different models listed below; and all other specifications, finishes, markings, etc., not directly affected by the conversion would be the same as previously described. From a collectible and investment standpoint, the Thuer Conversion is very desirable. Competent appraisal should be secured if acquisition is contemplated.

## Model 1849 Pocket Conversion

| Exc. | V.G. | Good | Fair | Poor |
|---|---|---|---|---|
| 5000 | 4000 | 3000 | 2250 | 1500 |

## Model 1851 Navy Conversion

| Exc. | V.G. | Good | Fair | Poor |
|---|---|---|---|---|
| 4000 | 3000 | 2250 | 1500 | 1250 |

## Model 1860 Army Conversion

| Exc. | V.G. | Good | Fair | Poor |
|---|---|---|---|---|
| 4000 | 3000 | 2250 | 1500 | 1250 |

## Model 1861 Navy Conversion

| Exc. | V.G. | Good | Fair | Poor |
|---|---|---|---|---|
| 5500 | 4500 | 3500 | 2500 | 1750 |

## Models 1862 Police Conversion

| Exc. | V.G. | Good | Fair | Poor |
|---|---|---|---|---|
| 5000 | 4000 | 3000 | 2250 | 1500 |

## Model 1862 Pocket Navy Conversion

| Exc. | V.G. | Good | Fair | Poor |
|---|---|---|---|---|
| 5000 | 4000 | 3000 | 2250 | 1500 |

## Richards Conversion, 1860 Army Revolver

This was Colt's second attempt at metallic cartridge conversion, and it met with quite a bit more success than the first. The Richards Conversion was designed for the .44 Colt cartridge and has a 6-shot cylinder and an integral ejector rod to replace the loading lever which had been removed. The other specifications pertaining to the 1860 Army Revolver remain as previously described if they are not directly altered by the conversion. The Richards Conversion adds a breechplate with a firing pin and its own rear sight. There were approximately 9,000 of these Conversions manufactured between 1873 and 1878.

### Martially Marked Variation

This variation is found with mixed serial numbers and a second set of conversion serial numbers. The "U.S." is stamped on the left side of the barrel lug, and inspectors cartouche appears on the grip.

| Exc. | V.G. | Good | Fair | Poor |
|---|---|---|---|---|
| 3250 | 2750 | 2250 | 1500 | 900 |

### Production Model

| Exc. | V.G. | Good | Fair | Poor |
|---|---|---|---|---|
| 2500 | 2000 | 1500 | 1000 | 750 |

## Richards-Mason Conversion, 1860 Army Revolver

This conversion is different from the Richards Conversion in a number of readily apparent aspects. The barrel was manufactured with a small lug much different in appearance than seen on the standard 1860 Army. The breechplate does not have its own rear sight, and there is a milled area to allow the hammer to contact the base of the cartridge. These Conversions were also chambered for the .44 Colt cartridge, and the cylinder holds 6 shots. There is an integral ejector rod in place of the loading lever. The barrels on some are stamped either "Address Col. Saml. Colt New-York U.S.America" or "Colt's Pt. F.A. Mfg.Co. Hartford,Ct." The patent dates 1871 and 1872 are stamped on the left side of the frame. The finish of these revolvers, as well as the grips, were for the most part the same as on the unconverted Armies; but for the first time, nickel-plated guns are found. There were approximately 2,100 of these Conversions produced in 1877 and 1878.

| Exc. | V.G. | Good | Fair | Poor |
|---|---|---|---|---|
| 2750 | 2250 | 1750 | 1250 | 750 |

## Richards-Mason Conversions 1851 Navy Revolver

These revolvers were converted in the same way as the 1860 Army previously described, the major difference being the caliber .38, either rimfire or centerfire. Finishes are mostly the same as on unconverted revolvers, but nickel-plated guns are not rare.

**Production Model Serial #1-3,800**

| Exc. | V.G. | Good | Fair | Poor |
|------|------|------|------|------|
| 2000 | 1750 | 1250 | 750 | 600 |

**U.S. Navy Model Serial 41,000-91,000 Range**
"USN" stamped on butt; steel grip frame.

| Exc. | V.G. | Good | Fair | Poor |
|------|------|------|------|------|
| 2500 | 2000 | 1500 | 1000 | 750 |

## Richards-Mason Conversion 1861 Navy Revolver

The specifications for this model are the same as for the 1851 Navy Conversion described above, with the base revolver being different. There were 2,200 manufactured in the 1870's.

**Production Model Serial #100-3,300 Range**

| Exc. | V.G. | Good | Fair | Poor |
|------|------|------|------|------|
| 2000 | 1750 | 1250 | 750 | 600 |

**U.S. Navy Model #1,000-9,999 Serial Range**

| Exc. | V.G. | Good | Fair | Poor |
|------|------|------|------|------|
| 2500 | 2000 | 1500 | 1000 | 750 |

## Model 1862 Police and Pocket Navy Conversions

The conversion of these two revolver models is the most difficult to catalogue of all the Colt variations. There were approximately 24,000 of these produced between 1873 and 1880. There are five basic variations with a number of sub-variations. The confusion is usually caused by the different ways in which these were marked. Depending upon what parts were utilized, caliber markings could be particularly confusing. One must also consider the fact that many of these conversion revolvers found their way into secondary markets, such as Mexico and Central and South America, where they were either destroyed or received sufficient abuse to obliterate most identifying markings. The five basic variations are all chambered for either the .38 rimfire or the .38 centerfire cartridge. All held 5 shots, and most were found with the round roll-engraved stagecoach holdup scene. The half-fluted cylinder from the 1862 Police is quite rare on the conversion revolver and not found at all on some of the variations. The finishes on these guns were pretty much the same as they were before conversion, but it is not unusual to find nickel-plated specimens. The basic variations are as follows.

**Round Barrel Pocket Navy with Ejector**

| Exc. | V.G. | Good | Fair | Poor |
|------|------|------|------|------|
| 2500 | 2000 | 1500 | 1000 | 750 |

**3.5" Round Barrel Without Ejector**

| Exc. | V.G. | Good | Fair | Poor |
|------|------|------|------|------|
| 1750 | 1250 | 1000 | 650 | 500 |

**4.5" Octagonal Barrel**

| Exc. | V.G. | Good | Fair | Poor |
|------|------|------|------|------|
| 2000 | 1750 | 1250 | 750 | 600 |

**Standard Configuration 1862 Police and Pocket Navy**
Half-fluted cylinder--Add 20 Percent.

| Exc. | V.G. | Good | Fair | Poor |
|------|------|------|------|------|
| 2000 | 1750 | 1250 | 750 | 600 |

**Round Barrel Model, with Ejector**

| Exc. | V.G. | Good | Fair | Poor |
|------|------|------|------|------|
| 2500 | 2000 | 1500 | 1000 | 750 |

## Model 1871-1872 open Top Revolver

This Model was the first revolver Colt manufactured especially for a metallic cartridge. It was not a conversion. The frame, 7.5" or 8" round barrel, and the 6-shot cylinder were produced for the .44 rimfire metallic cartridge. The gripframe and some internal parts were taken from the 1860 Army and the 1851 Navy. Although this Model was not commercially successful and was not accepted by the U.S. Ordnance Department, it did pave the way for the Single Action Army which came out shortly thereafter and was an immediate success. This Model is all blued, with a case-colored hammer. There are some with silver-plated brass grip frames, but most are blued steel. The one-piece grips are of varnished walnut. The cylinder is roll-engraved with the naval battle scene. The barrel is stamped "Address Col. Saml. Colt New-York U.S. America." The later-production revolvers are barrel stamped "Colt's Pt.F.A.Mfg.Co. Hartford, Ct. U.S.A." The first 1,000 revolvers were stamped "Colt's/Patent." After that, 1871 and 1872 patent dates appeared on the frame. There were 7,000 of these revolvers manufactured in 1872 and 1873.

**1860 Army Gripframe**

| Exc. | V.G. | Good | Fair | Poor |
|------|------|------|------|------|
| 8500 | 7000 | 5500 | 3000 | 1500 |

**1851 Navy Gripframe**

| Exc. | V.G. | Good | Fair | Poor |
|------|------|------|------|------|
| 9000 | 7500 | 6000 | 3500 | 1750 |

# DERRINGERS AND POCKET REVOLVERS

**First Model Derringer**
This is a very small all-metal single shot. It is chambered for the .44 rimfire cartridge. The 2.5" barrel pivots to the left and downward for loading. This model is engraved with a scroll pattern and has been noted blued, silver, or nickel-plated. The barrel is stamped "Colt's Pt.F.A. Mfg.Co/Hartford Ct. U.S.A/ No.1." ".41 Cal." is stamped on the frame under the release catch. There were approximately 6,500 of this Model manufactured from 1870-1890. It was the first single-shot pistol Colt produced.

| Exc. | V.G. | Good | Fair | Poor |
|------|------|------|------|------|
| 1000 | 750 | 600 | 400 | 250 |

**Second Model Derringer**
Although this Model has the same odd shape as the First Model, it is readily identifiable by the checkered varnished walnut grips and the "No 2" on the barrel after the address. It is also .41 rimfire and has a 2.5" barrel that pivots in the same manner as the First Model. There were approximately 9,000 of these manufactured between 1870 and 1890.

| Exc. | V.G. | Good | Fair | Poor |
|------|------|------|------|------|
| 750 | 500 | 450 | 300 | 150 |

**Third Model Derringer**
This Model was designed by Alexander Thuer who was also responsible for Colt's first metallic cartridge conversion. It is often referred to as the "Thuer Model" for this reason. It is also chambered for the .41 rimfire cartridge and has a 2.5" barrel that pivots to the right (but not down) for loading. The Third Model has a more balanced appearance than its predecessors, and its commercial success (45,000 produced between 1875 and 1910) reflects this. The barrel on this Model is stamped "colt" in very small block letters on the first 2,000 guns. The remainder of the production features the "COLT" in large italicized print. The ".41 Cal." is stamped on the left side of the frame. This Model will be found with the barrel blued or plated in either silver or nickel and the bronze frame plated. The grips are varnished walnut.

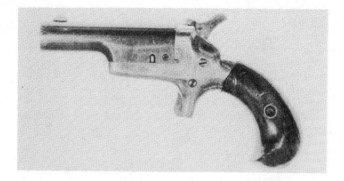

### First Variation, Early Production

This has a raised area on the underside of the frame through which the barrel screw passes, and the spur is not angled. Small block "colt" lettering on barrel.

| Exc. | V.G. | Good | Fair | Poor |
|------|------|------|------|------|
| 2000 | 1750 | 1250 | 750  | 500  |

### First Variation, Late Production

This is similar to Early Production but has large italicized "COLT" on barrel.

| Exc. | V.G. | Good | Fair | Poor |
|------|------|------|------|------|
| 1250 | 850  | 650  | 450  | 250  |

### Production Model

| Exc. | V.G. | Good | Fair | Poor |
|------|------|------|------|------|
| 600  | 500  | 400  | 300  | 200  |

### House Model Revolver

There are two basic versions of this model. They are both chambered for the .41 rimfire cartridge. The 4-shot version is known as the "Cloverleaf" due to the shape of the cylinder when viewed from the front. Approximately 7,500 of the nearly 10,000 House revolvers were of this 4-shot configuration. They are offered with a 1.5" or 3" barrel. The 1.5" length is quite rare, and some octagonal barrels in this length have been noted. The 5-shot round-cylinder version accounts for the rest of the production. It is found with serial numbers over 6,100 and is offered with a 2-7/8" length barrel only. This Model is stamped on the top strap "Pat. Sept.19, 1871." This Model has brass frames that were sometimes nickel-plated. The barrels are found either blued or plated. The grips are varnished walnut or rosewood. There were slightly fewer than 10,000 of both variations manufactured from 1871-1876.

### Cloverleaf with 1.5" Barrel

| Exc. | V.G. | Good | Fair | Poor |
|------|------|------|------|------|
| 1000 | 800  | 650  | 500  | 350  |

### Cloverleaf with 3" Barrel

| Exc. | V.G. | Good | Fair | Poor |
|------|------|------|------|------|
| 850  | 700  | 500  | 400  | 250  |

### House Pistol with 5-Shot Round Cylinder

| Exc. | V.G. | Good | Fair | Poor |
|------|------|------|------|------|
| 1150 | 1000 | 750  | 600  | 450  |

### Open Top Pocket Revolver

This is a .22-caliber rimfire, 7-shot revolver that was offered with either a 2-3/8" or a 2-7/8" barrel. The model was a commercial success, with over 114,000 manufactured between 1871 and 1877. There would undoubtedly have been a great deal more sold had not the cheap copies begun to flood the market at that time, forcing Colt to drop this model from the line. This revolver has a silver or nickel-plated brass frame and a nickel-plated or blued barrel and cylinder. The grips are varnished walnut. The cylinder bolt slots are found toward the front on this model. "Colt's Pt.F.A.Mfg. Co./Hartford, Ct.U.S.A." is stamped on the barrel and ".22 Cal." on the left side of the frame.

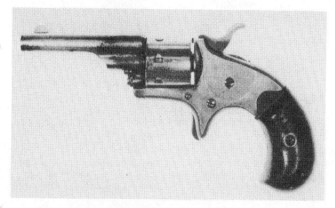

### Early Model With Ejector Rod

| Exc. | V.G. | Good | Fair | Poor |
|------|------|------|------|------|
| 650  | 550  | 450  | 300  | 175  |

### Production Model Without Ejector Rod

| Exc. | V.G. | Good | Fair | Poor |
|------|------|------|------|------|
| 500  | 400  | 350  | 250  | 125  |

### New Line Revolver .22

This was the smallest framed version of the five distinct New Line Revolvers. It has a 7-shot cylinder and a 2.25" octagonal barrel. The frame is nickel-plated, and the balance of the revolver is either nickel-plated or blued. The grips are of rosewood. There were approximately 55,000 of these made from 1873-1877. Colt also stopped production of the New Lines rather than try to compete with the "Suicide Specials." "Colt New .22" is found on the barrel; and ".22 Cal.," on the frame. The barrel is also stamped "Colt's Pt.F.A.Mfg.Co./Hartford, Ct. U.S.A."

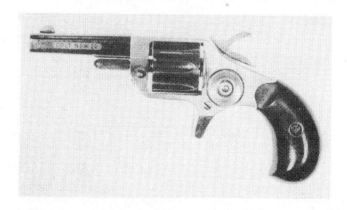

### 1st Model

Short cylinder flutes.

| Exc. | V.G. | Good | Fair | Poor |
|------|------|------|------|------|
| 550  | 450  | 400  | 350  | 200  |

## 2nd Model
Long cylinder flutes.

| Exc. | V.G. | Good | Fair | Poor |
|------|------|------|------|------|
| 500 | 400 | 350 | 250 | 125 |

## New Line Revolver .30
This is a larger version of the .22 New Line. The basic difference is the size, caliber, caliber markings, and the offering of a blued version with case-colored frame. There were approximately 11,000 manufactured from 1874-1876.

| Exc. | V.G. | Good | Fair | Poor |
|------|------|------|------|------|
| 600 | 500 | 400 | 300 | 250 |

## New Line Revolver .32
This is the same basic revolver as the .30 caliber except that it is chambered for the .32-caliber rimfire and .32-caliber centerfire and is so marked. There were 22,000 of this model manufactured from 1873-1884. This model was offered with the very rare 4" barrel, and this variation would be worth nearly twice the value of a standard model.

| Exc. | V.G. | Good | Fair | Poor |
|------|------|------|------|------|
| 500 | 400 | 300 | 250 | 200 |

## New Line Revolver .38
There were approximately 5,500 of this model manufactured between 1874 and 1880. It is chambered for either the .38 rimfire or .38 centerfire caliber and is so marked. This model in a 4" barrel would also bring twice the value.

| Exc. | V.G. | Good | Fair | Poor |
|------|------|------|------|------|
| 600 | 500 | 400 | 300 | 250 |

## New Line Revolver .41
This is the "Big Colt," as it was sometimes known in advertising of its era. It is chambered for the .41 rimfire and the .41 centerfire and is so marked. The large caliber of this variation makes this the most desirable of the New Lines to collectors. There were approximately 7,000 of this model manufactured from 1874-1879. A 4"-barrelled version would again be worth a 100 percent premium.

| Exc. | V.G. | Good | Fair | Poor |
|------|------|------|------|------|
| 600 | 500 | 400 | 300 | 250 |

## New House Model Revolver
This Revolver is similar to the other New Lines except that it features a square butt instead of the birdshead configuration, a 2.25" round barrel without ejector rod, and a thin loading gate. It is chambered for the .32 (rare), .38, and the .41 centerfire cartridges. The finish was either full nickel-plated or blued, with a case-colored frame. The grips are walnut, rosewood or (for the first time on a Colt revolver) checkered hard rubber, with an oval around the word "Colt." The barrel address is the same as on the other New Lines. The frame is marked "New House," with the caliber. There were approximately 4,000 manufactured between 1880-1886.
.32 Caliber Model Would Bring a 10 Percent Premium.

| Exc. | V.G. | Good | Fair | Poor |
|------|------|------|------|------|
| 1000 | 800 | 650 | 450 | 300 |

## New Police Revolver
This was the final revolver in the New Line series. It is chambered for .32, .38, and .41 centerfire caliber. The .32 and .41 are quite rare. It is offered in barrel lengths of 2.25", 4.5", 5.5", and 6.5". An ejector rod is found on all but the 2.5" barrel. The finish is either nickel or blued and case-colored. The grips are hard rubber with a scene of a policeman arresting a criminal embossed on them; thusly the model became known to collectors as the "Cop and Thug" model. The barrel stamping is as the other New Lines, and the frame is stamped "New Police .38." There were approximately 4,000 of these manufactured between 1882-1886.

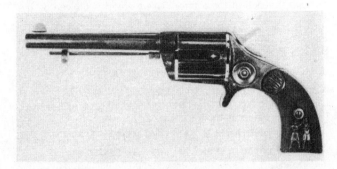

The .32 and .41 Caliber Versions of This Model Will Bring a 40-50 Percent Premium.

| Exc. | V.G. | Good | Fair | Poor |
|------|------|------|------|------|
| 1000 | 800 | 650 | 450 | 300 |

# COLT'S SINGLE ACTION ARMY REVOLVER

The Colt Single Action Army, or Peacemaker as it is sometimes referred to, is one of the most widely collected and recognized firearms in the world. With few interruptions or changes in design, it has been manufactured from 1873 until the present. It is still available on a limited production basis from the Colt Custom Shop. The variations in this model are myriad. It has been produced in 30 different calibers and barrel lengths from 2.5" to 16", with 4.75", 5.5", and 7.5" standard. The standard finish is blued, with a case-colored frame. Many are nickel-plated. Examples have been found silver- and gold-plated, with combinations thereof. The finest engravers in the world have used the SAA as a canvas to display their artistry. The standard grips from 1873-1883 were walnut, either oil-stained or varnished.

From 1883 to approximately 1897, the standard grips were hard rubber with eagle and shield. After this date, at serial number 165,000, the hard rubber grips featured the Rampant Colt. Many special-order grips were available, notably pearl and ivory, which were often checkered or carved in ornate fashion. The variables involved in establishing values on this model are extreme. Added to this, one must also consider historical significance, since the SAA played a big part in the formative years of the American West. Fortunately for those among us interested in the SAA, there are a number of fine publications available dealing exclusively with this model. It is my strongest recommendation that they be acquired and studied thoroughly to prevent extremely expensive mistakes. The Colt factory records are nearly complete for this model, and research should be done before acquisition of rare or valuable specimens.

For our purposes we will break down the Single Action Army production as follows:

Antique or Black Powder, 1873-1898, serial #1-175,000
The cylinder axis pin is retained by a screw in the front of the frame.

Pre-War, 1899-1940, serial #175,001-357,859
The cylinder axis pin is retained by a spring-loaded button through the side of the frame. This method is utilized on the following models, as well.

Post-War 2nd Generation, 1956-1978, serial #0001SA-99,999SA

3rd Generation, 1978-Present, serial SA1,001-

A breakdown of production by caliber will follow the chapter. It is important to note that the rarer calibers and the larger calibers bring higher values in this variation.

## ANTIQUE SINGLE ACTION ARMY REVOLVER
### 1st Year Production "Pinched Frame" 1873 Only
It is necessary to categorize this variation on its own. This is one of the rarest and most interesting of all the SAA's--not to mention that it is the first. On this model the top strap is pinched or constricted approximately one half inch up from the hammer to form the rear sight. The highest surviving serial number having this feature is #156, the lowest #1. From these numbers, it is safe to assume that the first run of SAA's were all pinched-frame models; but there is no way to tell how many there were, since Colt did not serial number the frames in the order that they were manufactured. An educated guess would be that there were between 50 and 150 pinched frame guns in all and that they were all made before mid-July 1873. The reason for the change came about on the recommendation of Capt. J. R. Edie, a government inspector who thought that the full fluted top strap would be a big improvement in the sighting capabilities of the weapon. The barrel length of the first model is 7.5"; the standard caliber, .45 Colt; and the proper grips were of walnut. The front sight blade is German silver. Needless to say, this model will rarely be encountered; and if it is, it should never be purchased without competent appraisal.

| Exc. | V.G. | Good | Fair | Poor |
|------|------|------|------|------|
| 15000 | 11000 | 7500 | 5000 | 4000 |

### Early Military Model 1873-1877
The serial number range on this first run of military contract revolvers extends to #24,000. The barrel address is in the early script style with the # symbol preceding and following. The frame bears the martial marking "US," and the walnut grips have the inspector's cartouche stamped on them. The front sight is steel as on all military models; the barrel length, 7.5". The caliber is .45 Colt, and the ejector rod head is the bullseye or donut style with a hole in the center of it. The finish features the military polish and case-colored frame, with the remainder blued. Authenticate any potential purchase; many spurious examples have been noted.

| Exc. | V.G. | Good | Fair | Poor |
|------|------|------|------|------|
| 10000 | 7500 | 6000 | 3750 | 2250 |

### Early Civilian Model 1873-1877
This Model is identical to the Early Military Model but has no military acceptance markings or cartouches. Some could have the German silver front sight blade. The early bullseye ejector rod head is used on this Model. The Civilian Model has a higher degree of polish than is found on the military models, and the finish on these early models could be plated or blued with a case-colored frame. The grips are standard one-piece walnut. Ivory-grip models are worth a premium.

| Exc. | V.G. | Good | Fair | Poor |
|------|------|------|------|------|
| 8500 | 6000 | 4000 | 2500 | 1750 |

### .44 Rimfire Model 1875-1880
This Model was made to fire the .44 Henry Rimfire Cartridge. It was to be used as a compatible companion sidearm to the Henry and Winchester 1866 rifles that were used extensively during this era. However, this was not the case; and the .44 Rimfire was doomed to economic failure as soon as it appeared on the market. By that time, it had already been established that large-caliber centerfire cartridges were a good deal more efficient than their rimfire counterparts. The large-caliber rimfires were deemed obsolete before this Colt ever hit the market. The result of this was that Colt's sales representatives sold most of the production to obscure Banana Republics in South and Central America, where this model received much abuse.

Most had the original 7.5" barrels cut down; and nearly all were denied even the most basic maintenance, making the survival rate of this Model quite low. All this adds to its desirability as a collector's item and makes the risk of acquiring a fake that much greater. This Model is unique in that it was the only SAA variation to have its own serial-number range, starting with #1 and continuing to #1892, the latest known surviving specimen. The block style barrel markings were introduced during this production run. At least 90 of these revolvers were converted by the factory to .22 rimfire, and one was shipped chambered for .32 rimfire.

| Exc. | V.G. | Good | Fair | Poor |
|------|------|------|------|------|
| 10000 | 7500 | 6000 | 3750 | 2250 |

### Late Military Model 1878-1891
The later Military Models are serial numbered to approximately #136,000. They bear the block-style barrel address without the # prefix and suffix. The frames are marked "US," and the grips have the inspector's cartouche. The finish is the military-style polish, case-colored frame; and the remainder, blued. Grips are oil-stained walnut. On the military-marked Colts, it is imperative that potential purchases be authenticated as many fakes have been noted.

| Exc. | V.G. | Good | Fair | Poor |
|------|------|------|------|------|
| 5000 | 4000 | 3000 | 2250 | 1500 |

### Artillery Model 1895-1903
A number of "US" marked SAA's were returned either to the Colt factory or to the Springfield Armory, where they were altered and refinished. These revolvers have 5.5" barrels and any combination of mixed serial numbers. They were remarked by the inspectors of the era and have a case-colored frame and a blued cylinder and barrel. Some have been noted all blued within this variation. This Model, as with the other military-marked Colts, should definitely be authenticated before purchase. Some of these revolvers fall outside the 1898 antique cutoff date that has been established by the Government and, in our experience, are not quite as desirable to investors. They are generally worth approximately 20 percent less.

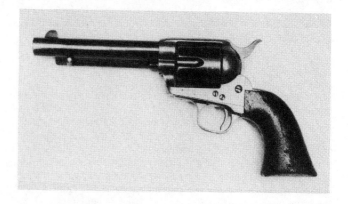

| Exc. | V.G. | Good | Fair | Poor |
|------|------|------|------|------|
| 3000 | 2500 | 2250 | 1750 | 1250 |

### London Model
These SAA's were manufactured to be sold through Colt's London Agency. The barrel is stamped "Colt's Pt.F.A. Mfg. Co.

Hartford, Ct. U.S.A. Depot 14 Pall Mall London." This model is available in various barrel lengths. They are generally chambered for .45 Colt, .450 Boxer, .450 Eley, .455 Eley, and rarely .476 Eley, the largest of the SAA chamberings. A good many of these London Models were cased and embellished, and they should be individually appraised. This Model should be authenticated as many spurious examples have been noted.

| Exc. | V.G. | Good | Fair | Poor |
|---|---|---|---|---|
| 3000 | 2500 | 2250 | 1750 | 1250 |

## Frontier Six-Shooter 1878-1882
Several thousand SAA's were made with the legend "Colt's Frontier Six Shooter" acid-etched into the left side of the barrel instead of being stamped. This etching is not very deep, and today collectors will become ecstatic if they discover a specimen with mere vestiges of the etched panel remaining. These acid-etched SAA's are serial-numbered #45,000-65,000. They have various barrel lengths and finishes, but all are chambered for the .44-40 caliber.

| Exc. | V.G. | Good | Fair | Poor |
|---|---|---|---|---|
| 9000 | 7500 | 5000 | 2500 | 1500 |

## Sheriff's or Storekeeper's Model 1882-1898
This Model was manufactured with a short barrel (2.5"-4.75"). Most have 4" barrels. It features no ejector rod or housing, and the frame is made without the hole in the right forward section to accommodate the ejector assembly. The Sheriff's or Storekeeper's Model is numbered above serial #73,000. It was manufactured with various finishes and chambered for numerous calibers. This Model continued after 1898 into the smokeless or modern era. Examples manufactured in the pre-war years are worth approximately 20 percent less. Although faking this Model is quite difficult, it has been successfully attempted.

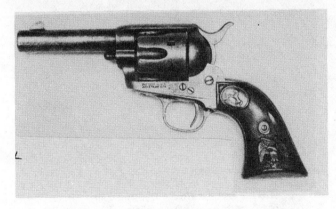

| Exc. | V.G. | Good | Fair | Poor |
|---|---|---|---|---|
| 12500 | 10000 | 7500 | 4500 | 2500 |

## Flattop Target Model 1888-1896
This Model is highly regarded and sought after by collectors. It is not only rare (only 925 manufactured) but is an extremely attractive and well finished variation. It is chambered for 22 different calibers from .22 rimfire to .476 Eley. The .22 rimfire, .38 Colt, .41 and .45 Colt are the most predominant chamberings. The 7.5" barrel length is the most commonly encountered. The serial-number range is between #127,000-162,000. Some have been noted in higher ranges. The finish is all blued, with a case-colored hammer. The checkered grips are either hard rubber or walnut. The most readily identifying feature of the flattop is the lack of a groove in the top strap and the sight blade dovetailed into the flattop. The front sight has a removable blade insert. The values given are for a standard production model chambered for the calibers previously mentioned as being the most common. It is important to have other calibers individually appraised as variance in values can be quite extreme.

| Exc. | V.G. | Good | Fair | Poor |
|---|---|---|---|---|
| 15000 | 12500 | 8500 | 5000 | 3750 |

## Bisley Model 1894-1915
This Model was named for the target range in Great Britain, where their National Target Matches were held since the nineteenth century. The Model was designed as a target revolver with an odd humped-back grip that was supposed to better fill the hand while target shooting. It is also easily identified by the wide low profile hammer spur, the wide trigger, and the name "Bisley" stamped on the barrel. The Bisley production fell within the serial-number range #165,000-331,916. There were 44,350 made. It was offered in 16 different chamberings from .32 Colt to .455 Eley. The most common calibers were .32-20, .38-40, .41, .44-40, and .45 Colt.

The barrel lengths are 4.75", 5.5", and 7.5". The frame and hammer are case-colored; the remainder, blued. Smokeless powder models produced after 1899 utilized the push-button cylinder pin retainer. The grips are checkered hard rubber. This Model was actually designed with English sales in mind; and though it did sell well over there, American sales accounted for most of the Bisley production. The values we provide here cover the standard calibers and barrel lengths. Rare calibers and/or other notable variations can bring greatly fluctuating values, and qualified appraisals should be secured in such cases.

Bisleys manufactured from 1898-1915 are worth approximately 20 percent less.

| Exc. | V.G. | Good | Fair | Poor |
|---|---|---|---|---|
| 3500 | 3000 | 2000 | 1250 | 750 |

## Bisley Model Flattop Target 1894-1913
This Model is quite similar to the Standard Bisley Model, with the flattop frame and dovetailed rear sight feature. It also has the removable front sight insert. It has an all-blued finish with case-colored hammer only and is available with a 7.5" barrel. Smokeless powder models produced after 1899 utilized the push-button cylinder pin retainer. The calibers are the same as the standard Bisley. Colt manufactured 976 of these revolvers. The advice regarding appraisal would also apply.

| Exc. | V.G. | Good | Fair | Poor |
|---|---|---|---|---|
| 8000 | 7000 | 4500 | 2500 | 1750 |

## Standard Civilian Production Models 1876-1898
This final designated category for the black powder or antique SAA's includes all the revolvers not previously categorized. They have barrel lengths from 4.75", 5.5", and 7.5" and are chambered for any one of 30 different calibers. The finishes could be blued, blued and case-colored, or plated in nickel, silver, gold, or combinations thereof. Grips could be walnut, hard rubber,

ivory, pearl, stag, or bone. The possibilities are endless. The values given here are for the basic model, and we again strongly advise securing qualified appraisal when not completely sure of any model variation.

| Exc. | V.G. | Good | Fair | Poor |
|------|------|------|------|------|
| 7500 | 5500 | 3500 | 2000 | 1000 |

At this time it is important to note that the Colt's Single Action Army Revolvers we have discussed to this point are in the antique category as established by our Federal Government. The arbitrary cutoff date of 1898 has been established, and any weapon made prior to this date is considered an antique and, as such, not subject to the restraints placed on collectors and dealers by the Gun Control Act of 1968. This is important because firearms falling into this category will usually bring higher values due to the demand by pure investors who do not relish paperwork on collectible investments. There will be those who disagree with on me this line of reasoning, but my experience tells me that it is correct.

# PRE-WAR SINGLE ACTION ARMY REVOLVER 1899-1940

### Standard Production Pre-War Models
The 1899 cutoff has been thoroughly discussed, but it is interesting to note that the actual beginning production date for smokeless models was 1900. The Pre-War Colts are, all in all, quite similar to the antiques--the finishes, barrel lengths, grips, etc. Calibers are also similar, with the exception of the obsolete ones being dropped and new discoveries added. The most apparent physical difference between the smokeless powder and black powder models is the previously discussed method of retaining the cylinder axis pin. The pre-war Colts utilized the spring-loaded button through the side of the frame. The black powder models utilized a screw in the front of the frame. The values we furnish for this model designation are for these standard models only. The serial-number range on the Pre-War SAA's is 175,001- 357,859. Note that any variation can have marked effects on value fluctuations, and qualified appraisal should be secured.

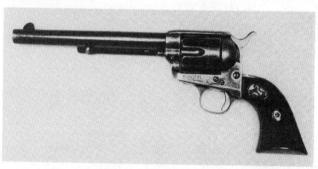

| Exc. | V.G. | Good | Fair | Poor |
|------|------|------|------|------|
| 5000 | 4000 | 3000 | 2000 | 1000 |

### Long Fluted Cylinder Model 1913-1915
Strange as it may seem, the Colt Company has an apparent credo they followed to never throw anything away. That credo was never more evident than with this Model. These Long Flute Cylinders were actually left over from the Model 1878 Double Action Army Revolvers. Someone in the hierarchy at Colt must have had an inspiration that drove the gunsmiths on the payroll slightly mad: to make these cylinders fit the SAA frames. There were 1,478 of these Long Flutes manufactured. They are chambered for the .45 Colt, .38-40, .32-20, .41 Colt, and the .44 Smith & Wesson Special. They were offered in the three standard barrel lengths and were especially well polished, having what has been described as Colt's "Fire Blue" on the barrel and cylinder. The frame and hammer are case-colored. They are fitted with checkered hard rubber grips and are particularly fine examples of Colt's craft.

| Exc. | V.G. | Good | Fair | Poor |
|------|------|------|------|------|
| 6000 | 4500 | 3500 | 2500 | 1500 |

# POST WAR SINGLE ACTION ARMY REVOLVER

### Standard Post-War Model 1956-1975
In 1956 the shooting and gun-collecting fraternity succeeded in convincing Colt that there was a market for a re-introduced SAA. The revolver was brought back in the same external configuration. The only changes were internal. The basic specifications as to barrel length and finish availability were the same. The calibers available were .38 Special, .357 Magnum, .44 Special, and .45 Colt.

The serial-number range of the re-introduced 2nd Generation, as it is sometimes known, Colt is #0001SA-73,000SA. Values for the standard post-war Colts are established by four basic factors: caliber (popularity and scarcity), barrel length, finish, and condition. Shorter barrel lengths are generally more desirable than the 7.5". The .38 Special is the rarest caliber, but the .45 Colt and .44 Special are more sought after than the .357 Magnum. Special feature revolvers, such as the 350 factory-engraved guns produced during this period, must be individually appraised. The ivory situation in the world today has become quite a factor, as ivory grips are found on many SAA's. We will attempt to take these factors into consideration and evaluate this variation as accurately and clearly as possible. Remember as always, when in doubt secure a qualified appraisal.
4.75" Barrel--Add 25 Percent.
5.5" Barrel--Add 15 Percent.
Nickel Finish--Add 20 Percent.
Ivory Grips--Add $250.

**Values for 7.5" Barrel Model**

.38 Special
| NIB | Exc. | V.G. | Good | Fair | Poor |
|-----|------|------|------|------|------|
| 1500 | 950 | 750 | 550 | 450 | 350 |

.357 Magnum
| NIB | Exc. | V.G. | Good | Fair | Poor |
|-----|------|------|------|------|------|
| 1000 | 750 | 650 | 500 | 400 | 300 |

.44 Special
| NIB | Exc. | V.G. | Good | Fair | Poor |
|-----|------|------|------|------|------|
| 1250 | 900 | 700 | 525 | 425 | 325 |

.45 Colt
| NIB | Exc. | V.G. | Good | Fair | Poor |
|-----|------|------|------|------|------|
| 1250 | 900 | 700 | 525 | 425 | 325 |

### Sheriff's Model 1960-1975
Between 1960 and 1975, there were approximately 500 Sheriff's Models manufactured. They have 3" barrels and no ejector rod assemblies. The frames were made without the hole for the ejector rod to pass through. They were blued, with case-colored frames; 25 revolvers were nickel-plated and would bring a sizeable premium if authenticated. The barrels are marked "Colt Sheriff's Model." The serial number has a "SM" suffix. They are chambered for the .45 Colt cartridge.
Nickel Finish--Add 20 Percent.

| NIB | Exc. | V.G. | Good | Fair | Poor |
|-----|------|------|------|------|------|
| 1500 | 1200 | 1000 | 750 | 600 | 500 |

### Buntline Special 1957-1975

The "Buntline Special" was named after a dime novelist named Ned Buntline, who supposedly gave this special long barrel revolver to Wyatt Earp. The story is suspected to be purely legend as no Colt records exist to lend it credence. Be that as it may, the Colt factory decided to take advantage of the market and produced the 12" barrelled SAA from 1957-1974. There were approximately 3,900 manufactured. They are chambered for the .45 Colt cartridge and are offered in the blued and case-colored finish. Only 65 Buntlines are nickel-plated, making this an extremely rare variation that definitely should be authenticated before purchase. Walnut grips are the most commonly noted, but they are also offered with the checkered hard rubber grips. The barrels are marked on the left side "Colt Buntline Special .45."

Nickel Finish--Add 60 Percent.

| NIB | Exc. | V.G. | Good | Fair | Poor |
|-----|------|------|------|------|------|
| 1000 | 800 | 650 | 550 | 400 | 350 |

### New Frontier 1961-1975

The New Frontier is readily identified by its flattop frame and adjustable sight. It also has a very high front sight. Colt manufactured approximately 4,200 of them. They are chambered for the .357 Magnum, .45 Colt, .44 Special (255 produced), and rarely (only 49 produced) in .38 Special. The 7.5" barrel length is by far the most common, but the 4.75" and 5.5" barrels are also offered. The standard finish is case-colored and blue. Nickel plating and full blue are offered but are rarely encountered. Standard grips are walnut. The barrel is stamped on the left side "Colt New Frontier S.A.A." The serial has the "NF" suffix.

4.75" Barrel--Add 25 Percent.
5.5" Barrel--Add 20 Percent.
Full Blue--Add 50 Percent.
.38 Special--Add 50 Percent.
.44 Special--Add 30 Percent.

| NIB | Exc. | V.G. | Good | Fair | Poor |
|-----|------|------|------|------|------|
| 750 | 650 | 500 | 450 | 400 | 300 |

### New Frontier Buntline Special 1962-1967

This model is very rare, as Colt only manufactured 70 during this five-year period. They are similar to the standard Buntline, with a 12" barrel. They are chambered for .45 Colt only.

| NIB | Exc. | V.G. | Good | Fair | Poor |
|-----|------|------|------|------|------|
| 1500 | 1200 | 1000 | 750 | 600 | 500 |

# THIRD GENERATION SINGLE ACTION ARMY 1976-1981

In 1976 Colt made some internal changes in the SAA. The external configuration was not altered. The serial-number range began in 1976 with #80,000SA, and in 1978 #99,999SA was reached. At this time the suffix became a prefix, and the new serial range began with #SA01001. This model's value is determined in much the same manner as was described in the section on the 2nd Generation SAA's. Caliber, barrel length, finish, and condition are once again the four main determining factors.

The prevalence of special-order guns was greater during this period, and many more factory-engraved SAA's were produced. Colt's Custom Shop was quite active during this period. We feel that it is not advisable to undertake evaluation of specially embellished guns and strongly advise that competent appraisal be secured on any firearms that deviate from the standard. There are, quite frankly, too many fraudulent Colt SAA's out there; and the financial risks are great.

4.75" Barrel--Add 25 Percent.
5.5" Barrel--Add 10 Percent.
Nickel Plated--Add 10 Percent.
Ivory Grips--Add $250.

### Values with 7.5" Barrel

.357 Magnum

| NIB | Exc. | V.G. | Good | Fair | Poor |
|-----|------|------|------|------|------|
| 800 | 600 | 550 | 450 | 350 | 300 |

.44-40

| NIB | Exc. | V.G. | Good | Fair | Poor |
|-----|------|------|------|------|------|
| 1000 | 750 | 650 | 550 | 450 | 400 |

.44-40 Black Powder Frame (Screw Retaining Cylinder Pin)

| NIB | Exc. | V.G. | Good | Fair | Poor |
|-----|------|------|------|------|------|
| 1250 | 1000 | 800 | 650 | 550 | 450 |

.44 Special

| NIB | Exc. | V.G. | Good | Fair | Poor |
|-----|------|------|------|------|------|
| 850 | 650 | 600 | 500 | 400 | 350 |

.45 Colt

| NIB | Exc. | V.G. | Good | Fair | Poor |
|-----|------|------|------|------|------|
| 850 | 650 | 600 | 500 | 400 | 350 |

### Sheriff's Model 3rd Generation

This Model is very similar to the 2nd Generation Sheriff's Model. The serial number and the fact that this Model is also chambered for the .44-40 are the only external differences. Colt offered this Model with interchangeable cylinders--.45 Colt/.45 ACP or .44-40/.44 Special--available in 3" barrel, blued and case-colored finish standard.

Interchangeable Cylinders--Add 30 Percent.
Nickel Finish--Add 10 Percent.
Ivory Grips--Add $250.

| NIB | Exc. | V.G. | Good | Fair | Poor |
|-----|------|------|------|------|------|
| 850 | 700 | 650 | 550 | 450 | 400 |

### Buntline Special 3rd Generation

This is the same basic configuration as the 2nd Generation with the 12" barrel. Standard finish blued and case-colored, it is chambered for .45 Colt and has checkered hard rubber grips.

Nickel Finish--Add 10 Percent.

| NIB | Exc. | V.G. | Good | Fair | Poor |
|-----|------|------|------|------|------|
| 850 | 700 | 600 | 500 | 400 | 350 |

### New Frontier 3rd Generation

This model is very similar in appearance to the 2nd Generation guns. The 3rd Generation New Frontiers have five-digit serial numbers; the 2nd Generation guns, four-digit numbers. That and the calibers offered are basically the only differences. The 3rd Generations are chambered for the .44 Special and .45 Colt and are rarely found in .44-40. Barrel lengths are 7.5" standard, with the 4.75" and 5.5" rarely encountered.

.44-40--Add 20 Percent.
4.75" Barrel--Add 35 Percent.
5.5" Barrel--Add 25 Percent.

| NIB | Exc. | V.G. | Good | Fair | Poor |
|-----|------|------|------|------|------|
| 650 | 550 | 450 | 400 | 300 | 250 |

## CURRENT PRODUCTION SINGLE ACTION ARMY 1982-PRESENT

### Standard Single Action Army

The SAA, it is sad to note, has all but faded from the firearms picture. They are currently available as a special-order custom shop proposition. The cost is great; and the availability, low. The heyday of one of the most venerable firearms of them all is pretty much at an end. The current SAA's are available in only .44-40, .44 Special, and .45 Colt. Barrels are available in 3" through 10" lengths. The finishes are nickel-plated and blued, with case-colored frames. A number of optional finishes are available on request. Grips are available on a custom-order basis. This model is available on special-order only.

The minimum order that the Colt custom shop will accept is $1,095 at retail, so anyone desiring to own a new Colt SAA must order options, as the base price of a new gun won't be acceptable.

Nickel Finish--Add $125.
Royal Blue Finish--Add $200.
Mirror Brite Finish--Add $225.
Gold Plate--Add $365.
Silver Plate--Add $365.
Class A Engraving--Add $875.
Class B Engraving--Add $1,200.
Class C Engraving--Add $1,500.
Class D Engraving--Add $1,750.
Buntline Engraving-- Add 15 Percent.

| NIB | Exc. | V.G. | Good | Fair | Poor |
|---|---|---|---|---|---|
| 1150 | 1000 | 600 | 450 | 400 | 300 |

## SCOUT MODEL SINGLE ACTION ARMY

### New Frontier Scout 1958-1972

This is a scaled-down version of the SAA that is chambered for the .22 l.r. with an interchangeable .22 Magnum cylinder. It is offered with a 4.25", 4.75", or a 9.5" barrel. The frame is alloy; and the finish, either blued or nickel-plated. The grips are hard rubber.

**Colt New Frontier 22**

9.5" Buntline--Add 50 Percent.
Extra Cylinder--Add 10 Percent.
Nickel Plated--Add 10 Percent.

| NIB | Exc. | V.G. | Good | Fair | Poor |
|---|---|---|---|---|---|
| 300 | 250 | 200 | 175 | 125 | 90 |

### Colt Single Action Army Production Breakdown by Caliber Antique and Pre-War

| CALIBER | SAA | FLATTOP SAA | BISLEY | FLATTOP BISLEY |
|---|---|---|---|---|
| .22 R.F. | 107 | 93 | 0 | 0 |
| .32 R.F. | 1 | 0 | 0 | 0 |
| .32 Colt | 192 | 24 | 160 | 44 |
| .32 S&W | 32 | 30 | 18 | 17 |
| .32-44 | 2 | 9 | 14 | 17 |
| .32-20 | 29,812 | 30 | 13,291 | 131 |
| .38 Colt (1914) | 1,011 | 122 | 412 | 96 |
| .38 Colt (1922) | 1,365 | 0 | 0 | 0 |
| .38 S&W | 9 | 39 | 10 | 5 |
| .38 Colt Sp. | 82 | 7 | 0 | 0 |
| .38 S&W Sp. | 25 | 0 | 2 | 0 |
| .38-44 | 2 | 11 | 6 | 47 |
| .357 Mag. | 525 | 0 | 0 | 0 |
| .380 Eley | 1 | 3 | 0 | 0 |
| .38-40 | 38,240 | 19 | 12,163 | 98 |
| .41 | 16,402 | 91 | 3,159 | 24 |
| .44 SmBr. | 15 | 0 | 1 | 0 |
| .44 R.F. | 1,863 | 0 | 0 | 0 |
| .44 Germ. | 59 | 0 | 0 | 0 |
| .44 Russ. | 154 | 51 | 90 | 62 |
| .44 S&W | 24 | 51 | 29 | 64 |
| .44 S&W Sp. | 506 | 1 | 0 | 0 |
| .44-40 | 64,489 | 21 | 6,803 | 78 |
| .45 Colt | 150,683 | 100 | 8,005 | 97 |
| .45 SmBr. | 4 | 0 | 2 | 0 |
| .45 ACP | 44 | 0 | 0 | 0 |
| .450 Boxer | 729 | 89 | 0 | 0 |
| .450 Eley | 2,697 | 84 | 5 | 0 |
| .455 Eley | 1,150 | 37 | 180 | 196 |
| .476 Eley | 161 | 2 | 0 | 0 |
| **Total** | **310,386** | **914** | **44,350** | **976** |

The above chart covers the production by caliber of the Single Action Army Revolvers manufactured between 1873 and 1940. These are the antique and the prewar forearms. This chart readily informs us as to which are the rare calibers.

## Peacemaker Scout 1970-1977
This model is quite similar to the New Frontier Scout, with a steel case-colored frame. The barrel lengths offered are 4.75", 6", or 7.5". It also has an interchangeable .22 Magnum cylinder.

Colt Peacemaker 22

| NIB | Exc. | V.G. | Good | Fair | Poor |
|---|---|---|---|---|---|
| 325 | 275 | 225 | 200 | 150 | 100 |

## Scout Model SAA
This is basically a scaled-down version of the SAA chambered for the .22 l.r. cartridge. This Model is offered with a 4.75", 6", or 7" barrel. The earlier production has case-colored frames with the remainder blued; later production is all blued. Grips are checkered hard rubber. This Model was discontinued in 1986.

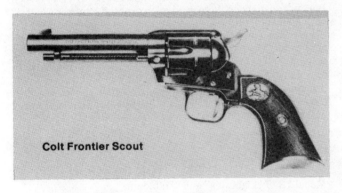
Colt Frontier Scout

| NIB | Exc. | V.G. | Good | Fair | Poor |
|---|---|---|---|---|---|
| 250 | 200 | 175 | 150 | 100 | 75 |

Anyone wishing to procure a factory letter authenticating a Single Action Army should do so by writing to: COLT HISTORIAN, P.O. BOX 1868, HARTFORD, CT 06101. There is a charge of $35 per serial number for this service. If Colt cannot provide the desired information, $10 will be refunded. Enclose the Colt model name, serial number, and your name and address, along with the check.

# COLT ANTIQUE LONG ARMS

## Berdan Single Shot Rifle
This is a very scarce rifle on today's market. There were approximately 30,200 manufactured, but nearly 30,000 of them were sent to Russia. This Rifle was produced from 1866-1870. It is a trapdoor-type action chambered for .42 centerfire. The standard model has a 32.5" barrel; the carbine, 18.25". The finish is blued, with a walnut stock. This rifle was designed and the patent held by Hiram Berdan, Commander of the Civil War "Sharpshooters" Regiment. This was actually Colt's first cartridge arm. The 30,000 rifles and 25 half-stocked carbines that were sent to Russia were in Russian Cyrillic letters. The few examples made for American sales have Colt's name and Hartford address on the barrel.

### Rifle Russian Order, 30,000 Manufactured
| Exc. | V.G. | Good | Fair | Poor |
|---|---|---|---|---|
| 1500 | 1250 | 1000 | 650 | 450 |

### Carbine Russian Order, 25 Manufactured
| Exc. | V.G. | Good | Fair | Poor |
|---|---|---|---|---|
| 4500 | 3750 | 3000 | 2000 | 1500 |

### Rifle U.S. Sales, 100 Manufactured
| Exc. | V.G. | Good | Fair | Poor |
|---|---|---|---|---|
| 2750 | 2000 | 1750 | 1250 | 1000 |

### Carbine U.S. Sales, 25 Manufactured
| Exc. | V.G. | Good | Fair | Poor |
|---|---|---|---|---|
| 5000 | 4000 | 3500 | 2500 | 2000 |

## Colt-Franklin Military Rifle
This is a rifle that was not a successful venture for Colt. The patents were held by William B. Franklin, a vice president of the company. This was a bolt-action rifle with a primitive, gravity-fed box magazine. It is chambered for the .45-70 Government cartridge, has a 32.5" barrel, and is blued, with a walnut stock. The rifle has the Colt Hartford barrel address and is stamped with an eagle's head and U.S. inspector's marks. There were only 50 of these rifles produced, and it is believed that they were prototypes intended for Government sales. This was not to be, and production ceased after approximately 50 were manufactured in 1887 and 1888.

| Exc. | V.G. | Good | Fair | Poor |
|---|---|---|---|---|
| 4500 | 3750 | 3000 | 2000 | 1500 |

## Colt-Burgess Lever Action Rifle
This represented Colt's only attempt to compete with Winchester for the lever-action rifle market. It is said that when Winchester started to produce revolving handguns for prospective marketing, Colt dropped the Burgess from their line. This Rifle is chambered for .44-40. It has a 25.5" barrel and a 15-shot tubular magazine. The Carbine version has a 20.5" barrel and 12-shot magazine. The finish is blued, with a case-colored hammer and lever. The stock is walnut with an oil finish. The Colt Hartford address is on the barrel, and "Burgess Patents" is stamped on the bottom of the lever. There were 3,775 rifles manufactured--1,219 with round barrels and 2,556 with octagonal barrels. There were also 2,593 Carbines. The Burgess was produced from 1883-1885.

### Rifle, Octagonal Barrel
| Exc. | V.G. | Good | Fair | Poor |
|---|---|---|---|---|
| 1750 | 1400 | 1000 | 750 | 550 |

### Rifle, Round Barrel
| Exc. | V.G. | Good | Fair | Poor |
|---|---|---|---|---|
| 2000 | 1650 | 1250 | 950 | 750 |

### Carbine
| Exc. | V.G. | Good | Fair | Poor |
|---|---|---|---|---|
| 2250 | 1850 | 1500 | 1250 | 950 |

### Baby Carbine, Lighter Frame and Barrel (RARE)
| Exc. | V.G. | Good | Fair | Poor |
|---|---|---|---|---|
| 2750 | 2000 | 1750 | 1500 | 1150 |

## Lightning Slide Action, Medium Frame
This was the first slide-action rifle Colt produced. It is chambered for .32-20, .38-40, and .44-40 and was intended to be a companion piece to the SAA's in the same calibers. The rifle has a 26" barrel with 15-shot tube magazine; the carbine, a 20" barrel with 12-shot magazine. The finish is blued, with case-colored hammer; the walnut stock is oil-finished; and the forend, usually checkered. The Colt name and Hartford address are stamped on the barrel along with the patent dates. There were approximately 89,777 manufactured between 1884 and 1902.

### Rifle

| Exc. | V.G. | Good | Fair | Poor |
|------|------|------|------|------|
| 1500 | 1250 | 950 | 650 | 400 |

### Carbine

| Exc. | V.G. | Good | Fair | Poor |
|------|------|------|------|------|
| 2000 | 1500 | 1250 | 800 | 500 |

### Military Rifle or Carbine

.44-40 caliber, short magazine tube, bayonet lug, and sling swivels.

| Exc. | V.G. | Good | Fair | Poor |
|------|------|------|------|------|
| 4500 | 3500 | 2750 | 2000 | 1500 |

### Baby Carbine, 1 lb., Lighter Version of Standard Carbine

| Exc. | V.G. | Good | Fair | Poor |
|------|------|------|------|------|
| 4500 | 3500 | 2750 | 2000 | 1500 |

### San Francisco Police Rifle

.44-40 caliber, SFP 1-SFP401 on bottom tang.

| Exc. | V.G. | Good | Fair | Poor |
|------|------|------|------|------|
| 2000 | 1500 | 1250 | 800 | 500 |

### Lightning Slide Action Small Frame

This is a very well-made rifle and the first of its type that Colt manufactured. It is chambered for the .22 Short and Long. The standard barrel length is 24"; the finish, blued with a case-colored hammer. The stock is walnut; some were checkered; some, not. The barrel is stamped with the Colt name and Hartford address and the patent dates. There were 89,912 manufactured between 1887 and 1904.

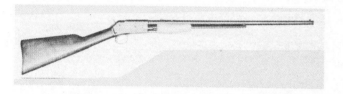

| Exc. | V.G. | Good | Fair | Poor |
|------|------|------|------|------|
| 1000 | 850 | 700 | 500 | 300 |

### Lightning Slide Action, Large Frame

This rifle is similar in appearance to the Medium Frame Lightning, though larger in size. It is chambered in larger rifle calibers of the era, from .38-56 up to .50-95 Express. The larger calibers are more desirable from a collector's standpoint. The rifle has a 28" barrel; the carbine, a 22" barrel. The finish is blued, with a case-colored hammer. The stock is oiled walnut; the forend, checkered. The Colt name and Hartford address are stamped on the barrel along with the patent dates. This rifle is quite large and has come to be known as the "Express Model." Colt manufactured 6,496 between 1887 and 1894.

### Rifle, 28" Octagonal Barrel

| Exc. | V.G. | Good | Fair | Poor |
|------|------|------|------|------|
| 2500 | 2000 | 1500 | 750 | 500 |

### Rifle, 28" Round Barrel

| Exc. | V.G. | Good | Fair | Poor |
|------|------|------|------|------|
| 2750 | 2250 | 1750 | 1000 | 600 |

### Carbine, 22" Barrel

| Exc. | V.G. | Good | Fair | Poor |
|------|------|------|------|------|
| 3500 | 3000 | 2250 | 1500 | 750 |

### Baby Carbine, 22" Barrel 1lb. Lighter

| Exc. | V.G. | Good | Fair | Poor |
|------|------|------|------|------|
| 8500 | 7500 | 6000 | 3000 | 1750 |

### Model 1878 Double Barrel Shotgun

This Model is chambered in 10 or 12 gauge and has 28", 30", or 32" barrels. It is a sidelock double-trigger hammer gun with case-colored locks and breech. The barrels are browned damacus-patterned. The checkered walnut stock is varnished or oil-finished. The Colt's Hartford address is stamped on the barrel rib; and Colt's name, on the lock. This has been regarded as one of the finest shotguns made in America, although Colt had difficulty competing with the less expensive European imports of the day. They ceased production after only 22,690 were manufactured between 1878 and 1889.

Fully Engraved Model--Add 80 Percent.

| Exc. | V.G. | Good | Fair | Poor |
|------|------|------|------|------|
| 3500 | 3000 | 2250 | 1250 | 650 |

### Model 1883 Double Barrel Shotgun

This Model is a hammerless boxlock, chambered for 10 or 12 gauge. The barrels are 28", 30", or 32"; and it features double triggers. The frame and furniture are case-colored; the barrels, browned with damascus pattern. The checkered walnut stock is varnished or oil-finished. Colt's Hartford address is stamped on the barrel rib. "Colt" is stamped on each side of the frame. Again, as in the Model 1878, this is rated as one of the finest of all American-made shotguns. There were many special orders, and they require individual appraisal. Colt manufactured 7,366 of these guns between 1883 and 1895.

Fully Engraved Model--Add 80 Percent.

| Exc. | V.G. | Good | Fair | Poor |
|------|------|------|------|------|
| 3800 | 3250 | 2500 | 1500 | 750 |

### Double Barrel Rifle

This is one of the rarest of all Colt firearms and is a prize for the Colt collector. There were only 35 of these guns manufactured. They were said to be the special interest of Caldwell Hart Colt, Samuel Colt's son, who was an avid arms collector. It is said that most of the 35 guns produced wound up in his collection or those of his friends. This gun is chambered for .45-70 or one of the larger variations thereof. It is an exposed hammer sidelock with double triggers. The locks, breech, and furniture are case-colored; the barrels, browned or blued. The barrels are 28" in length, and the checkered stock was oil-finished or varnished walnut. The barrel rib is stamped with the Colt name and Hartford address. The locks are also stamped "Colt." One must exercise extreme caution in dealing with this model as there have been Model 1878 Shotguns converted into double rifles. Colt manufactured the 35 guns over the period 1879-1885.

| Exc. | V.G. | Good | Fair | Poor |
|------|------|------|------|------|
| 15000 | 12500 | 8500 | 6500 | 5000 |

## COLT DOUBLE ACTION REVOLVERS

### Model 1877 "Lightning" and "Thunderer"

The Model 1877 was Colt's first attempt at manufacturing a double-action revolver. It shows a striking resemblance to the Single Action Army. Sales on this model were brisk, with over 166,000 produced between 1877 and 1909. In actuality this was an action that had inherent weaknesses and was quite prone to malfunction. It is chambered for two different cartridges. In .38 Colt, it is known as the "Lightning"; and in .41 Colt, as the "Thunderer." The standard finishes are blued, with case-colored frame and nickel plate. The birdshead grips are of checkered rosewood on the early guns and hard rubber on the majority of the production run.

The barrel lengths most often encountered are 2.5" and 3.5" without an ejector rod, and 4.5" and 6" with the rod. Other barrel lengths from 1.5" through 10" were offered. The Model 1877 holds 6 shots in either caliber. There were quite a few different variations found within this model designation. Values furnished are for the standard variations. Antiques made before 1898 would be more desirable from an investment standpoint.

.41 Caliber "Thunderer"--Add 10 Percent.
Over 7" Barrel--Add 10 Percent.
London Barrel Address--Add 20 Percent.
.32 Caliber--Add 25 Percent.
Rosewood Grips--Add 10 Percent.

**Without Ejector, 2.5" and 3.5" Barrel**

| Exc. | V.G. | Good | Fair | Poor |
|------|------|------|------|------|
| 1500 | 1200 | 750  | 500  | 350  |

**With Ejector, 4.5" and 6" Barrel**

| Exc. | V.G. | Good | Fair | Poor |
|------|------|------|------|------|
| 1750 | 1500 | 1000 | 750  | 450  |

## Model 1878 "Frontier"

This Model is a large and somewhat ungainly looking revolver. It has a solid frame with a removable triggerguard. The cylinder does not swing out, and there is a thin loading gate. It has birdshead grips made of checkered hard rubber; walnut would be found on the early models. The finish is either blued and case-colored or nickel-plated. The Model 1878 holds 6 shots, and the standard barrel lengths are 4.75", 5.5", and 7.5" with an ejector assembly and 3", 3.5", and 4" without. The standard chamberings for the Model 1878 are .32-20, 38-40, .41 Colt, .44-40, and .45 Colt. This Model was fairly well received because it is chambered for the large calibers that were popular in that era. Colt manufactured 51,210 between 1878 and 1905. Antique models made before 1898 would be more desirable from an investment standpoint.

### Model 1878 "Frontier" Standard

| Exc. | V.G. | Good | Fair | Poor |
|------|------|------|------|------|
| 1500 | 1200 | 750  | 500  | 350  |

## Model 1902

This is a U.S. Ordnance contract Model 1878. It has a 6" barrel and is chambered for .45 Colt. The finish is blued, and there is a lanyard swivel on the butt. This Model bears the U.S. inspector's marks. It is sometimes referred to as the Philippine or the Alaskan model. The triggerguard is quite a bit larger than standard.

| Exc. | V.G. | Good | Fair | Poor |
|------|------|------|------|------|
| 1750 | 1500 | 1000 | 700  | 500  |

## Model 1889 Navy

The 1889 Navy is a very important model from a historical standpoint as it was the first double-action revolver Colt manufactured with a swingout cylinder. They produced 31,000 of them between 1889 and 1894. The Model 1889 is chambered for the .38 Colt and the .41 Colt cartridges. The cylinder holds 6 shots. It is offered with a 3", 4.5", or 6" barrel; and the finish was either blued or nickel-plated. The grips are checkerd hard rubber with the "Rampant Colt" in an oval molded into them. The patent dates 1884 and 1888 appear in the barrel marking, and the serial numbers are stamped on the butt.

3" Barrel--Add 20 Percent.

| Exc. | V.G. | Good | Fair | Poor |
|------|------|------|------|------|
| 950  | 750  | 650  | 450  | 200  |

### U.S. Navy Model

This variation has a 6" barrel, is chambered for .38 Colt, and is offered in blued finish only. "U.S.N." is stamped on the butt. Most of the Navy models were altered at the Colt factory to add the Model 1895 improvements. An original unaltered specimen would be worth as much as 50 percent premium over the altered values shown.

| Exc. | V.G. | Good | Fair | Poor |
|------|------|------|------|------|
| 1000 | 800  | 700  | 500  | 250  |

## Model 1892 "New Army and Navy"

This Model is very similar in appearance to the 1889 Navy. The main differences are improvements to the lockwork function. It has double bolt stop notches, a double cylinder locking bolt, and shorter flutes on the cylinder. The .38 Smith & Wesson and the .32-20 were added to the .38 Colt and .41 Colt chamberings. The checkered hard rubber grips are standard, with plain walnut grips found on some contract series guns. Barrel lengths and finishes are the same as described for the Model 1889. The patent dates 1895 and 1901 appear stamped on later models. Colt manufactured 291,000 of these revolvers between 1892 and 1907. Antiques before 1898 are more desirable from an investment standpoint.

3" Barrel--Add 20 Percent.

| Exc. | V.G. | Good | Fair | Poor |
|------|------|------|------|------|
| 400  | 350  | 300  | 200  | 100  |

### U.S. Navy Model

| Exc. | V.G. | Good | Fair | Poor |
|------|------|------|------|------|
| 550  | 450  | 400  | 300  | 200  |

### U.S. Army Model

| Exc. | V.G. | Good | Fair | Poor |
|------|------|------|------|------|
| 500  | 400  | 350  | 250  | 150  |

## Model 1905 Marine Corps

This Model is a variation of the New Army and Navy Model. It was derived from the late production with its own serial range #10,001-10,926. With only 926 produced between 1905 and 1909, it is quite rare on today's market and is eagerly sought after by Colt Double Action collectors. This Model is chambered for the .38 Colt and the .38 Smith & Wesson Special cartridges. It holds 6 shots, has a 6" barrel, and is offered in a blued finish only. The grips are checkered walnut and are quite different than those found on previous models. "U.S.M.C." is stamped on the butt; patent dates of 1884, 1888, and 1895 are stamped on the barrel. One hundred twenty-five of these revolvers were earmarked for civilian sales and do not have the Marine Corps markings; these will generally be found in better condition. Values are very similar.

| Exc. | V.G. | Good | Fair | Poor |
|------|------|------|------|------|
| 750  | 650  | 500  | 350  | 200  |

## New Service Model

This Model was in continual production from 1898 through 1944. It is chambered for 11 different calibers--.38 Special, .357 Magnum, .38-40, .44 Russian, .44 Special, .44-40, .45ACP, .45 Colt, .450 Eley, .455 Eley, and .476 Eley. It is offered in barrel lengths from 2" to 7.5", either blued or nickel-plated. Checkered hard rubber grips were standard until 1928, and then checkered walnut grips were used with an inletted Colt medallion. This was the largest swingout cylinder double-action revolver that Colt ever produced, and approximately 356,000 were manufactured over the 46 years they were made. There are many different variations of this revolver, and one should consult a book dealing strictly with Colt for a thorough breakdown and description.

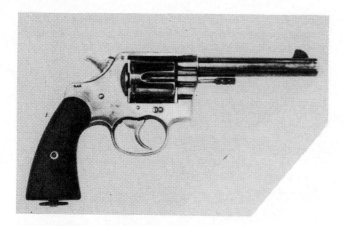

## Early Model, #1-12,000

| Exc. | V.G. | Good | Fair | Poor |
|------|------|------|------|------|
| 850 | 750 | 600 | 350 | 250 |

## Early Model Target, #6,000-15,000
Checkered walnut grips, flattop frame, 7.5" barrel.

| Exc. | V.G. | Good | Fair | Poor |
|------|------|------|------|------|
| 900 | 800 | 650 | 400 | 300 |

## Improved Model, #21,000-32,500
Has internal locking improvements.

| Exc. | V.G. | Good | Fair | Poor |
|------|------|------|------|------|
| 600 | 500 | 400 | 300 | 200 |

## Improved Target Model, #21,000-32,500

| Exc. | V.G. | Good | Fair | Poor |
|------|------|------|------|------|
| 750 | 650 | 500 | 350 | 250 |

## U.S. Army Model 1909, #30,000-50,000
5.5" barrel, .45 Colt, walnut grips, "U.S. Army Model 1909" on butt.

| Exc. | V.G. | Good | Fair | Poor |
|------|------|------|------|------|
| 600 | 500 | 400 | 300 | 200 |

## U.S. Navy Model 1909, #30,000-50,000
Same as above with "U.S.N." on butt.

| Exc. | V.G. | Good | Fair | Poor |
|------|------|------|------|------|
| 850 | 750 | 600 | 350 | 250 |

## U.S. Marine Corps Model 1909, 30,000-50,000
Checkered walnut rips, "U.S.M.C." on butt.

| Exc. | V.G. | Good | Fair | Poor |
|------|------|------|------|------|
| 1500 | 1200 | 800 | 650 | 450 |

## U.S. Army Model 1917, #150,000-301,000
Smooth walnut grips, 5.5" barrel, .45ACP and .45 Colt, model designation stamped on butt.

| Exc. | V.G. | Good | Fair | Poor |
|------|------|------|------|------|
| 550 | 450 | 400 | 300 | 225 |

## Model 1917 Civilian, #335,000-336,000
Approximately 1,000 made in .45ACP only from Army parts over-run. No military markings.

| Exc. | V.G. | Good | Fair | Poor |
|------|------|------|------|------|
| 900 | 800 | 650 | 400 | 300 |

## Late Model New Service, #325,000-356,000
Checkered walnut grips and internal improvements.

| Exc. | V.G. | Good | Fair | Poor |
|------|------|------|------|------|
| 600 | 500 | 400 | 300 | 200 |

## Shooting Master, #333,000-350,000
Round butt, checkered walnut grips with Colt medallion, 6" barrel, "Colt Shooting Master" on barrel, flattop frame with target sights.

| Exc. | V.G. | Good | Fair | Poor |
|------|------|------|------|------|
| 900 | 800 | 650 | 400 | 300 |

## Magnum Model New Service, Over #340,000
.357 Magnum, .38 Special.

| Exc. | V.G. | Good | Fair | Poor |
|------|------|------|------|------|
| 500 | 400 | 350 | 250 | 200 |

## New Pocket Model
This was the first swingout-cylinder, double-action pocket revolver made by Colt. It is chambered for .32 Colt and .32 Smith & Wesson. It holds 6 shots and is offered with barrel lengths of 2.5", 3.5", 5", and 6". The finish is blued or nickel-plated, and the grips are checkered hard rubber with the oval Colt molded into them. "Colt's New Pocket" is stamped on the frame. 1884 and 1888 patent dates are stamped on the barrel of later-production guns. There were approximately 30,000 of these manufactured between 1893 and 1905. Antiques made before 1898 are more desirable.
Early Production without Patent Dates--Add 25 Percent.
5" Barrel--Add 10 Percent.

| Exc. | V.G. | Good | Fair | Poor |
|------|------|------|------|------|
| 400 | 350 | 300 | 250 | 150 |

## Pocket Positive
Externally this is the same revolver as the New Pocket, but it has the positive lock feature. It was manufactured between 1905 and 1940.

| Exc. | V.G. | Good | Fair | Poor |
|------|------|------|------|------|
| 400 | 375 | 275 | 225 | 125 |

## New Police Model
This Model appears very similar to the New Pocket Model. The frame is stamped "New Police." It is chambered for the .32 Colt, .32 Colt New Police, and .32 Smith & Wesson cartridges. The barrel lengths are 2.5", 4", and 6". The finishes are blued or nickel-plated. Colt manufactured 49,5000 of this Model from 1896-1907. The New York City Police Department purchased 4,500 of these revolvers, and the backstraps are so marked. There was also a target model of this revolver, which

features a 6" barrel with a flattop frame and target sights, of which 5,000 were produced.
New York Police Marked--Add 10 Percent.
Target Model--Add 20 Percent.

| Exc. | V.G. | Good | Fair | Poor |
|------|------|------|------|------|
| 300 | 250 | 200 | 150 | 100 |

## Police Positive

This is externally the same as the New Police with the addition of the positive lock feature and two new chamberings--the .38 New Police and the .38 Smith & Wesson. They were manufactured from 1905-1947.

| Exc. | V.G. | Good | Fair | Poor |
|------|------|------|------|------|
| 350 | 300 | 250 | 200 | 150 |

## Police Positive Target

This is basically the same as the New Police Target with the positive lock feature. It is chambered in .22 l.r., as well as the other cartridges offered in the earlier model.

| Exc. | V.G. | Good | Fair | Poor |
|------|------|------|------|------|
| 550 | 500 | 400 | 300 | 200 |

## Police Positive Special

This model is very similar to the Police Positive but has a slightly larger frame to accept the longer cylinder needed to chamber more powerful cartridges such as the .38 Special, in addition to the original chamberings. They were manufactured from 1907-1973.

| Exc. | V.G. | Good | Fair | Poor |
|------|------|------|------|------|
| 300 | 275 | 225 | 150 | 100 |

## Army Special Model

This is a heavier-framed improved version of the New Army and Navy revolver. It is chambered for the .32-20, .38 Colt, .38 Smith & Wesson, and .41 Colt. It is offered with a 4", 4.5", 5", and 6" barrel. The finish is blue or nickel-plated, and the grips are checkered hard rubber. The serial-number range is #291,000-540,000, and they were manufactured between 1908-1927.

| Exc. | V.G. | Good | Fair | Poor |
|------|------|------|------|------|
| 350 | 300 | 250 | 200 | 150 |

## Officer's Model Target 1st Issue

This revolver is chambered for the .38 Special cartridge. It has a 6" barrel and is blued. It has a flattop frame with adjustable target sights. Colt manufactured this Model from 1904-1908.

| Exc. | V.G. | Good | Fair | Poor |
|------|------|------|------|------|
| 550 | 450 | 350 | 300 | 200 |

## Officer's Model Target 2nd Issue

This Model is very similar to the 1st Issue but is offered in .22 l.r. and .32 Police Positive caliber, as well as in .38 Special. It also is furnished with a 4", 4.5", 5", 6", and 7.5" barrel in .38 Special only. It has checkered walnut grips. Colt manufactured this Model between 1908 and 1940.

| Exc. | V.G. | Good | Fair | Poor |
|------|------|------|------|------|
| 500 | 400 | 300 | 250 | 150 |

## Camp Perry Single Shot

This model was created by modifying an Officer's Model frame to accept a special flat single-shot "cylinder." This flat chamber pivots to the left side and downward for loading. The pistol is chambered for .22 l.r. and is offered with an 8" or 10" barrel. The finish is blued, with checkered walnut grips. The name "Camp Perry Model" is stamped on the left side of the chamber; the caliber is on the barrel. Colt named this model after the site of the U.S. Target competition held annually at Camp Perry, Ohio. They manufactured 2,525 of these between 1920 and 1941.

| Exc. | V.G. | Good | Fair | Poor |
|------|------|------|------|------|
| 1250 | 1000 | 750 | 500 | 350 |

## Official Police

This was a very popular revolver in the Colt line for many years. It was manufactured from 1927 to 1969. It is chambered for .32-20 and .41 Colt. These calibers were discontinued in 1942 and 1930, respectively. The .38 Special was chambered throughout the entire production run, and .22 l.r. was added in 1930. This model holds 6 shots, has a square butt, and is offered with 2", 4", 5", and 6" barrel lengths. The grips are checkered walnut. The finish is either blued or nickel-plated.
Nickel-plated--Add 10 Percent.
.22 l.r.--Add 20 Percent.

| Exc. | V.G. | Good | Fair | Poor |
|------|------|------|------|------|
| 350 | 300 | 250 | 200 | 150 |

## Commando Model

This Model, for all intents and purposes, is an Official Police chambered for .38 Special, with a 2", 4", or 6" barrel. This Model is parkerized and stamped "Colt Commando" on the barrel. There were approximately 50,000 manufactured between 1942-1945 for use in WWII.

| Exc. | V.G. | Good | Fair | Poor |
|------|------|------|------|------|
| 300 | 275 | 225 | 150 | 100 |

## Marshall Model

This is an Official Police that is marked "Colt Marshall" on the barrel and has an "M" suffix in the serial number. It has a 2" or 4" barrel and a round butt. The finish is blued. There were approximately 2,500 manufactured between 1954 and 1956.

| Exc. | V.G. | Good | Fair | Poor |
|------|------|------|------|------|
| 500 | 400 | 300 | 250 | 150 |

## Bankers Special

The Bankers Special is a 2"-barrelled, easily concealed revolver. It was designed with bank employees in mind. It is chambered for .38 Special and was offered in blued finish. The grips are rounded but full-sized, and Colt utilized this feature in advertising this model. The U.S. Postal Service equipped its railway mail clerks with this model. There were approximately 35,000 manufactured between 1926 and 1943.

| Exc. | V.G. | Good | Fair | Poor |
|------|------|------|------|------|
| 500 | 400 | 300 | 250 | 150 |

## Detective Special 1st Issue

This model is actually a duplication, as it is nothing more than a Police Positive Special with a 2" barrel standard. It was originally chambered for .32 New Police, .38 New Police, (which were discontinued) and .38 Special, which continued until the end of the production run. The finish is blued, and it is offered with wood or plastic grips. There were over 400,000 manufactured between 1926 and 1972.

| Exc. | V.G. | Good | Fair | Poor |
|------|------|------|------|------|
| 375 | 300 | 250 | 175 | 100 |

## Detective Special 2nd Issue

This is basically a modernized, streamlined version of the 1st issue. It is very similar except that it has a 2" or 3" barrel with a shrouded ejector rod and wraparound checkered walnut grips and is chambered for .38 Special. It was finished in blue or nickel plate.

| Exc. | V.G. | Good | Fair | Poor |
|------|------|------|------|------|
| 350 | 275 | 225 | 150 | 100 |

## Cobra 1st Issue

The Cobra is simply an alloy-framed lightweight version of the Detective Special. It weighs only 15 ounces. The Cobra is chambered for .32, .38 Special, and .22 l.r. This model is available in either a round-butt or square-butt version with a 4" barrel only. They were manufactured between 1950 and 1973.

| Exc. | V.G. | Good | Fair | Poor |
|------|------|------|------|------|
| 350 | 275 | 225 | 150 | 100 |

## Cobra 2nd Issue

The same as the 1st Issue in .38 Special only, this is streamlined with wraparound walnut grips and shrouded ejector rod.

| Exc. | V.G. | Good | Fair | Poor |
|------|------|------|------|------|
| 300 | 250 | 200 | 125 | 100 |

## Agent 1st Issue

This revolver is basically the same as the 1st Issue Cobra with a shortened grip frame. This was done to make the Agent more concealable. Colt manufactured the Agent 1st Issue from 1955-1973.

| Exc. | V.G. | Good | Fair | Poor |
|------|------|------|------|------|
| 300 | 250 | 200 | 125 | 100 |

## Agent L.W. 2nd Issue

This is a streamlined version with the shrouded ejector rod. In the last four years of its production, it was matte finished. Colt manufactured this model between 1973 and 1986.

| Exc. | V.G. | Good | Fair | Poor |
|------|------|------|------|------|
| 250 | 200 | 175 | 125 | 100 |

## Border Patrol

This model is quite rare, as Colt manufactured only 400 of them in 1952. It is basically a Police Special with a heavy 4" barrel. It is chambered for .38 Special and was built to be very strong. The finish is blued and serial numbered in the 610,000 range.

| Exc. | V.G. | Good | Fair | Poor |
|------|------|------|------|------|
| 750 | 650 | 500 | 400 | 250 |

## Aircrewman Special

This model was especially fabricated for the Air Force to be carried by their pilots for protection. It is extremely lightweight at 11 ounces. The frame and the cylinder are made of aluminum alloy. It has a 2" barrel and is chambered for .38 Special. The finish was blued, with checkered walnut grips. There were approximately 1,200 manufactured in 1951, and they are marked "U.S." or "A.F."

| Exc. | V.G. | Good | Fair | Poor |
|------|------|------|------|------|
| 800 | 700 | 550 | 450 | 300 |

## Courier

This is another version of the Cobra. It features a shorter gripframe and a 03" barrel. This model is chambered for .32 and .22 rimfire. There were approximately 3,000 manufactured in 1955 and 1956.

.22 Rimfire--Add 20 Percent.

| Exc. | V.G. | Good | Fair | Poor |
|------|------|------|------|------|
| 850 | 750 | 600 | 500 | 350 |

## Trooper

This model was designed specifically by Colt to fill the need for a large, heavy-duty, powerful revolver that was accurate. The Trooper filled that need. It was offered with a 4" or 6" barrel and blued or nickel finishes with checkered walnut grips. The Trooper is chambered for .38 Special/.357 Magnum, and there is a .22 rimfire version for the target shooters. This model was manufactured between 1953 and 1969.

| Exc. | V.G. | Good | Fair | Poor |
|------|------|------|------|------|
| 300 | 250 | 200 | 150 | 100 |

## Colt .357 Magnum

This is a deluxe version of the Trooper. It is offered with a special target wide hammer and large target-type grips. The sights are the Accro target model. It features a 4" or 6" barrel and a blued finish and was manufactured between 1953 and 1961. There were less than 15,000 produced.

| Exc. | V.G. | Good | Fair | Poor |
|------|------|------|------|------|
| 400 | 350 | 300 | 200 | 150 |

## Diamondback

This model is a medium-frame, duty-type weapon suitable for target work. It has the short frame of the Detective Special with the ventilated-rib 2.5", 4", or 6" barrel. It is chambered for .38 Special and .22 rimfire for the target shooters. The finish is blued or nickel-plated, with checkered walnut grips. The Diamondback features adjustable target sights, wide target hammer, and a steel frame. It was manufactured between 1966 and 1986.
Nickel Finish--Add 15 Percent.

| NIB | Exc. | V.G. | Good | Fair | Poor |
|-----|------|------|------|------|------|
| 400 | 375 | 300 | 250 | 200 | 150 |

## Viper

This is an alloy-framed revolver chambered for the .38 Special. It has a 4" barrel and was manufactured between 1977 and 1984. The Viper is essentially a lightweight version of the Police Positive.

Colt Viper

| NIB | Exc. | V.G. | Good | Fair | Poor |
|-----|------|------|------|------|------|
| 275 | 225 | 200 | 175 | 125 | 100 |

## Python

The Python is the Cadillac of the Colt double-action line. It has been manufactured since 1955 and is still the flagship of the Colt line. It is chambered for the .357 Magnum cartridge, holds 6 shots, and has been offered in barrel lengths of 2.5", 3", 4", 6", and 8". This revolver is offered finished in high polished Colt Royal Blue, nickel plate, matte-finish stainless steel, or what is known as "The Ultimate"--a high polished stainless steel. The 3" barrel, as well as the nickel plating, has been discontinued. The grips are checkered walnut. It is possible that the nickel-

plated specimens may bring a 10 percent premium. In my experience this is not always the case as many potential purchasers have a definite preference for the blued finish.

| NIB | Exc. | V.G. | Good | Fair | Poor |
|-----|------|------|------|------|------|
| 750 | 550 | 450 | 350 | 275 | 225 |

### Matte Stainless Steel

| NIB | Exc. | V.G. | Good | Fair | Poor |
|-----|------|------|------|------|------|
| 825 | 650 | 550 | 450 | 350 | 275 |

### "The Ultimate"

| NIB | Exc. | V.G. | Good | Fair | Poor |
|-----|------|------|------|------|------|
| 875 | 675 | 575 | 475 | 375 | 300 |

## Python .38 Special

This is an 8"-barrelled Python chambered for .38 Special only. It was a limited-production venture that was not a success. It was offered in blue only.

| Exc. | V.G. | Good | Fair | Poor |
|------|------|------|------|------|
| 500 | 400 | 325 | 275 | 225 |

## Python Hunter

The Hunter was a special 8" .357 Magnum Python with an extended eye relief Leupold 2X scope. The grips are neoprene with gold Colt medallions. The revolver, with mounted scope and accessories, was fitted into a Haliburton extruded aluminum case. The Hunter was manufactured in 1981 only.

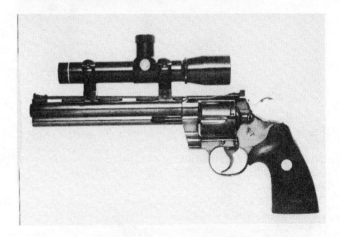

| NIB | Exc. | V.G. | Good | Fair | Poor |
|-----|------|------|------|------|------|
| 1000 | 800 | 650 | 500 | 400 | 300 |

## Metropolitan MK III

This revolver is basically a heavier-duty version of the Official Police. It is chambered for .38 Special and fitted with a 4" heavy barrel. It is finished in blue only and was manufactured from 1969-1972.

| NIB | Exc. | V.G. | Good | Fair | Poor |
|-----|------|------|------|------|------|
| 200 | 175 | 150 | 125 | 100 | 75 |

## Lawman MK III

This model is offered chambered for the .357 Magnum with a 2" or 4" barrel. It has checkered walnut grips and is either blued or nickel-plated. Colt manufactured the Lawman between 1969 and 1983.

| Exc. | V.G. | Good | Fair | Poor |
|------|------|------|------|------|
| 275  | 250  | 200  | 150  | 100  |

## Lawman MK V

This is an improved version of the MK III. It entailed a redesigned grip, a shorter lock time, and an improved double action. It was manufactured from 1982- 1985.

| NIB | Exc. | V.G. | Good | Fair | Poor |
|-----|------|------|------|------|------|
| 300 | 250  | 225  | 175  | 125  | 90   |

## Trooper MK III

This revolver was intended to be the target-grade version of the MK III series. It is offered with a 4", 6", or 8" vent-rib barrel with a shrouded ejector rod similar in appearance to the Python. It is chambered for the .22 l.r. and the .22 Magnum, as well as .357 Magnum. It features adjustable target sights, checkered walnut target grips, and is either blued or nickel- plated. This model was manufactured between 1969 and 1983.

| NIB | Exc. | V.G. | Good | Fair | Poor |
|-----|------|------|------|------|------|
| 325 | 275  | 250  | 200  | 150  | 100  |

## Trooper MK V

This improved version of the MK III was manufactured between 1982 and 1985.

| NIB | Exc. | V.G. | Good | Fair | Poor |
|-----|------|------|------|------|------|
| 325 | 275  | 250  | 200  | 150  | 100  |

## Boa

This is basically a deluxe version of the Trooper MK V. It has all the same features plus the high polished blue found on the Python. Colt manufactured 1,200 of these revolvers in 1985, and the entire production was purchased and marketed by Lew Horton Distributing Company in Southboro, Massachusetts.

| NIB | Exc. | V.G. | Good | Fair | Poor |
|-----|------|------|------|------|------|
| 450 | 400  | 350  | 300  | 250  | 150  |

## Peacekeeper

This model was designed as a duty-type weapon with target capabilities. It is offered with a 4" or 6" barrel chambered for .357 Magnum. It features adjustable sights and neoprene combat-style grips and has a matte-blue finish. This model was manufactured between 1985 and 1987.

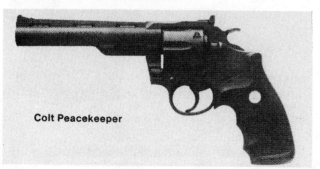

Colt Peacekeeper

| NIB | Exc. | V.G. | Good | Fair | Poor |
|-----|------|------|------|------|------|
| 300 | 275  | 225  | 200  | 150  | 100  |

## King Cobra

This model has replaced everything else Colt has manufactured to this point with the exception of the Python. The King Cobra is a large-framed, 4" or 6" solid-ribbed barrel revolver that weighs approximately 42 ounces. It is chambered for the .357 Magnum cartridge. It features adjustable outline sights and has black neoprene grips with gold Colt medallions. It is blued, matte finish, or high polish stainless steel. Colt introduced this model in 1988.

**Blued**

| NIB | Exc. | V.G. | Good | Fair | Poor |
|-----|------|------|------|------|------|
| 410 | 350  | 300  | 250  | 200  | 150  |

**Stainless Steel**

| NIB | Exc. | V.G. | Good | Fair | Poor |
|-----|------|------|------|------|------|
| 435 | 375  | 350  | 275  | 225  | 175  |

**High Polish Stainless Steel**

| NIB | Exc. | V.G. | Good | Fair | Poor |
|-----|------|------|------|------|------|
| 475 | 400  | 375  | 300  | 250  | 200  |

## Anaconda

Right view of the new Colt Anaconda, .44 Magnum double action revolver.

NEW Colt Anaconda Double Action Revolver
(.44 Rem Magnum), matte stainless steel, 6" barrel, with black neoprene "pebbled" wrap around combat style grips.
Model number MM3060

This is Colt's latest offering, a long-awaited double-action revolver chambered for the .44 Remington Magnum cartridge. It is currently offered with a 6" barrel and adjustable red-insert front and white-outline rear sights. It is constructed of matte-finished stainless steel and has black neoprene finger-groove grips with gold Colt medallions. At this writing, prices are not yet available.

## COLT SEMI-AUTOMATIC PISTOLS

The Colt Firearms Co. was the first of the American gun manufacturers to take the advent of the semi-automatic pistol seriously. This pistol design was becoming popular among European gunmakers in the late 1880's and early 1900's. In the United States, however, the revolver was firmly ensconced as the accepted design. Colt realized that if the semi-auto could be made to function reliably, it would soon catch on. The powers that be at Colt were able to negotiate with some of the noted inventors of the day, including Browning, and to secure or lease the rights to manufacture their designs. Colt also encouraged the creativity of their employees with bonuses and incentives and, through this innovative thinking, soon became the leader in semi-auto pistol sales--a position that they have never really relinquished to any other American gun maker. The Colt semiautomatic pistols represent a very interesting field for the collector of Colt handguns. There were many variations with high enough production to make it worthwhile to seek them out. There are a number of fine books on the Colt semi-automatics, and anyone wishing to do so will be able to learn a great deal about them. Collector interest is very high in this field, and values are definitely on the rise.

### Model 1900

This was the first of the Colt automatic pistols. It was actually a developmental model with only 3,500 being produced. The Model 1900 was not really a successful design. It was quite clumsy and out of balance in the hand and was not as reliable in function as it should have been. This Model is chambered for the .38 Rimless smokeless cartridge. It has a detachable magazine that holds seven cartridges. The barrel is 6" in length. The finish is blued, with a case-colored hammer and safety/sight combination. The grips are either plain walnut, checkered walnut, or hard rubber. This pistol is a Browning design, and the left side of the slide is stamped "Browning's Patent" with the 1897 patent date. Colt sold 200 pistols to the Navy and 200 to the Army for field trials and evaluation. The remaining 3,300 were sold on the civilian market. This Model was manufactured from 1900-1903.

Civilian Model with Sight/Safety Combination--Add 40 Percent.

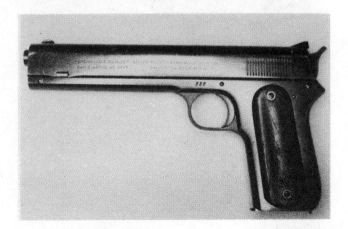

**Standard Civilian Production**

| Exc. | V.G. | Good | Fair | Poor |
|------|------|------|------|------|
| 3000 | 2500 | 1500 | 900 | 500 |

#### U.S. Navy Military Model

| Exc. | V.G. | Good | Fair | Poor |
|------|------|------|------|------|
| 5500 | 5000 | 3000 | 1750 | 1000 |

#### U.S. Army Military Model

| Exc. | V.G. | Good | Fair | Poor |
|------|------|------|------|------|
| 4750 | 3750 | 2200 | 1250 | 750 |

### Model 1902 Sporting Pistol

This Model is chambered for the .38 Rimless smokeless cartridge. It has a 7-round detachable magazine and a 6" barrel and is blued, with checkered hard rubber grips featuring the "Rampant Colt" molded into them. The most notable features of the 1902 Sporting Model are the rounded butt, rounded hammer spur, dovetailed rear sight, and the 1897-1902 patent dates. Colt manufactured approximately 7,500 of these pistols between 1903 and 1908.

| Exc. | V.G. | Good | Fair | Poor |
|------|------|------|------|------|
| 2750 | 2000 | 1250 | 750 | 450 |

### Model 1902 Military Pistol

This Model is a somewhat larger, heavier pistol than the 1902 Sporting Pistol. It has the same .38 ACP chambering and 6" barrel, but the detachable magazine holds 8 rounds. The grip of this model is larger and squared off, and it has a lanyard swivel on the butt. There were approximately 18,000 manufactured between 1902 and 1929.

**Early Model with Front of Slide Serrated**

| Exc. | V.G. | Good | Fair | Poor |
|------|------|------|------|------|
| 2750 | 2000 | 1250 | 750 | 450 |

**Standard Model with Rear of Slide Serrated**

| Exc. | V.G. | Good | Fair | Poor |
|------|------|------|------|------|
| 2500 | 1750 | 1000 | 500 | 400 |

**U.S. Army Marked, #15,001-15,200 with Front Serrations**

| Exc. | V.G. | Good | Fair | Poor |
|------|------|------|------|------|
| 6000 | 5000 | 2750 | 1500 | 800 |

### Model 1903 Pocket Pistol

This was the first automatic pocket pistol Colt produced. It is essentially identical to the 1902 Sporting Model with a shorter slide. The barrel length is 4.5", and it is chambered for the .38 Rimless smokeless cartridge. It is blued, with a case-colored hammer, with checkered hard rubber grips that have the "Rampant Colt" molded into them. The detachable magazine holds 7 rounds. There were approximately 26,000 manufactured between 1903 and 1929.

| Exc. | V.G. | Good | Fair | Poor |
|------|------|------|------|------|
| 950 | 750 | 450 | 300 | 200 |

### Model 1903 Hammerless, .32 Pocket Pistol

This was the second pocket automatic Colt manufactured. It was another of John Browning's designs, and it developed into one of Colt's most successful pistols. This pistol is chambered for the .32 ACP cartridge. Initially the barrel length was 4"; this was shortened to 3.75". The detachable magazine holds 8 rounds. The standard finish is blue, with quite a few nickel-plated. The early model grips are checkered hard rubber with the "Rampant Colt" molded into them. Many of the nickel-plated pistols had pearl grips. In 1924 the grips were changed to checkered walnut with the Colt medallions. The name of this Model can be misleading as it is not a true hammerless but a concealed hammer design. It features a slide stop and a grip safety. Colt manufactured 572,215 civilian versions of this pistol and approximately 200,000 more for military contracts. This Model was manufactured between 1903 and 1945.

Early Model 1897 Patent Date--Add 40 Percent.
Nickel Plated With Pearl Grips--Add $100.
4" Barrel to #72,000--Add 20 Percent.

| Exc. | V.G. | Good | Fair | Poor |
|------|------|------|------|------|
| 550 | 500 | 450 | 300 | 200 |

**U.S. Military Model**
Serial prefix M, marked "U.S. Property" on frame, parkerized finish.

| Exc. | V.G. | Good | Fair | Poor |
|------|------|------|------|------|
| 750 | 600 | 400 | 300 | 250 |

### Model 1908 Hammerless .380 Pocket Pistol

This Model is essentially the same as the .32 Pocket Pistol, chambered for the more potent .380 ACP, also known as the

9mm Browning short. Other specifications are the same. Colt manufactured approximately 138,000 in this caliber for civilian sales. An unknown number were sold to the military.

**Standard Civilian Model**
Nickel with Pearl Grips--Add $100.

| Exc. | V.G. | Good | Fair | Poor |
|------|------|------|------|------|
| 650 | 550 | 475 | 350 | 250 |

**Military Model**
Serial prefix M, marked "U.S. Property" on frame, parkerized finish.

| Exc. | V.G. | Good | Fair | Poor |
|------|------|------|------|------|
| 900 | 750 | 650 | 500 | 300 |

### Model 1908 Hammerless .25 Pocket Pistol

This was the smallest automatic Colt made. It is chambered for the .25 ACP cartridge, has a 2" barrel, and is 4.5" long overall. It weighs a mere 13 ounces. This is a true pocket pistol. The detachable magazine holds 6 shots. This Model was offered in blue or nickel plate, with grips of checkered hard rubber and checkered walnut on later versions. This Model has a grip safety, slide lock, and a magazine disconnector safety. This was another Browning design, and Fabrique Nationale manufactured this pistol in Belgium before Colt picked up the rights to make it in the U.S. This was a commercial success by Colt's standards, with approximately 409,000 manufactured between 1908 and 1941.

**Civilian Model**

| Exc. | V.G. | Good | Fair | Poor |
|------|------|------|------|------|
| 400 | 350 | 300 | 200 | 100 |

**Military Model**
"U.S. Property" marked on right frame. Very rare.

| Exc. | V.G. | Good | Fair | Poor |
|------|------|------|------|------|
| 1000 | 750 | 600 | 450 | 300 |

## Model 1905 .45 Automatic Pistol

The Spanish American War and the experiences with the Moro's in the Philippine campaign taught a lesson about stopping power or the lack of it. The United States Army was convinced that they needed a more powerful handgun cartridge. This led Colt to the development of a .45-caliber cartridge suitable for the semi-automatic pistol. The Model 1905 and the .45 Rimless round were the result. In actuality this cartridge was not nearly powerful enough to satisfy the need, but it led to the development of the .45 ACP. Colt believed that this pistol/cartridge combination would be a success and was geared up for mass production. The Army actually bought only 200 of them, and the total production was approximately 6,300 from 1905 to 1911.

The pistol has a 5" barrel and detachable 7-shot magazine and is blued, with a case-colored hammer. The grips are checkered walnut. The hammer was rounded on the first 3,600 pistols and was changed to a spur hammer on the later models. The right side of the slide is stamped "Automatic Colt/Calibre 45 Rimless Smokeless." This model was not a commercial success for Colt--possibly because it has no safety whatsoever except for the floating inertia firing pin. The 200 military models have grip safeties only. A very small number (believed to be less than 500) of these pistols were grooved to accept a shoulder stock. The stocks were made of leather and steel and made to double as a holster. These pistols have been classified "Curios and Relics" under the provisions of the Gun Control Act of 1968.

### Civilian Model

| Exc. | V.G. | Good | Fair | Poor |
|---|---|---|---|---|
| 1500 | 1200 | 800 | 550 | 300 |

### Military Model, Serial #1-201

Known as the 1907 Contract Pistol, it has a lanyard loop, a loaded chamber indicator, and a grip safety and bears the inspector's initials "K.M."

| Exc. | V.G. | Good | Fair | Poor |
|---|---|---|---|---|
| 2250 | 1750 | 1250 | 750 | 450 |

# COLT 1911

The Colt Government Model is one of the most recognizable handguns in the world. Its popularity is second only to the Single Action Army among firearm collectors in the world today. It was this pistol that established Colt as the leader among handgun manufacturers. Arguably the advent of this fine pistol was timely from a historic point of view. It appeared just in time for the begining of WWI and was able to prove its worth on the battlefields of Europe and the Pacific in both WWI and WWII. This was undoubtedly John Browning's crowning achievement, as this pistol shall always be the most respected of the Colt Auto line. There were over 200 factory variations and the production run from 1911 and still going strong is unsurpassed. There were approximately 336,000 civilian and 2,695,212 military versions of the 1911 and 1911A1 manufactured to this point.

This model was used in WWI, WWII, the Korean War and Vietnam. Its recent replacement still stirs controversy from some knowledgeable quarters. There are a number of excellent books specializing in this firearm, and one interested in collecting this pistol will have no trouble gaining an education in the field.

## Model 1911 Automatic Pistol Commercial Series

The commercial or civilian version of the 1911 is readily recognized by the "C" prefix in the serial number. This variation commenced production in 1911 with serial number C1 and was replaced in 1925 by its successor, the 1911A1 at serial number C130,000. The 1911 is a large-frame semi-automatic with a 5" barrel. The finish is a high polish blue with checkered walnut grips. The grips feature a raised diamond around the screw holes. The 1911 has a thin front sight blade, long trigger, short spur on the hammer, and the grip safety. The mainspring housing is flat, and there is no relief cut on the frame behind the trigger. The pistol is chambered for the .45 ACP and has a 7-round detachable magazine. The words "Government Model" were not stamped on this pistol until the 1911A1 Series after 1946. There are a number of variations of this Model. We list the major ones and advise those interested in collecting to procure one of the excellent volumes available on this pistol.

Early Models 1897, 1902, 1905 and 1911 Patent Dates
Serial numbers through C4,500
3 Digit Serial Number--Add 20 Percent.
2 Digit Serial Number--Add 40 Percent.

| Exc. | V.G. | Good | Fair | Poor |
|---|---|---|---|---|
| 1350 | 1000 | 750 | 500 | 400 |

### Standard 1911 Pistol

| Exc. | V.G. | Good | Fair | Poor |
|---|---|---|---|---|
| 1150 | 850 | 600 | 400 | 300 |

### Argentine Contract

This is part of the commercial serial range and falls between numbers C110,000 and C130,000. The pistols are marked "Pistola Automatica Sistema Colt, Calibre 11.25mm, Modelo 1916." They bear the Argentine Crest and were manufactured between 1917 and 1925.

| Exc. | V.G. | Good | Fair | Poor |
|---|---|---|---|---|
| 950 | 750 | 550 | 400 | 300 |

### 1911 Russian Order

This variation is chambered for .45ACP and has the Russian version of "Anglo Zakazivat" stamped on the frame. There were 14,500 of these blued pistols manufactured in 1915-1916. They are found between serial numbers C50,000 and C85,000. This variation is rarely encountered today, as they did go to Russia and a lot has happened over there since. One should be extremely cautious and secure qualified appraisal if contemplating a purchase, as fakes have been noted.

| Exc. | V.G. | Good | Fair | Poor |
|------|------|------|------|------|
| 2500 | 1750 | 1250 | 650 | 400 |

### WWI British Contract
This series is chambered for the British .455 cartridge and is so marked on the right side of the slide. The British "Broad Arrow" proofmark will also be found. These pistols were made in 1915-1916 and have their own serial range W10001 through W21000. They are commercial series pistols.

| Exc. | V.G. | Good | Fair | Poor |
|------|------|------|------|------|
| 1500 | 1000 | 750 | 550 | 450 |

### Model 1911 Automatic Pistol, Military Series
The military Model 1911 is basically identical to the commercial series except for the markings that appear on the military version. They both have the blued finish and the diamond-checkered walnut grips. The serial-number range on 1911 military pistols falls between 1 and 629,500 with no prefix. They were manufactured by other subcontractors as well as by Colt and are listed with appropriate values. The standard frame stamping is "United States Property." The right side of the slide is marked "Model of 1911" followed by "U.S. Army," "U.S. Navy," or "U.S.M.C." They were manufactured between 1912 and 1925.

### Colt Manufacture
U.S. Army marked throughout serial range.
Below Serial #10,000--Add 10 Percent.

| Exc. | V.G. | Good | Fair | Poor |
|------|------|------|------|------|
| 1150 | 1000 | 750 | 550 | 450 |

### U.S. Navy Marked

| Exc. | V.G. | Good | Fair | Poor |
|------|------|------|------|------|
| 1500 | 1000 | 750 | 550 | 450 |

### U.S.M.C. Marked
Approximately 13,500 produced in appropriate serial range.

| Exc. | V.G. | Good | Fair | Poor |
|------|------|------|------|------|
| 1500 | 1000 | 750 | 550 | 450 |

### Springfield Armory Manufacture
There were approximately 25,767 pistols produced by the Springfield Armory. They are within serial number 72,751 and #133,186. These pistols have the Springfield Eagle and the U.S. Ordnance Flaming Bomb stamped on the frame and slide.

| Exc. | V.G. | Good | Fair | Poor |
|------|------|------|------|------|
| 1250 | 900 | 700 | 500 | 400 |

### Springfield Armory D.C.M. Model
There were fewer than 100 of these pistols produced for sale through the Department of Civilian Marksmanship before the beginning of WWI. They are marked "NRA" on the frame. Expert authentication should be secured on this pistol!

| Exc. | V.G. | Good | Fair | Poor |
|------|------|------|------|------|
| 2500 | 1850 | 1250 | 800 | 600 |

### Remington-UMC Manufacture
There were 21,676 of these pistols produced in 1918 and 1919. They have their own serial-number range #1-21,676 and are stamped "Remington UMC" on the slide.

| Exc. | V.G. | Good | Fair | Poor |
|------|------|------|------|------|
| 1250 | 900 | 700 | 500 | 400 |

### North American Arms Co. Manufacture
This is the rarest variation of the military Colt 1911. Only 100 were produced in Quebec, Ontario, during 1918. These pistols are not serial numbered. A small number, used for recordkeeping, can be found on some of the pistols. It appears on the slide just after the serrations end. These pistols are also not marked "U.S Property." One must be very wary of fakes when dealing with this model, as it is extremely desirable to collectors.

| Exc. | V.G. | Good | Fair | Poor |
|------|------|------|------|------|
| 10000 | 7500 | 6000 | 400 | 2750 |

### British RAF Rework
These pistols were made from the British Contract pistols left at the end of WWI. They were simply refinished and stamped by hand "RAF" on the left side of the frame.

| Exc. | V.G. | Good | Fair | Poor |
|------|------|------|------|------|
| 1250 | 900 | 700 | 500 | 400 |

## Arsenal Reworked 1911 Military Models

After WWI the Armed Forces still had a need for handguns. It is estimated that over 50 percent of the 1911's went home in duffel bags as war souvenirs with the returning "Doughboys." The remaining 1911's were sent to Augusta Arsenal, Rock Island Arsenal, or Springfield Armory, where they were refurbished as needed. These guns were parkerized and bear the initials of the arsenal that reworked them, "AA", "RIA," or "SA".

| Exc. | V.G. | Good | Fair | Poor |
|------|------|------|------|------|
| 750 | 650 | 500 | 350 | 250 |

## Norwegian Automatisk Pistol Model 1912

Norway had been seriously considering the adoption of a semi-automatic pistol since 1904, when they established the "Permanent Gun Commission" to test the offerings available at that time. Eventually, after much testing and debate, including the Norwegian Parliament's involvement, the Colt 1911 was settled on. Due to legal ramifications around John Browning's involvement with Fabrique Nationale, the Norwegian government had to negotiate with F.N. instead of Colt. They desired to acquire the rights to manufacture the pistol themselves under license and not merely to purchase it outright. In 1917 the negotiations were complete, and the "Kongsberg Vapenfabrikk" delivered the first pistol. There were 500 pistols in the initial order. They have Norwegian acceptance markings and are designated "M/1912." In all other respects, they are identical to the Colt Model 1911. The last of the "M/1912" pistols was manufactured in 1919.

| Exc. | V.G. | Good | Fair | Poor |
|------|------|------|------|------|
| 1350 | 1000 | 800 | 600 | 500 |

## Norwegian Automatisk Pistol Model 1914

In 1919 the Norwegian service pistol was changed slightly. The slide lock lever was enlarged and extended downward, and the hammer spur was made slightly longer. The reasoning behind these modifications was to make the pistol easier to handle. Whether it accomplished this goal or not is debatable. The new model is marked "11.25m/m Aut.Pistol M/1914" on the left side of the slide. Production on the M/1914 continued until the early 1930's. Approximately 20,000 were manufactured.

| Exc. | V.G. | Good | Fair | Poor |
|------|------|------|------|------|
| 1000 | 750 | 650 | 450 | 300 |

## Pistole 657(n)-Norw. 14-

After Nazi Germany occupied Norway, the "Kongsberg Vapenfabrikk" was put into operation to produce the M/1914 to be issued to occupation troops. This production ceased in 1943, after approximately 10,000 pistols were produced. The above designation was assigned by the German Heereswaffenamt. These pistols do not exhibit the Norwegian crown cypher; and some, though not all, bear the WaA German Ordnance Office acceptance mark.

| Exc. | V.G. | Good | Fair | Poor |
|------|------|------|------|------|
| 1000 | 750 | 650 | 450 | 300 |

# MODEL 1911A1 AUTOMATIC PISTOL

After proving its worth in the trench warfare of WWI, the cessation of hostilities gave Colt time to sit back and re-evaluate the 1911 and see if there was room for improvement. A board of ordnance officers convened to document the changes that should be made. These changes were deemed relatively minor but quite necessary. The most important change was to lengthen the spur on the grip safety to eliminate the hammer pinch that was experienced by those with larger than normal hands. To improve the angle of the grip, an arched and checkered mainspring housing was added to the new design; and relief cuts were malled into the frame behind the triggerguard to make the trigger finger more comfortable. The diamond pattern was dropped from the grips. This was the extent of the redesign. The pistol was identical in all other aspects. The 1911A1 was produced by Colt from 1925 until 1970, when it was replaced by the Series 70 Government Model, which is essentially another minor modification of the time-tested design. During this period Colt produced approximately 281,000 commercial guns and either produced or licensed the production of nearly 2,000,000 military guns.

### Model 1911A1 Automatic Pistol Commercial Series

It is said that the period between the two wars saw the finest of the Colt Automatics produced. The 1911A1 was known as the "Government Model" in its civilian configuration; and with the exception of the fit, finish, and markings, it was identical to the military models. The "C" prefix still designated the commercial series and did so until 1950, when it was changed to a suffix. The "Government Model" is polished and blued. It has checkered walnut grips. There were a number of different commercial models manufactured. We individually list them.

### Pre-WWII Commercial

These pistols were manufactured by Colt from 1925-1942. They fall within the #C130,000-C215,000 serial range.

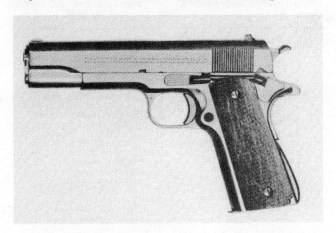

| Exc. | V.G. | Good | Fair | Poor |
|------|------|------|------|------|
| 1250 | 900 | 700 | 500 | 350 |

### Post WWII Commercial

Produced 1946-1969. "C" prefix until 1950, when it was changed to a suffix. Approximately 196,000 manufactured.

| Exc. | V.G. | Good | Fair | Poor |
|------|------|------|------|------|
| 650 | 550 | 450 | 350 | 250 |

### Super .38 1929 Model

This pistol is identical in outward physical configuration to the .45 ACP Colt Commercial. It is chambered for the .38 Super cartridge and has a magazine that holds 9 rounds. The right side of the slide is marked "Colt Super .38 Automatic" in two lines, followed by the "Rampant Colt."

| Exc. | V.G. | Good | Fair | Poor |
|------|------|------|------|------|
| 1750 | 1450 | 1000 | 700 | 600 |

## Super Match .38 1935 Model

Only 5,000 of these specially fit and finished target-grade pistols were manufactured. They have Stevens adjustable sights, and the top surfaces are matte-finished to reduce glare. Twelve hundred of these pistols were purchased and sent to Britain in 1939, at the then costly rate of $50 per unit.

| Exc. | V.G. | Good | Fair | Poor |
|------|------|------|------|------|
| 2750 | 2000 | 1500 | 1000 | 750 |

## 1st Model National Match .45

This pistol was produced so that Colt would have a factory-produced target-grade pistol for the 1932 National Matches at Camp Perry. The pistol was made up of specially selected hand-honed and fitted parts. It has a special "Match" grade barrel. The first pistols had fixed sights, but shortly thereafter the "Stevens Adjustable Rear Target Sight" was used. The right side of the slide is marked "National Match." This Model possessed exceptional shooting qualities. It was produced until 1941.

| Exc. | V.G. | Good | Fair | Poor |
|------|------|------|------|------|
| 1500 | 1250 | 950 | 650 | 450 |

## Ace Model .22 Pistol

In 1930 Colt purchased advertising which, in effect, requested the shooting public to let the Company know if they would be interested in a .22 rimfire pistol built similar to the Government Model. The response must have been positive because in 1931 the Colt Ace appeared on the market. The Ace uses the same frame as the Government Model with a modified slide and a heavy barrel. It is chambered for .22 l.r. The size is the same as the larger-caliber version, and the weight is 36 ounces. The operation is straight blowback. The Ace has a 10-round detachable magazine and features the "Improved Ace Adjustable Target Sight." The markings on the left side of the slide are the same as on the Government Model; the right side reads "Colt Ace 22 Long Rifle." At first the Army purchased a few pistols (totalling 206) through 1936. It was found, however, that the function of the Ace was less than perfect, as the .22 rimfire lacked the power to consistently and reliably blow back the slide. Approximately 11,000 Ace pistols were manufactured, and in 1941 they were discontinued.

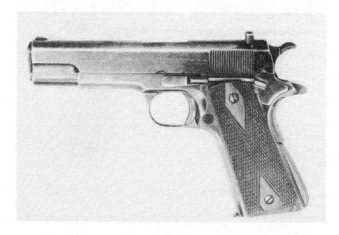

| Exc. | V.G. | Good | Fair | Poor |
|------|------|------|------|------|
| 1500 | 1250 | 950 | 650 | 450 |

## Service Model Ace .22 R.F. Pistol

In 1937 Colt introduced this improved version of the Ace Pistol. It utilizes a floating chamber invented by David "Carbine" Williams, the firearm's designer who invented the M1 carbine while serving time on a southern chain gang. This loading chamber gave the Service Model Ace the reliability and "feel" that the public wanted. The serial number is prefixed by the letters "SM." The external configuration is the same as the Ace, and the slide is marked "Colt Service Model Ace .22 Long Rifle." Colt sold some to the Army and some on a commercial basis. There was a total of 13,000 manufactured before production ceased in 1944.

| Exc. | V.G. | Good | Fair | Poor |
|------|------|------|------|------|
| 1700 | 1450 | 1100 | 800 | 600 |

## Conversion Units .22/.45, .45/.22

In 1938 Colt released a .22-caliber conversion unit. With this kit, one who already owned a Government Model could simply switch the top half and fire inexpensive .22 rimfire ammunition. The unit consists of a slide marked "Service Model Ace", barrel with floating chamber, ejector, slide lock, recoil spring, and 10-shot magazine. The Conversion Units feature the Stevens Adjustable Rear Sight. Later that same year, a kit to convert the Service Model Ace to .45 ACP was offered. In 1942 production of these units ceased. The .22 kit was reintroduced in 1947; the .45 kit was not brought back.

### Pre-War Service Model Ace Conversion Unit

| Exc. | V.G. | Good | Fair | Poor |
|------|------|------|------|------|
| 1000 | 750 | 500 | 400 | 300 |

### .45/.22 Conversion Unit

| Exc. | V.G. | Good | Fair | Poor |
|------|------|------|------|------|
| 300 | 250 | 200 | 150 | 100 |

### Post-War .22 Conversion Unit

| Exc. | V.G. | Good | Fair | Poor |
|------|------|------|------|------|
| 250 | 225 | 200 | 150 | 100 |

## Drake National Match Pistols

In the 1950's, Springfield Armory used some of these specially machined and hardened slides to construct highly accurate pistols for the Camp Perry Competition. The slides have "NM" and a number on the left side and the Drake name on the right. The "NM" number also appears on the barrel, and the bushing and "NM" is stamped on the triggerguard. "SA" (designating Springfield Armory) is stamped on the frame, along with the letter "S" on the barrel link. These high-grade pistols have either adjustable sights or high-profile fixed sights. They are quite scarce and should be authenticated.

| Exc. | V.G. | Good | Fair | Poor |
|------|------|------|------|------|
| 950 | 750 | 600 | 450 | 400 |

## National Match Reworks

These pistols were hand fitted by government armorers for use by the U.S. shooting teams. They have the letters "NM" on all the parts and are either blued or parkerized with target-type sights.

| Exc. | V.G. | Good | Fair | Poor |
|------|------|------|------|------|
| 800 | 700 | 600 | 450 | 350 |

## Gold Cup National Match

This model is chambered for the .45 ACP, features the flat mainspring housing of the 1911, and has a match-grade barrel and bushing. The parts were hand fitted to target tolerances, and the slide has an enlarged ejection port. The trigger is the long version with an adjustable trigger stop, and the sights are adjustable target type. The finish is blued, with checkered walnut grips and gold medallions. The slide is marked "Gold Cup National Match," and the serial number is prefixed by the letters "NM." This pistol was manufactured from 1957 until 1970.

| Exc. | V.G. | Good | Fair | Poor |
|------|------|------|------|------|
| 650 | 600 | 500 | 400 | 300 |

## Gold Cup MKIII National Match

This pistol is identical to the Gold Cup .45 except that it is chambered for the .38 Mid-Range Wad Cutter round. It was manufactured from 1961 until 1974.

| Exc. | V.G. | Good | Fair | Poor |
|------|------|------|------|------|
| 700 | 650 | 550 | 450 | 350 |

## Foreign Contract Commercial Pistols
## Mexican Contract Pistols

These pistols were manufactured before 1927. They are marked "Ejercito Mexicano," which translates to "Mexican Army." They have the "C" serial-number prefix, and most were well-used.

| Exc. | V.G. | Good | Fair | Poor |
|------|------|------|------|------|
| 900 | 750 | 600 | 500 | 350 |

## Argentine Contract Pistols

These pistols were delivered to Argentina in 1927. The right side of the slide is marked with the two-line inscription "Ejercito Argentino Colt .Cal.45 Mod. 1927." There is also the Argentine National Seal and the "Rampant Colt." Colt enjoyed a profitable relationship with Argentina through the late 1920's, delivering approximately 10,000 pistols before failing to meet a delivery date in the early 1930's. This brought about the licensing of the Argentine Government to manufacture the Colt Pistol on their own.

| Exc. | V.G. | Good | Fair | Poor |
|------|------|------|------|------|
| 550 | 500 | 400 | 300 | 200 |

## Model 1911A1 Automatic Pistol Military Model

As WWII loomed on the horizon and Germany's intentions became ever clearer, it became apparent that we would have an escalated need for weapons once again in this century. We were, however, now better able to fill this need than we had been the time before. Our gun manufacturers had already tooled up and were producing guns for the British "Lend Lease Program." Our Government awarded contracts to Colt, Remington-Rand, Ithaca, Union Switch & Signal, and Singer. Their collective efforts resulted in the manufacture of approximately 2,000,000 1911A1's. These pistols were used not only in WWII but in the Korean and Vietnam Wars.

It is only recently that the 1911A1 has been replaced, controversially, as our Nation's Service Pistol. Regardless of who manufactured these 1911A1's, they all have 5" barrels and 7-round detachable magazines and are chambered for the .45 ACP cartridge. All but the earliest Colt-produced guns are parkerized and have brown checkered plastic grips. The first 1911A1's produced were a bright polished blue with checkered walnut grips. The authenticity of a WWII 1911A1 can be checked by comparing the manufacturer to the assigned serial number chart that appears at the end of this chapter. There are a number of fine publications that specialize in this Model, and the serious student should acquire them and learn.

## Colt Manufacture

These pistols were produced from 1924 through 1945. They commenced with serial number 700,000, and there were approximately 1,627,000 manufactured.
Early Models with Polished and Blued Finish--Add 100 Percent.

| Exc. | V.G. | Good | Fair | Poor |
|------|------|------|------|------|
| 600 | 500 | 400 | 300 | 250 |

## Remington-Rand Manufacture

Approximate production 948,905; 1943-1945.

| Exc. | V.G. | Good | Fair | Poor |
|------|------|------|------|------|
| 600 | 500 | 400 | 300 | 250 |

## Ithaca Manufacture

Approximate production 441,557; 1943-1945.

| Exc. | V.G. | Good | Fair | Poor |
|------|------|------|------|------|
| 650 | 550 | 450 | 350 | 300 |

## Union Switch & Signal Manufacture
Approximate production 55,100; 1943 only.

| Exc. | V.G. | Good | Fair | Poor |
|---|---|---|---|---|
| 1000 | 800 | 600 | 400 | 350 |

## Singer Manufacture
Five hundred produced in 1942 only. Exercise caution if contemplating purchase, as the extreme rarity of this model has encouraged fakery.

| Exc. | V.G. | Good | Fair | Poor |
|---|---|---|---|---|
| 10000 | 7500 | 5500 | 4500 | 3500 |

## SERIAL NUMBERS ASSIGNED TO M1911 AND 1911A1 CONTRACTORS

| Year | Serial No. | Manufacturer |
|---|---|---|
| 1912 | 1-500 | Colt |
| | 501-1000 | Colt USN |
| | 1001-1500 | Colt |
| | 1501-2000 | Colt USN |
| | 2001 2500 | Colt |
| | 2501-3500 | Colt USN |
| | 3501-3800 | Colt USMC |
| | 3801-4500 | Colt |
| | 4501-5500 | Colt USN |
| | 5501-6500 | Colt |
| | 6501-7500 | Colt USN |
| | 7501 8500 | Colt |
| | 8501 9500 | Colt USN |
| | 9501-10500 | Colt |
| | 10501-11500 | Colt USN |
| | 11501-12500 | Colt |
| | 12501-13500 | Colt USN |
| | 13501-17250 | Colt |
| 1913 | 17251-36400 | Colt |
| | 36401-37650 | Colt USMC |
| | 37651-38000 | Colt |
| | 38001-44000 | Colt USN |
| | 44001-60400 | Colt |
| 1914 | 60401-72570 | Colt |
| | 72571-83855 | Springfield |
| | 83856-83900 | Colt |
| | 83901-84400 | Colt USMC |
| | 84401-96000 | Colt |
| | 96001-97537 | Colt |
| | 97538-102596 | Colt |
| | 102597-107596 | Springfield |
| 1915 | 107597-109500 | Colt |
| | 109501-110000 | Colt USN |
| | 110001-113496 | Colt |
| | 113497-120566 | Springfield |
| | 120567-125566 | Colt |
| | 125567-133186 | Springfield |
| 1916 | 133187-137400 | Colt |

## SERIAL NUMBERS ASSIGNED TO M1911 AND 1911A1 CONTRACTORS "continued"

| Year | Serial No. | Manufacturer |
|---|---|---|
| 1917 | 137401-151186 | Colt |
| | 151187-151986 | Colt USMC |
| | 151987-185800 | Colt |
| | 185801-186200 | Colt USMC |
| | 186201-209586 | Colt |
| | 209587-210386 | Colt USMC |
| | 210387-215386 | Colt Frames |
| | 215387-216186 | Colt USMC |
| | 216187-216586 | Colt |
| | 216587-216986 | Colt USMC |
| 1918 | 216987-217386 | Colt USMC |
| | 217387-232000 | Colt |
| | 232001-233600 | Colt USN |
| | 233601-594000 | Colt |
| 1918 | 1-13152 | Rem-UMC |
| 1919 | 13153-21676 | Rem-UMC |
| | 594001-629500 | Colt |
| | 629501-700000 | Unknown |
| 1924 | 700001-710000 | Colt |
| 1937 | 710001-712349 | Colt |
| 1938 | 712350-713645 | Colt |
| 1939 | 13646-717281 | Colt USN |
| 1940 | 717282-721977 | Colt |
| 1941 | 721978-756733 | Colt |
| 1942 | 756734-800000 | Colt |
| | S800001-S800500 | Singer |
| | 800501-801000 | H&R (Assigned) |
| 1943 | 801001-958100 | Colt |
| | 958101-1088725 | U.S. S.& S. |
| | 1088726-1208673 | Colt |
| | 1208674-1279673 | Ithaca |
| | 1279674-1279698 | Augusta Arsenal (Renumber) |
| | — | |
| | 1279699-1441430 | Remington-Rand |
| | 1441431-1471430 | Ithaca |
| | 1471431-1609528 | Remington-Rand |
| 1944 | 1609529-1743846 | Colt |
| | 1743847-1890503 | Ithaca |
| | 1890504-2075103 | Remington-Rand |
| 1945 | 2075104-2134403 | Ithaca |
| | 2134404-2244803 | Remington-Rand |
| | 2244804-2380013 | Colt |
| | 2380014-2619013 | Remington-Rand |
| | 2619014-2693613 | Ithaca |

## MKIV Series 70 Government Model
This Model is essentially a newer version of the 1911A1. It has the prefix "70G" from 1970-1976, "G70" from 1976-1980, and "70B" from 1980-1983, when production ceased. This Model is offered in blue or nickel-plate and has checkered walnut grips with the Colt medallion. It is chambered for .45 ACP, .38 Super, 9mm, and 9mm Steyr (foreign export only).

| NIB | Exc. | V.G. | Good | Fair | Poor |
|---|---|---|---|---|---|
| 450 | 400 | 350 | 300 | 250 | 200 |

## MKIV Series 70 Gold Cup National Match
This is the newer version of the 1957 National Match. It features a slightly heavier slide and Colt-Elliason sights. The chambering is .45 ACP only. The Accurizer barrel and bushing was introduced on this model. It was manufactured form 1970-1983.

**Colt Gold Cup 45**

| NIB | Exc. | V.G. | Good | Fair | Poor |
|-----|------|------|------|------|------|
| 600 | 550 | 475 | 400 | 300 | 250 |

## Commander

This is a shortened version of the Government Model. It has a 4.25" barrel, a lightweight alloy frame, and a rounded spur hammer. The total weight of the Commander is 27.5 ounces. The serial number has the suffix "LW." The Commander is chambered for the .45 ACP, 9mm, and .38 Super. The latter two have been discontinued. Some were chambered for 7.65 Parabellum for export only. The Commander was introduced in 1949 and is still being manufactured.

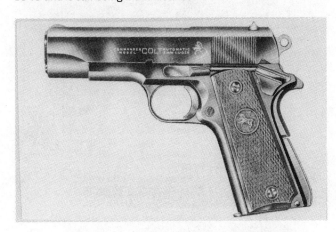

| NIB | Exc. | V.G. | Good | Fair | Poor |
|-----|------|------|------|------|------|
| 600 | 500 | 450 | 375 | 300 | 200 |

## Combat Commander

The Combat Commander was produced in response to complaints from some quarters about the excessive recoil and rapid wear of the alloy-framed Commander. This model is simply a Commander with a steel frame. The Combat Commander weighs 32 ounces and is offered in blue or satin nickel with walnut grips.

| NIB | Exc. | V.G. | Good | Fair | Poor |
|-----|------|------|------|------|------|
| 600 | 500 | 450 | 375 | 300 | 200 |

## MKIV Series 80 Government Model

This model was introduced in 1983. It is, for all purposes, the same externally as the Series 70. The basic difference is the addition of the new firing pin safety on this model.

**Blued**

| NIB | Exc. | V.G. | Good | Fair | Poor |
|-----|------|------|------|------|------|
| 600 | 500 | 400 | 350 | 300 | 250 |

**Nickel Plated**

| Exc. | V.G. | Good | Fair | Poor |
|------|------|------|------|------|
| 550 | 450 | 375 | 300 | 250 |

**Stainless Steel**

| NIB | Exc. | V.G. | Good | Fair | Poor |
|-----|------|------|------|------|------|
| 625 | 575 | 475 | 400 | 325 | 275 |

**Polished Stainless Steel**

| NIB | Exc. | V.G. | Good | Fair | Poor |
|-----|------|------|------|------|------|
| 700 | 600 | 500 | 450 | 350 | 300 |

## MKIV Series 80 Gold Cup National Match

Externally the same as the Series 70 Gold Cup with the new firing pin safety.

**Blued**

| NIB | Exc. | V.G. | Good | Fair | Poor |
|-----|------|------|------|------|------|
| 750 | 650 | 550 | 500 | 400 | 350 |

**Stainless Steel**

| NIB | Exc. | V.G. | Good | Fair | Poor |
|-----|------|------|------|------|------|
| 825 | 700 | 600 | 550 | 450 | 400 |

**Polished Stainless Steel**

| NIB | Exc. | V.G. | Good | Fair | Poor |
|-----|------|------|------|------|------|
| 875 | 750 | 650 | 600 | 500 | 450 |

## Officers ACP

This is a shortened version of the Government Model. It has a 3.5" barrel and weighs 37 ounces. It is chambered for the .45 ACP only and has checkered walnut grips. The Officers ACP was introduced in 1985.

**Blued**

| NIB | Exc. | V.G. | Good | Fair | Poor |
|-----|------|------|------|------|------|
| 600 | 500 | 400 | 375 | 300 | 200 |

**Matte Blued**

| NIB | Exc. | V.G. | Good | Fair | Poor |
|-----|------|------|------|------|------|
| 575 | 475 | 375 | 350 | 275 | 200 |

**Satin Nickel (Discontinued 1985)**

| Exc. | V.G. | Good | Fair | Poor |
|------|------|------|------|------|
| 450 | 350 | 300 | 250 | 200 |

**Stainless Steel**

| NIB | Exc. | V.G. | Good | Fair | Poor |
|-----|------|------|------|------|------|
| 625 | 500 | 400 | 350 | 300 | 250 |

### Lightweight Officers ACP

This is an alloy-framed version that weighs 24 ounces. It was introduced in 1986.

| NIB | Exc. | V.G. | Good | Fair | Poor |
|-----|------|------|------|------|------|
| 600 | 500 | 400 | 375 | 300 | 200 |

### Delta Elite

This model is chambered for the 10mm Norma cartridge. It is offered in blue or stainless steel. The grips are black neoprene with the Delta medallion. It features a high-profile three-dot combat sight system. The Delta Elite was introduced in 1987.

**Colt Delta Elite,** 10mm Semi-Automatic, "Ultimate" Stainless Steel, Model Number 02021

**Blued**

| NIB | Exc. | V.G. | Good | Fair | Poor |
|-----|------|------|------|------|------|
| 650 | 525 | 425 | 375 | 325 | 275 |

**Stainless Steel**

| NIB | Exc. | V.G. | Good | Fair | Poor |
|-----|------|------|------|------|------|
| 700 | 600 | 500 | 450 | 400 | 300 |

**Polished Stainless Steel**

| NIB | Exc. | V.G. | Good | Fair | Poor |
|-----|------|------|------|------|------|
| 775 | 675 | 575 | 500 | 450 | 350 |

### Double Eagle

This is a double-action semi-automatic pistol chambered for the 10mm Auto and the .45 ACP cartridges. It has a 5" barrel and an 8-round detachable box magazine. It is constructed of stainless steel and has checkered black synthetic grips. The sights are fixed and utilize the three-dot system.

Left View

Right View

**NEW Double Action Semiautomatic Pistol**
Caliber: 45 ACP, Stainless Steel, Model number DA1070

| NIB | Exc. | V.G. | Good | Fair | Poor |
|-----|------|------|------|------|------|
| 500 | 425 | 350 | 300 | 250 | 200 |

### Double Eagle Officer's Model

This is a compact version of the double-action Double Eagle pistol chambered for .45 ACP only.

Left View

Right View

**NEW Double Eagle Officer's Model**
Semi-Automatic, Double Action Pistol
Caliber: 45 ACP, Stainless Steel, Model number DA9180

| NIB | Exc. | V.G. | Good | Fair | Poor |
|-----|------|------|------|------|------|
| 480 | 425 | 375 | 300 | 250 | 200 |

### Double Eagle First Edition

This version of the double-action Double Eagle pistol is chambered for the 10mm Auto and is furnished with a Cordura holster, double-magazine pouch, and three magazines, as well as a zippered black Cordura case.

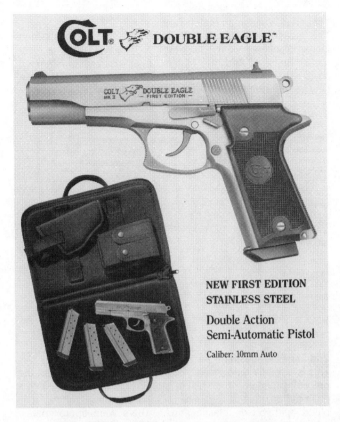

| NIB | Exc. | V.G. | Good | Fair | Poor |
|-----|------|------|------|------|------|
| 385 | 300 | 250 | 200 | 175 | 125 |

**Mustang Plus II**
This version of the Mustang pistol features the 2.75" barrel with the longer grip frame that accommodates a 7-round magazine. It was introduced in 1988 and is offered in blue, as well as stainless steel.
Stainless Steel--Add 10 Percent.

NEW FIRST EDITION
STAINLESS STEEL

Double Action
Semi-Automatic Pistol

Caliber: 10mm Auto

NEW Colt 380 Mustang Plus II, matte stainless steel finish with black composition stocks. Combines the full grip length of the 380 Government Model with the shorter compact barrel and slide of the Mustang. Model number 06092

| NIB | Exc. | V.G. | Good | Fair | Poor |
|-----|------|------|------|------|------|
| 700 | 650 | 550 | 475 | 375 | 300 |

| NIB | Exc. | V.G. | Good | Fair | Poor |
|-----|------|------|------|------|------|
| 385 | 300 | 250 | 200 | 175 | 125 |

**.380 Series 80 Government Model**
This is a single-action, blowback-operated semi-automatic pistol chambered for the .380 ACP cartridge. It has a 3.25" barrel and a 7-round magazine. The sights are fixed. It is available either blued, nickel-plated, or stainless steel. It has synthetic grips and was introduced in 1985.
Nickel Finish--Add 10 Percent.
Stainless Steel--Add 10 Percent.

**Mustang Pocket Lite**
This is a lightweight version of the Mustang, that features an aluminum-alloy receiver. The finish is blued only, and it has synthetic grips. It was introduced in 1987.

| NIB | Exc. | V.G. | Good | Fair | Poor |
|-----|------|------|------|------|------|
| 385 | 300 | 250 | 200 | 175 | 125 |

**Mustang**
This is a more compact version of the .380 Government Model. It has a 2.75" barrel and a 5-round detachable magazine.
Nickel Finish--Add 10 Percent.
Stainless Steel--Add 10 Percent.

*Colt 380s are becoming increasingly popular for home protection and with law enforcement agencies as back-up weapons because of their dependability, light weight and compact size.*

NEW Colt 380 Mustang, matte stainless steel finish with black composition stocks. Model number 06090

| NIB | Exc. | V.G. | Good | Fair | Poor |
|-----|------|------|------|------|------|
| 385 | 300 | 250 | 200 | 175 | 125 |

# .22 RIMFIRE SEMI-AUTOMATIC PISTOLS

## Colt Junior Pocket Model

This diminutive unit is only 4.5" long overall and weighs 12 ounces. Colt did not manufacture this pistol but rather had it made for them by Astra in Spain. The pistol was introduced in 1958 chambered for .25 ACP. One year later a .22 Short version appeared. Both had external hammers and detachable 6-round magazines. The passage of the 1968 Gun Control Act made import of a weapon of this size illegal, so Colt discontinued its relationship with Astra. The pistol was re-introduced in 1970 as an American-made product and was produced for two more years. Production ceased in 1972. Astra also made this pistol and called it the Cub.
.22 Short--Add 25 Percent.

| NIB | Exc. | V.G. | Good | Fair | Poor |
|-----|------|------|------|------|------|
| 300 | 250 | 200 | 175 | 125 | 75 |

## Pre-Woodsman Model

This pistol was designed by John Browning. The name Woodsman was not used until 1927, but some collectors use it to describe this pistol as it is of the same pattern. This pistol was designed for general purpose use, hunting, and informal target practice. The pistol has a 6.5" thin barrel and weighs 28 ounces. There is a 10- round detachable magazine, and the chambering is .22 Long Rifle standard velocity only. It has a concealed hammer and a sliding thumb safety. The finish is blue, with checkered plastic grips. It was manufactured between 1915 and 1927, and there were approximately 54,000 produced.

| Exc. | V.G. | Good | Fair | Poor |
|------|------|------|------|------|
| 750 | 550 | 450 | 300 | 200 |

## 1st Series Woodsman

This series was manufactured from 1927 until 1947. It was chambered for .22 l.r. standard velocity up to 1932. After that date it was redesigned to fire high-velocity ammunition. The mainspring housing on these high-velocity models is serrated instead of checkered. This change took place at serial number 83,790. All Woodsmans after this fired high-velocity ammunition. This model is blued, with checkered wood grips and the side of the frame is marked "The Woodsman." The 10-shot detachable magazine is released at the bottom. There were approximately 112,000 manufactured.

### Sport Model, 4.5" Barrel
| Exc. | V.G. | Good | Fair | Poor |
|------|------|------|------|------|
| 750 | 550 | 450 | 300 | 200 |

### Target Model, 6.5" Barrel
| Exc. | V.G. | Good | Fair | Poor |
|------|------|------|------|------|
| 650 | 475 | 375 | 275 | 200 |

## 1st Series Woodsman Match Target

This model has a special 6.5" heavy barrel, target sights, and longer checkered walnut target grips. The side of the receiver has a "Bullseye" and the "Match Target" designation stamped on it. There were only 16,000 of these pistols manufactured between 1938 and 1944. They are quite scarce today.

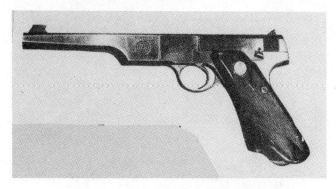

| Exc. | V.G. | Good | Fair | Poor |
|------|------|------|------|------|
| 1500 | 1250 | 850 | 500 | 400 |

## 2nd Series Woodsman

This is a totally redesigned pistol and is very different from the preceding models. It has a slide stop, a hold-open device, and a push-button magazine release behind the triggerguard. It is blued, with brown plastic grips. There were approximately 146,000 manufactured between 1948 and 1955.

### Sport Model, 4.5" Barrel
| Exc. | V.G. | Good | Fair | Poor |
|------|------|------|------|------|
| 550 | 450 | 350 | 250 | 200 |

### Target Model, 6" Barrel
| Exc. | V.G. | Good | Fair | Poor |
|------|------|------|------|------|
| 450 | 350 | 300 | 200 | 150 |

### Match Target Model, 4.5" Barrel
| Exc. | V.G. | Good | Fair | Poor |
|------|------|------|------|------|
| 700 | 600 | 500 | 400 | 300 |

### Match Target Model, 6" Barrel
| Exc. | V.G. | Good | Fair | Poor |
|------|------|------|------|------|
| 600 | 500 | 400 | 300 | 250 |

## 3rd Series Woodsman

This model is very similar to the 2nd Series except that the magazine catch is located at the bottom of the grip. It was manufactured from 1955-1960 with black plastic grips and from 1960-1977 with checkered walnut.

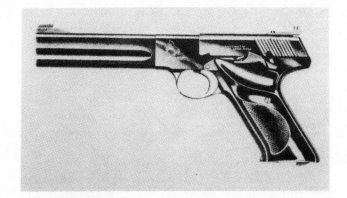

**Sport Model, 4.5" Barrel**

| Exc. | V.G. | Good | Fair | Poor |
|---|---|---|---|---|
| 400 | 300 | 250 | 175 | 125 |

**Target Model, 6" Barrel**

| Exc. | V.G. | Good | Fair | Poor |
|---|---|---|---|---|
| 375 | 325 | 250 | 175 | 125 |

**Match Target Model, 4.5" Barrel**

| Exc. | V.G. | Good | Fair | Poor |
|---|---|---|---|---|
| 500 | 400 | 300 | 200 | 150 |

**Match Target, 6" Barrel**

| Exc. | V.G. | Good | Fair | Poor |
|---|---|---|---|---|
| 450 | 350 | 300 | 200 | 150 |

**Challenger Model**

This pistol is simply a Woodsman with less expensive grips and sights. It has either a 4.5" or a 6" barrel, fixed sights, no hold-open device, and a bottom magazine release. It is chambered for .22 l.r. The production ran to 77,000. It was manufactured between 1950 and 1955.

| Exc. | V.G. | Good | Fair | Poor |
|---|---|---|---|---|
| 350 | 300 | 250 | 200 | 150 |

**Huntsman Model**

The only difference between the Huntsman and the Challenger is that the Huntsman utilizes a 3rd Series frame. The Huntsman had black plastic grips until 1960 and checkered walnut after that. There were approximately 100,000 manufactured between 1955 and 1977.

| Exc. | V.G. | Good | Fair | Poor |
|---|---|---|---|---|
| 300 | 250 | 200 | 150 | 100 |

**Targetsman Model**

This is essentially the Huntsman with adjustable target sights and a thumb-rest grip. It is offered with a 6" barrel only. There were approximately 65,000 manufactured between 1959 and 1977.

| Exc. | V.G. | Good | Fair | Poor |
|---|---|---|---|---|
| 350 | 300 | 250 | 200 | 150 |

## COLT MODERN LONG ARMS

**Colteer I-22**

This is a single-shot bolt-action rifle chambered for .22 l.r. or .22 Magnum. It has a plain uncheckered walnut stock, 20" barrel, and adjustable sights. There were approximately 50,000 manufactured between 1957 and 1966.

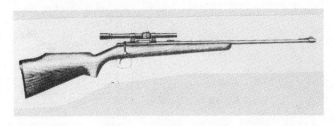

| Exc. | V.G. | Good | Fair | Poor |
|---|---|---|---|---|
| 250 | 200 | 175 | 125 | 90 |

**Stagecoach**

This is a semi-automatic, saddle ring carbine. It is chambered for .22 l.r. and has a 16.5" barrel and a 13-shot tubular magazine. The stock is fancy walnut, and the receiver has the stagecoach holdup scene roll-engraved on it. There were approximately 25,000 manufactured between 1965 and 1975.

| Exc. | V.G. | Good | Fair | Poor |
|---|---|---|---|---|
| 300 | 250 | 200 | 150 | 100 |

**Courier**

This model is very similar to the Stagecoach, with a pistolgrip stock and beavertail forearm. It was manufactured between 1970 and 1975.

| Exc. | V.G. | Good | Fair | Poor |
|---|---|---|---|---|
| 250 | 200 | 175 | 125 | 90 |

**Colteer**

This is a less expensive version of the Stagecoach. It features a 19.5" barrel, has a 15-shot tubular magazine, and is stocked in a plainer grade walnut. There is no roll-engraving. Approximately 25,000 were manufactured between 1965 and 1975.

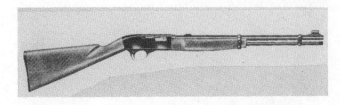

| Exc. | V.G. | Good | Fair | Poor |
|---|---|---|---|---|
| 250 | 200 | 175 | 125 | 90 |

**Colt "57" Bolt Action Rifle**

This rifle was manufactured for Colt by the Jefferson Mfg. Co of New Haven, Connecticut. It utilizes a Fabrique Nationale Mauser action and has a checkered American walnut stock with a Monte Carlo comb. The Rifle is offered with adjustable sights. It is chambered for .243 or .30-06. There is also a deluxe version that features higher-grade wood. There were approximately 5,000 manufactured in 1957.
Deluxe Version--Add 20 Percent.

| Exc. | V.G. | Good | Fair | Poor |
|---|---|---|---|---|
| 550 | 450 | 350 | 300 | 225 |

## Coltsman Bolt Action Rifle

The Coltsman was manufactured for Colt by Kodiak Arms. It utilizes either a Mauser or Sako action. The rifle is offered in .243, .308, .30-06, and .300 Winchester Magnum. It has a barrel length of 22", 24" in the Magnum chambering. The stock is checkered American walnut. There were approximately 10,000 manufactured between 1958 and 1966. There is a deluxe version that features a higher-grade, skipline-checkered walnut stock and rosewood forend tip; this is called "The Coltsman Custom."

Coltsman Custom--Add 50 Percent.

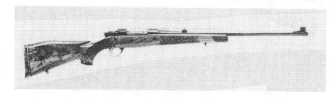

| Exc. | V.G. | Good | Fair | Poor |
|------|------|------|------|------|
| 650 | 550 | 450 | 350 | 250 |

## Coltsman Pump Shotgun

This model was manufactured by Jefferson Arms, utilizing an aluminum alloy frame made by Franchi. It is chambered for 12, 16, and 20 gauge and has a 26" or 28" plain barrel. There were approximately 2,000 manufactured between 1961 and 1965.

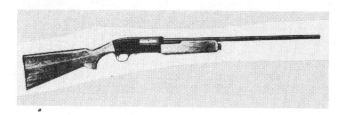

| Exc. | V.G. | Good | Fair | Poor |
|------|------|------|------|------|
| 350 | 300 | 275 | 200 | 150 |

## Semi-Auto Shotgun

The Semi-Auto Shotgun was manufactured for Colt by the firm of Luigi Franchi in Italy. It features an aluminum alloy receiver and is chambered for 12 or 20 gauge. The barrel length is 26", 28", 30", or 32"-- either vent-rib or plain. A deluxe version, "The Custom Auto," features a fancy walnut stock and a hand-engraved receiver. There were approximately 5,300 manufactured between 1962 and 1966.

Custom Auto--Add 25 Percent.

| Exc. | V.G. | Good | Fair | Poor |
|------|------|------|------|------|
| 375 | 325 | 300 | 225 | 175 |

## Double Barrel Shotgun

During 1961 and 1962. Colt had approximately 50 side-by-side shotguns made for them by a French gun manufacturer. They have the Colt name on the breech area of the barrels and are in the 467,000-469,000 serial range. There is very little information available on this gun, and Colt never went past the test-market stage.

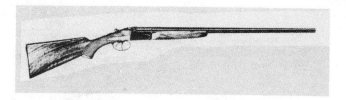

| Exc. | V.G. | Good | Fair | Poor |
|------|------|------|------|------|
| 1000 | 750 | 650 | 500 | 400 |

## Colt Sauer Bolt Action Rifle

This is a very high quality and unique rifle manufactured for Colt by the firm of J.P. Sauer & Son of Germany. The rifle features a non-rotating bolt that makes the Colt Sauer action smoother functioning than most. It has a 24" barrel, skipline-checkered walnut stock with rosewood forend tip, pistolgrip cap, and recoil pad. There are five basic configurations: the Standard Action, chambered for .25-06, .270 Winchester, and .30-06; the Short Action, chambered for .22-250, .243 Winchester, and .308 Winchester; the Magnum Action, chambered for .7mm Remington Magnum, .300 Winchester Magnum, and .300 Weatherby Magnum; also the "Grand Alaskan" and the "Grand African," heavier versions chambered for .375 Holland & Holland Magnum and 458 Winchester Magnum, respectively. These rifles were all discontinued by Colt in 1985.

### Colt Sauer Short Action

| Exc. | V.G. | Good | Fair | Poor |
|------|------|------|------|------|
| 900 | 750 | 500 | 400 | 350 |

Standard Action--Add $50.
Magnum Action-- Add $200.
"Grand Alaskan"--Add $400.
"Grand African"--Add $450.

## Colt Sauer Drilling

This is a rather unique firearm and one with which many American enthusiasts are not familiar--a 3- barrelled gun. It features a side-by-side shotgun in 12 gauge over a .30-06 or .243 rifle barrel. The name was based on the German word for three, as this is where the concept was developed. They are quite popular in Europe where the game preserve style of hunting is prevalent but have little use in America where our hunting seasons don't often overlap. This drilling has 25" barrels and pop-up sights for the rifle barrel and is nicely engraved. It was discontinued by Colt in 1985.

| Exc. | V.G. | Good | Fair | Poor |
|------|------|------|------|------|
| 3500 | 2750 | 2000 | 1500 | 1100 |

## Colt-Sharps Rifle

Introduced in 1970 as the last word in sporting rifles, the Colt-Sharps is a falling-block action that was advertised as a modern Sharps-Borchardt. This undertaking was first-class all the way. The finish is high polish blue with a deluxe-grade hand-checkered walnut stock and forend. This Rifle is chambered for .17 Remington, .22-250, .243, .25-06, 7mm Remington Magnum, .30-06, and .375 Holland & Holland Magnum; and it was offered cased with accessories. This model was manufactured between 1970 and 1977.

| Exc. | V.G. | Good | Fair | Poor |
|------|------|------|------|------|
| 2500 | 2000 | 1600 | 1200 | 750 |

## Colt AR-15/M16 Rifle

The semi-automatic AR-15 and its military, fully automatic counterpart, the M16, are Colt's unchallenged production leaders. It is estimated that over 8,000,000 have been sold to our Government, foreign governments, law enforcement departments, and civilians (AR-15 only). As I write this, Colt has restricted civilian sales and it is not possible to purchase from Colt a semi-automatic AR-15 because of the hysteria that has gripped our governing bodies. Prices have fluctuated wildly as a result of this hysteria. Assault rifle paranoia has caused these weapons in the AR-15 configuration to be selling for 3 to 4 times the retail rate in some metropolitan areas. They have become illegal to own in California. For this reason we will omit pricing on these models as it is impossible to be accurate for all readers or even a majority of them. We will list all semi-automatic variations and leave the pricing to you.

### AR-15 Sporter
The first civilian version of the M16, this is a semi-automatic gas-operated rifle with 20" barrel and black nylon stock and forend. It is chambered for the 5.56mm (.223) and has a 20- or 30-round detachable box magazine. It features a two-position aperature rear sight and a post front. It weighs 7 lbs. 8 oz. This model has the early-style sights and does not have the forward bolt assist.

### AR-15 A2 Sporter Model
This is virtually the same rifle with the addition of the forward bolt assist.

### AR-15 A2 Govt. Model
This variation features the new 800-meter rear sight system.

### AR-15 A2 H-Bar
This is another variation that is quite similar but has a heavy target-type barrel. The gun weighs 8 lbs. and was introduced in 1986.

### AR-15 A2 Delta H-Bar
This is a full target variation with a heavy barrel, 3X9-power rubber armored variable scope, and adjustable mounts. It has an adjustable cheekpiece and a leather sling and is furnished with a hard case. It was introduced in 1987.

### AR-15 A2 Carbine
This model is the same as the A2 Sporter with a 16" barrel, shortened forearm, and collapsible buttstock.

### AR-15 A2 Govt. Model Carbine
This model has the 800-meter rear sight and in all other respects is the same as the AR-15 A2 Carbine.

### AR-15 9mm Carbine
This model was manufactured in 1985 and 1986. It is identical to the A2 Carbine except that it is chambered for the 9mm Parabellum cartridge and has a 20-round magazine.

## COLT COMMEMORATIVES
The field of commemoratives can be fascinating and frustrating, depending on one's point of view. For someone who collects things from purely an aesthetic sense, commemoratives are quite desirable. Most are embellished and have had great care put into their fit and finish. They are attractively cased, and the proliferation of them makes acquisition relatively simple except from a financial standpoint. On the other hand, the collector who has an eye for the investment potential of his collections has found that the commemorative market has been soft and as investments they historically have not done well. The reason for this is twofold. The limited production appeal is not always what it seems. Many times the amounts produced are greater than one would consider limited.

It is also a fact that if one fires a commemorative, its collectibility is gone. Even excessive handling can cause this problem. This means that since the majority of these firearms are kept new in the original boxes, the supply will usually outstrip the demand. Very few commemoratives are ever lost or worn out. Collectors who seek firearms for their historic significance are usually not interested in the commemoratives, as even though they may have been issued to commemorate a specific historic person or event, they are not a part of the era and are regarded as "instant" collectibles. In some areas one will find that the Colt Commemoratives are not as desirable, saleable, or expensive as the plain out of the box versions. This is especially true in the Single Action Army models. We list the commemoratives made by Colt in chronological order.

Remember that the prices reflect new-in-the-box as it came from the factory--all papers, books, etc., intact and included. We also include the issue price for comparison. If the model with which you are concerned has been fired or is not in its original casing or box, deduct as much as 50 percent from these prices. It is interesting to note that in some areas shooters are taking advantage of the soft commemorative market and are buying SAA's at lower prices than the plain 3rd Generation guns--then shooting them. This can perhaps have a positive effect on appreciation.

## COLT COMMEMORATIVES

### 1961

| | Issue | NIB | Amount Mfg. |
|---|---|---|---|
| Geneseo, Illinois 125th Anniversary Derringer | $28 | $450 | 104 |
| Sheriff's Model (Blue & Case) | 130 | 1,250 | 478 |
| Sheriff's Model (Nickel) | 140 | 3,000 | 25 |
| Kansas Statehood Scout | 75 | 275 | 6,201 |
| 125th Anniversary Model SAA .45 | 150 | 725 | 7,390 |
| Pony Express Centennial Scout | 80 | 400 | 1,007 |
| Civil War Centennial Pistol | 75 | 125 | 24,114 |

### 1962

| | Issue | NIB | Amount Mfg. |
|---|---|---|---|
| Rock Island Arsenal Centennial Scout | $39 | $200 | 550 |
| Columbus, Ohio Sesquicentennial Scout | 100 | 500 | 200 |
| Ft. Findlay, Ohio Sesquicentennial Scout | 90 | 550 | 110 |
| Ft. Findlay Cased Pair | 185 | 1,500 | 20 |
| New Mexico Golden Anniversary Scout | 80 | 325 | 1,000 |
| Ft. McPherson, Nebraska Centennial Derringer | 29 | 300 | 300 |
| West Virginia Statehood Centennial Scout | 75 | 300 | 3,452 |

### 1963

| | Issue | NIB | Amount Mfg. |
|---|---|---|---|
| West Virginia Statehood Centennial SAA .45 | $150 | $750 | 600 |
| Arizona Terr. Cent. Scout | 75 | 325 | 5,355 |
| Arizona Terr. Cent. SAA .45 | 150 | 850 | 1,280 |
| Carolina Charter Tercent. Scout | 75 | 350 | 300 |
| Carolina Charter Tercent. 22/45 Comb. | 240 | 1,000 | 251 |
| H. Cook 1 to 100 22/45 Comb. | 275 | 1,000 | 100 |
| Ft. Stephenson, Ohio Sesquicentennial Scout | 75 | 450 | 200 |
| Battle of Gettysburg Centennial Scout | 90 | 350 | 1,019 |
| Idaho Terr. Cent. Scout | 75 | 300 | 902 |
| Gen. J.H. Morgan Indiana Raid Scout | 75 | 500 | 100 |
| Cherry's 35th Anniversary 22/45 Comb. | 275 | 1,400 | 100 |
| Nevada Statehood Centennial Scout | 75 | 275 | 3,984 |
| Nevada Statehood Centennial SAA .45 | 150 | 700 | 1,688 |
| Nevada Statehood Centennial 22/45 Comb. | 240 | 1,050 | 189 |
| Nevada Statehood Centennial 22/45 W/extra Cyls. | 350 | 1,150 | 577 |
| Nevada Battle Born Scout | 85 | 275 | 981 |
| Nevada Battle Born SAA .45 | 175 | 1,000 | 80 |
| Nevada Battle Born 22/45 Comb. | 265 | 2,200 | 20 |
| Montana Terr. Centennial Scout | 75 | 275 | 2,300 |
| Montana Terr. Centennial SAA .45 | 150 | 700 | 851 |
| Wyoming Diamond Jubilee Scout | 75 | 275 | 2,357 |
| General Hood Centennial Scout | 75 | 275 | 1,503 |
| New Jersey Terrcent. Scout | 75 | 350 | 1,001 |
| New Jersey Terrcent SAA .45 | 150 | 900 | 250 |
| St. Louis Bicentennial Scout | 75 | 275 | 802 |
| St. Louis Bicentennial SAA .45 | 150 | 700 | 200 |
| St. Louis Bicentennial 22/45 Comb. | 240 | 1,000 | 250 |
| California Gold Rush Scout | 80 | 300 | 500 |
| Pony Express Pres. SAA .45 | 250 | 850 | 1,004 |
| Chamizal Treaty Scout | 85 | 300 | 450 |
| Chamizal Treaty SAA .45 | 170 | 1,000 | 50 |
| Chamizal Treaty 22/45 Comb. | 280 | 1,550 | 50 |
| Col. Sam Colt Sesquicentennial SAA .45 | 225 | 700 | 4,750 |
| Col. Sam Colt Deluxe SAA .45 | 500 | 1,500 | 200 |
| Col. Sam Colt Special Deluxe SAA .45 | 1,000 | 3,250 | 50 |

### 1964

| | Issue | NIB | Amount Mfg. |
|---|---|---|---|
| Wyatt Earp Buntline SAA .45 | $250 | $1,750 | 150 |

### 1965

| | Issue | NIB | Amount Mfg. |
|---|---|---|---|
| Oregon Trail Scout | $75 | $300 | 1,995 |
| Joaquin Murietta 22/45 Comb. | 350 | 1,250 | 100 |
| Forty Niner Miner Scout | 85 | 300 | 500 |
| Old Ft. Des Moines Reconst. Scout | 90 | 300 | 700 |
| Old Ft. Des Moines Reconst. SAA.45 | 170 | 800 | 100 |
| Old Ft. Des Moines Reconst. 22/45 Comb. | 290 | 1,250 | 100 |
| Appomattox Centennial Scout | 75 | 275 | 1,001 |
| Appomattox Centennial SAA .45 | 150 | 750 | 250 |
| Appomattox Centennial 22/45 Comb. | 240 | 1,000 | 250 |
| General Meade Campaign Scout | 75 | 275 | 1,197 |
| St. Augustine Quadracentennial Scout | 85 | 300 | 500 |
| Kansas Cowtown Series Wichita Scout | 85 | 275 | 500 |

## COLT COMMEMORATIVES

| 1966 | Issue | NIB | Amount Mfg. |
|---|---|---|---|
| Kansas Cowtown Series Dodge City Scout | $85 | $275 | 500 |
| Colorado Gold Rush Scout | 85 | 275 | 1,350 |
| Oklahoma Territory Scout | 85 | 275 | 1,343 |
| Dakota Teritory Scout | 85 | 275 | 1,000 |
| General Meade SAA .45 | 165 | 900 | 200 |
| Abercrombie & Fitch Trailblazer New York | 275 | 875 | 200 |
| Abercrombie & Fitch Trailblazer Chicago | 275 | 875 | 100 |
| Abercrombie & Fitch Trailblazer San Francisco | 275 | 900 | 100 |
| Kansas Cowtown Series Abilene Scout | 95 | 275 | 500 |
| Indiana Sesquicentennial Scout | 85 | 250 | 1,500 |
| Pony Express 4-Square Set .45 4 Guns | 1,400 | 3,500 | N/A |
| California Gold Rush SAA .45 | 175 | 1,000 | 130 |

| 1967 | Issue | NIB | Amount Mfg. |
|---|---|---|---|
| Lawman Series Bat Masterson Scout | $90 | $350 | 3,000 |
| Lawman Series Bat Masterson SAA .45 | 180 | 800 | 500 |
| Alamo Scout | 85 | 325 | 4,250 |
| Alamo SAA .45 | 165 | 800 | 750 |
| Alamo 22/45 Comb. | 265 | 1,000 | 250 |
| Kansas Cowtown Series Coffeyville Scout | 95 | 275 | 500 |
| Kansas Trail Series Chisolm Trail Scout | 100 | 250 | 500 |
| WWI Series Chateau Thierry .45 Auto | 200 | 575 | 7,400 |
| WWI Series Chateau Thierry Deluxe | 500 | 1,250 | 75 |
| WWI Series Chateau Thierry Special Deluxe | 1,000 | 2,000 | 25 |

| 1968 | Issue | NIB | Amount Mfg. |
|---|---|---|---|
| Nebraska Cent. Scout | $100 | $300 | 7,001 |
| Kansas Trail Series Pawnee Trail Scout | 110 | 250 | 501 |
| WWI Series Belleau Wood .45 Auto | 200 | 550 | 7,400 |
| WWI Series Belleau Wood Deluxe | 500 | 1,250 | 75 |
| WWI Series Belleau Wood Special Deluxe | 1,000 | 2,000 | 25 |
| Lawman Series Pat Garrett Scout | 110 | 350 | 3,000 |
| Lawman Series Pat Garrett SAA .45 | 220 | 800 | 500 |

| 1969 | Issue | NIB | Amount Mfg. |
|---|---|---|---|
| Gen. Nathan B. Forrest Scout | $110 | $300 | 3,000 |
| Kansas Trail Series Santa Fe Trail Sct. | 120 | 250 | 501 |
| WWI Ser. 2nd Battle of Marne .45 Auto | 220 | 550 | 7,400 |
| WWI Ser. 2nd Battle of Marne Deluxe | 500 | 1,300 | 75 |
| WWI Ser. 2nd Battle of Marne Special Deluxe | 1,000 | 2,000 | 25 |
| Alabama Sesquicentennial Scout | 110 | 325 | 3,001 |
| Alabama Sesquicentennial SAA .45 | N/A | 15,000 | 1 |
| Golden Spike Scout | 135 | 275 | 11,000 |
| Kansas Trail Ser. Shawnee Trail Scout | 120 | 250 | 501 |
| WWI Ser. Meuse-Argonne .45 Auto | 220 | 500 | 7,400 |
| WWI Ser. Meuse-Argonne Deluxe | 500 | 1,250 | 75 |
| WWI Ser. Meuse-Argonne Special Deluxe | 1,000 | 2,000 | 25 |
| Arkansas Terr. Sesquicentennial Scout | 110 | 225 | 3,500 |
| Lawman Ser. Wild Bill Hickock Scout | 117 | 350 | 3,000 |
| Lawman Ser. Wild Bill Hickock SAA .45 | 220 | 800 | 500 |
| California Bicentennial Scout | 135 | 275 | 5,000 |

| 1970 | Issue | NIB | Amount Mfg. |
|---|---|---|---|
| Kansas Ft. Ser. Ft. Larned Scout | $120 | $250 | 500 |
| WWII Ser. European Theatre | 250 | 550 | 11,500 |
| WWII Ser. Pacific Theatre | 250 | 600 | 11,500 |
| Texas Ranger SAA .45 | 650 | 1,750 | 1,000 |
| Kansas Ft. Ser. Ft. Hays Scout | 130 | 275 | 500 |
| Marine Sesquicentennial Scout | 120 | 250 | 3,000 |
| Missouri Sesquicentennial Scout | 125 | 250 | 3,000 |
| Missouri Sesquicentennial SAA .45 | 220 | 650 | 900 |
| Kansas Ft. Ser. Ft. Riley Scout | 130 | 250 | 500 |
| Lawman Ser. Wyatt Earp Scout | 125 | 350 | 3,000 |
| Lawman Ser. Wyatt Earp SAA .45 | 395 | 1,250 | 500 |

## COLT COMMEMORATIVES

| 1971 | Issue | NIB | Amount Mfg. |
|---|---|---|---|
| NRA Centennial SAA .45 | $ 250 | $600 | 5,000 |
| NRA Centennial SAA .357 Magazine | 250 | 500 | 5,000 |
| NRA Centennial Gold Cup .45 Auto | 250 | 600 | 2,500 |
| U.S. Grant 1851 Navy | 250 | 400 | 4,750 |
| Robt. E. Lee 1851 Navy | 250 | 400 | 4,750 |
| Lee - Grant Set 1851 Navies | 500 | 850 | 250 |
| Kansas Ft. Ser. Ft. Scott Scout | 130 | 275 | 500 |

| 1973 | | | |
|---|---|---|---|
| Florida Terr. Sesquicentennial Scout | $125 | $250 | 2,001 |
| Arizona Ranger Scout | 135 | 275 | 3,001 |

| 1974 | | | |
|---|---|---|---|
| Peacemaker Centennial SAA .45 | $ 300 | $700 | 1,500 |
| Peacemaker Centennial SAA .44-40 | 300 | 750 | 1,500 |
| Peacemaker Centennial Cased Set | 625 | 1,500 | 500 |

| 1975 | | | |
|---|---|---|---|
| USS Texas Special Edition .45 Auto | N/A | $1,000 | 500 |
| Not Factory Issued | | | |

| 1976 | | | |
|---|---|---|---|
| U.S. Bicentennial Set | $1,695 | $1,800 | 1,776 |

| 1977 | | | |
|---|---|---|---|
| 2nd Amendment .22 | $ 195 | $350 | 3,020 |
| U.S.Cavalry 200th Anniversary Set | 995 | 1,000 | 3,000 |

| 1978 | | | |
|---|---|---|---|
| Statehood 3rd Model Dragoon | $12,500 | $10,000 | $52 |

| 1979 | | | |
|---|---|---|---|
| Ned Buntline SAA N.F. .45 | $ 895 | $800 | 3,000 |
| Ohio President's Special Edition .45 Auto | N/A | 800 | 250 |
| Tombstone Centennial .45 Auto | 550 | 650 | 300 |

| 1980 | | | |
|---|---|---|---|
| Drug Enforcement Agency .45 Auto | $ 550 | $1,100 | 910 |
| Olympics Ace Special Edition .22 | 1,000 | 1,150 | 200 |
| Heritage Walker .44 Percussion | 1,495 | 1,450 | 1,847 |

| 1981 | | | |
|---|---|---|---|
| John M. Browning .45 Auto | $1,100 | $800 | 3,000 |

| 1982 | | | |
|---|---|---|---|
| John Wayne SAA | $2,995 | $1,650 | 3,100 |
| John Wayne SAA Deluxe | 10,000 | 7,000 | 500 |
| John Wayne SAA Presentation | 20,000 | 15,000 | 100 |

| 1983 | | | |
|---|---|---|---|
| Buffalo Bill Wild West Show Centennial SAA | $1,350 | $1,250 | 500 |
| Armory Model Limited Production SAA .45 | 1,125 | 1,000 | 500 |
| (not a true commemorative) | | | |

| 1984 | | | |
|---|---|---|---|
| 1st Edition Government Model .380 ACP | $425 | $400 | 1,000 |
| Duke Frontier .22 | 475 | 475 | 1,000 |
| Winchester/Colt SAA .44-40 | N/A | 2,500 | 4,000 |
| USA Edition SAA .44-40 | 4,995 | 3,500 | 100 |
| Kit Carson New Frontier .22 | 550 | 450 | 1,000 |
| 2nd Edition Government Model .380 ACP | 525 | 500 | 1,000 |
| Officer's ACP Commencement Issue | 700 | 600 | 1,000 |
| Theodore Roosevelt SAA .44-40 | 1,695 | 1,500 | 500 |
| North American Oilmen Buntline SAA .45 | 3,900 | 3,500 | 200 |

### COLT COMMEMORATIVES

| 1986 | Issue | NIB | Amount Mfg. |
|---|---|---|---|
| 150th Anniversary SAA .45 | $1,595 | $1,400 | 1,000 |
| 150th Anniversary Engraving Sampler | 1,613 | 1,500 | N/A |
| 150th Anniversary Engraving Sampler .45 Auto | 1,155 | 1,000 | N/A |
| Texas 150th Sesquicentennial Sheriff's .45 | 836 | 1,000 | N/A |
| Mustang 1st Edition .380 ACP | 475 | 450 | 1,000 |
| Officer's ACP Heirloom Edition | 1,575 | 1,550 | N/A |
| Klay-Colt 1851 Navy | 1,850 | 1,850 | 150 |
| Klay-Colt 1851 Navy Engraved Edition | 3,150 | 3,150 | 50 |
| Double Diamond Set .357 & .45 Auto | 1,575 | 1,500 | 1,000 |
| **1987** | | | |
| Combat Elite Custom Edition .45 Auto | $ 900 | $750 | 500 |
| 12th Man Spirit of Aggieland .45 Auto | 950 | 750 | 999 |
| **1989** | | | |
| Snake Eyes Limited Edition 2-2.5" Pythons | $2,950 | $1,895 | 500 |

## COLUMBIA ARMORY
### Columbia, Tennessee

This company supposedly manufactured three pistols--the Columbian, Parker, and the Spencer--circa 1888-1889. Evidence exists that they were actually made by the John T. Smith Co. (holder of patents on all three) of Rock Falls, Connecticut. They were produced for and marketed by Maltby Henly & Co., a New York sporting goods dealer. The Columbia Armory marking was merely a marketing ploy, not uncommon in this era. The three pistols themselves are odd because they have a prominent screw head behind the barrel as on hinged-frame break open revolvers. In actuality these are solid frames; removing the screw allows the trigger unit to drop out for cleaning. The Columbian is chambered for the .22 rimfire and the .32; the Parker, .32; and the Spencer, .38. They are all of the Smith Co. "Hammerless Safety" design and are so marked.

| Exc. | V.G. | Good | Fair | Poor |
|---|---|---|---|---|
| 150 | 125 | 100 | 75 | 50 |

## COLUMBUS F. A. MFG. CO.
### Columbus, Georgia

**Columbus Revolver**
This Confederate revolver was privately produced by L. Haiman of Columbus. This weapon is chambered for .36-caliber percussion and has a 6-shot, unfluted cylinder. It is similar in appearance to the 1851 Colt Navy and has a 7.5" octagonal barrel. The pistol is browned steel, with brass gripstraps and walnut grips. The barrel is marked "Columbus Fire Arms Manuf. Co/Columbus, Ga." This company received a contract from the Confederate States of America in August of 1862 for 10,000 pistols, but this was never filled. Only 100 revolvers were manufactured in 1863 and 1864. In 1864 the Company was sold to the Confederate government, who wished to establish a major arsenal at the Columbus site. Union troops destroyed the facility in 1865, and no other weapons were ever produced there.

| Exc. | V.G. | Good | Fair | Poor |
|---|---|---|---|---|
| 15000 | 12500 | 10000 | 7500 | 5000 |

## COMBLAIN
### Belgium and Brazil

**Single Shot Rifle**
The Comblain Single Shot Rifle was designed in Belgium in 1870. It is a falling-block hammer-type action and is quite strong. There were a good many manufactured in Belgium, and they were used by the Home Guard as late as WWII. The Belgium Comblain is chambered for the 11 X 53R centerfire cartridge and is marked "Comblain Brevette" with a serial number below. The Brazilian government adopted the Comblain rifle as a service arm in 1874 and purchased them from Belgium. The Brazilian version is hammerless and is chambered for a slightly different version of the same basic cartridge. The manufacture was discontinued after 1874.

| Exc. | V.G. | Good | Fair | Poor |
|---|---|---|---|---|
| 750 | 650 | 500 | 350 | 250 |

## COMMANDO ARMS
### Knoxville, Tennessee

This company was formerly known as Volunteer Enterprises. The name change took place in 1978.

**Mark III Carbine**
This is a blowback-operated semi-automatic carbine patterned after the Thompson submachine gun. It is chambered for the .45 ACP cartridge and has a 16.5" barrel with a peep rear sight and a vertical foregrip. This model was manufactured between 1969 and 1976.

Commando Mark III

| Exc. | V.G. | Good | Fair | Poor |
|---|---|---|---|---|
| 300 | 275 | 225 | 175 | 125 |

**Mark 9 Carbine**
This model is similar to the Mark III except that it is chambered for the 9mm cartridge.

Commando Mark 9

| Exc. | V.G. | Good | Fair | Poor |
|---|---|---|---|---|
| 300 | 275 | 225 | 175 | 125 |

## Mark .45

This is simply the new designation for the Mark III after the company name change.

Commando Mark 45

| Exc. | V.G. | Good | Fair | Poor |
|------|------|------|------|------|
| 300 | 275 | 225 | 175 | 125 |

## CONNECTICUT ARMS CO.
### Norfolk, Connecticut

### Pocket Revolver

This was yet another of the many attempts at side stepping the Rollin White patent held by Smith & Wesson that gave them exclusive rights to manufacture bored-through cylinders. This model uses a cup-primed cartridge and is loaded from the front of the cylinder. There is a hinged hook on the side of the frame under the cylinder that acts as the extractor. The cartridge is .28 caliber, and the unfluted cylinder holds 6 rounds. The 3" barrel is octagonal, and the frame is made of silver-plated brass. The remainder is blued and the square butt has walnut grips. The barrel is marked "Conn. Arms Co. Norfolk, Conn." There were approximately 2700 manufactured in the 1860s.

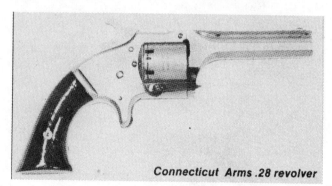

Connecticut Arms .28 revolver

| Exc. | V.G. | Good | Fair | Poor |
|------|------|------|------|------|
| 300 | 275 | 225 | 150 | 100 |

## CONNECTICUT VALLEY ARMS CO.
### Norcross, Georgia

### Express Rifle

This is a side-by-side, double-barrelled rifle chambered for .50-caliber percussion. It has 28" tapered barrels with a hooked breech for easy takedown. The finish is blued, and there is a deluxe model with a checkered walnut stock and an economy model with a hardwood stock. This rifle is available in kit form also.
Deluxe Version--Add 100 Percent.

| NIB | Exc. | V.G. | Good | Fair | Poor |
|-----|------|------|------|------|------|
| 525 | 450 | 400 | 350 | 300 | 225 |

### Over/Under Rifle

This model has 26" tapered Over/Under barrels and is chambered for .50-caliber percussion. It is blued, with stainless-steel nipples and a checkered walnut stock. This model is not available as a kit.

| NIB | Exc. | V.G. | Good | Fair | Poor |
|-----|------|------|------|------|------|
| 575 | 500 | 450 | 400 | 350 | 275 |

### Hawken Rifle

This is a percussion muzzleloader patterned after the original Hawken rifle. It is chambered for .50 caliber and has a 28" octagonal barrel, double set triggers, and a select walnut stock.

| NIB | Exc. | V.G. | Good | Fair | Poor |
|-----|------|------|------|------|------|
| 400 | 325 | 275 | 225 | 150 | 100 |

### Presentation Grade Hawken

This model is similar to the Standard Hawken with an engraved lock, fancy brass patchbox, and a select European walnut stock.

| NIB | Exc. | V.G. | Good | Fair | Poor |
|-----|------|------|------|------|------|
| 500 | 425 | 375 | 325 | 275 | 200 |

### Pennsylvania Long Rifle

This is a .50-caliber flintlock with a 40" octagonal barrel. It has double-set triggers and a select walnut stock.

| NIB | Exc. | V.G. | Good | Fair | Poor |
|-----|------|------|------|------|------|
| 475 | 400 | 350 | 300 | 250 | 175 |

### Kentucky Rifle

This model is chambered for .45 caliber percussion and has a 33.5" octagonal barrel and a hardwood stock.

| NIB | Exc. | V.G. | Good | Fair | Poor |
|-----|------|------|------|------|------|
| 275 | 225 | 175 | 150 | 100 | 75 |

### Mountain Rifle

This is a half-stock rifle chambered for either .50 or .54-caliber percussion, with a select walnut stock.

| NIB | Exc. | V.G. | Good | Fair | Poor |
|-----|------|------|------|------|------|
| 300 | 225 | 175 | 125 | 100 | 75 |

### Blazer Rifle

This is a modern rendering of the .50-caliber percussion rifle and is not a replica of a historic arm. It has a contemporary stock design, a 28" octagonal barrel, and a hardwood stock.

| NIB | Exc. | V.G. | Good | Fair | Poor |
|-----|------|------|------|------|------|
| 150 | 125 | 100 | 85 | 65 | 45 |

### Brittany II Shotgun

This is a side-by-side, .410 bore shotgun with 24" round barrels and percussion locks. It has double triggers and a hardwood pistolgrip stock.

| NIB | Exc. | V.G. | Good | Fair | Poor |
|-----|------|------|------|------|------|
| 170 | 150 | 125 | 100 | 75 | 50 |

### Trapper Shotgun

This is a single-barrel, 12-gauge percussion shotgun with a 28" round barrel and three screw-in choke tubes. It has a hardwood stock.

| NIB | Exc. | V.G. | Good | Fair | Poor |
|-----|------|------|------|------|------|
| 225 | 200 | 175 | 150 | 100 | 75 |

## PISTOLS
### Siber

This is a replica of the Swiss Siber pistol chambered for .45-caliber percussion, with an engraved lock and select walnut stock.

| NIB | Exc. | V.G. | Good | Fair | Poor |
|-----|------|------|------|------|------|
| 400 | 325 | 275 | 225 | 150 | 100 |

### Kentucky

This is a .45-caliber percussion pistol with a 10" barrel and a hardwood stock.

| NIB | Exc. | V.G. | Good | Fair | Poor |
|-----|------|------|------|------|------|
| 140 | 125 | 100 | 80 | 60 | 40 |

### Philadelphia Derringer

This is a replica chambered for .45-caliber percussion with a 3.25" barrel, engraved lock, and a hardwood stock.

| NIB | Exc. | V.G. | Good | Fair | Poor |
|-----|------|------|------|------|------|
| 75 | 65 | 50 | 40 | 30 | 20 |

### Sheriff's Model

This model is an engraved, nickle-plated replica of the 1860 Army percussion revolver. It is chambered for .36 caliber, has a one-piece walnut grip, and is furnished with a powder flask.

| NIB | Exc. | V.G. | Good | Fair | Poor |
|-----|------|------|------|------|------|
| 225 | 200 | 175 | 150 | 125 | 100 |

**3rd Model Dragoon**

This replica is chambered for .44 caliber and has walnut one-piece grips.

| NIB | Exc. | V.G. | Good | Fair | Poor |
|-----|------|------|------|------|------|
| 225 | 200 | 175 | 150 | 125 | 100 |

**Colt Walker Replica**

| NIB | Exc. | V.G. | Good | Fair | Poor |
|-----|------|------|------|------|------|
| 275 | 250 | 225 | 200 | 175 | 150 |

**Remington Bison**

| NIB | Exc. | V.G. | Good | Fair | Poor |
|-----|------|------|------|------|------|
| 250 | 225 | 200 | 175 | 150 | 125 |

**Pocket Police**

| NIB | Exc. | V.G. | Good | Fair | Poor |
|-----|------|------|------|------|------|
| 135 | 110 | 100 | 85 | 65 | 45 |

**Wells Fargo**

This model is chambered for .31-caliber percussion and is supplied with an extra cylinder. It has a 4" octagonal barrel and no rammer.

| NIB | Exc. | V.G. | Good | Fair | Poor |
|-----|------|------|------|------|------|
| 165 | 145 | 125 | 100 | 75 | 50 |

**1851 Navy**

| NIB | Exc. | V.G. | Good | Fair | Poor |
|-----|------|------|------|------|------|
| 135 | 110 | 100 | 85 | 65 | 45 |

**1861 Navy**

| NIB | Exc. | V.G. | Good | Fair | Poor |
|-----|------|------|------|------|------|
| 150 | 135 | 110 | 90 | 75 | 50 |

**1860 Army**

| NIB | Exc. | V.G. | Good | Fair | Poor |
|-----|------|------|------|------|------|
| 220 | 200 | 175 | 150 | 125 | 100 |

**1858 Remington**

| NIB | Exc. | V.G. | Good | Fair | Poor |
|-----|------|------|------|------|------|
| 175 | 150 | 125 | 100 | 75 | 50 |

**1858 Remington Target**

This is a replica of the original Remington with the addition of adjustable target sights.

| NIB | Exc. | V.G. | Good | Fair | Poor |
|-----|------|------|------|------|------|
| 235 | 200 | 175 | 125 | 100 | 75 |

## CONSTABLE, R.
### Philadelphia, Pennsylvania

**Pocket Pistol**

This company produced a derringer-style pocket pistol with a 3" round or octagonal barrel. The stock is of walnut with German-silver mountings. These pistols are marked "R. Constable Philadelphia" and were manufactured in the 1850s.

| Exc. | V.G. | Good | Fair | Poor |
|------|------|------|------|------|
| 650 | 550 | 450 | 350 | 250 |

## CONTENTO/VENTURA
### Importer--Ventura
### Seal Beach, California

This high-grade, double-barrel shotgun is no longer imported.

**Side By Side**

**Model 51**

This is a lower-priced double barrel chambered for 12, 16, 20, 28 gauge, and .410. It was offered with barrel lengths of 26", 28", 30", and 32", with various chokes. It is a boxlock with extractors and double triggers. The straight stock was of checkered walnut.

| Exc. | V.G. | Good | Fair | Poor |
|------|------|------|------|------|
| 400 | 350 | 300 | 225 | 150 |

**Model 52**

This Model is similar to the Model 51 except that it is chambered for 10 gauge.

| Exc. | V.G. | Good | Fair | Poor |
|------|------|------|------|------|
| 500 | 450 | 400 | 325 | 250 |

**Model 53**

This is a deluxe version of the Model 51. It features a scalloped receiver and automatic ejectors and is available with a single-selective trigger.

Single-Selective Trigger--Add 25 Percent.

| Exc. | V.G. | Good | Fair | Poor |
|------|------|------|------|------|
| 475 | 425 | 375 | 300 | 225 |

**Model 61**

This model features hand-detachable Holland & Holland-type sidelocks and is chambered for 12 and 20 gauge with various barrel lengths and chokes. It has automatic ejectors, cocking indicators, a floral engraved receiver, and a select, hand-checkered, walnut pistolgrip stock.

| Exc. | V.G. | Good | Fair | Poor |
|------|------|------|------|------|
| 875 | 800 | 750 | 600 | 450 |

**Model 65**

This is the top of the line--basically the same as the Model 61 with extensive engraving and a finer grade of walnut in the stock. This model has a finer overall finish.

| Exc. | V.G. | Good | Fair | Poor |
|------|------|------|------|------|
| 1150 | 1000 | 850 | 700 | 550 |

**Contento Over/Under**

This model is chambered for 12 gauge only and is in the trap configuration. It has 32" barrels with screw-in choke tubes, a high ventilated rib, and automatic ejectors. It features a standard single-selective trigger and a checkered, walnut Monte Carlo stock.

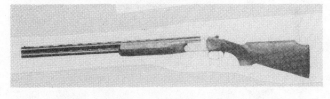

| Exc. | V.G. | Good | Fair | Poor |
|------|------|------|------|------|
| 1050 | 900 | 750 | 600 | 500 |

**Mark 2**

This is the same model with an extra single barrel and a fitted leather case.

| Exc. | V.G. | Good | Fair | Poor |
|------|------|------|------|------|
| 1350 | 1200 | 1050 | 900 | 800 |

**Mark 3**

This model is similar to the standard model with engraving and a select-grade walnut stock.

| Exc. | V.G. | Good | Fair | Poor |
|------|------|------|------|------|
| 1600 | 1500 | 1250 | 1100 | 950 |

**Mark 3 Combo**

This model has an extra single barrel and a fitted leather case.

| Exc. | V.G. | Good | Fair | Poor |
|------|------|------|------|------|
| 2800 | 2600 | 2250 | 1750 | 1300 |

## CONTINENTAL
### RWM
### Cologne, Germany

**Continental Pocket Pistol**

This is a blowback-operated, single-action, semi-automatic pocket pistol chambered for the 6.35mm cartridge. It has an internal hammer, 2" barrel, and a 7-shot detachable magazine. The finish is blued with plastic grips, and the slide is marked "Continental Kal.6.35."

| Exc. | V.G. | Good | Fair | Poor |
|------|------|------|------|------|
| 210 | 185 | 145 | 110 | 75 |

## CONTINENTAL ARMS CO.
### Liege, Belgium

**Double Rifle**

This high-grade, double-barrelled rifle utilized the Anson & Deeley boxlock system, that is known for its strength. It has either 24" or 26" barrels and is chambered for .270, .303, .30-40, .30-06, .348, 375 H&H, .400 Jeffreys, .465, .475, .500, and .600 Nitro Express. It features double triggers and a hand-checkered walnut stock.

| Exc. | V.G. | Good | Fair | Poor |
|------|------|------|------|------|
| 5000 | 4500 | 3750 | 3000 | 2250 |

## CONTINENTAL ARMS CO.
### Norwich, Connecticut

**Pepperbox**

This is a revolving, pepperbox-type pistol chambered for the .22-caliber rimfire cartridge. It has a 5-barrel cluster 2.5" in length. It features a spur trigger and single-action lockwork. The frame is iron with a blued finish and rosewood, flared grips. The barrels are marked, "Continental Arms Co. Norwich Ct. Patented Aug. 28, 1866." This model is also known as the "Ladies Companion." There were approximately 300 manufactured in the late 1860's.

| Exc. | V.G. | Good | Fair | Poor |
|------|------|------|------|------|
| 600  | 525  | 475  | 375  | 300  |

## COOK & BROTHER
### New Orleans, Louisiana

This company produced rifles for the Confederacy during the Civil War. The Cook brothers were English, and their rifles resembled the British Enfield. In 1861 the company was located in New Orleans; but by 1863 the advancing Union Army forced the company to relocate at Athens, Georgia, where they remained until 1864. This rifle was chambered for .58-caliber percussion and was produced in three lengths: the Musketoon with a 24" barrel, the rifle with a barrel length of 33" and a bayonet lug, and the carbine with a 21" barrel and a saddle ring. These weapons were left in the white; and the stocks were made of walnut, maple, or pecan. The stocks are full-length with two barrel bands, and the mountings are brass. There were approximately 2,000 manufactured between 1861 and 1864. All models have the same approximate value.

| Exc. | V.G. | Good | Fair | Poor |
|------|------|------|------|------|
| 3750 | 3500 | 3000 | 2250 | 1500 |

## COONAN ARMS CO.
### St. Paul, Minnesota

**Model A**

This pistol is constructed of stainless steel and is chambered for the .357 Magnum. It is a single-action semi-automatic similar to the Colt 1911 in appearance and function. It has a 5" barrel and a 7-shot, detachable magazine. It is furnished with fixed sights and smooth walnut grips. This model was introduced in 1981 and was discontinued at serial #2000 in 1984.

| NIB | Exc. | V.G. | Good | Fair | Poor |
|-----|------|------|------|------|------|
| 625 | 600  | 525  | 450  | 400  | 325  |

**Model B**

This is the improved version of the Coonan. It features a linkless barrel system, extended grip safety, enclosed trigger bar, and a more contoured grip. A 6" barrel is available, as are adjustable sights, as extra cost options. A .38 Special conversion is also available. This Model was introduced in 1985 and is now the standard production model.

6" Barrel-- Add $40.
Bomar Adjustable Sights--Add $130.
.38 Special Conversion-- Add $40.

| NIB | Exc. | V.G. | Good | Fair | Poor |
|-----|------|------|------|------|------|
| 680 | 650  | 600  | 525  | 450  | 375  |

**Comp I**

This model is similar to the Model B with an attached compensator and a stippled front grip strap. It was introduced in 1989.

| NIB  | Exc. | V.G. | Good | Fair | Poor |
|------|------|------|------|------|------|
| 1350 | 1200 | 1000 | 850  | 700  | 500  |

**Comp I Deluxe**

This is the compensator model with adjustable sights, a blued stainless-steel slide, checkered grip straps, and a finer degree of finishing.

| NIB  | Exc. | V.G. | Good | Fair | Poor |
|------|------|------|------|------|------|
| 1650 | 1350 | 1150 | 950  | 800  | 600  |

## COOPER, J. M. & CO.
### Philadelphia, Pennsylvania

**Pocket Revolver**

This revolver is chambered for .31-caliber percussion and has a 6-shot unfluted cylinder. The octagonal barrel is either 4", 5", or 6" in length. They were patterned after the 1849 Colt Pocket Model but were unique in that they were double-action. They are blued with walnut grips. During the first two years of production they were made in Pittsburgh, Pennsylvania, and were so marked. There were approximately 15,000 manufactured between 1864 and 1869.

Pittsburgh-Marked Models--Add 20 Percent.

| Exc. | V.G. | Good | Fair | Poor |
|------|------|------|------|------|
| 500  | 425  | 375  | 250  | 150  |

## COOPERATIVA OBRERA
### Eibar, Spain

**Longines**

This pistol is rare in that it is of relatively good quality for an "Eibar" pistol. It is chambered for the 7.65mm. Externally it looks very similar to a 1910 Browning, but it does not differ with other Eibar blowbacks internally. The slide is marked "Cal. 7.65 Automatic Pistol Longines."

| Exc. | V.G. | Good | Fair | Poor |
|------|------|------|------|------|
| 225  | 175  | 150  | 110  | 85   |

## COPELAND, FRANK
### Worcester, Massachusetts

**Copeland Pocket Revolver .22**

This is a 7-shot revolver with an unfluted cylinder with the lock notches on the front. The octagonal barrel is 2.5" and is chambered for .22-caliber rimfire. The frame is brass; the remainder, blued with a spur-type trigger and a birds head butt. The grips are of walnut or rosewood; and the barrel was marked "F.Copeland,Worcester, Mass." It was manufactured in the 1860's.

| Exc. | V.G. | Good | Fair | Poor |
|---|---|---|---|---|
| 275 | 225 | 175 | 125 | 100 |

**Copeland .32 Revolver**

This is a slightly larger revolver chambered for .32-caliber rimfire. It has a 5-shot fluted cylinder and an iron frame. The finish is nickel-plated, and the barrel is marked "F. Copland, Sterling, Mass." This revolver was manufactured in the 1860's.

| Exc. | V.G. | Good | Fair | Poor |
|---|---|---|---|---|
| 250 | 200 | 150 | 100 | 75 |

# COSMI, A. & F.
### Torretti, Italy
### Importer--New England Arms
### Kittery Pt., Maine

**Semi - Automatic**

This is a unique shotgun in that it loads from the rear of the stock. The action pivots and breaks open to cock. It is chambered for 12 and 20 gauge and has various barrel lengths and chokes. There is an 8-shot magazine, and a vent rib is standard. This is basically a custom-built, made-to-order gun. There is a standard and a deluxe model, with the differences being in the degree of embellishment.

**Standard Model**

| NIB | Exc. | V.G. | Good | Fair | Poor |
|---|---|---|---|---|---|
| 4000 | 3750 | 3250 | 2850 | 2200 | 1750 |

**Deluxe Model**

| NIB | Exc. | V.G. | Good | Fair | Poor |
|---|---|---|---|---|---|
| 5000 | 4750 | 4250 | 3500 | 2750 | 2000 |

# COSMOPOLITAN ARMS CO.
### Hamilton, Ohio

**Breech Loading Rifle**

This is a single-shot percussion rifle chambered for .52 caliber. It has a 31" round barrel and a falling breech block that pivots downward when the triggerguard is moved down. This rifle was produced for the military during the Civil War and has a bayonet lug on the side of the barrel. The finish is blued, and the walnut stock is varnished, with no forend. It is marked "Cosmopolitan Arms Co. Hamilton O. U.S./Gross Patent." This is a rare rifle as approximately 100 were manufactured between 1859 and 1862.

| Exc. | V.G. | Good | Fair | Poor |
|---|---|---|---|---|
| 1500 | 1300 | 1000 | 750 | 500 |

# COWLES & SON
### Chicopee, Massachusetts

**Single Shot**

This small, single-shot pocket pistol pivots sideways to load. It is chambered for the .22 or .30 caliber rimfire cartridges and has a 3.25" round barrel. The frame is silver-plated brass, with a blued barrel and a walnut birds head grip. There were approximately 200 manufactured in 1865.

| Exc. | V.G. | Good | Fair | Poor |
|---|---|---|---|---|
| 250 | 225 | 175 | 125 | 100 |

# CRESCENT F. A. CO.
### Norwich, Connecticut

This company manufactured good quality, inexpensive side-by-side shotguns between 1888 and 1893. Their products were purchased and resold by many companies of the day. In 1893 they were bought out by H.D. Folsom, who produced many of the so-called hardware store guns. In 1926 they were absorbed by Stevens Arms & Tool Co.

**Double Barrel Shotgun**

This side-by-side was made with various barrels and chokes, double triggers, and exposed hammers. The barrels are of Damascus laminated steel, and the stocks are of walnut. Prices varied, with the small gauges worth more than the larger. They are chambered for 12, 16, 20, and 28 gauge, and .410. Later there were hammerless models produced with fluid steel barrels, and they are worth a premium over the earlier models.

**12 and 16 Gauge**

| Exc. | V.G. | Good | Fair | Poor |
|---|---|---|---|---|
| 200 | 175 | 150 | 125 | 100 |

**20 Gauge**

| Exc. | V.G. | Good | Fair | Poor |
|---|---|---|---|---|
| 300 | 275 | 225 | 175 | 140 |

**28 Gauge and .410**

| Exc. | V.G. | Good | Fair | Poor |
|---|---|---|---|---|
| 400 | 350 | 300 | 250 | 200 |

**Hammerless, Fluid Steel Barrels--Add 25 Percent.**

# CRISPIN, SILAS
### New York, New York

**Crispin Revolver**

This was an effort to circumvent the Rollin White patent held by Smith & Wesson. It features a two-piece split cylinder and is chambered for its own belted .32-caliber rimfire cartridge that was reportedly quite unstable and dangerous to load. The revolver has a 5" octagonal barrel and an iron frame. The finish is blued. The frame is marked "Smith Arms Co., New York City. Crispin's Pat. Oct. 3, 1865." This 6-shot revolver is very rare, and the quantity manufactured in the latter part of the 1860's is unknown.

| Exc. | V.G. | Good | Fair | Poor |
|---|---|---|---|---|
| 4500 | 4250 | 3750 | 3000 | 2500 |

# CRUCELEGUI, HERMANOS
### Eibar, Spain

This company manufactured poor-quality "Velo-Dog" revolvers between 1900 and 1925. They chambered them for 5mm, 6.35mm, 7.65mm, and 8mm. The tradenames used were; Puppy, Velo-Mith, LeBrong, Bron-Sport, C.H., and Brong-Petit.

| Exc. | V.G. | Good | Fair | Poor |
|---|---|---|---|---|
| 125 | 100 | 80 | 60 | 35 |

# CUMMINGS, O. S.
### Lowell, Massachusetts

**Cummings Pocket Revolver**

This was an exact copy of the Smith & Wesson 1st Model 3rd Issue revolver. It is chambered for .22 rimfire and has a 7-shot fluted cylinder and a 3.5" ribbed round barrel. The frame is iron with a spur trigger, and the finish is nickel-plated. The barrel is stamped "O.S. Cummings Lowell, Mass." It has a rosewood birdshead grip. There were approximately 1,000 manufactured in the 1870's.

| Exc. | V.G. | Good | Fair | Poor |
|---|---|---|---|---|
| 250 | 225 | 175 | 150 | 125 |

# CUMMINGS & WHEELER
### Lowell, Massachusetts

**Pocket Revolver**

This revolver is quite similar to the Cummings Pocket revolver previously discussed, but there are subtle differences--such as the length of the flutes on the cylinder and the size and shape of the grip. The barrel is slightly longer and is marked "Cummings & Wheeler, Lowell, Mass."

| Exc. | V.G. | Good | Fair | Poor |
|---|---|---|---|---|
| 275 | 250 | 200 | 150 | 125 |

# CUSTOM GUN GUILD
### Doraville, Georgia

**Wood's Model IV**

This is a high quality, custom-built, single-shot rifle. It utilizes a falling-block action and was produced in a number of popular calibers. The barrel lengths offered were from 22" to 28", and the stock is of select checkered walnut. This is a very light-weight rifle, at approximately 5.5 lbs. It was manufactured for one year only, 1984, and is not often encountered on today's market.

| Exc. | V.G. | Good | Fair | Poor |
|------|------|------|------|------|
| 3000 | 2750 | 2500 | 1750 | 1000 |

# D.W.M.
### Berlin, Germany
### ALSO SEE--Luger & Borchardt

The firm of Deutsche Waffen und Munitions was a major producer of the German Luger pistol and also the company that made the Borchardt. At the close of WWI, the provisions of the Treaty of Versailles forbade the production of Parabellum pistols. D.W.M. was tooled up with a full complement of employees and were not allowed to produce their biggest seller. They decided to manufacture a pistol with very little possibility of military application. The 1910 Model Browning design was chosen. There was little done to change this pistol, and it was put on the market in 1921 as the Model 22.

## Model 22
This is a blowback-operated semi-automatic patterned after the 1910 Browning. It is chambered for the 7.65mm cartridge and has a 3.5" barrel and a blued finish. The grips were of wood at first and then changed to plastic soon afterward. There were approximately 40,000 manufactured between 1921 and 1931.

| Exc. | V.G. | Good | Fair | Poor |
|------|------|------|------|------|
| 750 | 675 | 500 | 400 | 350 |

# DAEWOO
### Korea

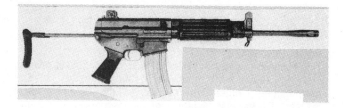

## Max I
This is a semi-automatic assault rifle produced by the Korean company that made M-16 rifles under license from Colt for the Korean armed forces. This rifle combines features of the M-16 with features found on other rifles. It is chambered for 5.56mm and has an 18" barrel, and a gas-operated rotary bolt action. The magazines are interchangeable with those from the M-16. The finish is black, and there is a retractable stock. This rifle was introduced in 1985 but is no longer imported. This is another assault-type rifle that is not possible to accurately appraise in this book. If a transaction is contemplated, please check current market prices in your given area.

## Max II
This rifle is quite similar to the Max I with a folding composite stock.

# DAISY
### Rogers, Arkansas

## V/L Rifle
This model is a single shot chambered for the .22- caliber caseless round. It is unique in that a concentrated blast of compressed air generates the heat needed to ignite the charge that is stuck to the back of the lead projectile. The barrel is 18" long with open sights, and the stock is wood-grained plastic. There were approximately 19,000 manufactured in 1968 and 1969.

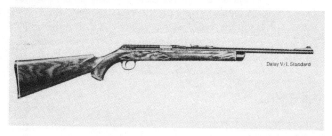

| NIB | Exc. | V.G. | Good | Fair | Poor |
|-----|------|------|------|------|------|
| 125 | 100 | 85 | 75 | 50 | 25 |

## V/L Presentation Model
This model is similar to the standard V/L rifle, with a walnut stock. There were 4,000 manufactured in 1968 and 1969.

| NIB | Exc. | V.G. | Good | Fair | Poor |
|-----|------|------|------|------|------|
| 175 | 150 | 125 | 100 | 75 | 50 |

## V/L Cased Presentation Model
This is the same as the Presentation rifle except that the rifle has a gold-colored plaque in the butt stock and comes in a fitted case with 300 rounds of ammunition.

| NIB | Exc. | V.G. | Good | Fair | Poor |
|-----|------|------|------|------|------|
| 250 | 200 | 175 | 125 | 100 | 75 |

# DAKIN GUN CO.
### San Francisco, California

## Model 100
This is a side-by-side shotgun offered in 12 and 20 gauge. The barrels are 26" or 28" in length, with various chokes. The action is a boxlock with extractors and double triggers. The finish is lightly engraved and blued, with a checkered walnut stock. This model was manufactured in the 1960's.

| Exc. | V.G. | Good | Fair | Poor |
|------|------|------|------|------|
| 350 | 325 | 280 | 210 | 150 |

## Model 147
This model is similar to the Model 100, with ventilated rib barrels.

| Exc. | V.G. | Good | Fair | Poor |
|------|------|------|------|------|
| 400 | 375 | 225 | 250 | 175 |

## Model 160
This model features a single-selective trigger. Otherwise it is the same as the Model 147.

| Exc. | V.G. | Good | Fair | Poor |
|------|------|------|------|------|
| 450 | 400 | 350 | 300 | 250 |

## Model 215

This model is a deluxe sidelock version that is heavily engraved and has a select-grade walnut stock.

| Exc. | V.G. | Good | Fair | Poor |
|------|------|------|------|------|
| 950 | 850 | 700 | 500 | 425 |

## Model 170

This is an Over/Under chambered for 12, 16, and 20 gauge. It has a boxlock action and 26" or 28" vent-rib barrels with various chokes. Double triggers are standard, and the blued receiver is lightly engraved. This Model was also discontinued in the 1960's.

| Exc. | V.G. | Good | Fair | Poor |
|------|------|------|------|------|
| 500 | 425 | 350 | 275 | 200 |

# DAKOTA ARMS, INC.
## Sturgis, South Dakota

This company was formed by Don Allen, Inc., and H. L. Grisel, Inc. Both were fine craftsmen in the field of custom rifles. They offer four basic models with a number of options to fit the customers' needs or wants. The workmanship and materials are of the highest quality. They have been in business since 1987.

## Dakota 76 Classic

This is a high-grade, bolt-action rifle that is a completely machined modern version of the Pre-64 Winchester Model 70. This action is a creation of Pete Grisel. It is chambered for the .257 Roberts, .270 Winchester, .280 Remington, .30-06, 7mm Remington Magnum, .338, .300 Winchester Magnum, and the .458 Winchester Magnum. The barrel is 23" long, and a Mauser-type extractor is used. The select, hand-checkered walnut stock is made by Don Allen. This rifle was first manufactured in 1987.

| NIB | Exc. | V.G. | Good | Fair | Poor |
|-----|------|------|------|------|------|
| 2000 | 1850 | 1650 | 1400 | 950 | 750 |

## Safari Grade

This rifle is similar except that it is chambered for .375 Holland & Holland and .458 Winchester Magnum. It has an ebony forend tip and one-piece magazine assembly and features open sights.

| NIB | Exc. | V.G. | Good | Fair | Poor |
|-----|------|------|------|------|------|
| 3000 | 2750 | 2450 | 2000 | 1350 | 1000 |

## Alpine Grade

This is a lighter-weight Mountain rifle with the short Classic action. The stock is slimmer; and the barrel, thinner. It is cham-

bered for .22-250, .243, .6mm, 250- 3000, 7mm/08, .308, and .358. This model was introduced in 1989.

| NIB | Exc. | V.G. | Good | Fair | Poor |
|-----|------|------|------|------|------|
| 1850 | 1750 | 1400 | 1250 | 850 | 500 |

## African Grade

This rifle is similar to the Safari Grade except that it is chambered for the .416 Rigby cartridge. The walnut is specially selected for strength, and there are crossbolts through the stock.

| NIB | Exc. | V.G. | Good | Fair | Poor |
|-----|------|------|------|------|------|
| 3500 | 3250 | 2750 | 2450 | 1500 | 1250 |

# DALY, CHARLES
## Dayton, Ohio

The firm of Charles Daly is a many-faceted entity that began as an importer of very high quality European shotguns manufactured purely for the American shooting public. These guns were produced by various fine German gun makers and utilized the finest materials and craftsmanship of the era. Production of these guns was stopped before WWII. In the early 1960's the Charles Daly name was resurrected as an importer of good quality guns manufactured by B. C. Miroku in Japan. The Miroku guns were not in the same league as the earlier Prussian guns but are becoming collectible in their own right. Production of the Japanese Dalys ceased in 1976. The last group of guns to bear the Daly name up to this point is the Italian-made guns that were imported by Outdoor Sports Headquarters of Dayton, Ohio. They picked up the flag in 1976 and, although the Italian-made guns were not as well received as the Miroku guns, managed to sell quite a few units while they were available.

## Charles Daly, Early Prussian Guns
## Commanidor Over/Under Model 100

This is a boxlock Over/Under with an Anson & Deeley action. It is chambered for all gauges, with choice of barrel length and chokes. It was offered with double triggers standard, but a single-selective trigger was available and would be worth an additional 20 percent. This model is blued with a checkered walnut stock and was manufactured in Belgium in the late 1930's.

| Exc. | V.G. | Good | Fair | Poor |
|------|------|------|------|------|
| 500 | 450 | 375 | 275 | 220 |

## Commanidor Over/Under Model 200

This gun is the same as the Model 100 with a better- grade walnut stock.

| Exc. | V.G. | Good | Fair | Poor |
|------|------|------|------|------|
| 650 | 600 | 500 | 375 | 275 |

## Superior Side By Side

This double barrel was chambered for all gauges and was offered with choice of barrel lengths and chokes. It features an Anson & Deeley boxlock action and double triggers and was blued with a walnut stock. This model was not manufactured after 1933.

| Exc. | V.G. | Good | Fair | Poor |
|------|------|------|------|------|
| 1000 | 850 | 650 | 450 | 400 |

## Empire Side By Side

This model is a more elaborately ornamented version of the Superior, with a better grade of walnut.

| Exc. | V.G. | Good | Fair | Poor |
|------|------|------|------|------|
| 2500 | 2000 | 1750 | 1250 | 1000 |

## Diamond Grade Side By Side

This is another model that is very similar to the superior but a good deal more deluxe. It is elaborately engraved and features a high grade walnut stock.

| Exc. | V.G. | Good | Fair | Poor |
|------|------|------|------|------|
| 5000 | 4500 | 3750 | 3000 | 2250 |

### Regent Diamond Grade Side By Side

This is the best grade in the Prussian Daly Side By Side series. It is of the highest quality throughout and has the most elaborate engraving and the best grade walnut the company offered. These guns were not manufactured after 1933.

| Exc. | V.G. | Good | Fair | Poor |
|------|------|------|------|------|
| 5500 | 4750 | 4000 | 3250 | 2500 |

### Empire Over/Under

This model is a high grade gun with an Anson & Deeley boxlock. It was offered in 12, 16, and 20 gauge, with choice of barrel length and choke. This model features double triggers and automatic ejectors, is engraved with fine quality scrollwork, and has a select-grade walnut stock. It was discontinued in 1933.

| Exc. | V.G. | Good | Fair | Poor |
|------|------|------|------|------|
| 2250 | 2000 | 1500 | 1150 | 900 |

### Diamond Grade Over/Under

This model is similar to the Empire but is a more deluxe version.

| Exc. | V.G. | Good | Fair | Poor |
|------|------|------|------|------|
| 5000 | 4500 | 3750 | 3000 | 2250 |

### Sextuple Single Barrel Trap
### Empire Grade

This is a single-barrel, break-open design of the highest quality. The action features six locking lugs and is very strong. This model was chambered for 12 gauge and was offered with 30"--34" full-choke barrels with a vent rib and automatic ejectors. This model is well engraved and has a select-grade walnut stock. It was not manufactured after 1933.

| Exc. | V.G. | Good | Fair | Poor |
|------|------|------|------|------|
| 2500 | 2250 | 1850 | 1500 | 1150 |

### Regent Diamond Grade

This single-barrel trap gun is similar to the Empire Grade, with a greater amount of engraving and a better-grade walnut stock.

| Exc. | V.G. | Good | Fair | Poor |
|------|------|------|------|------|
| 3500 | 3250 | 2850 | 2500 | 1750 |

### Drillings
### Superior Grade Drilling

The drilling, or three-barrelled gun, was very popular on the European game preserves where it was possible to hunt different species simultaneously. This type of gun never really caught on in the U.S., as there is really no need for this type of firearm in the type of hunting most Americans experience. The Daly Drillings are of the highest quality and are chambered for 12, 16, and 20 gauge Side-by-Side with a rifle barrel in .25-20, .25-35, or .30-30 running beneath them. The gun is engraved and has a select walnut stock. It was not manufactured after 1933.

| Exc. | V.G. | Good | Fair | Poor |
|------|------|------|------|------|
| 2500 | 2250 | 1800 | 1450 | 1000 |

### Diamond Grade Drilling

This model had similar specifications to the Superior Grade, with more engraving and a better grade of walnut in the stock.

| Exc. | V.G. | Good | Fair | Poor |
|------|------|------|------|------|
| 4500 | 4000 | 3750 | 3000 | 2400 |

### Regent Diamond Grade Drilling

This is the best quality drilling that was brought in under the Daly banner. It is similar to the Diamond Grade, with elaborate engraving and the highest quality walnut stock.

| Exc. | V.G. | Good | Fair | Poor |
|------|------|------|------|------|
| 5500 | 5000 | 4500 | 4000 | 3400 |

### Charles Daly, B. C. Miroku Guns
### Empire Grade Side-By-Side

This model is chambered for 12, 16, and 20 gauge, with 26", 28", and 30" barrels and various chokes. It has an Anson and Deeley boxlock action and a single trigger. Extractors are standard on this model. The finish is blued with a checkered walnut stock. This model was manufactured between 1968 and 1971. Add 10 Percent for Ventilated-Rib Barrels and/or 20 Gauge.

| Exc. | V.G. | Good | Fair | Poor |
|------|------|------|------|------|
| 550 | 500 | 450 | 375 | 300 |

### Superior Grade Single Barrel Trap

This break-open gun is chambered for 12 gauge with 32" or 34" vent-rib barrels with full choke. There is an automatic ejector, and the finish is blued. The walnut Monte Carlo stock was offered standard with a recoil pad. This model was manufactured between 1968 and 1976.

| Exc. | V.G. | Good | Fair | Poor |
|------|------|------|------|------|
| 550 | 500 | 450 | 350 | 300 |

### Over/Unders

These guns were manufactured between 1963 and 1976 by B. C. Miroku. They had boxlock actions and were chambered for 12, 20, and 28 gauge, and .410 Bore. They were offered with 26", 28", and 30" barrel lengths with vent ribs standard. Various choke combinations were offered. They have single-selective triggers and automatic ejectors. The finish is blued with select, hand-checkered walnut stocks. The differences between the grades are the degree and quality of the engraving and the grade of walnut used for the stock. The smaller-bore guns bring a premium as follows.

20 Gauge--Add 10 Percent.
28 Gauge--Add 20 Percent.
.410-- Add 30 Percent.

### Venture Grade

This is the base model with all specifications as mentioned above.

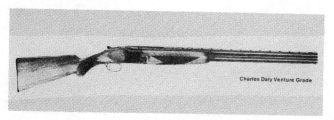

Charles Daly Venture Grade

| Exc. | V.G. | Good | Fair | Poor |
|------|------|------|------|------|
| 550 | 500 | 450 | 375 | 300 |

### Venture Grade Skeet or Trap

This model is offered in either 26" Skeet & Skeet or 30" full choke.

Charles Daly Venture Trap

| Exc. | V.G. | Good | Fair | Poor |
|------|------|------|------|------|
| 575 | 525 | 475 | 375 | 300 |

### Field Grade

This model is chambered for 12 and 20 gauge only.

| Exc. | V.G. | Good | Fair | Poor |
|------|------|------|------|------|
| 650 | 575 | 500 | 425 | 325 |

### Superior Grade

| Exc. | V.G. | Good | Fair | Poor |
|------|------|------|------|------|
| 750 | 675 | 600 | 525 | 400 |

### Superior Grade Trap

| Exc. | V.G. | Good | Fair | Poor |
|------|------|------|------|------|
| 650 | 575 | 500 | 425 | 325 |

## Diamond Grade

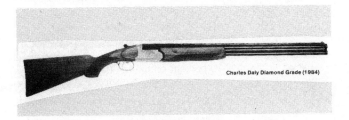

Charles Daly Diamond Grade (1984)

| Exc. | V.G. | Good | Fair | Poor |
|---|---|---|---|---|
| 1000 | 900 | 750 | 600 | 500 |

### Diamond Grade Trap or Skeet
These two models are competition guns with either 26" Skeet & Skeet or 30" full choke barrels and Monte Carlo stocks. Wide Rib--Add 5 Percent.

| Exc. | V.G. | Good | Fair | Poor |
|---|---|---|---|---|
| 1050 | 950 | 800 | 650 | 550 |

### Charles Daly, Italian Manufacture
The Italian Daly guns were manufactured by the firm of Breda in Milan, Italy. The semi-automatic "Novamatic" was produced in 1968. All other models began Italian production in 1976.

### Novamatic Lightweight
This is a recoil-operated semi-automatic shotgun chambered for 12 gauge only and was offered with a 26" or 28" vent-rib barrel with screw-in choke tubes. The receiver is alloy, and the stock is checkered walnut. This model was imported under the Daly name in 1968 only.

| Exc. | V.G. | Good | Fair | Poor |
|---|---|---|---|---|
| 300 | 275 | 225 | 175 | 125 |

### Novamatic Trap
This model is similar to the standard model, with a Monte Carlo stock and a 30" full choke barrel.

| Exc. | V.G. | Good | Fair | Poor |
|---|---|---|---|---|
| 350 | 300 | 250 | 200 | 150 |

### Charles Daly Field Grade Over/Under
This gun is an Over/Under chambered for 12 and 20 gauge with 26" or 28" chrome-lined vent-rib barrels. It has a cross-bolt boxlock action, single-selective trigger, and extractors. The finish is blued with a stamped checkered walnut stock. This model was introduced in 1989.

| Exc. | V.G. | Good | Fair | Poor |
|---|---|---|---|---|
| 450 | 400 | 350 | 275 | 225 |

### Charles Daly Deluxe Over/Under
This model is similar to the Field Grade with automatic ejectors, screw-in choke tubes, and a silver-finished receiver. The walnut stock is hand-checkered. This model was also introduced in 1989.

| Exc. | V.G. | Good | Fair | Poor |
|---|---|---|---|---|
| 650 | 600 | 500 | 400 | 300 |

### Diamond Grade Over/Under
This model is chambered for 12 and 20 gauge, 3" Magnum. It has various barrel lengths and screw-in choke tubes. It is a boxlock with single trigger, automatic ejectors, and select walnut stock. This model was discontinued in 1968.

| Exc. | V.G. | Good | Fair | Poor |
|---|---|---|---|---|
| 700 | 625 | 550 | 400 | 325 |

### Diamond Grade Trap or Skeet
Same as the Diamond Field with 26" or 30" barrels. This model was available in 1989 after the Field model was discontinued.

| Exc. | V.G. | Good | Fair | Poor |
|---|---|---|---|---|
| 1000 | 900 | 750 | 500 | 400 |

### Presentation Grade Over/Under
This model was similar to the Daly Deluxe with a Purdy-type

boxlock action with engraved false sideplates. The stock is of deluxe French walnut. This model was discontinued in 1986.

| Exc. | V.G. | Good | Fair | Poor |
|---|---|---|---|---|
| 1000 | 900 | 750 | 500 | 400 |

### Superior II Over/Under
This model is chambered for 12 and 20 gauge with 26" or 28" vent-rib barrels with various chokes. It has a boxlock action, single trigger, and automatic ejectors. The engraved receiver is blued, and the stock is walnut. This model was discontinued in 1988.

| Exc. | V.G. | Good | Fair | Poor |
|---|---|---|---|---|
| 675 | 600 | 500 | 375 | 300 |

### Superior Grade Side By Side
This is a side-by-side double barrel chambered for 12 and 20 gauge. It has 26" or 28" barrels with various chokes, a boxlock action, and single trigger. The finish is blued, with a walnut stock.

| Exc. | V.G. | Good | Fair | Poor |
|---|---|---|---|---|
| 500 | 425 | 375 | 300 | 225 |

### Charles Daly Automatic
This is a gas-operated semi-automatic chambered for 12 gauge with 3" Magnum chambers. The barrels are 26" or 28", with a vent rib. Screw-in choke tubes are standard on the later models. It has an alloy receiver and a five-shot magazine. There is a slug gun available with rifle sights. The stock is checkered walnut, and there are two versions--a pistol grip and an English-style straight grip. The choke-tube model would be worth a 10 percent premium.

| Exc. | V.G. | Good | Fair | Poor |
|---|---|---|---|---|
| 375 | 325 | 275 | 225 | 150 |

# DAN ARMS OF AMERICA
### Allentown, Pennsylvania
These Italian-made shotguns were manufactured by Silmer and imported by Dan Arms of America. They are no longer produced as of 1988.

### Side X Sides
### Field Grade
This model is chambered for all gauges with 26" or 28" barrels, with various choke combinations offered. It has double triggers and extractors, with a blued finish and a walnut stock.

| Exc. | V.G. | Good | Fair | Poor |
|---|---|---|---|---|
| 300 | 265 | 225 | 150 | 125 |

### Deluxe Field Grade
This model is similar to the Field Grade, with a single trigger and automatic ejectors.

| Exc. | V.G. | Good | Fair | Poor |
|---|---|---|---|---|
| 450 | 400 | 325 | 250 | 200 |

### Over/Unders
### Lux Grade I
This model is chambered for 12 and 20 gauge with 3" chambers and a 26", 28" or 30" vent-rib barrels. It features double triggers, extractors, and a blued finish with a walnut stock.

| Exc. | V.G. | Good | Fair | Poor |
|---|---|---|---|---|
| 275 | 250 | 200 | 150 | 100 |

### Lux Grade II
This model is similar to the Grade I except that it is chambered for 12 gauge only and has a single trigger.

| Exc. | V.G. | Good | Fair | Poor |
|---|---|---|---|---|
| 325 | 300 | 250 | 200 | 150 |

### Lux Grade III
This model is chambered for 20 gauge only and also features automatic ejectors.

| Exc. | V.G. | Good | Fair | Poor |
|---|---|---|---|---|
| 400 | 325 | 275 | 225 | 175 |

### Lux Grade IV

This model is chambered for 12 gauge only and features screw-in choke tubes.

| Exc. | V.G. | Good | Fair | Poor |
|------|------|------|------|------|
| 450 | 375 | 325 | 275 | 200 |

### Silver Snipe

This is the top of the line, made to customer specifications model. It is chambered for 12 or 20 gauge, with various barrel lengths and choke combinations. It has engraved false side-plates and a select walnut stock.

| Exc. | V.G. | Good | Fair | Poor |
|------|------|------|------|------|
| 1250 | 1000 | 800 | 600 | 450 |

## DANCE, J. H. & BROTHERS
### Columbia, Texas

The Dance revolver is a very important addition for any collector of Confederate arms. This weapon is similar in appearance to the Colt dragoon-type revolver and is chambered both in .36 and .44 caliber percussion. The major difference in appearance is that the Dance has no external recoil shield in back of the cylinder, giving it a flatter look than the Colt. Both calibers have 6-shot cylinders; and the heavier .44 caliber version has an 8", part-round/part-octagonal barrel, while the .36 caliber has a 7.5" barrel. Both models are blued, with polished brass frames and one-piece walnut grips. There were approximately 350 manufactured in .44 caliber and 150 in the smaller .36 caliber. They were produced in 1862 and 1863. One must be very wary of fakes if interested in this pistol, as they have been noted to be made from altered 1851 Colt Navy revolvers. If a transaction is contemplated, secure individual appraisal.

**.44 Caliber**

| Exc. | V.G. | Good | Fair | Poor |
|------|------|------|------|------|
| 7500 | 6500 | 5000 | 3750 | 3000 |

**.36 Caliber**

| Exc. | V.G. | Good | Fair | Poor |
|------|------|------|------|------|
| 10000 | 8500 | 7500 | 5000 | 3500 |

## DANSK
### Copenhagen, Denmark

### Schouboe 1903

Designed by Jens Schouboe, inventor of the Madsen light machine gun, this is a well-designed, well-made 7.65mm blow-back pistol that, for some unexplainable reason, did not do well commercially. Production came to an end in 1910, with less than 1,000 manufactured.

| Exc. | V.G. | Good | Fair | Poor |
|------|------|------|------|------|
| 4000 | 3500 | 3000 | 2500 | 2000 |

### Model 1907

This is a true oddity, an 11.35mm blowback pistol designed to fire a 55-grain, copper-aluminum-and-wood projectile at a velocity of 1625 ft./sec. This lightweight bullet at this velocity would actually function the slide. The pistol was submitted to various countries for field testing, but it always fell short due to the ineffectiveness of the bullet design. It simply has no stopping power. Only 500 were manufactured before production stopped in 1917. They are quite scarce today.

| Exc. | V.G. | Good | Fair | Poor |
|------|------|------|------|------|
| 5000 | 4500 | 4000 | 3500 | 3000 |

A wooden combination case and shoulder stock has been noted. This would bring a 40 percent premium due to its extreme rarity.

## DARDICK CORP.
### Hamden, Connecticut

The Dardick pistol came on the scene in 1954 and was the first major change in pistol design since the advent of the semi automatic. It was available in two models--the 1100 (with a small grip and a magazine capacity of 11 "trounds") and the 1500 (with a larger grip and a capacity of 15 "trounds"). The trounds are plastic triangular cases in which the cartridges are encased. As the pistol cylinder rotates, these trounds would pop into three cut-outs and would be carried into battery by the cylinder. The model 1100 has a 3" barrel; the 1500, a 6" barrel. The design is sound and the quality good; but the Dardick was considerably more expensive than Colt and Smith & Wesson, and the ammunition was not readily available. It was discontinued in 1962--a financial failure.

### Series 1100
**Chambered in .38 Dardick only.**

| Exc. | V.G. | Good | Fair | Poor |
|------|------|------|------|------|
| 750 | 650 | 550 | 400 | 350 |

### Series 1500
**Chambered for the .22, .30, and the .38 Dardick.**

| Exc. | V.G. | Good | Fair | Poor |
|------|------|------|------|------|
| 950 | 850 | 750 | 600 | 500 |

A carbine conversion consisting of a long barrel and shoulder stock was also available and would bring a premium of $250 to $400 depending on the condition.

## DARLING, B. & B. M.
### Belingham, Massachusetts

### Darling Pepperbox Pistol

This is a 6-shot pistol of the type referred to as a pepperbox. The barrels are all in one unit, making up one cluster. This model is chambered for .30-caliber percussion and has flutes running between the barrels. The barrels are 3.25" long, and the pistol is a single action with a large high hammer. The action is lightly engraved and browned. The grips are of walnut. This pistol was made at Shrewsbury, Massachusetts, and Woonsocket, Rhode Island, as well as Belingham. It is quite scarce, as an estimated 125 total were manufactured between 1835 and 1840. This is one of the most collectible and sought-after American pepperboxes. Be wary of fakes.

| Exc. | V.G. | Good | Fair | Poor |
|---|---|---|---|---|
| 2000 | 1750 | 1400 | 1000 | 750 |

# DARNE, S. A.
### St. Etienne, France
**Darne Side X Side Shotguns**

This shotgun is truly unique. It features a sliding breech activated by a release lever in the rear of the barrels. The breech block slides rearward, ejecting the empty shells and exposing the chambers for loading. This is a high grade gun of the finest materials and workmanship. It is lightweight, well balanced and a joy to carry in the field. This shotgun is chambered for 12, 16, 20, and 28 gauge, with a 27.5" barrel standard. Other lengths were available, and chokes were optional. The stock was available either straight or pistol-gripped, and the model designations differ in degree of engraving and grade of wood. This company manufactured firearms from 1881 through 1979. Their tradition is being carried on presently by Bruchet; these guns are listed separately.

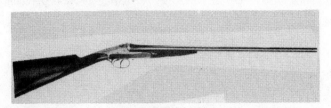

**Model R11**
| Exc. | V.G. | Good | Fair | Poor |
|---|---|---|---|---|
| 1000 | 900 | 750 | 600 | 450 |

**Model R15**
| Exc. | V.G. | Good | Fair | Poor |
|---|---|---|---|---|
| 2500 | 2000 | 1750 | 1500 | 1000 |

**Model V19**
| Exc. | V.G. | Good | Fair | Poor |
|---|---|---|---|---|
| 3250 | 3000 | 2750 | 2250 | 1750 |

**Model V22**
| Exc. | V.G. | Good | Fair | Poor |
|---|---|---|---|---|
| 3750 | 3500 | 3000 | 2500 | 2000 |

**Model V Hors Series No. 1**
| Exc. | V.G. | Good | Fair | Poor |
|---|---|---|---|---|
| 4500 | 4000 | 3750 | 3250 | 2500 |

# DAUDETEAU
### St. Denis, France
**Model 1896**

This is a bolt-action service rifle chambered for the 6.5mm Daudeteau cartridge. It has a 26" barrel with a full-length stock held on by two barrel bands. There is a cleaning rod mounted beneath the barrel. It has military-type sights and an integral box magazine located in front of the triggerguard. The finish is blued with a walnut stock. This rifle was never adopted by the French government because they were satisfied with the 8mm rifles that were already in use. The Daudeteau rifles were adopted by and exported to El Salvador, Portugal, and Uruguay.

| Exc. | V.G. | Good | Fair | Poor |
|---|---|---|---|---|
| 200 | 175 | 150 | 100 | 75 |

# DAVENPORT FIREARMS CO.
### Norwich, Connecticut
**Single Barrel Shotgun**

This is a break-open action, single-barrel shotgun that was once very common in the U.S.A. This company produced many of these serviceable arms chambered for the 10, 12, 16, and 20 gauge, with barrels from 26" to 36" in length. There are some with Damascus barrels and some with fluid steel. They have exposed hammers and extractors and feature utility-grade walnut stocks. These guns were manufactured between 1880 and 1910.

| Exc. | V.G. | Good | Fair | Poor |
|---|---|---|---|---|
| 200 | 150 | 125 | 100 | 75 |

**8 Gauge Goose Gun**

This model is basically similar to the other break-open single shots made by this company except that it is a good deal larger and is chambered for the 8 gauge shell. They were once fairly common when there were many more game birds in our skies. They were manufactured in the late 1890's and early 1900's.

| Exc. | V.G. | Good | Fair | Poor |
|---|---|---|---|---|
| 300 | 250 | 200 | 150 | 100 |

**Falling Block Single Shot Rifle**

This model is considerably rarer than the Davenport shotgun, and many collectors have never seen one. They are very similar to the more common Hopkins and Allen New Model Jr. Rifle. This rifle is chambered for .22, .25, and .32 rimfire cartridges. It has a 24" round barrel and open sights. The activating lever is hook-shaped, and there is an exposed hammer. The finish is blued with a plain, straight-gripped walnut stock. The barrel is marked "The W.H. Davenport FireArms Co. Norwich, Conn. U.S.A. Patented Dec. 15, 1891." They were manufactured between 1891 and 1910.

| Exc. | V.G. | Good | Fair | Poor |
|---|---|---|---|---|
| 550 | 500 | 425 | 325 | 250 |

# DAVIDSON F. A.
### Eibar, Spain

These guns were manufactured in Spain by Fabrica De Armas.

**Model 63B**

This is a side-x-side double barrel chambered for 12, 16, 20, 28 gauge, and .410, with barrel lengths from 25" to 30" and various choke combinations. It has an Anson & Deeley boxlock action that is engraved and nickel-plated. The walnut stock is hand checkered. This model was manufactured between 1963 and 1976.

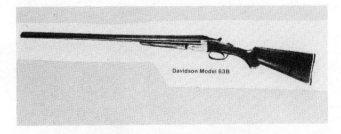
Davidson Model 63B

| Exc. | V.G. | Good | Fair | Poor |
|---|---|---|---|---|
| 275 | 225 | 200 | 150 | 125 |

**Model 69 SL**

This is a true detachable sidelock gun that is chambered for 12 and 20 gauge. The barrels are 26" or 28" with various chokes. The action is engraved and nickel-plated; the stock is checkered walnut. This model was manufactured between 1963 and 1976.

| Exc. | V.G. | Good | Fair | Poor |
|---|---|---|---|---|
| 400 | 350 | 300 | 225 | 150 |

## Stagecoach Model 73

This model has detachable sidelocks with exposed hammers. It is chambered for 12 and 20 gauge, with 20" barrels choked full and modified. It has 3" magnum chambers and a checkered walnut stock. It is no longer manufactured.

| Exc. | V.G. | Good | Fair | Poor |
|------|------|------|------|------|
| 275  | 225  | 175  | 150  | 125  |

## DAVIS, A. JR.
### Stafford, Connecticut

**Underhammer Pistol**

This is a common-appearing example of the underhammer or boot-type pistol. It is chambered for .31 caliber percussion and has a 7.5", part-round/part-octagonal barrel. It has a brass frame with a round butt with pointed tip and maple grips. The topstrap is stamped "A.Davis Jr./Stafford Conn."

| Exc. | V.G. | Good | Fair | Poor |
|------|------|------|------|------|
| 400  | 350  | 300  | 225  | 175  |

## DAVIS & BOZEMAN
### Central, Alabama

**Muzzle Loading Rifle**

This weapon of the Confederacy is chambered for .58 caliber percussion. It was patterned after the U.S. Model 1841 rifle, although there is no patchbox and the stock is fastened by two bands. The round barrel is 33" long and accepts a saber bayonet. The finish is white with a full-length walnut stock, brass mountings, and an iron ramrod. The lock is marked "D.& B. Ala." The serial number and date of manufacture are at the rear of the lock. There were approximately 750 produced during the Civil War.

| Exc. | V.G. | Good | Fair | Poor |
|------|------|------|------|------|
| 5500 | 4750 | 4000 | 3250 | 2500 |

## DAVIS INDUSTRIES
### Chino, California

**D-22 Derringer**

This is a small, two-barrel, over/under derringer with upward pivoting barrels similar in appearance to the Remington of Old West fame. It is chambered for .22 l. r. .22 WMR, .25 ACP and .32 ACP. The barrels are 2.4" long, and the finish is black teflon or chrome plate. The grips are laminated wood.

| NIB | Exc. | V.G. | Good | Fair | Poor |
|-----|------|------|------|------|------|
| 70  | 60   | 45   | 35   | 30   | 20   |

**P-32**

This is a blowback-operated semi-automatic chambered for the .32 ACP cartridge. It has a 2.8" barrel, fixed sights, and a 6-shot magazine. The finish is black teflon or chrome plate, and the grips are laminated wood. This model was introduced in 1987.

Davis P-32

| NIB | Exc. | V.G. | Good | Fair | Poor |
|-----|------|------|------|------|------|
| 85  | 75   | 60   | 45   | 35   | 25   |

**P-380**

This model is similar to the P-32 except that it is chambered for the .380 ACP. It was introduced in 1989.

| NIB | Exc. | V.G. | Good | Fair | Poor |
|-----|------|------|------|------|------|
| 100 | 80   | 65   | 50   | 40   | 30   |

## DAVIS WARNER
### Assonet, Massachusetts
### SEE--Warner Arms Corporation

## DAW, G.H.
### London, England

**Daw Revolver**

This revolver is a well-made, though somewhat fragile, double-action percussion model chambered for .38 caliber. It has a 5.5" barrel held on to the axis pin with a wedge like the Colt pistol of its day. The hinged rammer also resembles the type found on the Colt revolver. The barrel is round, with the top and the bottom flattened. This arm is unique in a couple of ways. The double action is one known as a hesitation lock, that can be brought back to the full-cock position with the trigger and held with only a very slight amount of additional pressure needed to fire the piece. It can also be cocked single-action. Safety studs in between the nipples, upon which the hammer can be rested, made this a safe revolver to carry loaded. The barrel is marked "George H. Daw, 57 Threadneedle St. London, Patent No.112." The finish is blued, and the wood grips are checkered. This revolver was manufactured in the 1860's.

| Exc. | V.G. | Good | Fair | Poor |
|------|------|------|------|------|
| 3500 | 3000 | 2500 | 1850 | 1400 |

## DEANE & ADAMS
### London, England
### SEE--Deane-Harding

## DEANE-HARDING
### London, England

**Deane - Harding Revolver**

This company was formed after the breakup of Deane-Adams and Deane. The maker of this pistol was the older of the two Deanes, and evidence suggests that the breakup was less than amicable. This large revolver is chambered for .44 caliber percussion and has a 5-shot unfluted cylinder. The octagonal barrel was 5.25" long, and the frame is made of blued iron. The grips are checkered walnut. According to accounts of the day, this was a flimsy pistol that was prone to malfunction. It never achieved commercial success. It was manufactured in 1858.

| Exc. | V.G. | Good | Fair | Poor |
|------|------|------|------|------|
| 2500 | 2000 | 1750 | 1250 | 800  |

## DECKER, WILHELM
### Zella St. Blasii, Germany

Decker manufactured a truly unique pocket revolver. It is a 6-shot, solid-frame, true hammerless, striker-fired revolver. It is chambered for the 6.35mm. Loading is accomplished through a gate, and empty cases are expelled via the same gate by the use of a pin. The right side of the pistol is covered by a thin sheet-metal plate, streamlining it for the pocket. WWI stopped production, and this revolver is rarely found today.

| Exc. | V.G. | Good | Fair | Poor |
|------|------|------|------|------|
| 900  | 800  | 700  | 500  | 350  |

## DEMIRETT, J.
### Montpelier, Vermont

**Underhammer Pistol**

This is an unusual departure from the usual boot-type pistol. It is chambered for .27-caliber percussion, with barrel lengths of 3" to 8". The barrel and frame are one piece, with a bend just behind the trigger. The barrels are octagonal, and the grips are made of stag horn. The barrel is stamped "J. Demerrit / Montpelior/Vermont."

| Exc. | V.G. | Good | Fair | Poor |
|------|------|------|------|------|
| 750 | 675 | 500 | 400 | 300 |

# DEMRO
## Manchester, Connecticut

### XF-7 Wasp Carbine
This is a blowback-operated, semi-automatic carbine chambered for .45 ACP or 9mm Luger. It has a 16.5" barrel, a black plastic pistol grip, and a folding stock. A fitted case was available for an additional charge.

| Exc. | V.G. | Good | Fair | Poor |
|------|------|------|------|------|
| 350 | 300 | 250 | 200 | 150 |

### T.A.C. Model 1
This model is similar to the Wasp, with a fixed stock.

| Exc. | V.G. | Good | Fair | Poor |
|------|------|------|------|------|
| 350 | 300 | 250 | 200 | 150 |

# DERINGER REVOLVER AND PISTOL CO.
## Philadelphia, Pennsylvania

After the death of Henry Deringer, the name was taken over by the above company run by I. J. Clark, who used it to manufacture conventional rimfire revolvers based on the patents owned by Charles Foehl. This company was operational between 1870 and 1879.

### Derringer Model I
This is a 7-shot, .22 rimfire revolver with a tip up action that was a copy of the then popular Smith & Wesson revolver. There were few of these manufactured in 1873.

| Exc. | V.G. | Good | Fair | Poor |
|------|------|------|------|------|
| 400 | 350 | 275 | 200 | 150 |

### Derringer Model II
This is similar to the Model I, with a round barrel instead of the octagonal one found on the Model I. It also has a simpler cylinder-rotation system and was made in a .32 rimfire 5-shot as well as the .22.

| Exc. | V.G. | Good | Fair | Poor |
|------|------|------|------|------|
| 375 | 325 | 250 | 175 | 150 |

### Centennial 1876
This is an unremarkable solid-frame revolver chambered for the .22, .32, and .38 caliber rimfire cartridges. The .22 holds 7 shots, and the .32 and .38 hold 5.

| Exc. | V.G. | Good | Fair | Poor |
|------|------|------|------|------|
| 400 | 350 | 275 | 200 | 150 |

# DERINGER, H.
## Philadelphia, Pennsylvania

### Derringer
This pocket pistol was designed and manufactured by Henry Deringer, who is credited for being the first to produce a pistol of this type. Hence, all small pocket pistols of this nature would be erroneously known as derringers. The original was usually chambered for .41 caliber percussion with a barrel length that ranged from 1.5" to 6". The dueling pistols that Deringer made generally had longer barrels from 6" to 9". The pistols were always single-barrelled, with German silver mountings and walnut stocks. They are marked "Deringer-Philadela". The locks are case-colored, with the other iron parts blued. There is no accurate record of the number produced, but estimates place total production at approximately 15,000 between 1830 and 1868. Values usually are greater for the larger pistols than for the smaller models. There are many fakes of this maker, and they will usually have a purposely misspelled name. Some were imported from Europe, and the quality is not the same as the genuine article.

### Small Pocket Models Under 3.5" Barrels

| Exc. | V.G. | Good | Fair | Poor |
|------|------|------|------|------|
| 1000 | 900 | 750 | 600 | 500 |

### Medium Sized Models 3.5"--6" Barrels

| Exc. | V.G. | Good | Fair | Poor |
|------|------|------|------|------|
| 1500 | 1350 | 1000 | 750 | 600 |

### Large Sized Models 7"--9" Barrels

| Exc. | V.G. | Good | Fair | Poor |
|------|------|------|------|------|
| 2500 | 2250 | 2000 | 1500 | 1200 |

# DESTROYER CARBINE
## Spain

### Destroyer Carbine
The Model 1921 Destroyer carbine was produced for the Spanish military police. It was based on a modified Mauser action and chambered for the 9mm Bayard pistol cartridge. It has a 20" barrel and holds 7 shots. It has a full-length stock with two barrel bands and sling swivels. It is a fairly rare weapon and desired by military collectors.

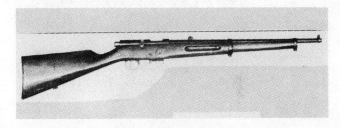

| Exc. | V.G. | Good | Fair | Poor |
|------|------|------|------|------|
| 275 | 250 | 200 | 150 | 100 |

# DETONICS MANUFACTURING CORP.
## Bellevue, Washington

The Detonics pistol was based on the Colt Model 1911 design. It basically started out as a smaller, more compact version of this time-proven concept. This concept has expanded to include a number of specialized combat and competition pistols as well. In 1988 the firm was sold to a group of investors, and it should be interesting to see in what direction this company turns.

### Mark I
This model is the first in the series of compact pistols based on the Model 1911. It is chambered for the .45 ACP cartridge and has a 3.25" barrel and a 6-shot detachable magazine. The barrel of the Detonics pistols do not use a bushing but have a self-centering cone system. The sights are the fixed combat type, and the finish is matte blued with checkered walnut grips. This model was discontinued in 1981.

| Exc. | V.G. | Good | Fair | Poor |
|------|------|------|------|------|
| 600 | 500 | 450 | 400 | 325 |

### Mark II
This model is satin nickel-plated and was discontinued in 1979.

| Exc. | V.G. | Good | Fair | Poor |
|------|------|------|------|------|
| 500 | 400 | 350 | 300 | 225 |

### Mark III
This model is hard chrome-plated and was discontinued in 1979.

| Exc. | V.G. | Good | Fair | Poor |
|------|------|------|------|------|
| 550 | 450 | 400 | 350 | 275 |

### Mark IV
This model has a polished blue finish and was discontinued in 1981.

| Exc. | V.G. | Good | Fair | Poor |
|------|------|------|------|------|
| 550 | 450 | 400 | 350 | 275 |

### Combat Master

This is the new designation for the Mark I; and except for the fact that it is chambered for 9mm and .38 Super as well as .45 ACP, there is no difference.

| NIB | Exc. | V.G. | Good | Fair | Poor |
|-----|------|------|------|------|------|
| 925 | 775 | 600 | 500 | 425 | 350 |

### Combat Master Mark V

This model is similar to the Combat Master except that it is made of stainless steel and is matte finished. It was discontinued in 1985.

| Exc. | V.G. | Good | Fair | Poor |
|------|------|------|------|------|
| 750 | 600 | 500 | 400 | 300 |

### Combat Master Mark VI

This version has adjustable sights, and the sides of the slide are polished. There was a limited production of 1,000 chambered for the .451 Detonics Magnum caliber.
.451 Detonics Magnum--Add 40 Percent.

| NIB | Exc. | V.G. | Good | Fair | Poor |
|-----|------|------|------|------|------|
| 800 | 725 | 650 | 550 | 450 | 350 |

### Combat Master Mark VII

This model is similar to the Mark VI but has no sights whatsoever. It was a special-order proposition.
.451 Detonics Magnum--Add 40 Percent.

| NIB | Exc. | V.G. | Good | Fair | Poor |
|-----|------|------|------|------|------|
| 900 | 800 | 750 | 650 | 550 | 450 |

### Military Combat MC2

This version is chambered for .45 ACP, 9mm, and .38 Super. The general specifications are similar to previously described pistols, with the dull finish and fixed sights. This model is furnished with a camo pistol rug and Pachmayr grips. It was discontinued in 1984.

| NIB | Exc. | V.G. | Good | Fair | Poor |
|-----|------|------|------|------|------|
| 625 | 575 | 500 | 425 | 350 | 275 |

### Scoremaster

This is a pistol designed for competition. It is chambered for .45 ACP or .451 Detonics Magnum. It has a 5" or 6" barrel, Millet adjustable sights, and a grip safety. The tolerances are held closer than on the other production models.

| NIB | Exc. | V.G. | Good | Fair | Poor |
|-----|------|------|------|------|------|
| 1150 | 1000 | 850 | 650 | 500 | 400 |

### Janus Competition Scoremaster

This version is similar to the standard Scoremaster except that it is chambered for .45 ACP only and compensated. This model was introduced in 1988.

| NIB | Exc. | V.G. | Good | Fair | Poor |
|-----|------|------|------|------|------|
| 1650 | 1450 | 1250 | 1000 | 750 | 500 |

### Servicemaster

This is a shortened version of the Scoremaster chambered for the .45 ACP only. It has a 4.25" barrel, interchangeable sights, and a non-glare finish. It was discontinued in 1986.

| Exc. | V.G. | Good | Fair | Poor |
|------|------|------|------|------|
| 900 | 750 | 600 | 400 | 325 |

### Pocket 9
This model is a double-action semi-automatic 9mm with a 3" barrel. It is made of matte-finished stainless steel, with a 6-shot detachable magazine. It was discontinued in 1986.

| Exc. | V.G. | Good | Fair | Poor |
|------|------|------|------|------|
| 450 | 400 | 325 | 275 | 200 |

## DEUTSCHE WERKE
### Erfurt, Germany

### Ortgies
Production of this pistol chambered for 7.65mm began in 1921. The 7.65mm and 9mm Kurz chamberings followed a year later. Perhaps the most unique feature of this pistol is the patented invisible method of attaching the grips. The Ortgies is marked "Deutsche Werke Erfurt" and has an ornate "D" monogram on the butt.

#### 6.35mm
| Exc. | V.G. | Good | Fair | Poor |
|------|------|------|------|------|
| 250 | 225 | 175 | 125 | 90 |

#### 7.65mm
| Exc. | V.G. | Good | Fair | Poor |
|------|------|------|------|------|
| 225 | 200 | 150 | 100 | 75 |

#### 9mm Kurz
| Exc. | V.G. | Good | Fair | Poor |
|------|------|------|------|------|
| 250 | 225 | 175 | 125 | 90 |

## DEVISME, F. P.
### Paris, France

### Devisme Revolver
This very well made revolver is chambered for the .41 rimfire cartridge and holds 6 shots. This is an odd design in that the barrel pivots down and allows access to the cylinder for loading. The ejector rod pivots to the right so it can be used to knock out the spent cases. The round barrel is 5.75" in length. The sights are fixed, and the gun is blued with a case-colored frame and checkered walnut grips. This revolver is marked "Devisme a Paris" on top of the barrel, and the frame is stamped "Devisme Bte." This revolver was first manufactured in 1867.

| Exc. | V.G. | Good | Fair | Poor |
|------|------|------|------|------|
| 1500 | 1250 | 1000 | 700 | 450 |

## DICKINSON
### SEE--Dickinson, E.L.

## DICKINSON, E. L. & J.
### Springfield, Massachusetts

### Ranger
This revolver was manufactured in 1871 and was one of many like it produced after the Rollin White patent restrictions were removed. It is purely a Smith & Wesson copy. A solid frame, 6-shot, round-barrelled revolver with birds head grips. It is chambered for .32 rimfire. Production ceased in the 1880's.

| Exc. | V.G. | Good | Fair | Poor |
|------|------|------|------|------|
| 200 | 175 | 150 | 110 | 80 |

### Single Shot
This is a single-shot, break-open loading pocket pistol chambered for .32 rimfire. It was made in the late 1870's. The lever used to open the action is located under the 3.75" barrel. The frame is silver-plated brass with a blued barrel, and the butt is square with walnut grips.

| Exc. | V.G. | Good | Fair | Poor |
|------|------|------|------|------|
| 400 | 350 | 300 | 225 | 150 |

## DICKSON, NELSON & CO.
### Dawson, Georgia

### Dickson, Nelson Rifle
This was a Confederate weapon produced by the partnership of William Dickson and Owen O. Nelson. They called their company The Shakanoosa Arms Co. and patterned this rifle after the U.S. Model 1841. This rifle is chambered for .58-caliber percussion, with a 34" barrel in the rifle configuration and a 24" carbine barrel. The mountings are brass; and the locks and barrels, iron. The full-length stocks are either walnut or cherry wood. The lock is marked "Dickson/Nelson & Co./C.S." The rear of the lock is stamped "Ala." and dated. There were very few of these weapons manufactured in 1864 and 1865.

| Exc. | V.G. | Good | Fair | Poor |
|------|------|------|------|------|
| 5000 | 4500 | 4000 | 3500 | 2750 |

## DIMICK, H. E.
### St. Louis, Missouri

### Belt Pistol
This is a large, single-shot percussion pistol chambered for .48 caliber. It has an 11", part-round/part-octagonal barrel and double-set triggers. The construction is of browned iron, and the stock is walnut. This pistol was manufactured between 1830 and 1849.

| Exc. | V.G. | Good | Fair | Poor |
|------|------|------|------|------|
| 2000 | 1850 | 1500 | 1150 | 900 |

## DOMINGO ACHA
### Eibar, Spain

### Looking Glass
This is a typical "Eibar"-type, blowback-operated, semi-automatic pistol. It is chambered for both 6.35mm and 7.65mm cartridges. The slides are marked "Looking Glass," and they are of the same poor quality as found on other Spanish guns manufactured before their civil war.

| Exc. | V.G. | Good | Fair | Poor |
|------|------|------|------|------|
| 150 | 125 | 100 | 75 | 50 |

## DOMINO
### Brescia, Italy
### Importer--Mandall Shooting Supplies
### Scottsdale, Arizona

### Model OP 601 Match Pistol
This is a high quality, semi-automatic target pistol chambered for the .22 short cartridge. It has a 5.6" barrel, with matched target sights. The barrel and slide are vented for recoil reduction. It has an adjustable and removable modular trigger. The finish is blued, with fully adjustable target grips.

| NIB | Exc. | V.G. | Good | Fair | Poor |
|-----|------|------|------|------|------|
| 1300 | 1150 | 1000 | 800 | 625 | 450 |

### Model SP 602 Match Pistol
This version is similar to the Model 601, except that it is chambered for the .22 l.r. cartridge. The values are the same.

# DORNHAUS & DIXON
## Huntington Beach, California
### SEE--Bren 10

# DORNHEIM, G. C.
## Suhl, Germany

### Gecado

Dornheim was a marketing company that never manufactured a firearm. Gecado was the tradename for a pair of mediocre "Eibar"-type semi-automatics chambered for 6.35mm and 7.65mm. They are stamped "Gecado" inside a diamond.

| Exc. | V.G. | Good | Fair | Poor |
|------|------|------|------|------|
| 200 | 150 | 125 | 75 | 50 |

# DREYSE
## SEE--Rheinmetall

# DRISCOLL, J. B.
## Springfield, Massachusetts

### Single Shot Pocket Pistol

This is a small pistol chambered for .22 rimfire. It has a 3.5" octagonal barrel that pivots downward for loading after a trigger-like hook under the breech is pulled. It has a spur trigger, silver-plated brass frame, and a blued barrel. The square butt is flared at the bottom, and the grips are walnut. There were approximately 200 manufactured in the late 1860's.

| Exc. | V.G. | Good | Fair | Poor |
|------|------|------|------|------|
| 350 | 300 | 250 | 200 | 150 |

# DUBIEL ARMS CO.
## Sherman, Texas

This company was established in 1975 by Joseph Dubiel and Dr. John Tyson. They are engaged in the manufacture of high quality, custom-built, bolt-action rifles. The rifles are constructed from patented Dubiel actions that feature a 5-lug bolt locking mechanism and a 36-degree bolt rotation. They are chambered for all calibers from .22-250 through .458 Winchester Magnum. Barrel lengths, weights, and stock styles are made to the customer's order. Douglas Premium barrels and Canjar triggers are used, and there are six basic stock designs available. The rifles are guaranteed to group in 1.5" at 100 yards with factory ammunition. The values listed are basic retail prices, and appraisal should be secured as options will drastically affect prices.

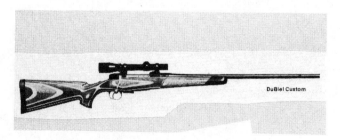

DuBiel Custom

| NIB | Exc. | V.G. | Good | Fair | Poor |
|-----|------|------|------|------|------|
| 2500 | 2250 | 2000 | 1750 | 1500 | 1200 |

# DUMOULIN
## Herstal, Belgium
# IMPORTER--MIDWEST GUNSPORT
## Zebulon, North Carolina

The guns produced by Ernest Dumoulin are essentially hand-made to the customer's order. They are of the highest quality, both in materials and workmanship. There are many options available that have a tremendous impact on value fluctuations. The models and values listed here are base prices. If a sale or purchase is contemplated, individual competent appraisal should be secured.

## Shotguns
### Europa Model

This is a side-by-side double barrel chambered for 12, 20, and 28 gauge and .410 bore. It is available in any length barrel and choke combination, with an Anson & Deeley boxlock action and automatic ejectors. One has the option of double or single-selective triggers and a choice of six different moderate engraving patterns. The select walnut stock is oil-finished. This model was introduced in 1989.
Basic Values

| NIB | Exc. | V.G. | Good | Fair | Poor |
|-----|------|------|------|------|------|
| 3350 | 3100 | 2750 | 2250 | 1800 | 1400 |

### Leige Model

This is a side-by-side double chambered for 12, 16, 20, and 28 gauge. It is similar to the Europa, with a greater degree of finish and more engraving. The walnut is of a higher grade. This model was introduced in 1986.

| NIB | Exc. | V.G. | Good | Fair | Poor |
|-----|------|------|------|------|------|
| 5300 | 5000 | 4500 | 4000 | 3500 | 3000 |

### Continental Model

This is a side by side chambered for 12, 20, and 28 gauge and .410. Barrel lengths and chokes are on a custom-order basis. This is a true sidelock action with automatic ejectors and choice of triggers. There are six different engraving patterns, and the stock is made of high grade, hand-checkered, oil-finished walnut. This model was introduced in 1989.

| NIB | Exc. | V.G. | Good | Fair | Poor |
|-----|------|------|------|------|------|
| 7500 | 7000 | 6500 | 5750 | 5000 | 4200 |

### Etendart Model

This is a side by side chambered for 12, 20, and 28 gauge. This best grade side by side is built on a purely made-to-order basis. It is profusely engraved and uses exhibition grade walnut in its stock. There are 12 different engraving patterns from which to choose, and the cost is according to embellishments chosen. Values given here are for the basic model.

| NIB | Exc. | V.G. | Good | Fair | Poor |
|-----|------|------|------|------|------|
| 14500 | 12500 | 10000 | 8000 | 6000 | 4500 |

### Superposed Express International

This model is an over/under chambered for 20 gauge and is furnished with a set of rifle barrels in the customer's choice of seven calibers. The walnut is of a deluxe grade, and engraving is available at extra cost. This is a made-to-order gun, and the value here is for the most basic model. This gun was discontinued in 1985.

| Exc. | V.G. | Good | Fair | Poor |
|------|------|------|------|------|
| 2500 | 2250 | 1750 | 1250 | 1000 |

### Boss Royal Model

This is the best grade Over/Under, chambered for 12, 20, and 28 gauge. It is a full sidelock gun that is made to the customer's specification using the finest materials and workmanship available. This model was introduced in 1987.

| NIB | Exc. | V.G. | Good | Fair | Poor |
|-----|------|------|------|------|------|
| 18500 | 15000 | 12500 | 10000 | 8000 | 6750 |

### Eagle Model Combination Gun

This model has a rifle barrel or the shotgun barrel which is chambered for 12 or 20 gauge. The rifle calibers available are .22 Hornet, .222 Remington, .222 Remington Magnum, 6mm, .243, .25-06, .30-06, 6.5 X 57R, 7 X 57R, 8 X 57JRS, and 9.3 X 74R. The action is a boxlock with automatic ejectors, and the other specifications are on a custom-order basis. This model was introduced in 1989.

| NIB | Exc. | V.G. | Good | Fair | Poor |
|-----|------|------|------|------|------|
| 2750 | 2500 | 2000 | 1750 | 1250 | 1000 |

## Double Rifles
### Europa I

This is a made-to-order, Over/Under, double-barrelled rifle available in the same calibers as the Eagle Combination gun. It has an Anson & Deeley boxlock and all other options to the customer's specifications.

| NIB | Exc. | V.G. | Good | Fair | Poor |
|---|---|---|---|---|---|
| 5000 | 4750 | 4000 | 3500 | 2900 | 2250 |

### Continental I Model
This is a more deluxe Over/Under rifle with a true sidelock action. The calibers are the same as the Europa. The specifications are to the customer's order with 12 engraving patterns to choose from at extra cost. This model was introduced in 1989.

| NIB | Exc. | V.G. | Good | Fair | Poor |
|---|---|---|---|---|---|
| 8500 | 7800 | 7000 | 5500 | 4500 | 3750 |

### Pionnier Express Rifle
This is a side-by-side double rifle chambered for the .22 Hornet through the .600 Nitro Express. It has the Anson & Deeley boxlock action and is quite deluxe throughout. The specifications are to the customer's order, and there are basically 12 models available (P-I through P-XII). The differences among these models are in the degree of ornamentation and quality of the walnut used for the stock. The prices of these models would have to be ascertained through appraisal, as a book of this nature could not possibly consider the variables that one could encounter with a gun of this type. Values range from approximately $8,000 to $12,000 for the basic models.

### Aristocrate Model
This model is a low-profile single shot chambered for all calibers up to .375 Holland & Holland. This is a deluxe, made-to-order rifle with exhibition-grade walnut and 12 engraving patterns available.

| Exc. | V.G. | Good | Fair | Poor |
|---|---|---|---|---|
| 9000 | 8000 | 7000 | 5500 | 4800 |

### Bolt Action Rifles
### Centurion Model
This is a custom-order rifle built on a Mauser or Sako action and chambered for all calibers from .270 to .458 Winchester Magnum. The barrel lengths available were 21.5", 24", and 25.5"; and there were many engraving options from which to choose. The stock is of deluxe French walnut, with rosewood forend tip and pistolgrip cap. This rifle was discontinued in 1986.

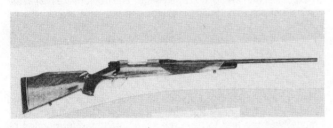

| Exc. | V.G. | Good | Fair | Poor |
|---|---|---|---|---|
| 675 | 600 | 500 | 400 | 325 |

### Centurion Classic
This model is similar to the Mauser-actioned Centurion chambered for the non-Magnum calibers only. The walnut used for the stock is a better grade.

| NIB | Exc. | V.G. | Good | Fair | Poor |
|---|---|---|---|---|---|
| 1500 | 1350 | 1100 | 900 | 650 | 550 |

### Diane
This is a more deluxe version of the Centurion Classic.

| NIB | Exc. | V.G. | Good | Fair | Poor |
|---|---|---|---|---|---|
| 1550 | 1400 | 1150 | 950 | 700 | 600 |

### Amazone
This is a 20"-barrelled, full-length stocked, upgraded version of the Diane.

| NIB | Exc. | V.G. | Good | Fair | Poor |
|---|---|---|---|---|---|
| 1750 | 1600 | 1250 | 1000 | 750 | 600 |

### Bavaria Deluxe
This model is similar to the Centurion, with the same barrel lengths and calibers available. The engraving styles available are more deluxe. This model was discontinued in 1985.

| NIB | Exc. | V.G. | Good | Fair | Poor |
|---|---|---|---|---|---|
| 1900 | 1750 | 1500 | 1250 | 1000 | 750 |

### Safari Model
This model is similar to the Bavaria Deluxe, but it is chambered for the heavy Magnum calibers only.

| NIB | Exc. | V.G. | Good | Fair | Poor |
|---|---|---|---|---|---|
| 2400 | 2000 | 1750 | 1500 | 1250 | 1000 |

### Safari Sportsman
This Model is built on a Magnum Mauser action and is chambered for the .375 Holland & Holland, .404 Jeffreys, .416 Rigby, and the .505 Gibbs. This is a true big game rifle that was made available in 1986.

| NIB | Exc. | V.G. | Good | Fair | Poor |
|---|---|---|---|---|---|
| 4000 | 3750 | 3250 | 2750 | 2500 | 2000 |

### African Pro
This is a more deluxe version of the Safari Sportsman, with a folding-leaf rear sight, hooded front sight, and an ebony or buffalo horn forend tip.

| NIB | Exc. | V.G. | Good | Fair | Poor |
|---|---|---|---|---|---|
| 4800 | 4500 | 4000 | 3250 | 2750 | 2500 |

NOTE:
Again we feel it is important to note that all values furnished in this section are estimates based on the most basic model in each designation. There are many options that will radically affect the values, and a competent appraisal should be secured if a sale or purchase is contemplated.

## DUSEK, F.
### Opocno, Czechoslovakia
Dusek commenced business in the mid-1920's and continued to make firearms through WWII. They manufactured pistols for Nazi Germany under the contract code "aek." After the War the communists took over, and Dusek's designs were relegated to the CZ factory.

### Duo
Introduced in 1926, this 6.35mm pistol is based on the 1906 Browning design. It has a 2.25" barrel and 6-shot detachable magazine. The Duo was very successful from a commercial standpoint and was exported throughout the world. During WWII the slide markings were in German; and the name "Eblen", Dusek's German sales agent, may sometimes be found on the slide. The Duo may also be found marked Ideal, Jaga, and Singer. Nazi-marked examples will bring a 25 percent premium.

| Exc. | V.G. | Good | Fair | Poor |
|---|---|---|---|---|
| 225 | 200 | 150 | 100 | 80 |

### Perla
This 6.35mm pistol has a fixed barrel and open-topped slide. It resembles a Walther design and is striker-fired. The slide is marked "Automat Pistole Perla 6.35mm"; the grips, "Perla 6.35." Dusek made this model from the early 1930's until WWII.

| Exc. | V.G. | Good | Fair | Poor |
|---|---|---|---|---|
| 225 | 200 | 150 | 100 | 80 |

## E.M.F. CO., INC.
### Santa Ana, California
### SEE--Uberti, Aldo
E.M.F. is an importer and distributer of quality Italian-made reproduction firearms. Their offerings are listed in the section dealing with Aldo Uberti firearms.

## EAGLE ARMS CO.
### New Haven, Connecticut
### SEE--Plant Manufacturing Co.

## ECHAVE & ARIZMENDI
### Eibar, Spain

This company was founded in 1911 and produced the usual poor-quality, early Spanish semi-automatic pistols. They did improve their quality later on and were permitted to return to gun manufacturing after the Spanish Civil War. They were one of the few pistol makers to survive this period. They imported many models, and their products are not particularly of interest to collectors.

### Basque, Echasa or Dickson Special Agent
These two pistols are the same under different names. They are chambered for 7.65mm and are double-action, blowback-operated, semi-automatic copies of the Walther PP. The disassembly methods and the quality are the two differences. The finish is blued, and the grips are checkered wood. The slides are marked either "Basque" or "Echasa" and "Made in Spain Cal. .32."

| Exc. | V.G. | Good | Fair | Poor |
|------|------|------|------|------|
| 200  | 150  | 125  | 100  | 75   |

### Bronco
This is a copy of the Browning 1906 chambered for 7.65mm and 6.35mm. It has a grip safety and is marked "1918 Model Automatic Pistol Bronco Patent No. 66130." This model was manufactured at the end of WWI.

| Exc. | V.G. | Good | Fair | Poor |
|------|------|------|------|------|
| 150  | 125  | 100  | 75   | 50   |

### Echasa
This is similar to the 6.35mm Bronco, without a grip safety. It is marked "Model 1916."

| Exc. | V.G. | Good | Fair | Poor |
|------|------|------|------|------|
| 150  | 125  | 100  | 75   | 50   |

### Fast
This model is similar to the Echasa except that it is chambered for the .22 l.r. and the 9mm short, as well as the 7.65mm and the 6.35mm. There is one version that is chrome-plated with white plastic grips.

| Exc. | V.G. | Good | Fair | Poor |
|------|------|------|------|------|
| 175  | 150  | 125  | 100  | 75   |

### Lightning
This is a renamed version of the Bronco in 6.35mm.

| Exc. | V.G. | Good | Fair | Poor |
|------|------|------|------|------|
| 150  | 125  | 100  | 75   | 50   |

### Lur Panzer
This model is a copy of the Luger toggle-lock action, chambered for .22 rimfire. This is an almost exact copy except for a different trigger assembly and a less robust mainspring. It is marked "Lur Cal.22 LR Made in Spain." The plastic grips have "Panzer" molded into them.

| Exc. | V.G. | Good | Fair | Poor |
|------|------|------|------|------|
| 225  | 200  | 150  | 125  | 100  |

### Pathfinder
This is the 6.35mm Bronco with another name for export purposes.

| Exc. | V.G. | Good | Fair | Poor |
|------|------|------|------|------|
| 150  | 125  | 100  | 75   | 50   |

### Protector
This model is similar to the Echasa, chambered for 6.35mm. There is a slight difference in the triggerguard and the magazine catch. The grips have molded flowers and the caliber in a circle.

| Exc. | V.G. | Good | Fair | Poor |
|------|------|------|------|------|
| 150  | 125  | 100  | 75   | 50   |

### Selecta
This model is similar to the Protector, chambered for 7.65mm.

| Exc. | V.G. | Good | Fair | Poor |
|------|------|------|------|------|
| 150  | 125  | 100  | 75   | 50   |

## ECHEVERRIA, STAR-BONIFACIO SA
### Eibar, Spain
### IMPORTER--INTERARMS
### Alexandria, Virginia

This is an old-line Spanish company that survived the Spanish civil war. It was founded in 1908 by Jean Echeverria, but the early records of the company were lost during the civil war. The early pistols the company produced were patterned after the Mannlicher designs, and the tradename Star was the closest thing to Steyr that could be used. After the close of WWI, the company began production of the open-topped slide Star for which they have become known. They also produced a large 1911-type pistol that was successful. During the civil war, the plant was damaged and the company records destroyed; but after the cessation of hostilities, they were one of only three gun companies that were allowed to remain in business. They survive to this day and are known for the manufacture of quality firearms.

### Star Model 1908
This was the first pistol produced under the Star banner. It is a Mannlicher copy that is chambered for 6.35mm. It has a 3" fixed barrel and an open-topped slide. The detachable magazine holds 8 shots. The finish is blued, and the grips are checkered plastic. The slide is marked "Automatic Pistol Star Patent."

| Exc. | V.G. | Good | Fair | Poor |
|------|------|------|------|------|
| 275  | 250  | 200  | 150  | 100  |

### Star Model 1914
This model is similar to the model 1908, with a 5" barrel and larger grips that have the Star name molded into them. This model was the first to have the six-pointed star surrounded by rays of light (that became the Star trademark) stamped on its slide.

| Exc. | V.G. | Good | Fair | Poor |
|------|------|------|------|------|
| 275  | 250  | 200  | 150  | 100  |

## Star Model 1919

This model is also a copy of a Mannlicher design and differs from its predecessors chiefly in the way the pistol is disassembled. This model has a spring catch at the top of the trigger guard. This model also has a small spur on the hammer, and the magazine release was relocated to a button behind the trigger guard instead of a catch at the bottom of the butt. This model was chambered for 6.35mm, 7.65mm and 9mm short, with various barrel lengths offered. The maker's name, as well as the Star trademark, is stamped into the slide. This model was produced until 1929.

| Exc. | V.G. | Good | Fair | Poor |
|------|------|------|------|------|
| 275 | 250 | 200 | 150 | 100 |

## Modelo Militar

This model represents the first pistol Star produced that was not a Mannlicher design copy. This model was copied from the Colt 1911. It was chambered initially for the 9mm Largo in hopes of securing a military contract. When this contract was awarded to Astra, Star chambered the Model 1919 for the .38 Super and the .45 ACP and put it on the commercial market. This model is like the Colt 1911--it has a Browning-type swinging link and the same type of lock up. However there is no grip safety, and the thumb safety functions differently. This model was produced until 1924.

| Exc. | V.G. | Good | Fair | Poor |
|------|------|------|------|------|
| 275 | 250 | 200 | 175 | 125 |

## Star Model A

This model is a modification of the Model 1919, chambered for the 7.63 Mauser, 9mm Largo, and the .45 ACP cartridge. The slide is similar in appearance to the 1911 Colt, and the spur hammer has a small hole in it. Early models had no grip safety, but later production added this feature. Some models are slotted for addition of a shoulder stock.

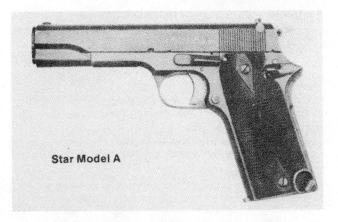

Star Model A

| Exc. | V.G. | Good | Fair | Poor |
|------|------|------|------|------|
| 250 | 225 | 175 | 150 | 100 |

## Star Model B

This model is similar to the Model A except that it is almost an exact copy of the Colt 1911. It is chambered for 9mm parabellum and has a spur hammer with no hole. This model was introduced in 1928.

| Exc. | V.G. | Good | Fair | Poor |
|------|------|------|------|------|
| 275 | 250 | 200 | 175 | 125 |

## Star Model C

This model is the Model B chambered for the 9mm Browning Long cartridge. It was manufactured in the 1920's.

| Exc. | V.G. | Good | Fair | Poor |
|------|------|------|------|------|
| 225 | 175 | 150 | 125 | 90 |

## Star Model CO

This model is a pocket pistol similar to the early open-topped Star pistols. It is chambered for the 6.35mm cartridge, and the finish is blued with checkered plastic grips that bear the Star name and logo. This model was manufactured between 1930 and 1957.

| Exc. | V.G. | Good | Fair | Poor |
|------|------|------|------|------|
| 200 | 150 | 125 | 100 | 75 |

## Star Model D

This is a medium-sized pistol that is similar in appearance to a smaller Model A. It is chambered for the .9mm short cartridge and was called the "Police and Pocket Model" after it was adopted by the Spanish police. It was manufactured between 1930 and 1941.

| Exc. | V.G. | Good | Fair | Poor |
|------|------|------|------|------|
| 200 | 175 | 150 | 110 | 80 |

## Star Model E

This model is a pocket pistol chambered for the 6.35mm cartridge. It has a 2.5" barrel and an external hammer. The detachable magazine holds 5 rounds, and the finish is blued with checkered plastic grips. This model was manufactured between 1932 and 1941.

| Exc. | V.G. | Good | Fair | Poor |
|------|------|------|------|------|
| 200 | 175 | 150 | 110 | 80 |

## Star Model F

This model was the first of the .22 caliber Star pistols. It has a 4" barrel, a 10-shot magazine, and fixed sights. The finish is blued, and the plastic grips are checkered. This model was manufactured between 1942 and 1967.

| Exc. | V.G. | Good | Fair | Poor |
|------|------|------|------|------|
| 175 | 150 | 125 | 100 | 75 |

## Star Model F Target

This model is similar to the Model F, with a 6" barrel.

| Exc. | V.G. | Good | Fair | Poor |
|------|------|------|------|------|
| 225 | 200 | 175 | 150 | 110 |

### Star Model F Sport

This model has a 5" barrel and was also manufactured between 1962 and 1967.

| Exc. | V.G. | Good | Fair | Poor |
|------|------|------|------|------|
| 200 | 175 | 150 | 125 | 100 |

### Star Model F Olympic

This version has a 6" barrel and adjustable sights. It is furnished with a muzzle brake and barrel weights. It was manufactured between 1942 and 1967.

| Exc. | V.G. | Good | Fair | Poor |
|------|------|------|------|------|
| 275 | 225 | 175 | 150 | 125 |

### Star Model F Olympic Rapid Fire

This model is similar to the Olympic but is chambered for .22 short only.

| Exc. | V.G. | Good | Fair | Poor |
|------|------|------|------|------|
| 275 | 225 | 175 | 150 | 125 |

### Star Model FR

This version has an adjustable sight and a slide stop. The 4" barrel is heavier, with flattened sides. It was manufactured between 1967 and 1972.

| Exc. | V.G. | Good | Fair | Poor |
|------|------|------|------|------|
| 185 | 165 | 145 | 125 | 100 |

### Star Model FRS

This model is similar to the Model FR, with a 6" barrel. It is also available chrome-plated with white checkered plastic grips. It was introduced in 1967 and is still in production.

| Exc. | V.G. | Good | Fair | Poor |
|------|------|------|------|------|
| 185 | 165 | 145 | 125 | 100 |

### Star Model FM

This is a heavier-framed version of the Model FRS. It has a 4.5" barrel and is available in blue or chrome-plated. It was introduced in 1972 and is still made.

| Exc. | V.G. | Good | Fair | Poor |
|------|------|------|------|------|
| 185 | 165 | 145 | 125 | 100 |

### Star Model H

This model is similar to the old Model CO--only larger in size. It is chambered for the 7.65mm cartridge and was manufactured between 1932 and 1941.

| Exc. | V.G. | Good | Fair | Poor |
|------|------|------|------|------|
| 165 | 145 | 125 | 100 | 75 |

### Star Model HF

This is a pocket-sized version of the Model F chambered for .22 short. It has a 2.5" barrel and is quite scarce on today's market.

| Exc. | V.G. | Good | Fair | Poor |
|------|------|------|------|------|
| 200 | 175 | 150 | 125 | 100 |

### Star Model HN

This model is simply the Model H chambered for the 9mm short cartridge. It was manufactured and discontinued at the same time as the Model H was.

| Exc. | V.G. | Good | Fair | Poor |
|------|------|------|------|------|
| 175 | 150 | 125 | 100 | 75 |

### Star Model I

This is an improved version of the Model H with a 4" barrel and a recontoured grip. It was chambered for 7.65mm and was produced until 1941. After the war it was resumed and survived until the mid-1950's, when it was replaced by the modernized Model IR which would be valued approximately the same.

Star Model I

| Exc. | V.G. | Good | Fair | Poor |
|------|------|------|------|------|
| 150 | 125 | 100 | 75 | 60 |

### Star Model M

This model is similar to the Model B, chambered for the .38 Auto cartridge.

Star Model M

| Exc. | V.G. | Good | Fair | Poor |
|------|------|------|------|------|
| 175 | 150 | 125 | 100 | 75 |

### Star Model P

This is the post-war version of the Model B, chambered for the .45 ACP cartridge.

| Exc. | V.G. | Good | Fair | Poor |
|------|------|------|------|------|
| 250 | 225 | 300 | 150 | 125 |

### Star Model CU "Starlet"

This model is similar to the Model CO, with an alloy frame that was anodized in black, blue, gray, green, or gold. It has a steel slide that is blued or chrome-plated. It has checkered, white plastic grips and is chambered for the .25ACP cartridge. It has a 2.5" barrel, fixed sights, and a 5-shot magazine. This model was introduced in 1975 and was not imported after the 1968 Gun Control Act made it unacceptable.

| Exc. | V.G. | Good | Fair | Poor |
|------|------|------|------|------|
| 175  | 150  | 125  | 100  | 75   |

## Star Model BKS "Starlight"

This model was the smallest locked-breech automatic chambered for the 9mm cartridge at the time. It has an alloy frame and a 4.25" barrel. It is similar in appearance to a scaled-down Colt 1911 without a grip safety. It has an 8-shot magazine and is either blued or chrome-plated, with checkered plastic grips. This model was manufactured between 1970 and 1981.

| Exc. | V.G. | Good | Fair | Poor |
|------|------|------|------|------|
| 250  | 225  | 200  | 150  | 125  |

## Star Model PD

This model is chambered for the .45 ACP cartridge and has a 4" barrel. It has an alloy frame and a 6-shot magazine and adjustable sights and is blued with checkered walnut grips. It was introduced in 1975.

| NIB | Exc. | V.G. | Good | Fair | Poor |
|-----|------|------|------|------|------|
| 400 | 325  | 275  | 225  | 175  | 125  |

## Star Model BM

This model is a steel-framed 9mm that is styled after the Colt 1911. It has an 8-shot magazine and a 4" barrel. It is available either blued or chrome-plated.

| NIB | Exc. | V.G. | Good | Fair | Poor |
|-----|------|------|------|------|------|
| 335 | 300  | 250  | 200  | 150  | 125  |

## Star Model BKM

This model is similar to the BM, with an alloy frame.

| NIB | Exc. | V.G. | Good | Fair | Poor |
|-----|------|------|------|------|------|
| 375 | 325  | 275  | 225  | 175  | 125  |

## Star Model 28

This was the first of Star's Super 9's. It is a double-action semi-automatic chambered for the 9mm Parabellum cartridge. It has a 4.25" barrel and a steel frame. The magazine holds 15 shots. The construction of this pistol was totally modular, and it has no screws at all in its design. It is blued with checkered synthetic grips and was manufactured in 1983 and 1984.

| NIB | Exc. | V.G. | Good | Fair | Poor |
|-----|------|------|------|------|------|
| 415 | 375  | 325  | 275  | 225  | 175  |

## Star Model 30M

This is an improved version of the Model 28, that is quite similar in appearance. It was introduced in 1985.

| NIB | Exc. | V.G. | Good | Fair | Poor |
|-----|------|------|------|------|------|
| 550 | 500  | 425  | 350  | 300  | 250  |

## Star Model 30/PK

This model is similar to the Models 28 and 30M, with a lightweight alloy frame.

| NIB | Exc. | V.G. | Good | Fair | Poor |
|-----|------|------|------|------|------|
| 550 | 500  | 425  | 350  | 300  | 250  |

‌‍‌‍‍‌‍

# ECLIPSE
## Pittsburgh, Pennsylvania
## Enterprise Gun Works

**Single Shot Derringer**
This pocket pistol was made by the firm of James Bown & Son, doing business as the Enterprise Gun Works. It is chambered for .22 or .32-caliber rimfire cartridges. A few in .25 rimfire have been noted and would add approximately 25 percent to the values listed. The barrel is 2.5" in length and is part-round/part-octagonal. It pivots sideways for loading. It has a spur trigger and a birdshead grip. The barrel is stamped "Eclipse." It is made of nickel-plated iron, with walnut grips. There were approximately 10,000 manufactured between 1870 and 1890.

| Exc. | V.G. | Good | Fair | Poor |
|------|------|------|------|------|
| 200 | 175 | 150 | 100 | 75 |

# 84 GUN CO.
## Eighty Four, Pennsylvania

This company was in business for a brief time in the early 1970's. They produced three basic bolt-action rifles--each in four grades that differ in amounts of embellishment and grades of wood. There is very little known about this company and their products. An accurate appraisal with hands-on would be the only proper way to place a value on these rifles as there are not enough traded in to establish correct values in a book of this nature. The basic models are as follows.

**Classic Rifle**
Grade 1--Grade 4 available
450--1600

**Lobo Rifle**
Grade 1--Grade 4 available.
425--2500

**Pennsylvania Rifle**
Grade 1--Grade 4 available.
425--2500

# ELGIN CUTLASS
## Springfield, Massachusetts

This weapon was manufactured by two companies--C. B. Allen of Springfield, Massachusetts, and Morill, Mosman and Blair of Amherst, Massachusetts. It is a unique pistol that has an integral knife attachment affixed to the gun barrel. It was designed and patented by George Elgin and simultaneously produced by the two companies. The inspiration for this weapon was supposedly Jim Bowie, who at that time had made a name as a knife fighter with his large "Bowie" knife. The blades for these pistols were supplied by N. P. Ames of the famed Ames Sword Co. These pistols are much sought after, and one must excercise caution as fraudulent examples have been noted.

**C. B. Allen-Made Pistols**
**U.S. Navy Elgin Cutlass Pistol**
This model is chambered for .54 caliber percussion and has a 5" octagonal smooth-bore barrel. The Bowie-style blade is 11" long by 2" wide and is forged together with the triggerguard and the knuckle guard that protects the grip. The handle is walnut. This pistol was issued to the U.S. Navy's Wilkes-South Sea Exploration Expedition, and the markings are "C.B.Allen / Springfield / Mass." "Elgin's Patent" and the letters "CB", "CBA" along with the date 1837. If the sheath that was issued with this knife pistol is included and in sound condition, it would add approximately $700 to the value. There were 150 manufactured for the U.S. Navy in 1838.

| Exc. | V.G. | Good | Fair | Poor |
|------|------|------|------|------|
| 12500 | 10000 | 8000 | 6500 | 4750 |

**Civilian Model**
This version is chambered for .35 or .41 caliber percussion and has a 4" octagonal barrel with a 7.5"--10" knife blade. It has a round triggerguard but does not have the knuckle bow across the grip, as found on the military model. They are marked "C.B.Allen Springfield, Mass." Blades marked "N.P.Ames" have been noted. There were approximately 100 manufactured in 1837.

| Exc. | V.G. | Good | Fair | Poor |
|------|------|------|------|------|
| 5000 | 4500 | 3750 | 3250 | 2750 |

**Morill, Mosman and Blair-Made Pistols**
**Small Model**
The main difference in the pistols of the two makers is that this model has a round barrel and a square-back triggerguard that comes to a point at the rear. This version is chambered for .32 caliber percussion and has a 2.75" barrel. The knife blade is 7.5" in length and is screwed to the frame. This Model is unmarked except for a serial number. The number produced is unknown, and they were manufactured in 1837.

| Exc. | V.G. | Good | Fair | Poor |
|------|------|------|------|------|
| 4000 | 3500 | 2750 | 2250 | 1750 |

**Large Model**
This model is chambered for .36 caliber percussion and has a 4" round barrel and a 9" knife blade. The pistol is usually marked "Cast Steel" and serial numbered. The blade is etched with an American eagle, stars, and an urn with flowers. "Elgin Patent" is etched in the center. This Model was also manufactured in 1837.

| Exc. | V.G. | Good | Fair | Poor |
|------|------|------|------|------|
| 4000 | 3500 | 3000 | 2500 | 2000 |

# ELLS, JOSIAH
## Pittsburgh, Pennsylvania

**Pocket Revolver**
There are three distinct variations of this percussion revolver. They are chambered for .28 and .31 caliber and have 6-shot unfluted cylinders. They have been noted with 2.5", 3", and 3.75" octagonal barrels.

**Model 1**
The first model has an open-topped frame and is chambered for .28 caliber. The cylinder holds 5 or 6 shots, and the hammer is of the bar type. It was offered with a 2.5" or 3" barrel. The markings are "J.Ells; Patent;1854." There were approximately 625 manufactured between 1857 and 1859.

| Exc. | V.G. | Good | Fair | Poor |
|------|------|------|------|------|
| 450 | 400 | 325 | 275 | 200 |

**Model 2**
The second Model is similar to the first, with a solid-topped frame. They have 5-shot cylinders and 3.75" long barrels. There were approximately 550 manufactured.

| Exc. | V.G. | Good | Fair | Poor |
|------|------|------|------|------|
| 450 | 400 | 325 | 275 | 200 |

**Model 3**
The third Model is radically different from its forerunners. It has a closed-top frame and a conventional spur-type hammer that strikes from the right side. It functions either as a double-or single-action. It is chambered for .28 caliber and has a 5-shot cylinder and a 3.75" barrel. There were only about 200 manufactured between 1857 and 1859.

| Exc. | V.G. | Good | Fair | Poor |
|------|------|------|------|------|
| 575 | 550 | 425 | 375 | 300 |

# ENFIELD ROYAL SMALL ARMS FACTORY
## Middlesex, England

In 1879 the British Army needed revolvers, and the Royal Small Arms Factory was commissioned to produce them. The result was that on August 11, 1880, the Enfield Mark I was accepted for duty.

**Enfield Mark I Revolver**
This model is a 6-shot, hinged-frame, break-open revolver. It has an odd ejection system--when the barrel is pulled down, the cylinder moves forward; and the extractor plate remains in place, retaining the spent cartridges. This revolver is chambered for the .476 cartridge and has a 6-shot cylinder. The

barrel is 6" long, and the finish is blued with checkered walnut grips.

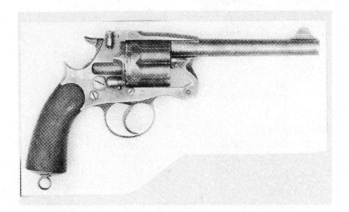

| Exc. | V.G. | Good | Fair | Poor |
|------|------|------|------|------|
| 250  | 225  | 175  | 140  | 100  |

**Enfield Mark 2**

The Mark 2 is similar externally, with some design improvements--such as a rounded front sight, taper-bored cylinders, an integral top strap, and plain grips. The Mark 2 was introduced in 1881 and was replaced by the Webley Mark I in 1887.

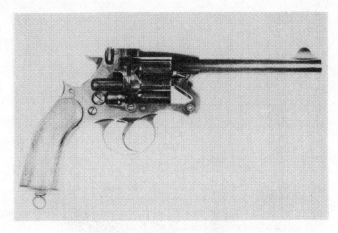

| Exc. | V.G. | Good | Fair | Poor |
|------|------|------|------|------|
| 250  | 225  | 175  | 140  | 100  |

**Enfield-Produced Webley Mark 6**

The Royal Small Arms Factory was out of the pistol business until 1921, when they produced a number of .455-caliber Webley Mark 6 revolvers. They are identical to the Webley-produced versions with "Enfield" stamped on the frame. This model was discontinued after WWI.

| Exc. | V.G. | Good | Fair | Poor |
|------|------|------|------|------|
| 225  | 200  | 175  | 140  | 100  |

**Enfield No. 2 Mark I**

This model was originally chambered for the .38 Webley Special. It is a 6-shot, break-open double action, with a 5" barrel. The finish is blued, with black plastic checkered grips. This model was actually a modified Webley design and was adopted in 1932. In 1938 the bullet was changed from a 200-grain lead "soft-nosed" to a 178-grain jacketed, in response to pressure from the Geneva Conference.

| Exc. | V.G. | Good | Fair | Poor |
|------|------|------|------|------|
| 200  | 175  | 150  | 125  | 100  |

**Enfield No. 2 Mark I***

This pistol is the same as the Mark I with the hammer spur and single action lockwork omitted in response to the Royal Tank Regiment's fear that the spur would catch on the tank as the crews were entering and exiting their confines.

| Exc. | V.G. | Good | Fair | Poor |
|------|------|------|------|------|
| 225  | 200  | 175  | 150  | 125  |

During WWII these pistols were manufactured by Albion Motors Ltd. of Glasgow, Scotland. These pistols were produced between 1941 and 1943, and approximately 24,000 were made. They are marked "Albion" on the right side of the frame. These examples would not be valued differently than Enfield-made pistols. Enfield pistols with the marking "SM" or "SSM" will also be noted, and this refers to various parts produced by Singer Sewing Machine Company of England. These pistols were assembled at Enfield.

These pistols were used until 1957, when the FN-Browning GP35 semi-automatic pistol replaced them.

**Enfield Rifles**
**Lee-Enfield Mark I**

This rifle is chambered for the .303 cartridge and has a 30" barrel. The attached box magazine holds 10 rounds, and the sights are military-styled. The stock is full-length walnut, and there is a cleaning rod beneath it. There are two barrel bands and a bayonet lug. This model was manufactured between 1895 and 1899.

| Exc. | V.G. | Good | Fair | Poor |
|------|------|------|------|------|
| 250  | 225  | 200  | 150  | 100  |

**Lee-Enfield Mark I***

This model is a Mark 3 Martini Henry with a .303-caliber barrel fitted to it. It was introduced in 1899.

| Exc. | V.G. | Good | Fair | Poor |
|------|------|------|------|------|
| 250  | 225  | 200  | 150  | 100  |

**Lee-Enfield Mark I****

This model is simply the Mark I with no attached cleaning rod. It was introduced in 1899.

| Exc. | V.G. | Good | Fair | Poor |
|------|------|------|------|------|
| 250  | 225  | 200  | 150  | 100  |

### Lee-Enfield Mark II SMLE

This model is the Mark I converted by fitting a shorter and lighter barrel, modifying the action to accept a stripper clip, and fitting new sights. The letters SMLE stand for Short Magazine, Lee-Enfield. It was introduced in 1903.

| Exc. | V.G. | Good | Fair | Poor |
|------|------|------|------|------|
| 225 | 200 | 175 | 150 | 100 |

### SMLE Mark III

This model is chambered for .303 British and has a 25" barrel with a 10-round magazine. The magazine has a cut off, and the sights are military-styled. The action is modified to accept a stripper clip and automatically eject it when the bolt is closed. This model was introduced in 1907.

| Exc. | V.G. | Good | Fair | Poor |
|------|------|------|------|------|
| 200 | 175 | 150 | 125 | 75 |

### SMLE No. 5 Mark I

This model is also known as the Jungle Carbine. It is chambered for the .303 British cartridge and has a 20.5" barrel with an attached flash suppressor and a shorter forend and handguard. It is furnished with a rubber buttpad and modified rear sight. This was not a popular weapon with the soldiers who carried it as the recoil was excessive due to the lighter weight.

| Exc. | V.G. | Good | Fair | Poor |
|------|------|------|------|------|
| 300 | 250 | 225 | 175 | 125 |

### No. 3 Mark I P1914

This rifle was built on a modified Mauser-type action and was chambered for the .303 British cartridge. It was a secondary-issue arm during WWI and was simpler to mass-produce than the SMLE. These rifles were also produced in the U.S.A. by Remington and Winchester.

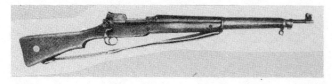

| Exc. | V.G. | Good | Fair | Poor |
|------|------|------|------|------|
| 225 | 200 | 175 | 125 | 90 |

### SMLE No. 4 Mark I

This model was an improved version that featured a stronger action with an aperture sight and was easier to mass produce. It was issued in 1939 and was used during WWII. There is a cased and scoped Sniper model of this variation.

| Exc. | V.G. | Good | Fair | Poor |
|------|------|------|------|------|
| 200 | 175 | 150 | 100 | 75 |

### Sniper Model Cased

| Exc. | V.G. | Good | Fair | Poor |
|------|------|------|------|------|
| 750 | 650 | 550 | 425 | 350 |

### No .3 Mark I

This is a single-shot, bolt-action training rifle that is chambered for the .22 rimfire cartridge.

| Exc. | V.G. | Good | Fair | Poor |
|------|------|------|------|------|
| 350 | 325 | 275 | 200 | 150 |

# ENFIELD AMERICAN, INC.
### Atlanta, Goergia

### MP-45

This is a blowback-operated, semi-automatic assault pistol chambered for the .45 ACP cartridge. It was offered with a barrel length of 4.5" through 18.5". The long barrel features a shroud. The finish is parkerized, and there were four different magazines available in 10, 20, 30, and 50-round capacities. This firearm was manufactured in 1985 only.

| Exc. | V.G. | Good | Fair | Poor |
|------|------|------|------|------|
| 300 | 275 | 225 | 175 | 125 |

# ERA
### Brazil

### Era Double Barrel Shotgun

This is an inexpensive side-by-side chambered for 12 and 20 gauge, as well as .410. It was offered with 26", 28", or 30" barrels with various choke combinations. It has double triggers and extractors, with a checkered hardwood pistolgrip stock. This gun is also available as a Quail model with a 20" barrel and as a Riot model with an 18" barrel. These two models are not offered in .410 bore.

| Exc. | V.G. | Good | Fair | Poor |
|------|------|------|------|------|
| 175 | 150 | 125 | 100 | 75 |

### Era Over/Under Shotgun

This gun is chambered for 12 or 20 gauge, with 28" ventilated-rib barrels that were choked full and modified. It is a boxlock with double triggers, extractors, and a hardwood stock. It was also offered in a Trap model and a Skeet model chambered for 12 gauge only and appropriately choked. These latter two models would be worth a 10 percent premium over the values shown.

| Exc. | V.G. | Good | Fair | Poor |
|------|------|------|------|------|
| 300 | 275 | 250 | 200 | 150 |

## ERICHSON, G.
### Houston, Texas

### Erichson Pocket Pistol
This small pistol is a very close copy of the Philadelphia-style Henry Deringer. It is chambered for .45-caliber percussion and has a 3.25" barrel. The mountings are German silver and not engraved; the stock is walnut. The hammer is deeply fluted; and the forend, carved. The barrel is marked "G.Erichson / Houston, Texas." The number produced is unknown, but examples are scarce. They were manufactured in the 1850's.

| Exc. | V.G. | Good | Fair | Poor |
|------|------|------|------|------|
| 2500 | 2250 | 2000 | 1500 | 1000 |

## ERMA WERKE WAFFENFABRIK
### Erfurt, Germany
### Post-War
### Dachau, Germany

This company is known primarily as a manufacturer of submachineguns, but they are also in the handgun and rifle business. In 1933 they answered the German Army's need for an inexpensive practice weapon by producing a .22 rimfire conversion unit for the Luger pistol. This was marketed commercially and was available for many years. The success of this unit led the company to produce other inexpensive target and plinking pistols. After the war they were reorganized in the western sector and resumed submachinegun production. In 1964 they returned to the sporting firearms business with the introduction of their .22 rimfire Luger-lookalike pistol. Since then, they have produced many like-quality firearms. They were imported by Excam of Hialeah, Florida. This association is now terminated, and they are currently imported by Beeman Precision in Santa Rosa, California, and Mandell Shooting Supplies in Scottsdale, Arizona.

### Erma .22 Luger Conversion Unit
This unit was produced for the German Army in 1933 and then became a successful commercial item. It would turn a standard 9mm or 7.65mm Luger into an inexpensive-to-shoot .22 rimfire. The unit consists of a barrel insert, a breech block, and toggle unit with its own lightened recoil spring, and a .22 magazine. This unit was furnished with a wooden box. There were many different sized units to fit various caliber and barrel-length Lugers, but all used the same parts and concept. These units have become very desirable to Luger collectors.

| Exc. | V.G. | Good | Fair | Poor |
|------|------|------|------|------|
| 500 | 425 | 350 | 275 | 200 |

### .22 Target Pistol (Old Model)
This is an inexpensive, blowback-operated, semi-automatic pistol chambered for the .22 rimfire cartridge. This model has a 4" barrel and an open-topped slide. The frame is made from a cast zinc alloy, and there is an external hammer. There are adjustable sights, and balance weights were available. This pistol was manufactured in 1936.

| Exc. | V.G. | Good | Fair | Poor |
|------|------|------|------|------|
| 250 | 225 | 175 | 125 | 100 |

### .22 Target Pistol (New Model)
This is an improved version of the Old Model, that features a new grip angle and a magazine and takedown device which is like that of the Luger. There were interchangeable barrels and three basic models--the "Sport," "Hunter," and the "Master." The difference was the length of the barrels --4", 5", and 6", respectively. These pistols were manufactured between 1937 and 1940, when they were discontinued due to Erma's involvement in the war effort.

| Exc. | V.G. | Good | Fair | Poor |
|------|------|------|------|------|
| 275 | 250 | 200 | 150 | 125 |

### KGP-Series
These pistols were made to resemble the Luger quite closely. They utilized the mechanical features of the .22 conversion unit and developed a pistol around it. There are many different versions of this pistol chambered for .22 rimfire, .32 ACP, and .380 ACP. The original designation was the KGP-68; but the Gun Control Act of 1968 required that a magazine safety be added, and the model was redesignated the KGP-68A. The last designations for the three calibers are KGP-22, KGP-32, and KGP-38. These pistols were manufactured between 1964 and 1986, and their values are as follows.

### KGP-68
This model has a 4" barrel and is chambered for the .32 ACP and the .380 ACP cartridges. It has a 6-shot magazine and an anodized alloy receiver. This model is also known as the Beeman MP-08.

| Exc. | V.G. | Good | Fair | Poor |
|------|------|------|------|------|
| 350 | 300 | 250 | 200 | 125 |

### KGP-69
This is a .22 rimfire version of this series, with an 8-shot magazine capacity. It is also known as the Beeman P-08.

| Exc. | V.G. | Good | Fair | Poor |
|------|------|------|------|------|
| 350 | 300 | 250 | 200 | 125 |

### ET-22 Luger Carbine
This is a rare firearm. According to some estimates only 375 were produced. It features a 11.75" barrel and is chambered for the .22 rimfire cartridge. It has an artillery Luger-type rear sight and checkered walnut grips, with a smooth walnut forend. The pistol was furnished with a red felt lined, black leatherette case.

| Exc. | V.G. | Good | Fair | Poor |
|------|------|------|------|------|
| 400 | 350 | 300 | 200 | 150 |

### KGP-22
This was the later version of the KGP-69 chambered for .22 rimfire.

| Exc. | V.G. | Good | Fair | Poor |
|------|------|------|------|------|
| 350 | 300 | 250 | 200 | 125 |

### KGP-32 & KGP-38
These two designations are the later versions of the KGP-68 and 68A.

| Exc. | V.G. | Good | Fair | Poor |
|------|------|------|------|------|
| 350 | 300 | 250 | 200 | 125 |

## ESP 85A

This is a high quality target pistol imported by Mandall Shooting Supply. It features an interchangable barrel system that converts the chambering from .22 rimfire to .32 S&W Long Wadcutter. The barrels are both 6" in length, and there are adjustable and interchangable sights and a 5-or 8-shot detachable magazine. The finish is blued, and the grips are stippled target types. The gun is furnished in a padded hard case with two extra magazines and takedown tools. This unit was introduced in 1989.

| NIB | Exc. | V.G. | Good | Fair | Poor |
|-----|------|------|------|------|------|
| 1100 | 1000 | 850 | 700 | 550 | 450 |

## RX-22

This pistol is a .22 rimfire copy of the Walther PPK. It has a 3.25" barrel, an 8-shot detachable magazine, and a blued finish with checkered black plastic grips. It was assembled in the U.S.A. from parts made in West Germany. It was discontinued in 1986.

| Exc. | V.G. | Good | Fair | Poor |
|------|------|------|------|------|
| 200 | 175 | 150 | 125 | 100 |

## Revolvers
## ER-772 Match

This is a target revolver chambered for the .22 rimfire and has a 6" shrouded barrel with a solid rib. The swing-out cylinder holds 6 shots, and the sights are adjustable. The finish is blued, with stippled target grips. This model was introduced in 1989.

| NIB | Exc. | V.G. | Good | Fair | Poor |
|-----|------|------|------|------|------|
| 500 | 450 | 400 | 350 | 250 | 200 |

## ER-773 Match

This revolver is similar to the ER-772 except that it is chambered for the .32 S&W long cartridge.

| NIB | Exc. | V.G. | Good | Fair | Poor |
|-----|------|------|------|------|------|
| 500 | 450 | 400 | 350 | 250 | 200 |

## ER-777

This is basically a similar revolver to the ER-773 except that it has a 4.5" or 5" barrel and is chambered for the .357 Magnum cartridge. The revolver is larger and has standard sport grips. This model was also introduced in 1989.

| NIB | Exc. | V.G. | Good | Fair | Poor |
|-----|------|------|------|------|------|
| 500 | 450 | 400 | 350 | 250 | 200 |

## Rifles
## EMI .22

This is a semi-automatic .22 rimfire version of the M1 Carbine. It has an 18" barrel and a 15-round magazine. It was manufactured between 1966 and 1976.

Erma Model EMI 22

| Exc. | V.G. | Good | Fair | Poor |
|------|------|------|------|------|
| 200 | 175 | 150 | 125 | 100 |

## EG-72, EG-722

This is a 15-shot slide-action carbine chambered for .22 rimfire, with a 18.5" barrel and open sights. The finish is blued, and it was manufactured between 1970 and 1985.

| Exc. | V.G. | Good | Fair | Poor |
|------|------|------|------|------|
| 135 | 110 | 100 | 75 | 50 |

## EG-712, EG-73

This model is a lever copy of the Winchester 94 Carbine chambered for the .22 rimfire or the .22 rimfire Magnum (EG-73). It has an 18.5" barrel and holds 15 shots in a tubular magazine. It was manufactured between 1973 and 1985.

| Exc. | V.G. | Good | Fair | Poor |
|------|------|------|------|------|
| 200 | 175 | 150 | 125 | 100 |

# ERQUIAGA
### Eibar, Spain

This is another Spanish company that commenced business during WWI as a subcontractor on the French "Ruby" contract. They manufactured the usual poor-quality, 7.65mm Eibar-type pistol.

## Fiel

This is the tradename found on the Ruby subcontract pistol described above. It is marked "Erquiaga y Cia Eibar Cal. 7.65 Fiel."

| Exc. | V.G. | Good | Fair | Poor |
|------|------|------|------|------|
| 175 | 150 | 125 | 100 | 75 |

## Fiel 6.35

After the end of WWI, a 1906 Browning copy was made. It is chambered for the 6.35mm cartridge. The markings are "Automatic Pistol 6.35 Fiel No.1." Later models had "EMC" molded into the grip.

| Exc. | V.G. | Good | Fair | Poor |
|------|------|------|------|------|
| 150 | 125 | 100 | 75 | 50 |

## Marte

This is another poor-quality "Eibar"-type pistol that is chambered for the 6.35mm and that was made in the early 1920's.

| Exc. | V.G. | Good | Fair | Poor |
|------|------|------|------|------|
| 150 | 125 | 100 | 75 | 50 |

# ERRASTI, A.
### Eibar, Spain

Errasti manufactured a variety of inexpensive yet serviceable pistols from the early 1900's until the Spanish Civil War.

## Velo-Dog

The usual cheap solid frame folding trigger revolvers one associates with the model designation. They were chambered in 5.5mm and 6.35mm and were made in the early 1900's.

| Exc. | V.G. | Good | Fair | Poor |
|------|------|------|------|------|
| 150 | 125 | 100 | 75 | 50 |

## M1889

In 1915-1916 Errasti produced the 10.4mm Italian army service revolver. The quality was reasonably good. They were marked "Errasti Eiber" on the right side of the frame.

| Exc. | V.G. | Good | Fair | Poor |
|------|------|------|------|------|
| 200 | 175 | 150 | 100 | 75 |

## Errasti

Two "Eibar" type Browning copies were made under this trade name. One was chambered for the 6.35mm, the other the 7.65mm. They were boty marked "Automatic Pistol Errasti."

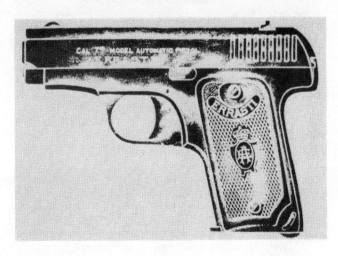

| Exc. | V.G. | Good | Fair | Poor |
|------|------|------|------|------|
| 150 | 125 | 100 | 75 | 50 |

## Errasti Oscillante

Manufactured in the 1920's, these revolvers were copied from the Smith & Wesson Military & Police design. They were chambered for the .32, .38, and .44 calibers with the .38 being the most frequently encountered.

| Exc. | V.G. | Good | Fair | Poor |
|------|------|------|------|------|
| 150 | 125 | 100 | 75 | 50 |

## Dreadnaught, Goliath and Smith Americano

These three trade names were found on a group of poor quality nickel-plated revolvers. They were made from 1905 through 1920 and were obvious copies of the Iver Johnson design. They had break open actions, ribbed barrel, and were chambered for .32, .38, and .44 calibers. They are scarce today, as most have long since fallen apart.

| Exc. | V.G. | Good | Fair | Poor |
|------|------|------|------|------|
| 150 | 125 | 100 | 75 | 50 |

# ESCODIN, M.
### Eibar, Spain

This company made a Smith & Wesson revolver copy from 1924 through 1931. It is chambered for the .32 and the .38 Special. The only marking is a coat of arms stamped on the left side of the frame.

| Exc. | V.G. | Good | Fair | Poor |
|------|------|------|------|------|
| 150 | 125 | 100 | 75 | 50 |

# ESPIRIN, HERMANOS
### Eibar, Spain

### Euskaro

This very poor-quality, often unsafe revolver was manufactured from 1906 until WWI. They are copies of the Iver Johnson-design break-open actions, chambered for .32, .38, and .44. This product epitomizes the worst Eibar had to offer during the pre-civil war era.

| Exc. | V.G. | Good | Fair | Poor |
|------|------|------|------|------|
| 125 | 100 | 75 | 50 | 25 |

# EUROARMS OF AMERICA
### Winchester, Virginia

This company is an importer of black powder muzzle-loading firearms, primarily replicas of early American weapons.

### Revolvers
### 1851 Navy

This is a replica of the Colt revolver chambered for .36 or .44 caliber percussion. It has a squareback, silver-plated trigger guard and a 7.5" barrel.

| NIB | Exc. | V.G. | Good | Fair | Poor |
|-----|------|------|------|------|------|
| 135 | 125 | 110 | 80 | 65 | 45 |

### 1851 Navy Police Model

This model is chambered for .36 caliber with a 5-shot, fluted cylinder and a 5.5" barrel.

| Exc. | V.G. | Good | Fair | Poor |
|------|------|------|------|------|
| 125 | 110 | 80 | 65 | 45 |

### 1851 Navy Sheriff's Model

This is a 5"-barrelled version of the Navy Model.

| NIB | Exc. | V.G. | Good | Fair | Poor |
|-----|------|------|------|------|------|
| 110 | 100 | 80 | 60 | 50 | 35 |

### 1851 "Schneider & Glassick" Navy

A replica of the Confederate revolver chambered for .36 or .44 caliber percussion.

| NIB | Exc. | V.G. | Good | Fair | Poor |
|-----|------|------|------|------|------|
| 110 | 100 | 80 | 60 | 50 | 35 |

## 1851 "Griswold & Gunnison" Navy

This is a replica of this Confederate revolver chambered for .36 or .44 caliber percussion.

| Exc. | V.G. | Good | Fair | Poor |
|---|---|---|---|---|
| 90 | 75 | 60 | 40 | 25 |

## 1862 Police

This is a replica of the Colt Model 1862 chambered for .36 caliber percussion, with a 7.5" barrel and a steel frame.

| Exc. | V.G. | Good | Fair | Poor |
|---|---|---|---|---|
| 125 | 110 | 90 | 65 | 45 |

## 1860 Army

This is a replica of the Colt revolver chambered for .44 caliber percussion. It was offered with a 5" or 8" barrel.

| NIB | Exc. | V.G. | Good | Fair | Poor |
|---|---|---|---|---|---|
| 150 | 125 | 100 | 75 | 50 | 30 |

## 1861 Navy

This is a replica of the Colt revolver chambered for .36 caliber percussion.

| NIB | Exc. | V.G. | Good | Fair | Poor |
|---|---|---|---|---|---|
| 160 | 135 | 110 | 80 | 60 | 40 |

## 1858 Remington Army or Navy

These are replicas of the Remington percussion revolvers chambered for .26 or .44 caliber.

| NIB | Exc. | V.G. | Good | Fair | Poor |
|---|---|---|---|---|---|
| 175 | 150 | 125 | 100 | 75 | 50 |

## Rifles

The following rifles are modern replicas of early American and British firearms. They are of good quality and are quite serviceable. There is no collector interest, and we list them along with their values.

## Cook & Brother Carbine

| NIB | Exc. | V.G. | Good | Fair | Poor |
|---|---|---|---|---|---|
| 375 | 325 | 250 | 200 | 150 | 100 |

## 1863 J. P. Murray

| NIB | Exc. | V.G. | Good | Fair | Poor |
|---|---|---|---|---|---|
| 360 | 310 | 225 | 175 | 125 | 100 |

## 1853 Enfield Rifled Musket

| NIB | Exc. | V.G. | Good | Fair | Poor |
|---|---|---|---|---|---|
| 400 | 350 | 300 | 250 | 175 | 125 |

## 1858 Enfield Rifled Musket

| NIB | Exc. | V.G. | Good | Fair | Poor |
|---|---|---|---|---|---|
| 375 | 325 | 250 | 200 | 150 | 100 |

## 1861 Enfield Musketoon

| NIB | Exc. | V.G. | Good | Fair | Poor |
|---|---|---|---|---|---|
| 350 | 300 | 225 | 175 | 125 | 90 |

## 1803 Harper's Ferry

| NIB | Exc. | V.G. | Good | Fair | Poor |
|---|---|---|---|---|---|
| 500 | 425 | 350 | 300 | 225 | 150 |

## 1841 Mississippi Rifle

| NIB | Exc. | V.G. | Good | Fair | Poor |
|---|---|---|---|---|---|
| 475 | 400 | 325 | 275 | 200 | 125 |

## Pennsylvania Rifle

| Exc. | V.G. | Good | Fair | Poor |
|---|---|---|---|---|
| 250 | 225 | 200 | 150 | 100 |

## Hawken Rifle

| NIB | Exc. | V.G. | Good | Fair | Poor |
|---|---|---|---|---|---|
| 300 | 250 | 200 | 150 | 100 | 80 |

## Cape Gun

| NIB | Exc. | V.G. | Good | Fair | Poor |
|---|---|---|---|---|---|
| 400 | 350 | 275 | 225 | 175 | 125 |

## Buffalo Carbine

| NIB | Exc. | V.G. | Good | Fair | Poor |
|---|---|---|---|---|---|
| 400 | 350 | 300 | 250 | 175 | 100 |

## 1862 Remington Rifle

| Exc. | V.G. | Good | Fair | Poor |
|---|---|---|---|---|
| 250 | 225 | 200 | 125 | 80 |

## Zouave Rifle

| NIB | Exc. | V.G. | Good | Fair | Poor |
|---|---|---|---|---|---|
| 325 | 275 | 225 | 175 | 125 | 90 |

## Shotguns

## Duck Gun

This is a single-barrelled percussion fowling piece chambered for 8, 10, or 12 gauge. It has a 33" smooth-bore barrel and a case-colored hammer and lock. The stock is walnut with brass mountings. This model was introduced in 1989.

| NIB | Exc. | V.G. | Good | Fair | Poor |
|---|---|---|---|---|---|
| 400 | 350 | 300 | 250 | 175 | 100 |

## Double Barrel Shotgun

This is a side-by-side, chambered for 12 gauge percussion. It has 28" barrels with engraved locks and a walnut stock.

| Exc. | V.G. | Good | Fair | Poor |
|---|---|---|---|---|
| 375 | 325 | 275 | 200 | 125 |

# EVANS REPEATING RIFLE CO.
## Mechanic Falls, Maine

### Lever Action Rifle

This rifle is totally unique for a number of reasons. It holds the most rounds of any repeating rifle that did not have a detachable magazine, with capacities up to 38 rounds on some models. This rifle was chambered for its own cartridge--the .44 Evans-- of which there were two versions: a 1" cartridge in the "Old Model" and the "Transition Model" and a 1.5" cartridge in the "New Model". The finish on these rifles is blued, with nickel-plated levers and buttplates noted on some examples. The stocks are walnut. There were approximately 12,250 of all models manufactured between 1873 and 1879.

### Old Model

This variation is chambered for the 1" .44 Evans cartridge and has a buttstock that covers only the top half of the revolving 34-shot magazine located in the butt of the rifle. The buttplate appears as if it is reversed, and the markings on the "Old Model" are "Evans Repeating Rifle/ Pat. Dec. 8, 1868 & Sept. 16, 1871." There are three versions of the Old Model as follows. They were manufactured between 1874 and 1876 and serial numbered 1--500.

### Military Musket

This version has a 30" barrel, with 2 barrel bands and provisions for a bayonet. There were only 50 estimated manufactured.

| Exc. | V.G. | Good | Fair | Poor |
|---|---|---|---|---|
| 1500 | 1250 | 900 | 750 | 500 |

### Sporting Rifle

There were approximately 300 of this model produced with a 26", 28", or 30" octagonal barrel.

| Exc. | V.G. | Good | Fair | Poor |
|---|---|---|---|---|
| 1100 | 900 | 750 | 500 | 400 |

### Carbine

This variation has a 22" barrel, with one barrel band and a sling swivel. There were 150 produced.

| Exc. | V.G. | Good | Fair | Poor |
|---|---|---|---|---|
| 1350 | 1150 | 800 | 650 | 550 |

## Transitional Model

This model has a buttstock that covers both the top and bottom of the rotary magazine, with an exposed portion in the middle of the butt. The buttplate does not have the backward appearance, and the barrel is marked "Evans Repeating Rifle Mechanic Falls Me./Pat Dec. 8, 1868 & Sept. 16, 1871." This version was manufactured in 1876 and 1877 and was serial numbered between 500--2185, for a total of approximately 1,650 manufactured.

## Military Musket

This version has a 30" barrel and two barrel bands. 150 were produced.

| Exc. | V.G. | Good | Fair | Poor |
|------|------|------|------|------|
| 1150 | 950 | 800 | 600 | 450 |

## Carbine

There were 450 of these produced, with a 22" barrel and one barrel band.

| Exc. | V.G. | Good | Fair | Poor |
|------|------|------|------|------|
| 1000 | 800 | 650 | 500 | 375 |

## Sporting Rifle

This version has a 26", 28", or 30" barrel. There were 1,050 produced.

| Exc. | V.G. | Good | Fair | Poor |
|------|------|------|------|------|
| 800 | 600 | 475 | 350 | 275 |

## "Montreal Carbine"

This is a special issue marked "Montreal," sold by R. H. Kilby, Evans' Canadian sales agent. There were between 50 and 100 produced.

| Exc. | V.G. | Good | Fair | Poor |
|------|------|------|------|------|
| 1150 | 950 | 800 | 600 | 450 |

## New Model

There were approximately 10,000 of the New Model produced, chambered for the 1.5" .44 Evans cartridge with a magazine capacity reduced to 28. The frame was redesigned and rounded at the top, and the forend fit flush to the receiver. The lever and hammer are streamlined, and there is a dust cover over the loading gate. The markings are the same as on the Transitional Model with "U.S.A." added to the last line. This version was not serial numbered, and any numbers found are assembly numbers only.

## Military Musket

There were 3,000 produced, with a 30" barrel and two barrel bands.

| Exc. | V.G. | Good | Fair | Poor |
|------|------|------|------|------|
| 1000 | 800 | 650 | 500 | 375 |

## Carbine

There were 4,000 produced with a 22" barrel, one barrel band, and a sling swivel.

| Exc. | V.G. | Good | Fair | Poor |
|------|------|------|------|------|
| 850 | 750 | 600 | 450 | 400 |

## Sporting Rifle

There were 3,000 produced with 26", 28", or 30" octagonal barrels.

| Exc. | V.G. | Good | Fair | Poor |
|------|------|------|------|------|
| 650 | 550 | 450 | 375 | 275 |

# EVANS, J. E.
### Philadelphia, Pennsylvania

## Evans Pocket Pistol

This pistol is a copy of the Philadelphia-made Henry Deringer pistol and is chambered for .41 caliber. It utilizes the percussion ignition system and has barrels from 2.5" to 3" in length. The stock is of walnut with a checkered grip, and the mountings are scroll-engraved German silver. The barrel is marked "J.E.Evans Philada." These pistols were manufactured in the 1850's.

| Exc. | V.G. | Good | Fair | Poor |
|------|------|------|------|------|
| 750 | 650 | 550 | 450 | 350 |

# EXCAM
### Hialeah, Florida
### SEE--Erma & Uberti

Excam is an importer of firearms and does not manufacture. The Erma and Uberti products they import are under their own heading in this book. The other products that they import are listed here.

## TA 76

This pistol is patterned after the Colt Single Action Army and is chambered for the .22 rimfire cartridge. It has a 4.75", 6", or 9" barrel and blue finish with wood grips. It is offered with brass triggerguard and backstrap and also offered chrome-plated. A combo model with an extra .22 Magnum cylinder is available and would add 10 percent to the listed values.

| Exc. | V.G. | Good | Fair | Poor |
|------|------|------|------|------|
| 90 | 75 | 65 | 40 | 25 |

## TA 38 Over/Uner Derringer

This pistol is a 2-shot derringer patterned after the Remington Derringer. It is chambered for the .38 Special cartridge, has 3" barrels that pivot upward for loading, and is blued with checkered nylon grips. This model was discontinued in 1985.

| Exc. | V.G. | Good | Fair | Poor |
|------|------|------|------|------|
| 90 | 75 | 65 | 40 | 25 |

## TA 90

This model is a double action, semi-automatic copy of the CZ-75 which some experts rate as the finest combat handgun in the world. It is chambered for the 9mm parabellum and has a 4.75" barrel. It is constructed of steel and is finished with a matte blue or chrome with checkered wood or rubber grips. The detachable magazine holds 15 rounds.

| NIB | Exc. | V.G. | Good | Fair | Poor |
|-----|------|------|------|------|------|
| 415 | 380 | 325 | 275 | 200 | 150 |

## BTA-90B

This is a compact version of the TA 90, that has a 3.5" barrel and a 12-round detachable magazine. It is similar in all other respects to the standard model, with rubber grips only.

| NIB | Exc. | V.G. | Good | Fair | Poor |
|-----|------|------|------|------|------|
| 425 | 400 | 350 | 300 | 225 | 175 |

## TA 90 SS

This is a competition version of the TA 90, that is similar to the standard model except that it is compensated and features adjustable sights. It is offered either blued or chrome-plated and was introduced in 1989.

| NIB | Exc. | V.G. | Good | Fair | Poor |
|-----|------|------|------|------|------|
| 650 | 575 | 500 | 400 | 325 | 225 |

## TA 41, 41C, and 41 SS

This series of pistols is identical to the TA 90 series except that they are chambered for the .41 Action Express cartridge. Their values are about 10 percent higher than the 9mm versions. They were introduced in 1989.

## Warrior Model W 722

This is a double-action revolver chambered for the .22 rimfire and the .22 rimfire magnum with an interchangeable cylinder. It has a 6" barrel, adjustable sights, and an 8-shot cylinder capacity. It is blued, with checkered plastic grips. This model was not imported after 1986.

| Exc. | V.G. | Good | Fair | Poor |
|------|------|------|------|------|
| 100  | 75   | 50   | 35   | 20   |

## Model W 384

This is a double-action revolver chambered for the .38 Special cartridge, with a 4" or 6" vent-rib barrel, blued finish, and plastic grips. It was discontinued in 1986.

| Exc. | V.G. | Good | Fair | Poor |
|------|------|------|------|------|
| 150  | 125  | 100  | 75   | 50   |

## Model W 357

This model is similar to the W 384 except that it is chambered for the .357 Magnum cartridge. It was discontinued in 1986.

| Exc. | V.G. | Good | Fair | Poor |
|------|------|------|------|------|
| 200  | 150  | 125  | 100  | 75   |

## Targa GT 26

This is a blowback-operated, semi-automatic pistol chambered for the .25 ACP cartridge. It has a 2.5" barrel and a 6-shot detachable magazine. It is finished in blue or matte chrome, with a choice of alloy or steel frame. The grips are wood.

**Steel Frame Version**

| NIB | Exc. | V.G. | Good | Fair | Poor |
|-----|------|------|------|------|------|
| 110 | 90   | 75   | 50   | 40   | 30   |

**Alloy Frame Version**

| NIB | Exc. | V.G. | Good | Fair | Poor |
|-----|------|------|------|------|------|
| 70  | 60   | 50   | 35   | 30   | 25   |

## GT 22

This is a semi-automatic pistol chambered for the .22 l.r. cartridge. It has a 4" barrel, fixed sights, and a 10-round magazine. It is available either blued or matte chrome-plated and has wooden grips.

| NIB | Exc. | V.G. | Good | Fair | Poor |
|-----|------|------|------|------|------|
| 200 | 175  | 150  | 125  | 90   | 70   |

## GT 22 T

This model is similar to the GT 22, with a 6" barrel and adjustable target-type sights.

| NIB | Exc. | V.G. | Good | Fair | Poor |
|-----|------|------|------|------|------|
| 225 | 200  | 175  | 150  | 100  | 75   |

## GT 32

This is a blowback-operated semi-automatic pistol chambered for the .32 ACP cartridge. It has a 7-round magazine and is either blued or matte chrome-plated with wood grips.

| NIB | Exc. | V.G. | Good | Fair | Poor |
|-----|------|------|------|------|------|
| 200 | 175  | 150  | 125  | 90   | 75   |

## GT 380

This pistol is similar to the GT 32 except that it is chambered for the .380 ACP cartridge.

| NIB | Exc. | V.G. | Good | Fair | Poor |
|-----|------|------|------|------|------|
| 215 | 185  | 175  | 135  | 110  | 85   |

## GT 380 XE

This model is similar to the the GT 380, with an 11-shot, high-capacity, detachable magazine.

| NIB | Exc. | V.G. | Good | Fair | Poor |
|-----|------|------|------|------|------|
| 225 | 200  | 185  | 150  | 125  | 100  |

# EXEL ARMS OF AMERICA
**Gardner, Massachusetts**
**SEE--Lanber**
**Laurona & Ugartechia**

This firm was engaged in the import of the above Spanish shotguns. They ceased importing them in 1967, and the specific models will be found listed under the manufacturers' names.

# F.A.S.
**Italy**
**Importer--Beeman Prec. Arms**
**Santa Rosa, California**
**Osbourne's**
**Cheboygan, Michigan**

## Model 601

This is a high-grade, competition target pistol chambered for the .22 short cartridge. It is a semi-automatic, with a 5.5" barrel and adjustable target sights. The detachable magazine holds 5 rounds, and the finish is blued with wraparound target grips. This model was discontinued in 1988.

| Exc. | V.G. | Good | Fair | Poor |
|------|------|------|------|------|
| 1000 | 900  | 750  | 575  | 400  |

## Model 602

This model is similar to the Model 601 except that it is chambered for the .22 l.r. It was discontinued in 1987.

| Exc. | V.G. | Good | Fair | Poor |
|------|------|------|------|------|
| 950  | 850  | 700  | 525  | 350  |

## Model 603

This model is chambered for the .32 S&W Wadcutter cartridge and features adjustable grips. It was discontinued in 1987.

| Exc. | V.G. | Good | Fair | Poor |
|------|------|------|------|------|
| 950  | 850  | 700  | 525  | 350  |

# FEG
**Budapest, Hungary**
**Importer--Interarms**
**Alexandria, Virginia**

## Model R-9

This model is a copy of the Browning Hi-Power semi-automatic pistol. It is chambered for 9mm parabellum and has a 4.75" barrel. The frame is steel, and the finish is blued with checkered wood grips. The detachable magazine holds 13 shots, and the sights are fixed. This model was imported in 1986 and 1987 only.

| Exc. | V.G. | Good | Fair | Poor |
|------|------|------|------|------|
| 275  | 225  | 200  | 150  | 125  |

## Model PPH

This pistol is a copy of the Walther PP, chambered for the .380 ACP cartridge. It is a double-action semi-automatic with a 3" barrel, alloy frame, and a blued finish, with thumbrest checkered plastic grips. It was imported in 1986 and 1987 only.

| Exc. | V.G. | Good | Fair | Poor |
|------|------|------|------|------|
| 225  | 175  | 150  | 110  | 90   |

# F.I.E.
**Hialeah, Florida**
**SEE--Franchi**

This company, Firearms Import and Export, is engaged in the business of importing the Franchi shotgun (which is listed under its own heading) and the Arminius revolver (which is made in Germany). They are also distributors for the Titan semi-automatic pistols, which are manufactured in the U.S.A. They are also importing a series of 9mm pistols from Italy that are produced by Tanfoglio and known as the TZ series.

## TZ 75

This is a copy of the CZ 75 Czechoslovakian combat pistol produced by Tanfoglio in Italy. It is a 9mm, double-action semi-automatic with a 4.75" barrel, all-steel construction, fixed sights, and a 15-shot magazine. It is offered either blued or matte chrome plated, with wood or rubber grips.

F.I.E. TZ-75

| NIB | Exc. | V.G. | Good | Fair | Poor |
|-----|------|------|------|------|------|
| 440 | 400 | 350 | 300 | 225 | 150 |

## TZ 75 Series 88

This is an improved version that is also chambered for the .41 Action Express cartridge. It has a firing pin safety and can be carried cocked and locked. There are a few other minor changes. It was introduced in 1988.

| NIB | Exc. | V.G. | Good | Fair | Poor |
|-----|------|------|------|------|------|
| 460 | 425 | 375 | 325 | 250 | 175 |

## KG-99

This is a blowback-operated, semi-automatic assault pistol chambered for the 9mm parabellum cartridge. It has a 36-round magazine. It was discontinued in 1984.

| Exc. | V.G. | Good | Fair | Poor |
|------|------|------|------|------|
| 450 | 400 | 350 | 250 | 175 |

## Spectre Assault Pistol

This is an assault-type semi-automatic pistol chambered for the 9mm parabellum. It has a 30-or 50-round magazine available. It was introduced in 1989.

| NIB | Exc. | V.G. | Good | Fair | Poor |
|-----|------|------|------|------|------|
| 650 | 575 | 475 | 400 | 300 | 200 |

## Titan II .22

This is a semi-automatic pistol chambered for the .22 l.r. It has a 10-shot magazine and a blued finish with walnut grips. It is made in the U.S.A.

F.I.E. Titan II

| NIB | Exc. | V.G. | Good | Fair | Poor |
|-----|------|------|------|------|------|
| 155 | 125 | 100 | 75 | 50 | 25 |

## Titan E32

This is a single-action, blowback-operated, semi- automatic pistol that was chambered for the .32 ACP and is now chambered for the .380 ACP cartridge. The finish is blue or chrome-plated, and the grips are walnut.

| NIB | Exc. | V.G. | Good | Fair | Poor |
|-----|------|------|------|------|------|
| 225 | 200 | 150 | 125 | 100 | 75 |

## Super Titan II

This model is similar to the Titan except that it has a 12-round, high-capacity magazine.

| NIB | Exc. | V.G. | Good | Fair | Poor |
|-----|------|------|------|------|------|
| 250 | 225 | 200 | 150 | 100 | 75 |

## Titan 25

This is a smaller version of the Titan Series chambered for the .25 ACP cartridge. It is blued or chrome-plated.

| NIB | Exc. | V.G. | Good | Fair | Poor |
|-----|------|------|------|------|------|
| 75 | 65 | 50 | 40 | 30 | 20 |

## Titan Tigress

This is similar to the Titan 25 except that it is gold-plated and cased.

| NIB | Exc. | V.G. | Good | Fair | Poor |
|-----|------|------|------|------|------|
| 165 | 145 | 125 | 100 | 50 | 30 |

## D38 Derringer

This is a 2-shot, Over/Under, Remington-style derringer chambered for the .38 Special cartridge. It is chrome-plated and was dropped from the line in 1985.

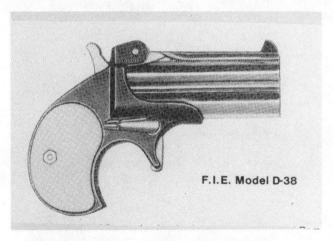

F.I.E. Model D-38

| Exc. | V.G. | Good | Fair | Poor |
|------|------|------|------|------|
| 75 | 60 | 45 | 30 | 20 |

## D86 Derringer

This is a single-shot derringer with a 3" barrel. It is chambered for the .38 Special cartridge and is chrome-plated. There is an ammunition storage compartment in the butt and a transfer bar safety that makes it safer to carry. This model was introduced in 1986.

| NIB | Exc. | V.G. | Good | Fair | Poor |
|-----|------|------|------|------|------|
| 95 | 80 | 65 | 50 | 35 | 20 |

There is a series of single action, .22-caliber revolvers that were patterned after the Colt Single Action Army. They were manufactured in the U.S.A. or Brescia, Italy. They are inexpensive and of fair quality. The differences between these models are basically barrel lengths, type of sights, and finish. They all are chambered for the .22 l.r. and have interchangeable .22 magnum cylinders. We list them for reference purposes.

### Cowboy

| NIB | Exc. | V.G. | Good | Fair | Poor |
|-----|------|------|------|------|------|
| 100 | 80 | 70 | 50 | 35 | 20 |

### Gold Rush

| NIB | Exc. | V.G. | Good | Fair | Poor |
|-----|------|------|------|------|------|
| 175 | 150 | 125 | 100 | 75 | 50 |

### Texas Ranger

| NIB | Exc. | V.G. | Good | Fair | Poor |
|-----|------|------|------|------|------|
| 100 | 85 | 75 | 50 | 35 | 20 |

### Buffalo Scout

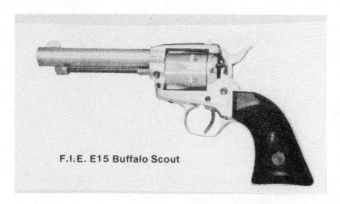

F.I.E. E15 Buffalo Scout

| NIB | Exc. | V.G. | Good | Fair | Poor |
|-----|------|------|------|------|------|
| 95 | 80 | 70 | 50 | 35 | 20 |

### Legend S.A.A.

| NIB | Exc. | V.G. | Good | Fair | Poor |
|-----|------|------|------|------|------|
| 125 | 110 | 85 | 65 | 50 | 30 |

### Hombre

This model is a single action made in Germany by Arminius. It is patterned after the Colt Single Action Army revolver. The Hombre is chambered for the .357 Magnum, .44 Magnum, and .45 Colt cartridges. It is offered with a 5.5", 6", or 7.5" barrel, case-colored frame, and blued barrel and cylinder, with smooth walnut grips. The backstrap and triggerguard are offered in brass and will bring a 10 percent premium.

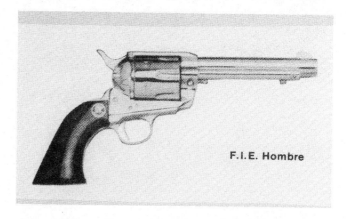

F.I.E. Hombre

| NIB | Exc. | V.G. | Good | Fair | Poor |
|-----|------|------|------|------|------|
| 250 | 225 | 200 | 175 | 110 | 75 |

### Arminius Revolvers
### 522TB

This is a swing-out cylinder, double-action revolver chambered for the .22 rimfire cartridge. It has a 4" barrel and is blued with wood grips.

| NIB | Exc. | V.G. | Good | Fair | Poor |
|-----|------|------|------|------|------|
| 150 | 125 | 100 | 75 | 50 | 30 |

### 722

This model is similar to the 522, with an 8-shot cylinder and a 6" barrel. It is available with a chrome finish.

| NIB | Exc. | V.G. | Good | Fair | Poor |
|-----|------|------|------|------|------|
| 150 | 125 | 100 | 75 | 50 | 30 |

### 532TB

This model is a 7-shot, double-action revolver chambered for the .32 S&W cartridge. It has a 4" barrel and adjustable sights and is finished in either blue or chrome.

| NIB | Exc. | V.G. | Good | Fair | Poor |
|-----|------|------|------|------|------|
| 160 | 130 | 110 | 80 | 60 | 40 |

### 732B

This model is similar to the 532TB, with a 6" barrel and fixed sights. It was discontinued in 1988.

| NIB | Exc. | V.G. | Good | Fair | Poor |
|-----|------|------|------|------|------|
| 120 | 100 | 80 | 65 | 50 | 35 |

### Standard Revolver

This is a double-action, swing-out cylinder revolver chambered for .32 Magnum or .38 Special. It has a 4" or 6" barrel and fixed sights and is blued with wood grips. This model is made in the U.S.A. and was introduced in 1989.

| NIB | Exc. | V.G. | Good | Fair | Poor |
|-----|------|------|------|------|------|
| 125 | 100 | 75 | 50 | 35 | 20 |

### Models 384TB and 386TB

These two models are double actions chambered for the .38 Special cartridge. The 384 has a 4" barrel; and the 386, a 6" barrel. They are available in blue or chrome plate and were discontinued in 1985.

| NIB | Exc. | V.G. | Good | Fair | Poor |
|-----|------|------|------|------|------|
| 185 | 160 | 140 | 110 | 85 | 60 |

## Model 357TB

This model is similar to the 384TB except that it is chambered for the .357 Magnum cartridge and is offered with a 3", 4", or 6" barrel.

| NIB | Exc. | V.G. | Good | Fair | Poor |
|---|---|---|---|---|---|
| 250 | 225 | 175 | 125 | 90 | 75 |

## 222, 232, and 382TB

These models are double-action swing-out cylinder revolvers chambered for .22 rimfire, .32 S&W, and .38 Special. They are 2"-barrelled snub-nosed revolvers, with either blued or chrome-plated finishes. They were discontinued in 1985.

| Exc. | V.G. | Good | Fair | Poor |
|---|---|---|---|---|
| 125 | 100 | 75 | 50 | 25 |

## Model 3572

This is a similar revolver to the 382TB except that it is chambered for the .357 Magnum cartridge. It was discontinued in 1984.

| Exc. | V.G. | Good | Fair | Poor |
|---|---|---|---|---|
| 225 | 200 | 175 | 125 | 100 |

## Shotguns and Rifle
## Model 122

This is a bolt-action rifle chambered for .22 rimfire, with a 21" barrel and adjustable sights. It has a 10-shot magazine and a walnut Monte Carlo stock. It was introduced in 1986.

| Exc. | V.G. | Good | Fair | Poor |
|---|---|---|---|---|
| 110 | 95 | 75 | 50 | 25 |

## Single Shot

This model is Brazilian made and chambered for 12 or 20 gauge and .410. It is a single-barrelled break open, with 25" through 30" barrel and various chokes. It is blued with a wood stock and was introduced in 1985.

| Exc. | V.G. | Good | Fair | Poor |
|---|---|---|---|---|
| 100 | 80 | 60 | 45 | 25 |

## S.O.B.

This model is similar to the single shot, with an 18.5" barrel and a pistol grip instead of a standard stock. This model was discontinued in 1984.

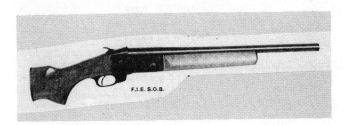

| Exc. | V.G. | Good | Fair | Poor |
|---|---|---|---|---|
| 100 | 80 | 60 | 45 | 25 |

## Sturdy Over/Under

This model is chambered for 12 and 20 gauge and has 3" chambers and 28" vent-rib barrels with various chokes. This is an Over/Under with double triggers and extractors. The frame is engraved and silver finished. It was manufactured in Italy by Maroccini and imported between 1985 and 1988.

| Exc. | V.G. | Good | Fair | Poor |
|---|---|---|---|---|
| 300 | 275 | 225 | 175 | 150 |

## Brute

This model is a side by side chambered for 12 and 20 gauge and .410. It has 19" barrels, double triggers, and extractors. It has a wood stock and was dropped from the line in 1984.

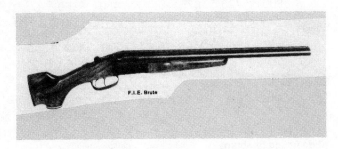

| Exc. | V.G. | Good | Fair | Poor |
|---|---|---|---|---|
| 200 | 175 | 125 | 100 | 75 |

## SPAS-12

This is a unique shotgun in that it can function as a pump or an automatic with the touch of a button. It is a paramilitary-type shotgun chambered for 12 gauge, with a 21.5" barrel and a 9-shot tube magazine. It has an alloy receiver and a folding stock. The finish is all black. This model is manufactured by Franchi in Italy.

| NIB | Exc. | V.G. | Good | Fair | Poor |
|---|---|---|---|---|---|
| 525 | 475 | 425 | 375 | 300 | 250 |

## Law-12

This is a paramilitary-type, 12-gauge, semi-automatic shotgun that is gas-operated and has a 9-shot tube magazine. The barrel is 21.5" in length and choked cylinder bore. It has a military special black finish and a black synthetic stock.

| NIB | Exc. | V.G. | Good | Fair | Poor |
|---|---|---|---|---|---|
| 425 | 375 | 325 | 275 | 200 | 150 |

## SAS-12

This is a paramilitary-type, slide-action shotgun chambered for 12 gauge. It has a 21.5" barrel, choked cylinder bore. The finish is similar to the LAW-12, and it is manufactured by Franchi in Italy.

| NIB | Exc. | V.G. | Good | Fair | Poor |
|---|---|---|---|---|---|
| 350 | 325 | 300 | 250 | 200 | 150 |

# FABARM
**Brescia, Italy**
**Importer--St. Lawrence Sales, Inc.**
**Lake Orion, Michigan**

## Semi-Automatic Shotguns
## Ellegi Standard

This is a gas-operated, semi-automatic shotgun chambered for 12 gauge. It has a 28" vent-rib barrel with choice of choke. The receiver is blue anodized alloy with a photo-etched gamescene, and the stock and forearm are checkered walnut. This model was introduced in 1989.

| NIB | Exc. | V.G. | Good | Fair | Poor |
|---|---|---|---|---|---|
| 700 | 625 | 525 | 450 | 350 | 250 |

The Ellegi Model is available in six other configurations. The differences are in the barrel length and choke, type of choke tubes, and finish. Basically the guns are quite similar to the standard model. These variations are as follows.

### Ellegi Multichoke

| NIB | Exc. | V.G. | Good | Fair | Poor |
|-----|------|------|------|------|------|
| 700 | 625 | 525 | 450 | 350 | 250 |

### Ellegi Innerchoke

| NIB | Exc. | V.G. | Good | Fair | Poor |
|-----|------|------|------|------|------|
| 725 | 650 | 550 | 475 | 375 | 275 |

### Ellegi Magnum

| NIB | Exc. | V.G. | Good | Fair | Poor |
|-----|------|------|------|------|------|
| 725 | 650 | 550 | 475 | 375 | 275 |

### Ellegi Super Goose

| NIB | Exc. | V.G. | Good | Fair | Poor |
|-----|------|------|------|------|------|
| 800 | 725 | 625 | 550 | 450 | 350 |

### Ellegi Slug

| NIB | Exc. | V.G. | Good | Fair | Poor |
|-----|------|------|------|------|------|
| 775 | 700 | 600 | 525 | 425 | 325 |

### Ellegi Police

| NIB | Exc. | V.G. | Good | Fair | Poor |
|-----|------|------|------|------|------|
| 575 | 500 | 450 | 400 | 300 | 225 |

## Slide Action Shotguns
### Model S.D.A.S.S.

This model is chambered for 12 gauge with a 3" chamber. It is offered with a 20" or 24.5" barrel threaded for external choke tubes. This model has an 8-shot tube magazine, twin action bars, an alloy receiver, and a matte black finish. It is a defensive-type shotgun and has been imported since 1989.

| NIB | Exc. | V.G. | Good | Fair | Poor |
|-----|------|------|------|------|------|
| 500 | 450 | 400 | 350 | 250 | 175 |

The Special Police and the Martial Model are variations of the basic slide action and differ in barrel length and choke. The Police Model has a shrouded barrel.

### Special Police

| NIB | Exc. | V.G. | Good | Fair | Poor |
|-----|------|------|------|------|------|
| 525 | 475 | 425 | 350 | 275 | 200 |

### Martial Model

| NIB | Exc. | V.G. | Good | Fair | Poor |
|-----|------|------|------|------|------|
| 475 | 425 | 375 | 300 | 225 | 175 |

## Single Shot Shotguns
### Omega Standard

This model has an alloy receiver and is chambered for 12 and 20 gauge, as well as .410. It has 26" or 28" barrels with various chokes. The finish is black with a beech stock. It was introduced in 1989.

| NIB | Exc. | V.G. | Good | Fair | Poor |
|-----|------|------|------|------|------|
| 150 | 125 | 100 | 75 | 50 | 40 |

### Omega Goose Gun

This version is chambered for 12 gauge only, with a 35.5" full-choke barrel.

| NIB | Exc. | V.G. | Good | Fair | Poor |
|-----|------|------|------|------|------|
| 160 | 140 | 125 | 100 | 75 | 50 |

## Side X Side Shotguns
### Beta Model

This double barrel is chambered for 12 gauge only, with choice of barrel length and choke. It has a boxlock action with false side plates. It has a single trigger and automatic ejectors, and the finish is blued with a checkered, select walnut stock. This model was introduced in 1989.

| NIB | Exc. | V.G. | Good | Fair | Poor |
|-----|------|------|------|------|------|
| 925 | 850 | 750 | 600 | 450 | 300 |

### Beta Europe

This is a deluxe version that features single-selective triggers and a gamescene-engraved, coin-finished receiver. The stock is the straight English style with a splinter forend. This model was introduced in 1989.

| NIB | Exc. | V.G. | Good | Fair | Poor |
|-----|------|------|------|------|------|
| 1750 | 1500 | 1250 | 1000 | 750 | 500 |

## Over/Under Shotguns
### Field Model

This model is chambered for 12 gauge and has 29" vent-rib barrels with various chokes. The receiver is coin-finished, and the stock is checkered walnut. This Model was discontinued in 1985.

| Exc. | V.G. | Good | Fair | Poor |
|------|------|------|------|------|
| 700 | 600 | 500 | 400 | 300 |

### Gamma Field

This model is chambered for 12 or 20 gauge and is offered with 26", 28", or 29" vent-rib barrels and various choke combinations. Screw-in choke tubes are available and would be worth a 10 percent premium. This model has a boxlock, coin-finished receiver that is moderately engraved and a checkered walnut stock.

| NIB | Exc. | V.G. | Good | Fair | Poor |
|-----|------|------|------|------|------|
| 925 | 850 | 775 | 650 | 500 | 350 |

### Gamma Paradox Gun

This model is chambered for 12 gauge only, and the top barrel is rifled for accurate placement of slugs. The barrels are 25" long with vent rib, and the bottom barrel has three screw-in choke tubes. This model has a single-selective trigger and automatic ejectors. The finish is similar to the Field Model. It was introduced in 1989.

| NIB | Exc. | V.G. | Good | Fair | Poor |
|-----|------|------|------|------|------|
| 1000 | 900 | 825 | 750 | 600 | 450 |

### Gamma Trap or Skeet

These are competition-grade guns with either a 27.5" barrel with five screw-in choke tubes on the skeet model or a 29" barrel with screw-in trap chokes. Both models feature single-selective triggers and automatic ejectors; and the trap model has a Monte Carlo stock. They have moderately engraved, coin-finished boxlock actions and were introduced in 1989.

| NIB | Exc. | V.G. | Good | Fair | Poor |
|-----|------|------|------|------|------|
| 1000 | 900 | 825 | 750 | 600 | 450 |

### Gamma Sporting Competition Model

This gun was designed for Sporting Clays and is chambered for 12 gauge only. The 29" barrel has a wide rib and is furnished with five screw-in choke tubes. It has a single-selective trigger, automatic ejectors, and a checkered walnut stock with a competition recoil pad. It is finished like the skeet and trap models and was introduced in 1989.

| NIB | Exc. | V.G. | Good | Fair | Poor |
|-----|------|------|------|------|------|
| 1000 | 900 | 825 | 750 | 600 | 450 |

## FABBRI ARMI
### Gardone V.T., Italy
### Importer--New England Arms
### Kittery Point, Maine

The firm of Fabbri Armi currently manufactures one of the best shotguns in the world. They are available as a custom made-to-order item, and they are not often seen in the used gun market. The values for guns of this nature and quality are impossible to accurately establish in a book of this nature as there are so many options and conditions that make the prices fluctuate greatly. We give an estimate figure as a base starting point but strongly urge individual appraisal should a transaction involving one of these fine firearms be contemplated.

**Side x Side Shotgun**
Chambered for 12 or 20 gauge with all other features on a custom-order basis.

| NIB | Exc. | V.G. | Good | Fair | Poor |
|-----|------|------|------|------|------|
| 22500 | 20000 | 17500 | 12500 | 8500 | 6000 |

**Over/Under Shotgun**
Chambered for 12 or 20 gauge with all other features on a custom-order basis.

| NIB | Exc. | V.G. | Good | Fair | Poor |
|-----|------|------|------|------|------|
| 25000 | 22500 | 20000 | 15000 | 10000 | 7500 |

# FABRIQUE NATIONALE
### Herstal, Belgium

In 1889 Fabrique Nationale (or FN) was founded by a group of Belgian investors for the purpose of manufacturing Mauser rifles for the Belgian army. This was to be accomplished under license from Mauser, with the technical assistance of Kudwig Loewe of Berlin. A few years later, in the 1890's, John Browning arrived in Europe seeking a manufacturer for his semi-automatic shotgun. He had severed his ties with Winchester after a disagreement. This led to a long association that worked out extremely well for both parties. Later Browning became associated with Colt, and the world market was divided--with the Eastern Hemisphere going to FN and the Western Hemisphere to Colt.

In this section, we list arms that bear the FN banner. The FN-manufactured firearms produced under the Browning banner are listed in the Browning section of this book.

### Model 1900
This is a blowback-operated semi-automatic pistol chambered for the 7.65mm cartridge. It has a 4" barrel and fixed sights and is blued with molded plastic grips. This model is notorious as the pistol that was used to assassinate Archduke Ferdinand, an event that touched off WWI. It was manufactured between 1899 and 1910. This model is referred to as the "Old Model."

**FN Browning Model 1900**

| Exc. | V.G. | Good | Fair | Poor |
|------|------|------|------|------|
| 350 | 325 | 275 | 200 | 150 |

### Model 1903
This model was a considerable improvement over the Model 1900. It is also a blowback-operated semi-automatic; but the recoil spring is located under the barrel, and the firing pin travels through the slide after being struck by a hidden hammer. The barrel is held in place by five locking lugs that fit into five grooves in the frame. This pistol is chambered for the 9mm Browning long cartridge and has a 5" barrel. The finish is blued

with molded plastic grips, and the detachable magazine holds seven rounds. There is a detachable shoulder stock/holster along with a 10-round magazine that was available for this model. These accesories are extremely rare and if present would make the package worth approximately five times that of the pistol alone. There were approximately 58,000 manufactured between 1903 and 1939. This model was one of the Browning patents that the Eibar Spanish gunmakers did so love to copy because of the simplicity of the design.

**FN Browning Model 1903**

| Exc. | V.G. | Good | Fair | Poor |
|------|------|------|------|------|
| 475 | 425 | 375 | 275 | 175 |

### Model 1906
This is a smaller version of the Model 1903, designed to be a pocket pistol and chambered for the 6.35mm cartridge. It became known as the "Vest Pocket" model and was also the basis for many Eibar copies. It has a 2.5" barrel and was produced in two distinct variations. The first variation had no safety lever or slide lock and relied on the grip safety. The second variation, that occurred at approximately serial number 100,000, added this safety lever and slide lock, which helped simplify dismantling of the pistol. This model was available either blued or nickel-plated. The plated models would bring a 10 percent premium. There were approximately 1,086,100 manufactured between 1906 and 1959.

**1st Variation Under Serial Number 100,000**

| Exc. | V.G. | Good | Fair | Poor |
|------|------|------|------|------|
| 350 | 300 | 250 | 200 | 125 |

**2nd Variation Over Serial Number 100,000**

| Exc. | V.G. | Good | Fair | Poor |
|------|------|------|------|------|
| 300 | 275 | 200 | 175 | 100 |

## Model 1910 "New Model"

This model is chambered for 7.65mm and 9mm short. It has a 3.5" barrel, is blued, and has molded plastic grips. The principal difference between this model and its predecessors is that the recoil spring on the Model 1910 is wrapped around the barrel. This gives the slide a more graceful tubular appearance instead of the old slab-sided look. This model has the triple safety features of the 1906 Model 2nd variation and is blued with molded plastic grips. This model was adopted by police forces around the world. It was manufactured between 1912 and 1954.

FN Browning Model 1910
Pocket Auto

| Exc. | V.G. | Good | Fair | Poor |
|------|------|------|------|------|
| 350 | 300 | 250 | 175 | 125 |

## Model 1922

This model is similar to the Model 1910, with a longer 4.5" barrel and correspondingly longer slide. This model was a military success, and approximately 200,000 were produced during the WWII German occupation of Belgium in 1940--1944. These pistols bear the Waffenamt acceptance marks, are known as the "Pistole Modell 626(b)," and are chambered for 7.65mm only. These pistols would bring a 10 percent premium. There were also contracts from France, Yugoslavia, and Holland, as well as Belgian military versions. They were manufactured between 1912 and 1959.

FN Browning Model 1922

| Exc. | V.G. | Good | Fair | Poor |
|------|------|------|------|------|
| 275 | 225 | 175 | 125 | 100 |

## "Baby" Model

This is a smaller and lighter version of the Model 1906. It is chambered for the 6.35mm cartridge and has a 2" barrel.

There is no grip safety or slide lock on this model, and it appears to be more square in shape than the Model 1906. This model was offered in blue, with molded plastic grips. Early models have the word "Baby" molded into the grips; post-1945 versions do not. There is also a nickel-plated version with pearl grips. There were over 500,000 of these manufactured between 1931 and 1983.

| Exc. | V.G. | Good | Fair | Poor |
|------|------|------|------|------|
| 400 | 325 | 300 | 225 | 150 |

## Model 1935

This model was the last design from John Browning and was developed between 1925 and 1935. This pistol is known as the Model 1935, the P-35, High-Power or HP, and also as the GP (which stood for "Grand Puissance") and was referred to by all those names at one time or another. The HP is essentially an improved version of the Colt 1911 design. The swinging link was replaced with a fixed cam, which was less prone to wear. It is chambered for the 9mm Parabellum and has a 13-round detachable magazine. The only drawback to the design is that the trigger pull is not as fine as that of the 1911, as there is a transfer bar instead of a stirrup arrangement. This is necessary due to the increased magazine capacity resulting in a thicker grip. The barrel is 4.75" in length. It has an external hammer with a manual and a magazine safety and was available with various finishes and sight options and was furnished with a shoulder stock. The Model 1935 was used by many countries as their service pistol--as such there are many variations. We list these versions and their approximate values. There are books available specializing in this model, and it would be beneficial to gain as much knowledge as possible if one contemplates acquisition of this fine and highly collectible pistol.

## Pre-War Commercial Model

This model is found with either a fixed sight or a sliding tangent rear sight and is slotted for a detachable shoulder stock. It was manufactured from 1935 until 1940.
Wood Holster Stock--Add 50 Percent.

**Fixed Sight Version**

| Exc. | V.G. | Good | Fair | Poor |
|------|------|------|------|------|
| 600 | 525 | 475 | 375 | 275 |

**Tangent Sight Version**

| Exc. | V.G. | Good | Fair | Poor |
|------|------|------|------|------|
| 1000 | 850 | 675 | 550 | 400 |

## Pre-War Military Contract

The Model 1935 was adopted by many countries as a service pistol, and they are as follows.

**Belgium**

| Exc. | V.G. | Good | Fair | Poor |
|------|------|------|------|------|
| 1200 | 1050 | 900 | 600 | 375 |

Canada and China (See John Inglis & Company)
**Denmark**

| Exc. | V.G. | Good | Fair | Poor |
|---|---|---|---|---|
| 1250 | 1100 | 950 | 650 | 400 |

**Great Britain**

| Exc. | V.G. | Good | Fair | Poor |
|---|---|---|---|---|
| 1150 | 1000 | 850 | 550 | 325 |

**Estonia**

| Exc. | V.G. | Good | Fair | Poor |
|---|---|---|---|---|
| 1200 | 1050 | 900 | 600 | 375 |

**Holland**

| Exc. | V.G. | Good | Fair | Poor |
|---|---|---|---|---|
| 1250 | 1100 | 950 | 650 | 400 |

**Latvia**

| Exc. | V.G. | Good | Fair | Poor |
|---|---|---|---|---|
| 1500 | 1350 | 1050 | 775 | 500 |

**Lithuania**

| Exc. | V.G. | Good | Fair | Poor |
|---|---|---|---|---|
| 1250 | 1100 | 950 | 650 | 400 |

**Romania**

| Exc. | V.G. | Good | Fair | Poor |
|---|---|---|---|---|
| 1500 | 1350 | 1050 | 775 | 500 |

## German Military Pistole Modell 640(b)

In 1940 Germany occupied Belgium and took over the FN plant. The production of the Model 1935 continued, with Germany taking the output. The FN plant was assigned the production code "ch," and many thousands were produced. The finish on these Nazi guns runs from as fine as the Pre-war Commercial series to downright crude, and it is possible to see how the war was progressing for Germany by the finish on their weapons.

One must be cautious with some of these guns as there have been fakes noted with their backstraps cut for shoulder stocks, producing what would appear to be a more expensive variation. Individual appraisal should be secured if any doubt exists.

**Fixed Sight Model**

| Exc. | V.G. | Good | Fair | Poor |
|---|---|---|---|---|
| 500 | 450 | 400 | 300 | 250 |

**Tangent Sight Model--50,000 Manufactured**

| Exc. | V.G. | Good | Fair | Poor |
|---|---|---|---|---|
| 800 | 750 | 700 | 550 | 400 |

**Captured Pre-War Commercial Model**

These pistols were taken over when the plant was occupied. They are slotted for stocks and have tangent sights. There were few produced between serial number 48,000 and 52,000. All noted have the Waa 613 Nazi proof mark. Beware of fakes!

| Exc. | V.G. | Good | Fair | Poor |
|---|---|---|---|---|
| 1500 | 1400 | 1150 | 750 | 500 |

**Post-War Military Contract**

These pistols were manufactured from 1946, and they embody some design changes--such as improved heat treating and barrel locking. Pistols produced after 1950 do not have barrels that can interchange with the earlier model pistols. The earliest models have an "A" prefix on the serial number and do not have the magazine safety. These pistols were produced for many countries, and there were many thousands manufactured.

**Fixed Sight**

| Exc. | V.G. | Good | Fair | Poor |
|---|---|---|---|---|
| 475 | 425 | 375 | 300 | 250 |

**Tangent Sight**

| Exc. | V.G. | Good | Fair | Poor |
|---|---|---|---|---|
| 750 | 675 | 575 | 400 | 300 |

**Slotted and Tangent Sight**

| Exc. | V.G. | Good | Fair | Poor |
|---|---|---|---|---|
| 1150 | 1050 | 750 | 500 | 400 |

## Post-War Commercial Model

This model was introduced in 1950 and in 1954. Those imported into the U.S.A. are marked Browning Arms Co. These pistols have the commercial polished finish.

**Fixed Sight**

| Exc. | V.G. | Good | Fair | Poor |
|---|---|---|---|---|
| 500 | 425 | 350 | 300 | 250 |

**Tangent Sight**

| Exc. | V.G. | Good | Fair | Poor |
|---|---|---|---|---|
| 750 | 650 | 500 | 400 | 350 |

**Slotted and Tangent Sight**

| Exc. | V.G. | Good | Fair | Poor |
|---|---|---|---|---|
| 1200 | 1100 | 800 | 550 | 450 |

## Rifles
## Model 1889

This is the Mauser rifle that FN was formed to manufacture. It is chambered for 7.65mm and has a 30.5" barrel. The magazine holds 5 rounds. The unique feature which set the Belgian rifle apart from the Mausers made by other countries is the thin steel tube that encases the barrel. The sights are of the military type. The finish is blued, with a walnut stock.

| Exc. | V.G. | Good | Fair | Poor |
|---|---|---|---|---|
| 275 | 250 | 200 | 125 | 100 |

## Model 1949

This is a gas-operated semi-automatic rifle chambered for 7x57, 7.92mm, and .30-06. It has a 23" barrel and military-type sights. The integral magazine holds 10 rounds. The finish is blued, and the stock is walnut. This is a very well-made gun that was actually designed before WWII. When the Germans were in the process of taking over Belgium, a group of FN engineers fled to England and took the plans for this rifle with them, preventing the German military from acquiring a very fine weapon. This model was introduced in 1949, after hostilities had ceased. This model was sold on contract to Egypt, chambered for 7.92mm; to Venezuela, chambered for 7x57; and to Columbia and Indonesia, chambered for the .30-06. The Egyptian model has recently been imported in large numbers and is worth approximately 20 percent less.
.30-06 caliber--Add 20 Percent.

| Exc. | V.G. | Good | Fair | Poor |
|---|---|---|---|---|
| 400 | 350 | 300 | 225 | 150 |

## Model 30-11 Sniper Rifle

This weapon is chambered for the 7.62 NATO cartridge. It has a 20" heavy barrel and Anschutz sights. There is a flash suppressor mounted on the muzzle. It is built on a highly precision-made Mauser bolt action fed by a 9-round, detachable box magazine. The walnut stock is rather unique in that the butt is made up of two parts, with the rear half being replaceable to suit the needs of different-sized shooters. It is issued with a shooting sling, bipod, and a foam-lined carrying case. This is a very rare firearm on the commercial market as it was designed and sold to the military and police markets.

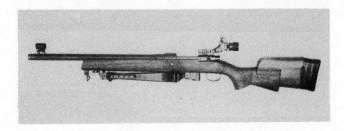

| Exc. | V.G. | Good | Fair | Poor |
|---|---|---|---|---|
| 5000 | 4500 | 3500 | 2750 | 2000 |

## FN-L.A.R.

This is a gas-operated, semi-automatic version of the famous FN battle rifle. This weapon has been adopted by more free world countries than any other. It is chambered for the 7.62 NATO or .308 and has a 21" barrel with an integral flash suppressor. The sights are adjustable with an aperture rear, and the detachable box magazine holds 20 rounds. The stock and forearm are made of wood or a black synthetic. This model has been discontinued by the company and is no longer manufactured. Sadly, this is another firearm that has been affected by the assault rifle hysteria; and it is virtually impossible to accurately place a cash value on it. If one is contemplating a transaction, qualified appraisal should be secured.

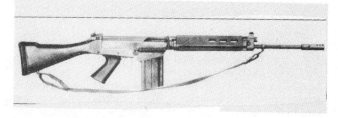

## Heavy Barrelled Model

This model is similar to the L.A.R. except that the barrel is much heavier in diameter, and there is a bipod furnished. The forend is shorter than on the standard model, and it is made of wood. This model was also discontinued in 1988 and also cannot accurately be appraised in a book of this nature.

## Paratroopers Model

This is a similar rifle to the standard L.A.R., with an 18" barrel and a folding stock. There is also a model that has the standard 21" barrel. This model should also be individually appraised due to radical market fluctuations.

## FNC

This is a lighter-weight assault-type rifle chambered for the 5.56mm cartridge. It is a gas-operated semi-automatic with a 18.5" barrel. It has a 30-round box magazine and is black, with either a fixed or folding stock. This model was also discontinued by FN. The same problem with fluctuating values applies to this weapon as to the L.A.R., and we strongly advise that one researches the market in a particular geographic location as prices can fluctuate radically.

## Sporting Rifles

### Musketeer

This is a bolt-action rifle built on the Mauser action chambered for various popular cartridges. It has a 24" barrel and is blued, with a checkered walnut stock. It was manufactured between 1947 and 1963.

| Exc. | V.G. | Good | Fair | Poor |
|------|------|------|------|------|
| 400 | 375 | 325 | 225 | 150 |

### Deluxe Sporte

This is a higher-grade version of the Musketeer with the same general specifications. It was also manufactured between 1947 and 1963.

| Exc. | V.G. | Good | Fair | Poor |
|------|------|------|------|------|
| 500 | 450 | 400 | 300 | 200 |

### FN Supreme

This model is chambered for the popular standard calibers and has a 24" barrel with an aperture sight and a checkered walnut stock. It was manufactured between 1957 and 1975.

| Exc. | V.G. | Good | Fair | Poor |
|------|------|------|------|------|
| 550 | 500 | 450 | 350 | 225 |

### Supreme Magnum Model

This version is similar to the standard Supreme except that it is chambered for .264 Win. Mag., 7mm Rem. Mag., and .300 Win. Mag. It is furnished with a recoil pad and was manufactured between the same years as the standard model.

| Exc. | V.G. | Good | Fair | Poor |
|------|------|------|------|------|
| 600 | 550 | 500 | 400 | 250 |

# FAIRBANKS, A. B.
## Boston, Massachusetts

### Fairbanks All Metal Pistol

This odd pistol was produced of all metal, with a one-piece cast brass frame and handle and an iron barrel and lock system. It is chambered for .33 caliber and utilizes the percussion ignition system. The barrel lengths noted are of 3" to 10". The barrels are marked "Fairbanks Boston.Cast Steel." They were manufactured between 1838 and 1841.

| Exc. | V.G. | Good | Fair | Poor |
|------|------|------|------|------|
| 350 | 300 | 250 | 200 | 150 |

# FALCON FIREARMS
## Northridge, California

### Portsider

This is a copy of the Colt 1911 built for a lefthanded individual. It is constructed of stainless steel and is similar in all other respects to the Colt. It was introduced in 1986.

Falcon Portsider

| NIB | Exc. | V.G. | Good | Fair | Poor |
|-----|------|------|------|------|------|
| 575 | 500 | 425 | 375 | 300 | 225 |

**Portsider Set**
This is a matching serial-numbered pair consisting of a lefthanded and a righthanded version of this model. It was cased, and there were only 100 manufactured in 1986 and 1987.

| NIB | Exc. | V.G. | Good | Fair | Poor |
|-----|------|------|------|------|------|
| 1400 | 1250 | 1000 | 750 | 600 | 475 |

**Gold Falcon**
The frame of this model was machined from solid 17-karat gold. The slide is stainless steel, and the sights have diamond inlays. It was engraved to the customer's order, and there were only 50 manufactured.

| NIB | Exc. | V.G. | Good |
|-----|------|------|------|
| 30000 | 25000 | 20000 | 15000 |

# FAMARS, A. & S.
## Brescia, Italy

The Famars shotgun is one of the world's finest and is available on a custom-order basis. This makes it quite difficult to accurately establish values in a book of this nature. Each individual gun must be appraised if a transaction is contemplated as the array of options available makes the values fluctuate greatly. They manufacture two basic models, and we list them and give an estimated value in their basic form only.

**External Hammer Shotgun**
This is a double-barrelled, side by side, with external hammers and double triggers. All other features are custom-ordered.

| Exc. | V.G. | Good | Fair | Poor |
|------|------|------|------|------|
| 7500 | 7000 | 6000 | 4000 | 2750 |

**Sidelock Shotgun**
This model is a side by side, with hand-detachable sidelocks. All other features are custom-ordered.

| Exc. | V.G. | Good | Fair | Poor |
|------|------|------|------|------|
| 10000 | 8500 | 7500 | 5000 | 3500 |

# FARQUHARSON, JOHN
## London, England

This was not a gunmaker but the designer of what is perhaps the finest single-shot action ever developed. It was patented on May 25, 1872, and has been used as the basis for some of the world's best single-shot rifles manufactured by top English gunmakers throughout the years. There will be references to this action under sections dealing with these makers.

# FARROW ARMS CO.
## Holyoke, Massachusetts
## Mason, Tennessee

**Farrow Falling Block Rifle**
This rifle was designed by W.M. Farrow, a target shooter who had worked on the Ballard rifles for the Marlin company. The Farrow rifles are chambered for various calibers and have barrel lengths from 28"--36" of octagonal configuration. They feature tang sights and are either all blued or have a nickel-plated receiver. The stocks are walnut. There were two grades offered that varied according to the grade of wood used. These rifles are quite scarce on today's market, and the number manufactured between 1885 and 1900 is unknown.

**No. 1 Model**
Fancy walnut with checkering and a Schutzen buttplate.

| Exc. | V.G. | Good | Fair | Poor |
|------|------|------|------|------|
| 4500 | 4000 | 3500 | 3000 | 1750 |

**No. 2 Model**
Plainer wood and no checkering.

| Exc. | V.G. | Good | Fair | Poor |
|------|------|------|------|------|
| 3750 | 3000 | 2750 | 2250 | 1400 |

# FAYETTEVILLE ARMORY
## Fayetteville, North Carolina

**Fayetteville Rifle**
This rifle was produced for the Confederate States of America during the Civil War. It was made up of parts captured at Harpers Ferry and then later from new manufactured parts. These rifles are chambered for .58 caliber and utilize the percussion ignition system. They have a 33" barrel and a full-length stock secured by two barrel bands. There is a bayonet lug on the barrel. They are either browned or in the white with brass mountings and walnut stocks. Early models are noted with patchboxes. The locks are marked "Fayetteville," and there is an eagle with the letters "C.S.A." The buttplate is marked "C.S.A."
There were approximately 2,000 manufactured between 1862 and 1865.

**Early Model**
There is no eagle or date on the lock, and "C.S.A / Fayetteville, N.C." is the lock marking.

| Exc. | V.G. | Good | Fair | Poor |
|------|------|------|------|------|
| 5000 | 4500 | 3750 | 3250 | 2250 |

**Second Model**
This version has the eagle and is dated 1862. The letters N.C. were deleted from the lock marking.

| Exc. | V.G. | Good | Fair | Poor |
|------|------|------|------|------|
| 4000 | 3500 | 3000 | 2500 | 1500 |

**Third Model**
This model is very similar in configuration to the U.S. Model 1861 Musket and is marked with the dates 1862 through 1865.

| Exc. | V.G. | Good | Fair | Poor |
|------|------|------|------|------|
| 3000 | 2500 | 2000 | 1750 | 1250 |

NOTE:
With this rifle, as well as with all Confederate arms, be very careful of fakes. Their construction was crude, and it is not uncommon to see spurious examples being misrepresented. Competent appraisal should be secured if a transaction is contemplated.

# FEATHER INDUSTRIES, INC.
## Boulder, Colorado

**AT-22**
This is a blowback-operated semi-automatic chambered for the .22 l.r. cartridge. It has a removable, shrouded 17" barrel and a folding metal stock. There are adjustable sights, and the finish is black. There is a detachable 20-round magazine. This model was introduced in 1986.

| NIB | Exc. | V.G. | Good | Fair | Poor |
|-----|------|------|------|------|------|
| 250 | 225 | 175 | 150 | 110 | 75 |

## AT-9

This is similar to the AR-22 except that it is chambered for the 9mm parabellum cartridge and has a 16" barrel and 32-round magazine. It was introduced in 1988.

| NIB | Exc. | V.G. | Good | Fair | Poor |
|-----|------|------|------|------|------|
| 500 | 450 | 375 | 325 | 275 | 200 |

## KG-9

This is a 9mm, semi-automatic assault rifle that was introduced in 1989.

| NIB | Exc. | V.G. | Good | Fair | Poor |
|-----|------|------|------|------|------|
| 575 | 500 | 425 | 375 | 300 | 250 |

## KG-22

This model is similar in appearance to the KG-9 except that it is chambered for .22 l.r. and has a 20-round detachable magazine. It was introduced in 1989.

| NIB | Exc. | V.G. | Good | Fair | Poor |
|-----|------|------|------|------|------|
| 300 | 275 | 225 | 175 | 125 | 100 |

## SAR-180

This model is the current incarnation of the old American 180, which was manufactured in Austria a number of years ago. It is chambered for .22 l.r. and has a 17.5" barrel. It is a blowback-operated semi-automatic that has a 165-round drum magazine that sits on top of the action on the flat side. The rear sight is adjustable, and the finish is blued with a walnut stock, pistol grip, and forend. This model was revived by Feather Industries in 1989.

| NIB | Exc. | V.G. | Good | Fair | Poor |
|-----|------|------|------|------|------|
| 500 | 450 | 400 | 350 | 275 | 200 |

## Mini-AT

This model is a blowback-operated semi-automatic pistol chambered for the .22 l.r. cartridge. It is a 5.5"-barrelled version of the AT-22 rifle and has a 20-round magazine. This model was manufactured between 1986 and 1989.

| Exc. | V.G. | Good | Fair | Poor |
|------|------|------|------|------|
| 200 | 175 | 150 | 125 | 100 |

## Guardian Angel

This model is a 2-shot, Over/Under, derringer-styled pistol. It is chambered for the 9mm parabellum and can be converted to fire the .38 Super cartridge. It is constructed of stainless steel and has an internal hammer and fully enclosed trigger. It was introduced in 1988.

| NIB | Exc. | V.G. | Good | Fair | Poor |
|-----|------|------|------|------|------|
| 150 | 125 | 100 | 75 | 50 | 40 |

# FEDERAL ENGINEERING CORP.
## Chicago, Illinois

### XC-220

This is a blowback-operated, semi-automatic rifle chambered for the .22 l.r. cartridge. It has a 16.5" barrel and a steel receiver that is blued. The stock is black synthetic. This model was introduced in 1984.

| NIB | Exc. | V.G. | Good | Fair | Poor |
|-----|------|------|------|------|------|
| 350 | 300 | 275 | 225 | 175 | 125 |

### XC-450

This model is similar in appearance to the XC-220 except that it is chambered for the .45 ACP cartridge. It has a 30-round detachable magazine.

| NIB | Exc. | V.G. | Good | Fair | Poor |
|-----|------|------|------|------|------|
| 600 | 525 | 450 | 400 | 300 | 250 |

### XC-900

This is a 9mm parabellum version of the same basic firearm. It has a 32-round magazine and was introduced in 1984.

| NIB | Exc. | V.G. | Good | Fair | Poor |
|-----|------|------|------|------|------|
| 550 | 500 | 425 | 350 | 275 | 200 |

# FEDERAL ORDNANCE, INC.
## South El Monte, California

Federal Ordnance is an importer as well as a manufacturer that basically fabricates new and custom firearms out of existing older military parts. The firearms they import are military surplus weapons that will be covered in their own sections of this book. The firearms covered here are of Federal Ordnance manufacture.

## M-14 Semi-Automatic

This model is a semi-automatic version of the M-14 service rifle. It is constructed of a newly manufactured receiver that has no selector and select surplus G.I. parts. The rifle is refinished to original specifications and furnished with a 20-round magazine and either a wood or fiberglass stock. This model was introduced in 1986. Although this model is a battle rifle and falls into the category affected by the wild price fluctuations we have been experiencing, prices for this gun have stayed fairly stable due to a fairly constant supply. This model has been manufactured since 1986.

| Exc. | V.G. | Good | Fair | Poor |
|------|------|------|------|------|
| 650 | 600 | 550 | 450 | 375 |

## Model 714 Broomhandle Mauser

This is a remanufactured C96-type pistol chambered for 7.63mm or 9mm parabellum. It utilizes a new manufactured frame and surplus parts. It features a 10-round detachable magazine, adjustable sights, and walnut grips. A Bolo Model with a smaller grip was produced in 1988 only.

| NIB | Exc. | V.G. | Fair | Poor |
|-----|------|------|------|------|
| 850 | 800 | 725 | 600 | 450 |

## Model 713 Mauser Carbine

This is a 16"-barrelled version of the Mauser with a fixed walnut stock. It has a standard magazine and is chambered for 7.63mm or 9mm parabellum. It is refinished and was introduced in 1987.

| Exc. | V.G. | Good | Fair | Poor |
|------|------|------|------|------|
| 1250 | 1000 | 900 | 700 | 575 |

### Model 713 Deluxe

This model is chambered for 7.63mm and has a 16" barrel with a detachable shoulder stock made of deluxe walnut. It has been modified to accept detachable magazines and is furnished with two 20-shot units. It has a 1000-meter adjustable sight and is furnished in a fitted leather case. There were only 1,500 manufactured in 1986.

| NIB | Exc. | V.G. | Good | Fair | Poor |
|-----|------|------|------|------|------|
| 2000 | 1750 | 1500 | 1250 | 1000 | 800 |

### Standard Broomhandle

This model is a refurbished surplus C-96 Mauser pistol with a new 7.63mm or 9mm barrel. All springs are replaced, and the entire gun is refinished. It is furnished with a shoulder stock/holster of Chinese manufacture.

| NIB | Exc. | V.G. | Good | Fair | Poor |
|-----|------|------|------|------|------|
| 725 | 650 | 525 | 450 | 350 | 275 |

### Ranger 1911A1

This is Federal Ordnance's version of the 1911A1 Colt service pistol. It is made of all steel, is chambered for .45 ACP, and has checkered walnut grips. It was introduced in 1988.

| NIB | Exc. | V.G. | Good | Fair | Poor |
|-----|------|------|------|------|------|
| 440 | 375 | 325 | 275 | 225 | 150 |

# FEGYVERGYAR
## Budapest, Hungary

Rudolf Frommer was a first-class engineer who became associated with Fegyvergyar in 1896. In 1900 he became the manager and held that position until his retirement in 1935. He died one year later in 1936. His designs were successful and prolific. They were used militarily and sold on the commercial market as well.

### Model 1901

This is an odd pistol that was not successful at all. It was chambered for an 8mm cartridge that was the forerunner of the 8mm Roth-Steyr. It has a long, slender barrel, which was actually a collar with the barrel within. It has a rotary bolt and external hammer and is recoil-operated. There is a 10-round integral magazine, and it is loaded from the top via a stripper clip. This pistol was manufactured from 1903 to 1905.

| Exc. | V.G. | Good | Fair | Poor |
|------|------|------|------|------|
| 1750 | 1500 | 1250 | 1000 | 750 |

### Model 1906

This is an improved version of the 1901, chambered for the 7.65mm Roth cartridge. It is, for all intents and purposes, the same action; but on later models a detachable 10-round magazine was adopted. It was manufactured between 1906 and 1910 in small quantity.

| Exc. | V.G. | Good | Fair | Poor |
|------|------|------|------|------|
| 1500 | 1350 | 1100 | 850 | 675 |

### Model 1910

This was the final version in this series of pistols and is similar with the addition of a grip safety.

| Exc. | V.G. | Good | Fair | Poor |
|------|------|------|------|------|
| 1250 | 1000 | 900 | 700 | 500 |

### Model "Stop"

This model was introduced in 1912 and took a whole new approach compared to any of the pistols this company had produced to that point. It is still unconventional as it uses two recoil springs in a tube above the barrel and resembles an air pistol in this way. It is chambered for 7.65mm or 9mm short and has a 3.75" barrel. The detachable magazine holds 7 rounds, and the sights are fixed. This locked-breech action, semi-automatic pistol was a commercial success. It was used widely by the Austro-Hungarian military during WWI. It was manufactured between 1912 and 1920.

| Exc. | V.G. | Good | Fair | Poor |
|------|------|------|------|------|
| 275 | 225 | 200 | 150 | 100 |

### Baby Model

This is a smaller version of the Stop that was designed as a pocket pistol with a 2" barrel and chambered for the same calibers. It was manufactured at the same time as the Stop Model.

| Exc. | V.G. | Good | Fair | Poor |
|------|------|------|------|------|
| 275 | 225 | 175 | 125 | 100 |

### Lilliput

This pocket pistol is chambered for 6.35mm and outwardly resembles the Baby. It is actually a simple, blowback-operated, semi-automatic pistol and was a good deal less complex to produce. This model was introduced in 1921.

| Exc. | V.G. | Good | Fair | Poor |
|------|------|------|------|------|
| 250 | 200 | 150 | 125 | 75 |

## Model 1929

This is a blowback-operated semi-automatic chambered for the 9mm short cartridge. It has an external hammer; and the barrel was retained, as the Browning was, by four lugs. This was a simple and reliable pistol, and it was adopted by the military as a replacement for the Stop. This model was manufactured between 1929 and 1937.

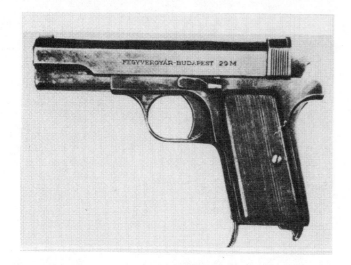

| Exc. | V.G. | Good | Fair | Poor |
|------|------|------|------|------|
| 225 | 190 | 175 | 125 | 100 |

## Model 1937

This was an improved version of the Model 1929 and was the last of Frommer's designs. It appeared a year after his death. This model is similar to the Model 1929, with a grooved slide to make cocking easier. It was adopted as the M1937 by the Hungarian Military, and in 1941 the German government ordered 85,000 pistols chambered for 7.65mm to be used by the Luftwaffe. These pistols were designated the "P Mod 37 Kal 7.65." They were also marked "jhv," which was the German code for the Hungarian company. These German pistols also have a manual safety, which is not found on the Hungarian military version and bears the Waffenamt acceptance marks. This model was manufactured from 1937 until the end of WWII.

### Nazi Proofed 7.65mm Version

| Exc. | V.G. | Good | Fair | Poor |
|------|------|------|------|------|
| 275 | 250 | 200 | 150 | 100 |

### 9mm Short Hungarian Military Version

| Exc. | V.G. | Good | Fair | Poor |
|------|------|------|------|------|
| 250 | 225 | 175 | 125 | 90 |

## FEINWERKBAU
### Oberndorf, Germany
### Importer--Beeman Precision Arms
### Santa Rosa, California

This company is known predominately for the production of high quality, extremely accurate air rifles and pistols. They also produce some of the most accurate target .22-caliber firearms in the world today. These firearms are listed.

### Model 2000 Universal

This is a single-shot, bolt-action target rifle chambered for the .22 rimfire cartridge. It has a 26.5" barrel with adjustable aperture sights and a fully adjustable trigger. There were four different stock configurations offered with stippled pistol grips and forearms. An electronic trigger was available as a $450 option. This model was discontinued in 1988.

| Exc. | V.G. | Good | Fair | Poor |
|------|------|------|------|------|
| 1200 | 1050 | 850 | 650 | 550 |

### Mini 2000

This version has a 22" barrel, and the electronic trigger was available at the additional cost.

| Exc. | V.G. | Good | Fair | Poor |
|------|------|------|------|------|
| 1000 | 850 | 750 | 550 | 450 |

### Running Boar Rifle

This version has a thumbhole stock with an adjustable cheekpiece and is furnished without sights. It was specially designed for the offhand Running Boar Competitions.

| Exc. | V.G. | Good | Fair | Poor |
|------|------|------|------|------|
| 1200 | 1050 | 850 | 650 | 550 |

### Match Rifle

This version has a 26.75" barrel and an adjustable cheekpiece stock.

| Exc. | V.G. | Good | Fair | Poor |
|------|------|------|------|------|
| 1100 | 950 | 750 | 550 | 450 |

### Model 2600 Ultra Match Free Rifle

This Model is similar to the Model 2000, with a laminated thumbhole stock and a heavy 26" barrel, fully adjustable sights, and trigger. It is offered with an electronic trigger for an additional $400. This model was introduced in 1986.

Fienwerkbau Model 2600 Target

| NIB | Exc. | V.G. | Good | Fair | Poor |
|-----|------|------|------|------|------|
| 1400 | 1200 | 1000 | 850 | 650 | 550 |

## FEMARU
### Budapest, Hungary

Hungary became a communist sattelite in the mid-1950's. At this time the Femaru company was designated to replace the firm of Fegyvergyar as the official Hungarian arms manufacturer. The products are of good quality.

### Hege

This model is a complete copy of the Walther PP. It is chambered for the 7.65mm and manufactured to be sold by Hegewaffen of Germany. The slide is so marked, along with a Pegasus in a circle. The designation "AP 66 Cal.7.65" also appears. The pistol was intended for export sales in the U.S. and other western countries.

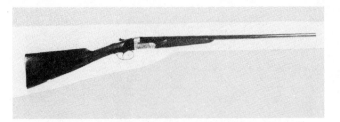

| Exc. | V.G. | Good | Fair | Poor |
|------|------|------|------|------|
| 250 | 225 | 175 | 125 | 100 |

### Tokagypt

There were 15,000 of these pistols built in 1958, under contract for the Egyptian army. It is a modified version of the Soviet TT-33 Tokarev chambered for the 9mm parabellum with a safety added. This is a very well-made, serviceable pistol; and it is difficult to understand why Egypt renigged on the contract. The balance were sold commercially--some under the trademark "Firebird."

| Exc. | V.G. | Good | Fair | Poor |
|------|------|------|------|------|
| 400 | 350 | 275 | 200 | 125 |

### Walam

This is another Walther PP copy of excellent quality chambered for the 9mm short or .380 ACP. Egypt was also to be the recipient of this contract, but again they mysteriously cancelled. The pistols were sold on the commercial market--some designated Model 48.

| Exc. | V.G. | Good | Fair | Poor |
|------|------|------|------|------|
| 250 | 225 | 175 | 125 | 100 |

## FERLIB
### Gardone V.T., Italy
### Importers--Quality Arms
### Houston, Texas
### New England Arms
### Kittery Point, Maine

### Model F.VI

This is a high-grade, side by side shotgun chambered for all gauges and is essentially custom-ordered. It is available in various barrel lengths and chokes and has an Anson and Deeley boxlock action, double triggers, and automatic ejectors. The action is case-colored, and the stock is hand-checkered select walnut. Single-selective triggers are available for an additional $375.
28 Gauge and .410--Add 10 Percent.

| NIB | Exc. | V.G. | Good | Fair | Poor |
|-----|------|------|------|------|------|
| 3800 | 3500 | 2800 | 2250 | 1700 | 1450 |

### Model F.VII

This model has a scroll-engraved, coin-finished frame but otherwise is similar to the Model F.VI. Single trigger option and small gauge premium are the same.

| NIB | Exc. | V.G. | Good | Fair | Poor |
|-----|------|------|------|------|------|
| 5000 | 4250 | 3750 | 3000 | 2400 | 1950 |

### Model F.VII/SC

This is a more deluxe version with gold inlays and a gamescene-engraved receiver. Options and premium are the same.

| NIB | Exc. | V.G. | Good | Fair | Poor |
|-----|------|------|------|------|------|
| 6100 | 5500 | 4500 | 3750 | 2800 | 2250 |

### Model F.VII Sideplate

This version features false sideplates that are completely covered with gamescene engraving. This model is standard with a single-selective trigger, but the small gauge premium is applicable.

| NIB | Exc. | V.G. | Good | Fair | Poor |
|-----|------|------|------|------|------|
| 5500 | 5000 | 4250 | 3500 | 2750 | 2200 |

### Model F.VII/SC Sideplate

This is the false sideplate model with gold inlays accenting the full coverage engraving.
28 Gauge and .410--Add 10 Percent.

| NIB | Exc. | V.G. | Good | Fair | Poor |
|-----|------|------|------|------|------|
| 7200 | 6500 | 5250 | 4500 | 3500 | 2750 |

### Hammer Gun

This model features a boxlock action with external hammers. Its other features are custom-ordered to the purchaser's specifications.

| NIB | Exc. | V.G. | Good | Fair | Poor |
|-----|------|------|------|------|------|
| 2900 | 2500 | 1850 | 1500 | 1000 | 750 |

## FERRY, ANDREWS & CO.
### Stafford, Connecticut

### Underhammer Pistol

This boot pistol is chambered for .36 caliber percussion and has a 3" part-round / part-octagonal barrel. They are very similar to the other underhammer pistols that were produced in Connecticut and Massachusetts. The topstrap was marked "Andrews Ferry & Co." The number manufactured is unknown. They were produced in the 1850's.

| Exc. | V.G. | Good | Fair | Poor |
|------|------|------|------|------|
| 400 | 350 | 300 | 225 | 125 |

## FIALA ARMS COMPANY
### New Haven, Connecticut

### Fiala Target Pistol

This is a different type of pistol than what is commonly encountered. Outwardly it resembles a semi-automatic Colt Woodsman; in actuality it is a manually operated firearm that must be cycled by hand after every shot. It was chambered for the .22 rimfire and was offered with interchangeable barrels in lengths of 3", 7.5", and 20". The finish is blued, and the grips are checkered walnut. They are marked "Fiala Arms and Equipment Co. Inc. / New Haven Conn. / Patents Pending." This pistol was furnished with a detachable shoulder stock in a leather trunk case that held the gun, three barrels, stock, and cleaning tools. The Government has classified this pistol with its stock as a "Curio and Relic"; and in its complete state it is a very desirable collectible.

Complete, Three barrels, Stock, Tools, and Case

| Exc. | V.G. | Good | Fair | Poor |
|------|------|------|------|------|
| 1250 | 1100 | 850 | 675 | 550 |

Gun Only

| Exc. | V.G. | Good | Fair | Poor |
|------|------|------|------|------|
| 500 | 425 | 350 | 250 | 150 |

## FINNISH LION
### Valmet, Sweden

**ISU Target Rifle**
This is a single-shot, bolt-action rifle chambered for the .22 rimfire cartridge. It has a 27" heavy barrel and a target stock with accessories. It features target adjustable sights and was manufactured between 1966 and 1977.

| Exc. | V.G. | Good | Fair | Poor |
|------|------|------|------|------|
| 350 | 300 | 250 | 200 | 125 |

**Champion Free Rifle**
This model has a 29" heavy barrel and double-set triggers. Otherwise it is similar to the ISU model. It was manufactured between 1965 and 1972.

Finnish Lion Champion Model

| Exc. | V.G. | Good | Fair | Poor |
|------|------|------|------|------|
| 600 | 525 | 450 | 375 | 275 |

**Match Rifle**
This model is similar to the Champion rifle, with a thumbhole stock and an adjustable buttplate. It was manufactured between 1937 and 1972.

Finnish Lion Match Model

| Exc. | V.G. | Good | Fair | Poor |
|------|------|------|------|------|
| 500 | 425 | 350 | 275 | 200 |

## FIOCCHI OF AMERICA, INC.
### Ozark, Missouri
### SEE--Pardini and A. Zoli

This company imports the above firearms, and they are listed in their own respective sections.

## FIREARMS INTERNATIONAL
### Washington, D.C.
### SEE--Star

This company was once the importer of the Star Model D as it was sold in the U.S.A. They also imported various other .25-caliber Colt copies that are not considered collectible and that would be valued in the $150-and-under range.

## FOEHL C.
### Philadelphia, Pennsylvania

**Foehl Derringer**
This pocket pistol is chambered for .41 caliber percussion and has a 2" barrel. The mountings are of German silver, and the stock is of walnut. The pistol is patterned after the Classic Henry Deringer design and is marked "C. Foehl" on the lock. This pistol was manufactured in the 1850's.

| Exc. | V.G. | Good | Fair | Poor |
|------|------|------|------|------|
| 750 | 700 | 600 | 450 | 300 |

## FOEHL & WEEKS
### Philadelphia, Pennsylvania

This company engaged in the manufacture of firearms from 1890 through 1894. They produced the following three revolvers.

**Columbian**
This is a solid-frame revolver with a cylinder that is removable for loading. It is chambered for the .32 and .38 caliber cartridges. The barrel bears the patent date "20 January 1891."

| Exc. | V.G. | Good | Fair | Poor |
|------|------|------|------|------|
| 150 | 125 | 100 | 75 | 50 |

**Columbian Automatic**
A typical break open revolver circa 1891, chambered for the .38 caliber cartridge only.

| Exc. | V.G. | Good | Fair | Poor |
|------|------|------|------|------|
| 175 | 150 | 125 | 100 | 75 |

**Perfect**
The Perfect is very similar to the Columbian automatic but features a concealed hammer for pocket carry. It is chambered for both .32 and .38 caliber.

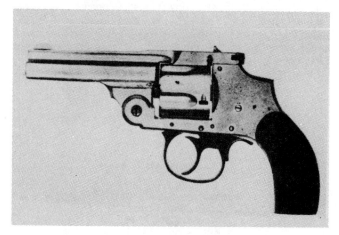

| Exc. | V.G. | Good | Fair | Poor |
|------|------|------|------|------|
| 175 | 150 | 125 | 100 | 75 |

## FOGARTY
### American Repeating Rifle Co.
### Boston, Massachusetts

**Fogarty Repeating Rifle**
This is a breech-loading rifle chambered for the .50-caliber rimfire cartridge. The barrel lengths are 32" in the rifle configuration and 20" as a carbine. The rifle has a walnut stock and full-length forend held in place by three barrel bands. The carbine has a short forend with one band. This is a lever action that is loaded through the butt. The action is case-colored, with the remainder blued. This weapon was invented by Valentine Fogarty and manufactured between 1866 and 1869, when it was sold to Winchester. Winchester made no effort to use the patents; they sold off the machinery and closed the company.

## Rifle

| Exc. | V.G. | Good | Fair | Poor |
|------|------|------|------|------|
| 2000 | 1850 | 1600 | 1250 | 950 |

## Carbine

| Exc. | V.G. | Good | Fair | Poor |
|------|------|------|------|------|
| 2500 | 2375 | 2000 | 1600 | 1250 |

# FOLSOM, H.
## St. Louis, Missouri
### SEE--Crescent Arms Co.

### Derringer

This company started business by producing a pocket pistol that was similar to the Philadelphia-type Derringer. It is .41-caliber percussion, with a 2.5" barrel and German silver mountings. The stock is walnut. The barrel is marked "H.Folsom." This company manufactured these pistols in the 1860's. Later they produced single-shot rifles, as well as double-barrelled and single-shot shotguns. These can be found in the Crescent arms section.

| Exc. | V.G. | Good | Fair | Poor |
|------|------|------|------|------|
| 650 | 575 | 450 | 350 | 275 |

# FOREHAND & WADSWORTH
## Worcester, Massachusetts

This company was formed after the death of Ethan Allen in 1871. Prior to that date he was in partnership with his sons-in-law, Sullivan Forehand and Henry Wadsworth. This company was in business as such until 1890, when Wadsworth retired. The name was changed to Forehand Arms Co. and remained in business until 1902, when Forehand's heirs sold out to Hopkins and Allen. This company produced a number of collectible pistols, as well as a considerable amount of "Suicide Specials"--cheap, double-action pocket pistols with no particular merit.

### Single Shot Derringer

This model is chambered for the .22 rimfire cartridge and has a 2" half round/half octagonal barrel that pivots to the side for loading. The frame is iron, either nickel-or siver-plated; and the barrel is blued or nickel-plated. The birdshead butt has walnut grips, and the barrel is marked "Forehand & Wadsworth-Worcester." There were only a few hundred manufactured between 1871 and 1890.

| Exc. | V.G. | Good | Fair | Poor |
|------|------|------|------|------|
| 300 | 250 | 200 | 150 | 100 |

### Single Shot .41 Derringer

This model is chambered for the .41 rimfire cartridge. It has a 2.5" rounded barrel which pivots to the side for loading. The frame is iron with a spur trigger, and the finish is blued. The barrel is marked "Forehand & Wadsworth/ Worcester. Mass. / Pat.Mch.7,1865." The birdshead butt has walnut grips. There were approximately 300 manufactured between 1871 and 1890.

| Exc. | V.G. | Good | Fair | Poor |
|------|------|------|------|------|
| 450 | 400 | 325 | 250 | 200 |

### Side Hammer .22

This model is chambered for the .22 rimfire cartridge and has a 2.25"--4" octagonal barrel. It has a 7-shot unfluted cylinder that is sometimes roll-engraved. The hammer is mounted on the right side of the iron frame, and the birdshead butt has walnut grips. The barrel is marked "Forehand & Wadsworth," and the finish is either blued or nickel-plated. There were approximately 1,000 manufactured between 1871 and 1879.

| Exc. | V.G. | Good | Fair | Poor |
|------|------|------|------|------|
| 300 | 250 | 200 | 150 | 100 |

### Center Hammer

This model is chambered for the .32 caliber rimfire cartridge. It has a 3.5" octagonal barrel and a 6-shot unfluted cylinder. The ejector rod is located inside the axis pin and can be removed by depressing a spring catch under the center pin. The frame is iron, and the revolver is finished in either blue or nickel-plate. The birdshead grips are of rosewood or walnut. The barrel is marked "Forehand & Wadsworth Worcester, Mass, U.S." The topstrap is marked in large stamped letters "TERROR." There were approximately 1,200 manufactured between 1871 and 1879.

| Exc. | V.G. | Good | Fair | Poor |
|------|------|------|------|------|
| 350 | 300 | 150 | 175 | 125 |

### Old Model Army Single Action Revolver

This Model is one of two large revolvers made by this company. It is chambered for the .44 Russian centerfire cartridge and has a 7.5" round barrel. The fluted cylinder holds 6 shots, and the finish is blued with walnut grips. The barrel is marked "Forehand & Wadsworth, Worcester, Mass. U.S. Patd. Oct. 22, '61, June 27, '71 Oct. 28, '73." There is no evidence that this pistol was ever used as a military weapon--although there have been examples with a bear stamped on the frame, and these revolvers have been associated with the California Militia; and if authentic, they should be worth a 20 percent premium. There were approximately 250 manufactured between 1872 and 1878.

| Exc. | V.G. | Good | Fair | Poor |
|------|------|------|------|------|
| 750 | 675 | 575 | 450 | 300 |

### New Model Army Single Action Revolver

This model is similar to the Old Model, with a 6.5" barrel and a half cock notch on the hammer. There is also an ejector-rod housing mounted on the side of the barrel and the frame. There were approximately 250 manufactured between 1878 and 1882.

| Exc. | V.G. | Good | Fair | Poor |
|------|------|------|------|------|
| 650 | 575 | 475 | 350 | 225 |

### Double Action Revolver.

This model is chambered for the .32 or .38 caliber rimfire cartridges. It has a 3.5" barrel and a 6-shot fluted cylinder. The finish is blued with birdshead walnut grips, and the topstrap is marked "Forehand & Wadsworth Double Action" on the .32 and "American Bulldog" on the .38. The number manufactured is not available, but they were produced between 1871 and 1890.

| Exc. | V.G. | Good | Fair | Poor |
|------|------|------|------|------|
| 250 | 225 | 175 | 125 | 75 |

### British Bulldog

This model is chambered for the .32 or .38 S&W cartridge and is a 6-shot, solid-frame double action that is either blued or nickel-plated, with checkered plastic grips. There were many manufactured in the 1890's.

| Exc. | V.G. | Good | Fair | Poor |
|------|------|------|------|------|
| 250 | 225 | 175 | 125 | 90 |

### British Bulldog .44

This is a larger 5-shot version chambered for the .44 S&W cartridge. It has a 5" barrel and is similar in appearance to the smaller Bulldog. This model was also manufactured in the 1890's.

| Exc. | V.G. | Good | Fair | Poor |
|------|------|------|------|------|
| 275 | 250 | 175 | 125 | 90 |

### Swamp Angel

This model is chambered for the .41 rimfire short and has a 3" barrel with a 5-shot cylinder. It is a single action that is either blued or nickel-plated, with checkered plastic grips. The topstrap is marked "Swamp Angel," and it was manufactured in the 1890's.

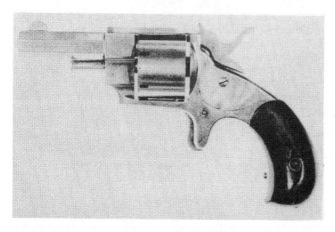

| Exc. | V.G. | Good | Fair | Poor |
|------|------|------|------|------|
| 200 | 175 | 150 | 100 | 75 |

### Forehand Arms Co. 1898-1902
### Perfection Automatic

This model is chambered for the .32 S&W or the .38 S&W cartridges and has round ribbed barrels in lengths from 3"--6". They are double-action topbreaks, with 5-shot fluted cylinders. The finish is either blue or nickel-plated, with checkered plastic grips. They are marked on the top of the barrel and were manufactured between 1898 and 1902.

| Exc. | V.G. | Good | Fair | Poor |
|------|------|------|------|------|
| 200 | 150 | 100 | 75 | 50 |

## FOWLER, B. JR.
### Connecticut

### Percussion Pistol

This is a very odd-looking pistol that is chambered for .38 caliber percussion. It has a 4" part round/part octagonal barrel, with silver bands inlaid in the octagon portion. The handle is at nearly right angles to the iron frame and has grips of maple.

There are engraved German silver mountings, and the barrel is marked "B.Fowler Jr." It was manufactured in the 1840's.

| Exc. | V.G. | Good | Fair | Poor |
|------|------|------|------|------|
| 375 | 350 | 300 | 225 | 150 |

## FOX, A. H.
### Philadelphia, Pennsylvania

This company was founded in 1903 by Ansley H. Fox. He had been in the business of manufacturing shotguns since 1896 in Baltimore, Maryland. This company was known as the Fox Gun Co. This venture was not a commercial success, and there are few examples known to exist from this early venture. The earliest guns produced by his new company were marked "Philadelphia Gun Co." The A. H. Fox banner was not used until 1905 and continued until 1930, when the Savage Arms Co. of Utica, New York, acquired them. Savage produced these high quality Fox guns until 1942, when all but the plainest utility model was discontinued. The A. H. Fox guns are considered by most to be on a par with the L. C. Smith and Parker as classic American shotguns, and the collector interest is quite high although they will not bring the price of the Parker and Smith guns. The guns manufactured between 1903 and 1930 are a bit more desirable from a collector's standpoint and will generally bring a premium of approximately 25 percent, all other things being equal.

### Sterlingworth

This model is a side-by-side double chambered for 12, 16, and 20 gauges. The barrels were offered in lengths of 26", 28", and 30" with various choke combinations. The action is a boxlock with double triggers and extractors. Automatic ejectors were available and would add approximately 30 percent to the respective values. The walnut stock has a checkered pistolgrip. This model was manufactured between 1903 and 1930.
20 Gauge--Add 50 Percent.

| Exc. | V.G. | Good | Fair | Poor |
|------|------|------|------|------|
| 1250 | 1000 | 800 | 500 | 275 |

### Sterlingworth Deluxe

This model is similar to the Sterlingworth, with an ivory bead, recoil pad, and the option of a 32" barrel. The automatic ejectors were an option that would add approximately 30 percent to the values shown.
20 Gauge--Add 50 Percent.

| Exc. | V.G. | Good | Fair | Poor |
|------|------|------|------|------|
| 1450 | 1250 | 1000 | 700 | 400 |

### SP Grade

This is a utility-grade boxlock that is chambered for 12 and 20 gauge. It is available with various barrel lengths and chokes. It has a boxlock action, double triggers, and extractors. The walnut stock has a checkered pistol grip and forend.
20 Gauge--Add 35 Percent.
Automatic Ejectors--Add 15 Percent.

| Exc. | V.G. | Good | Fair | Poor |
|------|------|------|------|------|
| 1000 | 850 | 750 | 450 | 225 |

### HE Grade

This model is similar to the Sterlingworth in appearance except that it was intended as a long-range model. It has 3" chambers and was offered with a 30" or 32" barrel, with full chokes and standard automatic ejectors. The original 3"-chambered guns are marked "Not Warranted" on the barrel; be wary of altered chamber specimens.
Single-Selective Trigger--Add 20 Percent.

| Exc. | V.G. | Good | Fair | Poor |
|------|------|------|------|------|
| 2400 | 2150 | 1750 | 1000 | 650 |

## High Grade Guns A-FE

These guns are similar in appearance and mechanics to the Sterlingworth guns. The difference is in the degree of engraving, the grade of wood used for the stock, the workmanship, checkering, etc. These are fine guns, and there are many options that alter the values. The 20-gauge guns would be worth approximately 50 percent more than a corresponding 12 gauge if built on the 20-gauge frame. The 20 gauge built on the 16-gauge frame would be worth 25 percent additional than the 12 gauge. Single-selective triggers, ventilated ribs, and beavertail forearms would add approximately $250 to $1,200. These high-grade guns should, without a doubt, be individually appraised as there are far too many variables to accurately grade and appraise in a book of this nature.

### A Grade

| Exc. | V.G. | Good | Fair | Poor |
|------|------|------|------|------|
| 1450 | 1150 | 850 | 600 | 400 |

### AE Grade (Automatic Ejectors)

| Exc. | V.G. | Good | Fair | Poor |
|------|------|------|------|------|
| 1750 | 1450 | 1150 | 900 | 700 |

### BE Grade

| Exc. | V.G. | Good | Fair | Poor |
|------|------|------|------|------|
| 2800 | 2500 | 2000 | 1500 | 900 |

### CE Grade

| Exc. | V.G. | Good | Fair | Poor |
|------|------|------|------|------|
| 3000 | 2600 | 2100 | 1550 | 950 |

### XE Grade

| Exc. | V.G. | Good | Fair | Poor |
|------|------|------|------|------|
| 5500 | 5000 | 3500 | 1850 | 1100 |

### DE Grade

| Exc. | V.G. | Good | Fair | Poor |
|------|------|------|------|------|
| 8500 | 7500 | 5000 | 3000 | 1500 |

### FE Grade

| Exc. | V.G. | Good | Fair | Poor |
|------|------|------|------|------|
| 25000 | 18500 | 10000 | 7000 | 5000 |

## Single Barrel Trapgun

This model is chambered for 12 gauge and has a 30" or 32" ventilated-rib barrel, with a boxlock action and automatic ejector. The stock is hand-checkered walnut, and some examples that were made between 1932 and 1942 have the Monte Carlo-type stock configuration. The four grades differ in the amount of ornamentation, grade of wood, and workmanship utilized.

### JE Grade

| Exc. | V.G. | Good | Fair | Poor |
|------|------|------|------|------|
| 1750 | 1450 | 950 | 750 | 450 |

### KE Grade

| Exc. | V.G. | Good | Fair | Poor |
|------|------|------|------|------|
| 2500 | 2000 | 1650 | 1250 | 750 |

### LE Grade

| Exc. | V.G. | Good | Fair | Poor |
|------|------|------|------|------|
| 3250 | 2500 | 2000 | 1500 | 1000 |

### ME Grade

| Exc. | V.G. | Good | Fair | Poor |
|------|------|------|------|------|
| 8000 | 6500 | 4500 | 3000 | 2000 |

## FOX
### SEE--Demro

## FRANCHI, L.
### Brescia, Italy
### Importer--FIE
### Hialeah, Florida
### American Arms, Inc.
### No. Kansas City, Missouri

## SxS Shotguns
### Astore

This model is chambered for 12 gauge and was offered in various barrel lengths and chokes. It has an Anson and Deeley boxlock action, double triggers, and automatic ejectors. It features a straight, hand-checkered walnut stock and was manufactured between 1937 and 1960.

| Exc. | V.G. | Good | Fair | Poor |
|------|------|------|------|------|
| 1000 | 900 | 750 | 500 | 350 |

### Astore II

This is a somewhat more elaborate version of the Astore. It was manufactured on contract in Spain for Franchi.

| Exc. | V.G. | Good | Fair | Poor |
|------|------|------|------|------|
| 1250 | 1100 | 900 | 700 | 450 |

### Astore 5

This is a more deluxe version of the Astore with fancier wood and more elaborate engraving. This model is no longer manufactured.

| Exc. | V.G. | Good | Fair | Poor |
|------|------|------|------|------|
| 2000 | 1750 | 1250 | 950 | 600 |

### Airone

This model is chambered for 12 gauge and is available in various barrel lengths and chokes. It is an Anson & Deeley boxlock, with double triggers and automatic ejectors. It is moderately engraved and features a straight, hand-checkered walnut stock. It was manufactured in the 1940's.

| Exc. | V.G. | Good | Fair | Poor |
|------|------|------|------|------|
| 1300 | 1050 | 950 | 750 | 500 |

## Sidelock Double Barrel Shotgun

This model was a strictly custom-made item. It was available in 12, 16, or 20 gauge with a self-opening, hand-detachable sidelock action. The barrel lengths and chokes were up to the customer, as were the style and dimensions of the stock. It features a single-selective trigger and automatic ejectors. This gun was offered in six grades, that differ only in the degree of engraving and the grade of walnut used in the stock. They have all been discontinued except for the Imperial Monte Carlo Extra, which is available on a custom-order basis.

### Condor

| Exc. | V.G. | Good | Fair | Poor |
|------|------|------|------|------|
| 7500 | 6500 | 4500 | 3500 | 2500 |

### Imperial

| Exc. | V.G. | Good | Fair | Poor |
|------|------|------|------|------|
| 10000 | 8500 | 6000 | 4500 | 3250 |

### Imperiales

| Exc. | V.G. | Good | Fair | Poor |
|------|------|------|------|------|
| 10500 | 9000 | 6500 | 5000 | 3500 |

### No. 5 Imperial Monte Carlo

| Exc. | V.G. | Good | Fair | Poor |
|------|------|------|------|------|
| 15000 | 12500 | 9000 | 7500 | 5000 |

### No. 11 Imperial Monte Carlo

| Exc. | V.G. | Good | Fair | Poor |
|------|------|------|------|------|
| 16000 | 13500 | 10000 | 8000 | 5500 |

### Imperial Monte Carlo Extra

| Exc. | V.G. | Good | Fair | Poor |
|------|------|------|------|------|
| 20000 | 17500 | 12500 | 9500 | 7500 |

## Over/Under Shotguns
### Priti Deluxe Model
This Over/Under is chambered for 12 or 20 gauge and has 26" or 28" barrels with a vent rib and various chokes. It has a single trigger and automatic ejectors. The action is a boxlock, and the stock is hand-checkered walnut. This model was introduced in 1988.

| NIB | Exc. | V.G. | Good | Fair | Poor |
|-----|------|------|------|------|------|
| 475 | 425  | 350  | 300  | 225  | 150  |

### Falconet
This model is chambered for all gauges and was offered with barrel lengths from 24" to 30" and various chokes. This model was made with an alloy receiver in three different anodized finishes--buckskin (tan), ebony, or silver. It has vent-rib barrels, a boxlock action, single-selective trigger, automatic ejectors, and light engraving. It was manufactured between 1968 and 1975.
Silver Receiver--Add 10 Percent.
28 Gauge and .410--Add 25 Percent.

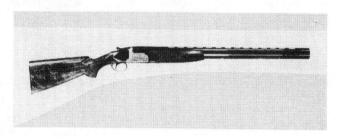

| Exc. | V.G. | Good | Fair | Poor |
|------|------|------|------|------|
| 550  | 500  | 425  | 350  | 250  |

### Falconet Skeet
This version has a case-colored steel receiver and 26" skeet-choked barrels, with a wide competition rib. It was manufactured between 1970 and 1974.

| Exc. | V.G. | Good | Fair | Poor |
|------|------|------|------|------|
| 950  | 850  | 700  | 550  | 450  |

### Falconet International Skeet
This is a deluxe version of the standard Skeet grade.

| Exc. | V.G. | Good | Fair | Poor |
|------|------|------|------|------|
| 1000 | 900  | 750  | 600  | 475  |

### Falconet Trap
This is a competition gun chambered for 12 gauge, with 30" modified and full chokes and a wide vent rib. The stock is of trap configuration. This model was manufactured between 1970 and 1974.

| Exc. | V.G. | Good | Fair | Poor |
|------|------|------|------|------|
| 950  | 850  | 700  | 550  | 450  |

### Falconet International Trap
This is a deluxe version of the standard Trap gun.

| Exc. | V.G. | Good | Fair | Poor |
|------|------|------|------|------|
| 1000 | 900  | 750  | 600  | 475  |

### Peregrine Model 451
This model is chambered for 12 gauge, with 26" or 28" vent-rib barrels. It was offered in various chokes with an alloy receiver, single-selective trigger, and automatic ejectors. The stock is hand-checkered walnut. This gun was manufactured in 1975.

| Exc. | V.G. | Good | Fair | Poor |
|------|------|------|------|------|
| 600  | 525  | 450  | 375  | 275  |

### Peregrine Model 400
This is a steel-framed version of the Model 451.

| Exc. | V.G. | Good | Fair | Poor |
|------|------|------|------|------|
| 650  | 575  | 500  | 400  | 300  |

### Aristocrat
This model is chambered for 12 gauge and has 26", 28", or 30" vent-rib barrels with a variety of choke combinations. This is a boxlock, with single-selective trigger and automatic ejectors. It has a hand-checkered walnut stock and was manufactured between 1960 and 1969.

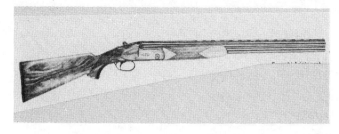

| Exc. | V.G. | Good | Fair | Poor |
|------|------|------|------|------|
| 650  | 575  | 500  | 400  | 300  |

### Aristocrat Magnum
This model is similar to the standard Aristocrat, with 32" full-choke barrels and 3" chambers.

| Exc. | V.G. | Good | Fair | Poor |
|------|------|------|------|------|
| 650  | 575  | 500  | 400  | 300  |

### Aristocrat Silver King
This version is similar to the Aristocrat except that it uses select walnut and has a coin-finished, engraved receiver. It was manufactured between 1962 and 1969. The Aristocrat designation is used for four more models that differ only in the degree of engraving and grade of walnut.

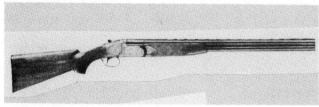

| Exc. | V.G. | Good | Fair | Poor |
|------|------|------|------|------|
| 750  | 675  | 575  | 475  | 350  |

### Aristocrat Deluxe

| Exc. | V.G. | Good | Fair | Poor |
|------|------|------|------|------|
| 1000 | 800  | 675  | 575  | 400  |

### Aristocrat Supreme

| Exc. | V.G. | Good | Fair | Poor |
|------|------|------|------|------|
| 1450 | 1200 | 850  | 700  | 575  |

### Aristocrat Imperial

| Exc. | V.G. | Good | Fair | Poor |
|------|------|------|------|------|
| 2750 | 2250 | 1750 | 1250 | 950  |

### Aristocrat Monte Carlo

| Exc. | V.G. | Good | Fair | Poor |
|------|------|------|------|------|
| 3500 | 3000 | 2750 | 2000 | 1500 |

### Model 2003 Trap
This gun is chambered for 12 gauge, with 30" or 32" competition vent-rib barrels. It is choked in the popular trap combinations. It has a boxlock action, with single-selective trigger and automatic ejectors. It was furnished in a fitted case and was manufactured in 1976.

| Exc. | V.G. | Good | Fair | Poor |
|------|------|------|------|------|
| 1250 | 1100 | 800  | 650  | 500  |

### Model 2004 Trap
This is a single-barrelled version of the Model 2003.

| Exc. | V.G. | Good | Fair | Poor |
|------|------|------|------|------|
| 1250 | 1100 | 800  | 650  | 500  |

## Model 2005 Combination Trap
This is a cased set which consists of a single barrel and a set of Over/Under barrels.

| Exc. | V.G. | Good | Fair | Poor |
|------|------|------|------|------|
| 2500 | 2200 | 1750 | 1200 | 950 |

## Model 3000 "Undergun"
This model has a very high rib and is furnished in a cased set of a single barrel and a set of Over/Under barrels.

| Exc. | V.G. | Good | Fair | Poor |
|------|------|------|------|------|
| 2750 | 2450 | 2000 | 1500 | 1200 |

## Alcione Model
This model is chambered for 12 gauge and has 28" vent-rib barrels with various chokes. The barrels are separated by a vent rib as well, and a single selective trigger and automatic ejectors are standard.

| NIB | Exc. | V.G. | Good | Fair | Poor |
|-----|------|------|------|------|------|
| 850 | 775 | 575 | 475 | 350 | 300 |

## Alcione SL
This is a more elaborately engraved version of the Alcione Over/Under. It has a coin-finished receiver and was furnished in a fitted case. This model was dropped from the line in 1986.

| Exc. | V.G. | Good | Fair | Poor |
|------|------|------|------|------|
| 1500 | 1200 | 950 | 700 | 500 |

## Black Magic Hunter
This model is currently imported by American Arms and is chambered for 12 gauge, 3" only. It has 28" vent-ribbed barrels that are separated and feature screw-in chokes. The gun has a single-selective trigger, automatic ejectors, and a blued finish with gold-plated parts. The stock is hand-checkered walnut. This model was introduced in 1989.

| NIB | Exc. | V.G. | Good | Fair | Poor |
|------|------|------|------|------|------|
| 1200 | 1050 | 850 | 700 | 550 | 450 |

## Black Magic Lightweight Hunter
This version has an alloy receiver with 26" or 2.75" chambered barrels. Otherwise it is similar to the standard gun.

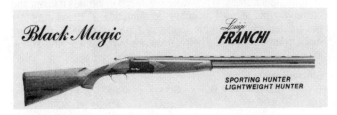

| NIB | Exc. | V.G. | Good | Fair | Poor |
|------|------|------|------|------|------|
| 1150 | 1000 | 800 | 650 | 500 | 400 |

## Semi-Automatic Shotguns
### Standard Model
This model is a recoil-operated semi-automatic chambered for 12 or 20 gauge. It is offered with a 24"-- 30" vent-rib barrel and a variety of chokes. After 1989 it featured screw-in choke tubes, and these guns would be worth approximately $75 more than the fixed-choke model. The frame is made of alloy, and the stock is hand-checkered walnut. This model has been manufactured since 1950 and is still available.
Magnum Model--Add 10 Percent.

| NIB | Exc. | V.G. | Good | Fair | Poor |
|-----|------|------|------|------|------|
| 525 | 475 | 425 | 350 | 250 | 175 |

## Hunter Model
This model is a deluxe version of the Standard with an etched receiver and fancier wood.
Magnum Model--Add 10 Percent.

| NIB | Exc. | V.G. | Good | Fair | Poor |
|-----|------|------|------|------|------|
| 575 | 500 | 450 | 375 | 275 | 200 |

## Eldorado
This is a fancier version of the Hunter with an engraved, gold-filled receiver and a higher-grade stock. It was manufactured between 1954 and 1975.

| Exc. | V.G. | Good | Fair | Poor |
|-----|------|------|------|------|
| 475 | 425 | 325 | 250 | 175 |

## Crown Grade, Diamond Grade, Imperial Grade
These three grades differ in the degree of engraving and the grade of walnut only. All were discontinued in 1975.

### Crown Grade

| Exc. | V.G. | Good | Fair | Poor |
|------|------|------|------|------|
| 1500 | 1250 | 1000 | 700 | 475 |

### Diamond Grade

| Exc. | V.G. | Good | Fair | Poor |
|------|------|------|------|------|
| 2000 | 1750 | 1250 | 900 | 675 |

### Imperial Grade

| Exc. | V.G. | Good | Fair | Poor |
|------|------|------|------|------|
| 2500 | 2250 | 1750 | 1250 | 950 |

## Model 500
This is a gas-operated, semi-automatic 12 gauge, with a 28" vent-rib barrel and a hand-checkered walnut stock. It was introduced in 1976.
Deluxe Version--Add 10 Percent.

| Exc. | V.G. | Good | Fair | Poor |
|-----|------|------|------|------|
| 350 | 325 | 275 | 200 | 150 |

## Model 520 "Eldorado Gold"
This is a gold-inlaid version of the Model 500, with fancy wood and a highly engraved receiver.

| Exc. | V.G. | Good | Fair | Poor |
|------|------|------|------|------|
| 1000 | 850 | 650 | 450 | 300 |

## Model 530 Trap
This version of the Model 500 features a 30" or 32" barrel and very high vent rib. The stock is in the Trap configuration.

| Exc. | V.G. | Good | Fair | Poor |
|-----|------|------|------|------|
| 675 | 600 | 500 | 400 | 300 |

## Prestige Model
This is a gas-operated, semi-automatic 12 gauge offered in various barrel lengths, with a vent rib and screw-in choke tubes standard after 1989. This gun has an alloy receiver and a hand-checkered walnut stock.

| NIB | Exc. | V.G. | Good | Fair | Poor |
|-----|------|------|------|------|------|
| 725 | 675 | 525 | 450 | 350 | 275 |

## Elite Model
This gun is similar to the Prestige, with an etched receiver and fancier wood.

| NIB | Exc. | V.G. | Good | Fair | Poor |
|-----|------|------|------|------|------|
| 750 | 700 | 550 | 475 | 375 | 300 |

## SPAS 12
This is a paramilitary-type shotgun that has the capability of functioning either as a slide action or as a semi-automatic with the touch of a button. It is chambered for 12 gauge and has a 21.5" barrel. The magazine holds 9 shots, and the receiver is alloy. The finish is matte black, with either a folding or fixed synthetic stock.

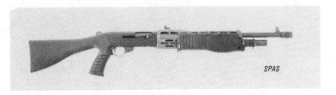

SPAS

| NIB | Exc. | V.G. | Good | Fair | Poor |
|-----|------|------|------|------|------|
| 600 | 475 | 400 | 350 | 300 | 250 |

## Black Magic Game Model

This is a gas-operated semi-automatic chambered for the 12 gauge 3" shell. It is offered with 24"--28" vent-rib barrels with screw-in choke tubes. The gun uses any shells interchangeably and has a black and gold anodized alloy receiver with a walnut stock. It is also available in a Trap and a Skeet Model and was introduced in 1989.
Skeet Model--Add 20 Percent.
Trap Model-- Add 25 Percent.

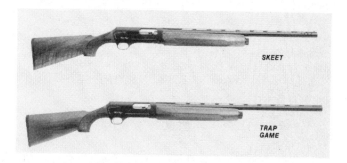

| NIB | Exc. | V.G. | Good | Fair | Poor |
|-----|------|------|------|------|------|
| 600 | 550 | 475 | 400 | 325 | 225 |

## Rifles
### Centennial Semi-Automatic

This model is a semi-automatic rifle chambered for .22 l.r. cartridge. It has a 21" barrel and an alloy receiver. The sights are adjustable and the rifle was manufactured in 1968 only, to commemorate the 100th Anniversary of the Franchi Company.
Deluxe Engraved Model--Add 20 Percent.

| Exc. | V.G. | Good | Fair | Poor |
|------|------|------|------|------|
| 350 | 300 | 250 | 175 | 125 |

# FRANCOTTE, A.
### Liege, Belgium
### Importer--Royal Arms International
### Woodland Hills, California

## Jubilee

This model is a side-by-side, double-barrel shotgun that features an Anson & Deeley boxlock action. It is available in 12, 16, 20, and 28 gauge with various barrel lengths and chokes. This model has automatic ejectors and comes standard with double triggers. There is the standard model and five higher grades that differ in the amount of engraving and the grade of wood and checkering.

| Exc. | V.G. | Good | Fair | Poor |
|------|------|------|------|------|
| 1500 | 1350 | 1100 | 850 | 700 |

### No. 14

| Exc. | V.G. | Good | Fair | Poor |
|------|------|------|------|------|
| 2000 | 1850 | 1600 | 1300 | 1100 |

### No. 18

| Exc. | V.G. | Good | Fair | Poor |
|------|------|------|------|------|
| 2500 | 2250 | 2000 | 1500 | 1300 |

### No. 20

| Exc. | V.G. | Good | Fair | Poor |
|------|------|------|------|------|
| 3000 | 2500 | 2250 | 1750 | 1500 |

### No. 25

| Exc. | V.G. | Good | Fair | Poor |
|------|------|------|------|------|
| 3500 | 3000 | 2750 | 2000 | 1750 |

### No. 30

| Exc. | V.G. | Good | Fair | Poor |
|------|------|------|------|------|
| 4500 | 4000 | 3500 | 3000 | 2500 |

## Eagle Grade No. 45

This is simply a more deluxe version of the Jubilee model.

| Exc. | V.G. | Good | Fair | Poor |
|------|------|------|------|------|
| 3500 | 3000 | 2500 | 2000 | 1500 |

## Knockabout

This model is quite similar in appearance to the Jubilee but is a more utility-grade gun. It is chambered for 12, 16, 20, and 28 gauge and .410.
20 Gauge--Add 20 Percent.
28 Gauge--Add 30 Percent.
.410-- Add 40 Percent.

| Exc. | V.G. | Good | Fair | Poor |
|------|------|------|------|------|
| 1250 | 1100 | 850 | 650 | 500 |

## Sidelock SxS

This gun is chambered for the 12, 16, 20, and 28 gauge and the .410. It is produced on a custom-order basis, with barrel lengths and chokes to the customer's specifications. It features a true sidelock action and extensive scroll engraving. The walnut is of a very deluxe grade and is finely hand-checkered. The .410 will bring a premium of from $1,200--$1,500.

| NIB | Exc. | V.G. | Good | Fair | Poor |
|-----|------|------|------|------|------|
| 12650 | 10000 | 8000 | 6500 | 5000 | 3500 |

## Deluxe Sidelock SxS

This version is similar to the standard sidelock, with gold-inlaid gamescenes.

| NIB | Exc. | V.G. | Good | Fair | Poor |
|-----|------|------|------|------|------|
| 15000 | 12500 | 10000 | 8000 | 5750 | 4800 |

# FRANKLIN, C. W.
### Liege, Belgium

This company produced single-shot, single-barrel shotguns and double-barrel guns around 1900. Their products were both hammerless and exposed-hammer guns with either Damascus or fluid-steel barrels. They were produced in various gauges and barrel lengths as well as choke combinations. These guns are not particularly collectible, and most are not suitable for firing modern ammunition. Their values are fairly similar and as follows:

**Single Barrel**

| Exc. | V.G. | Good | Fair | Poor |
|------|------|------|------|------|
| 100 | 75 | 50 | 35 | 20 |

**Damascus Barrel Double**

| Exc. | V.G. | Good | Fair | Poor |
|------|------|------|------|------|
| 175 | 150 | 125 | 100 | 65 |

**Steel Barrel Double**

| Exc. | V.G. | Good | Fair | Poor |
|------|------|------|------|------|
| 200 | 175 | 150 | 125 | 90 |

# FRANKONIA JAGD
### Germany

## Favorit

This is a bolt-action sporting rifle chambered for various European calibers. It has a 24" barrel and set triggers. The finish is blued, with a checkered walnut stock.

| Exc. | V.G. | Good | Fair | Poor |
|------|------|------|------|------|
| 300 | 275 | 250 | 175 | 125 |

## Favorit Deluxe

This model is similar, with a higher-grade walnut stock.

| Exc. | V.G. | Good | Fair | Poor |
|------|------|------|------|------|
| 325 | 300 | 275 | 200 | 150 |

### Safari Model
This version is chambered for the larger, Magnum-type calibers.

| Exc. | V.G. | Good | Fair | Poor |
|---|---|---|---|---|
| 475 | 425 | 375 | 275 | 200 |

### Heeren Rifle
This is a high-grade, single-shot rifle chambered for various popular European calibers. It has a 26" octagonal barrel, double-set triggers, and adjustable sights. It is heavily engraved with hand-checkered, high-grade walnut. The finish is blued.

| Exc. | V.G. | Good | Fair | Poor |
|---|---|---|---|---|
| 3000 | 2650 | 2200 | 1700 | 1250 |

## FRASER, DANIEL & SON
### Edinburgh, Scotland
The firm of Fraser & Son was founded in 1871, and they have produced some very high quality rifles.

### Falling Block Single Shot.
This was the first rifle built by this company, and it was constructed during the heyday of the British single-shot rifle. It is chambered for many calibers--from the smallest to the large African cartridges. The action is cycled by a lever on the right side of the frame. The barrel lengths are various, and the stock is made of select checkered walnut. This rifle was manufactured between 1871 and 1889.

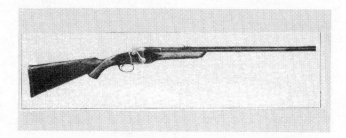

| Exc. | V.G. | Good | Fair | Poor |
|---|---|---|---|---|
| 8500 | 7500 | 5500 | 3500 | 2000 |

### Double Rifle
This is a side-by-side double that has exposed hammers and is chambered for all of the popular, early rimmed cartridges. It is engraved and could be custom ordered to the customer's specifications. It was furnished cased with accessories.

| Exc. | V.G. | Good | Fair | Poor |
|---|---|---|---|---|
| 12500 | 10000 | 8500 | 6500 | 4000 |

## FRASER F. A. CORP.
### Fraser, Michigan

### Fraser 25 cal.
This pocket pistol was formerly known as the Bauer and is a copy of the "Baby Browning." It is chambered for .25 ACP and has a 2.25" barrel and a 6-round magazine. It is made of stainless steel with black nylon grips. There is a 24 kt. gold-plated model that is worth approximately $100 additional.

| NIB | Exc. | V.G. | Good | Fair | Poor |
|---|---|---|---|---|---|
| 135 | 125 | 100 | 75 | 50 | 35 |

## FREEDOM ARMS
### Freedom, Wyoming

### Percussion Mini-Revolver
This all stainless-steel revolver is chambered for .22 caliber and utilizes the percussion ignition system. It is offered with a choice of 1", 1.75", and 3" barrel lengths. The cylinder holds 5 shots. It has a birdshead grip, and there is a belt buckle available that houses the pistol for an additional $40.

| NIB | Exc. | V.G. | Good | Fair | Poor |
|---|---|---|---|---|---|
| 200 | 180 | 165 | 125 | 100 | 75 |

### Patriot
This model is similar in appearance to the Percussion model, but it is chambered for the .22 l.r. cartridge. It has a polished stainless-steel finish.

| NIB | Exc. | V.G. | Good | Fair | Poor |
|---|---|---|---|---|---|
| 155 | 135 | 110 | 85 | 65 | 45 |

### Minuteman
This is the same revolver with a 3" barrel. It was discontinued in 1988.

| Exc. | V.G. | Good | Fair | Poor |
|---|---|---|---|---|
| 145 | 125 | 90 | 75 | 50 |

### Ironsides
This model is chambered for the .22 rimfire magnum cartridge and has a 1" or a 1.75" barrel.

| NIB | Exc. | V.G. | Good | Fair | Poor |
|---|---|---|---|---|---|
| 175 | 150 | 125 | 100 | 80 | 60 |

### Bostonian
This is simply the Ironsides with a 3" barrel.

| NIB | Exc. | V.G. | Good | Fair | Poor |
|---|---|---|---|---|---|
| 175 | 150 | 125 | 100 | 80 | 60 |

### Celebrity
This model includes the belt buckle that houses either the .22 l.r. or the .22 Magnum revolver.
.22 Magnum Model--Add $25.

| NIB | Exc. | V.G. | Good | Fair | Poor |
|---|---|---|---|---|---|
| 195 | 175 | 150 | 125 | 100 | 75 |

### Casull Field Grade
This is currently the most powerful production handgun in the world. It is a single action with a 5-shot cylinder chambered for the .454 Casull Magnum and fires a 225-grain bullet at over 2,000 feet per second. This version offers a 4.75", 7.5", and a 10" barrel. It comes standard with fixed sights, and adjustable sights are available as a $75 option. This model has a matte stainless-steel finish with black rubber "Pachmayr" grips. It was introduced in 1988.

| NIB | Exc. | V.G. | Good | Fair | Poor |
|---|---|---|---|---|---|
| 775 | 725 | 650 | 550 | 450 | 375 |

## Casull Premier Grade

This is the deluxe version of this formidable handgun. It is chambered for the .454 Mag., .44 Rem. Mag., .45 Win. Mag., and the .45 Colt. This model has a replaceable forcing cone and is also available with walnut grips. The adjustable sights are an extra cost option on this model as well.

| NIB | Exc. | V.G. | Good | Fair | Poor |
|------|------|------|------|------|------|
| 1050 | 1000 | 850 | 750 | 650 | 500 |

## Signature Edition

There were 2,000 of these produced with a high polished finish and rosewood grips. They have the 7.5" barrel only and were furnished with a fitted case and accessories. The serial numbers are DC1--DC2,000. The DC represents Dick Casull, the designer of the firearm.

| NIB | Exc. | V.G. | Good | Fair | Poor |
|------|------|------|------|------|------|
| 2000 | 1750 | 1500 | 1250 | 900 | 600 |

# FREEMAN, AUSTIN T.
### Hoard's Armory
### Watertown, New York

## Freeman Army Model Revolver

This revolver is chambered for .44 caliber and utilizes the percussion ignition system. It has a 7.5" round barrel and a 6-shot unfluted cylinder with recessed nipples. The revolver is made of iron and is blued, with a case-colored rammer and hammer. The one-piece grips are walnut. The frame is marked "Freeman's Pat. Dec. 9, 1862/Hoard's Armory, Watertown, N.Y." Although there is no concrete evidence, it is possible that some of these revolvers could have been used in the Civil War by state militias. There were several thousand manufactured in 1863 and 1864.

| Exc. | V.G. | Good | Fair | Poor |
|------|------|------|------|------|
| 1000 | 900 | 750 | 650 | 500 |

# FRENCH STATE
### Manufactured by MAS
### St. Etienne, France
### SACM
### Cholet, France
### MAC
### Catellerault, France
### MAT
### Tulle, France

France did not manufacture service revolvers until the 1880's. Up until that point, they purchased handguns from independent sources on a contract basis. Their first attempt was the Model 1885 revolver.

## Model 1885

This revolver is chambered for the 11mm cartridge. It has a solid frame and a 6-shot cylinder with a loading gate. The barrel is 5" in length, and the finish is blued with checkered walnut grips.

| Exc. | V.G. | Good | Fair | Poor |
|------|------|------|------|------|
| 300 | 250 | 200 | 150 | 100 |

## Model 1887

This model is similar to the Model 1885 but is chambered for the 8mm cartridge. This was not a satisfactory design and was in service only five years.

| Exc. | V.G. | Good | Fair | Poor |
|------|------|------|------|------|
| 300 | 250 | 200 | 150 | 100 |

## Model 1892

This model is chambered for the 8mm Lebel cartridge and has a 5" barrel. It is a solid-frame revolver, and the 6-shot cylinder swings out to the right for loading. The loading gate latch is a lever on the side of the frame that also serves to lock the hammer if the cylinder is not latched. This is a sound safety feature. The finish is blued, with checkered walnut grips and a lanyard swivel on the butt. This was a good service revolver, but the 8mm Lebel cartridge was pathetically inadequate in stopping power and was a poor choice for a military handgun.

| Exc. | V.G. | Good | Fair | Poor |
|------|------|------|------|------|
| 225 | 200 | 175 | 125 | 75 |

## Model 1892 "A Pompe"

This revolver is similar to the standard Model 1892 except that the cylinder latch is a sleeve around the ejector rod that is slid forward to release the cylinder. This is a very rare variation.

| Exc. | V.G. | Good | Fair | Poor |
|------|------|------|------|------|
| 225 | 200 | 175 | 125 | 75 |

## MAS Model 1935

After WWI the French military decided that they wanted a new semi-automatic service pistol; and the firm of SACM developed the Model 1935, which was adopted for service. It was a creation of Charles Petter and was actually a modification of the Browning swinging-link design. It was chambered for the 7.65mm Long--another cartridge that was nearly useless for military applications. The pistol itself was well made and well designed. It eventually became known as the Model 1935A, and there were some examples noted with German Waffenamts. These were procured after the Occupation in WWII.

### German Waffenamt Model

| Exc. | V.G. | Good | Fair | Poor |
|------|------|------|------|------|
| 225 | 175 | 150 | 100 | 75 |

### Standard Model

| Exc. | V.G. | Good | Fair | Poor |
|------|------|------|------|------|
| 175 | 150 | 125 | 100 | 75 |

## Model 1935S

This model was developed in 1938 and is simply a simplified version of the 1935A. It is chambered for the same anemic cartridge and has a straighter, less-contoured appearance. The locking ribs were eliminated in favor of a single lug on the barrel that fit into a single slot in the slide. The 1935S was manufactured by all of the firms listed at the beginning of this chapter.

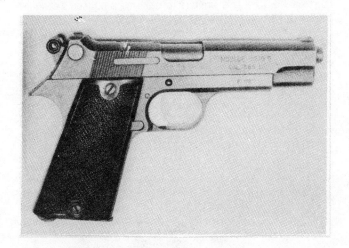

| Exc. | V.G. | Good | Fair | Poor |
|------|------|------|------|------|
| 175 | 150 | 125 | 100 | 75 |

## MAS Model 1950

This model was designed after WWII in response to the French military's request for a service pistol in an effective caliber. This model is chambered for the 9mm Parabellum and carries a 9-shot magazine. It is blued, with ribbed plastic grips. The Model 1950 was manufactured by MAS and MAC.

| Exc. | V.G. | Good | Fair | Poor |
|------|------|------|------|------|
| 475 | 425 | 350 | 275 | 200 |

## FRIGON
### Clay Center, Kansas

Frigon is an importer. These guns are manufactured by Marocchi located in Italy.

## FT 1

This model is a single-barrelled trap gun chambered for 12 gauge and has a 32" or 34" ventilated-rib barrel with full choke. It is a boxlock with automatic ejector and features a stock that can be interchanged rapidly. The finish is blued, and the model was introduced in 1986.

| NIB | Exc. | V.G. | Good | Fair | Poor |
|-----|------|------|------|------|------|
| 875 | 750 | 650 | 550 | 450 | 300 |

## FTC

This model is similar to the FT 1 except that it is offered with two sets of barrels--a single vent-rib trap barrel and a set of Over/Under vent-rib barrels. This model is furnished in a fitted case and was also introduced in 1986.

| NIB | Exc. | V.G. | Good | Fair | Poor |
|-----|------|------|------|------|------|
| 1600 | 1400 | 1150 | 800 | 650 | 500 |

## FS-4

This model is a 4-gauge set chambered for 12, 20, and 28 gauge and .410. Each barrel has its own forearm, and the set is furnished with a fitted case. This model was also introduced in 1986.

| NIB | Exc. | V.G. | Good | Fair | Poor |
|-----|------|------|------|------|------|
| 2350 | 2100 | 1750 | 1500 | 1100 | 750 |

## FROMMER
### SEE--Fegyvergyar.

## FRUHWIRTH
### Austria

### M.1872 Fruhwirth System Rifle

This rifle was developed by Fruhwirth, a well-known Austrian gunsmith. It is chambered for the 11mm centerfire and utilizes the same barrel that was formerly used on the single-shot Werndl carbine. This rifle has a 25" barrel and a 6-shot capacity. The finish is blued, and the stock is walnut. It was adopted for service by the Austrian military and used in the Tyrole and by various Gendarme units.

| Exc. | V.G. | Good | Fair | Poor |
|------|------|------|------|------|
| 350 | 300 | 250 | 175 | 100 |

## FURR ARMS
### Prescott, Arizona
### J. & G. Sale, Inc.
### Prescott, Arizona

This is a family-owned company that specializes in the production of very high quality reproductions of the Gatling gun, as well as the James 6-pound cannon and the H.M.S. Victory naval cannon. These reproductions are virtually handmade and are produced in 1/10, 1/6, 1/3, 1/2, 3/4, and full-sized. The prices on these creations run from $500 for a 1/10-scale cannon to $19,000 for a 3/4-scale carriage Gatling gun. This type of firearm should be evaluated by independent appraisal and is not in the preview of a book of this scope and nature. The distributor can be contacted for current values.

## FYRBURG, ANDREW
### Hopkinton, Massachusetts

After a lifetime of working on firearms designs and assigning them to other companies, Fyrburg in 1903 finally produced two revolvers under his own trademark. They are a 3"-barrelled .32 caliber and a 3.5" .38 caliber. They both have round ribbed barrels and round butts. They look very much like the contemporary Iver Johnson designs with the exception of a large catch on the frame lock, Fyrburg's own design. The grips bear the trademark, "AFCo."

| Exc. | V.G. | Good | Fair | Poor |
|------|------|------|------|------|
| 150 | 125 | 100 | 75 | 50 |

## GABBET - FAIRFAX, H.
### Leamington Spa, England

**Mars**

Hugh Gabbet-Fairfax was a noted inventor of semi-automatic firearms designs. During the period between 1895 and 1900 he patented both pistol and rifle mechanisms. In 1897 he submitted a prototype to Webley for possible manufacture. The pistol was called the Mars. Webley declined to adopt the design and produce it under their own banner but did agree to make them on a commission basis for the inventor. The pistol was tested by the British army and rejected, possibly for feeding problems but more likely due to excessive recoil. The Mars fired the most powerful cartridges of its day and was not surpassed for power in an auto-loader until the appearance of the .44 Auto-Mag, 70 years later. The three calibers were the 8.5mm, firing a 140-grain bullet at 1,750 feet per second; the 9mm, firing a 156-grain bullet at 1,650 feet per second; and the .45 Long, which fired a 220-grain bullet at 1,200 feet per second. The price for this impressive performance was said to be recoil at intolerable levels. Mars went bankrupt around 1904, and the pistol is now one of the rarest of all auto-loaders.

| Exc. | V.G. | Good | Fair | Poor |
|---|---|---|---|---|
| 5000 | 4750 | 4000 | 3250 | 2500 |

## GABILONDO Y URRESTI
### Guernica, Spain
### Elgoibar, Spain
Stoeger Industries South Hackensack, New Jersey

This company is one of the largest and certainly most successful of the old-line Spanish gun makers. They began producing firearms in 1904. Their first pistols were cheap "Velo-Dog" revolvers. In 1909 they made their first semi-automatic pistol. In 1914 they introduced the "Eibar-type" pistol that was known as the "Ruby" and one year later received an open-end contract for 10,000 pistols per month from the French. Within six months this contract was increased to 30,000 per month, and the subcontracting that was to lead to the proliferation of the Eibar-type pistol began. After WWI Gabilondo produced 1910 Browning copies and in 1931 began to manufacture the Llama pistol, based on the 1911 Colt design. These pistols are still being made today.

**Velo-Dog Revolver**

These early revolvers have a solid frame and are chambered for 6.35mm. They have short, 1.5" barrels, concealed hammers, and folding triggers. The finish is blued, with checkered wood grips. They were manufactured between 1904 and 1914.

| Exc. | V.G. | Good | Fair | Poor |
|---|---|---|---|---|
| 150 | 125 | 100 | 75 | 50 |

**Radium**

This was the first semi-automatic pistol produced by Gabilondo. It is chambered for 6.35mm and is based on the 1906 Brown-ing without a grip safety. It has a 2.5" barrel and is unusual in one respect--instead of a removable magazine, the righthand grip slides downward to reveal the box magazine. The cartridges are dropped into this grip magazine until it is loaded (it holds 6), and then the grip slides back into place. This reactivates the spring, placing the cartridges under pressure. The slide is marked "Fire Arms Manufacturing Automatic Pistol Radium Cal. 6.35." This unusual pistol was produced between 1909 and 1914.

| Exc. | V.G. | Good | Fair | Poor |
|---|---|---|---|---|
| 175 | 150 | 125 | 100 | 75 |

**Ruby**

This is the pistol that made Eibar famous. It is chambered for 7.65mm and is the pistol that the French contracted to Gabilondo and nearly every other gunmaker in Spain. It is a simple, blowback-operated pistol that was not very well made. This model remained in production off-and-on until 1930, when it was finally phased out to make room for the Llama.

| Exc. | V.G. | Good | Fair | Poor |
|---|---|---|---|---|
| 200 | 175 | 150 | 100 | 75 |

**Bufalo**

This model designation was used for a series of pistols chambered for the 6.35mm, 7.65mm, and 9mm short cartridges. They are all rather unremarkable copies of the Browning 1906 and 1910 with external hammers. They are blued with black plastic grips and are marked "Automatica Piastola Espana Bufalo." The caliber is also stamped on the slide. This model was manufactured between 1919 and 1925 under this name and for a number of years more under different names.

| Exc. | V.G. | Good | Fair | Poor |
|---|---|---|---|---|
| 175 | 150 | 125 | 100 | 75 |

**Danton**

This model is simply the Bufalo without the grip safety. The slide has the Danton name stamped on it, and the grips have it molded into them. This pistol was manufactured between 1925 and 1933.

| Exc. | V.G. | Good | Fair | Poor |
|---|---|---|---|---|
| 175 | 150 | 125 | 100 | 75 |

**Llama**

There were and are many different models produced under this banner. They are all based appearance-wise on the Colt 1911, although many differ internally. They are all marked in similar fashion: before 1945 "Gabilondo y Cia Elgoibar (Espana) Cal.---"; on the models produced after 1945, the name Llama appears in addition to the original marking.

**Model 1**

This pistol is chambered for the 7.65mm and is a blowback-operated design. It was introduced in 1933.

| Exc. | V.G. | Good | Fair | Poor |
|---|---|---|---|---|
| 200 | 175 | 150 | 100 | 75 |

### Model 2
This model is similar to the Model 1 except that it is chambered for the 9mm short cartridge.

| Exc. | V.G. | Good | Fair | Poor |
|------|------|------|------|------|
| 225 | 200 | 175 | 125 | 100 |

### Model 3
This model is simply the Model 2 with minor internal improvements. It was manufactured between 1936 and 1945.

| Exc. | V.G. | Good | Fair | Poor |
|------|------|------|------|------|
| 210 | 185 | 165 | 135 | 110 |

### Model 3A
This is simply the Model 3 with an added grip safety. It was introduced in 1955.

| Exc. | V.G. | Good | Fair | Poor |
|------|------|------|------|------|
| 225 | 200 | 175 | 125 | 100 |

### Model 4
This model is a locked-breech design chambered for the .380 ACP cartridge and was introduced in 1931. It has no grip safety and is actually the first pistol in the Llama line.

| Exc. | V.G. | Good | Fair | Poor |
|------|------|------|------|------|
| 200 | 175 | 150 | 100 | 75 |

### Model 5
This model is the same as the Model 4 but produced for import to the U.S.A. and marked "Made in Spain."

| Exc. | V.G. | Good | Fair | Poor |
|------|------|------|------|------|
| 200 | 175 | 150 | 100 | 75 |

### Model 6
This model is similar to the Model 4 without a grip safety.

| Exc. | V.G. | Good | Fair | Poor |
|------|------|------|------|------|
| 200 | 175 | 150 | 100 | 75 |

### Model 7
This model has a locked breech and is chambered for the .38 Super cartridge. It was manufactured from 1932 until 1954.

| Exc. | V.G. | Good | Fair | Poor |
|------|------|------|------|------|
| 250 | 225 | 200 | 150 | 110 |

### Model 8
This model is similar to the Model 7, chambered for .38 Auto or 9mm Largo. It also features a grip safety. It was introduced in 1955.

| Exc. | V.G. | Good | Fair | Poor |
|------|------|------|------|------|
| 275 | 250 | 225 | 175 | 125 |

### Model 9
This is a larger pistol chambered for the 9mm Largo, 7.65 Parabellum, and the .45 ACP cartridges. It has no grip safety and fires from a locked breech. It was manufactured between 1936 and 1954.

| Exc. | V.G. | Good | Fair | Poor |
|------|------|------|------|------|
| 300 | 275 | 250 | 200 | 125 |

### Model 9A
This model is similar to the Model 9, with a grip safety.

| Exc. | V.G. | Good | Fair | Poor |
|------|------|------|------|------|
| 300 | 275 | 250 | 200 | 125 |

### Model 10
This is a locked breech pistol chambered for 7.65mm or .32 ACP. It was manufactured between 1935 and 1954.

| Exc. | V.G. | Good | Fair | Poor |
|------|------|------|------|------|
| 200 | 175 | 150 | 125 | 75 |

### Model 10A
This model is similar to the Model 10, with an added grip safety. It was introduced in 1954.

| Exc. | V.G. | Good | Fair | Poor |
|------|------|------|------|------|
| 225 | 200 | 175 | 150 | 100 |

### Model 11
This model is a departure from the usual Llama designs. It is chambered for 9mm Parabellum and has a 5" barrel with a correspondingly longer slide. The grip is longer and has a finger rest at its base. The magazine holds 9 rounds. This model has no grip safety and has a ring-type hammer. The finish is blued, with grooved walnut grips. It was manufactured between 1936 and 1954.

| Exc. | V.G. | Good | Fair | Poor |
|------|------|------|------|------|
| 300 | 275 | 250 | 200 | 125 |

### Models 12, 13 and 14
See Ruby Extra.

### Model 15
This model is a blowback-operated pistol chambered for the .22 l.r. cartridge. It is finished in either blue, chrome, or nickel-plate, with a variety of grips offered. This model resembles a diminutive Colt Government Model.

| Exc. | V.G. | Good | Fair | Poor |
|------|------|------|------|------|
| 250 | 225 | 200 | 150 | 100 |

### Model 16
This model is a deluxe version of the Model 15, that features engraving, adjustable sights, a ventilated rib and fancy grips.

| Exc. | V.G. | Good | Fair | Poor |
|------|------|------|------|------|
| 325 | 275 | 250 | 200 | 150 |

## Model 17

This is a smaller, more streamlined version of the Model 16, chambered for .22 short.

| Exc. | V.G. | Good | Fair | Poor |
|------|------|------|------|------|
| 300 | 250 | 225 | 175 | 125 |

## Mugica

Most of the Llama pistols were also produced for Jose Mugica, an Eibar gun dealer. These pistols are marked "Mugica-Eibar-Spain," and their values would not be affected.

## Ruby Extra

This designation was given to a number of revolvers manufactured by Gabilondo after 1950. They were all S&W copies and are as follows;

## Model 12

This model is a 6-shot, swingout, double-action revolver chambered for the .38 long cartridge. It has a 5" barrel and is blued, with a square butt and checkered wood grips.

| Exc. | V.G. | Good | Fair | Poor |
|------|------|------|------|------|
| 175 | 150 | 125 | 100 | 75 |

## Model 13

This model has a round butt, 4" or 6" vent-rib barrel, and adjustable sights. It is chambered for the .38 Special cartridge.

| Exc. | V.G. | Good | Fair | Poor |
|------|------|------|------|------|
| 200 | 175 | 150 | 125 | 100 |

## Model 14

This Model is similar to the Model 13 except that it is chambered for .22 l.r. or .32 cartridges.

| Exc. | V.G. | Good | Fair | Poor |
|------|------|------|------|------|
| 200 | 175 | 150 | 125 | 100 |

## Llama Model 26

This is a double-action revolver based on the Smith & Wesson design. It is chambered for the .38 Special cartridge. It has a 4" vent-rib barrel and adjustable sights.

| Exc. | V.G. | Good | Fair | Poor |
|------|------|------|------|------|
| 200 | 175 | 150 | 125 | 100 |

## Llama Model 27

This model is similar to the Model 26 but is chambered for the .32 long cartridge and has a 2" barrel.

| Exc. | V.G. | Good | Fair | Poor |
|------|------|------|------|------|
| 200 | 175 | 150 | 125 | 100 |

## Llama Model 28

This model is chambered for the .22 l.r. cartridge and has a 6" barrel.

| Exc. | V.G. | Good | Fair | Poor |
|------|------|------|------|------|
| 200 | 175 | 150 | 125 | 100 |

## Llama Omni

This is a double-action semi-automatic pistol chambered for the .45 ACP and the 9mm cartridges. It has a 4.25" barrel and a 7-round detachable magazine in .45 caliber and a 13-round magazine in 9mm. It has a double sear bar and three distinct safeties. The construction is all steel, and the finish is blued. It was discontinued in 1986.

| Exc. | V.G. | Good | Fair | Poor |
|------|------|------|------|------|
| 400 | 350 | 275 | 200 | 150 |

## Llama Small Frame Semi-Automatic

This is a blowback-operated, single-action, semi-automatic pistol chambered for the .22 l.r., .32 ACP, and the .380 ACP cartridges. In appearance it resembles a miniature 1911 A1 Colt. It has a 3-11/16" barrel and a 7-round detachable magazine. It is available either blued or satin chrome finished.
Satin Chrome Finish--Add $75.

| NIB | Exc. | V.G. | Good | Fair | Poor |
|-----|------|------|------|------|------|
| 325 | 250 | 200 | 150 | 110 | 85 |

## Llama Compact Frame Semi-Automatic

This is a compact, semi-automatic, single-action pistol chambered for the 9mm or the .45 ACP cartridges. It has a 4.25" barrel and either a 7- or 9-round detachable magazine. The finish is blued. It was introduced in 1986.

LLAMA DEEP BLUE FINISH
COMPACT FRAME AUTOMATIC .45, 9MM & .38 SUPER

| NIB | Exc. | V.G. | Good | Fair | Poor |
|-----|------|------|------|------|------|
| 375 | 300 | 250 | 200 | 150 | 100 |

## Llama Large Frame Semi-Automatic

This is a full-size 1911 A1-type semi-automatic pistol chambered for the 9mm, .38 Super, or the .45 ACP cartridges. It has a 5.25" barrel and weighs 36 ounces. It is available with either a 7-round or a 9-round detachable magazine, depending on the caliber. The finish is either blued or satin chrome.
Satin Chrome Finish--Add $125.

LLAMA DEEP BLUE FINISH
LARGE FRAME AUTOMATIC .45

LLAMA SATIN CHROME FINISH
LARGE FRAME AUTOMATIC .45

| NIB | Exc. | V.G. | Good | Fair | Poor |
|-----|------|------|------|------|------|
| 375 | 300 | 250 | 200 | 150 | 100 |

## Llama Model 82

This is a double-action semi-automatic pistol chambered for 9mm Parabellum. It has a 4.25" barrel with a three-dot sighting system. It has a 15-round detachable magazine, a loaded-chamber indicator, and an ambidextrous safety. The finish is blued, with black plastic grips. It was introduced in 1988.

LLAMA M-82 MATTE BLUE FINISH
9MM DA AUTOMATIC

| NIB | Exc. | V.G. | Good | Fair | Poor |
|-----|------|------|------|------|------|
| 975 | 850 | 550 | 450 | 350 | 250 |

## Llama Model 87 Competition

This is a competition pistol chambered for the 9mm Parabellum cartridge. It is based on the Model 82, with a compensator, special barrel bushing, and a bevelled magazine well. It has an squared and checkered triggerguard with an adjustable trigger. The finish is blued, and it was introduced in 1989.

| NIB | Exc. | V.G. | Good | Fair | Poor |
|-----|------|------|------|------|------|
| 1450 | 1250 | 950 | 700 | 550 | 400 |

## Llama Martial

This is a double-action revolver chambered for the .22 l.r. or the .38 Special cartridges. It has a 6-round swingout cylinder and is offered with a 4" or 6" barrel with adjustable sights. The finish is blued, with checkered hardwood grips. It was manufactured between 1969 and 1976.

| Exc. | V.G. | Good | Fair | Poor |
|------|------|------|------|------|
| 225 | 175 | 150 | 110 | 85 |

## Llama Comanche I

This is similar to the Martial, chambered for the .22 l.r. cartridge. It was manufactured between 1977 and 1982.

| Exc. | V.G. | Good | Fair | Poor |
|------|------|------|------|------|
| 250 | 200 | 175 | 125 | 100 |

### Llama Comanche II

This version is chambered for the .38 Special cartridge and was manufactured between 1977 and 1982.

| Exc. | V.G. | Good | Fair | Poor |
|------|------|------|------|------|
| 250  | 200  | 175  | 125  | 100  |

### Llama Comanche III

This is a .357 Magnum version in the Comanche series, offered with a 4", 6", or 8.5" barrel. The finish is blued, with checkered walnut grips; and the revolver is equipped with adjustable sights. It was introduced in 1975.
Satin Chrome Finish--Add 20 Percent.

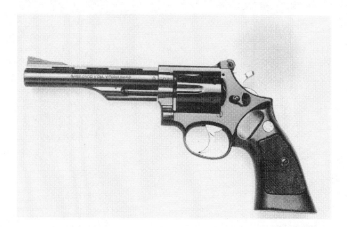

| NIB | Exc. | V.G. | Good | Fair | Poor |
|-----|------|------|------|------|------|
| 325 | 275  | 200  | 175  | 125  | 100  |

### Llama Super Comanche

This is a .44 Magnum, double-action version of the Comanche series. It is offered with a 6" or 8.5" vent-rib barrel with adjustable sights. The finish is blued, with checkered walnut grips.

| NIB | Exc. | V.G. | Good | Fair | Poor |
|-----|------|------|------|------|------|
| 425 | 325  | 250  | 225  | 175  | 125  |

# GALAND, C.F.
## Liege, Belgium

Charles Galand was a talented and well respected firearms inventor. In 1870 he patented a double-action lock that was accepted and used by Webley and Colt. He invented the "Velo-Dog" revolver, a design that was copied by more firearms companies than can be imagined. He produced weapons of his own under the trademark Galand Arms Factory. The Galand company went out of business during WWI.

### Galand, Galand & Sommerville, Galand Perrin

These three designations all apply to the same large, 6-shot, open-frame, double-action revolver made circa 1870. It features a unique ejection system which, by means of rotating a lever downward from the triggerguard; causes the barrel and cylinder to slide forward, leaving the ejector and the spent cases behind. This model is chambered for 7mm, 9mm, and 12mm. It was used briefly by the Russian navy and the Romanian army.

| Exc. | V.G. | Good | Fair | Poor |
|------|------|------|------|------|
| 350  | 325  | 275  | 200  | 150  |

### Velo-Dog

Galand actually invented this often copied revolver. It was originally open-top design with a fixed trigger and guard. Later models feature folding triggers and no triggerguards. The originals were chambered for the 5.5mm Velo-Dog cartridge. The .22 caliber and 6.35mm followed at a later date.

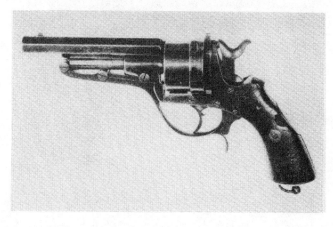

| Exc. | V.G. | Good | Fair | Poor |
|------|------|------|------|------|
| 150  | 125  | 100  | 75   | 50   |

### Le Novo

This was a very novel design for 1907. It is an open-topped, concealed hammer revolver chambered for 6.35mm. It has a folding trigger and a folding butt that covers and conceals the trigger. There is also a lever-actuated gear that removes the axis pin for ease of loading.

| Exc. | V.G. | Good | Fair | Poor |
|------|------|------|------|------|
| 200  | 175  | 125  | 100  | 75   |

### Tue-Tue

This is one of the best pocket revolver designs ever. It appeared in 1894, chambered for the .22 short, 5.5mm Velo-Dog, and 6.35mm. It has a solid frame, concealed hammer, folding trigger, and a swing-out cylinder with central extractor.

| Exc. | V.G. | Good | Fair | Poor |
|------|------|------|------|------|
| 200  | 175  | 150  | 100  | 75   |

## GALAND & SOMMERVILLE
Liege, Belgium
SEE--Galand

## GALEF
Zabala Hermanos & Antonio Zoli
Spain

### Zabala Double
This is an economical side by side chambered for 10, 12, 16, and 20 gauge. It was offered with barrel lengths from 22" to 30", with various chokes. It is a boxlock with extractors and has a checkered hardwood stock.

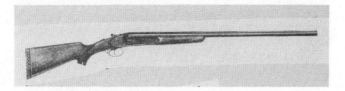

| Exc. | V.G. | Good | Fair | Poor |
|---|---|---|---|---|
| 225 | 200 | 150 | 100 | 75 |

### Companion
This model is a single-barrel break open with an underlever. It folds in half for transport. It is chambered for all gauges plus .410 and was offered with a 28" or 30" full-choke barrel. The design is hammerless, and the checkered stock has a pistol grip.

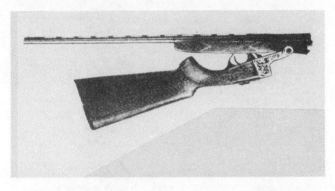

| Exc. | V.G. | Good | Fair | Poor |
|---|---|---|---|---|
| 125 | 100 | 75 | 50 | 25 |

### Monte Carlo Trap
This model is a single-barrelled break open chambered for 12 gauge, with a 32" vent-rib, full-choke barrel. It is hammerless with an underlever and has a checkered pistolgrip Monte Carlo stock.

| Exc. | V.G. | Good | Fair | Poor |
|---|---|---|---|---|
| 200 | 175 | 150 | 100 | 75 |

### Silver Snipe, Golden Snipe, and Silver Hawk
SEE--Antonio Zoli

## GALESI, INDUSTRIA ARMI
Brescia, Italy

The firm of Armi Galesi was founded in 1914 and was well known in Italy for a number of years. Their products were not imported until after WWII, and then they became known worldwide and especially in the U.S.A. The company was recently renamed "Rigarmi."

### Galesi
This was the first model produced back in 1914. It is a blowback-operated semi-automatic chambered for the 6.35mm

cartridge. It is basically a copy of the 1906 Browning, without a grip safety. This model was discontinued by WWI and was produced again after the war until it was finally dropped in 1923 in favor of a slightly improved model that was produced until 1930.

| Exc. | V.G. | Good | Fair | Poor |
|---|---|---|---|---|
| 230 | 225 | 175 | 125 | 100 |

### Model 1930
This totally redesigned model is chambered for the 6.35mm or the 7.65mm. It is based on the 1910 Browning design and was striker-fired with a groove on the top of the barrel for a sight. In 1936 a 9mm short version was introduced. This pistol is blued with checkered plastic grips, and the slide is marked "Brevetto Mod. 1930." The pre-war designation was the Model 6.

| Exc. | V.G. | Good | Fair | Poor |
|---|---|---|---|---|
| 250 | 225 | 175 | 125 | 100 |

### Model 9
This model is an improved version of the Model 6 and was introduced in 1950 and is chambered for the .22 rimfire, 6.35mm, and the 7.65mm cartridges. The Model 9 is finished in blue or plated. The distinct finger-groove grips make it easy to spot this model. This was the last variation before the name change. The Model 9 pistols that were imported into the U.S. are marked "Hijo" and imported by Sloan & Co. of New York.

| Exc. | V.G. | Good | Fair | Poor |
|---|---|---|---|---|
| 175 | 150 | 125 | 100 | 75 |

### Rigarmi
This pistol is a copy of the Walther PP, chambered for the .22 l.r., 6.35mm, and the 7.65mm cartridge. They are finished in a variety of ways and are marked "Rigarmi Brescia."

| Exc. | V.G. | Good | Fair | Poor |
|---|---|---|---|---|
| 125 | 100 | 75 | 50 | 25 |

## GALIL
Israel Military Industries
Israel
Importer--Action Arms, Ltd.
Philadelphia, Pennsylvania

This is the excellent Israeli-made military rifle in its civilian semi-automatic mode. Until recently this rifle was imported by Magnum research in Minneapolis, Minnesota. Sadly this firearm falls into the legislation-caused hysteria regarding "assault rifles" that has swept our country, and it presently cannot be imported. The price fluctuations from one part of the country to another preclude any accurate evaluation of this weapon at this time. We list the various models for reference purposes but recommend an independent appraisal if a transaction is contemplated.

## Model AR

This model is chambered in .223 or .308 and features either a 16" or a 19" barrel. It is gas-operated with a rotating bolt and has a gas piston system similar to the Soviet AK. The finish is parkerized, and it features the flip "Tritium" night sights. It has a folding stock. The .308 version would be higher priced.

## Model ARM

This version is similar to the AR. with a ventilated wood handguard and a folding bipod and carrying handle.

## Sniper Rifle

This is a precision-built version of the semi-automatic Galil design, that holds exacting tolerances for purposes of accuracy. It features a 20" heavy barrel and an adjustable wooden stock, and a 6x40 scope is furnished in addition to the Tritium night sights. It is supplied with two 25-shot magazines and a fitted carrying case. This is a very scarce commodity. There were very few imported.

## Hadar II

This version is simply the Galil action in a walnut, one-piece, thumbhole stock. It features a pistol grip and has an 18.5" barrel. This model has a 4-shot magazine and adjustable sight and is furnished with a recoil pad. This model was introduced in 1989.

| NIB | Exc. | V.G. | Good | Fair | Poor |
|-----|------|------|------|------|------|
| 1000 | 900 | 800 | 650 | 550 | 450 |

# GALLAGER
### Richardson & Overman
### Philadelphia, Pennsylvania

## Gallager Carbine

This is a breech-loading carbine chambered for .50-caliber percussion. The 22.25" round barrel slides forward to load. The last 5,000 produced are chambered for the .56-62 Spencer metallic cartridge. The frame is iron, as are the mountings and the patch box. There is a saddle ring on a slide bar, and the barrel is blued with the remaining metal case-colored. The stock is walnut, and there is no forend. This carbine was used extensively by union forces during the Civil War, although it was invented by M. J. Gallager of Savannah, Georgia. There were 28,000 manufactured (23,000 percussion and 5,000 using the Spencer cartridge) during the 1860's.

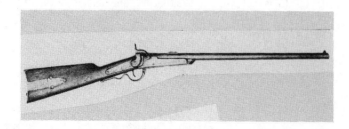

### Percussion Model

| Exc. | V.G. | Good | Fair | Poor |
|------|------|------|------|------|
| 750 | 675 | 550 | 450 | 350 |

### Spencer Cartridge Model

| Exc. | V.G. | Good | Fair | Poor |
|------|------|------|------|------|
| 650 | 575 | 450 | 350 | 300 |

# GAMBA, RENATO
### Gardone V. T., Italy

## Shotguns SxS
## Hunter Super

This side-by-side double-barrel is chambered for 12-gauge only. It was offered in a variety of barrel lengths and chokes. It has an Anson and Deeley boxlock action. The gun has double triggers and extractors. The receiver is engraved and silver-plated.

| NIB | Exc. | V.G. | Good | Fair | Poor |
|-----|------|------|------|------|------|
| 1500 | 1350 | 1050 | 850 | 650 | 500 |

## Principessa

This model is chambered for 12 or 20-gauge and is quite similar to the Hunter Super, with an English-style, hand-checkered stock and a higher degree of engraving.

| NIB | Exc. | V.G. | Good | Fair | Poor |
|-----|------|------|------|------|------|
| 2000 | 1850 | 1500 | 1250 | 900 | 700 |

## Oxford 90

This model is chambered for 12 or 20 gauge and is available in various barrel lengths and chokes. This is a full sidelock action that utilizes the Purdey locking system. It features double triggers, automatic ejectors, and a high-grade, hand-checkered, English-style walnut stock.

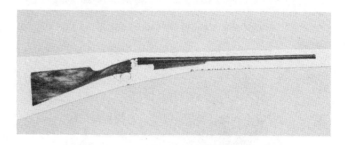

| NIB | Exc. | V.G. | Good | Fair | Poor |
|-----|------|------|------|------|------|
| 2750 | 2500 | 2000 | 1750 | 1250 | 950 |

## London

This model is chambered for 12 or 20 gauge and is offered in various barrel lengths and chokes. It features the Holland & Holland sidelock system, either double or single-selective trigger, automatic ejectors, and a high-grade, hand-checkered, English-style stock.

| NIB | Exc. | V.G. | Good | Fair | Poor |
|-----|------|------|------|------|------|
| 6750 | 6000 | 5000 | 4000 | 2500 | 2000 |

## London Royal

This model is quite similar to the standard London, with an engraved gamescene.

| NIB | Exc. | V.G. | Good | Fair | Poor |
|-----|------|------|------|------|------|
| 8000 | 6500 | 5500 | 4500 | 3000 | 2500 |

## Ambassador Golden Black

This model is chambered for 12 and 20 gauge and also features the Holland & Holland sidelock-type action. It is offered in various barrel lengths and chock combinations and has a single-selective trigger, automatic ejectors, and a single gold line engraved on the barrels and the frame. The stock is high-grade, hand-checkered walnut.

| NIB | Exc. | V.G. | Good | Fair | Poor |
|---|---|---|---|---|---|
| 14650 | 13500 | 10000 | 7500 | 6500 | 5500 |

### Ambassador Executive
This model is chambered for 12 and 20 gauge and is totally hand-built to the customer's specification. It is Gamba's best quality model.

| NIB | Exc. | V.G. | Good | Fair | Poor |
|---|---|---|---|---|---|
| 23500 | 20000 | 17500 | 14500 | 10000 | 7500 |

## Over and Under Shotguns
### Country Model
This gun is chambered for 12 and 20 gauge and has barrel lengths of 28" or 30", with a ventilated rib. The gun features double triggers, extractors, and a hand-checkered walnut stock.

| NIB | Exc. | V.G. | Good | Fair | Poor |
|---|---|---|---|---|---|
| 775 | 650 | 500 | 450 | 375 | 300 |

### Grifone Model
This model is chambered for 12 and 20 gauge and features 26", 28", or 30" vent-rib barrels, a single-selective trigger, and automatic ejectors. The boxlock action is silver-plated, and the gun features a deluxe, hand-checkered walnut stock. This model is available with screw-in chokes, and this would add 10 percent to the values.

| NIB | Exc. | V.G. | Good | Fair | Poor |
|---|---|---|---|---|---|
| 950 | 850 | 750 | 650 | 500 | 400 |

### Europa 2000
This model is chambered for 12 gauge only. It is available in various barrel lengths and choke combinations. It has an engraved, silver-plated, boxlock action with false sideplates. The gun has a single-selective trigger, automatic ejectors, and a hand-checkered walnut stock.

| NIB | Exc. | V.G. | Good | Fair | Poor |
|---|---|---|---|---|---|
| 1450 | 1250 | 1000 | 750 | 650 | 500 |

### Grinta Trap and Skeet
This model is chambered in 12 gauge and has either 26" skeet barrels or 30" full-choke barrels. It features a single selective trigger, automatic ejectors, and some engraving. The stock is hand-checkered walnut.

| NIB | Exc. | V.G. | Good | Fair | Poor |
|---|---|---|---|---|---|
| 1700 | 1500 | 1200 | 1000 | 750 | 500 |

### Victory Trap and Skeet
This model is similar to the Grinta, with fancier wood and a greater amount of engraving.

| NIB | Exc. | V.G. | Good | Fair | Poor |
|---|---|---|---|---|---|
| 1900 | 1700 | 1400 | 1200 | 900 | 700 |

### Edinburg Match
This model is similar to the Victory model, with slightly different engraving patterns.

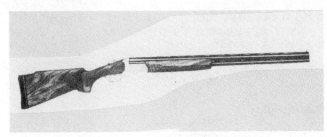

| NIB | Exc. | V.G. | Good | Fair | Poor |
|---|---|---|---|---|---|
| 1950 | 1750 | 1450 | 1250 | 950 | 750 |

### Boyern 88 Combination Gun
This model is an Over/Under with the top barrel chambered for 12 gauge over various rifle calibers. The action is gamescene-engraved and coin-finished. The gun features double triggers, extractors, and a fancy hand-checkered walnut stock with a recoil pad standard.

| NIB | Exc. | V.G. | Good | Fair | Poor |
|---|---|---|---|---|---|
| 1500 | 1300 | 1000 | 800 | 550 | 350 |

## Rifles
### Safari Express
This model is a double-barrelled rifle chambered for 7x65R, 9.3x74R, or .375 H&H. The barrels are 25" long and feature open sights. The action is an underlug with a Greener crossbolt. The gun features double triggers, automatic ejectors, and a coin-finished scroll-engraved receiver. It has a deluxe, hand-checkered walnut stock with a standard recoil pad.

| NIB | Exc. | V.G. | Good | Fair | Poor |
|---|---|---|---|---|---|
| 6600 | 6000 | 5500 | 4750 | 3750 | 2500 |

### Mustang
This gun is a sidelock single-barrel, chambered for 5.6x50, 6.5x57R, 7x65R, .222 Rem., .270 Win., or .30-06. This model has double-set triggers and a fully engraved sidelock action. It has the highest quality hand-checkered walnut stock.

| NIB | Exc. | V.G. | Good | Fair | Poor |
|---|---|---|---|---|---|
| 13000 | 12000 | 10000 | 7500 | 5000 | 4000 |

### RGZ 1000
This model uses a modified Mauser 98 bolt action with a 20.5" barrel. It is chambered for 7x64, .270 Win., 7mm Rem. Mag., and .300 Win. Mag. This rifle features a hand-checkered, walnut pistol-grip stock with a cheek piece.

| NIB | Exc. | V.G. | Good | Fair | Poor |
|---|---|---|---|---|---|
| 1300 | 1100 | 950 | 750 | 500 | 400 |

### RGX 1000 Express
This model is similar to the RGZ 1000, with double-set triggers and a 23.75" barrel.

| NIB | Exc. | V.G. | Good | Fair | Poor |
|---|---|---|---|---|---|
| 1450 | 1250 | 1000 | 800 | 600 | 500 |

## Pistols
### SAB G90
This model is a double-action semi-automatic chambered for either 7.65 Parabellum or 9 mm. It has a 4.75" barrel and features a 15-shot detachable magazine. The finish is either blued or chrome-plated with smooth, uncheckered walnut grips.

| NIB | Exc. | V.G. | Good | Fair | Poor |
|---|---|---|---|---|---|
| 675 | 625 | 550 | 500 | 350 | 275 |

### SAB G91 Compact
This model is similar to the SAB G90, with a 3.5" barrel and a 12-shot magazine.

| NIB | Exc. | V.G. | Good | Fair | Poor |
|---|---|---|---|---|---|
| 695 | 650 | 600 | 500 | 400 | 325 |

### Trident Fast Action
This is a 6-shot, swingout-cylinder revolver chambered for the .32 S&W or the .38 Special cartridge. It is offered with a 2.5" or 3" barrel and is double-actioned. The finish is blued, with checkered walnut grips.

| NIB | Exc. | V.G. | Good | Fair | Poor |
|---|---|---|---|---|---|
| 600 | 525 | 450 | 400 | 300 | 225 |

### Trident Super
This model is quite similar to the Trident Fast Action, with a 4" ventilated rib barrel.

| NIB | Exc. | V.G. | Good | Fair | Poor |
|---|---|---|---|---|---|
| 650 | 600 | 525 | 475 | 325 | 250 |

**Trident Match 900**
This model is similar to the Trident Super but is intended to be a match-grade target revolver. It features a 6" heavy barrel with adjustable sights and target-type, checkered walnut grips.

| NIB | Exc. | V.G. | Good | Fair | Poor |
|------|------|------|------|------|------|
| 1000 | 900 | 750 | 600 | 450 | 300 |

# GARAND
### Various

**Garand**
This was the service rifle of the U.S. Armed Forces, and it has the distinction of being the first semi-automatic rifle to be adopted as a service rifle. It was adopted in 1932 and actually came into service in 1936. It served with distinction until it was replaced in 1957 by the M14. It was used throughout WWII and the Korean conflict. There were M1 Garands used in Vietnam up to 1963. When the manufacture ceased in the 1950's, there had been over 5,500,000 produced. They were made by Springfield Armory, Springfield, Massachusetts; Winchester Arms Co., New Haven, Connecticut; Harrington & Richardson, Worcester, Massachusetts; and International Harvester Corp., various locations.

The Garand or M1, as it was designated, is chambered for the .30-06 cartridge and is a gas-operated, semi- automatic rifle. It has a 24" barrel, with adjustable military sights. It has an 8-round, internal box magazine that is fed with a clip that is automatically ejected after the rifle is emptied. This was the main criticism of the weapon--the limited capacity and the tell-tale ping that the empty clip emitted upon ejection. The Garand has a parkerized finish and a wood stock, with a forend and upper handguard. There are sling swivels and a bayonet lug. The collector should be aware that we are seeing recently imported Garand rifles on the market, and they are not to be confused with the collectible versions that are also sold. The recent models will have the importer's name and address stamped on the rifle, and this should be looked for before a purchase is made. These newly imported rifles are fine weapons, and most function in a totally satisfactory manner; but the collectibility, and therefore the value, is simply not there.

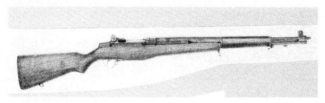

**Recent Imports**

| Exc. | V.G. | Good | Fair | Poor |
|------|------|------|------|------|
| 350 | 325 | 300 | 200 | 150 |

**Collectors Grade**

| Exc. | V.G. | Good | Fair | Poor |
|------|------|------|------|------|
| 750 | 650 | 550 | 450 | 350 |

**M1C or M1D Garand**
These were the designations for the first and second model snipers rifles issued during WWII. They are similar to the standard Garand, with either a Lyman or a Weaver scope in a detachable mount. There is also a detachable leather cheekpiece, as well as an added flash suppressor. There is also a recently imported snipers rifle available on the market, and the same cautions apply as on the standard model.

**Recent Import**

| Exc. | V.G. | Good | Fair | Poor |
|------|------|------|------|------|
| 800 | 700 | 600 | 500 | 400 |

**Collectors Grade**

| Exc. | V.G. | Good | Fair | Poor |
|------|------|------|------|------|
| 1600 | 1450 | 1200 | 1000 | 750 |

# GARATE, ANITUA
### Eibar, Spain

This company made many of the poor-quality "Eibar"-type pistols but were also awarded a contract by the British during WWI. They were able to produce quality work when the market called for it. The company went out of business at the beginning of the Spanish Civil War.

**Charola**
This very rare and early semi-automatic pistol was first made in 1897. It is the smallest-caliber locked-breech pistol ever made, chambered for the 5.5mm Clement--a bottlenecked, rimless cartridge. The Charola was also produced under license in Belgium.

| Exc. | V.G. | Good | Fair | Poor |
|------|------|------|------|------|
| 250 | 225 | 175 | 125 | 90 |

**Cosmopolite**
Made from 1920-1930, this is a .38 caliber copy of the Colt Police Positive.

| Exc. | V.G. | Good | Fair | Poor |
|------|------|------|------|------|
| 175 | 150 | 125 | 100 | 75 |

**El Lunar**
This revolver was made for the French army in 1915--1916. The revolver resembles a Colt Police Positive with the barrel of the French Mle 1892. It is chambered for the 8mm Lebel.

| Exc. | V.G. | Good | Fair | Poor |
|------|------|------|------|------|
| 200 | 175 | 150 | 125 | 100 |

**G.A.C.**
This is a copy of the Smith & Wesson Military & Police revolver. It was manufactured between 1930 and 1936, chambered for .32-20 caliber. There have been some noted in .38 caliber. They are marked "G.A.C. Firearms Mfg. Co." All were produced for export sales.

| Exc. | V.G. | Good | Fair | Poor |
|------|------|------|------|------|
| 175 | 150 | 125 | 100 | 75 |

**Garate, Anitua**
Produced under the company name, this is a typical 8-shot, 7.65mm, "Eibar" semi-automatic.

| Exc. | V.G. | Good | Fair | Poor |
|------|------|------|------|------|
| 150 | 125 | 100 | 75 | 50 |

## Garate, Anitua

This pistol was also produced under the company's own name but became known as "Pistol OP No. 1 Mark 1." It was accepted for duty by the British army November 8, 1915, and declared obsolete on November 15, 1921. It is a 5" ribbed-barrel, double-action, breakopen revolver. It weighs 1.5 lbs. and is chambered for the .455 cartridge. This was strictly a military item; it was never offered for commercial sale.

| Exc. | V.G. | Good | Fair | Poor |
|------|------|------|------|------|
| 275 | 250 | 200 | 150 | 100 |

## La Lira

This is a close-to-identical copy of the Mannlicher Model 1901 with three exceptions--the La Lira is chambered for the .32ACP; it is fed by a removable magazine; and the quality is not nearly as good as the Mannlicher. The pistol is marked "System La Lira" on the breech; "Para Cartoucho Browning 7.65mm," on the barrel; and "G.A.C.," on the grips. It was only produced prior to WWI and is quite rare.

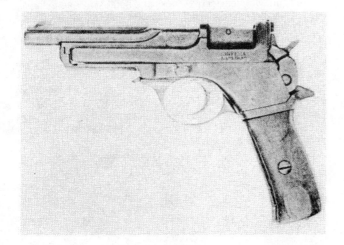

| Exc. | V.G. | Good | Fair | Poor |
|------|------|------|------|------|
| 200 | 175 | 150 | 125 | 100 |

## L'Eclair

This 6-shot, solid-frame revolver chambered for the 5.5mm Velo-Dog was made from 1900-1914.

| Exc. | V.G. | Good | Fair | Poor |
|------|------|------|------|------|
| 150 | 125 | 100 | 75 | 50 |

## Sprinter

This Browning 1906 copy is chambered for the 6.35mm cartridge. It was made before WWI and is marked "The Best Automatique Pistol Sprinter Patent 6.35mm Cartridge."

| Exc. | V.G. | Good | Fair | Poor |
|------|------|------|------|------|
| 150 | 125 | 100 | 75 | 50 |

## Triumph

This pistol is identical to the La Lira model but is marked "Triumph Automatic Pistol." The different designation probably meant an export model.

| Exc. | V.G. | Good | Fair | Poor |
|------|------|------|------|------|
| 200 | 175 | 150 | 125 | 100 |

# GARATE, HERMANOS
### Ermua, Spain

## Cantabria

This is a hinged-trigger, breakopen revolver chambered for the 6.35mm cartridge. The pistol has a concealed hammer with cocking spur and a peculiar short barrel that resembles the slide on a semi-automatic. The name "Cantabria" is stamped on the left side.

| Exc. | V.G. | Good | Fair | Poor |
|------|------|------|------|------|
| 175 | 150 | 125 | 100 | 75 |

## Velo-Stark

A typically poor-quality, solid-frame, "Velo-Dog" revolver with concealed hammer and folding trigger.

| Exc. | V.G. | Good | Fair | Poor |
|------|------|------|------|------|
| 150 | 125 | 90 | 65 | 40 |

# GARBI
### Eibar, Spain
**Importer--W. L. Moore and Co.Westlake Village, California**

## Model 51-A

This model is chambered for 12 gauge only. It has various barrel lengths and chokes, double triggers, extractors, a case-hardened receiver, and a checkered walnut straight-grip stock.

| Exc. | V.G. | Good | Fair | Poor |
|------|------|------|------|------|
| 475 | 450 | 400 | 300 | 225 |

## Model 51-B

This model is similar to the Model 51-A except that it is chambered for 16 and 20 gauge, as well as 12 gauge. It features automatic ejectors and has either a case-hardened or coin-finished receiver.

| Exc. | V.G. | Good | Fair | Poor |
|------|------|------|------|------|
| 800 | 725 | 650 | 500 | 375 |

## Model 60-A

This model is chambered for 12 gauge only and was offered with various barrel lengths and chokes. It has a true sidelock action, cocking indicators, and a scroll-engraved receiver. The hand-checkered walnut stock is offered in either a straight or pistol grip.

| Exc. | V.G. | Good | Fair | Poor |
|------|------|------|------|------|
| 700 | 625 | 550 | 400 | 275 |

## Model 60-B

This model is similar to the Model 60-A except that it is chambered for 16 and 20 gauge as well as 12 gauge. It has automatic ejectors, a greater degree of engraving, and is offered with the English-style grip only.

| Exc. | V.G. | Good | Fair | Poor |
|------|------|------|------|------|
| 1250 | 1100 | 900 | 700 | 500 |

### Model 62-A

This model is chambered in 12 gauge, with a choice of various barrel lengths and chokes. It features double triggers, extractors, and a true sidelock action that is moderately engraved. It features cocking indicators and a hand-checkered walnut stock.

| Exc. | V.G. | Good | Fair | Poor |
|------|------|------|------|------|
| 725 | 650 | 500 | 425 | 300 |

### Model 62-B

This model is similar to the Model 62-A except that it is chambered for 16 and 20 gauge as well as 12 gauge. It features various barrel lengths and chokes, double triggers, automatic ejectors, and a heavily engraved case-hardened or coin-finished receiver. The hand-checkered walnut stock is available with a straight grip only.

| Exc. | V.G. | Good | Fair | Poor |
|------|------|------|------|------|
| 1200 | 1050 | 850 | 650 | 450 |

### Model 71

This model is chambered for 12, 16, or 20 gauge. It is available in various barrel lengths and choke combinations. It features a Holland & Holland style, fully detachable sidelock with automatic ejectors and a single-selective trigger. It is engraved with fine English-style scrollwork and has a hand-rubbed, hand-checkered walnut stock. This model was discontinued in 1988.

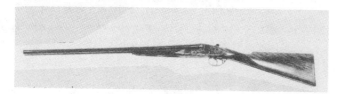

| Exc. | V.G. | Good | Fair | Poor |
|------|------|------|------|------|
| 2250 | 2000 | 1800 | 1500 | 1100 |

### Model 100

This model is available in 12, 16, or 20 gauge and also features the Holland & Holland detachable sidelock. It has chopper-lump barrels, automatic ejectors, and a single trigger. The engraving is in the Purdy style, and the hand-checkered walnut stock is oil-finished.

| NIB | Exc. | V.G. | Good | Fair | Poor |
|-----|------|------|------|------|------|
| 3500 | 3250 | 2750 | 2250 | 1750 | 1500 |

### Model 101

This model is very similar to the Model 100 except that the engraving style is in the floral pattern.

| NIB | Exc. | V.G. | Good | Fair | Poor |
|-----|------|------|------|------|------|
| 4000 | 3750 | 3250 | 2500 | 2000 | 1750 |

### Model 102

This model is similar to the Model 101 except that it is also available in 28 gauge and features the large scroll engraving seen on Holland & Holland firearms. This model was discontinued in 1988.

| Exc. | V.G. | Good | Fair | Poor |
|------|------|------|------|------|
| 4000 | 3750 | 3200 | 2500 | 2000 |

### Model 103A

This model differs from the Model 102 in the style and volume of engraving.

| NIB | Exc. | V.G. | Good | Fair | Poor |
|-----|------|------|------|------|------|
| 5500 | 5000 | 4500 | 3750 | 3000 | 2500 |

### Model 103B

This model is available in 12, 16, 20, or 28 gauge. It features various barrel lengths and choke combinations. The action is the Holland & Holland style sidelock. It has chopper-lump barrels and a Holland & Holland easy-opening mechanism, automatic ejectors, single-selective trigger, and Purdy-type scroll engraving.

| NIB | Exc. | V.G. | Good | Fair | Poor |
|-----|------|------|------|------|------|
| 7500 | 6750 | 6000 | 4250 | 3500 | 3000 |

### Model 120

This model is similar to the Model 103B but features gamescene engravings.

| NIB | Exc. | V.G. | Good | Fair | Poor |
|-----|------|------|------|------|------|
| 7000 | 6250 | 5500 | 3750 | 3000 | 2500 |

### Model 200

This model is similar to the Model 120 but is a magnum-proofed gun with heavier duty locks and floral-style engraving.

| NIB | Exc. | V.G. | Good | Fair | Poor |
|-----|------|------|------|------|------|
| 7250 | 6500 | 5750 | 4000 | 3250 | 2750 |

### Model Special AG

This model is available in 12, 16, 20, or 28 gauge with various barrel lengths and choke combinations. It has a single-selective trigger, automatic ejectors, and a hand-detachable Holland & Holland sidelock action. The gun is profusely covered with large scroll engraving and has a high-grade, hand-checkered walnut stock. This is Garbi's best quality gun.

| NIB | Exc. | V.G. | Good | Fair | Poor |
|-----|------|------|------|------|------|
| 7600 | 6800 | 6200 | 4500 | 3750 | 3200 |

# GARCIA
### SEE--Sako

This sporting goods dealer imported the fine line of Sako rifles, as well as others, for a number of years.

# GARRET, J.& F. CO.
### Greensboro, North Carolina

**Garrett Single Shot Pistol**

This pistol is chambered for .54 caliber and utilizes the percussion ignition system. It has an 8.5" round barrel with a flared-tip swivel ramrod mounted beneath it. The frame is polished brass, and the barrel is in the white. The round butt has two-piece walnut grips. There is no name marking on this pistol-- only the letters "G.W." or "S.R." on the breech. There were approximately 500 manufactured in 1862 and 1863. Some believe that this was a Confederate pistol, but others claim that it was not a Confederate arm at all but rather a secondary martial Union pistol. There is no definitive proof either way--so the controversy will continue.

| Exc. | V.G. | Good | Fair | Poor |
|------|------|------|------|------|
| 3000 | 2500 | 2000 | 1500 | 1000 |

# GASSER, LEOPOLD
### Ottakring, Austria

This company was a large revolver manufacturer that operated in the last half of the 1800's. They produced service revolvers for the Austrian army, as well as commercial models that were sold throughout Austria, Hungary, and the Balkan nations.

## M1870

This is a large, open-frame revolver. It is 14.75" long, with a 9.3" barrel. The weight is 52 ounces, and it is chambered for the 11mm cartridge. The cylinder holds 6 shots. The lock work is double action. The revolver is marked "Gasser Patent, Guss Stahl." It also bears an Austrian eagle and an apple pierced by an arrow, with the words "Schutz Mark."

| Exc. | V.G. | Good | Fair | Poor |
|------|------|------|------|------|
| 375 | 325 | 250 | 175 | 125 |

## M1870/74

This is an improved version of the M1870 with a steel frame instead of iron. Outwardly it is identical.

| Exc. | V.G. | Good | Fair | Poor |
|------|------|------|------|------|
| 375 | 325 | 250 | 175 | 125 |

## Gasser-Kropatschek M1876

This reduced-sized version of the M1870/74 weighs 1 lb. 11 ozs. It is chambered for the 9mm cartridge.

| Exc. | V.G. | Good | Fair | Poor |
|------|------|------|------|------|
| 300 | 225 | 175 | 125 | 100 |

## Montenegrin Gasser

This model designation is somewhat vague in that it encompasses many different variations rather than one specific revolver. These revolvers are usually breakopens with top straps chambered for the 10.7mm cartridge. They are somewhat smaller than other Gasser models, with 5"--6" barrels and cylinder capacity of only 5 rounds. They are often highly decorated with engraving, silver and gold inlay, and ivory or bone grips. This model was also made, under license, in Belgium.

Values given are for the plain, unadorned model. Embellished models will need individual appraisal.

| Exc. | V.G. | Good | Fair | Poor |
|------|------|------|------|------|
| 400 | 325 | 250 | 200 | 150 |

## Rast & Gasser M1898

This was the Austrian service revolver of its time and the last model to be made under the Gasser banner. This is an 8-shot, solid-frame revolver with a loading gate and an integral ejector rod. The barrel is 4.75" long; and the weight, 28 ounces. It is chambered for the 8mm cartridge. It is a well-made revolver, with an inspection plate on the left side that allows nearly total access to the double-action lock work. The downfall of the M1898 was the lack of stopping power in the anemic cartridge for which it was chambered.

| Exc. | V.G. | Good | Fair | Poor |
|------|------|------|------|------|
| 275 | 225 | 175 | 125 | 100 |

# GATLING ARMS CO.
### Birmingham, England

This company existed for only two years, 1888-1890. It was formed to market the American Gatling gun in Europe and the Far East. It was undercapitalized and never really got off the ground. They did manage to manufacture and market one revolver, but this did not alter their fortunes.

## Dimancea

Designed by a Romanian army captain, this 6-shot, true hammerless, double-action revolver is chambered for the .38 or .45 caliber cartridges. The loading system is rather unique--a spur that resembles a hammer is pulled down, allowing the barrel and cylinder to pivot and to be pulled forward. During this motion the empty cases are ejected and new ones could be inserted. All these weapons are marked "The Gatling Arms and Ammunition Co. Birmingham"; some are also marked "Dimancea Patent."

| Exc. | V.G. | Good | Fair | Poor |
|------|------|------|------|------|
| 900 | 800 | 675 | 500 | 425 |

# GAULOIS
### St. Etienne, France
### SEE--Le Francaise

# GAVAGE, A.
### Liege, Belgium

The Gavage company produced a small, 7.65mm semi-automatic pistol from the late 1930's until the early 1940's. It is very similar in appearance to the Clement. It has a fixed barrel and a concealed hammer. The only identifying markings are "AG" molded into the grips. Some have been found bearing German Waffenamts. This pistol is quite rare.

| Exc. | V.G. | Good | Fair | Poor |
|------|------|------|------|------|
| 350 | 275 | 225 | 150 | 100 |

# GAZTANAGA, ISIDRO
### Eibar, Spain

This was yet another Eibar company that engaged in the manufacture of inexpensive, rather poor-quality pistols from the early 1900's until the Spanish civil war.

## Destroyer M1913

This 1906 Browning copy chambered for 6.35mm was produced through WWI.

| Exc. | V.G. | Good | Fair | Poor |
|------|------|------|------|------|
| 150  | 125  | 100  | 75   | 50   |

## Destroyer M1916

This is a typical "Eibar" design chambered for 7.65mm. It was produced for the French and could be found with either a 7-or 9-shot magazine. They are marked "Pistolet Automatique Destroyer I Gaztanaga Eibar."

| Exc. | V.G. | Good | Fair | Poor |
|------|------|------|------|------|
| 150  | 125  | 100  | 75   | 50   |

## Destroyer Revolver

This is a reasonably good quality .38 caliber copy of the Colt Police Positive.

| Exc. | V.G. | Good | Fair | Poor |
|------|------|------|------|------|
| 175  | 150  | 125  | 100  | 75   |

## Super Destroyer

This pistol was manufactured in 1933 after the company had reorganized. Externally it is a close copy of the popular Walther PP; however, internally it is the usual 1910 Browning design found on all the "Eibar" copies. It is chambered for the 7.65mm, and the slide is stamped "Pistola Automatica 7.65 Super Destroyer." The quality and finish is above the usual "Eibar" norm.

| Exc. | V.G. | Good | Fair | Poor |
|------|------|------|------|------|
| 175  | 150  | 125  | 100  | 75   |

## Surete

This is a modified "Destroyer" chambered for 7.65mm. It is marked "Cal. 7.65 Pistolet Automatique Surete" with "IG" stamped on the frame.

| Exc. | V.G. | Good | Fair | Poor |
|------|------|------|------|------|
| 175  | 150  | 125  | 100  | 75   |

# GECO
### Moscow, Gustave
### Hamburg, Germany

# GEHA
### Germany

This firearm consists of a surplus Mauser 98 rifle that has been rebarrelled and altered to fire the 12 gauge shotgun shell. This was accomplished in Germany at the end of WWI. The Treaty of Versailles allowed the Germans to make sporting weapons; and this, coupled with the fact that there were many leftover Mauser 98 rifles available, caused the idea of producing a 2-shot shotgun to come to fruition. They were sold on the world market, and obviously a great many were produced as they are quite common to this day. This gun has a 26.5" barrel and a full choke. There is a brass bead front sight, and the buttstock has a brass medallion inletted into each side, that is marked "Geha." The magazine holds one shell, giving the gun a 2-shot capacity.

| Exc. | V.G. | Good | Fair | Poor |
|------|------|------|------|------|
| 225  | 200  | 150  | 100  | 75   |

# GEM
### Bacon Arms Company
### Norwich, Connecticut
### SEE--Bacon Arms Company under their separate listing.

## Gem Pocket Revolver

This single-action revolver is chambered for the .22 rimfire cartridge and has a 1.25" octagonal barrel and a spur trigger. The frame is iron, and it is scroll-engraved and nickel-plated. The grips are either walnut or ivory and are of the birdshead configuration. The barrel is marked "Gem." There were few manufactured between 1878 and 1883.

| Exc. | V.G. | Good | Fair | Poor |
|------|------|------|------|------|
| 500  | 450  | 400  | 300  | 200  |

# GENEZ, A. G.
### New York, New York

## Pocket Pistol

This pistol was styled after the Henry Deringer of Philadelphia. It is chambered for .41 caliber percussion and has a 3" barrel, with German silver mountings and a walnut stock. This pistol was manufactured in the 1850s.

| Exc. | V.G. | Good | Fair | Poor |
|------|------|------|------|------|
| 750  | 675  | 550  | 400  | 300  |

# GENSCHOW, G.
### Hamburg, Germany

Genshow is a large maker of ammunition and has been since the nineteenth century. Prior to WWI they marketed two revolvers manufactured for them by outside sources.

## Geco

A number of revolvers were sold under this trademark. They were made by Arizmendi and chambered for the 6.35mm, 7.65mm, .32 long, and 8mm Lebel. These are essentially "Velo-Dog" types, but some are larger in size. The quality is poor; and they hold very little, if any, interest for collectors.

| Exc. | V.G. | Good | Fair | Poor |
|------|------|------|------|------|
| 150  | 125  | 100  | 75   | 50   |

## German Bulldog

These are heavier double-action revolvers with solid frames, integral ejector rods, and loading gates. They are chambered for .32, .38, and .45 calibers. The proofmarks indicate Belgian manufacture.

| Exc. | V.G. | Good | Fair | Poor |
|------|------|------|------|------|
| 150  | 125  | 100  | 75   | 50   |

# GERING, H. M.& CO.
### Arnstadt, Germany

## Leonhardt

This pistol is identical to the "Beholla" made by Becker. It had to be produced from the same blueprints. Gering made no other firearms, and this weapon had to be the result of wartime pressure.

| Exc. | V.G. | Good | Fair | Poor |
|------|------|------|------|------|
| 275  | 250  | 200  | 150  | 100  |

# GERMAN WWII SERVICE PISTOL

## P-38

This pistol was developed by Walther and was first known as the model "HP" in 1939. This model evolved into the P-38; and at the end of 1939, they were marked with the Walther code

"480." In 1940 the code was changed to "AC" for the Walther plant, and in 1941 the Mauser plant began production using the code "byf." Mauser pistols manufactured after January, 1945 were marked "svw." Later the Spreewerke plant at Spandua began production, and they used the code "cyq" or "cxq." These weapons were produced in various forms until the end of the war, and commercial production was continued at Walther after the end of WWII and continous to this day.

## P-38

The Pistole Model 38--or Model HP (for "Heerespistole") as it is also known--is a double-action semi-automatic that is recoil-operated and fires from a locked breech by means of an external hammer. It is chambered for the 9mm Parabellum and has a 5" barrel. The detachable magazine holds 8 rounds, and the sights are adjustable for windage. The finish is blued, with synthetic grips. The wartime version was produced by various companies between 1939 and 1945. Each variation has its own distinct markings.

## O Series Heerespistol

This was the first of the wartime P-38's and has a high-polish finish. It features both the Walther banner and the designation P-38. The serial number has five digits with the "0" prefix. These were very well finished and were produced in three different issues during 1939 and early 1940.

**1st Issue 0 Series**

| Exc. | V.G. | Good | Fair | Poor |
|------|------|------|------|------|
| 3500 | 3000 | 2250 | 1500 | 950 |

**2nd Issue 0 Series**

| Exc. | V.G. | Good | Fair | Poor |
|------|------|------|------|------|
| 3000 | 2500 | 1750 | 1000 | 750 |

**3rd Issue 0 Series**

| Exc. | V.G. | Good | Fair | Poor |
|------|------|------|------|------|
| 1750 | 1500 | 1000 | 700 | 450 |

## 480 Code

This numerical code was assigned to Walther in late 1939, and a small number of pistols were produced with the code "480 P-38" marked on the slide before the code was changed to "ac" in 1940.

| Exc. | V.G. | Good | Fair | Poor |
|------|------|------|------|------|
| 1750 | 1500 | 1000 | 700 | 450 |

## "ac-40"

Pistols marked in this manner were manufactured by Walther in 1940. They are rare as the "480" code was not dropped until October of 1940.

| Exc. | V.G. | Good | Fair | Poor |
|------|------|------|------|------|
| 1000 | 850 | 650 | 500 | 375 |

## "ac-41" and "ac-42"

Manufactured by Walther in 1941 and 1942.

| Exc. | V.G. | Good | Fair | Poor |
|------|------|------|------|------|
| 550 | 475 | 375 | 275 | 200 |

## "ac", "byf" (Mauser) and "cyq" (Spreewerke) 1943--1945

These are the most common of the wartime P-38's and are by far the most often encountered.

| Exc. | V.G. | Good | Fair | Poor |
|------|------|------|------|------|
| 450 | 375 | 300 | 225 | 150 |

## "byf-44" Dual Tone Finish

This model is phosphate finished and has a different color to the slide than the frame.

| Exc. | V.G. | Good | Fair | Poor |
|------|------|------|------|------|
| 500 | 450 | 350 | 275 | 200 |

## 1945 Late War (Milled Finish)

These pistols have a very rough and almost unfinished appearance and were only produced for a short time in 1945. They have an 0 serial number prefix.

| Exc. | V.G. | Good | Fair | Poor |
|------|------|------|------|------|
| 750 | 650 | 500 | 400 | 300 |

## "svw 1945"

These pistols were manufactured by Mauser after January of 1945. Be aware that many of these pistols have recently been imported into the Country; and this has seriously affected the collector market, lowering the value of this model.

| Exc. | V.G. | Good | Fair | Poor |
|------|------|------|------|------|
| 350 | 300 | 250 | 200 | 150 |

# GERSTENBERGER & EBERWEIN
## Gussenstadt, Germany
### Em-Ge, G.& E., Omega & Pic

This series of cheap, poor-quality revolvers were widely sold in the U.S.A. before their import was banned by the Gun Control Act of 1968. They are chambered for .22 and .32 calibers. They have 2.25" barrels, solid frames, and loading gates and hold 6 shots. Some have spring-loaded ejector rods; others, removable axis pins that are used to push out the spent cases. All were very poor indeed and worth uniformly little today.

| Exc. | V.G. | Good | Fair | Poor |
|------|------|------|------|------|
| 125 | 100 | 75 | 50 | 25 |

# GEVARM
## St. Etienne, France
### E-1 Autoloading Rifle

This is a blowback-operated semi-automatic rifle that is chambered for the .22 l.r. cartridge. It has a 19" barrel, 10-round magazine, and a blued finish with a walnut pistolgrip stock.

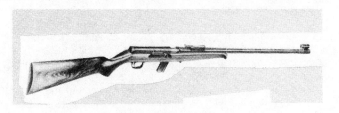

| Exc. | V.G. | Good | Fair | Poor |
|------|------|------|------|------|
| 175 | 150 | 125 | 100 | 75 |

## GIB
### Eibar, Spain

**10 Gauge Shotgun**

This is a side-by-side, double-barrel shotgun chambered for the 3.5" 10-gauge Magnum shell. It has 32" matte-ribbed barrels that are choked full-and-full. It features a boxlock action, with a case-colored receiver and blued barrels. The walnut pistolgrip stock is checkered, with a recoil pad standard.

| Exc. | V.G. | Good | Fair | Poor |
|------|------|------|------|------|
| 275 | 250 | 225 | 150 | 100 |

## GIBBS
### New York, New York

**Gibbs Carbine**

This firearm was manufactured by the firm of William F. Brooks. It is chambered for .52 caliber and utilizes the percussion ignition system. It is a breech-load single shot that has a 22" barrel that slides forward to load. The lock plates and the breech are case-colored, and the barrel is blued. The mountings are iron, and the stock is walnut with a saddle ring on the left side. The triggerguard is a lever that is used to open the sliding breech. The lock has the American eagle and "Wm. F. Brooks/Manf New York/1863." The breech is marked "L.H. Gibbs/Patd/Jany 8, 1856." This was a secondary U.S. military arm, and there was an order for 10,000 units. In 1863, the New York draft riots caused a fire that destroyed the Phoenix Armory, where this carbine was made. There were only 1,050 produced.

| Exc. | V.G. | Good | Fair | Poor |
|------|------|------|------|------|
| 2000 | 1750 | 1200 | 750 | 500 |

## GIBBS GUNS, INC.
### Greenback, Tennessee

**Mark 45 Carbine**

This blowback-operated semi-automatic was based on the Thompson Submachine Gun. It is chambered for .45 ACP and has a 16.5" barrel. It is available with a 5-, 15-, 30-, or 90-round magazine. The finish is blued, with a walnut buttstock and forend. A nickel-plated model was available as an option and would bring approximately $25 additional. This gun was manufactured in the U.S. and discontinued in 1988.

| NIB | Exc. | V.G. | Good | Fair | Poor |
|-----|------|------|------|------|------|
| 275 | 225 | 175 | 150 | 125 | 100 |

## GIBBS TIFFANY & CO.
### Sturbridge, Massachusetts

**Underhammer Pistol**

This is a typical underhammer "Boot" pistol chambered for .28 caliber. It utilizes the percussion ignition system. There have been examples noted with barrel lengths from 3" to 8". This model has a browned iron frame and either a walnut or maple pointed handle that is trimmed with brass. The topstrap is marked "Gibbs Tiffany & Co." This pistol is one of the most commonly found of its type. It was manufactured between the late 1830's and the late 1850's.

| Exc. | V.G. | Good | Fair | Poor |
|------|------|------|------|------|
| 500 | 425 | 350 | 275 | 175 |

## GILLESPIE
### New York, New York

**Derringer Type Pocket Pistol**

This company produced a small percussion pocket pistol that was similar to those manufactured by H. Deringer of Philadelphia. They were usually chambered for .41 caliber, with a 2.5" barrel and a walnut stock. They were manufactured in the 1840's.

| Exc. | V.G. | Good | Fair | Poor |
|------|------|------|------|------|
| 750 | 650 | 500 | 350 | 250 |

## GLAZE, W. & CO.
### Columbia, South Carolina
### SEE--B. & B. M. Darling

This company was sales agent for the Darling Pepperbox pistol, and as such had their names stamped on some noted examples. The values would be the same as the Darling pistols that were not marked in this manner.

## GLISENTI
### Tirin, Italy

**Glisenti Model 1910**

The Glisenti was the Italian service pistol from its inception in 1910 until 1934. Some were still in use during WWII. It has a 3.9" barrel, weighs 29 ounces, has fixed sights, and holds 7 rounds of 9mm Glisenti ammunition in its detachable magazine. The mechanics associated with the function of the Glisenti are quite complex and not very strong.

| Exc. | V.G. | Good | Fair | Poor |
|------|------|------|------|------|
| 550 | 500 | 425 | 300 | 225 |

## GLOCK
### Austria
### Importer--Glock Inc.
### Smyrna, Georgia

This is a unique pistol that caused quite a controversy among the anti-gun groups when it was first released. The frame of this pistol is made of a polymer plastic with steel inserts. The fear (unfounded as usual) was that metal detectors would not pick up the weapon at airports. Since the weapon is more than 50 percent metal, this concern was proven ridiculous.

**Glock 17**

This model is chambered for the 9mm Parabellum cartridge. It is a double-action semi-automatic that has a 5" barrel and a 17-shot detachable magazine. This pistol is offered with either fixed or adjustable sights at the same retail price. The finish is black with black plastic grips. It is furnished in a plastic case with an extra magazine. This pistol was introduced in 1985.

**GLOCK 17** 9mm Semi-Automatic
Double Action (Safe Action) Pistol
**GLOCK, INC.** Smyrna, Georgia

| NIB | Exc. | V.G. | Good | Fair | Poor |
|-----|------|------|------|------|------|
| 515 | 475 | 425 | 350 | 275 | 175 |

### Glock 17L Competition Model
This version features a 6" compensated barrel and adjustable sights. The trigger is fine-tuned to a 3.5 lbs. let off. This model was introduced in 1988.

**GLOCK 17L COMPETITION MODEL** 9mm Semi-Automatic
Double Action (Safe Action) Pistol
**GLOCK, INC.** Smyrna, Georgia

| NIB | Exc. | V.G. | Good | Fair | Poor |
|-----|------|------|------|------|------|
| 775 | 650 | 500 | 425 | 350 | 225 |

### Glock 19
This is similar to the Model 17 but is a compact version with a 4" barrel and a smaller grip that will accept either a 15-shot or the standard 17-round magazine that protrudes a bit. The grip straps on this model are serrated. It was introduced in 1988.

| NIB | Exc. | V.G. | Good | Fair | Poor |
|-----|------|------|------|------|------|
| 515 | 475 | 425 | 350 | 275 | 175 |

## GODDARD
### SEE--B. & B. M. Darling
Goddard was a sales agent for the Darling Pepperbox pistol and had their name stamped on the examples they sold. This would have no effect on the value of these pistols.

## GOLDEN EAGLE
### Tochigi, Japan
### Nikko Limited

**Shotguns**
### Golden Eagle Model 5000 Grade I
This model is an Over/Under with a boxlock action. It is chambered for 12 or 20 gauge and has barrel lengths of 26", 28", and 30" with ventilated ribs and various choke combinations. This gun has a single-selective trigger and automatic ejectors. The finish is blued, with a hand-checkered walnut stock that has an eagle's head inlaid into the pistolgrip cap. This model was manufactured between 1976 and the early 1980's.

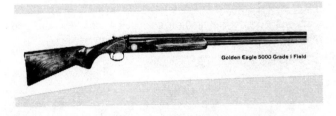

Golden Eagle 5000 Grade I Field

| Exc. | V.G. | Good | Fair | Poor |
|------|------|------|------|------|
| 850 | 750 | 600 | 475 | 300 |

### Grade I Skeet
This model is similar to the standard Model 5000 except that it has a 26" or 28" barrel with a wide competition rib and is choked skeet-and-skeet.

| Exc. | V.G. | Good | Fair | Poor |
|------|------|------|------|------|
| 950 | 800 | 700 | 550 | 375 |

### Grade I Trap
This model is similar to the Skeet model, with a 30" or 32" barrel that is choked for trap.

| Exc. | V.G. | Good | Fair | Poor |
|------|------|------|------|------|
| 950 | 800 | 700 | 550 | 375 |

## Model 5000 Grade II

This is a deluxe version of the Grade I with a fancier stock and more elaborate engraving. The eagle head is inlaid on the receiver in gold.

Golden Eagle 5000 Grade II

| Exc. | V.G. | Good | Fair | Poor |
|------|------|------|------|------|
| 1000 | 850 | 750 | 600 | 425 |

## Grandee Grade III

This model is heavily engraved and inlaid, with a high-grade walnut stock.

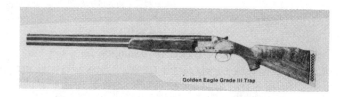

Golden Eagle Grade III Trap

| Exc. | V.G. | Good | Fair | Poor |
|------|------|------|------|------|
| 2500 | 2000 | 1750 | 1400 | 1000 |

## Rifles
### Model 7000 Grade I

This model was based on the Mauser bolt action and was chambered for all popular American calibers. It was offered with either a 24" or 26" barrel and features a high-gloss, skipline-checkered walnut stock with a rosewood pistolgrip cap and forend tip.

| Exc. | V.G. | Good | Fair | Poor |
|------|------|------|------|------|
| 500 | 425 | 375 | 275 | 200 |

## Model 7000 African

This is similar to the Grade I, chambered for .375 H&H and .458 Win. Mag. It has open sights.

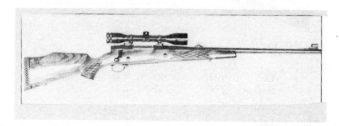

| Exc. | V.G. | Good | Fair | Poor |
|------|------|------|------|------|
| 550 | 475 | 400 | 325 | 250 |

## Model 7000 Grade II

This version features a better grade of walnut and scroll engraving on the action. It was furnished in a carrying case.

| Exc. | V.G. | Good | Fair | Poor |
|------|------|------|------|------|
| 625 | 550 | 475 | 375 | 300 |

# GONCZ CO.
### Hollywood, California

## GC Carbine

This model is chambered for the 7.63mm Mauser, 9mm Parabellum, .38 Super, and the .45 ACP cartridges. The barrel is 16.1" in length, and the action is totally unique to this company and is not based on any other. The finish is black, and the stock is plain walnut.

| NIB | Exc. | V.G. | Good | Fair | Poor |
|-----|------|------|------|------|------|
| 450 | 400 | 325 | 275 | 200 | 125 |

## GC Stainless

This is an entirely stainless-steel version of the Model GC Carbine. It was introduced in 1987.

| NIB | Exc. | V.G. | Good | Fair | Poor |
|-----|------|------|------|------|------|
| 550 | 450 | 375 | 325 | 250 | 175 |

## GC Collectors Edition

This is a low serial-numbered limited edition of completely hand-polished stainless steel.

| NIB | Exc. | V.G. | Good | Fair | Poor |
|-----|------|------|------|------|------|
| 800 | 600 | 500 | 425 | 350 | 225 |

## Halogen Carbine

This version is furnished with a powerful light source mounted under the barrel. It is chambered for 9mm and .45 ACP only.

| NIB | Exc. | V.G. | Good | Fair | Poor |
|-----|------|------|------|------|------|
| 550 | 450 | 375 | 325 | 250 | 175 |

## Laser Carbine

This version has a laser sighting system that is effective to 400 yards, mounted under the barrel.

| NIB | Exc. | V.G. | Good | Fair | Poor |
|------|------|------|------|------|------|
| 1500 | 1250 | 1000 | 750 | 650 | 500 |

## GA Pistol

This model is chambered for the same calibers as the carbine. It has a 9.5" shrouded barrel and a 16-or 18-shot detachable magazine. The finish is black with a one-piece grip. This model was manufactured between 1985 and 1987, when the use of stainless steel became standard. All current production models are now stainless steel.

| NIB | Exc. | V.G. | Good | Fair | Poor |
|-----|------|------|------|------|------|
| 425 | 350 | 275 | 200 | 150 | 100 |

## GAT-9 Pistol

This version is similar to the Model GA except that it is chambered for 9mm only and features an adjustable trigger and hand-honed action.

| NIB | Exc. | V.G. | Good | Fair | Poor |
|-----|------|------|------|------|------|
| 550 | 475 | 375 | 300 | 225 | 150 |

## GA Collectors Edition

This is a hand-polished stainless-steel version that was limited in production.

| NIB | Exc. | V.G. | Good | Fair | Poor |
|-----|------|------|------|------|------|
| 750 | 675 | 600 | 500 | 400 | 300 |

## GS Pistol

This model has a 5" barrel without the shroud; otherwise it is quite similar to the GA Pistol. In 1987 all production became stainless steel.

| NIB | Exc. | V.G. | Good | Fair | Poor |
|-----|------|------|------|------|------|
| 350 | 275 | 225 | 175 | 125 | 75 |

### GS Collectors Edition
This is a hand-polished, limited-production, stainless-steel version of the GS.

| NIB | Exc. | V.G. | Good | Fair | Poor |
|-----|------|------|------|------|------|
| 725 | 625 | 550 | 475 | 350 | 250 |

# GOVERNOR
## Norwich, Connecticut

### Governor Pocket Revolver
This model was manufactured by the Bacon Arms Co. and was chambered for the .22 caliber rimfire cartridge. These pistols were made by altering the Bacon Pepperbox after the Rollin White patent expired. It has a 7-shot cylinder and a 3" round barrel. There is a spur trigger, and the frame is blued iron. The grips are of walnut and in the birdshead configuration. "Governor" is stamped on the topstrap. These pistols were manufactured between 1869 and 1874 and were of fair quality. It is important to note that Norwich, Connecticut, was the Eibar, Spain, of the U.S. and as such was the home of many mediocre firearms.

| Exc. | V.G. | Good | Fair | Poor |
|------|------|------|------|------|
| 200 | 175 | 125 | 75 | 50 |

# GRABNER, G.
## Rehberg, Austria

### Kolibri
The Kolibri system was the smallest semi-automatic pistol and cartridge ever manufactured. It fires a 3-grain bullet at approximately 500 feet per second. This is hardly dangerous and surely not an effective weapon for any purpose. There are actually two versions--a 2.7mm and a 3mm. The barrels have no rifling, and accuracy is not good. A detachable 5-round magazine feeds the pistol, which was made from 1914 until the mid-20's.

| Exc. | V.G. | Good | Fair | Poor |
|------|------|------|------|------|
| 675 | 600 | 500 | 400 | 300 |

# GRAND PRECISION
## Eibar, Spain

This was a trading company established solely for the purpose of making sales in Europe by having a name that sounded French or Belgian instead of Spanish. All the pistols found stamped as such will not be affected value-wise and are covered elsewhere in this text. They are all poor-quality firearms with little collector interest.

# GRANGER, G.
## St. Etienne, France
## Importer--Wes Gilpin
## Dallas, Texas

### Side x Side Shotgun
This company manufactures very high-grade double-barrel shotguns chambered for 12, 16, and 20 gauge. Every other feature--barrel length, stock, choke, choice of triggers, and ornamentation--are on a custom-order basis. This company has produced high-grade guns since 1902.

| Exc. | V.G. | Good | Fair | Poor |
|------|------|------|------|------|
| 15000 | 12500 | 10000 | 7500 | 5000 |

# GRANT, STEPHEN
## London, England

### Side x Side Shotguns
This company produced very high quality firearms on a custom-order, limited-production basis. Their guns are chambered for 12, 16, and 20 gauge and are extremely scarce on today's market. The workmanship and materials were of the highest order. Manufacture has been discontinued. It is not possible to estimate the values of this rare firearm. Individual qualified appraisal should be secured.

# GRAS
## France

### Model 1874
This rifle is chambered for the 11mm cartridge and has a 32" barrel. The earlier models were converted from the Chassepot system by adding a sleeve to the chamber that allows the 11mm cartridge to be fired. A new bolt and new sights were also added. Latter specimens were newly manufactured. There is a full-length walnut stock, with a barrel band and a metal tip. The bayonet is a spike blade with a wood handle and a brass buttcap.

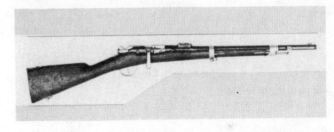

| Exc. | V.G. | Good | Fair | Poor |
|------|------|------|------|------|
| 275 | 250 | 200 | 150 | 75 |

# GREEN, E.
## Cheltenham, England

### Green
The Green is a military-type, break open, automatic extracting revolver chambered for .450 and .455 caliber. It is double-action, very well made, and quite popular with its military users in the late 1800's.

| Exc. | V.G. | Good | Fair | Poor |
|------|------|------|------|------|
| 450 | 400 | 350 | 275 | 200 |

# GREENE
## Milbury, Massachusetts
### Greene Breechloading Rifle
This rifle was manufactured by the A. H. Waters Armory and is chambered for .53 caliber and utilizes the percussion ignition system. The round barrel is 35" in length, and it is fired by an underhammer. The breech is opened by a bolt action far too complex to be practical. The rifling of this weapon was designed by Lancaster of London and is unique in that it appears to be a smoothbore and is actually oval in configuration. The mountings are of iron, and the finish is blued with a case-colored hammer. The full-length stock is walnut, with three barrel bands. The front sight is also the bayonet lug, and the rifle is marked "Greene's Patent/ Nov.17,1857. There were 4,000 manufactured between 1859 and 1862. Under 1,000 were used by Union forces in the Civil War, and the rest were purchased by state militias.

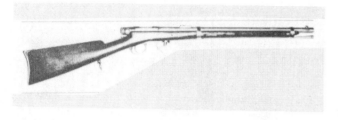

| Exc. | V.G. | Good | Fair | Poor |
|---|---|---|---|---|
| 1500 | 1350 | 1000 | 750 | 500 |

# GREENER, W. W. LTD.
## Birmingham, England
### General Purpose Model
This model is a single barrel built on the single-shot, improved Martini action. It was chambered for 12 gauge only and was offered with a 26", 30", or 32" barrel that was choked either full or modified. This action automatically ejects the empty shell. The finish is case-colored and blue, and the walnut stock is in the straight English style. Greener also manufactured this model as a harpoon gun that was quite popular with the whalers of its day.

| Exc. | V.G. | Good | Fair | Poor |
|---|---|---|---|---|
| 350 | 300 | 250 | 175 | 125 |

### Empire
This model is a side-by-side double that is chambered for 12 gauge only. It was offered with either 2.75" or 3" chambers, and the barrel length is 28" through 32" with various choke combinations. This is a boxlock action with double triggers. Automatic ejectors were available for additional cost. The stock was offered in either the straight style or with a pistol grip.
Automatic Ejectors--Add 20 Percent.

| Exc. | V.G. | Good | Fair | Poor |
|---|---|---|---|---|
| 1750 | 1500 | 1250 | 1000 | 750 |

### Empire Deluxe
This model is similar to the Empire, with higher-grade walnut.
Automatic Ejectors--Add 20 Percent.

| Exc. | V.G. | Good | Fair | Poor |
|---|---|---|---|---|
| 2000 | 1750 | 1500 | 1250 | 950 |

### F35 Grade Farkiller
This is a hammerless side-by-side that was chambered for 12 gauge only. It was offered with barrel lengths from 28"--32", with various choke combinations. It has double triggers and has automatic ejectors as an option. The stock is walnut, and it is either straight or with a pistol grip.
Automatic Ejectors--Add 20 Percent.

| Exc. | V.G. | Good | Fair | Poor |
|---|---|---|---|---|
| 2500 | 2250 | 2000 | 1500 | 1200 |

### F35 Farkiller Large Bore
This model is similar to the standard Farkiller except that it is chambered for either 8 or 10 gauge.
Automatic Ejectors--Add 20 Percent.

| Exc. | V.G. | Good | Fair | Poor |
|---|---|---|---|---|
| 2750 | 2500 | 2250 | 1750 | 1500 |

### Jubilee Grade DH35
This model is available in 12, 16, 20, and 28 gauge and .410. It was offered with barrel lengths from 26" to 30", with various choke combinations. It features automatic ejectors and double triggers standard, with a single-selective trigger available which adds approximately $500 to the value. The hand-checkered walnut stock is available with either a straight or pistolgrip stock.

| Exc. | V.G. | Good | Fair | Poor |
|---|---|---|---|---|
| 2500 | 2250 | 2000 | 1500 | 1250 |

### Sovereign Grade DH40
This model is similar to the Jubilee, with more engraving and a better grade of walnut.

| Exc. | V.G. | Good | Fair | Poor |
|---|---|---|---|---|
| 2750 | 2500 | 2250 | 1750 | 1500 |

### Crown Grade DH55
This is a more deluxe version of the Sovereign, with more elaborate engraving and fancier walnut.

| Exc. | V.G. | Good | Fair | Poor |
|---|---|---|---|---|
| 3500 | 3000 | 2750 | 2000 | 1750 |

### Royal Grade DH75
This is the best grade Greener and is similar to the Crown Grade, with more ornamentation and the best grade of walnut.

| Exc. | V.G. | Good | Fair | Poor |
|---|---|---|---|---|
| 4500 | 4000 | 3750 | 3000 | 2750 |

# GREIFELT & CO.
## Suhl, Germany
### Over/Under Shotguns
### Grade No. 1
This model was chambered for 12, 16, 20, and 28 gauge and .410. It was offered with vent-rib barrels from 26"-- 32" in length. There are various choke combinations, as well as automatic ejectors. Double triggers are standard. A single-selective trigger was available and would increase the value approximately 15 percent. The action is an Anson & Deeley boxlock, and the hand-checkered walnut stock is available either with a straight or pistolgrip stock. The values are for the standard 12-gauge version.
28 Gauge and .410--Add 25 Percent.

| Exc. | V.G. | Good | Fair | Poor |
|---|---|---|---|---|
| 3500 | 3150 | 2750 | 1750 | 1450 |

### Grade No.3
This model is similar to the No. 1, with less engraving. It was manufactured prior to WWII.
28 Gauge and .410--Add 25 Percent.

| Exc. | V.G. | Good | Fair | Poor |
|---|---|---|---|---|
| 2750 | 2300 | 1850 | 1450 | 1000 |

## Model 143E

This is the post-war version of the No. 1. It is not quite as fine a shotgun as the earlier model and is not offered in 28 gauge or .410.

| Exc. | V.G. | Good | Fair | Poor |
|------|------|------|------|------|
| 2500 | 2150 | 1750 | 1300 | 850 |

## Combination Gun

This Over/Under has a shotgun barrel chambered for 12, 16, 20, and 28 gauge and .410 plus a rifle barrel chambered for any rimmed cartridge that was available at that time. It was offered in a 24" or 26" barrel length, with a solid rib. The pricing of this model has a great deal to do with the availability of ammunition for the rifle barrel as well as the options on the particular gun. This is a pre-WWII firearm.

Deduct 40 Percent if rifle caliber is obsolete.
28 Gauge and .410-- Add 25 Percent.
Automatic Ejectors--Add 15 Percent.

| Exc. | V.G. | Good | Fair | Poor |
|------|------|------|------|------|
| 5000 | 4500 | 4000 | 3000 | 2250 |

## Side x Side Shotguns
## Model 22

This model was chambered for 12 and 20 gauge and was offered with 28" or 30" barrels choked full and modified. It has a boxlock action with false sideplates, double triggers, and extractors. The hand-checkered walnut stock was offered with an English-style straight grip or a pistol grip. This model was manufactured after WWII.

| Exc. | V.G. | Good | Fair | Poor |
|------|------|------|------|------|
| 2000 | 1800 | 1500 | 1200 | 950 |

## Model 22E

This model is similar to the Model 22, with the addition of automatic ejectors.

| Exc. | V.G. | Good | Fair | Poor |
|------|------|------|------|------|
| 2500 | 2200 | 1750 | 1500 | 1150 |

## Model 103

This model is chambered for 12 and 16 gauge and has either a 28" or a 30" barrel that is choked full and modified. It has a boxlock action, with double triggers and extractors. The checkered walnut stock has a pistol or straight English-style grip. This was a post-war model.

| Exc. | V.G. | Good | Fair | Poor |
|------|------|------|------|------|
| 2000 | 1800 | 1500 | 1200 | 950 |

## Model 103E

This model is similar to the Model 103, with automatic ejectors.

| Exc. | V.G. | Good | Fair | Poor |
|------|------|------|------|------|
| 2250 | 2000 | 1500 | 1250 | 1000 |

## Drilling

This model features a side-by-side shotgun chambered for 12, 16, or 20 gauge over a single rifle barrel chambered for any rimmed cartridge. It has 26" barrels with various chokes. The action is a boxlock with extractors, double triggers, and a rifle sight that pops up when the rifle barrel is selected. This gun was manufactured prior to WWII.

Deduct 40 Percent if rifle caliber is obsolete.
20 Gauge--Add 10 Percent.

| Exc. | V.G. | Good | Fair | Poor |
|------|------|------|------|------|
| 3500 | 3150 | 2750 | 2250 | 1750 |

# GRENDEL, INC.
### Rockledge, Florida

## P-10 Pistol

This is a blowback-operated, double-action, semi-automatic pistol chambered for the .380 Auto. It has a 3" barrel and holds 11 rounds, that are loaded from the top either by hand or with a stripper clip. The pistol features all-steel construction and has a matte-black finish with black plastic grips. It is offered in electroless nickel plate, as well as a green teflon finish for a slightly higher price.

Green Finish--Add $5.
Electroless Nickel--Add $15.

| NIB | Exc. | V.G. | Good | Fair | Poor |
|-----|------|------|------|------|------|
| 150 | 125 | 100 | 75 | 65 | 50 |

## SRT-20F Compact Rifle

This is a bolt action rifle built on the Sako action. It is chambered for the .308 cartridge and has a 20" finned match-grade barrel and a folding synthetic stock. It is furnished with an integral bipod and no sights. The magazine holds 9 rounds.

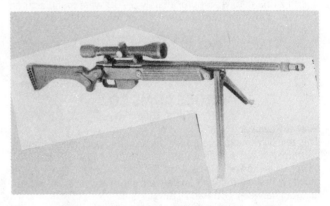

| NIB | Exc. | V.G. | Good | Fair | Poor |
|-----|------|------|------|------|------|
| 525 | 475 | 400 | 325 | 250 | 150 |

## SRT-24

This model is similar to the SRT-20F, with a 24" barrel. It was discontinued in 1988.

| Exc. | V.G. | Good | Fair | Poor |
|------|------|------|------|------|
| 450 | 375 | 300 | 225 | 125 |

# GRIFFON & HOWE
### New York, New York

This very well respected firm specializes in the production of the highest-grade bolt-action rifles America had to offer. They were strictly custom gunsmiths who built one-of-a-kind, made-to-order rifles based on the U.S. Springfield or the German Mauser 98 actions. They produced only 2,700 rifles from 1923 until 1966, and they were made in many different calibers. The list of options was long, and many were engraved and inlaid. They offered their own unique scope-mounting system, that was different than anything else available. It is impossible to price these rifles in a book such as this due to the many variables that must be considered. If one contemplates a transaction, an independent appraisal should definitely be secured.

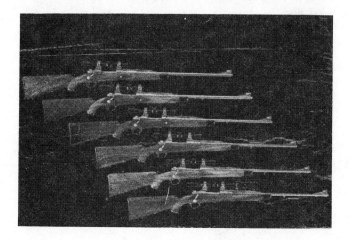

## GRISWOLD & GUNNISON
### Griswoldville, Georgia

**1851 Navy Type**
This Confederate manufactured revolver was copied from the Colt Navy and was chambered for .36 caliber. It utilized the percussion ignition system and had a six shot unfluted cylinder. It had a 7.5" barrel and a barrel wedge that had no spring to hold it in place. The frame and gripstraps were of brass and the rest was blue iron. The one piece grip was of walnut. This was the best quality revolver purchased by the C.S.A. and was also the most numerous. Approximately 3,700 were manufactured between 1862 and 1864, when Union forces totally destroyed the facility.

| Exc. | V.G. | Good | Fair | Poor |
|------|------|------|------|------|
| 7500 | 6500 | 5000 | 4000 | 2750 |

## GROSS ARMS CO.
### Tiffin, Ohio

**Pocket Revolver**
This revolver is chambered for the .25- and .30-caliber rimfire cartridge. It has a 7-shot unfluted cylinder and a 6" octagonal barrel. It is marked "Gross Arms Co., Tiffin, Ohio." The finish is blued, with walnut grips. There were only a few hundred manufactured between 1864 and 1866.

| Exc. | V.G. | Good | Fair | Poor |
|------|------|------|------|------|
| 750 | 700 | 600 | 475 | 325 |

## GRUBB, J. C. & CO.
### Philadelphia, Pennsylvania

**Pocket Pistol**
This pistol is chambered for the .41 caliber and utilizes the percussion-ignition system. It was produced with various length barrels and was patterned after the Philadelphia derringer-type pistol. It is mounted with German silver and has an engraved lock and triggerguard. The stock is walnut, and the lock is marked "J.C.Grubb." There were several hundred manufactured between 1850 and 1860.

| Exc. | V.G. | Good | Fair | Poor |
|------|------|------|------|------|
| 650 | 575 | 475 | 375 | 275 |

## GUEDES-CASTRO
### Steyr, Austria

**Model 1885**
This was one of the last of the military single-shot rifles, and it was rendered obsolete by the bolt action almost at the same time that it was introduced. This rifle was invented by Castro Guedes, a Portuguese, and was built in Austria under contract for the Portuguese military. This rifle was chambered for the 8x60 Guedes, one of the first small-bore military cartridges that also became obsolete quickly. This rifle has a 28" barrel and military-type sights. The action is a short-travel, falling breech-block type that is activated by the finger-lever triggerguard. This was one of the few single shots that has a manual safety. This rifle was manufactured for a very short time circa 1885 and is quite scarce on today's market. The cartridges are even less available than the rifle.

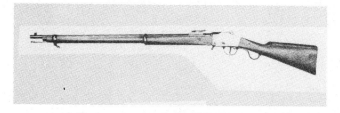

| Exc. | V.G. | Good | Fair | Poor |
|------|------|------|------|------|
| 500 | 400 | 350 | 250 | 125 |

## GUIDE LAMP
### Detroit, Michigan
### Division General Motors

**Liberator**
Guide Lamp made automotive headlamps. In 1942, amid the production crunch caused by WWII, they were pressed into service to manufacture a last-ditch, assassin's type pistol for the sole reason that they were proficient at stamping sheet metal. They produced about 3 million in three months. It is said that one could be made faster than it could be loaded. The pistol is 5.5"" long, with a 3.5" smooth bore barrel chambered for the .45ACP. It holds one cartridge, with extras packed into the grip. It weighs 16 ounces. Materials and construction were quite cheap, and each Liberator cost our Government $2.10. They were packed in a waterproof plastic bag with a comic-strip instruction sheet and were air-dropped to the resistance groups behind enemy lines in the Pacific Theatre. They are fairly plentiful but very popular among military weapons collectors.

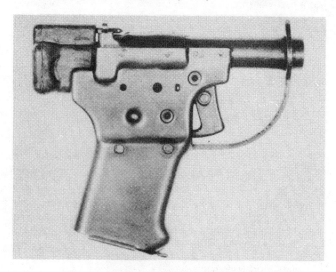

| Exc. | V.G. | Good | Fair | Poor |
|------|------|------|------|------|
| 500 | 425 | 375 | 300 | 225 |

# GUION, T. F.
### New Orleans, Louisiana

**Pocket Pistol**

This pistol is a copy of the Henry Deringer of Philadelphia. It is chambered for .41-caliber percussion and has a 2.5" barrel, German silver mountings, and a walnut stock. It was manufacured in the 1850s.

| Exc. | V.G. | Good | Fair | Poor |
|------|------|------|------|------|
| 650  | 575  | 500  | 400  | 275  |

# GUNWORKS LTD.
### Buffalo, New York

**Model 9 Derringer**

This is an Over/Under derringer chambered for 9mm, .38 Special, .38 Super, and .357 Magnum. It has 2.5" barrels, with a spur trigger and Millet sights. The finish is electroless nickel-plate, and the grips are walnut. This company ceased to manufacture this gun in 1986.

| Exc. | V.G. | Good | Fair | Poor |
|------|------|------|------|------|
| 125  | 100  | 90   | 75   | 50   |

# GUSTAF, CARL
### Eskilstuna, Sweden

**Bolt Action Rifle**

This is an above-average rifle based on a Mauser action. It is chambered for 6.5x55, 7x64, .270, 7mm Magnum, .308, .30-06, and 9.3x62. It features a 24" barrel and is blued with a hand-checkered walnut stock in either the classic style or with a Monte Carlo cheekpiece. This rifle was manufactured between 1970 and 1977.

| Exc. | V.G. | Good | Fair | Poor |
|------|------|------|------|------|
| 500  | 425  | 350  | 275  | 200  |

**Grade II**

This model is similar to the standard model but features better-grade walnut and a rosewood pistolgrip cap and forend tip.

| Exc. | V.G. | Good | Fair | Poor |
|------|------|------|------|------|
| 600  | 525  | 450  | 375  | 300  |

**Grade III**

This version is similar to the Grade II, with a high gloss finish and high-grade walnut.

| Exc. | V.G. | Good | Fair | Poor |
|------|------|------|------|------|
| 700  | 625  | 550  | 475  | 400  |

**Deluxe Bolt Action**

This model has an engraved floorplate and triggerguard, a damascened bolt, and a high-grade French walnut stock. It was manufactured between 1970 and 1977.

| Exc. | V.G. | Good | Fair | Poor |
|------|------|------|------|------|
| 800  | 725  | 650  | 575  | 500  |

**Varmint Model**

This model is a bolt action with an improved rapid lock time. It is chambered for .222, .22-250, .243, and 6.5x55. It features a heavy 27" barrel and a large bolt knob made of Bakelite. The rifle was furnished without open sights and has a heavy target-type stock. It was manufactured in 1970 only.

| Exc. | V.G. | Good | Fair | Poor |
|------|------|------|------|------|
| 500  | 425  | 350  | 275  | 200  |

**Grand Prix Target**

This model is a single-shot, bolt-action rifle chambered for the .22 l.r. It features a rapid lock time and has a heavyweight 27" barrel with adjustable weights. The rifle was furnished without sights and with an adjustable butt target stock. It was manufactured in 1970 only.

| Exc. | V.G. | Good | Fair | Poor |
|------|------|------|------|------|
| 550  | 475  | 400  | 325  | 300  |

**Model 2000**

This model was built on a Mauser action and was chambered for 6.5x55, .243, .270, .308, and .30-06. It features a 60-percent bolt lift and a cold swaged barrel and action. It was furnished with open sights, and the finish is blued. The walnut stock is hand-checkered and has a Monte Carlo cheekpiece. This Model was manufactured until 1985.

| Exc. | V.G. | Good | Fair | Poor |
|------|------|------|------|------|
| 600  | 500  | 400  | 300  | 200  |

# GWYN & CAMPBELL
### Hamilton, Ohio

**Union Carbine**

This weapon is also known as the Grapevine carbine and the Gwyn and Campbell Carbine. It is chambered for .52 caliber and utilizes the percussion ignition system. It has a falling-block action that is activated by the triggerguard lever. The part-round/part-octagonal barrel is 20" in length. The lock is marked "Gwyn & Campbell/Patent/1862/ Hamilton,O." The mountings are iron; and the frame is case-colored, with the rest blued. The stock is walnut, and there was a forearm. There were approximately 8,500 of these carbines manufactured between 1862 and 1865. They were used by the Union forces during the Civil War.

| Exc. | V.G. | Good | Fair | Poor |
|------|------|------|------|------|
| 1000 | 800  | 600  | 450  | 350  |

# HDH, SA.
### Liege, Belgium

**Cobold**

This was a popular double-action revolver produced around the turn of the century. It has a solid-frame octagonal barrel and an odd safety catch that locks the cylinder. It was chambered for the 9.4mm Dutch, 10.6mm German, .38, and .45 caliber. It was relatively well made for a Liege pistol of this time period.

| Exc. | V.G. | Good | Fair | Poor |
|------|------|------|------|------|
| 200  | 175  | 125  | 100  | 75   |

**Puppy**

HDH originated this very popular trade name and affixed it to many different cheap revolvers. There are various types in calibers from 5.5mm to 7.65mm. Most are "Velo-Dogs." Values are so similar and low that, for our purposes, we will regard them together. Collector interest is quite thin.

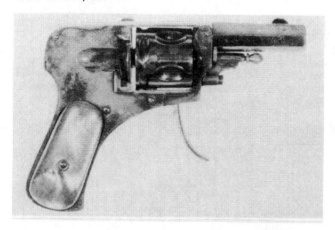

| Exc. | V.G. | Good | Fair | Poor |
|------|------|------|------|------|
| 150 | 125 | 100 | 75 | 50 |

### Lincoln
This vest-pocket .22-caliber revolver has a solid frame, folding trigger, imitation pearl or ivory grips, and ornate but coarse engraving.

| Exc. | V.G. | Good | Fair | Poor |
|------|------|------|------|------|
| 150 | 125 | 100 | 75 | 50 |

### Lincoln-Bossu
This is a hammerless, solid-frame, folding-trigger, "Velo-Dog"-type revolver. It is chambered for the 5.5mm or 6.35mm cartridge.

| Exc. | V.G. | Good | Fair | Poor |
|------|------|------|------|------|
| 150 | 125 | 100 | 75 | 50 |

### Left Wheeler
This is a Colt Police Positive copy chambered for the .32 or .38 caliber cartridge. This was the last revolver HDH manufactured.

| Exc. | V.G. | Good | Fair | Poor |
|------|------|------|------|------|
| 175 | 150 | 125 | 100 | 75 |

HDH was prolific in the number of models they manufactured, and it is not uncommon to find the initials on many different firearms of this period. This has little to no effect on the value of these pistols.

## H.J.S. INDUSTRIES, INC.
### Brownsville, Texas

### Frontier Four Derringer
This model is a four-barrelled pocket pistol chambered for the .22 l.r. The barrels are 2.5" long and slide forward to load. The construction is of stainless steel with wood grips, and the design is loosely based on the Sharps derringer.

| Exc. | V.G. | Good | Fair | Poor |
|------|------|------|------|------|
| 125 | 100 | 75 | 50 | 25 |

### Lone Star Derringer
This is a break open, single-shot pocket pistol chambered for the .38 Special cartridge. It has a 2.5" barrel and is made of stainless steel with wood grips.

| Exc. | V.G. | Good | Fair | Poor |
|------|------|------|------|------|
| 150 | 125 | 100 | 75 | 50 |

## HWP INDUSTRIES
### Milwaukee, Wisconsin

### Sledgehammer
This is a 5-shot, swingout-cylinder, double-action revolver chambered for the .500 HWP cartridge. This caliber is a creation of the manufacturer and is not available in other firearms. This extremely powerful revolver has a shrouded 4" barrel that has a quick change feature. The revolver is made of stainless steel and features Pachmayr grips. It was introduced in 1989.

| Exc. | V.G. | Good | Fair | Poor |
|------|------|------|------|------|
| 1300 | 1000 | 900 | 650 | 450 |

## HAENEL, C. G.
### Suhl, Germany

This company was formed in 1840 but did not become involved with the manufacture of firearms until the M1879 and M1883 Commission revolvers which will be covered later in the text. Hugo Schmeisser joined the firm in 1921, as head engineer and designer. This opened the door for Haenel to enter modern weapon production.

### Model 1
This is a 6.35mm, blowback semi-automatic pistol. It is 4.72" overall with a 2.48" barrel. The pistol weighs 13.5 ounces, is striker fired and has a 6-round detachable magazine. The left side of the slide is stamped "C.G. Haenel Suhl-Schmeisser Patent." Each grip panel is marked "HS"in an oval.

| Exc. | V.G. | Good | Fair | Poor |
|------|------|------|------|------|
| 300 | 275 | 225 | 175 | 100 |

### Model 2
The Model 2 is very similar to the Model 1 but is slightly shorter and lighter. The word "Schmeisser" is molded into the grips. It is scarcer than the Model 1.

| Exc. | V.G. | Good | Fair | Poor |
|------|------|------|------|------|
| 325 | 300 | 250 | 200 | 125 |

## HAFDASA
### Buenos Aires, Argentina

### Ballester-Molina
Brought out in the 1930's, this was a close copy of the Colt Model 1911, the only differences being the skip-spaced grooves on the slide, the slightly smaller grip, and the absence of a grip safety. This was the official pistol of the Argentine, and many were bought by the British during WWII. The slide is stamped "Pistola Automatica Cal. .45 Fabricado por HAFDASA Patentes Internacional Ballester Molina Industria Argentina."

| Exc. | V.G. | Good | Fair | Poor |
|------|------|------|------|------|
| 475 | 425 | 325 | 225 | 150 |

## Criolla

This is simply a .22-caliber version of the Ballester-Molina. It is physically identical except for caliber and weight. Much like our Colt Ace, they were used as training waepons. Some were sold commercially under the trademark "La Criolla."

| Exc. | V.G. | Good | Fair | Poor |
|------|------|------|------|------|
| 1000 | 850 | 650 | 500 | 350 |

## Hafdasa

This is an unusual .22-caliber blowback made with a tubular receiver. It is a true hammerless, striker-fired, with an angled grip. The pistol is cocked by grabbing the bolt through a double cut-out ejection port. The quality of the pistol is excellent. The only markings are "HA" on the butt.

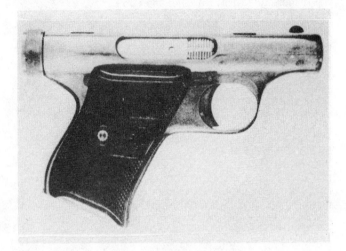

| Exc. | V.G. | Good | Fair | Poor |
|------|------|------|------|------|
| 350 | 325 | 275 | 200 | 150 |

## Zonda

This is identical to the Hafdasa with the name "Zonda" stamped on the frame. This was probably an export trademark.

| Exc. | V.G. | Good | Fair | Poor |
|------|------|------|------|------|
| 350 | 325 | 275 | 200 | 150 |

## HAKIM
### Egypt

This rifle is chambered for the 7.92x57mm and is a gas-operated semi-automatic copied from the Swedish Model 42 Ljungman. This is a well-made rifle that is obsolete in Egypt and was sold on the surplus arms market after 1986. It was manufactured by Maadi Military and Civil Industries Co.

| Exc. | V.G. | Good | Fair | Poor |
|------|------|------|------|------|
| 250 | 225 | 200 | 150 | 100 |

## HAHN, WILLIAM
### New York, New York

**Pocket Pistol**

This pistol is styled after the Philadelphia Derringer and is chambered for .41 caliber percussion. It has a 2.5" round barrel, German silver mountings, and a walnut stock. This pistol was manufactured in the 1850's.

| Exc. | V.G. | Good | Fair | Poor |
|------|------|------|------|------|
| 650 | 575 | 500 | 400 | 300 |

## HALE, H. J.
### Bristol, Connecticut

**Underhammer Pistol**

This pistol is chambered for the .31 caliber and utilizes the percussion ignition system. It has a 5" or 6" part-round/part-octagonal barrel and an iron frame with either a pointed or a round walnut butt. The markings read "H.J.Hale/Warranted/Cast Steel." There were quite a few of these manufactured during the 1850's.

| Exc. | V.G. | Good | Fair | Poor |
|------|------|------|------|------|
| 600 | 500 | 400 | 300 | 200 |

## HALE & TULLER
### Hartford, Connecticut

**Underhammer Pistol**

This pistol is chambered for .44 caliber and utilizes the percussion ignition system. It has a 6" tapered round barrel and a pointed walnut grip. The interesting fact regarding this weapon is that they were manufactured at the Connecticut State Prison between 1837 and 1840. The quantity produced is not known.

| Exc. | V.G. | Good | Fair | Poor |
|------|------|------|------|------|
| 600 | 525 | 450 | 350 | 250 |

## HALL, ALEXANDER
### New York, New York

**Revolving Rifle**

This extremely rare rifle is chambered for .58 caliber and utilizes the percussion ignition system. It has a 15-shot magazine that is hung from the frame on a hinge in front of the trigger guard. The frame is brass, and the buttstock is walnut. There is no forend. These rifles were manufactured in the 1850's, and the number produced is not known.

| Exc. | V.G. | Good | Fair | Poor |
|------|------|------|------|------|
| 11500 | 9500 | 7500 | 5000 | 3750 |

## HALL-NORTH
### Middletown, Connecticut

**Model 1840 Carbine**

This carbine was manufactured by Simeon North and was chambered for .52-caliber percussion. It is a single-shot, breech-loading, smooth bore with a 21" round barrel. It has a full-length stock held on by two barrel bands. There is a ramrod mounted under the barrel, and the mountings are of iron. The lock is case-hardened, and the barrel is brown. The stock is walnut. The markings are "US/S. North/Midltn/Conn". There are two distinct variations, both produced under military contract.

**Type 1 Carbine**

This model has a squared, right-angled breech lever mounted on the trigger plate. There were 500 of these manufactured in 1840.

| Exc. | V.G. | Good | Fair | Poor |
|------|------|------|------|------|
| 3200 | 2750 | 2200 | 1600 | 1200 |

### Type 2 Carbine

This variation features a curved, breech-operating lever that is known as a fishtail. There were approximately 6,000 of these manufactured from 1840 to 1843. Some have an 8" bar and ring.

| Exc. | V.G. | Good | Fair | Poor |
|------|------|------|------|------|
| 2400 | 1850 | 1400 | 1100 | 750 |

# HAMBUSH, JOSEPH
### Ferlach, Austria

### Boxlock SxS Shotgun

This is a high-grade, custom-order gun that is chambered for all gauges. It features workmanship of a very high order, and all specifications could vary with the customer's wishes. The gun was available with a single-selective or double trigger and automatic ejectors and was usually gamescene engraved. This is a rare gun and is not often encountered on today's market. Pricing is only estimated as not enough are traded to provide accurate values.

| Exc. | V.G. | Good | Fair | Poor |
|------|------|------|------|------|
| 1250 | 1000 | 800 | 550 | 350 |

### Sidelock SxS Shotgun

This model is similar in all repects to the boxlock except that it features a full sidelock action. It is usually found with gamescene engraving.

| Exc. | V.G. | Good | Fair | Poor |
|------|------|------|------|------|
| 2250 | 2000 | 1800 | 1500 | 1250 |

# HAMMERLI, SA
### Lenzburg, Switzerland

This company has been in the business of making superbly accurate target rifles and pistols for many years. Their reputation has earned for them a place in nearly every serious shooting match held anywhere in the world. They have produced many different models over the years--some one-of-a-kind built for a specific shooter. Lately their products have become more standardized, and they have branched out to manufacture Western frontier-styled revolvers and, in partnership with SIG Neuhausen, a double-action, large-caliber semi-automatic pistol. They have also allied with the firm of Walther to produce a line of target pistols.

### Rifles
### Model 45 Smallbore rifle

This precision single-shot, bolt-action rifle is chambered for the .22 l.r. cartridge and features a 27.5" heavy barrel with an aperture rear and globe target front sight. It has a match rifle-type thumbhole stock and was manufactured between 1945 and 1957.

| Exc. | V.G. | Good | Fair | Poor |
|------|------|------|------|------|
| 675 | 600 | 525 | 425 | 325 |

### Model 54 Smallbore Rifle

This model is similar to the Model 45, with an adjustable buttplate. It was manufactured between 1954 and 1957.

| Exc. | V.G. | Good | Fair | Poor |
|------|------|------|------|------|
| 700 | 625 | 550 | 450 | 350 |

### Model 503 Smallbore Free Rifle

This model is similar to the Model 54, with a free rifle style stock.

| Exc. | V.G. | Good | Fair | Poor |
|------|------|------|------|------|
| 650 | 575 | 500 | 400 | 300 |

### Model 506 Smallbore Match Rifle.

This is the later version of the Smallbore target series and is similar to the previous model. It was manufactured between 1963 and 1966.

| Exc. | V.G. | Good | Fair | Poor |
|------|------|------|------|------|
| 700 | 625 | 650 | 550 | 450 |

### Olympic 300 Meter

This is a large-bore, bolt-action, single-shot, free rifle chambered for the 7x57, .30-06, or .300 H&H Magnum cartridge. It has a 20.5" heavy barrel with an aperture rear and globe target front sight. It features double-set triggers and a free rifle-type, adjustable thumbhole stock with a wide beavertail forearm and Schutzen-style buttplate. This is a long-range target rifle that was manufactured between 1945 and 1959.

| Exc. | V.G. | Good | Fair | Poor |
|------|------|------|------|------|
| 900 | 800 | 650 | 500 | 400 |

### Sporting Rifle

This is a bolt-action, single-shot hunting rifle chambered for many popular calibers, both American and European. It features double-set triggers and a classic- style stock.

| Exc. | V.G. | Good | Fair | Poor |
|------|------|------|------|------|
| 650 | 575 | 500 | 400 | 325 |

### Pistols
### Model 100 Free Pistol

This model features a trigger-guard-activated, Martini single-shot action and is chambered for the .22 l.r. cartridge. It has a 11.5" octagonal barrel, with adjustable target-type sights. The finish is blued, and it has a single-set trigger and a walnut target grip and forend. This pistol was manufactured between 1933 and 1949.

| Exc. | V.G. | Good | Fair | Poor |
|------|------|------|------|------|
| 850 | 725 | 650 | 500 | 400 |

### Model 101

This model is similar to the Model 100, with a heavy round barrel and more sophisticated target sights. It features a matte-blued finish and was manufactured between 1956 and 1960.

| Exc. | V.G. | Good | Fair | Poor |
|------|------|------|------|------|
| 850 | 725 | 650 | 500 | 400 |

### Model 102

This model is essentially the Model 101 with a high-polished blue finish. It was manufactured between 1956 and 1960.

| Exc. | V.G. | Good | Fair | Poor |
|------|------|------|------|------|
| 850 | 725 | 650 | 500 | 400 |

### Model 103

This model is similar to the Model 101, with a lighter-weight octagonal barrel that features a high polished and blued finish. It was manufactured between 1956 and 1960.

| Exc. | V.G. | Good | Fair | Poor |
|------|------|------|------|------|
| 950 | 825 | 750 | 600 | 500 |

### Model 104

This is the Model 103 with a lightweight round barrel. It was manufactured between 1961 and 1965.

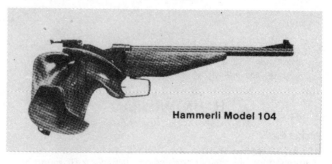

Hammerli Model 104

| Exc. | V.G. | Good | Fair | Poor |
|------|------|------|------|------|
| 750 | 625 | 550 | 450 | 350 |

## Model 105
This model features a redesigned stock and an improved action and was manufactured between 1962 and 1965.

| Exc. | V.G. | Good | Fair | Poor |
|------|------|------|------|------|
| 950  | 825  | 750  | 600  | 500  |

## Model 107
This is basically the same as the Model 105 with an improved trigger.

| Exc. | V.G. | Good | Fair | Poor |
|------|------|------|------|------|
| 1000 | 900  | 750  | 600  | 475  |

## Model 107 Deluxe
This version has an engraved action, and the stock features hand carving.

| Exc. | V.G. | Good | Fair | Poor |
|------|------|------|------|------|
| 1350 | 1250 | 900  | 800  | 600  |

## Model 120-1 Free Pistol
This is a bolt-action, single-shot pistol chambered for the .22 l.r. This pistol has a 9.9" barrel and is activated for loading and cocking by an alloy lever on the side of the bolt. The finish is blued, with checkered walnut grips. It features adjustable, target-type sights.

Hammerli Model 120

| Exc. | V.G. | Good | Fair | Poor |
|------|------|------|------|------|
| 450  | 375  | 300  | 225  | 150  |

## Model 120-2
This model features contour grips and otherwise is quite similar to the Model 120-1.

| Exc. | V.G. | Good | Fair | Poor |
|------|------|------|------|------|
| 475  | 400  | 325  | 250  | 175  |

## Model 120 Heavy Barrel
This model is similar to the Model 120-1, with a 5.7" heavy barrel.

| Exc. | V.G. | Good | Fair | Poor |
|------|------|------|------|------|
| 450  | 375  | 300  | 225  | 150  |

## Model 150
This model has a single-shot, Martini-type action and is chambered for .22 l.r. It has an 11.25" barrel with adjustable sights and grips that are contoured to fit the hand. It features a single-set trigger and is blued with walnut stocks.

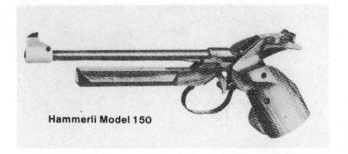

Hammerli Model 150

| Exc. | V.G. | Good | Fair | Poor |
|------|------|------|------|------|
| 1950 | 1800 | 1500 | 1250 | 1000 |

## Model 152
This model is at the top of the line. It is chambered for .22 l.r. and has an 11.25" barrel, a Martini action, and an electronic release trigger.

| Exc. | V.G. | Good | Fair | Poor |
|------|------|------|------|------|
| 2150 | 1950 | 1750 | 1500 | 1200 |

## International Model 206
This is a semi-automatic target pistol chambered for the .22 l.r. cartridge. It has a 7.5" barrel with an integral muzzle brake, adjustable sights, and walnut grips. It was manufactured between 1962 and 1969.

| Exc. | V.G. | Good | Fair | Poor |
|------|------|------|------|------|
| 700  | 600  | 475  | 375  | 275  |

## International Model 207
This model is similar to the Model 206, with adjustable grips.

| Exc. | V.G. | Good | Fair | Poor |
|------|------|------|------|------|
| 725  | 625  | 500  | 400  | 300  |

## International Model 208
This is a blowback-operated semi-automatic pistol chambered for the .22 l.r. cartridge. It has a 6" barrel with adjustable sights and an 8-shot magazine. The trigger is adjustable, as are the target grips. The barrel is drilled and tapped for the addition of barrel weights. This pistol was manufactured between 1966 and 1988.

| Exc. | V.G. | Good | Fair | Poor |
|------|------|------|------|------|
| 1750 | 1550 | 1250 | 1000 | 750  |

## International Model 208 Deluxe
This version features an extensively engraved receiver, as well as hand-carved grips. It was also discontinued in 1988.

| Exc. | V.G. | Good | Fair | Poor |
|------|------|------|------|------|
| 3000 | 2750 | 2500 | 2000 | 1500 |

## International Model 209
This is also a blowback-operated semi-automatic chambered for the .22 short cartridge. It has a 4.75" barrel with a muzzle brake and adjustable target sights. It has a 5-shot magazine and is blued, with walnut grips. It was manufactured between 1966 and 1970.

| Exc. | V.G. | Good | Fair | Poor |
|------|------|------|------|------|
| 800  | 700  | 600  | 450  | 350  |

## International Model 210
This model is similar to the Model 109, with adjustable grips.

| Exc. | V.G. | Good | Fair | Poor |
|------|------|------|------|------|
| 800  | 700  | 600  | 450  | 350  |

## International Model 211
This model is similar to the Model 210, with non-adjustable thumbrest grips.

Hammerli International Model 211

| Exc. | V.G. | Good | Fair | Poor |
|------|------|------|------|------|
| 1750 | 1550 | 1250 | 1000 | 750  |

## Model 212

This blowback-operated semi-automatic pistol is chambered for the .22 l.r. cartridge. It has a 5" barrel with adjustable sights and was designed for hunting small game. The finish is blued with walnut grips.

| Exc. | V.G. | Good | Fair | Poor |
|------|------|------|------|------|
| 1500 | 1275 | 1000 | 750 | 650 |

## Model 230

This model is a blowback-operated semi-automatic chambered for the .22 short cartridge. It has a 6.3" barrel and a 5-shot magazine. The sights are adjustable, as is the walnut grip. This pistol was designed to shoot the 25-meter Silhouette competition. It was manufactured between 1970 and 1983.

Hammerli Model 230-1

| Exc. | V.G. | Good | Fair | Poor |
|------|------|------|------|------|
| 700 | 600 | 500 | 400 | 300 |

## Model 232

This model is the current rapid-fire target pistol and is chambered for .22 short. It has a 5" barrel, adjustable sights, and a 6-shot magazine. The grips are contoured walnut. This model was introduced in 1984.

Hammerli Model 232

| Exc. | V.G. | Good | Fair | Poor |
|------|------|------|------|------|
| 1500 | 1300 | 1150 | 850 | 650 |

## Model 280

This is the new state-of-the-art target pistol from Hammerli. It features a modular design and has a frame of carbon fiber material. It has a 4.6" barrel with adjustable sights, trigger, and grips. It is chambered for .22 l.r. or .32 Wadcutter. The magazine holds 5 rounds, and the pistol was introduced in 1988.

| Exc. | V.G. | Good | Fair | Poor |
|------|------|------|------|------|
| 1800 | 1500 | 1350 | 1000 | 800 |

## Dakota

This is a single-action revolver based on the Colt SAA design. It has a solid frame and is loaded through a gate. It is chambered for .22 l.r.,.357 Magnum .44-40, and .45 Colt and was offered with barrel lengths of 5", 6", and 7.5". It has a 6-shot cylinder and is blued, with a brass triggerguard and walnut grips.

### .22 Caliber

| Exc. | V.G. | Good | Fair | Poor |
|------|------|------|------|------|
| 150 | 125 | 100 | 75 | 50 |

### Large Calibers

| Exc. | V.G. | Good | Fair | Poor |
|------|------|------|------|------|
| 225 | 175 | 150 | 125 | 100 |

## Super Dakota

This model is similar to the Dakota but is chambered for .41 and .44 Magnum, with adjustable sights.

| Exc. | V.G. | Good | Fair | Poor |
|------|------|------|------|------|
| 250 | 225 | 175 | 150 | 100 |

## Virginian

This is basically a more deluxe version of the Dakota. It is chambered for the .357 and .45 Colt cartridge. The triggerguard and back strap are chrome plated, with the frame case-colored and the remainder blued. This model features the "Swissafe" safety system that allows the cylinder axis pin to be locked back to prevent the hammer from falling.

| Exc. | V.G. | Good | Fair | Poor |
|------|------|------|------|------|
| 275 | 250 | 200 | 175 | 125 |

# HAMMERLI-WALTHER
## Lenzburg, Switzerland

These target pistols were produced by Hammerli under license from Walther after WWII. This project continued until approximately 1963, when production was ceased.

## Olympia Model 200 Type 1952

This model is chambered for the .22 short or l.r. cartridge. It is a blowback-operated semi-automatic that has a 10-round magazine. It has a 7.5" barrel that is tapped for weights, adjustable target sights, and a blued finish with walnut grips. It was manufactured between 1952 and 1958.

| Exc. | V.G. | Good | Fair | Poor |
|------|------|------|------|------|
| 650 | 575 | 475 | 375 | 300 |

## Model 200 Type 1958

This model is similar to the 1952 Type but has an integral muzzle brake. It was manufactured between 1958 and 1963.

| Exc. | V.G. | Good | Fair | Poor |
|------|------|------|------|------|
| 700 | 625 | 525 | 425 | 325 |

## Model 201

This is a Model 200 Type 1952 with a 9.5" barrel. It was manufactured between 1955 and 1957.

| Exc. | V.G. | Good | Fair | Poor |
|------|------|------|------|------|
| 650 | 575 | 475 | 375 | 300 |

## Model 202

This model was similar to the Model 201 with adjustable walnut grips. It was manufactured between 1955 and 1957.

| Exc. | V.G. | Good | Fair | Poor |
|------|------|------|------|------|
| 700 | 625 | 525 | 425 | 325 |

## Model 203

This model was similar to the Model 200 with the adjustable grips. It was available with or without a muzzle brake and the Type 1958 with the integral muzzle brake would be worth approximately 10% additional.

| Exc. | V.G. | Good | Fair | Poor |
|------|------|------|------|------|
| 700 | 625 | 525 | 425 | 325 |

## Model 204

This model was chambered for .22 l.r. only and had a 7.5" barrel, a muzzle brake, and barrel weights. It was manufactured between 1956 and 1963.

| Exc. | V.G. | Good | Fair | Poor |
|------|------|------|------|------|
| 750 | 675 | 575 | 475 | 375 |

## Model 205

This model was similar to the Model 204 with adjustable target grips. It was manufactured between 1956 and 1963.

| Exc. | V.G. | Good | Fair | Poor |
|------|------|------|------|------|
| 850  | 775  | 675  | 575  | 450  |

# HAMMOND BULLDOG
## Connecticut Arms & Mfg. Co.
### Naubuc, Connecticut

### Hammond Bulldog

This is a single-shot weapon chambered for the .44 rimfire cartridge. It has a 4" octagonal barrel that pivots to the left for loading. It is a very solid, spur-triggered, derringer-type weapon constructed of blued iron, with checkered walnut grips. It was manufactured in 1864 and was carried as a backup by many Union soldiers during the Civil War.

| Exc. | V.G. | Good | Fair | Poor |
|------|------|------|------|------|
| 750  | 600  | 500  | 375  | 250  |

# HAMMOND, GRANT MFG. CO.
## New Haven, Connecticut

### Military Automatic Pistol

This is an extremely rare semi-automatic pistol chambered for the .45 ACP cartridge. It has a 6.75" barrel and an 8-shot magazine. The finish is blued, and the grips are checkered walnut. This pistol is marked on the right of the slide "Grant Hammond Mfg. Corp. New Haven, Conn." The left side shows the patent dates. This pistol was manufactured in 1917 only and was submitted for the U.S. Government trials. There were no others produced.

| Exc. | V.G. | Good | Fair | Poor |
|------|------|------|------|------|
| 8500 | 7850 | 6750 | 5000 | 4000 |

# HANKINS, WILLIAM
## Philadelphia, Pennsylvania

### Pocket Revolver

This small revolver is chambered for .26 caliber and utilizes the percussion ignition system. It has a 3" octagonal barrel and a 5-shot unfluted cylinder. It is a single action with a spur trigger, and the finish is blued with walnut grips. This company went into partnership with Sharps in 1861 and produced a number of other firearms that will be listed under the Sharps-Hankins section of this book. There were approximately 650 manufactured in 1860 and 1861.

| Exc. | V.G. | Good | Fair | Poor |
|------|------|------|------|------|
| 750  | 650  | 550  | 425  | 275  |

# HARRINGTON & RICHARDSON, INC.
## Worcester, Massachusetts

G. H. Harrington and W. A. Richardson founded this company in 1877 for the purpose of manufacturing revolvers. Initially the company produced cheap, solid-frame, spur-trigger revolvers under the trade name of Aetna. They were typical of the products manufactured during this era. They produced this type of revolver until 1897, when a line of break-open, automatic-ejecting revolvers was introduced. They were also of a design that was typical in their era. A number of hammerless revolvers were also produced. Gradually, their line evolved to include many inexpensive, yet serviceable, sporting pistols, rifles, and shotguns. The company endured for many years.

### Model No. 1

This is a spur-trigger, solid-frame, single-action revolver chambered for the .32 or .38 rimfire cartridges. It has a 3" octagonal barrel and either a 7-shot or a 5-shot cylinder, depending on the caliber. The finish is nickel-plated with checkered rubber bird-shead grips. The barrel is marked "Harrington & Richardson Worchester, Mass." There were approximately 3,000 manufactured in 1877 and 1878.

| Exc. | V.G. | Good | Fair | Poor |
|------|------|------|------|------|
| 300  | 250  | 200  | 125  | 75   |

### Model 1-1/2

This is a spur-trigger, single-action revolver chambered for the .32 rimfire cartridge. It has a 2.5" octagonal barrel and a 5-shot cylinder. The finish is nickel-plated with round-butt rubber grips with a "H&R" emblem molded in. There were approximately 10,000 manufactured between 1878 and 1883.

| Exc. | V.G. | Good | Fair | Poor |
|------|------|------|------|------|
| 175  | 150  | 125  | 75   | 50   |

### Model 2-1/2

This version has a 3.25" barrel and a 7-shot cylinder. Otherwise it was similar to the Model 1-1/2. There were approximately 5,000 manufactured between 1878 and 1883.

| Exc. | V.G. | Good | Fair | Poor |
|------|------|------|------|------|
| 175  | 150  | 125  | 75   | 50   |

### Model 3-1/2

This version is similar to the Model 2-1/2 except that it is chambered for the .38 rimfire cartridge. It has a 3.5" barrel and a 5-shot cylinder. There were approximately 2,500 manufactured.

| Exc. | V.G. | Good | Fair | Poor |
|------|------|------|------|------|
| 200  | 175  | 150  | 100  | 75   |

### Model 4-1/2

This version is chambered for the .41 rimfire cartridge and has a 2.5" barrel and a 5-shot cylinder. There were approximately 1,000 manufactured.

| Exc. | V.G. | Good | Fair | Poor |
|------|------|------|------|------|
| 250  | 200  | 175  | 125  | 90   |

### Model 1880

This is a double-action revolver chambered for either the .32 or the .38 S&W centerfire cartridges. It has a 3" round barrel and a solid frame. It features a 5-or 6-shot cylinder, depending on the caliber. The finish is nickel-plated with hard rubber grips. The barrel is marked "Harrington & Richardson Worchester, Mass." There were approximately 4,000 manufactured between 1880 and 1883.

| Exc. | V.G. | Good | Fair | Poor |
|------|------|------|------|------|
| 250  | 200  | 175  | 125  | 90   |

### The American Double Action

This is a double-action revolver chambered for the .32, .38, or .44 centerfire cartridges. It has either a 2.5", 4.5", or 6" round or octagonal barrel. It has either a 5-or 6-shot fluted cylinder, depending on the caliber. It has a solid frame and is nickel-plated, with some blue models noted. The grips are of hard rubber. It is marked "The American Double Action." Some noted are marked "H&R Bulldog." There were approximately 850,000 manufactured between 1883 and 1940.

| Exc. | V.G. | Good | Fair | Poor |
|------|------|------|------|------|
| 125  | 100  | 85   | 65   | 40   |

### The Young America Double Action

This is a solid-frame, double-action revolver chambered for the .22 rimfire or .32 S&W centerfire cartridges. It has either 2", 4.5", or 6" round or octagonal barrels. It has either a 5-shot or 7-shot cylinder, depending on the caliber. It is either blued or nickel-plated, with hard rubber grips. It is marked "Young America Double Action" or "Young America Bulldog." There were approximately 1,500,000 manufactured between 1884 and 1941.

| Exc. | V.G. | Good | Fair | Poor |
|------|------|------|------|------|
| 125 | 100 | 85 | 65 | 40 |

**First Model Hand Ejector**

This was the first top-break revolver this company manufactured. It is a double action chambered for the .32 or .38 centerfire cartridges. It has a 3.25" ribbed round barrel. This version does not feature the automatic ejection found on later models. Empty cartridges are ejected by means of a protruding center pin under the barrel. The finish is nickel-plated, with hard rubber grips. The company name is marked on the barrel. There were approximately 6,000 manufactured between 1886 and 1888.

| Exc. | V.G. | Good | Fair | Poor |
|------|------|------|------|------|
| 200 | 150 | 125 | 90 | 65 |

**Model 1 Double Action Revolver**

This is a top-break, automatic-ejecting double action chambered for the .32, .32 long, and the .38 S&W cartridges. It has a 3.25" ribbed round barrel with either a 5-or 6-shot cylinder, depending on the caliber. The finish is nickel-plated, with hard rubber grips. There were approximately 5,000 manufactured between 1887 and 1889.

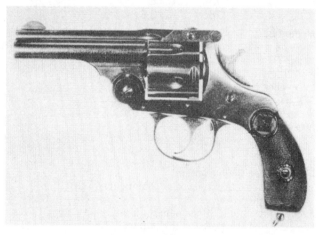

| Exc. | V.G. | Good | Fair | Poor |
|------|------|------|------|------|
| 175 | 145 | 110 | 80 | 50 |

**Model 2**

This version is similar to the Model 1, available with a 2.5", 3.25", 4", 5", or 6" barrels. The grips feature the H&R target logo. There were approximately 1,300,000 manufactured between 1889 and 1940.

| Exc. | V.G. | Good | Fair | Poor |
|------|------|------|------|------|
| 125 | 100 | 80 | 65 | 40 |

**Knife Model**

This version of the Model 2 has a 4" ribbed round barrel with a folding 2.25" double-edged knife mounted under the barrel. It was available either blued or nickel-plated, and there were approximately 2,000 manufactured between 1901 and 1917.

| Exc. | V.G. | Good | Fair | Poor |
|------|------|------|------|------|
| 450 | 400 | 350 | 250 | 150 |

**Self-Loader**

This is a blowback-operated semi-automatic pistol chambered for either 6.35mm or the 7.65mm cartridges. It has either a 2" or 3.5" barrel with a 6-shot or 8-shot magazine. The larger 7.65 model has a grip safety. These pistols were designed by Webley & Scott and were manufactured by H&R under license. They are either blued or nickel-plated with checkered, hard rubber grips that bear the H&R monogram. The slide is marked, "H&R Self-Loading" with 1907 or 1909 patent dates. There were approximately 16,500 manufactured in 6.35mm between 1912 and 1916 and 34,500 in 7.65mm manufactured between 1916 and 1924.

| Exc. | V.G. | Good | Fair | Poor |
|------|------|------|------|------|
| 350 | 300 | 250 | 175 | 100 |

**Hunter**

This is a double-action revolver chambered for the .22 l.r. cartridge. It has a 10" octagonal barrel and a 9-shot fluted cylinder. The finish is blued, with checkered walnut grips.

| Exc. | V.G. | Good | Fair | Poor |
|------|------|------|------|------|
| 150 | 125 | 100 | 75 | 50 |

**Trapper**

This version features a 6" octagonal barrel and a 7-shot cylinder. Otherwise it is similar to the Hunter.

| Exc. | V.G. | Good | Fair | Poor |
|------|------|------|------|------|
| 150 | 125 | 100 | 75 | 50 |

**Model 922 First Issue**

This is a double-action revolver chambered for the .22 rimfire cartridge. It has a 2.5", 4", or 6" barrel. The finish is blued, with checkered walnut grips.

| Exc. | V.G. | Good | Fair | Poor |
|------|------|------|------|------|
| 150 | 125 | 100 | 75 | 50 |

**Target Model**

This is a 7-shot, double-action revolver chambered for either .22 l.r. or the .22 rimfire Magnum cartridge. It has a break-open frame and a 6" barrel with fixed sights. The finish is blued, with checkered walnut grips.

| Exc. | V.G. | Good | Fair | Poor |
|------|------|------|------|------|
| 150 | 125 | 100 | 75 | 50 |

**.22 Special**

This is a larger, double-action, break-open revolver chambered for the .22 l.r. or the .22 rimfire Magnum cartridge. It has a 6" barrel and a 7-shot cylinder. The finish is blued, with checkered walnut grips.

| Exc. | V.G. | Good | Fair | Poor |
|------|------|------|------|------|
| 175 | 150 | 125 | 90 | 65 |

### Expert
This version is similar to the .22 Special except that it has a 10" barrel.

| Exc. | V.G. | Good | Fair | Poor |
|---|---|---|---|---|
| 150 | 125 | 100 | 75 | 50 |

### No. 199 Sportsman
This is a single-action, break-open revolver chambered for .22 l.r. It has a 6" barrel with adjustable target sights and a 9-round cylinder. The finish is blued, with checkered walnut grips.

| Exc. | V.G. | Good | Fair | Poor |
|---|---|---|---|---|
| 200 | 175 | 150 | 100 | 75 |

### Ultra Sportsman
This is an improved, more deluxe version of the Sportsman. It has a special, wide target hammer and an improved action.

| Exc. | V.G. | Good | Fair | Poor |
|---|---|---|---|---|
| 225 | 200 | 175 | 125 | 90 |

### Defender
This model is a double-action, break-open revolver chambered for the .38 S&W cartridge. It was available with a 4" or 6" barrel and fixed sights. The finish is blued, with plastic grips. During WWII this model was used by factory guards and some police units.

| Exc. | V.G. | Good | Fair | Poor |
|---|---|---|---|---|
| 150 | 125 | 100 | 75 | 50 |

### New Defender
This is a double-action, break-open revolver chambered for the .22 l.r. cartridge. It has a 2" barrel and a 9-shot cylinder. The finish is blued with checkered, walnut round-butt grips.

| Exc. | V.G. | Good | Fair | Poor |
|---|---|---|---|---|
| 225 | 200 | 175 | 125 | 90 |

### USRA Target Pistol
This is a single-shot, break-open pistol chambered for the .22 l.r. cartridge. It was offered with a 7", 8", or 10" barrel with adjustable target sights. The finish is either blued or nickel-plated, with checkered walnut grips. It was manufactured between 1928 and 1941.

| Exc. | V.G. | Good | Fair | Poor |
|---|---|---|---|---|
| 450 | 400 | 350 | 250 | 150 |

### Model 504
This is a double-action, swing-out-cylinder revolver chambered for the .32 H&R Mag. cartridge. It has a 4" or 6" heavy barrel with adjustable sights. The cylinder holds five shots. The finish is blued, with either black plastic or walnut grips. A smaller version with a 3" or 4" barrel and a round butt was also made. Values are the same.

H&R Model 504

| Exc. | V.G. | Good | Fair | Poor |
|---|---|---|---|---|
| 175 | 150 | 125 | 90 | 65 |

### Model 532
This is a solid-frame revolver similar to the Model 504 except that the cylinder has to be removed for loading. It was manufactured in 1984 and 1985.

H&R Model 532

| Exc. | V.G. | Good | Fair | Poor |
|---|---|---|---|---|
| 100 | 75 | 50 | 40 | 25 |

### Model 586
This is a double-action revolver made in the Western style. It is chambered for the .32 H&R Magnum cartridge. It has a 4.5", 5.5", 7.5", or 10" barrel with adjustable sights. It has a 5-round cylinder. The finish is blued, with either black plastic or walnut grips.

| Exc. | V.G. | Good | Fair | Poor |
|---|---|---|---|---|
| 175 | 150 | 125 | 100 | 75 |

### Model 603
This version is a double-action revolver chambered for the .22 rimfire Magnum cartridge, with a 6" flat-sided barrel and swing-out 6-shot cylinder. The finish is blued, with smooth walnut grips.

| Exc. | V.G. | Good | Fair | Poor |
|---|---|---|---|---|
| 165 | 140 | 110 | 85 | 60 |

### Model 604
This is similar to the Model 603, with a 6", ribbed, heavy barrel.

| Exc. | V.G. | Good | Fair | Poor |
|---|---|---|---|---|
| 175 | 150 | 125 | 90 | 65 |

## Model 622

This is a solid-frame double-action revolver chambered for the .22 l.r. cartridge. It has a 2.5" or 4" barrel. The finish is blued, with round-butt plastic grips.

H&R Model 622

| Exc. | V.G. | Good | Fair | Poor |
|------|------|------|------|------|
| 100 | 80 | 65 | 50 | 25 |

## Model 623

This is a nickel-plated version of the Model 622.

| Exc. | V.G. | Good | Fair | Poor |
|------|------|------|------|------|
| 125 | 100 | 80 | 60 | 40 |

## Model 632

This is a .32 centerfire version of the Model 622.

| Exc. | V.G. | Good | Fair | Poor |
|------|------|------|------|------|
| 110 | 90 | 75 | 60 | 30 |

## Model 642

This is the Model 622 chambered for the .22 rimfire Magnum cartridge.

| Exc. | V.G. | Good | Fair | Poor |
|------|------|------|------|------|
| 100 | 80 | 65 | 50 | 25 |

## Model 649

This version is similar to the Model 622, with a 5.5" or 7.5" barrel. It features hardwood grips.

H&R Model 649

| Exc. | V.G. | Good | Fair | Poor |
|------|------|------|------|------|
| 150 | 125 | 100 | 75 | 50 |

## Model 650

This is a nickel-plated version of the Model 649.

| Exc. | V.G. | Good | Fair | Poor |
|------|------|------|------|------|
| 150 | 125 | 100 | 75 | 50 |

## Model 660

This is a solid-frame, Western-style revolver chambered for the .22 l.r. cartridge. It has a 5.5" barrel and is a double action. The finish is blued, with walnut grips. It is also known as the "Gunfighter."

| Exc. | V.G. | Good | Fair | Poor |
|------|------|------|------|------|
| 100 | 80 | 65 | 45 | 25 |

## Model 666

This is a double-action revolver chambered for the .22 l.r. or .22 rimfire Magnum cartridges. It has a 6" barrel with a 6-shot cylinder. The finish is blued, with plastic grips. It was manufactured between 1976 and 1982.

| Exc. | V.G. | Good | Fair | Poor |
|------|------|------|------|------|
| 100 | 80 | 65 | 45 | 25 |

## Model 676

This version features side loading and has an ejector rod on the barrel. The finish is blued, with a case-colored frame. It has walnut grips. It was manufactured between 1976 and 1982.

| Exc. | V.G. | Good | Fair | Poor |
|------|------|------|------|------|
| 150 | 125 | 100 | 75 | 50 |

## Model 686

This is similar to the Model 660 "Gunfighter" except that it was offered with a 4.5", 5.5", 7.5", 10", and 12" barrel.

| Exc. | V.G. | Good | Fair | Poor |
|------|------|------|------|------|
| 175 | 150 | 125 | 100 | 75 |

## Model 732

This is a double-action, solid-frame revolver with a swing-out cylinder. It is chambered for the .32 cartridge and has a 2.5" or 4" barrel. The cylinder holds six shots. The finish is blued, with black plastic grips. It is also known as the "Guardsman."

| Exc. | V.G. | Good | Fair | Poor |
|------|------|------|------|------|
| 125 | 100 | 80 | 65 | 45 |

## Model 733

This is a nickel-plated version of the 732 with a 2.5" barrel.

| Exc. | V.G. | Good | Fair | Poor |
|------|------|------|------|------|
| 150 | 125 | 100 | 75 | 50 |

## Model 900

This is a solid-frame revolver with a removable cylinder chambered for the .22 l.r. cartridge. It has a 2.5" or 4" barrel and a 9-shot cylinder. The finish is blued, with black plastic grips. It was manufactured between 1962 and 1973.

| Exc. | V.G. | Good | Fair | Poor |
|------|------|------|------|------|
| 100 | 90 | 80 | 60 | 40 |

## Model 901

This version is chrome-plated, with white plastic grips. It was manufactured in 1962 and 1963 only.

| Exc. | V.G. | Good | Fair | Poor |
|------|------|------|------|------|
| 100 | 90 | 80 | 60 | 40 |

## Model 903

This version has a swing-out cylinder and is chambered for the .22 l.r. cartridge. It has a flat-sided, 6" barrel and a 9-shot cylinder. The finish is blued, with smooth walnut grips.

| Exc. | V.G. | Good | Fair | Poor |
|------|------|------|------|------|
| 125 | 100 | 90 | 75 | 50 |

## Model 904

This version has a ribbed heavy barrel.

| Exc. | V.G. | Good | Fair | Poor |
|------|------|------|------|------|
| 150 | 125 | 100 | 75 | 50 |

## Model 905

This is a nickel-plated version of the Model 904.

| Exc. | V.G. | Good | Fair | Poor |
|------|------|------|------|------|
| 165 | 140 | 110 | 80 | 65 |

## Model 922 Second Issue

This is a solid-frame revolver chambered for the .22 rimfire cartridge. It features a 2.5", 4", or 6" barrel. The finish is blued, with black plastic grips. It was manufactured between 1950 and 1982.

| Exc. | V.G. | Good | Fair | Poor |
|------|------|------|------|------|
| 100 | 90 | 80 | 60 | 40 |

## Model 923
This is a nickel-plated version of the Model 922.

| Exc. | V.G. | Good | Fair | Poor |
|------|------|------|------|------|
| 110 | 95 | 85 | 65 | 45 |

## Model 925
This is a double-action, break-open, hand-ejector revolver chambered for the .38 S&W cartridge. It has a 2.5" barrel with adjustable sights and a 5-shot cylinder. The finish is blued, with a one-piece wrap-around grip. It was manufactured between 1964 and 1984.

H&R Model 925

| Exc. | V.G. | Good | Fair | Poor |
|------|------|------|------|------|
| 150 | 125 | 100 | 75 | 50 |

## Model 935
This is a nickel-plated version of the Model 925.

| Exc. | V.G. | Good | Fair | Poor |
|------|------|------|------|------|
| 150 | 125 | 100 | 75 | 50 |

## Model 929
This is a solid-frame, swing-out revolver chambered for the .22 rimfire cartridge. It has a 2.5", 4", or 6" barrel and a 9-shot cylinder. The finish is blued, with plastic grips. It is also known as the "Sidekick" and was manufactured between 1956 and 1985.

| Exc. | V.G. | Good | Fair | Poor |
|------|------|------|------|------|
| 125 | 100 | 85 | 65 | 45 |

## Model 930
This is the nickle-plated version of the Model 929. It was not available in the 6" barrel configuration.

| Exc. | V.G. | Good | Fair | Poor |
|------|------|------|------|------|
| 125 | 100 | 85 | 65 | 45 |

## Model 939 Ultra Sidekick
This is a deluxe version of the Sidekick with a ventilated-rib, 6" barrel. It features adjustable sights and a flat-sided barrel. It has thumbrest grips and features a safety device whereby the pistol could not be fired unless it was unlocked by a furnished key. It was manufactured between 1958 and 1982.

H&R Model 939

| Exc. | V.G. | Good | Fair | Poor |
|------|------|------|------|------|
| 125 | 100 | 85 | 65 | 45 |

## Model 940
This is a round-barrelled version of the Model 939.

| Exc. | V.G. | Good | Fair | Poor |
|------|------|------|------|------|
| 100 | 90 | 80 | 65 | 45 |

## Model 949
This is a double-action, Western-type revolver chambered for the .22 l.r. cartridge. It has a 5.5" barrel with an ejector rod. It has a 9-shot, gate-loaded cylinder and adjustable sights. The finish is blued, with walnut grips. It was manufactured between 1960 and 1985.

| Exc. | V.G. | Good | Fair | Poor |
|------|------|------|------|------|
| 125 | 100 | 80 | 65 | 40 |

## Model 950
This is the nickel-plated version of the Model 949.

| Exc. | V.G. | Good | Fair | Poor |
|------|------|------|------|------|
| 125 | 100 | 80 | 65 | 40 |

## Model 976
This version of the Model 949 has a case-colored frame.

| Exc. | V.G. | Good | Fair | Poor |
|------|------|------|------|------|
| 100 | 80 | 65 | 45 | 30 |

## Model 999 Sportsman
This is a double-action, break-open, self-ejecting revolver chambered for the .22 rimfire cartridge. It has a 6" vent-rib barrel with adjustable sights. The finish is blued, with walnut grips. It was manufactured between 1950 and 1985.

H&R Model 999

| Exc. | V.G. | Good | Fair | Poor |
|------|------|------|------|------|
| 200 | 150 | 125 | 90 | 65 |

## Engraved Model 999
This is a fully engraved version of the Model 999.

| Exc. | V.G. | Good | Fair | Poor |
|------|------|------|------|------|
| 425 | 350 | 300 | 200 | 125 |

## Hammerless Double
This is a side-by-side, double-barrel shotgun chambered for 10 or 12 gauge. It has 28", 30", or 32" Damascus barrels with various choke combinations. It features a hammerless Anson & Deeley boxlock action. It has double triggers and extractors. This gun was designed by Anson & Deeley in England and manufactured under license by H&R. The barrels are Damascus. The receiver is engraved and case-colored. The stock is checkered, select-grain walnut. There were four grades available. They differ in the amount of engraving and the quality of materials and workmenship utilized. There were approximately 3,500 manufactured between 1882 and 1885.

### D Grade

| Exc. | V.G. | Good | Fair | Poor |
|------|------|------|------|------|
| 650 | 550 | 425 | 300 | 175 |

### C Grade

| Exc. | V.G. | Good | Fair | Poor |
|------|------|------|------|------|
| 750 | 650 | 500 | 400 | 275 |

**B Grade**

| Exc. | V.G. | Good | Fair | Poor |
|------|------|------|------|------|
| 900 | 750 | 600 | 500 | 350 |

**A Grade**

| Exc. | V.G. | Good | Fair | Poor |
|------|------|------|------|------|
| 2000 | 1750 | 1500 | 1000 | 550 |

**Harrich No. 1**

This is a single-barrel, break-open trap gun that was manufactured in Austria and marketed by Harrington & Richardson. It is chambered for 12 gauge and has either a 32" or 34", vent-rib, full-choke barrel. It features an automatic ejector and is heavily engraved and blued with a checkered, select walnut stock. It was imported between 1971 and 1975.

| Exc. | V.G. | Good | Fair | Poor |
|------|------|------|------|------|
| 1750 | 1500 | 1150 | 850 | 650 |

Harrington & Richardson manufactured a series of single-barrel, break-open shotguns between 1908 and 1942. They were chambered for various gauges and had various barrel lengths and chokes. The finishes were blued with walnut stocks. There is little collector interest in these guns and, if in sound condition, are desirable as shooters only. They are the Models 3, 5, 6, 7, 8, and 9, as well as a hinged-frame, folding design. Values are as follows:

| Exc. | V.G. | Good | Fair | Poor |
|------|------|------|------|------|
| 125 | 100 | 85 | 65 | 40 |

**Topper**

This is a single-shot, break-open shotgun chambered for various gauges with various barrel lengths and chokes. The finish is blued, with a hardwood stock. It was introduced in 1946.

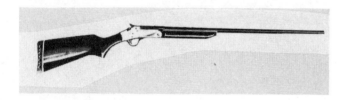

| Exc. | V.G. | Good | Fair | Poor |
|------|------|------|------|------|
| 110 | 95 | 75 | 60 | 40 |

**Model 088**

This is a single-shot, break-open shotgun chambered for all gauges with various barrel lengths and chokes. It has an external hammer and an automatic ejector. The barrel is blued, with a case-colored frame and hardwood stock.

| Exc. | V.G. | Good | Fair | Poor |
|------|------|------|------|------|
| 100 | 85 | 65 | 45 | 30 |

**Model 099**

This is a matte, electroless, nickel-plated version of the Model 088.

| Exc. | V.G. | Good | Fair | Poor |
|------|------|------|------|------|
| 110 | 95 | 75 | 60 | 40 |

**Model 162**

This version has a 24" barrel with rifle sights. It is chambered for 12 or 20 gauge only.

| Exc. | V.G. | Good | Fair | Poor |
|------|------|------|------|------|
| 125 | 100 | 80 | 65 | 45 |

**Model 176**

This version is chambered for the 10-gauge, 3.5" Magnum shell. It has a heavy-weight 36" barrel with a full choke. It was manufactured between 1977 and 1985.

| Exc. | V.G. | Good | Fair | Poor |
|------|------|------|------|------|
| 125 | 100 | 80 | 65 | 45 |

**Model 400**

This is a slide-action shotgun chambered for 12, 16, or 20 gauge. It has a 28" full-choke barrel. The finish is blued, with a hardwood stock. It was made between 1955 and 1967.

| Exc. | V.G. | Good | Fair | Poor |
|------|------|------|------|------|
| 150 | 125 | 100 | 75 | 50 |

**Model 401**

This version features the H&R variable-choke device. It was manufactured between 1956 and 1963.

| Exc. | V.G. | Good | Fair | Poor |
|------|------|------|------|------|
| 175 | 150 | 125 | 90 | 65 |

**Model 402**

This version is chambered for the .410 shell. It was manufactured between 1959 and 1967.

| Exc. | V.G. | Good | Fair | Poor |
|------|------|------|------|------|
| 175 | 150 | 125 | 90 | 65 |

**Model 440**

This is a slide-action shotgun chambered for 12, 16, or 20 gauge with a 26", 28", or 30" barrel in various chokes. The finish is blued, with a hardwood stock. It was made between 1968 and 1973.

| Exc. | V.G. | Good | Fair | Poor |
|------|------|------|------|------|
| 150 | 125 | 100 | 75 | 50 |

**Model 442**

This version features a vent-rib barrel and a checkered stock. It was manufactured between 1969 and 1973.

| Exc. | V.G. | Good | Fair | Poor |
|------|------|------|------|------|
| 175 | 150 | 125 | 90 | 65 |

**Model 403**

This is an auto-loading shotgun chambered for .410 with a 26", full-choke barrel. The finish is blued, with a hardwood stock. It was manufactured in 1964.

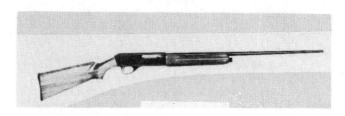

| Exc. | V.G. | Good | Fair | Poor |
|------|------|------|------|------|
| 200 | 175 | 150 | 100 | 75 |

**Model 404**

This is a side-by-side, double-barrel shotgun manufactured by Rossi in Brazil. It is chambered for 12 and 20 gauge, as well as .410. It has 26" or 28" barrels and a boxlock action with double triggers and extractors. The finish is blued, with a hardwood stock. It was imported between 1969 and 1972. A checkered-stock version is known as the Model 404C and would be worth approximately 10 percent additional.

| Exc. | V.G. | Good | Fair | Poor |
|------|------|------|------|------|
| 175 | 150 | 125 | 90 | 65 |

## Model 1212

This is an Over/Under, field-grade shotgun chambered for 12 gauge. It has 28" vent-rib barrels with various choke combinations. The finish is blued, with a checkered walnut stock. It was manufactured in Spain by Landbar Arms. It was imported after 1976. A waterfowl version with 3" chambers and a 30" full-choke barrel was available and would be worth approximately $10 additional.

| Exc. | V.G. | Good | Fair | Poor |
|------|------|------|------|------|
| 300  | 250  | 200  | 150  | 100  |

## Model 058

This is an interchangeable rifle/shotgun combination gun. It was supplied with a 20-gauge barrel as well as one in either .22 Hornet, .30-30, .357 Magnum, or .44 Magnum. The finish is blued, with a hardwood stock.

| Exc. | V.G. | Good | Fair | Poor |
|------|------|------|------|------|
| 125  | 100  | 80   | 65   | 40   |

## Model 258

This is a more deluxe version furnished in matte, electroless nickel plate.

| Exc. | V.G. | Good | Fair | Poor |
|------|------|------|------|------|
| 175  | 150  | 125  | 90   | 75   |

## Reising Model 60

This is a semi-automatic version of the Model 50 submachine gun. It is chambered for the .45 ACP cartridge. It has an 18.25" barrel and is furnished with a 12-or 20-round detachable magazine. The finish is blued, with a walnut stock. It operates on a retarded blowback system and was developed to be used as a police weapon. It was tested by a number of military agencies but not accepted. It was manufactured between 1944 and 1946.

| Exc. | V.G. | Good | Fair | Poor |
|------|------|------|------|------|
| 375  | 325  | 250  | 175  | 100  |

## Model 65 Military

This is a blowback-operated, .22 l.r., semi-automatic rifle that has a 23" barrel and Redfield peepsights. The finish is blued, with a walnut stock. It was manufactured between 1944 and 1946 as a training rifle for the United States Marine Corps.

| Exc. | V.G. | Good | Fair | Poor |
|------|------|------|------|------|
| 250  | 200  | 175  | 125  | 90   |

## Model 150

This is a blowback-operated, semi-automatic rifle chambered for the .22 l.r. cartridge. It has a 20" barrel and a 5-round magazine. The finish is blued, with a walnut stock. It was manufactured between 1949 and 1953.

| Exc. | V.G. | Good | Fair | Poor |
|------|------|------|------|------|
| 100  | 80   | 60   | 45   | 30   |

## Model 155

This is a single-shot, break-open rifle chambered for the .44 Magnum or the .45-70 cartridge. It has a 20" barrel with fixed sights. The finish is blued, with a walnut stock. It was introduced in 1972.

| Exc. | V.G. | Good | Fair | Poor |
|------|------|------|------|------|
| 125  | 100  | 80   | 60   | 40   |

## Model 157

This version is chambered for the .22 Magnum, .22 Hornet, and the .30-30 cartridges. It is similar to the Model 155.

| Exc. | V.G. | Good | Fair | Poor |
|------|------|------|------|------|
| 125  | 100  | 80   | 60   | 40   |

## Model 158

This version is also chambered for the .357 Magnum and the .44 Magnum cartridges. The action is activated by a side lever. It has an automatic ejector and a case-colored frame. The barrel length is 22". It was not manufactured after 1985. A combination version that was supplied with an interchangeable 26" 20-gauge barrel was available and would be worth an additional 20 percent.

| Exc. | V.G. | Good | Fair | Poor |
|------|------|------|------|------|
| 100  | 80   | 60   | 45   | 30   |

## Model 171

This is a reproduction of the Model 1873 Trapdoor Springfield Carbine. It is chambered for the .45-70 cartridge and has a 22" barrel. The barrel is blued, with a case-colored receiver and a walnut stock.

| Exc. | V.G. | Good | Fair | Poor |
|------|------|------|------|------|
| 300  | 250  | 200  | 150  | 100  |

## Model 171-DL

This is a deluxe version of the Model 171.

| Exc. | V.G. | Good | Fair | Poor |
|------|------|------|------|------|
| 350  | 300  | 250  | 200  | 125  |

## Model 300 Ultra

This is a high-quality, bolt-action sporting rifle chambered for various popular calibers from .22-250 up to the .300 Winchester Magnum cartridges. It has a 22" or 24" barrel and was furnished without sights. The finish is high-polish blue with a select, checkered walnut stock. It was manufactured between 1965 and 1978.

H&R Model 300

| Exc. | V.G. | Good | Fair | Poor |
|------|------|------|------|------|
| 450  | 400  | 350  | 275  | 175  |

## Model 301 Carbine

This version has an 18" barrel and a full-length, Mannlicher-type stock.

| Exc. | V.G. | Good | Fair | Poor |
|------|------|------|------|------|
| 450  | 400  | 350  | 275  | 175  |

## Model 317 Ultra Wildcat

This version was built on a short Sako bolt action. It is chambered for the .17 Rem., .17-223, .222 Rem., and the .223 Rem. cartridges. It has a 20" barrel that was furnished without sights. The finish is blued, with a checkered walnut stock. It was manufactured between 1968 and 1976.

| Exc. | V.G. | Good | Fair | Poor |
|------|------|------|------|------|
| 450 | 400 | 350 | 275 | 175 |

## Model 317P

This is a deluxe version that features high-grade walnut and basketweave checkering. It was manufactured between 1968 and 1976.

| Exc. | V.G. | Good | Fair | Poor |
|------|------|------|------|------|
| 550 | 500 | 450 | 375 | 250 |

## Model 333

This is a plain utility version of the Model 300 chambered for the 7mm Mag. cartridge. It was manufactured in 1974.

| Exc. | V.G. | Good | Fair | Poor |
|------|------|------|------|------|
| 250 | 200 | 175 | 125 | 100 |

## Model 340

This is a bolt-action sporting rifle chambered for various popular calibers from .243 to .308 Winchester. It has a 22" barrel and a 5-shot magazine. The finish is blued, with a checkered walnut stock.

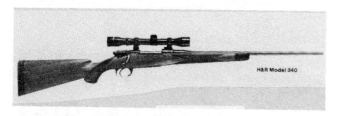

H&R Model 340

| Exc. | V.G. | Good | Fair | Poor |
|------|------|------|------|------|
| 400 | 350 | 300 | 225 | 150 |

## Model 360 Ultra Automatic

This is a semi-automatic sporting rifle chambered for the .243 Win. and the .308 Win. cartridges. It has a 22" barrel with adjustable sights and a 3-shot detachable magazine. The finish is blued, with a checkered walnut stock. It was manufactured between 1965 and 1978.

| Exc. | V.G. | Good | Fair | Poor |
|------|------|------|------|------|
| 350 | 300 | 250 | 175 | 100 |

## Model 451 Medalist

This is a bolt-action sporting rifle chambered for the .22 l.r. cartridge. It has a 26" barrel with open sights and a 5-shot detachable magazine. The finish is blued, with a walnut stock. It was manufactured between 1948 and 1961.

| Exc. | V.G. | Good | Fair | Poor |
|------|------|------|------|------|
| 175 | 150 | 125 | 100 | 75 |

## Model 700

This is a semi-automatic sporting rifle chambered for the .22 rimfire Magnum cartridge. It has a 22" barrel with adjustable sights and a 5-round, detachable magazine. The finish is blued, with a checkered walnut stock. It was manufactured between 1977 and 1985.

| Exc. | V.G. | Good | Fair | Poor |
|------|------|------|------|------|
| 175 | 150 | 125 | 100 | 75 |

## Model 700 DL

This version features a higher-grade, checkered walnut stock and was furnished with a 4X scope. It was manufactured until 1985.

| Exc. | V.G. | Good | Fair | Poor |
|------|------|------|------|------|
| 300 | 250 | 200 | 150 | 100 |

## Model 750

This is a bolt-action single-shot rifle chambered for the .22 l.r. cartridge. It has a 22" barrel with sights and a short stock designed for young shooters. The finish is blued, and the stock is hardwood.

H&R Model 750

| Exc. | V.G. | Good | Fair | Poor |
|------|------|------|------|------|
| 100 | 80 | 60 | 45 | 25 |

## Model 865

This is a bolt-action repeating rifle chambered for the .22 l.r. cartridge. It has a 22" barrel with open sights and a 5-round detachable magazine. The finish is blued, with a hardwood stock.

| Exc. | V.G. | Good | Fair | Poor |
|------|------|------|------|------|
| 100 | 80 | 60 | 45 | 25 |

## Model 5200

This is a bolt-action, single-shot target rifle chambered for the .22 l.r. cartridge. It has a 28" heavy barrel that was furnished without sights. It has an adjustable trigger and is blued, with a target-type walnut stock.

| Exc. | V.G. | Good | Fair | Poor |
|------|------|------|------|------|
| 400 | 350 | 300 | 225 | 125 |

## Model 5200 Sporter

This is a bolt-action repeater that is chambered for the .22 l.r. cartridge. It has a 24" barrel that was furnished with adjustable sights. It has a 5-round detachable magazine. The finish is blued with a checkered, select walnut stock. It was not manufactured after 1983.

| Exc. | V.G. | Good | Fair | Poor |
|------|------|------|------|------|
| 400 | 350 | 300 | 225 | 125 |

## 100th Anniversary Officer's Model

This was a commemorative replica of the Officer's Model 1873 Trapdoor Springfield Rifle. It is chambered for the .45-70 cartridge. It has a 26" barrel. It is engraved, and there is an anniversary plaque mounted on the stock. The finish is blued, with a case-colored receiver and a pewter forend tip. There were 10,000 manufactured in 1971. As with all commemoratives, this model is desirable only when NIB with all supplied material.

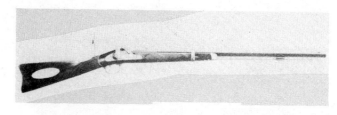

| NIB | Exc. | V.G. | Good | Fair | Poor |
|-----|------|------|------|------|------|
| 450 | 350 | 300 | 275 | 200 | 125 |

## Custer Memorial Issue

This is a limited-production issue commemorating George Armstrong Custer's Battle of the Little Bighorn. It is a very deluxe version of the .45-70 Trapdoor Springfield Carbine. It is heavily engraved and gold-inlaid with a very high-grade checkered walnut stock. It was furnished in a mahogany display case that included two books dealing with the subject. There were two versions produced--an Officer's Model, of which 25 were issued commemorating the 25 officers that fell with Custer, and another version commemorating the 243 enlisted men who lost their lives at the Little Bighorn. As with all commemoratives, in order to be collectible, they must be NIB with all furnished material.

### Officer's Model--25 Manufactured

| NIB | Exc. | V.G. | Good | Fair | Poor |
|-----|------|------|------|------|------|
| 2700 | 2000 | 1500 | 1000 | 600 | 400 |

### Enlisted Men's Model--243 Manufactured

| NIB | Exc. | V.G. | Good | Fair | Poor |
|-----|------|------|------|------|------|
| 1500 | 1000 | 750 | 500 | 350 | 250 |

## Model 174

This is a commercial version called the Little Bighorn Carbine. It is chambered for the .45-70 cartridge and has a 22" barrel. It was manufactured in 1972.

| Exc. | V.G. | Good | Fair | Poor |
|------|------|------|------|------|
| 400 | 350 | 300 | 250 | 175 |

## Model 178

This is a replica of the Trapdoor Infantry Musket. It is chambered for the .45-70 cartridge and has a 32" barrel with a full-length walnut stock. It was manufactured between 1973 and 1984.

| Exc. | V.G. | Good | Fair | Poor |
|------|------|------|------|------|
| 325 | 300 | 250 | 200 | 125 |

# HARTFORD ARMS & EQUIPMENT CO.
## Hartford, Connecticut

This company was founded to produce .22-caliber pistols. They manufactured four different models from 1929 until 1932, when they filed for bankruptcy. The High Standard Co. purchased the assets and used the pistols as a basis for their own production.

## Single Shot Target

This .22-caliber single shot resembles a semi-automatic in appearance and function. It has a 6.75" round barrel, blued with a case-colored frame and slide. It features target sights, with either wood or rubber grips. There is no magazine or place for one. The markings on the frame are "Manfd. by the Hartford Arms and Equip. Co. Hartford, Conn. Patented .22 cal. Long Rifle."

| Exc. | V.G. | Good | Fair | Poor |
|------|------|------|------|------|
| 750 | 650 | 500 | 350 | 275 |

## Repeating Pistol

This is similar to the single shot in appearance, with a 10-shot magazine fitted into the butt. The slide could be worked manually to feed successive shots. The finish is all blued.

| Exc. | V.G. | Good | Fair | Poor |
|------|------|------|------|------|
| 750 | 650 | 500 | 350 | 275 |

## Semi-Auto 1st Model

Although the same in appearance to the repeater and the single shot, this is an actual semi-automatic in function. The finish is all blued.

| Exc. | V.G. | Good | Fair | Poor |
|------|------|------|------|------|
| 700 | 600 | 450 | 375 | 300 |

## Semi-Auto 2nd Model

This is a similar pistol to the 1st Model, with a heavier slab-sided barrel, reminiscent of the Colt Match Target Woodsman.

| Exc. | V.G. | Good | Fair | Poor |
|------|------|------|------|------|
| 700 | 600 | 450 | 375 | 300 |

# HATFIELD RIFLE COMPANY
## St. Joseph, Missouri

## Squirrel Rifle

This rifle is available from Hatfield in a flintlock or a percussion ignition system. The calibers chambered are .32, .36, .45, or .50. They have 39" barrels and feature double-set triggers and adjustable sights. The mountings are brass;, and the stocks, of maple. These rifles are very high quality and essentially hand-built. There are many options--such as fancy-grade wood and engraving, etc. The values represented here are for a standard rifle. Custom features can have a drastic effect on the value. Independent appraisal is definitely warranted.

| NIB | Exc. | V.G. | Good | Fair | Poor |
|-----|------|------|------|------|------|
| 475 | 400 | 350 | 300 | 225 | 150 |

## Shotguns
## Uplanded Grade I

This is a side-by-side double that is chambered for 20 gauge only. It has 3" chambers and a 26" improved cylinder and modified barrel with a matte raised rib. This is a boxlock action with single-selective trigger and automatic ejectors. The action is case-colored; and the remainder, blue with a deluxe-grade, hand-checkered walnut stock. This model was introduced in 1987.

| NIB | Exc. | V.G. | Good | Fair | Poor |
|-----|------|------|------|------|------|
| 1150 | 1050 | 750 | 600 | 475 | 400 |

## Uplander Pigeon Grade II

This version is similar to the Grade I, with scroll engraving and furnished with a fitted leather case.

| NIB | Exc. | V.G. | Good | Fair | Poor |
|-----|------|------|------|------|------|
| 2000 | 1750 | 1275 | 900 | 650 | 500 |

## Uplander Super Pigeon Grade III

This model is completely covered with deep-relief engraving and also has the leather case.

| NIB | Exc. | V.G. | Good | Fair | Poor |
|-----|------|------|------|------|------|
| 2500 | 2200 | 1700 | 1400 | 1000 | 700 |

## Uplander Golden Quail Grade IV

This model is more elaborately engraved and has six gold inlays and two gold barrel bands. It also is leather-cased.

| NIB | Exc. | V.G. | Good | Fair | Poor |
|-----|------|------|------|------|------|
| 4000 | 3500 | 2750 | 2000 | 1700 | 1300 |

## Uplander Woodcock Grade V

This is the best-grade double that Hatfield offers. It has seven 24 kt. gold inlays and is very elaborately engraved. It is also furnished in the leather case.

| NIB | Exc. | V.G. | Good | Fair | Poor |
|-----|------|------|------|------|------|
| 5600 | 5000 | 4250 | 3500 | 2750 | 2000 |

## HAVILAND & GUNN
### Ilion, New York

### Gallery Pistol

This single-shot pistol is chambered for a .17 caliber rimfire cartridge and was used for indoor target practice. It has a 5" round barrel with an octagonal breech and was entirely cast in one piece of iron and then nickel plated. The loop triggerguard is also the hammer spring. The hammer is case-colored, and there are no grips. These pistols are not marked, and their origin is unknown. They were manufactured circa 1870.

| Exc. | V.G. | Good | Fair | Poor |
|------|------|------|------|------|
| 400  | 350  | 300  | 225  | 125  |

## HAWES
### Los Angeles, California

This company was not a manufacturer but imported handguns and distributed them under the Hawes trademark. The quality of the pistols is mediocre, and collector interest is minimal.

### Courier

This is a .25-caliber, blowback, semi-automatic pocket pistol manufactured by Galesi.

| Exc. | V.G. | Good | Fair | Poor |
|------|------|------|------|------|
| 125  | 100  | 75   | 50   | 25   |

### Diplomat

This is a .380ACP blowback pistol with an external hammer.

| Exc. | V.G. | Good | Fair | Poor |
|------|------|------|------|------|
| 150  | 125  | 100  | 75   | 50   |

### Trophy

Made in Germany by J. P. Sauer & Sohn, this is a solid-frame revolver with a swing-out cylinder and a 6" barrel. It is chambered for the .22 l.r. and the .38 Special. It features adjustable sights.

| Exc. | V.G. | Good | Fair | Poor |
|------|------|------|------|------|
| 250  | 200  | 175  | 125  | 90   |

### Medalion

This is the service version of the Trophy with a 3", 4", or 6" barrel and fixed sights.

| Exc. | V.G. | Good | Fair | Poor |
|------|------|------|------|------|
| 200  | 175  | 125  | 100  | 75   |

J. P. Sauer also made a Western-styled series for Hawes based in appearance on the Colt Single Action Army.

### Silver City Marshal

This 6-shot, 5.5"-barrel, single-action revolver with fixed sights is chambered for .22 l.r. or .22 rimfire Magnum.

Hawes Silver City Marshal

| Exc. | V.G. | Good | Fair | Poor |
|------|------|------|------|------|
| 125  | 100  | 75   | 50   | 25   |

### Western Marshal

This is a large-frame single action chambered for .357 Magnum, .44 Magnum .45 Colt, .45ACP, 44-40, 9mm, .22 l.r., and .22 rimfire Magnum. It has fixed sights, and the finish is blued.

| Exc. | V.G. | Good | Fair | Poor |
|------|------|------|------|------|
| 175  | 150  | 125  | 100  | 75   |

### Chief Marshal

This is a 6.5"-barrel, 6-shot, blued single action with adjustable sights. It is chambered for the .357 Magnum, .44 Magnum, and the .45 Colt.

| Exc. | V.G. | Good | Fair | Poor |
|------|------|------|------|------|
| 175  | 150  | 125  | 100  | 75   |

### Texas Marshal

The same as the Western Marshal with a nickel-plated finish.

| Exc. | V.G. | Good | Fair | Poor |
|------|------|------|------|------|
| 185  | 160  | 135  | 100  | 75   |

### Montana Marshal

The same as the Western Marshal with a brass backstrap and triggerguard.

| Exc. | V.G. | Good | Fair | Poor |
|------|------|------|------|------|
| 175  | 150  | 125  | 100  | 75   |

### Deputy Marshal

A 5.5", 6-shot single action chambered for .22 l.r. and .22 rimfire Magnum.

| Exc. | V.G. | Good | Fair | Poor |
|------|------|------|------|------|
| 125  | 100  | 75   | 50   | 25   |

### Federal Marshal

A 6-shot single action chambered for the .357 Magnum, .44 Magnum, and the .45 Colt.

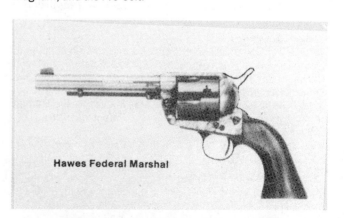

Hawes Federal Marshal

| Exc. | V.G. | Good | Fair | Poor |
|------|------|------|------|------|
| 175  | 150  | 125  | 100  | 75   |

## HAWES & WAGGONER
### Philadelphia, Pennsylvania

**Pocket Pistol**
This pistol was copied from the Henry Deringer. It is chambered for .41-caliber percussion and has a 3" barrel, German silver mountings, and a walnut stock. It was manufactured in the 1850's.

| Exc. | V.G. | Good | Fair | Poor |
|------|------|------|------|------|
| 650  | 550  | 450  | 350  | 250  |

## HAWKEN
### St. Louis, Missouri

The Hawken Brothers of St. Louis, Missouri, have come to be known as the originators of the "Plains" or "Mountain" rifles that were produced in the Midwest from 1815 until approximately 1870. The brothers, Jacob and Samuel Hawken, produced flintlocks at first and then percussion locks. Their rifles were produced in various calibers and styles, with either full or half stocks. The Hawken name on a rifle of this period drastically raises its value. The variety and diversity of the rifles produced by this company preclude accurate evaluation. The likelihood of encountering a fake is not uncommon, and individual appraisal should definitely be procured if a transaction is contemplated.

## HECHLER & KOCH
### Oberndorf/Neckar, Germany

At the end of WWII, the French dismantled the Mauser factory as part of their reparations; and the buildings remained idle until 1950, when firearms production was again allowed in Germany. Hechler & Koch was formed and occupied the vacant Mauser plant. They began to produce the G3 automatic rifle based on the Cetme design and progressed to machine guns and submachine guns and eventually to the production of commercial civilian rifles and pistols. Today they are a very successful company that sells their products throughout the world.

**Model 91**
This rifle is recoil-operated, with a delayed-roller lock bolt. It is chambered for the .308 Winchester cartridge and has a 17.7" barrel with military style aperture sights. It is furnished with a 20-round detachable magazine and is finished in matte black with a black plastic stock. This rifle is one that has fallen under the assault rifle cloud in which our country is currently engulfed, and as such will not be priced. If one plans a transaction involving one of these fine weapons, an individual appraisal should be secured as there are wide variations in prices around the country. Some areas have made their ownership illegal.

**Model 91 A3**
This model is simply the Model 91 with a retractable metal stock.

**Model 93**
This model is similar to the Model 91 except that it is chambered for the .223 cartridge and has a 16.4" barrel. The magazine holds 25 rounds, and the status is the same as the Model 91.

**Model 93 A3**
This is the Model 93 with the retractable metal stock.

**Model 94**
This is a carbine version chambered for the 9mm Parabellum cartridge, with a 16.5" barrel. It is a smaller-scaled weapon that has a 15-shot magazine. This model should also be appraised in one's given area before purchase.

**Model 94 A3**
This model has a retractable metal stock.

**Model 270**
This model is chambered for the .22 l.r. cartridge. It is a sporting-styled rifle with a 16.5" barrel. It is furnished with either a 5-or a 20-round magaine and is blued, with a checkered walnut stock. This rifle was discontinued in 1985.

| Exc. | V.G. | Good | Fair | Poor |
|------|------|------|------|------|
| 350  | 300  | 250  | 200  | 125  |

**Model 300**
This model is similar to the Model 270 except that it is chambered for the .22 rimfire Magnum cartridge. It was not imported after 1988.

| Exc. | V.G. | Good | Fair | Poor |
|------|------|------|------|------|
| 450  | 400  | 300  | 250  | 175  |

**Model 630**
This model is chambered for the .223 and features the same roller-delayed semi-automatic action as found on the paramilitary-type weapons. This is a sporting style rifle that has a polished blue finish and a checkered walnut stock. The barrel is 17.7" long, and the magazines offered hold either 4 or 10 rounds. Import was discontinued in 1986.

| Exc. | V.G. | Good | Fair | Poor |
|------|------|------|------|------|
| 700  | 650  | 600  | 475  | 350  |

**Model 770**
This model is similar to the Model 630 except that it is chambered for the .308 Winchester cartridge and has a 19.7" barrel. It was not imported after 1986.

| Exc. | V.G. | Good | Fair | Poor |
|------|------|------|------|------|
| 750  | 700  | 650  | 525  | 400  |

**Model 940**
This model is essentially the same as the Model 770 except that it is chambered for the .30-06 cartridge. It has a 21" barrel and was not imported after 1986.

| Exc. | V.G. | Good | Fair | Poor |
|------|------|------|------|------|
| 800  | 725  | 675  | 550  | 425  |

**Model SL6**
This is Hechler & Koch's current sporting rifle chambered for the .223 cartridge. It has a 17.7" barrel and features the same basic action as the military versions. It has a matte black finish and a walnut stock with a vented walnut hand guard. The magazine holds 4 rounds.

| Exc. | V.G. | Good | Fair | Poor |
|------|------|------|------|------|
| 600  | 525  | 475  | 375  | 275  |

**Model SL7**
This model is similar to the SL6 except that it is chambered for the .308 Winchester cartridge and has a 3-round magazine.

Heckler & Koch SL7

| Exc. | V.G. | Good | Fair | Poor |
|------|------|------|------|------|
| 600  | 525  | 475  | 375  | 275  |

230 • HECHLER & KOCH

## PSG-1

This rifle is a high precision sniping rifle that features the delayed-roller semi-automatic action. It is chambered for the .308 Winchester cartridge and has a 5-shot magazine. It is furnished with a complete array of accessories including a 6x42-power Hensholdt scope and mounting system. A fully adjustable buttstock is available and would add approximately $500 to the values.

| NIB | Exc. | V.G. | Good | Fair | Poor |
|---|---|---|---|---|---|
| 8750 | 7200 | 6000 | 4500 | 3250 | 2750 |

## BASR Model

This is a bolt-action rifle chambered for various popular calibers. It has a stainless-steel barrel and was essentially custom built to the customer's specifications. The stock is of Kevlar. This model is quite rare since only 100 were manufactured in 1968.

| Exc. | V.G. | Good | Fair | Poor |
|---|---|---|---|---|
| 1750 | 1500 | 1200 | 900 | 750 |

## Pistols
## HK4

This is a blowback-operated semi-automatic pistol based on the Mauser HSc design. It is chambered for .22 l.r., .25 ACP, .32 ACP, and .380. These calibers were easily converted by switching the barrels, recoil springs and magazines. The rimfire model could be changed by rotating the breechface. The conversion kits were available for all calibers. The barrel is 3" long; and the finish is blued, with molded plastic thumbrest grips. This pistol was sold from 1968-1973 as the Harrington & Richardson HK4 and is so marked. It was completely discontinued in 1984.

### .22 Caliber or .380 Caliber

| Exc. | V.G. | Good | Fair | Poor |
|---|---|---|---|---|
| 450 | 375 | 300 | 200 | 125 |

### .25 Caliber or .32 Caliber

| Exc. | V.G. | Good | Fair | Poor |
|---|---|---|---|---|
| 325 | 275 | 225 | 150 | 100 |

### Conversion Units

| Exc. | V.G. | Good | Fair | Poor |
|---|---|---|---|---|
| 50 | 40 | 35 | 30 | 25 |

## P9

This is a single-action, delayed-blowback semi-automatic pistol chambered for 9mm or 7.65mm Parabellum. The action is based on the G-3 rifle mechanism. The barrel is 4" in length, and the pistol has an internal hammer and a thumb-operated hammer drop and recocking lever. There is also a manual safety and a loaded-chamber indicator. The finish is parkerized, and the grips are molded plastic and well contoured. It has fixed sights. This model was manufactured between 1977 and 1984.

| Exc. | V.G. | Good | Fair | Poor |
|---|---|---|---|---|
| 400 | 375 | 300 | 225 | 125 |

## P9S

This model is similar to the Model P9 except that the action features a double-action capability and it is chambered for the .45 ACP and the 9mm Parabellum. This model was also manufactured between 1977 and 1984.

| Exc. | V.G. | Good | Fair | Poor |
|---|---|---|---|---|
| 400 | 350 | 300 | 225 | 150 |

## P9S Target Model

This version is similar to the Model P9S, with a 5.5" barrel, adjustable sights, and an adjustable trigger. It was discontinued in 1984.

| Exc. | V.G. | Good | Fair | Poor |
|---|---|---|---|---|
| 450 | 375 | 325 | 250 | 175 |

## VP 70Z

This is a blowback-operated semi-automatic chambered for the 9mm Parabellum cartridge. It is striker-fired and double-action only. The barrel is 4.5" long, and the double-column magazine holds 18 rounds. The finish is blued, and the receiver and grip are molded from plastic. This model was discontinued in 1984.

| Exc. | V.G. | Good | Fair | Poor |
|---|---|---|---|---|
| 375 | 325 | 275 | 200 | 125 |

## P7 PSP

This was the first of the squeeze-cocked H&K pistols. It is a single-action semi-automatic that is placed in the firing position by pressure on the front of the gripstrap. This moves the striker into battery; and firing is then accomplished by a single-action pressure on the trigger, releasing the gripstrap cocking device and decocking the mechanism. This particular model does not have the extended finger guard on the trigger and also does not have an ambidextrous safety. It was discontinued in 1984.

| Exc. | V.G. | Good | Fair | Poor |
|---|---|---|---|---|
| 650 | 600 | 500 | 400 | 275 |

## P7 M8

This is the 8-shot newer version of the "squeeze cocker." It has the heat-shield finger guard and the ambidextrous safety. It has a 4" barrel and a 3-dot sight system. The finish is matte blue with stippled black plastic grips.

| NIB | Exc. | V.G. | Good | Fair | Poor |
|-----|------|------|------|------|------|
| 900 | 750 | 650 | 600 | 500 | 375 |

## P7 M13

This version is similar to the P7 M8 except that it has a double-column 13-shot magazine.

| NIB | Exc. | V.G. | Good | Fair | Poor |
|------|------|------|------|------|------|
| 1100 | 900 | 750 | 675 | 550 | 425 |

## P7 K3

This is the "Squeeze Cocker" chambered for the .380 cartridge. It has a recoil buffer that is oil-filled and a 3.8" barrel. The magazine holds 8 rounds. This model was introduced in 1988.

| NIB | Exc. | V.G. | Good | Fair | Poor |
|-----|------|------|------|------|------|
| 900 | 750 | 600 | 500 | 400 | 325 |

## .22 Caliber Conversion Unit

This unit will convert the P7 K3 to fire the .22 l.r. rimfire cartridge.

| NIB | Exc. | V.G. | Good | Fair | Poor |
|-----|------|------|------|------|------|
| 465 | 400 | 350 | 300 | 200 | 150 |

# HEINZELMANN, C.E.
## Plochigen am Neckar, Germany

### Heim

This is a 6.35mm, blowback pocket pistol that appears quite similar to a Mauser WTP. It has a fixed barrel and recoil spring secured by a bushing at the muzzle. The pistol is quite rare. It was made in the 1930's. The left side of the frame is stamped "C.E.Heinzelmann Plochingen A.N. Patent Heim-6.35."

| Exc. | V.G. | Good | Fair | Poor |
|------|------|------|------|------|
| 750 | 675 | 550 | 400 | 300 |

# HELFRICHT
## Germany

### Model 3 Pocket Pistol

This is a striker-fired, blowback-operated semi-automatic pistol chambered for the 6.35mm cartridge. It has a 2" barrel with a rudimentary groove sight and a 6-shot magazine. The finish is blued, with black plastic grips bearing the molded logo "KH". This model has a short tubular extension to the barrel that is supposed to improve the accuracy.

| Exc. | V.G. | Good | Fair | Poor |
|------|------|------|------|------|
| 450 | 400 | 350 | 275 | 200 |

### Model 4 Pocket Pistol

This pistol is identical to the Model 3 without the barrel extension.

| Exc. | V.G. | Good | Fair | Poor |
|------|------|------|------|------|
| 400 | 350 | 300 | 225 | 150 |

# HENRION & DASSY
## Liege, Belgium

### Semi-automatic

This pistol is chambered for the .25 ACP cartridge. It has a 2.5" barrel and a 5-round detachable magazine. The finish is blued, and it has black checkered plastic grips that are marked "H&D." This firearm was manufactured in the early 1900's.

| Exc. | V.G. | Good | Fair | Poor |
|------|------|------|------|------|
| 600 | 500 | 450 | 375 | 275 |

# HENRY
## SEE--Winchester

# HENRY, ALEX
## Edinburgh, Scotland

### Single Shot Rifle

This is a high-grade single shot that features a true falling-block action that is activated by a side lever on the action. It was available in the popular European cartridges of the era, and the barrel length varies from 22" to 28" in length. This rifle exhibits fine quality materials and workmanship. The select-grade walnut stock and schnabel forend are hand checkered. The finish of the rifle is scroll-engraved and blued. This company manufactured firearms from 1869 until 1895.

| Exc. | V.G. | Good | Fair | Poor |
|------|------|------|------|------|
| 2500 | 2250 | 1750 | 1250 | 800 |

### Double Rifle

This model is a side-by-side, double-barrelled Express Rifle chambered for the .500/450 Black Powder Express cartridge. It has damascus barrels and double triggers. This gun is hammerless and features ornate scroll engraving as well as a high-grade hand-checkered walnut stock and forend. It was furnished with a fitted leather case and accessories. This rifle was manufactured in the 1890's.

| Exc. | V.G. | Good | Fair | Poor |
|------|------|------|------|------|
| 5000 | 4500 | 3750 | 2900 | 1850 |

# HEROLD
**Franz Jaeger**
**Suhl, Germany**

**Bolt Action Rifle**
This rifle was built on a smaller version of the basic Mauser 98 commercial style action. It is chambered for the .22 Hornet cartridge and is offered with a 24" round ribbed barrel. It features a folding-leaf rear and a ramp-type front sight. There are double-set triggers. and the finish is blued. The stock is hand-checkered select-grade walnut. This rifle was manufactured prior to WWII and imported by Charles Daly and Stoeger Arms.

| Exc. | V.G. | Good | Fair | Poor |
|------|------|------|------|------|
| 1000 | 850 | 700 | 550 | 475 |

# HERTERS
**Waseca, Minnesota**

This company was in the business of importing and distributing firearms manufactured by various companies in Europe. They were also a source of parts and supplies for the gunsmithing trade. They ceased operations in the early 1980's.

**Revolvers**
**Guide**
This model is a solid-frame, swing-out cylinder double-action revolver chambered for the .22 rimfire cartridge. It is offered with a 6" barrel and holds 6 shots. The finish is blued, and the grips are checkered walnut.

| Exc. | V.G. | Good | Fair | Poor |
|------|------|------|------|------|
| 100 | 80 | 50 | 35 | 25 |

**Power-Mag Revolver**
This is a Western-style single-action revolver chambered for .357 Magnum, .401 Herters Power Magnum, and .44 Magnum. The barrel lengths are 4" and 6". The cylinder holds 6 shots; and the finish is blued, with wood grips.

| Exc. | V.G. | Good | Fair | Poor |
|------|------|------|------|------|
| 150 | 125 | 80 | 60 | 50 |

**Western**
This is a single-action, Western-style revolver chambered for .22 l.r. It has a 6-shot cylinder and is blued, with wood grips.

| Exc. | V.G. | Good | Fair | Poor |
|------|------|------|------|------|
| 85 | 75 | 60 | 45 | 25 |

**Rifles**
**J-9 or U-9 Hunter**
These rifles are both bolt-action Mausers chambered for various popular calibers. The J-9 was manufactured in England; and the U-9, in Yugoslavia. The barrels are 24" in length;, and the finish is blued with a plain, Monte Carlo-style walnut stock.

| Exc. | V.G. | Good | Fair | Poor |
|------|------|------|------|------|
| 225 | 185 | 135 | 100 | 75 |

**J-9 or U-9 Presentation or Supreme**
These models are similar to the Hunter except that they feature checkering and sling swivels. They are basically the same rifles with different designations, and the values are the same.

| Exc. | V.G. | Good | Fair | Poor |
|------|------|------|------|------|
| 250 | 225 | 200 | 150 | 100 |

# HEYM, F. W.
**Suhl, Germany**
**Importer--Heym America**
**Ft. Wayne, Indiana**

This company specializes in the production of high-grade sporting rifles and shotguns. They were founded in 1934 and operated from Suhl, Germany, until the end of WWII--when they ceased operations at that location and recommenced the manufacture of firearms in the early 1950's in Munnerstadt, West Germany. Prior to the formation of Heym America, they were imported by Paul Jaeger of Grand Junction, Tennessee.

**Single Shot Rifles**
**Model HR-30**
This rifle is built on the Ruger No. 1 falling-block action. It is chambered for most calibers and features a 24" round barrel or a 26" barrel in the magnum calibers. There is a quarter rib with express sights, and the single-set trigger is made by Canjar. The rifle is engraved with a gamescene motif, and the stock is deluxe, hand-checkered French walnut with a classic European-style cheekpiece. The receiver is coin-finished, and the remainder is blued.

| Exc. | V.G. | Good | Fair | Poor |
|------|------|------|------|------|
| 3000 | 2750 | 2250 | 1750 | 1250 |

**Model HR-38**
This model is similar to the HR-30, with an octagonal barrel. The other specifications are the same.

| Exc. | V.G. | Good | Fair | Poor |
|------|------|------|------|------|
| 3500 | 3250 | 2500 | 2000 | 1500 |

**Double Rifle**
**Model 77B/55B Over/Under Rifle**
This model is chambered for many popular calibers, both American and European. It has 25" barrels with open sights and a boxlock action with Kersten double crossbolts. The action is heavily engraved with a gamescene motif and is silver-plated. The gun features double triggers, cocking indicators, and automatic ejectors. The stock is select European walnut with hand checkering. The barrels are machined to accept a Zeiss scope in claw mounts.

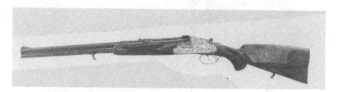

| Exc. | V.G. | Good | Fair | Poor |
|------|------|------|------|------|
| 5000 | 4500 | 4000 | 3250 | 2500 |

**Model 55BSS**
The specifications for this model are similar to the Model 55B except that it features a full sidelock action and more elaborate engraving.

| Exc. | V.G. | Good | Fair | Poor |
|------|------|------|------|------|
| 9500 | 8500 | 7500 | 5000 | 3500 |

**Model 55BF/77BF**
This model is similar to the 55B except that it has one barrel rifled and the other smooth and chambered for 12, 16, or 20-gauge shotgun.

| Exc. | V.G. | Good | Fair | Poor |
|------|------|------|------|------|
| 5000 | 4500 | 4000 | 3250 | 2500 |

## Model 55BFSS
This model is a full sidelock version of the combination gun.

| Exc. | V.G. | Good | Fair | Poor |
|---|---|---|---|---|
| 9500 | 8500 | 7500 | 5000 | 3500 |

## Model 88 B
This model is a side-by-side, double-barrelled rifle chambered for many calibers up to the .375 H&H. It features a boxlock action with a Greener crossbolt and double underlugs. It has 24" Krupp steel barrels and double triggers with automatic ejectors. This was very much a made-to-order weapon, and the engraving patterns vary. The stock is select walnut with hand checkering and dimensions to fit the customer.

| Exc. | V.G. | Good | Fair | Poor |
|---|---|---|---|---|
| 9500 | 8750 | 7750 | 5500 | 4000 |

## Model 88 BSS
This model is similar to the Model 88 B, with a full sidelock action.

| Exc. | V.G. | Good | Fair | Poor |
|---|---|---|---|---|
| 14000 | 12500 | 9500 | 6500 | 5250 |

## Model 88 Safari
This model is chambered for the .375 H&H, .458 Win. Mag., .470, or .500 Nitro Express calibers and has 25" barrels with a considerably larger-sized action. This was also a made-to-order firearm.

| Exc. | V.G. | Good | Fair | Poor |
|---|---|---|---|---|
| 13500 | 12000 | 9000 | 6000 | 4750 |

## Model 22 Safety
This is an Over/Under combination gun chambered for 16 or 20 gauge over .22 Hornet, .22 WMR, .222 Rem.,.222 Rem. Mag., .223, 5.6x50R, 6.5x57R, and 7x57R. The solid-ribbed barrels are 24" in length. This gun has a boxlock action with a single trigger and automatic ejectors. This gun has a feature that automatically decocks the action if the gun is dropped or bumped hard. The receiver is coin-finished, and the remainder is blued. The hand-checkered stock is of select European walnut.

| Exc. | V.G. | Good | Fair | Poor |
|---|---|---|---|---|
| 2500 | 2000 | 1750 | 1200 | 900 |

## Drillings
## Model 33
This is a boxlock drilling chambered for the 16x16 or 20x20 gauge over a rifled barrel chambered for various popular European or American cartridges. The barrels are 25" long and choked full and modified. The model features a Greener crossbolt with double underlugs, double triggers, and engraving with coin finishing. The stock is hand-checkered European walnut.

| Exc. | V.G. | Good | Fair | Poor |
|---|---|---|---|---|
| 6000 | 5000 | 4250 | 3250 | 2500 |

## Model 37
This model is a true sidelock chambered for all the calibers and gauges as the Model 33 is and also chambered for the 12 gauge, as well. It features hand detachable sidelocks and a select French walnut stock.

| Exc. | V.G. | Good | Fair | Poor |
|---|---|---|---|---|
| 9500 | 8500 | 7500 | 6000 | 4250 |

## Bolt Action Rifles
## Model SR-20
This model is built on a Mauser action and is chambered for many popular calibers up to the .375 H&H. It has a 21", 24", or 26" barrel with open sights. It features a hinged floorplate and an adjustable trigger. A single-set trigger is available. The finish is blued, with a hand checkered walnut stock.

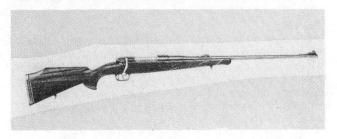

| NIB | Exc. | V.G. | Good | Fair | Poor |
|---|---|---|---|---|---|
| 1450 | 1250 | 950 | 750 | 600 | 450 |

## Model SR-20 Alpine
This is a mountain rifle with Mannlicher-style, full-length stock and schnabel forend. It is chambered for various calibers and has a 20" barrel. The finish is blue, and the stock is hand-checkered walnut. This model was introduced in 1989.

| NIB | Exc. | V.G. | Good | Fair | Poor |
|---|---|---|---|---|---|
| 2650 | 2250 | 1750 | 1250 | 850 | 600 |

## Model SR-20 Classic Safari
This model is chambered for the .404 Jeffries, .425 Express, and the .458 Winchester Magnum. It features a 24" barrel with express sights. This is a generally more deluxe model with select, high-grade walnut used for the stock. This model was introduced in 1989.

| NIB | Exc. | V.G. | Good | Fair | Poor |
|---|---|---|---|---|---|
| 3500 | 3000 | 2750 | 2250 | 1750 | 1450 |

# HIGGINS, J. C.
### Chicago, Illinois
The trademark J. C. Higgins was used by Sears, Roebuck of Chicago on the firearms and other sporting goods products that they marketed between 1946 and 1962. The guns sold by this company under the Higgins banner numbered in the hundreds. They were, for the most part, products of domestic manufacturers who produced rifles and shotguns under the Higgins name. The guns were usually a less deluxe version of the model that was sold under the maker's own name, and the Sears guns were usually less expensive than those of the competition. There is little or no collector interest in the J. C. Higgins line, and models encountered are often sold as starter firearms for young shooters. As such, they occupy a special place in the hearts of many enthusiasts, including myself, who vividly remember that the first rifle they ever owned was a J. C. Higgins .22 given to them by their dad. The evaluation of these firearms would be out of the purview of a book of this nature. A rule to follow is that the Higgins version of a particular firearm is usually worth a bit less than the same gun with its manufacturer's name upon it.

# HIGH STANDARD MFG. CO.
## New Haven, Connecticut

The High Standard Company was founded in 1926 as a tool-manufacturing company that produced gun-barrel drills. In 1932 they purchased the bankrupt Hartford Arms Company and found themselves in the pistol-manufacturing business. The first models were similar to the Hartford, but they very quickly improved and produced their own designs. Very quickly they earned a reputation for producing extremely accurate .22 automatic pistols. They produced military-training pistols during the war years and also a silenced version for use by special forces. After the war their production continued; and they added shotguns and rifles, as well as a line of utility-grade revolvers. The company finally went out of business in 1984, and their high-grade semi-automatic pistols are becoming desirable from a collector's standpoint.

### Model A
This model is identical to the last Hartford pistol. It is a blowback-operated, semi-automatic pistol with an internal hammer. It is chambered for the .22 l.r. cartridge and has a 4.5" or 6.75" barrel with adjustable sights. It has a 10-round detachable magazine. The finish is blued, with checkered walnut grips. There were approximately 7,300 manufactured between 1932 and 1942.

| Exc. | V.G. | Good | Fair | Poor |
|------|------|------|------|------|
| 425 | 375 | 325 | 250 | 175 |

### Model B
This version has fixed sights and hard rubber grips. There were approximately 65,000 manufactured between 1932 and 1942.

| Exc. | V.G. | Good | Fair | Poor |
|------|------|------|------|------|
| 400 | 350 | 300 | 225 | 150 |

### U.S. Marked Model B
This version was manufactured in 1942 and 1943 as part of the WWII effort. It is marked "Property of U.S." on the frame. There were approximately 14,000 manufactured.

| Exc. | V.G. | Good | Fair | Poor |
|------|------|------|------|------|
| 475 | 400 | 350 | 275 | 200 |

### Model C
This version is chambered for the .22 short cartridge. There were approximately 5,000 manufactured between 1935 and 1942.

| Exc. | V.G. | Good | Fair | Poor |
|------|------|------|------|------|
| 500 | 425 | 375 | 300 | 225 |

### Model D
This model is similar to the Model A, with a heavy barrel. There were 2,500 manufactured between 1938 and 1942.

| Exc. | V.G. | Good | Fair | Poor |
|------|------|------|------|------|
| 475 | 400 | 350 | 275 | 200 |

### Model E
This is a high-grade target version of the Model A with a heavy barrel and thumbrest grips. There were approximately 2,500 manufactured between 1938 and 1942.

| Exc. | V.G. | Good | Fair | Poor |
|------|------|------|------|------|
| 600 | 550 | 475 | 375 | 275 |

### Model H-A
This version is the Model A with an external hammer and no external safety. There were approximately 1,000 made between 1940 and 1942.

| Exc. | V.G. | Good | Fair | Poor |
|------|------|------|------|------|
| 500 | 425 | 375 | 300 | 225 |

### Model H-B
This version is the Model B with an external hammer. There were approximately 25,000 manufactured between 1940 and 1954.

| Exc. | V.G. | Good | Fair | Poor |
|------|------|------|------|------|
| 475 | 400 | 350 | 275 | 200 |

### Model H-D
This is a version of the Model D with an external hammer and no external safety. There were approximately 7,000 manufactured between 1940 and 1949.

| Exc. | V.G. | Good | Fair | Poor |
|------|------|------|------|------|
| 450 | 375 | 325 | 250 | 175 |

### Model H-D--USA
This is a bull-barrelled, fixed-sight version of the Model H-D. The finish is either blued or parkerized, and it is marked "Property of U.S.A." There were approximately 44,000 manufactured between 1943 and 1946. The early blued guns are worth approximately 20 percent additional.

| Exc. | V.G. | Good | Fair | Poor |
|------|------|------|------|------|
| 425 | 350 | 300 | 225 | 150 |

### Model H-D Military
This is similar to the Model H-D, with the addition of an external thumb safety. There were approximately 150,000 manufactured between 1946 and 1955.

| Exc. | V.G. | Good | Fair | Poor |
|------|------|------|------|------|
| 400 | 350 | 300 | 225 | 125 |

### Model H-E
This is the external-hammer version of the Model E. There were approximately 1,000 manufactured between 1940 and 1942. This is the rarest of the semi-automatic High Standard pistols. It is very desirable from a collector's standpoint.

| Exc. | V.G. | Good | Fair | Poor |
|------|------|------|------|------|
| 800 | 700 | 600 | 450 | 300 |

### Model G
This is a semi-automatic pistol chambered for the .380 ACP cartridge. It was the first of the lever-takedown models and has a 5" barrel with fixed sights. There is a catch in front of the triggerguard that holds the barrel unit. When this catch is released, the barrel is removed and the slide could be slid forward off the frame. It features an external hammer, as well as an external safety on the frame. The finish is blued, with checkered plastic grips. There were approximately 7,400 manufactured between 1947 and 1950.

| Exc. | V.G. | Good | Fair | Poor |
|------|------|------|------|------|
| 550 | 450 | 400 | 275 | 200 |

### Model G-B
This is a blowback-operated semi-automatic pistol chambered for the .22 l.r. cartridge. It has 4.5" or 6.75" interchangeable barrels. It has a 10-shot detachable magazine. This model also features the takedown lever in front of the triggerguard. This is an internal-hammer pistol with a blued finish and checkered plastic grips. There were approximately 5,000 manufactured between 1949 and 1950. If both barrels are present, add approximately 15 percent to the value.

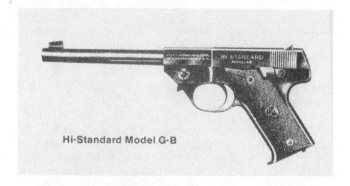

Hi-Standard Model G-B

| Exc. | V.G. | Good | Fair | Poor |
|------|------|------|------|------|
| 425 | 375 | 325 | 250 | 150 |

## Model G-D

This version has a heavy barrel and adjustable sights. Otherwise, it is similar to the Model G-B. There were approximately 3,300 manufactured between 1948 and 1951. Both barrels would increase the values approximately 15 percent.

| Exc. | V.G. | Good | Fair | Poor |
|------|------|------|------|------|
| 425 | 375 | 325 | 250 | 150 |

## Model G-E

This is a high quality target version that has an even heavier barrel and adjustable sights. There were approximately 3,000 manufactured in 1949 and 1950. Both barrels on this model would add approximately 15 percent to the value.

| Exc. | V.G. | Good | Fair | Poor |
|------|------|------|------|------|
| 600 | 500 | 400 | 300 | 200 |

## 1st Model Olympic

This model is similar to the Model G-E but is chambered for the .22 short cartridge and has a lightweight, alloy slide. The takedown lever was changed to a pushbutton on this model, and there are thumbrest grips. There were approximately 1,200 manufactured in 1949 and 1950. The extra barrel would add approximately 15 percent to the value.

Hi-Standard Model Olympic

| Exc. | V.G. | Good | Fair | Poor |
|------|------|------|------|------|
| 700 | 600 | 500 | 375 | 275 |

## 1st Model Sport King

This is a blowback-operated semi-automatic pistol chambered for the .22 l.r. cartridge. It has an interchangeable 4.5" or 6.75" barrel with fixed sights. It features the pushbutton takedown and is blued, with checkered plastic grips. It was manufactured between 1951 and 1958. The extra barrel would add approximately 15 percent.

| Exc. | V.G. | Good | Fair | Poor |
|------|------|------|------|------|
| 375 | 325 | 250 | 175 | 100 |

## 1st Model Flite King

This is an alloy-framed version of the Sport King chambered for the .22 short cartridge. It was manufactured between 1953 and 1958. The extra barrel would add approximately 15 percent to the value.

| Exc. | V.G. | Good | Fair | Poor |
|------|------|------|------|------|
| 350 | 300 | 225 | 150 | 100 |

## Field King

This is the Sport King with a heavy barrel and adjustable sights. It was manufactured between 1951 and 1958. The extra barrel would add approximately 15 percent to the value.

| Exc. | V.G. | Good | Fair | Poor |
|------|------|------|------|------|
| 375 | 325 | 250 | 175 | 100 |

## Supermatic

This is a blowback-operated, semi-automatic target pistol chambered for the .22 l.r. cartridge. It has a 4.5" or 6.75" barrel with adjustable target sights. It has a 10-shot detachable magazine and is furnished with barrel weights. The finish is blued, with checkered plastic grips. It was manufactured between 1951 and 1958. The additional barrel would be worth approximately 15 percent.

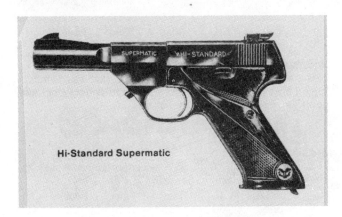

Hi-Standard Supermatic

| Exc. | V.G. | Good | Fair | Poor |
|------|------|------|------|------|
| 400 | 350 | 300 | 225 | 125 |

## 2nd Model Olympic

This model is similar to the Supermatic with a lightweight, alloy slide and chambered for the .22 short cartridge. It was manufactured between 1951 and 1958. The additional barrel would be worth approximately 15 percent.

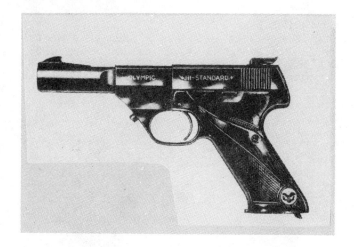

| Exc. | V.G. | Good | Fair | Poor |
|------|------|------|------|------|
| 500 | 400 | 350 | 250 | 175 |

### Duramatic

This is a blowback-operated sporting pistol chambered for the .22 l.r. cartridge. It has interchangeable 4.5" or 6.5" barrels with fixed sights. This model features a screw-activated take-down mechanism in front of the triggerguard. It is blued, with checkered wood grips. It was manufactured between 1954 and 1970. The extra barrel would add approximately 15 percent to the value.

| Exc. | V.G. | Good | Fair | Poor |
|------|------|------|------|------|
| 375 | 325 | 250 | 175 | 100 |

### 2nd Model Sport King

This is an improved version of the Sport King that was manufactured between 1958 and 1970. The extra barrel would add approximately 15 percent to the value.

| Exc. | V.G. | Good | Fair | Poor |
|------|------|------|------|------|
| 350 | 300 | 225 | 150 | 100 |

### 3rd Model Sport King

This version is similar to the 2nd Model but available in nickel plate. It was manufactured between 1974 and 1984.

| Exc. | V.G. | Good | Fair | Poor |
|------|------|------|------|------|
| 300 | 250 | 200 | 125 | 100 |

### Sport King M

This version has the military-style, straighter grip.

| Exc. | V.G. | Good | Fair | Poor |
|------|------|------|------|------|
| 300 | 250 | 200 | 125 | 100 |

### 2nd Model Flite King

This version is similar to the 2nd Model Sport King with a lightweight, alloy slide and chambered for the .22 short cartridge. It was manufactured between 1958 and 1966.

| Exc. | V.G. | Good | Fair | Poor |
|------|------|------|------|------|
| 300 | 250 | 200 | 125 | 100 |

### Sharpshooter

This version has a 5.5" heavy barrel with adjustable sights. It features the pushbutton takedown mechanism and is blued with brown, checkered plastic grips. It was manufactured between 1971 and 1981.

| Exc. | V.G. | Good | Fair | Poor |
|------|------|------|------|------|
| 300 | 250 | 200 | 125 | 100 |

### Supermatic Tournament

This version has either a 5.5" or 6.75" heavy barrel. It is furnished with barrel weights and adjustable target-type sights. The finish is blued with checkered walnut grips. It was manufactured between 1958 and 1966.

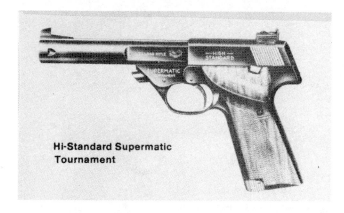

Hi-Standard Supermatic Tournament

| Exc. | V.G. | Good | Fair | Poor |
|------|------|------|------|------|
| 400 | 350 | 300 | 200 | 125 |

### Supermatic Citation

This model has a 5.5" bull barrel with adjustable target sights. It has a blued finish with thumbrest grips.

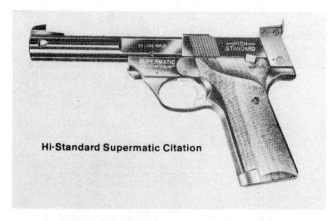

Hi-Standard Supermatic Citation

| Exc. | V.G. | Good | Fair | Poor |
|------|------|------|------|------|
| 450 | 400 | 350 | 250 | 175 |

**Supermatic Citation Military**

This version is similar to the Citation except that it has the straighter, military-type grip frame.

| Exc. | V.G. | Good | Fair | Poor |
|------|------|------|------|------|
| 450 | 400 | 350 | 250 | 175 |

**Supermatic Trophy**

This version is similar to the Supermatic Citation, with either a 5.5" bull barrel or a 7.5" fluted barrel. The rear sight is mounted on the frame and straddles the slide. It has an adjustable trigger pull and over-travel adjustment. The finish is blued with checkered, walnut, thumbrest grips.

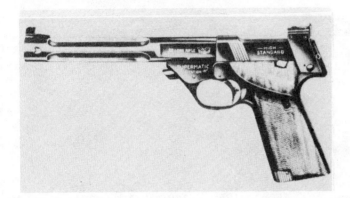

| Exc. | V.G. | Good | Fair | Poor |
|------|------|------|------|------|
| 475 | 425 | 375 | 275 | 200 |

**Supermatic Trophy Military**

This version features the straighter, military-type grip frame. It was manufactured between 1965 and 1984.

| Exc. | V.G. | Good | Fair | Poor |
|------|------|------|------|------|
| 475 | 425 | 375 | 275 | 200 |

**3rd Model Olympic**

This is similar to the Supermatic Trophy model with a lightweight, alloy slide. It is chambered for the .22 short cartridge. A straight-grip, military model is also available. The values are the same. It was manufactured between 1963 and 1966.

| Exc. | V.G. | Good | Fair | Poor |
|------|------|------|------|------|
| 500 | 450 | 400 | 300 | 225 |

**Olympic ISU**

This model is similar to the Supermatic Citation, with a 6.75" or 8" barrel furnished with weights. It is chambered for the .22 short cartridge. A military model with the straight grip is also available. The values are the same. It was manufactured between 1958 and 1984.

| Exc. | V.G. | Good | Fair | Poor |
|------|------|------|------|------|
| 500 | 450 | 400 | 300 | 225 |

**1972 Olympic Commemorative**

This is a limited edition issued to commemorate the only American-manufactured .22 pistol used to win an Olympic Gold Medal. It is heavily engraved with gold-inlaid Olympic Rings and furnished in a fitted presentation case. It was manufactured in 1972 and, as with all commemoratives, must be NIB with all furnished material to be desirable from a collector's standpoint.

| NIB | Exc. | V.G. | Good | Fair | Poor |
|-----|------|------|------|------|------|
| 1000 | 850 | 600 | 450 | 350 | 250 |

**1980 Olympic Commemorative**

This version features five Olympic Rings on the receiver. There were 1,000 manufactured, and the serial number has a USA prefix. It was manufactured in 1980 and was furnished with a presentation case. As with all commemorative pistols, it must be NIB with all furnished material to be desirable from a collector's standpoint.

| NIB | Exc. | V.G. | Good | Fair | Poor |
|-----|------|------|------|------|------|
| 600 | 500 | 375 | 300 | 225 | 150 |

**Victor**

This is a blowback-operated, semi-automatic target pistol chambered for the .22 l.r. cartridge. It has either a 4.5" or 5.5" ribbed barrel with adjustable target sights. It features either a pushbutton or screw-activated takedown mechanism and has a 10-round detachable magazine. The finish is blued, with checkered walnut grips.

Hi-Standard Victor

| Exc. | V.G. | Good | Fair | Poor |
|------|------|------|------|------|
| 500 | 425 | 350 | 275 | 175 |

**10-X**

This is a high-grade target pistol designed for serious match competition. It was produced with parts specially selected by one of High Standard's master gunsmiths who hand-assembled and initialed each unit. It has a matte-blue finish with checkered walnut grips. There are two versions--one with an Allen-screw barrel release; and the earlier pushbutton barrel-release system, which would be worth approximately 40 percent additional. This model was manufactured between 1982 and 1984.

| Exc. | V.G. | Good | Fair | Poor |
|------|------|------|------|------|
| 850 | 775 | 700 | 550 | 425 |

**Sharpshooter-M**

This model has a 5.5" bull barrel and adjustable sights. It is blued, with military-style plastic grips. It was manufactured between 1982 and 1984.

| Exc. | V.G. | Good | Fair | Poor |
|------|------|------|------|------|
| 350 | 300 | 250 | 175 | 100 |

## Derringer

This is an Over/Under, double-action-only pocket pistol chambered for the .22 l.r. or the .22 rimfire Magnum cartridges. It has 3.5" barrels and is furnished either blued or nickel-plated, with plastic grips. This firearm was widely utilized as a law enforcement backup weapon in the Magnum chambering. The nickel-finish model is worth approximately 10 percent additional.

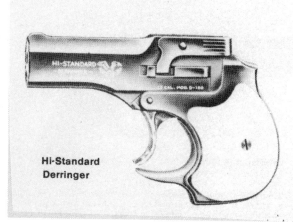

Hi-Standard
Derringer

| Exc. | V.G. | Good | Fair | Poor |
|------|------|------|------|------|
| 200  | 165  | 145  | 100  | 75   |

**Silver Plated Derringer with Presentation Case**

| Exc. | V.G. | Good | Fair | Poor |
|------|------|------|------|------|
| 250  | 200  | 150  | 125  | 100  |

**Gold Plated Derringer with Presentation Case**

| Exc. | V.G. | Good | Fair | Poor |
|------|------|------|------|------|
| 275  | 225  | 175  | 150  | 100  |

## Sentinel Series

These revolvers are double-action, solid-frame, swing-out cylinder models chambered for the .22 l.r. cartridge. They are offered with 3", 4", or 6" barrels. They have anodized aluminum frames and a 9-shot cylinder. They are offered in finishes of blue and nickel-plate, as well as pink and yellow anodized. They have either wood or plastic grips.

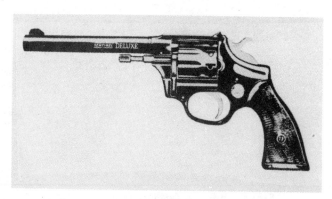

**Sentinel**

| Exc. | V.G. | Good | Fair | Poor |
|------|------|------|------|------|
| 150  | 125  | 100  | 75   | 50   |

**Sentinel Imperial--Adjustable Sights**

| Exc. | V.G. | Good | Fair | Poor |
|------|------|------|------|------|
| 165  | 145  | 110  | 90   | 75   |

**Sentinel Deluxe**

| Exc. | V.G. | Good | Fair | Poor |
|------|------|------|------|------|
| 165  | 145  | 110  | 90   | 75   |

## Sentinel Snub--2.5" Barrel, Round Butt

| Exc. | V.G. | Good | Fair | Poor |
|------|------|------|------|------|
| 150  | 125  | 100  | 75   | 50   |

## Durango

This is a Western-style, double-action revolver chambered for the .22 l.r. cartridge. It is offered with a 4.5" or 5.5" barrel, has a steel frame, and is either blued or nickel-plated with wood grips. It was manufactured between 1971 and 1973.

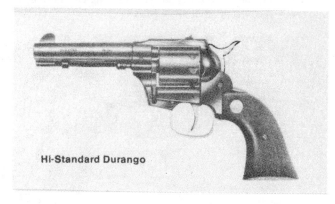

Hi-Standard Durango

| Exc. | V.G. | Good | Fair | Poor |
|------|------|------|------|------|
| 150  | 125  | 100  | 75   | 50   |

## Double Nine

This is a Western-style, double-action revolver chambered for the .22 l.r. cartridge. It has a 5.5" barrel and an alloy frame. It is either blued or nickel-plated with simulated-ivory, ebony, or stag grips. It was manufactured between 1959 and 1984.

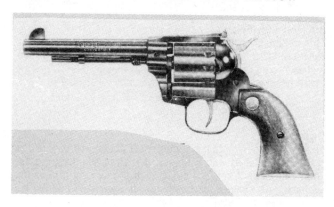

| Exc. | V.G. | Good | Fair | Poor |
|------|------|------|------|------|
| 150  | 125  | 100  | 75   | 50   |

## Longhorn

This is a 9.5"-barrelled version of the Double Nine.

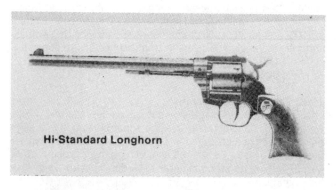

Hi-Standard Longhorn

| Exc. | V.G. | Good | Fair | Poor |
|------|------|------|------|------|
| 200  | 175  | 125  | 100  | 75   |

### Hombre

This is a 4.5"-barrelled version of the Double Nine with a steel frame.

| Exc. | V.G. | Good | Fair | Poor |
|------|------|------|------|------|
| 150 | 125 | 100 | 75 | 50 |

### High Sierra

This version has a 7" octagonal barrel and a gold-plated grip frame.

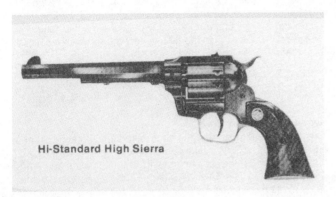

Hi-Standard High Sierra

| Exc. | V.G. | Good | Fair | Poor |
|------|------|------|------|------|
| 200 | 175 | 125 | 100 | 75 |

### Posse

This version has a 3.5" barrel and a brass grip frame with walnut grips. It was manufactured between 1961 and 1966.

| Exc. | V.G. | Good | Fair | Poor |
|------|------|------|------|------|
| 125 | 100 | 75 | 50 | 25 |

### Natchez

This version features rounded birdshead grips.

| Exc. | V.G. | Good | Fair | Poor |
|------|------|------|------|------|
| 125 | 100 | 75 | 50 | 25 |

### Kit Gun

This is a double-action, swing-out-cylinder revolver chambered for the .22 l.r. cartridge. It has a 4" barrel with adjustable sights and a 9-shot cylinder. The finish is blued, with walnut grips. It was manufactured between 1970 and 1973.

| Exc. | V.G. | Good | Fair | Poor |
|------|------|------|------|------|
| 150 | 125 | 100 | 75 | 50 |

### Sentinel I

This is a double-action revolver chambered for the .22 l.r. cartridge. It is offered with a 2", 3", or 4" barrel and a 9-shot swing-out cylinder. It has adjustable sights and is either blued or nickel-plated, with walnut grips.

| Exc. | V.G. | Good | Fair | Poor |
|------|------|------|------|------|
| 225 | 175 | 125 | 100 | 75 |

### Sentinel Mark IV

This model is similar to the Sentinel I but is chambered for the .22 rimfire Magnum cartridge.

| Exc. | V.G. | Good | Fair | Poor |
|------|------|------|------|------|
| 150 | 125 | 100 | 75 | 50 |

### Sentinel Mark II

This is a double-action revolver chambered for the .357 Magnum cartridge. It is offered with a 2.5", 4", or 6" barrel with fixed sights. The finish is blued, with walnut grips. It was manufactured between 1974 and 1976.

| Exc. | V.G. | Good | Fair | Poor |
|------|------|------|------|------|
| 225 | 175 | 125 | 100 | 75 |

### Sentinel Mark III

This version is similar to the Mark II, with adjustable sights.

| Exc. | V.G. | Good | Fair | Poor |
|------|------|------|------|------|
| 250 | 200 | 150 | 125 | 100 |

### Crusader

This is a large-frame double-action revolver chambered for the .357 Magnum, .44 Magnum, or the .45 Colt cartridges. It has a 7.5" barrel and a 6-shot, swing-out cylinder. It has adjustable sights and is blued, with walnut grips. This model was limited in its production and is not often encountered on today's market.

| Exc. | V.G. | Good | Fair | Poor |
|------|------|------|------|------|
| 550 | 500 | 450 | 350 | 275 |

### Supermatic Field Grade

This is a gas-operated semi-automatic shotgun chambered for 12 gauge. It has either a 28" modified or 30" full- choke barrel. The finish is blued, with a plain walnut stock. It was manufactured between 1960 and 1966.

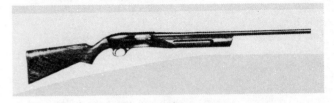

| Exc. | V.G. | Good | Fair | Poor |
|------|------|------|------|------|
| 200 | 175 | 150 | 100 | 65 |

### Supermatic Special

This version has a 27" barrel and an adjustable choke manufactured by Harrington & Richardson.

| Exc. | V.G. | Good | Fair | Poor |
|------|------|------|------|------|
| 200 | 175 | 150 | 100 | 65 |

### Supermatic Deluxe

This version is similar to the Field Grade, with a vent-rib barrel and a checkered walnut stock. It was manufactured between 1961 and 1966.

| Exc. | V.G. | Good | Fair | Poor |
|------|------|------|------|------|
| 250 | 200 | 175 | 125 | 85 |

### Supermatic Trophy

This version features the adjustable choke with a ventilated-rib barrel and checkered walnut stock.

| Exc. | V.G. | Good | Fair | Poor |
|------|------|------|------|------|
| 225 | 175 | 150 | 100 | 75 |

### Supermatic Deer Gun

This version has a 22" barrel with rifle sights and a recoil pad. It was manufactured in 1965 only.

| Exc. | V.G. | Good | Fair | Poor |
|------|------|------|------|------|
| 225 | 175 | 150 | 100 | 75 |

### Supermatic Skeet

This version has a 26" vent-rib barrel that is bored skeet. It was manufactured between 1962 and 1966.

| Exc. | V.G. | Good | Fair | Poor |
|------|------|------|------|------|
| 300 | 250 | 200 | 150 | 100 |

### Supermatic Trap

This version is similar to the Skeet model, with a 30" full-choke barrel and a trap-style stock with recoil pad. It was manufactured between 1962 and 1966.

| Exc. | V.G. | Good | Fair | Poor |
|------|------|------|------|------|
| 250 | 200 | 150 | 100 | 75 |

### Flite King Field Grade

This is a slide-action shotgun chambered for 12 or 20 gauge. It is offered with 26", 28", or 30" barrels with various chokes. The finish is blued, with a plain walnut stock. It was manufactured between 1960 and 1966.

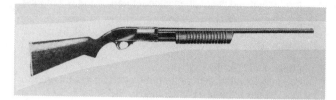

| Exc. | V.G. | Good | Fair | Poor |
|------|------|------|------|------|
| 175 | 150 | 125 | 100 | 75 |

### Flite King Special

This version has a 27" barrel with an adjustable choke.

| Exc. | V.G. | Good | Fair | Poor |
|------|------|------|------|------|
| 175 | 150 | 125 | 100 | 75 |

### Flite King Deluxe

This version has a ventilated-rib barrel and a checkered walnut stock. It was manufactured between 1961 and 1966.

| Exc. | V.G. | Good | Fair | Poor |
|------|------|------|------|------|
| 200 | 175 | 150 | 125 | 100 |

### Flite King Trophy

This version features a 27" ventilated-rib barrel with the adjustable choke. It was manufactured between 1960 and 1966.

| Exc. | V.G. | Good | Fair | Poor |
|------|------|------|------|------|
| 200 | 175 | 150 | 125 | 100 |

### Flite King Brush

This version has an 18" or 20" cylinder-bore barrel with rifle sights. It was manufactured between 1962 and 1964.

| Exc. | V.G. | Good | Fair | Poor |
|------|------|------|------|------|
| 175 | 150 | 125 | 100 | 75 |

### Flite King Brush Deluxe

This version features an adjustable peepsight and checkered walnut stock with recoil pad and was furnished with sling swivels and a sling. It was manufactured between 1964 and 1966.

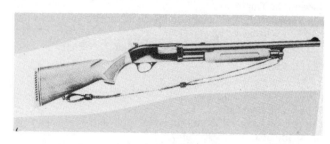

| Exc. | V.G. | Good | Fair | Poor |
|------|------|------|------|------|
| 250 | 200 | 175 | 125 | 100 |

### Flite King Skeet

This is a 12-gauge version with a 26" ventilated-rib barrel that is skeet-bored. It was manufactured between 1962 and 1966.

| Exc. | V.G. | Good | Fair | Poor |
|------|------|------|------|------|
| 275 | 225 | 200 | 150 | 125 |

### Flite King Trap

This version has a 30", ventilated-rib, full-choke barrel and a trap-type stock with recoil pad. It was manufactured between 1962 and 1966.

| Exc. | V.G. | Good | Fair | Poor |
|------|------|------|------|------|
| 250 | 200 | 175 | 125 | 100 |

### Model 10B

This is a unique semi-automatic shotgun that features a bullpup-type action. It is chambered for 12 gauge and has an 18" barrel. It has a pistol grip mounted at the front of the receiver with a shoulder pad mounted at its rear. The finish is matte blue with a black plastic stock and pistol grip. It has a folding carrying handle and a space to attach a flashlight to the top of the receiver. This was rated as an excellent combat shotgun but was never produced in great numbers. It carried a warning on the receiver that the weapon should not be fired left-handed as the ejecting empty case would strike a left-hander in the side of the face. This model has become somewhat collectible recently.

| Exc. | V.G. | Good | Fair | Poor |
|------|------|------|------|------|
| 650 | 575 | 450 | 350 | 250 |

### Supermatic Shadow Seven

This is an Over/Under shotgun chambered for 12 gauge. It has either a 27.5" or 29.5" vent-rib barrel with various choke combinations. It has a boxlock action with a single trigger and automatic ejectors. The finish is blued, with a checkered walnut stock. This model was manufactured in Japan and imported in 1974 and 1975.

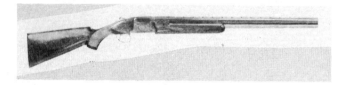

| Exc. | V.G. | Good | Fair | Poor |
|------|------|------|------|------|
| 675 | 600 | 500 | 425 | 350 |

### Supermatic Indy

This is a more deluxe version of the Shadow Seven that features a heavily engraved receiver with a skipline-checkered stock furnished with a recoil pad and a ventilated forearm. It was also manufactured in Japan and imported in 1974 and 1975.

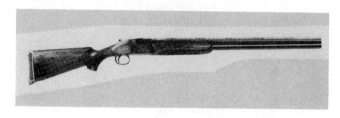

| Exc. | V.G. | Good | Fair | Poor |
|------|------|------|------|------|
| 800 | 700 | 600 | 500 | 425 |

### Supermatic Shadow

This is a gas-operated semi-automatic shotgun chambered for 12 or 20 gauge with either 2.75" or 3" chambers. It has a 26", 28", or 30" ventilated-rib barrel with various chokes. The finish is blued, with a checkered walnut stock. This model was manufactured in Japan and imported in 1974 and 1975.

| Exc. | V.G. | Good | Fair | Poor |
|------|------|------|------|------|
| 350 | 300 | 275 | 200 | 125 |

### Sport King Rifle

This is a blowback-operated semi-automatic rifle chambered for the .22 rimfire cartridges. It features a 22" barrel with open sights and a tubular magazine. The finish is blued, with a plain walnut stock. It was manufactured between 1960 and 1966.

| Exc. | V.G. | Good | Fair | Poor |
|------|------|------|------|------|
| 100 | 90 | 75 | 50 | 25 |

## Sport King Special

This version has a Monte Carlo-type stock and beavertail forearm.

| Exc. | V.G. | Good | Fair | Poor |
|------|------|------|------|------|
| 150  | 125  | 100  | 60   | 40   |

## Sport King Deluxe

This version has a checkered walnut stock. It was manufactured between 1966 and 1975.

| Exc. | V.G. | Good | Fair | Poor |
|------|------|------|------|------|
| 175  | 150  | 125  | 100  | 75   |

## Sport King Carbine

This is a compact version of the Field model with an 18" barrel and a straight-grip stock with a barrel band holding on the forearm. It was furnished with a sling. It was manufactured between 1964 and 1973.

| Exc. | V.G. | Good | Fair | Poor |
|------|------|------|------|------|
| 175  | 150  | 125  | 100  | 75   |

## Flite King

This is a slide-action rifle chambered for the .22 rimfire cartridges. It has a 24" barrel with a tubular magazine. It features open sights and an internal hammer. The finish is blued, with a Monte Carlo-type stock. It was manufactured between 1962 and 1975.

| Exc. | V.G. | Good | Fair | Poor |
|------|------|------|------|------|
| 125  | 100  | 80   | 60   | 40   |

## Hi-Power Field Grade

This is a bolt-action sporting rifle built on a Mauser-type action. It is chambered for the .270 and the .30-06 cartridges. It has a 22" barrel furnished with open sights. It has a 4-round magazine and is blued, with a plain walnut stock. It was manufactured between 1962 and 1966.

Hi-Standard Hi-Power Field

| Exc. | V.G. | Good | Fair | Poor |
|------|------|------|------|------|
| 300  | 250  | 225  | 150  | 100  |

## Hi-Power Deluxe

This version is similar to the Field Grade but features a checkered, Monte Carlo-type stock. It was manufactured between 1962 and 1966.

| Exc. | V.G. | Good | Fair | Poor |
|------|------|------|------|------|
| 350  | 300  | 275  | 200  | 150  |

## HILL, W.J.
### Birmingham, England

**Hill's Self Extracting Revolver**

This is a folding-trigger double-action revolver that utilizes a novel double-hinge tip-up design to facilitate loading. It is chambered for .32 caliber rimfire and has an unfluted 6-shot cylinder. The round barrel is 3.75" in length and is marked "Hill's Patent Self-Extracor." The finish is blued, with checkered walnut grips. This revolver was manufactured circa 1880.

| Exc. | V.G. | Good | Fair | Poor |
|------|------|------|------|------|
| 500  | 400  | 350  | 250  | 150  |

## HILLIARD, D. H.
### Cornish, New Hampshire

**Underhammer Pistol**

This is a larger-than-normal underhammer or boot pistol that is chambered for .34 caliber and utilizes the percussion ignition system. It has a 12" part-octagonal barrel and features fine peep sights. It is clear that this pistol was intended for target work. The finish is blued, and the walnut handle has a large knob on the butt end. This pistol is sometimes found with "Remington" marked on the barrel. This pistol was manufactured in the 1850's.

| Exc. | V.G. | Good | Fair | Poor |
|------|------|------|------|------|
| 500  | 400  | 325  | 250  | 200  |

## HINO-KOMURA
### Tokyo, Japan

This is an exremely rare and unusual pistol. There were approximately 500 manufactured between 1905 and 1912. They were chambered for the 7.65mm, but one has been reported chambered for the 8mm Nambu. The action of this pistol is a blow-forward design. To cock the action, the muzzle is pulled forward until the slide engages a catch on the trigger assembly. Pulling the trigger at this point allows the barrel to move back and engage the cartridge nose into the chamber. Squeezing the grip safety then allows the barrel to slam back into the fixed firing pin on the breech block. After this point it then functions like a conventional semi- automatic. Very few of these pistols have been observed and hardly ever outside of Japan.

| Exc. | V.G. | Good | Fair | Poor |
|------|------|------|------|------|
| 3500 | 3250 | 2750 | 2000 | 1500 |

## HODGKINS, D. C. & SONS
### Macon, Georgia

**Percussion Carbine**

This was a Confederate copy of the Model 1855 Springfield Carbine. It is chambered for .58 caliber and utilizes the percussion ignition system. It has a 22" barrel and a half stock of walnut that is held in place by one barrel band and a pewter end cap. There is a swivel-mounted ramrod and a sling swivel on the bow of the triggerguard. The letters "CSA" are stamped on the barrel over the letter "P". There were approximately 100 manufactured in 1862 and 1863. All were contracted for by the Confederate government. As with all CSA weapons, these Carbines are quite crude and appear as if they were handmade. They are extremely rare, and collector interest is very high. Be wary of fakes.

| Exc. | V.G. | Good | Fair | Poor |
|------|------|------|------|------|
| 5000 | 4250 | 3500 | 2750 | 2000 |

## HOFFMAN, LOUIS
### Vicksburg, Mississippi

**Pocket Pistol**

This pistol was based on the Henry Deringer Philadelphia design. It is chambered for .41 caliber percussion and has a 3" barrel, German silver mountings, and a walnut stock. It was manufactured in the 1850's.

| Exc. | V.G. | Good | Fair | Poor |
|------|------|------|------|------|
| 600  | 500  | 400  | 300  | 225  |

## HOFER, P.
### Ferlach, Austria

This is a custom maker of high-grade double rifles. They are available on a made-to-order basis and characteristically feature only the best grade of materials and workmanship. There are too few of these firearms traded to establish realistic values, and any encountered should be individually appraised. The prices for a new model begin at approximately $10,000.

# HOLDEN, C. B.
## Worcester, Massachusetts

### Open Frame Rifle
This rifle is also known as the Model 1862. It is a single-shot, breech-loading rifle chambered for the .44 rimfire cartridge. This is a unique rifle in that the entire side of the action is open so that one could lower the triggerguard and open the breech, then reach in and load and then cock the hammer. The barrel is octagonal and 28" in length, with open sights. The frame is bronze, and the blue barrel is marked "C.B.Holden Worcester-,Mass." There were very few of these rifles produced (several hundred at most) between 1862 and 1870.

| Exc. | V.G. | Good | Fair | Poor |
|------|------|------|------|------|
| 750 | 675 | 600 | 475 | 325 |

# HOLLAND & HOLLAND, LTD.
## London, England
## Importer--New England Arms
## Kittery Point, Maine

The firm of Holland & Holland was founded in 1835 and has had a long and illustrious history of producing the very finest firearms the world has ever known. They have supplied rifles and shotguns to the wealthy and titled. Their products have been used to hunt the largest, most dangerous of game. The cost of these weapons is quite high, and it would be essential to secure a qualified independent appraisal before considering a transaction. The early black-powder arms with exposed hammers are usually worth a good deal less than their modern hammerless counterparts. However, they are very difficult to evaluate in a book of this nature due to the variations in features and the vast range of condition in which they are usually found. We list the Holland & Hollands and give an estimated value for reference purposes only. It would be irresponsible to attempt to influence the purchase of a firearm of this nature without a hands-on professional appraisal.

### Over/Under Shotguns
### Old Model Royal Grade
This model is chambered for 12 gauge and features hand-detachable sidelocks, automatic ejectors, and a hand-checkered, English-style straight-grip stock. These were about the only standard features; all other specifications were to the customer's order. The materials and workmanship were of the finest quality. These guns are quite rare, as only 30 were manufactured prior to 1951.

| Exc. | V.G. | Good | Fair | Poor |
|------|------|------|------|------|
| 22000 | 18500 | 15000 | 11000 | 8500 |

### New Model Royal Grade
This is an improved version that feature a slimmer action. It was manufactured between 1951 and 1960.

| Exc. | V.G. | Good | Fair | Poor |
|------|------|------|------|------|
| 25000 | 20000 | 17500 | 12500 | 10000 |

### Royal Grade Game Gun
This is the latest creation from Holland & Holland. It is a strictly custom-built-to-order proposition and was introduced in 1990. This firearm incorporates the finest features available today.

| Exc. | V.G. | Good | Fair | Poor |
|------|------|------|------|------|
| 45000 | 38000 | 32500 | 25000 | 20000 |

### Side x Side Shotguns
### Northwood Boxlock
This model is chambered for 12 gauge through 28 gauge and has 28" or 30" solid-ribbed barrels. The action is a scalloped boxlock that is case-colored. It features double trigger standard and automatic ejectors. The high-grade, hand-checkered walnut stock was available either in the English style or with a pistol grip.
20 or 28 Gauge--Add 10 Percent.
Deluxe Version with Engraving--Add 10 Percent.

| Exc. | V.G. | Good | Fair | Poor |
|------|------|------|------|------|
| 7500 | 6500 | 5250 | 4000 | 3000 |

### Cavalier Boxlock
This model is similar to the Northwood but is in a better overall grade. It was chambered for 12, 20, and 28 gauge and was also built to the customer's specifications.
20 or 28 Gauge--Add 10 Percent.
Deluxe Model with More Engraving--Add 20 Percent.

| Exc. | V.G. | Good | Fair | Poor |
|------|------|------|------|------|
| 12500 | 10000 | 7500 | 5500 | 4500 |

### Dominion Sidelock
This model is chambered for 12, 16, or 20 gauge. It is a true sidelock gun with double triggers, automatic ejectors, and an English-style stock. All other features were on a custom-order basis. This older-model gun was discontinued.

| Exc. | V.G. | Good | Fair | Poor |
|------|------|------|------|------|
| 5000 | 4250 | 3500 | 2750 | 2000 |

### Dominion Game Gun
This is the currently produced version of the Dominion. It is manufactured in 12 gauge only, to customer's specifications.

| Exc. | V.G. | Good | Fair | Poor |
|------|------|------|------|------|
| 30000 | 25000 | 20000 | 15000 | 10000 |

### Royal Ejector Grade Hammerless Sidelock
This model was produced in all gauges, with all other features to the customer's specifications. It was manufactured from 1885 and is considered one of the best shotguns ever produced.
20 Gauge--Add 25 Percent.
28 Gauge--Add 35 Percent.
.410--Add 70 Percent.

| Exc. | V.G. | Good | Fair | Poor |
|------|------|------|------|------|
| 12500 | 10000 | 7500 | 6000 | 5000 |

### Deluxe Model
This model is similar to the Royal Ejector, with a greater amount of engraving and a self-opening action. The wood used is the highest grade obtainable.

| Exc. | V.G. | Good | Fair | Poor |
|------|------|------|------|------|
| 15000 | 12500 | 10000 | 7500 | 5500 |

### Badminton Grade
This model is similar to the Royal Deluxe, without the self-opening action. It was introduced in 1902.
20 Gauge--Add 25 Percent.
28 Gauge--Add 35 Percent.
.410--Add 50 Percent.

| Exc. | V.G. | Good | Fair | Poor |
|------|------|------|------|------|
| 11000 | 8500 | 7500 | 5500 | 4000 |

### Riviera Grade
This is essentially the Badminton model supplied with an extra set of barrels and furnished in a fitted leather case. It was discontinued in 1967.
20 Gauge--Add 25 Percent.
28 Gauge--Add 35 Percent.
.410--Add 50 Percent.

| Exc. | V.G. | Good | Fair | Poor |
|------|------|------|------|------|
| 15000 | 12500 | 10000 | 7500 | 5500 |

### Centenary Grade
This is a lightweight version of the offered sidelock models. It is chambered for a special 12-gauge shell and only has a 2" chamber. The Centenary feature would reduce the values of the respective models by approximately 10 percent. One should be wary of altered chambers in this model.

## Royal Game Gun

This is Holland & Holland's best quality sidelock gun. It is chambered for all gauges, has hand-detachable locks, and is totally built to the customer's specifications.
20 and 28 Gauges--Add 10 Percent.

| Exc. | V.G. | Good | Fair | Poor |
|------|------|------|------|------|
| 42500 | 32500 | 25000 | 17500 | 10000 |

## Single Barrel Trap Gun

This discontinued model was offered in 12 gauge with a 30" or 32" full-choke ventilated-rib barrel. It features an automatic ejector and a boxlock action. The hand-checkered walnut stock has a Monte Carlo comb and a recoil pad. This model was available in the three following grades, that differ in the degree of engraving and grade of walnut used in the stock.

### Standard Grade

| Exc. | V.G. | Good | Fair | Poor |
|------|------|------|------|------|
| 5000 | 4500 | 3750 | 2500 | 2000 |

### Deluxe Grade

| Exc. | V.G. | Good | Fair | Poor |
|------|------|------|------|------|
| 7500 | 6500 | 5500 | 4750 | 3000 |

### Exhibition Grade

| Exc. | V.G. | Good | Fair | Poor |
|------|------|------|------|------|
| 9000 | 8000 | 7000 | 5500 | 3750 |

## Double Rifles
### No. 2 Grade Double Rifle

This side-by-side Side model features a sidelock action and is chambered for popular American and British cartridges. It has 24" barrels with folding-leaf-type express sights. This model has automatic ejectors and double triggers. It features a hand-checkered European Walnut stock.
Obsolete cartridges could be worth less.

| Exc. | V.G. | Good | Fair | Poor |
|------|------|------|------|------|
| 15000 | 12500 | 8500 | 7000 | 6000 |

### Royal Side x Side Rifle

This is a more deluxe, heavily engraved version of the No. 2 Double Rifle. It has many made to order features.

| Exc. | V.G. | Good | Fair | Poor |
|------|------|------|------|------|
| 50000 | 40000 | 30000 | 22500 | 15000 |

### Royal Deluxe Side x Side Rifle

This was the best-grade double rifle that was completely built to order using the finest quality materials and workmanship.

| Exc. | V.G. | Good | Fair | Poor |
|------|------|------|------|------|
| 56000 | 45000 | 35000 | 25000 | 17500 |

### H&H 700 Bore Side x Side Rifle

This is the latest offering from this firm. It is chambered for a new cartridge that will surpass any previous sporting caliber. It is called the .700 H&H and fires a 1000-grain projectile. This would have sufficient energy to drop a tyrannosaurus if one were to be resurrected. This rifle weighs 19 pounds and has 26" barrels. All other features are of the highest quality and made to the customer's specifications. This model has not officially been released, and there is no official price. One can only wonder for now.

## Bolt Action Rifles
### Best Quality Rifle

This is a bolt-action rifle built on a Mauser or Enfield action. It is chambered for various calibers up to the .375 H&H Magnum cartridge. It features a 24" barrel with a folding-leaf express sight and has a 4-shot box magazine. The finish is blued, and the hand-checkered stock is select French Walnut. There were many options that could be ordered on this rifle, and they would reflect greatly on the value. Independent appraisal is necessary. The values given here are estimates for the basic firearm only.

| Exc. | V.G. | Good | Fair | Poor |
|------|------|------|------|------|
| 7500 | 6500 | 5000 | 3500 | 2250 |

### Deluxe Magazine Rifle

This rarely encountered version is similar to the Best Quality Rifle, with the best grade walnut available and more elaborate engraving. There were also many custom options offered on this model that would affect the value. Appraisal is highly recomended.

| Exc. | V.G. | Good | Fair | Poor |
|------|------|------|------|------|
| 10500 | 8500 | 7000 | 5000 | 3000 |

# HOLLOWAY ARMS CO.
## Ft. Worth, Texas

### HAC Model 7

This is a paramilitary-styled rifle that barely saw the light of day before the company ceased production. It is chambered for the .308 cartridge and is a gas-operated, semi-automatic "Assault Type Rifle" It has a 20" barrel with adjustable sights and was furnished with a scope mount. The receiver is alloy and black-anodized, with a side fold stock. The magazine holds 20 rounds, and the rifle came with a belt buckle that was serial-numbered the same as the rifle. There were only a few hundred manufactured in 1984 and 1985. The values of this rifle, as with other assault rifles, varies to such a degree in different geographic locales that it is not possible to accurately price in this publication. Independent appraisal should be secured.

### HAC Model 7C

This is similar to the HAC 7, with a 16" carbine-length barrel.

### HAC Model 7S

This is a heavy-barrelled "Sniper's Model."

# HOLMES FIREARMS
## Wheeler, Arkansas

### MP-22

This is a blowback-operated, semi-automatic, assault-type pistol chambered for the .22 l.r. cartridge. It has a 6" barrel and an alloy receiver. The finish is black with a walnut grip. This weapon was manufactured in 1985.

| NIB | Exc. | V.G. | Good | Fair | Poor |
|-----|------|------|------|------|------|
| 350 | 300 | 275 | 225 | 200 | 150 |

### MP-83

This model is similar in appearance to the MP-22 except that it is larger in size and is chambered for either 9mm or .45ACP. It was also manufactured in 1985 only.

| NIB | Exc. | V.G. | Good | Fair | Poor |
|-----|------|------|------|------|------|
| 400 | 350 | 325 | 275 | 250 | 200 |

## HOOD F. A. CO.
### Norwich, Connecticut

This company manufactured firearms from 1873 until 1882. Everything they made falls into the category sometimes known as "Suicide Specials." There are slight variations among the revolvers as to barrel length, butt style, finish, etc.; but they are all basically the same. They are poorly made, spur-trigger, solid-frame revolvers chambered in either .22 or .32 rimfire. The barrels are smooth bore with bogus rifling cut into the last half inch to fool the customer. They were marketed through various different retailers, and this is the reason for the long list of trade names. Values are the same regardless of the marketing name.

| Exc. | V.G. | Good | Fair | Poor |
|------|------|------|------|------|
| 200  | 175  | 125  | 100  | 75   |

## HOPKINS & ALLEN
### Norwich, Connecticut
### ALSO SEE--Bacon Arms Co.
### Merwin Hulbert & Co.

This company was founded in 1868 in Norwich, Connecticut. They produced a large number of inexpensive revolvers that were sold under a number of trade names. They did produce a small number of quality revolvers that are considered to be valuable and have a good deal of collector interest today. They also produced revolvers that were sold by other companies, most notably the Merwin Hulbert Company. These revolvers can be found in their own section of this text.

The trade names used by this company are as follows: Acme, Blue Jacket, Captain Jack, Chichester, Defender, Dictator, Hopkins & Allen, Imperial Arms Co., Monarch, Mountain Eagle, Ranger, Tower's Police Safety, Universal, and XL. Most of these are single-action, solid-frame, spur-trigger revolvers chambered for either .22, .32, .38, or the .41 rimfire cartridges. They were commonly referred to as "Suicide Specials," and all would be worth a similar amount.

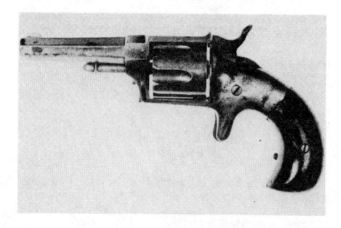

| Exc. | V.G. | Good | Fair | Poor |
|------|------|------|------|------|
| 175  | 150  | 125  | 100  | 75   |

Certain of these revolvers are hinge-frame, double-action break opens with round ribbed barrels of various lengths. They are either blued or nickel-plated, with checkered plastic grips. They are similar to other revolvers of their type manufactured during this era and are all quite similar in value.

| Exc. | V.G. | Good | Fair | Poor |
|------|------|------|------|------|
| 150  | 125  | 100  | 75   | 50   |

### Dictator

This is a single-action revolver chambered for the .36 caliber percussion and later converted to the .38 rimfire cartridge. It has a 4" round barrel with an integral loading lever and a 5-shot unfluted cylinder that is roll-engraved. The finish is blued, with walnut grips. The barrel is marked, "Dictator." There were approximately 6,000 manufactured in the late 1860's and early 1870's. Approximately 5,000 were converted to the .38 rimfire chambering. Values given are for the conversion model, with percussion pistols bringing approximately double these values.

| Exc. | V.G. | Good | Fair | Poor |
|------|------|------|------|------|
| 500  | 400  | 350  | 250  | 150  |

### Falling Block Rifle

This is a single-shot falling-block rifle. The action is activated by a lever. It is chambered for a number of calibers that were popular during that era, from .22 rimfire to .38-55. The frames are various sizes to accommodate the calibers chambered. The barrels offered are 24", 26", or 28" octagonal. The finish is blued, with a checkered walnut stock. There were several thousand manufactured between 1888 and 1892.

| Exc. | V.G. | Good | Fair | Poor |
|------|------|------|------|------|
| 500  | 400  | 300  | 225  | 125  |

### Schuetzen Rifle

This is a deluxe target version chambered for the .22 rimfire or the .25-20 cartridge. It has a 26" octagonal barrel and is available with double-set triggers. The finish is blued, and it has a select, checkered walnut stock with a Swiss Schuetzen-type buttplate.

| Exc. | V.G. | Good | Fair | Poor |
|------|------|------|------|------|
| 850  | 750  | 650  | 500  | 400  |

### Navy Revolver

This is a large single-action revolver chambered for the .38 rimfire cartridge. It has a 6.5" round barrel and a 6-shot cylinder. It is either blued or nickel-plated, with square-butt walnut grips. The barrel is marked, "Hopkins & Allen Mfg. Co., Pat. Mar. 28, 71, Apr. 27, 75." The topstrap is marked, "XL Navy." This is one of two revolvers rated as the finest revolvers this company produced. There were a few hundred manufactured between 1878 and 1882.

| Exc. | V.G. | Good | Fair | Poor |
|---|---|---|---|---|
| 500 | 425 | 350 | 250 | 175 |

**Army Revolver**
This model is similar to the Navy Revolver except that it is chambered for the .44 rimfire cartridge. It has barrel lengths of 4.5", 6", or 7.5". The barrel markings are the same, and the topstrap is marked, "XL No. 8." There were several hundred manufactured between 1878 and 1882.

| Exc. | V.G. | Good | Fair | Poor |
|---|---|---|---|---|
| 650 | 575 | 475 | 325 | 225 |

**Derringer**
This is a single-shot pocket pistol chambered for the .22 rimfire cartridge. It has a 1.75" barrel that pivoted downward for loading. It features an internal hammer with a unique folding trigger. The finish is either blued or nickel-plated, with walnut birdshead grips. It is scroll-engraved. Occasionally, this model will be found with ivory or pearl grips, which would be worth approximately a 10 percent premium. This model is marked, "Hopkins & Allen Arms Co., Norwich, Conn. U.S.A." The grips have a gold-plated Hopkins & Allen medallion inlaid into them. One should be aware that there have been a number of modern copies produced recently in Europe that are very close reproductions. If in doubt, secure a qualified appraisal. There were a few hundred manufactured in the 1880's and 1890's.

| Exc. | V.G. | Good | Fair | Poor |
|---|---|---|---|---|
| 800 | 700 | 600 | 475 | 350 |

# HOTCHKISS
**Winchester Arms Co.**
**New Haven, Connecticut**

This rifle was designed by Benjamin B. Hotchkiss, who sold the rights to manufacture to Winchester in 1877. This rifle was placed on the market in 1883 and was the first bolt-action rifle ever produced by Winchester. It was intended for use by the military, as well as for sporting purposes. This rifle is chambered for the .45-70 Govt. cartridge and is unique in being the first rifle with a magazine in the butt, which consisted of a tube that holds 6 rounds. The model is divided into three distinct types, and all feature blued finish with straight-grip, oil-stained walnut stocks. The 3 variations were as follows.

**1st Model Sporting Rifle Serial No's. 1-6419**
This model consists of a "Sporting Rifle" that has a 26" barrel and adjustable sights. This Model has a crescent butt with an ebony forend tip. The Winchester name and address are marked on the barrel.

| Exc. | V.G. | Good | Fair | Poor |
|---|---|---|---|---|
| 1100 | 1000 | 800 | 600 | 400 |

**1st Model Carbine**
This version features a 24" round barrel with one barrel band and a carbine-style buttplate. There is a saddle ring on the left side of the stock, and the sights are military style.

| Exc. | V.G. | Good | Fair | Poor |
|---|---|---|---|---|
| 1000 | 850 | 700 | 500 | 350 |

**1st Model Musket**
This version has a 32" round barrel, two barrel bands, and a bayonet lug. The buttplate is a carbine type, and the sights are military styled.

| Exc. | V.G. | Good | Fair | Poor |
|---|---|---|---|---|
| 1000 | 850 | 700 | 500 | 350 |

**2nd Model Sporting Rifle Serial No.'s 6420-22521**
The difference between the 1st and the 2nd Model was the addition of a magazine cutoff and a safety. All other features remained the same.

| Exc. | V.G. | Good | Fair | Poor |
|---|---|---|---|---|
| 1100 | 1000 | 800 | 600 | 400 |

**2nd Model Carbine**
This version has a 22.5" round barrel.

| Exc. | V.G. | Good | Fair | Poor |
|---|---|---|---|---|
| 1000 | 850 | 700 | 500 | 350 |

**2nd Model Musket**
This model has a 28" round barrel.

| Exc. | V.G. | Good | Fair | Poor |
|---|---|---|---|---|
| 1000 | 850 | 700 | 500 | 350 |

**3rd Model Sporting Rifle Serial No.'s 22522-84555**
This model has a two-piece stock.

| Exc. | V.G. | Good | Fair | Poor |
|---|---|---|---|---|
| 1200 | 1100 | 900 | 700 | 500 |

**3rd Model Carbine**
This model has the two-piece stock and a 20" round barrel.

| Exc. | V.G. | Good | Fair | Poor |
|---|---|---|---|---|
| 3000 | 2250 | 1750 | 1300 | 900 |

**3rd Model Musket**
This model is similar to the 2nd Model, with a two-piece stock.

| Exc. | V.G. | Good | Fair | Poor |
|---|---|---|---|---|
| 1100 | 1000 | 800 | 600 | 400 |

# HOWA MACHINE COMPANY
**Japan**

This company produced bolt-action rifles for Smith & Wesson up until 1985 and then for Mossberg in 1986 and 1987. These rifles are listed under those respective headings in this book. Currently the Howa line is imported by Interarms of Alexandria, Virginia.

## Model 1500 Hunter

This model is chambered for .22-250, .223, .243, .270, 7mm Remington Magnum .308, .30-06, and .300 Winchester Magnum. The barrel length is 22" or 24", and the magazine holds 5 shots--or 3 in the Magnum calibers. The rifle features iron sights and a blued finish, with a checkered walnut stock. It was imported by Interarms in 1988 only.

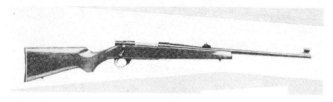

| Exc. | V.G. | Good | Fair | Poor |
|------|------|------|------|------|
| 350 | 325 | 300 | 225 | 150 |

## Model 1500 Trophy

This Model is similar to the Hunter and is chambered for the same calibers. It features a better-grade walnut stock with skip-line checkering. This Model was introduced in 1988.

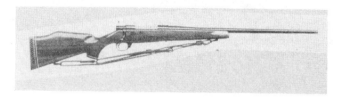

| NIB | Exc. | V.G. | Good | Fair | Poor |
|-----|------|------|------|------|------|
| 500 | 400 | 350 | 325 | 250 | 175 |

## Model 1500 Varmint

This is a 24" heavy-barrelled version chambered for the .22-250 or .223. It does not feature iron sights and was introduced in 1988.

| NIB | Exc. | V.G. | Good | Fair | Poor |
|-----|------|------|------|------|------|
| 525 | 475 | 425 | 375 | 275 | 200 |

## Model 1500 Lightning

This version is chambered for the .270, 7mm Remington Magnum, and .30-06. It features a synthetic stock and is slightly lighter in weight. This Model was introduced in 1988.

| NIB | Exc. | V.G. | Good | Fair | Poor |
|-----|------|------|------|------|------|
| 500 | 450 | 400 | 350 | 250 | 175 |

# HOWARD-WHITNEY
### New Haven, Connecticut
### SEE--Whitney Arms Co.

# HUNT
### New Haven, Connecticut

## Volition Repeater

This was actually the very first firearm attributable to the firm of Winchester. It was chambered for a unique round that was known as the "Rocket Ball" and consisted of a .44-caliber hollow-based projectile that was filled with propellant and covered by a disk with a hole in it that permitted the flash of a separate priming device to reach the powder and ignite it. This rifle and cartridge combination was invented by Walter Hunt and was manufactured in 1849 in very limited quantities. The progression of the Winchester firm can be traced directly back to this rifle. There is only one known to exist in the Winchester Museum, and the value would be literally impossible to determine.

# HUNTER ARMS CO.
### Fulton, New York
### SEE--L. C. Smith

# HUSQVARNA
### Husqvarna, Sweden

**Pistols**
**Lahti**

Swedish Model 40 pistol, also known as the Lahti, is a heavy-duty, well-made service pistol that was manufactured between 1940 and 1944. It is chambered for the 9mm parabellum cartridge and has a 5.5" barrel. This pistol was designed by Aino Lahti, using the P-08 as a starting point. It has a locked-breech, recoil-operated action that has an accelerator to aid to the recoil operation. This pistol was noted for its reliability, especially in the cold climate in which it was used. This pistol has a blue finish, with checkered plastic grips and an 8-shot detachable magazine. The loster rig would add approximately 15 percent to the values listed.

| Exc. | V.G. | Good | Fair | Poor |
|------|------|------|------|------|
| 400 | 350 | 275 | 225 | 150 |

**Bolt Action Rifles**
**Hi-Power**

This rifle was built on a modified Mauser action and is chambered for various American and European calibers. It has a 24" barrel with open sights and a checkered beechwood stock. It was manufactured between 1946 and 1951.

| Exc. | V.G. | Good | Fair | Poor |
|------|------|------|------|------|
| 350 | 300 | 275 | 200 | 150 |

## Model 1100 Deluxe

This Model is similar to the Hi-Power with a high comb stock made of European walnut. It was manufactured between 1952 and 1956.

| Exc. | V.G. | Good | Fair | Poor |
|------|------|------|------|------|
| 450 | 400 | 325 | 250 | 200 |

## Model 1000 Super Grade

This Model is similar to the Model 1100, with a Monte Carlo cheekpiece. It was manufactured between 1952 and 1956.

| Exc. | V.G. | Good | Fair | Poor |
|------|------|------|------|------|
| 450 | 400 | 325 | 250 | 200 |

## Model 3100 Crown Grade

This Model features a Mauser-type action, 24" barrel, and a walnut stock with black forend tip and pistol grip cap. It is chambered from .243 up to the .308 Winchester. It was manufactured between 1954 and 1972.

| Exc. | V.G. | Good | Fair | Poor |
|------|------|------|------|------|
| 475 | 425 | 350 | 300 | 250 |

## Model 4100 Lightweight

This Model is similar to the Model 3100 except that it features a lighter weight walnut stock with a Schnabel forearm. It was manufactured between 1954 and 1972.

| Exc. | V.G. | Good | Fair | Poor |
|------|------|------|------|------|
| 475 | 425 | 350 | 300 | 250 |

## Model 456

This model is similar to the Model 4100, with a Mannlicher-style full-length stock. It was manufactured between 1959 and 1970.

| Exc. | V.G. | Good | Fair | Poor |
|------|------|------|------|------|
| 500 | 450 | 375 | 325 | 275 |

## Model 6000

This model is similar to the Model 4100 except that it features select-grade walnut and has an express-type folding-leaf rear sight. It was manufactured between 1968 and 1970.

| Exc. | V.G. | Good | Fair | Poor |
|------|------|------|------|------|
| 600 | 550 | 475 | 400 | 300 |

## Model 9000 Crown Grade

This model has a new Husqvarna Mauser-type action and is now chambered for the .300 Winchester Magnum in addition to the standard calibers that were available. It has a 23.5" barrel with open sights and an adjustable trigger. The stock is select walnut. This model was manufactured in 1971 and 1972.

| Exc. | V.G. | Good | Fair | Poor |
|------|------|------|------|------|
| 475 | 425 | 350 | 300 | 250 |

## Model 8000 Imperial Grade

This model is similar to the Crown Grade except that it features an engraved floorplate, jeweled bolt, and a higher grade walnut stock. It was manufactured in 1971 and 1972.

| Exc. | V.G. | Good | Fair | Poor |
|------|------|------|------|------|
| 600 | 550 | 475 | 400 | 300 |

# HY-HUNTER, INC.
### Burbank, California

## Chicago Cub

This is 6-shot double-action revolver chambered for the .22 short cartridge. It has a 2" barrel and is blued, with checkered plastic grips. It features a folding trigger.

| Exc. | V.G. | Good | Fair | Poor |
|------|------|------|------|------|
| 50 | 40 | 30 | 25 | 20 |

## Detective

This is a 6-shot double-action revolver chambered for .22 l.r. or .22 WMR. It has a 2.5" barrel and is blued, with checkered plastic grips.

| Exc. | V.G. | Good | Fair | Poor |
|------|------|------|------|------|
| 65 | 50 | 40 | 30 | 25 |

## Frontier Six Shooter

This is a 6-shot, Western-style single-action revolver chambered for the .22 l.r. or .22 WMR cartridge.

| Exc. | V.G. | Good | Fair | Poor |
|------|------|------|------|------|
| 75 | 65 | 50 | 40 | 30 |

## Frontier Six Shooter

This model is a 6-shot, single-action, Western-style revolver chambered for the .357 Magnum, .44 Magnum and the .45 Colt cartridge. It is blued and has checkered walnut grips.

| Exc. | V.G. | Good | Fair | Poor |
|------|------|------|------|------|
| 125 | 100 | 85 | 75 | 50 |

## Maxim

This is a blowback-operated semi-automatic chambered for the .25 ACP cartridge. It has a 2" barrel and a 5-shot detachable magazine.

| Exc. | V.G. | Good | Fair | Poor |
|------|------|------|------|------|
| 75 | 65 | 50 | 40 | 30 |

## Militar

This is a blowback-operated, double-action semi-automatic chambered for the .22 l.r.,.32 ACP, and the .380. It has a 4" barrel and a 6-round magazine.

| Exc. | V.G. | Good | Fair | Poor |
|------|------|------|------|------|
| 100 | 80 | 60 | 50 | 40 |

## Stingray

This is a blowback-operated semi-automatic chambered for the .25 ACP cartridge. It has a 2.5" barrel and a 5-shot magazine.

| Exc. | V.G. | Good | Fair | Poor |
|------|------|------|------|------|
| 75 | 65 | 50 | 40 | 30 |

## Panzer

This is a blowback-operated semi-automatic chambered for the .22 l.r. cartridge. It has a 4" barrel and a 7-shot magazine.

| Exc. | V.G. | Good | Fair | Poor |
|------|------|------|------|------|
| 75 | 65 | 50 | 40 | 30 |

## Stuka

This is a .22 l.r. semi-automatic that has a 4" barrel and a 7-shot magazine.

| Exc. | V.G. | Good | Fair | Poor |
|------|------|------|------|------|
| 75 | 65 | 50 | 40 | 30 |

## Automatic Derringer

This model is an Over/Under pocket pistol styled after the Remington Derringer. It is chambered for the .22 l.r. cartridge and is blued, with plastic grips.

| Exc. | V.G. | Good | Fair | Poor |
|------|------|------|------|------|
| 50 | 40 | 30 | 25 | 20 |

## Accurate Ace

This is a single-shot, Flobert-type action pistol chambered for the .22 short cartridge.

| Exc. | V.G. | Good | Fair | Poor |
|------|------|------|------|------|
| 50 | 40 | 30 | 25 | 20 |

## Favorite

This model is a copy of the Stevens break-open single-shot pistol. It is chambered for the .22 l.r. or .22 WMR cartridge and has a 6" blued barrel on a nickel-plated action, with checkered white plastic grips.

| Exc. | V.G. | Good | Fair | Poor |
|------|------|------|------|------|
| 100 | 80 | 70 | 50 | 25 |

### Gold Rush Derringer

This is a single-shot, spur-trigger pocket pistol with a break-open action. The barrel is 2.5" in length, and it is chambered for the .22 l.r. cartridge.

| Exc. | V.G. | Good | Fair | Poor |
|------|------|------|------|------|
| 50 | 40 | 30 | 25 | 20 |

### Target Model

This was a bolt-action target pistol chambered for .22 l.r. or .22 WMR. It has a 10" barrel and adjustable sights. The stock is wood.

| Exc. | V.G. | Good | Fair | Poor |
|------|------|------|------|------|
| 50 | 40 | 30 | 25 | 20 |

# HYDE & SHATTUCK
## Hatfield, Massachusetts

### Queen Derringer

This pocket pistol is rarely encountered on today's market. It is chambered for the .22 rimfire cartridge and has a 2.5" part-octagonal barrel. The barrel pivots to the side for loading, and the brass frame has a distinctive cutaway that exposes nearly the entire hammer. It is a single action and features a spur trigger. The barrel is either blued or nickel-plated and marked "Queen." Occasionally they are found marked "Hyde & Shattuck." It has birdshead grips. There were very few manufactured between 1876 and 1879.

| Exc. | V.G. | Good | Fair | Poor |
|------|------|------|------|------|
| 300 | 250 | 200 | 150 | 100 |

# HYPER
## Jenks, Oklahoma

### Single Shot Rifle

This is a high quality single shot with a falling-block action. It was chambered for any caliber the customer desired and features a combination triggerguard action lever similar to the one found on the Ruger No. 1 rifle. The barrel length and barrel maker could be chosen by the customer, as well as the weight and barrel contour. The trigger is fully adjustable, and the striker that fires the rifle rotates on a bronze bearing and is powered by dual springs. The safety is located on the tang. The stock was made to the customer's specifications and features hand-checkered AA grade American walnut. This rifle was manufactured until 1984.

| Exc. | V.G. | Good | Fair | Poor |
|------|------|------|------|------|
| 2500 | 2000 | 1750 | 1450 | 1250 |

# IAB
## Brescia, Italy
## Industria Armi Bresciane

This company manufactured high-grade competition guns that were imported by Puccinelli & Co. of San Anselmo, California, and by Sporting Arms International of Indianola, Mississippi.

### S-300

This is a single-barrel trap gun chambered for 12 gauge. It was offered with a 30" or 32" barrel, with a wide competition-style vent rib. The trap-style stock is of hand-checkered walnut.

| Exc. | V.G. | Good | Fair | Poor |
|------|------|------|------|------|
| 1500 | 1250 | 1000 | 850 | 650 |

### C-300 Combo

This model is an Over/Under double that is chambered for 12 gauge. It features 30" or 32" barrels, with a wide competition vent rib. It has a single-selective trigger and automatic ejectors. This model has a checkered walnut trap-style stock and was furnished with two extra single barrels in a fitted case.

| Exc. | V.G. | Good | Fair | Poor |
|------|------|------|------|------|
| 2500 | 2250 | 1850 | 1500 | 1250 |

### C-300 Super Combo

This model is the same as the C-300 Combo with more engraving and a select walnut stock.

| Exc. | V.G. | Good | Fair | Poor |
|------|------|------|------|------|
| 3000 | 2750 | 2250 | 1750 | 1500 |

# IGA
## Veranopolis, Brazil
## Importer--Stoeger Industries
## Hackansack, New Jersey

### Single Barrel Shotgun

This is a break-open, exposed-hammer single shot chambered for 12 and 20 gauge and .410. It has a 28" barrel with a full choke and a hardwood stock. The finish is blued.

| NIB | Exc. | V.G. | Good | Fair | Poor |
|-----|------|------|------|------|------|
| 110 | 90 | 75 | 50 | 40 | 30 |

### Coach Gun

This model is a side-by-side double barrel chambered for 12 or 20 gauge with modified-and-improved cylinder chokes. The barrels are 20" in length, and there are double triggers and extractors. The chambers are 3", and the stock is hardwood.

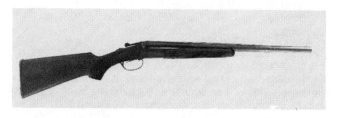

| NIB | Exc. | V.G. | Good | Fair | Poor |
|-----|------|------|------|------|------|
| 285 | 225 | 175 | 150 | 100 | 75 |

### Standard SxS

This model is similar to the Coach Gun except that it is chambered for the 28 gauge and .410, with 28" barrels with various chokes available, as well as the 12 and 20 gauge offering.

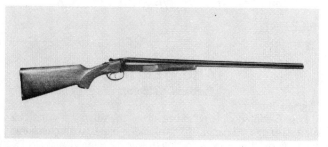

| NIB | Exc. | V.G. | Good | Fair | Poor |
|-----|------|------|------|------|------|
| 300 | 250 | 200 | 175 | 125 | 100 |

## Standard O/U
This model is an Over/Under chambered for 12 or 20 gauge. It features 28" separated vent-rib barrels with a sliding underlug. There are double triggers, and the chambers are 3". The stock is checkered walnut. This model was discontinued in 1986.

| NIB | Exc. | V.G. | Good | Fair | Poor |
|-----|------|------|------|------|------|
| 250 | 200 | 175 | 150 | 100 | 75 |

### Deluxe O/U
This model is a better-grade version of the Standard model. It features a single-selective trigger and automatic ejectors, as well as chrome-lined bores and select checkered walnut for the stock.

| NIB | Exc. | V.G. | Good | Fair | Poor |
|-----|------|------|------|------|------|
| 450 | 400 | 350 | 300 | 200 | 125 |

## I.G.I.
### Zingone de Tressano, Italy
### Italguns International

### Domino
This is a high quality, blowback-operated, semi-automatic target pistol chambered for the .22 l.r. cartridge. It is a conventional-appearing firearm but is actually quite a novel design. The slide is a casting that is locked onto the frame and houses a reciprocating bolt and barrel assembly. It has an adjustable trigger and a 5-shot magazine that is inserted and removed from the top of the pistol. The finish is blued, and the grips are designed to be customized by the individual shooter. There are two basic models--the SP 602 (chambered for the .22 l.r.) and the OP 601 (chambered for .22 Short). They both have 6" barrels and have a respectable record winning international shooting competitions. This pistol was imported by Mandall Shooting Supplies and is no longer available.

| Exc. | V.G. | Good | Fair | Poor |
|------|------|------|------|------|
| 800 | 700 | 600 | 450 | 350 |

## INDIAN ARMS CORP.
### Detroit, Michigan

### Indian Arms .380

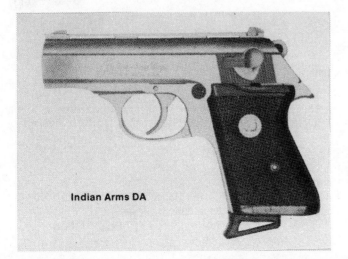

Indian Arms DA

This is a blowback-operated semi-automatic pistol styled after the Walther PPK. It is chambered for the .380 ACP cartridge and has a 3.25" barrel. This pistol is constructed of stainless steel and has a 6-shot magazine. The finish is either white stainless or blue stainless, and the early models have a unique key-locked safety system not found on the later production guns. The grips are checkered walnut. There were approximately 1,000 manufactured between 1975 and 1977.

| Exc. | V.G. | Good | Fair | Poor |
|------|------|------|------|------|
| 475 | 400 | 350 | 275 | 200 |

## INGLIS, JOHN & COMPANY
### Toronto, Canada
This company manufactured under license from Fabrique Nationale the Browning Pattern .35 hi-power pistol. They supply this pistol under contract to China, as well as to the Canadian military. Be aware that the Chinese-contract Inglis pistols are currently being imported into the United States, and these recent imports will be marked with the importer's name and should not be valued the same as the original collectible pistols. If a doubt exists, secure an independent appraisal.

### Chinese Contract Pattern .35
This pistol is very similar to the FN-manufactured hi-power. It is chambered for 9mm Parabellum cartridge. It has a 5" barrel and a 13-shot detachable magazine. The finish is a black phosphate, with checkered black plastic grips. It has sliding tangent sights, and the butt is slotted for a wooden, holster-type shoulder stock. The markings are in Chinese characters, and they were manufactured in 1944 and 1945.
Wooden Shoulder Stock--Add $200.

| Exc. | V.G. | Good | Fair | Poor |
|------|------|------|------|------|
| 1750 | 1500 | 1250 | 800 | 700 |

### Canadian Military
### Mk. 1 No. 1
This pistol is similar to the Chinese Contract, with Canadian markings, a tangent sight, and a slotted butt.
Wooden Shoulder Stock--Add $200.

| Exc. | V.G. | Good | Fair | Poor |
|------|------|------|------|------|
| 1200 | 1000 | 800 | 600 | 450 |

### Mk. 1 No. 2
This pistol is similar to the Mk. 1 No. 1 but has a fixed sight and is not slotted for the shoulder stock.

| Exc. | V.G. | Good | Fair | Poor |
|------|------|------|------|------|
| 600 | 500 | 450 | 350 | 250 |

### Mk. 1 No. 2
This variation has fixed sights but features the slotted butt. It is necessary to be aware of fakes when dealing with this model.

| Exc. | V.G. | Good | Fair | Poor |
|------|------|------|------|------|
| 1200 | 1000 | 800 | 600 | 450 |

## INDUSTRIA ARMI GALESI
### Brescia, Italy
### SEE--Galesi

## INGRAM
### Atlanta, Georgia
### Military Armament Corp.

### MAC 10
This is a blowback-operated, semi-automatic pistol that fires from the open-bolt position. It is chambered for the 9mm Parabellum, as well as the .45 ACP cartridges. The barrel is 5.75" in

length, and the detachable magazine holds 32 rounds. The pistol is constructed of all metal and is parkerized a black color. This is a semi-automatic version of the popular MAC 10 Submachinegun. It was discontinued in 1982. There were accessories available for this gun, consisting of a barrel extension case and extra magazine.

Accessory Kit--Add 20 Percent.

| Exc. | V.G. | Good | Fair | Poor |
|------|------|------|------|------|
| 800 | 700 | 600 | 500 | 400 |

## MAC 10A1

This model is similar to the MAC 10 except that it fires from a closed-bolt position.

Accessory Kit--Add 20 Percent.

| Exc. | V.G. | Good | Fair | Poor |
|------|------|------|------|------|
| 300 | 275 | 225 | 175 | 150 |

## MAC 11

This is a smaller version of the MAC 10, chambered for the .380 ACP cartridge.

Accessory Kit--Add 20 Percent.

| Exc. | V.G. | Good | Fair | Poor |
|------|------|------|------|------|
| 700 | 600 | 500 | 400 | 300 |

# INTERARMS
### Alexandria, Virginia

This company is the premier importer of firearms in the world today. They have imported many different firearms which are listed under their own headings in this text. They consist of Astra, Howa Machine, Star, Walther, and Rossi. The firearms listed under this section are basically known as Interarms products and are not listed elsewhere.

## Rifles
### Mark X Viscount

This is a Mauser bolt-action rifle chambered for most popular calibers up to .300 Winchester Magnum. It has a 24" barrel with open sights and an adjustable trigger. The magazine holds 5 shots--3 shots on the Magnum model--and the finish is blued, with a checkered walnut stock. The Mark X series is manufactured in Yugoslavia.

| NIB | Exc. | V.G. | Good | Fair | Poor |
|-----|------|------|------|------|------|
| 475 | 425 | 350 | 275 | 200 | 150 |

### Mark X Lightweight

This is a 20"-barrelled version of the Mark X, with a lightweight synthetic stock. It is chambered for .270, .7mm Remington Magnum, and .30-06. This model was introduced in 1988.

| NIB | Exc. | V.G. | Good | Fair | Poor |
|-----|------|------|------|------|------|
| 485 | 440 | 375 | 300 | 200 | 150 |

### Mini Mark X

This is a miniaturized version of the Mauser action that is chambered for the .223 caliber only. It has a 20" barrel, open sights, a 5-shot magazine, and an adjustable trigger. The stock is made of checkered hardwood. This model was introduced in 1987.

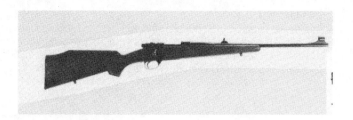

| NIB | Exc. | V.G. | Good | Fair | Poor |
|-----|------|------|------|------|------|
| 385 | 325 | 300 | 275 | 175 | 125 |

### Mark X American Field

This model is similar to the standard Mark X but is a deluxe version with a select walnut stock, ebony forend tip and pistol grip cap, sling swivels, and a recoil pad. This model was introduced in 1984.

| NIB | Exc. | V.G. | Good | Fair | Poor |
|-----|------|------|------|------|------|
| 575 | 525 | 450 | 400 | 300 | 200 |

### Whitworth Express Rifle

This is an English-manufactured Mauser bolt-action rifle chambered for the .375 H&H and the .458 Win. Mag. cartridges. The barrel is 24" in length, with a three-leaf express sight. The magazine holds 3 rounds, and the stock is a classic-style checkered walnut. This model was introduced in 1974.

| NIB | Exc. | V.G. | Good | Fair | Poor |
|-----|------|------|------|------|------|
| 700 | 650 | 600 | 550 | 425 | 300 |

### Whitworth Mannlicher Carbine

This English-made carbine is chambered for the .243, .270, .7x57mm, .308, and the .30-06 cartridges. It has a 20" barrel with open sights and a Mannlicher-styled full-length stock with sling swivels. This model was manufactured between 1984 and 1987.

| Exc. | V.G. | Good | Fair | Poor |
|------|------|------|------|------|
| 550 | 500 | 450 | 350 | 200 |

### Cavalier

This model is a former version of the Viscount made in England and no longer imported. It was offered in the same calibers but has a modernistic-styled stock with a rollover cheekpiece and a recoil pad. It is no longer imported.

| Exc. | V.G. | Good | Fair | Poor |
|------|------|------|------|------|
| 375 | 325 | 275 | 325 | 150 |

### Mannlicher Carbine

This model is similar to the Cavalier, with a 20" barrel and a full-length Mannlicher-styled stock. It has been discontinued.

| Exc. | V.G. | Good | Fair | Poor |
|------|------|------|------|------|
| 375 | 325 | 275 | 225 | 150 |

### Continental Carbine

This model is similar to the Mannlicher Carbine, with double-set triggers. It is no longer imported.

| Exc. | V.G. | Good | Fair | Poor |
|------|------|------|------|------|
| 400 | 350 | 300 | 250 | 175 |

## Alaskan Model
This model is similar to the Mark X, chambered for the .375 H&H and the .458 Win. Mag. It has a 24" barrel with an extra recoil lug in the stock and a recoil pad. This model was not imported after 1984.

| Exc. | V.G. | Good | Fair | Poor |
|---|---|---|---|---|
| 450 | 400 | 350 | 300 | 200 |

## 22-ATD
This is a semi-automatic copy of the Browning takedown rifle, with a 19.4" barrel and open sights. It has an 11-round magazine and a blued finish with a checkered hardwood stock. This rifle is manufactured in the Peoples Republic of China by Norinco. It was introduced in 1987.

| NIB | Exc. | V.G. | Good | Fair | Poor |
|---|---|---|---|---|---|
| 175 | 150 | 125 | 100 | 75 | 50 |

## Helwan Brigadier
This is an Egyptian copy of a Beretta design. It is a semi-automatic single action chambered for the 9mm Parabellum cartridge. It has a 4.5" barrel and fixed sights. The construction is all steel; and it is blued, with black plastic grips and an 8-shot magazine. It was introduced in 1988.

| NIB | Exc. | V.G. | Good | Fair | Poor |
|---|---|---|---|---|---|
| 260 | 225 | 200 | 175 | 125 | 100 |

## FEG R-9
This line of pistols was imported from Hungary. The R-9 is a copy of the Browning High-Power except that it is double-action. It is chambered for the 9mm Parabellum and features all-steel construction with fixed sights and a 13-shot magazine. The finish is blued, with checkered wood grips. This model was manufactured in 1986 and 1987 only.

| Exc. | V.G. | Good | Fair | Poor |
|---|---|---|---|---|
| 275 | 225 | 185 | 145 | 100 |

## FEG PPH
This model was copied from the Walther PP and is chambered for the .380 ACP cartridge. It has a 3.5" barrel and a 6-shot magazine. The construction is all steel, and it is a double action. The finish is blued, with checkered thumbrest plastic grips.

| Exc. | V.G. | Good | Fair | Poor |
|---|---|---|---|---|
| 200 | 175 | 150 | 125 | 100 |

## Virginian Dragoon
This model is a Western-style single action imported from Switzerland and then manufactured in the U.S.A. from 1976 until 1984. This model is chambered for the .44 Magnum cartridge and has a 6", 7.5", 8.75", or a 12" buntline-styled barrel. The cylinder holds 6 rounds, and the sights are adjustable. The finish is blued, with walnut grips. This model was discontinued in 1984.

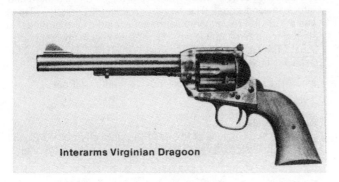

**Interarms Virginian Dragoon**

| Exc. | V.G. | Good | Fair | Poor |
|---|---|---|---|---|
| 250 | 200 | 175 | 150 | 100 |

## Stainless Dragoon
This is a stainless-steel version of the .44-Magnum Dragoon.

| Exc. | V.G. | Good | Fair | Poor |
|---|---|---|---|---|
| 275 | 225 | 200 | 175 | 125 |

## Virginian .22 Convertible
This model is a .22-rimfire, single-action, Western-styled revolver. It has a 5.5" barrel, adjustable sights, and a blue finish with walnut grips.

| Exc. | V.G. | Good | Fair | Poor |
|---|---|---|---|---|
| 175 | 150 | 125 | 100 | 75 |

## Virginian Stainless .22 Convertible
This revolver is the stainless-steel version of the standard rimfire convertible.

| Exc. | V.G. | Good | Fair | Poor |
|---|---|---|---|---|
| 200 | 175 | 150 | 100 | 80 |

## Mauser Parabellum Karabiner
This is an extremely high-quality modern version of the Luger Carbine. It is chambered for the 9mm Parabellum cartridge and has an 11.75" barrel with a finely checkered walnut forend and detachable shoulder stock. The carbine is furnished in a fitted leather case and is limited to 100 imported into the U.S.A. This firearm must be registered as a short-barrelled rifle. Check with the dealer for procedure to be followed for legal ownership.

| NIB | Exc. | V.G. | Good | Fair | Poor |
|---|---|---|---|---|---|
| 6500 | 5750 | 5000 | 4000 | 3000 | 2250 |

## Mauser Parabellum Cartridge Counter
This is a high-quality modern version of the famed and rare cartridge-counter Luger. It is chambered for the 9mm Parabellum cartridge and has a specially designed grip that allows one to see at a glance how many cartridges remain in the weapon. This deluxe version was limited to 100 imported into the U.S.A. and is furnished in a fitted leather case.

| NIB | Exc. | V.G. | Good | Fair | Poor |
|---|---|---|---|---|---|
| 3600 | 3000 | 2500 | 2000 | 1500 | |

# INTERDYNAMICS OF AMERICA
### Miami, Florida
## KG-9
This is a blowback-operated semi-automatic chambered for the 9mm Parabellum. It is an assault-type pistol that fires from a closed bolt. The barrel is 3" in length, and the detachable magazine holds 36 rounds. It was manufactured between 1981 and 1983.

| Exc. | V.G. | Good | Fair | Poor |
|---|---|---|---|---|
| 700 | 625 | 575 | 500 | 400 |

## KG-99
This version is similar to the KG-9 except that it fires from the closed bolt and has a shrouded barrel. This model was manufactured between 1981 and 1984.

| Exc. | V.G. | Good | Fair | Poor |
|---|---|---|---|---|
| 275 | 225 | 175 | 125 | 100 |

## KG-99 Stainless
This is a stainless-steel version that was manufactured in 1984 only.

| Exc. | V.G. | Good | Fair | Poor |
|---|---|---|---|---|
| 325 | 275 | 225 | 150 | 125 |

## KG-99M
This is a miniaturized version of the KG-99. It was manufactured in 1984.

| Exc. | V.G. | Good | Fair | Poor |
|---|---|---|---|---|
| 210 | 185 | 165 | 145 | 100 |

# INTRATEC USA, INC.
### Miami, Florida

## TEC-9
This is a blowback-operated, semi-automatic assault pistol chambered for the 9mm Parabellum. It features a 5" barrel with a vented shroud and has a 36-round detachable magazine. The finish is matte black. This pistol was introduced in 1985.

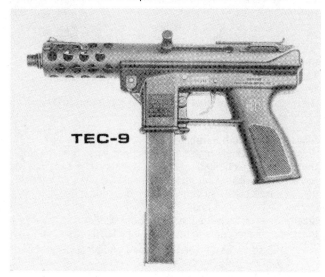

| NIB | Exc. | V.G. | Good | Fair | Poor |
|-----|------|------|------|------|------|
| 270 | 225 | 200 | 175 | 125 | 100 |

## TEC-9C
This is a 16"-barrelled carbine version that features a folding stock. It was manufactured in 1987 only.

| Exc. | V.G. | Good | Fair | Poor |
|------|------|------|------|------|
| 275 | 225 | 200 | 150 | 100 |

## TEC-9M
This version is miniaturized, with a 3" barrel and a 20-shot magazine. There is a stainless-steel version available, and it would be worth approximately 40 percent additional.

| NIB | Exc. | V.G. | Good | Fair | Poor |
|-----|------|------|------|------|------|
| 250 | 200 | 175 | 150 | 100 | 75 |

## TEC-22 "Scorpion"
This version is chambered for the .22 l.r. cartridge. It features a 4" barrel and is also matte black finished, with adjustable sights and a 30-shot detachable magazine.

| NIB | Exc. | V.G. | Good | Fair | Poor |
|-----|------|------|------|------|------|
| 175 | 150 | 125 | 100 | 75 | 50 |

## TEC-38
This modernized Over/Under derringer is chambered for the .38 Special cartridge. It is double-actioned, and the barrels are 3" in length. The finish is blued. It was manufactured between 1986 and 1988.

| Exc. | V.G. | Good | Fair | Poor |
|------|------|------|------|------|
| 125 | 100 | 80 | 65 | 45 |

# IRVING, W.
### New York, New York

## Single Shot Derringer
This pistol is chambered for the .22 rimfire cartridge and has a 2.75" part-octagonal barrel that pivots to the side for loading. The frame is made of brass with a spur trigger and a square butt with rosewood grips. The barrel is marked "W.Irving." There was a .32 rimfire version also manufactured, but this model is rarely encountered and is worth approximately 40 percent additional. The barrel of the .32-caliber version is 3" in length. This pistol was manufactured in the 1860's.

| Exc. | V.G. | Good | Fair | Poor |
|------|------|------|------|------|
| 500 | 400 | 300 | 200 | 125 |

## Pocket Revolver
There are two versions of this revolver, both chambered for .31 caliber percussion and each having a 6-shot unfluted cylinder.

## 1st Model
This revolver has a 3" octagonal barrel and a brass frame. The cylinder stops are in the front of the cylinder, and it has a spur

trigger. The barrel is marked "W.Irving." There were only 50 of these produced between 1858 and 1862.

| Exc. | V.G. | Good | Fair | Poor |
|---|---|---|---|---|
| 700 | 600 | 500 | 350 | 250 |

## 2nd Model
The 2nd Model is a more conventional-appearing revolver with a 4.5" round barrel and a triggerguard similar to the Colt-type revolvers of the day. The cylinder stops are in the rear of the cylinder, and there is an integral hinged ramrod. The barrel is marked "Address W.Irving. 20 Cliff St. N-Y." There were approximately 600 manufactured with a brass frame and 1500 with a frame of iron. The brass-frame version will bring a premium of about 35 percent.

| Exc. | V.G. | Good | Fair | Poor |
|---|---|---|---|---|
| 550 | 500 | 400 | 300 | 200 |

## IRWINDALE ARMS, INC.
### Irwindale, California
### SEE--AMT
These firearms were previously manufactured by AMT and are found listed under that heading.

## ISRAELI MILITARY INDUSTRIES
### Israel
I.M.I. is the State of Israel's primary manufacturer of small arms. They produce the weapons used by the Israeli armed forces as well as many fine weapons that are exported for military and commercial sales around the world. They manufacture the Galil assault rifle and the Uzi submachinegun, as well as the semi-automatic carbine and pistol that are offered for civilian sales by Action Arms Ltd. of Philadelphia, Pennsylvania. They are also the maker of the unique Desert Eagle semi-automatic pistol, sold by Magnum Research of Minneapolis, Minnesota. The quality firearms this company manufactures are found listed in their own respective sections of this book.

## ITHACA GUN CO.
### Ithaca, New York
This company was founded by William H. Baker and several other partners. The first Ithaca shotgun was produced in 1883. The company was originally known as W. H. Baker & Co. Gunworks. In October of 1889 when Baker died, the name was changed to Ithaca Gun Co. The first models were robust shotguns with damascus barrels and a boxlock action that had the hammers mounted at the extreme rear of the frame. This differed from the usual sidelock external-hammer guns. The first Ithaca shotguns had a dollshead extension on the barrel rib, and the locking mechanism was similar to the early British shotguns. They earned a well deserved reputation for manufacturing excellent and reliable shotguns that fit the needs of the American sportsman.

## Crass Model
This is a damascus-barrelled, side-by-side double with external hammers. It is chambered for 10 or 12 gauge and features double triggers, extractors, and a checkered walnut stock. There were approximately 77,000 manufactured between 1893 and 1903.

| Exc. | V.G. | Good | Fair | Poor |
|---|---|---|---|---|
| 750 | 675 | 600 | 500 | 350 |

## Lewis Model
This is an improved version of the Crass Model that was manufactured until 1906.

| Exc. | V.G. | Good | Fair | Poor |
|---|---|---|---|---|
| 750 | 675 | 600 | 500 | 350 |

## Marien Model
This is still another improved version of the Crass Model that was manufactured between 1906 and 1908.

| Exc. | V.G. | Good | Fair | Poor |
|---|---|---|---|---|
| 750 | 675 | 600 | 500 | 350 |

## Flues Model
This side-by-side, double-barrel shotgun is still another improvement of the original Crass Model. It was introduced in 1908 and was manufactured until 1926. There were approximately 100,000 produced.

| Exc. | V.G. | Good | Fair | Poor |
|---|---|---|---|---|
| 850 | 750 | 675 | 550 | 400 |

## Hammerless Double
In 1925 the company changed its production to a hammerless, fluid-steel side by side chambered for all gauges with 26", 28", 30", or 32" barrels with various choke combinations. This model features a boxlock action and is standard with double triggers and extractors. The gun was offered in a number of configurations that differ predominantly in the amount of ornamentation and general quality of the materials and workmanship utilized in their construction. The shotguns produced in this series were manufactured between 1925 and 1948. There were a number of options available that have a drastic effect on the value of these guns. They are quite collectible; and although we are furnishing general values, we strongly recommend securing a qualified appraisal, especially on the higher-grade models, if an acquisition is contemplated. The options available and their approximate values to be added to the respective models are as follows:

Non-selective Single Trigger--Add $150
Single-selective Trigger--Add $200
Ventilated Rib--Add $200
Vent Rib, High-grade Models-- Add $350
Automatic Ejectors--Add 35 Percent
Beavertail Forearm--Add $175.

Models that were manufactured prior to 1925 are considerably less valuable since they are not considered safe to fire modern ammunition.

The values we supply are for 12-and 16-gauge guns.

20-gauge guns are worth approximately 20 percent additional.

10-gauge, 20-gauge, and .410 guns are worth approximately 100 percent additional.

### Field Grade
| Exc. | V.G. | Good | Fair | Poor |
|---|---|---|---|---|
| 1000 | 850 | 650 | 450 | 250 |

### Grade No. 2
| Exc. | V.G. | Good | Fair | Poor |
|---|---|---|---|---|
| 1500 | 1250 | 950 | 650 | 350 |

### Grade No. 3
| Exc. | V.G. | Good | Fair | Poor |
|---|---|---|---|---|
| 1750 | 1500 | 1000 | 650 | 350 |

28-gauge and .410 models are extremely rare on the following high-grade models, and the formula formerly used cannot be applied. Please seek independent appraisals on small-bore, high-grade models.

### Grade No. 4E--Auto Ejectors
| Exc. | V.G. | Good | Fair | Poor |
|---|---|---|---|---|
| 3250 | 2750 | 2000 | 1250 | 550 |

### Grade No. 5E--Auto Ejectors

| Exc. | V.G. | Good | Fair | Poor |
|------|------|------|------|------|
| 4000 | 3250 | 2500 | 1500 | 750 |

### Grade No. 6E--Auto Ejectors

| Exc. | V.G. | Good | Fair | Poor |
|------|------|------|------|------|
| 4750 | 4000 | 3000 | 1750 | 900 |

### Grade No. 7E--Auto Ejectors

| Exc. | V.G. | Good | Fair | Poor |
|------|------|------|------|------|
| 9500 | 8000 | 5500 | 3500 | 1850 |

### $1,000 Grade

This is a side-by-side double barrel chambered for 12 gauge. 16-gauge and 20-gauge models have been noted but are so rare that they must be independently appraised. This gun has all the features of the 7E Grade with a higher degree of ornamentation and higher quality materials and workmanship. It was manufactured before WWII.

| Exc. | V.G. | Good | Fair | Poor |
|------|------|------|------|------|
| 12500 | 10000 | 7000 | 4000 | 2500 |

### $2,000 Grade

This is another extremely high-grade double that should be independently appraised. It features a great degree of ornamentation and the highest quality materials and workmanship.

| Exc. | V.G. | Good | Fair | Poor |
|------|------|------|------|------|
| 10000 | 7500 | 5000 | 3250 | 1800 |

### Sousa Grade

This is Ithaca's absolute top-of-the-line model. It supposedly was developed with the help of John Phillip Sousa, the famous composer. There were only 11 examples manufactured, and it is too rare to even attempt to evaluate in a publication of this nature. Should one ever run across this model, a qualified, independent appraisal would be essential.

### Single Barrel Trap Guns

These are break-open, single-barrel, single-shot, competition-type guns chambered for 12 gauge. They were offered with 30", 32", or 34", ventilated-rib, full-choke barrels. They feature a boxlock action with an automatic ejector. The various grades listed differ in the amount of engraving and the general quality of the workmanship and materials utilized in their construction. There were many options available that have a drastic effect on the value, and we strongly recommend a qualified appraisal if a transaction is contemplated. Models manufactured before 1921 having serial numbers under 400,000 are called Flues Models and are worth considerably less than the values shown, as they are not considered safe to fire with modern ammunition.

### Victory Grade

| Exc. | V.G. | Good | Fair | Poor |
|------|------|------|------|------|
| 1000 | 800 | 675 | 500 | 400 |

### Knick Model

| Exc. | V.G. | Good | Fair | Poor |
|------|------|------|------|------|
| 1400 | 1100 | 850 | 650 | 550 |

### No. 4E

| Exc. | V.G. | Good | Fair | Poor |
|------|------|------|------|------|
| 1500 | 1200 | 950 | 750 | 650 |

### No. 7E

| Exc. | V.G. | Good | Fair | Poor |
|------|------|------|------|------|
| 4000 | 3050 | 2500 | 2000 | 1600 |

### $5,000 Grade

| Exc. | V.G. | Good | Fair | Poor |
|------|------|------|------|------|
| 9500 | 8250 | 6750 | 5500 | 4750 |

### Sousa Grade

This model is too rare to evaluate. Independent appraisal should be secured.

### Century Grade Trap

This is a single-barrel trap gun chambered for 12 gauge with a 32" or 34", vent-rib, full-choke barrel. It has an engraved boxlock action and an automatic ejector. The finish is blued, with a checkered walnut stock. It was manufactured in the 1970's by SKB.

| Exc. | V.G. | Good | Fair | Poor |
|------|------|------|------|------|
| 600 | 500 | 450 | 350 | 300 |

### Century II

This version has a Monte Carlo-type trap stock. It was also manufactured by SKB.

| Exc. | V.G. | Good | Fair | Poor |
|------|------|------|------|------|
| 650 | 550 | 500 | 400 | 350 |

### 5E Grade

This is a single-barrel trap gun chambered for 12 gauge with a 32" or 34" vent-rib barrel. It was manufactured on a custom-order basis and features a heavily engraved boxlock action. This is a very high quality gun that was manufactured between 1925 and 1986. Production was resumed in 1988.

| NIB | Exc. | V.G. | Good | Fair | Poor |
|-----|------|------|------|------|------|
| 7500 | 3500 | 2500 | 2000 | 1750 | 1450 |

### Dollar Grade

This is the top-of-the-line, single-barrel trap gun. It is hand-built on an individual basis. Production was continued in 1988.

| NIB | Exc. | V.G. | Good | Fair | Poor |
|-----|------|------|------|------|------|
| 10000 | 6000 | 5000 | 4250 | 3250 | 2500 |

### Model 66

This is an inexpensive, single-shot, lever-action shotgun. It is chambered for 20 gauge or .410. It has a 24" barrel with a full choke. The finish is blued, with a hardwood stock. It was manufactured between 1963 and 1978. The .410 model would be worth approximately 30 percent additional.

Ithaca Model 66

| Exc. | V.G. | Good | Fair | Poor |
|------|------|------|------|------|
| 125 | 100 | 75 | 50 | 25 |

### Model 66 RS

This is a 20-gauge deer gun that has a 22" barrel and rifle sights.

| Exc. | V.G. | Good | Fair | Poor |
|------|------|------|------|------|
| 150 | 125 | 100 | 75 | 50 |

### Model 37 Featherlight

This slide-action shotgun is chambered for 12, 16, or 20 gauge. It features a 26", 28", or 30" barrel with various chokes. It has a 4-shot magazine and ejects the empties out the bottom of the receiver, making it an ambidextrous shotgun. It has an internal hammer and a takedown feature. The finish is blued, with a walnut stock. It was manufactured between 1937 and 1986. It has recently been re-introduced by the new Ithaca Acquisition Corp. as the Model 87. There are many versions of the Model 37 gun that differ basically as to options, ornamentation, and quality of materials. The values are as follows:

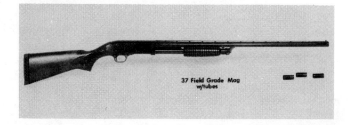

37 Field Grade Mag w/tubes

| Exc. | V.G. | Good | Fair | Poor |
|------|------|------|------|------|
| 275 | 250 | 200 | 150 | 100 |

### Model 37V--Vent Rib

| Exc. | V.G. | Good | Fair | Poor |
|------|------|------|------|------|
| 325 | 300 | 250 | 200 | 150 |

### Model 37D--Deluxe

| Exc. | V.G. | Good | Fair | Poor |
|------|------|------|------|------|
| 350 | 325 | 275 | 225 | 175 |

### Model 37DV--Deluxe, Vent Rib

| Exc. | V.G. | Good | Fair | Poor |
|------|------|------|------|------|
| 400 | 350 | 300 | 250 | 200 |

### Model 37 Magnum--3" Chamber

| Exc. | V.G. | Good | Fair | Poor |
|------|------|------|------|------|
| 325 | 300 | 250 | 200 | 150 |

### Model 37 Ultralite--English Stock

| Exc. | V.G. | Good | Fair | Poor |
|------|------|------|------|------|
| 350 | 325 | 275 | 225 | 175 |

### Model 37 Bicentennial

This is an engraved, high-grade version chambered for 12 gauge and furnished in a case along with a pewter belt buckle. There were 1,776 manufactured in 1976. This is a commemorative model and must be NIB to achieve collector interest.

| NIB | Exc. | V.G. | Good | Fair | Poor |
|-----|------|------|------|------|------|
| 400 | 350 | 300 | 250 | 200 | 125 |

### Model 37 Ducks Unlimited Commemorative

| NIB | Exc. | V.G. | Good | Fair | Poor |
|-----|------|------|------|------|------|
| 375 | 300 | 250 | 200 | 175 | 100 |

### Model 37 2500 Series Centennial

This is a high-grade version chambered for 12 gauge, with an etched receiver that was antique-finished with silver-plated parts. It commemorated Ithaca's 100th anniversary and has a deluxe walnut stock. It was manufactured between 1980 and 1984. As with all commemoratives, it must be NIB with all supplied material to command collector interest.

| NIB | Exc. | V.G. | Good | Fair | Poor |
|-----|------|------|------|------|------|
| 800 | 650 | 550 | 450 | 300 | 175 |

### Model 37 $1,000 Grade

This is a pre-WWII shotgun that features high-grade engraving and checkering. It is gold-inlaid and has a high-grade walnut stock. It is chambered for all gauges. It was manufactured between 1937 and 1940.

| Exc. | V.G. | Good | Fair | Poor |
|------|------|------|------|------|
| 6000 | 5000 | 4000 | 3000 | 2250 |

### Model 37 $5,000 Grade

This gun is similar to the $1,000 Grade but was made between 1947 and 1967. This was the post-WWII version.

| Exc. | V.G. | Good | Fair | Poor |
|------|------|------|------|------|
| 5500 | 4500 | 3500 | 2500 | 2000 |

### Model 87 Magnum

This slide-action shotgun is the latest designation for the re-introduced Model 37. It is chambered for 12 and 20 gauge with 3" chambers. It has a 25" barrel with screw-in chokes and a ventilated rib. The finish is blued, with a checkered walnut stock.

| NIB | Exc. | V.G. | Good | Fair | Poor |
|-----|------|------|------|------|------|
| 450 | 400 | 350 | 300 | 225 | 150 |

The new Model 87 Series that has been re-introduced by the Ithaca Acquisition Co. in 1989 is available in a number of different configurations. These versions differ in the options and the ornamentation utilized in their construction. They are as follows:

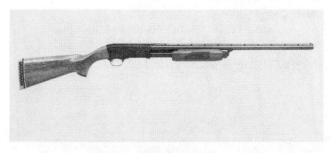

### Model 87 Field Grade--Economy Model

| NIB | Exc. | V.G. | Good | Fair | Poor |
|-----|------|------|------|------|------|
| 475 | 375 | 325 | 275 | 200 | 125 |

### Model 87 Camo

| NIB | Exc. | V.G. | Good | Fair | Poor |
|-----|------|------|------|------|------|
| 525 | 475 | 425 | 375 | 300 | 200 |

### Model 87 Turkey Gun

| NIB | Exc. | V.G. | Good | Fair | Poor |
|-----|------|------|------|------|------|
| 400 | 350 | 300 | 250 | 175 | 100 |

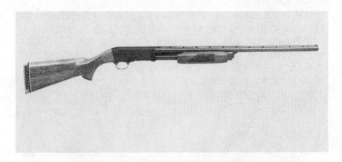

### Model 87 Deluxe

| NIB | Exc. | V.G. | Good | Fair | Poor |
|-----|------|------|------|------|------|
| 500 | 450 | 400 | 350 | 275 | 175 |

### Model 87 Ultralite

| NIB | Exc. | V.G. | Good | Fair | Poor |
|-----|------|------|------|------|------|
| 485 | 425 | 350 | 300 | 225 | 150 |

### Model 87 Ultralite Deluxe

| NIB | Exc. | V.G. | Good | Fair | Poor |
|-----|------|------|------|------|------|
| 525 | 475 | 425 | 375 | 300 | 200 |

### Model 87 Supreme Grade

| NIB | Exc. | V.G. | Good | Fair | Poor |
|-----|------|------|------|------|------|
| 825 | 750 | 675 | 500 | 400 | 300 |

### Model 87 Deerslayer

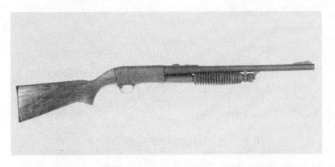

| NIB | Exc. | V.G. | Good | Fair | Poor |
|-----|------|------|------|------|------|
| 390 | 325 | 250 | 200 | 150 | 100 |

### Model 87 Deluxe Deerslayer

| NIB | Exc. | V.G. | Good | Fair | Poor |
|-----|------|------|------|------|------|
| 425 | 350 | 300 | 250 | 200 | 150 |

## Monte Carlo Deerslayer II

| NIB | Exc. | V.G. | Good | Fair | Poor |
|-----|------|------|------|------|------|
| 525 | 450 | 400 | 350 | 250 | 175 |

## Model 87 Military & Police

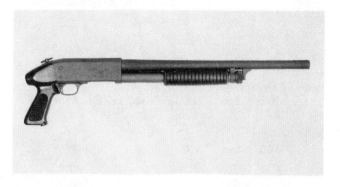

| NIB | Exc. | V.G. | Good | Fair | Poor |
|-----|------|------|------|------|------|
| 400 | 350 | 300 | 275 | 200 | 100 |

## Model 51 Series

This is a gas-operated semi-automatic shotgun chambered for 12 or 20 gauge. It was offered with 26", 28", or 30" barrels with various chokes and ventilated ribs. The finish is blued, with a checkered walnut stock. It was manufactured between 1970 and 1985. The various models differ because of options, the degree of ornamentation, and the quality of materials utilized in their constructions. Values are as follows:

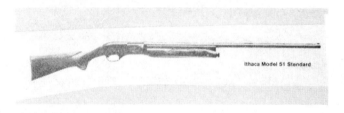

Ithaca Model 51 Standard

### Model 51A Standard--Plain Barrel
Vent Rib--Add $100.

| Exc. | V.G. | Good | Fair | Poor |
|------|------|------|------|------|
| 275 | 225 | 200 | 150 | 100 |

### Model 51A Magnum--3" Chamber
Vent Rib--Add $100.

| Exc. | V.G. | Good | Fair | Poor |
|------|------|------|------|------|
| 300 | 250 | 225 | 175 | 125 |

### Model 51A Waterfowler--Matte Finished

| Exc. | V.G. | Good | Fair | Poor |
|------|------|------|------|------|
| 425 | 375 | 325 | 250 | 175 |

### Model 51A Deerslayer

| Exc. | V.G. | Good | Fair | Poor |
|------|------|------|------|------|
| 325 | 275 | 225 | 150 | 100 |

### Model 51A Turkey Gun

| Exc. | V.G. | Good | Fair | Poor |
|------|------|------|------|------|
| 325 | 275 | 225 | 150 | 100 |

### Model 51A Supreme Trap

| Exc. | V.G. | Good | Fair | Poor |
|------|------|------|------|------|
| 425 | 375 | 325 | 250 | 175 |

### Model 51A Supreme Skeet

| Exc. | V.G. | Good | Fair | Poor |
|------|------|------|------|------|
| 450 | 400 | 350 | 275 | 200 |

### Model 51 Ducks Unlimited Commemorative

| NIB | Exc. | V.G. | Good | Fair | Poor |
|-----|------|------|------|------|------|
| 475 | 400 | 375 | 325 | 275 | 200 |

## Model 51 Presentation--Engraved Receiver

| NIB | Exc. | V.G. | Good | Fair | Poor |
|-----|------|------|------|------|------|
| 1500 | 1250 | 1000 | 750 | 500 | 300 |

## Mag-10 Series

This is a gas-operated semi-automatic shotgun chambered for the 10-gauge, 3.5" Magnum shell. It was offered in various barrel lengths and chokes with a plain or vent-rib barrel. Screw-in chokes were available in 1986 and would add $60 to the listed values. It was available with either a high-polish or matte-blued finish with a gloss-or matte-finish stock made of select walnut. The models vary in their value due to options or quality of materials and workmanship. This model was manufactured between 1975 and 1986.

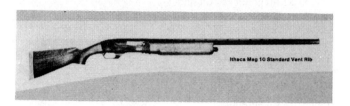

Ithaca Mag 10 Standard Vent Rib

### Standard Grade

| Exc. | V.G. | Good | Fair | Poor |
|------|------|------|------|------|
| 750 | 700 | 650 | 500 | 400 |

### Standard Vent-Rib Grade

| Exc. | V.G. | Good | Fair | Poor |
|------|------|------|------|------|
| 850 | 775 | 700 | 550 | 450 |

### Deluxe Vent-Rib Grade

| Exc. | V.G. | Good | Fair | Poor |
|------|------|------|------|------|
| 1000 | 850 | 775 | 600 | 500 |

### Supreme Grade

| Exc. | V.G. | Good | Fair | Poor |
|------|------|------|------|------|
| 1200 | 1050 | 850 | 700 | 600 |

### Roadblocker--Military and Police Model

| Exc. | V.G. | Good | Fair | Poor |
|------|------|------|------|------|
| 650 | 575 | 500 | 400 | 300 |

### Presentation Grade--Engraved, Gold-Inlaid, 200 Made

| NIB | Exc. | V.G. | Good | Fair | Poor |
|-----|------|------|------|------|------|
| 1875 | 1500 | 1100 | 900 | 750 | 600 |

### National Wild Turkey Federation--1985 Manufacture

| NIB | Exc. | V.G. | Good | Fair | Poor |
|-----|------|------|------|------|------|
| 850 | 700 | 600 | 550 | 450 | 350 |

For a number of years, Ithaca imported the SKB Over/Under and side-by-side shotguns from Japan, as well as the Perazzi competition guns from Italy. These firearms are listed in their own respective sections of this text.

## Model X5-C

This is a blowback-operated semi-automatic rifle chambered for the .22 l.r. cartridge. It has a 7-round, detachable magazine and is blued, with a walnut stock. It was manufactured between 1958 and 1964.

| Exc. | V.G. | Good | Fair | Poor |
|------|------|------|------|------|
| 100 | 80 | 70 | 60 | 45 |

## Model X-15

This is similar to the X5-C but was manufactured between 1964 and 1967.

| Exc. | V.G. | Good | Fair | Poor |
|------|------|------|------|------|
| 100 | 80 | 70 | 60 | 45 |

## Model 49 Saddlegun

This is a single-shot, lever-action rifle chambered for the .22 l.r. cartridge. It has an 18.5" barrel with fixed sights. It is blued with an anodized alloy receiver and has a hardwood stock. It was manufactured between 1961 and 1978.

| Exc. | V.G. | Good | Fair | Poor |
|------|------|------|------|------|
| 100  | 80   | 70   | 60   | 45   |

## Model 72 Saddlegun

This is a lever-action repeater chambered for the .22 or .22 rimfire Magnum cartridges. It has an 18.5" barrel with open sights. It is blued, with a walnut stock. This model was manufactured by Erma in Germany between 1973 and 1978.

| Exc. | V.G. | Good | Fair | Poor |
|------|------|------|------|------|
| 200  | 150  | 125  | 100  | 75   |

## LSA-55 or 65 Series

These are bolt-action sporting rifles manufactured in Finland by the firm of Tikka. They were based on a Mauser-type action and chambered for various popular cartridges. The standard barrel length is 22", furnished with a folding-leaf sight. It has a 3-shot magazine. The finish is blued, with a checkered Monte Carlo stock. This Series was imported between 1969 and 1977, and the variations differ in the options offered, calibers chambered, and quality of materials utilized.

### LSA-55 Standard

| Exc. | V.G. | Good | Fair | Poor |
|------|------|------|------|------|
| 400  | 350  | 300  | 250  | 175  |

### LSA-55 Deluxe

| Exc. | V.G. | Good | Fair | Poor |
|------|------|------|------|------|
| 425  | 375  | 325  | 275  | 200  |

### LSA-55 Varmint--Heavy Barrel

| Exc. | V.G. | Good | Fair | Poor |
|------|------|------|------|------|
| 450  | 400  | 350  | 300  | 225  |

### LSA-65--Long Action

| Exc. | V.G. | Good | Fair | Poor |
|------|------|------|------|------|
| 400  | 350  | 300  | 250  | 175  |

### LSA-65 Deluxe

| Exc. | V.G. | Good | Fair | Poor |
|------|------|------|------|------|
| 425  | 375  | 325  | 275  | 200  |

## LSA-55 Turkey Gun

This is an Over/Under combination gun chambered for 12 gauge and .222 Remington. It has a 24.5" ribbed barrel with a folding sight. It has double triggers and an exposed hammer. The finish is blued; and it has a checkered, walnut, Monte Carlo-type stock. It was manufactured in Finland by Tikka between 1970 and 1981.

| Exc. | V.G. | Good | Fair | Poor |
|------|------|------|------|------|
| 600  | 525  | 450  | 350  | 275  |

## X-Caliber

This is a break-open single-shot pistol chambered for the .22 l.r. through .44 Magnum cartridges. It is offered with a 10" or 15" barrel. It features a dual firing-pin system for rimfire and centerfire cartridges. The barrels are interchangeable, and the finish is either blued on the Model 20 Target Model or matte Teflon-coated on the Model 30 Hunting Model. The grips are either Goncalo Alves or walnut. It was introduced in 1988.

| NIB | Exc. | V.G. | Good | Fair | Poor |
|-----|------|------|------|------|------|
| 275 | 225  | 200  | 175  | 145  | 100  |

# IVER JOHNSON ARMS, INC.
### Middlesex, New Jersey
### ALSO SEE--AMAC

This company was founded in 1883 as an offshoot of the Johnson Bye Company. It was once located in Fitchburg, Massachusetts. It developed into one of the old-line gun companies that produced a number of different revolvers, as well as shotguns. They produced many inexpensive revolvers typical of the era. The earliest productions were sold under tradenames and usually were not marked with the company logo. They were sold under the names Encore, Eclipse, Favorite, Tycoon, and Eagle. These were inexpensive, solid-frame, spur-trigger revolvers that have little collector interest or utility value on today's market. Their values are similar and as follows:

| Exc. | V.G. | Good | Fair | Poor |
|------|------|------|------|------|
| 125  | 100  | 75   | 50   | 25   |

## Safety Automatic Double Action

This is a double-action, break-open pistol chambered for the .22 rimfire, .32 centerfire, and the .38 centerfire cartridge. They have various-length, round ribbed barrels and are offered either with external hammers or internal hammers. They feature automatic ejection of the spent cases as the pistol is broken open. They were very popular revolvers and were advertised with this slogan, "Hammer the Hammer." This refers to the fact that they utilize a transfer bar that prevents the hammer from reaching the firing pin unless the trigger is fully depressed. These pistols were manufactured between 1893 and 1950; and there were many, many thousands produced.

| Exc. | V.G. | Good | Fair | Poor |
|------|------|------|------|------|
| 150  | 125  | 100  | 75   | 50   |

## Model 1900

This is a double-action, solid-frame revolver that does not feature an ejecting mechanism. It is chambered for the .22 rimfire, .32 rimfire, or the .38 centerfire cartridges. It is offered with a 2.5", 4.5", or 6" barrel. The finish is either blued or nickel, with black rubber grips. It was manufactured between 1900 and 1947.

| Exc. | V.G. | Good | Fair | Poor |
|------|------|------|------|------|
| 150  | 125  | 100  | 75   | 50   |

## Safety Cycle Automatic

This is a hinged-frame, break-open revolver similar to Iver Johnson's first revolver. It has a 2" barrel.

| Exc. | V.G. | Good | Fair | Poor |
|------|------|------|------|------|
| 150  | 125  | 100  | 75   | 50   |

## Petite

This is a double-action, solid-frame revolver that is chambered for the .22 short cartridge. It features an internal hammer and a 7-shot cylinder. The barrel is 1" in length, and it has a folding trigger. The finish is nickel-plated, with black rubber grips. It was introduced in 1909 and was not a commercial success.

| Exc. | V.G. | Good | Fair | Poor |
|------|------|------|------|------|
| 250  | 200  | 175  | 125  | 75   |

## Supershot Sealed 8

This is a double-action revolver chambered for the .22 l.r. high-velocity cartridge. It has a 6" barrel and an 8-shot cylinder that is counterbored to enclose the cartridge rims, circumventing problems that could arise from the occasional burst case. It features the safety hammer and is a hinge-frame break-open revolver with automatic ejection. The finish is blued, with black rubber grips. It was manufactured between the end of WWI and 1957.

| Exc. | V.G. | Good | Fair | Poor |
|------|------|------|------|------|
| 150  | 125  | 100  | 50   | 25   |

## Protector Sealed 8

This is simply a 2.5"-barrelled pocket or defense model. Otherwise, it is similar to the Supershot.

| Exc. | V.G. | Good | Fair | Poor |
|------|------|------|------|------|
| 150  | 125  | 100  | 50   | 25   |

## Supershot 9

This model is similar to the Supershot Sealed 8 except that it has a 9-shot cylinder and is not counterbored. It was manufactured between 1929 and 1949.

| Exc. | V.G. | Good | Fair | Poor |
|------|------|------|------|------|
| 150  | 125  | 100  | 50   | 25   |

## Trigger Cocker Single Action

This is a unique single-action, break-open revolver that is chambered for the .22 l.r. cartridge and has a 6" round ribbed barrel. It features the counterbored 8-shot cylinder. The hammer is cocked by pulling the trigger. The second pull on the trigger fires the pistol. The finish is blued, with checkered wood grips. It was manufactured between 1940 and 1947.

| Exc. | V.G. | Good | Fair | Poor |
|------|------|------|------|------|
| 150  | 125  | 100  | 50   | 25   |

## .22 Target Single Action

This is a single-action break-open revolver chambered for the .22 l.r. cartridge. It has a 6" round ribbed barrel with adjustable sights. It has an 8-shot, counterbored cylinder. The finish is blued with adjustable, checkered walnut grips. It was manufactured between 1938 and 1948.

| Exc. | V.G. | Good | Fair | Poor |
|------|------|------|------|------|
| 150  | 125  | 100  | 75   | 50   |

## Model 844

This is a break-open double-action revolver chambered for the .22 l.r. cartridge. It has a 4.5" or 6" round ribbed barrel and features adjustable sights. It has an 8-shot cylinder. The finish is blued, with wood grips. It was manufactured in the 1950's.

| Exc. | V.G. | Good | Fair | Poor |
|------|------|------|------|------|
| 125  | 100  | 75   | 50   | 25   |

## Model 855

This is a single-action pistol chambered for the .22 l.r. cartridge. It has a 6" barrel and an 8-shot cylinder. It features a break-open frame and adjustable sights. The finish is blued, with wood grips. It was manufactured in the 1950's.

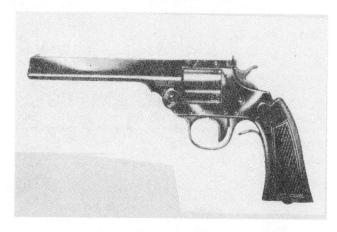

| Exc. | V.G. | Good | Fair | Poor |
|------|------|------|------|------|
| 125  | 100  | 75   | 50   | 25   |

## Model 55A Sportsmen Target

This is a solid-frame, non-ejecting revolver chambered for the .22 l.r. cartridge. It has a 4.75" or 6" barrel with fixed sights. It has an 8-shot cylinder that is loaded through a gate. The finish is blued, with wood grips.

| Exc. | V.G. | Good | Fair | Poor |
|------|------|------|------|------|
| 100  | 75   | 65   | 50   | 25   |

## Model 55S-A Cadet

This is a solid-frame, non-ejecting pocket revolver chambered for the .22 l.r., .22 WMR, .32 S&W, or .38 S&W cartridges. It has a 2.5" barrel and fixed sights. The finish is blued, with checkered plastic grips. It was introduced in 1955.

| Exc. | V.G. | Good | Fair | Poor |
|------|------|------|------|------|
| 100  | 75   | 65   | 50   | 25   |

## Model 57A Target

This revolver is similar to the Model 55A Cadet, with a 4.5" or 6' barrel and adjustable sights. It was manufactured between 1955 and 1975.

| Exc. | V.G. | Good | Fair | Poor |
|------|------|------|------|------|
| 100  | 75   | 65   | 50   | 25   |

## Model 66 Trailsman

This is a break-open double-action revolver chambered for the .22 l.r. cartridge. It has a 6" heavy ribbed barrel with adjustable sights. It features an 8-shot cylinder and does not have the safety hammer. The finish is blued, with wood grips. It was manufactured between 1958 and 1975.

Iver Johnson Model 66
Trailsman

| Exc. | V.G. | Good | Fair | Poor |
|---|---|---|---|---|
| 100 | 75 | 65 | 50 | 25 |

## Model 67 Viking
This pistol is similar to the Trailsman but features the "Hammer the Hammer" design.

| Exc. | V.G. | Good | Fair | Poor |
|---|---|---|---|---|
| 100 | 75 | 65 | 50 | 25 |

## Model 50
This was a solid-frame single-action revolver chambered for the .22 l.r. or the .22 rimfire Magnum cartridges. It has a 4.75" or 6" barrel and is made in the Western style. It has an 8-shot, gate-loaded cylinder and is offered with either fixed or adjustable sights. It is also known as the Sidewinder and was manufactured between 1961 and 1975.

| Exc. | V.G. | Good | Fair | Poor |
|---|---|---|---|---|
| 100 | 75 | 65 | 50 | 25 |

## American Bulldog
This is a double-action revolver chambered for the .22 l.r., .22 WRM, or the .38 Special cartridge. It is offered with a 2.5" or 4" barrel and adjustable sights. The finish is either blued or nickel-plated. It has plastic grips. It was manufactured between 1974 and 1976.

| Exc. | V.G. | Good | Fair | Poor |
|---|---|---|---|---|
| 125 | 100 | 75 | 50 | 25 |

## Rookie
This is a solid-frame revolver chambered for the .38 Special cartridge. It has a 4" barrel and a 5-shot cylinder. It is either blued or nickel-plated, with plastic grips.

Iver Johnson Rookie

| Exc. | V.G. | Good | Fair | Poor |
|---|---|---|---|---|
| 125 | 100 | 75 | 50 | 25 |

## Cattleman Series
This is a series of single-action, Western-style revolvers that were patterned after the Colt SAA. They are chambered for various cartridges between .22 l.r. and the .44 Magnum. They feature various barrel lengths, finishes, and grip materials. They are offered with fixed or adjustable sights. This series of pistols was manufactured in Italy by the firm of Aldo Uberti and was imported by Iver Johnson in the 1970's and early 1980's. Values for this model will be found in the Uberti section of this text.

## Model X300 Pony
This is a locked-breech, single-action, semi-automatic pistol chambered for the .380 ACP cartridge. It has a 3" barrel and a 6-round, detachable magazine. It is constructed of steel. The finish is blued. It was introduced in 1975.

Iver Johnson Pony

| Exc. | V.G. | Good | Fair | Poor |
|---|---|---|---|---|
| 175 | 150 | 125 | 100 | 75 |

## Trailsman
This is a blowback-operated, single-action semi-automatic chambered for the .22 l.r. cartridge. It has a 4.5" or 6" barrel and a 10-round, detachable magazine. It features all-steel construction and is blued, with black checkered plastic grips. A deluxe version with a polished finish and hardwood grips is also available and would increase the values by approximately 15 percent.

Iver Johnson Trailsman

| Exc. | V.G. | Good | Fair | Poor |
|---|---|---|---|---|
| 175 | 150 | 125 | 100 | 75 |

## TP Pistol
This is a double-action, semi-automatic, blowback-operated pistol chambered for either the .22 l.r. or the .25 ACP cartridge. It has a 2.8" barrel with a 7-round, detachable magazine with extension. It is either blued or nickel-plated, with black plastic grips. This model is currently offered by AMAC.

| NIB | V.G. | Good | Fair | Poor |
|-----|------|------|------|------|
| 195 | 150  | 125  | 100  | 75   |

## Champion

This is a single-barrel, break-open shotgun chambered for all gauges, as well as the .44 or .45 caliber as a rifle. It has a 26"-32" full-choke barrel with an external hammer and automatic ejector. The finish is blued, with a plain walnut stock. It was manufactured between 1909 and 1956.

| Exc. | V.G. | Good | Fair | Poor |
|------|------|------|------|------|
| 125  | 100  | 75   | 50   | 25   |

## Matted Rib Grade

This version is chambered for 12, 16, or 20 gauge and has a solid, matte-rib barrel. The finish is blued, with a checkered walnut stock. It was manufactured between 1909 and 1948.

| Exc. | V.G. | Good | Fair | Poor |
|------|------|------|------|------|
| 150  | 125  | 100  | 75   | 50   |

## Trap Grade

This version has a 32", vent-rib, full-choke barrel. It is chambered for 12 gauge only and was manufactured between 1909 and 1942.

| Exc. | V.G. | Good | Fair | Poor |
|------|------|------|------|------|
| 275  | 225  | 175  | 125  | 100  |

## Hercules Grade

This is a side-by-side, double-barrel shotgun chambered for all gauges. It is offered with barrel lengths from 26"- 32" with various choke combinations. It features a hammerless, boxlock action with double triggers and extractors. The finish is blued, with a checkered walnut stock. It was manufactured until 1948. Various options increase the value as follows:
Automatic Ejectors--Add 15 Percent.
Single-Selective Trigger--Add 15 Percent.

| Exc. | V.G. | Good | Fair | Poor |
|------|------|------|------|------|
| 550  | 450  | 375  | 300  | 250  |

## Skeeter Model

This more deluxe version of the Hercules was discontinued in 1946. Values for options are similar.

| Exc. | V.G. | Good | Fair | Poor |
|------|------|------|------|------|
| 1100 | 950  | 700  | 500  | 375  |

## Super Trap

This is a single-barrel trap gun chambered for 12 gauge with a 32", full-choke, vent-rib barrel. It features a boxlock action with an extractor. The finish is blued, with a checkered walnut stock. It was discontinued in 1942. The values for options are similar to the Hercules and Skeeter Models.

| Exc. | V.G. | Good | Fair | Poor |
|------|------|------|------|------|
| 1100 | 950  | 700  | 500  | 375  |

## Silver Shadow

This is an Over/Under shotgun chambered for 12 gauge with 26" or 28" vent-rib barrels with various choke combinations. It features double triggers and extractors. The finish is blued, with a checkered walnut stock. A single trigger was available and would increase the value by 25 percent. This model was manufactured in Italy and imported by Iver Johnson.

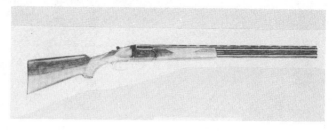

| Exc. | V.G. | Good | Fair | Poor |
|------|------|------|------|------|
| 350  | 300  | 275  | 200  | 150  |

# IXL
### New York, New York

## Pocket Revolver

This revolver is chambered for .31 percussion and has a 4" octagonal barrel. The unfluted cylinder holds 6 shots. This is a double-action revolver with a center-mounted spurless hammer. There were also some produced with a side-mounted spurred hammer, and these would be worth approximately 40 percent additional. The finish of this model is blued, with a large trigger guard and walnut grips. This model is marked "IXL N.York." There were approximately 750 of the spurless hammer version and 150 of the model with the side-mounted hammer manufactured in the late 1850's.

| Exc. | V.G. | Good | Fair | Poor |
|------|------|------|------|------|
| 450  | 400  | 350  | 275  | 150  |

## Navy Revolver

This model has a 7" barrel and is chambered for .36 caliber percussion. There is one version that features a center-mounted spurless hammer that would be worth approximately 40 percent more than the standard side-mounted spurred-hammer version. Both of these revolvers have a large triggerguard and are blued, with wood grips. They have serial numbers but no other markings. There were approximately 100 total Navy models manufactured in the late 1850's.

| Exc. | V.G. | Good | Fair | Poor |
|------|------|------|------|------|
| 1200 | 950  | 750  | 500  | 400  |

# JACQUEMART, JULES
### Liege, Belgium

## Le Monobloc

This is a blowback-operated semi-automatic pistol that is chambered for the 6.35mm cartridge. This model has a rigid barrel of 2" in length. The magazine holds 6 rounds; and the finish is blued, with checkered plastic grips. The slide is marked "Le Monobloc/Pistolet Automatique/Brevette." The grips have a floral motif intertwined "JJ" molded into them. This pistol was manufactured before WWI. Production ceased in 1914.

| Exc. | V.G. | Good | Fair | Poor |
|------|------|------|------|------|
| 350  | 300  | 250  | 200  | 125  |

## JACQUITH, ELIJAH
### Brattleboro, Vermont

### Revolving Underhammer Rifle
This extremely rare rifle is chambered for .40-caliber percussion and has a 34" part-octagonal barrel. This unique rifle has a large cylinder that holds 8 charges mounted in front of and above the trigger area. The center of this cylinder is open to allow sighting, and the bottom chambers feed the barrel. There is a loading lever mounted on the barrel, and there is no triggerguard. The cylinder and the receiver are case-colored, and the barrel is browned with a walnut stock that features a brass patchbox and a crescent buttplate. The barrel is marked "E. Jaquith Brattleboro. Vt." There were approximately 25 of these manufactured in 1838 and 1839.

| Exc. | V.G. | Good | Fair | Poor |
|------|------|------|------|------|
| 8000 | 7000 | 5500 | 4000 | 3000 |

## JAGER WAFFENFABIK
### Suhl, Germany

### Jager Semi-Automatic Pistol
This unique pistol was designed expressly for manufacturing simplicity. All parts except the barrel, breechblock, recoil spring and striker, were stampings. This pistol is chambered for the 7.65mm cartridge, and the barrel is 3" in length. It features a 7-round detachable magazine; and the finish is blued, with checkered black plastic grips. The sights are fixed, and there is a manual safety at the left rear of the frame. The left side of the slide is marked "Jager-Pistole DRP Angem." There is a serial number in front of the triggerguard. This was a good pistol and very easy to manufacture. It is remarkable that it was ever adopted for military use. According to the serial numbers encountered, there were approximately 5,500 manufactured prior to WWI.

| Exc. | V.G. | Good | Fair | Poor |
|------|------|------|------|------|
| 400 | 300 | 250 | 175 | 100 |

## JAPANESE STATE MILITARY WEAPONS
### Japan

The collecting of Japanese martial material has become a very desirable and popular pastime. There was a time when the firearms of Japan did not have the appeal for the collector that they now enjoy. This is not the case at this time, and these arms are rapidly gaining value. There are a number of fine books on the subject, and one who chooses to enter this field of collecting would find it both enjoyable and potentially profitable to learn all that he could about this fascinating subject.

### Rifles
Japanese military rifles are often crude in appearance and poorly made because of lack of quality materials. They are basically strong guns but should be checked by a competent gunsmith before they are fired. They are often found with the national crest, a chrysanthemum, ground off of the receiver. This was due to the vagaries of the occupational forces. If the crest is not intact, the values would be approximately 25 percent less than shown.

### Murata Type 20
This bolt-action rifle was chambered for an 8mm cartridge and was adopted for military service in 1887. They were used extensively in the Sino-Japanese war of 1894. This rifle has a 32" barrel with a full-length stock held on by two barrel bands. It has a bayonet lug and an 8-shot tubular magazine that is mounted under the barrel. After the Sino-Japanese War this rifle was considered obsolete, and Colonel Arisaka was appointed to research and develop a replacement service rifle. This rifle is not often found in good or better condition.

| Exc. | V.G. | Good | Fair | Poor |
|------|------|------|------|------|
| 300 | 250 | 200 | 125 | 75 |

### Murata Shotgun
These are rather crudely fashioned smoothbores made from surplus Murata rifles during the 1920's. These weapons were modified for commercial sales on an export basis. Many of them were sold to Japanese settlers in South America.

| Exc. | V.G. | Good | Fair | Poor |
|------|------|------|------|------|
| 150 | 125 | 100 | 75 | 50 |

### Arisaka Type 30 Rifle
This rifle was the result of Colonel Arisaka's research. It is chambered for 6.5mm Arisaka and has a 31.5" barrel. It has a 5-shot internal box magazine that is loaded through the action by means of a stripper clip. The ejector and the extractor are both mounted on the bolt, and the cocking piece has a distinctive hook protruding from it. This rifle is often referred to as the "Hook Safety". It was used extensively during the Russo-Japanese war. It has a full-length stock with a top handguard held on by two barrel bands. This model was manufactured between 1897 and 1905.

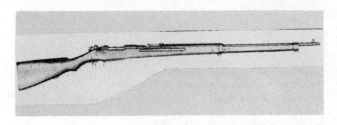

| Exc. | V.G. | Good | Fair | Poor |
|------|------|------|------|------|
| 175 | 150 | 125 | 90 | 65 |

## Arisaka Type 30 Carbine

This model is similar to the Type 30 Rifle, with a 19" barrel and no upper handguard.

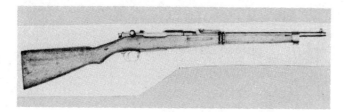

| Exc. | V.G. | Good | Fair | Poor |
|------|------|------|------|------|
| 175 | 150 | 125 | 90 | 65 |

## Arisaka Type 38 Rifle

This model was a considerably improved rifle. It is also chambered for the 6.5mm cartridge, but the action is more similar to the Mauser, and the ejector is mounted on the receiver. The hook was removed and replaced by a large knob-head saftey. It also has a larger bolt handle to facilitate cocking. It has a 31.5" barrel with a full-length stock and upper handguard held on by two barrel bands. It has a 5-round internal box magazine. This model was manufactured between 1905 and 1911.

| Exc. | V.G. | Good | Fair | Poor |
|------|------|------|------|------|
| 175 | 150 | 125 | 90 | 65 |

## Arisaka Type 38 Carbine

This model is similar to the Type 38 rifle, with a 19" barrel and no upper handguard.

| Exc. | V.G. | Good | Fair | Poor |
|------|------|------|------|------|
| 200 | 175 | 150 | 125 | 85 |

## Arisaka Type 44 Carbine

This version was introduced in 1911 and was intended for use by the cavalry. It is similar to the Model 38 except that it features an 18.5" barrel with a bayonet that is attached at the muzzle and folds under the barrel.

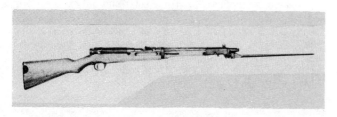

| Exc. | V.G. | Good | Fair | Poor |
|------|------|------|------|------|
| 250 | 200 | 150 | 100 | 75 |

## Japanese "Siamese Mauser" Rifle

These rifles were chambered for the 8x52R mm cartridge. They are essentially a modified Mauser action with a dust cover. They were manufactured in Japan and sold to the Siamese government in the 1920's. The cartridge has been obsolete for many years, and sadly many have been destroyed for collectors by gunsmiths using the action to build large-bore sporting rifles.

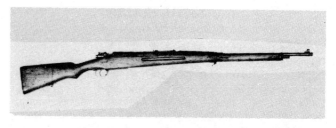

| Exc. | V.G. | Good | Fair | Poor |
|------|------|------|------|------|
| 125 | 100 | 80 | 60 | 40 |

## Arisaka Type 97 "Sniper's Rifle"

This rifle is similar to the Type 38, with the addition of a 4X telescopic sight and a bipod. The scope is mounted to the left side so that the stripper clip could still be used for loading. The bolt handle is bent downward so that it would clear the scope. This model was introduced in 1937.

| Exc. | V.G. | Good | Fair | Poor |
|------|------|------|------|------|
| 350 | 300 | 250 | 175 | 125 |

## Arisaka Type 99 Rifle

The Manchurian campaign of the Sino-Japanese War of the 1930's illustrated to the Japanese the failings of the 6.5mm Arisaka cartridge. This new rifle was chambered for the 7.7mm cartridge that was also used in the Japanese machine guns. The barrel is 25" in length, and the full-length stock and handguard are held on by two barrel bands. This model has a sight with two bars that fold out to the sides that were supposed to be used to lead aircraft. This was very ambitious thinking at best. This rifle was also fitted with a very flimsy wire monopod. This rifle was introduced in 1939 and was used in WWII.

| Exc. | V.G. | Good | Fair | Poor |
|------|------|------|------|------|
| 150 | 125 | 100 | 80 | 60 |

## Type 99 Parachute Rifle

This is a Type 99 hinged at the wrist of the stock so that it could be folded. This model was joined by an interrupted screw thread and was not successful.

| Exc. | V.G. | Good | Fair | Poor |
|------|------|------|------|------|
| 300 | 250 | 225 | 175 | 125 |

## Type 2 Parachute Rifle

This version features a sliding wedge instead of the screw joint, and it worked quite well. These are scarce rifles.

| Exc. | V.G. | Good | Fair | Poor |
|------|------|------|------|------|
| 300 | 250 | 225 | 175 | 125 |

## Type 99 Takedown Rifle

This rifle is similar to the standard Type 99 Rifle, with a takedown joint just in front of the receiver. There is a key that screws in, which when removed allows the barrel to be removed and the rifle to be separated into two pieces. This was not a good idea as it weakened the receiver and negatively affected accuracy.

| Exc. | V.G. | Good | Fair | Poor |
|------|------|------|------|------|
| 250 | 200 | 175 | 125 | 80 |

### Type 99 "Snipers Rifle"

This model is chambered for the 7.7mm cartridge and has a 25.5" barrel. It was fitted with a 4X telescopic sight and was adopted in 1942.

| Exc. | V.G. | Good | Fair | Poor |
|------|------|------|------|------|
| 350 | 300 | 250 | 200 | 125 |

### Type 5 Semi-automatic Rifle

This rifle was chambered for the 7.7mm cartridge and was basically a copy of the M1 Garand with a detachable box magazine. It was made at the Kure naval arsenal in 1945. There were only an estimated 75 rifles completed before the end of the war, and they were not functioning well due to metallurgical problems. This model is very seldom seen and is too rare to evaluate without individual appraisal.

### Handguns

In 1893 the Japanese government decided that they should produce their own service pistols. Prior to that they had been using the S&W New Model No. 3 revolver. The new Japanese-produced handguns would be made at either the Tokyo Arsenal (these are stamped with four interlocking rings) or the Nagoyo Arsenal (these are marked by figure 8 in a circle).

### Type 26 Revolver

This model is chambered for a 9mm rimmed cartridge that is unique to this pistol. It has a 4" barrel and is a hinged, top-break design. The cylinder holds 6 shots, and the lockwork is double action only. This pistol is similar to several revolvers used by other countries at that time. It is shaped like a Nagant, hinged like the S&W, has a hinged sideplate like the French Model 1892, and has lockwork similar to the Galand. This revolver has no hammerspur and could not be hand cocked. This was generally a good quality revolver, and it was manufactured between 1893 and 1924. It was actually used by backup troops until the end of the WWII.

| Exc. | V.G. | Good | Fair | Poor |
|------|------|------|------|------|
| 275 | 250 | 200 | 150 | 100 |

### 4th Year Type Nambu Pistol

This was the first of the Nambu semi-automatic pistols. It was adopted for service in 1915. It is chambered for the 8mm Nambu cartridge and has a 4.7" barrel. This model was manufactured predominantly at the Tokyo Arsenal and was used during WWI. This model has a grip safety and an 8-shot detach-

able magazine. The finish is blued and quite well executed on this model, and the grips are checkered wood.

| Exc. | V.G. | Good | Fair | Poor |
|------|------|------|------|------|
| 1000 | 800 | 650 | 450 | 350 |

### Baby Nambu

This is a smaller, compact version of the 4th Year Type pistol. It was also known as the Type B Pistol and was produced for use by staff officers. The barrel is 3.5" long, and the overall length is 2.5" shorter than the standard pistol. These Nambus are quite scarce, and their value reflects this rarity.

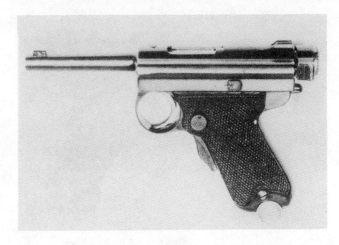

| Exc. | V.G. | Good | Fair | Poor |
|------|------|------|------|------|
| 2250 | 2000 | 1500 | 1000 | 750 |

### 14th Year Type Nambu Pistol

This model was introduced in 1925 and is basically an improved version of its forerunner. It is chambered for the 8mm Nambu cartridge and does not have the grip safety. The grips are thinner and grooved instead of checkered. The cocking piece was modified, and the sights were changed from adjustible to fixed. A manual safety was added to the left side of the frame, and also a magazine safety was utilized. There are two basic versions--one with a standard triggerguard, and a large ring version often referred to as the "Manchurian triggerguard" that was large enough to allow access with a heavy glove. The early models were manufactured at the Kokura Arsenal, formerly known as the Tokyo Arsenal. In 1927 they were made at the Nagoyo Arsenal, and in the 30's Nagoyo became the sole producer. This pistol declined noticeably in quality as the war years progressed. They were manufactured until the end of WWII in 1945.

| Exc. | V.G. | Good | Fair | Poor |
|------|------|------|------|------|
| 475 | 400 | 350 | 250 | 175 |

## Type 94 Pistol

This pistol was chambered for the 8mm cartridge and was smaller in size than the other Japanese designs. It was introduced in 1937 as a military weapon althuogh it was offered commercially before this date. This was a weak design that was inherently unsafe as it could be fired by applying pressure to the exposed sear bar on the side of the pistol. This pistol could also fire before the breech was locked--with potentially disasterous results. The barrel is 3.3" in length, and the detachable magazine holds 6 rounds. This model was manufactured up to the end of WWII, with those made in 1944 and 1945 being unbelievably crude.

| Exc. | V.G. | Good | Fair | Poor |
|------|------|------|------|------|
| 250 | 200 | 175 | 125 | 90 |

# JEFFERY, W. J. & CO. LTD.
## London, England

This company produced very high quality shotguns and rifles. Their products have been used by wealthy sportsmen for many years. They produced guns under their own banner and also as contractors for other distributors. They made the guns sold by the Army & Navy Departmant Store in London. Guns of this type were basically custom-ordered and as such are extremely hard to evaluate on a general basis. We supply an estimated value for a standard model but strongly urge that one secure an individual appraisal if a transaction is contemplated.

## Shotguns
### Boxlock

These guns were produced in all gauges, with barrel lengths and choke combinations to the customer's specifications. They were available with any trigger option and automatic extractors or ejectors. The materials and workmanship were of the highest order, and values would be based on options. This model was produced with exposed hammers and damascus barrels and would be worth approximately 50 percent less in that configuration. Small gauges would add approximately 50 percent.

| Exc. | V.G. | Good | Fair | Poor |
|------|------|------|------|------|
| 4000 | 3500 | 2500 | 1600 | 900 |

### Sidelock

The quality of this model is similar to that of the boxlock, with the added value of the sidelock action. This was also a made-to-order gun, and values cannot be accurately estimated without an individual appraisal. Hammerguns with damascus barrels would bring approximately 50 percent less. Small gauges would add approximately 50 percent.

| Exc. | V.G. | Good | Fair | Poor |
|------|------|------|------|------|
| 9000 | 7500 | 5000 | 3250 | 1650 |

## Rifles
### Single Shot

This model was built on the Farquharson Falling Block action and was chambered for many calibers up to the .600 Nitro Express. This was also a custom-order gun, and the barrel length was optional. There are usually folding express sights; and the finish is usually blued with a select, hand-checkered walnut stock. These were high quality firearms; and the values would be determined, for the most part, by the options and embellishments on the particular specimen. Individual appraisal is definitely advised. The caliber in which a rifle is chambered will also have an effect on the value. Obsolete calibers bring less, and the larger express calibers bring more.

| Exc. | V.G. | Good | Fair | Poor |
|------|------|------|------|------|
| 4000 | 3250 | 2500 | 1750 | 900 |

### Boxlock Double Rifle

This model is a boxlock chambered for many different calibers. It can be found with either a top or underlever action and has folding express sights. The stock and forearm are select, hand-checkered walnut; and the finish is usually blue. This was a custom-order proposition, and values can be affected by many variables--such as caliber, options, and embellishment. Damascus-barreled hammer guns are worth approximately 50 percent less.

| Exc. | V.G. | Good | Fair | Poor |
|------|------|------|------|------|
| 8000 | 6500 | 4500 | 3500 | 2500 |

### Sidelock Double Rifle

This version has detachable sidelocks and otherwise is comparable to the boxlock version. Individual appraisal is recommended.

| Exc. | V.G. | Good | Fair | Poor |
|------|------|------|------|------|
| 12500 | 10000 | 7500 | 5000 | 4000 |

# JENISON, J. & CO.
## Southbridge, Connecticut

### Underhammer Pistol

This is a underhammer or boot pistol that is chambered for .28 caliber percussion and has a 4" part-octagonal barrel with brass-mounted, pointed wooden handle that is sometimes made of oak. The frame is iron and is marked "J.Jenison & Co./Southbridge,Mass." There were a fair number of these manufactured in the 1850's.

| Exc. | V.G. | Good | Fair | Poor |
|------|------|------|------|------|
| 500 | 425 | 350 | 250 | 150 |

## JENKS CARBINE
### Springfield, Massachusetts
### N. P. Ames Manufacturer

### Jenks "Mule Ear Carbine"

This carbine was chambered for .54-caliber percussion and has a 24.5" round barrel and a full-length stock held on by two barrel bands. This is a single-shot breechloader that is activated by a hooked lever on the breech block. The hammer is mounted on the side of the receiver. The trim is brass; and the lock and lever are case colored, with the remainder browned. The stock is walnut, and there is no ramrod. The lock is marked "N.P.Ames / Springfield / Mass." The barrel is stamped "Wm.Jenks / USN" followed by the inspector's initials. The buttstock carries an inspector's cartouche. There were very few that were marked "USR" for the "U.S. Revenue Cutter Service," and these would bring an 80 percent premium--be wary of fakes! There were approximately 4,250 of this military Carbine manufactured between 1841 and 1846.

| Exc. | V.G. | Good | Fair | Poor |
|------|------|------|------|------|
| 1000 | 850 | 750 | 500 | 375 |

### Jenks Navy Rifle

This model is similar to the Mule Ear Carbine, with a 30" round barrel and the full stock held on by three barrel bands. The markings are the same, and there were 1,000 manufactured on contract to the U.S. Navy in 1841.

| Exc. | V.G. | Good | Fair | Poor |
|------|------|------|------|------|
| 1500 | 1250 | 950 | 700 | 500 |

## JENKS-HERKIMER
### New York
### Manufacturer--E. Remington & Son

### Jenks Carbine

This carbine, sometimes referred to as the "Mule- ear," is chambered for .54 caliber percussion. It is a breechloader with the hammer mounted on the right side. The action of this carbine is identical to the Jenks carbine manufactured by N. P. Ames. It has a 24.25" round barrel and a full-length stock held on by two bands. The lock is marked "Remington's / Herkimer / N.Y." The barrel is marked "W. Jenks / USN / RC / P / Cast Steel." The major difference between the Remington Jenks and the Ames Jenks is that the Remington utilizes the Maynard tape primer mechanism. There were approximately 1,000 of these carbines manufactured circa 1846.

| Exc. | V.G. | Good | Fair | Poor |
|------|------|------|------|------|
| 1250 | 1000 | 800 | 650 | 450 |

## JENKS-MERRILL
### Baltimore, Maryland

This was actually an experimental alteration that was accomplished by James H. Merrill. The Jenks carbine was converted to fire the .54-caliber Merrill combustible cartridge. The hammer was changed to a conventional design, and the markings were "J. H. Merrill Balto./Pat.July 1858." The breech was still marked "Wm.Jenks/USN." All other specifications were similar to the Jenks carbine. There were approximately 300 of these converted between 1858 and 1860.

| Exc. | V.G. | Good | Fair | Poor |
|------|------|------|------|------|
| 1850 | 1650 | 1400 | 900 | 650 |

## JENNINGS
### Windsor, Vermont
### Manufacturer--Robbins & Lawrence

### Jennings Rifle

The Jennings rifle is also part of the Winchester story. It followed the Hunt Repeater. B. Tyler Henry was the foreman at this company, and he later was responsible for development for the Vocanic, New Haven, and the Winchester Arms Company. Mr. Henry, along with Smith & Wesson, combined their efforts in the production of this rifle. There were three basic versions of the Jennings rifle, with a total production of approximatley 5,000.

### First Model

This breech-loading, single-shot rifle is chambered for .54 caliber percussion. It has a long oval triggerguard with a ring trigger. It features an automatic priming device and has an integral ramrod mounted under the barrel. It was manufactured in 1850 and 1851.

| Exc. | V.G. | Good | Fair | Poor |
|------|------|------|------|------|
| 2250 | 2000 | 1750 | 1500 | 1000 |

### Second Model

This model is actually quite different than the First Model. It was intended to be a repeater and has a magazine tube mounted under the barrel. It is also chambered for .54 caliber percussion, and the frame is more contoured than the straight frame of the First Model. It still has the ring trigger but does not feature a triggerguard. The stock is walnut, with a crescent buttplate. This model was manufactured in 1851 and 1852.

| Exc. | V.G. | Good | Fair | Poor |
|------|------|------|------|------|
| 5500 | 4750 | 4000 | 3250 | 2500 |

### Muzzle-Loading Rifle

This model was also chambered for .54 caliber percussion and was made up of parts that were left from the First and Second Models' production. It has the straight frame of the First Model and a conventionally curved trigger with a bow-type guard. There is a ramrod mounted under the barrel. This model was manufactured in 1852.

| Exc. | V.G. | Good | Fair | Poor |
|------|------|------|------|------|
| 1500 | 1250 | 950 | 800 | 600 |

## JENNINGS F. A., INC.
### Carson City, Nevada

Jennings distributes pistols manufactured by Calwestco in Chino, California, and Bryco Firearms in Carson City, Nevada.

**J-22**

This is a blowback-operated, semi-automatic pocket pistol chambered for the .22 l.r. cartridge. It has a 2.5" barrel and is constructed of cast aluminum with a choice of three finishes: bright chrome, teflon, or satin nickel-plated. The detachable magazine holds 6 shots, and the grips are either checkered plastic or smooth walnut. The sights are fixed.

| Exc. | V.G. | Good | Fair | Poor |
|------|------|------|------|------|
| 75   | 65   | 50   | 35   | 25   |

## Bryco Model 25

This is a single-action, blowback-operated, semi-automatic pistol chambered for the .25 ACP cartridge. It has a 2.5" barrel and holds 6 rounds. It is constructed of cast aluminum and finished similarly to the J-22, with resin impregnated wood grips.

| Exc. | V.G. | Good | Fair | Poor |
|------|------|------|------|------|
| 90   | 75   | 65   | 50   | 35   |

## Bryco Model 38

This is a single-action semi-automatic chambered for the .22 l.r., .32 ACP, or the .380 ACP cartridge. It has a 2.8" barrel and is similar in all other respects to the Model 25 except that it is slightly larger and heavier.

| Exc. | V.G. | Good | Fair | Poor |
|------|------|------|------|------|
| 110  | 90   | 75   | 65   | 50   |

## Bryco Model 48

This is a slightly larger sporter version of the Model 38. It has a reverse hooked triggerguard for the two-hand hold and is otherwise similar to the Model 38. This pistol was introduced in 1988.

| Exc. | V.G. | Good | Fair | Poor |
|------|------|------|------|------|
| 140  | 110  | 95   | 85   | 75   |

# JERICHO
**Harrisburg, Pennsylvania**
**Israeli Military Industries**
**Israel**

## Jericho

This is a double-action semi-automatic pistol chambered for the 9mm and the .41 Action Express cartridges on an interchangeable basis. The barrels are 4.72" in length and have polygonal rifling. The construction is all steel, and there is an ambidextrous safety. The sights are the three-dot system; and the finish is matte-blued, with black polymer grips. The pistol is furnished in a case with a cleaning kit. This model was introduced in 1989. It is imported by K.B.I. in Harrisburg, Pennsylvania.

| Exc. | V.G. | Good | Fair | Poor |
|------|------|------|------|------|
| 850  | 750  | 575  | 450  | 375  |

# JIEFFCO
**Robar et Cie**
**Liege, Belgium**

## Pocket Pistol

This model is a blowback-operated semi-automatic chambered for both the .25 ACP and the .32 Auto cartridge. It has a 3" barrel and a 6-shot magazine. The finish is blued, with checkered plastic grips. This model was manufactured between 1912 and 1914.

| Exc. | V.G. | Good | Fair | Poor |
|---|---|---|---|---|
| 275 | 250 | 200 | 150 | 100 |

**New Model Melior**

This is a blowback-operated, semi-automatic pocket pistol chambered for the .25 ACP cartridge. It has a 2" barrel and a 6-shot magazine. This model is blued, with checkered black plastic grips. It was manufactured in the early 1920's and was marketed by Davis-Warner.

| Exc. | V.G. | Good | Fair | Poor |
|---|---|---|---|---|
| 250 | 225 | 175 | 125 | 90 |

## JOHNSON AUTOMATIC RIFLE
### Cranston Arms Co.
### Providence, Rhode Island

**Model 1941**

This is a recoil-operated semi-automatic rifle chambered for the .30-06 and the 7mm cartridge. It has a 22" barrel and a 10-round rotary magazine that has lips machined into the receiver. This protects these normally delicate parts. The Johnson rifle was tested after the Garand went into mass production, and it really never did have a chance for success. But in 1941, with WWII creating a need for any and all rifles available, there were several thousand purchased by the Marine Corps for use by their special units. The Dutch government also purchased some to be used in Sumatra and Java. The 7mm versions were ordered from South America. The Johnson Rifle has a removable barrel, that was covered by a ventilated handguard, and a walnut stock. This rifle did not prove to be as dependable as it should have been, and it passed totally out of production in 1945.

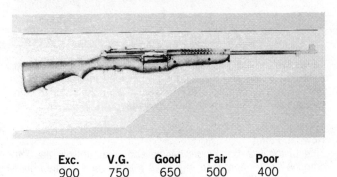

| Exc. | V.G. | Good | Fair | Poor |
|---|---|---|---|---|
| 900 | 750 | 650 | 500 | 400 |

## JOHNSON, BYE & CO.
### Worcester, Massachusetts

This company was a partnership between Iver Johnson and Martin Bye. It was the forerunner of the Iver Johnson Firearms Co. This firm was organized for the purpose of manufacturing cheap handguns, the type of revolvers often referred to as suicide specials. They operated from 1871 until 1883, when Bye sold out to Johnson and the Iver Johnson Co. was formed. There were a number of trademarks used by this company, but they were all applied to only three different pistols.

**Defender, Eagle, Encore, Eureka, Favorite, Lion, Smoker and Tycoon**

All of these names are used to describe the same basic pistol. It is chambered for the .22 r.f., .32 centerfire, .38, and .44 centerfire cartridges. They are single-action, solid-framed revolvers with spur triggers and no ejector rods. They have octagonal barrels of various lengths, and the tradename is stamped on the barrel. These were usually nickel-plated with checkered plastic grips and were very cheaply made.

| Exc. | V.G. | Good | Fair | Poor |
|---|---|---|---|---|
| 125 | 100 | 75 | 50 | 25 |

**Eclipse**

This was a departure from the normal product of this company. It is a very small, single-shot, derringer-type pistol that has a 1.5" barrel that pivots to the side for loading. It has a spur trigger and was also very cheaply made. It is chambered for the .22 short rimfire.

| Exc. | V.G. | Good | Fair | Poor |
|---|---|---|---|---|
| 125 | 100 | 75 | 50 | 25 |

**American Bulldog**

This model is slightly better than the others in that it has a triggerguard and features a double-action lock mechanism. It is chambered for the .32 and the .38 centerfires, as well as the .22 and .32 rimfire cartridges. It has a 3" barrel and is also a solid frame without an ejector rod.

| Exc. | V.G. | Good | Fair | Poor |
|---|---|---|---|---|
| 125 | 100 | 75 | 50 | 25 |

## JOSLYN
### Milbury, Massachusetts
### A. H. Waters-- Manufacturer

**Model 1855 Carbine**

This military carbine is chambered for .54 caliber percussion and has a 22.5" round barrel. This is a single-shot breechloader that has a ring-shaped breech lever on the upper wrist of the stock. The half-length walnut stock is held on by one barrel band; and the lock and the breech lever are case-colored, with the remainder blued with brass trim. The lock is marked "A.H.Waters & Co./Milbury, Mass." The patent dates are stamped on the breech lever. There were approximately 1,000 manufactured in 1855 and 1856.

| Exc. | V.G. | Good | Fair | Poor |
|---|---|---|---|---|
| 2250 | 1950 | 1600 | 1200 | 950 |

**Model 1855 Rifle**

This is a .58-caliber, 38"-barrelled version of the Joslyn Carbine. It has three barrel bands on a full-length stock and a bayonet lug. There were only a few hundred manufactured in 1856.

| Exc. | V.G. | Good | Fair | Poor |
|---|---|---|---|---|
| 2500 | 2200 | 1800 | 1400 | 1100 |

## JOSLYN FIREARMS COMPANY
### Stonington, Connecticut

### Model 1862 Carbine
This military carbine is chambered for the .52 rimfire cartridge. It is a single-shot breechloader that operates by pivoting the breechblock upwards and to the left. It has a 22" round barrel and a half stock that is held on by one barrel band. The lock is case colored; and the barrel blued. The mountings are made of brass. The lock is marked "Joslyn Firearms Co. / Stonington / Conn." The patent date is marked on the barrel. The trigger plate is 8" long, and the upper tang measures 4.5". There were approximately 4,000 manufactured in 1862, and they were used by Union forces during the Civil War.

| Exc. | V.G. | Good | Fair | Poor |
|------|------|------|------|------|
| 1500 | 1250 | 1000 | 700 | 400 |

### Model 1864 Carbine
This model is similar to the Model 1862, but the mountings are case-hardened iron instead of brass. The trigger plate is 7" long, and the upper tang measures 2". It has a round latch on the breechblock and an improved firing pin. This model is marked the same with the addition of 1864. There were approximately 12,000 of these manufactured in 1864 and 1865, and it was very widely used by Union forces during the Civil War.

| Exc. | V.G. | Good | Fair | Poor |
|------|------|------|------|------|
| 1400 | 1150 | 900 | 800 | 500 |

### Army Model Revolver
This single-action, side-hammer revolver is chambered for .44 caliber percussion and has an 8" octagonal barrel and a 5-shot unfluted cylinder. The finish is blued, with a case-colored integral loading lever and hammer. It has checkered walnut grips. The barrel is marked "B. F. Joslyn/ Patd. May 4, 1858." There are two basic versions of the Joslyn Army Revolver.

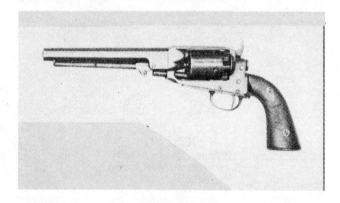

### First Model
This Model features a brass triggerguard and has an iron buttcap. There were approximately 500 manufactured in 1861.

| Exc. | V.G. | Good | Fair | Poor |
|------|------|------|------|------|
| 1750 | 1500 | 1200 | 800 | 550 |

### Second Model
This Model is very similar to the First Model, with an iron triggerguard and no buttcap. There were approximately 2,500 manufactured in 1861 and 1862. Joslyn revolvers of both types are often found with U.S. inspector's marks, as approximately half were purchased by the military and used in the Civil War. These martially marked specimens would bring approximately a 20 percent premium.

| Exc. | V.G. | Good | Fair | Poor |
|------|------|------|------|------|
| 1500 | 1250 | 1000 | 700 | 400 |

## JOSLYN
### Springfield, Massachusetts
### Manufacturer--Springfield Armory

### Joslyn Breechloading Rifle
This was the first mass-produced, true breechloading cartridge firearm manufactured in a national armory. The actions were supplied by the Joslyn Firearms Company, and the rifles were chambered for the .56-50 rimfire cartridge. This rifle has a 35.5" round barrel and a full-length stock that is held on by three barrel bands. The lock is marked "U.S./Springfield" with "1864" at the back. The barrel is marked "B. F. Joslyn's Patent / Oct. 8th, 1861 / June 24th, 1862." There were approximately 3,000 of these manufactured circa 1865. They were probably issued to Union forces, but it is unknown if they saw action before the end of the Civil War.

| Exc. | V.G. | Good | Fair | Poor |
|------|------|------|------|------|
| 1500 | 1250 | 1000 | 700 | 500 |

### .50-70 Alteration
Approximately 1,600 Joslyn rifles were re-chambered to fire the .50-70 centerfire cartridge. The conversion consisted of re-chambering and drilling a new firing pin hole after the rimfire pin was sealed. There was no specific serial-number range in which these conversions were done. Most of these weapons were eventually converted to smooth bores and sold in Africa. The original military specimens are extremely scarce.

| Exc. | V.G. | Good | Fair | Poor |
|------|------|------|------|------|
| 2000 | 1750 | 1400 | 1000 | 750 |

## JURRAS, LEE
### Prescott, Arizona
### SEE--Auto-Mag

Jurras was instrumental in the last incarnation of the famed Automag pistol, and these guns are covered in their own section. He also produces the Howdah Pistol that is marketed through J. & G. Sales in Prescott, Arizona.

### Howdah Pistol
This pistol is a break-open single shot that utilizes the Thompson Center contender frame as a basis for a custom-built hand cannon that is chambered for a series of ammunition designed explicitly for these high-powered pistols. It is loaded and marketed by R. Davis of Athens, Tennessee. These cartridges are the .375, .416, .460, .475, .500, and the .577. They are very powerful handgun cartridges and were designed for hunting the largest of game. This pistol has a 12" barrel and adjustable sights. It has a Nitex finish and is a limited-production item.

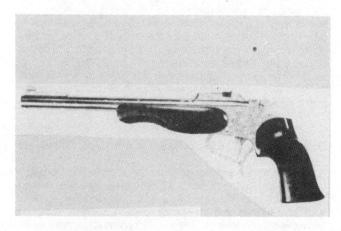

| Exc. | V.G. | Good | Fair | Poor |
|------|------|------|------|------|
| 1200 | 1000 | 800 | 650 | 500 |

## JUSTICE, P. S.
### Philadelphia, Pennsylvania

### Percussion Rifle
This is a single-shot, muzzle-loading rifle with a 35" round barrel. It is chambered for .58 caliber percussion and has a full-length stock held on by two barrel bands. There is a bayonet lug on the side of the muzzle. This rifle has a polished iron lock and a browned barrel. There is a brass patchbox and trim. The Justice rifle utilized locks from other rifles, and it is not uncommon to find evidence of the original markings being removed before "P.S.Justice/Philada." was added. This was the first military weapon produced for the Union Army at the beginning of the Civil War, and the quality was not what it should have been. There were approximately 2,500 produced in 1861.

| Exc. | V.G. | Good | Fair | Poor |
|------|------|------|------|------|
| 1500 | 1250 | 1000 | 750 | 450 |

## KBI, INC.
### Harrisburg, Pennsylvania

This company imports firearms and is currently importing the Jericho pistol from I.M.I. (that has been covered under its own section), as well as distributing the American-made pistol covered here.

### PSP-25
This is a blowback-operated, semi-automatic pocket pistol patterned after the Baby Browning. It is chambered for the .25 ACP cartridge and has a 2" barrel. The construction is all steel; and the finish is blued, with checkered plastic grips. This pistol is manufactured in the U.S.A. under license from Fabrique Nationale. It was introduced in 1989.

| NIB | Exc. | V.G. | Good | Fair |
|-----|------|------|------|------|
| 250 | 225 | 200 | 175 | 125 |

## KDF, INC.
### Seguin, Texas
### Kleinguenther Distinctive Firearms

This company formerly imported the Voere bolt-action rifle and since Voere's absorption by Mauser, has become the sole importer of Mauser rifles in the U.S. They also import a line of Italian shotguns.

### Condor
This is an Over/Under shotgun chambered for 12 gauge. It has 28" barrels with various choke combinations and a wide vent rib. It has a boxlock action with a single-selective trigger and automatic ejectors. The finish is blued, with a checkered walnut stock. It is manufactured in Italy.

| Exc. | V.G. | Good | Fair | Poor |
|------|------|------|------|------|
| 650 | 600 | 525 | 375 | 275 |

### Brescia
This is a side-by-side, double-barrel shotgun chambered for 12 gauge. It has 28" full and modified barrels with a boxlock action with double triggers and extractors. The finish is blued, with a checkered walnut stock. It is manufactured in Italy.

| Exc. | V.G. | Good | Fair | Poor |
|------|------|------|------|------|
| 350 | 325 | 300 | 200 | 125 |

### K-14 Insta Fire Rifle
This is a bolt-action sporting rifle chambered for various popular calibers. It has a 24" or 26" barrel furnished without sights. This rifle is known to have an extremely fast lock time and features a concealed, detachable box magazine. The finish is blued with a checkered walnut, Monte Carlo-type stock furnished with a recoil pad.

| Exc. | V.G. | Good | Fair | Poor |
|------|------|------|------|------|
| 600 | 550 | 450 | 325 | 250 |

### K-15
This is a high-grade, bolt-action sporting rifle chambered for various popular calibers. It is offered with a 24" or 26" barrel without sights. It also features the fast lock time and a 60-degree lift bolt. It has a 3- or 5- round detachable magazine depending on the caliber and is blued with a select walnut, checkered, Monte Carlo-type stock. This rifle comes with a guarantee that it will fire a .5" group at 100 yards. There are a number of options available that would increase the value, and we recommend a qualified appraisal.

| Exc. | V.G. | Good | Fair | Poor |
|------|------|------|------|------|
| 1000 | 850 | 750 | 550 | 400 |

### K-15 Pro-Hunter
This version is either matte-blued or electroless nickel-plated with a fiberglas stock.

| Exc. | V.G. | Good | Fair | Poor |
|------|------|------|------|------|
| 1400 | 1250 | 1000 | 700 | 500 |

### K-15 Swat Rifle
This version is chambered for the .308 cartridge and is offered with a 24" or 26" barrel without sights. It features a 4-shot detachable magazine. The finish is parkerized with a dull, oil-finished, target-type walnut stock.

| Exc. | V.G. | Good | Fair | Poor |
|------|------|------|------|------|
| 1500 | 1300 | 1100 | 800 | 550 |

### K-15 Dangerous Game
This version is chambered for the .411 KDF cartridge that was designed for this rifle only. It is a heavy-duty Magnum-type rifle designed to be used on the very large African and Alaskan game.

| Exc. | V.G. | Good | Fair | Poor |
|------|------|------|------|------|
| 2000 | 1600 | 1300 | 1000 | 700 |

### K-16
This is a bolt-action sporting rifle based on the Remington Model 700 action. It has been modified to incorporate the insta-fire ignition. It is chambered for various popular American calibers and is offered with a 24" or 26" barrel without sights. It features a single-stage, adjustable trigger and KDF accurizing.

There is a choice of finishes, and it has a Dupont Rynite stock in either tan or grey. It is standard with a recoil pad and quick-detachable sling swivels. There are a number of options available which have a drastic effect on the values. We recommend securing a competent appraisal when in doubt.

| Exc. | V.G. | Good | Fair | Poor |
|------|------|------|------|------|
| 775  | 675  | 500  | 400  | 300  |

## Titan Menor

This is a bolt-action sporting rifle chambered for .222 or the .223 cartridges. It features a short action and is offered with a 24" or 26" barrel without sights. The finish is high-polish blue with a select checkered Monte Carlo-type stock. A classic stock with Schnabel forend is available and would increase the values approximately 15 percent.

| Exc. | V.G. | Good | Fair | Poor |
|------|------|------|------|------|
| 650  | 600  | 550  | 400  | 300  |

## Titan II Standard

This is the medium-action version chambered for various popular calibers. Otherwise, it is similar to the Titan Menor. It is a generally larger rifle.

| Exc. | V.G. | Good | Fair | Poor |
|------|------|------|------|------|
| 900  | 800  | 700  | 500  | 400  |

## Titan II Magnum

This is the large-action version chambered for Magnum calibers between 7mm Rem. Mag. and .375 H&H. This model was discontinued in 1988.

| Exc. | V.G. | Good | Fair | Poor |
|------|------|------|------|------|
| 1000 | 850  | 750  | 550  | 450  |

## Titan .411 KDF Mag.

This version is chambered for the dangerous-game cartridge. It is offered with a 26" barrel with an integral muzzle break. It has a blued or electroless nickel finish. This model was discontinued in 1988.

| Exc. | V.G. | Good | Fair | Poor |
|------|------|------|------|------|
| 1200 | 1050 | 850  | 650  | 550  |

## K-22

This is a bolt action repeating rifle chambered for the .22 l.r. cartridge. It has a 21" free floating barrel that is furnished without sights. It has a five-round detachable magazine and a fully adjustable trigger. The finish is blued with a select walnut stock. It is offered with a guarantee of 1" groups at 100 yards. There are three deluxe versions that differ in quality of materials and workmanship only. This is also known as the Mauser 201 rifle.

| Exc. | V.G. | Good | Fair | Poor |
|------|------|------|------|------|
| 300  | 275  | 250  | 175  | 125  |

### K-22 Deluxe

| Exc. | V.G. | Good | Fair | Poor |
|------|------|------|------|------|
| 400  | 375  | 350  | 275  | 225  |

### K-22 Deluxe Custom

| Exc. | V.G. | Good | Fair | Poor |
|------|------|------|------|------|
| 650  | 550  | 450  | 375  | 325  |

### K-22 Deluxe Special Select

| Exc. | V.G. | Good | Fair | Poor |
|------|------|------|------|------|
| 1000 | 850  | 750  | 650  | 525  |

## Model 2005

This was a blow back operated semi-automatic rifle chambered for the .22 l.r. cartridge. It had a 19.5" barrel with open sights. It had a five-round detachable magazine, a blued finish, and a walnut stock. It was imported in 1986 only. Its import was disallowed by the BATF. A deluxe version was available, valued at approximately 20% additional.

| NIB | Exc. | V.G. | Good | Fair | Poor |
|-----|------|------|------|------|------|
| 125 | 100  | 80   | 60   | 40   | 30   |

## Model 2107

This was a bolt-action sporting rifle chambered for the .22 l.r. or the .22 rimfire Mag. cartridges. It has a 19.5" barrel with open sights and a five-round detachable magazine. The finish was blued with a walnut stock. A deluxe version was available and valued at approximately 10% additional.

| Exc. | V.G. | Good | Fair | Poor |
|------|------|------|------|------|
| 175  | 150  | 125  | 100  | 75   |

## Model 2112

This is a deluxe version of the Model 2107.

| Exc. | V.G. | Good | Fair | Poor |
|------|------|------|------|------|
| 250  | 200  | 175  | 125  | 90   |

# K.F.C.

**Japan**
**Importer--LaPaloma Marketing**
**Tucson, Arizona**

## E-1 Trap or Skeet Over/Under

This model is chambered for 12 gauge and has either 30" full-and-full choked barrels or 26" skeet-and-skeet choked barrels. The barrels feature a wide competition rib. The action is a boxlock, and it has a single-selective trigger with automatic ejectors. The finish is blued; and the stock is select, oil-finished, hand-checkered walnut. The receiver is engraved. This model was manufactured until 1986.

| Exc. | V.G. | Good | Fair | Poor |
|------|------|------|------|------|
| 950  | 800  | 700  | 500  | 400  |

## E-2 Trap or Skeet Over/Under

This model is similar to the E-1, with more elaborate engraving.

| Exc. | V.G. | Good | Fair | Poor |
|------|------|------|------|------|
| 1400 | 1250 | 1000 | 750  | 500  |

## Field Grade Over/Under

This gun is similar to the competition guns except that the vent rib is narrower and the barrels are 26" or 28" in length with various chokes. The select walnut stock is dimensioned as a hunting gun--not a competition model. This model was discontinued in 1986.

| Exc. | V.G. | Good | Fair | Poor |
|------|------|------|------|------|
| 650  | 575  | 500  | 400  | 275  |

## Model 250

This was a semi-automatic shotgun chambered for 12 gauge only. It has vent rib barrels of 26", 28" or 30" in length and was finished in a matte-blue with a select hand-checkered walnut stock. This model was available with screw-in choke tubes. It was manufactured between 1980 and 1986.

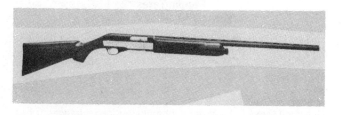

| Exc. | V.G. | Good | Fair | Poor |
|------|------|------|------|------|
| 350  | 300  | 275  | 200  | 100  |

## KASSNAR IMPORTS, INC.
### Harrisburg, Pennsylvania

This company has been an importer of firearms for many years, and many of the products that they market have been covered under their own sections. Churchill shotguns were imported by Kassnar until 1988; they are listed separately. Kassnar imported the Hungarian Pistols of FEG until recently. They are listed in the Interarms section. The following firearms are currently imported by Kassnar.

### Omega Shotguns
### Standard Over/Under
This gun is chambered for 12, 20, 28 gauges, and .410. It is a folding boxlock action offered with vent-rib barrels either 26" or 28" in length. This gun has a single trigger and extractors. The finish is blue. with a walnut stock; and the choke combinations are varied.

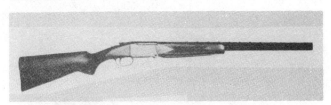

| NIB | Exc. | V.G. | Good | Fair | Poor |
|-----|------|------|------|------|------|
| 320 | 275 | 225 | 200 | 150 | 100 |

### Deluxe Over/Under
This model is the same as the standard model with a better grade of walnut.

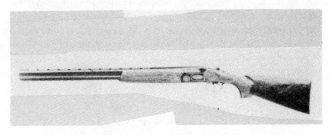

| NIB | Exc. | V.G. | Good | Fair | Poor |
|-----|------|------|------|------|------|
| 375 | 325 | 250 | 225 | 175 | 125 |

### Standard SxS
This is a boxlock folding gun chambered for 20, 28 gauge, and .410. It has double triggers, extractors, and 26" barrels. The finish is blue, and the stock is made of hardwood.

| NIB | Exc. | V.G. | Good | Fair | Poor |
|-----|------|------|------|------|------|
| 225 | 200 | 175 | 150 | 100 | 75 |

### Deluxe SxS
This model is chambered for .410 only and has better wood.

| NIB | Exc. | V.G. | Good | Fair | Poor |
|-----|------|------|------|------|------|
| 250 | 225 | 200 | 175 | 125 | 100 |

## KEBERST INT.
### Kendall International
### Paris, Kentucky

### Keberst Model 1A
This is a high-grade, custom-built bolt-action rifle chambered for .338 Lapua Magnum, .338-416 Rigby, and the .338-06 cartridges. This rifle has a patented muzzle brake and recoil pad system that is quite effective in controlling the sizeable recoil generated by the cartridges for which it was chambered. The barrel is 24", and the finish is matte blue with a camouflaged synthetic stock. It was furnished with a 3X-9X Leupold scope and cleaning tools in a specially fitted case. This rifle was manufactured in 1987 and 1988.

| Exc. | V.G. | Good | Fair | Poor |
|------|------|------|------|------|
| 3500 | 3000 | 2500 | 1800 | 1200 |

## KENDALL, INTERNATIONAL
### Paris, Kentucky
### SEE--Keberst International

## KENDALL, NICANOR
### Windsor, Vermont

### Underhammer Pistol
This boot pistol is chambered for .31-.41 caliber percussion and features a part-octagonal barrel in lengths of 4" to 10". These rather formidable pistols are larger than most of the other underhammers of the era. They were virtually handmade, so they vary from one example to another. Most of them are found with brass trim and maple handles. They are marked "N. Kendall / Windsor, VT." They were manufactured in the 1850's.

| Exc. | V.G. | Good | Fair | Poor |
|------|------|------|------|------|
| 550 | 500 | 400 | 300 | 175 |

## KENO
### Unknown

### Derringer
This obscure little single-shot pocket pistol is rarely encountered. It is chambered for the .22 rimfire cartridge and has a 2.5" barrel. The barrel swings to the side to load, and the frame is made of brass. The barrel is either blued or nickel-plated and marked "Keno." The birdshead grips are walnut. The maker and number manufactured are unknown.

| Exc. | V.G. | Good | Fair | Poor |
|------|------|------|------|------|
| 300 | 250 | 200 | 150 | 100 |

## KEPPLINGER, I. HANNES
### Kufstein, Austria

### 3-S Rifle System
This is a short-action rifle chambered for all popular American and European cartridges. The major parts are constructed of a high-strength alloy, and it features a de-cocking lever that allows manual cocking and de-cocking of the firing-pin spring. The barrel is 23" in length, and the detachable magazine holds 3 rounds. This is essentially a custom-built gun and is rarely encountered on the market. The engraving varies with the customer's wishes; and the walnut stock, either full-length Mannlicher style or with a Schnabel forend, is made of the highest-grade wood available. This company does not have an importer at this time. We are not able to evaluate, as there are too few traded. It is listed for reference only.

## KERR
### London, England

### Kerr Revolver
This is a solid-frame revolver that is not really a solid frame. The barrel and the top strap are forged together and screwed to the frame so that the patent held by Adams would not be violated. This revolver is chambered for .44 caliber percussion, and the barrel is 5.5" in length. The unfluted cylinder holds 6 shots, and the lockwork is removable. This revolver has a new-type ramrod mounted under the barrel that was an invention of Kerr's; and the finish is browned, with checkered walnut grips. The frame is marked "Kerr's Patent 648"; and on the reverse side, "London Armoury Bermondsey." The Kerr revolvers were very popular in the British Colonies, and there were also a number sold to the Confederate States that were used during the Civil War. If it

were possible to identify one of the CSA pistols, they would bring a very sizeable premium. They are extremely difficult to identify and verify.

| Exc. | V.G. | Good | Fair | Poor |
|------|------|------|------|------|
| 1500 | 1250 | 1000 | 750 | 500 |

## KESSLER ARMS CORPORATION
### Silver Creek, New York

**Bolt Action Shotgun**
This is an inexpensive shotgun that is chambered for 12, 16, or 20 gauge and has a 26" or 28" full-choke barrel. The gun has a takedown feature and is blued, with a plain walnut stock. It was manufactured between 1951 and 1953.

| Exc. | V.G. | Good | Fair | Poor |
|------|------|------|------|------|
| 100 | 75 | 50 | 30 | 20 |

**Levermatic Shotgun**
This is a lever-action shotgun chambered for 12, 16, and 20 gauge. It has either a 26" or 28" full-choke barrel, a takedown feature, and a plain walnut stock. It was manufactured between 1951 and 1953.

| Exc. | V.G. | Good | Fair | Poor |
|------|------|------|------|------|
| 125 | 100 | 75 | 50 | 25 |

## KETTNER, EDWARD
### Suhl, Germany

**Drilling**
This is a high quality three-barrelled firearm chambered for 12x12 gauge or 16x16 gauge over various metric rifle cartridges. The barrels are 25" in length and feature ejectors, selective triggers, and pop-up rifle sights that appear when the rifle barrel is selected. This gun is deep-relief engraved in the German style and has a high-grade checkered walnut stock. It was manufactured between 1922 and 1939.

| Exc. | V.G. | Good | Fair | Poor |
|------|------|------|------|------|
| 2250 | 2000 | 1750 | 1400 | 950 |

## KIMBALL ARMS COMPANY
### Detroit, Michigan

**Semi-Automatic Pistol**
This is a unique pistol in that it is a delayed blowback-operated semi-automatic pistol chambered for the .30 Carbine cartridge. This model has a 5" or 3.5" barrel and looks very much like a .22 target automatic externally. The design was innovative and utilizes a grooved chamber that holds the cartridge momentarily to aid the delayed blowback action. The pistol, however, had little chance to be successful in its era as the cartridge was designed for a rifle and was not at all efficient in so short a barrel. The military was not interested, and the hunting fraternity was not a fan of the .30 Carbine cartridge. There is supposed to be a .22 Hornet and a .357 Magnum version, and some were actually produced in the Hornet chambering. The pistol was reportedly unsafe and could possibly blow the slide back into the shooter's face. This is supposedly the reason that Kimball Arms was in business from only 1955 to 1958 and that there were only 238 of the pistols manufactured.

| Exc. | V.G. | Good | Fair | Poor |
|------|------|------|------|------|
| 850 | 750 | 650 | 500 | 375 |

## KIMBER OF OREGON, INC.
### Clackamas, Oregon

This company was founded in 1980 and has earned a deserved reputation for re-introducing the very high quality bolt-action sporting rifle.

**Model 82 Classic**
This bolt-action sporting rifle features a Mauser-type action. It is chambered for .22 l.r., .22 Magnum, or the .22 Hornet cartridges. It has a 22" barrel and was furnished without sights. It has a 4-or 5-round magazine. The finish is blued with a select, claro walnut stock that features a checkered steel buttplate. This is a very high quality rimfire rifle that was discontinued in 1988.

| Exc. | V.G. | Good | Fair | Poor |
|------|------|------|------|------|
| 600 | 550 | 500 | 350 | 250 |

**Cascade Model**
This version has a Monte Carlo-type stock. Otherwise, it is similar to the Model 82 Classic.

| Exc. | V.G. | Good | Fair | Poor |
|------|------|------|------|------|
| 650 | 600 | 550 | 400 | 300 |

**Custom Classic Model**
This is a higher-grade version also chambered for the .218 Bee and the .25-20 cartridges. It is also discontinued.

| Exc. | V.G. | Good | Fair | Poor |
|------|------|------|------|------|
| 800 | 725 | 650 | 400 | 300 |

**Mini Classic**
This version has an 18" barrel and was produced in 1988 only.

| Exc. | V.G. | Good | Fair | Poor |
|------|------|------|------|------|
| 510 | 475 | 425 | 300 | 200 |

## Deluxe Grade
This version is similar to the Custom Classic and was introduced in 1989.

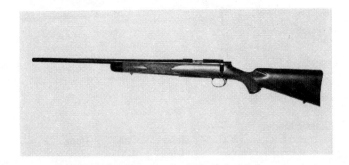

| NIB | Exc. | V.G. | Good | Fair | Poor |
|------|------|------|------|------|------|
| 1000 | 850 | 650 | 550 | 450 | 350 |

## Model 82A Government
This is a military-style target rifle chambered for the .22 l.r. cartridge and designed as a training rifle for the U.S. Army. It has a 25" heavy target-type barrel which features scope-mounting blocks. The finish is matte-blued, with a heavy walnut target stock. It was introduced in 1987.

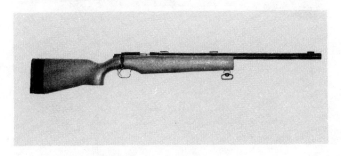

| NIB | Exc. | V.G. | Good | Fair | Poor |
|-----|------|------|------|------|------|
| 575 | 525 | 450 | 375 | 300 | 200 |

## Continental
This is a bolt-action sporting rifle chambered for the .22 l.r., .22 Magnum, and the .22 Hornet cartridges. It features a 20" barrel with open sights and a full-length, walnut, Mannlicher-type stock. The finish is blued. It was introduced in 1987.

| NIB | Exc. | V.G. | Good | Fair | Poor |
|-----|------|------|------|------|------|
| 850 | 750 | 650 | 500 | 400 | 300 |

## Super Continental
This is a deluxe version with very high-grade walnut. It was discontinued in 1988.

| Exc. | V.G. | Good | Fair | Poor |
|------|------|------|------|------|
| 1200 | 1100 | 1000 | 750 | 600 |

## Super America
This is a very high-grade rimfire sporter that is similar to the other Model 82 rifles except that it was offered with the highest quality materials and workmanship available. It was discontinued in 1988.

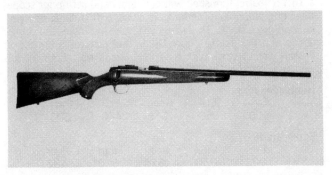

| Exc. | V.G. | Good | Fair | Poor |
|------|------|------|------|------|
| 1000 | 850 | 750 | 500 | 400 |

## Super Grade
This is the successor to the Super America model. It was introduced in 1989.

| NIB | Exc. | V.G. | Good | Fair | Poor |
|------|------|-----|------|------|------|
| 1100 | 1000 | 900 | 750 | 600 | 475 |

## Centennial
This commemorative rifle is moderately engraved and includes a special match barrel, skeleton buttplate, hand-selected walnut stock, and light engraving. It was issued to commemorate the 100th anniversary of the 22 l.r. cartridge. There were 100 manufactured in 1987. As with all commemoratives, it must be NIB with all supplied materials to command collector interest. It was serial-numbered C1-C100.

| NIB | Exc. | V.G. | Good | Fair | Poor |
|------|------|------|------|------|------|
| 2500 | 2250 | 2000 | 1750 | 1500 | 1150 |

## Brownell
There were 500 commemorative rifles produced in honor of the late Leonard Brownell. This model features a very high-grade, Mannlicher-type, full-length walnut stock. It was produced in 1986 only. As with all commemoratives, it must be NIB with all supplied materials to command collector interest.

| NIB | Exc. | V.G. | Good | Fair | Poor |
|------|------|------|-----|------|------|
| 1500 | 1250 | 1000 | 800 | 600 | 500 |

## Model 84 Series
This Series of rifles is similar in quality and configuration to the Model 82 Rimfire Series except that it is chambered for the smaller centerfire cartridges from .17 Remington through the .223 Remington caliber. The cartridges chambered included a number of small-bore wildcat cartridges. This Series features a Mauser-type bolt action, was offered with either a 22" or 24" barrel, has a 5-round magazine, and is blued with deluxe claro walnut stocks. The differences in the various models are basically in the quality of materials and workmanship utilized in their construction. They are as follows:

### Classic Model
| Exc. | V.G. | Good | Fair | Poor |
|------|------|------|------|------|
| 700 | 650 | 600 | 400 | 250 |

### Custom Classic Model
| Exc. | V.G. | Good | Fair | Poor |
|------|------|------|------|------|
| 950 | 800 | 700 | 500 | 350 |

### Deluxe Grade Sporter
| NIB | Exc. | V.G. | Good | Fair | Poor |
|------|------|-----|------|------|------|
| 1200 | 1000 | 850 | 750 | 500 | 400 |

### Continental
| NIB | Exc. | V.G. | Good | Fair | Poor |
|-----|------|-----|------|------|------|
| 975 | 900 | 800 | 700 | 500 | 350 |

### Super Continental
| Exc. | V.G. | Good | Fair | Poor |
|------|------|------|------|------|
| 1300 | 1100 | 850 | 700 | 575 |

**Super America**

| Exc. | V.G. | Good | Fair | Poor |
|------|------|------|------|------|
| 1000 | 925 | 825 | 600 | 450 |

**Super Grade**

| NIB | Exc. | V.G. | Good | Fair | Poor |
|-----|------|------|------|------|------|
| 1250 | 1100 | 1000 | 850 | 650 | 450 |

### Ultra Varmint

This version has a 24" stainless-steel barrel of medium weight. It is chambered for .17 Remington, .221 Remington, and the .223 Remington cartridges. It features a laminated birch stock. It was introduced in 1989.

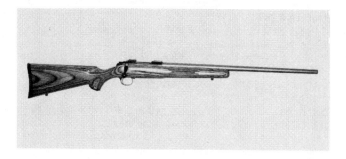

| NIB | Exc. | V.G. | Good | Fair | Poor |
|-----|------|------|------|------|------|
| 1150 | 1000 | 900 | 750 | 550 | 400 |

### Super Varmint

This version is similar to the Ultra Varmint, with a fancy walnut stock. It was introduced in 1989.

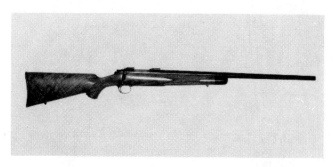

| NIB | Exc. | V.G. | Good | Fair | Poor |
|-----|------|------|------|------|------|
| 1250 | 1100 | 1000 | 850 | 650 | 500 |

### Model 89 Series

This version is also known as the "Big Game Rifle." It features a long action based on the Mauser 98 and the pre-'64 Winchester Model 70 action. It is chambered for the larger hunting calibers between .270 Win. and the .375 H&H cartridges. It is offered with a 22" or 24" barrel. The finish is blued, with deluxe walnut utilized in the stock. The variations differ as to the quality of materials and workmanship used in their construction. The .375 H&H chambering adds an additional $200 to the value.

### Classic Model

| Exc. | V.G. | Good | Fair | Poor |
|------|------|------|------|------|
| 800 | 650 | 550 | 400 | 300 |

### Custom Classic Model

| Exc. | V.G. | Good | Fair | Poor |
|------|------|------|------|------|
| 1000 | 850 | 650 | 450 | 350 |

### Deluxe Grade

| NIB | Exc. | V.G. | Good | Fair | Poor |
|-----|------|------|------|------|------|
| 1400 | 1250 | 1000 | 750 | 650 | 500 |

### Super America

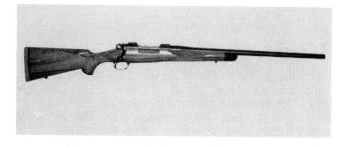

| Exc. | V.G. | Good | Fair | Poor |
|------|------|------|------|------|
| 1100 | 900 | 700 | 500 | 400 |

### Super Grade

| NIB | Exc. | V.G. | Good | Fair | Poor |
|-----|------|------|------|------|------|
| 1500 | 1350 | 1100 | 800 | 700 | 600 |

### Predator

This is a single-shot, bolt-action hunting pistol based on the Model 84 action. It is chambered for the .221 Fireball, .223 Rem., 6mm TCU, 7mm TCU, or the 6x45mm cartridges. It has a 14.75" barrel furnished without sights and set up for scope-mounting purposes. The finish is blued, with a contoured walnut one-piece stock. There are two grades available--the Hunter Grade and the deluxe Super Grade that features a checkered French walnut stock with an ebony forend tip. Both models were manufactured in 1987 and 1988 only.

### Hunter Grade

| Exc. | V.G. | Good | Fair | Poor |
|------|------|------|------|------|
| 800 | 650 | 575 | 400 | 300 |

### Super Grade

| Exc. | V.G. | Good | Fair | Poor |
|------|------|------|------|------|
| 1000 | 850 | 675 | 500 | 400 |

# KING PIN
### Unknown

**Derringer**

This is a diminutive, single-shot pocket pistol chambered for the .22 rimfire cartridge. It has a 2.5" barrel that swings to the side for loading. The construction of this pistol is 100% brass, including the barrel. The birdshead grips are walnut. This pistol was manufactured in the 1880's, but the maker and quantity produced is unknown.

| Exc. | V.G. | Good | Fair | Poor |
|------|------|------|------|------|
| 300 | 250 | 200 | 150 | 90 |

# KIRRIKALE, ENDUSTRISI
### Ankara, Turkey

**Kirrikale Pistol**

This model is a copy of the Walther PP type pistol. It is chambered for the 7.65mm and the 9mm short cartridges. It has a 3.5" barrel and a 6-round magazine. The finish is blue, and the grips are checkered plastic. The slide is marked "MKE"; and on the other side, "Kirrikale Tufek Fb Cal.---." This pistol was imported by Firearms Center in Victoria, Texas, and also by Mandall Shooting Supplies.

| NIB | Exc. | V.G. | Good | Fair | Poor |
|-----|------|------|------|------|------|
| 400 | 350 | 275 | 225 | 150 | 100 |

# KLEPZIG & COMPANY
### San Francisco, California

**Pocket Pistol**

This company produced a pistol that was copied from the Henry Deringer, Philadelphia type. It is chambered for .41-caliber percussion and has a 2.5" barrel, German silver mountings, and a walnut stock. They were manufactured from the late 1850's to early 1860's.

| Exc. | V.G. | Good | Fair | Poor |
|------|------|------|------|------|
| 600 | 500 | 400 | 300 | 200 |

# KOHOUT & SPOLECNOST
### Kdyne, Czechoslovakia

**Mars**

This is a blowback-operated semi-automatic chambered for either the 6.35mm or the 7.65mm cartridges. The 7.56mm is a copy of the 1910 Browning without the grip safety; and the 6.35mm is a copy of the 1906 Browning, also without the grip safety. The quality of these pistols was good, and they are both marked "Mars 7.65 (or 6.35) Kohout & Spol. Kdyne." The finish is blued, with plastic grips that are vertically ribbed with the word "Mars" molded into them. These pistols were manufactured between 1928 and 1945.

| Exc. | V.G. | Good | Fair | Poor |
|------|------|------|------|------|
| 275 | 250 | 200 | 150 | 100 |

**Niva, PZK**

These two pistols are the Mars chambered for the 6.35mm cartridge and marketed under different names.

| Exc. | V.G. | Good | Fair | Poor |
|------|------|------|------|------|
| 275 | 250 | 200 | 150 | 100 |

# KOLB, HENRY M.
### Philadelphia, Pennsylvania

**Baby Hammerless**

This is a solid-framed, folding-trigger, double-action revolver that has a concealed hammer and a 5-shot cylinder. It is chambered for the .22 shot rimfire cartridge and was produced with very few changes between 1892 and 1912 under the ownership of Henry Kolb and Charles Foehl. When Foehl died in 1912, Reginald F. Sedgely took over as a partner; and eventually the company became known as Sedgely in 1930.

| Exc. | V.G. | Good | Fair | Poor |
|------|------|------|------|------|
| 250 | 225 | 200 | 150 | 100 |

**New Baby Hammerless**

This was an important version of this model that was introduced in 1910. It has a hinged breakopen frame and is easier to load. This model has the ribbed barrel and the latch found on the Iver Johnson revolvers. This model is also chambered for the .22 short rimfire cartridge and was produced until the early 1920's.

| Exc. | V.G. | Good | Fair | Poor |
|------|------|------|------|------|
| 250 | 225 | 200 | 150 | 100 |

# KOLIBRI
### SEE--Grabner

# KOMMER, THEODORE WAFFENFABRIK
### Zella Mehils, Germany

**Model 1**

This is a blowback-operated semi-automatic pocket pistol chambered for the 6.35mm cartridge. It is a good quality copy of the 1906 Browning desing. It has an enlarged and knurled muzzle that facilitates takedown and an 8-round magazine. The finish was blued, with rounded grips of checkered plastic. It was introduced in the early 1920's.

| Exc. | V.G. | Good | Fair | Poor |
|------|------|------|------|------|
| 275 | 250 | 200 | 150 | 100 |

**Model 2**

This model is similar to the Model 1, with straight grips instead of the contoured ones and a 7-shot magazine. It was introduced in the early 1920's.

| Exc. | V.G. | Good | Fair | Poor |
|------|------|------|------|------|
| 275 | 250 | 200 | 150 | 100 |

**Model 3**

This model was introduced in 1927 and is similar to the two preceding models, with an 8-round magazine. All three of these pistols are marked "Kommer Pistole 6.35". The maker's name is also found on these pistols. The Models 3 and 4 have the Roman numerals representing their model number after the manufacturer's name.

| Exc. | V.G. | Good | Fair | Poor |
|------|------|------|------|------|
| 250 | 225 | 175 | 125 | 90 |

## Model 4

This model is chambered for the 7.65mm cartridge and is larger than the ones that preceded it. It is a striker-fired copy of the 1910 Browning without the grip safety, and it has a 7-round magazine. This was a good quality pistol, and it is marked "Waffenfabrik Kommer Zella Mehlis Kal. 7.65". The finish is blued, and the grips are checkered plastic. This model was manufactured between 1936 and 1940.

| Exc. | V.G. | Good | Fair | Poor |
|------|------|------|------|------|
| 275 | 250 | 200 | 150 | 100 |

# KORRIPHILIA
### West Germany
### Importer--Osborne's
### Cheboygan, Michigan

## HSP Type 1

This is a very high quality, double-action, semi-automatic pistol chambered for the 7.65mm Luger, .38 Special, 9mm Police, 9mm Luger, 9mm Steyr, 10mm ACP, and the .45 ACP cartridges. The construction is part stainless steel, and the barrel is 4" in length. The finish is either blue or satin stainless. This firearm is very rarely encountered.

| NIB | Exc. | V.G. | Good | Fair | Poor |
|-----|------|------|------|------|------|
| 2400 | 2050 | 1600 | 1000 | 850 | 700 |

## HSP Type II

This version has a 5" barrel; otherwise it is the same as the Type I.

| NIB | Exc. | V.G. | Good | Fair | Poor |
|-----|------|------|------|------|------|
| 2600 | 2250 | 1750 | 1100 | 950 | 750 |

## HSP Type III

This model is a single action; otherwise it is similar to the Type II.

| NIB | Exc. | V.G. | Good | Fair | Poor |
|-----|------|------|------|------|------|
| 2800 | 2500 | 2000 | 1650 | 1250 | 775 |

# KORTH
### West Germany
### Importer--Beeman Precision Arms
### Santa Rosa, California

## Semi-automatic Pistol

This high quality, double-action semi-automatic pistol is chambered for the 9mm Parabellum cartridge and has a 4.5" barrel. It features combat adjustable sights and a 13-shot detachable magazine. It is available with either a matte or a high polished blue finish and has checkered walnut grips. It was introduced in 1985.

| NIB | Exc. | V.G. | Good | Fair | Poor |
|-----|------|------|------|------|------|
| 3000 | 2750 | 2500 | 2000 | 1750 | 1400 |

## Revolver

This is a high quality, precision-made, solid frame, swingout-cylinder revolver chambered for .22 l.r., .22 Magnum, .357 Magnum, and 9mm Parabellum. It has a 6-shot cylinder and barrel lengths of 3", 4", or 6". The cylinders and barrels are interchangeable for caliber conversions, and the finish is either a matte or a high-polished blue. The grips are checkered walnut.

| NIB | Exc. | V.G. | Good | Fair | Poor |
|-----|------|------|------|------|------|
| 2450 | 2100 | 1750 | 1500 | 1200 | 900 |

# KRAG JORGENSEN
### Springfield, Massachusetts

This was the first small-bore, bolt-action repeating rifle that used smokeless powder that was adopted by the U.S. Government as a service rifle. It was adopted as the Model 1892 and was very similar to the rifle being used by Denmark as a service rifle. All of the Krag-Jorgensens were manufactured at the Springfield Armory. There are 11 basic variations of Krag Rifles, and all except one are chambered for the .30-40 Govt. cartridge. They are bolt actions that hold 5 rounds in the unique side-mounted hinged magazine. All of the Krags have walnut stocks and handguards that are oil-finished. They all have dark gray case-hardened receivers and blued barrels. One should be aware that there have been many alterations based on the Krag rifle by many gunsmiths through the years, and the one consistency is that all of these conversions lowered the value of the rifle and rendered it uncollectible. Please be warned.

## Model 1892

There were approximately 24,500 of these rifles produced, dated 1894, 1895, and 1896. They have 30" barrels and are serial numbered from 1--24,562. Nearly all were converted to the later Model 1896, and the original 1st Type is extremely scarce.

### 1st Type

This version is serial numbered from 1--1,500 and is dated 1894 only. It features a wide upper barrel band and an iron one-piece cleaning rod mounted under the barrel. There is no compartment in the butt, and the muzzle is not crowned and appears flat. The upper handguard does not extend over the receiver, and the buttplate is flat, without a compartment. One should be wary of fakes and secure expert appraisal if a transaction is contemplated. Unaltered specimens are extremely rare.

| Exc. | V.G. | Good | Fair | Poor |
|------|------|------|------|------|
| 4000 | 3750 | 3500 | 3000 | 2500 |

### 2nd Type

This model is similar to the 1st Type, with a front barrel band that is cut out in the center and does not appear solid. The serial range is 1,500-- 24,562, and the dates 1894 or 1895 are stamped on the receiver and the stock. Again--be wary of fakes. This is a very rare rifle.

| Exc. | V.G. | Good | Fair | Poor |
|------|------|------|------|------|
| 1800 | 1500 | 1000 | 750 | 600 |

### Altered to 1896 Model

This model encompassed very nearly the entire production run of the Model 1892 Krag rifle. They still bear the dates 1894, 1895, and 1896 on the receiver; but they do not have the cleaning rod, and the hole in the stock has been plugged. The front barrel band was changed, and the butt has a compartment for a cleaning kit. The top handguard covers the receiver, and the buttplate is curved at the bottom.

| Exc. | V.G. | Good | Fair | Poor |
|------|------|------|------|------|
| 300 | 250 | 200 | 150 | 100 |

## Model 1896 Rifle

This Model is similar to the altered Model 1892 and has a 30" barrel with the cleaning kit in the butt. The rear sight was improved, and the receiver is marked "U.S.Model 1896" and "Springfield Armory." The serial range runs from 35,000-- 110,000; and the stock is dated 1896, 1897, and 1898.

There were many of these altered to the later stock configurations--in the field or at the Springfield Armory. These changes would lower the value, and one should secure expert appraisal on this Model.

| Exc. | V.G. | Good | Fair | Poor |
|------|------|------|------|------|
| 450 | 400 | 350 | 275 | 175 |

### Model 1896 Carbine
This Model is similar to the 1896 Rifle, with a 22" barrel and half-length stock held on by one barrel band. There were approximately 19,000 manufactured between 1896 and 1898, and the serial number range is 35,000--90,000. There were many rifles cut to carbine dimensions--be wary of these alterations!

| Exc. | V.G. | Good | Fair | Poor |
|------|------|------|------|------|
| 650 | 600 | 500 | 400 | 250 |

### Model 1895 Carbine (Variation)
This Model is marked "1895" and "1896" on the receiver -- without the word Model. They were produced before the Model 1896 was officially adopted, and they are serial numbered from 25,000--35,000. They are similar to the Model 1896 Carbine, with a smaller safety and no oiler bottle in the butt.

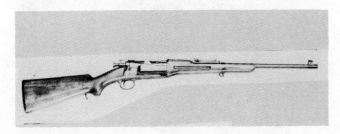

| Exc. | V.G. | Good | Fair | Poor |
|------|------|------|------|------|
| 900 | 700 | 600 | 500 | 400 |

### Model 1896 Cadet Rifle
This is a very rare variation produced for use by the Military Academy at West Point. The dimensions are the same as the 1896 Rifle with a one-piece cleaning rod under the barrel and the 1896-type front band. There were 400 manufactured, and most were altered to standard configuration when they were phased out in 1898.

| Exc. | V.G. | Good | Fair | Poor |
|------|------|------|------|------|
| 3000 | 2500 | 2200 | 1750 | 1250 |

### Model 1898 Rifle
This model is similar to the Model 1896 in appearance except that the receiver is marked "U.S./Model 1898." The bolt handle was modified, and the sights and handguards were improved. There were 330,000 manufactured between 1898 and 1903, and the serial number range is 110,000--480,000.

| Exc. | V.G. | Good | Fair | Poor |
|------|------|------|------|------|
| 450 | 400 | 350 | 250 | 150 |

### Model 1898 Carbine
This model is similar to the rifle, with a 22" barrel and a bar and ring on the left side of the receiver. There were approximately 5,000 manufactured in 1898 and 1899. The serial range is 125,000--135,000. Again, be aware that many of the rifles have been converted to carbine dimensions over the years. When in doubt secure an independent appraisal.

| Exc. | V.G. | Good | Fair | Poor |
|------|------|------|------|------|
| 1500 | 1250 | 1000 | 700 | 500 |

### Model 1898 Carbine 26" Barrel
This was an attempt to satisfy both the infantry and the cavalry. There were 100 manufactured for trial, and the serial range is between 387,000--389,000. Be very wary of fakes.

| Exc. | V.G. | Good | Fair | Poor |
|------|------|------|------|------|
| 3000 | 2500 | 2200 | 1750 | 1250 |

### Model 1898 Practice Rifle
This was the only Krag not chambered for the .30-40 cartridge. It is chambered for the .22 rimfire and was designed as a target-practice rifle. It has a 30" barrel and is identical in exterior appearance to the Model 1898 Rifle. The receiver is marked the same as the standard model--with "Cal.22" added. There were approximately 840 manufactured in 1906 and 1907.

| Exc. | V.G. | Good | Fair | Poor |
|------|------|------|------|------|
| 2000 | 1750 | 1500 | 1100 | 850 |

### Model 1899 Carbine
This was the last of the Krags; and it is similar to the 1898, with the "Model 1899" stamped on the receiver and a 2" longer stock. There were approximately 36,000 manufactured between 1899 and 1902.

| Exc. | V.G. | Good | Fair | Poor |
|------|------|------|------|------|
| 650 | 550 | 500 | 400 | 275 |

### Model 1899 Philippine Constabulary Carbine
There were approximately 8,000 altered to accept the knife bayonet at the Springfield Armory and the Rock Island Arsenal. The Springfield pieces are marked "J.F.C." on the stock. This Model has a 22" barrel, with the full stock of the rifle held on with two barrel bands. One must exercise extreme care as many rifles were altered in a similar manner at later dates.

| Exc. | V.G. | Good | Fair | Poor |
|------|------|------|------|------|
| 1000 | 850 | 750 | 600 | 475 |

### Benicia Arsenal Conversion
In the 1920's the Department of Civilian Marksmanship had a number of Krag rifles converted for their use. These are Model 1898 rifles shortened and fitted with Model 1899 Carbine stocks. These conversions are beginning to be regarded as legitimate variations by some collectors of Krag rifles.

| Exc. | V.G. | Good | Fair | Poor |
|------|------|------|------|------|
| 350 | 300 | 250 | 175 | 100 |

# KRAUSER, ALFRED
## Zella Mehlis, Germany

### Helfricht or Helkra
This is another case where there was more than one name for a single-model pistol. This company actually manufactured four versions of the same pistol under the above names. The pistol was patented in 1920 by Hugo Helfrucht, and it is a blowback-operated, semi-automatic pocket pistol chambered for the 6.35mm cartridge. It has a 2" barrel; and the finish is blued, with checkered plastic grips. The Models 1, 2, and 3 are virtually identical, and the one identifying feature that separates them from the Model 4 is that the slide ends in front of the triggerguard and the barrel protrudes about 1". The safety of these three pistols is also unusual in that it is a lever that rides under the grip with a large checkered head. The Model 4 has no exposed barrel. Otherwise these pistols are rather similar. They were manufactured between 1921 and 1929.

| Exc. | V.G. | Good | Fair | Poor |
|------|------|------|------|------|
| 450 | 400 | 350 | 250 | 150 |

# KRICO
## Stuttgart, West Germany
### Importer--Beeman's Precision Arms
### Santa Rosa, California

## Sporting Rifle

This is a bolt action built on a small Mauser action, that was chambered for the .22 Hornet and the .22 Remington cartridge. It has a 22", 24", or a 26" barrel and is offered with either single or double-set triggers. It has a 4-round box magazine and adjustable sights. The walnut stock is hand-checkered, with a pistol grip. This model was manufactured between 1956 and 1962.

| Exc. | V.G. | Good | Fair | Poor |
|------|------|------|------|------|
| 600 | 550 | 475 | 375 | 275 |

## Sporting Carbine

This model is similar to the rifle, with a 20" barrel and a full-length Mannlicher-style stock.

| Exc. | V.G. | Good | Fair | Poor |
|------|------|------|------|------|
| 625 | 575 | 500 | 400 | 300 |

## Varmint Special Rifle

This version is similar to the Sporting Rifle, with a heavier-weight barrel.

| Exc. | V.G. | Good | Fair | Poor |
|------|------|------|------|------|
| 600 | 550 | 475 | 375 | 275 |

## Model 300

This model is chambered for the .22 rimfire cartridge and has a 23.5" barrel. It has a 5-shot magazine, and the receiver is grooved for mounting a scope. The stock was of select checkered walnut. This rifle was imported until 1988.

| Exc. | V.G. | Good | Fair | Poor |
|------|------|------|------|------|
| 675 | 600 | 550 | 400 | 300 |

## Model 302 and 304

These are similar to the Model 300 but are designated differently. The features are the same. These designations were discontinued in 1986.

| Exc. | V.G. | Good | Fair | Poor |
|------|------|------|------|------|
| 675 | 600 | 550 | 400 | 300 |

## Model 311 Smallbore

This is a bolt-action sporter chambered for the .22 l.r. cartridge. It has a 22" barrel and a 5-or 10-round detachable magazine. This model features double-set triggers and adjustable sights. The finish is blued, with a hand-checkered walnut stock. This model was not imported after 1988.

| Exc. | V.G. | Good | Fair | Poor |
|------|------|------|------|------|
| 325 | 275 | 225 | 150 | 100 |

## Model 320

This Model is similar to the Model 320, with a 19.5" barrel and a full-length Mannlicher-style stock. It was discontinued in 1988.

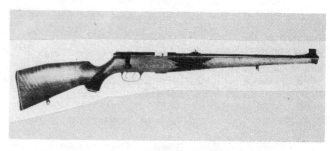

| Exc. | V.G. | Good | Fair | Poor |
|------|------|------|------|------|
| 675 | 600 | 550 | 400 | 300 |

## Model 340

This is a silhouette rifle chambered for the .22 l.r. cartridge. It has a 21" heavy barrel and was furnished without sights. It has a match-grade trigger and a 5-round magazine. The walnut stock is stippled rather than checkered. This model was not imported after 1988.

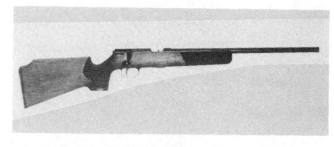

| Exc. | V.G. | Good | Fair | Poor |
|------|------|------|------|------|
| 700 | 625 | 575 | 425 | 325 |

## Model 340 Mini-Sniper

This model is similar to the Model 340, with an overall matte finish and a ventilated handguard. The barrel has a muzzle brake, and the stock was furnished with a raised cheekpiece.

| Exc. | V.G. | Good | Fair | Poor |
|------|------|------|------|------|
| 1000 | 850 | 750 | 500 | 400 |

## Model 340 Kricotronic

This version of the Model 340 is similar to the standard 340, with an electronic trigger. It was not imported after 1988.

| Exc. | V.G. | Good | Fair | Poor |
|------|------|------|------|------|
| 1250 | 1000 | 850 | 600 | 500 |

## Model 400 Sporter

This is a bolt-action Sporter chambered for the .22 Hornet cartridge. It has a 23.5" barrel and was furnished with open sights and a 5-shot magazine. The finish is blued, with a European-styled checkered walnut stock. This model was not imported after 1988.

| Exc. | V.G. | Good | Fair | Poor |
|------|------|------|------|------|
| 700 | 625 | 550 | 425 | 325 |

## Model 420

This version is similar to the Model 400, with a 19.5" barrel and a full-length Mannlicher-styled stock. It features double-set triggers and was discontinued in 1988.

| Exc. | V.G. | Good | Fair | Poor |
|------|------|------|------|------|
| 875 | 750 | 675 | 500 | 400 |

## Model 440

This is a centerfire version of the Model 340 silhouette rifle, that was chambered for the .22 Hornet cartridge. This model was not imported after 1988.

| Exc. | V.G. | Good | Fair | Poor |
|------|------|------|------|------|
| 900 | 800 | 700 | 500 | 375 |

## Model 600 Sporter

This model is a bolt-action Sporter chambered for popular centerfire calibers from 17 Remington to the .308 Winchester cartridges. The barrel is 23.5" in length, and there are open sights and a 3-round magazine. The finish is blued, with a European-style checkered walnut stock. This model was not imported after 1988.

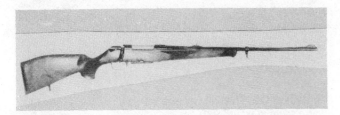

| Exc. | V.G. | Good | Fair | Poor |
|------|------|------|------|------|
| 1100 | 950 | 875 | 700 | 575 |

## Model 620

This version has a 20.5" barrel and a full-length Mannlicher-styled stock. It features double-set triggers.

| Exc. | V.G. | Good | Fair | Poor |
|------|------|------|------|------|
| 1150 | 1000 | 900 | 750 | 600 |

## Model 640 Varmint Rifle

This model is chambered for the .22-250, .222 Remington, and the .223 Remington cartridges and has a 23.5" heavyweight barrel. It features double-set triggers and a high combed Monte Carlo-style stock. The magazine holds 4 rounds; and the finish is blued, with a checkered walnut stock. This model was not imported after 1988.

| Exc. | V.G. | Good | Fair | Poor |
|------|------|------|------|------|
| 1175 | 1025 | 925 | 775 | 625 |

## Model 640 Sniper Rifle

This model has an overall matte finish and was discontinued in 1988.

| Exc. | V.G. | Good | Fair | Poor |
|------|------|------|------|------|
| 1300 | 1100 | 950 | 750 | 600 |

## Model 640 Deluxe Sniper Rifle

This version is chambered for the .223 or .308 cartridges and has a 23" barrel. The select walnut stock features an adjustable cheekpiece and a ventilated handguard. The stock is stippled instead of checkered, and it has a match-grade trigger with a 3-round magazine and a jeweled bolt. This model was also not imported after 1988.

| Exc. | V.G. | Good | Fair | Poor |
|------|------|------|------|------|
| 1500 | 1250 | 1000 | 750 | 650 |

## Model 700 Sporter

This bolt-action Sporter is chambered for the .270 and .30-06 cartridges and has a 23.5" barrel. The rifle features a single-set trigger, open sights, and a 3-round magazine. It has a European-styled hand-checkered walnut stock. This model was discontinued in 1988.

| Exc. | V.G. | Good | Fair | Poor |
|------|------|------|------|------|
| 1000 | 850 | 750 | 600 | 500 |

## Model 720

This version is similar to the Model 700, with a 20.5" barrel and a full-length Mannlicher-styled stock. It also features double-set triggers and was discontinued in 1988.

| Exc. | V.G. | Good | Fair | Poor |
|------|------|------|------|------|
| 1000 | 850 | 750 | 600 | 500 |

## Model 720 Limited Edition

This model is chambered for the .270 cartridge only and features gold-plated trim as well as gold scrollwork on various parts of the gun. The serial number is inlaid in gold. This model was not imported after 1988.

| Exc. | V.G. | Good | Fair | Poor |
|------|------|------|------|------|
| 2250 | 2000 | 1750 | 1400 | 900 |

# KRIDER, J. H.
### Philadelphia, Pennsylvania

## Pocket Pistol

This pistol is a copy of the Philadelphia-style Henry Deringer Pistol. It is chambered for .41 caliber percussion and has a 3" barrel marked "Krider Phila." The lock and barrel are browned, and the stock is walnut. There are German silver mountings. This pistol was manufactured between 1855 and 1865.

| Exc. | V.G. | Good | Fair | Poor |
|------|------|------|------|------|
| 750 | 650 | 500 | 400 | 300 |

## Militia Rifle

This rifled musket is chambered for .58 caliber percussion. It is a single-shot muzzleloader and has a 39" round barrel with a full-length walnut stock, that was fastened by two barrel bands on the rifle and three bands on the musket. The mountings are brass; the lock is case-colored, and the barrel is browned. The lock is marked "Krider." There were only a few hundred manufactured in 1861, and they went to the Philadelphia militia to be used in the Civil War. These were very well-made rifles.

| Exc. | V.G. | Good | Fair | Poor |
|------|------|------|------|------|
| 1750 | 1500 | 1350 | 1000 | 750 |

# KRIEGHOFF, HEINRICH, GUN CO.
### Suhl, Germany

**Krieghoff Lugers are listed in the Luger section.**

Krieghoff guns are very high-grade collectible firearms. There were many options available that make the values fluctuate greatly. We strongly recommend that an individual appraisal be secured when a transaction involving a gun of this nature is contemplated.

## Drillings and Combination Guns
### Plus Model
This three-barrel gun features side-by-side shotgun barrels chambered for 12 or 20 gauge over a rifle barrel chambered for the .222 Remington, .243 Winchester, .270, and the .30-06 cartridges. It was designed primarily for import to the U.S.A. The barrels are 25" in length, and there are double triggers and a boxlock action with automatic ejectors. The gun is lightly engraved and is blued, with a hand-checkered walnut stock. It was introduced in 1988.

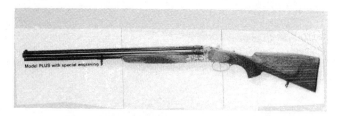

| NIB | Exc. | V.G. | Good | Fair | Poor |
|---|---|---|---|---|---|
| 3800 | 3500 | 3000 | 2500 | 1850 | 1250 |

### Trumpf Model
This Over/Under combination gun is chambered for 12, 16, or 20 gauge over a rifle barrel chambered for many calibers, both European and American. It has a boxlock action, 25" barrels, and double triggers standard. It is engraved and blued, with a hand-checkered walnut stock.

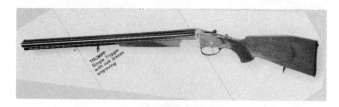

| Exc. | V.G. | Good | Fair | Poor |
|---|---|---|---|---|
| 7000 | 6000 | 4750 | 3200 | 2400 |

### Trumpf Dural
This model is similar to the Trumpf except that it is offered with a lightweight Duraluminum frame.

| Exc. | V.G. | Good | Fair | Poor |
|---|---|---|---|---|
| 7000 | 6000 | 4750 | 3200 | 2400 |

### Neptun Model
This is a very high-grade, heavily engraved sidelock combination Over/Under gun. It has the same basic features as the Trumpf Model but is of a more deluxe nature--both in materials and workmanship. It is available chambered for 12 and 20 gauge and various rifle calibers.

| Exc. | V.G. | Good | Fair | Poor |
|---|---|---|---|---|
| 11750 | 10000 | 7750 | 5000 | 4000 |

### Neptun Dural
This is the sidelock Neptun with a lightweight Duraluminum frame.

| Exc. | V.G. | Good | Fair | Poor |
|---|---|---|---|---|
| 11750 | 10000 | 7750 | 5000 | 4000 |

### Neptun Primus Model
This Model is similar to the Neptun, with elaborate deep-relief engraving and hand-detachable sidelocks.

| Exc. | V.G. | Good | Fair | Poor |
|---|---|---|---|---|
| 15000 | 12500 | 9500 | 7000 | 5250 |

### Neptun Primus Dural
This model is similar to the Neptun Primus Model, with a lightweight Duraluminum frame.

| Exc. | V.G. | Good | Fair | Poor |
|---|---|---|---|---|
| 15000 | 12500 | 9500 | 7000 | 5250 |

## Double Rifles
### Teck Over/Under
This is an Over/Under rifle chambered for various American and metric cartridges. It has 25" barrels with a boxlock action, double triggers, and extractors. This gun features the Kersten double crossbolt and double underlug locking system. It has express sights and a checkered walnut stock. Popular calibers would be worth a premium.

| Exc. | V.G. | Good | Fair | Poor |
|---|---|---|---|---|
| 7500 | 6500 | 5000 | 3750 | 3000 |

### Ulm Model
This Model is a more deluxe sidelock version of the Teck. There are many options available that make values fluctuate. Individual appraisal is recommended.

| Exc. | V.G. | Good | Fair | Poor |
|---|---|---|---|---|
| 12500 | 10000 | 8000 | 6750 | 5000 |

### Ulm Primus
This is a generally higher-grade version of the Ulm with hand-detachable sidelocks.

| Exc. | V.G. | Good | Fair | Poor |
|---|---|---|---|---|
| 15000 | 12500 | 10000 | 7500 | 6000 |

### Model 32 Standard
This is an Over/Under boxlock shotgun chambered for 12, 20, and 28 gauge and .410. It has barrel lengths from 26.5" to 32". It features a single-selective trigger and automatic ejectors. The finish is blued, with a select walnut stock. This Model was discontinued in 1980.
28 Gauge or .410 Two-Barrel Set--Add 50 Percent.

| Exc. | V.G. | Good | Fair | Poor |
|---|---|---|---|---|
| 2000 | 1750 | 1500 | 1000 | 750 |

### Model 32 Single-Barrel Trap Gun
The specifications for this Model are similar to the Model 32 Standard except that it is offered with a single 32" to 34" barrel only.

| Exc. | V.G. | Good | Fair | Poor |
|---|---|---|---|---|
| 1750 | 1400 | 1100 | 750 | 600 |

### KS-5 Single-Barrel Trap Gun
This shotgun is chambered for 12 gauge only, with screw-in choke tubes available as an option, and a 32" or 34" barrel with an adjustable rib and trigger. The finish is blued, with a select walnut stock. It was introduced in 1985.
Screw-In Chokes--Add $350.

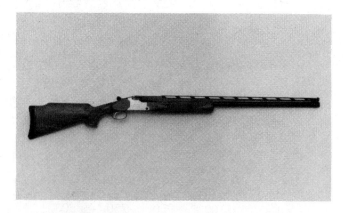

| NIB | Exc. | V.G. | Good | Fair | Poor |
|---|---|---|---|---|---|
| 2900 | 2550 | 2000 | 1550 | 1000 | 700 |

### KS-5 Special
This model is similar to the KS-5, but it is cased and comes with an adjustable comb stock.

| NIB | Exc. | V.G. | Good | Fair | Poor |
|---|---|---|---|---|---|
| 3800 | 3250 | 2750 | 2250 | 1750 | 1100 |

## K-80 Trap Gun

This is a 12-gauge competition shotgun that is available as either an Over/Under or a single-barrel shotgun. It is offered with barrel lengths from 30" to 34". The standard finish is blued, with a silver receiver. There are three options available in addition to the standard K-80 model. They are the Bavaria, the Danube, and the Gold Target models. These models differ in the amount and type of embellishment only. Values given are for the standard model.

Bavaria model--Add 70%.
Danube model--Add 110%.
Gold Target model--Add 180%.
Standard Model

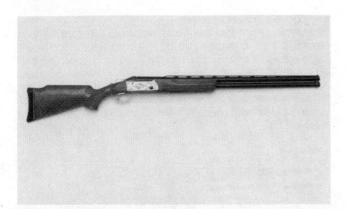

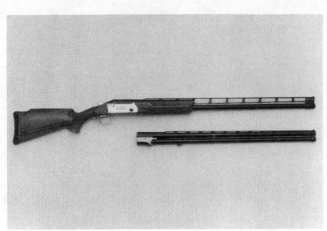

| NIB | Exc. | V.G. | Good | Fair | Poor |
|-----|------|------|------|------|------|
| 5750 | 4800 | 4000 | 3250 | 2500 | 2000 |

## K-80 Sporting Clays

This is a 12-gauge Over/Under with 28" barrels supplied with five screw-in choke tubes. It is furnished with a choice of three different rib dimensions. The stock is made especially for sporting clay shooting. It was introduced in 1988.

Bavaria model--Add 70 Percent.
Danube model--Add 110 Percent.
Gold Target model--Add 180 Percent.

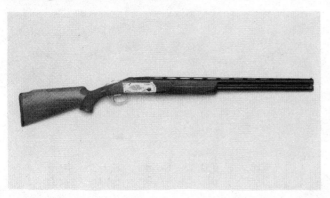

**Standard Model**

| NIB | Exc. | V.G. | Good | Fair | Poor |
|-----|------|------|------|------|------|
| 5800 | 4850 | 4000 | 3250 | 2500 | 2000 |

## K-80 Skeet Gun

This model is similar to the other K-80 guns except that it is especially dimensioned for the sport of skeet shooting. It is also available as a four-barrel set chambered for 12, 20, and 28 gauge, as well as .410.

Bavaria model--Add 70 Percent.
Danube model--Add 110 Percent.
Gold Target model--Add 180 Percent.
Four-Barrel Set--Values for all the above doubled.

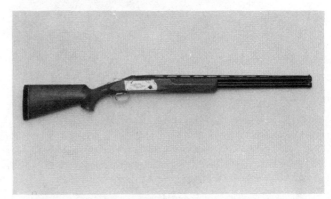

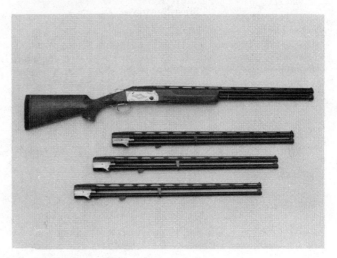

**Standard Model**

| NIB | Exc. | V.G. | Good | Fair | Poor |
|-----|------|------|------|------|------|
| 5200 | 4500 | 3500 | 3000 | 2500 | 2000 |

# KRNKA, KAREL
### Vienna, Austria

Karel Krnka was a very talented firearms inventor born in 1858. He began his career in firearms design as a member of the Austro-Hungarian army. He made many improvements to their service rifle design. After he left the military, he took the job of head engineer with the ill-fated and short-lived "Gatling Gun Co." This company ceased operations in 1890, and then Krnka went to work for the patent office and remained there for a few years. In 1898 he became foreman of the Roth Cartridge Co. and worked with Roth on firearms designs until the death of Roth in 1909. After this he became associated with the Hertenberger Cartridge Company; and finally in 1922 he moved to Czechoslovakia, where he became a firearms designer for the firm of C.Z. He remained at this post until his death in 1926. He recorded his first firearm patent in 1888 for a mechanical repeater with a ring trigger. His best known innovations are the internal butt magazine that is loaded by means of a stripper clip and the rotating locked bolt with internal firing pin. These designs were never actually turned into a mass-marketed pistol but were major contributions in the development of a practical semi-automatic pistol design.

## KROPATSCHEK
### Steyr-Werke
### Steyr, Austria

**Model 1878**
This is a Marine Model rifle chambered for the 11mm cartridge. It has a 32" barrel and a 7 round-magazine. The cleaning rod is mounted on the left side of the full-length stock, that is held on by three barrel bands. This rifle was issued in the white with a polished finish and a walnut stock.

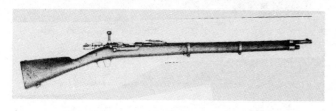

| Exc. | V.G. | Good | Fair | Poor |
|------|------|------|------|------|
| 250 | 225 | 200 | 125 | 75 |

## KUFAHL, G. L.
### Sommerda, Germany

**Kufahl Needle-Fire Revolver**
This revolver was designed and patented in Britain in 1852 by G. L. Kufahl, who tried unsuccessfully to interest a British company in producing it. He then went to the firm of Rheinmettal Dreyse, where a needle-fire gun was produced in 1838. This company manufactured his design. This revolver was chambered for a unique, totally consumed .30-caliber "cartridge." A lead projectile had the ignition percussion cap affixed to its base, with the propellant powder in the rear. The firing pin had to be long enough to penetrate the powder charge and hit the percussion cap. This does not sound efficient, but realize that these were the days before cartridges. This revolver has a 3.2" barrel and an unfluted cylinder that holds 6 shots. It is not bred all the way through but is loaded from the front. The finish is blued, with a modicum of simple engraving and checkered wood grips that protrude all the way over the trigger. The markings are "Fv.V. Dreyse Sommerda."

| Exc. | V.G. | Good | Fair | Poor |
|------|------|------|------|------|
| 1500 | 1250 | 950 | 600 | 450 |

## KYNOCH GUN FACTORY
### Birmingham, England

The firm of Kynoch was known for the manufacture of ammunition, but this was a separate and distinct company that was started by the same man. George Kynoch quit the ammunition company that he founded and started this firearms company in 1888. He occupied the factory formerly used to manufacture the Tranter revolver until William Tranter retired in 1885. This venture was not, however, to be long-lived as George Tranter died in 1890 and the company ceased operations.

**Early Double Trigger Revolver**
This unique revolver is chambered for the .45 Colt cartridge and has a 6" barrel. It features two triggers, one being located under the triggerguard and used to cock the weapon. The second trigger inside of the guard fires the revolver. It has a concealed hammer and a 6-shot fluted cylinder. This model has a hinged top-break frame and features a self-extracting ratchet. This revolver is blued, with checkered walnut grips, and was manufactured in 1885.

| Exc. | V.G. | Good | Fair | Poor |
|------|------|------|------|------|
| 850 | 750 | 600 | 450 | 350 |

**Late Double Trigger Revolver**
This model is an improvement of the early model and is similar except that it is chambered for .32 and .38 caliber as well as the .45. The cocking trigger was modified so that it is enclosed within the lower portion of the triggerguard. There were under 600 of these revolvers manufactured between 1896 and 1890.

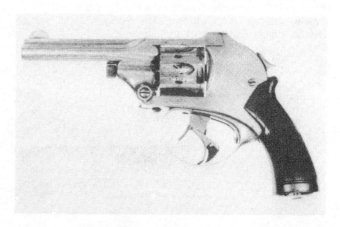

| Exc. | V.G. | Good | Fair | Poor |
|------|------|------|------|------|
| 950 | 850 | 700 | 550 | 450 |

## LAR MFG. CO.
West Jordan, Utah

### Grizzly Mark I
This is a large, single-action semi-automatic pistol that is similar in design and function to the Colt 1911. It is chambered for the .45 Winchester Magnum or the .357 Magnum cartridges. There are conversion units available that will convert the pistol to 10mm, as well as .45 ACP and .357 Magnum. The barrel is 6.5", 8", or 10" in length. The sights are adjustable Milletts, and the safety is of the ambidextrous type. The magazine holds 7 rounds; and the standard finish is parkerized, with checkered rubber grips. Hard chrome plating is available and adds approximately $180 to the cost of a NIB example. The conversion units are valued at approximately $175 per unit. There is also a scope mount available at $88 and a compensator that replaces the barrel bushing for $75. This is a well-made handgun designed for the handgun hunter and silouette shooter. It was introduced in 1984.

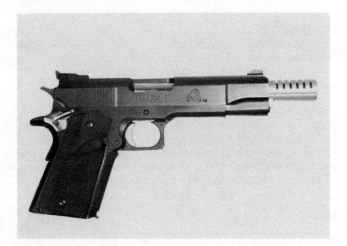

| NIB | Exc. | V.G. | Good | Fair | Poor |
|---|---|---|---|---|---|
| 750 | 675 | 600 | 500 | 400 | 350 |

### Grizzly Mark II
This model is similar to the Mark I without the ambidextrous safety and features a fixed sight. It was manufactured in 1986 only.

| Exc. | V.G. | Good | Fair | Poor |
|---|---|---|---|---|
| 600 | 550 | 450 | 400 | 350 |

## LES, INC.
Skokie, Illinois

### Rogak P-18
This is a very large, locked-breech, double-action semi-automatic pistol chambered for the 9mm Parabellum cartridge. It has a 5.5" barrel and is constructed from stainless steel. This was one of the first 9mm pistols to be called high capacity as it has a double column, 18-round detachable magazine. This pistol was not a commercial success and has been discontinued.

| Exc. | V.G. | Good | Fair | Poor |
|---|---|---|---|---|
| 350 | 300 | 275 | 200 | 150 |

## LABEAU-CORALLY
Liege, Belgium
Importer--Midwest Gun Sport
Zebulon, North Carolina

These are high grade guns that are, to a great extent, custom built; and, therefore, we recommend individual appraisal before purchase.

### Shotguns SxS
### Sologne Model
This is a side-by-side double that is chambered for 12, 16, or 20 gauge. It features an Anson & Deeley boxlock action, with false sideplates optional. It is furnished in barrel lengths from 26" to 30" with various choke combinations. It has automatic ejectors and a single trigger. The select walnut stock is hand-checkered. This is a high-grade double.

| Exc. | V.G. | Good | Fair | Poor |
|---|---|---|---|---|
| 7500 | 6750 | 5000 | 4200 | 3750 |

### Grand Russe Model
This is a more deluxe version of the Sologne, with better walnut and light engraving.

| Exc. | V.G. | Good | Fair | Poor |
|---|---|---|---|---|
| 8500 | 7500 | 6500 | 4500 | 4000 |

### Sidelock Ejector Grade
This high-grade, true sidelock gun is chambered for 12, 16, 20, or 28 gauge, and .410. It is furnished with 26" through 30" barrels, with various choke combinations. It has automatic ejectors and double triggers. This model is heavily engraved with an optional choice of patterns. The stock is of hand-checkered select French walnut.
28 Gauge and .410--Add 10 Percent.

| Exc. | V.G. | Good | Fair | Poor |
|---|---|---|---|---|
| 20000 | 17500 | 12500 | 7500 | 6500 |

### Over/Unders
### Sidelock Over/Under
This model features a true sidelock action and is chambered for 12 or 20 gauge. The barrel length and choke specifications are to the customer's order. The action is patterned after the Boss pattern low-profile sidelock, and the select French walnut is hand-checkered.

| Exc. | V.G. | Good | Fair | Poor |
|---|---|---|---|---|
| 20000 | 17500 | 12500 | 7500 | 6500 |

### Boss Model
This is the Best-grade gun in the Over/Under line and is similar to the Sidelock Over/Under except that it is heavily engraved and has the highest-grade wood available. It is strictly a custom-order proposition and should be individually appraised.

| Exc. | V.G. | Good | Fair | Poor |
|---|---|---|---|---|
| 30000 | 25000 | 20000 | 15000 | 11500 |

### Double Rifles
### Boxlock Ejector Grade
This is a high-grade side-by-side double rifle chambered for the 8x57JRS, 9.3x74R, .375 H&H, and the .458 Win. Mag. The action is an Anson and Deeley boxlock, and the barrels are 25" in length. There is a quarter rib with folding express sights, double triggers, and automatic ejectors. The finish is engraved and blued, with a hand-checkered French walnut stock. This model was not imported after 1988.

| Exc. | V.G. | Good | Fair | Poor |
|---|---|---|---|---|
| 9000 | 8000 | 6000 | 4500 | 3500 |

### Sidelock Ejector Grade
This model is essentially a true sidelock action, but otherwise it is quite similar to the Boxlock gun. The calibers chambered are the same. The general quality of materials and workmanship is higher, and there is more engraving.

| Exc. | V.G. | Good | Fair | Poor |
|---|---|---|---|---|
| 22500 | 18500 | 15000 | 10000 | 7500 |

# LAGRESE
## Paris, France

**Lagrese Revolver**

This is a large ornate revolver chambered for the .43 rimfire cartridge. It has a 6.25" barrel and a 6-shot fluted cylinder. This revolver has no top strap; and the frame, as well as the grip straps, are cast in one piece with the barrel screwed into the frame. It is loaded through a gate and has double-action lockwork. The outstanding feature about this well-made revolver is its extremely ornate appearance. There are more sweeps and curves than could be imagined. It is engraved and blued, with well-figured curved walnut grips. It is marked "Lagrese Bte a Paris" and was manufactured in the late 1860's.

| Exc. | V.G. | Good | Fair | Poor |
|------|------|------|------|------|
| 2000 | 1750 | 1500 | 1150 | 800 |

# LAHTI
## Finland
### SEE--Husqvarna

**Lahti**

This pistol was designed by Aimo Lahti and produced by Valtion, the Finnish State Arms Factory. It was also made by Husqvarna in Sweden, and this model is found in the Husqvarna section of this book. This pistol is a locked-breech semi-automatic that features a bolt accelerator which does much to make this a very reliable firearm. It is chambered for the 9mm Parabellum cartridge and has a 4.7" barrel. The detachable magazine holds 8 rounds; and the finish is blued, with checkered plastic grips. This pistol was designed to function in extreme cold and has a reputation for reliability. The Swedish version known as the M40 is a fine pistol but is not considered on a par with the Finnish version. It was introduced in 1935.

| Exc. | V.G. | Good | Fair | Poor |
|------|------|------|------|------|
| 1250 | 1000 | 800 | 550 | 450 |

# LAMB, H. C. & CO.
## Jamestown, North Carolina

**Muzzle Loading Rifle**

This rifle is chambered for .58 caliber and utilizes the percussion ignition system. It has a 33" barrel and a full-length oak stock held on by two barrel bands. There is a ramrod mounted under the barrel that is made of iron. All other trim is brass, and there is a bayonet lug at the muzzle. This rifle was made for the Confederacy; and the workmanship was crude, as it was on most CSA weapons. The stock is marked "H.C.Lamb & Co.,N.C." There were supposedly 10,000 rifles ordered, but actually there were approximately 250 manufactured between 1861 and 1863. The rarity of the guns of the Confederacy gives them a great deal of collector appeal. One should always be aware that there have been fraudulent examples noted, and a qualified independent appraisal is definitely advisable when dealing with weapons of this nature.

| Exc. | V.G. | Good | Fair | Poor |
|------|------|------|------|------|
| 6500 | 5500 | 4000 | 3250 | 2500 |

# LAMES
## Chiavari, Italy

**Skeet or Trap Grade**

This is an Over/Under shotgun chambered for 12 gauge with either 26" skeet-and-skeet barrels or 30" or 32" full-choked barrels. It has a competition-style wide vent rib and automatic ejectors. The trigger is single-selective, and the finish is blued. The trap gun has a Monte Carlo stock of checkered walnut. Both models feature recoil pads.

| Exc. | V.G. | Good | Fair | Poor |
|------|------|------|------|------|
| 600 | 525 | 450 | 350 | 275 |

**California Trap Grade**

This Over/Under is similar to the standard Trap model, with separated barrels. All other features are the same.

| Exc. | V.G. | Good | Fair | Poor |
|------|------|------|------|------|
| 700 | 600 | 550 | 450 | 325 |

**Field Grade**

This model is similar in design to the standard Trap model, with 3" chambers and barrel lengths of 26", 28", or 30" and a field dimensioned stock. It features various choke combinations and was also available with the separated barrels of the California Trap for an additional 20 percent in cost.

| Exc. | V.G. | Good | Fair | Poor |
|------|------|------|------|------|
| 400 | 350 | 300 | 225 | 150 |

# LANBER ARMAS S.A.
## Vizcaya, Spain
### Lanber Arms of America
### Adrian, Michigan

**Model 844 ST**

This is a 12-gauge Over/Under shotgun with 26" or 28" vent-rib barrels. The chokes vary, and the gun features a single-selective trigger, extractors, and an engraved receiver with a blued finish and a walnut stock. This gun was manufactured until 1986, when the entire line was no longer imported.

| Exc. | V.G. | Good | Fair | Poor |
|------|------|------|------|------|
| 400 | 350 | 300 | 250 | 175 |

**Model 844 MST**

This model is similar to the Model 844 ST except that it is chambered for 3" Magnum and has 30" full-and-modified barrels.

| Exc. | V.G. | Good | Fair | Poor |
|------|------|------|------|------|
| 400 | 350 | 300 | 250 | 175 |

**Model 844 EST**

This model is similar to the others, but it features automatic ejectors.

| Exc. | V.G. | Good | Fair | Poor |
|------|------|------|------|------|
| 450 | 400 | 350 | 300 | 200 |

**Model 844 EST CHR**

This model has automatic ejectors and double triggers. All other features are the same as the EST.

| Exc. | V.G. | Good | Fair | Poor |
|------|------|------|------|------|
| 425 | 375 | 325 | 275 | 175 |

## Model 2004 LCH

This model is an Over/Under chambered for 12 gauge and features 28" vent-rib barrels with screw-in choke tubes. It has a single-selective trigger, automatic ejectors, and an engraved boxlock action that is matte finished, with a hand-checkered walnut stock. This model was also discontinued in 1986.

| Exc. | V.G. | Good | Fair | Poor |
|------|------|------|------|------|
| 750 | 650 | 550 | 475 | 375 |

## Model 2008 LCH and Model 2009 LCH

These are the Trap and Skeet versions of the series. The basic differences are in the barrel lengths and the stock dimensions.

| Exc. | V.G. | Good | Fair | Poor |
|------|------|------|------|------|
| 850 | 750 | 650 | 575 | 475 |

# LANCASTER, CHARLES
## London, England

### 4 Barrelled Pistol

This is a unique pistol for several reasons. It is chambered for the .476 rimfire cartridge and has four 6.25" barrels. The bore has a slightly twisted oval pattern that imparts a spin to the bullet. The barrels are hinged at the bottom and break downward for loading. It is a double-action type lockwork with a very long, difficult trigger pull. The pistol is well made; and the caliber, suitably heavy to insure stopping power. The primary goal was military; and it was successful, seeing action in the Sudan campaigns of 1882 and 1885. This powerful weapon was also popular with big game hunters as a backup sidearm. The finish is blued, with checkered walnut grips. It is marked "Charles Lancaster (Patent) 151 New Bond St. London." This model was introduced in 1881. There are smaller-caliber versions of this pistol with shorter barrels. They are not as well known as the large-caliber version, and the values would be similar as their rarity would be balanced by the desirability of the large-bore models.

| Exc. | V.G. | Good | Fair | Poor |
|------|------|------|------|------|
| 2500 | 2000 | 1600 | 1000 | 750 |

### 2 Barrelled Pistol

This model is similar to the 4-barrelled version, with only two superposed barrels chambered for the .476 rimfire cartridge. The advantage to the 2-barrelled pistol is that it is lighter and better balanced.

| Exc. | V.G. | Good | Fair | Poor |
|------|------|------|------|------|
| 2000 | 1750 | 1300 | 900 | 600 |

### 4 Barrelled Shotgun

This company also produced a shotgun in the 4-barrel configuration. It is chambered for 12 or 16 gauge and has 28" barrels. The gun is, as one would imagine, quite heavy and poorly balanced; and it was not a great success.

| Exc. | V.G. | Good | Fair | Poor |
|------|------|------|------|------|
| 2000 | 1750 | 1300 | 900 | 600 |

### Bolt Action Rifle

This is a high-grade sporting rifle chambered for various different calibers. The barrel is 24" in length; and the finish is blued with a classic-styled, hand-checkered walnut stock. This rifle was discontinued in 1936.

| Exc. | V.G. | Good | Fair | Poor |
|------|------|------|------|------|
| 1250 | 1000 | 800 | 550 | 400 |

# LANG, J.
## London, England

### Percussion Pistol

This pistol is chambered for .60-caliber percussion. It is a single-barrelled, muzzle-loading pistol with a 3.25" barrel. This is essentially a defensive weapon that was very well made, with damascus barrels and an ornate engraved hammer and frame. The grips are finely checkered walnut, and there is a hinged ramrod under the barrel. There is a spring steel belt hook mounted to the left side of the frame. This pistol was manufactured circa 1836 and was marked "J.Lang."

| Exc. | V.G. | Good | Fair | Poor |
|------|------|------|------|------|
| 3000 | 2500 | 2000 | 1500 | 1000 |

### Gas Seal Revolver

This revolver is chambered for the .42-caliber percussion and has a 4.75" barrel. The unfluted cylinder holds 6 shots and is spring-loaded to be forced into the barrel when cocked, in order to obtain the "Gas Seal" feature desired. This revolver was very well made and finished. It is lightly engraved, with a case-colored cylinder and a blued barrel and frame. The grips are finely checkered walnut, and the markings are "J.Lang 22 Cockspur St. London." This type of firearm was the forerunner of later designs such as the Russian Nagant. This revolver was manufactured in the 1850's.

| Exc. | V.G. | Good | Fair | Poor |
|------|------|------|------|------|
| 1750 | 1500 | 1250 | 900 | 550 |

# LANGENHAN, FRIEDRICH
## Zella Mehlis, Germany

### Langenhan Army Model

This is a blowback-operated semi-automatic pistol chambered for the 7.65mm Auto Pistol cartridge. It has a 4" barrel and a detachable magazine that holds 8 rounds. The pistol was made with a separate breech block that is held into the slide by a screw. This feature doomed this pistol to eventual failure as when this screw became worn, it could loosen when firing and allow the breech block to pivot upwards--and the slide would then be propelled rearward and into the face of the shooter. This is not a comforting thought. This pistol was produced and used in WWI only and was never offered commercially. It is marked "F.L.Selbstlade DRGM." The finish is blued, and the grips are molded rubber, with "F.L." at the top.

| Exc. | V.G. | Good | Fair | Poor |
|------|------|------|------|------|
| 250 | 225 | 200 | 150 | 100 |

## Model 2

This is a blowback-operated semi-automatic pistol chambered for the 6.35mm cartridge. It has a 3" barrel and an 8-round detachable magazine. The pistol fires by means of a concealed hammer, and the breech block is separate from the rest of the slide and is held in place by a heavy crossbolt. The finish is blued, and the grips are molded checkered black plastic with the monogram "F.L." at the top. The slide is marked "Langenhan 6.35." This model was manufactured between 1921 and 1936.

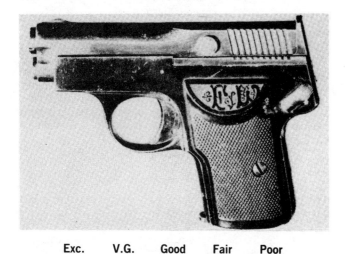

| Exc. | V.G. | Good | Fair | Poor |
|------|------|------|------|------|
| 300 | 250 | 225 | 175 | 125 |

## Model 3

This model is similar to the Model 2 except that it is somewhat smaller. The barrel is 2.25" in length, and the butt is only large enough to house a 5-round detachable magazine. The markings are the same with the addition of "Model III" on the slide. This model was also manufactured until 1936.

| Exc. | V.G. | Good | Fair | Poor |
|------|------|------|------|------|
| 325 | 275 | 250 | 200 | 150 |

# LASALLE
### France
### Manufrance

## Slide Action Shotgun

This slide action is chambered for 12 or 20 gauge and is offered with a 26", 28", or 30" barrel with improved-cylinder, modified, or full chokes. The receiver is alloy, anodized blue; and the vent-rib barrel is blued. The stock is checkered walnut.

| Exc. | V.G. | Good | Fair | Poor |
|------|------|------|------|------|
| 275 | 250 | 200 | 150 | 100 |

## Semi-automatic Shotgun

This is a gas-operated semi-automatic shotgun chambered for 12 gauge only, with the same barrel length and choke combinations as are available on the Slide Action model. The receiver is also alloy, and the stock is checkered walnut.

| Exc. | V.G. | Good | Fair | Poor |
|------|------|------|------|------|
| 325 | 275 | 225 | 175 | 125 |

# LAURONA
### Eibar, Spain
### Importer--Galaxy Imports
### Victoria, Texas

## Model 67G

This is an Over/Under chambered for 12 gauge, with double triggers and 28" vent-rib barrels with extractors. The boxlock action and barrels are blued, and the stock is checkered walnut.

| Exc. | V.G. | Good | Fair | Poor |
|------|------|------|------|------|
| 250 | 225 | 200 | 150 | 100 |

## Model 82

This model is similar to the Model 67 except that it features a double-selective trigger system that would function either as a single or double triggers.

| Exc. | V.G. | Good | Fair | Poor |
|------|------|------|------|------|
| 550 | 500 | 400 | 300 | 225 |

## Model 82 G Super Game

This is a higher-grade model that is chambered for 12 or 20 gauge and features 28" barrels with various chokes. The twin single triggers was offered, as well as automatic ejectors and a good deal of fine scroll engraving. The finish is black chrome-plated, and the stock is hand-checkered select walnut.

| Exc. | V.G. | Good | Fair | Poor |
|------|------|------|------|------|
| 1000 | 950 | 850 | 600 | 450 |

## Model 83 Super Game

This model is similar to the Model 82 except that it features screw-in choke tubes.

| Exc. | V.G. | Good | Fair | Poor |
|------|------|------|------|------|
| 1000 | 800 | 650 | 400 | 300 |

## Model 84 Super Game

This variation has a single-selective trigger and 3" magnum chambers.

| Exc. | V.G. | Good | Fair | Poor |
|------|------|------|------|------|
| 1000 | 800 | 650 | 400 | 300 |

# LAW ENFORCEMENT ORDNANCE CORP.
### Ridgeway, Pennsylvania

## Striker 12

This is a semi-automatic shotgun designed for social encounters. It is chambered for 12 gauge and has an 18.25" cylinder bored barrel. The unique feature about this gun is its 12-round drum magazine. The barrel is shrouded, and the stock folds. A fixed-stock model is also available. This gun was introduced primarily as a law enforcement tool, and the original models had 12" barrels and were legal for law enforcement agencies and Class 3 licensed individuals only. The 18.25" version is legal for private ownership and was introduced in 1986.

| Exc. | V.G. | Good | Fair | Poor |
|------|------|------|------|------|
| 750 | 650 | 525 | 450 | 350 |

# LEBEL
### French State

The Lebel system was invented by Nicolas Lebel in 1886. The French replaced the single-shot Gras Model 1874 rifle with this weapon. This was the first successful small-bore rifle and sent the rest of the European continent into a dash to emulate it. The Lebel system was used until it was made obsolete by the Berthier rifle in the 1890's.

## Model 1886 "Lebel"

The Lebel rifle is chambered for the 8mm Lebel cartridge. It has a 31" barrel and holds 8 shots in a tubular magazine that runs beneath the barrel. This design is very long and heavy and was not in use for very long before being replaced by the more efficient box magazine weapons, such as those from Mauser. This rifle has a two-piece stock with no upper hand guard. It is held on by two barrel bands, and a cruciform bayonet could be fixed under the muzzle. Although this rifle was made obsolete rather quickly, it did have the distinction of being the first successful smokeless-powder small-bore rifle; and there were shortened examples in use until the end of WWII.

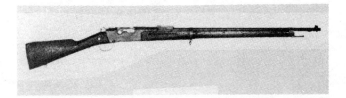

| Exc. | V.G. | Good | Fair | Poor |
|------|------|------|------|------|
| 150  | 125  | 100  | 75   | 50   |

## Revolver Model 1892

This revolver is chambered for an 8mm centerfire cartridge and has a 4.5" barrel with a 6-shot cylinder. It is referred to as a "Lebel," but there is no certainty that Nicolas Lebel had anything to do with its design or production. This revolver is a simple double-action, with a swing-out cylinder that swings to the right side for loading. The design of this weapon is similar to the Italian Model 1889. There is one redeeming feature on this revolver, and that is a hinged sideplate on the left side of the frame that could be swung away after unlocking so that repairs or cleaning of the lockwork could be performed with relative simplicity. The cartridge for which this weapon was chambered was woefully inadequate. This revolver remained in use from its introduction in 1893 until the end of WWII in 1945, mainly because the French never got around to designing a replacement.

| Exc. | V.G. | Good | Fair | Poor |
|------|------|------|------|------|
| 175  | 150  | 125  | 100  | 75   |

## LEE FIREARMS CO.
### Milwaukee, Wisconsin

### Lee Single Shot Carbine

This is a very rare single-shot break-open carbine that pivots to the right side for loading. It is chambered for the .44 rimfire cartridge and has a 21.5" barrel with a hammer mounted in the center of the frame. The carbine has a walnut buttstock but no forearm and is marked "Lee's Firearms Co. Milwaukee, Wisc." There were approximately 450 manufactured between 1863 and 1865. There are very few surviving examples, and one should be wary of fakes.

| Exc. | V.G. | Good | Fair | Poor |
|------|------|------|------|------|
| 1500 | 1250 | 1000 | 750  | 500  |

### Lee Sporting Rifle

This model is similar to the military carbine except that it has a longer octagonal barrel. The barrel length was varied, and there were more of these manufactured. The survival rate appears to have been better than for the Carbine model.

| Exc. | V.G. | Good | Fair | Poor |
|------|------|------|------|------|
| 650  | 550  | 450  | 300  | 175  |

## LEE-ENFIELD
### Middlesex, England
### Royal Small Arms Factory

This was the British service rifle from 1895 through WWII. There are a number of minor variations, and it would behoove the potential collector to avail oneself of the material written on this weapon. We furnish descriptions and values of most of these variations.

### Mark 1

This rifle was introduced on the 11th of November, 1895. Its outward appearance is similar to that of the Lee-Metford Mark 2* Rifle. The method of rifling is different, since smokeless powder had been developed. It is chambered for the .303 British cartridge and has a 30.2" barrel and a full-length stock held on by two barrel bands. There is a cleaning rod mounted under the barrel. It has military-type sights and a box magazine located in front of the triggerguard. The finish is blued, with a walnut stock with sling swivels and a stacking swivel.

| Exc. | V.G. | Good | Fair | Poor |
|------|------|------|------|------|
| 250  | 225  | 175  | 125  | 90   |

### Mark 1*

This version was produced by fitting a .303 British barrel to a Mark 3 Martini-Henry action. It has a 30.2" barrel and features a stripper-clip guide on the receiver. It was introduced in 1899.

| Exc. | V.G. | Good | Fair | Poor |
|------|------|------|------|------|
| 250  | 225  | 175  | 125  | 90   |

### Mark 1**

This model is similar to the Mark 1 except that the cleaning rod was removed. It was introduced in 1899.

| Exc. | V.G. | Good | Fair | Poor |
|------|------|------|------|------|
| 250  | 225  | 175  | 125  | 90   |

### Short Magazine Mark 1 Rifle

This is a carbine-length version that is chambered for the .303 British cartridge and has a 25" barrel with a 10-round, detachable box magazine. Upon its introduction it was intended to be the perfect infantryman's rifle. At first, it was not accepted because its short length was deemed to be detrimental from an accuracy standpoint. It did, however, survive; and the "SMLE" earned the reputation of one of the finest bolt-action service rifles ever produced. The finish is blued, and it has a full-length walnut stock held on by two barrel bands. The stock extended very nearly to the muzzle, creating a snubnose effect with the protruding barrel. It was introduced in 1903.

| Exc. | V.G. | Good | Fair | Poor |
|------|------|------|------|------|
| 225  | 200  | 150  | 100  | 75   |

### Mark 2

This version is similar to the SMLE Mark 1 except that it has a shorter, lighter barrel, improved sights, and a stripper-clip guide on the receiver. It was also introduced in 1903.

| Exc. | V.G. | Good | Fair | Poor |
|------|------|------|------|------|
| 225  | 200  | 150  | 100  | 75   |

### Mark 3

This version is similar to the Mark 1, with the addition of improved sights. It was introduced in 1907.

| Exc. | V.G. | Good | Fair | Poor |
|------|------|------|------|------|
| 225  | 200  | 150  | 100  | 75   |

### Mark 4

This is a Mark 2 rifle converted by adding the features of the Mark 3. It was introduced in 1907.

| Exc. | V.G. | Good | Fair | Poor |
|------|------|------|------|------|
| 200  | 175  | 150  | 100  | 75   |

### No. 4 Mark 1

This version features the addition of a hinged aperture rear sight. The nose cap was removed from the stock. It was introduced in 1942.

| Exc. | V.G. | Good | Fair | Poor |
|------|------|------|------|------|
| 200  | 175  | 150  | 100  | 75   |

### No. 4 Mark 2

This version is similar to the No. 4 Mark 1, with an improved trigger mechanism. It was introduced in 1949.

| Exc. | V.G. | Good | Fair | Poor |
|------|------|------|------|------|
| 200  | 175  | 150  | 100  | 75   |

## No. 5 Mark 1

This version is known as the "Jungle Carbine." It is chambered for the .303 British cartridge and has an 18.5" barrel with a flash-hider on the muzzle. It has a shortened stock, with a rear handguard held on by one barrel band. The stock has a rubber recoil pad. The finish is blued.

Although the weapon was light and compact for carrying, it had an excessive recoil and muzzle blast and was not popular with the soldiers who used it.

| Exc. | V.G. | Good | Fair | Poor |
|------|------|------|------|------|
| 300 | 250 | 200 | 150 | 100 |

# LEE-METFORD
## Great Britain

### Mark 1

This is a bolt-action service rifle chambered for the .303 British cartridge. It was designed by James Lee and incorporated rifling developed by William Metford. This rifling was specifically designed to alleviate the problem of black powder fouling. It has a 30.2" barrel and a 10-round, detachable box magazine located in front of the triggerguard. It features military-type sights and a cleaning rod mounted underneath the barrel. The finish is blued, with a full-length walnut stock held on by two barrel bands. It was introduced in 1888.

| Exc. | V.G. | Good | Fair | Poor |
|------|------|------|------|------|
| 200 | 175 | 150 | 100 | 75 |

### Mark 1*

This version is similar to the Mark 1 except that the safety catch was removed from the cocking piece and a brass disc was inletted into the buttstock for regimental markings. There were a number of internal improvements, as well as the fitting of a different, blade-type front sight. It was introduced in 1892.

| Exc. | V.G. | Good | Fair | Poor |
|------|------|------|------|------|
| 175 | 150 | 125 | 100 | 75 |

### Mark 2

This version has a modified magazine that holds 10 rounds in a double column. It was introduced in 1892.

| Exc. | V.G. | Good | Fair | Poor |
|------|------|------|------|------|
| 175 | 150 | 125 | 100 | 75 |

### Mark 2*

This version has a lengthened bolt, with the addition of a safety catch. It was introduced in 1895.

| Exc. | V.G. | Good | Fair | Poor |
|------|------|------|------|------|
| 200 | 175 | 150 | 100 | 75 |

### Mark 1 Carbine

This version has a 20.75" barrel, and the receiver was modified to accept a stripper-clip guide. It was introduced in 1894.

| Exc. | V.G. | Good | Fair | Poor |
|------|------|------|------|------|
| 200 | 175 | 150 | 100 | 75 |

# LEECH & RIGDON
## Greensboro, Georgia

### Leech & Rigdon Revolver

This Confederate revolver was patterned after the 1851 Colt Navy. It is chambered for .36 caliber percussion and has a 6-shot unfluted cylinder. The 7.5" barrel is part-octagonal and has a loading lever beneath it. The frame is open-topped; and the finish is blued, with brass grip straps and walnut one-piece grips. The barrel is marked "Leech & Rigdon CSA." There were approximately 1,500 revolvers manufactured in 1863 and 1864. These were all contracted for by the Confederacy and are considered to be a prime acquisition for collectors. Be wary of fakes, and trust in qualified independent appraisals only.

| Exc. | V.G. | Good | Fair | Poor |
|------|------|------|------|------|
| 5000 | 4000 | 3500 | 2500 | 2000 |

# LEFAUCHAUX, CASIMER & EUGENE
## Paris, France

### Pinfire Revolver

The pinfire ignition system was invented by Casimir Lefauchaux in 1828 but was not widely used until the 1850's. It consists of a smooth rimless case which contains the powder charge and a percussion cap. A pin protrudes from the side of this case at the rear and when struck by the hammer is driven into the cap, thereby igniting the charge and firing the weapon. The pistols for this cartridge are slotted at the end of the cylinder to allow the pins to protrude and be struck by the downward blow of the hammer. This particular revolver is chambered for .43 caliber and has a 5.25" barrel. The cylinder holds 6 shots; and the finish is blued, with checkered walnut grips. This revolver was manufactured after 1865 and was selected for service by the French military.

| Exc. | V.G. | Good | Fair | Poor |
|------|------|------|------|------|
| 375 | 300 | 275 | 200 | 125 |

# LEFEVER ARMS CO.
## Syracuse, New York

This firm was founded by Dan Lefever, who was a pioneer in the field of breech-loading firearms. This company was founded in 1884, with Lefever as the president. He was referred to as "Uncle Dan" within the firearms industry. He was responsible for many improvements in the double-barrel shotgun design. He developed the automatic hammerless system in the late 1880's. He also developed a compensating action that allowed simple adjustments to compensate for action wear. In 1901 he was forced out of the company and organized another company--the D. M. Lefever, Sons & Company--also in Syracuse. Dan Lefever died in 1906, and his new company went out of business. The original company was acquired by Ithaca in 1916. They continued to produce Lefever guns until 1948.

### Sidelock Shotgun

This is a double-barrel, side-by-side shotgun chambered for 10, 12, 16, or 20 gauge. It was offered with 26", 28", 30", or 32" barrels with various choke combinations. The barrels are either damascus or fluid steel. Damascus guns have become very collectible and in better condition--very good to excellent--can bring nearly the same price as the fluid-steel guns. It features a full sidelock action. Double triggers are standard. The finish is blued, with a checkered walnut stock. There are a number of variations that differ in the amount of ornamentation and the quality of materials and workmanship utilized in their construction. Automatic ejectors are represented by the letter "E" after the respective grade designation. This shotgun was manufactured between 1885 and 1919. We strongly recommend that a qualified appraisal be secured if a transaction is contemplated.
20 Gauge--Add 25 Percent.
Single Selective Trigger--Add 10 Percent.

### DS Grade

| Exc. | V.G. | Good | Fair | Poor |
|------|------|------|------|------|
| 1200 | 1050 | 800 | 600 | 400 |

### DSE Grade

| Exc. | V.G. | Good | Fair | Poor |
|------|------|------|------|------|
| 1600 | 1450 | 1100 | 750 | 500 |

### H Grade

| Exc. | V.G. | Good | Fair | Poor |
|------|------|------|------|------|
| 1400 | 1250 | 950 | 650 | 550 |

### HE Grade

| Exc. | V.G. | Good | Fair | Poor |
|------|------|------|------|------|
| 1800 | 1650 | 1300 | 1000 | 750 |

### G Grade

| Exc. | V.G. | Good | Fair | Poor |
|------|------|------|------|------|
| 1500 | 1300 | 1000 | 750 | 500 |

## GE Grade
| Exc. | V.G. | Good | Fair | Poor |
|------|------|------|------|------|
| 2000 | 1800 | 1500 | 1200 | 850 |

## F Grade
| Exc. | V.G. | Good | Fair | Poor |
|------|------|------|------|------|
| 1750 | 1550 | 1250 | 950 | 650 |

## FE Grade
| Exc. | V.G. | Good | Fair | Poor |
|------|------|------|------|------|
| 2250 | 2000 | 1750 | 1250 | 950 |

## E Grade
| Exc. | V.G. | Good | Fair | Poor |
|------|------|------|------|------|
| 2000 | 1800 | 1550 | 1000 | 800 |

## EE Grade
| Exc. | V.G. | Good | Fair | Poor |
|------|------|------|------|------|
| 2750 | 2450 | 1800 | 1300 | 1000 |

## D Grade
| Exc. | V.G. | Good | Fair | Poor |
|------|------|------|------|------|
| 2500 | 2200 | 1650 | 1050 | 800 |

## DE Grade
| Exc. | V.G. | Good | Fair | Poor |
|------|------|------|------|------|
| 3250 | 2800 | 2250 | 1500 | 1200 |

## C Grade
| Exc. | V.G. | Good | Fair | Poor |
|------|------|------|------|------|
| 4000 | 3400 | 2850 | 2000 | 1500 |

## CE Grade
| Exc. | V.G. | Good | Fair | Poor |
|------|------|------|------|------|
| 6000 | 5000 | 4000 | 3000 | 2250 |

## B Grade
| Exc. | V.G. | Good | Fair | Poor |
|------|------|------|------|------|
| 6000 | 5000 | 4000 | 3000 | 2250 |

## BE Grade
| Exc. | V.G. | Good | Fair | Poor |
|------|------|------|------|------|
| 10000 | 9000 | 6500 | 4500 | 3000 |

## A Grade
| Exc. | V.G. | Good | Fair | Poor |
|------|------|------|------|------|
| 20000 | 16000 | 11000 | 7000 | 3500 |

## AA Grade
| Exc. | V.G. | Good | Fair | Poor |
|------|------|------|------|------|
| 30000 | 22500 | 15000 | 8000 | 4500 |

There was also an Optimus Grade and a Thousand Dollar Grade offered. These are extremely high-grade, heavily ornamented firearms inlaid with precious metals. They are extremely rare, and evaluating them on a general basis is impossible.

## Nitro Special
This is a side-by-side, double-barrel shotgun chambered for 12, 16, or 20 gauge, as well as .410. The barrels were offered in lengths of 26" to 32" with various choke combinations. It features a boxlock action with double triggers and extractors standard. The finish is blued, with a case-colored receiver and a checkered walnut stock. This model was manufactured between 1921 and 1948; and incredible as it may seem, its price at introduction was $29.
20 Gauge--Add 25 Percent.
.410--Add 100 Percent.
Single Selective Trigger--Add 20 Percent.
| Exc. | V.G. | Good | Fair | Poor |
|------|------|------|------|------|
| 450 | 375 | 300 | 250 | 175 |

## A Grade
This is a more deluxe version of the Nitro Special. It was manufactured between 1934 and 1942. The additional values for small gauges and single-selective triggers would apply, as well as an optional automatic ejector which would add 30 percent to the value.

| Exc. | V.G. | Good | Fair | Poor |
|------|------|------|------|------|
| 900 | 775 | 550 | 450 | 375 |

## A Grade Skeet
This is a higher-grade competition version with 26" skeetbored barrels. It was offered standard with a single trigger, automatic ejectors, and a beavertail forearm. The additional values for the small bore options would apply.
| Exc. | V.G. | Good | Fair | Poor |
|------|------|------|------|------|
| 1200 | 1000 | 850 | 725 | 600 |

## Long Range Single Barrel
This is a field-grade single-shot shotgun chambered for all gauges and offered with 26" through 32" barrel lengths. It has a boxlock action with an extractor. The finish is blued, with a checkered walnut stock. It was discontinued in 1942.
| Exc. | V.G. | Good | Fair | Poor |
|------|------|------|------|------|
| 350 | 300 | 250 | 175 | 125 |

## Single Barrel Trap
This is a single-shot, competition-grade gun chambered for 12 gauge with a 30" or 32" full-choke vent-rib barrel. It has a boxlock action and features an automatic ejector. The finish is blued, with a checkered walnut stock. It was discontinued in 1942.
| Exc. | V.G. | Good | Fair | Poor |
|------|------|------|------|------|
| 550 | 450 | 350 | 250 | 175 |

# LEFEVER, D. M., SONS & COMPANY
## Syracuse, New York

"Uncle Dan" Lefever founded the Lefever Arms Company in 1884. In 1901 he was forced out of his company and founded the D. M. Lefever, Sons & Company. He continued to produce high-grade, side-by-side, double-barrel shotguns until his death in 1906, when the company ceased operations. There were approximately 1,200 shotguns of all variations produced during this period, making them extremely rare and difficult to evaluate on a general basis. We list the models and average values but strongly suggest securing qualified appraisal if a transaction is contemplated.

## Lefever Double Barrel Shotgun
This is a side-by-side, double-barrel shotgun chambered for 12, 16, or 20 gauge. It was offered with various-length barrels and choke combinations that were made to order. It features double triggers and automatic ejectors. A single-selective trigger was available as an option. The finish is blued, with a checkered walnut stock. The individual grades differ in the amount of ornamentation and the general quality of the materials and workmanship utilized in their construction. This model was discontinued in 1906.
Single Selective Trigger--Add 10 Percent.
20 Gauge--Add 25 Percent.

### O Excelsior Grade--Extractors
| Exc. | V.G. | Good | Fair | Poor |
|------|------|------|------|------|
| 2400 | 2000 | 1650 | 950 | 700 |

### Excelsior Grade--Auto Ejectors
| Exc. | V.G. | Good | Fair | Poor |
|------|------|------|------|------|
| 2700 | 2500 | 2000 | 1250 | 900 |

### F Grade, No. 9
| Exc. | V.G. | Good | Fair | Poor |
|------|------|------|------|------|
| 3000 | 2750 | 2250 | 1500 | 1100 |

### G Grade--10 Gauge, Damascus Barrels
| Exc. | V.G. | Good | Fair | Poor |
|------|------|------|------|------|
| 3500 | 3100 | 2600 | 2000 | 1350 |

### E Grade, No. 8
| Exc. | V.G. | Good | Fair | Poor |
|------|------|------|------|------|
| 4000 | 3500 | 3000 | 2400 | 1700 |

**D Grade, No. 7**

| Exc. | V.G. | Good | Fair | Poor |
|------|------|------|------|------|
| 4500 | 3900 | 3400 | 2750 | 2000 |

**C Grade, No. 6**

| Exc. | V.G. | Good | Fair | Poor |
|------|------|------|------|------|
| 5000 | 4500 | 3750 | 3000 | 2500 |

**B Grade, No. 5**

| Exc. | V.G. | Good | Fair | Poor |
|------|------|------|------|------|
| 6500 | 5750 | 4800 | 3500 | 3000 |

**AA Grade, No. 4**

| Exc. | V.G. | Good | Fair | Poor |
|------|------|------|------|------|
| 9000 | 7800 | 6500 | 4200 | 2750 |

There is an "Uncle Dan" grade, which is the top-of-the-line version, that features extremely high quality in materials and workmanship and a great deal of ornamentation. This firearm is extremely rare and seldom found in today's market. It is impossible to evaluate it on a general basis.

# LE FORGERON
**Liege, Belgium**
**Importer--Midwest Guns**
**Zebulon, North Carolina**

### Model 6020 Double Rifle
This is a boxlock-actioned side-by-side rifle that is chambered for the 9.3x74R cartridge. It has 25" barrels with double triggers and automatic ejectors. The finish is blued, and the pistol grip stock is checkered walnut.

| Exc. | V.G. | Good | Fair | Poor |
|------|------|------|------|------|
| 5000 | 4500 | 4000 | 3000 | 2500 |

### Model 6040
This Model is simply the Model 6020 with false sideplates. All other specifications are the same.

| Exc. | V.G. | Good | Fair | Poor |
|------|------|------|------|------|
| 5750 | 5200 | 4500 | 3500 | 3000 |

### Model 6030
This Model is a double rifle that has a true sidelock action and is engraved. It has a deluxe French walnut stock.

| Exc. | V.G. | Good | Fair | Poor |
|------|------|------|------|------|
| 9000 | 8000 | 7250 | 5500 | 4200 |

### Boxlock Shotgun
This is a side-by-side, double barrelled shotgun chambered for 20 or 28 gauge. The barrel lengths are optional, as are the choke combinations. This gun has a single-selective trigger and automatic ejectors. It is engraved and blued, with a deluxe French walnut stock.
False Sideplates--Add 20 Percent.

| Exc. | V.G. | Good | Fair | Poor |
|------|------|------|------|------|
| 4500 | 4000 | 3250 | 2250 | 1750 |

### Sidelock Shotgun
This shotgun has similar specifications to the boxlock except that it has a true sidelock action and is generally more deluxe in materials and workmanship.

| Exc. | V.G. | Good | Fair | Poor |
|------|------|------|------|------|
| 11500 | 10500 | 8500 | 6500 | 5500 |

# LE FRANCAIS
**St. Etienne, France**
**Francais D'Armes et Cycles**

### Le Francais Model 28
This is a unique pistol chambered for the 9mm Browning cartridge. It is a large pistol, with a 5" barrel that was hinged with a tip-up breech. This is a blowback-operated semi-automatic pistol that has no extractor. The empty cases are blown out of the breech by gas pressure. The one feature about this pistol that is desirable is that it is possible to tip the barrel breech forward like a shotgun and load cartridges singly, while holding the contents of the magazine in reserve. This weapon has fixed sights and a blued finish, with checkered walnut grips. It was manufactured between 1928 and 1938.

| Exc. | V.G. | Good | Fair | Poor |
|------|------|------|------|------|
| 1250 | 1050 | 850 | 650 | 450 |

### Police Model
This model is a blowback-operated, double action semi-automatic that is chambered for the .32 ACP cartridge. It has a 3.5" barrel and a 7-round magazine. It has the same hinged-barrel feature of the Model 28 and is blued, with fixed sights and molded rubber grips. This model was manufactured between 1914 and 1938.

| Exc. | V.G. | Good | Fair | Poor |
|------|------|------|------|------|
| 800 | 700 | 550 | 375 | 275 |

### Officers Model
This model is also a blowback-operated semi-automatic chambered for the .25 ACP cartridge. It has a 2.5" barrel and a concealed hammer. It has fixed sights, and the finish is blued. The grips are molded rubber. This Model was manufactured between 1914 and 1938.

| Exc. | V.G. | Good | Fair | Poor |
|------|------|------|------|------|
| 300 | 250 | 200 | 150 | 100 |

# LEMAN, H. E.
**Lancaster, Pennsylvania**

### Leman Militia Rifle
This is a .58 caliber percussion muzzleloader that has a 33" round barrel. The stock is full-length and is held on by two barrel bands. There is a ramrod mounted under the barrel. The trim is brass; and the barrel is browned, with a case-colored lock. The lock is marked "H.E.Leman/ Lancaster, Pa." There were approximately 500 manufactured between 1860 and 1864. They are believed to have been used by the Pennsylvania State Militia in the Civil War.

| Exc. | V.G. | Good | Fair | Poor |
|------|------|------|------|------|
| 2000 | 1800 | 1500 | 900 | 650 |

# LE MAT
**Paris, France**

### Le Mat
This revolver has a somewhat unique background that makes it a bit controversial among collectors. It is a foreign-made firearm manufactured in Paris, France, as well as in Birmingham, England. It was designed and patented by an American, Jean Alexander LeMat of New Orleans, Louisiana; and it was purchased for use by the Confederate States of America and used in the Civil War. This is a curious firearm as it is a huge weapon that has two barrels. The top 6.5" barrel is chambered for .42 caliber percussion and is supplied by a 6-shot unfluted cylinder that revolves on a 5", .63-caliber, smooth-bore barrel that doubles as the cylinder axis pin. These two barrels are held together by a front and a rear ring. The rear sight is a notch in the nose of the hammer, and there is an attached ramrod on the side of the top barrel. The weapon is marked "Lemat and Girards Patent, London." The finish is blued, with checkered walnut grips. There were fewer than 3,000 manufactured, of which approximately one half were purchased by the Confederate States of America. They were made between 1856 and 1865.

| Exc. | V.G. | Good | Fair | Poor |
|------|------|------|------|------|
| 5000 | 4000 | 3250 | 2400 | 1750 |

#### Baby LeMat
This model is similar in appearance (though a good deal smaller in size) to the standard model pistol. It is chambered for .32 caliber percussion and has a 4.25" top barrel and a .41-caliber smooth-bore lower barrel. The cylinder is unfluted and holds 9 shots. The barrel is marked "Systeme Le Mat Bte s.g.d.g. Paris." It has British proofmarks and is blued, with checkered walnut grips. This is the scarcest model Le Mat, as there were only an estimated 100 manufactured and used by the Confederate States of America in the Civil War.

| Exc. | V.G. | Good | Fair | Poor |
|------|------|------|------|------|
| 6500 | 5500 | 4500 | 3250 | 2500 |

## LEONARD, G.
### Charlestown, Massachusetts

#### Pepperbox
This is a .31-caliber, four-barrelled pepperbox with a concealed hammer. The barrels are 3.25" in length. There is a ring trigger used to cock the weapon, while a smaller trigger located outside the ring is used to fire the weapon. The barrels on this pistol do not revolve. There is a revolving striker inside the frame that turns to fire each chamber. The barrels must be removed for loading and capping purposes. The frame is iron and blued, with engraving. The rounded grips are walnut. The barrel is stamped "G.Leonard Jr. Charlestown." There were fewer than 200 manufactured in 1849 and 1850.

| Exc. | V.G. | Good | Fair | Poor |
|------|------|------|------|------|
| 1000 | 850 | 650 | 450 | 300 |

## LE PAGE SA.
### Liege, Belgium

#### Pinfire Revolver
This company was in the business of revolver manufacture in the 1850's, producing a .40-caliber pinfire revolver that was very similar to the Lefauchaux and other pinfires of the day. The barrel lengths vary, and the unfluted cylinder holds 6 shots. These pistols are double action and sometimes are found with ornate but somewhat crude engraving. The finish is blued, with wood grips. The quality of these weapons is fair. They were serviceable; but the ammunition created somewhat of a problem, as it is rather fragile and difficult to handle with the protruding primer pin to contend with.

| Exc. | V.G. | Good | Fair | Poor |
|------|------|------|------|------|
| 350 | 300 | 250 | 200 | 125 |

#### Semi-Automatic Pistol
The company was dormant for many years and was revived in 1925 to produce this blowback-operated semi-automatic with an open-topped slide and exposed barrel. It is chambered for the 7.65mm, 9mm Short, and the 9mm Browning Long cartridges. The barrel is 4" in length, and the grip is oversized, has finger grooves, and houses a 12-shot magazine. The pistol was

not a commercial success, and there were not a great many manufactured.

| Exc. | V.G. | Good | Fair | Poor |
|------|------|------|------|------|
| 300 | 250 | 200 | 150 | 100 |

## LIDDLE & KAEDING
### San Francisco, California

#### Pocket Revolver
This revolver was manufactured by Forehand and Wadsworth and stamped with the above name. This company was a dealer in California and had nothing whatever to do with the production of this revolver. It is chambered for the .32 rimfire cartridge and has a 3.25" octagonal barrel and a 5-shot fluted cylinder. The frame is iron; and the finish is blued, with walnut grips. There were a few hundred manufactured between 1880 and 1886. The dealer's name is marked on the top strap.

| Exc. | V.G. | Good | Fair | Poor |
|------|------|------|------|------|
| 300 | 250 | 200 | 150 | 100 |

## LIEGEOISE D ARMES
### Liege, Belgium

#### SxS Boxlock Shotgun
This double-barrelled gun is chambered for 12 and 20 gauge. The barrels are 28" or 30" in length, and the choke combinations are varied. It has a single trigger and automatic ejectors. The action is moderately engraved; and the finish is blued, with a checkered walnut stock.

| Exc. | V.G. | Good | Fair | Poor |
|------|------|------|------|------|
| 750 | 675 | 600 | 450 | 350 |

## LIGNOSE
### Suhl, Germany

#### Einhand Model 2A
This unique design was based on the Chelewski. It allows the shooter to cock and fire this blowback-operated semi-automatic pistol with one hand (Einhand). It is chambered for the 6.35mm cartridge and has a 2" barrel. The magazine holds 6 shots; and the finish is blued, with molded rubber grips marked "Lignose." The triggerguard on this pistol has a reverse curve that fits the finger, and it moves backward to cock the slide. It was manufactured in 1917 by the Bergman Company, but the rights were then sold to Lignose where it was produced after 1921.

| Exc. | V.G. | Good | Fair | Poor |
|------|------|------|------|------|
| 250 | 225 | 200 | 150 | 100 |

### Einhand Model 3A

This model is similar to the Model 2A, with a longer grip that houses a 9-shot magazine. All other specifications are the same as the Model 2A.

| Exc. | V.G. | Good | Fair | Poor |
|------|------|------|------|------|
| 250 | 225 | 200 | 150 | 100 |

### Model 2

This model was similar to the Model 2A, with the extended grip and 9-shot capacity but no provision for one-hand cocking.

| Exc. | V.G. | Good | Fair | Poor |
|------|------|------|------|------|
| 200 | 175 | 150 | 100 | 75 |

## LILLIPUT
### SEE--Menz

## LINDE A.
### Memphis, Tennessee

**Pocket Pistol**

This company manufactured a small, concealable firearm patterned after the Henry Deringer Philadelphia-type pistol. It is chambered for .41-caliber percussion and has a 2.5" barrel, German silver mountings, and a walnut stock. It was manufactured in the 1850's.

| Exc. | V.G. | Good | Fair | Poor |
|------|------|------|------|------|
| 650 | 600 | 500 | 400 | 300 |

## LINDSAY, JOHN P.
### Naugatuck, Connecticut
### Union Knife Company

The Union Knife Co. manufactured the Lindsay 2-shot pistols for the inventor, John P. Lindsay. There are three separate and distinct models as follows.

### 2 Shot Belt Pistol

This pistol is an oddity. It is a single-barrelled, .41-caliber percussion pistol with a double chamber that contains two powder charges and projectiles that are simultaneously fired by two separate hammers. The hammers are released by a single trigger that allows them to fall in the proper sequence. The 5.5" octagonal barrel is contoured into a radical stepped-down shape, and there is a spur trigger. The frame is brass and has scroll engraving. The barrel is blued and is marked "Lindsay's Young America." There were estimated to be fewer than 100 manufactured between 1860 and 1862.

| Exc. | V.G. | Good | Fair | Poor |
|------|------|------|------|------|
| 2000 | 1750 | 1500 | 1150 | 900 |

### 2 Shot Pocket Pistol

This is a smaller version of the Belt Pistol. It is chambered for the same caliber but has a 4" barrel. There were approximately 200 manufactured between 1860 and 1862.

| Exc. | V.G. | Good | Fair | Poor |
|------|------|------|------|------|
| 1500 | 1250 | 1000 | 750 | 500 |

### 2 Shot Martial Pistol

This is a large version of the Lindsay design. It is chambered for .45-caliber smooth-bore and has an 8.5" part-round/part-octagonal barrel. In other respects it is similar to the smaller models. The inventor tried to sell this pistol to the government but was unsuccessful. It was estimated that there were 100 manufactured between 1860 and 1862.

| Exc. | V.G. | Good | Fair | Poor |
|------|------|------|------|------|
| 2500 | 2250 | 1800 | 1450 | 1200 |

## LINS, A. F.
### Philadelphia, Pennsylvania

**Pocket Pistol**

This pistol is chambered for .41 caliber percussion and is a copy of the Henry Deringer pistol. It has a 3" barrel and a walnut stock and is marked "A.Fred. Lins. Philada." This pistol was manufactured between 1855 and 1860.

| Exc. | V.G. | Good | Fair | Poor |
|------|------|------|------|------|
| 850 | 750 | 650 | 450 | 350 |

**Rifled Musket**

This is a single-shot, muzzleloading, percussion rifle chambered for .58 caliber. It has a 39" barrel and a full-length walnut stock held on by three barrel bands. There is an iron ramrod mounted under the barrel. The mountings are iron, and there is a bayonet lug combined with the front sight. The lock is marked "A. Fred. Lins/Philada." This is a rare weapon that was used by Union forces in the Civil War. There were approximately 200 manufactured in 1861 and 1862.

| Exc. | V.G. | Good | Fair | Poor |
|------|------|------|------|------|
| 2000 | 1750 | 1450 | 1100 | 750 |

## LITTLE ALL RIGHT FIREARMS CO.
### Lawrence, Massachusetts

### Little All Right Palm Pistol
This is an unusual-appearing pocket-sized palm pistol. It is chambered for the .22 short rimfire cartridge and has a 1.75" barrel. The cylinder holds 5 shots. The trigger is mounted on the top of the barrel at the muzzle and is hinged and connected to a rod that cocks the concealed hammer, cycles the cylinder, and fires the weapon in double-action fashion. The grip was designed to be fit into the palm and not gripped as in a conventional pistol. The finish is nickel-plated, and the grips are pearl.

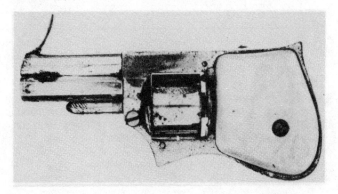

| Exc. | V.G. | Good | Fair | Poor |
|------|------|------|------|------|
| 500 | 400 | 350 | 275 | 175 |

## LJUNGMAN
### Eskilstuna, Sweden
### Carl Gustav

### Ljungman AG-42
This rifle was designed by Eril Eklund and was placed in service with the Swedish military in 1942--less than one year after it was designed. The rifle is a direct gas-operated design with no piston or rod. It is chambered for the 6.5mm cartridge and has a 24.5" barrel with a 10-round detachable magazine. This rifle has military-type sights and a full-length stock and handguard held on by barrel bands. There are provisions for a bayonet. There is also an Egyptian version of this rifle known as the "Hakim" and a Danish version that was manufactured by Madsen. Our AR-15 rifles use the same type of gas system.

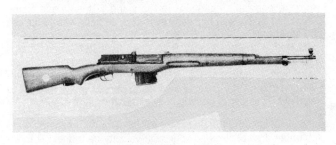

| Exc. | V.G. | Good | Fair | Poor |
|------|------|------|------|------|
| 750 | 675 | 500 | 400 | 275 |

### Egyptian Hakim
| Exc. | V.G. | Good | Fair | Poor |
|------|------|------|------|------|
| 300 | 250 | 200 | 150 | 100 |

## LJUTIC INDUSTRIES
### Yakima, Washington

### Bi-Matic Semi-Automatic
This is a custom-built, gas-operated, semi-automatic shotgun that is known for its low level of felt recoil. It is chambered for 12 gauge and has 26" to 32" barrels choked for either Skeet or Trap. The stock specifications are to the customer's order. There are options available that affect the value, so we recommend an individual appraisal.

| Exc. | V.G. | Good | Fair | Poor |
|------|------|------|------|------|
| 2000 | 1800 | 1500 | 1200 | 900 |

### Dynatrap Single Barrel
This is a single-shot trap gun chambered for 12 gauge. It has a 33" vent-rib full-choke barrel and features a push-button opener and a manual extractor. The stock is made to Trap specifications. There are many options that affect the value; independent appraisal is recommended.

| Exc. | V.G. | Good | Fair | Poor |
|------|------|------|------|------|
| 2000 | 1800 | 1500 | 1200 | 900 |

### Model X-73 Single Barrel
This model has similar features to the Dynatrap, with a very high competition rib. Appraisal is recommended.

| Exc. | V.G. | Good | Fair | Poor |
|------|------|------|------|------|
| 2500 | 2250 | 1750 | 1400 | 1100 |

### Mono Gun Single Barrel
This gun is chambered for 12 gauge and has a 34" vent-rib barrel. It is essentially a custom-order proposition that is available with a standard, as well as a release, trigger. There are many value-affecting options available. Appraisal is recommended.

| NIB | Exc. | V.G. | Good | Fair | Poor |
|-----|------|------|------|------|------|
| 3800 | 3500 | 3000 | 2500 | 2000 | 1750 |

### LTX Model
This is a deluxe version of the Mono Gun with a 33" medium-height vent rib and a high-grade walnut stock with fine hand checkering. Options raise values drastically. Appraisal is recommended.

| NIB | Exc. | V.G. | Good | Fair | Poor |
|-----|------|------|------|------|------|
| 5000 | 4500 | 4000 | 3500 | 2500 | 2000 |

### Space Gun
This is a unique single-barrel gun chambered for 12 gauge, with Trap choking. It has a stock and forearm that reminds one of a crutch in appearance but which allows the shooter to have in-line control with very little felt recoil. The barrel, forearm, and stock are all on one line. There is a recoil pad and a very high ventilated rib.

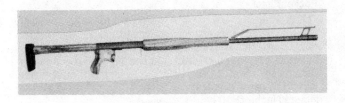

| NIB | Exc. | V.G. | Good | Fair | Poor |
|-----|------|------|------|------|------|
| 3750 | 3450 | 3050 | 2400 | 1750 | 1500 |

### Bi-Gun O/U

This model is an Over/Under double chambered for 12 gauge. It has 30" or 32" vent-ribbed barrels that are separated. The choking is to Trap specifications, and the stock is deluxe hand-checkered walnut.

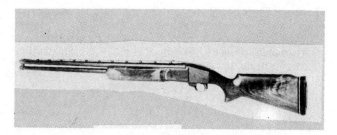

| NIB | Exc. | V.G. | Good | Fair | Poor |
|-----|------|------|------|------|------|
| 10000 | 8500 | 7000 | 6000 | 5000 | 4000 |

### Bi Gun Combo

This model is the Over/Under Bi Gun supplied with a high-ribbed single barrel in addition to the separated Over/Under barrels. It is furnished in a fitted case, and the walnut is of exhibition grade.

| NIB | Exc. | V.G. | Good | Fair | Poor |
|-----|------|------|------|------|------|
| 17000 | 15000 | 11000 | 9000 | 7500 | 6500 |

## LLAMA
### Spain
### SEE Gabilondo

## LOEWE, LUDWIG & CO.
### Berlin, Germany
### SEE--Borchardt

The firm of Ludwig Loewe was noted as the first manufacturer of the famed Borchardt semi-automatic pistol in 1893. They merged with DWM shortly after the introduction of the Borchardt and faded from the fireams scene. Before the introduction of the Borchardt, they manufactured Smith & Wesson "Russian" revolvers under license from Smith & Wesson for sale to the Imperial Russian government. These revolvers are identical to the products of Smith & Wesson except that they are marked "Ludwig Loewe Berlin" on the top of the barrel.

### Loewe Smith & Wesson Russian Revolver

| Exc. | V.G. | Good | Fair | Poor |
|------|------|------|------|------|
| 250 | 225 | 200 | 125 | 75 |

## LOHNER, C.
### Philadelphia, Pennsylvania

### Pocket Pistol

This is a percussion single-shot pistol patterned after the Henry-type derringer. It is chambered for .44 caliber and has a 5" round barrel that is flattened at the top. This model has a walnut stock with a round checkered handle. The mountings are German silver with an engraved iron triggerguard, hammer and lock. The barrel is marked "C.Lohner." This pistol was manufactured in the 1850's.

| Exc. | V.G. | Good | Fair | Poor |
|------|------|------|------|------|
| 850 | 750 | 650 | 450 | 350 |

## LOMBARD, H. C. & CO.
### Springfield, Massachusetts

### Pocket Pistol

This is a single-shot Pocket Pistol chambered for the .22 caliber rimfire cartridge. It has a 3.5" octagonal barrel that swings to the right side for loading. The frame is silver-plated brass, and the barrel is blued. There is a spur trigger, and the square butt has walnut grips. The barrel is marked "H.C.Lombard & Co. Springfield, Mass." There were only a few hundred manufactured in the 1860's.

| Exc. | V.G. | Good | Fair | Poor |
|------|------|------|------|------|
| 350 | 300 | 250 | 150 | 100 |

## LORCIN ENGINEERING CO., INC.
### Riverside, California

### Model L-25

This is a blowback-operated, semi-automatic pocket pistol chambered for the .25 ACP cartridge. It has a 2.5" barrel and a 7-shot magazine. It is finished in various manners, with contoured grips that were designed to better fill the hand. This model was introduced in 1989.

| NIB | Exc. | V.G. | Good | Fair | Poor |
|-----|------|------|------|------|------|
| 85 | 75 | 65 | 50 | 40 | 25 |

## LOWELL ARMS CO.
### SEE--Rollin White Arms Co.

## LOWER, J. P.
### SEE--Slotter & Co.

## LUGERS
### Various Manufacturers

The name "Luger" as applied to this handgun is technically a misnomer. The Luger name was copyrighted by the New York firm of A. F. Stoeger & Co. and should be applied to pistols marked as such and sold by them only. For our purposes, however, we will label it the "Luger" for the sake of simplicity and expedience. The correct name for this pistol is the Parabellum; and it is, along with the Colt's Single Action Army, one of the most recognizable handguns in the world. This unique pistol, identified as German by nearly everyone, actually was conceived by an American. Hugo Borchardt lived in Connecticut and was affiliated with the Sharps Rifle Co. In 1881 when Sharps ceased production, Hugo Borchardt began work on a semi-automatic handgun design. He had no luck marketing his invention in the U.S.A., so he traveled to Europe where he went to work with the firm of Ludwig Loewe in Berlin, Germany.

His pistol became the first commercial semi-automatic pistol to chamber a smokeless-powder high-velocity cartridge. This association lasted for two years and saw the manufacture of approximately 1,100 pistols before a merger with DMK, a firm from Karlsruhe, resulted in the formation of the Deutsche Waffen und Munitions Company known as DWM. Borchardt was affiliated with DWM, and in 1897 the company produced 1,900 of the pistols that bear his name.

The company sought out foreign markets for their products, and in 1897 another expatriate American named Georg Luger was chosen to return to the U.S.A. to demonstrate the Borchardt pistol to the U.S. Army. Georg Luger was a top-flight engineer, who possessed a great deal of ability and drive. He went to work for DWM in 1895. The Americans found problems with the Borchardt design and submitted criticism and recommendations for design changes. DWM assigned this work to Luger, and he began on the course that would make his name live forever. The main problem with the Borchardt design was the ungainly and complex coiled recoil spring. Luger changed this to a simplified leaf spring that connected to the toggle and was located in the butt of the pistol. He raked the grip angle and streamlined a few other points and chambered it initially for the 7.63mm cartridge that was used in the Borchardt.

The Swiss Army was solicited as a potential customer, and they suggested that the pistol be chambered for a less potent cartridge. The 7.65 Parabellum, also known as the .30 Luger, was developed; and the pistol was chambered for it. The Swiss adopted this pistol as their service weapon in 1900, and the Luger Legend was launched.

This handgun has captured the imagination of many collectors and has become extremely popular and, in the case of the rarer variations, quite valuable. There are approximately 300 variations of the Luger pistol. They were manufactured by seven different companies:

1. DWM - Deutsch Waffen und Munitions - Karlsruhe, Germany
2. The Royal Arsenal of Erfurt Germany
3. Simson & Co. - Suhl,Germany
4. Mauser - Oberndorf, Germany
5. Vickers Ltd. - England
6. Waffenfabrik Bern - Bern,Switzerland
7. Heinrich Krieghoff - Suhl,Germany

The "Luger" was commercially manufactured from 1900 until 1943. Some have been observed dated 1945. There were approximately 3,000,000 produced. Ten percent were for contract sales to countries outside of Germany; and the rest saw service in the German military, either in WWI or WWII. The standard Luger was chambered in either 7.65mm Parabellum or 9mm Parabellum. Barrel lengths noted have been 3-3/4", 4", and 4-3/4" on standard commercial and military models; 6" on commercial and military naval models; 8" on commercial and military artillery models; 11-3/4" on the Luger Carbine; and 12"--20" on 1920 commercial models. The rarest of the Luger variations is the .45 ACP model used in the 1907 U.S. Army trials. The most common is either the 1920 Commercial or the WWI DWM military model.

The new collector of Luger pistols is quite fortunate in many respects. First and foremost, there are a number of fine publications available on this fascinating firearm. It is not difficult to garner detailed information. Our bibliography lists many which we feel are quite beneficial. The next advantage is that there are so many different Lugers out there that there seem to be plenty to go around; and the prices, though steadily rising, vary enough so that there seems to be something in everyone's range, within limits. There are also many interesting accessories, stocks, holsters, caliber conversion units, drum magazines, etc. One must excerise caution when collecting Lugers--especially the rarer variations--as many spurious examples have been noted. The difference between a rare Luger and a common variation may be only a proof mark; and this can amount to hundreds, even thousands, of dollars' difference in value. Again--be cautious.

Lugers are classified into models and types for identifying purposes. There are two models: the old model, having the dished toggles and toggle lock; and the new model, with the checkered toggles and no lock. There are three types: the 1900 Type, an old model with a grip safety; the 1906 Type, a new model with a grip safety; and the 1908 Type, a new model with no grip safety. This is admittedly a simplification but is a good rule of thumb for basic breakdown and identification. There are other variations, such as trigger widths, frame lengths, etc.; but this can be learned from specialized publications.

The value of a Luger is determined by ascertaining that the finish is original. All serial numbers must match; the last two digits of the serial number must appear on the small parts of the guns that were so marked. Another number negates collector interest and greatly reduces the value of the pistol. The rarity of the particular model determines the value.

For our purposes, we list the Lugers chronologically within the particular manufacturer. The few later model Lugers made and marketed after the WWII, as well as the custom Lugers on the market, will follow. Then we list the accessories.

## Deutsch Waffen und Munitions
### 1899/1900 Swiss Test Model
This is an old model, 1900 Type, with no stock lug. It has a 4.75" barrel and is chambered for the 7.65mm cartridge. The Swiss Cross in sunburst is stamped over the chamber. The serial range runs to three digits. With less than 100 manufactured and only one known to exist, it is one of the rarest of the Lugers and the first true Luger that was produced. This model is far too rare to estimate an accurate value.

### 1900 Swiss Contract
An old model, 1900 Type, with no stock lug, this model has a 4.75" barrel and is chambered for the 7.65mm cartridge. The Swiss Cross in Sunburst is stamped over the chamber. The military serial number range is 2001--5000; the commercial range, 01--21250. There were approximately 2,000 commercial and 3,000 military models manufactured.
Wide Trigger--Add 20 Percent.

| Exc. | V.G. | Good | Fair | Poor |
|------|------|------|------|------|
| 2650 | 2000 | 1450 | 950 | 700 |

### 1900 Commercial
This is an old model, 1900 Type, with no stock lug. It has a 4.75" barrel and is chambered for the 7.65mm cartridge. The area above the chamber is blank. The serial range is 01--19000, and there were approximately 5,500 manufactured for commercial sale in Germany or other countries. Some have "Germany" stamped on the frame. These pistols were imported into the U.S., and some were even stamped after blueing.

| Exc. | V.G. | Good | Fair | Poor |
|------|------|------|------|------|
| 2650 | 2000 | 1450 | 950 | 700 |

### 1900 American Eagle
This is an old model, 1900 Type. with no stock lug. It has a 4.75" barrel and is chambered for the 7.65mm cartridge. The American Eagle Crest is stamped over the chamber. The serial range is between 2000--200000, and there were approximately 11,000--12,000 commercial models marked "Germany" and 1,000 military test models without the commercial import stamp. The serial numbers of this military lot have been estimated at between 6100--7100.

| Exc. | V.G. | Good | Fair | Poor |
|------|------|------|------|------|
| 2400 | 1850 | 1250 | 800 | 600 |

### 1900 Bulgarian Contract

This is an old model, 1900 Type, with no stock lug. It has a 4.75" barrel and is chambered for the 7.65mm cartridge. The Bulgarian crest is stamped over the chamber, and the safety is marked in Bulgarian letters. The serial range is 20000-21000, with 1,000 manufactured. This is a military test model and is quite rare as most were rebarreled to 9mm during the time they were used. Even with the 9mm versions, approximately 10 are known to exist. It was the only variation to feature a marked safety before 1904.

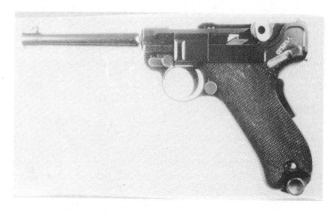

| Exc. | V.G. | Good | Fair | Poor |
|------|------|------|------|------|
| 7500 | 5000 | 3500 | 2250 | 1750 |

### 1900 Carbine

This is an old model, 1900 Type, with a stock lug. It has an 11.75" barrel and is chambered for the 7.65mm cartridge. The Carbines have a gracefully contoured and finely checkered walnut forearm and detachable shoulder stock. The rear sight on this extremely rare variation is a five-position sliding model located on the rear link. The area above the chamber is blank. The serial range is three digits or under, and this may have been a prototype as less than 100 were produced with only one known to exist today. This model is far too rare to estimate an accurate value.

### 1902 Prototype

This is an old model, 1900 Type, with no stock lug. It has a 6" barrel and is chambered for the 7.65mm cartridge. The serial numbers are in the 10000 range with a capital B, and the chamber is blank. The 6" barrel is of a heavy contour, and there were less than 10 manufactured. The rarity of this variation precludes estimating value.

### 1902 Carbine

This is an old model, 1900 Type, with a stock lug. It has an 11.75" barrel and is chambered for the 7.65mm cartridge. The sight has four positions and is silver-soldered to the barrel. A stock and forearm was sold with this weapon. The serial range was 21000--22100 and 23500--24900. There were approximately 2,500 manufactured for commercial sale in and out of Germany. Many were imported into the U.S., but none here have been noted with the "Germany" import stamp.
With Stock--Add 50 Percent.

| Exc. | V.G. | Good | Fair | Poor |
|------|------|------|------|------|
| 6500 | 5000 | 3250 | 2500 | 1950 |

### 1902 Commercial

This is an old model, 1900 Type, with no stock lug. It has a 4" barrel that is thicker in diameter. Among collectors this is referred to as a "Fat" barrel. The area above the chamber is blank. It is chambered for the 9mm cartridge, and the serial numbers fall within the 22300--22400 and the 22900--23500 range. There were approximately 600 manufactured, and the greater part of those noted were marked "Germany" for export purposes.

| Exc. | V.G. | Good | Fair | Poor |
|------|------|------|------|------|
| 5000 | 3750 | 2800 | 2000 | 1500 |

### 1902 American Eagle

This is an old model, 1900 Type, with no stock lug. It has a 4" "Fat" barrel, with the American Eagle crest stamped over the chamber. It is chambered for the 9mm cartridge, and the serial numbers fall within the 22100--22300 and the 22450--22900 range. This model was solely intended for export sales in the U.S.A., and all are marked "Germany" on the frame. There were approximately 700 manufactured.

| Exc. | V.G. | Good | Fair | Poor |
|------|------|------|------|------|
| 5000 | 3750 | 2800 | 2000 | 1500 |

### 1902 American Eagle Cartridge Counter

This is simply a 1902 American Eagle Luger that has the "Powell Indicating Devise" added to the left grip. This is an American invention and consists of a slotted magazine and a numbered window that allows visual access to the number of cartridges remaining. There were 50 lugers altered in this way at the request of the U.S. Board of Ordnance, for U.S. Army evaluation. The serial numbers are 22401--22450. Be especially wary of fakes!

| Exc. | V.G. | Good | Fair | Poor |
|------|------|------|------|------|
| 15000 | 10000 | 7500 | 4000 | 3000 |

### 1902 Presentation Carbine

This is an old model, 1900 Type, with a stock lug. It has an 11.75" barrel and is chambered for the 7.65mm cartridge. These carbines have the initials of the owner gold-inlaid above the chamber. They are furnished with a checkered walnut stock and forearm. Only four have been noted in the 9000C serial number range. They have the initials "GL" for **Georg Luger** on the back of the rear toggle. They are too rare to estimate value.

### 1902/06 Carbine (Transitional)

These carbines were made of parts left over from the 1902 series and the new-type toggle assembly. They have 11.75" barrels and are chambered for the 7.65mm cartridge. They have the four-position sliding sight, silver-soldered to the barrel, and a checkered walnut stock and forearm. There were approximately 100 manufactured in the 23600 serial-number range. With Stock--Add 25 Percent.

| Exc. | V.G. | Good | Fair | Poor |
|------|------|------|------|------|
| 9500 | 7500 | 4750 | 3750 | 2800 |

### 1903 Commercial

This is an old model, 1906 Type, transitional with no stock lug. It has a 4" barrel and is chambered for the 7.65mm cartridge. The chamber area is blank. There were approximately 50 manufactured for export to France, serial- numbered 25000--25050. The extractor on this model is marked "CHARGE."

| Exc. | V.G. | Good | Fair | Poor |
|------|------|------|------|------|
| 9500 | 7500 | 4750 | 3750 | 2800 |

### 1904 Navy

This variation has the old model frame and the 1906 transitional toggle assembly. It has a 6" "Fat" barrel and is chambered for the 9mm cartridge. The chamber area is blank, and the extractor is marked "Geladen." The safety is marked "Gesichert." There were approximately 1,500 manufactured in the one- to four-digit serial range, for military sales to the German navy.

| Exc. | V.G. | Good | Fair | Poor |
|-------|-------|------|------|------|
| 13500 | 10000 | 7500 | 5000 | 3250 |

### 1906 Navy Commercial

This is a new model, 1906 Type, with stock lug. It has a 6" barrel and is chambered for the 9mm cartridge. The chamber is blank, and the extractor is marked "Geladin." The safety is marked "Gesichert," and some have the "Germany" export stamp. The proper magazine has a wood bottom with concentric circles on the sides. There were approximately 2,500 manufactured in the 25050--65000 serial range. They were produced for commercial sales in and outside of Germany.

| Exc. | V.G. | Good | Fair | Poor |
|------|------|------|------|------|
| 3500 | 2750 | 1750 | 1200 | 850 |

### 1906 Commercial

This is a new model, 1906 Type, with no stock lug. It has a 4" barrel and is chambered for the 9mm cartridge. The extractor is marked "Geladin," and the area of the frame under the safety in its lower position is polished and not blued. The chamber is blank. There were approximately 4,000 manufactured for commercial sales. Some have the "Germany" export stamp. The serial range is 26500--68000.

| Exc. | V.G. | Good | Fair | Poor |
|------|------|------|------|------|
| 1750 | 1350 | 900 | 650 | 500 |

### 1906 Commercial (Marked Safety)

This model is identical to the 1906 Commercial except that the area of the frame under the safety in its lowest position is marked "Gesichert" and the barrel is 4.75" in length and chambered for the 7.65mm cartridge. There were approximately 750 manufactured, serial-numbered 25050-- 26800.

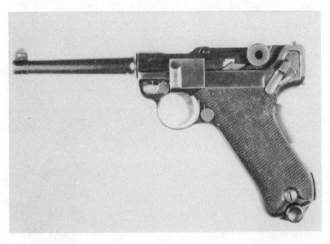

| Exc. | V.G. | Good | Fair | Poor |
|------|------|------|------|------|
| 2500 | 1800 | 1250 | 800 | 650 |

### 1906 American Eagle

This model has a 4" barrel and is chambered for the 9mm cartridge. The chamber area has the American Eagle crest stamped upon it. The extractor is marked "Loaded," and the frame under the safety at its lowest point is polished and not blued. This model has no stock lug. There were approximately 3,000 manufactured for commercial sale in the U.S.A. in the serial range 26500--69000.

| Exc. | V.G. | Good | Fair | Poor |
|------|------|------|------|------|
| 2000 | 1500 | 950 | 650 | 450 |

### 1906 American Eagle (Marked Safety)

This is very similar to the previous model, with a 4.75" barrel chambered for the 7.65mm cartridge. The frame under the safety at its lowest point is marked "Gesichert." There were approximately 750 manufactured in the 25100-- 26500 serial number range.

| Exc. | V.G. | Good | Fair | Poor |
|------|------|------|------|------|
| 2500 | 2000 | 1600 | 1150 | 800 |

### 1906 American Eagle 4.75" barrel

This model is the same as the Marked Safety model with the unmarked polished frame area. There were approximately 8,000 manufactured in the 26500--69000 serial range.

| Exc. | V.G. | Good | Fair | Poor |
|------|------|------|------|------|
| 1850 | 1450 | 850 | 550 | 450 |

### 1906 U.S. Army Test Luger .45 Caliber

This model is acknowledged as the rarest of all the Lugers. The frame is larger than standard, and the barrel is 5" in length. It is chambered for the .45 ACP cartridge and was sent to the U.S. for testing in 1907. The chamber is blank; the extractor is marked "Loaded," and the frame is polished under the safety lever. The trigger on this model has an odd hook at the bottom. There were reportedly only two of these impressive Lugers manufactured. Serial no. 1 has never been located, and it was rumored to have been destroyed after the tests were concluded. Serial no. 2 is in a collection in the U.S.A.

In any condition, Serial no. 1 would be priceless.

### 1906 Swiss Commercial

This variation has a 4.75" barrel and is chambered for the 7.65mm cartridge. The Swiss Cross in sunburst appears over the chamber. The extractor is marked "Geladen," and the frame under the safety is polished. There is no stock lug, and the proof marks are commercial. There were approximately 1,000 manufactured in the 35000--55000 serial- number range.

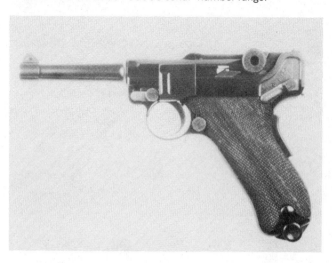

| Exc. | V.G. | Good | Fair | Poor |
|------|------|------|------|------|
| 2750 | 2000 | 1600 | 1150 | 850 |

### 1906 Commercial

This model has a 4.75" barrel and is chambered for the 7.65mm cartridge. It had no stock lug. The chamber area is blank, and the extractor is marked "Geladen." The frame under the safety is polished and unmarked. There were approximately 5,000 manufactured for commercial sales both in and outside of Germany. They will be found in the 26500--69000 serial-number range.

| Exc. | V.G. | Good | Fair | Poor |
|------|------|------|------|------|
| 1750 | 1250 | 900 | 700 | 550 |

### 1906 Swiss Military

This model is identical to the previously mentioned Swiss Commercial. The small Geneva Cross appears on all major parts.

| Exc. | V.G. | Good | Fair | Poor |
|------|------|------|------|------|
| 2400 | 1850 | 1450 | 950 | 650 |

### 1906 Swiss Military Cross in Shield

This is identical to the above variation with the cross replacing the sunburst on the chamber marking. There were 10,215 of both models combined. They are in the 5000-- 15215 serial-number range.

| Exc. | V.G. | Good | Fair | Poor |
|------|------|------|------|------|
| 2500 | 1950 | 1500 | 1000 | 700 |

### 1906 Dutch Contract

This model has a 4" barrel and is chambered for the 9mm cartridge. It has no stock lug, and the chamber is blank. The extractor is marked "Geladen" on both sides, and the safety is marked "RUST" with a curved upward pointing arrow. This pistol was manufactured for military sales to the Netherlands, and a date will be found on the barrel of most examples encountered. The Dutch refinished their pistols on a regular basis and marked the date on the barrels. There were approximately 4,000 manufactured, serial-numbered between 1 and 4000.

| Exc. | V.G. | Good | Fair | Poor |
|------|------|------|------|------|
| 1750 | 1400 | 950 | 700 | 550 |

### 1906 Royal Portugese Navy

This model has a 4" barrel, is chambered for the 9mm cartridge, and has no stock lug. The Royal Portuguese Naval crest, an anchor under a crown, is stamped above the chamber. The extractor is marked "CARREGADA" on the left side. The frame

under the safety is polished. There were approximately 1,000 manufactured with one- to four-digit serial numbers.

| Exc. | V.G. | Good | Fair | Poor |
|------|------|------|------|------|
| 7500 | 6000 | 4500 | 4000 | 3250 |

### 1906 Royal Portuguese Army

This model has a 4.75" barrel and is chambered for the 7.65mm cartridge. It has no stock lug. The chamber area has the Royal Portuguese crest stamped upon it. The extractor is marked "CARREGADA." There were approximately 5,000 manufactured, with one- to four-digit serial numbers.

| Exc. | V.G. | Good | Fair | Poor |
|------|------|------|------|------|
| 1250 | 1000 | 800 | 600 | 450 |

### 1906 Republic of Portugal Navy

This model has a 4" barrel and is chambered for the 9mm cartridge. It has no stock lug, and the extractor was marked "CAR-REGADA." This model was made after 1910, when Portugal had become a republic. The anchor on the chamber is under the letters "R.P." There were approximately 1,000 manufactured, with one- to four-digit serial numbers.

| Exc. | V.G. | Good | Fair | Poor |
|------|------|------|------|------|
| 7500 | 6000 | 4500 | 4000 | 3250 |

### 1906 Brazilian Contract

This model has a 4.75" barrel and is chambered for the 7.65mm cartridge. It has no stock lug, and chamber area is blank. The extractor is marked "CARREGADA," and the frame under the safety is polished. There were approximately 5,000 manufactured for military sales to Brazil. Most saw very rough use, and good- or better-condition specimens are quite scarce. There have been 9mm examples noted, and they may be arsenal-refurbished pistols. The serial numbers are from one to four digits.

| Exc. | V.G. | Good | Fair | Poor |
|------|------|------|------|------|
| 2000 | 1600 | 1200 | 1000 | 850 |

### 1906 Bulgarian Contract

This model has a 4.75" barrel and is chambered for the 7.65mm cartridge. It has no stock lug, and the extractor and safety are marked in cyrillic letters. The Bulgarian crest is stamped above the chamber. Nearly all of the examples located have the barrels replaced with 4" 9mm units. This was done after the later 1908 model was adopted. Some were refurbished during the Nazi era, and these pistols bear Waffenamts and usually mismatched parts. There were approximately 1,500 manufactured, with serial numbers of one to four digits.

| Exc. | V.G. | Good | Fair | Poor |
|------|------|------|------|------|
| 5000 | 4000 | 3200 | 2250 | 1500 |

### 1906 Russian Contract

This model has a 4" barrel and is chambered for the 9mm cartridge. It has no stock lug, and the extractor and safety are marked with cyrillic letters. Crossed Nagant rifles are stamped over the chamber. There were approximately 1,000 manufactured, with one- to four-digit serial numbers; but very few survive. This is an extremely rare variation, and caution should be excercised if purchase is contemplated.

| Exc. | V.G. | Good | Fair | Poor |
|------|------|------|------|------|
| 10000 | 8000 | 6500 | 4000 | 2500 |

### 1906 Navy 1st Issue

This model has a 6" barrel and is chambered for the 9mm cartridge. The safety and extractor are both marked in German, and the chamber area is blank. There is a stock lug, and the unique two-position sliding navy sight is mounted on the rear toggle link. There were approximately 12,000 manufactured for the German navy, with serial numbers of one to five digits. The wooden magazine bottom features concentric rings.

| Exc. | V.G. | Good | Fair | Poor |
|------|------|------|------|------|
| 2850 | 2000 | 1500 | 1100 | 850 |

### 1906 Navy 2nd Issue

This model is identical to the 1st Issue except that the safety position is downward, and on the 1st Issue the lever needs to be upward. Many 1st Issues were altered to function as the 2nd Issue. Alteration to the marking can be noted on these pistols. There were approximately 11,000 2nd Issue navies manufactured, with one- to five-digit serial numbers--some with an "a" suffix. They were produced for sale to the German navy.

| Exc. | V.G. | Good | Fair | Poor |
|------|------|------|------|------|
| 2500 | 1850 | 1250 | 950 | 700 |

### 1908 Commercial

This model marked the first of the 1908 types and the elimination of the grip safety that had been standard on all models up to this point. The 1908 Commercial has a 4" barrel and is chambered for the 9mm cartridge. It has no stock lug, and the chamber area is blank. The extractor and the safety are both marked in German, and many examples are marked with the "Germany" export stamp. There were approximately 9,000 manufactured in the 39000--71500 serial-number range.

| Exc. | V.G. | Good | Fair | Poor |
|------|------|------|------|------|
| 1250 | 1000 | 750 | 600 | 450 |

### 1908 Navy Commercial

This model has a 6" barrel and is chambered for the 9mm cartridge. It has a stock lug, no grip safety, and the characteristic two-position sliding sight mounted on the rear toggle link. The chamber area is blank, and the safety and extractor are both marked. The "Germany" export stamp appears on some examples. There were approximately 1,500 manufactured, in the 44000--50000 serial-number range.

| Exc. | V.G. | Good | Fair | Poor |
|------|------|------|------|------|
| 4500 | 3500 | 2500 | 1750 | 1250 |

### 1908 Navy Military

This model is similar in appearance to the 1908 Commercial Navy but has the "Crown M" military proof. They may or may not have the concentric rings on the magazine bottom. There were approximately 40,000 manufactured, with one- to five-digit serial numbers with an "a" or "b" suffix. These Lugers are quite scarce as many were destroyed during and after WWI.

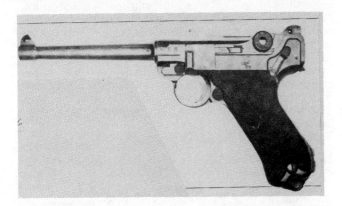

| Exc. | V.G. | Good | Fair | Poor |
|------|------|------|------|------|
| 2750 | 1900 | 1400 | 1000 | 750 |

### 1914 Navy

This model is the same as the 1908 Navy with the exception of a date from 1914--1918 stamped above the chamber. Most noted are dated 1916--1918. There were approximately 40,000 manufactured, with one- to five-digit serial numbers with an "a" or "b" suffix. They are scarce as many were destroyed as a result of WWI.

| Exc. | V.G. | Good | Fair | Poor |
|------|------|------|------|------|
| 2500 | 1850 | 1250 | 950 | 700 |

### 1908 Military 1st Issue

This model was the 1st Luger adopted for service by the German army. It has a 4" barrel and is chambered for the 9mm cartridge. It has no stock lug, and the extractor and safety are both marked in German. The chamber is blank. There were approximately 20,000 manufactured, with one- to five-digit serial numbers--some with an "a" suffix.

| Exc. | V.G. | Good | Fair | Poor |
|------|------|------|------|------|
| 950 | 750 | 600 | 500 | 350 |

### 1908 Military Dated Chamber

This model is quite similar to the 1908 Military 1st Issue except that the date of manufacture from 1910--1913 is stamped over the chamber. This model qualifies as one of the most common variations, with many thousands produced.

| Exc. | V.G. | Good | Fair | Poor |
|------|------|------|------|------|
| 950 | 750 | 600 | 500 | 350 |

### 1914 Military

This model is also quite similar to the 1908 model, except that it has a stock lug and the year 1913--1918 stamped on the chamber. Another very common variation, many thousands were produced and used in WWI.

| Exc. | V.G. | Good | Fair | Poor |
|------|------|------|------|------|
| 1000 | 800 | 650 | 500 | 350 |

### 1913 Commercial

This is an unusual model in that it is a 1908 type with a grip safety. The barrel is 4" in length, and it is chambered for the 9mm cartridge. The chamber is blank, and the extractor and safety are marked in German. The reason for the grip safety is unclear--perhaps it was made to use up existing parts. There were approximately 1,000 manufactured, with serial numbers 71000--72000; but very few have been noted, and it is considered to be quite rare.

| Exc. | V.G. | Good | Fair | Poor |
|------|------|------|------|------|
| 1250 | 1450 | 1100 | 850 | 600 |

### 1914 Artillery

This model has an 8" barrel and is chambered for the 9mm cartridge. It features a nine-position adjustable sight that has a base that is an integral part of the barrel. This model has a stock lug and was furnished with a military-style flat board stock and holster rig (see Accessories). The chamber is dated from 1914--1918, and the safety and extractor are both marked. This model was developed for artillery and machinegun crews; and many thousands were manufactured, with one- to five-digit serial numbers--some have letter suffixes. This model is quite desirable from a collector standpoint and is rarer than its production figures would indicate. After the war many were destroyed as the allies deemed them more insidious than other models, for some reason.

| Exc. | V.G. | Good | Fair | Poor |
|------|------|------|------|------|
| 1750 | 1350 | 1100 | 800 | 600 |

### DWM Double Dated

This model has a 4" barrel and is chambered for the 9mm cartridge. The date 1920 or 1921 is stamped over the original chamber date of 1910--1918, creating the double-date nomenclature. These are arsenal-reworked WWI military pistols and were then issued to the German army and/or police units within the provisions of the Treaty of Versailles. Many thousands of these Lugers were produced.

| Exc. | V.G. | Good | Fair | Poor |
|------|------|------|------|------|
| 900 | 700 | 550 | 400 | 300 |

### 1920 Police Rework

This model is quite similar to the Double Date rework except that the original manufacture date was removed before the rework date was stamped. There were many thousands of these produced.

| Exc. | V.G. | Good | Fair | Poor |
|------|------|------|------|------|
| 800 | 650 | 500 | 350 | 300 |

### 1920 Commercial

This model is probably the most common of the Luger variations. Many thousands were produced. They have barrel lengths from 3.5" through and including 6". They are chambered for both the 7.65mm and the 9mm cartridge. Many are marked "Germany" or "Made in Germany" for export. Others are unmarked and were produced for commercial sale inside Germany. Some of these pistols are military reworks with the markings and the proofmarks removed; others were newly manufactured. The extractors and safety are both marked, and the chamber is blank. The serial-number range is one to five digits, and letter suffixes often appear.

| Exc. | V.G. | Good | Fair | Poor |
|------|------|------|------|------|
| 650 | 550 | 450 | 350 | 300 |

### 1920 Commercial Navy

This model has a 6" barrel and is chambered for the 9mm cartridge. Some have a stock lug; others have been noted without. The chamber area is generally blank, but some have been found with 1914--1918 dates stamped upon them. These were reworked by DWM from Military Navy Lugers after WWI for commercial sales. They are marked "Germany" or "Made in Germany" and were sold by Stoeger Arms, among others. The extractor and safety are both marked, and the unique Navy sight is on the rear toggle link. No one knows exactly how many were produced, but they are quite scarce.

| Exc. | V.G. | Good | Fair | Poor |
|------|------|------|------|------|
| 2200 | 1800 | 1450 | 900 | 700 |

### 1920 Commercial Artillery

This model was the military artillery model that was reworked after WWI by DWM. The chamber is blank in most cases, and the 8" barrel is chambered for the 9mm cartridge. Erfurt-manufactured pistols, as well as DWM-manufactured pistols, were reworked in this manner. The export markings "Germany" or "Made in Germany" are found on most examples. The amount produced is not known, but examples are quite scarce.

| Exc. | V.G. | Good | Fair | Poor |
|------|------|------|------|------|
| 1500 | 1200 | 850 | 650 | 450 |

### 1920 Long Barrel Commercial

This model was made for commercial sale in Germany or to be exported and was so marked. It has a barrel from 10"--24" in length and is chambered for the 7.65mm or the 9mm cartridge. The extractor and safety are both marked, and an artillery model rear sight is used. This model was often built to a customer's specifications. They are very rare, and the number manufactured is not known. One must be extremely cautious of fakes when dealing with this model, and competent appraisal should always be secured.

| Exc. | V.G. | Good | Fair | Poor |
|------|------|------|------|------|
| 2000 | 1600 | 1250 | 750 | 550 |

### 1920 Carbine

This later-type Carbine has an 11.75" barrel and is chambered for the 7.65mm cartridge. The chamber is blank, and the extractor is marked either "Geladen" or "Loaded." The safety is not marked. The Carbine has a checkered walnut forearm and stock, and most have the "Germany" or "Made in Germany" export stamp. There were very few of these Carbines manufactured for commercial sales in and outside of Germany, and they are highly prized by collectors.
With Stock-Add 25 Percent.

| Exc. | V.G. | Good | Fair | Poor |
|------|------|------|------|------|
| 6000 | 4500 | 3500 | 2500 | 1750 |

### 1920 Navy Carbine

This model was built from surplus navy Luger parts. They were produced for commercial sales in and outside of Germany. In appearance they are quite similar to the 1920 Carbine with the distinctive two-position, sliding navy sight on the rear toggle link. Most are marked with the export stamp and have the Naval Military proof marks still in evidence. The safety and extractor are marked, and rarely one is found chambered for the 9mm cartridge. There were very few manufactured, and they are quite rare on today's market.

| Exc. | V.G. | Good | Fair | Poor |
|------|------|------|------|------|
| 2750 | 2250 | 1750 | 1000 | 800 |

### 1920 Swiss Commercial

This model was produced for commercial sale in Switzerland. They have no stock lug and feature a grip safety. They were newly manufactured, as well as being made from surplus military pistol reworked to specifications. The barrel length is from 3.5"--6", and they are chambered for both the 7.65mm and the 9mm cartridge. The Swiss Cross in sunburst is stamped over the chamber, and the extractor is marked "Geladen." The frame under the safety is polished. There were a few thousand produced, with serial numbers in the one- to five-digit range, sometimes with a letter suffix.

| Exc. | V.G. | Good | Fair | Poor |
|------|------|------|------|------|
| 1750 | 1250 | 900 | 700 | 550 |

### 1923 Stoeger Commercial

This model is found with barrel lengths from 3.5" up to 24", chambered for the 7.65mm or the 9mm cartridge. There is a stock lug. The chamber area is either blank or has the American eagle stamped on it. The export stamp and "A.F.Stoeger Inc. New York" is found on the right side of the receiver. The extractor and safety are marked in German or English. This was the model that Stoeger registered with the U.S. Patent office to secure the Luger name, and some examples will be so marked. There were less than 1,000 manufactured, with one- to five-digit serial numbers without a letter suffix. Individual appraisal must be secured on barrel lengths above 6". Be wary as fakes have been noted. The values given here are for the shorter-barrelled models.
Barrel Lengths Over 8"--Add 25 Percent.

| Exc. | V.G. | Good | Fair | Poor |
|------|------|------|------|------|
| 2500 | 2000 | 1500 | 950 | 700 |

## Abercrombie & Fitch Commercial

The noted sporting firm imported 100 Swiss Lugers for commercial sale in the U.S. "Abercrombie & Fitch Co. New York. Mde in Switzerland."--in either one or two lines--is stamped on the top of the barrel. The barrel is 4.75" in length, and there were 49 chambered for 9mm and 51 chambered for the 7.65mm cartridge. This pistol has a grip safety and no stock lug. The Swiss Cross in sunburst is stamped over the chamber. The extractor is marked, but the safety area is polished. The serial range is four digits--some with a letter suffix. This is a very rare and desirable Luger. Be very careful of fakes on models of this type and rarity.

| Exc. | V.G. | Good | Fair | Poor |
|------|------|------|------|------|
| 5000 | 4000 | 3250 | 2250 | 1750 |

## 1923 Commercial

This model has a 3.75" barrel and is chambered for the 7.65mm cartridge. It has a stock lug, and the chamber area is blank. The extractor and safety are both marked in German. These pistols were manufactured for commercial sales in and outside of Germany. There were approximately 18,000 produced, with serial numbers in the 73500--96000 range.

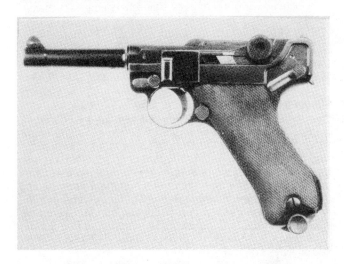

| Exc. | V.G. | Good | Fair | Poor |
|------|------|------|------|------|
| 800 | 600 | 500 | 400 | 300 |

## 1923 Commercial Safe & Loaded

This model is identical to the previous 1923 Commercial except that the extractor and safety are marked in English "Safe" & "Loaded." There were approximately 7,000 manufactured in the 73500--96000 serial-number range.

| Exc. | V.G. | Good | Fair | Poor |
|------|------|------|------|------|
| 1500 | 1200 | 950 | 750 | 500 |

## 1923 Dutch Commercial & Military

This model has a 4" barrel and is chambered for the 9mm cartridge. It has a stock lug, and the chamber area is blank. The extractor is marked in German, and the safety is marked "RUST" with a downward pointing arrow. This model was sold commercially and to the military in the Netherlands. There were approximately 1,000 manufactured in the one- to three-digit serial range, with no letter suffix.

| Exc. | V.G. | Good | Fair | Poor |
|------|------|------|------|------|
| 1500 | 1200 | 950 | 750 | 500 |

## Royal Dutch Air Force

This was the last Luger produced by DWM. In 1930 they were absorbed by Mauser, before this 4,000-unit contract was complete. Mauser completed the contract, but the toggle links were stamped DWM. They bear the Mauser Oberndorf proof mark instead of the nitro proof. These Mauser pistols fall in the 14000 serial range. This model has a 4" barrel and is chambered for the 9mm cartridge. The chamber area is blank. The extractor is marked "Geladen"; the safety, marked "RUST" with an upward pointing arrow. There is no stock lug, and a grip safety was used. There were 4,000 manufactured in the 10100--14100 serial-number range.

| Exc. | V.G. | Good | Fair | Poor |
|------|------|------|------|------|
| 1500 | 1200 | 950 | 750 | 500 |

## Vickers Ltd.
## 1906 Vickers Dutch

This model was ordered from the English firm of Vickers Ltd. by Holland in the 1915-1917 era because at that time there was a state of war between Germany and the Netherlands. This pistol has a 4" barrel and is chambered for the 9mm cartridge. There is no stock lug, and it uses a grip safety. The chamber is blank, and the extractor is marked "Geladen." "Vickers Ltd." is stamped on the front toggle link. The safety is marked "RUST" with an upward pointing arrow. Examples have been found with an additional date as late as 1933 stamped on the barrel. These dates indicate arsenal refinishing and in no way detract from the value of this variation. Arsenal reworks are matte-finished, and the originals are a higher-polished rust blue. There were approximately 10,000 manufactured in the 1--10100 serial-number range.

| Exc. | V.G. | Good | Fair | Poor |
|------|------|------|------|------|
| 2500 | 2000 | 1500 | 950 | 700 |

## Erfurt Royal Arsenal
## 1908 Erfurt

In 1910 the Erfurt Royal Arsenal was commissioned by the German government to begin Luger production. DWM was not able to produce sufficient quantities to keep the armed forces satisfied. The noted characteristic of the Erfurt-produced Luger is the poor finish. Toolmarks are much more in evidence than on the DWM product. The 1908 model has a 4" barrel and is chambered for the 9mm cartridge. It has no stock lug; and the year of manufacture, from 1910--1913, is stamped above the chamber. The extractor and safety are both marked in German, and "ERFURT" under a crown is stamped on the front toggle link. There were many thousands produced as Germany was involved in WWI. They are found in the one-to five-digit serial range, sometimes with a letter suffix.

| Exc. | V.G. | Good | Fair | Poor |
|------|------|------|------|------|
| 700 | 550 | 450 | 350 | 300 |

### 1914 Erfurt Military

This model has a 4" barrel and is chambered for the 9mm cartridge. It has a stock lug and the date of manufacture over the chamber, 1914-1918. The extractor and safety are both marked in German, and the front link is marked "ERFURT" under a crown. The finish on this model is very rough; and as the war progressed in 1917 and 1918, the finish got worse. There were many thousands produced with one- to five-digit serial numbers, some with letter suffixes.

| Exc. | V.G. | Good | Fair | Poor |
|------|------|------|------|------|
| 700 | 550 | 450 | 350 | 300 |

### 1914 Erfurt Artillery

This model has an 8" barrel and is chambered for the 9mm cartridge. It has a stock lug and was issued with a flat board-type stock and other accessories which will be covered in the section of this book dealing with same. The sight is a nine-position adjustable model soldered to the barrel. The chamber is dated 1914-1918, and the extractor and safety are both marked in German. "ERFURT" under a crown is stamped on the front toggle link. There were a great many manufactured with one- to five-digit serial numbers, some with a letter suffix. This model is similar to the DWM Artillery except that the finish is not as fine.

| Exc. | V.G. | Good | Fair | Poor |
|------|------|------|------|------|
| 1750 | 1250 | 900 | 700 | 550 |

### Double Date Erfurt

This model was reworked after WWI and issued to the German army and police forces within the provisions of the Treaty of Versailles. The barrel is 4" in length, and they are chambered for the 9mm cartridge. The area above the chamber has two dates: the original 1910-1918, and the date of rework, 1920 or 1921. The extractor and safety are both marked in German, and this model can be found with or without a stock lug. "ERFURT" under a crown is stamped on the front toggle link. Police or military unit markings are found on the front of the grip straps more often than not. There were thousands of these produced by DWM as well as Erfurt.

| Exc. | V.G. | Good | Fair | Poor |
|------|------|------|------|------|
| 700 | 550 | 450 | 350 | 300 |

## WAFFENFABRIK BERN
### See separate section on Bern.
### Simson & Co. Suhl, Germany

The firm of Simson & Company received the contract to produce Lugers for the German army after the end of WWI. This army was limited to 100,000 men by the Treaty of Versailles. Simson was to be the sole military producer from 1922-1932. For the most part, Simson began by reworking surplus military Lugers but soon started manufacturing them. They even produced some commercial variations. These Lugers are stamped "SIMSON & CO.Suhl" on the front toggle link. Reworks are easy

to note as the DWM or Erfurt marking was removed and Simson was added. The toggle links on original Simson-manufactured weapons do not have the beveled edges.

### Simson & Co. Rework

This model is encountered quite frequently as there were many thousands produced after WWI. They are military Lugers reworked and bearing the "Simson & Co. Suhl" stamp on the front toggle link. They have 4" barrels and are chambered for the 7.65 and the 9mm cartridge. The chamber is blank, but some examples are dated 1917 or 1918. The extractor and safety are marked in German. Most examples have stock lugs; some have been noted without them. The only difference between military models and commercial models is the proofmarks.

| Exc. | V.G. | Good | Fair | Poor |
|------|------|------|------|------|
| 1250 | 1000 | 800 | 650 | 500 |

### Simson Grip Safety Rework

This very rare model is a WWI Luger to which a new 4" barrel chambered for the 9mm cartridge and a grip safety was added. There is a stock lug. The chamber area is blank; the extractor is marked but the safety is not. There were only a few of these commercial reworks manufactured, and caution should be taken to avoid fakes.

| Exc. | V.G. | Good | Fair | Poor |
|------|------|------|------|------|
| 2500 | 1750 | 1450 | 950 | 650 |

### Simson Dated Military

This model was actually manufactured by Simson and is not a rework. It has a 4" barrel and is chambered for the 9mm cartridge. There is a stock lug, and the year of manufacture from 1925-1928 is stamped above the chamber. The extractor and the safety are both marked in German. The checkered walnut grips of Simson-made Lugers are noticeably thicker than others. This is an extremely rare variation. Approximately 2,000 were manufactured with one- to three-digit serial numbers, and very few seem to have survived.

| Exc. | V.G. | Good | Fair | Poor |
|------|------|------|------|------|
| 2250 | 1850 | 1400 | 950 | 700 |

### Simson S Code

This model was, in all probability, the first Luger produced for the Nazi Military. The front toggle link is stamped with a gothic "S" instead of the usual marking. This was the begining of the Nazi practice of assigning manufacturers' codes. This was also the last Luger produced by Simson. This model has a 4" barrel and is chambered for the 9mm cartridge. It has a stock lug, and the area above the chamber is blank. The extractor and the safety are both marked. The grips are also thicker. There were approximately 12,000 manufactured with one- to five-digit serial numbers--some with the letter "a" suffix. This pistol is quite rare on today's market.

| Exc. | V.G. | Good | Fair | Poor |
|------|------|------|------|------|
| 2750 | 2000 | 1650 | 1000 | 750 |

### Early Nazi Era Reworks Mauser

These Lugers were reworked in the 1930-1933 period and are sometimes referred to as "Sneak Lugers," as they were reworked for issue in violation of the Treaty of Versailles. There are a great many different examples of these pistols, and to this day not all have been catalogued. They generally have the Nazi acceptance mark or Waffenamt, "WaA66", stamped on them.

**Deaths Head Rework**
This model has an arsenal-replaced 4" barrel chambered for the 9mm cartridge. It has a stock lug; and a skull and crossbones are stamped, in addition to the date of manufacture, on the chamber area. This date was from 1914-1918. The extractor and safety are both marked. The Waffenamt proof is present. It is thought that this variation was produced for the 1930-1933 era "SS" division of the Nazi Party. Mixed serial numbers are encountered on this model and do not lower the value. This is a very rare Luger on today's market, and caution should be exercised if purchase is contemplated.

| Exc. | V.G. | Good | Fair | Poor |
|---|---|---|---|---|
| 1150 | 850 | 650 | 550 | 450 |

**Kadetten Institut Rework**
This Mauser rework has a 4" barrel and is chambered for the 9mm cartridge. It has a stock lug, and the chamber area is stamped "K.I." above the date 1933. This stood for Cadets Institute, an early "SA" and "SS" officers' training school. The extractor and safety are both marked, and the Waffenamt is present. There were only a few hundred reworked, and the variation is quite scarce. Be wary of fakes.

| Exc. | V.G. | Good | Fair | Poor |
|---|---|---|---|---|
| 1150 | 850 | 650 | 550 | 450 |

**Mauser Unmarked Rework**
This model has a 4" barrel and is chambered for the 9mm cartridge. The entire weapon is void of identifying markings. There is extensive refurbishing, removal of all markings, rebarrelling, etc. The stock lug is present, and the extractor and safety are marked. The Waffenamt proof mark is on the right side of the receiver. The number manufactured is not known.

| Exc. | V.G. | Good | Fair | Poor |
|---|---|---|---|---|
| 1000 | 800 | 600 | 500 | 400 |

**Mauser Manufactured Lugers 1930--1942**
In 1930 DWM merged with the firm of Mauser of Oberndorf, Germany. Mauser took over all the manufacturing of the Luger pistol. Up to 1934 most of the Luger work centered on the reworks. After that date Germany began to rearm in preparation for its future military goals. Mauser increased its Luger production. In 1938 the P-38 replaced the Luger as the German service pistol, but production continued until late 1942. The Mauser Lugers produced for the German military were coded and were not marked with the Mauser "Banner" and name. The Mauser marked-pistols were commercial models.

**DWM - Mauser Oberndorf**
This model has a 4" barrel and is chambered for the 9mm cartridge. It has a stock lug, blank chamber area and a marked extractor and safety. This is an early example of Mauser Luger, and the front toggle link is still marked DWM as leftover parts were intermixed with new Mauser parts in the production of this pistol. This is one of the first Lugers to be finished with the "Salt" blue process. There were approximately 500 manufactured with one- to four-digit serial numbers with the letter "v" suffix. This is a very rare variation.

| Exc. | V.G. | Good | Fair | Poor |
|---|---|---|---|---|
| 2800 | 2450 | 1850 | 1450 | 1000 |

**1934/06 Swiss Commercial Mauser**
This model has a 4.75" barrel and is chambered for the 7.65mm cartridge. There is no stock lug, but it has a grip safety. The Swiss Cross in sunburst is stamped above the chamber. The extractor and safety are marked in German. The front toggle link is marked with the Mauser banner. There were approximately 200 manufactured for commercial sale in Switzerland. This variation is very well finished, and the serial numbers are all four digits with a "v" suffix.

| Exc. | V.G. | Good | Fair | Poor |
|---|---|---|---|---|
| 4500 | 3250 | 2500 | 1500 | 950 |

**1935/06 Portugese "GNR"**
This model has a 4.75" barrel and is chambered for the 7.65mm cartridge. It has no stock lug but has a grip safety. The chamber is marked "GNR," representing the Republic National Guard. The extractor is marked "Carregada"; and the safety, "Seguranca." On the front toggle link the Mauser banner is stamped. There were exactly 564 manufactured according to the original contract records which the Portuguese government made public. They all have four-digit serial numbers with a "v" suffix.

| Exc. | V.G. | Good | Fair | Poor |
|---|---|---|---|---|
| 2500 | 1750 | 1100 | 800 | 600 |

**1934 Mauser Commercial**
This model has a 4" barrel and is chambered for the 7.65mm or the 9mm cartridge. It has a stock lug, and the chamber area is blank. The extractor and the safety are marked. The Mauser banner is stamped on the front toggle link. The finish on this pistol was very good, and the grips are either checkered walnut or black plastic on the later models. There were a few thousand manufactured for commercial sales in and outside of Germany.

| Exc. | V.G. | Good | Fair | Poor |
|---|---|---|---|---|
| 2750 | 2000 | 1450 | 1100 | 800 |

**S/42 K Date**
This model has a 4" barrel and is chambered for the 9mm cartridge. It has a stock lug, and the extractor and safety are marked. This was the first Luger that utilized codes to represent maker and date of manufacture. The front toggle link is marked S/42 in either gothic or script; this was the code for Mauser. The chamber area is stamped with the letter "K," the code for 1934, the year of manufacture.

**S/42 K Date**
There were approximately 10,500 manufactured with one- to five-digit serial numbers--some with letter suffixes.

| Exc. | V.G. | Good | Fair | Poor |
|---|---|---|---|---|
| 3000 | 2000 | 1500 | 1000 | 700 |

**S/42 G Date**
This model is identical to the K Date except that the chamber area is stamped "G", the code for the year 1935. The gothic lettering was eliminated, and there were many thousands of this model produced.

| Exc. | V.G. | Good | Fair | Poor |
|---|---|---|---|---|
| 950 | 650 | 500 | 400 | 300 |

**Dated Chamber S/42**
This model has a 4" barrel and is chambered for the 9mm cartridge. The chamber area is dated 1936--1940, and there is a stock lug. The extractor and safety are marked. In 1937 the rust blue process was eliminated entirely, and all subsequent pistols were salt blued. There were many thousands manufactured with one- to five-digit serial numbers--some with the letter suffix.

| Exc. | V.G. | Good | Fair | Poor |
|---|---|---|---|---|
| 900 | 600 | 450 | 400 | 300 |

**S/42 Commercial Contract**
This rare and unusual variation has a 4" barrel and is chambered for the 9mm cartridge. It has a stock lug, and the chamber area is dated. It has a marked extractor and safety. The unusual feature is that, although this was a commercial pistol, the front toggle link is stamped S/42, which was the military code for Mauser. There were only a few hundred manufactured, so perhaps the toggles were left over from previous military production runs. The serial-number range is four digits with the letter "v."

| Exc. | V.G. | Good | Fair | Poor |
|---|---|---|---|---|
| 1750 | 1000 | 850 | 650 | 450 |

### Code 42 Dated Chamber

This model has a 4" barrel and is chambered for the 9mm cartridge. The new German code for Mauser, the number 42, is stamped on the front toggle link. There is a stock lug. The chamber area is dated 1939 or 1940. Some are found with walnut grips; others, with black plastic. There were at least 50,000 manufactured with one- to five-digit serial numbers; some have letter suffixes.

| Exc. | V.G. | Good | Fair | Poor |
|------|------|------|------|------|
| 850 | 600 | 500 | 400 | 300 |

### 41/42 Code

This model is identical to the 42 Code-dated chamber except that the date of manufacture is represented with two digits--41, not 1941. There were approximately 20,000 manufactured with the one- to five-digit serial-number range.

| Exc. | V.G. | Good | Fair | Poor |
|------|------|------|------|------|
| 900 | 650 | 500 | 400 | 300 |

### byf Code

This model is very similar in appearance to the foregoing WWII military Lugers with the exception that this model features the new German letter code "byf" that represented Mauser. The year of manufacture, either 41 or 42, is stamped on the chamber. This model was also made with black plastic, as well as walnut grips. There were many thousands produced with the one- to five-digit serial numbers--some with a letter suffix.

| Exc. | V.G. | Good | Fair | Poor |
|------|------|------|------|------|
| 800 | 600 | 450 | 400 | 300 |

### Persian Contract 4"

This model has a 4" barrel and is chambered for the 9mm cartridge. It has a stock lug, and the Persian crest is stamped over the chamber. All identifying markings on this variation--including extractor, safety and toggle--are marked in Farsi, the Persian alphabet. There were 1,000 manufactured. The serial numbers are also in Farsi.

| Exc. | V.G. | Good | Fair | Poor |
|------|------|------|------|------|
| 6000 | 5000 | 3500 | 2750 | 2250 |

### Persian Contract Artillery

This model features all the Farsi markings of the 4" Persian model but it has an 8" barrel and nine-position adjustable sight on the barrel. This model is supplied with a flat board stock. There were 1,000 manufactured and sold to Persia.

| Exc. | V.G. | Good | Fair | Poor |
|------|------|------|------|------|
| 3000 | 2250 | 1750 | 1250 | 1000 |

### 1934/06 Dated Commercial

This model has a 4.75" barrel and is chambered for the 7.65mm cartridge. It has a grip safety but no stock lug. The year of manufacture, from 1937-1942, is stamped above the chamber, and the Mauser banner is stamped on the front link. The extractor is marked, but the safety is not. There were approximately 1,000 manufactured with one- to three-digit serial nimbers--some with the letter suffix.

| Exc. | V.G. | Good | Fair | Poor |
|------|------|------|------|------|
| 1500 | 1250 | 850 | 650 | 500 |

### 1934 Mauser Dutch Contract

This model has a 4" barrel and is chambered for the 9mm cartridge. The year of manufacture, 1936-1940, is stamped above the chamber. The extractor is marked "Geladen," and the safety is marked "RUST" with a downward pointing arrow. The Mauser banner is stamped on the front toggle link. This was a military contract sale, and approximately 1,000 were manufactured with four-digit serial numbers with a letter "v" suffix.

| Exc. | V.G. | Good | Fair | Poor |
|------|------|------|------|------|
| 1750 | 1450 | 1000 | 800 | 600 |

### 1934 Mauser Swedish Contract

This model has a 4.75" barrel and is chambered for the 9mm and the 7.65mm cartridge. The chamber is dated 1938 or 1939. The extractor and safety are both marked in German, and there is a stock lug. The front toggle link is stamped with the Mauser banner. There were only 275 dated 1938 and 25 dated 1939 in 9mm. There were only 30 chambered for 7.65mm dated 1939. The serial-number range is four digits with the letter "v" suffix.

| Exc. | V.G. | Good | Fair | Poor |
|------|------|------|------|------|
| 2000 | 1650 | 1250 | 900 | 700 |

### 1934 Mauser Swedish Commercial

This model has a 4" barrel and is chambered for the 7.65mm cartridge. 1940 is stamped over the chamber; "Kal. 7.65" is stamped on the left side of the barrel. The extractor and safety are both marked, and the Mauser banner is stamped on the front toggle link. There is a stock lug. This model is very rare as there were only a few hundred manufactured with four digit serial numbers with the letter "w" suffix.

| Exc. | V.G. | Good | Fair | Poor |
|------|------|------|------|------|
| 2000 | 1650 | 1250 | 900 | 700 |

### 1934 Mauser German Contract

This model has a 4" barrel and is chambered for the 9mm cartridge. The chamber is dated 1939-1942, and the front toggle link is stamped with the Mauser banner. There is a stock lug, and the extractor and safety are both marked. The grips are either walnut or black plastic. There were several thousand manufactured with one- to five-digit serial numbers--some with letter suffixes. They were purchased for issue to police or paramilitary units.

| Exc. | V.G. | Good | Fair | Poor |
|------|------|------|------|------|
| 1750 | 1450 | 1000 | 800 | 600 |

### Austrian Bundes Heer (Federal Army)

This model has a 4" barrel and is chambered for the 9mm cartridge. The chamber is blank, and there is a stock lug. The extractor and safety are marked in German, and the Austrian Federal Army proof is stamped on the left side of the frame above the trigger guard. There were approximately 200 manufactured with four digit serial numbers and no letter suffix.

| Exc. | V.G. | Good | Fair | Poor |
|------|------|------|------|------|
| 1750 | 1450 | 1000 | 800 | 600 |

### Mauser 2 Digit Date

This model has a 4" barrel and is chambered for the 9mm cartridge. The last two digits of the year of manufacture--41 or 42--are stamped over the chamber. There is a stock lug, and the Mauser banner is on the front toggle link. The extractor and safety are both marked, and the proof marks were commercial. Grips are either walnut or black plastic. There were approximately 2,000 manufactured for sale to Nazi political groups. They have one- to five- digit serial numbers; some have the letter suffix.

| Exc. | V.G. | Good | Fair | Poor |
|------|------|------|------|------|
| 950 | 750 | 600 | 500 | 400 |

### Krieghoff Manufactured Lugers

The firm of H. K. Krieghoff of Suhl, Germany began the manufacture of Luger pistols in 1935. The company obtained the contract to produce pistols for the Luftwaffe. Hermann Goering supposedly had both a financial interest in the firm and a friendship with Heinrich Krieghoff.

## 1923 DWM Krieghoff Commercial

This model has a 4" barrel and is chambered for both the 7.65mm and 9mm cartridge. The chamber is dated 1921 or left blank. There is a stock lug. The front toggle is marked DWM, as they manufactured this Luger to be sold by Krieghoff. "Krieghoff Suhl" is stamped on the back above the lanyard loop. The second "F" in Krieghoff was defective, and all specimens have this distinctive die strike. The safety and extractor are marked in German. There were only a few hundred manufactured with four-digit serial numbers with the letter "i" suffix.

| Exc. | V.G. | Good | Fair | Poor |
|------|------|------|------|------|
| 1750 | 1450 | 1000 | 800 | 600 |

## DWM/Krieghoff Commercial

This model is quite similar to the 1923 Krieghoff/DWM except that it is marked "Heinrich Krieghoff Waffenfabrik Suhl" on the right side of the frame. Some examples have the "Germany" export stamp. There were several hundred manufactured with four-digit serial numbers with a letter suffix.

| Exc. | V.G. | Good | Fair | Poor |
|------|------|------|------|------|
| 2750 | 2250 | 1850 | 1300 | 900 |

## Krieghoff Commercial Inscribed Side Frame

This was the first Luger manufactured by Krieghoff. It has a 4" or 6" barrel and is chambered for either the 7.65mm or 9mm cartridge. 1,000 were marked "Heinrich Krieghoff Waffenfabrik Suhl" on the right side of the frame, and 500 were devoid of this marking. All have the dagger and anchor trademark over "H.K. Krieghoff Suhl" on the front toggle link. The extractor and safety are both marked. There is a stock lug, and the grips are of brown checkered plastic. There were approximately 1,500 manufactured with one- to four-digit serial numbers with a "P" prefix.

| Exc. | V.G. | Good | Fair | Poor |
|------|------|------|------|------|
| 3000 | 2500 | 2000 | 1500 | 1000 |

## S Code Krieghoff

This model has a 4" barrel and is chambered for the 9mm cartridge. The Krieghoff trademark is stamped on the front toggle link, and the letter "S" is stamped over the chamber. There is a stock lug, and the extractor and safety are both marked. The grips are brown checkered plastic. There were approximately 4,500 manufactured for the Luftwaffe with one- to four-digit serial numbers.

| Exc. | V.G. | Good | Fair | Poor |
|------|------|------|------|------|
| 2500 | 2000 | 1500 | 1000 | 750 |

## Grip Safety Krieghoff

This model has a 4" barrel and is chambered for the 9mm cartridge. The chamber area is blank, and the front toggle link is stamped with the Krieghoff trademark. There is a stock lug and a grip safety. The extractor is marked "Geladen," and the safety is marked "FEUER" (fire) in the lower position. The grips are checkered brown plastic. This is a very rare Luger, and the number produced is not known.

| Exc. | V.G. | Good | Fair | Poor |
|------|------|------|------|------|
| 3500 | 2750 | 2250 | 1750 | 1300 |

## 36 Date Krieghoff

This model has a 4" barrel and is chambered for the 9mm cartridge. It has a stock lug and the Krieghoff trademark on the front toggle link. The safety and extractor are marked, and the grips are brown plastic. The two-digit year of manufacture, 36, is stamped over the chamber. There were approximately 700 produced in the 3800 -4500 serial-number range.

| Exc. | V.G. | Good | Fair | Poor |
|------|------|------|------|------|
| 2750 | 2250 | 1850 | 1300 | 900 |

## 4 Digit Dated Krieghoff

This model is quite similar in appearance to the 36 Date model, with the year of production, 1936-1940, stamped above the chamber. There were approximately 9,000 manufactured within the 4500--14000 serial-number range.

| Exc. | V.G. | Good | Fair | Poor |
|------|------|------|------|------|
| 2250 | 1850 | 1250 | 850 | 650 |

## 2nd Series Krieghoff Commercial

This model has a 4" barrel and is chambered for the 9mm cartridge. There is a stock lug, and the Krieghoff trademark is stamped on the front link. The chamber area is blank, and the extractor and safety are marked. There were approximately 500 manufactured for commercial sales inside Germany. The date of manufacture is estimated at 1939-1940, as this variation has the dark finish that results from blueing without polishing the surface, which was done during these years. The grips are coarsely checkered black plastic. The serial-number range is one to three digits with a "P" prefix.

| Exc. | V.G. | Good | Fair | Poor |
|------|------|------|------|------|
| 2750 | 2250 | 1850 | 1300 | 900 |

## Post War Krieghoff

This model has a 4" barrel and is chambered for the 9mm cartridge. There is a stock lug, and the chamber area is blank. The extractor and safety are marked, and the serial numbers in the one- to three-digit range are unusually large--about 3/16ths of an inch. There were 300 of these post-war Lugers produced for the occupation forces. They were assembled from leftover parts, and only 150 have the Krieghoff trademark on the front toggle link--the second 150 have blank links.

| Exc. | V.G. | Good | Fair | Poor |
|------|------|------|------|------|
| 1650 | 1400 | 950 | 750 | 650 |

## Krieghoff Post War Commercial

This model is very similar in appearance to the unmarked Post War previously mentioned except that this model is chambered for the 7.65mm cartridge and the extractor is not marked. There were approximately 200 manufactured with standard-sized two- or three-digit serial numbers. They were supposedly sold to the occupation forces in the PX stores.

| Exc. | V.G. | Good | Fair | Poor |
|------|------|------|------|------|
| 1500 | 1350 | 900 | 700 | 600 |

## Luger Accessories

There were a number of interesting accessories issued with military Lugers and as options on the commercial variations. They are in some cases as collectible and valuable as the pistols themselves. One must be extremely careful in purchasing some of these items as fakes have been noted.

## Detachable Stocks

There are basically four stocks available for the Luger. The Carbine stock is a fully contoured and checkered walnut stock that is approximately 13" in length. There is a sling swivel and a horn buttplate. Finding one to purchase would be very difficult; but if this were possible, the value would be as follows:

| Exc. | V.G. | Good | Fair | Poor |
|------|------|------|------|------|
| 1250 | 950 | 800 | 700 | 550 |

## Artillery Stock with Holster

The artillery rig is a flat board-type stock approximately 13.75" in length. There is a holster and magazine pouches with straps attached. This is a very desirable addition to the Artillery Luger. A word of caution--one must check federal laws regarding detachable stocks and short-barrelled pistols; there are a number of restrictions that must be observed.

| Exc. | V.G. | Good | Fair | Poor |
|------|------|------|------|------|
| 450 | 400 | 350 | 300 | 200 |

## Navy Stock

This stock is similar in appearance to the Artillery stock but is 12.75" in length and has a brass disk inlaid in the left side.

| Exc. | V.G. | Good | Fair | Poor |
|------|------|------|------|------|
| 650  | 550  | 450  | 350  | 250  |

## Ideal Stock/Holster

This is a telescoping metal tube stock with an attached leather holster. It is used in conjunction with a metal-backed set of plain grips that correspond to the metal hooks on the stock and allow attachment. This Ideal stock is U.S. patented and is so marked.

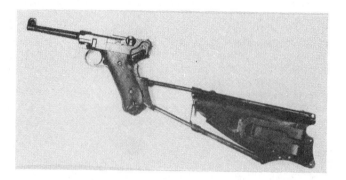

| Exc. | V.G. | Good | Fair | Poor |
|------|------|------|------|------|
| 1250 | 950  | 800  | 700  | 550  |

## Drum Magazine  1st Issue

This is a 32-round, snail-like affair that is used with the Artillery Luger. It is also used with an adapter in the German 9mm submachine gun. The 1st Issue has a telescoping tube that is used to wind the spring. There is a dust cover that protects the interior from dirt.

| Exc. | V.G. | Good | Fair | Poor |
|------|------|------|------|------|
| 650  | 550  | 450  | 350  | 300  |

## Drum Magazine  2nd Issue

This is similar in appearance to the 1st Issue but with a folding spring winding lever.

| Exc. | V.G. | Good | Fair | Poor |
|------|------|------|------|------|
| 550  | 450  | 400  | 300  | 250  |

## Drum Magazine Loading Tool

This tool is slipped over the magazine and allows the spring to be compressed so that cartridges could be inserted.

| Exc. | V.G. | Good | Fair | Poor |
|------|------|------|------|------|
| 450  | 400  | 350  | 300  | 200  |

## Drum Magazine Unloading Tool

This tool allows the single stripping of cartridges from the heavily tensioned drum magazine. This is a very rare accessory, and some are of the opinion that an original issue model never existed and that the few observed were made from loading tools. Qualified appraisal should be secured.

## Drum Carrying Case

This is another controversial item--a fitted leather pouch that was made for the 32-round snail drum. There are experts who state that this was never a genuine German accessory and that they were made in Italy or the Middle East in the 1920's. But they are listed in some of the very finest of publications as a Luger accessory. Again--use your judgment after securing qualified appraisal.

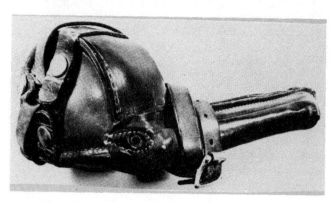

| Exc. | V.G. | Good | Fair | Poor |
|------|------|------|------|------|
| 200  | 150  | 125  | 100  | 50   |

## Holster/Rigs

The variations in Luger leather are almost as diverse as the pistols themselves. The values given here are for the standard military rig with extra magazine and takedown tool. When considering the rarer variations of holsters, it is best to secure individual appraisal.

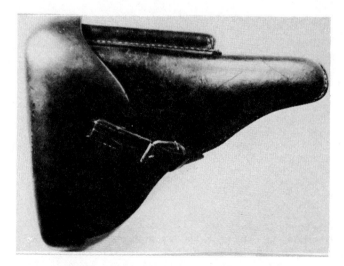

| Exc. | V.G. | Good | Fair | Poor |
|------|------|------|------|------|
| 125  | 100  | 75   | 50   | 40   |

## Late Production Mauser Lugers

These Lugers were manufactured by Mauser in the 1970's, and they were imported by Interarms. The quality of these later versions is exceptional, and they do have the importer's name stamped on them.

## P.08 Interarms

This model has a 4" or 6" barrel and is chambered for either 7.65mm or 9mm.

| NIB | Exc. | V.G. | Good | Fair | Poor |
|-----|------|------|------|------|------|
| 750 | 650  | 500  | 400  | 350  | 300  |

## Swiss Eagle Interarms
This model has the Swiss-style straight front grip strap and the American Eagle crest over the chamber. It is chambered for 7.65mm or 9mm and is offered with a 4" or 6" barrel.

| NIB | Exc. | V.G. | Good | Fair | Poor |
|---|---|---|---|---|---|
| 650 | 550 | 450 | 350 | 325 | 300 |

## Commemorative Bulgarian
This model has the Bulgarian crest over the chamber. There were only 100 produced.

| NIB | Exc. | V.G. | Good | Fair | Poor |
|---|---|---|---|---|---|
| 1750 | 1500 | 1200 | 950 | 650 | 450 |

## Commemorative Russian
This model has the Crossed Nagant Rifles over the chamber. There were 100 produced.

| NIB | Exc. | V.G. | Good | Fair | Poor |
|---|---|---|---|---|---|
| 1750 | 1500 | 1200 | 950 | 650 | 450 |

## Modern Production Carbine
This splendid reproduction was produced on a limited basis. The workmenship is excellent, and the Carbine and stock are furnished in a case.

| NIB | Exc. | V.G. | Good | Fair | Poor |
|---|---|---|---|---|---|
| 6500 | 5500 | 4000 | 3200 | 2500 | 2000 |

## John Martz Custom Lugers
For a number of years John Martz has been engaged in the business of customizing existing Lugers. His is truly a labor of love-- as the workmanship, in both quality and ingenuity, is excellent.

## Martz Luger Carbine
This is a reproduction of the original, with 16" legal barrel length. There were approximately 60 manufactured.

| NIB | Exc. | V.G. | Good | Fair | Poor |
|---|---|---|---|---|---|
| 4500 | 3500 | 2500 | 2250 | 1850 | 1250 |

## Navy .45 ACP
This is a 6"-barrelled Navy-style Luger chambered for the .45 ACP cartridge. In order to accommodate the larger cartridge, Martz splits two Lugers apart lengthwise and then welds them back together, giving him a thicker frame with which to work. On the examples examined it is nearly impossible to detect the weld. This is a unique weapon.

| NIB | Exc. | V.G. | Good | Fair | Poor |
|---|---|---|---|---|---|
| 3500 | 3000 | 2250 | 2000 | 1750 | 1100 |

## Baby Luger 9mm
This is a cut-down version chambered for the 9mm cartridge. There were approximately 96 produced.

| NIB | Exc. | V.G. | Good | Fair | Poor |
|---|---|---|---|---|---|
| 1500 | 1250 | 1000 | 850 | 750 | 650 |

## Baby Luger .380 ACP
This cut-down version is chambered for the .380 ACP cartridge. There were approximately five manufactured.

| NIB | Exc. | V.G. | Good | Fair | Poor |
|---|---|---|---|---|---|
| 3000 | 2500 | 1750 | 1500 | 1250 | 1000 |

# LUNA
### Zella-Mehlis, Germany

## Model 200 Free Pistol
This is a high-grade target pistol built by the firm of E. F. Buchel. It features a Martini falling-block action and is chambered for the .22 rimfire cartridge. It has an 11" barrel and adjustable target sights. The finish is blued, with checkered walnut grips. It was manufactured before WWII.

| Exc. | V.G. | Good | Fair | Poor |
|---|---|---|---|---|
| 1250 | 1000 | 800 | 600 | 500 |

## Target Rifle
This model was also built on the Martini falling-block single-shot action. It is chambered for the .22 rimfire cartridge, as well as the .22 Hornet. It has a 20" barrel and adjustable target sights. The finish is blued, with a walnut target-type stock. This model was manufactured by E. F. Buchel prior to WWII.

| Exc. | V.G. | Good | Fair | Poor |
|---|---|---|---|---|
| 1000 | 850 | 650 | 500 | 400 |

# MAB
### SEE--Bayonne

# MAC
### SEE--Ingram

# MAS
### St. Etienne, France
### Manufacture s'Armes de St. Etienne

## MAS 36
This is a bolt-action French service rifle chambered for the 7.5mm cartridge. It has a 22.6" barrel and a 5- round integral magazine. This rifle is essentially a modifed Mauser action with a shorter stroke but a slightly weaker action. The bolt handle has a strange bend to it that allows it to be conveniently accessed. The stock is of two-piece design, and there is no safety of any kind. This was the last bolt action to be adopted for military service. It was used in WWII.

| Exc. | V.G. | Good | Fair | Poor |
|---|---|---|---|---|
| 200 | 175 | 150 | 100 | 75 |

## MAS 36 CR39
This is a paratroopers' version of the MAS 36 with a folding stock made of hollow aluminum. All other specifications are the same.

| Exc. | V.G. | Good | Fair | Poor |
|---|---|---|---|---|
| 225 | 200 | 175 | 125 | 90 |

## Model 1917
This was an early gas-operated semi-automatic rifle that is very awkward and unwieldy in appearance. It is chambered for the 8mm Lebel cartridge and has a 31.4" barrel. The integral magazine holds 5 rounds. The full length stock is walnut. This rifle saw limited service in WWI.

| Exc. | V.G. | Good | Fair | Poor |
|---|---|---|---|---|
| 375 | 325 | 250 | 175 | 125 |

## Model 1918
This is simply a shorter and lighter version of the Model 1917 with a 23.1" barrel. It was introduced after the close of WWI.

| Exc. | V.G. | Good | Fair | Poor |
|---|---|---|---|---|
| 375 | 325 | 250 | 175 | 125 |

## MAS 49

This is a gas-operated semi-automatic rifle chambered for the 7.5mm cartridge. It used the same stock, forend, and sights as the bolt-action MAS 36. The MAS 49 is a very robust design that is somewhat heavy but very strong. The finish is blued, with a walnut stock and full-length forend that is held on by one barrel band. There is no provision for a bayonet. This rifle was one of the first semi-automatics to be adopted by a European country in 1949. It has been replaced by the FA MAS 5.56mm Bullpup select- fire carbine.

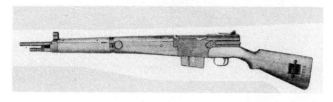

| Exc. | V.G. | Good | Fair | Poor |
|------|------|------|------|------|
| 325  | 275  | 225  | 150  | 100  |

## MBA GYROJET
### San Ramon, California

This pistol is a unique firearm. In actuality it is not really a pistol but a hand-held rocket launcher that fires small spin-stabilized rockets. This venture was put together in 1960 by R. Maynard and Art Biehl who were looking for new and novel ideas that they could financially sponsor. The Gyrojet was actually not an original idea, as the Germans had produced a shoulder-held rocket launcher in 1945 that had nine barrels and was used as an anti-aircraft weapon. The Gyrojet ammunition was 13mm before 1968; and after the Gun Control Act of 1968 made projectiles larger than .50 caliber destructive devises, the rockets were cut to 12mm, to about 1.5" in length. The launcher resembles a semi-automatic pistol and holds six rockets in the butt. The barrel is 5" in length; and the finish is either black or satin nickel-plate, with walnut grips. This weapon was placed on the market in 1965 and disappeared before 1975. The cost factor, as well as the inaccuracy and rapid fall-off of velocity, contributed to its premature demise. These pistols, as well as the rockets, are sought-after collector items today.

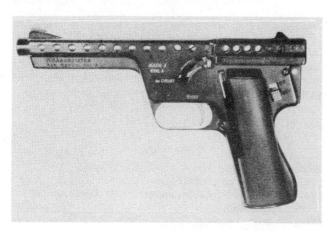

### Mark I Pistol
| Exc. | V.G. | Good | Fair | Poor |
|------|------|------|------|------|
| 700  | 600  | 500  | 400  | 300  |

### Mark I Carbine
This model is similar to the Pistol except that it has an 18" barrel and a buttstock with a pistol grip.

| Exc. | V.G. | Good | Fair | Poor |
|------|------|------|------|------|
| 1250 | 1050 | 850  | 600  | 500  |

## MK ARMS, INC.
### Irvine, California

### MK 760
This is a semi-automatic carbine that fires from the closed-bolt position and is chambered for the 9mm cartridge. It has a 16" barrel with a ventilated shroud and features fixed open sights. The magazines offered hold 14, 24, or 36 rounds; and there is a metal skeleton-type folding stock. The finish is parkerized. This model was introduced in 1983.

| NIB | Exc. | V.G. | Good | Fair | Poor |
|-----|------|------|------|------|------|
| 500 | 450  | 375  | 300  | 250  | 200  |

## MKE
### Ankara, Turkey
### Importer--Mandall Shooting Supplies
### Scottsdale, Arizona

### Kirrikale
This double-action semi-automatic is blowback-operated and patterned closely after the Walther PP. It is chambered for the 7.65mm or the .380 ACP cartridge. This pistol has a 4" barrel and a 7-round detachable magazine. The sights are fixed; and the finish is blued, with checkered plastic grips. This pistol is used by Turkey as their military service pistol.

| NIB | Exc. | V.G. | Good | Fair | Poor |
|-----|------|------|------|------|------|
| 400 | 350  | 275  | 225  | 150  | 100  |

## M.O.A. CORP.
### Dayton, Ohio

### Maximum
This is a single-shot, falling-block target pistol chambered for 21 popular cartridges between .22 Hornet and the .44 Mag. It has barrel lengths of 8.5", 10", and 14"; and the action is activated by a lever. There is a transfer-bar safety device and open adjustable sights. The finish is blued, with a walnut grip and forearm. This model was introduced in 1986.

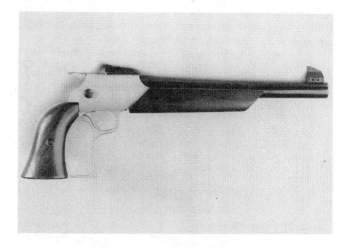

| NIB | Exc. | V.G. | Good | Fair | Poor |
|-----|------|------|------|------|------|
| 500 | 425  | 375  | 300  | 250  | 200  |

### Carbine
This model is similar to the Maximum, with an 18" barrel. It was manufactured in 1986 and 1987.

| NIB | Exc. | V.G. | Good | Fair | Poor |
|-----|------|------|------|------|------|
| 500 | 425  | 375  | 300  | 250  | 200  |

## MAGNUM RESEARCH, INC.
### Minneapolis, Minnesota
### Desert Eagle
This pistol is a gas-operated semi-automatic chambered for the .357 Magnum, .41 Magnum, and the .44 Magnum cartridges. The barrel lengths are 6", 10", and 14"; and the magazines hold 8 or 9 shots, depending on the caliber. This very large firearm is very effective when used for the purpose for which it was intended--hunting or silhouette shooting. There are a number of finishes available: matte blue, polished blue, nickel-plated, hardchrome-plated, either matte or polished, as well as a stainless-steel version. This pistol was introduced in 1983.

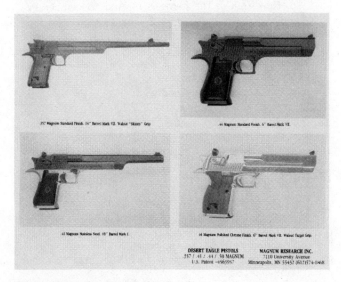

Choice of finishes--Add $130.
14" barrel--Add $170.
6" Conversion Unit--Add $495.
10" or 14" Conversion Unit--Add $675.
Stainless Steel Version--Add $40.

**Basic .357 Magnum**

| NIB | Exc. | V.G. | Good | Fair | Poor |
|---|---|---|---|---|---|
| 630 | 550 | 500 | 450 | 400 | 350 |

**Basic .41 Magnum**

| NIB | Exc. | V.G. | Good | Fair | Poor |
|---|---|---|---|---|---|
| 740 | 675 | 600 | 550 | 450 | 400 |

**Basic .44 Magnum**

| NIB | Exc. | V.G. | Good | Fair | Poor |
|---|---|---|---|---|---|
| 750 | 700 | 650 | 600 | 500 | 450 |

### Hunter Edition
This is a deluxe version that is chambered for the .357 or the .44 Magnum cartridge and has a 6" barrel. It is furnished with 2x20 Simmons scope and comes in a fitted cherrywood case. It was introduced in 1987.

| NIB | Exc. | V.G. | Good | Fair | Poor |
|---|---|---|---|---|---|
| 1150 | 1000 | 800 | 600 | 500 | 400 |

## MAKAROV
### Soviet Union
### Makarov Pistol
This was the standard service pistol of the Communist Bloc countries and is still in service in many parts of the world. It is chambered for the 9x18mm Soviet cartridge and is manufactured not only in the Soviet Union but in East Germany and China as well. It has an 8-round magazine. Basically this pistol is patterned after the Walther PP but is larger. It is blowback-operated and is at about the top limit of power for a blowback

design. The finish is blued, with brown checkered plastic grips that have a star molded into them. It is impossible to estimate how many were manufactured as the Soviets do not allow access to their records.

| Exc. | V.G. | Good | Fair | Poor |
|---|---|---|---|---|
| 850 | 800 | 725 | 600 | 450 |

## MALIN, F. E.
### London, England
### Importer--Cape Horn Outfitters
### Charlotte, North Carolina
This company manufactured high-grade shotguns made to the customer's specifications. They featured the highest-grade materials and workmanship and were priced accordingly. They were furnished with fitted leather cases. These guns are not manufactured under the Malin name at this time but have been taken over by the firm of Charles Bosworth.

### Boxlock
This model features an Anson & Deeley action and high-grade walnut. All other specification were on a custom-order basis. This gun should definitely be individually appraised as values will fluctuate greatly with options.

**Basic Model Estimated Value Only**

| NIB | Exc. | V.G. | Good | Fair | Poor |
|---|---|---|---|---|---|
| 4000 | 3500 | 3000 | 2500 | 1850 | 1450 |

### Sidelock
This model features a Holland & Holland-type detachable sidelock action, and all other features (as on the boxlock) were on a custom-order basis. This model should also be appraised individually.

**Basic Model Estimated Value Only**

| NIB | Exc. | V.G. | Good | Fair | Poor |
|---|---|---|---|---|---|
| 5500 | 5000 | 4250 | 3000 | 2500 | 1850 |

## MALTBY, HENLEY AND CO.
### New York, New York
### Spencer Safety Hammerless Revolver
This is a double-action pocket revolver chambered for the .32-caliber centerfire cartridge. It has a 3" ribbed round barrel and has a 5-shot cylinder. The frame is solid, and loading is accomplished by means of a groove milled into the frame that allows access to the cylinder chambers. The most unique thing about this revolver is that it was constructed completely of brass with

the exception of the cylinder. The grips are wood, and the barrel is marked "Spencer Safety Hammerless Pat. Jan. 24, 1888 & Oct.29, 1889." There were estimated to be several thousand manufactured in the 1890's.

| Exc. | V.G. | Good | Fair | Poor |
|------|------|------|------|------|
| 250 | 225 | 175 | 125 | 75 |

# MANHATTAN FIREARMS COMPANY
## Norwich, Connecticut
## Newark, New Jersey

### Bar Hammer Pistol

This is a double-action, single-shot pistol chambered for .31, .34, or .36 caliber percussion. It was offered with a half-octagonal barrel between 2" and 4" in length. It has a centrally mounted bar hammer and a large loop trigger guard. The finish is blued with round-shaped, two-piece walnut grips. The hammer is marked "Manhattan F.A. Mfg. Co. New York." The frame is engraved. There were approximately 1,500 manufactured in Norwich, Connecticut, in the late 1850's.

| Exc. | V.G. | Good | Fair | Poor |
|------|------|------|------|------|
| 500 | 425 | 350 | 250 | 150 |

### Shotgun Hammer Pistol

This is a single-shot, single-action pistol chambered for .36 caliber percussion. It was offered with a 5.5" half-octagonal barrel. It features a spurred shotgun-style hammer and a round trigger guard. The receiver is engraved, with a blued finish and round two-piece walnut grips. It is marked "Manhattan F.A. Mfg. Co. New York." There were approximately 500 manufactured in Norwich, Connecticut, in the late 1850's.

| Exc. | V.G. | Good | Fair | Poor |
|------|------|------|------|------|
| 550 | 450 | 375 | 225 | 175 |

### Pepperbox

This is a revolving, double-action, pepperbox-type pistol chambered for the .28 or .31 caliber percussion. It has barrel clusters that are 3", 4", or 5" in length. There are three basic variations--a 3-barrel, 5-barrel, or 6-barrel version. They all feature a bar hammer and a large ring trigger guard. The barrel clusters are unfluted, and the frames are scroll-engraved. The finishes of all variations are blued, with case-colored receivers and round two-piece walnut grips. They are all marked "Manhattan F.A. Mfg. Co. New York." The words "Cast Steel" appear on the barrels. There were a total of approximately 3,000 manufactured in Norwich, Connecticut, in the late 1850's. The variations and values are as follows:

### Three-shot with 3" Barrel

| Exc. | V.G. | Good | Fair | Poor |
|------|------|------|------|------|
| 750 | 675 | 600 | 450 | 350 |

### Five-shot with 3" Barrel

This is a very rare model with manually rotated barrels.

| Exc. | V.G. | Good | Fair | Poor |
|------|------|------|------|------|
| 750 | 675 | 600 | 450 | 350 |

### Five-shot with 3", 4", 5" Barrel

The barrels automatically rotate when the trigger is pulled.

| Exc. | V.G. | Good | Fair | Poor |
|------|------|------|------|------|
| 600 | 525 | 450 | 350 | 250 |

### Six-shot with 3" or 4" Barrel

Automatic rotation.

| Exc. | V.G. | Good | Fair | Poor |
|------|------|------|------|------|
| 600 | 525 | 450 | 350 | 250 |

### Six-shot W/5" Barrel

Automatic rotation; rarest version.

| Exc. | V.G. | Good | Fair | Poor |
|------|------|------|------|------|
| 750 | 675 | 600 | 450 | 350 |

### Pocket Revolver

This is a single-action pocket revolver chambered for .31 caliber percussion. It has octagonal barrels that are 4", 5", or 6" in length, with an integral loading lever mounted under the barrel. There are two distinct versions --one with a 5-shot cylinder, the other with a 6-shot cylinder. The finish is blued, with a case-colored hammer and loading lever. The receiver is scroll-engraved. The grips are two-piece walnut. This firearm is quite similar to Colt's Model 1849 Pocket Revolver. It is marked, "Manhattan Firearms/Manufg. Co. New-York" on the 5-shot model. The serial numbers run from No. 1 to approximately 1,000. The 6-shot version is marked "Manhattan Firearms Mf'g. Co. New York". The frame is marked "December 27, 1859"; and the serial numbers run from approximately 1,000 to 4,800. The grip frame is plated on the 6-shot model. There was a total of approximately 4,800 manufactured in Newark, New Jersey, between 1858 and 1862.

### First Model--5-Shot

| Exc. | V.G. | Good | Fair | Poor |
|------|------|------|------|------|
| 500 | 425 | 350 | 250 | 150 |

### Second Model--6-Shot

| Exc. | V.G. | Good | Fair | Poor |
|------|------|------|------|------|
| 450 | 400 | 300 | 200 | 100 |

### London Pistol Company

This variation is comprised of pocket-model revolvers that were produced with cosmetic defects. Rather than scrap them, Manhattan marked the barrels "London Pistol Company" and sold them as second-quality revolvers. They were not marked "Manhattan" so the lesser quality had no negative effect on their company image. There were approximately 200 manufactured between 1859 and 1861.

| Exc. | V.G. | Good | Fair | Poor |
|------|------|------|------|------|
| 450 | 400 | 300 | 200 | 100 |

### .36 Caliber Percussion Revolver

This is a single-action percussion revolver that is outwardly similar in appearance to the Colt Model 1851 Navy. It does have a number of design features that contribute to its commercial success. It is chambered for .36 caliber percussion and was offered with a 4", 5", or 6.5" octagonal barrel with a loading lever mounted beneath it. It has a 5- shot or 6-shot cylinder that is roll-engraved with military and naval scenes. The finish is blued, with a case-colored frame, hammer, and loading lever. The grip straps are silver-plated brass, and the grips are one-piece walnut. There are five distinct variations of this model--for a total of approximately 78,000 manufactured in Newark, New Jersey, between 1859 and 1868.

### Model I

This version has a 5-shot cylinder and is marked "Manhattan Firearms Mfg. Co. New York." The serial numbers are from no. 1 through 4200. The 6"-barrelled version would be worth a 15 percent premium.

| Exc. | V.G. | Good | Fair | Poor |
|------|------|------|------|------|
| 750 | 675 | 600 | 450 | 350 |

### Model II

This version is similar to the Model I but has an 1859 patent date marked on the barrel. The serial range is 4200 to 14500.

| Exc. | V.G. | Good | Fair | Poor |
|------|------|------|------|------|
| 600 | 525 | 450 | 350 | 250 |

### Model III

This version has a 5-shot cylinder and is marked, "Manhattan Firearms Co. Newark NJ." It also has the 1859 patent date. The serial numbers are from 14500 to 45200.

| Exc. | V.G. | Good | Fair | Poor |
|------|------|------|------|------|
| 500 | 425 | 350 | 250 | 150 |

## Model IV

This version has similar markings with a March 8, 1864, patent date. It was modified with a plate on the recoil shield to reduce the risk of chain-fires. The serial numbers are from 45200 to 69200.

| Exc. | V.G. | Good | Fair | Poor |
|------|------|------|------|------|
| 500 | 475 | 350 | 250 | 150 |

## Model V

This version has a 6-shot cylinder and is marked in a similar manner to the Model IV variation. It is serial numbered in its own series from no. 1 to 9000.

| Exc. | V.G. | Good | Fair | Poor |
|------|------|------|------|------|
| 600 | 525 | 450 | 350 | 250 |

## .22 Caliber Pocket Revolver

This is a spur-trigger, single-action pocket revolver chambered for the .22 rimfire cartridge. It was patterned after the Smith & Wesson first model 1st issue revolver. It has a 3" ribbed octagonal barrel and a 7-shot unfluted cylinder. The barrel pivots upward for loading. The finish is blued, with a silver-plated frame that features scroll-engraving. The square-butt grips are either walnut or rosewood. There were approximately 17,000 manufactured in Newark, New Jersey, between 1860 and 1873. There are a number of subvariations with similar values.

| Exc. | V.G. | Good | Fair | Poor |
|------|------|------|------|------|
| 450 | 400 | 300 | 200 | 100 |

## Manhattan-American Standard Hero

This is a spur-trigger, single-shot pocket pistol chambered for .34 caliber percussion. It has a 2" or 3" round smooth-bore barrel that screws off the frame for breech loading. The frame is brass with a blued barrel and case-colored hammer. The grips are two-piece rounded walnut. This pistol was introduced in 1868, which was the last year that the Manhattan Firearms Company was in existence. For the remainder of its production, it was marked "A.S.T. Co./HERO" and was produced by the American Standard Tool Company, Manhattan's successor. This company existed only until 1873. There were approximately 30,000 manufactured by both companies in Newark, New Jersey, between 1868 and 1873.

## Manhattan Manufactured

This version is marked, "HERO/M.F.A.Co." There were approximately 5,000 produced.

| Exc. | V.G. | Good | Fair | Poor |
|------|------|------|------|------|
| 350 | 300 | 250 | 150 | 100 |

## American Standard Manufactured

There were approximately 25,000 produced.

| Exc. | V.G. | Good | Fair | Poor |
|------|------|------|------|------|
| 300 | 250 | 200 | 100 | 75 |

# MANN, FRITZ
### Suhl, Germany

## 6.35mm Pocket Pistol

This is an unusual blowback operated semi-automatic pistol. It is chambered for the 6.35mm cartridge and has a 1.65" barrel. The unusual feature is that the frame and slide are one piece with a removable barrel and separate bolt. The barrel is knurled at the muzzle and rotates 90 degrees to remove. The magazine holds 5 rounds; and the finish is blue, with checkered plastic grips that have "Mann" molded into them. The frame is marked with the maker's name and the caliber. This is one of the smallest firearms ever produced; it weighs only 9 ounces. It was manufactured between 1920 and 1922.

| Exc. | V.G. | Good | Fair | Poor |
|------|------|------|------|------|
| 300 | 250 | 200 | 150 | 100 |

## 7.65mm Pocket Pistol

This is a more conventional blowback-operated semi-automatic pistol that is chambered for the 7.65mm and the 9mm Short cartridge. It has a 2.35" barrel and is striker fired. The magazine holds 5 rounds. This is basically similar to the Browning-style pistol, with an unusual magazine catch that is part of the safety. The finish is blued, with black plastic grips with "Mann" molded into them. The maker's name is marked on the slide. This model was manufactured in fairly substantial amounts between 1924 and 1929, when the company ceased operations.

| Exc. | V.G. | Good | Fair | Poor |
|------|------|------|------|------|
| 350 | 300 | 250 | 200 | 125 |

# MANNLICHLER PISTOL
### Steyr, Austria
### SEE--Steyr

# MANNLICHER SCHOENAUER
### Steyr, Austria

## Model 1903 Mountain Carbine

This model is a bolt-action carbine chambered for the 6.5x54mm Mannlicher Schoenauer cartridge. It has a 17.7" barrel and a 5-shot rotary magazine. Its bolt handle is the characteristic Mannlicher spoon type. It has a folding-leaf rear sight and double-set triggers. The walnut stock is the full-length style that has become synonymous with the Mannlicher Carbine, with a metal end cap.

| Exc. | V.G. | Good | Fair | Poor |
|------|------|------|------|------|
| 1000 | 875 | 750 | 500 | 350 |

### Model 1905 Carbine
This model is similar to the Model 1903 except that it is chambered for the 9x56mm cartridge.

| Exc. | V.G. | Good | Fair | Poor |
|------|------|------|------|------|
| 1150 | 1000 | 900 | 750 | 450 |

### Model 1908 Carbine
This model is chambered for the 7x57 or the 8x56mm cartridges. It is similar to the Model 1903 in its other features.

| Exc. | V.G. | Good | Fair | Poor |
|------|------|------|------|------|
| 1000 | 875 | 750 | 500 | 350 |

### Model 1910 Carbine
This is also a similar model except for the caliber, 9.5x57mm.

| Exc. | V.G. | Good | Fair | Poor |
|------|------|------|------|------|
| 1000 | 875 | 750 | 500 | 350 |

### Model 1924 Carbine
This is the Model 1905 chambered for the .30-06 cartridge.

| Exc. | V.G. | Good | Fair | Poor |
|------|------|------|------|------|
| 1150 | 1000 | 900 | 750 | 450 |

### High Velocity Rifle
This version of the bolt-action Mannlicher Schoenauer is chambered for the 7x64 Brenneke, .30-06, 8x60S Magnum, 9.3x62mm, and the 10.75x68mm cartridges. It has a 23.5" barrel with a folding-leaf sight. The walnut stock is half- length. Takedown Model--Add 75 Percent.

| Exc. | V.G. | Good | Fair | Poor |
|------|------|------|------|------|
| 2250 | 2000 | 1750 | 1000 | 700 |

All of the above models were discontinued prior to WWII.

### Model 1950
This model is also the classic Mannlicher Schoenauer bolt action chambered for the .257 Roberts, .270 Winchester, and the .30-06 cartridges. It has a 24" barrel and a 5-shot rotary magazine. This model has provisions for conventionally mounting a scope. The walnut stock is half-length, with an ebony forend tip. It was manufactured between 1950 and 1952.

| Exc. | V.G. | Good | Fair | Poor |
|------|------|------|------|------|
| 800 | 700 | 550 | 450 | 375 |

### Model 1950 Carbine
This version is similar to the Model 1950 rifle except that it has a 20" barrel and a full-length stock.

| Exc. | V.G. | Good | Fair | Poor |
|------|------|------|------|------|
| 1000 | 900 | 750 | 600 | 450 |

### Model 1950 6.5 Carbine
This model is chambered for the 6.5x54mm Mannlicher Schoenauer cartridge and has a 18.5" barrel with the full-length stock.

| Exc. | V.G. | Good | Fair | Poor |
|------|------|------|------|------|
| 1000 | 900 | 750 | 600 | 450 |

### Model 1952
This version is similar to the Model 1950 except that it features a turned-back bolt handle. This model was manufactured between 1952 and 1956,

| Exc. | V.G. | Good | Fair | Poor |
|------|------|------|------|------|
| 800 | 700 | 550 | 450 | 375 |

### Model 1952 Carbine
This model is similar to the full stocked Model 1950 carbine except that it is chambered for 7x57mm in addition to the other calibers that were chambered in the Model 1950. The bolt handle is also turned back. This model was manufactured between 1952 and 1956.

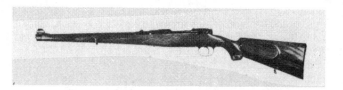

| Exc. | V.G. | Good | Fair | Poor |
|------|------|------|------|------|
| 1000 | 900 | 750 | 600 | 450 |

### Model 1952 6.5mm Carbine
This version is chambered for the 6.5x54mm Mannlicher Schoenauer cartridge and has the turned-back bolt handle and an 18.5" barrel. It was manufactured between 1952 and 1956.

| Exc. | V.G. | Good | Fair | Poor |
|------|------|------|------|------|
| 1000 | 900 | 750 | 600 | 450 |

### Model 1956 Rifle
This model is chambered for the .243 and the .30-06 cartridges and has a more modern, less classic European appearance than the Model 1952. The stock features a Monte Carlo comb that is higher for scoped shooting, and the barrel is 22" in length. The stock is half-length. This model was manufactured between 1956 and 1960.

| Exc. | V.G. | Good | Fair | Poor |
|------|------|------|------|------|
| 800 | 700 | 550 | 450 | 375 |

### Model 1956 Carbine
This model is similar to the Model 1956 rifle, with a 20" barrel and a full-length stock. It was manufactured between 1956 and 1960.

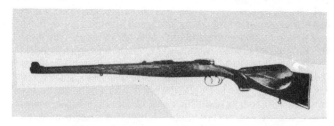

| Exc. | V.G. | Good | Fair | Poor |
|------|------|------|------|------|
| 1000 | 900 | 750 | 600 | 450 |

### Model 1961 MCA Rifle
This is an improved version of the Model 1956. It has a more modern appearance and is set up for easier scope mounting.

| Exc. | V.G. | Good | Fair | Poor |
|------|------|------|------|------|
| 800 | 700 | 550 | 450 | 375 |

### Model 1961 MCA Carbine.
This model is similar to the rifle, with a 20" barrel and a half-length stock.

| Exc. | V.G. | Good | Fair | Poor |
|------|------|------|------|------|
| 1000 | 900 | 750 | 600 | 450 |

### Model M72 LM Rifle
This version has a 23" fluted barrel and the full-length walnut stock. It is available with double-set triggers or a conventional single trigger. It is chambered for various popular cartridges and was manufactured between 1972 and 1980.

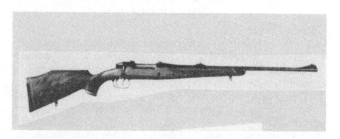

| Exc. | V.G. | Good | Fair | Poor |
|------|------|------|------|------|
| 800 | 700 | 550 | 450 | 375 |

## MANUFRANCE
### St. Etienne, France
### SEE--Le Francais

In addition to the "LeFancais Pistol" that is covered in its own section, this company made other firearms that are of interest.

### Auto Stand
This is a blowback-operated semi-automatic chambered for the .22 l.r. cartridge. It is a target pistol that was manufactured by Pyrenees and marketed by Manufrance. It is identical to the Pyrenees Model E-1.

| Exc. | V.G. | Good | Fair | Poor |
|---|---|---|---|---|
| 250 | 225 | 200 | 150 | 100 |

### Buffalo Stand
This is a bolt-action pistol that has a 12" barrel. It has adjustable sights; and the finish is blued, with a walnut stock. It is chambered for the .22 l.r. cartridge and was manufactured before 1914.

| Exc. | V.G. | Good | Fair | Poor |
|---|---|---|---|---|
| 250 | 225 | 200 | 150 | 100 |

### Le Agent
This is a solid-frame double-action revolver that has no ejector. It is chambered for the 8mm French service cartridge, has a 5" barrel, and is blued with checkered walnut grips. This revolver saw service with some French government agencies in the 1890's.

| Exc. | V.G. | Good | Fair | Poor |
|---|---|---|---|---|
| 200 | 175 | 150 | 100 | 75 |

### Le Colonial
This is a commercial model that is chambered for the 8mm French service cartridge and has a 5" barrel. It is a solid-framed, concealed-hammer revolver with no ejector. It looks similar to a large "Velo-Dog" revolver. The quality of this model is mediocre. It was manufactured around the turn of the century.

| Exc. | V.G. | Good | Fair | Poor |
|---|---|---|---|---|
| 200 | 175 | 150 | 100 | 75 |

## MANURHIN
### Mulhouse, France

This company is predominately in the business of manufacturing machine tools and producing loading tools for the ammunition industry. After WWII they obtained a license to produce Walther pistols from Fritz Walther. These pistols are very similar to the German versions but are marked "Manufacture de Machines du Haut-Rhin" on the left front of the slide and "Lic Excl. Walther" on the left rear. The grips have the name of the company molded into them. These pistols are chambered for .22,

7.65mm, and 9mm Short. They were imported into the U.S.A. in the early 1950's by Thalson Import Co. of San Francisco, California. Later models were imported by Interarms, but these pistols are simply marked "Mark II" and "Made in France." The pistols manufactured are the entire line of PP and PPK models, and the values would be approximately 25 percent less than a comparable Walther-manufactured pistol.

### New Production
The Matra Manurhin Defense Corp. is currently manufacturing this line of handguns, and they are imported by Atlantic Business Organizations of New York. Importation was resumed in 1988.

### Model 73 Defense Revolver
This is a double action, swingout-cylinder, solid-framed revolver that is extremely well made. It is chambered for the .357/.38 Special cartridges and has barrel lengths of 2.5", 3", or 4" with fixed sights. The finish is blued, and the grips are checkered walnut.

| NIB | Exc. | V.G. | Good | Fair | Poor |
|---|---|---|---|---|---|
| 1150 | 1000 | 850 | 750 | 500 | 350 |

### Model 73 Gendarmerie
This model is similar to the Defense Revolver except that it has adjustable sights and is also offered with a 5.5", 6", and an 8" long barrel.

| NIB | Exc. | V.G. | Good | Fair | Poor |
|---|---|---|---|---|---|
| 1250 | 1100 | 900 | 800 | 550 | 400 |

### Model 73 Sport
This model has a release trigger, target-type adjustable sights, and a special, short lock time action. Otherwise the features are the same as on the Gendarmerie model.

| NIB | Exc. | V.G. | Good | Fair | Poor |
|---|---|---|---|---|---|
| 1250 | 1100 | 900 | 800 | 550 | 400 |

### Model 73 Convertible
This model is similar to the Gendarmerie model except that it is available in three interchangeable calibers--.22 rimfire, .32, and .38. Values are for complete unit with three barrels and cylinder.

| NIB | Exc. | V.G. | Good | Fair | Poor |
|---|---|---|---|---|---|
| 2250 | 1850 | 1600 | 1400 | 950 | 750 |

### Model 73 Silhouette
This model is similar to the Sport model and is chambered for the .22 l.r. or the .357 Magnum cartridges. It has a 10" or a 10.75" heavy full-shrouded barrel and walnut grips that are fitted to fill the hand.

| NIB | Exc. | V.G. | Good | Fair | Poor |
|---|---|---|---|---|---|
| 1200 | 1050 | 850 | 750 | 500 | 350 |

### Model PP
This is a newly manufactured French version of the Walther Model PP. It is very similar to the German version and has a new steel hammer-block safety.

| Exc. | V.G. | Good | Fair | Poor |
|---|---|---|---|---|
| 400 | 350 | 300 | 225 | 150 |

### Model PPK/S
This also is a French version of the Walther with the hammer-block safety.

| Exc. | V.G. | Good | Fair | Poor |
|---|---|---|---|---|
| 400 | 350 | 300 | 225 | 150 |

314 • MARATHON PRODUCTS

## MARATHON PRODUCTS, INC.
### Santa Barbara, California

**.22 First Shot**
This is a small bolt-action single-shot rifle that was designed to be a first gun for a small and young shooter. It has a 16.5" barrel with open sights. The finish is blued, with a hardwood stock. The total length of this rifle is 31". It was manufactured between 1985 and 1987.

| Exc. | V.G. | Good | Fair | Poor |
|------|------|------|------|------|
| 65   | 55   | 45   | 30   | 25   |

**.22 Super Shot**
This rifle is similar to the First Shot, with a 24" barrel and a full-sized stock. It was manufactured between 1985 and 1987.

| Exc. | V.G. | Good | Fair | Poor |
|------|------|------|------|------|
| 65   | 55   | 45   | 30   | 25   |

**.22 Hot Shot Pistol**
This is a bolt-action pistol that is chambered for .22 l.r. and has a 14.5" barrel. The finish is blued, with a hardwood stock. It was manufactured in 1986 and 1987.

| Exc. | V.G. | Good | Fair | Poor |
|------|------|------|------|------|
| 65   | 55   | 45   | 30   | 25   |

**Centerfire Rifle**
This model is based on a Mauser bolt action and is chambered for various popular centerfire cartridges. It has a 24" barrel and a 5-shot magazine. It features open sights and an adjustable trigger. The finish is blued, with a walnut stock. This model was manufactured in 1985 and 1986.

| Exc. | V.G. | Good | Fair | Poor |
|------|------|------|------|------|
| 300  | 250  | 200  | 150  | 125  |

## MARBLES GAME GETTER
### Gladstone, Michigan

**Game Getter**
The Marble Manufacturing Company produced many products for the sportsman from 1907 until 1929. They made compasses, axes, and some very collectible knives. They also produced the Game Getter, an Over/Under pistol that features a rifled barrel chambered for .22 caliber rimfire over a smooth-bore barrel chambered for .44-40 Game Getter/ .410 in a 2" or 2.5" chambering. This pistol is available with barrel lengths of 12", 15", or 18". The Over/Under barrels are separated, and there is a folding skeleton steel stock. The barrels break open for loading, and the hammer automatically selects the barrel to be fired. The finish is blued, and the grips are either rubber or walnut. There was a leather holster offered with this pistol, that would be worth $100 additional. The problem with this firearm is that it is not legal to own if the barrel length is 12" or 15" unless it has been properly registered during the 1968 BATF Amnesty. The values shown are for the 18"-barrelled version only. If a short-barrelled version is encountered, be sure that it is legally registered and that you are dealing with a Class 3 licensed individual or business. Then seek individual appraisal.

| Exc. | V.G. | Good | Fair | Poor |
|------|------|------|------|------|
| 800  | 700  | 650  | 500  | 400  |

## MARGOLIN
### Soviet State Arsenal

**Model MTs-1**
This is a blowback-operated, semi-automatic target pistol chambered for the .22 l.r. cartridge. It has a 7.5" barrel and a 6-shot detachable magazine. The finish is blue, with checkered walnut grips. This pistol is seldom encountered in the U.S.A.

| Exc. | V.G. | Good | Fair | Poor |
|------|------|------|------|------|
| 800  | 700  | 600  | 450  | 350  |

**Target Model**
This Model is similar to the Model MTs-1 except that the barrel length is 6".

| Exc. | V.G. | Good | Fair | Poor |
|------|------|------|------|------|
| 800  | 700  | 600  | 450  | 350  |

## MARIETTE BREVETTE
### Liege, Belgium

**Pepperbox**
This is a revolving, 6-barrelled, pepperbox-type pistol that was made from the patent of Mariette. This type of pepperbox was manufactured both in Belgium and France. It is chambered for .38 caliber percussion, and the barrels were made separately and screwed into a block that holds the 6 chambers. Other pepperboxes were usually made by boring one block with all the barrels. This pistol is of the double-action type, with a ring trigger that operates an internal hammer. The barrels are 2.8" in length; and the finish is blued, with floral engraving. The grips are ebony. The markings are "Mariette Brevette." This model was manufactured after 1837.

| Exc. | V.G. | Good | Fair | Poor |
|------|------|------|------|------|
| 1850 | 1600 | 1250 | 900  | 650  |

**4 Barrelled Pepperbox**
This model is similar to the 6-barrelled version except that it is chambered for .35 caliber percussion and has only four barrels.

| Exc. | V.G. | Good | Fair | Poor |
|------|------|------|------|------|
| 1600 | 1300 | 1000 | 750  | 500  |

## MARLIN FIREARMS CO.
### New Haven, Connecticut

**Ballard Rifles**
John Mahlon Marlin was born in Connecticut in 1836. There is not much known about his life until the time he became a pistol maker in 1863. There is information to indicate that he was employed as a machinist at the Colt factory. Although not confirmed, it is certain that he was a machinist, as the apprentice agreement he signed with the American Machine Works when he was 18 years of age is still in existence. He was listed in the city directory of New Haven, Connecticut, in 1863 as a pistol maker. The first rifle of his own design was not patented until 1879, although he manufactured Ballard rifles from 1875.

Under his leadership the Marlin Firearms Co. became quite successful and produced a number of high quality firearms. During his years at Marlin he had in his employ Andrew Burgess and Lewis Hepburn, two of the foremost firearms designers and inventors of their time. Through their efforts John M. Marlin was able to build a successful firearms company that endures to this day. John Mahlon Marlin died in 1901. There are currently a great many collectors of Marlin firearms; and in this writer's opinion, these firearms are definitely a desirable proposition, as they have not peaked in value and probably will not do so for some time. One is able to purchase high-grade and significant Marlin firearms at substantially less than a comparable Winchester.

There is one disadvantage of collecting Marlin firearms--the factory records are far less than complete, and there are not as many published works to enable collectors to catalog the products as well as some of the other companies. For our purposes we list the firearms chronologically in respective categories including the Ballards and Marlin-Ballards.

The Ballard single-shot rifle was invented by C. H. Ballard of Worcester, Massachusetts. It was patented in 1861. The first of the Ballard rifles was manufactured by the Ball and Williams Co. of Worchester, Massachusetts. In 1866 Merwin and Bray purchased the firm, calling it Merrimack Arms Co., and operated until 1869, when they sold it to the Brown Manufacturing Co. of New York City. This venture took a decidedly negative turn, and in 1873 mortgage foreclosure forced the sale to Schoverling and Daly of New York City. These gentlemen were arms dealers, not manufacturers, so they entered into an agreement with John M. Marlin to produce the Ballard rifle.

The rifles produced during this period are regarded as some of the finest single shots ever made, and the venture finally became successful. In 1881 the business became incorporated as the Marlin Firearms Co., and the Ballard was produced under this banner until it was discontinued around the year 1891. The popularity of the repeating rifle simply eroded the demand for the fine single shot until it was no longer a profitable venture.

## Ball & Williams Ballards
### First Model
This model was the first Ballard produced. It was introduced in 1861 and was offered with a 24" or 28" octagonal barrel. The frame is case-colored, and the barrel is blued. The walnut stock is varnished. The major identifying feature of this model is the inside extractor. This was the only Ballard that had this feature before Marlin began to manufacture the rifle in 1875. The barrel is stamped "Ball & Williams/Worchester, Mass." and "Ballards Patent/Nov.5,1861." There were approximately 100 manufactured and serial numbered from 1-100.

| Exc. | V.G. | Good | Fair | Poor |
|------|------|------|------|------|
| 1500 | 1300 | 1000 | 800 | 550 |

### Military Rifle
There is not enough known about these rifles and probably never will be. They were chambered most frequently for the .44 and .54 rimfire cartridges and feature the outside tangs and extractors. They were offered with a 30" round barrel and full-length forearm. There are three barrel bands and sling swivels. The government ordered only 35 of these for use in the Civil War; and if one was to be definitely authenticated as a genuine martial specimen, it would be quite valuable. Many of these rifles were marked "Kentucky" on top of the receiver because the militia of that state armed its men with the Ballard rifles and carbines. This marking was a sales aid used by the company and does not indicate militia ownership. The amount manufactured is not known. Barrel markings are as on the first model.

| Exc. | V.G. | Good | Fair | Poor |
|------|------|------|------|------|
| 900 | 750 | 650 | 500 | 350 |

### Civil War Military Carbine
This model has a 22" part-round/part-octagonal barrel and is chambered for the .44 rimfire cartridge. It has the outside tang and extractor. The stock and forearm are walnut with a barrel-band sling swivel. The buttstock bears an oval cartouche surrounding the inspector's marks, "MM." These letters also appear stamped on major metal parts. There were 1,509 ordered by the government for use in the Civil War. The barrel was marked the same as the rifle.

| Exc. | V.G. | Good | Fair | Poor |
|------|------|------|------|------|
| 1500 | 1300 | 1000 | 800 | 550 |

### Sporting Rifle
This model is chambered for the .32, .38, and .44 rimfire cartridges. The octagonal barrel is 24", 26", or 28" in length and is blued. The frame is case-colored. The stock and forearm are varnished walnut, and there is a knob that protrudes in front of the frame to operate the outside manual extractor. There is a crescent buttplate standard. There were approximately 6,500 manufactured, and barrel markings are the same as on the first model.

| Exc. | V.G. | Good | Fair | Poor |
|------|------|------|------|------|
| 800 | 650 | 550 | 400 | 300 |

### Sporting Carbine
This model is similar in appearance to the Sporting Rifle with a 22" part-round/part-octagon barrel. It is chambered for the .44 and .54 caliber cartridge, and the sling swivel is found on a barrel band in the front. The knob on the bottom activates the outside extractor. There have been some encountered with "Kentucky" stamped on the top, but this does not affect the value. The markings are the same as on the previous models. There are no production figures available, but some estimate approximately 2,000 were manufactured.

| Exc. | V.G. | Good | Fair | Poor |
|------|------|------|------|------|
| 900 | 750 | 650 | 500 | 350 |

### Dual Ignition System
This system allows the use of the rimfire cartridge or percussion method by simply turning the striker on the hammer from one position to the other. This model features a percussion nipple mounted on the breech block, and the hammer is marked "Patented Jan.5,1864." The patent was held by Merwin and Bray. This swivel system is usually found on the sporting models and would increase the value of the weapon by 20 percent.

## Merrimack Arms Co. and Brown Manufacturing Co.
The values for the Ballard rifles manufactured by these two firms are the same, and the specifications are similar. The identifying difference is in the markings, "Merrimack Arms & Mfg. Co. / Newburyport Mass." or "Brown Mfg.Co. Newburyport, Mass." Merrimack produced approximately 3,000 of these rifles between 1867 and 1869 serial numbered in the 18000-20000 range. Brown produced approximately 1,800 between 1869 and 1873 in the 20000-22000 serial number range.

### Sporting Rifle
This model was produced in .22 (rare), .32, .38, .44, .46, and .52 caliber rimfire or percussion, as most encountered featured the dual ignition system and had the nipple in the breech block. They have either a round or octagonal barrel in 24", 26", or 28" lengths. The appearance and finish is similar to the Ball & Williams rifles; and the major difference is the inside tang. The extractor was still outside mounted and manually activated. Exact production breakdown is unknown. There is no premium for the dual ignition system on these later guns.

| Exc. | V.G. | Good | Fair | Poor |
|------|------|------|------|------|
| 850 | 700 | 550 | 450 | 300 |

### Sporting Carbine
This model is quite similar in appearance to the Sporting Rifle, with a 22" part-round/part-octagonal barrel.

| Exc. | V.G. | Good | Fair | Poor |
|------|------|------|------|------|
| 950 | 800 | 650 | 550 | 400 |

### Military Rifle
The Military Rifle is similar to the sporting version except that it has a 30" round barrel and full-length forearm with three barrel bands. It is chambered for the .44 and .52 caliber rimfire or percussion with the dual ignition system.

| Exc. | V.G. | Good | Fair | Poor |
|------|------|------|------|------|
| 950 | 800 | 650 | 550 | 400 |

### Shotgun
This model is similar to the Sporting Rifle in appearance but is chambered for 24 gauge, with a 30" round barrel. There is a groove milled in the top of the frame to use as a sight. The buttplate is shotgun-style instead of the usual crescent shape.

| Exc. | V.G. | Good | Fair | Poor |
|------|------|------|------|------|
| 650 | 550 | 450 | 350 | 250 |

## Marlin-Ballard Rifles

Commencing in 1875 the Ballard single-shot rifle was made by John Marlin for Schoverling and Daly. In 1881 the business was incorporated and became the Marlin Firearms Co. All the Ballards made from then until 1891, when they were discontinued, were produced under this banner. The only real difference in the rifles manufactured during these periods was in the markings. The earlier rifles are stamped "J.M.Marlin New Haven. Conn. U.S.A./Ballards Patent. Nov.5,1861"; and the post-1881 models are stamped "Marlin Firearms Co. New Haven Ct. U.S.A. / Patented Feb.9,1875 / Ballards Patent Nov.5,1861." The major difference between Marlin-made Ballards and the earlier models is the inside tang and the internal extractor on the Marlin-made rifles. All of the Marlin-made Ballards have an octagonal frame top, and the Marlin Firearms Co. models have grooved receiver sides.

The standard finish on all these later rifles is case-colored frames and blued octagonal or part-round/part-octagonal barrels. There are many variations in these rifles as to types of sights, stock, engraving, and other special-order features--such as barrel lengths, weights, and contours. These rifles must be considered individually and competently appraised. There is also the fact that many of these Ballards have been rebarrelled and rechambered over the years, as they were known for their shooting ability and were used quite extensively.

This can seriously affect the value in a negative manner unless it can be authenticated that the work was done by the likes of Harry Pope or George Schoyen and other noted and respected gunsmiths of that era. This can add considerably to the value of the rifle. One must approach this model with caution and learn all that can be learned before purchasing.

## Ballard Hunters Rifle

This model resembles the earlier Brown Mfg. Co. rifles, and it utilizes many leftover parts acquired by Marlin. It is chambered for the .32, .38, and .44 rimfire and centerfire and features John Marlin's unique reversible firing pin that allows the same gun to use both rimfire and centerfire ammunition simply by rotating the firing pin in the breech block. This model still had the external ejector and bears the J. M. Marlin markings. There were approximately 500 manufactured in the 1 to 500 serial range. They were produced in 1875 and 1876.

| Exc. | V.G. | Good | Fair | Poor |
|------|------|------|------|------|
| 1500 | 1300 | 1000 | 800 | 550 |

## Ballard No. 1 Hunters Rifle

This model bears the early J. M. Marlin marking only, as it was manufactured from 1876 until 1880 and was discontinued before the incorporation. It has a 26", 28", and 30" barrel and is chambered for the .44 rimfire or centerfire cartridge. It has the reversible firing pin and also the new internal extractor. Production figures are not available, but the serial-number range is between 500 and 4000.

| Exc. | V.G. | Good | Fair | Poor |
|------|------|------|------|------|
| 900 | 750 | 650 | 500 | 375 |

## Ballard No. 1-1/2 Hunters Rifle

This model is similar to the No. 1 except that it is chambered for the .45-70, .40-63, and the .40-65 cartridges and does not have the reversible firing pin. The barrel length is 30" and 32". It was manufactured between 1879 and 1883. This model is found with both early and later markings.

| Exc. | V.G. | Good | Fair | Poor |
|------|------|------|------|------|
| 1100 | 950 | 850 | 700 | 500 |

## Ballard No. 1-3/4 "Far West" Hunters Rifle

This model was made by J. M. Marlin only and is similar to the 1-1/2, the difference being the addition of double-set triggers and a ring on the opening lever. It was manufactured in 1880 and 1881.

| Exc. | V.G. | Good | Fair | Poor |
|------|------|------|------|------|
| 1000 | 850 | 750 | 600 | 400 |

## Ballard No. 2 Sporting Rifle

This model is chambered for the .32, .38 rimfire or centerfire cartridges, and the .44 centerfire. It has the reversible firing pin and was offered in 26", 28", and 30" barrel lengths. This model features "Rocky Mountain" sights and was manufactured between 1876 and 1891. It is found with both early and late markings.

| Exc. | V.G. | Good | Fair | Poor |
|------|------|------|------|------|
| 850 | 750 | 600 | 450 | 300 |

## Ballard No. 3 Gallery Rifle

This model is similar to the No. 2 rifle but is chambered for the .22 rimfire cartridge and has a manually operated external extractor. The sights are the same; and a 24" barrel was offered in addition to the 26", 28", and 30". This rifle was manufactured between 1876 and 1891.

| Exc. | V.G. | Good | Fair | Poor |
|------|------|------|------|------|
| 950 | 850 | 700 | 400 | 250 |

## Ballard No. 3F Gallery Rifle

This is a deluxe version of the No. 3. It has a pistol grip stock, a nickel-plated Schutzen-style buttplate, and an opening lever like a repeating rifle. It features a 26" octagonal barrel and an oil-finished stock. It was manufactured in the late 1880's and is quite scarce in today's market.

| Exc. | V.G. | Good | Fair | Poor |
|------|------|------|------|------|
| 1300 | 1150 | 1000 | 850 | 650 |

## Ballard No. 4 Perfection Rifle

This model is chambered for a number of centerfire calibers from .32-40 to .50-70. The barrel lengths are from 26" to 30", and the sights are of the "Rocky Mountain" type. This model was manufactured between 1876 and 1891.

| Exc. | V.G. | Good | Fair | Poor |
|------|------|------|------|------|
| 850 | 750 | 650 | 500 | 350 |

## Ballard No. 3-1/2 Target Rifle

This model is similar to the No. 4 Perfection Rifle except that it has a checkered stock with a shotgun-style buttplate, a 30" barrel, and a tang peep sight with globe front sight. It was chambered for the .40-65 cartridge and was manufactured from 1880-1882.

| Exc. | V.G. | Good | Fair | Poor |
|------|------|------|------|------|
| 1200 | 1050 | 800 | 650 | 450 |

## Ballard No. 4-1/2 Mid Range Rifle

This model is also a variation of the No. 4 Perfection model. It has a higher-grade checkered stock with a shotgun buttplate. It has a 30" part-round/part-octagonal barrel and is chambered for the .38-40, .40-65, and the .45-70 cartridges. It features a Vernier tang peep sight and a globe front sight. It was manufactured between 1878 and 1882.

| Exc. | V.G. | Good | Fair | Poor |
|------|------|------|------|------|
| 1500 | 1300 | 1150 | 950 | 675 |

## Ballard No. 4-1/2 A-1 Mid Range Target Rifle

This is a deluxe version of the No. 4-1/2 rifle. It features scroll engraving on the frame--with "Ballard A-1" on the left and "Mid-Range" on the right. It is chambered for the .38-50 and the .40-65 cartridge and has a high- grade checkered stock with a horn forend tip. The sights are the highest-grade Vernier tang sight and a spirit lever front sight. The shotgun or rifle-style butt was optional. This model was manufactured between 1878 and 1880.

| Exc. | V.G. | Good | Fair | Poor |
|------|------|------|------|------|
| 2000 | 1800 | 1500 | 1150 | 850 |

## Ballard No. 5 Pacific Rifle

This model has a 30" or 32" medium- to heavy-weight barrel, with a ramrod mounted underneath. It is chambered for many different calibers from .38-50 to .50-70. This model features "Rocky Mountain" sights, a crescent butt, double-set triggers, and a ring-style opening lever. It was manufactured between 1876 and 1891.

| Exc. | V.G. | Good | Fair | Poor |
|------|------|------|------|------|
| 1800 | 1650 | 1300 | 950 | 650 |

## Ballard No. 5-1/2 Montana Rifle

This model is similar to the Pacific Rifle, with an extra heavy-weight barrel, and is chambered for the .45 Sharps cartridge only. It features a checkered steel shotgun-style buttplate. It was manufactured from 1882- 1884 and has the late markings only.

| Exc. | V.G. | Good | Fair | Poor |
|------|------|------|------|------|
| 2500 | 2250 | 1750 | 1300 | 1000 |

## Ballard No. 6 Schuetzen Off Hand Rifle

This model has a 30" or 32" octagonal barrel and is chambered for the .40-65, .44-75, and the .38-50 cartridges. The stock is of select walnut in the high-combed Schuetzen style. The buttplate is nickel-plated, and the receiver is not engraved. The sights are Vernier tang type on the rear and a spirit lever front. The triggers are double set, and the opening lever has a ring and a spur. This model is marked J. M. Marlin only and was manufactured between 1876 and 1880.

| Exc. | V.G. | Good | Fair | Poor |
|------|------|------|------|------|
| 2200 | 2000 | 1750 | 1300 | 1100 |

## Ballard No. 6 Schuetzen Rifle

This model is similar to the Off Hand model but was produced by the later Marlin Firearms Co. and was so marked. It is a more deluxe version with checkered stock, horn forend tip, and a fully engraved receiver. This model was chambered for the .32-40 and the .38-55 cartridges and was manufactured between 1881 and 1891.

| Exc. | V.G. | Good | Fair | Poor |
|------|------|------|------|------|
| 2500 | 2250 | 1750 | 1300 | 1000 |

## Ballard No. 6-1/2 Off Hand Mid Range Rifle

This model is chambered for the .40-54 Everlasting cartridge only. It has a 28" or 30" part-round/part-octagonal barrel, a Schuetzen-style stock, and a plain non-engraved receiver. It was manufactured between 1880 and 1882.

| Exc. | V.G. | Good | Fair | Poor |
|------|------|------|------|------|
| 2000 | 1800 | 1500 | 1150 | 850 |

## Ballard No. 6-1/2 Rigby Off Hand Mid Range Rifle

This model is chambered for the .38-50 and the .40-65 cartridges. It features the Rigby ribbed-style barrel in 26" and 28" lengths, with Vernier rear and globe front sights and a high-grade, checkered walnut, Schuetzen-style stock with horn forend tip, and pistolgrip cap. The buttplate is nickel-plated, and the opening lever is of the ring type with a single trigger and extensively engraved receiver. This model was manufactured from 1880 to 1882.

| Exc. | V.G. | Good | Fair | Poor |
|------|------|------|------|------|
| 2500 | 2250 | 1750 | 1300 | 1000 |

## Ballard No. 6-1/2 Off Hand Rifle

This model is chambered for the .32-40 and .38-55 cartridges and features barrel lengths of 28" and 30". It has a checkered, high-grade walnut, Schuetzen-style stock with nickel-plated buttplate. The forend tip and pistolgrip cap are of horn, and the receiver is engraved. This model has a single trigger, full-ring opening lever, Vernier tang rear sight, and spirit lever front sight. The 6-1/2 Off Hand was made by the Marlin Firearms Co. between 1883 and 1891 and is found with the later markings only.

| Exc. | V.G. | Good | Fair | Poor |
|------|------|------|------|------|
| 2250 | 1850 | 1550 | 1200 | 900 |

## Ballard No. 7 "Creedmore A-1" Long Range Rifle

This model is commonly chambered for the .44-100 or the .45-100 cartridges. It has a 34" part-round/part-octagonal barrel and a high-grade checkered pistolgrip stock, with a horn forend tip and shotgun-style butt. The sights are a special 1300-yard Vernier tang rear and a spirit level front. There is another sight base on the heel of the stock for mounting the rear sight for ultra long-range shooting. The opening lever is similar to a repeating rifle, and a single trigger is featured. The receiver is engraved and marked "Ballard A-1" on the left and "Long Range" on the right. This model was manufactured between 1876 and 1886 and is found with both early and late markings.

| Exc. | V.G. | Good | Fair | Poor |
|------|------|------|------|------|
| 3000 | 2750 | 2250 | 1500 | 1200 |

## Ballard No. 7 Long Range Rifle

This model is similar to the "Creedmore A-1" but is slightly less deluxe. The engraving is less elaborate, and the lettering on the receiver is absent. This model was manufactured between 1883 and 1890 and is found with the later markings only.

| Exc. | V.G. | Good | Fair | Poor |
|------|------|------|------|------|
| 2750 | 2500 | 2000 | 1250 | 1000 |

## Ballard No. 7A-1 Long Range Rifle

This model is a higher-grade version of the "Creedmore A-1," with fancier walnut and a checkered straight stock. Better sights and deluxe engraving are also featured. This model was manufactured between 1879 and 1883 and is found with both markings.

| Exc. | V.G. | Good | Fair | Poor |
|------|------|------|------|------|
| 3500 | 3250 | 2750 | 2000 | 1500 |

## Ballard No. 7A-1 Extra Long Range Rifle

This is the highest-grade version of the No. 7 rifles. It features a 34" "Rigby"-type ribbed, round barrel. This was usually a special-order rifle with most features to customer specifications. The model was manufactured in very limited numbers between 1879 and 1883. It is found with both markings.

| Exc. | V.G. | Good | Fair | Poor |
|------|------|------|------|------|
| 4000 | 3500 | 3000 | 2250 | 1700 |

## Ballard No. 8 Union Hill Rifle

This model has a 28" and 30" part-round/part-octagonal barrel and is chambered for the .32-40 and the .38-55 cartridges. It has a checkered pistolgrip stock with nickel-plated buttplate; and the opening lever is fully enclosed ring, as on the repeaters. There is a double-set trigger and a tang peep with globe front sight. The receiver is not engraved. This model was manufactured between 1884 and 1890 and is found only with the late markings. This was one of the most popular rifles in the Ballard line.

| Exc. | V.G. | Good | Fair | Poor |
|------|------|------|------|------|
| 1500 | 1250 | 1000 | 750 | 500 |

## Ballard No. 9 Union Hill Rifle

This model is similar to the No. 8 except that it features a single trigger and better sights. It was manufactured between 1884 and 1891 and has the later markings only.

| Exc. | V.G. | Good | Fair | Poor |
|------|------|------|------|------|
| 1800 | 1600 | 1250 | 1000 | 700 |

## Ballard No. 10 Schuetzen Junior Rifle

This model is simply a heavier-barrelled version of the No. 9. The barrel is 32" long, and the checkered pistolgrip stock is of the off-hand style. The rear sight is a Vernier mid range model, and the front sight is a spirit-level type. This was a popular model that was manufactured between 1885 and 1891. It is found with the later markings only.

| Exc. | V.G. | Good | Fair | Poor |
|------|------|------|------|------|
| 2000 | 1800 | 1500 | 1150 | 850 |

## Marlin Handguns

The first firearm that was manufactured by John M. Marlin was actually a derring-type single shot that was small enough to be hidden in the palm of the hand. From this beginning evolved the company that became known for its highly accurate and dependable rifles. The Marlin Company manufactured handguns up to the turn of the centry, discontinuing their last and only double-action model in 1899.

## 1st Model Derringer

This was the first handgun produced by Marlin. The barrel is 2-1/16" long and pivots to the side for loading. There is a plunger under the frame that is depressed to free the barrel. This device is a Ballard patent. This pistol is chambered for the .22 rimfire cartridge, and there is no extractor. The frame is brass and usually nickel-plated. It has two grooves milled beneath the blued barrel. The grips are of rosewood. The barrel is stamped "J.M.Marlin, New Haven, Ct." There were approximately 2,000 manufactured between 1863 and 1867. They are quite scarce on today's market.

| Exc. | V.G. | Good | Fair | Poor |
|------|------|------|------|------|
| 500 | 425 | 350 | 250 | 175 |

## O.K. Model Derringer

The O.K. Model is chambered for .22, .30, and .32 rimfire cartridges. The barrel is 2-1/8" or 3-1/8" on the .32. There is no extractor, and it functions as the 1st Model. The frame is plated brass with flat sides, and the barrel is found either blued or nickel-plated. The grips are rosewood. The markings are the same as on the 1st Model but are located on the right side of the barrel. The top of the barrel is marked "O.K." There were approximately 5,000 manufactured between 1863 and 1870.

| Exc. | V.G. | Good | Fair | Poor |
|------|------|------|------|------|
| 450 | 400 | 325 | 225 | 150 |

## Victor Model Derringer

This Model is similar in appearance to the "O.K." Model but is larger in size and is chambered for the .38-caliber rimfire cartridge. The barrel is 2-11/16" long; and there was, for the first time, an extractor. The finish and function were unchanged. The right side of the barrel is stamped "J.M.Marlin/New Haven.Ct./Pat.April 5.1870." "Victor" is stamped on the top of the barrel. There were approximately 4,000 manufactured between 1870 and 1881.

| Exc. | V.G. | Good | Fair | Poor |
|------|------|------|------|------|
| 500 | 425 | 350 | 250 | 175 |

## Nevermiss Model Derringer

This model was made in three different sizes chambered for the .22, .32, and .41 rimfire cartridges. The barrel is 2.5" long and swings sideways for loading. The frame is plated brass, and the barrels are either blued or nickel-plated. The grips are rosewood. The frame is grooved under the barrels as on the 1st Model. There is an extractor on this Model. The barrel markings are the same as on the "Victor," with the top of the barrel marked "Nevermiss." There were approximately 5,000 manufactured between 1870 and 1881.

### .22 and .32 Caliber Models

| Exc. | V.G. | Good | Fair | Poor |
|------|------|------|------|------|
| 300 | 250 | 200 | 150 | 100 |

### .41 Caliber Model

| Exc. | V.G. | Good | Fair | Poor |
|------|------|------|------|------|
| 400 | 350 | 300 | 250 | 175 |

## Stonewall Model Derringer

This Model is identical to the .41-caliber "Nevermiss," but the top of the barrel is marked "Stonewall." It is very rarely encountered.

| Exc. | V.G. | Good | Fair | Poor |
|------|------|------|------|------|
| 500 | 450 | 400 | 350 | 225 |

## O.K. Pocket Revolver

This is a solid-frame, spur-trigger, single-action revolver chambered for the .22 rimfire short. The round barrel is 2.25", and the 7-shot cylinder is unfluted. The frame is nickel-plated brass with a blue or nickel-plated barrel, and the birdshead grips are rosewood. The cylinder pin is removable and is used to knock the empty cases out of the cylinder. The top of the barrel is marked "O.K." and "J.M.Marlin. New Haven, Conn. U.S.A." There were approximately 1,500 manufactured between 1870 and 1875.

| Exc. | V.G. | Good | Fair | Poor |
|------|------|------|------|------|
| 350 | 300 | 250 | 200 | 150 |

## Little Joker Revolver

This model is similar in appearance to the "O.K." model except that it features engraving and ivory or pearl grips. There were approximately 500 manufactured between 1871 and 1873.

| Exc. | V.G. | Good | Fair | Poor |
|------|------|------|------|------|
| 400 | 350 | 300 | 250 | 175 |

## J. M. Marlin Standard Pocket Revolvers

In 1872 Marlin began production of its Smith & Wesson look-alike. The Manhattan Firearms Co. had developed a copy of the Model 1 S&W .22 cartridge revolver. In 1868 the company ceased business, and the revolvers were produced by the American Standard Tool Co. until their dissolution in 1873.

In 1872 Marlin had entered into an agreement with this company to manufacture these revolvers which were no longer protected by the Rollin White patent after 1869. The Marlin revolvers are very similar to those made by American Standard, the only real difference being that Marlin grips are of the birdshead round configuration. A contoured grip frame and a patented pawl spring mechanism is utilized on the Marlin revolvers.

## Marlin XXX Standard 1872 Pocket Revolver

This is the first in the series of four Standard model revolvers. It is chambered for the .30 caliber rimfire. The earlier model has an octagonal 3-1/8" barrel; and the later, a round 3" barrel. There are round and octagonal barrel variations (with unfluted cylinder) and round barrel variations (with short and long fluted cylinders). All of the barrels are ribbed and tip up for loading. They have plated brass frames, and the barrels are nickel-plated.

The birdshead grips are of rosewood or hard rubber, bearing the monogram "M.F.A. Co." inside a star. There is a spur trigger. The markings "J.M.Marlin-New Haven Ct." appear on the earlier octagonal barrelled models. "U.S.A. Pat. July 1.1873" was added to the later round-barrelled models. All barrels are marked "XXX Standard 1872." There were approximately 5,000 of all types manufactured between 1872 and 1887.

**Octagon Barrel--Early Variation**

| Exc. | V.G. | Good | Fair | Poor |
|------|------|------|------|------|
| 400 | 350 | 300 | 250 | 175 |

**Round Barrel--Non-Fluted Cylinder**

| Exc. | V.G. | Good | Fair | Poor |
|------|------|------|------|------|
| 375 | 325 | 275 | 225 | 150 |

**Round Barrel--Short Fluted Cylinder**

| Exc. | V.G. | Good | Fair | Poor |
|------|------|------|------|------|
| 350 | 300 | 250 | 200 | 125 |

**Round Barrel--Long Fluted Cylinder**

| Exc. | V.G. | Good | Fair | Poor |
|------|------|------|------|------|
| 300 | 250 | 200 | 150 | 100 |

## Marlin XX Standard 1873 Pocket Revolver

This model is similar in appearance to the XXX 1872 model except that it is chambered for the .22 long rimfire and is marked "XX Standard 1873." There are three basic variations--the early octagonal barrel model with non-fluted cylinder, the round-barrel model with non-fluted cylinder, and the round barrel with fluted cylinder. Function and features are the same as described for the "XXX Standard 1872" model. There were approximately 5,000 manufactured between 1873 and 1887.

**Early Octagon Barrel Model**

| Exc. | V.G. | Good | Fair | Poor |
|------|------|------|------|------|
| 350 | 300 | 250 | 200 | 150 |

**Round Barrel--Non-Fluted Cylinder**

| Exc. | V.G. | Good | Fair | Poor |
|------|------|------|------|------|
| 300 | 250 | 200 | 150 | 100 |

**Round Barrel--Fluted Cylinder**

| Exc. | V.G. | Good | Fair | Poor |
|------|------|------|------|------|
| 275 | 225 | 175 | 125 | 80 |

## Marlin No. 32 Standard 1875 Pocket Revolver

This model is also similar in appearance to the "XXX Standard 1872" model except that it is chambered for the .32 rimfire cartridge. The 3" barrel is round with a rib, and the 5-shot cylinder is fluted and is in two different lengths to accommodate either the .32 short or long cartridge. The finish, function, and most markings are the same as on previous models with the exception of the barrel top marking "No.32 Standard 1875." There were approximately 8,000 manufactured between 1875 and 1887.

| Exc. | V.G. | Good | Fair | Poor |
|------|------|------|------|------|
| 275 | 225 | 175 | 125 | 80 |

## Marlin 38 Standard 1878 Pocket Revolver

This model is different than its predecessors in that it features a steel frame and flat bottom butt, with hard rubber monogram grips. There was still a spur trigger, and the 3.25" ribbed round barrel still tipped up for loading. This model is chambered for the .38 centerfire cartridge. The finish is full nickel plate, and the top of the barrel is marked "38 Standard 1878." There were approximately 9,000 manufactured between 1878 and 1887.

| Exc. | V.G. | Good | Fair | Poor |
|------|------|------|------|------|
| 300 | 250 | 200 | 150 | 100 |

## Marlin 1887 Double Action Revolver

This is the last handgun that Marlin produced and the only double action. It is chambered for the .32 or the .38 caliber centerfire cartridges and is of the break-open auto-ejector type. The fluted cylinder holds 6 shots in .32 and 5 shots in .38 caliber. The round ribbed barrel is 3.25" in length, and the frame is made of steel. The standard finish is nickel-plated with a blued triggerguard. Many full-blued examples have been noted. The round butt grips are hard rubber, and the top of the barrel is marked "Marlin Firearms Co. New Haven Conn. U.S.A./Patented Aug.9 1887." There were approximately 15,000 manufactured between 1887 and 1899.

| Exc. | V.G. | Good | Fair | Poor |
|------|------|------|------|------|
| 325 | 275 | 225 | 150 | 100 |

## Early Production Marlin Rifles

### Model 1881 Lever Action Rifle

This was the first of the Marlin lever-action rifles and has always been regarded as a high quality rifle. It is capable of handling the large calibers and was well received by the shooting public. The rifle is chambered for the .32-40, .38-55, .40-60, .45-70, and the .45-85. The 24", 28" or 30" octagonal barrel is standard. Round barrels were offered and are scarce today. There is a tubular magazine beneath the barrel, and the rear sight is the buckhorn type with a blade on the front. This model ejects its empty cartridges from the top. The finish is blued, with a case-colored hammer, lever, and buttplate. The walnut stock is varnished. There were approximately 20,000 manufactured between 1881 and 1892; but this is not easy to ascertain, as the factory records on Marlin rifles are quite incomplete.

**Early Model Produced in 1881 with a Removable Trigger Plate**

| Exc. | V.G. | Good | Fair | Poor |
|------|------|------|------|------|
| 4000 | 3500 | 3000 | 2250 | 1750 |

**Standard Model Made 1882-1892--Trigger Plate Non-Removable**

| Exc. | V.G. | Good | Fair | Poor |
|------|------|------|------|------|
| 2000 | 1750 | 1500 | 1000 | 700 |

**Lightweight Model--Thinner Frame, Lever, and Barrel--.32-40 and .38-55 Caliber Only--24" and 28" Barrel**

| Exc. | V.G. | Good | Fair | Poor |
|------|------|------|------|------|
| 2250 | 2000 | 1750 | 1250 | 900 |

### Model 1888 Lever Action Rifle

This Model is chambered for the .32-20, .38-40, and the .44-40 cartridges. This is a shorter action that was designed (chiefly by Lewis Hepburn) to handle the pistol cartridges for which it was chambered. The standard barrel was octagonal, but round barrels were available as special-order items. This is a top-ejecting action. It has a buckhorn rear and a blade front sight. The finish is blued with a case-colored hammer, lever, and buttplate. The walnut stock is varnished. There were approximately 4,800 manufactured in 1888 and 1889. As with most of these fine old rifles, many special-order options were available that affect today's market value. Individual appraisal would be necessary for these special models, to ascertain both value and authenticity.

| Exc. | V.G. | Good | Fair | Poor |
|------|------|------|------|------|
| 2250 | 2000 | 1750 | 1250 | 900 |

### Model 1889 Lever Action Rifle

This was Marlin's first side-eject, solid-top rifle. It is chambered for .25-20, .32-20, .38-40, and the .44-40 cartridges. It features either octagonal or round barrels in lengths from 24" to 32" with buckhorn rear and blade front sights. The finish is blued with a case-colored hammer, lever, and buttplate. The plain walnut stock is varnished. The barrel is stamped "Marlin Fire-Arms Co.New Haven Ct. U.S.A./Patented Oct.11 1887 April 2.1889."

This model features a lever latch, and many options were offered. Again one must urge individual appraisal on such variations. Values fluctuate greatly due to some seemingly insignificant variation. There were approximately 55,000 manufactured between 1889 and 1899.

**Production Model 24" Barrel**

| Exc. | V.G. | Good | Fair | Poor |
|------|------|------|------|------|
| 800 | 700 | 550 | 400 | 250 |

**Carbine 20" Barrel and Saddle Ring on Left Side of Receiver**

| Exc. | V.G. | Good | Fair | Poor |
|------|------|------|------|------|
| 1500 | 1300 | 1000 | 750 | 500 |

**Musket 30" Barrel with Full-length Stock--68 Made in .44-40**

| Exc. | V.G. | Good | Fair | Poor |
|------|------|------|------|------|
| 3500 | 3250 | 2750 | 2250 | 1500 |

## Model 1891 Lever Action Rifle

This was Marlin's first rifle designed to fire the .22 rimfire and the first repeating rifle to accept the .22 short, long, and long-rifle cartridges interchangeably. It was also chambered for the .32 rimfire and centerfire. The 24" octagonal barrel is standard, with a buckhorn rear and blade front sight. The finish is blued with a case-colored hammer, lever, and buttplate. The stock is plain walnut. The first variation is marked "Marlin Fire-Arms Co. New Haven, Ct. U.S.A./Pat'd Nov.19.1878.April 2.1889.Aug.12 1890" on the barrel, with the solid-topped frame marked "Marlin Safety." The second variation was marked the same with "March 1,1892" added. There were approximately 18,650 manufactured between 1891 and 1897.

### 1st Variation .22 Rimfire Only--Side Loading--Appr. 5,000

| Exc. | V.G. | Good | Fair | Poor |
|------|------|------|------|------|
| 1500 | 1250 | 1000 | 750 | 500 |

### 2nd Variation--.22 and .32 Rimfire, .32 Centerfire, Tube Loading, Model 1891 on Later Model Tangs

| Exc. | V.G. | Good | Fair | Poor |
|------|------|------|------|------|
| 750 | 650 | 500 | 400 | 275 |

## Model 1892 Lever Action Rifle

This is basically an improved version of the Model 1891 and is similar to the second variation of the 1891. The only notable exceptions were the tang marking "Model 1892" and "Model 92" on later models. The .22 rimfire was scarce in the Model 1892. There were approximately 45,000 manufactured between 1895 and 1916. There were many options, and these special-order guns must be individually appraised to ascertain value and authenticity.
Antique (Pre-1898)--Add 20 Percent.

| Exc. | V.G. | Good | Fair | Poor |
|------|------|------|------|------|
| 1050 | 900 | 700 | 500 | 400 |

### .32 Rimfire and Centerfire

| Exc. | V.G. | Good | Fair | Poor |
|------|------|------|------|------|
| 950 | 800 | 600 | 400 | 300 |

## Model 1893 Lever Action Rifle

This Model was the first rifle Marlin designed for the then new smokeless powder cartridges. It is chambered for the .25-36, .30-30, .32 Special, .32-40, and the .38-55. It was offered standard with either a round or octagonal barrel, in lengths of 24" to 32". Buckhorn rear and blade front sights were also standard. The receiver, lever, hammer, and buttplate are case-colored, and the rest is blued. The stock is varnished walnut.

As with all of these early Marlins, many options were offered and, when encountered, will drastically alter the value of the particular rifle. For this reason we supply the values for the basic model and urge securing competent appraisal on non-standard specimens. The barrel on earlier guns is marked "Marlin Fire-Arms Co. New Haven,Ct.U.S.A./Patented Oct.11.1887.April 2.1889.Aug.1.1893." In 1919 the markings were changed to "The Marlin Firearms Corporation/New Haven,Conn.U.S.A.-Patented." The rifles manufactured after 1904 are marked "Special Smokeless Steel" on the left side of the barrel. The upper tang is marked "Model 1893" on early guns; and "Model 93," on later specimens. There were approximately 900,000 manufactured between 1893 and 1935. Factory records are incomplete on the Model 1893.

**Antique Production Pre-1898**

| Exc. | V.G. | Good | Fair | Poor |
|------|------|------|------|------|
| 1000 | 800 | 650 | 450 | 275 |

**Modern Production 1899-1935**

| Exc. | V.G. | Good | Fair | Poor |
|------|------|------|------|------|
| 800 | 600 | 450 | 350 | 225 |

## Model 1894 Lever Action Rifle

This model is similar to the Model 1893, with a shorter action. It is chambered for the .25-20, .32-20, .38-40, and the .44-40. 24" to 32" round or octagonal barrels with full-length magazine tubes are standard, as are buckhorn rear and blade front sights. The finish is case-colored receiver, lever, hammer, and buttplate, with the rest blued. The walnut stock is varnished. The first versions were marked "Marlin Fire-Arms Co.,New Haven,Ct.U.S.A./Patented Oct.11,1887.April 2,1889." The top of the frame is marked "Marlin Safety," and the model designation is not stamped on the tang. These early rifles were chambered for .38-40 and .44-40 only. The later rifles added the patent date "Aug.1,1893"; and "Model 1894" was stamped on the tang. On the latest versions this was shortened to "Model 94." There were approximately 250,000 manufactured between 1894 and 1935. This model was also produced with a great many options. Individual appraisal should be secured when confronted with these features.

### Antique Production (Pre-1898)

| Exc. | V.G. | Good | Fair | Poor |
|------|------|------|------|------|
| 1000 | 800 | 650 | 450 | 275 |

### Modern Production (1899-1935)

| Exc. | V.G. | Good | Fair | Poor |
|------|------|------|------|------|
| 800 | 600 | 450 | 350 | 225 |

## Model 1895 Lever Action Rifle

This is a large rifle designed to fire the larger hunting cartridges. It is chambered for the .33 W.C.F., .38-56, .40-65, .40-70, .40-83, .45-70, and the .45-90. It came standard with round or octagonal barrels from 26" to 32" in length. A bull-length magazine tube was also standard, as were buckhorn rear and blade front sights. The finish is case-colored receiver, lever, and hammer; the rest is blued with a varnished walnut stock. The barrel markings are the same as the Model 1894, and the top tang is marked "Model 1895." After 1896 "Special Smokeless Steel" was stamped on the barrel. There were also many options available for this model, and they have a big effect on the value. There were approximately 18,000 manufactured between 1895 and 1917.

### Antique Production (Pre-1898)

| Exc. | V.G. | Good | Fair | Poor |
|------|------|------|------|------|
| 1250 | 1100 | 850 | 550 | 400 |

### Modern Production (1899-1917)

| Exc. | V.G. | Good | Fair | Poor |
|------|------|------|------|------|
| 1000 | 900 | 650 | 350 | 225 |

## Model 1897 Lever Action Rifle

This model is an improved version of the Model 1892. It was chambered for the .22 rimfire only and came standard with a 24", 26", or 28" round, octagonal, or part-round/ part-octagonal barrel. The standard sights are buckhorn rear and blade front, and all were manufactured as takedown rifles. They have case-colored receiver, lever, and hammer. The rest is blued, and the walnut stock is varnished. There were approximately 125,000 manufactured between 1897 and 1917. In 1922 production was begun with the designation changed to Model 39 which is produced to this day. There were also options offered with this rifle that have great effect on the value; take this into consideration and seek qualified appraisal.
For First Year Production Antique--Add 40 Percent.

**Standard Production Rifle**

| Exc. | V.G. | Good | Fair | Poor |
|------|------|------|------|------|
| 2000 | 1800 | 1500 | 1150 | 850 |

**Modern Production Marlin Rifles**
**Model 18 Slide Action Rifle**
This model is chambered for the .22 rimfire cartridges. It was offered standard with a 20" round or octagonal barrel, open sights, and a straight walnut stock. It has an exposed hammer and blued finish with blued steel buttplate. There is a half-length tubular magazine, and the stock features a quick take-down screw on the top tang which was marked "Model 18." This rifle was manufactured between 1906 and 1909.

| Exc. | V.G. | Good | Fair | Poor |
|------|------|------|------|------|
| 350 | 300 | 250 | 150 | 100 |

**Model 20 Slide Action Rifle**
The Model 20 was chambered for the .22 rimfire cartridges and was offered standard with a 24" octagonal barrel and open sight, with an exposed hammer. This rifle was only made as a "Take-Down" receiver model and is blued, with a straight walnut stock. It was manufactured between 1907 and 1909.

| Exc. | V.G. | Good | Fair | Poor |
|------|------|------|------|------|
| 350 | 300 | 250 | 150 | 100 |

**Model 25 Slide Action Rifle**
This Model was chambered for the .22 short only and was not a commercial success. The 23" round or octagonal barrel is standard, as are open sights. It is called a takedown model, but only the stock is removable--the receiver does not separate. It has an exposed hammer, tubular magazine, and straight walnut stock. The finish is blued. This rifle was manufactured in 1910.

| Exc. | V.G. | Good | Fair | Poor |
|------|------|------|------|------|
| 375 | 325 | 275 | 175 | 125 |

**Model 27 Slide Action Rifle**
This is a centerfire rifle chambered for the .25-20 and .32-20 cartridges. It features a 24" octagonal barrel with 2/3-length magazine tube that holds 7 shots. It has open sights, a blued finish, and straight walnut stock with crescent buttplate. It was manufactured between 1910 and 1932.

| Exc. | V.G. | Good | Fair | Poor |
|------|------|------|------|------|
| 350 | 300 | 250 | 150 | 100 |

**Model 27S Slide Action Rifle**
The Model 17S is similar to the Model 27 but was offered with a round or octagonal 24" barrel. The .25 rimfire cartridge was added to those already available. This model was introduced in 1913 and was manufactured until 1932.

| Exc. | V.G. | Good | Fair | Poor |
|------|------|------|------|------|
| 350 | 300 | 250 | 150 | 100 |

**Model 29 Slide Action Rifle**
This model is identical to the Model 20 with a 23" round barrel and smooth walnut forend instead of a grooved one as found on the Model 20. It was manufactured between 1913 and 1916.

| Exc. | V.G. | Good | Fair | Poor |
|------|------|------|------|------|
| 350 | 300 | 250 | 150 | 100 |

**Model 32 Slide Action Rifle**
This model was the first of the hammerless slide-action rifles. It is chambered for the .22 rimfire and has a 24" octagonal barrel and half-length magazine tube. The Model 32 is a takedown rifle with adjustable sights and features "Ballard" rifling. It is blued, with a pistolgrip walnut stock. The advent of WWI and the need for Marlin to produce military arms cut short the production of this model. It was manufactured in 1914 and 1915 only.

| Exc. | V.G. | Good | Fair | Poor |
|------|------|------|------|------|
| 350 | 300 | 250 | 150 | 100 |

**Model 37 Slide Action Rifle**
This model is the same as the Model 29 with a 24" round barrel and full-length magazine tube. It was manufactured between 1913 and 1916.

| Exc. | V.G. | Good | Fair | Poor |
|------|------|------|------|------|
| 350 | 300 | 250 | 150 | 100 |

**Model 38 Slide Action Rifle**
This was the hammerless model introduced after the end of WWI to replace the Model 32. It is similar in appearance but features a Rocky Mountain adjustable rear and an ivory bead front sight instead of the distinctive round Swebilius sight on the Model 32. The Model 38 was manufactured between 1920 and 1930.

| Exc. | V.G. | Good | Fair | Poor |
|------|------|------|------|------|
| 350 | 300 | 250 | 150 | 100 |

**Model 40 Slide Action Rifle**
This model is identical to the Model 27S centerfire rifle except that the barrel is marked "Marlin-Rockwell." The top tang is stamped "Marlin/Mod. 40." This is a very rare model, and not many marked in this manner have been noted.

| Exc. | V.G. | Good | Fair | Poor |
|------|------|------|------|------|
| 350 | 300 | 250 | 150 | 100 |

**Model 47 Slide Action Rifle**
This model is similar to the Model 20, with a 23" round barrel and an improved magazine tube. The Model 47 has a case-colored receiver and a checkered buttstock. This model was not offered for sale nor was it listed in Marlin's catalog but was offered free of charge to anyone purchasing four shares of Marlin stock for $100. One other fact about this model is that it was the first Marlin to be case-colored with the new cyanide method; this created a tiger-striped pattern that is peculiar to the Model 47 Rifle.

| Exc. | V.G. | Good | Fair | Poor |
|------|------|------|------|------|
| 350 | 300 | 250 | 150 | 100 |

**Model 1936 Lever Action Carbine**
This model is a direct descendant of the Model 1893. It is chambered for the .30-30 and the .32 Special cartridge. The stock is streamlined with a pistol grip added and a 20" round barrel. A barrel band and improved sights are utilized. It has a 7-shot tube magazine and a semi-beavertail forearm. The receiver, lever, and hammer are case-colored; and the rest is blued. This model was manufactured between 1936 and 1948. It was designated the Model 36 in 1937.

| Exc. | V.G. | Good | Fair | Poor |
|------|------|------|------|------|
| 300 | 250 | 200 | 150 | 100 |

**Model 36 Lever Action Rifle**
This model is similar to the Model 1936 Carbine, with a 24" barrel, 2/3-length magazine tube, and steel forend tip instead of the barrel band.

| Exc. | V.G. | Good | Fair | Poor |
|------|------|------|------|------|
| 325 | 275 | 225 | 175 | 125 |

**Model 36A or Sporting Carbine**
This model is similar to the 1936 Carbine, with a 24" barrel. It features a 2/3-length magazine tube and holds 6 shots instead of 7. The front sight is the "Huntsman" non-glare type with a silver bead.

| Exc. | V.G. | Good | Fair | Poor |
|------|------|------|------|------|
| 325 | 275 | 225 | 175 | 125 |

**Model 36A-DL Lever Action Rifle**
This model is similar to the Model 36A, with a deluxe checkered stock. It features slight swivels and is furnished with a leather sling.

| Exc. | V.G. | Good | Fair | Poor |
|------|------|------|------|------|
| 350 | 300 | 250 | 200 | 150 |

## Model 336 Carbine

This model was introduced in 1948 and was an improved version of the Model 36. It features a new-type round bolt, chrome-plated with improved extractor and redesigned cartridge carrier that improved feeding. It is chambered for the .30-30 and the .32 Special cartridges and has a 20" tapered round barrel with Ballard-type rifling. The finish is blue, with the receiver top matted to reduce reflections. The pistolgrip stock and semi-beavertail forend are of American walnut. It features Rocky Mountain style rear and bead front sights, and the hammer is lowered to facilitate scope mounting.

| Exc. | V.G. | Good | Fair | Poor |
|---|---|---|---|---|
| 250 | 200 | 175 | 125 | 100 |

## Model 336C

The same as the Model 336 Carbine. In 1951 the catalog model designation was changed. In 1953 the .35 Remington cartridge was added to the line.

| Exc. | V.G. | Good | Fair | Poor |
|---|---|---|---|---|
| 250 | 200 | 175 | 125 | 100 |

## Model 336A

This model is similar to the 336C, with a 24" barrel and steel forend tip instead of a barrel band. The magazine tube is 2/3-length and holds 6 shots. This model was introduced in 1948.

| Exc. | V.G. | Good | Fair | Poor |
|---|---|---|---|---|
| 250 | 200 | 175 | 125 | 100 |

## Model 336 ADL

This model differs from the Model 336A by having a checkered stock and forend, swivels, and a sling.

| Exc. | V.G. | Good | Fair | Poor |
|---|---|---|---|---|
| 275 | 225 | 200 | 150 | 125 |

## Model 336 SC

This is basically a 336A with forend tip and 2/3 magazine but has a 20" barrel instead of the 24" found on the 336A.

| Exc. | V.G. | Good | Fair | Poor |
|---|---|---|---|---|
| 275 | 225 | 200 | 150 | 100 |

## Model 336 SD

This is the 336 SC in a deluxe checkered stock version, with swivels and supplied with a sling.

| Exc. | V.G. | Good | Fair | Poor |
|---|---|---|---|---|
| 300 | 250 | 225 | 175 | 125 |

## Model 336 Zipper

This model was advertised as a fast-handling, lever-action carbine chambered for the .219 Zipper cartridge--a flat trajectory, varmint-type round. It has a 20" barrel, which was the feature that doomed it to failure as this was too short to coax the maximum performance and accuracy from the cartridge. The "Micro-Groove" rifling that was used did not yield long barrel life; and the model survived from 1955 through 1959, when it was discontinued. It is externally similar to the 336 SC.

| Exc. | V.G. | Good | Fair | Poor |
|---|---|---|---|---|
| 400 | 350 | 300 | 200 | 150 |

## Model 336T (Texan)

This is a straight-stock version of the 336 C, chambered for the .30-30 cartridge, with an 18.5" barrel. It was manufactured from 1954-1983.

| Exc. | V.G. | Good | Fair | Poor |
|---|---|---|---|---|
| 250 | 200 | 175 | 125 | 100 |

## Model 336 DT

A deluxe-stock version of the "Texan," with the map of Texas and a longhorn carved on the butt. It was manufactured between 1962 and 1964.

| Exc. | V.G. | Good | Fair | Poor |
|---|---|---|---|---|
| 300 | 250 | 225 | 175 | 125 |

## Model 336 "Marauder"

This is simply a 336 T with a 16.25" barrel and a slimmer forend. It is chambered for either the .30-30 or .35 Remington cartridges, has a gold trigger, and is drilled and tapped for both scope mounts and receiver sights. It was manufactured in 1963 and 1964.

| Exc. | V.G. | Good | Fair | Poor |
|---|---|---|---|---|
| 275 | 250 | 200 | 150 | 100 |

## Model 336 .44 Magnum

This is the 336 "Marauder" with a 20" Micro-Groove barrel chambered for the .44 Magnum cartridge. It holds 10 shots and was introduced in 1963.

| Exc. | V.G. | Good | Fair | Poor |
|---|---|---|---|---|
| 275 | 250 | 200 | 150 | 100 |

## Model 336 T "Centennial"

In 1970 a 100th year medallion was embedded into the buttstock of every rifle manufactured.

| Exc. | V.G. | Good | Fair | Poor |
|---|---|---|---|---|
| 275 | 250 | 200 | 150 | 100 |

## 1970 100th Year Commemorative Matched Pair

This is a deluxe octagonal barrelled .30-30 with an engraved receiver and deluxe wood with an inlaid medallion, accompanied by a matching Model 339 .22 rimfire rifle. They are numbered the same and are furnished in a deluxe luggage case. There were 1,000 sets manufactured in 1970. These are commemoratives, and as such it should be noted that collectors usually will only show interest if they are new and uncocked in the original packaging. All accessories and brochures should be included for them to be worth top dollar. Once a commemorative has been used, it has no more value than as a shooter.

| NIB | Exc. | V.G. | Good | Fair | Poor |
|---|---|---|---|---|---|
| 1000 | 850 | 650 | 500 | 400 | 300 |

## Model 336 "Zane Grey Century"

This Model was introduced in 1972, the 100th anniversary of the birth of Zane Grey, the famous Western author. This model has a 22" octagonal barrel chambered for the .30-30. The stock is high-grade walnut and features a brass buttplate and pistolgrip cap. A Zane Grey medallion is inlaid into the receiver. There were 10,000 manufactured in 1972. This is a commemorative rifle and must be new in the box to generate the top collector appeal.

| NIB | Exc. | V.G. | Good | Fair | Poor |
|---|---|---|---|---|---|
| 350 | 300 | 250 | 200 | 150 | 100 |

## Model 336 Octagon

This model was introduced to utilize the octagonal barrel making equipment that was on hand from the manufacture of the commemoratives. It is essentially a 336T with a 22" tapered octagonal barrel chambered for .30-30 only. It features a full-length magazine tube, slim forend with steel cap, and a classic-style hard rubber buttplate. The walnut stock is straight, and the lever is square. The finish, including the trigger, is blued. This model was made in 1973 only.

| Exc. | V.G. | Good | Fair | Poor |
|---|---|---|---|---|
| 250 | 200 | 175 | 150 | 100 |

## Model 336 ER (Extra Range)

This model was introduced in 1983 and was advertised as being chambered for the .307 Winchester and the .356 Winchester cartridges. The .307 was never produced. The .356 Winchester was supposed to add new capabilities to this classic rifle, but it never caught on with the shooting public and was discontinued in 1986 after only 2,441 Model ER's were manufactured. It has a 20" barrel and 5-shot tube magazine.

| Exc. | V.G. | Good | Fair | Poor |
|---|---|---|---|---|
| 275 | 250 | 225 | 175 | 125 |

## Model 336 CS

This is the current carbine model of this line. It has a hammer-block safety and is chambered for the .30-30, .35 Remington, and until 1988 the .375 Winchester. The barrel is 20", and the magazine tube holds 6 shots. The pistolgrip stock and semi-beavertail forearm are American walnut. This model has been manufactured since 1984. The 1983 model was known as the 336 C and had no hammer-block safety.

| NIB | Exc. | V.G. | Good | Fair | Poor |
|-----|------|------|------|------|------|
| 350 | 300 | 250 | 200 | 150 | 100 |

## Model 336 LTS

This is the latest version of the old "Marauder" carbine. It was dubbed the LTS or "Lightweight" model instead of the Marauder as it was feared that the latter designation would be inappropriate in today's society. The model features a 16.5" barrel with full-length tube magazine that holds 5 shots. The walnut stock has a straight grip, and there is a barrel band on the forearm. The butt has a rubber rifle pad. This model was introduced in 1988.

| NIB | Exc. | V.G. | Good | Fair | Poor |
|-----|------|------|------|------|------|
| 350 | 300 | 250 | 200 | 150 | 100 |

## Model 30 AS

This model is similar to the 336 CS, but the stock is made of walnut-finished hardwood instead of genuine American walnut. It is chambered for .30-30 only.

| NIB | Exc. | V.G. | Good | Fair | Poor |
|-----|------|------|------|------|------|
| 285 | 250 | 200 | 175 | 125 | 100 |

## Model 375 Lever Action

This model was introduced in 1980. It has a 20" Micro-Groove barrel and is chambered for the .375 Winchester cartridge. This should have been a popular rifle; but perhaps because of difficulty in obtaining ammunition, it was not a commercial success. Its appearance is much the same as the Model 336, with walnut pistolgrip stock and steel forend tip. This model was discontinued in 1983 after 16,315 were manufactured.

| Exc. | V.G. | Good | Fair | Poor |
|------|------|------|------|------|
| 250 | 225 | 175 | 125 | 100 |

## Model 444 Lever Action

This model was introduced in 1965. It is chambered for the .444 Marlin, a large and powerful cartridge that has the capability of dropping any game in North America, theoretically speaking. The rifle is essentially a Model 336 action modified to accept the larger cartridge. It has a 24" round barrel that was cut back to 22" in 1971. It holds 5 shots total and, when introduced, featured a straight-gripped Monte Carlo stock and semi-beavertail forend with barrel band. Another band holds the 2/3-length magazine tube in place. In 1971 the stock was changed to a pistolgrip without the Monte Carlo comb.

| Exc. | V.G. | Good | Fair | Poor |
|------|------|------|------|------|
| 200 | 175 | 150 | 125 | 100 |

## Model 444 S

This model was introduced in 1972 and is essentially the later 444 with a steel forend tip instead of the barrel bands.

| Exc. | V.G. | Good | Fair | Poor |
|------|------|------|------|------|
| 250 | 200 | 175 | 150 | 125 |

## Model 444 SS

In 1984 the company added a crossbolt hammer-block safety to the 444 S and redesignated it the 444 SS. This model is currently in production.

| NIB | Exc. | V.G. | Good | Fair | Poor |
|-----|------|------|------|------|------|
| 400 | 325 | 275 | 225 | 175 | 125 |

## Model 1894 Lever Action

The production of the Model 336 in .44 Magnum was a frustrating experience as the action was simply too long for a short-pistol case. In 1969 Marlin reintroduced the Model 1894 chambered for the .44 Magnum cartridge. The barrel is 20", and the full-length magazine tube holds 10 rounds. It features an adjustable rear and a ramp-type front sight. The finish is blued, with a matted receiver top. The walnut stock has a straight grip; and the forend, a barrel band. From 1969 to 1971 there was a brass saddle ring.

| Exc. | V.G. | Good | Fair | Poor |
|------|------|------|------|------|
| 275 | 225 | 175 | 125 | 100 |

## Model 1894 Octagon Barrel

This is basically the same as the Model 1894, with a 20" octagonal barrel and a steel forend tip instead of the barrel band. There were 2,957 manufactured in 1973 only.

| Exc. | V.G. | Good | Fair | Poor |
|------|------|------|------|------|
| 275 | 225 | 175 | 125 | 100 |

## Model 1894 Sporter

This variation has a 20" round barrel, half-length magazine tube that holds 6 shots, and a hard rubber classic-style butt plate. Only 1,398 were manufactured in 1973.

| NIB | Exc. | V.G. | Good | Fair | Poor |
|-----|------|------|------|------|------|
| 375 | 325 | 275 | 225 | 150 | 100 |

## Model 1894 C Lever Action

This model is chambered for the .38 Special and .357 Magnum cartridges. It features an 18.5 round barrel, with full-length magazine tube and two barrel bands. It holds 9 shots and has a walnut straight-grip stock. This model was manufactured between 1969 and 1984. In 1984 a hammer-block crossbolt safety was added, and the model number was changed to 1894 CS. All other specifications remained the same.

| Exc. | V.G. | Good | Fair | Poor |
|------|------|------|------|------|
| 275 | 225 | 175 | 125 | 100 |

## Model 1894 M Lever Action Rifle

This model is similar to the other 1894 rifles except that it is chambered for the .22 Magnum cartridge and features an outside loading tube magazine that holds 11 shots. The barrel is 20" long, and there is a steel forend tip instead of a barrel band.

It is important to note that this model will not function properly with any cartridge except the .22 Magnum and that injury could result from attempting to chamber and fire the shorter .22 l.r. This model was manufactured between 1983 and 1988 and was only produced with the crossbolt safety.

| Exc. | V.G. | Good | Fair | Poor |
|------|------|------|------|------|
| 275 | 225 | 175 | 150 | 100 |

## Model 1894 S Lever Action Rifle

This model was introduced in 1984. It is chambered for the .41 Magnum and the .44 Special/.44 Magnum cartridges. In 1988 the .45 Colt chambering was offered. This model has a 20" barrel and a straight-grip stock. The forend has a steel cap. This model is currently produced and features the hammer-block safety.

| NIB | Exc. | V.G. | Good | Fair | Poor |
|-----|------|------|------|------|------|
| 375 | 325 | 250 | 200 | 175 | 125 |

Marlin 1894CL
Calibers 32/20, 25/20
and 218 Bee

## Model 1894 CL (Classic) Lever Action Rifle

This Model was introduced in 1988 and is the same basic rifle chambered for the old .25-20 and .32-20 cartridges. The barrel is 22", and the half-length magazine tube holds 6 shots. The walnut stock has no white spacers and has a black buttplate.

| NIB | Exc. | V.G. | Good | Fair | Poor |
|-----|------|------|------|------|------|
| 400 | 325 | 250 | 200 | 175 | 125 |

Marlin 1895SS
Cal. 45/70 Gov't.

## Model 1895 Lever Action

The Model 1895 was reintroduced on the Model 336 action that had been modified to handle the .45-70 cartridge. This was done to capitalize on the nostalgia wave that descended on the country in the early 1970's. This model features a 22" round barrel with a 2/3-length magazine tube that holds 4 shots. The walnut stock had a straight grip until the Model 1895 S was released in 1980, when a pistolgrip stock was used. In 1983 the Model 1895 SS with the crossbolt hammer-block safety was added; and it is currently produced in this configuration.

| Exc. | V.G. | Good | Fair | Poor |
|------|------|------|------|------|
| 300 | 250 | 200 | 150 | 100 |

## Marlin Glenfield Lever Action Rifles

The Glenfield line of rifles was designed to be sold in large outlet chainstores and were simply cheaper versions that were to be sold for less money. The rifles functioned fine, but birch was used instead of walnut and pressed checkering instead of hand-cut. These rifles were manufactured under the Glenfield name between 1964 and 1983. There are five models of Lever Action Glenfields--the 36G, 30, 30A, 30 GT, and the 30 AS. They are chambered for the .30-30 cartridge, and the basic differences are slight and, in most cases, merely cosmetic. They are good, serviceable rifles but have little or no collector interest or investment potential.

| NIB | Exc. | V.G. | Good | Fair | Poor |
|-----|------|------|------|------|------|
| 150 | 125 | 100 | 90 | 75 | 50 |

## Model 39 Lever Action Rifle

This model originally evolved from the Model 1891 invented by L. L. Hepburn. The 1891 rifle became the 1892 and eventually developed into the takedown Model 1897. The latter two were produced until 1915, when they were discontinued in favor of machine gun production for WWI. In 1922, when the company was sold to John Moran and became the Marlin Firearms Corp., the .22 rimfire lever action was reintroduced as the Model 39. It has been in production in one form or another ever since.

## Model 39

As it was introduced in 1922, the Model 39 was chambered for the .22 rimfire and had a 22" octagonal barrel and a takedown receiver. It has a full-length magazine tube which holds 25 shorts, 20 longs, or 18 long-rifle cartridges. It has a solid top frame and side ejection, a Rocky Mountain rear, and ivory bead front sight. The receiver, lever, and hammer are case-colored; the barrel is blued. The pistolgrip stock and steel-capped forearm are varnished walnut. This model was manufactured in this form between 1922 and 1947 with a number of options that could affect value and would warrant individual appraisal.

**NOTE:** Model 39's made prior to 1932 which have either no prefix or the prefix S to the serial number should not be used with high-speed ammunition. The prefix HS indicates the improved bolt that is safe for this ammunition.

| Exc. | V.G. | Good | Fair | Poor |
|------|------|------|------|------|
| 800 | 650 | 500 | 350 | 175 |

## Model 39A Lever Action Rifle

This is an improved version of the Model 39. It has a heavier, tapered round barrel and semi-beavertail forearm and a redesigned pistolgrip stock. The rubber buttplate was replaced by one of a synthetic fiber; otherwise, specifications were similar to the Model 39. This model was manufactured from 1938 to 1960.

| Exc. | V.G. | Good | Fair | Poor |
|------|------|------|------|------|
| 275 | 225 | 175 | 125 | 100 |

## Model 39A Mountie

This is basically a carbine version of the Model 39A. It features a 20" tapered round barrel, straight-grip walnut stock, and slimmed-down forearm. It was manufactured between 1953 and 1960.

| Exc. | V.G. | Good | Fair | Poor |
|------|------|------|------|------|
| 275 | 225 | 175 | 125 | 100 |

## Model 39A 1960 Presentation Model

Released in 1960, this was Marlin's 90th Anniversary model. It is similar to the 39A but has a chrome-plated barrel and receiver with a high-grade, checkered walnut stock and forend. There is a squirrel carved on the right side of the buttstock. There were 500 produced in 1960. This is a commemorative and as such will be desirable to collectors only if NIB with all boxes and papers with which it was originally sold. Once used, it becomes a shooter and is not easily sold.

| NIB | Exc. | V.G. | Good | Fair | Poor |
|-----|------|------|------|------|------|
| 600 | 500 | 400 | 300 | 175 | 125 |

## Model 39M Mountie 1960 Presentation Model

This is the carbine version of the 90th Anniversary model. This is the same as the 39A with a 20" barrel and straight-grip stock. There were 500 of this model manufactured in 1960.

| NIB | Exc. | V.G. | Good | Fair | Poor |
|-----|------|------|------|------|------|
| 600 | 500 | 400 | 300 | 175 | 125 |

## Model 39A-DL Lever Action Rifle

This model is the same as the 90th Anniversary issue except that it is blued instead of chrome-plated. There were 3,306 manufactured between 1960 and 1963.

| Exc. | V.G. | Good | Fair | Poor |
|------|------|------|------|------|
| 250 | 200 | 150 | 100 | 75 |

## Golden 39A Lever Action Rifle

This model is similar to the 39A, with a gold-plated trigger and sling swivels. It was manufactured between 1960 and 1983.

| Exc. | V.G. | Good | Fair | Poor |
|------|------|------|------|------|
| 200 | 175 | 150 | 100 | 75 |

## Model 39 Carbine

This is a slimmer, lighter version of the Model 39A. It features a slimmer forend and thinner barrel. There were 12,140 manufactured between 1963 and 1967.

| Exc. | V.G. | Good | Fair | Poor |
|------|------|------|------|------|
| 175 | 150 | 125 | 90 | 60 |

## Model 39 Century Limited

The introduction of this model marked the 100th Anniversary of the Marlin Company. This model features a 20" octagonal barrel with semi-buckhorn rear and brass blade front sight. The stock is fancy walnut, with a straight grip and a brass forend tip and buttplate. There is a medallion inlaid into the right side of the receiver and a brass plate on the stock. There were 34,197 manufactured in 1970. As a commemorative this model needs to be as it came from the factory to command collector interest.

| NIB | Exc. | V.G. | Good | Fair | Poor |
|-----|------|------|------|------|------|
| 300 | 250 | 200 | 150 | 125 | 100 |

## Model 39A Article II

This model commemorated the National Rifle Association's 100th Anniversary in 1971. It has a 24" octagonal barrel, high-grade walnut pistolgrip stock, and brass forend tip and buttplate. The right side of the receiver has the NRA's Second Amendment "Right to Keep and Bear Arms" medallion inlaid. There were 6,244 of these .22 rifles manufactured in 1971.

| NIB | Exc. | V.G. | Good | Fair | Poor |
|-----|------|------|------|------|------|
| 300 | 250 | 200 | 150 | 125 | 100 |

## Model 39M Article II

This model is the same as the Model 39A Article II except that it is a carbine version with a 20" octagonal barrel and a straight-grip stock. There were 3,824 manufactured in 1971. As commemoratives NIB condition is essential to collector interest.

| NIB | Exc. | V.G. | Good | Fair | Poor |
|-----|------|------|------|------|------|
| 300 | 250 | 200 | 150 | 125 | 100 |

## Model 39A Octagon

This model was produced because the company had the machinery and some leftover barrels from the two commemorative models produced in 1970 and 1971. This was a regular production run which was meant to be used and was not a special issue. It has a 24", tapered octagonal barrel and is chambered for the .22 rimfire cartridges. It has a pistolgrip walnut stock, with steel forend tip. There were 2,551 manufactured in 1972 and 1973. This was not a commercially successful model, and it was discontinued for that reason.

| Exc. | V.G. | Good | Fair | Poor |
|------|------|------|------|------|
| 200 | 175 | 150 | 100 | 75 |

## Model 39M Octagon

This is the 20", octagonal-barrelled carbine version with a straight-grip stock. There were 2,140 manufactured in 1973.

| Exc. | V.G. | Good | Fair | Poor |
|------|------|------|------|------|
| 200 | 175 | 150 | 100 | 75 |

## Model 39D Lever Action Rifle

This is essentially the Model 39M carbine, 20"-barrel version with a pistolgrip stock. It was manufactured between 1970 and 1974.

| Exc. | V.G. | Good | Fair | Poor |
|------|------|------|------|------|
| 175 | 150 | 125 | 75 | 50 |

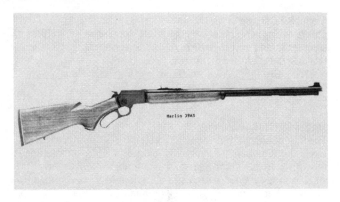

## Model 39AS Lever Action Rifle

This is the current production model of this extremely popular .22 rifle. It features the hammer-block crossbolt safety and sling swivel studs. It is similar in appearance to its predecessors and still boasts a genuine walnut pistolgrip stock and the same quality fit and finish we have come to expect from Marlin.

| NIB | Exc. | V.G. | Good | Fair | Poor |
|-----|------|------|------|------|------|
| 340 | 275 | 225 | 200 | 150 | 100 |

## Model 39TDS Lever Action Rifle

This is another current production model. It is similar to the Model 39AS, with a 20" carbine barrel and straight-grip stock. It replaced the Model 39M and was introduced in 1988.

| NIB | Exc. | V.G. | Good | Fair | Poor |
|-----|------|------|------|------|------|
| 375 | 325 | 250 | 225 | 150 | 100 |

## Model 56 Levermatic Rifle

This is a streamlined version of the lever action. It features a very short lever throw and a one-piece walnut stock. The 22" barrel is round and is chambered for the .22 rimfire cartridges. There are a 7-shot detachable magazine, open sights, and a gold-plated trigger. The receiver on this model was made of aluminum after 1956. There were 31,523 manufactured between 1955 and 1964.

| Exc. | V.G. | Good | Fair | Poor |
|------|------|------|------|------|
| 150 | 125 | 100 | 75 | 50 |

## Model 56 "Clipper King" Levermatic

This is the same as the Model 56 except that it is specially packaged and comes with a 4X .22 scope. The name "Clipper King" is stamped on the barrel, and the buttplate is red hard rubber. There were only 152 of these manufactured in 1959.

| Exc. | V.G. | Good | Fair | Poor |
|------|------|------|------|------|
| 175 | 150 | 125 | 100 | 75 |

## Model 57 Levermatic Rifle

This model is similar to the Model 56, with a tube magazine and Monte Carlo stock. In 1960 Marlin went back to a steel receiver on this model. There were 34,628 manufactured from 1959 to 1965.

| Exc. | V.G. | Good | Fair | Poor |
|------|------|------|------|------|
| 150 | 125 | 100 | 75 | 50 |

## Model 57M Levermatic Rifle

This is the Model 57 chambered for the .22 Magnum cartridge. There were 66,889 manufactured between 1959 and 1969.

| Exc. | V.G. | Good | Fair | Poor |
|------|------|------|------|------|
| 175 | 150 | 125 | 100 | 75 |

## Model 62 Levermatic Rifle

This model is similar in appearance to the Model 57 except that it is chambered for the centerfire .256 Magnum cartridge and has a 4-shot magazine. In 1966 the .30 carbine cartridge was added. This model has a 23" "Micro-Groove" barrel with open sights and a walnut one-piece stock. The first 4,000 Model 62's were shipped without serial numbers in violation of federal law. The company recalled the rifles for numbering; and, to this day, the owner of a centerfire Model 62 can return the rifle for numbering. There were 15,714 manufactured between 1963 and 1969.

| Exc. | V.G. | Good | Fair | Poor |
|------|------|------|------|------|
| 175 | 150 | 125 | 100 | 75 |

It is important to note that the year of manufacture of Marlin modern production rifles made between 1946 and 1968 can be ascertained by the letter prefix on the serial number. The prefixes are as follows:

| | | | | |
|------|------|------|------|-------|
| 1946 - C | 1951 - H | 1956 - N | 1961 - U | 1966 - AB |
| 1947 - D | 1952 - J | 1957 - P | 1962 - V | 1967 - AC |
| 1948 - E | 1953 - K | 1958 - R | 1963 - W | 1968 - AD |
| 1949 - F | 1954 - L | 1959 - S | 1964 - Y,Z | |
| 1950 - G | 1955 - M | 1960 - T | 1965 - AA | |

The Marlin Firearms Company produced a great many bolt-action rifles, both single shot and repeaters, starting in 1930 and continuing today. These rifles were low-priced and designed primarily as utility rifles. They also manufactured many auto-loaders of the same type during these years. The Glenfield name will also be found on these models, as many were produced to be marketed by the large chain outlets. These rifles have no collectible value of which I am aware, and they sell for under $100 in today's market. This list is for reference purposes, and I will not attempt to evaluate them.

| BOLT ACTIONS | AUTOLOADERS |
|--------------|-------------|
| Model 65 - SS- 1935-37 | Model 50 - 1931-34 |
| Model 65E - SS- 1935-37 | Model 50E - 1931-34 |
| Model 100 - SS- 1935-59 | Model A-1 - 1935-46 |
| Model 80 - Rep-1935-59 | Model A-1E - 1935-46 |
| Model 80E - Rep-1935-39 | Model A-1C - 1940-46 |
| Model 100S - SS- 1937-38 | Model A-1DL - 1940-46 |
| Model 81 - Rep-1939 | Model 88-C - 1947-56 |
| Model 81E - Rep-1939 | Model 88-DL - 1953-56 |
| Model 80B - Rep-1940 | Model 89-C - 1950-61 |
| Model 80BE - Rep-1940 | Model 89-DL - 1950-61 |
| Model 81B - Rep-1940 | Model 98 - 1950-61 |
| Model 81BE - Rep-1940 | Model 99 - 1959-61 |
| Model 101 - SS- 1941-77 | Model 99C - 1962-78 |
| Model 101DL - SS- 1941-45 | Model 99G - 1960-65 |
| Model 80C - Rep-1941-71 | Model DL - 1960-65 |
| Model 80DL - Rep-1941-64 | Model 60 - 1960-Pres. |
| Model 80 CSB - Rep-1941 | Model 49 - 1968-71 |
| Model 100 SB - SS- 1941 | Model 49DL - 1971-78 |
| Model 101 - SS- 1959 | Model 990 - 1979-87 |
| Model 122 - SS- 1962-65 | Model 995 - 1979-Pres. |
| Model 980 - Rep-1966-71 | |
| Model 780 - Rep-1971-88 | |
| Model 781 - Rep-1971-88 | |
| Model 782 - Rep-1971-88 | |
| Model 783 - Rep-1971-88 | |
| Model 880 - Rep-1988- | |
| Model 881 - Rep-1988- | |
| Model 882 - Rep-1988- | |
| Model 883 - Rep-1988- | |

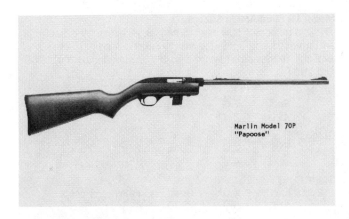

Marlin Model 70P "Papoose"

## Model 70P "Papoose"
This model is quite unique in that it is a total package concept. It is a semi-automatic takedown carbine chambered for the .22 rimfire family of cartridges. It has a 16.25" barrel and a 7-shot detachable magazine. It is supplied with 4X scope and bright red case that will float if dropped overboard. The stock is walnut-finished birch, with a pistol grip and rubber buttplate. It was introduced in 1986.

| NIB | Exc. | V.G. | Good | Fair | Poor |
|-----|------|------|------|------|------|
| 160 | 140 | 110 | 85 | 75 | 50 |

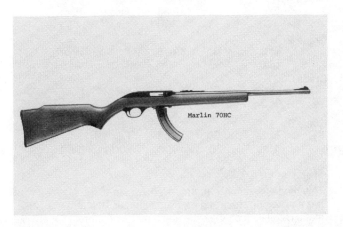

Marlin 70HC

## Model 70HC
This is the Model 70 .22 rimfire that has been produced since 1983 with a high-capacity, 25-round "Banana" magazine.

| Exc. | V.G. | Good | Fair | Poor |
|------|------|------|------|------|
| 160 | 125 | 100 | 75 | 50 |

MARLIN MODEL 9

## Model 9 Camp Carbine
This model has a 16.5 barrel and is chambered for the 9mm Parabellum pistol cartridge. It has a 12 or 20 shot detachable

magazine, walnut-finished hardwood pistolgrip stock, and a sandblasted matte-blued finish. There are open sights, and the receiver is drilled and tapped for scope mounting. This model was introduced in 1985.

| NIB | Exc. | V.G. | Good | Fair | Poor |
|-----|------|------|------|------|------|
| 310 | 275 | 225 | 175 | 125 | 100 |

MARLIN MODEL 45

## Model 45 Carbine
This is the same as the 9mm version but is chambered for the .45 ACP cartridge and has a 7-shot detachable magazine.

| NIB | Exc. | V.G. | Good | Fair | Poor |
|-----|------|------|------|------|------|
| 310 | 275 | 225 | 175 | 125 | 100 |

## Model 322 Bolt Action Rifle
This model is chambered for the .222 cartridge and has a 24" medium-weight barrel with Micro-Groove rifling. It has a checkered walnut pistolgrip stock. The magazine holds 4 shots, and the adjustable trigger and sights are Sako products. The Sako receiver is fitted for Sako scope-mounting bases. The Micro-Groove rifling in the barrel was not successful for this caliber, and accuracy fell off after as few as 500 shots--so this model was dropped and replaced. The serial numbers were Sako, and there were 5,859 manufactured between 1954 and 1959.

| Exc. | V.G. | Good | Fair | Poor |
|------|------|------|------|------|
| 375 | 325 | 250 | 175 | 125 |

## Model 422 Bolt Action Rifle
This model is the successor to the Model 322. It is simply the same rifle fitted with a 24", featherweight, stainless steel barrel and named the "Varmint King." The stock features a Monte Carlo stock with a cheekpiece. There were only 354 manufactured between 1956 and 1958.

| Exc. | V.G. | Good | Fair | Poor |
|------|------|------|------|------|
| 375 | 325 | 275 | 175 | 125 |

## Model 455 Bolt Action Rifle
This model is built on the Fabrique Nationale Belgian Mauser action. It is chambered for the .308 and the .30-06 cartridges. It has a stainless-steel barrel made by Marlin and has a 5-shot magazine. It has a Bishop checkered walnut stock with detachable sling swivels and a leather sling. The rear sight is a Lyman 48, and the front is a ramp type with a detachable hood. The receiver is drilled and tapped for scope mounts. The trigger is an adjustable Sako unit. There were 1,079 manufactured in .30-06 and only 59 in .308 between 1955 and 1959.

| Exc. | V.G. | Good | Fair | Poor |
|------|------|------|------|------|
| 375 | 325 | 275 | 175 | 125 |

## Marlin Shotguns

### Model 1898 Slide Action Shotgun

This model was made in 12 gauge, with an exposed hammer. It has a takedown receiver and walnut pistolgrip stock and forend. There is a 5-shot tube magazine, and the barrel lengths are from 26" and 32". They were manufactured between 1989 and 1905.

### Grade A

This variation has a 38", 30", or 32" barrel, is full choke, and is the plainest grade.

| Exc. | V.G. | Good | Fair | Poor |
|------|------|------|------|------|
| 500  | 450  | 400  | 300  | 175  |

### Grade A Brush or Riot

This is the same shotgun with a 26" cylinder-bore barrel.

| Exc. | V.G. | Good | Fair | Poor |
|------|------|------|------|------|
| 500  | 450  | 400  | 300  | 175  |

### Grade B

This is the same as the Grade A with a special smokeless steel barrel and a checkered stock.

| Exc. | V.G. | Good | Fair | Poor |
|------|------|------|------|------|
| 600  | 550  | 500  | 400  | 275  |

### Model 1898 Grade C

This is a more deluxe version with engraving and fancier wood.

| Exc. | V.G. | Good | Fair | Poor |
|------|------|------|------|------|
| 800  | 725  | 650  | 500  | 400  |

### Grade D

This variation has a Damascus barrel and the greatest amount of engraving.

| Exc. | V.G. | Good | Fair | Poor |
|------|------|------|------|------|
| 1800 | 1600 | 1250 | 900  | 700  |

### Model 16 Slide Action Shotgun

This Model is exactly the same as the Model 1898 except that it is chambered for 16 gauge only. The four grades are the same also. They were manufactured between 1903 and 1910.

### Grade A

| Exc. | V.G. | Good | Fair | Poor |
|------|------|------|------|------|
| 400  | 350  | 300  | 250  | 150  |

### Grade B

| Exc. | V.G. | Good | Fair | Poor |
|------|------|------|------|------|
| 500  | 450  | 400  | 350  | 225  |

### Grade C

| Exc. | V.G. | Good | Fair | Poor |
|------|------|------|------|------|
| 650  | 575  | 500  | 425  | 300  |

### Grade D

| Exc. | V.G. | Good | Fair | Poor |
|------|------|------|------|------|
| 1400 | 1200 | 1000 | 700  | 550  |

### Model 17 Slide Action Shotgun

This model is an exposed-hammer gun with a solid frame and a straight-grip stock. It is chambered for 12 gauge, with a 30" or 32" barrel. The Model 17 was manufactured between 1906 and 1908.

| Exc. | V.G. | Good | Fair | Poor |
|------|------|------|------|------|
| 450  | 400  | 350  | 275  | 175  |

### Model 17 Brush Gun

This variation is similar to the standard Model 17, with a 26" cylinder-bore barrel.

| Exc. | V.G. | Good | Fair | Poor |
|------|------|------|------|------|
| 475  | 425  | 375  | 300  | 200  |

### Model 17 Riot Gun

This variation has a 20" cylinder-bore barrel.

| Exc. | V.G. | Good | Fair | Poor |
|------|------|------|------|------|
| 400  | 350  | 300  | 225  | 125  |

### Model 19 Slide Action Shotgun

This is a takedown gun, chambered for 12 gauge. It is basically an improved and lightened version of the Model 1898. It is available in the same four grades. It was manufactured in 1906 and 1907.

### Grade A

| Exc. | V.G. | Good | Fair | Poor |
|------|------|------|------|------|
| 400  | 350  | 300  | 250  | 150  |

### Grade B

| Exc. | V.G. | Good | Fair | Poor |
|------|------|------|------|------|
| 500  | 450  | 400  | 350  | 225  |

### Grade C

| Exc. | V.G. | Good | Fair | Poor |
|------|------|------|------|------|
| 650  | 575  | 500  | 425  | 300  |

### Grade D

| Exc. | V.G. | Good | Fair | Poor |
|------|------|------|------|------|
| 1400 | 1200 | 1000 | 700  | 550  |

### Model 21 "Trap" Slide Action Shotgun

This model is basically the same as the Model 19 with a straight-grip stock. The 1907 catalog listed it as a Trap model. This model was manufactured in 1907 and 1908. The four grades are similar to the previous models.

### Grade A

| Exc. | V.G. | Good | Fair | Poor |
|------|------|------|------|------|
| 400  | 350  | 300  | 250  | 150  |

### Grade B

| Exc. | V.G. | Good | Fair | Poor |
|------|------|------|------|------|
| 500  | 450  | 400  | 350  | 225  |

### Grade C

| Exc. | V.G. | Good | Fair | Poor |
|------|------|------|------|------|
| 650  | 575  | 500  | 425  | 300  |

### Grade D

| Exc. | V.G. | Good | Fair | Poor |
|------|------|------|------|------|
| 1400 | 1200 | 1000 | 700  | 550  |

### Model 24 Slide Action Shotgun

This model is actually an improved version of the Model 21. It has a pistolgrip stock and exposed hammer. It features an automatic recoil lock on the slide and a matte rib barrel. Otherwise, it is quite similar to its predecessor. It was manufactured between 1908 and 1917.

### Grade A

| Exc. | V.G. | Good | Fair | Poor |
|------|------|------|------|------|
| 350  | 300  | 250  | 200  | 100  |

### Grade B

| Exc. | V.G. | Good | Fair | Poor |
|------|------|------|------|------|
| 500  | 450  | 400  | 350  | 225  |

### Grade C

| Exc. | V.G. | Good | Fair | Poor |
|------|------|------|------|------|
| 650  | 575  | 500  | 425  | 300  |

### Grade D

| Exc. | V.G. | Good | Fair | Poor |
|------|------|------|------|------|
| 1400 | 1200 | 1000 | 700  | 550  |

### Marlin "Trap Gun"

This model is unique in that it has no numerical designation and is simply known as the "Trap Gun." It is a takedown gun with interchangeable barrels from 16" to 32". It has a straight-grip buttstock and is quite similar in appearance to the Model 24. It was manufactured between 1909 and 1912.

| Exc. | V.G. | Good | Fair | Poor |
|------|------|------|------|------|
| 450  | 400  | 350  | 250  | 175  |

### Model 26 Slide Action Shotgun

This model is similar to the Model 24 Grade A, with a solid frame. It has 30" or 32" barrels.

| Exc. | V.G. | Good | Fair | Poor |
|------|------|------|------|------|
| 275  | 225  | 175  | 125  | 100  |

## Model 26 Brush Gun
This model has a 26" cylinder-bored barrel.

| Exc. | V.G. | Good | Fair | Poor |
|------|------|------|------|------|
| 300 | 250 | 200 | 150 | 125 |

## Model 26 Riot Gun
This variation has a 20" cylinder-bored barrel.

| Exc. | V.G. | Good | Fair | Poor |
|------|------|------|------|------|
| 250 | 200 | 150 | 100 | 75 |

## Model 28 Hammerless Slide Action Shotgun
This model was the first of the Marlin hammerless shotguns. It is a takedown 12 gauge, with barrels from 26" to 32" in length. The stock has a pistol grip, and it comes in four grades like its predecessors. The Model 28 was manufactured between 1913 and 1922.

### Grade A
| Exc. | V.G. | Good | Fair | Poor |
|------|------|------|------|------|
| 400 | 350 | 300 | 250 | 150 |

### Grade B
| Exc. | V.G. | Good | Fair | Poor |
|------|------|------|------|------|
| 500 | 450 | 400 | 350 | 225 |

### Grade C
| Exc. | V.G. | Good | Fair | Poor |
|------|------|------|------|------|
| 650 | 575 | 500 | 425 | 300 |

### Grade D
| Exc. | V.G. | Good | Fair | Poor |
|------|------|------|------|------|
| 1400 | 1200 | 1000 | 700 | 550 |

## Model 28 TS Trap Gun
This variation is the same as the Model 28 with a 30" full-choke barrel with matted rib and a high-comb straight-grip stock. It was manufactured in 1915.

| Exc. | V.G. | Good | Fair | Poor |
|------|------|------|------|------|
| 425 | 375 | 300 | 225 | 175 |

## Model 28T Trap Gun
This variation is the deluxe model, similar to the Model 28TS, with engraving, high-grade walnut, and hand checkering. It was manufactured in 1915.

| Exc. | V.G. | Good | Fair | Poor |
|------|------|------|------|------|
| 600 | 525 | 450 | 375 | 250 |

## Model 30 Slide Action Shotgun
This model is an improved version of the Model 16, 16-gauge shotgun. Its features are similar, with the addition of the improved takedown system and the automatic recoil lock on the slide. This model was manufactured between 1910 and 1914.

### Grade A
| Exc. | V.G. | Good | Fair | Poor |
|------|------|------|------|------|
| 400 | 350 | 300 | 250 | 150 |

### Grade B
| Exc. | V.G. | Good | Fair | Poor |
|------|------|------|------|------|
| 500 | 450 | 400 | 350 | 225 |

### Grade C
| Exc. | V.G. | Good | Fair | Poor |
|------|------|------|------|------|
| 650 | 575 | 500 | 425 | 300 |

### Grade D
| Exc. | V.G. | Good | Fair | Poor |
|------|------|------|------|------|
| 1400 | 1200 | 1000 | 700 | 550 |

## Model 30 Field Grade
This model is similar to the Model 30 Grade B, with a 25" modified-choke barrel and a straight-grip stock. It was manufactured in 1913 and 1914.

| Exc. | V.G. | Good | Fair | Poor |
|------|------|------|------|------|
| 400 | 350 | 300 | 225 | 150 |

## Model 31 Slide Action Shotgun
This model is a smaller version of the Model 28 hammerless takedown shotgun, chambered for 16 and 20 gauge. It was produced with barrel lengths of 26" and 28" and was available in the usual four grades, with various different chokes. This model was manufactured between 1915 and 1922.

### Grade A
| Exc. | V.G. | Good | Fair | Poor |
|------|------|------|------|------|
| 400 | 350 | 300 | 250 | 150 |

### Grade B
| Exc. | V.G. | Good | Fair | Poor |
|------|------|------|------|------|
| 500 | 450 | 400 | 350 | 225 |

### Grade C
| Exc. | V.G. | Good | Fair | Poor |
|------|------|------|------|------|
| 650 | 575 | 500 | 425 | 300 |

### Grade D
| Exc. | V.G. | Good | Fair | Poor |
|------|------|------|------|------|
| 1400 | 1200 | 1000 | 700 | 550 |

## Model 42/42A Slide Action Shotgun
This model was originally listed as the Model 42; but in the second year of production, the designation was changed to 42/A for no more apparent reason other than standardization of models. This model is similar to the Model 24 except that the barrel markings are different. It is still an exposed hammer takedown gun chambered for 12 gauge. It was manufactured between 1922 and 1933.

| Exc. | V.G. | Good | Fair | Poor |
|------|------|------|------|------|
| 275 | 250 | 200 | 150 | 100 |

## Model 43A Slide Action Shotgun
This hammerless model was quite similar to the Model 28, with different markings and less attention to finishing detail. It was manufactured between 1923 and 1930.

| Exc. | V.G. | Good | Fair | Poor |
|------|------|------|------|------|
| 350 | 300 | 250 | 200 | 150 |

## Model 43T Slide Action Shotgun
This model is the same as the Model 43A takedown hammerless with a 30" or 32" matte-rib barrel. The straight-grip stock is of high-grade walnut, with a non-gloss oil finish and fitted recoil paid. This model was manufactured between 1922 and 1930.

| Exc. | V.G. | Good | Fair | Poor |
|------|------|------|------|------|
| 400 | 350 | 300 | 250 | 200 |

## Model 43TS Slide Action Shotgun
This is a custom-order version of the Model 43T, the same in all respects except that the stock could be ordered to any specifications the shooter desired. It was manufactured between 1922 and 1930.

| Exc. | V.G. | Good | Fair | Poor |
|------|------|------|------|------|
| 600 | 550 | 500 | 350 | 275 |

## Model 44A Slide Action Shotgun
This model is similar to the Model 31 and was advertised as its successor. It is a hammerless takedown chambered for the 20 gauge. It features an improved bolt-opening device located in the triggerguard area instead of at the top of the receiver and has a shorter 4-shot magazine tube. The model was manufactured from 1922 until 1933.

| Exc. | V.G. | Good | Fair | Poor |
|------|------|------|------|------|
| 375 | 325 | 275 | 225 | 175 |

## Model 44S Slide Action Shotgun
This model is similar to the Model 44A, with a higher-grade walnut stock that featured hand-cut checkering.

| Exc. | V.G. | Good | Fair | Poor |
|------|------|------|------|------|
| 450 | 400 | 350 | 300 | 225 |

### Model 49 Slide Action Shotgun

This model is a 12-gauge, exposed-hammer takedown that combines features of the Model 42 and the Model 24. It is basically a lower-priced model that was never listed in the Marlin catalog. This model was part of Frank Kenna's money-raising program--anyone who purchased four shares of stock for $25 per share was given one free of charge. This model was manufactured between 1925 and 1928.

| Exc. | V.G. | Good | Fair | Poor |
|------|------|------|------|------|
| 450 | 400 | 350 | 275 | 200 |

### Model 53 Slide Action Shotgun

This model is a hammerless, takedown, 12 gauge that was not in production for very long. It is theorized that the Model 53 was produced to use up old parts on hand when the Model 43 was introduced. It was manufactured in 1929 and 1930.

| Exc. | V.G. | Good | Fair | Poor |
|------|------|------|------|------|
| 350 | 300 | 250 | 175 | 125 |

### Model 63 Slide Action Shotgun

This was the last of the slide-action shotguns produced by Marlin until the Model 120 in 1971. It is a hammerless, takedown 12 gauge and replaced the Model 43A in the Marlin catalog. This model had improvements over the earlier guns, but its introduction during the Depression did little to bolster sales. This model was also offered free of charge to anyone purchasing four shares of Marlin stock at $25 per share. It was manufactured between 1931 and 1933.

| Exc. | V.G. | Good | Fair | Poor |
|------|------|------|------|------|
| 350 | 300 | 250 | 175 | 125 |

### Model 63T Slide Action Shotgun

This is the trap-grade version of the Model 63. It has a better-grade hand-checkered stock, with a fitted recoil pad and oil finish. It was manufactured between 1931 and 1933.

| Exc. | V.G. | Good | Fair | Poor |
|------|------|------|------|------|
| 375 | 325 | 275 | 200 | 150 |

### Model 63TS Slide Action Shotgun

This variation is the same as the Model 63T except that the stock dimensions were custom-made to the customer's specifications. It was manufactured between 1931 and 1933.

| Exc. | V.G. | Good | Fair | Poor |
|------|------|------|------|------|
| 400 | 350 | 300 | 225 | 175 |

### Model 60 Single Barrel Shotgun

This is a break-open, exposed-hammer, top lever-opening 12 gauge with either 30" or 32" full-choke barrel. It has a pistolgrip stock. There were approximately 60 manufactured in 1923.

| Exc. | V.G. | Good | Fair | Poor |
|------|------|------|------|------|
| 200 | 175 | 150 | 125 | 100 |

### Model .410 Lever Action Shotgun

This was a unique venture for the Marlin Company--a lever-action shotgun based on the Model 1893 action with a longer loading port, modified tube magazine that held 5 shots, and a smooth-bore barrel chambered for the .410 shot shell. The finish of this gun is blued, with a walnut pistolgrip stock and grooved beavertail forend. It has a hard rubber rifle-type buttplate. The model was available with either a 22" or 26" full-choke barrel. This gun was also part of the stock-purchase plan and was given free of charge to anyone purchasing four shares at $25 per share. It was also cataloged for sale and was manufactured between 1929 and 1932.

| Exc. | V.G. | Good | Fair | Poor |
|------|------|------|------|------|
| 600 | 500 | 400 | 300 | 250 |

### Model .410 Deluxe

This variation was never cataloged and is essentially the same as the standard version with a hand-checkered stock. The forend does not have the grooves found on the standard model. Be wary of fakes!

| Exc. | V.G. | Good | Fair | Poor |
|------|------|------|------|------|
| 850 | 750 | 650 | 550 | 400 |

### Model 90 Over/Under Shotgun

This gun was produced in response to a request from Sears Roebuck that Marlin should manufacture an Over/Under shotgun for Sears to market in their stores. The guns produced for Sears have the prefix 103 in their serial numbers and were marked "Ranger" before WWII and "J.C.Higgins" after the War. Prior to 1945 they were not marked Marlin; after that date Sears requested that the company stamp their name on the guns. They were also produced as the Marlin Model 90 during the same period and were chambered for 12, 16, and 20 gauge, as well as .410 bore. The barrels are either 26", 28", or 30", with various chokes. The action is a boxlock with extractors. Guns made prior to 1949 had a space between the barrels; after that date they were solid. They can be found with double or single triggers and a checkered walnut stock. There were approximately 34,000 Model 90's manufactured between 1937 and 1963.

Single Trigger--Add 35 Percent.

| Exc. | V.G. | Good | Fair | Poor |
|------|------|------|------|------|
| 500 | 425 | 350 | 275 | 200 |

### Premier Mark I Slide Action Shotgun

This model was made by Manufrance and called the LaSalle. Marlin was able to purchase them without the barrels at a good enough price for them to barrel and market them under their own name. This model is 12 gauge only, with an alloy receiver and seven interchangeable barrels in 26"-30" lengths and various chokes. The plain stock is French walnut. The biggest problem with this gun is that the light weight (six pounds) produced very bad recoil, and it was less than enjoyable to shoot. This model was in production from 1959 through 1963, with approximately 13,700 sold.

| Exc. | V.G. | Good | Fair | Poor |
|------|------|------|------|------|
| 225 | 175 | 150 | 100 | 75 |

### Premier Mark II

This model is similar to the Mark I, with light engraving and a checkered stock.

| Exc. | V.G. | Good | Fair | Poor |
|------|------|------|------|------|
| 250 | 200 | 175 | 125 | 100 |

### Premier Mark IV

This model is similar to the Mark II, with more engraving on the receiver.

| Exc. | V.G. | Good | Fair | Poor |
|------|------|------|------|------|
| 300 | 250 | 200 | 150 | 125 |

### Model 120 Slide Action Shotgun

This model was styled to resemble the Winchester Model 12 and was advertised as an all steel and walnut shotgun. It was offered with interchangeable barrels from 26"-40", and various chokes were available. The checkered stock is of walnut, with a fitted recoil pad. The tube magazine holds 5 shots, 4 in 3". There was a Trap model available (1973-1975), as well as a slug gun (1974-1984). This model was manufactured between 1971 and 1985.

| Exc. | V.G. | Good | Fair | Poor |
|------|------|------|------|------|
| 300 | 250 | 200 | 150 | 125 |

**Model 778 Slide Action Shotgun (Glenfield)**
This model is similar to the Model 120, with a walnut-finished hardwood stock instead of walnut, and the Glenfield name stamped on it. It was manufactured between 1979 and 1984.

| Exc. | V.G. | Good | Fair | Poor |
|------|------|------|------|------|
| 225 | 175 | 150 | 125 | 100 |

**Model 55 Bolt Action Shotgun**
This model is chambered for 12, 16, and 20 gauge, with full or adjustable choke and barrels of 26" or 28". It is a bolt action with 2-shot box magazine. The pistolgrip stock is plain. This model was manufactured between 1950 and 1965.

| Exc. | V.G. | Good | Fair | Poor |
|------|------|------|------|------|
| 100 | 75 | 50 | 35 | 25 |

**Model 55 Swamp Gun**
This is simply the Model 55 with a 3" Magnum, 20" barrel and an adjustable choke. It was manufactured between 1963 and 1965.

| Exc. | V.G. | Good | Fair | Poor |
|------|------|------|------|------|
| 110 | 80 | 65 | 45 | 25 |

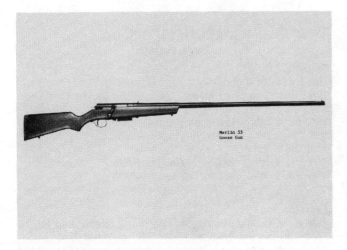

Marlin 55 Goose Gun

**Model 55 Goose Gun**
This is the Model 55 with a 3" chambered, 36" full-choke barrel and a recoil pad and sling. It was introduced in 1962 and is still manufactured.

| NIB | Exc. | V.G. | Good | Fair | Poor |
|-----|------|------|------|------|------|
| 230 | 175 | 140 | 125 | 100 | 75 |

**Model 55S Slug Gun**
This is the Model 55 with a 24" cylinder-bore barrel and rifle sights. It was manufactured between 1974 and 1983.

| Exc. | V.G. | Good | Fair | Poor |
|------|------|------|------|------|
| 150 | 125 | 100 | 75 | 50 |

**Model 5510 Bolt Action Shotgun**
This model is chambered for the 3.5" 10 gauge. It has a 34" full-choke barrel and a recoil pad and sling. It was manufactured between 1976 and 1985.

| Exc. | V.G. | Good | Fair | Poor |
|------|------|------|------|------|
| 200 | 150 | 125 | 100 | 75 |

## MARROCHI, ARMI
### Brescia, Italy
### Importer--Sile Distributors Inc.New York, New York

**Model 2000**
This model is a break-open single-shot that is chambered for 12 gauge with a 3" chamber. The barrel is 28" in length, with various chokes. There is an exposed hammer and an automatic ejector. The finish is blued, with a walnut stock.

| Exc. | V.G. | Good | Fair | Poor |
|------|------|------|------|------|
| 100 | 80 | 65 | 50 | 35 |

**Field Master I**
This is an Over/Under shotgun chambered for 12 gauge only. It has 26" or 28" vent-rib barrels with screw-in choke tubes. It features a single trigger that is non-selective and automatic ejectors. It is coin-finished, with a checkered walnut stock.

| Exc. | V.G. | Good | Fair | Poor |
|------|------|------|------|------|
| 400 | 350 | 300 | 200 | 150 |

**Field Master II**
This model is similar to the Field Master I except that it has a single-selective trigger.

| Exc. | V.G. | Good | Fair | Poor |
|------|------|------|------|------|
| 425 | 375 | 325 | 225 | 175 |

## MARS
### SEE--Gabbet-Fairfax

## MARSTON, S.W.
### New York, New York

**Double Action Pepperbox**
This is a double-action, pepperbox-type revolving pistol that is chambered for .31 caliber percussion and has a ring trigger. The 6-barrel cluster is 5" in length, and the frame is made of iron and is scroll engraved. The round handle has walnut grips. These pistols were unmarked, and very few were manufactured between 1850 and 1855.

| Exc. | V.G. | Good | Fair | Poor |
|------|------|------|------|------|
| 1000 | 850 | 750 | 500 | 350 |

**Two Barrel Pistol**
This is a 2-barrel pocket pistol that has Over/Under barrels that manually revolve to the side for loading. It is chambered for .31 or .36 caliber percussion and has a ring-type trigger. The barrels are flat-sided and of various lengths. The frame is engraved brass, and the barrels are blued and are marked "J.Cohn & S.W.Marston-New York." There were very few manufactured in the 1850's.

| Exc. | V.G. | Good | Fair | Poor |
|------|------|------|------|------|
| 1250 | 1000 | 850 | 600 | 450 |

## MARSTON, W. W. & Co.
### New York, New York

The W. W. Marston & Co. was a very prolific manufacturer of varied types of firearms. They used many tradenames--such as Union Arms Co., Phoenix Armory, Western Arms Co., Washington Arms Co., Sprague and Marston, and Marston and Knox. They operated between the 1850's and approximately 1872 and produced quite a large number of firearms, including percussion and metallic cartridge arms.

**Pocket Revolver**
This is a solid frame single action revolver chambered for .31 caliber percussion. It has an octagonal barrel that is from 3.25" to 7.5" in length. The cylinder holds 6 shots, and there is a loading lever under the barrel. The finish is blued, and the grips are walnut. The barrel is marked with one of Marston's tradenames. There are actually seven variations of this model with similar values. Independent appraisal should be secured on this model.
There were approximately 13,000 manufactured between 1857 and 1862.

| Exc. | V.G. | Good | Fair | Poor |
|------|------|------|------|------|
| 550 | 450 | 400 | 300 | 200 |

### Navy Revolver

This is a larger revolver chambered for .36 caliber percussion. It has a 7.5" or 8.5" octagonal barrel with an integral loading lever. The roll-engraved cylinder holds 6 shots; and the finish is blued, with walnut grips. The barrel is marked with one of the Marston tradenames, and there were approximately 1,000 manufactured between 1857 and 1862.

| Exc. | V.G. | Good | Fair | Poor |
|------|------|------|------|------|
| 1150 | 1000 | 800 | 550 | 400 |

### Double Action Single Shot Pistol

This was a bar-hammer pistol that is chambered for .31 or .36 caliber percussion and has a part-octagonal barrel that is between 2.5" and 5" in length. It has a scroll-engraved iron hammer and is blued, with walnut grips. The barrel is marked with one of Marston's tradenames. They were manufactured in the 1850's.

| Exc. | V.G. | Good | Fair | Poor |
|------|------|------|------|------|
| 450 | 375 | 325 | 250 | 175 |

### Single Action Pistol

This is a single shot that is chambered for .31 or .36 caliber and has a part octagonal barrel between 4" and 6" in length. It is marked with one of Marston's tradenames; and the finish is blued, with walnut grips. This model was manufactured in the 1860's.

| Exc. | V.G. | Good | Fair | Poor |
|------|------|------|------|------|
| 500 | 400 | 350 | 275 | 200 |

### Breech Loading Pistol

This is a single-shot breechloader that is chambered for .35 caliber and has either a part-octagonal or a full-octagonal barrel between 4" and 8.5" in length. The lever that opens the breech is located inside the grip frame, with a ring at its base. The finish is blued, with either a silver-plated brass or a case-colored iron frame. There were approximately 1,000 manufactured in the 1850's.

**Brass Frame**

| Exc. | V.G. | Good | Fair | Poor |
|------|------|------|------|------|
| 2000 | 1800 | 1500 | 1200 | 800 |

**Iron Frame**

| Exc. | V.G. | Good | Fair | Poor |
|------|------|------|------|------|
| 2250 | 2000 | 1700 | 1400 | 1000 |

### Double Action Pepperbox

This is a 6-barrelled, pepperbox type revolving pistol that is chambered for .31 caliber percussion and has a barrel cluster either 4" or 5" in length. It has a bar hammer and conventional triggerguard. The iron frame is engraved and blued. The grips are walnut. Some barrel clusters are fluted, and some are ribbed. They are marked with one of the Marston tradenames. They were manufactured during the 1850's.

| Exc. | V.G. | Good | Fair | Poor |
|------|------|------|------|------|
| 650 | 550 | 450 | 350 | 200 |

### 3 Barrelled Derringer

This is a strange little pocket pistol that has three barrels--one on top of the other. There are two basic models. One has a sliding knife blade that is mounted on the side of the barrels and that protrudes forward and locks with a spring clip. The blade is either spear-pointed or a clipped-point "Bowie" style. There is another model that has no knife blade. This pistol is chambered for the .22-caliber rimfire cartridge and has barrels 3" in length that pivot downward for loading. The frame is silver-plated brass; and the barrels are blued, with walnut grips. The frame has scroll engraving, and the barrel is marked "Wm.W. Marston/New York City." There were approximately 1,500 manufactured between 1858 and 1864.

### Knife Bladed Model

| Exc. | V.G. | Good | Fair | Poor |
|------|------|------|------|------|
| 1000 | 850 | 650 | 450 | 350 |

### Model Without Knife

| Exc. | V.G. | Good | Fair | Poor |
|------|------|------|------|------|
| 850 | 750 | 500 | 350 | 300 |

### .32 Caliber 3 Barrel Derringer

This model has no knife blade and is chambered for the .32-caliber rimfire cartridge. It has three barrels (one on top of the other) that are either 3" or 4" in length. They pivot downward for loading. The frame is silver-plated brass, and the barrels are blued. The grips are walnut. The barrel is marked "Wm. W. Marston/New York City." There were approximately 3,000 manufactured between 1864 and 1872.

| Exc. | V.G. | Good | Fair | Poor |
|------|------|------|------|------|
| 750 | 650 | 450 | 300 | 200 |

# MASQUELIER S. A.
## Liege, Belgium

### Carpathe

This is a single-shot rifle with a unique push-button cocking system. It is chambered for the .243, .270, .7x57mm, 7x65R, and the .30-06 cartridges. It has a 24" barrel and adjustable trigger and sights. The finish is blued, with an engraved receiver and hand-checkered walnut stock. This model was imported until 1986.

| Exc. | V.G. | Good | Fair | Poor |
|------|------|------|------|------|
| 3500 | 3250 | 2750 | 2000 | 1500 |

### Express

This is an Over/Under double rifle that is chambered for the .270, .30-06, 8x57JRS, and 9.3x74R cartridges. It has ribbed 24" barrels and features a single-selective trigger and automatic ejectors. The receiver is engraved and blued, with a hand-checkered walnut stock. This model was not imported after 1986.

| Exc. | V.G. | Good | Fair | Poor |
|------|------|------|------|------|
| 3500 | 3250 | 2750 | 2000 | 1500 |

### Ardennes

This was the best-grade Over/Under rifle that was made by this company. It was available as a custom-order item only, and the materials and workmanship are of a very high quality. This model was also discontinued in 1986.

| Exc. | V.G. | Good | Fair | Poor |
|------|------|------|------|------|
| 6500 | 5750 | 5000 | 4000 | 3250 |

### Boxlock SxS Shotgun

This model is chambered for 12 gauge only, with 2.75" chambers. It has an Anson & Deeley action that is scroll-engraved. There are automatic ejectors and a single-selective trigger. The finish is blued, with a hand-checkered French walnut stock. Import ceased after 1986.

| Exc. | V.G. | Good | Fair | Poor |
|------|------|------|------|------|
| 4500 | 3750 | 3000 | 2500 | 2000 |

### Sidelock SxS Shotgun

This model is similar to the Boxlock except that it features hand-detachable Holland & Holland-type sidelocks, and is elaborately engraved, with the best grade of French walnut. This model was not imported after 1986.

| Exc. | V.G. | Good | Fair | Poor |
|------|------|------|------|------|
| 13000 | 11500 | 8500 | 5000 | 4000 |

# MASSACHUSETTS ARMS CO.
## Chicopee Falls, Massachusetts

### Wesson & Leavitt Dragoon

This is a large percussion revolver that is chambered for .40 caliber and has a 6-shot cylinder and a 7" round barrel. The hammer is side-mounted, and the maker's name and the patent holder with dates is stamped on many major parts. The finish is blued, with a case-colored frame and walnut grips. There were approximately 800 manufactured in 1850 and 1851.

### Early Model with 6" Barrel--Approximately 30 Made

| Exc. | V.G. | Good | Fair | Poor |
|------|------|------|------|------|
| 2500 | 2000 | 1750 | 1300 | 1000 |

### Full Marked 7" Barrel Standard Model

| Exc. | V.G. | Good | Fair | Poor |
|------|------|------|------|------|
| 2250 | 1800 | 1500 | 1100 | 850 |

### Wesson & Leavitt Belt Revolver

This .31-caliber percussion revolver was similar in appearance but smaller than the Dragoon. The barrel lengths are 3" to 7", and the 6-shot cylinder is roll-engraved. There were approximately 1,000 manufactured in 1850 and 1851.

| Exc. | V.G. | Good | Fair | Poor |
|------|------|------|------|------|
| 1000 | 850 | 700 | 500 | 350 |

### Maynard Primed Belt Revolver

This model is similar to the Standard Belt Revolver, with the addition of the Maynard automatic priming device.
There were approximately 1,000 manufactured between 1851 and 1857.

| Exc. | V.G. | Good | Fair | Poor |
|------|------|------|------|------|
| 1000 | 850 | 700 | 500 | 350 |

### Maynard Primed Pocket Revolver

This model is a smaller version of the Belt revolver. It is chambered for .28 or .30 caliber percussion and was manufactured in two ways. The early type has a manually revolved cylinder, and the later type revolves automatically when the hammer is cocked. Barrel lengths are from 2.5" to 3.5" and either octagonal or round. There were approximately 3,000 manufactured between 1851 and 1860.

### Early Model .28 Caliber Only--Manually Revolved

| Exc. | V.G. | Good | Fair | Poor |
|------|------|------|------|------|
| 850 | 750 | 600 | 400 | 300 |

### Automatic Cylinder Model

| Exc. | V.G. | Good | Fair | Poor |
|------|------|------|------|------|
| 800 | 700 | 550 | 350 | 250 |

### Adams Patent Pocket Revolver

This is a double-action revolver chambered for .31 caliber percussion. It has a 3.25" octagonal barrel and a 5-shot cylinder. It has a solid frame and a loading lever on the left side of the barrel. The finish is blued, with walnut grips. There were approximately 4,500 manufactured between 1857 and 1861.

| Exc. | V.G. | Good | Fair | Poor |
|------|------|------|------|------|
| 750 | 650 | 500 | 350 | 250 |

### Adams Patent Navy Revolver

This larger version is chambered for .36 caliber percussion and has a 6" octagonal barrel. There were approximately 1,000 manufactured between 1856 and 1861. Approximately 600 were U.S. martially marked and will bring an added 20 percent.

| Exc. | V.G. | Good | Fair | Poor |
|------|------|------|------|------|
| 1100 | 950 | 800 | 500 | 400 |

### Single Shot Pocket Pistol

This diminutive pistol is chambered for .31 caliber percussion and has a part-octagonal barrel 2.5" to 3.5" in length. It uses the Maynard primer system and has a hammer mounted in the center of the frame. The barrel is marked "Mass. Arms Co/Chicopee Falls." The primer magazine door is marked "Maynard's Patent Sept. 22, 1845." It is also scroll-engraved. The finish is blued, and the grips are walnut. This model was manufactured in the 1850's.

| Exc. | V.G. | Good | Fair | Poor |
|------|------|------|------|------|
| 750 | 650 | 500 | 350 | 250 |

### Maynard Carbine

This is a single-shot breechloader chambered for .35 or .50 caliber percussion. The barrel is round and 20" in length. The triggerguard is the lever that pivots the barrel in break-open fashion when it is lowered. The finish is blued, with a case-colored frame. The buttstock is walnut, and there is no forend. This carbine was designed by the same Maynard who invented the tape primer system. There are two models--a 1st and a 2nd. They were made for both sporting use and as a U.S. Martial carbine. The 2nd model was used considerably during the Civil War.

### 1st Model

This model is marked "Maynard Patentee/May 27, 1851/June 17, 1856." It has an iron patchbox and a curved buttplate. It has a Maynard tape primer system and a tang sight. Later production was fitted with a sling swivel. There are approximately 400 of these carbines that are U.S. marked, but the total manufactured in the late 1850's is unknown.

### U.S. Martially Marked and AUTHENTICATED

| Exc. | V.G. | Good | Fair | Poor |
|------|------|------|------|------|
| 2000 | 1700 | 1500 | 1150 | 850 |

### Commercial Model

| Exc. | V.G. | Good | Fair | Poor |
|------|------|------|------|------|
| 1100 | 950 | 750 | 600 | 450 |

### 2nd Model

This model is chambered for .50 caliber only and does not have the tape primer system or the tang sight. There is no patchbox, and the buttplate is not as curved as on the 1st model. It is marked "Manufactured By/Mass. Arms Co./Chicopee Falls." There were approximately 20,000 manufactured between 1860 and 1865. This model was used by Union forces during the Civil War.

| Exc. | V.G. | Good | Fair | Poor |
|------|------|------|------|------|
| 950 | 850 | 750 | 550 | 350 |

### Maynard Patent Sporting Rifles

There are a great many variations of this firearm produced in virtually all popular calibers from .22 rimfire up to and including the .50/100. There is also a smooth-bore .64 caliber and 20-gauge model. There are three basic models--the 1865 (which is a percussion model chambered for .35, .40, and .50 caliber and made up of unfinished parts left over from government orders after the Civil War), the 1873, and the 1882--with many variations within these last two designations. Barrel lengths run between 20" and 32"; and the finishes used are case-colored frame with the rest blued, nickel-plated frame with the remainder blued, or completely blued. The stocks are oil-finished walnut with no forends except on two models--the 15 and the 16. Values on the Maynards are established by condition (the variation with the higher-grade models worth considerably more) and finally by the caliber (with the .22 rimfire and the .45-70 being the most popular). There were a large number manufactured between 1865 and 1890. We feel that the myriad of variations preclude accurate appraisal in a book of this nature. Individual appraisal should be secured in order to establish a realistic valuation.

## MATRA MANURHIN DEFENSE
### Mulhouse, France
### SEE--Manurhin

This is the technical name for the company that manufactured the Manurhin French versions of the Walther pistols. They are listed under Manurhin.

## MAUSER-WERKE
### Oberndorf-am-Neckar, Germany

This company was founded in 1869 by Peter and Wilhelm Mauser. Its original function was the manufacture of rifles. Over the years the name Mauser became synonymous with high-quality bolt-action rifles. They also became known for a number of pistol designs but were never quite as respected in that field as they were for their rifles. In 1874 the company became a corporation, and they received their first government contract. They became instrumental from that point on in arming the German military. In 1887 the firm of Ludwig Loewe and Company of Berlin became the controlling force in the Mauser corporation. In 1896, as the result of a merger, Ludwig Loewe evolved into the firm of DWM. At that time they fully controlled the Mauser firm. In 1897 DWM purchased all of the remaining Mauser stock. In 1914 Peter Paul Mauser died. He had been honored many times by the firearms fraternity.

The collecting of Mauser firearms is a fascinating field. There is literally something for everyone. Production figures are sufficient on most models to make it worthwhile to seek them. There are a number of excellent texts written on the subject, and it is quite simple for an interested individual to gain the necessary education needed to become a collector. Some variations, especially within the C96 pistol category, are quite rare and valuable. We advise securing qualified appraisals if a transaction is contemplated.

### Model 1871

This is a single-shot, bolt-action military rifle chambered for the 11mm cartridge. It has a 33.5" barrel with a full-length stock held on by two barrel bands and an end cap. There is a cleaning rod mounted beneath the barrel and a bayonet lug at the muzzle. The finish is blued, with a walnut stock. It is marked "Mod. 71" and features the year of production and the name of the manufacturer, as well as a crown. It was adopted as a service rifle by Prussia in February of 1872.

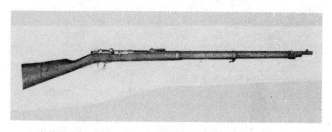

| Exc. | V.G. | Good | Fair | Poor |
|------|------|------|------|------|
| 400 | 350 | 300 | 200 | 125 |

### Model 1871 Jaeger Rifle

This version, the Scout Rifle, is similar to the standard version except that it has a 29.4" barrel.

| Exc. | V.G. | Good | Fair | Poor |
|------|------|------|------|------|
| 500 | 450 | 400 | 300 | 200 |

### Model 1871 Carbine

This variation has a 20" barrel and a full-length stock held on by one barrel band. It has no provision for adding a bayonet.

| Exc. | V.G. | Good | Fair | Poor |
|------|------|------|------|------|
| 500 | 450 | 400 | 300 | 200 |

### Serbian Model 78/80

This is a single-shot, bolt-action service rifle chambered for the 10.15mm cartridge. It has a 30.7" barrel and a full-length stock held on by two barrel bands and an end cap. There is a cleaning rod under the barrel and a bayonet lug at the muzzle. It is marked with Cyrillic letters. It was adopted as a service rifle by Yugoslavia in 1881.

| Exc. | V.G. | Good | Fair | Poor |
|------|------|------|------|------|
| 350 | 300 | 250 | 150 | 100 |

### Model 71/84 Rifle

This is a bolt-action repeating rifle chambered for the 11mm cartridge. It has a 31.5" barrel and a tubular magazine inside of the forend. It has a cleaning rod under the barrel and a bayonet lug at the muzzle. The finish is blued, with a full-length walnut stock held on by two barrel bands. It is marked with the name of the manufacturer, year of production, and a crown, as well as "Mod. 71/84." By 1886 the entire German army was armed with the Model 71/84 Rifle. It was produced by a number of German arsenals.

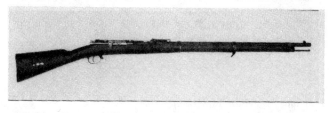

| Exc. | V.G. | Good | Fair | Poor |
|------|------|------|------|------|
| 400 | 350 | 300 | 200 | 125 |

### Serbian Model 71/84

There were approximately 4,000 repeating rifles produced for the Serbians. They features a 7-round, tubular magazine in the forend. The barrel length is 18.3". The finish is blued, and a full-length walnut stock is held on by one barrel band. It is marked in Cyrillic letters.

| Exc. | V.G. | Good | Fair | Poor |
|------|------|------|------|------|
| 350 | 300 | 250 | 150 | 100 |

### Turkish Model 87 Rifle

This is a bolt-action repeating rifle chambered for the 9.5mm cartridge. It has a 30" barrel with an 8-round, tubular magazine in the forend. The finish is blued, with a full-length walnut stock held on by one barrel band. Some models are marked with conventional lettering; and others, in the Turkish alphabet. It was adopted by the Turkish government in 1887.

| Exc. | V.G. | Good | Fair | Poor |
|------|------|------|------|------|
| 300 | 250 | 200 | 125 | 80 |

### Model 88 Commission Rifle

This is a bolt-action repeating rifle chambered for the 7.9mm cartridge. It has a 29" barrel and utilizes a 5-round, integral box magazine. The finish is blued, with a full-length walnut stock held on by one barrel band. It has a cleaning rod under the barrel and a bayonet lug near the muzzle. It is marked "GEW. 88." It also has the year of production, the name of the arsenal that manufactured it, and a crown. It was developed as a result of the German Small Arms Commission that met at Spandau, Germany.

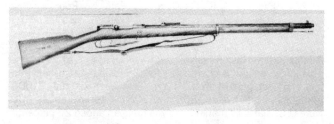

| Exc. | V.G. | Good | Fair | Poor |
|------|------|------|------|------|
| 225 | 175 | 150 | 100 | 75 |

## Belgian Model 1889 Rifle

This is a bolt-action repeating rifle chambered for the 7.65mm cartridge. It has a 30.6" barrel with a 5-round, integral box magazine. The finish is blued, with a full-length walnut stock held on by two barrel bands. It is marked with the name of the manufacturer and has a cleaning rod beneath the barrel and a bayonet lug at the muzzle. This was the first rifle that featured stripper-clip loading. A carbine version with a 21.65" barrel was also available.

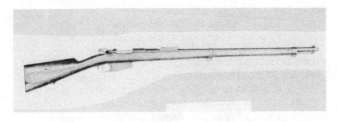

| Exc. | V.G. | Good | Fair | Poor |
|------|------|------|------|------|
| 225 | 175 | 150 | 100 | 75 |

## Argentine Model 91 Rifle

This is a bolt-action repeating rifle chambered for the 7.65mm cartridge. It was offered with a 29" barrel and, in the carbine configuration, a 17.6" barrel. It has a full-length walnut stock held on by one barrel band. There is a cleaning rod beneath the barrel, as well as a bayonet lug near the muzzle. The carbine lacks these features. This was the first of the South American contract Mausers, and there were approximately 180,000 rifles and 30,000 carbines produced in 1891. They feature the model designation and maker's name, as well as the Argentine coat of arms.

| Exc. | V.G. | Good | Fair | Poor |
|------|------|------|------|------|
| 250 | 200 | 175 | 125 | 90 |

## Spanish Model 91

This version is similar to the Argentine except that it features the Spanish coat of arms.

| Exc. | V.G. | Good | Fair | Poor |
|------|------|------|------|------|
| 250 | 200 | 175 | 125 | 90 |

## Spanish Model 93

This rifle represented a milestone in Mauser development. It is chambered for the 7x57mm cartridge and has a 29" barrel length. It was the first model that featured a staggered-column, integral box magazine that is flush with the bottom of the stock. This gives the rifle a more graceful appearance and simplified carrying. There were a number of other modifications that made this an extremely popular rifle in its day. It was adopted by the Spanish government in December of 1893.

| Exc. | V.G. | Good | Fair | Poor |
|------|------|------|------|------|
| 250 | 200 | 175 | 125 | 90 |

## Brazilian Model 94

This is a bolt-action repeating rifle that is similar in appearance to the Spanish Model 93. It is chambered for the same caliber and features the same length barrel. It is marked with the Brazilian coat of arms. It was manufactured by Ludwig Loewe and Company, as well as Fabrique Nationale in Herstel, Belgium.

| Exc. | V.G. | Good | Fair | Poor |
|------|------|------|------|------|
| 250 | 200 | 175 | 125 | 90 |

## Chilean Model 1895

This version is similar to the Brazilian Model 94, manufactured by Ludwig Loewe, and marked "Mauser-Chileno Modelo 1895."

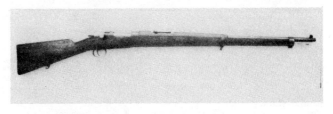

| Exc. | V.G. | Good | Fair | Poor |
|------|------|------|------|------|
| 250 | 200 | 175 | 125 | 90 |

## Siamese Mauser Rifle

This is a bolt-action repeating rifle chambered for the 8mm Siamese rimmed cartridge. It has a 29" barrel and a 5-round box magazine. The finish is blued, with a full-length walnut stock held on by one barrel band. This is essentially a Model 98 action. Most were manufactured in Japan. There is a sheet-metal cover over the ejection port designed to keep dirt out of the action. It is marked with what was known as the "Charkra" along with other Siamese markings. The Tokyo arsenal symbol is on the left side of the receiver. Ammunition for this rifle is nearly impossible to secure, and many are being cannibalized by custom gunsmiths manufacturing .45-70-caliber, bolt-action sporting rifles.

| Exc. | V.G. | Good | Fair | Poor |
|------|------|------|------|------|
| 200 | 150 | 100 | 80 | 65 |

## Swedish Model 94 Carbine

This is a bolt-action repeating rifle chambered for the 6.5mm cartridge. It has a 17.7" barrel and is blued, with a full-length stock and handguard held on by a single barrel band. It has a 5-round, integral box magazine and a bayonet lug. It is marked with the name of the manufacturer, date of production, and the Swedish crown.

| Exc. | V.G. | Good | Fair | Poor |
|------|------|------|------|------|
| 250 | 200 | 175 | 125 | 90 |

## Swedish Model 96 Rifle

This version is similar to the carbine, with a 29" barrel.

| Exc. | V.G. | Good | Fair | Poor |
|------|------|------|------|------|
| 250 | 200 | 175 | 125 | 90 |

## Swedish Model 38 Rifle

This version has a 23.6" barrel and lacks the Swedish crown marking.

| Exc. | V.G. | Good | Fair | Poor |
|------|------|------|------|------|
| 225 | 175 | 150 | 100 | 75 |

## Model 98 Rifle

This is the improved Mauser rifle for which the company's reputation has been based. It cocks on the bolt opening rather than closing. It features large, gas-escape holes for safety and has an enlarged receiver ring for extra strength. It is chambered for the 7.9mm cartridge and has a 29" barrel and a 5-round, integral magazine. It features military sights and is blued, with a full-length walnut stock and hand guard held on by two barrel bands. There is a cleaning rod and a bayonet lug. It is marked "GEW. 98" along with the name of the manufacturer, year of production, and a crown. Germany adopted this rifle on April 5, 1898.

| Exc. | V.G. | Good | Fair | Poor |
|------|------|------|------|------|
| 275 | 250 | 200 | 150 | 100 |

### Model 98a Carbine
This is similar to the Model 98 rifle, with a 23.6" barrel. It is marked "KAR. 98" along with the manufacturer, year of production, and a crown. It has no cleaning rod but features a bayonet lug. The stock is held on by one barrel band.

| Exc. | V.G. | Good | Fair | Poor |
|------|------|------|------|------|
| 275 | 250 | 200 | 150 | 100 |

### Model 98k Carbine
This version is similar to the Model 98a but is marked "Mod. 98" and is encountered with a laminated stock. This version was widely utilized by German forces in WWII.

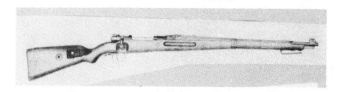

| Exc. | V.G. | Good | Fair | Poor |
|------|------|------|------|------|
| 300 | 250 | 225 | 175 | 125 |

There are several sniper versions of the WWII Mauser rifle with different types of mounting systems and scopes. It would behoove one interested in acquiring such a weapon to secure a competent appraisal as fraudulent examples have been noted.

### Model 33/40 Carbine
This is a 19.2"-barrel, modified carbine chambered for the 7.9mm cartridge. It was used by the Germans in WWII and is marked "G. 33/40" with the manufacturer's code and the year of production.

| Exc. | V.G. | Good | Fair | Poor |
|------|------|------|------|------|
| 650 | 550 | 450 | 300 | 200 |

### Czech Model 98 VZ24
This version is similar to the German Model 98, with a large, stamped steel triggerguard and magazine cover. The floorplate is permanently affixed and not removable. This version was assembled from Model 98k parts manufactured during WWII. The German markings were ground off and replaced by CZ markings.

| Exc. | V.G. | Good | Fair | Poor |
|------|------|------|------|------|
| 350 | 300 | 275 | 225 | 175 |

### French Occupation Model
This version was also produced from modified WWII German-production rifles. It has no bayonet lug but features a hexagon extension with a rod protruding from it for arsenal stacking. The barrel bands are stampings and are screwed directly into the stock.

| Exc. | V.G. | Good | Fair | Poor |
|------|------|------|------|------|
| 275 | 225 | 200 | 150 | 100 |

### Colombian Model 98
This version has a 29" barrel and is chambered for the .30-06 cartridge. Otherwise, it is similar to the other South American contract rifles.

| Exc. | V.G. | Good | Fair | Poor |
|------|------|------|------|------|
| 275 | 225 | 200 | 150 | 100 |

### Iranian Model 98
This version is chambered for the 7.92mm cartridge and was offered as a long model with a 29" barrel or as a short rifle with an 18" barrel. It features Farsi lettering.

| Exc. | V.G. | Good | Fair | Poor |
|------|------|------|------|------|
| 275 | 225 | 200 | 150 | 100 |

### Peruvian Model 1935 Rifle
This South American contract Model 98 is chambered for the .30-06 cartridge and has a 23" barrel. It features the Peruvian crest.

| Exc. | V.G. | Good | Fair | Poor |
|------|------|------|------|------|
| 250 | 200 | 175 | 125 | 90 |

### Polish Model 29
This version is chambered for the 7.9mm cartridge, has a 23.6" barrel, and is marked with the Polish eagle and the name "F. B. Radom," the manufacturer, as well as the date of production.

| Exc. | V.G. | Good | Fair | Poor |
|------|------|------|------|------|
| 375 | 325 | 300 | 250 | 200 |

### Standard Mauser Banner Rifle
This version is chambered for the 7.9mm cartridge and has a 23.6" barrel. It is blued, with a full-length stock held on by one barrel band, and is marked with the Mauser Banner trademark. It has also been noted chambered for 7mm, as well as 7.65mm. The left side of the receiver is marked "Standard-Modell."

| Exc. | V.G. | Good | Fair | Poor |
|------|------|------|------|------|
| 375 | 325 | 300 | 250 | 200 |

### Mexican Model 1936
This version is chambered for the 7x57mm cartridge, has a 23.2" barrel, and is blued, with a full-length walnut stock and hand guard held on by one barrel band. It has a 5-round magazine, features a cleaning rod and bayonet lug, and has the manufacturer's name, year, and the Mexican coat of arms marked on the receiver.

| Exc. | V.G. | Good | Fair | Poor |
|------|------|------|------|------|
| 250 | 200 | 175 | 125 | 90 |

### Spanish Model 43
This version is chambered for the 7.9mm cartridge, has a 23.6" barrel, and features the Spanish coat of arms and year and name of manufacturer. Many specimens feature a fascist symbol marked on the receiver. It was manufactured at the La Coruna arsenal.

| Exc. | V.G. | Good | Fair | Poor |
|------|------|------|------|------|
| 225 | 175 | 150 | 100 | 75 |

### Early Sporting Rifle
The Model 98 action has been used through the years to produce some extremely high quality sporting rifles. What we are dealing with here were the products of the Mauser Werke originally owned by Peter Paul Mauser at Oberndorf. They were chambered for various metric calibers and were built on the Mauser Model 98 action. For the most part, they were offered with 23.5" ribbed lightweight barrels and were offered with either single or double-set triggers. They feature open sights and a 5-round, integral box magazine. The finish is blued, with a walnut semi-pistolgrip stock and Schnabel forend. They were

furnished with sling swivels and a checkered black buttplate that bears the early Mauser crest. There are a number of sub-variations within this grouping that differ basically in the length of action, calibers chambered, and options offered. These variations and their values are as follows:

**Type A--Short Action**

| Exc. | V.G. | Good | Fair | Poor |
|---|---|---|---|---|
| 450 | 400 | 350 | 250 | 175 |

**Type A--Medium Action**

| Exc. | V.G. | Good | Fair | Poor |
|---|---|---|---|---|
| 450 | 400 | 350 | 250 | 175 |

**Type A--Long Action**

| Exc. | V.G. | Good | Fair | Poor |
|---|---|---|---|---|
| 475 | 425 | 375 | 275 | 200 |

**Type B**

| Exc. | V.G. | Good | Fair | Poor |
|---|---|---|---|---|
| 450 | 400 | 350 | 250 | 175 |

**Type K--21.65" Barrel**

| Exc. | V.G. | Good | Fair | Poor |
|---|---|---|---|---|
| 450 | 400 | 350 | 250 | 175 |

**Type M--Full-length Stock, Spoon Bolt Handle**

| Exc. | V.G. | Good | Fair | Poor |
|---|---|---|---|---|
| 475 | 425 | 375 | 275 | 200 |

**Type S--Full-length Stock, No Forend Cap**

| Exc. | V.G. | Good | Fair | Poor |
|---|---|---|---|---|
| 475 | 425 | 375 | 275 | 200 |

**Model 1896 "Broomhandle Mauser Pistol"**

This is a rather unusual-appearing, recoil-operated, locked-bolt pistol that first began commercial production in 1896. It was produced for 43 years, with the final examples being manufactured at Oberndorf, Germany, in 1939. During this period this pistol was left relatively unchanged except for some modifications to its physical appearance. This was an extremely complicated pistol that was invented and produced by some of the finest craftsmen that were ever involved in the firearms trade. The biggest contributors to the development of this model were the Feederle brothers, who were closely associated with Paul Mauser and were heavily involved in the operation of his experimental workshop in the final years of the Nineteenth Century. There are many variations within this model designation. Many are very slight yet have a drastic effect on the value of the respective pistol. We strongly recommend securing competent, individual appraisals if a transaction is contemplated. It is fortunate for potential collectors that several excellent volumes have been written on this subject. These volumes should be secured so that the potential collector can educate oneself before making a costly mistake.

**Six-Shot Step-Barrel Cone Hammer**

This is a very rare and early version of the C-96 pistol. It is chambered for the 7.63mm Mauser cartridge and has a 5.5" barrel. It features a fixed rear sight. It is blued, with checkered walnut grips, and is marked "Ruecklauf Pistole System Mauser, Oberndorf am/Neckar 1896." There were fewer than 200 manufactured.

| Exc. | V.G. | Good | Fair | Poor |
|---|---|---|---|---|
| 6500 | 5500 | 4250 | 3000 | 2000 |

**Twenty-Shot Step-Barrel Cone Hammer**

This is an extremely rare early variation that is similar to the 6-shot version, with an extended, 20- round magazine.

| Exc. | V.G. | Good | Fair | Poor |
|---|---|---|---|---|
| 15000 | 12500 | 9000 | 6500 | 4000 |

**System Mauser Cone Hammer**

This version features a tapered-barrel design, is chambered for the 7.63mm cartridge, and has a 5.5" barrel with an adjustable sight. It features the cone-type hammer with machined concentric rings. The finish is blued, with 22-groove wooden grips. It has a 10- round magazine.

| Exc. | V.G. | Good | Fair | Poor |
|---|---|---|---|---|
| 5500 | 4500 | 3500 | 2500 | 1750 |

**Six-Shot Cone Hammer**

This version is chambered for 7.63mm Mauser and has a 4.75" barrel. It features a fixed rear sight and a 6-round magazine. The finish is blued, with 21- groove walnut grips. It was the first Model 1896 pistol that was marked "Waffenfabrik Mauser, Oberndorf A/N" over the chamber.

| Exc. | V.G. | Good | Fair | Poor |
|---|---|---|---|---|
| 5000 | 4000 | 3250 | 2250 | 1500 |

**Twenty-Shot Cone Hammer**

This is an extremely rare version that is similar to the Six-Shot Cone Hammer except that it features an extended 10-round magazine.

| Exc. | V.G. | Good | Fair | Poor |
|---|---|---|---|---|
| 10000 | 8000 | 6000 | 4200 | 2500 |

**Standard Cone Hammer**

This version is similar to the Twenty-Shot Cone Hammer but features a 10-round magazine and 23-groove wooden grips.

| Exc. | V.G. | Good | Fair | Poor |
|---|---|---|---|---|
| 2750 | 2250 | 1750 | 1400 | 1000 |

**Turkish Contract Cone Hammer**

This version is similar to the Standard Cone Hammer except that it features Farsi markings along with the crest of the Turkish Sultan Abdul-Hamid II on the left side of the frame. There were approximately 1,000 produced.

| Exc. | V.G. | Good | Fair | Poor |
|---|---|---|---|---|
| 6500 | 5500 | 4250 | 3000 | 2000 |

**Early Transitional Large Ring Hammer**

This version is similar to its predecessors except that it features a large, ring-type hammer with a large hole in the center. This model is sometimes engraved with a dealer's name on the left side of the frame. Otherwise, it has the standard Mauser chamber markings. The grips have 23 grooves.

| Exc. | V.G. | Good | Fair | Poor |
|---|---|---|---|---|
| 3000 | 2400 | 1850 | 1150 | 800 |

### Model 1899 Flat Side--Italian Contract

This version is chambered for the 7.63mm Mauser cartridge and has a 5.5" barrel with adjustable sights. The sides of the frame are totally flat and lack the mill marks normally found on this pistol. The finish is blued, with 23-groove walnut grips. It features the standard chamber markings and is also marked "Pistole Automatiche Modello 1899." There were approximately 5,000 manufactured in 1899.

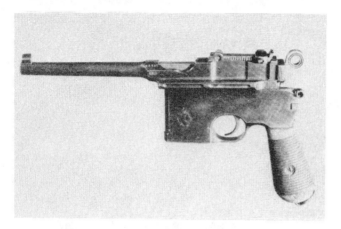

| Exc. | V.G. | Good | Fair | Poor |
|------|------|------|------|------|
| 3250 | 2750 | 2000 | 1400 | 1150 |

### Early Flat Side

This version is similar to the Italian-contract Flat Side but has an early-type adjustable sight and lacks the Italian markings.

| Exc. | V.G. | Good | Fair | Poor |
|------|------|------|------|------|
| 2750 | 2450 | 1800 | 1200 | 900 |

### Late Flat Side

This is the most common of the Flat Side pistols. It is similar to the early variation except that it features the lighter-type adjustable sight. Many are marked "Von Lengerke & Detmold, New York" on the left side of the frame.

| Exc. | V.G. | Good | Fair | Poor |
|------|------|------|------|------|
| 2250 | 1900 | 1500 | 1000 | 750 |

### Flat Side Bolo

This rare variation is chambered for 7.63mm and features a 3.9" barrel with fixed sights. It features the flat, unmilled frame. It has the small, checkered walnut bolo-type grip. It also features the large ring hammer.

| Exc. | V.G. | Good | Fair | Poor |
|------|------|------|------|------|
| 2500 | 2250 | 1850 | 1300 | 1000 |

### Early Large Ring Hammer Bolo

This compact version has a 3.9" barrel and the standard milled frame. It has late adjustable sights and is blued with black hard rubber grips molded into a floral pattern. It features standard chamber markings and a 10-round magazine.

| Exc. | V.G. | Good | Fair | Poor |
|------|------|------|------|------|
| 3400 | 3000 | 1600 | 1000 | 650 |

### Shallow-Milled Panel Model

This is a full-size version with a 5.5" barrel and the late adjustable sights. The panels that were milled in the frame are only one half as deep as those found on earlier models. Many are marked "Von Lengerke & Detmold." The finish is blued, with the 23-groove walnut or checkered hard rubber grips.

| Exc. | V.G. | Good | Fair | Poor |
|------|------|------|------|------|
| 2000 | 1500 | 1000 | 750 | 500 |

### Deep-Milled Panel Model

This version features panels milled deeper than on the Shallow-Milled Model. It still features the large ring hammer and has the standard chamber markings that are also marked on the center of the right rear frame.

| Exc. | V.G. | Good | Fair | Poor |
|------|------|------|------|------|
| 2000 | 1500 | 1000 | 750 | 500 |

### Late Large Ring Hammer Bolo

This was the last of the large ring pistols. It has a 3.9" barrel with the late adjustable sight. The finish is blued, with black hard rubber floral grips. It features the standard markings.

| Exc. | V.G. | Good | Fair | Poor |
|------|------|------|------|------|
| 2000 | 1500 | 1000 | 750 | 500 |

### Early Small Hammer Model

This version is chambered for the 7.63mm Mauser cartridge and has a 5.5" barrel. It was the first model that utilized the small ringed hammer with the small hole in the center. This version has the late adjustable sight, is blued, and has 34-groove walnut grips. It has the standard chamber marking, which is also marked on the right rear frame.

| Exc. | V.G. | Good | Fair | Poor |
|------|------|------|------|------|
| 1850 | 1450 | 950 | 600 | 400 |

### Early Small Hammer Bolo Model

This version is similar to its predecessor except that it has a 3.9" barrel. It is furnished with black hard rubber floral grips that are smaller in configuration than on the full-sized pistol.

| Exc. | V.G. | Good | Fair | Poor |
|------|------|------|------|------|
| 2250 | 1750 | 1400 | 950 | 600 |

### Six-Shot Small Hammer Model

This version is chambered for the 7.63mm Mauser cartridge and has a 3.9" barrel with fixed sights and a 6-round magazine. The finish is blued, with 27-groove walnut grips. It has the standard Mauser markings.

| Exc. | V.G. | Good | Fair | Poor |
|------|------|------|------|------|
| 5500 | 4500 | 3250 | 2250 | 1600 |

### Standard Pre-War Commercial

This is the most common of all the Broomhandle Mauser pistols. It is chambered for the 7.63mm Mauser cartridge and has a 5.5" barrel with the late adjustable sights. The finish is blued, with either checkered black hard rubber or 34-groove walnut grips. It has the standard Mauser markings, and many are marked "Von Lengerke & Detmold."

| Exc. | V.G. | Good | Fair | Poor |
|------|------|------|------|------|
| 1350 | 1000 | 750 | 500 | 400 |

### Mauser Banner Model

This version is similar in appearance to the Pre-War Commercial except that it has the Mauser Banner trademark marked on the top of the chamber and the standard Mauser marking on the right rear frame. The finish is blued, with 32-groove walnut grips. There were approximately 10,000 manufactured.

| Exc. | V.G. | Good | Fair | Poor |
|------|------|------|------|------|
| 2000 | 1500 | 1150 | 800 | 600 |

### Persian Contract

This version is similar in appearance to the Pre-War Commercial but features the distinctive Persian "Rising Sun" stamped on the left side of the barrel extension. It has the standard chamber marking, as well as the standard marking on the right rear frame. The Persian Lion Crest is marked on the left rear frame. Beware of fakes.

| Exc. | V.G. | Good | Fair | Poor |
|------|------|------|------|------|
| 3600 | 3000 | 2250 | 1400 | 750 |

### 9mm Export Model

This version is similar in appearance to its predecessors except that it is chambered for the 9mm Mauser Export cartridge. The flat-milled chamber area of the barrel is brought forward further than on any other model. It has the standard Mauser markings and is blued, with 34-groove walnut grips.

| Exc. | V.G. | Good | Fair | Poor |
|------|------|------|------|------|
| 1200 | 950 | 700 | 550 | 400 |

### Standard Wartime Commercial

This version is second only to the Pre-War Commercial in production. It is similar in appearance but was the first model that used the new safety. It has the standard Mauser markings along with the letters "NS" stamped on the back of the hammer. This denotes the New Safety. The finish is blued, with 30-groove walnut grips.

| Exc. | V.G. | Good | Fair | Poor |
|------|------|------|------|------|
| 1100 | 800 | 600 | 500 | 375 |

### 9mm Parabellum Military Contract

This version is similar in appearance to the Wartime Commercial except that it is chambered for the 9mm Parabellum cartridge. The finish shows many tool marks and little polishing. The walnut, 24-groove grips are usually marked with a large number "9" filled with red paint, although this is not always the case. It features the standard Mauser markings and is blued.

| Exc. | V.G. | Good | Fair | Poor |
|------|------|------|------|------|
| 1250 | 1000 | 750 | 600 | 450 |

### 1920 Rework

This version is chambered for either 7.63mm Mauser or the 9mm Parabellum cartridge. It has a 3.9" barrel and was produced to conform to the provisions of the Treaty of Versailles necessitating a barrel length less than four inches. The adjustable sight was removed and a fixed rear sight added. The finish is blued with walnut grips. It is not uncommon to find police unit markings stamped on the front grip strap.

| Exc. | V.G. | Good | Fair | Poor |
|------|------|------|------|------|
| 1000 | 750 | 500 | 400 | 350 |

### Luger Barrelled 1920 Rework

This Rework was created by turning down a 9mm Luger barrel and threading it into the sawed-off Mauser barrel. It is difficult to spot the joint, as this work was so expertly accomplished. The barrel length is 4". It has a fixed sight and is chambered for the 9mm Parabellum cartridge. The 23-groove walnut grips were often stamped with the red "9." It has the standard Mauser markings.

| Exc. | V.G. | Good | Fair | Poor |
|------|------|------|------|------|
| 1250 | 1000 | 750 | 500 | 450 |

### French Gendarme Model

This is a large-frame model with a 3.9" bolo-length barrel. It has adjustable sights and is blued, with checkered hard rubber grips. It has the standard Mauser markings; and although reputed to be a special French order, this has never been confirmed.

| Exc. | V.G. | Good | Fair | Poor |
|------|------|------|------|------|
| 2500 | 2000 | 1300 | 800 | 500 |

### Early Post-War Bolo Model

This version is chambered for the 7.63mm Mauser cartridge and has a 3.9" barrel. It features the bolo-style grip frame and adjustable sights and is blued, with 22-groove walnut grips. It features the standard Mauser markings.

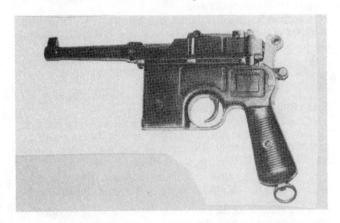

| Exc. | V.G. | Good | Fair | Poor |
|------|------|------|------|------|
| 1500 | 1200 | 900 | 650 | 400 |

### Late Post-War Bolo Model

This version is similar to the Early Model but features the Mauser Banner trademark over the chamber. The finish is a high-polished bright blue, similar to early Colt guns.

| Exc. | V.G. | Good | Fair | Poor |
|------|------|------|------|------|
| 1750 | 1500 | 1000 | 750 | 500 |

### Early Model 1930

This version is chambered for the 7.63mm Mauser cartridge and has a 5.2" stepped barrel. It has the standard Mauser chamber markings and right rear frame marking along with the letters "D.R.P. u. A.P." This was German patent information. The Mauser Banner appears on the left rear frame panel. This version is blued, with 12-groove walnut grips, and features the late universal-type safety.

| Exc. | V.G. | Good | Fair | Poor |
|------|------|------|------|------|
| 1600 | 1300 | 850 | 550 | 400 |

### Late Model 1930

With the exception of changes in the milling characteristics of the frame and the addition of solid receiver rails, this version is quite similar to the Early Model. It is marked the same.

| Exc. | V.G. | Good | Fair | Poor |
|------|------|------|------|------|
| 1500 | 1200 | 750 | 500 | 350 |

### Model 1930 Removable Magazine

This is a semi-automatic version of the Model 1896 Select-Fire pistol. It is similar in appearance to the Late 1930 Model except that it has a removable magazine. Be extremely wary of fakes created by welding the selector cuts on a Schnellfeuer.

| Exc. | V.G. | Good | Fair | Poor |
|------|------|------|------|------|
| 10000 | 7500 | 5000 | 3000 | 2000 |

### Cone Hammer Flat Side Carbine

This model is chambered for the 7.63mm Mauser cartridge and has an 11.75" barrel with an early-type adjustable sight. It has the flat, unmilled frame and a walnut buttstock integral with the grip. This is an extremely rare firearm.

| Exc. | V.G. | Good | Fair | Poor |
|------|------|------|------|------|
| 12500 | 9000 | 6500 | 3500 | 2500 |

### Large Ring Hammer Transitional Carbine
This version is similar to the Flat Side Carbine except that it has the milled frame panels. The finish is blued, with a walnut stock and forend.

| Exc. | V.G. | Good | Fair | Poor |
|------|------|------|------|------|
| 10000 | 7500 | 5500 | 3250 | 2500 |

### Large Ring Hammer Carbine
This version has a 14.5" barrel with adjustable sights and the standard Mauser markings. The finish is blued, with a walnut stock and forend.

| Exc. | V.G. | Good | Fair | Poor |
|------|------|------|------|------|
| 10000 | 7500 | 5500 | 3250 | 2500 |

### Small Ring Hammer Carbine
This version is similar in appearance to the Large Ring Hammer Carbine except that it features the small ring hammer with the small hole in the center. The finish is blued, with a walnut stock and forearm. It features the standard Mauser markings.

| Exc. | V.G. | Good | Fair | Poor |
|------|------|------|------|------|
| 8500 | 6000 | 4250 | 3000 | 2500 |

A large number of Broomhandle Mausers were exported to China over the years. Recently these firearms have been imported into the U.S.A. at various prices starting as low as $89. Please be aware that these recently imported guns in no way reflect on the collectibility and value of the pistols that have been described in this text. As a result of the Chinese fascination with the Broomhandle pistol, a number of comparatively crude Chinese-manufactured versions of this pistol have been produced over the years. They are as follows:

### Chinese Marked, Handmade Copies
These are usually quite poor in quality and should not be fired. Their value lies in the fact that they are a curiosity and reflect the ingenuity and talent of their makers.

| Exc. | V.G. | Good | Fair | Poor |
|------|------|------|------|------|
| 500 | 400 | 350 | 250 | 175 |

### Taku-Naval Dockyard Model
This is a slightly better quality Chinese reproduction with a flat-side frame. There were approximately 6,000 manufactured. Values given include correct shoulder stock and holster.

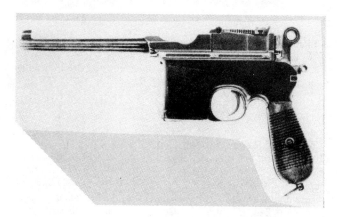

| Exc. | V.G. | Good | Fair | Poor |
|------|------|------|------|------|
| 1250 | 850 | 750 | 500 | 400 |

### Shansei Arsenal Model
This version is chambered for the .45 ACP cartridge. It is larger than a standard Mauser and has a magazine extended to hold ten rounds. The markings, unlike the Handmade Copies, are in Chinese characters. The finish is blued, with walnut grips. There were approximately 8,000 manufactured.

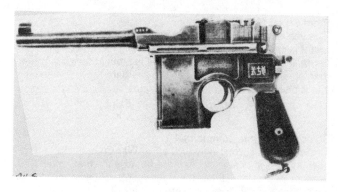

| Exc. | V.G. | Good | Fair | Poor |
|------|------|------|------|------|
| 4000 | 3000 | 2250 | 1500 | 1300 |

There were also a number of Spanish copies of the Model 1896 pistol. Some were of good quality; others, merely mediocre. They were produced by Unceta (Astra) and Zulaica y Cia (Royal) and marketed by the firm of Beistegui Hermanos. These copies are covered in their own sections of this text.

### Model 1910
This is a blowback-operated, semi-automatic pocket pistol chambered for the 6.35mm cartridge. It has a 3" barrel with fixed sights and a 9-round detachable magazine. The finish is blued, with either checkered walnut or hard rubber grips. It is marked "Waffenfabrik Mauser A.-G. Oberndorf A.N. Mauser's Patent." It was manufactured between 1910 and 1934. There are a number of variations within this model designation that would add to the value of the standard version. The variations are chiefly contract-series production; and it would behoove one to secure a qualified, individual appraisal if in doubt.

| Exc. | V.G. | Good | Fair | Poor |
|------|------|------|------|------|
| 350 | 275 | 225 | 150 | 100 |

### Model 1914
This is a blowback-operated, semi-automatic pocket pistol chambered for the 7.65mm cartridge. It has a 3.5" barrel with fixed sights. It utilizes a detachable box magazine and is blued, with checkered walnut wrap-around grips. It is marked "Waffenfabrik Mauser A.G. Oberndorf A.N. Mauser's Patent" on the slide. The frame has the Mauser Banner stamped on its left side. It was manufactured between 1914 and 1934. There were a number of variations produced that would have an effect on the value. We recommend securing a qualified, individual appraisal on this variation. WWI Eagle proof marks would add approximately 10 percent to the values given.

| Exc. | V.G. | Good | Fair | Poor |
|------|------|------|------|------|
| 350 | 275 | 225 | 150 | 100 |

## WTP Model I Vest Pocket Pistol

This is a blowback-operated semi-automatic pistol chambered for the 6.35mm cartridge. It has a 2.5" barrel with rudimentary sights and a 6-round detachable magazine. The finish is blued, with checkered black rubber or plastic grips that feature the Mauser Banner molded into them. The slide is marked "Mauser-Werke A.G. Oberndorf A.N." It also is marked "D.R.P. u. A.P." This Pistol was manufactured between 1922 and 1937. There are a number of variations within the model, and we suggest securing a qualified appraisal if in doubt.

| Exc. | V.G. | Good | Fair | Poor |
|------|------|------|------|------|
| 400 | 350 | 275 | 200 | 100 |

## WTP Model II Vest Pocket Pistol

This Pistol is similar to the Model I but is actually slightly smaller and more compact. The rear of the triggerguard is relieved to allow a better finger grip. It is chambered for the 6.35mm cartridge and has a 2" barrel. The finish is blued, with checkered black plastic Mauser-Banner grips. This model was manufactured between 1938 and 1940. There are many variations within this model designation that were basically the result of design improvements and contract orders. We recommend securing a qualified appraisal if in doubt.

| Exc. | V.G. | Good | Fair | Poor |
|------|------|------|------|------|
| 425 | 375 | 300 | 225 | 125 |

## Model 1934

This version is similar to the Model 1914 except that it features one-piece wrap-around grips. It is chambered for the 7.65mm cartridge and has a 3.5" barrel with fixed sights. The slide is marked "Mauser-Werke A.G. Oberndorf A.N." It has the Mauser

Banner stamped on the frame. The reverse side is marked with the caliber and "D.R.P. u A.P." This pistol was manufactured between 1934 and 1939, and some have Nazi markings. A Waffenamt version would be worth approximately 20 percent more than the values given. This version was also utilized by the Nazi navy, and an example that bears the Eagle over letter "M" on the sideplate would be worth approximately twice the value given. There are also a number of other variations that would add considerably to the value of this Model. We recommend securing a qualified appraisal if in doubt.

| Exc. | V.G. | Good | Fair | Poor |
|------|------|------|------|------|
| 350 | 275 | 225 | 150 | 100 |

## Model HSc

This is a blowback-operated, double-action semi-automatic pocket pistol that was quite modern in its styling. It is chambered for the 7.65mm and the .380 ACP cartridges. It has a 3.4" barrel and is either blued or nickel-plated. It features checkered walnut grips. It was introduced in 1938, and over the years a number of variations have been produced. This pistol has been finished in blue or nickel-plated and has fixed sights and a 7- or 8-round detachable magazine, depending on the caliber. We list the more commonly encountered variations and their values but recommend securing a qualified appraisal if in doubt.

## Early Commercial Model

This version features a high-polished blued finish, checkered walnut grips, the standard Mauser address on the slide, and the Eagle N proofmark. The floorplate of the magazine has the Mauser Banner stamped upon it.

| Exc. | V.G. | Good | Fair | Poor |
|------|------|------|------|------|
| 450 | 400 | 350 | 250 | 175 |

## Transition Model

This version lacks the high quality polish of the Early Commercial Model and has a matted sight channel.

| Exc. | V.G. | Good | Fair | Poor |
|------|------|------|------|------|
| 400 | 350 | 300 | 200 | 125 |

## Early Nazi Army Model

This version is similar in appearance to its predecessors except that it features the Waffenamt No. 135 or 655 marking. The finish is high-polish blued, with checkered walnut grips. The acceptance marks are located on the left side of the trigger guard.

| Exc. | V.G. | Good | Fair | Poor |
|------|------|------|------|------|
| 400 | 350 | 300 | 200 | 125 |

### Late Nazi Army Model
This version is either blued or parkerized, with walnut or plastic grips, and features the 135 acceptance mark only. It also has the Eagle N proof. Otherwise, it is similar to the Early version.

| Exc. | V.G. | Good | Fair | Poor |
|------|------|------|------|------|
| 350 | 300 | 250 | 150 | 100 |

### Early Nazi Navy Model
This version features the distinctive Kriegsmarine Eagle over M marking on the front grip strap. The finish is high-polish blued, with checkered walnut grips.

| Exc. | V.G. | Good | Fair | Poor |
|------|------|------|------|------|
| 800 | 700 | 550 | 400 | 300 |

### Wartime Nazi Navy Model
This version features a navy acceptance mark on the side of the triggerguard. It is blued, with either checkered walnut or plastic grips. It has the standard Mauser address and Banner and also the Eagle N proof.

| Exc. | V.G. | Good | Fair | Poor |
|------|------|------|------|------|
| 400 | 350 | 300 | 200 | 125 |

### Early Nazi Police Model
This version features a high-polish blued finish with checkered walnut grips. It has the standard Mauser markings and Banner on the slide, as well as the Eagle N proof. It also has the Eagle L procurement office stamp on the left side of the triggerguard.

| Exc. | V.G. | Good | Fair | Poor |
|------|------|------|------|------|
| 450 | 400 | 350 | 250 | 175 |

### Wartime Nazi Police Model
This version is blued, with either checkered walnut or plastic grips. It has the late, three-line Mauser address and Banner and also bears the procurement office Eagle L stamp.

| Exc. | V.G. | Good | Fair | Poor |
|------|------|------|------|------|
| 450 | 400 | 350 | 250 | 175 |

### Wartime Commercial Model
This version is blued, with checkered walnut grips, and has the late, three-line address. There are no acceptance marks on the left side of the triggerguard, and it bears the Eagle N proof.

| Exc. | V.G. | Good | Fair | Poor |
|------|------|------|------|------|
| 400 | 350 | 300 | 200 | 125 |

### Low Grip Screw Model
This version has the screws that attached the grip located near the bottom of the grip. The finish is high-polished blued, with checkered walnut grips. It has the early barrel address without the lines and has the Eagle N proof. Some have been observed with Nazi Kreigsmarine markings. There were approximately 2,000 manufactured.

| Exc. | V.G. | Good | Fair | Poor |
|------|------|------|------|------|
| 2000 | 1750 | 1150 | 750 | 650 |

### French Manufactured Model
At the end of WWII, the French manufactured HSc pistols to supply their troops that were fighting in Indochina. The finish of these pistols is either blued or parkerized; the grips, either walnut or plastic. They have the three-line slide address, and the left side of the triggerguard is marked with the intertwined letters "MR." They are chambered for the 7.65mm cartridge and are very rarely observed in better than poor condition due to the jungle conditions in which they were used.

| Exc. | V.G. | Good | Fair | Poor |
|------|------|------|------|------|
| 300 | 275 | 225 | 150 | 100 |

### Late Mauser Production Model
This version is similar in configuration to the earlier Commercial and Wartime Models. It is chambered for either .32 ACP or the .380 ACP cartridges. They are either blued or nickel-plated, with checkered walnut grips. They were manufactured between 1968 and 1981.

| Exc. | V.G. | Good | Fair | Poor |
|------|------|------|------|------|
| 350 | 300 | 250 | 200 | 150 |

### Interarms Import Models
This version of the HSc pistol was manufactured under license by Gamba in Italy. They are similar in appearance and calibers to the late Mauser-production models. They were imported by Interarms of Alexandria, Virginia, between 1983 and 1985.

| Exc. | V.G. | Good | Fair | Poor |
|------|------|------|------|------|
| 300 | 275 | 250 | 175 | 100 |

### Mauser Lugers
The parabellum pistols manufactured by the Mauser company are located in the Luger section of this text.

Mauser rifles are currently imported into the U.S.A. by the firm of KDF, Inc., located in Seguin, Texas. Many of the Mauser-produced sporting rifles currently available will be found in the section of this text dealing with KDF products.

### Model 2000
This is a bolt-action sporting rifle chambered for .270, .308, or the .30-06 cartridges. It has a 24" barrel with open sights and a 5-round magazine. The finish is blued, with a checkered walnut stock. It was manufactured between 1969 and 1971.

| Exc. | V.G. | Good | Fair | Poor |
|------|------|------|------|------|
| 350 | 300 | 250 | 200 | 150 |

### Model 3000
This version features a 22" barrel and was furnished without sights. It has a select walnut Monte Carlo-type stock with a rosewood forend tip and pistolgrip cap. It is skip-line checkered and was furnished with a recoil pad. It was manufactured between 1971 and 1974.

| Exc. | V.G. | Good | Fair | Poor |
|------|------|------|------|------|
| 450 | 400 | 350 | 300 | 250 |

### Model 3000 Magnum
This is similar to the Model 3000 except that it is chambered for 7mm Rem. Mag., .300 Win. Mag. and the .375 H&H Mag. cartridges. It has a 26" barrel and a 3-round integral magazine. The finish is blued, with a checkered walnut stock.

| Exc. | V.G. | Good | Fair | Poor |
|------|------|------|------|------|
| 500 | 450 | 400 | 350 | 300 |

### Model 4000
This is a bolt-action Varmint rifle chambered for .222 or the .223 cartridges. It is similar to the Model 3000 but was furnished with folding open sights.

| Exc. | V.G. | Good | Fair | Poor |
|------|------|------|------|------|
| 400 | 350 | 300 | 250 | 200 |

## Model 66S

This is a short-action rifle that features interchangeable caliber barrels. It is chambered for various cartridges between the .243 and the .30-06. It has a 24" barrel with open sights and was furnished with either single or double-set triggers. The finish is blued, with a checkered deluxe walnut stock. It was introduced in 1974. It is offered in a number of variations that differ in the calibers chambered, options offered, and the quality of materials and workmanship utilized. These models and their values are as follows:

| NIB | Exc. | V.G. | Good | Fair | Poor |
|-----|------|------|------|------|------|
| 1450 | 1200 | 1000 | 750 | 550 | 450 |

**Magnum Model--28" Barrel**

| NIB | Exc. | V.G. | Good | Fair | Poor |
|-----|------|------|------|------|------|
| 1550 | 1250 | 1050 | 800 | 600 | 500 |

**Mannlicher Model--21" Barrel, Full Stock**

| NIB | Exc. | V.G. | Good | Fair | Poor |
|-----|------|------|------|------|------|
| 1550 | 1250 | 1050 | 800 | 600 | 500 |

**Big Game Rifle--.375 H&H and .458 Win. Mag.**

| NIB | Exc. | V.G. | Good | Fair | Poor |
|-----|------|------|------|------|------|
| 1850 | 1500 | 1250 | 1000 | 800 | 700 |

## Model 66 SM

This version of the Model 66 is similar to the Model 66S with the same interchangeable-barrel capabilities. It is at present a custom-order rifle available through KDF, Inc. It is a more deluxe version of the Model 66S.

| NIB | Exc. | V.G. | Good | Fair | Poor |
|-----|------|------|------|------|------|
| 1800 | 1600 | 1250 | 1000 | 750 | 550 |

**Mannlicher Model--Full Stock**

| NIB | Exc. | V.G. | Good | Fair | Poor |
|-----|------|------|------|------|------|
| 1900 | 1700 | 1350 | 1100 | 800 | 600 |

**Magnum Model--26" Barrel**

| NIB | Exc. | V.G. | Good | Fair | Poor |
|-----|------|------|------|------|------|
| 1900 | 1700 | 1350 | 1100 | 800 | 600 |

**Model 66 SL Diplomat--Gamescene Engraved**

| NIB | Exc. | V.G. | Good | Fair | Poor |
|-----|------|------|------|------|------|
| 3200 | 2750 | 1850 | 1400 | 1200 | 1000 |

## Model 66A

This version is similar to the Model 66S except that it features an American-style laminated stock. It was introduced in 1988.

| NIB | Exc. | V.G. | Good | Fair | Poor |
|-----|------|------|------|------|------|
| 2150 | 2000 | 1750 | 1500 | 1000 | 750 |

**Magnum Model**

| NIB | Exc. | V.G. | Good | Fair | Poor |
|-----|------|------|------|------|------|
| 2250 | 2100 | 1850 | 1600 | 1250 | 1000 |

**Big Game Model**

| NIB | Exc. | V.G. | Good | Fair | Poor |
|-----|------|------|------|------|------|
| 2750 | 2500 | 2000 | 1750 | 1500 | 1200 |

## Model 225

This is a bolt-action sporting rifle that features a 60-degree lift bolt and three locking lugs. It is chambered for various cartridges between the .243 Winchester and the .300 Weatherby Magnum. It has a 24" or 26" barrel furnished without sights. It has a fully adjustable trigger and either a 3- or 5-round magazine, depending on the caliber. The finish is blued, with a select checkered walnut stock.

| NIB | Exc. | V.G. | Good | Fair | Poor |
|-----|------|------|------|------|------|
| 1400 | 1250 | 1000 | 750 | 600 | 500 |

## Model ES340

This is a single-shot bolt-action rifle chambered for the .22 l.r. cartridge. It has a 25.5" barrel with open sights. The finish is blued, with a checkered walnut stock. It was manufactured pre-WWII.

| Exc. | V.G. | Good | Fair | Poor |
|------|------|------|------|------|
| 300 | 250 | 225 | 175 | 125 |

## Model DSM34

This was a pre-war training rifle chambered for the .22 l.r. cartridge. It has a 25" barrel with open sights and is blued, with a walnut stock. It appeared military in configuration and was manufactured pre-WWII.

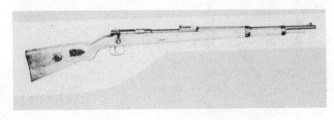

| Exc. | V.G. | Good | Fair | Poor |
|------|------|------|------|------|
| 325 | 275 | 250 | 200 | 150 |

## Model MS420B

This is a bolt-action repeating rifle chambered for the .22 l.r. cartridge. It has a 25" barrel with open sights and utilizes a 5-round detachable magazine. The finish is blued, with a walnut stock. It was manufactured before WWII.

| Exc. | V.G. | Good | Fair | Poor |
|------|------|------|------|------|
| 375 | 325 | 300 | 275 | 200 |

## Model ES350

This is a single-shot bolt-action rifle chambered for the .22 l.r. cartridge. It has a 27.5" barrel with target- type sights. The finish is blued, with a checkered walnut target stock. It was manufactured prior to WWII.

| Exc. | V.G. | Good | Fair | Poor |
|------|------|------|------|------|
| 450 | 400 | 375 | 350 | 275 |

## Model M410

This is a bolt-action sporting rifle chambered for the .22 l.r. cartridge. It has a 23.5" barrel with open sights and a 5-round detachable magazine. The finish is blued, with a checkered walnut stock. It was manufactured pre- WWII.

| Exc. | V.G. | Good | Fair | Poor |
|------|------|------|------|------|
| 375 | 325 | 300 | 275 | 200 |

## Model M420

This is a bolt-action repeating rifle chambered for the .22 l.r. cartridge. It has a 25.5" barrel with adjustable sights and a 5-round detachable magazine. The finish is blued, with a checkered walnut stock. It was manufactured before WWII.

| Exc. | V.G. | Good | Fair | Poor |
|------|------|------|------|------|
| 375 | 325 | 300 | 275 | 200 |

### Model EN310

This is a single-shot bolt-action rifle chambered for the .22 l.r. cartridge. It has a 19.75" barrel with open sights. The finish is blued, with a plain walnut stock. It was manufactured before WWII.

| Exc. | V.G. | Good | Fair | Poor |
|------|------|------|------|------|
| 250 | 225 | 200 | 150 | 100 |

### Model EL320

This version is similar to the Model EN310, with a 23.5" barrel and a checkered stock.

| Exc. | V.G. | Good | Fair | Poor |
|------|------|------|------|------|
| 275 | 250 | 225 | 175 | 125 |

### Model KKW

This was a single-shot, bolt-action target rifle chambered for the .22 l.r. cartridge. It has a 26" heavy barrel with a tangent-type sight. The finish is blued, with a military-type stock. This was used as a training rifle prior to WWII. It was also manufactured by Walther and Anschutz.

| Exc. | V.G. | Good | Fair | Poor |
|------|------|------|------|------|
| 400 | 350 | 300 | 225 | 150 |

### Model MS350B

This is a bolt-action repeating rifle chambered for the .22 l.r. cartridge. It has a 26.75" barrel with a micrometer rear sight. It has a 5-round detachable magazine. The finish is blued, with a checkered walnut stock.

| Exc. | V.G. | Good | Fair | Poor |
|------|------|------|------|------|
| 475 | 400 | 350 | 275 | 200 |

### Model ES340B

This is a single-shot bolt-action rifle chambered for the .22 l.r. cartridge. It has a 26.75" barrel with adjustable sights. The finish is blued, with a plain walnut stock.

| Exc. | V.G. | Good | Fair | Poor |
|------|------|------|------|------|
| 375 | 300 | 250 | 175 | 100 |

### Model MM410BN

This is a bolt-action sporting rifle chambered for the .22 l.r. cartridge. It has a 23.5" barrel with adjustable sights. It has a 5-round detachable magazine and is blued, with a checkered walnut stock.

| Exc. | V.G. | Good | Fair | Poor |
|------|------|------|------|------|
| 400 | 350 | 300 | 200 | 125 |

### Model MS420B

This is a target version of the Model MM410BN. It features a 26.75" heavy barrel and a target-type stock.

| Exc. | V.G. | Good | Fair | Poor |
|------|------|------|------|------|
| 400 | 350 | 300 | 200 | 125 |

The modern-production Models 107 and 201 are also known as the KDF Model 2107 and K-22 and will be found in the KDF section of this text.

## MAVERICK ARMS, INC.
### Eagle Pass, Texas

### Model 88

This is a slide-action shotgun chambered for 3" 12-gauge only. It is offered with 28" or 30" barrels with various chokes. The receiver is black anodized alloy, and the stock is a black synthetic material with a recoil pad. This model was introduced in 1989.

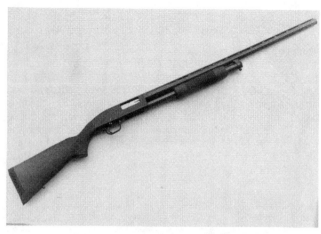

| NIB | Exc. | V.G. | Good | Fair | Poor |
|-----|------|------|------|------|------|
| 175 | 150 | 125 | 100 | 75 | 50 |

## MAYNARD
### Danville, Virginia

### Brass Framed Carbine

This carbine is also known as the Perry, and it was manufactured by Keen Walker & Co. for use in the Civil War by Confederate forces. It is a breechloader that is activated by the triggerguard and is chambered for .54 caliber percussion. It has a 21.5" round barrel and a brass frame. The barrel is blued, and the buttstock is walnut. There is no forend. There is a bar and sling ring on the side of the frame. There were very few manufactured in 1861 and 1862. As with all highly collectible Confederate weapons, we strongly recommend individual appraisal.

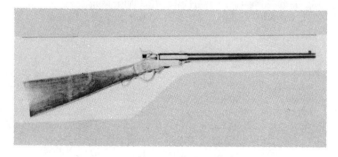

| Exc. | V.G. | Good | Fair | Poor |
|------|------|------|------|------|
| 5000 | 4250 | 3500 | 2750 | 1750 |

## MCMILLAN, G. & CO. INC.
### Phoenix, Arizona

This company is known as a manufacturer of high quality synthetic stocks. They also produce high-grade, high performance rifles on a custom-order basis.

### Competition Model

This is a custom bolt-action rifle chambered for the .308, 7mm/08, and the .300 Winchester Magnum cartridges. The barrel lengths, stock type, and dimensions are to the customer's specifications. This model was introduced in 1988.

| NIB | Exc. | V.G. | Good | Fair | Poor |
|-----|------|------|------|------|------|
| 1600 | 1500 | 1150 | 800 | 600 | 500 |

### Model 86 Snipers Rifle

This is a custom-order rifle that is chambered for the .308 Winchester or the .300 Winchester Magnum cartridges. It is offered with a synthetic stock and a choice of scope systems. It was introduced in 1988.

| NIB | Exc. | V.G. | Good | Fair | Poor |
|-----|------|------|------|------|------|
| 1600 | 1500 | 1150 | 800 | 600 | 500 |

## Model 86 System
This version includes the rifle, Ultra scope and mounting system, bipod, and a fitted case. This model was introduced in 1988,

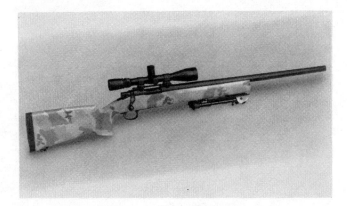

| NIB | Exc. | V.G. | Good | Fair | Poor |
|-----|------|------|------|------|------|
| 2700 | 2200 | 1850 | 1600 | 1100 | 950 |

## Model 87 Long Range Snipers Rifle
This is a large stainless-steel, single-shot bolt action that is chambered for the .50 BMG cartridge. It has a 29" barrel with an integral muzzle brake and a camouflaged synthetic stock. This rifle weighs 21 lbs. and is accurate to 1,500 meters. It was introduced in 1988.

| NIB | Exc. | V.G. | Good | Fair | Poor |
|-----|------|------|------|------|------|
| 3000 | 2750 | 2250 | 2000 | 1700 | 1450 |

## Model 87 System
This version is furnished with a bipod and a 20X Ultra scope and mounting system with a fitted case. It was introduced in 1988.

| NIB | Exc. | V.G. | Good | Fair | Poor |
|-----|------|------|------|------|------|
| 4200 | 3800 | 3250 | 2750 | 2200 | 1900 |

## Signature Model
This is a high quality bolt-action rifle that is available chambered for most popular calibers up to .375 Holland & Holland. It has a 22" or 24" button rifled stainless-steel barrel and a 3- or 4-shot magazine. The stock is synthetic, and this model was introduced in 1988.

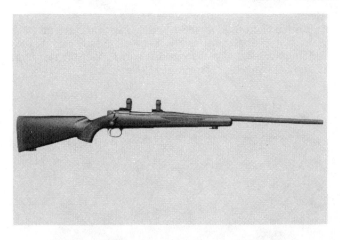

| NIB | Exc. | V.G. | Good | Fair | Poor |
|-----|------|------|------|------|------|
| 1500 | 1400 | 1150 | 1000 | 800 | 600 |

# MEAD & ADRIANCE
### St. Louis, Missouri

## Underhammer Pistol
This company did not manufacture firearms but were large dealers in St. Louis. This pistol was produced by Ethan Allen of Grafton, Massachusetts, and is chambered for calibers from .31 to .44, with varied barrel lengths. The frame is iron, and the saw-shaped grips are either rosewood or walnut. This pistol is marked "Mead & Adriance" and was manufactured in the 1840's.

| Exc. | V.G. | Good | Fair | Poor |
|------|------|------|------|------|
| 700 | 600 | 500 | 400 | 300 |

# MEIJA
### SEE--Japan State

# MENDENHALL, JONES & GARDNER
### Greensboro, North Carolina

## Muzzle Loading Rifle
This is a very rare muzzleloading rifle that was patterned after the U.S. Model 1841. It is chambered for .58 caliber percussion and has a 33" barrel with a full-length walnut stock held on by two barrel bands. It has an iron ramrod mounted under the barrel and is finished in the white. It has a bayonet lug, and the lock is marked "M.J.& G.,N.C." This rifle was made for use by Confederate forces in the Civil War and is very desirable from a collector standpoint. Be wary of fakes.

| Exc. | V.G. | Good | Fair | Poor |
|------|------|------|------|------|
| 5000 | 4000 | 3500 | 3000 | 2250 |

# MENZ, AUGUST
### Suhl, Germany

The firm of Menz entered the firearms business at the beginning of WWI, with a contract to build the Beholla pistol that was developed by Becker and Hollander and licensed to other companies for the war effort. After the war this company stayed in business and produced various pocket automatic designs. In 1937 the firm was purchased by Lignose.

## Menta

This is the name used for this company's version of the Beholla pistol. It is the same as the Beholla, chambered for the 7.65mm cartridge and marked differently. After the war this design was marketed commercially by Menz.

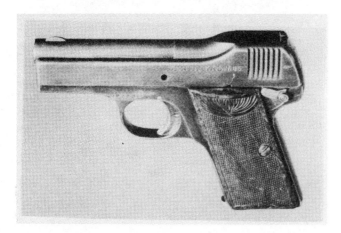

| Exc. | V.G. | Good | Fair | Poor |
|------|------|------|------|------|
| 300 | 250 | 200 | 150 | 100 |

## Liliput

This was a blowback-operated semi-automatic pistol chambered for the 4.25mm cartridge, and later in 1925 a 6.35mm version was offered. The barrel of this pistol is 2" in length, and the magazine holds 6 rounds. This is a very small pistol (only 3.5" in overall length) and weighs only 10 ounces. The 6.35mm version is slightly longer (4" overall). The slide is marked "Liliput Kal. 4.25 (or 6.35)." The finish is blued, with molded plastic grips bearing medallions with the caliber on one side and a logo on the other.

| Exc. | V.G. | Good | Fair | Poor |
|------|------|------|------|------|
| 350 | 300 | 250 | 200 | 125 |

## Menz Model II

This is a larger version of the Liliput chambered for the 7.65mm cartridge.

| Exc. | V.G. | Good | Fair | Poor |
|------|------|------|------|------|
| 350 | 300 | 250 | 200 | 125 |

## Menz VP Model

This "Vest Pocket Model" is similar to the Model II-- only chambered for the 6.35mm cartridge. It has a 2.35" barrel and a 6-round magazine. This model features a cocking indicator.

| Exc. | V.G. | Good | Fair | Poor |
|------|------|------|------|------|
| 350 | 300 | 250 | 200 | 125 |

## Model III

This pistol was a total redesign. It has a closed-top slide, and the quality is much better than the previous Menz pistols. It has a fixed barrel and is similar to the Model 1910 Browning with an exposed hammer. This model was produced until 1937.

| Exc. | V.G. | Good | Fair | Poor |
|------|------|------|------|------|
| 400 | 350 | 300 | 250 | 150 |

# MERCURY
### Liege, Belgium

## Model 622 VP

This is a semi-automatic rifle chambered for the .22 l.r. cartridge. It has a 20" barrel and a detachable 7- round magazine. The frame is constructed of steel; and the finish is blued, with a walnut stock. This rifle was manufactured by the firm of Robar & Son.

| Exc. | V.G. | Good | Fair | Poor |
|------|------|------|------|------|
| 300 | 275 | 250 | 200 | 125 |

# MERCURY
### Eibar, Spain

## Double Barreled Shotgun

This is a side-by-side double that is chambered for 10, 12, and 20 gauge. They are all chambered for the magnum loads. The barrels offered are 28" and 32" in length, with various choke combinations. This is a boxlock-actioned gun with double triggers and extractors. The frame is lightly engraved, and the finish is blued. The stock is checkered and features a pistol grip.
10 Gauge--Add 25 Percent.

| Exc. | V.G. | Good | Fair | Poor |
|------|------|------|------|------|
| 325 | 250 | 225 | 175 | 125 |

# MERKEL, GEBRUDER
### Suhl, Germany
### Importer--Armes de Chasse
### Chadds Ford, Pennsylvania

## Model 130

This is a very high-grade, side-by-side, double-barrel shotgun chambered for all gauges and offered in various barrel lengths and choke combinations. It has an Anson & Deeley boxlock action with false sideplates. It features automatic ejectors and is heavily engraved with gamescenes. The finish is blued, with a high-grade hand-checkered walnut stock. It was discontinued before WWII.

| Exc. | V.G. | Good | Fair | Poor |
|------|------|------|------|------|
| 12500 | 9500 | 6500 | 5000 | 4000 |

## Model 127

This is a higher-grade version that features Holland & Holland-type hand-detachable sidelocks. This is Merkel's top-of-the-line side-by-side gun and is ornately engraved and produced with the highest quality materials and workmanship. It was discontinued before WWII.

| Exc. | V.G. | Good | Fair | Poor |
|------|------|------|------|------|
| 22000 | 17500 | 12500 | 8500 | 6500 |

## Model 100 Series

This is an Over/Under double chambered for 12, 16, or 20 gauge and offered with various barrel lengths and choke combinations. It features a boxlock action with a Greener crossbolt. It has double triggers and extractors. It is blued, with a checkered walnut stock. A vent-rib barrel version is available that would be worth approximately 10 percent additional. This model is offered in two other variations that differ in the options offered only. It was discontinued before WWII.

| Exc. | V.G. | Good | Fair | Poor |
|------|------|------|------|------|
| 1500 | 1250 | 950 | 700 | 550 |

## Model 101--Ribbed Barrel with Engraving

| Exc. | V.G. | Good | Fair | Poor |
|------|------|------|------|------|
| 1650 | 1400 | 1100 | 900 | 700 |

## Model 101E--Auto Ejectors

| Exc. | V.G. | Good | Fair | Poor |
|------|------|------|------|------|
| 1750 | 1500 | 1200 | 1000 | 800 |

## Model 400 Series

This Series of Over/Under shotguns is similar to the Model 100 Series except that it is more elaborately ornamented and features a Kersten double-crossbolt system. It was discontinued before WWII.

| Exc. | V.G. | Good | Fair | Poor |
|------|------|------|------|------|
| 1700 | 1450 | 1150 | 950 | 750 |

## Model 400E--Auto Ejectors

| Exc. | V.G. | Good | Fair | Poor |
|------|------|------|------|------|
| 2000 | 1750 | 1400 | 1150 | 900 |

## Model 410

| Exc. | V.G. | Good | Fair | Poor |
|------|------|------|------|------|
| 1750 | 1500 | 1200 | 950 | 700 |

## Model 410E--Auto Ejectors

| Exc. | V.G. | Good | Fair | Poor |
|------|------|------|------|------|
| 2000 | 1750 | 1400 | 1150 | 900 |

## Model 200 Series

This is a more deluxe version of the Model 400 chambered for all gauges and offered with various-length ribbed barrels with various choke combinations. It features a scalloped boxlock receiver with the Kersten double-crossbolt system. It is standard with double triggers, extractors, and cocking indicators. The finish is blued, with a select, checkered walnut stock. The variations differ in the amount of ornamentation and the quality of materials and workmanship utilized. This Series was discontinued prior to WWII.

| Exc. | V.G. | Good | Fair | Poor |
|------|------|------|------|------|
| 1750 | 1500 | 1200 | 950 | 700 |

## Model 210

| Exc. | V.G. | Good | Fair | Poor |
|------|------|------|------|------|
| 2000 | 1750 | 1400 | 1150 | 900 |

## Model 201--Greener Crossbolt

| Exc. | V.G. | Good | Fair | Poor |
|------|------|------|------|------|
| 2000 | 1750 | 1400 | 1150 | 900 |

## 201E--Auto Ejectors

| Exc. | V.G. | Good | Fair | Poor |
|------|------|------|------|------|
| 2400 | 2000 | 1750 | 1300 | 1050 |

## Model 202--False Sideplates

| Exc. | V.G. | Good | Fair | Poor |
|------|------|------|------|------|
| 3000 | 2500 | 2100 | 1700 | 1250 |

## Model 202E--Auto Ejectors

| Exc. | V.G. | Good | Fair | Poor |
|------|------|------|------|------|
| 3250 | 2750 | 2350 | 1850 | 1500 |

## Model 203E--Auto Ejectors

| Exc. | V.G. | Good | Fair | Poor |
|------|------|------|------|------|
| 4000 | 3500 | 2750 | 2000 | 1750 |

## Model 204E--Sidelock Gun

| Exc. | V.G. | Good | Fair | Poor |
|------|------|------|------|------|
| 5700 | 5000 | 4250 | 3250 | 2400 |

## Model 300 Series

These are Over/Under shotguns chambered for all gauges, with various-length ribbed barrels with various choke combinations. It features a Merkel-Anson boxlock action with a Kersten double-crossbolt system and two underlugs. It has a scalloped frame and extractors. It also features cocking indicators. The finish is blued, with a checkered walnut stock. The variations differ in the options offered, amount of ornamentation, and quality of materials and workmanship utilized in their construction. This model was discontinued prior to WWII.

| Exc. | V.G. | Good | Fair | Poor |
|------|------|------|------|------|
| 2000 | 1600 | 1300 | 1000 | 750 |

## Model 300E--Auto Ejectors

| Exc. | V.G. | Good | Fair | Poor |
|------|------|------|------|------|
| 2500 | 2100 | 1750 | 1400 | 1000 |

## Model 301

| Exc. | V.G. | Good | Fair | Poor |
|------|------|------|------|------|
| 5000 | 4000 | 3500 | 2750 | 2000 |

## Model 301E--Auto Ejectors

| Exc. | V.G. | Good | Fair | Poor |
|------|------|------|------|------|
| 6000 | 5000 | 4500 | 3750 | 3000 |

## Model 302E--False Sideplates

| Exc. | V.G. | Good | Fair | Poor |
|------|------|------|------|------|
| 10000 | 8500 | 6000 | 4750 | 3900 |

## Model 303E

| Exc. | V.G. | Good | Fair | Poor |
|------|------|------|------|------|
| 12500 | 10000 | 8000 | 6000 | 5000 |

## Model 304E--Best Grade Merkel Over/Under

| Exc. | V.G. | Good | Fair | Poor |
|------|------|------|------|------|
| 16000 | 12500 | 10000 | 7500 | 6000 |

## Merkel-Anson Model 145 Drilling

This is a three-barrel gun that consists of side-by-side shotgun barrels over a rifle barrel. The shotgun barrels are chambered for 12, 16, or 20 gauge; and the rifle barrel, for various European rifle cartridges. It was offered with either a 21.5" or 25.5" barrel. It features an Anson & Deeley boxlock action with double triggers and extractors. The finish is blued, with a checkered walnut stock. It was manufactured prior to WWII.

| Exc. | V.G. | Good | Fair | Poor |
|------|------|------|------|------|
| 3500 | 2750 | 2250 | 1800 | 1500 |

## Model 142

This version is similar but features a higher degree of ornamentation.

| Exc. | V.G. | Good | Fair | Poor |
|------|------|------|------|------|
| 4500 | 3750 | 3250 | 2800 | 2500 |

## Model 140

This version is heavily engraved.

| Exc. | V.G. | Good | Fair | Poor |
|------|------|------|------|------|
| 5500 | 4750 | 4250 | 3800 | 3500 |

The firm of Merkel also manufactured a combination gun, as well as a series of double-barrelled rifles. They are rarely encountered on today's market since they were manufactured in an Eastern Bloc country and were not exported commercially to the U.S.A. They are very high-grade guns. The values can easily exceed five figures. We strongly recommend securing a qualified appraisal if a transaction is contemplated.

## Model 8

This is a side-by-side, double-barrel shotgun chambered for 12, 16, or 20 gauge. It has various-length barrels and choke combinations. It was offered with an engraved, case-colored, scalloped boxlock action with a Greener crossbolt and chopper-lump barrels. It has double triggers and extractors. The barrels are blued, with a checkered walnut stock that has a cheekpiece and is furnished with sling swivels. It was discontinued in 1987.

| Exc. | V.G. | Good | Fair | Poor |
|------|------|------|------|------|
| 900 | 800 | 600 | 475 | 400 |

## Model 47E

This gun is similar to the Model 8 but features automatic ejectors. It is currently imported.

| NIB | Exc. | V.G. | Good | Fair | Poor |
|-----|------|------|------|------|------|
| 1500 | 1250 | 1000 | 750 | 600 | 500 |

## Model 147E

This is a gamescene-engraved version of the Model 47E.

| NIB | Exc. | V.G. | Good | Fair | Poor |
|-----|------|------|------|------|------|
| 1950 | 1650 | 1400 | 1100 | 900 | 800 |

## Model 122

This is a more elaborately ornamented version of the 147E with a coin-finished sidelock action with a Greener crossbolt. It also features cocking indicators. It is currently imported.

| NIB | Exc. | V.G. | Good | Fair | Poor |
|-----|------|------|------|------|------|
| 3250 | 2750 | 2200 | 1850 | 1500 | 1250 |

## Model 147S

This is a more deluxe sidelock-action gun that is similar to the Model 122.

| NIB | Exc. | V.G. | Good | Fair | Poor |
|-----|------|------|------|------|------|
| 5500 | 4500 | 3750 | 3000 | 2500 | 2000 |

## Model 247S

This version is similar to the Model 147S except that it is more elaborately ornamented and features higher quality materials and workmanship.

| NIB | Exc. | V.G. | Good | Fair | Poor |
|-----|------|------|------|------|------|
| 5500 | 4500 | 3750 | 3000 | 2500 | 2000 |

## Model 347S

This is a more elaborately engraved version of the Model 247S.

| NIB | Exc. | V.G. | Good | Fair | Poor |
|-----|------|------|------|------|------|
| 6000 | 5000 | 4250 | 3500 | 3000 | 2500 |

## Model 447S

This is Merkel's current top-of-the-line SxS shotgun.

| NIB | Exc. | V.G. | Good | Fair | Poor |
|-----|------|------|------|------|------|
| 7000 | 6000 | 5250 | 4500 | 4000 | 3500 |

## Model 200E Series

These are the current-production Over/Under shotguns chambered for 12, 16, or 20 gauge. They are offered in various vent-rib barrel lengths with various choke combinations. They feature either a case-colored, scalloped boxlock action or, in the highest grade, a full H&H-type sidelock action. It is standard with double triggers and automatic ejectors. It is either blued or coin-finished, with a checkered walnut stock. The models differ in the degree of ornamentation and the quality of materials and workmanship utilized in their construction. They are currently manufactured. We recommend qualified appraisal on this very high-grade Series.

| NIB | Exc. | V.G. | Good | Fair | Poor |
|-----|------|------|------|------|------|
| 4000 | 3500 | 3000 | 2500 | 1800 | 1500 |

## Model 201E--Coin-finished

| NIB | Exc. | V.G. | Good | Fair | Poor |
|-----|------|------|------|------|------|
| 4400 | 3900 | 3400 | 2900 | 2200 | 1900 |

## Model 203E--Sidelock

| NIB | Exc. | V.G. | Good | Fair | Poor |
|-----|------|------|------|------|------|
| 10500 | 9500 | 8000 | 7000 | 5000 | 3500 |

## Model 303E--Hidden Detachable Sidelock Screws

| NIB | Exc. | V.G. | Good | Fair | Poor |
|-----|------|------|------|------|------|
| 17000 | 15000 | 12500 | 10000 | 7000 | 5000 |

## Model 304E Luxus Grade

This is Merkel's top-of-the-line, best-grade model designation. It is available as a SxS, Over/Under, Drilling, or Combination gun. It features the highest quality materials and workmanship and extremely elaborate engraving. It is impossible to generalize the values on a firearm of this status, and we strongly recommend securing a qualified appraisal if a transaction is contemplated.

# MERIDEN FIREARMS CO.
### Meriden, Connecticut

**Pocket Pistol**

This company was in the business of producing inexpensive, mediocre-quality double-action revolvers that are sometimes categorized as "Suicide Specials." They are chambered for the .32 and the .38 centerfire cartridges, and they are of the break-open, self-extracting type that was very common to this era. There were two basic types produced--a concealed and an exposed-hammer model. They are marked "Meriden Firearms Co. Meriden, Conn. USA." The finish is nickel-plated, and the grips are checkered molded rubber. The workmanship of these revolvers was quite shabby, and they were sold usually by mail for a few dollars at most. They were manufactured in fairly large quantities between 1895 and 1915.

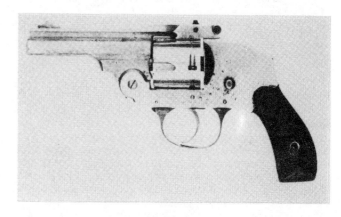

| Exc. | V.G. | Good | Fair | Poor |
|------|------|------|------|------|
| 150 | 125 | 100 | 75 | 50 |

# MERRILL
### Fullerton, California

**Sportsman**

This is a single-shot, break-open pistol chambered for various popular cartridges, including rifle and wildcat calibers. It has a 9" or a 12" octagonal barrel with a wide vent rib. The sights are adjustable, and the barrel is grooved to facilitate scope mounting. The finish is polished blue, with walnut grips. These barrels are interchangeable, and there is an optional wrist support for long-range handgun hunting.

Interchangeable Barrels--Add $75.
Wrist Support--Add $25.

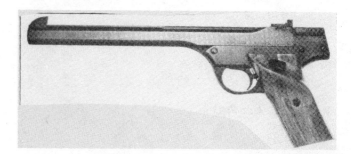

| Exc. | V.G. | Good | Fair | Poor |
|------|------|------|------|------|
| 5500 | 4750 | 4000 | 3000 | 2000 |

## MERRILL, JAMES H.
### Baltimore, Maryland

**Merrill Rifle**
This is a single-shot breechloading rifle that is chambered for .54 caliber and utilizes the percussion ignition system. The breech opens for loading by lifting and pulling back on a lever. The barrel is 33" in length, and there is a full-length walnut stock held on by two barrel bands. The mountings and patchbox are brass; and the lock is case-colored, with a browned barrel. The lock is marked "J.H.Merrill Balto./Pat. July 1858." There are military acceptance marks on the stock. There were approximately 775 of these rifles manufactured and purchased by the Government for use during the Civil War. They were made in 1864 and 1865.

| Exc. | V.G. | Good | Fair | Poor |
|------|------|------|------|------|
| 2000 | 1750 | 1450 | 1000 | 750 |

**Merrill Carbine**
The Merrill Carbine is similar in appearance to the rifle except that the barrel length is 22" and the stock is only half-length with one barrel band. There are some variations that are quite subtle in appearance but which have a considerable effect on values. We recommend that an independent appraisal be secured. The values given are for the standard 1st and 2nd Types. There were approximately 15,000 total manufactured, and most were used in the Civil War.

**1st Type**
There is no Eagle stamped on the lock, and the breech lever is flat.

| Exc. | V.G. | Good | Fair | Poor |
|------|------|------|------|------|
| 1500 | 1250 | 1000 | 750 | 500 |

**2nd Type**
There is an Eagle stamped on the lock, and the stock has no patchbox. The breech lever has a round tip.

| Exc. | V.G. | Good | Fair | Poor |
|------|------|------|------|------|
| 1750 | 1500 | 1250 | 850 | 650 |

## MERRILL, LATROBE & THOMAS
### S. Remington--Maker
### Ilion, New York

**Carbine**
This is a very rare carbine chambered for .58 caliber percussion. It is a breechloading single shot with a 21" barrel. It functions by lifting and pulling forward on a lever that opens the breech. This model has brass mountings and a blued barrel and lock that is marked "S.Remington/ Ilion, N.Y." The barrel is marked "Merrill, Latrobe & Thomas/Baltimore, Md./Patent Applied For." This model is quite desirable to collectors of Civil War weapons and should be independently appraised. There were approximately 170 manufactured in 1855.

| Exc. | V.G. | Good | Fair | Poor |
|------|------|------|------|------|
| 300 | 275 | 225 | 175 | 125 |

## MERRIMACK ARMS
### SEE--Brown Manufacturing Co.

## MERWIN & BRAY
### Worcester, Massachusetts

This was a sales agency owned and operated by Joseph Merwin and Edward Bray. They marketed the Plant revolver and the Ballard carbine during the 1860's. They sold pistols under their own name and eventually evolved into the firm of Merwin and Hulbert. Under this name they marketed the products of the Hopkins and Allen Company of Norwich, Connecticut.

**Merwin & Bray Pocket Pistol**
This is a single shot pistol chambered for the .32 rimfire cartridge and has a 3.5" barrel that swings to the right side for loading. It has a brass frame that is silver-plated, and the barrel is blued. The grips are walnut, and the barrel is stamped "Merwin & Bray New York." There were approximately 300 believed to have been manufactured by the Bacon Firearms Co. between 1865 and 1872.

| Exc. | V.G. | Good | Fair | Poor |
|------|------|------|------|------|
| 300 | 250 | 200 | 150 | 100 |

## MERWIN & HULBERT & CO.
### New York, New York

This firm evolved from Merwin and Bray and was a marketing company that never actually manufactured firearms. They were the sales agents for firearms manufactured by the Hopkins and Allen Co. of Norwich, Connecticut.

**Army Revolver**
This is a large martial-type revolver chambered for the .44-40 or the .44 Merwin & Hulbert cartridge. It has a 7" round ribbed barrel and a 6-shot cylinder. This revolver is unique in that the barrel and the topstrap turn to the side; and the whole unit, including the cylinder, pulls forward to eject the empty cases. This company aggressively courted government contracts for this weapon but were unsuccessful. There are basically five variations of this unusual revolver--four are single-action, and one is a double-action. They are all marked with both "Merwin Hulbert & Co." and "Hopkins & Allen Manufacturing Co." on the barrel. There were several thousand manufactured between 1876 and 1880.

**Open Top Frame with the Square Butt**

| Exc. | V.G. | Good | Fair | Poor |
|------|------|------|------|------|
| 750 | 650 | 550 | 400 | 300 |

**Open Top Frame with Birdshead Butt**

| Exc. | V.G. | Good | Fair | Poor |
|------|------|------|------|------|
| 700 | 600 | 500 | 350 | 250 |

**Square Butt with Topstrap**

| Exc. | V.G. | Good | Fair | Poor |
|------|------|------|------|------|
| 700 | 600 | 500 | 350 | 250 |

**Birdshead Grip with Topstrap**

| Exc. | V.G. | Good | Fair | Poor |
|------|------|------|------|------|
| 600 | 500 | 400 | 300 | 200 |

**Double Action Model**

| Exc. | V.G. | Good | Fair | Poor |
|------|------|------|------|------|
| 600 | 500 | 400 | 300 | 200 |

## Pocket Army Revolver

This model is similar to the Army Model except that it is chambered for the .44 Russian cartridge as well as the .44-40 and the .44 Merwin & Hulbert cartridges. The barrels are only 3.5" in length, and the butts are all in the birdshead configuration. There were approximately 9,000 manufactured in the 1880's. The .44-40 is the most commonly encountered.

| Exc. | V.G. | Good | Fair | Poor |
|------|------|------|------|------|
| 600 | 500 | 400 | 300 | 200 |

## Single Action Pocket Revolver

This is a smaller revolver chambered for the .32 and the .38 centerfire cartridges. It has a barrel length of from 3.5" to 5.5", and the cylinder holds either 5 or 6 rounds. It is loaded in the same manner as the Army revolver and has a spur type trigger. The finish is nickel-plated, and the grips are hard rubber. The barrel is marked "Merwin & Hulbert & Co." with the patent dates. There are some marked with the Hopkins & Allen name, and some are not. There were approximately 2,500 manufactured in the 1880's.

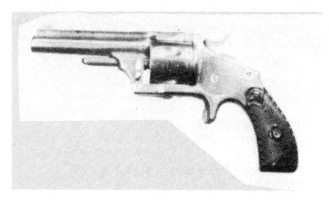

| Exc. | V.G. | Good | Fair | Poor |
|------|------|------|------|------|
| 350 | 300 | 250 | 200 | 100 |

## Single Action .22 Revolver

This model is chambered for the .22 rimfire cartridge and is quite similar to the Smith & Wesson 1st model. It has a 3.5" ribbed barrel, and the fluted cylinder holds 7 rounds. The barrel is marked "Merwin & Hulbert & Co." The finish is nickel-plated, and the birdshead grips are hard rubber. There were several thousand manufactured in the 1880's.

| Exc. | V.G. | Good | Fair | Poor |
|------|------|------|------|------|
| 400 | 350 | 300 | 250 | 150 |

## Double Action Pocket Revolver

This model is chambered for the .32 and the .38 centerfire cartridges. The .32 caliber has a 7-shot cylinder, and the .38 has one that holds 5 shots. The barrels are round with ribs and are between 3.5" and 5.5" in length. They have double-action lockwork and are nickel-plated, with hard rubber grips. The barrels are marked "Merwin & Hulbert," and Hopkins & Allen is not marked anywhere on the pistol. There is a variation with a folding hammer spur, and this model will bring approximately 10 percent additional. There were several thousand manufactured in each caliber in the 1880's.

| Exc. | V.G. | Good | Fair | Poor |
|------|------|------|------|------|
| 300 | 250 | 200 | 150 | 100 |

# METROPOLITAN ARMS CO.
## New York, New York

### 1851 Navy Revolver

This revolver is a copy of the Colt 1851 Navy revolver. It is chambered for the .36 caliber percussion and has a 6-shot unfluted cylinder that is roll-stamped on some examples and plain on others. The barrel is octagonal and is 7.5" in length. The finish is blued, with case-colored frame and one-piece walnut grips. These revolvers are very close copies of the Colt products; and except for the markings "Metropolitan Arms Co. New York," they would be difficult to differentiate. There were approximately 6,000 of this model manufactured between 1864 and 1866. The first 300 were manufactured for the firm of H. E. Dimick of St Louis. There are approximately 100 that were so marked. These revolvers will bring a great deal more from collectors and, therefore, will be valued on their own.

**H.E.Dimick Navy Model**

| Exc. | V.G. | Good | Fair | Poor |
|------|------|------|------|------|
| 3500 | 3000 | 2850 | 2250 | 1400 |

**Standard Navy Model**

| Exc. | V.G. | Good | Fair | Poor |
|------|------|------|------|------|
| 1200 | 1000 | 800 | 600 | 400 |

### 1861 Navy Revolver

This gun is a copy of the 1861 Colt Navy Revolver and is extremely rare. It is chambered for .36 caliber percussion and has a 6-shot roll-marked cylinder. The barrel is 7.5" in length; and the loading lever is the only difference from the Colt, as it is a pivoting instead of a rack-and-pinion type like that found on the Colt revolver. The finish is blued and case-colored, with one-piece walnut grips; and the barrel is marked "Metropolitan Arms Co.New York." There were approximately 50 manufactured in 1864 and 1865.

| Exc. | V.G. | Good | Fair | Poor |
|------|------|------|------|------|
| 5000 | 4250 | 3500 | 2750 | 1800 |

### Police Revolver

This model is a copy of the Colt Model 1862 Police. It is chambered for .36 caliber percussion and has a 4.5", 5.5", or 6.5" round barrel. The fluted cylinder holds 5 shots; and the finish is blued and case-colored, with one-piece walnut grips. This model is found both unmarked (which will bring approximately 20 percent additional) and also marked "Metropolitan Arms Co. New York." There were approximately 2,750 manufactured between 1864 and 1866, of which approximately 1,100 were unmarked.

| Exc. | V.G. | Good | Fair | Poor |
|------|------|------|------|------|
| 1000 | 850 | 700 | 500 | 400 |

# MIIDA
## Japan
### Marubena America Corp.

### Model 612

This is an Over/Under shotgun chambered for 12 gauge. It is offered with 26" or 28" vent-rib barrels with various choke combinations. It features a boxlock action, single-selective trigger, and automatic ejectors. The finish is blued and the walnut stock is hand-checkered, with a pistol grip. This model was imported between 1972 and 1974.

| Exc. | V.G. | Good | Fair | Poor |
|------|------|------|------|------|
| 900 | 800 | 750 | 600 | 450 |

## Model 612 Skeet
This Model is similar to the Model 612, with 27" barrels that are choked for Skeet. It features a greater degree of ornamentation. The Skeet model was also imported between 1972 and 1974.

| Exc. | V.G. | Good | Fair | Poor |
|------|------|------|------|------|
| 1000 | 900 | 850 | 700 | 500 |

## Model 2200 Trap or Skeet
This Model is similar to the Model 612, with either a 30" improved-modified-and-full choked barrel (Trap) or a 27" skeet-and-skeet barrel. They are both heavily engraved and feature select, hand-checkered walnut stocks. They were imported between 1972 and 1974.

| Exc. | V.G. | Good | Fair | Poor |
|------|------|------|------|------|
| 1100 | 1000 | 900 | 800 | 600 |

## Model 2300 Trap or Skeet
This Model is simply a more deluxe version of the Model 2200. It was imported from 1972 until 1974.

| Exc. | V.G. | Good | Fair | Poor |
|------|------|------|------|------|
| 1350 | 1250 | 1100 | 1000 | 750 |

## Model GRT Trap or GRS Skeet
These two models are chambered for 12 gauge and have either a 29" full-and-full choked barrel or a 27" skeet-and-skeet barrel. They feature competition vent ribs and a boxlock action with false sideplates that are heavily engraved and gold-inlaid. The breeches of the barrels are also engraved. This Model has a single-selective trigger and automatic ejectors, as well as a very high-grade walnut stock. These guns were imported between 1972 and 1974.

| Exc. | V.G. | Good | Fair | Poor |
|------|------|------|------|------|
| 2250 | 1850 | 1650 | 1200 | 1000 |

# MINNEAPOLIS F.A. CO.
### Minneapolis, Minnesota

## Palm Pistol
This was a unique design that was one of three pistols that were made in this particular manner. This pistol was actually made by the firm of James Duckworth in Springfield, Massachusetts. It was built on a patent held by the inventor James Turbiaux of Paris, France, who called his version "Le Protector." There was also a somewhat larger, more elaborate version known as the "Chicago Palm Pistol." This weapon was chambered for the .32 center fire cartridge and had a 1.75" round barrel that protruded between the fingers when the round body of the weapon was held in the palm for firing. There was a lever that was squeezed to cycle the double action lock work and fire the pistol. There was a rotary chamber that was removed from inside the body of the pistol for loading. The finish was nickel plated and the round grips were hard rubber. The side plate was marked "Minneapolis Firearms Co." and "The Protector." There were several thousand manufactured in 1891 and 1892.

| Exc. | V.G. | Good | Fair | Poor |
|------|------|------|------|------|
| 850 | 750 | 550 | 400 | 300 |

# MIROKU B. C.
### Miroku Japan
This company has manufactured good quality double-barrelled shotguns--both side-by-sides and Over/Unders--for companies such as Charles Daly, Browning, Winchester, and SKB. Although their products are of excellent quality, they have never become particularly collectible. The products of this company will be found under the respective companies' headings for which they were produced.

# MITCHELL ARMS, INC.
### Santa Ana, California
This company imports and distributes foreign-manufactured firearms.

## M-16
This is a .22 rimfire version of Colt's AR-15 rifle. It was introduced in 1987.

| NIB | Exc. | V.G. | Good | Fair | Poor |
|-----|------|------|------|------|------|
| 275 | 225 | 200 | 175 | 125 | 100 |

## MAS
This is a blowback-operated, semi-automatic rifle chambered for the .22 l.r. or the .22 Magnum cartridges. It is patterned after the French MAS Bullpup Service Rifle. It was introduced in 1987.

| NIB | Exc. | V.G. | Good | Fair | Poor |
|-----|------|------|------|------|------|
| 275 | 225 | 200 | 175 | 125 | 100 |

## Galil
This is a blowback-operated semi-automatic version of the Israeli Galil rifle. It is chambered for the .22 l.r. or the .22 Magnum cartridges. It was introduced in 1987.

| NIB | Exc. | V.G. | Good | Fair | Poor |
|-----|------|------|------|------|------|
| 275 | 225 | 200 | 175 | 125 | 100 |

## AK-22
This is a blowback-operated semi-automatic version of the Russian AK-47 rifle. It is chambered for the .22 l.r. or the .22 Magnum cartridges. It is furnished with a 20-round magazine and was introduced in 1985.

| NIB | Exc. | V.G. | Good | Fair | Poor |
|-----|------|------|------|------|------|
| 275 | 225 | 200 | 175 | 125 | 100 |

## PPS-50
This is a blowback-operated, semi-automatic version of the Russian PPSh WWII submachine gun. It is chambered for the .22 l.r. or the .22 Magnum cartridges and has a shrouded barrel and a 20-round curved magazine. A 50-round drum magazine is available and would be worth approximately $60.

| NIB | Exc. | V.G. | Good | Fair | Poor |
|-----|------|------|------|------|------|
| 275 | 225 | 200 | 175 | 125 | 100 |

This company also imported Yugoslavian-manufactured semi-automatic versions of the Russian AK-47 rifle chambered for the 7.62x39, as well as the .308 cartridges. They also imported a version called the R.P.K., which is a longer, heavy barrel version. With the current hysteria in our Country, it is no longer possible for weapons of this nature to be imported; and the values on examples that are already here have soared out of proportion. We strongly advise securing qualified local appraisals if a transaction on one of these weapons is contemplated.

## Skorpion
This is a blowback-operated, single-action, assault-type pistol chambered for the .32 ACP cartridge. It has a 4.75" barrel and utilizes a 20- or 30-round detachable magazine. The finish is blued, with a synthetic grip. It was imported from Yugoslavia in 1987 and 1988 only.

| Exc. | V.G. | Good | Fair | Poor |
|------|------|------|------|------|
| 600 | 500 | 425 | 350 | 300 |

## Spectre
This is a single-action, semi-automatic, assault-type pistol that is chambered for the 9mm Parabellum cartridge. It has an 8" shrouded barrel with an integral cooling system. It is offered with either a 30- or 50-round detachable magazine. The finish is blued, with a synthetic grip. A carbine version with an 18" barrel and folding buttstock is also available and is valued the same. It was imported from Yugoslavia in 1987 and 1988.

| Exc. | V.G. | Good | Fair | Poor |
|------|------|------|------|------|
| 600 | 500 | 425 | 350 | 300 |

Mitchell also imports a line of single-action, Western-style revolvers that are patterned after the Colt Single Action Army. These revolvers are imported from Italy and manufactured by Aldo Uberti. They are high quality firearms that are covered under the Uberti section of this text.

## MODESTO SANTOS CIA.
### Eibar, Spain

**Action, Corrientes, and M.S.**
These are essentially the same pistols that were marketed under different names depending upon where they were sold. This practice was very common among the Eibar companies in business around and shortly after WWI. These pistols are blowback-operated semi-automatic copies of the 1906 Browning design. They are chambered for 6.35mm amd the 7.65mm cartridges and are of the usual mediocre quality that was associated with Spanish guns of this period. The markings are all "Pistolet Automatique Model 1920." They are all blued, with checkered plastic grips with the letters "M.S." molded into them. These pistols were manufactured between 1920 and the Spanish Civil War.

| Exc. | V.G. | Good | Fair | Poor |
|---|---|---|---|---|
| 150 | 125 | 100 | 75 | 50 |

## MONDRAGON
### Sante Fe, Mexico

The Mondragon rifle was designed by Manuel Mondragon, who was perhaps Mexico's foremost ordnance genius. This rifle and its cartridge system are quite unique; and the concept was also applied by Mondragon, in conjunction with the Swiss designer Colonel Rubin, to artillery as well as rifle cartridges. The cartridge is known as a "Piston Cartridge" and is either 6.5x48mm or 6.5x52mm. Mondragon was born in 1858 and was educated at the Military College of Mexico and later studied at the French Military College at St. Cyr, France. He was placed in charge of military procurement by Porfirio Diaz, president of Mexico. It was during this time that he designed the "Automatic" Mondragon Rifle.

**Mondragon "Automatic" Rifle**
This rifle, also known as the Model 1893 and 1894, is actually a bolt action that resembles the more familiar Schmidt-Rubin Swiss rifle. The Rifle is chambered for the "Piston Cartridges" in 6.5mm. There is a switch on the right side of the stock above the triggerguard, which has three positions--one for a safety lock, one for regular operation, and the final position for automatic fire which actually allows the shooter to discharge the rifle by simply closing the bolt. It is said that this works rather effectively although accuracy does suffer when fired in this mode. The differences between the models is basically barrel lengths, with examples found between 21.75" and 34.5" in length.

| Exc. | V.G. | Good | Fair | Poor |
|---|---|---|---|---|
| 850 | 750 | 600 | 450 | 350 |

## MONTENEGRAN-GASSER
### SEE--Gasser, Leopold

## MOORE-ENFIELD
### J. P. Moore's Sons
### New York, New York

**Rifled Musket**
This is a muzzleloading rifle that is chambered for .58 caliber percussion and has a 39" round barrel. It has a full-length walnut stock held on by three barrel bands. The front sight is also the bayonet lug. This rifle has iron mountings, and the finish

was left in the white. There is a ramrod mounted under the barrel. The lockplate is marked with an eagle and the letter "M" (for Moore). There were several thousand manufactured between 1861 and 1863. They were used by Union forces in the Civil War.

| Exc. | V.G. | Good | Fair | Poor |
|---|---|---|---|---|
| 1500 | 1250 | 950 | 750 | 450 |

## MOORES PATENT FIREARMS CO.
### Brooklyn, New York

**No. 1 Derringer**
This model is chambered for the .41 rimfire cartridge and has a 2.5" barrel that pivots to the side for loading. This pistol was cast of all brass or iron, and there are no separate grip panels. The finish is either silver-plated or blued, and there is scroll engraving of a rather coarse nature covering the entire pistol. This pistol was first produced by Moore, and then the National Arms Company took over their facility and continued production. Eventually this Company was sold to Colt, and the No. 1 Derringer was produced under the Colt banner for a short time. There are five distinct variations which must be valued separately. There were approximately 10,000 manufactured overall between 1860 and 1865.

**1st Variation Marked "Patent Applied For"**

| Exc. | V.G. | Good | Fair | Poor |
|---|---|---|---|---|
| 950 | 850 | 700 | 600 | 450 |

**2nd Variation Marked "D.Moore Patented Feb. 19 1861"**

| Exc. | V.G. | Good | Fair | Poor |
|---|---|---|---|---|
| 750 | 650 | 500 | 400 | 250 |

**Standard Model Marked "Moore's Pat F.A.Co."**

| Exc. | V.G. | Good | Fair | Poor |
|---|---|---|---|---|
| 550 | 475 | 400 | 250 | 150 |

**National Arms Co. Production**

| Exc. | V.G. | Good | Fair | Poor |
|---|---|---|---|---|
| 550 | 475 | 400 | 250 | 150 |

**Iron Model**

| Exc. | V.G. | Good | Fair | Poor |
|---|---|---|---|---|
| 750 | 475 | 400 | 250 | 150 |

**Pocket Revolver**
This is a single-action revolver chambered for a .32- caliber teat-fire cartridge that was specially designed for this pistol by D. Moore and loaded from the front to circumvent the Rollin White Patent. It has a 3.25" barrel and a 6-shot unfluted cylinder. There is a spur-type trigger. The frame is silver-plated brass, and the birdshead grips are walnut. This was a very successful revolver from a commercial standpoint and was one of Smith & Wesson's strongest competitors during the Rollin White days. There were over 30,000 manufactured between 1864 and 1870.

| Exc. | V.G. | Good | Fair | Poor |
|---|---|---|---|---|
| 500 | 400 | 325 | 250 | 150 |

**Belt Revolver**
This model is chambered for the .32 rimfire cartridge and has a 4", 5", or 6" octagonal barrel. It has a 7-shot unfluted cylinder and single-action lockwork with a conventional trigger with guard. The barrel and the cylinder of this model pivot to the right for loading, and there is an ejector rod mounted under the barrel. The frame is scroll engraved and made of brass. The cylinder and the barrel are blued, and the grips are walnut. The barrel is marked "D.Moore Patent Sept. 18,1860." There were a few thousand manufactured between 1861 and 1863, and more than a few were privately purchased by officers in the Un-

ion Army and used in the Civil War. This Company lost an infringement suit to Smith & Wesson, and this cut short the production of this Revolver.

| Exc. | V.G. | Good | Fair | Poor |
|------|------|------|------|------|
| 500 | 400 | 325 | 250 | 150 |

## MORGAN & CLAPP
### New Haven, Connecticut
**Single Shot Pocket Pistol**
This small pistol is chambered for the .22 and .32 rimfire cartridges. It has a 3.5" octagonal barrel that swings to the right side for loading. The frame is silver-plated brass, and the barrel is blued. The grips are walnut. The trigger is of the spur type, and the barrel is marked "Morgan & Clapp New Haven." There were approximately 300 manufactured between 1854 and 1866.

| Exc. | V.G. | Good | Fair | Poor |
|------|------|------|------|------|
| 300 | 250 | 200 | 150 | 100 |

## MORINI
### Italy
### Importer--Osborne's
### Cheboygan, Michigan
**C-80 Standard**
This is a very high-grade, single-shot target pistol that is chambered for the .22 l.r. cartridge. The barrel is 10" in length and is totally free-floating. This model is built for serious competition and features an adjustable frame, as well as adjustable walnut grips. The sights are match grade and adjustable for radius.

| Exc. | V.G. | Good | Fair | Poor |
|------|------|------|------|------|
| 1000 | 850 | 675 | 550 | 450 |

**CM-80 Super Competition**
This model has a higher-polished finish and a unique sighting system that incorporates a Plexiglass front sight. The trigger is fully adjustable from 5 to 120 grams. The other specifications are similar to the Standard model.

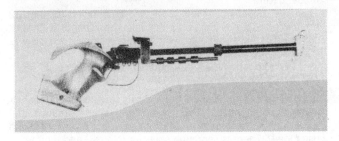

| Exc. | V.G. | Good | Fair | Poor |
|------|------|------|------|------|
| 1200 | 1000 | 850 | 750 | 600 |

## MORRONE
### Hope Valley, Rhode Island
### SEE--Rhode Island Arms Company

## MORSE
### Greenville, South Carolina
**Morse Carbine**
This is a breech-loading single-shot carbine chambered for an unusual .50-caliber cartridge which was actually a predecessor of the centerfire cartridge. This model has a 20" barrel with a tilting breech block that is operated by a lever behind the trigger-guard. The frame is brass, with a blued barrel and a wood stock. There were approximately 1,000 manufactured for the State Militia of South Carolina to use during the Civil War. Most

were unmarked; very few were marked "Morse," and these would bring a premium of approximately 35 percent over a standard late-production model. This was a Confederate weapon and as such is very collectible. We recommend that independent appraisal be secured on firearms of this nature.

| Exc. | V.G. | Good | Fair | Poor |
|------|------|------|------|------|
| 4500 | 3750 | 2750 | 2000 | 1750 |

## MOSIN-NAGANT
### Russia
**Model 1891**
This was the first Russian magazine rifle to utilize a high-velocity small-caliber cartridge, the 7.62mm. It has a 28.75" barrel and a 5-round internal magazine. The rifle has military-type sights, a bayonet lug, and a full-length stock held on by two barrel bands. The bolt of this rifle was thought to be overly complex, but the rifle was quite serviceable. It was based on a combination of the designs of the Belgian engineers Emile and Leon Nagant and the Russian Ivonovitch Mosin. It was adopted in 1891.

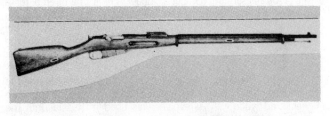

| Exc. | V.G. | Good | Fair | Poor |
|------|------|------|------|------|
| 175 | 150 | 125 | 100 | 75 |

**Model 1910 Carbine**
This Model is similar to the Model 1891, with a 20" barrel and improved sights.

| Exc. | V.G. | Good | Fair | Poor |
|------|------|------|------|------|
| 175 | 150 | 125 | 100 | 75 |

**Model 1930 Rifle**
This Model was the first rifle designed after the revolution, and it was not all that different from the Model 1891. The receiver was made round instead of hexagonal to simplify manufacture, and the sights were modernized to a tangent-type adjustable leaf with a hooded, tapered-post front sight. The barrel is 28.75" in length, and the caliber and the magazine capacity remained the same.

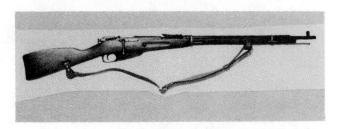

| Exc. | V.G. | Good | Fair | Poor |
|------|------|------|------|------|
| 175 | 150 | 125 | 100 | 75 |

**Model 1938 Carbine**
This Model is similar to the Model 1930, with a 20" carbine-length barrel.

| Exc. | V.G. | Good | Fair | Poor |
|------|------|------|------|------|
| 175 | 150 | 125 | 100 | 75 |

## Model 1944 Carbine
This Model is simply the Model 1938 Carbine with a hinged cruciform bayonet mounted at the muzzle. This rifle was copied by the Chinese as their Model 53.

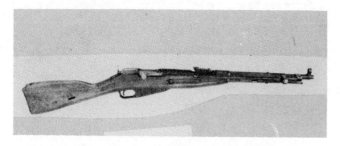

| Exc. | V.G. | Good | Fair | Poor |
|---|---|---|---|---|
| 150 | 125 | 100 | 75 | 50 |

## Model 1895 "Gas Seal" Revolver
This Revolver was adopted by the Russian Imperial government in 1895. It was designed by the Belgian Nagant brothers and was offered in two versions--a single-action (Troopers) model and a double-action (Officers) model. It is chambered for a unique 7.62mm cartridge that has a brass case that extends past the projectile to the mouth of the cylinder chamber. When the hammer is cocked, the cylinder is pushed forward into the barrel; and the case actually enters the barrel creating the "Gas Seal" when fired. It is effective but overly complex for the velocity gained. The barrel on this revolver is 4.35" in length, and the cylinder holds 7 rounds. The finish is blued, and the grips are checkered wood. This revolver was used in Russia until the development of the Tokarev Semi-automatic in 1933.

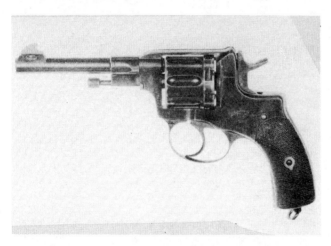

| Exc. | V.G. | Good | Fair | Poor |
|---|---|---|---|---|
| 300 | 250 | 200 | 150 | 100 |

# MOSSBERG, O. F. & SONS, INC.
### North Haven, Connecticut
This firm was founded by Oscar F. Mossberg in 1892 at Fitchburg, Massachusetts. For a time he operated at Chicopee Falls, Massachusetts, and since 1919 it has been located at North Haven, Connecticut.

## Brownie
This is a break-open, 4-barrelled repeating pistol chambered for the .22 l.r. cartridge. It was designed as a "palm squeezer"-type pistol that is held in the hand with the barrels protruding between the fingers. The four barrels are located in a two-over-two cluster, with a revolving firing pin that is activated by squeezing the grip in double-action fashion. Examples of this pistol have been noted chambered for the .32 short rimfire cartridge. Mossberg assigned the patent to the C. S. Shattuck Company of Hat-field, Massachusetts; and it was produced by them for a number of years. It was introduced in 1906, and manufacture continued on an on-and-off basis until it finally ceased during WWII. Later versions featured a trigger and a triggerguard and resembled a semi-automatic pistol in appearance.

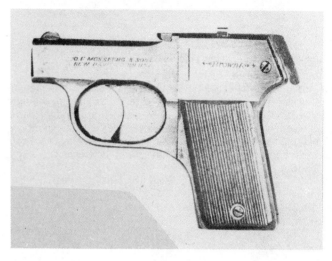

| Exc. | V.G. | Good | Fair | Poor |
|---|---|---|---|---|
| 350 | 325 | 300 | 225 | 150 |

## Model K Rifle
This is a slide-action rifle chambered for the .22 rimfire cartridge. It has a 22" barrel with a tubular magazine. It has a take-down feature and is fired by an internal hammer. It was offered with open sights. The finish is blued, with a plain walnut stock. It was discontinued in 1931.

| Exc. | V.G. | Good | Fair | Poor |
|---|---|---|---|---|
| 175 | 150 | 125 | 75 | 50 |

## Model M Rifle
This version is similar to the Model K, with a 24" octagonal barrel. It was manufactured between 1928 and 1931.

| Exc. | V.G. | Good | Fair | Poor |
|---|---|---|---|---|
| 175 | 150 | 125 | 75 | 50 |

## Model L Rifle
This is a single-shot falling-block rifle chambered for the .22 rimfire cartridge. It features a 24" take-down barrel with open sights. The finish is blued, with a plain walnut stock. It was manufactured between 1927 and 1932.

| Exc. | V.G. | Good | Fair | Poor |
|---|---|---|---|---|
| 300 | 250 | 200 | 150 | 100 |

In 1930 Mossberg began manufacturing single-shot and repeating bolt-action rifles. These were utility-grade firearms that were quite serviceable and reasonably priced. Many are still in use today. There is very little collector interest, and their value would be determined by the serviceability in which they remain. There is also a series of semi-automatic rifles for which the same criteria would apply. The values for all of these models are quite similar, and we will list them for reference purposes only.

### Bolt Action Rifles

| Model 10 | Model 25 | Model 340M |
|---|---|---|
| Model 14 | Model 25A | Model 341 |
| Model 140B | Model 26B | Model 342K |
| Model 140K | Model 26C | Model 346B |
| Model 142A | Model 30 | Model 346K |
| Model 142K | Model 320B | Model 352K |
| Model 144 | Model 320K | Model 450 |
| Model 144LS | Model 321K | Model 432 |
| Model 146B | Model 340B | Model 50 |
| Model 20 | Model 340K | Model 51 |
| | | Model 51M |

| Exc. | V.G. | Good | Fair | Poor |
|---|---|---|---|---|
| 100 | 80 | 65 | 45 | 20 |

## Semi-Automatic Rifles

| Model 151K | Model 350K |
| Model 151M | Model 351C |
| Model 152 | Model 351K |
| Model 152K | |

| Exc. | V.G. | Good | Fair | Poor |
|---|---|---|---|---|
| 125 | 100 | 80 | 60 | 40 |

## Model 400 Palomino

This is a lever-action rifle chambered for the .22 rimfire cartridges. It has a 22" barrel furnished with open sights and a tubular magazine. The finish is blued, with a checkered walnut stock. A carbine model with an 18.5" barrel is also available. The values are the same. It was manufactured between 1959 and 1964.

| Exc. | V.G. | Good | Fair | Poor |
|---|---|---|---|---|
| 150 | 125 | 100 | 75 | 50 |

## Model 800

This is a bolt-action sporting rifle chambered for various popular calibers. It has a 22" barrel with a folding-leaf sight. The finish is blued, with a checkered walnut stock. It was introduced in 1967.

| Exc. | V.G. | Good | Fair | Poor |
|---|---|---|---|---|
| 225 | 200 | 150 | 100 | 75 |

## Model 800D

This is a deluxe version with a roll-over comb stock. It has a rosewood forend tip and pistol-grip cap. It was manufactured between 1970 and 1973.

| Exc. | V.G. | Good | Fair | Poor |
|---|---|---|---|---|
| 300 | 250 | 200 | 150 | 100 |

## Model 800V

This version is furnished with a 24" heavy barrel and no sights. It is chambered for the smaller varmint calibers. It was introduced in 1968.

| Exc. | V.G. | Good | Fair | Poor |
|---|---|---|---|---|
| 225 | 200 | 150 | 100 | 75 |

## Model 800M

This version features a full-length, Mannlicher-type stock.

| Exc. | V.G. | Good | Fair | Poor |
|---|---|---|---|---|
| 275 | 250 | 200 | 150 | 100 |

## Model 800SM

This version is furnished with a 4X scope.

| Exc. | V.G. | Good | Fair | Poor |
|---|---|---|---|---|
| 300 | 275 | 225 | 150 | 100 |

## Model 810

This is a long-action version chambered for various calibers from .270 to the .338 Winchester Magnum cartridges. It is offered with a 22" or 24" barrel with a folding rear sight. The finish is blued, with a checkered walnut Monte Carlo-type stock. It was introduced in 1970.

| Exc. | V.G. | Good | Fair | Poor |
|---|---|---|---|---|
| 275 | 250 | 200 | 150 | 100 |

## Model 472C

This is a lever-action carbine chambered for the .30-30 or the .35 Remington cartridges. It has a 20" barrel with open sights and a tubular magazine. The finish is blued, with a walnut straight stock. It has a saddle ring on the left side of the receiver. It was introduced in 1972.

| Exc. | V.G. | Good | Fair | Poor |
|---|---|---|---|---|
| 200 | 175 | 150 | 100 | 75 |

## Model 472P

This version is similar to the Model 427C, with a pistol-grip stock and no saddle ring.

| Exc. | V.G. | Good | Fair | Poor |
|---|---|---|---|---|
| 200 | 175 | 150 | 100 | 75 |

## Model 472 One In Five Thousand

This version is similar to the Model 472C, with an etched receiver featuring an Indian scene. The buttplate is made of brass, as are the saddle ring and barrel band. The stock is of select-grade walnut. There were 5,000 manufactured in 1974.

| Exc. | V.G. | Good | Fair | Poor |
|---|---|---|---|---|
| 400 | 350 | 300 | 200 | 150 |

## Model 479 PCA

This is a lever-action carbine chambered for the .30-30 cartridge. It has a 20" barrel and a 6-round tubular magazine. The finish is blued, with a walnut stock.

| Exc. | V.G. | Good | Fair | Poor |
|---|---|---|---|---|
| 200 | 175 | 150 | 100 | 75 |

## Model 479 RR

This was a limited-production model designated the "Roy Rogers" signature model. It is similar in configuration to the Model 479 PCA, with a gold-plated trigger and barrel bands. There were 5,000 manufactured in 1983.

| Exc. | V.G. | Good | Fair | Poor |
|---|---|---|---|---|
| 300 | 250 | 200 | 150 | 100 |

The Mossberg company manufactured utility-grade, bolt-action shotguns beginning with the post-WWII period. There is little collector interest, and they are evaluated on their serviceability only. They are chambered for 12, 16, and 20 gauge, as well as .410. We list them for reference purposes.

## Bolt Action Shotguns

| Model 173 | Model 195K |
| Model 173Y | Model 385K |
| Model 183D | Model 385T |
| Model 183K | Model 390K |
| Model 183T | Model 390T |
| Model 185D | Model 395K |
| Model 185K | Model 395S |
| Model 190D | Model 395T |
| Model 190K | Model 73 |
| Model 195D | |

| Exc. | V.G. | Good | Fair | Poor |
|---|---|---|---|---|
| 75 | 65 | 50 | 40 | 25 |

## Model 200K

This is a slide-action shotgun chambered for 12 gauge, with a 28" barrel and a Mossberg select-choke device. The finish is blued, with a synthetic slide handle and a plain walnut buttstock. It was manufactured between 1955 and 1959.

| Exc. | V.G. | Good | Fair | Poor |
|---|---|---|---|---|
| 150 | 125 | 100 | 75 | 50 |

## Model 500 Series

This is a series of slide-action shotguns that are chambered for 12 or 20 gauge, as well as .410. They are offered with various-length vent-rib barrels and feature screw-in choke tubes. The finishes are blued, with select checkered walnut stocks. They were imported from Japan. The values of the individual variations are determined by the options and the quality of materials and workmanship utilized in their construction.

### Model 500 Regal

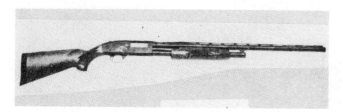

| Exc. | V.G. | Good | Fair | Poor |
|---|---|---|---|---|
| 250 | 200 | 150 | 100 | 75 |

### Model 500 Field Grade

| Exc. | V.G. | Good | Fair | Poor |
|---|---|---|---|---|
| 250 | 200 | 150 | 100 | 75 |

### Model 500 Steel Shot--Chrome Bore

| Exc. | V.G. | Good | Fair | Poor |
|---|---|---|---|---|
| 300 | 250 | 200 | 125 | 100 |

### Model 500 Slugster--Iron Sights

| Exc. | V.G. | Good | Fair | Poor |
|---|---|---|---|---|
| 275 | 250 | 200 | 150 | 100 |

### Model 500 Camper--18.5" Barrel, Camo Case

| Exc. | V.G. | Good | Fair | Poor |
|---|---|---|---|---|
| 295 | 275 | 225 | 175 | 125 |

### Model 500 Hi-Rib Trap

| Exc. | V.G. | Good | Fair | Poor |
|---|---|---|---|---|
| 275 | 250 | 200 | 150 | 100 |

### Model 500 Super Grade

| Exc. | V.G. | Good | Fair | Poor |
|---|---|---|---|---|
| 200 | 175 | 150 | 100 | 75 |

### Model 500 Pigeon Grade

| Exc. | V.G. | Good | Fair | Poor |
|---|---|---|---|---|
| 375 | 300 | 250 | 200 | 125 |

### Model 500 Pigeon Grade Trap

| Exc. | V.G. | Good | Fair | Poor |
|---|---|---|---|---|
| 450 | 375 | 300 | 250 | 175 |

### Model 500 Persuader--Riot Gun

| NIB | Exc. | V.G. | Good | Fair | Poor |
|---|---|---|---|---|---|
| 250 | 200 | 175 | 150 | 125 | 100 |

### Model 500 Mariner--Marinecote Finish

| NIB | Exc. | V.G. | Good | Fair | Poor |
|---|---|---|---|---|---|
| 350 | 300 | 225 | 200 | 150 | 125 |

### Model 500 Cruiser--Pistol Grip Only

| NIB | Exc. | V.G. | Good | Fair | Poor |
|---|---|---|---|---|---|
| 250 | 200 | 175 | 150 | 125 | 100 |

### Model 500 Bullpup

This model is chambered for 12 gauge with either an 18.5" or 20" shrouded barrel. It is a bullpup shotgun with a matte black finish and a synthetic slide handle, stock, and carrying handle. It was popularized on an episode of "Miami Vice" and is constructed in an assault-type configuration. It was introduced in 1986.

| NIB | Exc. | V.G. | Good | Fair | Poor |
|---|---|---|---|---|---|
| 400 | 325 | 250 | 200 | 150 | 100 |

### Model 590

This version is similar to the Model 500 Persuader except that it has a 20" shrouded barrel and a 9-round tubular magazine. It features a bayonet lug and is either blued or parkerized. It was introduced in 1987.

| NIB | Exc. | V.G. | Good | Fair | Poor |
|---|---|---|---|---|---|
| 325 | 275 | 200 | 175 | 125 | 100 |

### Model 590 Mariner--Marinecote Finish

| NIB | Exc. | V.G. | Good | Fair | Poor |
|---|---|---|---|---|---|
| 425 | 350 | 275 | 225 | 150 | 100 |

### Model 590 Bullpup

This version is similar to the Model 500 Bullpup, with a 20" barrel and a 9-round tubular magazine. It was introduced in 1989.

| NIB | Exc. | V.G. | Good | Fair | Poor |
|---|---|---|---|---|---|
| 475 | 400 | 325 | 250 | 200 | 125 |

### Model 835 Ulti-Mag

This is a slide-action shotgun chambered for the 12-gauge, 3.5" Magnum shell. It has a 28" vent-rib barrel with screw-in choke tubes and a 6-round tubular magazine. The finish is blued, with either a synthetic or checkered hardwood stock. It was introduced in 1988.

| NIB | Exc. | V.G. | Good | Fair | Poor |
|---|---|---|---|---|---|
| 425 | 350 | 275 | 225 | 150 | 100 |

### Model 835 Wild Turkey Federation

This is a limited-edition version of the Model 835 Ulti-Mag that is furnished with a medallion inlaid in the stock and a 10-round package of Federal Turkey Loads. It was introduced in 1989.

| NIB | Exc. | V.G. | Good | Fair | Poor |
|---|---|---|---|---|---|
| 475 | 400 | 325 | 250 | 200 | 125 |

## Model 3000

This is a slide-action shotgun formerly known as the S&W Model 3000. It is chambered for 12 or 20 gauge and is offered with various barrel lengths and chokes. It features a ventilated-rib barrel. The receiver is made of steel, with double-action slide bars. The finish is blued, with a checkered walnut stock. It was only offered in a field-grade version in 1986 and 1987.

| Exc. | V.G. | Good | Fair | Poor |
|------|------|------|------|------|
| 325 | 250 | 175 | 125 | 75 |

## Model 3000 Waterfowler

This is a matte-finished version of the Model 3000 that was furnished with sling swivels and a camo sling. It was produced in 1986.

| Exc. | V.G. | Good | Fair | Poor |
|------|------|------|------|------|
| 350 | 275 | 200 | 150 | 100 |

## Model 3000 Law Enforcement

This is the riot-gun configuration offered with an 18.5" or 20" cylinder-bore barrel. It was offered in 1986 and 1987.

| Exc. | V.G. | Good | Fair | Poor |
|------|------|------|------|------|
| 325 | 250 | 175 | 125 | 75 |

## Model 1000

This is a gas-operated semi-automatic shotgun formerly known as the S&W Model 1000. It is chambered for 12 or 20 gauge and is offered with various-length vent-rib barrels and chokes. Screw-in choke tubes were also available as an option. The receiver is made of aluminum alloy. The finish is blued, with a checkered walnut stock. It was offered in 1986 and 1987.

| Exc. | V.G. | Good | Fair | Poor |
|------|------|------|------|------|
| 400 | 325 | 250 | 200 | 125 |

## Model 1000 Slug

This version is offered with a 22" barrel with rifle sights and a recoil pad standard. It was offered in 1986 and 1987.

| Exc. | V.G. | Good | Fair | Poor |
|------|------|------|------|------|
| 400 | 325 | 250 | 200 | 125 |

## Model 1000 Super Series

This is a gas-operated semi-automatic shotgun chambered for 12 or 20 gauge. It features a self-regulating, gas-operated action that allows interchangeable firing of 2.75" and 3" shells. It is offered with various-length vent-rib barrels and screw-in chokes. The receiver is constructed of steel. The finish is blued, with a checkered walnut stock. This Model was offered by Mossberg in 1986 and 1987.

| Exc. | V.G. | Good | Fair | Poor |
|------|------|------|------|------|
| 500 | 450 | 400 | 300 | 200 |

## Model 1000 Super Waterfowler--Matte Finish

| Exc. | V.G. | Good | Fair | Poor |
|------|------|------|------|------|
| 500 | 450 | 400 | 300 | 200 |

## Model 1000 Super Slug--Rifle Sights

| Exc. | V.G. | Good | Fair | Poor |
|------|------|------|------|------|
| 500 | 450 | 400 | 300 | 200 |

## Model 1000 Super Trap--30" High Rib Barrel

| Exc. | V.G. | Good | Fair | Poor |
|------|------|------|------|------|
| 475 | 425 | 350 | 250 | 175 |

## Model 1000 Super Skeet--25" Barrel

| Exc. | V.G. | Good | Fair | Poor |
|------|------|------|------|------|
| 575 | 525 | 450 | 350 | 225 |

## Model 5500 MKII

This is a gas-operated semi-automatic shotgun chambered for 12 gauge. It is furnished with two vent-rib barrels-- one 26" in length and chambered for the 2.75" shell, and the other 28" in length and chambered for the 3" Magnum shell. It is supplied with screw-in choke tubes. The finish is blued, with a checkered hardwood stock. It was introduced in 1989.

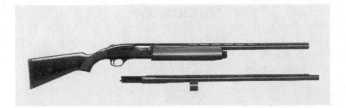

| NIB | Exc. | V.G. | Good | Fair | Poor |
|-----|------|------|------|------|------|
| 435 | 375 | 275 | 225 | 175 | 125 |

## Model 1500 Series

This is a bolt-action sporting rifle that was manufactured by Howa in Japan. It was previously known as the S&W Model 1500 rifle. It is chambered for various popular calibers between .223 and the .338 Win. Mag. It is offered with either a 22" or 24" barrel and utilizes a 5- or 6-round magazine, depending on the caliber. There are variations furnished with or without sights. The finish is blued, with either a hardwood or genuine walnut stock. The models differ in the calibers chambered and options offered. They were offered in 1986 and 1987.

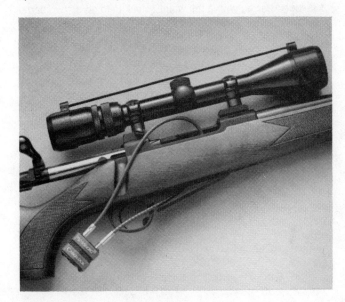

## Model 1500 Mountaineer Grade I

| Exc. | V.G. | Good | Fair | Poor |
|------|------|------|------|------|
| 300 | 250 | 225 | 150 | 125 |

## Model 1500 Mountaineer Grade II

| Exc. | V.G. | Good | Fair | Poor |
|------|------|------|------|------|
| 325 | 275 | 250 | 175 | 125 |

## Model 1500 Varmint--24" Heavy Barrel

| Exc. | V.G. | Good | Fair | Poor |
|------|------|------|------|------|
| 350 | 300 | 275 | 200 | 150 |

## Model 1550

This version is similar to the Model 1500 except that it is chambered for the .243, .270, and the .30-06 cartridges. It features a detachable box magazine and was offered in 1986 and 1987.

| Exc. | V.G. | Good | Fair | Poor |
|------|------|------|------|------|
| 325 | 275 | 250 | 175 | 125 |

## Model 1700 LS

This is a bolt-action sporting rifle chambered for the .243, .270, and the .30-06 cartridges. It has a 22" barrel that was furnished without sights. It features a detachable box magazine. The bolt is jeweled and the bolt handle was knurled. The finish is blued, with a select, checkered walnut stock with a schnabel forend. It was offered in 1986 and 1987.

| Exc. | V.G. | Good | Fair | Poor |
|------|------|------|------|------|
| 400 | 350 | 275 | 200 | 150 |

# MUGICA, JOSE
### Eibar, Spain
### SEE--Gabilondo

This is a tradename used on Llama pistols manufactured by Gabilondo and are found under that heading in this book.

# MURATA
### SEE--Japan State

# MURRAY, J. P.
### Columbus, Georgia

**Percussion Rifle**

This is a copy of the U.S. Model 1841. It was manufactured by the firm of E. S. Greenwood & William C. Gray. This single-shot muzzleloader is chambered for .58 caliber percussion and has a 33" round barrel, with a full walnut stock held on by two barrel bands. It has a bayonet lug and the finish is in the white, with brass mountings. There is an iron ramrod mounted under the barrel. This rifle is marked "J.P.Murray/Columbus Ga.," and it was used by the Confederacy during the Civil War. There were several hundred made between 1862 and 1864, and the prospective purchaser should secure independent appraisal.

| Exc. | V.G. | Good | Fair | Poor |
| --- | --- | --- | --- | --- |
| 4500 | 3750 | 3000 | 2500 | 1800 |

# MURPHY & O'CONNEL
### New York, New York

**Pocket Pistol**

This pistol is a copy of the Henry Deringer Philadelphia-style pistol. It is chambered for .41 caliber percussion and has a 3" barrel with German silver mountings and a walnut stock. It was manufactured in the 1850's.

| Exc. | V.G. | Good | Fair | Poor |
| --- | --- | --- | --- | --- |
| 650 | 575 | 450 | 350 | 250 |

# MUSGRAVE
### Republic of South Africa

Due to the problems that are now occurring in South Africa, these fine rifles are not currently being imported.

**RSA NR1 Single Shot Target Rifle**

This single-shot bolt-action rifle is chambered for .308 Winchester. The heavy barrel is 26" in length and features an adjustable aperture rear sight and a tunnel front sight that takes Anschutz-type inserts. The top of the action is closed for strength, and the trigger is fully adjustable. The stock is a target type, with upper handguard and beavertail forearm. It is made of select walnut. It was manufactured between 1971 and 1976.

| Exc. | V.G. | Good | Fair | Poor |
| --- | --- | --- | --- | --- |
| 325 | 275 | 225 | 175 | 125 |

**Valiant NR6**

This is a bolt-action repeating rifle that is chambered for .243, .270, .308, .30-06, and 7mm Remington Magnum. It has a 24" medium-weight barrel and features open sights. It was built on an improved Mauser action and has a hinged floorplate. The straight comb stock is made of select walnut and is skip-line checkered. It was furnished with a recoil pad and sling swivel studs. This model was imported between 1971 and 1976.

| Exc. | V.G. | Good | Fair | Poor |
| --- | --- | --- | --- | --- |
| 300 | 250 | 200 | 150 | 100 |

**Premier NR5**

This model is similar to the Valiant, with a 26" barrel and a Monte Carlo stock with a rosewood forend tip and pistol grip cap. The stock is hand-rubbed and oil-finished, with fine line hand-checkering. This model was also discontinued in 1976.

| Exc. | V.G. | Good | Fair | Poor |
| --- | --- | --- | --- | --- |
| 350 | 300 | 250 | 200 | 150 |

# MUSKETEER RIFLES
### Washington, D.C.
### Importer--Firearms International

**Sporter**

This is a Fabrique Nationale Mauser bolt-action rifle that is chambered for various popular cartridges between .243 and .300 Winchester Magnum. It has a 24" barrel without sights and features a blued finish with a checkered walnut Monte Carlo stock. It was imported between 1963 and 1972.

| Exc. | V.G. | Good | Fair | Poor |
| --- | --- | --- | --- | --- |
| 300 | 250 | 200 | 175 | 125 |

**Deluxe Sporter**

This version is similar to the standard Sporter, with an adjustable trigger, skipline checkering, and select walnut.

| Exc. | V.G. | Good | Fair | Poor |
| --- | --- | --- | --- | --- |
| 350 | 300 | 250 | 200 | 150 |

**Carbine**

This model is similar to the standard Sporter, with a 20" barrel.

| Exc. | V.G. | Good | Fair | Poor |
| --- | --- | --- | --- | --- |
| 325 | 275 | 225 | 175 | 125 |

# NAGANT, EMILE & LEON
### Liege, Belgium
### SEE--Mosin-Nagant

These were two brothers engaged in the design of revolvers in Belgium from 1878 until 1910. Their designs were, for the most part, rather unspectacular and not all that original until 1892 when Leon Nagant obtained the patent for his "Gas Seal" revolver, that was actually the only revolver of this type that worked. It is described in detail in the Mosin-Nagant section of this book. The Russians were already associated with the brothers Nagant through their work on the Tsarist service rifle, so it was not difficult to sell the design for the Gas Seal revolver. The first Russian revolvers were made in Liege; but in 1900 the Tula Arsenal commenced production, and the Russians bought all rights to produce this design. The Nagants could no longer manufacture their Gas Seal design, so they went back to producing conventional revolvers and in 1910 dropped firearms manufacture to begin the production of automobiles. They were not very successful in this endeavor and went out of business during WWI.

## Model 1878 Officers Revolver

This is a double-action revolver chambered for the 9mm cartridge. It has a 5" octagonal barrel and a solid frame with a
gate-loaded 6-shot cylinder. The finish is blued, and the grips
are checkered walnut. This model was adopted by Argentina,
Brazil, and the Norwegian army as their Model 1883. The
Swedish military adopted a 7.5mm version and designated it
the Model 1893. Except for the markings, these revolvers are
very similar.

| Exc. | V.G. | Good | Fair | Poor |
|------|------|------|------|------|
| 250 | 225 | 200 | 150 | 100 |

## NAMBU
### SEE--Japan State

## NATIONAL ARMS CO.
### Brooklyn, New York
### SEE--Moore's Patent Firearms Co.

This company purchased the Moore's Patent Firearms Co. in
1865, and all production after that date bears the National
Arms Co. banner. In 1870 this company was sold to Colt. The
early production is listed in the section on the Moore firearms.

## Large Frame Teat-Fire Revolver

This is large militia-type revolver chambered for the .45-caliber
teat-fire cartridge that was designed by D. Moore for this revolver. It has a 7.5" barrel and a 6-shot cylinder that loads from
the front. It has a siver-plated brass frame, and the barrel and
the cylinder are blued. The grips are of walnut, and the barrel is
marked "National Arms Co.,Brooklyn." There were very few of
these revolvers manufactured in 1865 and 1866. The production figures are not known.

| Exc. | V.G. | Good | Fair | Poor |
|------|------|------|------|------|
| 2000 | 1750 | 1500 | 1000 | 750 |

## No. 2 Derringer

This model is similar to the Moore's No. 1 Derringer except that
it has walnut grips. It is chambered for the .41 rimfire cartridge
and has a 2.5" barrel that pivots to the side for loading. The
frame is either silver-plated brass or iron, and the surface is
scroll-engraved. There were approximately 5,000 manufactured between 1865 and 1870 when Colt purchased the company. This model was produced as the Colt No. 2 Derringer for
a short time after the sale.

| Exc. | V.G. | Good | Fair | Poor |
|------|------|------|------|------|
| 450 | 400 | 350 | 275 | 200 |

## NAVY ARMS COMPANY
### Ridgefield, New Jersey
### ALSO SEE--Aldo Uberti

This company has for many years imported high-grade, Italian-
made replicas of Western-style, early-American firearms. Values and descriptions of these weapons will be found in the section of this text dealing with Aldo Uberti. They also import a line
of Italian shotguns, as well as used military firearms and modern
centerfire rifles. The values for these firearms are as follows:

## Model 83

This is an Over/Under shotgun chambered for 12 or 20 gauge
with 3" chambers. It has various-length, separated vent-rib barrels with various choke combinations. It features double triggers, extractors, and an engraved, chrome-finished boxlock action. The barrels are blued, with a checkered walnut stock. It
was introduced in 1985.

| NIB | Exc. | V.G. | Good | Fair | Poor |
|-----|------|------|------|------|------|
| 385 | 325 | 275 | 200 | 175 | 125 |

## Model 93

This version is similar to the Model 83 but features automatic
ejectors.

| NIB | Exc. | V.G. | Good | Fair | Poor |
|-----|------|------|------|------|------|
| 450 | 400 | 325 | 275 | 225 | 175 |

## Model 95

This version is similar to the Model 93, with a single trigger and
screw-in choke tubes.

| NIB | Exc. | V.G. | Good | Fair | Poor |
|-----|------|------|------|------|------|
| 475 | 425 | 350 | 300 | 250 | 200 |

## Model 96 Sportsman

This version is chambered for 12 gauge only, with 3" chambers,
and features a gold-plated receiver.

| NIB | Exc. | V.G. | Good | Fair | Poor |
|-----|------|------|------|------|------|
| 575 | 525 | 450 | 400 | 350 | 300 |

## Model 100

This is an Over/Under shotgun chambered for 12, 20, and 28
gauge, as well as .410. It features 26" vent-rib barrels and has
an engraved, chromed boxlock action. It features a single trigger
with extractors. The barrels are blued, with a checkered walnut
stock. It was introduced in 1989.

| NIB | Exc. | V.G. | Good | Fair | Poor |
|-----|------|------|------|------|------|
| 300 | 250 | 225 | 200 | 150 | 100 |

## Model 100 SxS

This version is a side-by-side double-barrel shotgun that shares
its designation with the Over/Under Model 100. It is chambered for 12 and 20 gauge with 3" chambers and has a 27.5"
barrel with various choke combinations. It has double triggers
and extractors. The finish is blued, with a checkered walnut
stock. It was imported between 1985 and 1987.

| Exc. | V.G. | Good | Fair | Poor |
|------|------|------|------|------|
| 375 | 325 | 275 | 200 | 125 |

## Model 150

This Model is similar to the Model 100 except that it features
automatic ejectors.

| Exc. | V.G. | Good | Fair | Poor |
|------|------|------|------|------|
| 450 | 400 | 325 | 225 | 150 |

## Model 105

This is a single-barrel, folding shotgun chambered for 12 and 20
gauge, as well as .410. It features a 26" or 28" full-choke barrel with an engraved chromed receiver, a blued barrel, and
checkered hardwood stock. It was introduced in 1985.

| NIB | Exc. | V.G. | Good | Fair | Poor |
|-----|------|------|------|------|------|
| 100 | 80 | 75 | 65 | 50 | 35 |

## Model 105 Deluxe
This version features a vent-rib barrel and a checkered walnut stock.

| NIB | Exc. | V.G. | Good | Fair | Poor |
|-----|------|------|------|------|------|
| 120 | 100  | 85   | 75   | 60   | 45   |

## Martini Target Rifle
This is a single-shot rifle based on the falling-block Martini action. It is chambered for the .444 or the .45-70 cartridges. It has a 26" or 30" octagonal barrel with a tang sight. The finish was blued, with a walnut stock. It was offered between 1972 and 1984.

| Exc. | V.G. | Good | Fair | Poor |
|------|------|------|------|------|
| 475  | 425  | 350  | 275  | 175  |

## Parker-Hale Sniper Rifle
See Parker-Hale section of this text.

## RPKS-74
This is a Chinese-manufactured semi-automatic version of the RPK Squad Automatic Weapon. It is chambered for the .223 or the 7.62x39mm cartridges. It has a 19" barrel and features the same gas-piston action as the other AK-type weapons. It has a hardwood stock and is furnished with an integral folding bipod. This is an assault-type weapon and cannot be accurately evaluated in a text of this type at this time. We strongly suggest seeking a qualified, local appraisal if a transaction is contemplated.

Navy Arms also imports a wide variety of surplus military weapons that are currently legal to bring into this country. They include the Browning Hi-Power, Smith & Wesson Model 1917, Mauser Broomhandle, Japanese Nambu, and 1911 Colt, as well as a number of foreign bolt-action and semi-automatic service rifles and surplus American weapons that have been overseas since WWII. These weapons are covered in their own respective sections of this text. Be advised that currently imported surplus military weapons must by law have the importer's name prominently and permanently stamped upon them. This has a serious detrimental effect on the collector status and subsequent value of these weapons. We advise securing qualified appraisal when in doubt.

## Luger
This is a toggle-lock action pistol chambered for the .22 l.r. cartridge. It is offered with a 4", 6", or 8" barrel with fixed sights and a 10-round detachable magazine. The finish is blued, with checkered walnut grips. This pistol was manufactured in the U.S.A. in 1986 and 1987.

| Exc. | V.G. | Good | Fair | Poor |
|------|------|------|------|------|
| 175  | 150  | 125  | 100  | 75   |

## Grand Prix Silhouette Pistol
This is a single-shot, long-range target pistol chambered for the .30-30, .44 Magnum, 7mm Special, and the .45-70 cartridges. It has a 13.75" barrel with adjustable target sights and an aluminum, heat-disbursing rib. The finish is matte-blue, with walnut grips and forearm. It was manufactured in 1985.

| Exc. | V.G. | Good | Fair | Poor |
|------|------|------|------|------|
| 325  | 275  | 225  | 175  | 125  |

# NEAL, W.
### Bangor, Maine

## Underhammer Pistol
This bootleg-type pistol is chambered for .31 caliber and utilizes the underhammer percussion-ignition system. It is offered with a 5" to 8" barrel length. The frame is iron, and it has a large, saw-shaped, walnut one-piece handle. The barrel is marked "Wm. Neal/Bangor,Me." This model was manufactured in the 1850's.

| Exc. | V.G. | Good | Fair | Poor |
|------|------|------|------|------|
| 550  | 475  | 400  | 300  | 200  |

# NEPPERHAN FIREARMS CO.
### Yonkers, New York

## Pocket Revolver
This model is chambered for .31-caliber percussion and is offered with octagonal barrels from 3.5" to 6" in length. The unfluted cylinder holds 5 shots. The finish is blued and case-colored, with one-piece walnut grips. The barrel is marked "Nepperhan/Fire Arms Co" on the bulk of the production run, with slight variances (the addition of "Yonkers New York") on an estimated 500 revolvers. This would add a premium of approximately 10 percent to the values shown. The total manufactured was approximately 5,000 in the first part of the 1860's.

| Exc. | V.G. | Good | Fair | Poor |
|------|------|------|------|------|
| 600  | 525  | 450  | 350  | 225  |

# NEWBURY ARMS CO.
### Catskill, New York
### Albany, New York

## Pocket Pistol
This single shot pistol was chambered for the .25 caliber rimfire cartridge and had a 4" octagonal barrel that swung to the left side for loading. It had a silver plated brass frame and the barrel was blued. It had a spur type trigger and walnut grips. This model had no integral extractor and was unmarked. There were several hundred manufactured in the 1850's.

| Exc. | V.G. | Good | Fair | Poor |
|------|------|------|------|------|
| 550  | 475  | 400  | 300  | 200  |

## Pocket Revolver
This is a very rare revolver that was chambered for .26 caliber percussion and had a 5" barrel that tipped up to reveal the nipples hidden under a shield. The cylinder held six shots and the trigger was shaped like a letter C with no guard. The barrel was marked "Newbury Arms Co. Albany." The hammer was a small (almost bobbed) affair also marked "Newbury." The frame was brass or iron and the finish was blued. There were two piece walnut grips. The exact production figures are unknown but this was a very scarce revolver manufactured between 1855 and 1860.

| Exc. | V.G. | Good | Fair | Poor |
|------|------|------|------|------|
| 2500 | 2000 | 1500 | 1000 | 750  |

# NEW ENGLAND FIREARMS CO.
### Gardner, Massachusetts

## Model R22
This is an inexpensive revolver chambered for .22 l.r., .22 Magnum, and .32 H&R Magnum. It has a 2.5", 4", or 6" barrel; and the cylinder holds 9 shots in .22 and 6 shots in the other calibers. It is a swingout-cylinder, solid-frame double-action revolver that is available in blue or nickel-plated, with hardwood grips. This company began production in 1988.

| NIB | Exc. | V.G. | Good | Fair | Poor |
|-----|------|------|------|------|------|
| 110 | 95   | 80   | 70   | 60   | 40   |

## Pardner
This is a single-shot breakopen shotgun chambered for 12, 16, and 20 gauge, plus .410. It has an exposed hammer with a transfer bar for safety, and the barrel is offered in lengths of 24", 26", and 28", with various chokes. The stock is of walnut, and the gun was introduced in 1987.

| NIB | Exc. | V.G. | Good | Fair | Poor |
|-----|------|------|------|------|------|
| 100 | 85   | 75   | 65   | 50   | 35   |

## Handi-Rifle

This model is similar in appearance to the Pardner but has a 22" rifle barrel with adjustable open sights. It is chambered for the .22 Hornet, .223, .30-30, and the .45-70 cartridges. The finish is blued, with a walnut stock. This model was introduced in 1989.

| NIB | Exc. | V.G. | Good | Fair | Poor |
|-----|------|------|------|------|------|
| 150 | 125 | 100 | 75 | 65 | 40 |

## Handi-Gun

This is a combination set that includes a shotgun barrel as well as a rifle barrel, in a choice of the offered calibers and gauges. This model was introduced in 1988.

| NIB | Exc. | V.G. | Good | Fair | Poor |
|-----|------|------|------|------|------|
| 200 | 175 | 150 | 125 | 100 | 75 |

# NEWCOMB, H. G.
### Natchez, Mississippi

## Pocket Pistol

This pistol is a copy of the Philadelphia derringer manufactured by the Henry Deringer Co. It is chambered for .41-caliber percussion and has a 2.5" barrel and a walnut stock. The mountings are German silver. This pistol was manufactured in the 1850's.

| Exc. | V.G. | Good | Fair | Poor |
|------|------|------|------|------|
| 650 | 550 | 450 | 350 | 250 |

# NEWTON ARMS CO.
### Buffalo, New York

This company was also known as the Buffalo Newton Rifle Co. and the Chas. Newton Rifle Co. They manufactured fine sporting rifles between 1913 and 1932. They made great advances in the field of ballistics, and some consider their cartridges that were manufactured before WWI to be the first Magnum chamberings. These rifles have become quite collectible.

## Newton-Mauser Rifle

This was the first of the Newton rifles, and it was built on an Oberndorf Mauser bolt action. It has a 24" barrel and is chambered for the .256 Newton cartridge. The rifle features double-set triggers and a blued finish. The hand-checkered pistol grip stock is made of walnut. This model was produced before WWI.

| Exc. | V.G. | Good | Fair | Poor |
|------|------|------|------|------|
| 750 | 675 | 550 | 400 | 275 |

## Standard Rifle First Type

This model is built on the company's own bolt action and is chambered for the Newton calibers, which consisted of the .22, .256, .280., 30, .33, and .35. It is also chambered for .30-06. It has a 24" barrel, with either regular or aperture sights and double-set triggers. The stock is hand-checkered walnut. This rifle was manufactured by the Newton Arms Co. between 1916 and 1918.

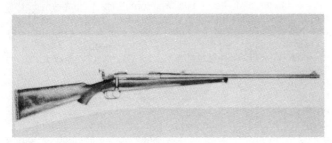

| Exc. | V.G. | Good | Fair | Poor |
|------|------|------|------|------|
| 1200 | 1000 | 750 | 550 | 400 |

## Standard Rifle Second Model

This model is similar to the First Type, with an improved Newton action with an Enfield-type bolt handle. It is chambered for .30-06, as well as the .256, .30, and the .35 Newton cartridges. This model has open sights and a walnut stock and was manufactured by the Charles Newton Co. after the close of WWI.

| Exc. | V.G. | Good | Fair | Poor |
|------|------|------|------|------|
| 1000 | 800 | 650 | 400 | 350 |

## Buffalo Newton Rifle

This rifle is similar to the Second-type Standard Rifle, but it was manufactured between 1922 and 1932 by what had become known as the Buffalo Newton Company--hence, the name change of the model.

| Exc. | V.G. | Good | Fair | Poor |
|------|------|------|------|------|
| 1000 | 800 | 650 | 400 | 350 |

# NICHOLS & CHILDS
### Conway, Massachusetts

## Percussion Belt Revolver

This is a very rare revolver that is chambered for .34-caliber percussion. It has a 6" round barrel and a 6-shot cylinder that functions in a different manner than most conventional revolvers. The outside hammer mounted on the right side of the frame pushes against the cylinder and causes it to revolve. There is a lever on the left side of the frame that puts tension on the cylinder and forms a gas seal with the barrel. The finish is browned, and the rounded grips are walnut. This is a very early percussion revolver and one of the rarest as there were only 25 manufactured in 1838.

| Exc. | V.G. | Good | Fair | Poor |
|------|------|------|------|------|
| 7500 | 6500 | 5000 | 3250 | 2500 |

## Revolving Percussion Rifle

This rare and ornate rifle is chambered for .36- and .40-caliber percussion, with a 26" round barrel. Some have part-round/part-octagonal barrels of 30" in length and 22" round carbine length. The cylinder functions much like the Belt Revolver. The stock is walnut with a crescent buttplate and ornate patchbox in one of two styles. There is no forend, and the barrel has to be removed to remove the cylinder. The cylinder on this rifle has been noted with capacities of 5, 6, 7, and 9 shots. There were approximately 150 manufactured between 1838 and 1840.

| Exc. | V.G. | Good | Fair | Poor |
|------|------|------|------|------|
| 7500 | 6500 | 5000 | 3250 | 2500 |

# NOBLE
### Haydenville, Massachusetts

This company was in the business of producing serviceable, inexpensive firearms. They operated between 1950 and 1971. Their products included a bolt-action sporter based on a Mauser action; single-shot, lever-action, slide-action, and semi-automatic .22 rifles; and double-barrelled, semi-automatic, and slide-action shotguns. In all, they manufactured approximately 50 different models. None of them have any collector interest;

and the most valuable model--the side-by-side double-barrelled shotgun--would be worth an estimated $150 in excellent condition. All the other models would each bring less than that. Therefore, we are not individually listing them.

# NORINCO
## Peoples Republic of China
## China North Industries Corp.

This is a Chinese arms conglomerate that started importing assault rifles in 1988 and has now branched out into the sporting arms field. They are imported and distributed by China Sports, as well as Interarms of Alexandria, Virginia.

## ATD .22

This is a semi-automatic takedown rifle patterned after the Browning model. It is chambered for .22 l.r. and has a 19.4" barrel. It has an 11-round magazine that loads through the stock. It has adjustable sights, a blued finish, and a checkered hardwood stock. Importation began in 1987.

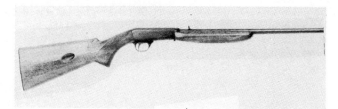

| NIB | Exc. | V.G. | Good | Fair | Poor |
|-----|------|------|------|------|------|
| 180 | 150  | 125  | 100  | 75   | 50   |

## EM-321

This is a slide-action rifle chambered for the .22 l.r. cartridge. It has a 19.5" barrel and a 10-round tubular magazine located under the barrel. The finish is blued, with a hardwood stock. It was introduced in 1989.

| NIB | Exc. | V.G. | Good | Fair | Poor |
|-----|------|------|------|------|------|
| 125 | 100  | 85   | 75   | 65   | 50   |

## Model HL-12-203 Shotgun

This is an Over/Under double-barrelled shotgun chambered for the 12-gauge, 2.75" shell only. It has 30" vent-ribbed barrels with screw-in choke tubes. The action is a boxlock with a single trigger and automatic ejectors. The finish is blued, with a checkered hardwood stock. This model was introduced in 1989.

| NIB | Exc. | V.G. | Good | Fair | Poor |
|-----|------|------|------|------|------|
| 375 | 325  | 275  | 225  | 175  | 125  |

## Model HL-12-102 Shotgun

This is a slide-action shotgun that is chambered for 12 gauge only and has a 28" barrel with various chokes. The tube magazine holds 3 rounds; and the finish is blued, with a hardwood stock. It was introduced in 1989.

| NIB | Exc. | V.G. | Good | Fair | Poor |
|-----|------|------|------|------|------|
| 250 | 225  | 200  | 175  | 125  | 100  |

## Model 213 Pistol

This is a single-action semi-automatic pistol patterned after the Browning Hi-Power. It is chambered for the 9mm Parabellum cartridge and has a blued finish, with checkered hardwood grips. It was sold in 1988 only.

| Exc. | V.G. | Good | Fair | Poor |
|------|------|------|------|------|
| 175  | 150  | 125  | 100  | 75   |

## Type 54-1 Tokarev

This is a single-action semi-automatic pistol chambered for the 7.62x25mm cartridge. The barrel is 4.6" in length. It has an 8-round detachable magazine and fixed sights. The finish is blued, with plastic grips. It is based on the Soviet design and was imported in 1989.

| Exc. | V.G. | Good | Fair | Poor |
|------|------|------|------|------|
| 175  | 150  | 125  | 100  | 80   |

## Type 59 Makarov

This is a blowback-operated semi-automatic chambered for the 9mm Makarov cartridge or the .380 ACP. The barrel is 3.5" in length, and the magazine holds 8 rounds. It is based on the Soviet design which was based on the Walther PP. It is blued, with brown plastic grips.

| Exc. | V.G. | Good | Fair | Poor |
|------|------|------|------|------|
| 275  | 250  | 225  | 175  | 125  |

## SKS Rifle

This is a newly manufactured version of a time-tested Communist Bloc design. The SKS has been used for many years, and our Vietnam veterans are not strangers to this rifle. It is chambered for the 7.62x39mm cartridge. The barrel is 20.5" in length. Some newer models have a 30-round detachable magazine, but current legislation will force a return to the standard 10-round fixed magazine of the original Siminov design. The military-type sights are adjustable, and there is a folding spike bayonet. The stock is made of hardwood. Importation began in 1988.

| Exc. | V.G. | Good | Fair | Poor |
|------|------|------|------|------|
| 250  | 225  | 200  | 150  | 100  |

The other semi-automatic weapons imported by this company fall into the "Assault Rifle" category and as such are part of a very volatile market. It is impossible to accurately estimate values at this point due to extreme fluctuations in various geographical locations. We list the offered firearms for reference purposes but feel that an individual local appraisal should be secured if a transaction is contemplated.

## Type 84S AK

This is a semi-automatic version of the AKS chambered for the .223 cartridge. It has a 16" barrel and is gas-operated. It has an adjustable military-type sight and a 30-round detachable magazine. The finish is blued, with a hardwood stock and forend.

## Type 84S-1

This model is similar except that it has an underfolding metal stock.

## Type 84S-3

This model has a synthetic red stock and is longer than the standard version.

## Type 84S-5

This version features a stock that folds to the side and has no provision for a bayonet.

## Type 81S

This model is chambered for the 7.62x39mm cartridge; otherwise it is similar to the Type 84S.

## Type 81S-1

This version has a metal stock that folds under the weapon.

# NORTH AMERICAN ARMS CORP.
## Toronto, Canada

### Brigadier

This is a large, alloy-framed semi-automatic pistol patterned after the Browning High Power in appearance. It is chambered for the .45 NAACO cartridge, which was made from a shortened .30-06 case and used a standard .45-caliber bullet. This load developed 1,600 ft./sec and a muzzle energy of 1,307 ft./lbs. The pistol has a removable trigger group and, in spite of the alloy frame, weighs 4.5 lbs. It has a 5" barrel and an 8-round detachable magazine. The finish is blued, and the grips are checkered walnut. This pistol was intended to be used as a military weapon but was not accepted by the Canadian government. It is very rarely encountered as only a few were manufactured between 1948 and 1951.

| Exc. | V.G. | Good | Fair | Poor |
|------|------|------|------|------|
| 1250 | 1000 | 800  | 600  | 500  |

## NORTH AMERICAN ARMS
### Spanish Fork, Utah

**Mini-Revolver**

This model is a very small, stainless-steel single-action revolver chambered for .22 short, long, or l.r., as well as the .22 rimfire magnum cartridge. It is offered with barrel lengths of 1", 2", and 2.5". The cylinder holds 5 rounds. The grips are either plastic or laminated rosewood. This Revolver has been manufactured since 1975. There are a number of options as follows:

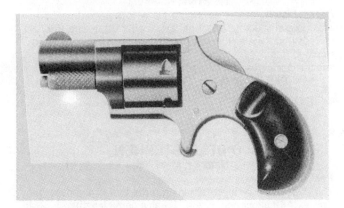

**Standard Rimfire Version**

| NIB | Exc. | V.G. | Fair | Poor |
|---|---|---|---|---|
| 140 | 125 | 110 | 85 | 60 |

**Magnum Version**

| NIB | Exc. | V.G. | Fair | Poor |
|---|---|---|---|---|
| 160 | 145 | 125 | 100 | 75 |

**Two Cylinder Magnum Convertible Version**

| NIB | Exc. | V.G. | Fair | Poor |
|---|---|---|---|---|
| 185 | 165 | 150 | 125 | 100 |

**Viper Belt Buckle Version**

| NIB | Exc. | V.G. | Fair | Poor |
|---|---|---|---|---|
| 165 | 140 | 120 | 100 | 75 |

**Standard Three Gun Set**

| NIB | Exc. | V.G. | Fair | Poor |
|---|---|---|---|---|
| 575 | 500 | 400 | 300 | 225 |

**Deluxe Three Gun Set**

| NIB | Exc. | V.G. | Fair | Poor |
|---|---|---|---|---|
| 625 | 550 | 450 | 350 | 275 |

**Cased .22 Magnum**

| NIB | Exc. | V.G. | Fair | Poor |
|---|---|---|---|---|
| 285 | 250 | 200 | 150 | 125 |

**Single Action Revolver**

This is a polished stainless-steel single-action revolver chambered for the .45 Winchester Magnum and the .450 Magnum Express cartridge. It has a 7.5" barrel and a 5-shot cylinder. There is a transfer bar safety, and the grips are walnut. This model was discontinued in 1988.

| Exc. | V.G. | Good | Fair | Poor |
|---|---|---|---|---|
| 850 | 775 | 650 | 500 | 400 |

## NORTH AMERICAN SAFARI EXPRESS
### Liege, Belgium
### SEE--Francotte

This is a tradename used by Francotte for their side-by-side double rifles that are imported and distributed by Armes De Chasse of Chads Ford, Pennsylvania.

## NORTH & COUCH
### New York, New York

**Animal Trap Pepperbox**

This is a revolving pepperbox type that was actually designed to be tied down as a trap for animals. It is fired by a cord tied to the trigger when used in this manner. It could also be fired from the hand-held position as well. It is chambered for .28 or .30 caliber percussion, and there are two basic versions. One has a 1.75" barrel cluster and disk-type circular hammer. It is marked "North & Couch, Middletown, Conn." The second type has a 2.12" and a spur-type hammer. It is marked "North & Couch New York." They were both manufactured in the 1860's.

**Disk Hammer Model**

| Exc. | V.G. | Good | Fair | Poor |
|---|---|---|---|---|
| 750 | 650 | 550 | 400 | 300 |

**Spur Hammer Model**

| Exc. | V.G. | Good | Fair | Poor |
|---|---|---|---|---|
| 800 | 700 | 600 | 450 | 350 |

## NORTON ARMS CO.
### Mt. Clemens, Michigan
### SEE--Budischowsky

This company manufactured the Budischowsky semi-automatic pistol prior to 1979. They were succeeded by the American Arms & Ammunition Co. after that date, who unsuccessfully continued the production of this pistol for a short time. Values for the Norton and the American Arms versions are considerably lower than for the original pistols.

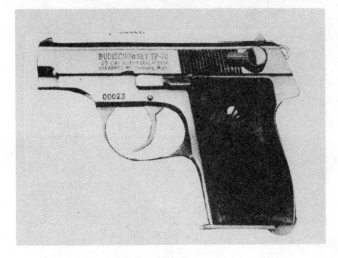

| Exc. | V.G. | Good | Fair | Poor |
|---|---|---|---|---|
| 300 | 250 | 200 | 125 | 100 |

## NORWICH PISTOL CO.
### Norwich, Connecticut

This company was founded in 1875 by Maltby, Curtis & Co., a New York sportings goods company, for the sole purpose of manufacturing inexpensive revolvers. The Norwich Pistol Co. operated as a separate unit and produced a long list of cheaply made revolvers that are all of solid-frame, spur-trigger, single-action design. They are chambered for calibers from .22 rimfire up to .44 rimfire and have various barrel lengths. This company contributed greatly to Norwich, Connecticut's reputation as the Eibar of America. There is little collector interest in these guns and little detailed information available for students of this type of weapon to research. The common denominator for all the products of this company is the patent date of April 23, 1878. This date should appear on all the products of this company regardless of the markings that appear on the weapon. These revolvers are all worth approximately the same, and we list them for reference purposes with a general value. The company went out of business in 1881.

America, Bulldozer, Challenge, Chieftain, Crescent, Defiance, Hartford Arms, Maltby Henley, Metropolitan Police, Nonpariel, Norwich Arms, Parole, Patriot, Pinafore, Prairie King, Protector, Spy, True Blue, U.M.C. Winfield Arms

| Exc. | V.G. | Good | Fair | Poor |
|------|------|------|------|------|
| 150 | 125 | 100 | 75 | 50 |

### O.D.I.
#### Midland Park, New Jersey

**Viking**
This is a semi-automatic pistol patterned after the Colt Model 1911. It is chambered for the .45 ACP cartridge and has a 5" barrel. The pistol is constructed of stainless steel and features the Seecamp double-action conversion. The grips are teakwood, and the magazine holds 7 rounds. This model was manufactured in 1981 and 1982.

| Exc. | V.G. | Good | Fair | Poor |
|------|------|------|------|------|
| 600 | 550 | 450 | 325 | 225 |

**Viking Combat**
This model is similar to the standard Viking but is sized like the Colt Commander, with a 4.24" barrel.

| Exc. | V.G. | Good | Fair | Poor |
|------|------|------|------|------|
| 600 | 550 | 450 | 325 | 225 |

### O.K.
#### Unknown

**O.K. Derringer**
This pocket pistol is chambered for the .22 rimfire cartridge and has a 2.75" barrel that pivots to the side for loading. It has a spur trigger and a brass frame. The barrel is blued and marked "O.K." The grips are walnut. The maker and quantity manufactured are unknown. They were produced in the late 1860's and the early 1870's.

| Exc. | V.G. | Good | Fair | Poor |
|------|------|------|------|------|
| 300 | 250 | 200 | 125 | 90 |

### OBREGON
#### Mexico City, Mexico

**Obregon**
This is a single-action semi-automatic pistol patterned externally after the Colt Model 1911. The internal lockup is considerably different and resembles that of the Steyr. It is chambered for the .45 ACP and has a rounder-appearing slide than the Colt. The barrel length is 5"; and the finish is blued, with checkered walnut grips. The slide is marked "Systema Obregon Cal.

11.35mm." This pistol was manufactured by Fabrica de Armas Mexico in small numbers for commercial sale in Mexico after WWII.

| Exc. | V.G. | Good | Fair | Poor |
|------|------|------|------|------|
| 450 | 400 | 350 | 250 | 175 |

### O'CONNELL, DAVID
#### New York, New York

**Pocket Pistol**
This is a single-shot pistol patterned after the Henry Deringer Philadelphia-type pistol. It is chambered for .41 caliber percussion and has a 2.5" barrel. The mountings are German silver, and the stock is walnut. It was manufactured in the 1850's.

| Exc. | V.G. | Good | Fair | Poor |
|------|------|------|------|------|
| 650 | 550 | 450 | 350 | 250 |

### O'DELL, STEPHEN
#### Natchez, Mississippi

**Pocket Pistol**
This is a Henry Deringer-patterned pistol that is chambered for .34- to .44-caliber percussion. It has a barrel length from 2" to 4", with gold bands inlaid at the breech end. The mountings are German silver, and the stock is walnut. The lock is marked "O'Dell." This is a very collectible maker, and one should be wary of fakes. This pistol was manufactured in the 1850's.

| Exc. | V.G. | Good | Fair | Poor |
|------|------|------|------|------|
| 2250 | 2000 | 1750 | 1400 | 1150 |

### OJANGUREN Y VIDOSA
#### Eibar, Spain

This typical Eibar company produced mediocre firearms from the early 1920's and was forced out of business during the Spanish Civil War.

**Apache**
This model is a typical Eibar Browning copy that is chambered for the 6.35mm cartridge. It is of the typical low quality associated with most Spanish arms of this era. The slide is marked "Pistole Browning Automatica Cal.6.35 Apache." The finish is blued, and the plastic grips have a head with a beret and the word "Apache" molded into them.

| Exc. | V.G. | Good | Fair | Poor |
|------|------|------|------|------|
| 175 | 150 | 125 | 75 | 50 |

**Ojanguren**
This is the trade name this company used to cover the line of revolvers they produced in the 1930's. They produced two in .32 caliber and two chambered for the .38 Special cartridge. They are similar in appearance and have barrel lengths of either 3" or 6". The finishes are blued, and they have plastic grips. One of the .38 caliber models --the "Legitimo Tanque"--is a reasonably well-made gun that was very popular with the Spanish target shooters. These guns have very little collector value and little practical value and are all valued alike.

| Exc. | V.G. | Good | Fair | Poor |
|------|------|------|------|------|
| 150 | 125 | 100 | 75 | 50 |

**Tanque**
This is a blowback-operated semi-automatic chambered for the 6.35mm cartridge. It has a 1.5" barrel and is actually an original design, which was rarely found on Eibar guns of this period. It has an oddly shaped slide, and the barrel is retained by means of a screw in the front of the frame. It has a 6-shot magazine, and the slide is marked "6.35 Tanque Patent." The plastic grips have a tank molded into them and the word "Tanque," as well as the letters "O&V."

| Exc. | V.G. | Good | Fair | Poor |
|------|------|------|------|------|
| 150 | 125 | 100 | 75 | 50 |

## OLD WEST GUN CO.
### Houston, Texas

This was an importer of Western-style reproduction firearms primarily manufactured by Aldo Uberti of Italy. This company purchased the inventory of Allen firearms in 1987 and later that year changed their name to Cimarron Arms. Their offerings are listed in the Uberti section of this book.

## OLYMPIC ARMS, INC.
### Olympia, Washington

**Black Widow**
This is a single-action semi-automatic pistol patterned after the Colt Model 1911. It is reduced in size and chambered for the .45 ACP cartridge. The barrel is 3.9" in length, and the magazine holds 6 rounds. The finish is electroless nickel plate, and the grips are ivory Micarta with a spider scrimshawed on them. The grip strap has finger grooves contoured into them.

| Exc. | V.G. | Good | Fair | Poor |
|------|------|------|------|------|
| 575 | 500 | 450 | 350 | 300 |

**Enforcer**
This is an alloy-framed semi-automatic pistol patterned after the Colt 1911. It has a 3.8" barrel and is chambered for the .45 ACP cartridge. The grip frame is shortened, and the magazine holds 6 rounds. It has adjustable sights, an ambidexstrous safety, and checkered rubber grips. The finishes offered are parkerized, anodized, or electroless nickel plate.

| NIB | Exc. | V.G. | Good | Fair | Poor |
|-----|------|------|------|------|------|
| 630 | 575 | 500 | 425 | 350 | 300 |

**Match Master**
This model is similar to the Enforcer except that it is a full-sized pistol with a 5" barrel and regular-length grip frame, with a 7-round magazine.

| NIB | Exc. | V.G. | Good | Fair | Poor |
|-----|------|------|------|------|------|
| 650 | 600 | 525 | 450 | 375 | 300 |

**SGW Ultra Match**
This is a precision-built version of the AR-15, that is designed for extreme accuracy. It is chambered for the .223 cartridge and has a 20" or 24" heavy match-grade stainless-steel barrel. The carrying handle is milled off, and a scope or target sights are mounted directly at receiver level. It has an adjustable set trigger, and the stock is longer than the original AR-15. It is finished in black and is furnished with scope mounts or (for an additional $130) target sights.

| NIB | Exc. | V.G. | Good | Fair |
|-----|------|------|------|------|
| 1000 | 850 | 750 | 500 | 400 |

## OMEGA
### Harrisburg, Pennsylvania
### Importer--Kassnar

**Over/Under Shotgun**
This model was made in Spain and is chambered for 12, 20, 28 gauge, and .410. It features a boxlock action and 26" or 28" vent-rib barrels. The chokes are varied, and there is a single trigger with extractors. The finish is blued, and the stock is checkered walnut. A deluxe model with better-grade wood is available at 20 percent additional.

| Exc. | V.G. | Good | Fair | Poor |
|------|------|------|------|------|
| 325 | 275 | 250 | 200 | 125 |

**Side X Side Double Barrel Shotgun**
This is a boxlock side-by-side that is chambered for 20 or 28 gauge, as well as .410. The barrels are 26" in length with various choke combinations. This model has double triggers and extractors. The finish is blued, with a hardwood stock. There is a deluxe model in .410 only, with a walnut stock for an additional 10 percent.

| Exc. | V.G. | Good | Fair | Poor |
|------|------|------|------|------|
| 250 | 200 | 150 | 100 | 75 |

**Single Barrel Shotgun**
This is a breakopen single shot that is chambered for 12 and 20 gauge, as well as .410. It is offered with various barrel lengths and chokes and has an extractor. The finish is a matte blue, with a hardwood stock.

| Exc. | V.G. | Good | Fair | Poor |
|------|------|------|------|------|
| 100 | 85 | 65 | 50 | 35 |

## OMEGA
### Eibar, Spain
### SEE--Armero Especialistas

## OMEGA
### Geneseo, Illinois
### Springfield Armory

**Omega Pistol**
This is a high-grade target-type pistol that is patterned after the Colt Model 1911 type pistol, with marked improvements. It is chambered for the .38 Super, 10mm, and the .45 ACP cartridges. The barrel is either 5" or 6" in length and has polygonal rifling. The barrels are furnished either ported or plain and feature a lockup system that eliminates the barrel link and bushing associated with the normal Browning design. This pistol has a dual extractor system, adjustable sights, and Pachmayr grips. It was introduced in 1987.

| NIB | Exc. | V.G. | Good | Fair | Poor |
|-----|------|------|------|------|------|
| 850 | 775  | 675  | 575  | 400  | 300  |

## OMEGA FIREARMS CO.
### Flower Mound, Texas

**Bolt Action Rifle**

This is a bolt-action rifle chambered for various calibers from .25-06 up to .358 Norma Magnum. It has a 22" or 24" barrel and choice of three types of stock--classic, Monte Carlo, and thumbhole sporter. The stocks are two-piece and are made of Claro or English Walnut or laminated. The bolt is octagonal, with a fully enclosed face and a 50-degree lift. It has a fully adjustable trigger and a dual safety system. There were no sights furnished. The magazine is rotary and holds five standard or four belted magnum cartridges. This rifle was discontinued in the mid-1970's.

| Exc. | V.G. | Good | Fair | Poor |
|------|------|------|------|------|
| 750  | 650  | 550  | 400  | 300  |

## OPUS SPORTING ARMS, INC.
### Long Beach, California

**Opus One**

This is a high-grade bolt-action rifle built on a U.S. Repeating Arms Model 70 action. It is chambered for .243, .270, and the .30-06 cartridges and has a 24" barrel. The stock is deluxe hand-checkered walnut, with an ebony pistolgrip cap and forend tip. The accuracy was guaranteed up to 100 yards, and it was furnished with a Halliburton aluminum case. This rifle was manufactured in 1987 and 1988.

| Exc. | V.G. | Good | Fair | Poor |
|------|------|------|------|------|
| 2400 | 2000 | 1750 | 1000 | 800  |

**Opus Two**

This model is similar to the Opus One except that it is chambered for the .7mm Remington Magnum and the .300 Winchester Magnum.

| Exc. | V.G. | Good | Fair | Poor |
|------|------|------|------|------|
| 2400 | 2000 | 1750 | 1000 | 800  |

**Opus Three**

This Magnum version is chambered for the .375 Holland & Holland and the .458 Winchester Magnum.

| Exc. | V.G. | Good | Fair | Poor |
|------|------|------|------|------|
| 2600 | 2250 | 1850 | 1150 | 850  |

## ORBEA & CIA
### Eibar, Spain

**Pocket Pistol**

This is a typical Eibar-quality, blowback-operated semi-automatic pistol chambered for the 6.35mm cartridge. The barrel is 2.5" in length;, and there is a grip safety, but no other safety is used on the pistol. The slide is marked "Orbea y Cia Eibar Espana Pistola Automatica Cal. 6.35." The finish is blued, and the grips are plastic. This pistol was manufactured between the end of WWI and the Spanish Civil War.

| Exc. | V.G. | Good | Fair | Poor |
|------|------|------|------|------|
| 175  | 150  | 125  | 75   | 50   |

## ORTGIES, HEINRICH & CO.
### Erfurt, Germany

**Ortgies Pistol**

This is a blowback-operated, single-action semi-automatic pistol that was chambered originally for the 7.65mm cartridge and later for the 6.35mm as well. There were a number also chambered for the .380 ACP. The 6.35mm version has a 2.75" barrel, and the larger caliber models have a 3.25" barrel. The original model was made by the Ortgies firm. Later the firm of Deutsche Werke bought the rights to produce the pistol, and after 1921 all were made by them. This was a very popular pistol--and well made and finished as well. The only real drawback is the lack of a safety device other than the grip safety. The finish is blued, with walnut grips that have a bronze medallion inlaid with the company logo upon it. The original models are marked "Ortgies & Co. Erfurt." The Deutsche Werke guns are so marked. There were approximately 10,000 of the original production produced between 1918 and 1921, and Deutsche Werke produced many thousands more after 1921.

| Exc. | V.G. | Good | Fair | Poor |
|------|------|------|------|------|
| 275  | 225  | 175  | 125  | 85   |

## ORVIS
### Dallas, Texas

This importer also retails and distributes many foreign sporting arms, as well as other types of sporting equipment. Models labeled "Orvis" would have no particular collector interest and would be valued as shooters by the maker of the firearm in question.

## OSBORN, S.
### Canton, Connecticut

**Underhammer Pistol**

This is a conventional-appearing, underhammer, bootleg-type pistol chambered for .34 caliber percussion. It has a 7" part-octagonal barrel and a brass-trimmed walnut handle. It is marked "S.Osborn/Canton, Conn."

| Exc. | V.G. | Good | Fair | Poor |
|------|------|------|------|------|
| 450 | 400 | 350 | 250 | 175 |

## OSGOOD GUN WORKS
### Norwich, Connecticut

**Duplex Revolver**

This is an oddity in that it is a single-action breakopen revolver that has Over/Under barrels and an 8-shot cylinder that supplies the top barrel. The lower barrel is a single shot and doubles as the center axis pin for the cylinder. The cylinder is chambered for .22 rimfire, and the lower barrel is chambered for the .32 rimfire cartridge. The hammer features a selective fire striker that fires either barrel. The finish is blued or nickel-plated, with round walnut grips. The barrel is marked "Osgood Gun Works-Norwich Conn." They are also marked "Duplex." There were at most a few hundred manufactured in the 1880's.

| Exc. | V.G. | Good | Fair | Poor |
|------|------|------|------|------|
| 550 | 500 | 450 | 350 | 250 |

## OWA
### Vienna, Austria
### Osterreiche Werke Anstalt

**OWA Pocket Pistol**

This is a small, blowback-operated semi-automatic pistol chambered for the .25 ACP cartridge. It was the only pistol that this company produced and was of an original design. The entire slide pivots forward, and the barrel is 2" in length. The name "OWA" is molded into the plastic grips and is not marked elsewhere on the pistol. The finish is blued. There is very little known about this company or their product. This pistol was manufactured between 1920 and 1925.

| Exc. | V.G. | Good | Fair | Poor |
|------|------|------|------|------|
| 250 | 200 | 175 | 100 | 75 |

## P-38
### SEE--German Military

## P.A.F.
### Pretoria, South Africa
### Pretoria Small Arms Factory

**P.A.F. Junior**

This is a blowback-operated semi-automatic pistol that is based on the Browning 1906 design but lacks the grip safety. It has a 2" barrel and a 6-shot magazine. This is a well-made pistol that is blued, with checkered plastic grips that have two crossed cartridges in a wreath molded into them. The slide is marked the same way, with "Junior Verwaardig in Suid Afrika Made in South Africa" stamped on it as well. There were approximately 10,000 manufactured in the early 1950's.

| Exc. | V.G. | Good | Fair | Poor |
|------|------|------|------|------|
| 400 | 350 | 300 | 225 | 150 |

## P.S.M.G. GUN CO.
### Arlington, Massachusetts

**Six In One Supreme**

This is a single-action semi-automatic pistol that is chambered for the .22 l.r., .30 Luger, .38 Super, .38 Special, 9mm, and the .45ACP cartridges with interchangeable-caliber capabilties. The barrel has a solid rib and is offered in 3.5", 5", or 7.5"

lengths. The sights are adjustable, and the finish is blued or satin nickel-plated. This model was introduced in 1988. The caliber conversion kits are valued at $450 per unit.

| NIB | Exc. | V.G. | Good | Fair | Poor |
|-----|------|------|------|------|------|
| 900 | 800  | 650  | 500  | 400  | 350  |

## PTK INTERNATIONAL, INC.
### Atlanta, Georgia
### SEE--Poly-Technologies

## PAGE-LEWIS ARMS CO.
### Chicopee Falls, Massachusetts

**Model A Target**

This is a single-shot rifle chambered for the .22 rimfire cartridge. It has a swinging-block action that is activated by a trigger guard lever. It has a 20" round tapered barrel and open sights. The finish is blued, and the stock and forearm are walnut. This is a lightweight boy's rifle--and not a target rifle as the name states. This well-made rifle was manufactured between 1920 and 1926, when the company was purchased by Stevens Arms Co.

| Exc. | V.G. | Good | Fair | Poor |
|------|------|------|------|------|
| 250  | 225  | 175  | 125  | 100  |

**Model B Sharpshooter**

This model is similar to the Model A except that it has a 24" barrel and a longer forend.

| Exc. | V.G. | Good | Fair | Poor |
|------|------|------|------|------|
| 250  | 225  | 175  | 125  | 100  |

**Model C Olympic**

This is the top of the line, which features a 24" tapered round barrel and a dual front sight with both a bead and a blade. All other features are the same as the Model B.

| Exc. | V.G. | Good | Fair | Poor |
|------|------|------|------|------|
| 300  | 250  | 200  | 150  | 100  |

## PALMER
### Windsor, Vermont
### E. G. Lamson & Co.

**Palmer Bolt Action Carbine**

This is a single shot and the first bolt action accepted for military service. It is chambered for the .50-caliber rimfire cartridge and has a 20" round barrel. It is a full sidelock, with a hammer mounted on the right side that directly strikes the primer. The breech is opened for loading by turning the bolt handle at the rear. There is a walnut half-length stock held on by one barrel band; and the lock is case-colored, with all other metal parts blued. The receiver is marked "Wm. Palmer/Patent/Dec.22, 1863." The lock is marked "G.Lamson & Co./ Windsor, Vt." There were approximately 1,000 manufactured in 1865. They were ordered for use in the Civil War but were delivered after the cease fire. All specimens will be U.S. marked.

| Exc. | V.G. | Good | Fair | Poor |
|------|------|------|------|------|
| 1500 | 1250 | 1000 | 750  | 500  |

## PARA-ORDNANCE MFG. INC.
### Scarborough, Ontario, Canada

**Semi-automatic Pistol**

This model is a single-action semi-automatic pistol patterned after the Colt Model 1911, with a wide alloy frame that is able to accept a double-column 13-round magazine. It is chambered for the .45 ACP cartridge and has a 5" barrel. It was introduced in 1989. The frame is also available for those interested in converting their own Colt- type pistol.

| NIB | Exc. | V.G. | Good | Fair | Poor |
|-----|------|------|------|------|------|
| 650 | 600  | 550  | 475  | 400  | 300  |

## PARDINI
### Italy
### Importer--Fiocchi of America
### Ozark, Missouri

**Standard Target Pistol**

This is a high quality, semi-automatic target pistol chambered for the .22 l.r. cartridge. It has a 4.9" barrel and fully adjustable sights and trigger. The finish is blued, and the adjustable target grips are walnut. This pistol was introduced in 1986. A ladies' model is available that has smaller grips. It is furnished with a locking case.

| NIB | Exc. | V.G. | Good | Fair | Poor |
|-----|------|------|------|------|------|
| 950 | 875  | 700  | 600  | 500  | 375  |

**Rapidfire Pistol**

This is a similar pistol except that it is chambered for the .22 Short cartridge and has an enclosed grip and a lightweight alloy bolt to speed up lock time. The barrel is 5.1" in length, and it is furnished with a locking case.

| NIB | Exc. | V.G. | Good | Fair | Poor |
|-----|------|------|------|------|------|
| 950 | 875  | 700  | 600  | 500  | 375  |

**Centerfire Pistol**

This model is similar in appearance to the Standard model except that it is chambered for the .32 Smith & Wesson Long cartridge and features a recoil shock-absorbing system for stability. It is furnished with a locking case and was introduced in 1986.

| NIB | Exc. | V.G. | Good | Fair | Poor |
|-----|------|------|------|------|------|
| 950 | 875  | 700  | 600  | 500  | 375  |

**Free Pistol**

This single-shot pistol is chambered for the .22 l.r. cartridge. It has a 9" barrel and a sliding rotary bolt action. The finish is blued, and the fully adjustable enclosed grips are walnut. The pistol is furnished with barrel weights and a fitted locking case.

| NIB  | Exc. | V.G. | Good | Fair | Poor |
|------|------|------|------|------|------|
| 1100 | 950  | 800  | 700  | 600  | 450  |

## PARKER
### Springfield, Massachusetts

**Four Shot Pistol**

This is a unique firearm for its time. It is chambered for .33-caliber percussion and has a 4" part-octagonal barrel. There is a magazine that is removable which holds four separate charges contained in the breech. Cocking the hammer aligns the chambers with the barrel. The markings are "Albert Parker/Patent Secured/Springfield, Mass." This is a rare pistol, and the number manufactured is unknown. They were produced in the late 1840's to the early 1850's.

| Exc. | V.G. | Good | Fair | Poor |
|------|------|------|------|------|
| 5500 | 4500 | 3500 | 2750 | 2000 |

## PARKER BROS.
### Meriden, Connecticut

This company was founded by Charles Parker. It evolved from the Parker Snow Brooks Company, a hardware-manufacturing concern in the 1860's. They produced a number of muzzle-loading muskets that were used in the Civil War. In 1868 Parker experimented with a breech-loading, 14-gauge shotgun that was never actually commercially produced. In 1874 Charles King joined the firm and took over the development and design departments. He developed the lifter-type actions that were manufactured over the next few decades. He was also instrumental in developing the first internal-hammer guns for the company. King eventually developed a new bolt system where a true hammerless design was utilized. These hammers were cocked by opening the barrels. This model featured a dollshead extension on the top of the rib that was part of the locking system. This locking system worked so well that it remained a part of the Parker design for the next fifty years. The completed design was finally developed in 1910. Parkers are known as American shotguns, but the early damascus barrels were manufactured in Belgium--and were finished in this Country. There are a number of different grades of Parkers, and they are all extremely collectible. We list them and supply general values but would offer an extreme caution that anyone contemplating a transaction secure a qualified and trustworthy, recommended appraisal, as there have been a number of fakes and upgrades noted. The value of these guns has become so great that to proceed without qualified assistance would be foolhardy.

Examples noted with external hammers and/or damascus barrels are also extremely collectible on today's market and are worth nearly as much as their fluid-steel, hammerless counterparts if they are in very good or excellent condition. We also recommend securing a qualified appraisal on the early damascus guns as well.

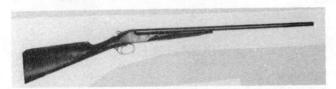

### Trojan
This is Parker's utility-grade gun. It is chambered for 12, 16, or 20 gauge and is offered with various barrel lengths and choke combinations. It was available with either a single or double trigger and extractors. The finish is blued, with a case-colored receiver and a checkered walnut stock. There were approximately 48,000 manufactured. The values given are for 12- or 16-gauge models.
20 Gauge--Add 40 Percent.

| Exc. | V.G. | Good | Fair | Poor |
|---|---|---|---|---|
| 2000 | 1500 | 1150 | 700 | 500 |

### VH
This is Parker's bread-and-butter gun. It is available with all of their offered options and is chambered for 12, 16, 20, and 28 gauge, as well as .410. It is offered with various barrel lengths and choke combinations. The finish is blued, with a case-colored receiver and a checkered walnut stock. It has double triggers and extractors. An automatic-ejector model is known as the VHE and would be worth approximately 40 percent additional. There were approximately 60,000 manufactured. Values furnished are for 12 and 16 gauge.
20 Gauge--Add 45 Percent.
28 Gauge--Add 100 Percent.
.410--Add 500 Percent.

| Exc. | V.G. | Good | Fair | Poor |
|---|---|---|---|---|
| 2500 | 1650 | 1250 | 800 | 600 |

### PH
This version is similar to the VH but was not produced in .410. Most of the PH models have damascus barrels. The values shown here are for fluid-steel barrels. There is a PHE model with automatic ejectors available, that would be worth approximately 40 percent additional. There were approximately 8,500 PH models manufactured. Values shown are for 12- and 16-gauge versions.
20 Gauge--Add 45 Percent.
28 Gauge--Add 100 Percent.

| Exc. | V.G. | Good | Fair | Poor |
|---|---|---|---|---|
| 3200 | 2400 | 1250 | 850 | 500 |

### GH
This model is similar to the VH but is moderately ornamented. It was available with all options and has barrels that are marked, "Parker Special Steel." There were approximately 28,500 manufactured. An automatic-ejector model known as the GHE

is available and would add approximately 35 percent to the values shown. Values are for 12-gauge version only.
16 Gauge--Add 15 Percent.
20 Gauge--Add 40 Percent.
28 Gauge--Add 75 Percent.
.410--Add 500 Percent.

| Exc. | V.G. | Good | Fair | Poor |
|---|---|---|---|---|
| 4000 | 3500 | 2000 | 1150 | 750 |

### DH
This version was the first of the higher-grade guns. It is moderately engraved and exhibits a very high degree of workmanship. The walnut used is very nicely figured. There were approximately 48,000 manufactured. An automatic ejector model known as the DHE is available and would add approximately 35 percent to the values given. The values furnished reflect the 12-gauge chambering.
16 Gauge--Add 10 Percent.
20 Gauge--Add 25 Percent.
28 Gauge--Add 100 Percent.
.410--Add 700 Percent.

| Exc. | V.G. | Good | Fair | Poor |
|---|---|---|---|---|
| 5000 | 4500 | 3000 | 1400 | 800 |

### CH
This version features Acme steel barrels and is similar to the DH model in ornamentation. A CHE model with automatic ejectors is available and would add approximately 35 percent to the values given. There were approximately 5,000 manufactured. Values shown are for 12-gauge chambering.
16 Gauge--Add 5 Percent.
20 Gauge--Add 25 Percent.
28 Gauge--Add 350 Percent.
.410--Add 800 Percent.

| Exc. | V.G. | Good | Fair | Poor |
|---|---|---|---|---|
| 6500 | 5500 | 4000 | 2000 | 1000 |

### BH
This is a very high-grade shotgun that is offered with four distinctive engraving styles. It features Acme steel barrels and is available with automatic ejectors as the model BHE, which would be worth approximately 35 percent additional. There were approximately 13,000 manufactured. The values given are for the 12-gauge chambering.
16 Gauge--Add 5 Percent.
20 Gauge--Add 40 Percent.
28 Gauge--Add 350 Percent.
.410--Add 550 Percent.

| Exc. | V.G. | Good | Fair | Poor |
|---|---|---|---|---|
| 9000 | 7500 | 5000 | 3000 | 1600 |

### AH
This is a highly ornamented shotgun that features very high quality workmanship and materials. It is rarely encountered on today's market. It features Acme steel barrels. There is an automatic-ejector version known as the AHE that would add approximately 30 percent to the value. There were approximately 5,500 manufactured. The values are for the 12-gauge chambering.
16 Gauge--Add 10 Percent.
20 Gauge--Add 40 Percent.
28 Gauge--Add 125 Percent.
.410--Add 300 Percent.

| Exc. | V.G. | Good | Fair | Poor |
|---|---|---|---|---|
| 25000 | 20000 | 12500 | 6500 | 3500 |

### AAH

This is an extremely high-grade gun that is elaborately orna-mented. It features the highest-grade materials and workman-ship available. Early models are furnished with Whitworth bar-rels; later ones feature Peerless barrels. An automatic-ejector model, the AAHE, is available and would add approximately 30 percent to the value. There were only 340 AAH models manu-factured. Values given are for the 12-gauge chambering. It was not offered in .410.

16 Gauge--Add 10 Percent.
20 Gauge--Add 40 Percent.
28 Gauge--Add 250 Percent.

| Exc. | V.G. | Good | Fair | Poor |
|---|---|---|---|---|
| 35000 | 27500 | 18500 | 9000 | 5000 |

### A-1 Special

This totally engraved version was completely custom-ordered. An example was not allowed to leave the factory before it was inspected by the company president. This is rated by some ex-perts as the finest shotgun ever manufactured anywhere. There were only 320 manufactured. This firearm is so rare and desir-able that most of us will only dream of seeing one. Values are for the 12-gauge chambering. A .410 version was not offered.

16 Gauge--Add 5 Percent.
20 Gauge--Add 40 Percent.
28 Gauge--Add 100 Percent.

| Exc. | V.G. | Good | Fair | Poor |
|---|---|---|---|---|
| 60000 | 50000 | 35000 | 13500 | 9000 |

### Single Barrel Trap

These break-open, single-shot, single-barrel trap guns were manufactured to a high degree of quality. They feature a boxlock action with an automatic ejector. They are chambered for 12 gauge only and are offered with a 30", 32", or 34" barrel with any choke. The finish is blued, with a select, checkered walnut stock. The differences in the grades are the degree of ornamentation and the quality of the materials and workman-ship utilized in their construction. Although they are rarer than the side-by-side, double-barrel models, they are nowhere near as collectible or valuable. We still recommend securing a quali-fied, individual appraisal if a transaction is contemplated.

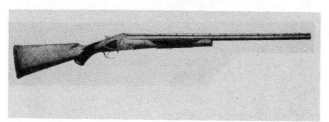

#### S.C. Grade
| Exc. | V.G. | Good | Fair | Poor |
|---|---|---|---|---|
| 2500 | 1750 | 1250 | 850 | 500 |

#### S.B. Grade
| Exc. | V.G. | Good | Fair | Poor |
|---|---|---|---|---|
| 3500 | 2750 | 2250 | 1000 | 750 |

#### S.A. Grade
| Exc. | V.G. | Good | Fair | Poor |
|---|---|---|---|---|
| 5000 | 3750 | 2500 | 1400 | 900 |

#### S.A.A. Grade
| Exc. | V.G. | Good | Fair | Poor |
|---|---|---|---|---|
| 7000 | 4750 | 3000 | 1950 | 1100 |

#### S.A-1 Special Grade
| Exc. | V.G. | Good | Fair | Poor |
|---|---|---|---|---|
| 10000 | 7500 | 5000 | 3200 | 2000 |

### Under Lifter Hammer Gun

This was the earliest commercial Parker that is chambered for various gauges and features damascus barrels and external hammers. The action is opened by means of a lifter located in front of the triggerguard protruding from the bottom of the ac-tion. These guns have become quite collectible as of late and are becoming increasingly more valuable. They are often en-countered in the large 10-gauge version.

| Exc. | V.G. | Good | Fair | Poor |
|---|---|---|---|---|
| 1000 | 850 | 750 | 500 | 400 |

## PARKER FIELD & SONS
### London, England

**Gas Seal Revolver**

This is a large, well-made revolver chambered for .42-caliber percussion. It has a 6" barrel and a 8-shot full- fluted cylinder. The hammer is centrally mounted and quite ornate in appear-ance. There is a loading lever under the barrel. The finish is blued and case-colored, with checkered walnut grips. This pis-tol was manufactured in the 1850's.

| Exc. | V.G. | Good | Fair | Poor |
|---|---|---|---|---|
| 1500 | 1250 | 950 | 650 | 450 |

## PARKER HALE LTD.
### Birmingham, England

**S&W Victory Conversion**

This is a Smith & Wesson Victory Model revolver that was con-verted to .22 rimfire by Parker Hale after WWII. It has a 4" barrel, and the cylinder holds 6 shots. The finish is blued, and the grips are checkered walnut.

| Exc. | V.G. | Good | Fair | Poor |
|---|---|---|---|---|
| 250 | 200 | 150 | 100 | 75 |

**Model 1200**

This is a bolt-action rifle chambered for many popular calibers between .22-250 and .300 Winchester Magnum. It has a 24" barrel with open sights and is blued, with a skip line checkered walnut stock.

| NIB | Exc. | V.G. | Good | Fair | Poor |
|---|---|---|---|---|---|
| 700 | 600 | 450 | 400 | 350 | 300 |

**Model 1100 Lightweight**

This Model is similar to the Model 1200 except that it has a 22" barrel in a lighter configuration. It has a 4-shot magazine and was introduced in 1985.

| NIB | Exc. | V.G. | Good | Fair | Poor |
|---|---|---|---|---|---|
| 600 | 500 | 400 | 350 | 300 | 250 |

**Model 81 Classic**

This model is a classic-styled bolt action that is chambered for 11 calibers between .22-250 and 7mm Remington Magnum. It has a 24" barrel with open sights. The finish is blued, and the walnut stock is hand-checkered. It was introduced in 1985.

| NIB | Exc. | V.G. | Good | Fair | Poor |
|---|---|---|---|---|---|
| 875 | 750 | 600 | 500 | 400 | 350 |

**Model 81 African**

This model is similar to the Model 81 Classic except that it is chambered for the .375 Holland & Holland cartridge. It was introduced in 1986.

| NIB | Exc. | V.G. | Good | Fair | Poor |
|---|---|---|---|---|---|
| 1200 | 950 | 800 | 700 | 600 | 500 |

**Model 84 Target**

This is a match-grade bolt-action rifle chambered for the .308 cartridge. It has target-adjustable sights and an adjustable cheekpiece on the walnut stock.

| NIB | Exc. | V.G. | Good | Fair | Poor |
|---|---|---|---|---|---|
| 1300 | 1000 | 900 | 750 | 650 | 550 |

## Model 85 Sniper
This Model is similar to the Model 84 Target except that it is furnished with a mounted scope and a bipod. It was imported in 1986 only.

| Exc. | V.G. | Good | Fair | Poor |
|---|---|---|---|---|
| 1700 | 1550 | 1050 | 800 | 700 |

## Model 640E Shotgun
This is a side-by-side double-barrel shotgun chambered for 12, 16, or 20 gauge. It has a boxlock action and is available in various barrel lengths and choke combinations. It has double triggers and extractors. The barrel features a concave rib. The barrels are blued; and the receiver, silver-finished. The straight-grip stock is hand-checkered walnut. This Model was introduced in 1986.

| NIB | Exc. | V.G. | Good | Fair | Poor |
|---|---|---|---|---|---|
| 575 | 500 | 450 | 400 | 300 | 225 |

## Model 640A
This Model is similar to the 640E, with a pistolgrip stock, single trigger, and a beavertail forend. It was introduced in 1986.

| NIB | Exc. | V.G. | Good | Fair | Poor |
|---|---|---|---|---|---|
| 675 | 600 | 550 | 500 | 400 | 325 |

## Model 645E
This is a moderately engraved version of the Model 640E.

| NIB | Exc. | V.G. | Good | Fair | Poor |
|---|---|---|---|---|---|
| 700 | 625 | 575 | 525 | 425 | 350 |

## Model 670E
This is a custom-order model that has a full sidelock action. It is highly engraved and has a silver-plated receiver. This Model was introduced in 1986.

| NIB | Exc. | V.G. | Good | Fair | Poor |
|---|---|---|---|---|---|
| 3000 | 2750 | 2250 | 1750 | 1250 | 950 |

## Model 680E-XXV
This Model is similar to the Model 670E except that the side plates are case-colored and the barrel length is 25" only.

| NIB | Exc. | V.G. | Good | Fair | Poor |
|---|---|---|---|---|---|
| 3000 | 2750 | 2250 | 1750 | 1250 | 950 |

# PARKER REPRODUCTIONS
## Japan
### Importer--Regent Chemical & Research
### Middlesex, New Jersey
This high-grade reproduction of the Parker Bros. side-by-side shotgun is manufactured by Winchester in Japan and is being distributed by Parker Reproductions of Webb City, Missouri. They are truly authentic reproductions.

## D Grade
This side-by-side is chambered for 12, 20, and 28 gauge and is an authentic reproduction of the original Parker D Grade gun. It is furnished with a fitted leather and canvas case and snap caps. This model was introduced in 1986.

| NIB | Exc. | V.G. | Good | Fair | Poor |
|---|---|---|---|---|---|
| 3000 | 2750 | 2050 | 1650 | 1300 | 1050 |

## DHE Grade Steel Shot Special
This model is similar to the D Grade except that it has reinforced chrome-lined barrels and 3" chambers.

| NIB | Exc. | V.G. | Good | Fair | Poor |
|---|---|---|---|---|---|
| 3100 | 2800 | 2100 | 1700 | 1400 | 1100 |

## B Grade Limited Edition
This model is chambered for 12, 20, and 28 gauge, as well as .410. It is an authentic reproduction of the Parker B Grade SxS. The engraving is extensive as on the original, and there were only 100 produced in 1987.

| NIB | Exc. | V.G. | Good | Fair | Poor |
|---|---|---|---|---|---|
| 4000 | 3500 | 2950 | 2250 | 1750 | 1250 |

## A-1 Special
This is a replica of the top-of-the-line production Parker gun. It is a very well executed firearm and is furnished cased with all accessories. It was introduced in 1988.

| NIB | Exc. | V.G. | Good | Fair | Poor |
|---|---|---|---|---|---|
| 9000 | 8000 | 6500 | 5000 | 4000 | 3250 |

# PEABODY
## Providence, Rhode Island
### Providence Tool Company

## Peabody Rifle
This is a single-shot, breech-loading rifle that is activated by the combination triggerguard and breechlever. It is chambered for the .443, .43 Spanish, .45 Peabody rimfire, .50 rimfire, .45-70, and the .50-70 centerfire cartridges. It is also chambered for a few European cartridges. The barrel is 33" in length and features a front sight that also acts as a bayonet lug. The receiver is marked "Peabody's Patent July 22, 1862/ Mann'f'd by Providence Tool Co. Prov. R.I." The finish is blued, with a case-colored receiver and a full-length walnut stock held on by two barrel bands. A carbine version with a 20" barrel, one barrel band, and a sling ring mounted on the left side of the frame is also available and would be worth approximately 50 percent additional. These weapons are most desirable when chambered for the .45-70 or the .50-70 cartridges. They would be worth approximately 10 percent additional in these calibers. They were manufactured in the late 1860's and 1870's.

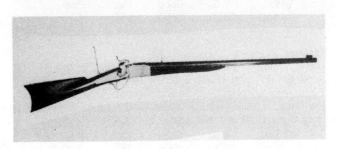

| Exc. | V.G. | Good | Fair | Poor |
|---|---|---|---|---|
| 750 | 650 | 550 | 400 | 300 |

## Sporting Rifle
This is a single-shot, breech-loading rifle that was chambered for the .44 rimfire and .45-70, as well as other calibers available at the time. It was offered with either a 26" or 28" round barrel in various weights, with the heavier models more desirable. The frame is marked, "Peabody's Patent, July 22, 1862/Man'f'd by Providence Tool Co., Prov. R.I." The finish is blued, with a case-colored receiver and a select walnut stock. It was manufactured between 1866 and 1875. This rifle was available with several finish options and should be individually appraised if in doubt.

| Exc. | V.G. | Good | Fair | Poor |
|---|---|---|---|---|
| 1000 | 850 | 750 | 500 | 400 |

## Peabody-Martini Rifles

These are high-grade, sporting and target, single-shot, breech-loading rifles. Their falling-block Martini actions are activated by a lever behind the triggerguard. They are chambered for a number of large bore cartridges that were popular during this era and are available in a number of different models that are readily identified as they are engraved in large Gothic letters on the left side of the frame. The right side of the frame is marked, "Peabody & Martini Patents." The barrel was marked, "Manufactured by the Providence Tool Co. Providence R.I. U.S.A." These rifles were manufactured between 1875 and the mid-1890's.

### Creedmoor

This version is chambered for the .40-90 and the .44-100 cartridges. It features a 32" part-octagonal barrel with a two-position Vernier peepsight mounted at the heel of the butt and the tang. It features a globe front sight with a wind gauge and spirit level. It features a select, checkered walnut stock with a shotgun-type buttplate.

| Exc. | V.G. | Good | Fair | Poor |
|------|------|------|------|------|
| 2500 | 2250 | 1850 | 1100 | 850 |

### Creedmoor Mid-Range

This version is chambered for the .40-70 and the .40-90 cartridges. It features a 28" part-octagonal barrel and has a Vernier tang sight with a wind gauge front sight. The stock is checkered, select walnut with a crescent buttplate.

| Exc. | V.G. | Good | Fair | Poor |
|------|------|------|------|------|
| 1850 | 1650 | 1250 | 850 | 600 |

### What Cheer

This is a straight-stock version of the long-range Creedmoor rifle.

| Exc. | V.G. | Good | Fair | Poor |
|------|------|------|------|------|
| 2500 | 2250 | 1850 | 1100 | 850 |

### What Cheer Mid-Range

This is a straight-stock version of the Mid-Range Creedmoor rifle.

| Exc. | V.G. | Good | Fair | Poor |
|------|------|------|------|------|
| 1850 | 1650 | 1250 | 850 | 600 |

### Kill Deer

This is a Martini-action sporting rifle chambered for the .45-70 cartridge. It is offered with a 28" or 30" part-octagonal barrel. It features a peepsight with interchangeable globe front sights. The finish is blued, with a case-colored receiver and a plain straight-grip stock with a shotgun-type buttplate.

| Exc. | V.G. | Good | Fair | Poor |
|------|------|------|------|------|
| 1750 | 1500 | 1000 | 750 | 500 |

## PEAVY, A. J.
### South Montville, Maine

### Knife-Pistol

This strange item consists of a folding knife with a brass single-shot pistol barrel concealed in the handle. It is chambered for .22 caliber rimfire and is quite heavy as, with the exception of the blade and the essential steel mechanical parts, the construction is all brass. The hammer resembles a second blade; and when it is cocked, a folding trigger snaps into position for firing. The markings are "A.J.Peavy-Pat.Sept.5,'65 & Mar.27,'66." The number manufactured is unknown, but they were produced between 1865 and 1870.

| Exc. | V.G. | Good | Fair | Poor |
|------|------|------|------|------|
| 1000 | 850 | 750 | 500 | 400 |

## PECARE & SMITH
### New York, New York

### Pepperbox

This is a 4-shot, pepperbox-type revolving arm that is chambered for .28 caliber percussion. It has a bar hammer and a folding trigger, and the barrel cluster is 4" in length. The lock work is double-action, and the frame is brass with browned barrels and walnut grips. The barrel is marked "Pecare & Smith," and there is a front sight pin on each barrel. The frame has broad scroll engraving. These Pepperboxes were manufactured in the late 1840's to the early 1850's.

| Exc. | V.G. | Good | Fair | Poor |
|------|------|------|------|------|
| 1750 | 1500 | 1250 | 900 | 650 |

## PEDERSEN CUSTOM GUNS
### North Haven, Connecticut

This was a division of the O. F. Mossberg Company that operated between 1973 and 1975. They were engaged in the business of producing a higher grade of firearm than the standard Mossberg line.

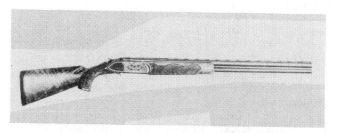

### Model 4000 Shotgun

This is essentially a Mossberg Model 500 slide-action shotgun that was modified into a higher-grade firearm. It is offered in 12 and 20 gauge, as well as .410. It has 26", 28", or 30" vent-rib barrels with various chokes. The receiver is floral engraved and blued, and the select walnut stock is hand-checkered. This model was manufactured in 1975.

| Exc. | V.G. | Good | Fair | Poor |
|------|------|------|------|------|
| 450 | 375 | 300 | 250 | 200 |

### Model 4500

This model is similar to the Model 4000 except that it features a lesser degree of ornamentation.

| Exc. | V.G. | Good | Fair | Poor |
|------|------|------|------|------|
| 400 | 350 | 275 | 225 | 175 |

### Model 1500

This is an Over/Under shotgun chambered for 12 gauge with a 3" chamber. It has 26", 28", or 30" vent-rib barrels with various choke combinations. It features a boxlock action, with automatic ejectors and a single-selective trigger. The finish is blued, and the walnut stock is hand-checkered. It was manufactured between 1973 and 1975.

| Exc. | V.G. | Good | Fair | Poor |
|------|------|------|------|------|
| 750 | 600 | 500 | 400 | 300 |

### Model 1000

This version of the Model 1500 features more engraving and silver inlays. It has a better grade of walnut and is available in two versions that differ only in the degree of ornamentation. This Model was manufactured between 1973 and 1975.

### Grade I

| Exc. | V.G. | Good | Fair | Poor |
|------|------|------|------|------|
| 2250 | 2000 | 1750 | 1450 | 1300 |

### Grade II

| Exc. | V.G. | Good | Fair | Poor |
|------|------|------|------|------|
| 1850 | 1500 | 1350 | 1150 | 950 |

## Model 200

This side-by-side double-barrelled shotgun is chambered for 12 and 20 gauge. It has 26", 28", or 30" barrels with various choke combinations. It has a boxlock action, with automatic ejectors and a single-selective trigger. There are two versions that differ only in the degree of ornamentation. This Model is blued, with a high-grade, hand-checkered walnut stock. This Model was manufactured in 1973 and 1974.

### Grade I

| Exc. | V.G. | Good | Fair | Poor |
|---|---|---|---|---|
| 2500 | 2000 | 1750 | 1250 | 1000 |

### Grade II

| Exc. | V.G. | Good | Fair | Poor |
|---|---|---|---|---|
| 2250 | 1850 | 1500 | 1000 | 800 |

## Model 2500

This is a utility model, side-by-side shotgun chambered for 12 and 20 gauge. It has 26" or 28" barrels with various choke combinations, double triggers, automatic ejectors, and a boxlock action. The finish is blued, and the hand-checkered stock is walnut.

| Exc. | V.G. | Good | Fair | Poor |
|---|---|---|---|---|
| 450 | 400 | 350 | 275 | 200 |

## Model 3000

This bolt-action rifle is chambered for .270 through .338 Magnum. It was built on a Mossberg 810 action and has either a 22" or a 24" barrel with open sights. There are three grades available that differ only in the degree of engraving and grade of walnut used for the hand-checkered stock.

### Grade III Plain

| Exc. | V.G. | Good | Fair | Poor |
|---|---|---|---|---|
| 550 | 475 | 400 | 350 | 300 |

### Grade II

| Exc. | V.G. | Good | Fair | Poor |
|---|---|---|---|---|
| 650 | 575 | 500 | 450 | 400 |

### Grade I

| Exc. | V.G. | Good | Fair | Poor |
|---|---|---|---|---|
| 1000 | 800 | 650 | 550 | 475 |

## Model 4700

This is a higher-grade version of the Mossberg Model 472 chambered for the .30-30 or the .35 Remington cartridges. It has a 24" barrel with a 5-shot tubular magazine and open sights. The finish is blued, and the stock is walnut.

| Exc. | V.G. | Good | Fair | Poor |
|---|---|---|---|---|
| 250 | 200 | 150 | 125 | 100 |

# PERAZZI
### Brescia, Italy
### Importer--Perazzi USA, Inc.
### Monrovia, California

This company is known primarily as a manufacturer of high-grade competition shotguns. In the past they were imported by Winchester and Ithaca, but they have developed their own distribution facilities and have expanded their product line to include sporting arms.

## Competition One Trap

This is a single-shot, break-open shotgun chambered for 12 gauge. It is offered with a 30" or 32" vent-rib, full-choke barrel. The finish is blued, with a hand-checkered, select walnut stock. This is a high-grade trap gun furnished with a fitted case.

| Exc. | V.G. | Good | Fair | Poor |
|---|---|---|---|---|
| 1700 | 1500 | 1200 | 850 | 650 |

## Competition One O/U Trap

This is an Over/Under double-barrel version of the Competition One single shot.

| Exc. | V.G. | Good | Fair | Poor |
|---|---|---|---|---|
| 1500 | 1350 | 1000 | 750 | 550 |

## MX-8

This is a high-grade Over/Under trap gun chambered for 12 gauge. It is offered with 30" or 32" vent-rib barrels choked full and modified. It has a boxlock action and features a non-selective single trigger with an automatic ejector. The finish is blued, with a checkered walnut trap-type stock with recoil pad. It was furnished with a fitted case and was introduced in 1969.

| Exc. | V.G. | Good | Fair | Poor |
|---|---|---|---|---|
| 4000 | 3500 | 2750 | 2000 | 1500 |

## MX-8 Combo

This version is similar to the MX-8 with the inclusion of a single barrel that is 32" or 34" in length. It has a competition vent rib and is full-choked. It was introduced in 1973.

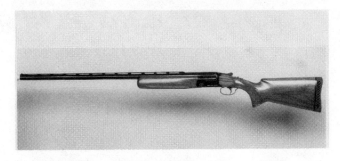

| Exc. | V.G. | Good | Fair | Poor |
|---|---|---|---|---|
| 6000 | 5000 | 3500 | 2750 | 2000 |

## Mirage

This version is similar to the MX-8, with a tapered competition rib.

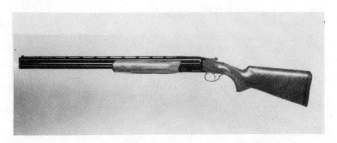

| Exc. | V.G. | Good | Fair | Poor |
|---|---|---|---|---|
| 3800 | 3000 | 2500 | 1750 | 1250 |

## Mirage Skeet

This version is offered with a 28" barrel, skeet-choked. It has an integral muzzle-break.

| Exc. | V.G. | Good | Fair | Poor |
|---|---|---|---|---|
| 3800 | 3000 | 2500 | 1750 | 1250 |

## MT-6

This is a trap-grade competition gun chambered for 12 gauge. It has either a 30" or 32" barrel with interchangeable choke tubes. It features a competition-type vent rib, a boxlock action, and automatic ejectors. It has a single trigger. The finish is blued, with a checkered walnut stock. It was discontinued in 1983.

| Exc. | V.G. | Good | Fair | Poor |
|---|---|---|---|---|
| 3500 | 2750 | 2250 | 1500 | 1000 |

## Light Game Model

This is a field-grade Over/Under shotgun chambered for 12 gauge. It has 27.5" vent-rib barrels with various choke combinations. It features a boxlock action with automatic ejectors and a single trigger. The finish is blued, with a checkered walnut stock. It was manufactured between 1972 and 1974.

| Exc. | V.G. | Good | Fair | Poor |
|---|---|---|---|---|
| 1500 | 1250 | 1000 | 800 | 650 |

Perazzi has expanded its line recently to include a great many new shotguns, both in the competition and hunting configuration. We list them broken down under their basic headings and supply general values. The models differ in value chiefly due to the amount of ornamentation and the quality of materials and workmanship utilized in their construction. It would be advisable for anyone contemplating a transaction on these new and very high-grade guns to contact the importer or secure a qualified appraisal if a transaction is contemplated.

## Single Barrel Trap Shotguns

These are high-grade, break-open, single-barrel shotguns manufactured for the sophisticated trapshooting competitor. They are chambered for 12 gauge and feature 32" or 34" barrels with a high competition rib. They have a boxlock action with automatic ejector. The finish is blued, with a select, checkered walnut stock. They are all currently manufactured.

### MX-3

| NIB | Exc. | V.G. | Good | Fair | Poor |
|---|---|---|---|---|---|
| 3500 | 3000 | 2250 | 2000 | 1500 | 1250 |

### TMX Special

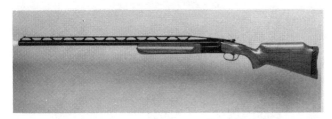

| NIB | Exc. | V.G. | Good | Fair | Poor |
|---|---|---|---|---|---|
| 3700 | 3200 | 2500 | 2200 | 1700 | 1400 |

### TM1 Special--Adjustable Trigger

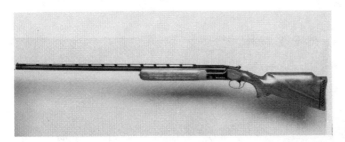

| NIB | Exc. | V.G. | Good | Fair | Poor |
|---|---|---|---|---|---|
| 3700 | 3200 | 2500 | 2200 | 1700 | 1400 |

### MX 3L--Engraving

| NIB | Exc. | V.G. | Good | Fair | Poor |
|---|---|---|---|---|---|
| 4400 | 3850 | 3000 | 2500 | 1950 | 1650 |

### MX 8 Special

| NIB | Exc. | V.G. | Good | Fair | Poor |
|---|---|---|---|---|---|
| 5000 | 4450 | 3650 | 3000 | 2450 | 1950 |

### Grand America Special

| NIB | Exc. | V.G. | Good | Fair | Poor |
|---|---|---|---|---|---|
| 5000 | 4450 | 3650 | 3000 | 2450 | 1950 |

### MX3S SC3

| NIB | Exc. | V.G. | Good | Fair | Poor |
|---|---|---|---|---|---|
| 7000 | 6250 | 5500 | 4250 | 3250 | 2250 |

### MX3 SCO--Heavily Engraved, Coin-Finished

| NIB | Exc. | V.G. | Good | Fair | Poor |
|---|---|---|---|---|---|
| 10000 | 8500 | 7500 | 5650 | 4500 | 3500 |

### TMXS SCO

| NIB | Exc. | V.G. | Good | Fair | Poor |
|---|---|---|---|---|---|
| 10000 | 8500 | 7500 | 5650 | 4500 | 3500 |

### MX3 Gold--Gold Inlaid Gamescenes

| NIB | Exc. | V.G. | Good | Fair | Poor |
|---|---|---|---|---|---|
| 11500 | 10000 | 8500 | 6500 | 5500 | 4500 |

### TMXS Gold--Top-of-the-Line Single Barrel

| NIB | Exc. | V.G. | Good | Fair | Poor |
|---|---|---|---|---|---|
| 11750 | 10500 | 9000 | 7000 | 6000 | 5000 |

## Over/Under Combination Trap Shotguns

This series of currently imported competition firearms is chambered for 12 gauge and is offered with a single 32" or 34" barrel, as well as a set of Over/Under barrels in 29.5" or 31.5" lengths. They both feature high-post competition ribs and trap chokings. These are high-grade guns, and the models offered vary in the amount of ornamentation and quality of workmanship and materials utilized in their construction. They all have checkered walnut stocks and are currently imported.

### MX 3 Combo

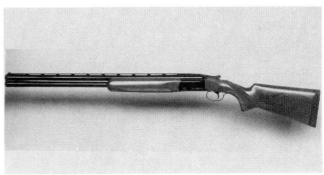

| NIB | Exc. | V.G. | Good | Fair | Poor |
|---|---|---|---|---|---|
| 5000 | 4250 | 3500 | 3000 | 2450 | 1850 |

### MX 3L Combo

| NIB | Exc. | V.G. | Good | Fair | Poor |
|---|---|---|---|---|---|
| 6500 | 5600 | 4500 | 3750 | 3000 | 2500 |

### MX 8 Special Combo

| NIB | Exc. | V.G. | Good | Fair | Poor |
|---|---|---|---|---|---|
| 7000 | 6250 | 5000 | 4250 | 3500 | 3000 |

### Grand America Special Combo

| NIB | Exc. | V.G. | Good | Fair | Poor |
|---|---|---|---|---|---|
| 7000 | 6250 | 5000 | 4250 | 3500 | 3000 |

**DB 81 Combo**

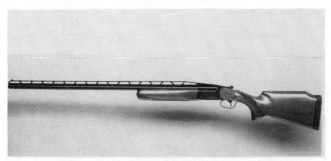

| NIB | Exc. | V.G. | Good | Fair | Poor |
|-----|------|------|------|------|------|
| 7000 | 6250 | 5000 | 4250 | 3500 | 3000 |

**DB 81S SC3 Combo**

| NIB | Exc. | V.G. | Good | Fair | Poor |
|-----|------|------|------|------|------|
| 10500 | 9000 | 7500 | 6000 | 4500 | 3750 |

**MX3 Gold Combo**

| NIB | Exc. | V.G. | Good | Fair | Poor |
|-----|------|------|------|------|------|
| 14500 | 13000 | 11500 | 9500 | 8000 | 5500 |

**SCOS Combo**

| NIB | Exc. | V.G. | Good | Fair | Poor |
|-----|------|------|------|------|------|
| 16000 | 14000 | 12000 | 10000 | 8500 | 7500 |

**SCOS Gold Combo**

| NIB | Exc. | V.G. | Good | Fair | Poor |
|-----|------|------|------|------|------|
| 17500 | 15500 | 13500 | 11000 | 9500 | 8500 |

**SCO Sideplate Combo**

| NIB | Exc. | V.G. | Good | Fair | Poor |
|-----|------|------|------|------|------|
| 22000 | 18500 | 15000 | 12500 | 11000 | 9500 |

**SCO Gold Sideplate Combo**

| NIB | Exc. | V.G. | Good | Fair | Poor |
|-----|------|------|------|------|------|
| 25000 | 22500 | 17500 | 15000 | 12500 | 10500 |

## Over/Under Hunting Guns

These Over/Under shotguns are designed for sporting purposes. They are chambered for 12, 20, and 28 gauge, as well as .410. They are offered with 26", 26.75", or 27.75" barrels with various choke combinations. They feature single-selective triggers and automatic ejectors. They are basically boxlock guns, with the two highest-grade versions featuring full sidelocks. The difference in the models offered is basically the degree of ornamentation as well as the quality of materials and workmanship utilized in their construction. They are currently imported.

**MX 5**

| NIB | Exc. | V.G. | Good | Fair | Poor |
|-----|------|------|------|------|------|
| 3250 | 2850 | 2500 | 2000 | 1500 | 1200 |

**MX 3**

| NIB | Exc. | V.G. | Good | Fair | Poor |
|-----|------|------|------|------|------|
| 3750 | 3250 | 3000 | 2500 | 2000 | 1750 |

**MX 12**

| NIB | Exc. | V.G. | Good | Fair | Poor |
|-----|------|------|------|------|------|
| 4500 | 4000 | 3750 | 3000 | 2500 | 2000 |

**SC3--Silver-Plated, Gamescene-Engraved**

| NIB | Exc. | V.G. | Good | Fair | Poor |
|-----|------|------|------|------|------|
| 6400 | 5750 | 5000 | 4250 | 3500 | 2750 |

**MX 12 SC3**

| NIB | Exc. | V.G. | Good | Fair | Poor |
|-----|------|------|------|------|------|
| 8000 | 7000 | 6000 | 5000 | 3500 | 3000 |

**MX 20 SC3**

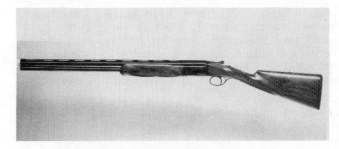

| NIB | Exc. | V.G. | Good | Fair | Poor |
|-----|------|------|------|------|------|
| 8000 | 7000 | 6000 | 5000 | 3500 | 3000 |

**MX 3C Gold--Gold-Inlaid Gamescenes**

| NIB | Exc. | V.G. | Good | Fair | Poor |
|-----|------|------|------|------|------|
| 12500 | 11500 | 9500 | 7500 | 5500 | 4500 |

**MX 12 Gold--Best-Grade Boxlock**

| NIB | Exc. | V.G. | Good | Fair | Poor |
|-----|------|------|------|------|------|
| 15000 | 12750 | 11500 | 9500 | 7500 | 6000 |

**MX 20 Gold--Best-Grade Small-Bore Boxlock**

| NIB | Exc. | V.G. | Good | Fair | Poor |
|-----|------|------|------|------|------|
| 15000 | 12750 | 11500 | 9500 | 7500 | 6000 |

**MX 12 SCO Sideplate**

| NIB | Exc. | V.G. | Good | Fair | Poor |
|-----|------|------|------|------|------|
| 19000 | 17500 | 15000 | 12500 | 10000 | 8500 |

**MX 12 Gold Sideplate--Gold-Inlaid Gamescenes**

| NIB | Exc. | V.G. | Good | Fair | Poor |
|-----|------|------|------|------|------|
| 22000 | 20000 | 17500 | 15000 | 12500 | 10000 |

**SHO--Full Sidelock Gun**

| NIB | Exc. | V.G. | Good | Fair | Poor |
|-----|------|------|------|------|------|
| 27500 | 25000 | 20000 | 17500 | 15000 | 12500 |

**SHO Gold--Gold-Inlaid Sidelock Gun**

| NIB | Exc. | V.G. | Good | Fair | Poor |
|-----|------|------|------|------|------|
| 32000 | 30000 | 25000 | 20000 | 17500 | 15000 |

**SHO Gold Extra--Best-Grade, Over/Under Sidelock Gun**

| NIB | Exc. | V.G. | Good | Fair | Poor |
|-----|------|------|------|------|------|
| 37500 | 32500 | 30000 | 22500 | 20000 | 17500 |

## Sidelock SxS Hunting Guns

Perazzi currently produces three extremely high-grade, side-by-side, double-barrel shotguns. They are essentially special-order items and are offered in all gauges with any barrel length and choke combination. They are extensively engraved with multiple gold inlays and the highest quality materials and workmanship available. We list them and their general values for reference purposes but strongly advise securing a qualified appraisal if a transaction is contemplated.

**DHO**

| NIB | Exc. | V.G. | Good | Fair | Poor |
|-----|------|------|------|------|------|
| 28500 | 24000 | 18500 | 14500 | 12000 | 10000 |

**DHO Gold--Gold-Inlaid, Gamescene-Engraved, Coin-Finished**

| NIB | Exc. | V.G. | Good | Fair | Poor |
|-----|------|------|------|------|------|
| 32000 | 27500 | 22000 | 16500 | 14500 | 12000 |

**DHO Extra--Perazzi's Best-Grade Gun**

| NIB | Exc. | V.G. | Good | Fair | Poor |
|---|---|---|---|---|---|
| 57000 | 49500 | 42000 | 32500 | 25000 | 20000 |

## PERRY PATENT FIREARMS CO.
### Newark, New Jersey

**Perry Single Shot Pistol**

This breech-loading pistol is chambered for .52 caliber percussion. It has a 6" round barrel that is tapered. Much longer barreled examples (up to 28") have been noted. The triggerguard acts as the breech-opening lever, and a paper cartridge is used. The finish is blued, with walnut grips. The barrel is marked "Perry Patent Firearms Co./Newark, N.J." There are two basic types, with a total manufactured of approximately 200 between 1854 and 1856.

**1st Type-Long, Contoured Triggerguard,Opening Lever**

| Exc. | V.G. | Good | Fair | Poor |
|---|---|---|---|---|
| 3500 | 2850 | 2000 | 1500 | 1000 |

**2nd Type S Curved Shorter Triggerguard and an Automatic Primer Feed that Protrudes from the Butt**

| Exc. | V.G. | Good | Fair | Poor |
|---|---|---|---|---|
| 3000 | 2500 | 1750 | 1250 | 850 |

**Perry Carbine**

This is a breech-loading single shot carbine chambered for .54 caliber percussion. It has a 20.75" round barrel and a half-length walnut stock held on by one barrel band. It features a tubular magazine in the butt, that holds primers for the automatic primer feed. The finish is blued and case-colored, and the mountings are iron. This is a very scarce military carbine as only 200 were known to have been purchased for use by Union forces in the Civil War. The barrel is marked "Perry Patent Arms Co." or a derivative thereof. An individual appraisal would be advised on this carbine.

| Exc. | V.G. | Good | Fair | Poor |
|---|---|---|---|---|
| 2000 | 1750 | 1500 | 1250 | 850 |

## PERRY & GODDARD
## RENWICK ARMS CO.
### New York, New York

**Derringer**

This strange little pistol had a barrel that swivels in a complete circle and either end could be loaded. It was chambered for the .44 rimfire cartridge and the barrel was octagonal and 2" in length. There was a post front sight at both ends of the barrel. The finish was blued and the grips were either hard rubber or wood. The barrel was marked "Double Header/E.S. Renwick." The barrel and the frame were scroll engraved There were very few manufactured in the late 1860's. There was really no practical reason for this system.

| Exc. | V.G. | Good | Fair | Poor |
|---|---|---|---|---|
| 4000 | 3500 | 3000 | 2250 | 1500 |

## PERUGINI & VISINI
### Brescia, Italy

This is a manufacturer of high-grade sporting arms. They were imported by W. L. Moore of Westlake Village, California, and Armes De Chasse of Chadds Ford, Pennsylvania. All importation ceased as of 1989.

**Liberty Model**

This is a side-by-side double-barrelled shotgun chambered for 12, 20, and 28 gauge, as well as .410. It has 28" barrels with various choke combinations. The action is an Anson & Deeley with a double Purdy-type lock. It has a single trigger and auto-matic ejectors and is engraved. The finish is blued, with a hand-checkered walnut stock. This model was furnished with a fitted leather case.

| Exc. | V.G. | Good | Fair | Poor |
|---|---|---|---|---|
| 5000 | 4250 | 3500 | 2750 | 2000 |

**Classic Model**

This is the top-of-the-line side-by-side shotgun. It is chambered for 12 and 20 gauge and has 28" barrels with various choke combinations. It features a full Holland & Holland-type sidelock action with a double Purdy-type lock. It has a single trigger and automatic ejectors. It is extensively engraved and blued. The walnut used for the hand-checkered stock and forend is of the highest quality. It was furnished with a fitted leather case.

| Exc. | V.G. | Good | Fair | Poor |
|---|---|---|---|---|
| 11000 | 8500 | 7000 | 5500 | 4750 |

**Bolt Action Rifle**

This is a high quality rifle that was built on a Mauser action and chambered for all popular U.S. and foreign calibers. It has a 24" or 26" barrel without sights and has a 3-shot magazine. The select, hand-checkered walnut stock is oil finished, and the metal is high polished and blued.

| Exc. | V.G. | Good | Fair | Poor |
|---|---|---|---|---|
| 4000 | 3500 | 2750 | 2000 | 1500 |

**Deluxe Bolt Action Rifle**

This model is similar to the standard rifle except that it features better walnut and is cased.

| Exc. | V.G. | Good | Fair | Poor |
|---|---|---|---|---|
| 4500 | 3750 | 3000 | 2250 | 1750 |

**Eagle Single Shot**

This model features an Anson & Deeley single-shot action and is chambered for all popular calibers. The barrel is 24" or 26" in length and made by Hammerli. It has open sights, an automatic ejector, and an adjustable trigger. The finish is blued, and the hand-checkered stock is of European Walnut.

| Exc. | V.G. | Good | Fair | Poor |
|---|---|---|---|---|
| 5000 | 4250 | 3500 | 2750 | 2000 |

**Boxlock Express Rifle**

This is a side-by-side rifle chambered for the .444 Marlin or 9.3x74R cartridges. It has 24" barrels with express sights. The action is an Anson & Deely, and it has double triggers and automatic ejectors. The receiver is case-colored, and the rest is blued. The hand-checkered stock is of walnut.

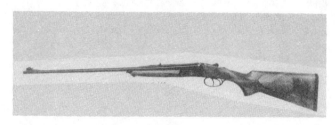

| Exc. | V.G. | Good | Fair | Poor |
|---|---|---|---|---|
| 3250 | 2750 | 2200 | 1750 | 1450 |

**Magnum O/U**

This is an Over/Under double rifle chambered for the .270, .375 Holland & Holland, and the .458 Winchester Magnum cartridges. It has 24" barrels with express sights and an Anson & Deeley boxlock action. It has double triggers and automatic ejectors. The finish is blued, and the hand-checkered stock is of select walnut.

| Exc. | V.G. | Good | Fair | Poor |
|---|---|---|---|---|
| 5500 | 4750 | 3900 | 2750 | 2250 |

## Super Express Rifle

This is a full sidelock, side-by-side double that is chambered for the large "African Calibers." It has 24" barrels with folding express sights and a Holland & Holland-type sidelock action. The receiver is engraved and either case-colored or coin-finished. The barrels are blued. The stock is of hand-checkered walnut.

| Exc. | V.G. | Good | Fair | Poor |
|------|------|------|------|------|
| 9500 | 8500 | 6750 | 5500 | 4850 |

## Victoria SxS Rifle

This double rifle is chambered for the .30-06, 7x65R, or the 9.3x74 cartridges. It has an Anson & Deeley boxlock action and 24" or 26" barrels with a folding express sight. It has double triggers and automatic ejectors. The finish is blued, with engraved borders; and the stock is select walnut.

| Exc. | V.G. | Good | Fair | Poor |
|------|------|------|------|------|
| 6500 | 5750 | 4850 | 3900 | 2750 |

## Selous SxS Rifle

This was the best grade model. It is chambered for the "African Calibers" and has 24" or 26" barrels with folding exprss sights. It has a full Holland & Holland detachable sidelock action. It has double triggers and automatic ejectors. The finish is engraved and blued, with best-grade walnut used in the hand-checkered stock and forend. This model was furnished with a fitted leather case.

| Exc. | V.G. | Good | Fair | Poor |
|-------|-------|-------|------|------|
| 20000 | 16500 | 13500 | 9000 | 6500 |

# PETTINGILL C. S.
### New Haven, Connecticut
### Rogers, Spencer & Co.
### Willowvale, New York

## Pocket Revlover

This is a hammerless, double-action revolver chambered for .31-caliber percussion. It has a 4" octagonal barrel and a 6-shot cylinder, with an integral loading lever. The frame is made of brass or iron; and the finish is blued, with walnut grips. The 1st and the 2nd Models are marked "Pettingill's Patent 1856" and also "T.K.Austin." The 3rd Model is marked with the Pettengill patent but is also marked "Raymond and Robitaille Patented 1858." There were approximately 400 manufactured in the late 1850's.

### 1st Model with Brass Frame

| Exc. | V.G. | Good | Fair | Poor |
|------|------|------|------|------|
| 1400 | 1250 | 1000 | 800 | 600 |

### 2nd Model with Iron Frame

| Exc. | V.G. | Good | Fair | Poor |
|------|------|------|------|------|
| 1000 | 850 | 700 | 500 | 400 |

### 3rd Model, Iron Frame and Improved Action

| Exc. | V.G. | Good | Fair | Poor |
|------|------|------|------|------|
| 1000 | 850 | 700 | 500 | 400 |

## Navy Revolver

This is a larger, belt-model, double-action, hammerless revolver chambered for .34-caliber percussion. It has a 4.5" barrel and a 6-shot cylinder. There is an integral loading lever. The frame is made of iron; the finish is blued, and the grips are walnut. This model is marked "Pettengill's Patent 1856" and also "Raymond & Robitaille Patented 1858." There were approximately 900 manufactured in the late 1850's.

| Exc. | V.G. | Good | Fair | Poor |
|------|------|------|------|------|
| 1500 | 1250 | 1000 | 750 | 500 |

## Army Model Revolver

This was the largest variation of this double-action hammerless revolver, and it is chambered for .44 caliber percussion. It has a 7.5" octagonal barrel with an integral loading lever. The frame is iron and is case-colored along with the loading lever; the rest is blued, with walnut grips. The early production models are marked the same as the Navy models, and the later production is marked "Petingill's Patent 1856, pat'd July 22, 1856 and July 27, 1858." There are some versions with government inspector's markings and some without. The government-inspected revolvers would be worth approximately 25 percent additional. There were approximately 3,400 manufactured in the 1860's.

| Exc. | V.G. | Good | Fair | Poor |
|------|------|------|------|------|
| 1500 | 1250 | 1000 | 750 | 500 |

# PFANNL, FRANCOIS
### Krems, Austria

## Erika

This is an unusual little pistol, to say the least. It is chambered for the tiny 4.25mm cartridge and has either a 1.5" or 2.25" barrel. It is a blowback-operated semi-automatic with a hinged barrel. The butt is raked at a very radical angle, and the magazine is inserted in front of the grip but behind the triggerguard, giving the grip a stepped appearance. There were a number of modifications to this design during its years of production, but the grips are all marked "Erika." The finish is blued, and the grips are molded plastic. There were approximately 3,500 manufactured between 1912 and 1926. There was an arrangement with Grabner, who produced a very similar design as the "Kolibri."

| Exc. | V.G. | Good | Fair | Poor |
|------|------|------|------|------|
| 400 | 350 | 300 | 200 | 125 |

# PHOENIX
### Lowell, Massachusetts

## Pocket Pistol

This is a very rare blowback-operated semi-automatic pistol that is chambered for the .25 ACP cartridge. It has a 2.25" barrel and a 6-round detachable magazine. The finish is blued, and the grips are checkered hard rubber. The name and address of the company are stamped on the slide. This pistol was manufactured in the 1920's.

| Exc. | V.G. | Good | Fair | Poor |
|------|------|------|------|------|
| 500 | 450 | 400 | 300 | 200 |

# PHOENIX ARMS CO.
### Liege, Belgium
### SEE--Robar et DeKerkhove

# PICKERT, FRIEDRICH
### Zella-Mehlis, Germany
### Arminius Waffenfabrik

In the first years of this century, the inexpensive revolver market was all but cornered by the gunmakers of Belgium. One exception was the German firm of Pickert. They produced reasonably good quality, reliable weapons at a very reasonable cost. Their designs were far from innovative, but they represented a good value for their time. The trade name "Arminius" was used on the entire line. Arminius was a German folk hero, and his head appeared on all the grips made by this company. After the onset of WWII in 1939, this company ceased operations; and in 1945 the trade name was acquired by the firm of Hermann Wiehauch. All of the revolvers produced by Pickert are double-action, either with exposed hammers or hammerless with a safety catch. They are solid-framed with a loading gate. Some models have an ejector rod mounted under the barrel; others have a removable cylinder. There are models with folding triggers; and some feature a compartment in the butt, in which extra cartridges are carried. Barrel lengths vary, and finishes are either blued or nickel-plated. The calibers chambered range from .22 rimfire to the .380 ACP. It would be extremely difficult to list completely the products of this company as the list is quite confusing. There are many different models with varying barrel lengths, finishes, etc. They are only moderately collectible, and the values for all are quite similar. We furnish an estimated value that could apply to the entire line.

| Exc. | V.G. | Good | Fair | Poor |
|------|------|------|------|------|
| 175 | 150 | 125 | 100 | 75 |

# PIEPER, HENRI & NICOLAS
### Liege, Belgium

This company was founded by Henri Pieper in 1859 and was concerned with the manufacture of components for rifles until 1898, when Henri died and his son Nicolas reorganized the company and began production of the Pieper semi-automatic pistol. In 1908 they moved their facilities to Herstal, Belgium, where they survived both World Wars.

### Pieper
This is a blowback-operated semi-automatic chambered for the 6.35mm or the 7.65mm cartridge. It features a unique tip-down barrel design, with a barrel length of 2.5". The finish is blued, and the grips are molded plastic with the company logo on them. There are a number of variations on this design, and they are designated the Model 1907 (which is not a tip-up de-

sign but resembles one), the Model 1908 (which was listed in their catalog as the "Basculant"), and the Model 1918 or "Demontant". These high quality tip-up pistols were expensive to manufacture, and they fell victim to the cheap simple pistols that were produced in Europe in the 1920's.

| Exc. | V.G. | Good | Fair | Poor |
|------|------|------|------|------|
| 175 | 150 | 125 | 100 | 75 |

### Pieper Bayard Revolver
This "Gas Seal" design was developed by Pieper in 1886. This well-made revolver was superior to the Nagant gas-seal revolver. It is chambered for 8mm and has a 5" barrel. There are two versions. The first, that was built by Pieper at Liege, is a 7-shot solid-frame revolver that features an automatic ejection system. The cartridge is of the familiar gas-seal design with the bullet seated deep within the case. The second version was actually built by Steyr and uses a swingout cylinder instead of the automatic ejection system of the earlier model. Both of these revolvers are well made and finished. They are blued, with molded plastic grips. The reason for their commercial failure is not evident.

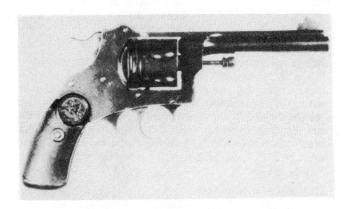

| Exc. | V.G. | Good | Fair | Poor |
|------|------|------|------|------|
| 275 | 250 | 200 | 150 | 100 |

### Legia
This is a blowback-operated semi-automatic chambered for the 6.35mm cartridge. It is patterned after the "Baby Browning" design, with a 2" barrel and a grip safety. The magazine holds 6 rounds, but an extended 10-round version with grip panels that match the pistol is also available. This model is also known as the "New Pieper" and was manufactured in the 1920's at a factory that Pieper owned in Paris, France.

| Exc. | V.G. | Good | Fair | Poor |
|------|------|------|------|------|
| 175 | 150 | 125 | 100 | 75 |

### Bayard

This is a fixed-barrel, blowback-operated semi-automatic pistol chambered for the 6.35mm, 7.65mm, and the 9mm short cartridge. It has an exposed barrel and a concealed hammer that was suspended upside down inside the slide. The barrel is 2.5" in length, and all the calibers use the same parts except the barrel and breech face. The magazine holds 6 rounds, and the pistol is very small for the calibers chambered. The finish is blued, with "Anciens Etablissement Pieper Liege, Belgium" stamped on the slide of all variations. It was manufactured with modifications from 1908 until 1940.

| Exc. | V.G. | Good | Fair | Poor |
|------|------|------|------|------|
| 175 | 150 | 125 | 100 | 75 |

## PILSEN, ZBROVKA
### Pilsen, Czechoslovakia

### Pocket Pistol

This company was affiliated with the firm of Skoda, a well known maker of artillery. The pistol produced is a blowback-operated semi-automatic that is based on the 1910 Browning design without the grip safety. It is chambered for the 7.65mm cartridge and has a 3.5" barrel and a 6-round magazine. The slide is marked "Akciova Spolecnost drive Skodovny zavody Zbrovka Plzen." The finish is blued, with molded plastic grips. It was manufactured in the 1920's.

| Exc. | V.G. | Good | Fair | Poor |
|------|------|------|------|------|
| 225 | 200 | 150 | 125 | 100 |

## PIOTTI
### Brescia, Italy
### Importer--W. L. Moore
### Westlake Village, California

This is a very high-grade, well-made shotgun; and most models have custom-order options that will radically affect the value. We list the models and give an estimated value but strongly recommend an individual appraisal if a transaction is being considered. The difference between the models is basically ornamentation and quality of workmanship and materials used.

### Piuma

This is a side-by-side chambered for the 12, 16, 20, or 28 gauge, as well as the .410. It is available in various barrel length and choke combinations. There is a solid rib and an Anson & Deeley boxlock action. This model is standard with double triggers and automatic ejectors and has a floral-engraved scalloped receiver. The finish is blued, with a select, hand-checkered walnut stock.

| NIB | Exc. | V.G. | Good | Fair | Poor |
|-----|------|------|------|------|------|
| 6500 | 5500 | 3750 | 2500 | 2000 | 1750 |

### Westlake

This model is similar to the Piuma, with a full sidelock action.

| Exc. | V.G. | Good | Fair | Poor |
|------|------|------|------|------|
| 7500 | 6500 | 5500 | 3750 | 2800 |

### Monte Carlo

This is also a sidelock with elaborate engraving.

| NIB | Exc. | V.G. | Good | Fair | Poor |
|-----|------|------|------|------|------|
| 11500 | 9500 | 8000 | 6500 | 5500 | 4000 |

### King Number 1

This model is heavily engraved and has some gold inlay.

| NIB | Exc. | V.G. | Good | Fair | Poor |
|-----|------|------|------|------|------|
| 14000 | 12000 | 9500 | 7000 | 6000 | 4250 |

### Lunik

This model has more gold inlay and deep-relief scroll engraving.

| NIB | Exc. | V.G. | Good | Fair | Poor |
|-----|------|------|------|------|------|
| 14500 | 12500 | 10000 | 7500 | 6500 | 4500 |

### King Extra

This model is gamescene-engraved and gold-inlaid.

| NIB | Exc. | V.G. | Good | Fair | Poor |
|-----|------|------|------|------|------|
| 15000 | 13500 | 11000 | 8500 | 7000 | 5000 |

### Monaco Series

This is the best-grade top of the line and is essentially a custom-order proposition. This model is very rarely encountered and should definitely be appraised by a qualified professional.

| NIB | Exc. | V.G. | Good | Fair | Poor |
|-----|------|------|------|------|------|
| 17500 | 15000 | 12500 | 10000 | 8500 | 6000 |

## PLAINFIELD MACHINE CO.
### Dunellen, New Jersey

### Super Enforcer

This is a cut-down version of the M1 Carbine. It has a 12" barrel and a pistol grip. It is fed by a detachable magazine; and the finish is blued, with a walnut stock.

| Exc. | V.G. | Good | Fair | Poor |
|------|------|------|------|------|
| 225 | 200 | 175 | 125 | 100 |

### M1 Carbine

This is a commercial reproduction of the military M1 Carbine. The specifications are the same. The finish is blued, with a walnut stock.

| Exc. | V.G. | Good | Fair | Poor |
|------|------|------|------|------|
| 200 | 175 | 150 | 100 | 75 |

### M1 Paratrooper Carbine.

This is a folding-stock version of the M1 Carbine. The finish is blued, with a metal wire stock and walnut forend.

| Exc. | V.G. | Good | Fair | Poor |
|------|------|------|------|------|
| 225 | 200 | 175 | 125 | 100 |

## PLAINFIELD ORDNANCE CO.
### Middlesex, New Jersey

### Model 71

This is a stainless-steel, blowback-operated semi-automatic pistol chambered for the .22 l.r. cartridge. It has a 10-shot detachable magazine and a 1" barrel. The grips are checkered walnut. This model is also available chambered for the .25 ACP cartridge, and there was a conversion kit available.

### Conversion Kit

| Exc. | V.G. | Good | Fair | Poor |
|------|------|------|------|------|
| 50 | 40 | 30 | 25 | 20 |

### .22 or .25 Caliber Pistol

| Exc. | V.G. | Good | Fair | Poor |
|------|------|------|------|------|
| 150 | 125 | 100 | 75 | 50 |

## Model 72

This model is similar to the Model 71, with an alloy frame.

| Exc. | V.G. | Good | Fair | Poor |
|------|------|------|------|------|
| 150 | 125 | 100 | 75 | 50 |

# PLANT'S MANUFACTURING CO.
## New Haven, Connecticut

### Front Loading Revolver

This is a large single-action revolver that is chambered for a .42-caliber cup-primed cartridge designed for this revolver. It has a 6" octagonal ribbed barrel, and the unfluted cylinder holds 6 rounds. It has a spur trigger and either a brass or iron frame; and the finish is blued, with walnut or rosewood grips. This system of ignition was intended to side step the Rollin White Patent; and it consists of a front-loading cylinder, as well as an interchangeable percussion cylinder. If the interchangeable percussion cyilinder is found with the revolver, the values would be increased approximately 30 percent. This revolver was marketed by Merwin & Bray, and there were approximately 1,500 of the 1st and 2nd Models manufactured and 10,000 of the 3rd Model in the 1860's.

### 1st Model Brass Frame

Marked "Plant's Mfg. Co. New Haven, Ct." on the barrel, "M & B" on the side of the frame, and "Patented July 12, 1859" on the cylinder. Under 100 manufactured.

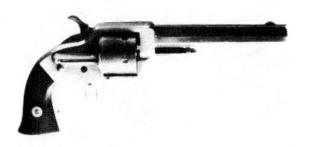

| Exc. | V.G. | Good | Fair | Poor |
|------|------|------|------|------|
| 950 | 850 | 750 | 600 | 450 |

### 1st Model Iron Frame

This model is identical to Brass Frame Model, with an iron frame. There were 500 manufactured.

| Exc. | V.G. | Good | Fair | Poor |
|------|------|------|------|------|
| 850 | 750 | 650 | 500 | 350 |

### 2nd Model Rounded Brass Frame

Marked same as 1st Model on barrel top and "Merwin & Bray, New York" on frame. "July 21, 1863" added to patent date. 300 manufactured.

| Exc. | V.G. | Good | Fair | Poor |
|------|------|------|------|------|
| 850 | 750 | 650 | 550 | 350 |

### 2nd Model Iron Frame

The model appears similar to the Brass Framed Model, with an iron frame.

| Exc. | V.G. | Good | Fair | Poor |
|------|------|------|------|------|
| 750 | 650 | 550 | 450 | 275 |

### 3rd Model

This model is similar to the 2nd Model, with a flat brass frame. It is marked the same as the 2nd Model.

| Exc. | V.G. | Good | Fair | Poor |
|------|------|------|------|------|
| 600 | 500 | 400 | 300 | 200 |

### Pocket Revolver

This model is a smaller version of the larger-framed "Army" model described above. It is chambered for a .30-caliber cup-primed cartridge. It has a 3.5" ribbed octagonal barrel and a 5-shot cylinder. It has a spur trigger and a silver-plated brass frame, with the remainder blued. The grips are walnut or rosewood, and the markings are varied. "Eagle Arms Co., New York," "Reynolds, Plant & Hotchkiss, New Haven,Ct.," and "Merwin & Bray Firearms Co., N.Y." have all been noted. There were approximately 20,000 manufactured in the 1860's.

| Exc. | V.G. | Good | Fair | Poor |
|------|------|------|------|------|
| 500 | 400 | 350 | 275 | 200 |

# POLY-TECHNOLOGIES, INC.
## China
## Importer--Keng's
## Riverdale, Georgia
## Distributor--PTK Int.
## Atlanta, Georgia

Poly-Tech builds semi-automatic versions of Chinese military weapons. They are built to military specifications and are of excellent quality. For the most part, they fall within the category of the "Assault" rifle that has been victimized by the anti-gun press as of late. It is impossible to accurately place a value on firearms of this type at this time. If one is contemplating a transaction, it would be advisable to secure an individual appraisal in your geographical area.

### SKS

This is a semi-automatic rifle chambered for the 7.62x39mm cartridge. It has a 20.5" barrel and a 10-shot fixed magazine. This is a newly manufactured version of the original Soviet Siminov carbine, and it is built to military specifications. The finish is blue, and the stock and handguard are made of a Chinese hardwood.

| NIB | Exc. | V.G. | Good | Fair | Poor |
|-----|------|------|------|------|------|
| 225 | 200 | 175 | 150 | 125 | 100 |

### AKS-762

This is a semi-automatic version of the Chinese-type 56 Assault rifle. It is chambered for the 7.62x39mm cartridge. It has a 16.5" barrel and is gas-operated. It is furnished with a 20-round magazine and a Chinese bayonet. The finish is blued, and the stock is hardwood.

### AK-47/S

This model is similar to the AKS-762, with the Soviet-style bayonet.

### M-14/S

This is the Chinese version of our M-14 Battle Rifle. It has a 22" barrel and is chambered for the .308 cartridge. It has the M-14 sight and a 20-round magazine. The finish is blued, and the stock is hardwood.

# POINTER
## Hopkins & Allen
## Norwich, Connecticut

### Single Shot Derringer

This is a small pocket pistol that is chambered for the .22-caliber rimfire cartridge. The round barrel is 2.75" in length and pivots sideways for loading. It is made without an ejector and has a spur trigger, nickel-plated brass frame, and round-bottomed walnut grips. The barrel is marked "Pointer," and the Hopkins & Allen name does not appear on the pistol at all. There were approximately 2,500 manufactured between 1870 and 1890.

| Exc. | V.G. | Good | Fair | Poor |
|------|------|------|------|------|
| 300 | 250 | 200 | 150 | 100 |

# POND, LUCIUS W.
### Worcester, Massachusetts

## Pocket Revolver

This is a single-action revolver chambered for the .32-caliber rimfire cartridge. It has been noted with octagonal barrels in lengths of 4", 5", or 6". It has a 6-round unfluted cylinder. This model is hinged at the topstrap and pivots upward for loading. There is a brass-framed version, as well as an iron-framed one. The finish is blued, with walnut grips. There is a screwdriver fitted into the butt. This was an infringement on the Rollin White patent, and Pond lost a lawsuit brought by Smith & Wesson. There are many revolvers that are marked "Manuf'd. for Smith & Wesson Pat'd. April 5, 1855." Versions so marked would bring a 20 percent premium. They were manufactured between 1861 and 1870.

### Brass Framed Revolver

| Exc. | V.G. | Good | Fair | Poor |
|------|------|------|------|------|
| 500 | 400 | 300 | 200 | 125 |

### Iron Framed Revolver

| Exc. | V.G. | Good | Fair | Poor |
|------|------|------|------|------|
| 375 | 300 | 200 | 150 | 100 |

## Separate Chamber Revolver

This is an unusual revolver that came about because of an attempt around the Rollin White patent. It is chambered for the .22- and .32-caliber rimfire cartridge and has separate steel-chamber inserts that are removed from the front for loading. The .22-caliber version has a 3.5" octagonal barrel and a 7-round unfluted cylinder, and the .32-caliber version has a 4", 5", or 6" octagonal barrel and a 6-round unfluted cylinder. The frame is silver-plated brass; and the remainder is blued, with walnut grips. The barrel is marked "L.W. Pond, Worcester, Mass." along with the patent dates. There were approximately 2,000 manufactured in .22 caliber and 5,000 in .32 caliber between 1963 and 1870.

### .22 Caliber Version

| Exc. | V.G. | Good | Fair | Poor |
|------|------|------|------|------|
| 600 | 500 | 400 | 300 | 200 |

### .32 Caliber Version

| Exc. | V.G. | Good | Fair | Poor |
|------|------|------|------|------|
| 450 | 400 | 300 | 250 | 150 |

# PORTER, P. W.
### New York, New York

## Turret Revolver

This is a very rare revolver that is chambered for .41-caliber percussion. It has a 5.25" round barrel and a vertical turret that holds 9 shots. The trigger guard is a ringed lever that turns the turret and cocks the hammer. The primer system is automatic. It has an iron frame and a loading lever under the barrel. The finish is blued, with walnut grips. There are no markings, and this is considered to be one of the rarest of all the firearms made in this era. It was manufactured in the 1850's.

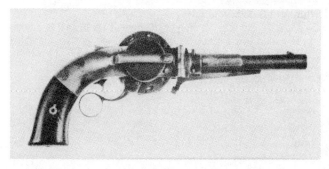

| Exc. | V.G. | Good | Fair | Poor |
|------|------|------|------|------|
| 8500 | 7500 | 6000 | 4000 | 3000 |

## Turret Rifle

This is a rifle version of the Turret Revolver, that is chambered for .44-caliber percussion and has a 26" to 28" octagonal barrel. It has a 9-shot vertical turret that functions similar to the revolver described earlier. This rifle is marked "Address P.W. Porter/New York," and there is a crescent butt and walnut stock with no forend. There are actually four distinct versions of this weapon, as well as a 22"-barrelled carbine that will bring a premium of approximately 25 percent. There were approximately 1,250 manufactured in the 1850's.

## 1st Model with Cannister Magazine

This version has a large round cannister over the turret, that is an automatic 30-shot magazine. This model was made in Tennessee and is very rare; most found have been without the cannister intact. Values given reflect this condition. There were only an estimated 25 of these produced.

| Exc. | V.G. | Good | Fair | Poor |
|------|------|------|------|------|
| 7500 | 6500 | 5500 | 4500 | 3500 |

## 2nd Model (New York)

| Exc. | V.G. | Good | Fair | Poor |
|------|------|------|------|------|
| 4500 | 3500 | 2750 | 2000 | 1500 |

## 3rd Model (New York)

This model has a screw-off cover over the magazine.

| Exc. | V.G. | Good | Fair | Poor |
|------|------|------|------|------|
| 4750 | 3750 | 3000 | 2250 | 1750 |

## 4th Model (New York)

This model has no automatic primer magazine, and the nipples are visible.

| Exc. | V.G. | Good | Fair | Poor |
|------|------|------|------|------|
| 3500 | 3000 | 2500 | 1750 | 1250 |

# POWELL, W. & SON LTD.
### Birmingham, England
### Importer--Jaqua's
### Findlay, Ohio

## Number 3 Boxlock

This is a custom-order side-by-side shotgun chambered for 12, 16, and 20 gauge, as well as .410. The barrel length and choke combinations are optional. It is standard with a single trigger and automatic ejectors. The finish is engraved and blued with a high-grade French walnut stock. This model should definitely be individually appraised as there are too many options that affect value for anything but an educated estimate.

| Exc. | V.G. | Good | Fair | Poor |
|------|------|------|------|------|
| 7500 | 6500 | 5250 | 4000 | 3250 |

## Number 1 Sidelock
This is a full sidelock version of the Powell artistry. It is a best-grade gun in every sense of the word, with extensive engraving and gold inlay. The materials and craftsmanship are of the highest order. This gun should also be individually appraised.

| Exc. | V.G. | Good | Fair | Poor |
|------|------|------|------|------|
| 17500 | 16000 | 12000 | 9000 | 7500 |

## PRAGA, ZBROVKA
### Prague, Czechoslovakia

This company was founded in 1918 by A. Novotny and produced two pistols. One has been said to be the worst firearm ever to be made; the other was rather unremarkable. This firm was not a financial success and ceased operations in 1926.

## Vz21
This is a blowback-operated semi-automatic pistol chambered for the 7.65mm cartridge. It is a modified 1910 Browning design without a grip safety. The barrel was 3.5", and the finish is blue. The magazine holds 6 rounds, and the grips are ribbed wood. The slide is marked "Zbrojowka Praga Praha." This was basically a military and police pistol, but a commercial model was made in 1923 that had molded plastic grips. This model was manufactured until 1926.

| Exc. | V.G. | Good | Fair | Poor |
|------|------|------|------|------|
| 300 | 250 | 200 | 150 | 100 |

## Praga 1921
This is the model that some say was the worst firearm ever made. It is a blowback operated semi-automatic chambered for the 6.35mm cartridge. The slide is of stamped steel, and there is a finger groove in the front. The trigger folds, and the barrel is 2" in length. The slide is marked "Zbrojowka Praga Praha Patent Cal 6.35." The grips are molded plastic, with the name "Praga" on them. The feature that makes this such a bad design is that it is striker-fired with no hammer and is intended to be carried fully loaded and cocked in the pocket with absolutely no safety of any kind. The folding trigger does not spring out until the slide is drawn back slightly by using the finger groove in the front of it. This is potentially a very hazardous situation. This model was also manufactured until 1926.

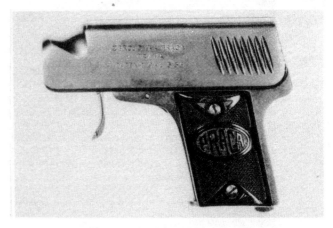

| Exc. | V.G. | Good | Fair | Poor |
|------|------|------|------|------|
| 250 | 225 | 200 | 150 | 100 |

## PRANDELLI & GASPARINI
### Brescia, Italy
### Importer--Richland Arms Co.
### Blissfield, Michigan

### Boxlock SxS Shotgun
This is a good quality double-barrelled shotgun that is chambered for 12 and 20 gauge and has 26"and 28" barrels with various choke combinations. It has a single-selective trigger, automatic ejectors, and an Anson & Deeley boxlock action. The finish is blued, and the stock is select walnut.

| Exc. | V.G. | Good | Fair | Poor |
|------|------|------|------|------|
| 1500 | 1250 | 1000 | 750 | 450 |

### Sidelock SxS Shotgun
This model is similar to the Boxlock, with a full sidelock action. It is slightly more deluxe regarding workmanship and materials than the Boxlock model.

| Exc. | V.G. | Good | Fair | Poor |
|------|------|------|------|------|
| 2500 | 2250 | 1750 | 1250 | 700 |

### Boxlock O/U Shotgun
This model is an Over/Under double, with a boxlock action and 26" or 28" vent-rib barrels with various choke combinations. It is chambered for 12 and 20 gauge and has a single trigger and automatic ejectors. The finish is blued, and the hand-checkered stock is select walnut.

| Exc. | V.G. | Good | Fair | Poor |
|------|------|------|------|------|
| 1750 | 1500 | 1250 | 900 | 650 |

### Sidelock O/U Shotgun
This model is similar to the Boxlock O/U, with a full sidelock action. It is slightly more deluxe overall.

| Exc. | V.G. | Good | Fair | Poor |
|------|------|------|------|------|
| 3000 | 2500 | 2250 | 1800 | 1200 |

## PRATT, GEORGE
### Middletown, Connecticut

### Trap Gun
This is a twin-barrelled, stationary-mounted burglar alarm or animal trap gun that is chambered for .38-caliber centerfire. The barrels are 4" in length; and the whole unit is cast of iron, with a rust-retarding galvanized finish. There are two cast-iron hammers that are spring-loaded and mounted in a straight line to the bores. There is a flat swivel arm that acts as a trigger.

The entire unit is mounted on a round swivel base, that allows a full 360 degrees of adjustment. The patent date "Dec. 18, 1883" is marked on the gun. There were many manufactured between 1880 and the early 1890's.

| Exc. | V.G. | Good | Fair | Poor |
|------|------|------|------|------|
| 400 | 350 | 300 | 200 | 100 |

# PRATT, H.
## Roxbury, Massachusetts

### Underhammer Pistol
This is an underhammer with a conventional hammer and a trigger guard that doubles as the mainspring. It is chambered for .31-caliber percussion and has an 8.5" octagonal barrel. There is a brass sideplate; and the rest is blued, with a walnut grip. The frame is marked "H.Pratt's/Patent." This pistol was manufactured in the 1850's.

| Exc. | V.G. | Good | Fair | Poor |
|------|------|------|------|------|
| 550 | 450 | 400 | 300 | 200 |

# PREMIER
## Italy and Spain

The Premier was a trade name used by various distributors to merchandise a number of shotguns that were manufactured in Italy and Spain. These guns were of reasonable utility quality and, with the exception of one model, quite reasonably priced. They have all been discontinued. They were imported in the late 1950's to the early 1960's.

### Regent SxS Shotgun
This side-by-side is chambered for 12, 16, 20, and 28 gauge. as well as .410. It has 26" through 30" barrels with various choke combinations. The finish is blued, and the walnut stock is checkered. It has a pistol grip and a beavertail forend.

| Exc. | V.G. | Good | Fair | Poor |
|------|------|------|------|------|
| 300 | 275 | 225 | 175 | 100 |

### Regent Magnum
This is a slightly larger version of the Regent, that is chambered for the 10-gauge 3.5" Magnum. The barrels are 32" in length and choked full-and-full.

| Exc. | V.G. | Good | Fair | Poor |
|------|------|------|------|------|
| 350 | 300 | 250 | 200 | 150 |

### Brush King
This model is similar to the Regent except that it has 22" modified-and-improved-cylinder barrels and a straight-grip English-style stock.

| Exc. | V.G. | Good | Fair | Poor |
|------|------|------|------|------|
| 275 | 250 | 200 | 150 | 100 |

### Ambassador Model
This is also a side-by-side double chambered for all gauges. It is similar to the Regent except generally more deluxe throughout.

| Exc. | V.G. | Good | Fair | Poor |
|------|------|------|------|------|
| 400 | 350 | 300 | 250 | 175 |

### Presentation Custom Grade
This is a custom-order gun with gamescene engraving and gold and silver inlays.

| Exc. | V.G. | Good | Fair | Poor |
|------|------|------|------|------|
| 1000 | 750 | 600 | 500 | 400 |

# PRESCOTT, E. A.
## Worcester, Massachusetts

### Percussion Pocket Revolver
This is a single-action spur-trigger revolver that is chambered for .31-caliber percussion. It has a 4" or 4.25" octagonal barrel with a 6-shot unfluted cylinder. It has a brass frame; and the rest is blued, with walnut grips. There were very few manufactured. This is a rare firearm, as there were approximately 100 manufactured in 1860 and 1861.

| Exc. | V.G. | Good | Fair | Poor |
|------|------|------|------|------|
| 800 | 650 | 550 | 450 | 300 |

### Pocket Revolver
This is a single-action, spur-trigger pocket revolver chambered for the .22 or .32 rimfire cartridges. It has octagonal barrels in lengths of 3" to 4". The unfluted cylinders hold 7 rounds in .22, and 6 rounds in .32. There are a number of different variations regarding the size of the frame and the type of butt--square or birdshead style. The values of these variations are very similar. They are all marked "E.A.Prescott Worcester Mass. Pat. Oct. 2, 1860." There were approximately 1,000 manufactured between 1862 and 1867.

| Exc. | V.G. | Good | Fair | Poor |
|------|------|------|------|------|
| 650 | 550 | 450 | 350 | 225 |

### Belt Revolver
This model is similar in appearance to the early Smith & Wesson revolvers; however, they have a solid brass frame and no hinges. They are chambered for the .22 and .32 rimfire cartridges and have ribbed octagonal barrels in lengths of 3" in the 7-shot .22, and 5.75" in the 6-shot .32. The frames are brass, with blued barrels and walnut or rosewood grips. The barrel is marked "E.A.Prescott, Worcester, Mass. Pat. Oct. 2, 1860." There were only a few hundred estimated manufactured between 1861 and 1863.

| Exc. | V.G. | Good | Fair | Poor |
|------|------|------|------|------|
| 650 | 550 | 450 | 350 | 225 |

### Navy Revolver
This is a single-action revolver with a conventional trigger. It is chambered for the .38-rimfire cartridge and has a 7.25" octagonal barrel. The unfluted cylinder holds 6 shots. The frame is silver-plated brass or blued iron; and the barrel and the cylinder are blued, with walnut grips. The barrel is marked "E.A.Prescott, Worcester, Mass. Pat. Oct. 2, 1860." There were a few hundred estimated manufactured between 1861 and 1863.

| Exc. | V.G. | Good | Fair | Poor |
|------|------|------|------|------|
| 650 | 550 | 450 | 350 | 225 |

# PRETORIA
## Pretoria, South Africa
### SEE--PAF

384 • PRINZ

# PRINZ
### Germany
### Importer--Helmut Hofmann
### Placitas, New Mexico

**Grade 1 Bolt Action Rifle**
This is a high quality rifle chambered for the .243, .30-06, .308, .7mm Remington Magnum and the .300 Winchester Magnum. It has a 24" barrel, and double-set triggers are available. The finish is blued, and the oil-finished stock is of select walnut. It was introduced in 1989.

| NIB | Exc. | V.G. | Good | Fair | Poor |
|-----|------|------|------|------|------|
| 500 | 450 | 400 | 350 | 300 | 225 |

**Grade 2 Bolt Action Rifle**
This is a slightly more deluxe version with a rosewood forend tip and pistolgrip cap.

| NIB | Exc. | V.G. | Good | Fair | Poor |
|-----|------|------|------|------|------|
| 550 | 500 | 450 | 400 | 350 | 250 |

**Tip Up Rifle**
This is a high quality single-shot rifle chambered for various popular American cartridges. It has a 24" barrel and is furnished without sights. The finish is blued, and the stock is select walnut.

| NIB | Exc. | V.G. | Good | Fair | Poor |
|-----|------|------|------|------|------|
| 2200 | 1850 | 1500 | 1150 | 950 | 750 |

**Model 85 "Princess"**
This is a combination gun that is available chambered for 12 gauge and a choice of various popular calibers. It has 24" or 26" barrels, with double triggers and automatic ejectors. The finish is blued, and the stock is select walnut.

| NIB | Exc. | V.G. | Good | Fair | Poor |
|-----|------|------|------|------|------|
| 1500 | 1250 | 1000 | 800 | 750 | 600 |

# PROTECTION
### Unknown

**Protection Pocket Revolver**
This is a single-action spur-trigger revolver chambered for .28-caliber percussion. It has a 3.25" octagonal barrel and a 6-shot unfluted cylinder with a roll-engraved police arrest scene on it. The frame is brass; and the rest is blued, with walnut grips. "Protection" is marked on the cylinder. There were two models produced, for a total estimated at 1,000 manufactured in the late 1850's.

**1st Model Roll Engraved Cylinder**

| Exc. | V.G. | Good | Fair | Poor |
|------|------|------|------|------|
| 650 | 600 | 500 | 400 | 250 |

**2nd Model Plain Cylinder Above Serial No. 650**

| Exc. | V.G. | Good | Fair | Poor |
|------|------|------|------|------|
| 550 | 500 | 400 | 300 | 200 |

# PURDEY, J. & SONS LTD.
### London, England

This company manufactures some of the finest sporting arms the world has ever known. They produce shotguns, as well as bolt-action rifles and double-barrelled express rifles. The materials and workmanship are at the top of the craft; and the values, as well might be imagined, are on a par with the quality. The majority of the firearms that Purdey produced through their many years in the field were strictly on a made-to-order basis, with options and ornamentation having a drastic effect on values. It is virtually impossible to establish a general value on firearms of this nature. We feel that an independent and highly qualified appraisal on this type of firearm is absolutely essential. There are not enough transactions to even intelligently estimate values for the products of this firm.

# PYRENEES
### Hendaye, France

This company was founded in 1923 and has manufactured semi-automatic pistols since. They have specialized in the "Unique" series of pistols and have produced many variations on this design. There were many tradenames utilized for this pistol, depending on the retailer. The tradenames were used prior to 1939, and pistols produced after this date are simply the "Unique. These tradenames are as follows: Superior, Capitan, Cesar, Chantecler, Chimere Renoir, Colonial, Prima, Rapid-Maxima, Reina, Demon, Demon-marine, Ebac, Elite, Gallia, Ixor, Le Majestic, St. Hubert, Selecta, Sympathique, Touriste, Le Sanspariel, Le Tout Acier, Mars, Perfect, Triomphe Francais, Unis & Vindex. Values for the above pistols would be comparable to the corresponding Unique model.

**Model 10 Unique**
This was the first of the series and is chambered for 6.35mm. It is a blowback-operated semi-automatic patterned after the 1906 Browning design. It has a safety catch above the trigger like the Eibar pistols and is blued, with grips of molded plastic that bear the Unique name. The slide is marked "Le Veritable Pistolet Francais Unique." This model was introduced in 1923.

| Exc. | V.G. | Good | Fair | Poor |
|------|------|------|------|------|
| 200 | 175 | 150 | 100 | 75 |

**Model 11**
This is the Model 10 with a grip safety and loaded-chamber indicator.

| Exc. | V.G. | Good | Fair | Poor |
|------|------|------|------|------|
| 250 | 200 | 175 | 125 | 100 |

**Model 12**
This model has a grip safety but no loaded-chamber indicator.

| Exc. | V.G. | Good | Fair | Poor |
|------|------|------|------|------|
| 225 | 185 | 165 | 110 | 90 |

**Model 13**
This model has a larger grip that accommodates a 7-round magazine instead of the 6-round capacity of the Model 10.

| Exc. | V.G. | Good | Fair | Poor |
|------|------|------|------|------|
| 225 | 185 | 165 | 110 | 90 |

**Model 14**
This model has a still larger grip and a 9-round magazine.

| Exc. | V.G. | Good | Fair | Poor |
|------|------|------|------|------|
| 225 | 185 | 165 | 110 | 90 |

**Model 15**
This model is an enlarged version of the Model 10 chambered for the 7.65mm cartridge. It was also introduced in 1923.

| Exc. | V.G. | Good | Fair | Poor |
|------|------|------|------|------|
| 250 | 175 | 150 | 100 | 75 |

**Model 16**
This is similar to the Model 15, with a larger butt and a 7-round magazine.

| Exc. | V.G. | Good | Fair | Poor |
|------|------|------|------|------|
| 250 | 175 | 150 | 100 | 75 |

## Model 17
This is the same as the Model 16, with a still larger butt and a 9-round magazine.

| Exc. | V.G. | Good | Fair | Poor |
|------|------|------|------|------|
| 300 | 250 | 200 | 150 | 100 |

## Model 18
This is a departure from the previous models. It is chambered for the 7.65mm cartridge and is patterned after the 1920 Browning, without a grip safety. It has a lanyard ring on the butt.

| Exc. | V.G. | Good | Fair | Poor |
|------|------|------|------|------|
| 250 | 175 | 150 | 100 | 75 |

## Model 19
This model has a larger butt than the Model 18 and a 7-round magazine.

| Exc. | V.G. | Good | Fair | Poor |
|------|------|------|------|------|
| 250 | 175 | 150 | 100 | 75 |

## Model 20
This model is similar to the Model 19, with a still larger butt and a 9-round magazine.

| Exc. | V.G. | Good | Fair | Poor |
|------|------|------|------|------|
| 275 | 200 | 175 | 125 | 100 |

## Model 21
This is the same as the Model 19 except that it is chambered for the 9mm Short cartridge.

| Exc. | V.G. | Good | Fair | Poor |
|------|------|------|------|------|
| 275 | 200 | 175 | 125 | 100 |

The preceding models were all pre-WWII and were in production when the Nazis occupied France in 1940. They took over the factory and modified the design to their own liking by adding exposed hammers. There were many with the Waffenamt inspector's marks and also many without that were sold commercially in Germany during the war years. The German military models would be worth approximately 25 percent more than the like model without the inspector's marks.

## Post War Unique
### Model Bcf66
This is a blowback-operated semi-automatic that is chambered for the 9mm Short cartridge and has a fixed 3.5" barrel with an open-topped slide and an external hammer. The slide is marked "Armes Unique Hendaye BP France." The finish is blued, and the grips are molded plastic.

| Exc. | V.G. | Good | Fair | Poor |
|------|------|------|------|------|
| 225 | 185 | 165 | 125 | 100 |

## Model C
This model is nearly identical to the pre-war Model 17 chambered for the 7.65mm cartridge. The slide is marked "7.65 Court 9 coups Unique." The finish is blued, with plastic grips that have a "PF" molded into a circle.

| Exc. | V.G. | Good | Fair | Poor |
|------|------|------|------|------|
| 200 | 150 | 125 | 100 | 75 |

## Model D
This was the first of the .22 rimfire models and was offered with a four different barrel lengths from 4" to 7.5". It has a fixed barrel and an open-topped slide. The long-barrelled version has a muzzle brake. The magazines hold 10 rounds, and there were a number of sight options offered. The hammer is external; and the finish is blued, with plastic grips.

| Exc. | V.G. | Good | Fair | Poor |
|------|------|------|------|------|
| 225 | 185 | 165 | 125 | 100 |

## Model Des 69
This deluxe version of the Model D was intended for formal target competition. It has better sights, grips, and a special trigger. It enjoys a reputation for extreme accuracy.

| Exc. | V.G. | Good | Fair | Poor |
|------|------|------|------|------|
| 275 | 250 | 200 | 175 | 125 |

## Model E

This model is the same as the Model D chambered for .22 short only.

| Exc. | V.G. | Good | Fair | Poor |
|------|------|------|------|------|
| 225 | 185 | 165 | 125 | 100 |

## Model F

This model is similar to the Model C except that it is chambered for the 9mm short and has an 8-round magazine.

| Exc. | V.G. | Good | Fair | Poor |
|------|------|------|------|------|
| 225 | 185 | 165 | 125 | 100 |

## Model L

This is an open-side model similar to the Model D except that it is chambered for the .22 rimfire, .32 ACP, and the 9mm Short cartridges. This model is offered with an alloy frame, as well as steel.

| Exc. | V.G. | Good | Fair | Poor |
|------|------|------|------|------|
| 250 | 225 | 200 | 150 | 125 |

## QUACKENBUSH
### Herkimer, New York

### .22 Rifle

This is a single-shot, take-down boy's rifle that is chambered for the .22-rimfire cartridge. It has an 18" barrel and is nickel-plated. The breech swings to the side for loading. The stock is walnut, and there were many manufactured in the 1880's.

| Exc. | V.G. | Good | Fair | Poor |
|------|------|------|------|------|
| 300 | 250 | 200 | 150 | 100 |

## QUINABAUG MFG. CO.
### Southridge, Massachusetts

### Underhammer Pistol

This is a standard underhammer-type pistol that is chambered for .31-caliber percussion and has barrels from 3" to 8" in length. The frame is blued iron, and the grips are walnut or maple. The top of the frame is marked "Quinabaug Rifle M'g Co. Southbridge, Mass." "E. Hutchings & Co. Agents" also appears on the barrel. This model was manufactured in the 1850's.

| Exc. | V.G. | Good | Fair | Poor |
|------|------|------|------|------|
| 650 | 550 | 450 | 350 | 250 |

## R. G. INDUSTRIES
### Miami, Florida
### Rohm Gmbh
### Sontheim/Brenz, Germany

This was an importer of inexpensive, moderate-quality handguns. They ceased operations in 1986.

### RG-25

This is a blowback-operated semi-automatic chambered for the .25 ACP cartridge. It is blued or chrome-plated, with plastic grips.

| Exc. | V.G | Good | Fair | Poor |
|------|-----|------|------|------|
| 75 | 65 | 50 | 35 | 25 |

### RG-16

This is a twin-barrelled derringer, patterned after the Remington in appearance. It is chambered for .22 rimfire. The finish is chrome-plated, with plastic grips.

| Exc. | V.G. | Good | Fair | Poor |
|------|------|------|------|------|
| 75 | 65 | 50 | 35 | 25 |

### RG-17

This derringer is similar to the RG-16--only larger and chambered for the .38 Special cartridge.

| Exc. | V.G. | Good | Fair | Poor |
|------|------|------|------|------|
| 90 | 80 | 70 | 50 | 25 |

### RG-14

This is a double-action revolver chambered for the .22 rimfire cartridge. It has a 4" barrel and a 6-shot cylinder. The finish is blued, with plastic grips.

| Exc. | V.G. | Good | Fair | Poor |
|------|------|------|------|------|
| 90 | 80 | 70 | 50 | 25 |

### RG-30

This is a double-action, swingout-cylinder revolver chambered for either the .22 rimfire or the .22 rimfire Magnum cartridge. It is blued, with plastic grips.

| Exc. | V.G. | Good | Fair | Poor |
|------|------|------|------|------|
| 75 | 65 | 50 | 35 | 25 |

### RG-40

This is a double-action, swingout-cylinder revolver chambered for the .38 Special cartridge. It is blued, with plastic grips.

| Exc. | V.G. | Good | Fair | Poor |
|------|------|------|------|------|
| 90 | 80 | 70 | 50 | 25 |

### RG-57

This is a double-action revolver chambered for .357 or .44 Magnum. It holds 6 shots and is blued, with checkered wood grips.

| Exc. | V.G. | Good | Fair | Poor |
|------|------|------|------|------|
| 125 | 100 | 80 | 65 | 50 |

## RG-63

This is a 6-shot double-action revolver made in the Western style. It is chambered for the .22 rimfire cartridge.

| Exc. | V.G. | Good | Fair | Poor |
|------|------|------|------|------|
| 60 | 50 | 40 | 35 | 25 |

## RG-66

This is a single-action, Western-style revolver chambered for the .22/.22 Magnum in a two-cylinder convertible model.

| Exc. | V.G. | Good | Fair | Poor |
|------|------|------|------|------|
| 60 | 50 | 40 | 35 | 25 |

## RG-66T

This model is similar to the RG-66, with adjustable sights.

| Exc. | V.G. | Good | Fair | Poor |
|------|------|------|------|------|
| 65 | 55 | 45 | 35 | 25 |

## RG-74

This is a double-action, swingout-cylinder model chambered for the .22 rimfire cartridge.

| Exc. | V.G. | Good | Fair | Poor |
|------|------|------|------|------|
| 75 | 65 | 55 | 45 | 35 |

## RG-88

This is a double-action, swingout-cylinder revolver chambered for the .357 Magnum cartridge.

| Exc. | V.G. | Good | Fair | Poor |
|------|------|------|------|------|
| 90 | 80 | 70 | 60 | 40 |

# RWS
## Nurenberg, Germany
### Dynamit Nobel

## Model 820 S

This is a high quality target rifle chambered for the .22 l.r. cartridge. It has a 24" heavy barrel and adjustable aperture sights. It has a fully adjustable trigger and a three-position adjustable match stock made of oil-finished walnut, with a stippled pistol grip and forend. It was discontinued in 1986.

| Exc. | V.G. | Good | Fair | Poor |
|------|------|------|------|------|
| 800 | 700 | 550 | 450 | 350 |

## Model 820 SF

This is a heavier-barrelled version of the Model 820 S. It was also discontinued in 1986.

| Exc. | V.G. | Good | Fair | Poor |
|------|------|------|------|------|
| 825 | 725 | 575 | 475 | 375 |

## Model 820 K

This is the offhand "Running Boar" version of the Model 820 SF. It has a lighter barrel and was furnished without sights. It was also discontinued in 1986.

| Exc. | V.G. | Good | Fair | Poor |
|------|------|------|------|------|
| 775 | 675 | 525 | 425 | 325 |

# RADOM
## Radom, Poland
### Fabryka Broni w Radomu

This company was founded after WWI and produced military rifles for Poland. In 1930 they began to produce a revolver that was the same as the Russian Nagant. In 1936 the VIS semi-automatic pistol production began. In 1939 Poland fell to Germany, and the Radom plant was occupied. The VIS pistol was continued and used by the Nazis. There was never a production code assigned to the Radom plant. After the war, weapons construction continued at this factory.

## Ng 30

This is simply a Polish copy of the Russian Nagant revolver. It is chambered for the 7.62 Russian cartridge, and the only difference is that the Polish version has a round front sight and on the Russian version the sight is undercut. There were approximately 20,000 manufactured between 1930 and 1936.

| Exc. | V.G. | Good | Fair | Poor |
|------|------|------|------|------|
| 300 | 250 | 200 | 150 | 100 |

## VIS-35

This is a fine service pistol that was Polish-designed. It was based on a modified Browning design, without the swinging link. There is a recoil spring guide and a grip safety. There is no manual safety, but there is a decocking lever that allows the hammer to be safely lowered on a loaded chamber. There is also a stripping catch that greatly simplifies takedown. This pistol is chambered for the .99 Parabellum cartridge and has a 4.5" barrel with fixed sights and an 8-shot magazine. The finish is blued, with black plastic grips on the earlier models and wood grips on Nazi guns made after 1943. The early Polish guns were very well made, with the Polish Eagle engraved on the slide. "FB" and "VIS" were molded into the grips on the earlier guns. Nazi guns were another story--the quality of the finish went downhill at a rapid pace. The decocking lever was eliminated first; then the stripping catch was eliminated in order to simplify and cheapen construction. The Eagle was not used on the Nazi guns, but they were stamped with the "P-35" German designation and also the Waffenamt inspector's mark "WaA77." Production of this pistol ceased in 1944, when the Russians destroyed the factory.

**Polish Eagle Model-1936 through 1939**

| Exc. | V.G. | Good | Fair | Poor |
|------|------|------|------|------|
| 800 | 650 | 500 | 350 | 200 |

**Nazi Captured Polish Eagle--Waffenamt Marked**

| Exc. | V.G. | Good | Fair | Poor |
|------|------|------|------|------|
| 950 | 750 | 600 | 450 | 300 |

**Nazi Production Model**

| Exc. | V.G. | Good | Fair | Poor |
|------|------|------|------|------|
| 450 | 350 | 250 | 200 | 175 |

# RANDALL FIREARMS CO.
## Sun Valley, California

This is a high quality, stainless-steel pistol patterned after the Colt Model 1911 Government Model. The company ceased production in 1985. In some areas this pistol is enjoying a surge in popularity among collectors of modern weapons.

## Service Model

This is a single-action semi-automatic pistol patterned after the Colt Model 1911 A1 design. It is chambered for the 9mm, .38 Super, and the .45 ACP cartridges. It has a 5" barrel and is constructed of stainless steel. The standard model was offered with fixed sights; but a ribbed, adjustable-sight model was also available. This model was available for either right- or left-handed shooters. It was discontinued in 1985.
Adjustable-Sight Model--Add $150.

| Exc. | V.G. | Good | Fair | Poor |
|------|------|------|------|------|
| 500  | 450  | 400  | 350  | 300  |

## Combat Model

This version is similar to the Service Model, with a ribbed slide with fixed, high-visibility sights. The right-hand model is furnished with Pachmayr rubber grips; and the left-hand model, with Herret walnut grips.

| Exc. | V.G. | Good | Fair | Poor |
|------|------|------|------|------|
| 550  | 500  | 450  | 400  | 350  |

## Service Model C (A/K/A Raider)

This version is patterned after the Colt Combat Commander. It is chambered for the 9mm or .45 ACP cartridges. It has a 4.25" barrel and is available with either fixed sights or a ribbed slide with adjustable sights. It is constructed of stainless steel and available for either right-handed or left-handed shooters. It was known as the Service Model C in 1983 and the Raider in 1984.
Adjustable-Sight Model--Add $150.

| Exc. | V.G. | Good | Fair | Poor |
|------|------|------|------|------|
| 500  | 450  | 400  | 350  | 300  |

## Curtis E. LeMay 4-Star Model

This version was designed by General Curtis E. LeMay. It is chambered for the 9mm or .45 ACP cartridges. It has a 4.25" barrel and features a compact construction with a .5" shorter grip frame and a squared trigger guard for two-hand hold. It is constructed of stainless steel and is available for either right-handed or left-handed shooters. An adjustable-sight, ribbed model is also available.
Adjustable-Sight Model--Add $100.

| Exc. | V.G. | Good | Fair | Poor |
|------|------|------|------|------|
| 600  | 550  | 500  | 450  | 400  |

# RANGER ARMS, INC.
### Gainesville, Texas

## Statesman

This is a bolt-action sporting rifle that is chambered for various popular calibers and has a 22" barrel. It was furnished without sights and is blued, with a checkered walnut stock. A recoil pad and sling swivels are standard. This model was manufactured in the early 1970's.

| Exc. | V.G. | Good | Fair | Poor |
|------|------|------|------|------|
| 325  | 300  | 250  | 200  | 125  |

## Statesman Magnum

This model is similar to the Statesman except that it is chambered for the magnum calibers and has a 24" barrel.

| Exc. | V.G. | Good | Fair | Poor |
|------|------|------|------|------|
| 350  | 325  | 300  | 250  | 150  |

## Senator

This is a more deluxe version, with select walnut and finer checkering.

| Exc. | V.G. | Good | Fair | Poor |
|------|------|------|------|------|
| 400  | 350  | 325  | 275  | 175  |

## Senator Magnum

This is the Senator chambered for magnum cartridges.

| Exc. | V.G. | Good | Fair | Poor |
|------|------|------|------|------|
| 425  | 375  | 350  | 300  | 200  |

## Governor

This was the top-of-the-line model, with better walnut and finer checkering.

| Exc. | V.G. | Good | Fair | Poor |
|------|------|------|------|------|
| 450  | 400  | 375  | 325  | 225  |

## Governor Magnum

This is the Governor model chambered for magnum cartridges.

| Exc. | V.G. | Good | Fair | Poor |
|------|------|------|------|------|
| 475  | 425  | 400  | 350  | 250  |

# RASHID
### Egypt

## Rashid Carbine

This is a gas-operated semi-automatic carbine that is based on the Swedish Ljungman system. It is chambered for the 7.62x39mm cartridge. It has a 20.5" barrel and in many aspects resembles the Soviet SKS rifle, which also had a big influence on its design. It had a 10-round integral magazine, and the sights are of the military adjustable type. It is blued, with a hardwood stock and an upper handguard. The folding bayonet is basically the same as that of the SKS. This rifle was adopted in 1954 and was used until phased out by the AK-47. There are a number of these fine rifles available due to the recent relaxation of import regulations.

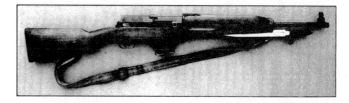

| Exc. | V.G. | Good | Fair | Poor |
|------|------|------|------|------|
| 300  | 250  | 200  | 150  | 100  |

# RAST & GASSER
### SEE--Gasser

# RAVELL
### Barcelona, Spain

## Maxim Double Rifle

This is a side-by-side double-barrelled rifle chambered for the .375 H&H or the 9.3x74R cartridges. It has 23" barrels with express sights and a Holland & Holland-type sidelock action. It features double triggers, automatic ejectors, and scroll engraving. The stock is hand-checkered select walnut, and a recoil pad is standard.

| Exc. | V.G. | Good | Fair | Poor |
|------|------|------|------|------|
| 4500 | 4000 | 3500 | 2750 | 2000 |

# RAVEN ARMS
### Industry, California

## P-25

This is a utilitarian, blowback-operated semi-automatic pocket pistol chambered for the .25 ACP cartridge. It has a 2.75" barrel and a 6-round detachable magazine. The finish is blued, chrome, or nickel-plated, with walnut grips. It was not manufactured after 1984.

| Exc. | V.G. | Good | Fair | Poor |
|------|------|------|------|------|
| 75   | 65   | 50   | 35   | 25   |

## MP-25

This model is similar to the P-25, with a die-cast frame and imitation-ivory grips.

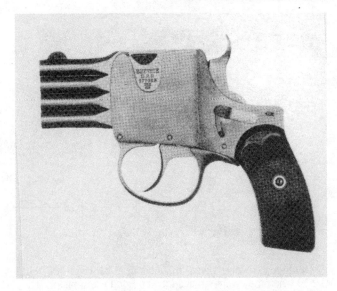

| Exc. | V.G. | Good | Fair | Poor |
|------|------|------|------|------|
| 550 | 500 | 400 | 300 | 225 |

| NIB | Exc. | V.G. | Good | Fair | Poor |
|-----|------|------|------|------|------|
| 75 | 65 | 55 | 45 | 35 | 25 |

## RECORD-MATCH ANSCHUTZ
### Zella-Mehlis, Germany

### Model 210 Free Pistol

This is a high quality single-shot target pistol that is built on a Martini falling-block action. It is chambered for the .22 l.r. cartridge and has an 11" barrel. It features an adjustable set trigger and adjustable target sights. The finish is blued, with checkered walnut grips and forend. This pistol was manufactured prior to WWII.

| Exc. | V.G. | Good | Fair | Poor |
|------|------|------|------|------|
| 1250 | 1000 | 850 | 750 | 600 |

### Model 210A

This model is similar to the Model 210, with a lightweight alloy frame.

| Exc. | V.G. | Good | Fair | Poor |
|------|------|------|------|------|
| 1200 | 950 | 800 | 700 | 550 |

### Model 200 Free Pistol

This is a less-deluxe version that does not have the set trigger.

| Exc. | V.G. | Good | Fair | Poor |
|------|------|------|------|------|
| 950 | 850 | 750 | 550 | 400 |

## REFORM
### Suhl, Germany
### August Schuler

### Reform Pistol

This was a unique attempt to produce a repeating pistol that is more concealable than a revolver. It is chambered for the 6mm cartridge and has four separate barrels and chambers, which are removed from the pistol, loaded, and then pushed down into the frame much like a top-loading magazine. As the double-action trigger is pulled, the barrels are moved upward and the empty cartridge is expelled. The hammer is made to deflect the casing from the shooter's face. The finish of the pistol is blued, and the grips are composite. It was manufactured between 1900 and 1905.

## REICHSREVOLVER
### Germany

This revolver was designed by the Small Arms Commission of the Prussian army in the late 1870's. There are two basic versions, and they were produced by the Erfurt Royal Arsenal, F. Dreyse of Sommerda, Sauer & Sohn, Spangenberg & Sauer, and C. H. Haenel of Suhl. The maker's initials are stamped in an oval above the trigger guard. The backstrap of this revolver is often marked with the regiment to which the revolver was originally issued.

### Model 1879

This version is chambered for the 10.55mm German Ordnance cartridge and has a 7.20" barrel. It has a 6-round cylinder and is a solid-frame, gate-loaded revolver with a removable cylinder and no integral ejection system. It has fixed sights; and the finish is blued, with plain round, flat-bottomed walnut grips, with a lanyard ring at the base. Oddly on a single-action revolver, there is a safety catch located on the left side of the frame--a superfluous feature on a revolver of this type. This model is also known as the Cavalry or Troopers Model.

| Exc. | V.G. | Good | Fair | Poor |
|------|------|------|------|------|
| 450 | 400 | 350 | 250 | 175 |

### Model 1883

This model is similar to the Model 1879, with a 5" barrel and a round-bottom walnut grip, with a lanyard ring at its base. It is also known as the Officers Model.

| Exc. | V.G. | Good | Fair | Poor |
|------|------|------|------|------|
| 400  | 350  | 300  | 225  | 150  |

Both of these revolvers were manufactured between 1880 and 1909 when they were replaced by the Parabellum pistol. They were, however, used in WWI extensively and by the Home Guard as late as WWII. The ammunition was available commercially up to 1939 but is quite scarce today.

# REID, JAMES
## New York, New York

**Model 1 Revolver**
This is a single-action, spur-trigger revolver chambered for the .22 rimfire cartridge. It has a 3.5" octagonal barrel and a 7-shot unfluted cylinder. The finish is blued, with walnut grips. The barrel is marked "J.Reid New York." There were approximately 500 manufactured between 1862 and 1865.

| Exc. | V.G. | Good | Fair | Poor |
|------|------|------|------|------|
| 500  | 400  | 350  | 250  | 150  |

**Model 2 Revolver**
This model is similar in appearance to the Model 1 except that it is larger and is chambered for the .32 rimfire cartridge. The barrel is marked "Address W. Irving 20 Cliff St. N.Y." or "James P. Fitch N.Y." There were approximately 1,300 manufactured between 1862 and 1865.

| Exc. | V.G. | Good | Fair | Poor |
|------|------|------|------|------|
| 500  | 400  | 350  | 250  | 150  |

**Model 3 Revolver**
This model is similar in appearance to the Model 2 except that the grip angle is more drastic and the grip more rounded. It is chambered for the .32 rimfire cartridge, and the barrel is 4.75" in length. The cylinders are threaded to use with percussion nipples in converting to percussion. This model is marked "J.Reid N.Y.City." It has an integral ejector rod mounted under the right side of the barrel. This is a very rare revolver, with an estimated 50 manufactured between 1862 and 1865.

| Exc. | V.G. | Good | Fair | Poor |
|------|------|------|------|------|
| 800  | 700  | 600  | 450  | 300  |

**Model 4 Revolver**
This model is also convertible for cartridge and percussion. It is chambered for the .32 rimfire cartridge and has barrel lengths of 3.75" to 8" It is a single action with a spur trigger and has a blued finish with walnut grips. The markings are the same as on the Model 3. There were approximately 1,600 manufactured between 1862 and 1865.

| Exc. | V.G. | Good | Fair | Poor |
|------|------|------|------|------|
| 450  | 375  | 325  | 225  | 125  |

**"My Friend" Knuckle Duster**
This is a unique firearm in that it has no barrel. The cylinder is chambered for the .22 rimfire cartridge and holds 7 shots. The construction is all metal, with the frame silver-plated brass or blued iron. The frame is scroll-engraved and is marked "My Friend Patd. Dec. 26, 1865." The frame has a hole in it for a finger so that it could double as a brass-knuckle type fighting weapon. There were over 10,000 manufactured between 1869 and 1884.

**Brass Frame**

| Exc. | V.G. | Good | Fair | Poor |
|------|------|------|------|------|
| 600  | 500  | 450  | 350  | 250  |

**Iron Frame**

| Exc. | V.G. | Good | Fair | Poor |
|------|------|------|------|------|
| 750  | 650  | 550  | 450  | 350  |

**.32 Caliber Knuckle Duster**
This model is similar to the .22-caliber version but is larger in size. There were approximately 3,400 manufactured between 1869 and 1884.

**Brass Frame**

| Exc. | V.G. | Good | Fair | Poor |
|------|------|------|------|------|
| 650  | 550  | 500  | 400  | 300  |

**Iron Frame**

| Exc. | V.G. | Good | Fair | Poor |
|------|------|------|------|------|
| 800  | 700  | 600  | 500  | 400  |

**.41 Caliber Knuckle Duster**
This is a still larger version of the Knuckle Duster. It has a brass frame and rifled chambers and is marked "J.Reid's Derringer." There were only 300 estimated manufactured between 1875 and 1878.

| Exc. | V.G. | Good | Fair | Poor |
|------|------|------|------|------|
| 2250 | 1750 | 1500 | 1250 | 950  |

**Model No. 1 Knuckle Duster**
This model has a 3" round barrel. The frame is brass. There were approximately 350 manufactured between 1875 and 1880.

| Exc. | V.G. | Good | Fair | Poor |
|------|------|------|------|------|
| 1000 | 850  | 750  | 600  | 450  |

**Model No. 2 Knuckle Duster**
This model is similar to the Model No. 1, with a 1.75" barrel. There were approximately 150 manufactured between 1875 and 1880.

| Exc. | V.G. | Good | Fair | Poor |
|------|------|------|------|------|
| 1100 | 950  | 850  | 700  | 500  |

**Model No. 3 Derringer**
This is a more conventional-appearing firearm that is chambered for the .41 rimfire cartridge. It is all metal and has a 3" octagonal barrel and a 5-shot fluted cylinder. The iron frame is silver plated, and the rest of the metal is blued. There were approximately 75 manufactured between 1880 and 1884.

| Exc. | V.G. | Good | Fair | Poor |
|------|------|------|------|------|
| 1400 | 1250 | 1000 | 800  | 600  |

**Model No. 4 Derringer**
This model is similar to the Model No. 3 except that it has a brass frame and walnut grips. It is marked "Ried's Extra." There were approximately 200 manufactured in 1883 and 1884.

| Exc. | V.G. | Good | Fair | Poor |
|------|------|------|------|------|
| 1250 | 1000 | 800  | 600  | 450  |

## New Model Knuckle Duster

This model is chambered for the .32 rimfire cartridge and has a 2" round barrel. The fluted cylinder holds 5 shots. The frame is silver-plated brass and has the finger hole for use as a fighting weapon. The barrel is marked "Reids New Model .32 My Friend." There were approximately 150 manufactured in 1884.

| Exc. | V.G. | Good | Fair | Poor |
|------|------|------|------|------|
| 750 | 650 | 550 | 450 | 350 |

# REISING ARMS CO.
### Hartford, Connecticut

## Target Pistol

This is a semi-automatic target pistol chambered for the .22 l.r. cartridge. It has a 6.5" barrel. There is an exposed hammer, and the barrel pivots upward for cleaning. It has a 10-round magazine and is actually a very well made pistol. The competition at the time was great--the Colt Woodsman had just appeared--and this company simply couldn't compete with Colt. The finish is blued, with the patent dates stamped on the slide; and the grips are checkered hard rubber, with a bear's head motif and the words "Riesing It's A Bear" molded into them. There were very few manufactured in the early 1920's. Early models were manufactured in New York City and are worth a premium. It is unwise to fire high-velocity ammunition in this pistol as the slides have been known to fracture from this practice.

### New York Manufacture

| Exc. | V.G. | Good | Fair | Poor |
|------|------|------|------|------|
| 400 | 350 | 300 | 200 | 150 |

### Hartford Manufacture

| Exc. | V.G. | Good | Fair | Poor |
|------|------|------|------|------|
| 375 | 325 | 275 | 175 | 125 |

# REMINGTON ARMS COMPANY, INC.
### Bridgeport, Connecticut

This company was founded by Eliphalet Remington. It was originally located in Ilion, New York. Beginning in the 1850's, they produced a number of rifles, shotguns, revolvers, derringers, and pistols. In 1888 the company was reorganized financially because of difficulties that they had experienced. At this time their interest in handguns tapered off; and for a number of years, they exclusively produced long arms. Since 1856 the company has been known by four different names: between 1856 and 1888--E. Remington & Sons; 1888-1910--Remington Arms Co.; 1910-1925--Remington Arms U.M.C. Co. (Union Metallic Cartridge Company); and 1925 to the present--Remington Arms Co. Early Remington firearms are very collectible and quite valuable on today's market. The problem with collecting these firearms is that they are not as well documented as some of the other major manufacturers' products. Beginning in 1816 Eliphalet Remington produced a number of flintlock and percussion sporting rifles. It is extremely difficult to catalog or evaluate any of his weapons from this era. As with any historically significant collectible and valuable firearm, we recommend securing a qualified appraisal if a transaction is contemplated.

## 1st Model Remington-Beals Revolver

This is a single-action pocket revolver chambered for .31 caliber percussion. It has a 3" octagonal barrel and a 5-shot unfluted cylinder. It is unique in that it has the mechanism that revolves the cylinder on the outside of the frame. The finish is blued and case-colored with a silver-plated brass triggerguard and smooth, gutta percha grips. The barrel is marked, "F. Beal's Patent,

June 24, '56 & May 26, '57." The frame is marked, "Remington's Ilion, N.Y." There were approximately 5,000 manufactured in 1857 and 1858.

| Exc. | V.G. | Good | Fair | Poor |
|------|------|------|------|------|
| 900 | 750 | 550 | 400 | 300 |

## 2nd Model Remington-Beals Revolver

This single-action pocket revolver is chambered for .31 caliber percussion. It has a 3" octagonal barrel and a 5-shot round cylinder. The main differences between this and the 1st model are the spur trigger and the squared butt with checkered rubber grips. The 1st model has a conventional trigger and guard and round-butt grips. This pistol is blued and case-colored. The barrel is marked, "Beals Patent 1856 & 57, Manufactured by Remingtons Ilion, N.Y." There were approximately 1,000 manufactured between 1858 and 1860.

| Exc. | V.G. | Good | Fair | Poor |
|------|------|------|------|------|
| 4500 | 3750 | 2500 | 1850 | 1500 |

## 3rd Model Remington-Beals Revolver

This version is also chambered for .31 caliber percussion. It has a 4" octagonal barrel and a 5-shot unfluted cylinder. It is larger than its predecessors and is the only version that features an integral loading lever mounted under the barrel. It has a spur trigger and checkered, rubber, square-butt grips. The finish is blued. The barrel is marked, "Beals Pat. 1856, 57, 58" and also "Manufactured by Remingtons, Ilion, N.Y." There were approximately 1,500 manufactured in 1859 and 1860.

| Exc. | V.G. | Good | Fair | Poor |
|------|------|------|------|------|
| 1200 | 1000 | 750 | 600 | 475 |

## Remington-Rider Revolver

This is a double-action pocket revolver chambered originally for .31 caliber percussion and later converted at the factory to fire the .32 rimfire cartridge. This conversion took place after 1873. The octagonal barrel is 3" in length. It has a 5-shot cylinder. This pistol features a very small butt and a large, brass, oval triggerguard, giving it a somewhat odd profile. It is either blued, nickel-plated, or two-toned with checkered, hard rubber grips. The barrel is marked, "Manufactured by Remingtons, Ilion, N.Y., Riders Pt. Aug, 17, 1858 May 3, 1859." There were approximately 20,000 manufactured between 1860 and 1873. The metallic cartridge conversion is sometimes found with a shorter barrel and is worth approximately 10 percent more than the percussion original version.

| Exc. | V.G. | Good | Fair | Poor |
|------|------|------|------|------|
| 700 | 550 | 425 | 300 | 225 |

## Remington-Beals Army Revolver

This is a large, single-action revolver chambered for .44 caliber percussion. It has a closed-top frame and an 8" octagonal barrel and uses a 6-shot, unfluted cylinder. It has a loading lever mounted beneath the barrel and is blued and case-colored. The square-butt grips are of two-piece walnut. The barrel is marked "Beals Patent Sept. 14, 1858 Manufactured by Remington's Ilion, New York." This pistol was designed to be competitive with the Colt percussion revolvers of this era, and actually they did quite well in the market. There were approximately 2,500 manufactured between 1860 and 1862. A martially marked version would be extremely rare and worth approximately 35 percent additional.

| Exc. | V.G. | Good | Fair | Poor |
|------|------|------|------|------|
| 3250 | 2750 | 1850 | 1100 | 800 |

## Remington-Beals Navy Revolver

This version is quite similar in appearance to the Army model but is slightly smaller. It is chambered for .36 caliber percussion and has a 7.5" octagonal barrel and a 6-shot, unfluted cylinder. The finish, as well as the markings, are the same as found on the Army model. The early models are worth approximately 80 percent more than the standard variations and are identified by the fact that the loading lever was built in a manner that would not allow the cylinder pin to be completely removed. This variation is quite rare. There were approximately 1,000 martially marked standard versions that would be worth approximately 40 percent more than the standard models. There were approximately 15,000 total manufactured between 1860 and 1862.

| Exc. | V.G. | Good | Fair | Poor |
|---|---|---|---|---|
| 1100 | 900 | 750 | 575 | 425 |

## 1861 Army Revolver

This is a single-action, military-type revolver chambered for .44 caliber percussion. It has an 8" octagonal barrel with a 6-shot, unfluted cylinder. This version is similar in appearance to the Beals model Army revolver except that there is a groove cut into the top of the loading lever that permits the cylinder to be removed without the lever being lowered. This feature, which was to be an improvement, was not accepted by the military service; and many were returned to have this channel filled in by a screw. It has the same closed-top frame. The finish is blued and case-colored with square-butt, two-piece, walnut grips. The barrel is marked "Patented Dec. 17, 1861 Manufactured by Remington's, Ilion, N.Y." There was a factory conversion to the .46 caliber rimfire cartridge, which would be worth approximately 20 percent less than the original, martially marked, standard percussion model. There were approximately 12,000 manufactured in 1862. This model is also known as the "Old Army Model."

| Exc. | V.G. | Good | Fair | Poor |
|---|---|---|---|---|
| 1750 | 1500 | 1050 | 650 | 450 |

## 1861 Navy Revolver

This is a smaller version of the 1861 Army Revolver, chambered for .36 caliber percussion. It has a 7.25" octagonal barrel with a 6-shot, unfluted cylinder. This version was finished and marked similarly to the Army model and was also factory-converted to the .38 cartridge. The cartridge conversion would be worth approximately 35 percent less than the original, martially marked, percussion model. There were approximately 8,000 manufactured in 1862.

| Exc. | V.G. | Good | Fair | Poor |
|---|---|---|---|---|
| 1750 | 1500 | 1050 | 650 | 450 |

## New Model Army Revolver

This improved version of the 1861 Army is similar in most respects but features safety notches between the nipples on the cylinder. The finish is blued and case-colored with two-piece walnut grips. The front sight screws into the barrel. The barrel is marked "Patented Sept. 14, 1858 E. Remington & Sons, Ilion, New York, U.S.A. New Model." This pistol gave the Colt 1860 Army its greatest competition and was used quite extensively by Union forces in the Civil War. There were approximately 132,000 manufactured between 1863 and 1875. There were a number of variations within this model designation.

### Standard Model--Military Version

| Exc. | V.G. | Good | Fair | Poor |
|---|---|---|---|---|
| 1400 | 1150 | 800 | 550 | 350 |

### Civilian Model--No Government Inspector's Markings

| Exc. | V.G. | Good | Fair | Poor |
|---|---|---|---|---|
| 1400 | 1150 | 800 | 500 | 350 |

### .44 or .46 Cartridge Conversion

| Exc. | V.G. | Good | Fair | Poor |
|---|---|---|---|---|
| 1250 | 1000 | 700 | 500 | 300 |

## New Model Navy Revolver

This version appears similar to the New Model Army but is smaller in size. It is chambered for .36 caliber percussion and has a 7.25" octagonal barrel and a 6-shot, unfluted cylinder with safety notches between the nipples. The finish and mark-ings were the same as on the Army Revolver, and this too provided the Colt Navy with its greatest competition. There were approximately 22,000 manufactured between 1863 and 1875.

### Military Version

| Exc. | V.G. | Good | Fair | Poor |
|---|---|---|---|---|
| 1850 | 1600 | 1250 | 900 | 650 |

### Civilian Version

| Exc. | V.G. | Good | Fair | Poor |
|---|---|---|---|---|
| 1200 | 950 | 650 | 450 | 300 |

### .38 Cartridge Conversion--1873 to 1888

| Exc. | V.G. | Good | Fair | Poor |
|---|---|---|---|---|
| 1000 | 750 | 500 | 400 | 250 |

## New Model Belt Revolver

This is a single-action revolver chambered for .36 caliber percussion. It has a 6.5" barrel with a 6-shot, unfluted cylinder with safety notches between the nipples. It is similar in appearance to the New Model Navy but is slightly smaller with a shorter barrel. The finish is similar, with some versions being nickel-plated. The markings were the same. There was a metallic cartridge conversion chambered for the .38 cartridge available. It would be worth approximately 25 percent less than the original percussion revolver. There were approximately 3,000 manufactured between 1863 and 1873.

| Exc. | V.G. | Good | Fair | Poor |
|---|---|---|---|---|
| 1150 | 900 | 600 | 400 | 275 |

## Remington-Rider Double Action Belt Revolver

This is a double-action version of the New Model Belt Revolver that is similar in appearance, chambered the same and finished alike. It is marked, "Manufactured by Remington's, Ilion, N.Y. Rider's Pt. Aug. 17, 1858, May 3, 1859." There was a factory conversion to the .38 cartridge that featured a two-piece cylinder. This version would be worth approximately 20 percent less than the standard percussion model. A fluted-cylinder version was also available but is extremely rare as there were only several hundred manufactured. Total production was approximately 5,000 manufactured between 1863 and 1873.

| Exc. | V.G. | Good | Fair | Poor |
|---|---|---|---|---|
| 1250 | 1000 | 700 | 500 | 350 |

## New Model Police Revolver

This is a smaller version of the Remington Navy Model. It was chambered for .36 caliber percussion, was offered with barrel lengths from 3.5" to 6.5", and has a 5-shot, unfluted cylinder with safety notches between the nipples. The finish is either blued and case-colored or nickel-plated, with two-piece walnut grips. There was a .38 caliber cartridge conversion available with a two-piece cylinder that would be worth approximately 20 percent less than the original percussion version. There were approximately 18,000 manufactured between 1863 and 1873.

| Exc. | V.G. | Good | Fair | Poor |
|---|---|---|---|---|
| 1000 | 750 | 600 | 450 | 300 |

## New Model Pocket Revolver

This is a single-action, spur-trigger revolver chambered for .31 caliber percussion. It features an octagonal barrel between 3" and 4.5" in length. It has a 5-shot, unfluted cylinder with safety notches between the nipples. The finish is either blued and case-colored or nickel-plated, with two-piece walnut grips. The barrel is marked, "Patented Sept. 14, 1858, March 17, 1863 E. Remington & Sons, Ilion, New York U.S.A. New Model." There were approximately 25,000 manufactured between 1863 and 1873. There are several variations within this model designation.

### 1st Version--Brass Frame and Trigger

| Exc. | V.G. | Good | Fair | Poor |
|---|---|---|---|---|
| 2500 | 1850 | 1500 | 1150 | 850 |

**2nd Version--Iron Frame, Brass Trigger**

| Exc. | V.G. | Good | Fair | Poor |
|---|---|---|---|---|
| 1250 | 1000 | 750 | 525 | 375 |

**3rd Version--Iron Frame, Iron Trigger**

| Exc. | V.G. | Good | Fair | Poor |
|---|---|---|---|---|
| 1000 | 750 | 600 | 450 | 300 |

**.32 Cartridge Conversion**

| Exc. | V.G. | Good | Fair | Poor |
|---|---|---|---|---|
| 850 | 700 | 550 | 400 | 275 |

**Remington-Rider Derringer**

This is a diminutive, single-shot pocket pistol chambered for .17 caliber percussion. It is entirely made of brass, with a 3" round barrel and a two-piece breech. It has brass grips, the barrel frame and grips produced integrally. It is silver-plated and marked, "Rider's Pt. Sept 13, 1859." There were approximately 1,000 manufactured between 1860 and 1863. This is an extremely rare and valuable little pistol, and we caution our readers to be wary of fakes.

| Exc. | V.G. | Good | Fair | Poor |
|---|---|---|---|---|
| 5500 | 4750 | 4000 | 3000 | 2000 |

**Zig-Zag Derringer**

This is a double-action, ring-trigger pocket pistol chambered for the .22 short cartridge. It has a 6-shot barrel cluster and resembles a pepperbox. The barrels have zig-zag grooves in the breech end that contribute to the revolving mechanism. The barrels are 3.25" in length. The finish is blued, with hard rubber grips. It is marked "Elliot's Patent Aug. 17, 1858 May 29, 1860." It is also marked "Manufactured by Remington's Ilion, N.Y." This was the first handgun manufactured by Remington that was originally designed as a metallic-cartridge pistol. There were approximately 1,000 manufactured in 1861 and 1862.

| Exc. | V.G. | Good | Fair | Poor |
|---|---|---|---|---|
| 3000 | 2500 | 1850 | 1100 | 750 |

**Remington-Elliot Derringer**

This is a ring-trigger, pepperbox-type pistol chambered for either the .22 or the .32 rimfire cartridges. It has a 5-shot barrel cluster that is 3" in length and fluted. The firing pin revolves, and the barrels pivot forward for loading. The finish is either blued or nickel-plated, with hard rubber grips. The barrel is marked "Manufactured by E. Remington & Sons, Ilion, N.Y. Elliot's Patents May 19, 1860 -Oct.1, 1861." There were approximately 25,000 totally manufactured between 1863 and 1888.

| Exc. | V.G. | Good | Fair | Poor |
|---|---|---|---|---|
| 1200 | 950 | 750 | 475 | 300 |

**Vest Pocket Pistol**

This is a single-shot derringer chambered for the .22 rimfire cartridge. It has a 3.25", round barrel with an octagonal breech. The finish is either blued or nickel-plated, with walnut grips. It is marked "Remington's Ilion, N.Y. Patent Oct. 1, 1861." Early versions have been noted with no markings at all. There were approximately 25,000 manufactured between 1865 and 1888. It is also known as the "Saw Handle Deringer."

| Exc. | V.G. | Good | Fair | Poor |
|---|---|---|---|---|
| 775 | 600 | 500 | 350 | 225 |

**Large-Bore Vest Pocket Pistol**

This is a larger version of the Vest Pocket Pistol chambered for the .30, .32, and the .41 caliber rimfire cartridges. It has either a 3.5" or 4", part-octagonal barrel. It is either blue or nickel-plated, with two-piece rosewood grips. The barrel was marked similarly to the smaller version with the addition of a Nov. 15, 1864 patent date. The .30 and .32 caliber version would be worth approximately 20 percent more than the standard .41 rimfire version. There were approximately 10,000 manufactured between 1865 and 1888.

| Exc. | V.G. | Good | Fair | Poor |
|---|---|---|---|---|
| 1100 | 850 | 650 | 500 | 375 |

**Remington-Elliot Derringer**

This is a single-action, single-shot pocket pistol chambered for the .41 rimfire cartridge. It has a 2.5", round barrel that screws into the frame. It features a combination hammer and breech block. The finish is blued or nickel-plated. It was standard with walnut grips but has been noted with grips of ivory or pearl. These would be worth a small premium. The barrel is marked "Remingtons, Ilion, N.Y. Elliot Pat. Aug. 27, 1867." There were approximately 10,000 manufactured between 1867 and 1888.

| Exc. | V.G. | Good | Fair | Poor |
|---|---|---|---|---|
| 1500 | 1250 | 950 | 700 | 500 |

**Remington Over/Under Derringer**

This is an Over/Under, double-barrel pocket pistol chambered for the .41 short rimfire cartridge. It has 3" round barrels that pivot upward for loading. There is a lock bar to release the barrels on the right side of the frame. The firing pin raises and lowers automatically to fire each respective barrel. It has a spur trigger and birdshead grip. The finish is either blued or nickel-plated; and it is featured with walnut, rosewood, or checkered hard rubber grips. Examples with factory pearl or ivory grips would be worth a small premium. This pistol is undoubtedly the most popular of all the American derringers and has become synonymous with the "Mississippi Riverboat Gambler." The numbers located on the underside of the bottom barrel of this model are assembly numbers, not serial numbers. There are a number of variations within this model designation. There were approximately 150,000 manufactured between 1866 and 1935.

**Early Type I**

This version has no extractor between the barrels and is marked "E. Remington & Sons, Ilion, N.Y." on one side and "Elliot's Patent Dec. 12, 1865" on the other side. There were only a few hundred manufactured in 1866.

| Exc. | V.G. | Good | Fair | Poor |
|---|---|---|---|---|
| 1500 | 1250 | 800 | 650 | 400 |

**Type I Mid-Production**

This version is marked the same as the early model but has a manual extractor between the barrels. It was manufactured in the late 1860's.

| Exc. | V.G. | Good | Fair | Poor |
|---|---|---|---|---|
| 1750 | 1400 | 1000 | 800 | 550 |

**Type I Late Production**

This version has an extractor and the same markings on the top of the barrel. It was manufactured between the late 1860's and 1888.

| Exc. | V.G. | Good | Fair | Poor |
|---|---|---|---|---|
| 750 | 600 | 500 | 400 | 300 |

**Type II**

This version is marked "Remington Arms Co., Ilion, N.Y." on the barrel rib. It was manufactured between 1888 and 1911.

| Exc. | V.G. | Good | Fair | Poor |
|---|---|---|---|---|
| 600 | 475 | 375 | 300 | 225 |

**Type III**

This version is marked "Remington Arms -U.M.C. Co., Ilion, N.Y." on the barrel rib. It was manufactured between 1912 and 1935.

| Exc. | V.G. | Good | Fair | Poor |
|---|---|---|---|---|
| 600 | 475 | 375 | 300 | 225 |

**Model 1865 Navy Rolling Block Pistol**

This is a single-action, single-shot, spur-trigger pistol with a rolling block-type action. It is chambered for the .50 caliber rimfire cartridge and has an 8.5", round barrel. The finish is blued and case-colored, with walnut grips and forend. The barrel is marked "Remingtons, Ilion N.Y. U.S.A. Pat. May 3d Nov. 15th, 1864 April 17th, 1866." This was Remington's first Rolling

Block Pistol. Military-marked versions would be worth approximately 25 percent more than the values for the civilian model shown. Centerfire conversions are often encountered with later breech blocks added, and they would be worth approximately 10 percent less than the standard civilian version. There were approximately 6,500 manufactured between 1866 and 1870.

| Exc. | V.G. | Good | Fair | Poor |
|------|------|------|------|------|
| 2400 | 2000 | 1650 | 1000 | 750 |

## Model 1867 Navy Rolling Block Pistol

This version is similar to the 1865 except that it has a conventional trigger and triggerguard and is chambered for the .50 caliber centerfire cartridge. It has a 7" round barrel. It was finished and marked similarly, and there are some who feel that all of these are converted 1865 models. The quantity manufactured is unknown, but they were produced in the early 1870's. Civilian specimens are worth approximately 30 percent more than the standard, Navy-marked version evaluated here.

| Exc. | V.G. | Good | Fair | Poor |
|------|------|------|------|------|
| 2000 | 1750 | 1450 | 850 | 600 |

## Remington-Rider Magazine Pistol

This is a rather unique pocket pistol chambered for the .32 rimfire extra-short cartridge. It has a 3" octagonal barrel with a 5-round, tubular magazine beneath it. It has a spur trigger and a combination breech block cartridge carrier positioned in front of the hammer. The magazine is loaded from the front. The finish is either blued and case-colored or, more commonly, nickel-plated. It has either walnut, pearl, or ivory grips and is marked "E. Remington & Sons, Ilion, N.Y. Riders Pat. Aug. 15, 1871." There were approximately 10,000 manufactured between 1871 and 1888. Most encountered will have some sort of engraved embellishment, but they will not be worth a premium over the rarer plain versions.

| Exc. | V.G. | Good | Fair | Poor |
|------|------|------|------|------|
| 750 | 600 | 450 | 350 | 225 |

## Model 1871 Army Rolling Block Pistol

This is a single-shot, rolling-block breechloader chambered for the .50 centerfire cartridge. It has an 8", round barrel and a conventional trigger and triggerguard. The finish is blued and case-colored, with walnut grips and forearm. The markings are similar to the Model 1867 Rolling Block with the letters "P S." added. It has a humpback, square-butt grip that set it apart from its predecessors. There were approximately 6,000 manufactured between 1872 and 1888.

| Exc. | V.G. | Good | Fair | Poor |
|------|------|------|------|------|
| 1750 | 1500 | 1250 | 750 | 500 |

## Remington-Smoot No. 1 Revolver

This is a spur-trigger, single-action pocket revolver chambered for the .30 short rimfire cartridge. It has a 2.75" ribbed octagonal barrel and a 5-round, fluted cylinder. The finish is either blued or nickel-plated, with walnut or checkered rubber grips. There is an ejector-rod housing mounted under the barrel. It is marked, "E. Remington & Sons, Ilion, N.Y. Pat. W. S. Smoot Oct. 21, 1873." The early version of this revolver featured a revolving recoil shield that turned with the cylinder. This version is extremely rare and would bring a 300 percent premium over the standard model.

| Exc. | V.G. | Good | Fair | Poor |
|------|------|------|------|------|
| 400 | 300 | 250 | 175 | 125 |

## Remington-Smoot No. 2 Revolver

This version is similar in appearance to the No. 1 Revolver except that it is chambered for the .32 short rimfire cartridge. There were approximately 20,000 manufactured between 1878 and 1888.

| Exc. | V.G. | Good | Fair | Poor |
|------|------|------|------|------|
| 375 | 275 | 225 | 150 | 100 |

## Remington-Smoot No. 3 Revolver

There are two basic versions of this spur-trigger, single-action revolver--one with a birdshead grip and no barrel rib, and the other with a humpbacked, square-butt grip that had the barrel rib. They are both chambered for the .38 short rimfire cartridge; examples in .38 centerfire have been noted and would be worth 10 percent additional. The finish is blued or nickel-plated, with checkered rubber grips. The markings are the same as the Model No. 1. There were approximately 25,000 manufactured totally between 1878 and 1888.

| Exc. | V.G. | Good | Fair | Poor |
|------|------|------|------|------|
| 500 | 400 | 325 | 250 | 175 |

## No. 4 Revolver

This is a spur-trigger, single-action revolver chambered for either the .38 or .41 short rimfire or centerfire cartridges. It has a 2.5", round barrel that screws into the frame. There is no ejector rod. It features a 5-round, fluted cylinder and is either blued or nickel-plated with checkered rubber grips. The barrel is marked "E. Remington & Sons, Ilion, N.Y." There were approximately 10,000 manufactured between 1877 and 1888.

| Exc. | V.G. | Good | Fair | Poor |
|------|------|------|------|------|
| 375 | 275 | 225 | 150 | 100 |

## Remington Iroquois Revolver

This is a spur-trigger, single-action pocket revolver chambered for the .22 rimfire cartridge. It has a 2.25" round barrel and no integral ejector rod. It has either a 7-shot, fluted or unfluted cylinder and is blued or nickel-plated with checkered, hard rubber, birdshead grips. The barrel is marked "Remington, Ilion, N.Y." with "Iroquois" marked on the top of the barrel. Occasionally an example will be noted without the Remington markings. There were approximately 10,000 manufactured between 1878 and 1888.

| Exc. | V.G. | Good | Fair | Poor |
|------|------|------|------|------|
| 400 | 300 | 250 | 175 | 125 |

## Model 1875 Single Action Army

This is a single-action revolver chambered for the .44 Remington cartridge and rarely encountered in .44-40. .45 government chamberings have been noted but are rarely encountered and would be worth a great deal more than the standard versions; this variation should definitely be appraised. This pistol has a 7.5" round barrel, but a 5.5" version has been rarely encountered and should also definitely be appraised. There is an integral ejector rod with a long triangular brace mounted between the barrel and the frame. The finish is either blued and case-colored or nickel-plated, with smooth walnut grips. Examples have been noted with a lanyard ring on the butt. The barrel is marked "E. Remington & Sons Ilion, N.Y. U.S.A." This pistol was designed to give the Colt Single Action Army competition; and although the quality was comparable, Remington had not made the government connections that Colt had; and none were sold for United States military use, although 1,300 were purchased by the Department of Interior for use by Indian reservation police. There were 10,000 purchased by the Egyptian government. There were 25,000 total manufactured between 1875 and 1889.

Blued Version--Add 40 Percent.

| Exc. | V.G. | Good | Fair | Poor |
|------|------|------|------|------|
| 4000 | 3000 | 2000 | 1250 | 600 |

## Model 1890 Single Action Army

This is a single-action revolver chambered for the .44-40 cartridge. It is offered with a 5.5" or 7.5" round barrel, with an integral ejector-rod housing. The triangular brace found on the Model 1875 is missing on this model. It has a 6-round, fluted cylinder and is either blued or nickel-plated, with checkered rubber grips that feature the letters "RA" molded at the top. The barrel is marked "Remington Arms Co., Ilion, N.Y." There have been some noted among the earliest versions with the 1875

model markings. This is a very rare version, as there were approximately 2,000 manufactured between 1891 and 1894. We strongly recommend securing a qualified appraisal as there have been spurious examples noted. It is not difficult for a talented forger to alter one of the more common Model 1875's to the Model 1890 configuration.
Blued Version--Add 40 Percent.

| Exc. | V.G. | Good | Fair | Poor |
|------|------|------|------|------|
| 4500 | 3500 | 2500 | 1750 | 1000 |

## Model 1891 Target Rolling Block Pistol

This is a rolling-block, single-shot, breechloading pistol chambered for the .22 rimfire, .25 Stevens, and the .32 S&W cartridges. It features a 10" half-octagonal barrel with target-type grips. The finish is blued and case-colored with walnut grips and forend. The barrel is marked "Remington Arms Co. Ilion, N.Y." The frame is marked "Remingtons Ilion N.Y. U.S.A. Pat. May 3 Nov. 15, 1864 April 17, 1866 P S." This is an extremely rare pistol, with slightly over 100 manufactured between 1892 and 1898. One should secure a competent appraisal as it would not be difficult to forge this variation.

| Exc. | V.G. | Good | Fair | Poor |
|------|------|------|------|------|
| 2000 | 1800 | 1250 | 775 | 575 |

## Model 1901 Target Rolling Block

This version is quite similar to the Model 1891 Target Model except that the thumb protrusion on the breech block was moved so that it was out of the line of sight. The rear sight is mounted on the frame instead of the barrel, and the front sight features an ivory bead. It is similar in all other respects and is also extremely rare. We recommend competent appraisal as spurious specimens have been noted. There were approximately 735 manufactured between 1901 and 1909.

| Exc. | V.G. | Good | Fair | Poor |
|------|------|------|------|------|
| 2000 | 1800 | 1250 | 775 | 575 |

## Mark III Signal Pistol

This is a single-shot, single-action, spur-trigger pistol chambered for a 10-gauge, flare-type signal cartridge. It has a 9" round barrel that breaks open for loading. It features a brass frame and an iron barrel that is finished in a matte black. The grips are two-piece walnut. The barrel is marked "The Remington Arms -Union Metallic Cartridge Co., Inc. Mark III, Remington Bridgeport Works Bridgeport, Connecticut U.S.A." There were approximately 25,000 manufactured between 1915 and 1918.

| Exc. | V.G. | Good | Fair | Poor |
|------|------|------|------|------|
| 350 | 275 | 200 | 125 | 75 |

## Remington 1911 and 1911A1

Remington manufactured service pistols for the U.S. Government. These models are listed in the Colt section of this text.

## Model 51

This is a single-action, semi-automatic pocket pistol that is blowback-operated. It is chambered for the .32 or the .380 ACP cartridges. It has a 3.5", round barrel. It utilizes either a 7-or 8-round, detachable magazine depending on the caliber. The finish is blued with checkered, hard rubber grips that have "Remington UMC" molded in a circle at their top. The slide is marked "The Remington Arms -Union Metallic Cartridge Co., Inc. Remington Ilion Wks. Ilion, N.Y. U.S.A. Pedersen's Patents Pending." Later versions carried a 1920 and a 1921 patent date. The early versions have nine cocking grooves on the slide; later models have 15 grooves with the frame marked "Remington Trademark." Early versions are worth approximately 10 percent additional. .32 caliber versions are worth approximately 25 percent additional, as they are rarer. There were approximately 65,000 manufactured between 1918 and 1934. The value for a standard, late-model, .380-caliber version is as follows:

| Exc. | V.G. | Good | Fair | Poor |
|------|------|------|------|------|
| 400 | 350 | 275 | 200 | 125 |

## Model 1841 "Mississippi Rifle"

This is a single-shot, muzzle-loading rifle chambered for .54 caliber percussion. It has a 33" round barrel, with a full-length stock held on by two barrel bands. It features brass furnishings, a browned barrel, and a case-colored lock. There is a steel ramrod mounted beneath the barrel that has a brass tip. The stock is walnut, with a brass patchbox on the right side. This rifle was produced by a number of contractors. Remington manufactured approximately 20,000 between 1846 and 1855. The lock plate was marked "Remington's Herkimer N.Y."

| Exc. | V.G. | Good | Fair | Poor |
|------|------|------|------|------|
| 1500 | 1250 | 950 | 675 | 450 |

## Model 1861 U.S. Rifle Musket

This is a single-shot, muzzle-loading rifle chambered for .58 caliber percussion. It has a 40" round barrel with a full-length stock held on by three barrel bands and a steel ramrod mounted beneath the barrel. The mountings are of iron. The metal is in the white with a walnut stock. This rifle was produced by a number of contractors. Remington manufactured approximately 40,000 between 1864 and 1866. The lock is marked "Remington's Ilion, N.Y."

| Exc. | V.G. | Good | Fair | Poor |
|------|------|------|------|------|
| 1250 | 1000 | 750 | 500 | 400 |

## Model 1863 Zouave Rifle

This is a single-shot muzzleloader chambered for .58 caliber percussion. It has a 33" round barrel with a full-length stock held on by two barrel bands. It has brass mountings and a blued and case-colored finish. There is a full-length, steel ramrod and a walnut stock. It features a brass patchbox in the buttstock. The lock is marked "Remington's Ilion N.Y." and dated 1863. This was one of the finest military rifles that came out of the Civil War era. Most encountered are in very good or better condition. There were approximately 12,500 manufactured between 1862 and 1865.

| Exc. | V.G. | Good | Fair | Poor |
|------|------|------|------|------|
| 1500 | 1250 | 950 | 675 | 450 |

## Breech-Loading Carbine

This is a single-shot, breech-loading rifle that was the forerunner of the famous Rolling-Block Action. It is chambered for the .46 or .50 rimfire cartridges. It has a 20" round barrel, with a half-length forend fastened by one barrel band. The .50 caliber version is quite a bit larger than the .46 caliber version. The finish is blued and case-colored with a walnut stock and iron mountings. The tang is marked "Remington's Ilion, N.Y. Pat. Dec. 23, 1863 May 3 & Nov. 16, 1864." The .50 caliber version is worth approximately 15 percent more than the .46 caliber version shown. There were approximately 15,000 .50-caliber versions produced; but most of them were not used by our government and were sold to France, which accounts for their rarity. There were approximately 5,000 produced in the .46 rimfire caliber. They were manufactured between 1864 and 1866 and were delivered prior to the end of the Civil War.

| Exc. | V.G. | Good | Fair | Poor |
|------|------|------|------|------|
| 1500 | 1250 | 950 | 675 | 450 |

## Revolving Rifle

This is a single-action revolving rifle chambered for either .36 or .44 percussion. It was offered with either a 24" or 28" octagonal barrel. It has a 6-shot, unfluted cylinder with safety notches between the nipples. It features a fancy, scroll-type trigger-guard with a spur under the bow. The stock is walnut with a crescent brass buttplate. The finish is blued and case-colored. The frame is similar to that of the New Model Revolver, with a slightly longer cylinder. It features a longer-length loading lever mounted under the barrel. There were factory conversions to the .38 rimfire cartridge that would be worth approximately 25 percent less than the standard percussion version. The .36-caliber version is more common than the .44-caliber version and would be worth approximately 10 percent less. The values given here are for the standard .44 caliber percussion model. The barrel is marked "Patented Sept. 14, 1858 E. Remington &

Sons, Ilion, New York, U.S.A. New Model." There were approximately 1,000 manufactured between 1866 and 1879.

| Exc. | V.G. | Good | Fair | Poor |
|------|------|------|------|------|
| 4000 | 3250 | 2500 | 1800 | 1250 |

### Remington-Beals Rifle

This is a single-shot, sliding-breech rifle chambered for the .32 or the .38 rimfire cartridges. It was offered with barrel lengths of 24", 26", or 28", that were part-octagonal in configuration. It features a folding rear sight. The triggerguard lever slides the barrel forward for loading. The finish is blued, with a straight-grip walnut stock and no forend. The frame is brass, although iron-framed versions are occasionally encountered and will bring approximately a 20 percent premium. The barrel is marked "Beals Patent June 28, 1864 Jan. 30, 1866 E. Remington & Sons, Ilion, New York." There were approximately 800 manufactured between 1866 and 1888.

| Exc. | V.G. | Good | Fair | Poor |
|------|------|------|------|------|
| 700  | 550  | 425  | 350  | 225  |

### U.S. Navy Rolling Block Carbine

This is a rolling-block, breech-loading, single-shot carbine chambered for the .50-70 cartridge. It has a 23.25" round barrel with a half-length forend held on by one barrel band. It has a folding-leaf rear sight and features a sling ring on the left side of the frame. The finish is blued and case-colored with iron mountings. The stock is oil-finished walnut. There are sling swivels mounted on the barrel band and the bottom of the butt. It is marked "Remington's Ilion, N.Y. U.S.A." along with the patent dates. There are U.S. inspector's markings on the right side, as well as a cartouche on the stock. There were approximately 5,000 manufactured in 1868 and 1869.

| Exc. | V.G. | Good | Fair | Poor |
|------|------|------|------|------|
| 1500 | 1250 | 950  | 675  | 450  |

### Model 1867 Navy Cadet Rifle

This is a single-shot, rolling-block, breech-loading rifle chambered for the .50/45 centerfire cartridge. It has a 32.5" round barrel, with a full-length forend held on by two barrel bands. The action is similar to the Navy Carbine; and it is either blued and case-colored or all-blued, with a walnut stock. There are no sling swivels. The markings were the same as the Navy Carbine, with the addition of the letters "U.S." on the buttplate. There were approximately 500 manufactured in 1868.

| Exc. | V.G. | Good | Fair | Poor |
|------|------|------|------|------|
| 1750 | 1450 | 1100 | 750  | 525  |

### Rolling Block Military Rifles

There were over 1,000,000 military rolling-block rifles and carbines produced for domestic and foreign sales between 1867 and 1902. They were all built on the large, No. 1 size action. They were produced in many different calibers with barrel lengths from 19" to 39", with either short or full-length forearms held on by as many as three barrel bands. They were produced for many foreign markets; and markings will be encountered in Arabic, Chinese, Danish, Egyptian, English, Spanish, Swedish, and Turkish, as well as a few others. It was also adopted by Argentina in 1879. There are a great many of these; and although they are collectible, they are not as valuable as the other rolling-block variations. The carbines are worth approximately 40 percent more than the full-stocked military rifles and should be inspected carefully so that they have not been shortened. Values for the full-length rifle are as follows:

| Exc. | V.G. | Good | Fair | Poor |
|------|------|------|------|------|
| 500  | 400  | 300  | 175  | 100  |

### No. 1 Rolling Block Sporting Rifle

This is a high-quality sporting weapon that was offered in a number of variations. It was built on the large size action and produced with many optional features that have a distinct effect on the value. They were offered in many popular calibers of the era, with various-length barrels that were either round or octago-

nal. Stocks varied in configuration and quality of walnut utilized. Different versions featured different sights. The standard finishes on all the variations were blued with a case-colored action. The barrels were marked "E. Remington & Sons Ilion, N.Y." It is important to note that the condition of the bore has a definite effect on the value. The .45-70 and the .50-70 are perhaps the most desirable calibers and may be worth a small premium to a collector. There were many thousands manufactured overall between 1868 and 1902. Variations and values are as follows:

### Standard No. 1 Sporting Rifle

This is the most commonly encountered version. It is chambered for various calibers from .40-50 to the .50-70 centerfire cartridges, as well as the .44 and the .46 rimfire cartridges. It was offered with 28" or 30" octagonal barrels and has been noted with round barrels, as well. It featured a folding-leaf rear sight. There were many options available that would increase the value. Secure an appraisal if in doubt.

| Exc. | V.G. | Good | Fair | Poor |
|------|------|------|------|------|
| 950  | 800  | 600  | 375  | 200  |

### Long-Range Creedmoor Rifle

This is a high-quality version chambered for the .44-90, .44-100, and the .44-105 centerfire cartridges. Other calibers have been noted but are rarely encountered. It was offered with a 34" part-octagonal barrel and has a long-range, Vernier tang sight, along with a globe front sight. The walnut stock features a checkered pistol grip and a plain forend with an iron cap. Again, be aware that there were many options offered (including special sights, fancy wood, and buttplates) that will have an increased effect on values. Secure an appraisal if in doubt. There were several thousand manufactured between 1873 and 1890.

| Exc. | V.G. | Good | Fair | Poor |
|------|------|------|------|------|
| 3500 | 2750 | 2000 | 1150 | 600  |

### Mid-Range Target Rifle

This version is similar to the Long-Range Rifle except that it is chambered for the .40-70, the .44-77, the .45-70, and the .50-70 cartridges. It has a 28" or 30" part-octagonal barrel with various stock configurations. It features a Vernier tang sight with a globe front. The stock is checkered, as well as the forearm. There were a number of options available that would affect the value. This model was produced between 1875 and 1890.

| Exc. | V.G. | Good | Fair | Poor |
|------|------|------|------|------|
| 3000 | 2250 | 1750 | 950  | 500  |

### Short-Range Rifle

This version was produced in various centerfire calibers between the .38 extra long and the .44 extra long, as well as several rimfire cartridges. It was offered with either a 26" or 30" round or octagonal barrel, with various sights. The standard version has an open rear sight and a beach-type front sight. The stock is checkered. There are many options available that would increase the value of this model. There were a few thousand manufactured between 1875 and 1890.

| Exc. | V.G. | Good | Fair | Poor |
|------|------|------|------|------|
| 2500 | 1800 | 1250 | 800  | 450  |

### Black Hills Rifle

This is a utility-grade rifle designed specifically for hunting purposes. It is chambered for the .45-60 centerfire cartridge and has a 28" round barrel with open sights. It features a plain, straight-grip stock and was manufactured between 1877 and 1882.

| Exc. | V.G. | Good | Fair | Poor |
|------|------|------|------|------|
| 2200 | 1600 | 1050 | 650  | 400  |

### Shotgun

There were several thousand 16-gauge rolling-block shotguns manufactured between 1870 and 1892. They were offered with 30" or 32" Damascus or fluid-steel barrels.

| Exc. | V.G. | Good | Fair | Poor |
|------|------|------|------|------|
| 700  | 600  | 450  | 325  | 200  |

**Baby Carbine**
This is a lightweight sporting carbine chambered for the .44-40 cartridge. It has a 20", thin round barrel and a half-length forearm held on by one barrel band. The finish is blued, and it features a saddle ring on the left side of the frame. It has a walnut stock with a carbine-type buttplate. There were several thousand manufactured between 1892 and 1902.

| Exc. | V.G. | Good | Fair | Poor |
|---|---|---|---|---|
| 3000 | 2250 | 1750 | 950 | 500 |

**Model 1-1/2 Sporting Rifle**
This is a lightweight version built on the 1.25"-wide, No. 1 rolling block action. It is chambered for rimfire cartridges from .22 to the .38 extra long, as well as centerfire cartridges from .32-20 to the .44-40. It has medium-weight octagonal barrels from 24" to 28" in length, with open rear and a blade-type front sight. The finish is blued and case-colored with a straight-grip, plain walnut stock. There were several thousand manufactured between 1888 and 1897.

| Exc. | V.G. | Good | Fair | Poor |
|---|---|---|---|---|
| 800 | 650 | 500 | 375 | 225 |

**Model 2 Sporting Rifle**
This single-shot breechloader was built on the 1.125"-wide, No. 2 rolling-block action and was chambered for various rimfire and centerfire cartridges between .22 and .38. It was offered with 24" or 26" octagonal barrels and features open, sporting-type rear sights. The finish is blued and case-colored with a walnut, "perch-belly"-type stock. There were many special-order features available that would affect values, and we recommend securing an appraisal if in doubt. It is smaller in appearance than the preceding models and was manufactured in fairly large quantities between 1873 and 1910. Antique variations manufactured before 1898 would be more desirable from a collector's standpoint and would be worth approximately 10 percent additional.

| Exc. | V.G. | Good | Fair | Poor |
|---|---|---|---|---|
| 800 | 650 | 500 | 375 | 225 |

**No. 4 Rolling Block Rifle**
This single-shot was built on the lightweight, No. 4 action and was chambered for the .22 rimfire, .25 Stevens rimfire, and the .32 short or long rimfire cartridges. It was offered with a 22.5" or 24" octagonal barrel. Later models were available with a round barrel. It features open sights. The finish is blued and case-colored. The straight-grip stock and forearm are walnut. There was a takedown model available that would be worth approximately 10 percent additional. This is the smallest of the rolling-block sporting rifles. There were approximately 50,000 manufactured between 1890 and 1933. Antique variations produced before 1898 would be more desirable and would bring approximately 10 percent additional.

| Exc. | V.G. | Good | Fair | Poor |
|---|---|---|---|---|
| 500 | 400 | 300 | 200 | 125 |

**Model No. 4 S Sporting Rifle**
This is a military-style sporting rifle built on the smaller, No. 4 frame. It is chambered for the .22 rimfire cartridge and has a 28" round barrel with a full-length forend held on by one barrel band. It also features a half-length handguard. There is a stud at the muzzle for attaching a knife-type bayonet. This version was initially marked "Boy Scout." At a later date, the marking was changed to "Military Model." This version was undoubtedly produced to be used by military academies as training rifles for their cadets. There were approximately 15,000 manufactured between 1913 and 1923.

| Exc. | V.G. | Good | Fair | Poor |
|---|---|---|---|---|
| 850 | 650 | 500 | 400 | 275 |

**No. 5 Rolling Block Rifle**
This single-shot was built on a No. 5 action, which is similar in size to the No. 1 but designed for high-pressure, smokeless cartridges. It was available in a number of variations and barrel

lengths, as well as a carbine version. The finish is blued and case-colored, with walnut stocks and various-length forearms held on with either one or two barrel bands. Some feature wooden handguards on the top of the barrel. The variations are as follows:

**Sporting or Target Rifle**
This version is chambered for the .30-30, .303 British, 7mm, .30 U.S., .32-40, .32 U.S., and the .38-55 cartridges. It was offered with 28" or 30" round barrels and features a plain, straight-grip stock with a half-length forend. It has open rear sights and was available with double-set triggers that would add approximately 10 percent to the value. It was manufactured between 1898 and 1905.

| Exc. | V.G. | Good | Fair | Poor |
|---|---|---|---|---|
| 850 | 650 | 500 | 400 | 275 |

**Model 1897**
This is a full-length, musket-type rolling block chambered for the 7x57 and the .30 U.S. cartridges. It has a full-length forend with a handguard held on by two barrel bands, with a bayonet lug at the muzzle. It features sling swivels and was chiefly exported to South and Central America. There was a later model known as the Model 1902 that was identical except for an automatic ejector. This version was manufactured between 1897 and 1902. Most encountered are in fairly poor condition because of the jungle climate in which they were used and stored.

| Exc. | V.G. | Good | Fair | Poor |
|---|---|---|---|---|
| 550 | 450 | 300 | 200 | 125 |

**Carbine**
This version is similar to the military rifle, chambered for the same calibers, except that it has a 20" round barrel with a half-length forend held on by one barrel band. It also features a handguard and a saddle ring on the left side of the frame. This version was also exported to Central and South America.

| Exc. | V.G. | Good | Fair | Poor |
|---|---|---|---|---|
| 850 | 700 | 500 | 400 | 300 |

**No. 6 Rolling Block Rifle**
This is a very lightweight, small rifle designed expressly to be used by young boys. It is chambered for the .22 rimfire cartridge, as well as the .32 short or long. It was also produced with a smooth-bore barrel to be used with shot cartridges. The round barrel is 20" in length. It has a takedown action with a barrel held on by a knurled knob underneath the frame. It is a very lightweight rolling block, with a thin operating knob on the breech. The finish is blued overall. Very early models featured a case-colored frame, and these versions would be worth approximately 10 percent additional. It has a straight-grip walnut stock with a small forearm. There were over 250,000 manufactured between 1902 and 1903.

| Exc. | V.G. | Good | Fair | Poor |
|---|---|---|---|---|
| 350 | 300 | 225 | 125 | 75 |

**No. 7 Rolling Block Rifle**
This unique version features a full checkered pistolgrip and forend that resembles a rolling-block pistol with the butt portion added to the back of the gripstrap. This is not the case, as it is all one piece; but it appeared as such. It is chambered for the .22 rimfire, as well as the .25-10 Stevens rimfire cartridges. It was offered with a 24", 26", or 28" part-octagonal barrel. It was built on the Model 1871 Rolling Block pistol action. It features a tang-mounted aperture sight and is blued and case-colored, with a checkered walnut stock. It is marked "Remington Arms Co. Ilion, N.Y. U.S.A." There were approximately 1,000 manufactured between 1903 and 1911. This was Remington's last rolling-block firearm.

| Exc. | V.G. | Good | Fair | Poor |
|---|---|---|---|---|
| 2750 | 2250 | 1750 | 1250 | 850 |

## Remington-Hepburn No. 3 Rifle

This is a falling-block, breech-loading, single-shot rifle that is activiated by a lever mounted on the right side of the frame. It is a simple action that is quite strong in its construction. It was designed by Lewis Hepburn, who was an employee of Remington for a number of years. This version is chambered for a number of calibers between the .22 Winchester centerfire and the .50-90 Sharps cartridges. It was offered with either a round or octagonal barrel that is 26", 28", or 30" in length. It has an open-type rear sight. The finish is blued with a case-colored receiver and a checkered, pistolgrip walnut stock. There were a number of options available which would increase values. We recommend securing an appraisal if in doubt. There were approximately 10,000 manufactured between 1883 and 1907. Antique versions manufactured before 1898 would be more desirable and worth approximately a 10 percent premium.

| Exc. | V.G. | Good | Fair | Poor |
|------|------|------|------|------|
| 1500 | 1250 | 1000 | 700 | 450 |

## No. 3 Match Rifle

This version is similar to the Sporting Model except that it features a high-comb buttstock with a nickel-plated, Schuetzen-type buttplate. It was made for target matches at short-or mid-range. It was chambered for various cartridges between the .25-20 Stevens and the .40-65. It was offered with a 30" part-octagonal barrel. There are two variations--the "A Quality" that has a plain stock and a tang-mounted peepsight with a Beach front sight, and the "B Quality" that features a fancy checkered walnut stock with a cheekrest and a matching checkered forend. It features a Vernier tang sight with a front sight that has a wind gauge and spirit level. Double-set triggers were offered and would be worth approximately 10 percent. There were approximately 1,000 of both variations manufactured between 1883 and 1907. Antique variations manufactured before 1898 would be more desirable and would bring approximately a 10 percent premium.

### A Quality
| Exc. | V.G. | Good | Fair | Poor |
|------|------|------|------|------|
| 1750 | 1500 | 1250 | 900 | 650 |

### B Quality
| Exc. | V.G. | Good | Fair | Poor |
|------|------|------|------|------|
| 2000 | 1750 | 1500 | 1100 | 850 |

## No. 3 Long-Range Creedmoor Rifle

This is a high-grade target version chambered for the .44 caliber centerfire cartridge. It was offered with a 32" or 34" part-octagonal barrel and features a long-range, Vernier tang-mounted sight with a wind gauge, spirit level front sight. It is blued and case-colored with a checkered, deluxe walnut stock and forend, with a hard rubber, shotgun-type buttplate. There were options offered on this model that would affect the values, and a qualified appraisal should be secured if in doubt. There were very few manufactured between 1880 and 1907. The antique versions manufactured prior to 1898 would be more desirable and would add approximately a 10 percent premium.

| Exc. | V.G. | Good | Fair | Poor |
|------|------|------|------|------|
| 2500 | 2200 | 1750 | 1200 | 800 |

## No. 3 Mid-Range Creedmoor Rifle

This version is similar to the Long-Range model except that it has a 28" barrel with a shorter Vernier sight. It is chambered for the .40-65 cartridge.

| Exc. | V.G. | Good | Fair | Poor |
|------|------|------|------|------|
| 2250 | 2000 | 1500 | 1000 | 650 |

## No. 3 Long-Range Military Rifle

This is a very rare variation that is chambered for the .44-75-520 Remington cartridge. It has a round 34" barrel and a full-length forearm held on by two barrel bands. The finish is blued and case-colored, and the stock is walnut. There are two basic versions. The plain grade has an uncheckered, straight-grip stock with military-type sights. There is also a fancy grade that features a high-grade, checkered, pistolgrip stock with a full-

length, checkered forend, Vernier tang sight, and wind gauge, spirit lever front sight. There were very few manufactured in the 1880's.

### Plain Grade
| Exc. | V.G. | Good | Fair | Poor |
|------|------|------|------|------|
| 3500 | 2800 | 2000 | 1400 | 900 |

### Fancy Grade
| Exc. | V.G. | Good | Fair | Poor |
|------|------|------|------|------|
| 4250 | 3500 | 2750 | 1850 | 1250 |

## No. 3 Schuetzen Match Rifle

This version is quite unique in that the action is activated by a fancy, scroll, triggerguard underlever. It was chambered for various popular cartridges and was offered with a 30" or 32" part-octagonal, heavy barrel. It features a Vernier tang sight with a hooded front sight. It was standard with double-set triggers and a palmrest. The finish is blued and case-colored, with a very high grade checkered walnut stock and forend. It has an ornate, Swiss-type Schuetzen buttplate and is also known as the "Walker-Hepburn Rifle." There were two versions available--one, a standard breechloader with the Remington Walker-marked barrel; and the other, a muzzleloading variation that was fitted with a removable false muzzle. This version was supplied with a brass bullet starter and other accessories. Values hinge upon these accessories being present. This is a very rare Remington rifle, and one should be extremely careful of fakes.

### Breechloading Version
| Exc. | V.G. | Good | Fair | Poor |
|------|------|------|------|------|
| 5000 | 4250 | 3250 | 2250 | 1750 |

### Muzzleloading Version
| Exc. | V.G. | Good | Fair | Poor |
|------|------|------|------|------|
| 6000 | 5250 | 4250 | 3250 | 2750 |

## No. 3 High-Power Rifle

This version was designed as a sporting and hunting rifle and was chambered for the .30-30, .30 Government, .32 Special, .32-40, and the .38-55 cartridges. It was offered with 26", 28", or 30" round barrels and has open sights. There were a number of options offered that would increase the value. We recommend a qualified appraisal if in doubt. There were very few produced between 1900 and 1907.

| Exc. | V.G. | Good | Fair | Poor |
|------|------|------|------|------|
| 1500 | 1250 | 1000 | 700 | 500 |

## Remington-Keene Magazine Rifle

This is a bolt-action rifle chambered for the .40, .43, and the .45-70 centerfire cartridges. It has a 22", 24.5", 29.25", or 32.5" barrel depending on the variation. It is a unique action in that it is a bolt action with an exposed hammer. The finish is blued, with a case-colored hammer and iron mountings. The stock is of walnut. It is marked "E. Remington & Sons, Ilion, N.Y." along with the patent date 1874, 1876, and 1877. It was the first bolt-action rifle that Remington produced and has a tubular magazine mounted under the barrel. It features a magazine cutoff so that it could be used as a single shot. There were five basic variations and a total of approximately 5,000 manufactured between 1880 and 1888. The variations and their values are as follows:

### Sporting Rifle--24.5" Barrel
| Exc. | V.G. | Good | Fair | Poor |
|------|------|------|------|------|
| 1050 | 850 | 650 | 450 | 325 |

### Army Rifle

This version features a 32.5" barrel with a full-length stock held on by two barrel bands and a forend tip. It features sling swivels and is quite rare.

| Exc. | V.G. | Good | Fair | Poor |
|------|------|------|------|------|
| 1150 | 950 | 750 | 500 | 425 |

## Navy Rifle

This version is quite similar to the Army Rifle except it features a 29.25" barrel. It is also quite rare.

| Exc. | V.G. | Good | Fair | Poor |
|------|------|------|------|------|
| 1150 | 950 | 750 | 550 | 425 |

## Carbine

This version features a 22" barrel with a full-length stock held on by two barrel bands and an iron forend tip. It has a 7-round tubular magazine and a leaf-type rear sight. It is also quite rare.

| Exc. | V.G. | Good | Fair | Poor |
|------|------|------|------|------|
| 1150 | 950 | 750 | 550 | 425 |

## Frontier Model

This version has a 24" barrel with a full-length forearm held on by one barrel band. It features sling swivels and a carbine-type buttplate. It was purchased by the United States Department of the Interior for arming Indian police on the reservations. The frame is marked "U.S.I.D."

| Exc. | V.G. | Good | Fair | Poor |
|------|------|------|------|------|
| 1500 | 1250 | 900 | 750 | 450 |

## Remington-Lee Magazine Rifle

This is a bolt-action military rifle designed by and contracted to James P. Lee for the U.S. Navy. It was originally contracted to the Sharps Rifle Company for manufacture in 1880. In 1881 Sharps ceased operations, and all parts and tooling were turned over to Remington so that the contract could be completed. Remington also produced this Rifle for export purposes with some action modifications. This Rifle is chambered for the .45-70 cartridge as well as others and has various barrel lengths depending on the version. It features a detachable box magazine located in front of the triggerguard. The finish is blued, with various-length walnut stocks. There were approximately 100,000 manufactured between 1880 and 1907. Most were exported. Antique versions produced before 1898 are more desirable and would bring approximately a 10 percent premium. The variations and their values are as follows:

## Model 1879--Sharps Mfg.

This version features a 28" barrel with a full-length stock held on by two barrel bands. The barrel is marked "Sharps Rifle Co. Bridgeport, Conn." The rectangular cartouche with "Old Reliable" is also present. There were approximately 300 produced prior to 1881.

| Exc. | V.G. | Good | Fair | Poor |
|------|------|------|------|------|
| 3000 | 2400 | 1850 | 1250 | 700 |

## Model 1879--Remington Mfg.

This model was produced in three distinct versions. They are all marked "Lee Arms Co. Bridgeport, Conn. U.S.A." as well as "Patented Nov. 4, 1879."

## U.S. Navy Model

This version has a 28" round barrel and a full-length stock held on by two barrel bands. It is chambered for the .45-70 cartridge and has U.S. Navy inspector's marks and an anchor on the barrel. There were approximately 1,300 manufactured.

| Exc. | V.G. | Good | Fair | Poor |
|------|------|------|------|------|
| 1500 | 1250 | 950 | 650 | 450 |

## Sporting Rifle

This version is chambered for the .45-70 and the .45-90 cartridges. It has a 28" or 30" part-octagonal barrel and a checkered pistolgrip stock with a half-length forearm. There were approximately 450 manufactured.

| Exc. | V.G. | Good | Fair | Poor |
|------|------|------|------|------|
| 1800 | 1550 | 1250 | 850 | 600 |

## Military Rifle

This version is quite similar to the Navy Model except that it has no United States military markings and is also produced in the .43 Spanish chambering. There were approximately 1,000 manufactured. Most were exported. The .43 Spanish version is worth approximately 25 percent less than the .45-70 version for which we furnish values.

| Exc. | V.G. | Good | Fair | Poor |
|------|------|------|------|------|
| 1250 | 1000 | 750 | 500 | 350 |

## Model 1882 Army Contract

This version has two grooves on each side of the magazine and is marked "Lee Arms Co. Bridgeport Conn., U.S.A." Some versions are marked "E. Remington & Sons, Ilion, N.Y. U.S.A. Sole Manufactured & Agents." It is chambered for the .45-70 cartridge and has a 32", round barrel with a blued finish and a full-length walnut stock held on by two barrel bands. There are U.S. inspector's marks at the breech and on the stock. There were approximately 750 manufactured.

| Exc. | V.G. | Good | Fair | Poor |
|------|------|------|------|------|
| 1750 | 1400 | 1100 | 800 | 650 |

## Model 1885 Navy Contract

This version is similar to the Army Model, with the U.S. inspector's markings on the left side of the stock and on the receiver ring. There is also an anchor stamped under the inspector's initials. There were approximately 1,500 manufactured.

| Exc. | V.G. | Good | Fair | Poor |
|------|------|------|------|------|
| 1500 | 1250 | 950 | 650 | 450 |

## Model 1882 & 1885 Military Rifles

These versions were produced for export purposes and civilian sales. Many are found with foreign military markings. They are chambered for the .45-70, .43 Spanish, .42 Russian, and the .45 Gardner cartridges. They feature a 32" barrel and a full-length stock held on by two barrel bands. The calibers other than .45-70 would be worth approximately 25 percent less than the values shown. There were approximately 10,000 manufactured in the Model 1882 configurations and 60,000 in the Model 1885. They are worth the same. The only difference between the Models is that the cocking knob is larger on the bolt of the model 1885. They are found with either of the barrel markings shown on the Model 1882 description.

| Exc. | V.G. | Good | Fair | Poor |
|------|------|------|------|------|
| 1000 | 800 | 600 | 450 | 325 |

## Model 1882 & 1885 Sporting Rifle

This version is chambered for the .45-70 and the .45-90 cartridges. It features a 26" or 30" octagonal barrel, with a walnut stock and half-length forend. There were approximately 200 manufactured.

| Exc. | V.G. | Good | Fair | Poor |
|------|------|------|------|------|
| 950 | 750 | 600 | 400 | 300 |

## Model 1882 & 1885 Carbine

This version features a 24" round barrel and a shorter, military-type forend held on by one barrel band. It is a very rare variation, and one should be aware of fraudulent examples.

| Exc. | V.G. | Good | Fair | Poor |
|------|------|------|------|------|
| 1500 | 1250 | 950 | 650 | 450 |

## Model 1899

This version is similar to its predecessors except that it was produced to handle the high pressure of the new smokeless powder cartridges. The extractor was modified for use with rimless cartridges, and the magazine features three grooves on each side. The finish is blued with walnut stocks, and all three versions are marked "Remington Arms Co. Ilion, N.Y. Patented Aug. 26, 1884 - Sept. 9, 1884 - March 17, 1885 - Jan 18, 1887." This model was manufactured between 1889 and 1907. The variations and their values are as follows:

## Military Rifle

This version is chambered for the 6mm USN, the .30-40, .303 British, 7x57, and the 7.65mm cartridge. It is similar in appearance to the Model 1885, with an improved forend designed to fit a bayonet. There is a wooden handguard, and the barrel is 29" in length. It has a full-length forearm held on by two barrel bands.

| Exc. | V.G. | Good | Fair | Poor |
|------|------|------|------|------|
| 900 | 700 | 550 | 425 | 300 |

## Military Carbine

This version is quite similar to the rifle except that it has a 20" barrel with a three-quarter length carbine stock held on by one barrel band. It also features a handguard.

| Exc. | V.G. | Good | Fair | Poor |
|------|------|------|------|------|
| 1000 | 750 | 600 | 475 | 350 |

## Sporting Rifle

This version was chambered for various popular calibers and was offered with a 24", 26", or 28" round or octagonal barrel. It has a blued finish and a checkered pistolgrip stock with a half-length forearm. It features open-type sporting sights. Examples chambered for the more popular calibers that are not obsolete are worth approximatey 20 percent more than the standard values furnished here. There were approximately 7,000 manufactured.

| Exc. | V.G. | Good | Fair | Poor |
|------|------|------|------|------|
| 1000 | 750 | 600 | 475 | 350 |

## Remington Lebel Bolt Action Rifle

This is a bolt-action military rifle manufactured specifically for the French government. It is chambered for the 8mm Lebel cartridge. It has a 31.5" barrel with a full stock held on by two barrel bands. The finish is blued. The stock is walnut. The barrel is marked "RAC 1907-15." The left side of the receiver is marked "Remington M'LE 1907-15." There were several thousand manufactured between 1907 and 1915.

| Exc. | V.G. | Good | Fair | Poor |
|------|------|------|------|------|
| 375 | 300 | 225 | 150 | 100 |

## Remington Mosin-Nagant Bolt Action Rifle

This is a bolt-action military rifle manufactured by Remington for the Russian government. It is chambered for the 7.62mm Russian cartridge and has a 32" barrel with a full-length stock held on by two barrel bands. The finish is blued, with a walnut stock. The top of the barrel is marked "Remington Armory" and dated. It also features the crest of Czar Nicholas II. There were 1,000,000 ordered, but the contract was terminated by the Russian revolution in 1918. There were at least 500,000 manufactured between 1916 and 1918.

| Exc. | V.G. | Good | Fair | Poor |
|------|------|------|------|------|
| 300 | 250 | 175 | 125 | 75 |

## U.S. Model 1917 Magazine Rifle

In 1917 when the United States entered WWI, there was a rifle shortage. We were already tooled up to produce the British Pattern 1914 rifle. It was re-designed quickly to fire the .30-06 cartridge and was re-named the Model 1917. The name Enfield was retained in honor of its birthplace. This is a heavy-duty, bolt-action rifle with a 26" barrel and a full-length walnut stock held on by two barrel bands. It has a 5-round, integral box magazine; and it is blued. This rifle was used throughout WWI and carried over to WWII. A million or more were sold to the British government to be used by the home guard. These versions would have a 2" red stripe around the butt to draw attention to the fact that they were chambered for the .30-06 instead of the .303 British, as was the 1914 Model. Remington was one of the companies that produced this firearm.

| Exc. | V.G. | Good | Fair | Poor |
|------|------|------|------|------|
| 350 | 275 | 200 | 150 | 100 |

## Remington-Whitmore Model 1874

This is a side-by-side, double-barrelled firearm produced as a smooth-bore shotgun, as a combination shotgun/rifle, and as a double-barrelled rifle. This was produced as a utility- grade rifle that features an unusual breech mechanism operated by pushing forward on the top lever. It was chambered for various gauges and calibers and was offered with 28" or 30" fluid-steel barrels. Damascus barrels were available as an option, and the value for both is approximately the same. The finish is blued and case-colored with a walnut, straight-grip or semi-pistolgrip stock. The barrels are marked "A. E. Whitmore's Patent Aug. 8, 1871, April 16, 1872." The rib between the barrels is marked "E. Remington & Sons, Ilion, N.Y." There were a few thousand manufactured between 1874 and 1882.

**Shotgun**

| Exc. | V.G. | Good | Fair | Poor |
|------|------|------|------|------|
| 800 | 650 | 500 | 400 | 275 |

**Combination Gun**

| Exc. | V.G. | Good | Fair | Poor |
|------|------|------|------|------|
| 2000 | 1750 | 1250 | 900 | 650 |

**Double Rifle--Be Very Wary of Fakes With Lined Smooth-Bore Barrels**

| Exc. | V.G. | Good | Fair | Poor |
|------|------|------|------|------|
| 5000 | 4000 | 2750 | 1850 | 1000 |

## Model 1882 Shotgun

This is a side-by-side, double-barrelled shotgun chambered for 10 or 12 gauge. It was offered with 28" or 30" fluid-steel or Damascus barrels. It features a sidelock action with external hammers and double triggers. The finish is blued and case-colored with a checkered, pistolgrip walnut stock and a hard rubber buttplate. The barrels are marked "E. Remington & Sons, Ilion, N.Y." The lock is marked "Remington Arms Co." This version features a conventional top lever that moves to the side. It was offered with optional engraving, and ornamented models should be individually appraised. There were approximately 7,500 manufactured between 1882 and 1889.

| Exc. | V.G. | Good | Fair | Poor |
|------|------|------|------|------|
| 800 | 650 | 500 | 400 | 275 |

## Model 1883 through 1889 Shotgun

This is also a side-by-side, double-barrelled shotgun with a sidelock action and exposed hammers. It is chambered for 10, 12, or 16 gauge, with barrel lengths from 28" to 32" in either fluid steel or Damascus. It is similar in appearance to the Model 1892 and was available with many degrees of ornamentation. The finish is blued and case-colored, with a checkered pistolgrip stock that features a pistolgrip cap. This version and the Model 1885, 1887, and 1889 shotguns are all quite similar. The only difference is the shape of their hammers and some slight improvements in the action. There were approximately 30,000 total of these four models manufactured between 1883 and 1909. The values for the standard variations are similar and furnished. Ornamented versions should be individually appraised.

| Exc. | V.G. | Good | Fair | Poor |
|------|------|------|------|------|
| 800 | 650 | 500 | 400 | 275 |

## Hammerless Shotgun Model 1894

This was a side-by-side, double-barrelled shotgun chambered for 10, 12, or 16 gauge. It features either steel or Damascus barrels from 26" to 32" in length. It is similar in appearance to its predecessors except that it has internal hammers. There were several thousand produced between 1894 and 1900. The values given are for a plain grade. There were many options and grades of ornamentation available that should be individually appraised.

| Exc. | V.G. | Good | Fair | Poor |
|------|------|------|------|------|
| 800 | 650 | 500 | 400 | 275 |

**Model 1900 Shotgun**
This version is similar to the Model 1894, with some internal improvements. It was offered in 12 and 16 gauge only. Higher-grade versions should be individually appraised.

| Exc. | V.G. | Good | Fair | Poor |
|---|---|---|---|---|
| 800 | 650 | 500 | 400 | 275 |

**Model 8**
This is a semi-automatic rifle chambered for the .25, .30, .32, and the .35 Remington cartridges. It has a 22" barrel with open sights. The recoil spring surrounds the barrel and is covered by a metal, full-length shroud. It has a 5-round, integral box magazine. The finish is blued, with a plain walnut stock. There were approximately 60,000 manufactured between 1906 and 1936. There are various versions that differ in the amount of ornamentation and the quality of materials and workmanship utilized. These variations and their values are as follows:

**Standard Grade**

| Exc. | V.G. | Good | Fair | Poor |
|---|---|---|---|---|
| 400 | 325 | 250 | 175 | 125 |

**Model 8A--Checkered Stock**

| Exc. | V.G. | Good | Fair | Poor |
|---|---|---|---|---|
| 450 | 375 | 300 | 225 | 150 |

**Model 8C**

| Exc. | V.G. | Good | Fair | Poor |
|---|---|---|---|---|
| 525 | 450 | 375 | 300 | 200 |

**Model 8D Peerless--Light Engraving**

| Exc. | V.G. | Good | Fair | Poor |
|---|---|---|---|---|
| 1000 | 750 | 500 | 400 | 300 |

**Model 8E Expert**

| Exc. | V.G. | Good | Fair | Poor |
|---|---|---|---|---|
| 1200 | 1100 | 850 | 600 | 450 |

**Model 8F Premier--Heavily Engraved**

| Exc. | V.G. | Good | Fair | Poor |
|---|---|---|---|---|
| 1500 | 1275 | 900 | 750 | 550 |

**Model 81 Woodsmaster**
This version is chambered for the same cartridges as the Model 8, as well as the .300 Savage cartridge. It is basically an improved version of the Model 8, with a 22" round barrel with open sights and a 5-round integral magazine. The finish is blued, with a walnut stock. There are a number of variations that differ in the amount of ornamentation and the quality of materials and workmanship utilized. It was manufactured between 1936 and 1950.

**Standard Model**

| Exc. | V.G. | Good | Fair | Poor |
|---|---|---|---|---|
| 400 | 325 | 250 | 175 | 125 |

**Model 81A--Takedown**

| Exc. | V.G. | Good | Fair | Poor |
|---|---|---|---|---|
| 450 | 375 | 300 | 225 | 150 |

**Model 81D Peerless--Engraved**

| Exc. | V.G. | Good | Fair | Poor |
|---|---|---|---|---|
| 1000 | 750 | 500 | 400 | 300 |

**Model 81F Premier--Heavily Engraved**

| Exc. | V.G. | Good | Fair | Poor |
|---|---|---|---|---|
| 1500 | 1275 | 900 | 750 | 550 |

**Model 12A**
This is a slide-action rifle chambered for the .22 rimfire cartridge. It features a 22" round barrel with open sights and a tubular magazine under the barrel. The finish is blued, with a plain walnut stock. It was manufactured between 1909 and 1936. There are a number of different versions that vary according to the options and the degree of ornamentation offered. This model was originally designated the Model 12. They are as follows:

**Model 12A**

| Exc. | V.G. | Good | Fair | Poor |
|---|---|---|---|---|
| 450 | 375 | 300 | 225 | 150 |

**Model 12B--.22 Short, Gallery Model**

| Exc. | V.G. | Good | Fair | Poor |
|---|---|---|---|---|
| 450 | 375 | 300 | 225 | 150 |

**Model 12C--24" Octagon Barrel**

| Exc. | V.G. | Good | Fair | Poor |
|---|---|---|---|---|
| 500 | 425 | 350 | 250 | 175 |

**Model 12CS--.22 Remington Special**

| Exc. | V.G. | Good | Fair | Poor |
|---|---|---|---|---|
| 475 | 400 | 325 | 250 | 175 |

**Model 12D Peerless--Light Engraving**

| Exc. | V.G. | Good | Fair | Poor |
|---|---|---|---|---|
| 550 | 475 | 400 | 300 | 225 |

**Model 12E Expert**

| Exc. | V.G. | Good | Fair | Poor |
|---|---|---|---|---|
| 1200 | 1000 | 750 | 600 | 450 |

**Model 12F Premier--Heavily Engraved**

| Exc. | V.G. | Good | Fair | Poor |
|---|---|---|---|---|
| 1500 | 1250 | 900 | 750 | 550 |

**Model 121A**
This is a hammerless, slide-action rifle chambered for the .22 rimfire cartridges. It was offered with a 24" round barrel with a tubular magazine mounted beneath it. It has a blued finish and a plain walnut stock. It was manufactured between 1936 and 1954. It was originally designated as the Model 121. There are a number of different grades available. They feature various degrees of ornamentation. The values are as follows:

**Standard Grade**

| Exc. | V.G. | Good | Fair | Poor |
|---|---|---|---|---|
| 375 | 300 | 250 | 175 | 100 |

**Model 121D Peerless--Engraved**

| Exc. | V.G. | Good | Fair | Poor |
|---|---|---|---|---|
| 500 | 400 | 350 | 250 | 175 |

**Model 121F Premier--Heavily Engraved**

| Exc. | V.G. | Good | Fair | Poor |
|---|---|---|---|---|
| 1200 | 1000 | 750 | 600 | 450 |

**Model 121S--.22 WRF**

| Exc. | V.G. | Good | Fair | Poor |
|---|---|---|---|---|
| 450 | 375 | 300 | 200 | 125 |

**Model 121SB--Smooth Bore**

| Exc. | V.G. | Good | Fair | Poor |
|---|---|---|---|---|
| 450 | 375 | 300 | 200 | 125 |

**Model 14**
This is a slide-action sporting rifle chambered for the .25 through .35 Remington cartridges. It has a 22" round barrel with open sights. The finish is blued, with a plain walnut stock. It was manufactured between 1912 and 1935. It was also designated the Model 14A.

| Exc. | V.G. | Good | Fair | Poor |
|---|---|---|---|---|
| 350 | 275 | 225 | 150 | 100 |

**Model 14R**
This version is similar to the Model 14 except that it has an 18.5" barrel and a straight-grip stock.

| Exc. | V.G. | Good | Fair | Poor |
|---|---|---|---|---|
| 400 | 325 | 275 | 200 | 125 |

**Model 14-1/2**
This is a slide-action rifle similar to the Model 14A except that it is chambered for the .38-40 and the .44-40 cartridges. It has a 22.5" barrel and was manufactured between 1912 and 1922. A carbine version with an 18.5" barrel is known as the Model 14-1/2R and would be worth approximately 10 percent additional.

| Exc. | V.G. | Good | Fair | Poor |
|---|---|---|---|---|
| 450 | 375 | 300 | 200 | 125 |

## Model 141

This is a slide-action sporting rifle chambered for the .30, .32, and the .35 Remington cartridges. It is a takedown rifle with a 24" barrel with open sights. It has a tubular magazine under the barrel and is blued with a plain walnut stock. It was manufactured between 1936 and 1950. Later models were designated the 141A.

| Exc. | V.G. | Good | Fair | Poor |
|------|------|------|------|------|
| 400 | 325 | 275 | 200 | 125 |

## Model 25

This is a slide-action sporting rifle chambered for the .25-30 and the .32-30 cartridges. It features a 24" barrel with open sights and a tubular magazine beneath it. The finish is blued with a walnut stock. It was manufactured between 1923 and 1936. Later models were designated 25A. A carbine model with an 18" barrel and a straight-grip stock was designated the Model 25R and would be worth approximately 10 percent additional.

| Exc. | V.G. | Good | Fair | Poor |
|------|------|------|------|------|
| 350 | 275 | 225 | 150 | 100 |

## Model 16

This is a semi-automatic rifle chambered for the .22 automatic cartridge. It has a 22" barrel with open sights and a tubular magazine in the buttstock. It is blued with a straight-grip walnut stock. It was manufactured between 1914 and 1928. Later versions were designated the Model 16A.

| Exc. | V.G. | Good | Fair | Poor |
|------|------|------|------|------|
| 300 | 225 | 175 | 125 | 75 |

## Model 24

This is a semi-automatic sporting rifle chambered for the .22 rimfire cartridge. It features a takedown design and was patterned after the Browning semi-auto rifle. It has a 19" barrel with open sights and a tubular magazine in the buttstock. The finish is blued with a walnut pistolgrip stock. It was manufactured between 1922 and 1935. Later versions were designated the Model 24A.

| Exc. | V.G. | Good | Fair | Poor |
|------|------|------|------|------|
| 325 | 250 | 200 | 150 | 100 |

## Model 241 Speedmaster

This is a semi-automatic sporting rifle chambered for the .22 rimfire cartridge. It has a 24" round barrel with open sights. It is a takedown rifle with a tubular magazine in the butt. The finish is blued, with a plain walnut stock. There were approximately 56,000 manufactured between 1935 and 1949. Later models were designated the Model 241A. There are three deluxe versions that vary as to the amount of ornamentation and the quality of the materials and workmanship utilized. The models and their values are as follows:

### Model 241

| Exc. | V.G. | Good | Fair | Poor |
|------|------|------|------|------|
| 375 | 300 | 250 | 200 | 150 |

### Model 241D Peerless--Engraved

| Exc. | V.G. | Good | Fair | Poor |
|------|------|------|------|------|
| 450 | 375 | 325 | 275 | 200 |

### Model 241E Expert

| Exc. | V.G. | Good | Fair | Poor |
|------|------|------|------|------|
| 850 | 775 | 650 | 450 | 350 |

### Model 241F Premier--Heavily Engraved

| Exc. | V.G. | Good | Fair | Poor |
|------|------|------|------|------|
| 1000 | 800 | 600 | 500 | 425 |

## Model 550A

This semi-automatic sporting rifle is able to fire the .22 s., l., or l.r. cartridges interchangeably. It has a 24" barrel with open sights, with a tubular magazine beneath it. It is blued with a one-piece, walnut pistolgrip stock. There were approximately 220,000 manufactured between 1941 and 1971.

| Exc. | V.G. | Good | Fair | Poor |
|------|------|------|------|------|
| 200 | 175 | 150 | 100 | 75 |

## Model 550P

This similar rifle features an aperture sight.

| Exc. | V.G. | Good | Fair | Poor |
|------|------|------|------|------|
| 225 | 200 | 175 | 125 | 100 |

## Model 55-2G

This rifle is similar to the Model 550A except that it was designed for use in shooting galleries. It features a shell deflector and a screw eye for chaining it to a shooting gallery counter.

| Exc. | V.G. | Good | Fair | Poor |
|------|------|------|------|------|
| 200 | 175 | 150 | 100 | 75 |

## Model 30A

This is a bolt-action sporting rifle based on the Model 1917 Enfield action. It is chambered for the Remington cartridges in .25 through .35 caliber, as well as 7x57 and .30-06. It features a 22" barrel with open sights and an integral box magazine. The finish is blued with a checkered walnut stock. It was manufactured between 1921 and 1940. A carbine model with a 20" barrel was designated the Model 30R and would have the same value.

| Exc. | V.G. | Good | Fair | Poor |
|------|------|------|------|------|
| 375 | 325 | 250 | 175 | 100 |

## Model 30S

This is a deluxe version of the Model 30A, chambered for the .257 Roberts, 7x57, and the .30-06 cartridges. It has a 24" barrel with a Lyman receiver sight and a select checkered walnut stock. It was manufactured between 1930 and 1940.

| Exc. | V.G. | Good | Fair | Poor |
|------|------|------|------|------|
| 450 | 375 | 300 | 225 | 150 |

Between the years 1930 and 1970, Remington manufactured many utility-grade, bolt-action, .22-caliber rifles. They were single shots as well as repeating rifles and were excellent quality, serviceable designs that were very similar with minor variations. There is no heavy collector interest in these models, and they are valued essentially for their value as shooters. We list them for reference purposes.

**Model 33**
**Model 33 NRA**
**Model 34**
**Model 34 NRA**
**Model 341 A**
**Model 341 P**
**Model 341 SB**
**Model 510 A**
**Model 510 P**
**Model 510 SB**
**Model 510 X**
**Model 511 A**
**Model 511 P**
**Model 511 X**
**Model 512 A**
**Model 512 P**
**Model 512 X**
**Model 514**
**Model 514 P**
**Model 514 BC**

Smooth-Bore Models--Add 20 Percent.

| Exc. | V.G. | Good | Fair | Poor |
|------|------|------|------|------|
| 125 | 100 | 75 | 50 | 25 |

## Model 37

This is a high-grade, bolt-action target rifle chambered for the .22 rimfire cartridge. It was offered with a 28" heavy barrel with target sights and scope bases. It has a 5-round magazine with a special single-shot adapter. The finish is blued with a walnut, target-type stock. It was manufactured between 1937 and 1940.

| Exc. | V.G. | Good | Fair | Poor |
|------|------|------|------|------|
| 400 | 325 | 250 | 175 | 100 |

## Model 37-1940
This is an improved version of the Model 37. It has a faster lock time, better trigger pull, and a redesigned stock. It was manufactured between 1940 and 1954.

| Exc. | V.G. | Good | Fair | Poor |
|------|------|------|------|------|
| 450 | 375 | 300 | 200 | 125 |

## Model 511 Scoremaster
This is a bolt-action, magazine-fed sporting rifle chambered for the .22 rimfire cartridge. It has a 22", round barrel and is blued with a walnut stock.

| Exc. | V.G. | Good | Fair | Poor |
|------|------|------|------|------|
| 250 | 200 | 175 | 125 | 75 |

## Model 513 TR
This is a bolt-action target rifle chambered for the .22 l.r. cartridge. It features a 27" heavy barrel with a Redfield aperture sight. It has a 6-round, detachable magazine. The finish is blued with a walnut, target-type stock that features sling swivels. It was manufactured between 1940 and 1969.

| Exc. | V.G. | Good | Fair | Poor |
|------|------|------|------|------|
| 300 | 250 | 200 | 150 | 100 |

## Model 513 S
This version is similar to the Model 513 TR except that it features Marble's open sights and a checkered, walnut, sporter-style stock. It was manufactured between 1941 and 1956.

| Exc. | V.G. | Good | Fair | Poor |
|------|------|------|------|------|
| 375 | 300 | 250 | 200 | 150 |

## Model 521 TL Jr.
This is a target rifle chambered for the .22 l.r. cartridge. It has a 25" heavy barrel and features Lyman target sights. This is a takedown rifle with a 6-round, detachable magazine. The finish is blued, and it has a walnut, target-type stock. It was manufactured between 1947 and 1969.

| Exc. | V.G. | Good | Fair | Poor |
|------|------|------|------|------|
| 250 | 200 | 175 | 125 | 75 |

## Model 760
This is a slide-action sporting rifle chambered for various popular centerfire cartridges from the .222 up to the .35 Remington cartridge. It has a 22" round barrel with open sights. It features a detachable box magazine. The finish is blued with a checkered, walnut, pistolgrip stock. It was manufactured between 1952 and 1982. Examples of this rifle chambered for the .222, .223, .244, and the .257 Roberts are worth a rather large premium over the other chamberings. We firmly believe that examples in these calibers should be individually appraised, as it would not be difficult for a qualified individual to create a re-barrelled, re-marked fake. There are a number of different versions that vary as to the amount of ornamentation and quality of materials and workmanship utilized. They are as follows:

### Standard Model
| Exc. | V.G. | Good | Fair | Poor |
|------|------|------|------|------|
| 250 | 200 | 175 | 125 | 100 |

### Model 760 Carbine--18.5" Barrel
| Exc. | V.G. | Good | Fair | Poor |
|------|------|------|------|------|
| 275 | 225 | 200 | 150 | 125 |

### Model 760D Peerless--Engraved
| Exc. | V.G. | Good | Fair | Poor |
|------|------|------|------|------|
| 1000 | 850 | 650 | 550 | 450 |

### Model 760F Premier--Gamescene Engraved
| Exc. | V.G. | Good | Fair | Poor |
|------|------|------|------|------|
| 2500 | 2000 | 1500 | 1200 | 1000 |

### Model 760F Gold Inlaid
| Exc. | V.G. | Good | Fair | Poor |
|------|------|------|------|------|
| 5000 | 4000 | 3000 | 2200 | 1750 |

### Model 760 Bicentennial--1976 Only
| Exc. | V.G. | Good | Fair | Poor |
|------|------|------|------|------|
| 350 | 300 | 250 | 175 | 100 |

## Model 760 ADL
| Exc. | V.G. | Good | Fair | Poor |
|------|------|------|------|------|
| 275 | 225 | 175 | 125 | 75 |

## Model 760 BDL--Basketweave Checkering
| Exc. | V.G. | Good | Fair | Poor |
|------|------|------|------|------|
| 300 | 250 | 200 | 150 | 100 |

## Model 552A Speedmaster
This is a semi-automatic rifle chambered for the .22 rimfire cartridge. It has a 23" barrel with open sights and a tubular magazine. It is blued, with a pistolgrip walnut stock. It was manufactured between 1959 and 1988.

| Exc. | V.G. | Good | Fair | Poor |
|------|------|------|------|------|
| 150 | 125 | 100 | 75 | 50 |

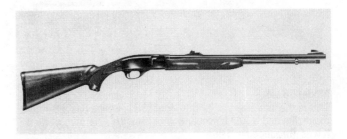

## Model 552 BDL
This version is similar to the Model 552, with a better grade stock and impressed checkering. It was introduced in 1966.

| NIB | Exc. | V.G. | Good | Fair | Poor |
|-----|------|------|------|------|------|
| 200 | 175 | 150 | 125 | 100 | 75 |

## Model 572 Fieldmaster
This is a slide-action rifle chambered for the .22 rimfire cartridge. It has a 21" barrel with open sights and a tubular magazine. It is blued with a walnut stock. It was manufactured between 1955 and 1988.

| Exc. | V.G. | Good | Fair | Poor |
|------|------|------|------|------|
| 150 | 125 | 100 | 75 | 50 |

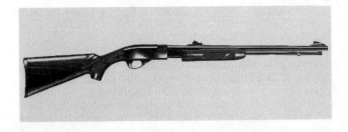

## Model 572 BDL
This version is similar to the Model 572 except that it features a better-grade stock with impressed checkering. It was introduced in 1966.

| NIB | Exc. | V.G. | Good | Fair | Poor |
|-----|------|------|------|------|------|
| 210 | 185 | 165 | 145 | 110 | 85 |

## Model 580
This is a single-shot, bolt-action rifle chambered for the .22 rimfire cartridge. It has a 24" barrel with open sights. The finish is blued with a Monte Carlo-type stock. It was manufactured between 1968 and 1978. A one-inch shorter-stocked model is known as the Model 580BR and would be worth approximately 10 percent additional.

| Exc. | V.G. | Good | Fair | Poor |
|------|------|------|------|------|
| 100 | 80 | 60 | 50 | 25 |

## Model 581
This is a bolt-action repeating rifle chambered for the .22 l.r. cartridge. It has a 24" round barrel with a 6-round, detachable magazine. It is blued, with a walnut stock. It was manufactured between 1967 and 1983.

| Exc. | V.G. | Good | Fair | Poor |
|---|---|---|---|---|
| 150 | 125 | 100 | 75 | 50 |

## Model 582
This version is similar to the Model 581, with a tubular magazine under the barrel. It was manufactured between 1967 and 1983.

| Exc. | V.G. | Good | Fair | Poor |
|---|---|---|---|---|
| 150 | 125 | 100 | 75 | 50 |

## Model 581-S
This is the latest version of the Model 581, which has a 5-round magazine and a 24" barrel and is blued with a hardwood stock. It was introduced in 1986.

| Exc. | V.G. | Good | Fair | Poor |
|---|---|---|---|---|
| 185 | 165 | 145 | 110 | 85 |

## Model 591
This is a bolt-action repeating rifle chambered for the obsolete 5mm rimfire Magnum cartridge. It has a 24" barrel with open sights and a 5-round, detachable magazine. The finish is blued, with a Monte Carlo-type stock. There were approximately 20,000 manufactured between 1970 and 1973. Collectors will currently pay $30 per box for original Remington 5mm ammunition.

| Exc. | V.G. | Good | Fair | Poor |
|---|---|---|---|---|
| 175 | 150 | 125 | 100 | 75 |

## Model 592
This version is simply the Model 591 with a tubular magazine under the barrel. There were approximately 7,000 manufactured.

| Exc. | V.G. | Good | Fair | Poor |
|---|---|---|---|---|
| 300 | 250 | 200 | 150 | 100 |

## Model 740
This is a gas-operated, semi-automatic sporting rifle chambered for the .308 and .30-06 cartridges. It has a 22" barrel with open sights and uses a detachable box magazine. It is blued with a plain walnut stock. A carbine version with an 18.5" barrel was available and would be worth approximately 10 percent additional. This model was manufactured between 1955 and 1960.

| Exc. | V.G. | Good | Fair | Poor |
|---|---|---|---|---|
| 250 | 225 | 200 | 150 | 100 |

## Model 740 ADL
This is similar to the Model 740 or 740A with a checkered walnut stock and a pistolgrip cap. A carbine version with an 18.5" barrel would be worth approximately 10 percent additional.

| Exc. | V.G. | Good | Fair | Poor |
|---|---|---|---|---|
| 275 | 250 | 225 | 150 | 100 |

## Model 740 BDL
This version is more deluxe with select walnut. The carbine version would be worth approximately 10 percent additional.

| Exc. | V.G. | Good | Fair | Poor |
|---|---|---|---|---|
| 300 | 275 | 250 | 150 | 100 |

## Model 742
This is a gas-operated, semi-automatic sporting rifle chambered for the 6mm Remington, .243, .280, .30-06, and the .308 cartridges. It has a 22" barrel with open sights and utilizes a 4-round, detachable magazine. The finish is blued, with a checkered walnut stock. A carbine version, chambered in .30-06 and .308 with an 18" barrel, would be worth approximately 10 percent additional. This model was manufactured between 1960 and 1980.

| Exc. | V.G. | Good | Fair | Poor |
|---|---|---|---|---|
| 300 | 275 | 250 | 150 | 100 |

## Model 742 BDL
This version features select walnut with a basketweave, Monte Carlo-type stock. It has a black pistolgrip cap and forend tip. It was manufactured between 1966 and 1980. There are several more-deluxe versions that differ in the amount of ornamentation and the quality of workmanship and materials utilized. They are as follows:

**Standard Grade**

| Exc. | V.G. | Good | Fair | Poor |
|---|---|---|---|---|
| 325 | 275 | 225 | 175 | 125 |

**Model 742D Peerless--Engraved**

| Exc. | V.G. | Good | Fair | Poor |
|---|---|---|---|---|
| 2100 | 1750 | 1500 | 1150 | 800 |

**Model 742F Premier--Gamescene Engraved**

| Exc. | V.G. | Good | Fair | Poor |
|---|---|---|---|---|
| 4000 | 3500 | 2750 | 1850 | 1300 |

**Model 742F Premier--Gold Inlaid**

| Exc. | V.G. | Good | Fair | Poor |
|---|---|---|---|---|
| 6500 | 5500 | 4000 | 3000 | 2250 |

**Model 742 Bicentennial--Mfg. 1976 Only**

| Exc. | V.G. | Good | Fair | Poor |
|---|---|---|---|---|
| 340 | 300 | 250 | 175 | 125 |

## Model 76 Sportsman
This is a slide-action sporting rifle chambered for the .30-06 cartridge. It has a 22" barrel and a 4-round, detachable magazine. The finish is blued with a plain hardwood stock. This is a utility-grade rifle manufactured between 1985 and 1987.

| Exc. | V.G. | Good | Fair | Poor |
|---|---|---|---|---|
| 250 | 225 | 175 | 125 | 75 |

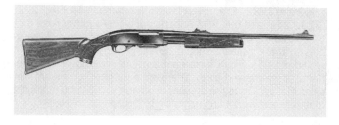

## Model 7600
This is a slide-action sporting rifle chambered for various popular cartridges between 6mm Remington and the .35 Whelen cartridges. It has a 22" barrel and a detachable box magazine. The finish is blued with an impressed, checkered walnut stock. A carbine version with an 18.5" barrel is also available and would be valued the same. This version was introduced in 1981. There are three high-grade versions that differ in the amount of ornamentation and quality of materials and workmanship. These variations and their values are as follows:

**Standard Grade**

| NIB | Exc. | V.G. | Good | Fair | Poor |
|---|---|---|---|---|---|
| 440 | 400 | 325 | 250 | 200 | 125 |

**Model 7600D Peerless--Engraved**

| NIB | Exc. | V.G. | Good | Fair | Poor |
|---|---|---|---|---|---|
| 2250 | 1800 | 1400 | 1200 | 950 | 750 |

**Model 7600F Premier--Gamescene Engraved**

| NIB | Exc. | V.G. | Good | Fair | Poor |
|------|------|------|------|------|------|
| 4750 | 4000 | 3500 | 2750 | 1850 | 1250 |

**Model 7600 Premier--Gold Inlaid**

| NIB | Exc. | V.G. | Good | Fair | Poor |
|------|------|------|------|------|------|
| 7000 | 6250 | 5000 | 4000 | 2750 | 1850 |

## Model Six

This is a slide-action sporting rifle chambered for various popular calibers, with a 22" barrel with open sights. It has a 4-round, detachable box magazine. The finish is blued, with a walnut stock. It was manufactured between 1981 and 1987.

| Exc. | V.G. | Good | Fair | Poor |
|------|------|------|------|------|
| 400 | 350 | 275 | 200 | 125 |

## Model 74 Sportsman

This is a utility-grade, gas-operated, semi-automatic sporting rifle chambered for the .30-06 cartridge. It has a 22" barrel with open sights and utilizes a 4-round, detachable magazine. The finish is blued with a plain, hardwood stock. It was manufactured between 1985 and 1987.

| Exc. | V.G. | Good | Fair | Poor |
|------|------|------|------|------|
| 300 | 250 | 175 | 125 | 75 |

## Model Four

This is a gas-operated, semi-automatic sporting rifle chambered for various popular cartridges. It has a 22" barrel with open sights and a 4-round, detachable magazine. The finish is blued with a select walnut, Monte Carlo-type stock. It was manufactured between 1982 and 1987.

| Exc. | V.G. | Good | Fair | Poor |
|------|------|------|------|------|
| 450 | 400 | 350 | 275 | 175 |

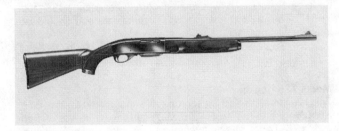

## Model 7400

This is a gas-operated, semi-automatic sporting rifle chambered for various popular calibers. It has a 22" barrel with open sights and a 4-round, detachable magazine. The finish is blued with an impressed, checkered walnut stock. It was introduced in 1982. A carbine version with an 18.5" barrel is also available. The values are the same.

| NIB | Exc. | V.G. | Good | Fair | Poor |
|------|------|------|------|------|------|
| 450 | 400 | 325 | 275 | 200 | 125 |

## Model 11

This is a bolt-action repeating rifle chambered for the .22 l.r. cartridge. It has a 20" barrel with open sights and utilizes either a 6- or 10-round, detachable magazine. The finish is blued with a nylon stock. It was manufactured between 1962 and 1964.

| Exc. | V.G. | Good | Fair | Poor |
|------|------|------|------|------|
| 150 | 125 | 100 | 75 | 50 |

## Model 12

This version is similar to the Model 11 except that it utilizes a tubular magazine mounted under the barrel. It was also manufactured between 1962 and 1964.

| Exc. | V.G. | Good | Fair | Poor |
|------|------|------|------|------|
| 175 | 150 | 125 | 100 | 75 |

## Model 10

This is a bolt-action, single-shot rifle that features the nylon stock. It was manufactured between 1962 and 1964.

| Exc. | V.G. | Good | Fair | Poor |
|------|------|------|------|------|
| 125 | 100 | 75 | 50 | 25 |

## Model 66

This is a blowback-operated, semi-automatic sporting rifle chambered for the .22 l.r. cartridge. It has a 20" barrel with open sights and features a tubular magazine in the buttstock. It was offered with a black or chrome-plated finish and either a black or brown checkered nylon stock. This model was manufactured between 1959 and 1988.

| Exc. | V.G. | Good | Fair | Poor |
|------|------|------|------|------|
| 150 | 125 | 100 | 75 | 50 |

## Model 77

This version is similar to the nylon Model 66 except that it utilizes a 5-round, detachable box magazine. It was manufactured in 1970 and 1971.

| Exc. | V.G. | Good | Fair | Poor |
|------|------|------|------|------|
| 150 | 125 | 100 | 75 | 50 |

## Model 76

This is a short-throw, lever-action rifle that is very similar in outward appearance to the Model 66. It also features the nylon stock. It was manufactured between 1962 and 1964.

| Exc. | V.G. | Good | Fair | Poor |
|------|------|------|------|------|
| 175 | 150 | 125 | 100 | 75 |

## Model 541S Custom

This is a high-grade, bolt-action repeating rifle chambered for the .22 rimfire cartridge. It has a 24" barrel and was furnished without sights. It utilizes a 5-round, detachable magazine. The finish is high-polish blued with a scroll-engraved receiver and triggerguard. The select, checkered walnut stock features a rosewood pistolgrip cap and forend tip. It was manufactured between 1972 and 1984.

| Exc. | V.G. | Good | Fair | Poor |
|------|------|------|------|------|
| 400 | 325 | 275 | 200 | 125 |

## Model 541T

This is a high-quality, bolt-action repeating rifle chambered for the .22 l.r. cartridge. It features a 24" barrel furnished without sights and drilled and tapped for scope mounting. The finish is blued, with a checkered walnut stock. It was introduced in 1986.

| NIB | Exc. | V.G. | Good | Fair | Poor |
|------|------|------|------|------|------|
| 335 | 275 | 200 | 175 | 125 | 75 |

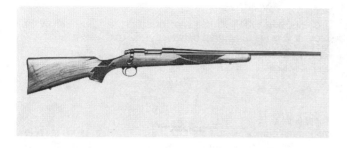

## Model 40X Sporter

This is a very high-grade, bolt-action sporting rifle chambered for the .22 l.r. cartridge. It features a 24" barrel with adjustable sights and a 5-round, detachable magazine. The finish is blued, with a custom walnut stock. There were fewer than 700 manufactured between 1969 and 1980.

| Exc. | V.G. | Good | Fair | Poor |
|------|------|------|------|------|
| 1500 | 1250 | 950 | 750 | 550 |

## Model 40X

This is a bolt-action, single-action target rifle chambered for the .22 l.r. cartridge. It has a 28" heavy barrel and was furnished with either Redfield Olympic sights or scope bases. The finish is blued with a select walnut, target-type stock. It has a hard rubber buttplate. It was manufactured between 1955 and 1964. The version without sights is worth approximately 10 percent less than the values given.

| Exc. | V.G. | Good | Fair | Poor |
|------|------|------|------|------|
| 500 | 400 | 325 | 250 | 150 |

## Model 40X Centerfire

This is a centerfire version chambered for .22, .22 Mag., .308, and .30-06. It was manufactured between 1961 and 1964. The version furnished without sights is worth approximately 10 percent less than the values furnished here.

| Exc. | V.G. | Good | Fair | Poor |
|------|------|------|------|------|
| 550 | 450 | 350 | 300 | 200 |

## Model 720A

This is a bolt-action sporting rifle based on an Enfield-type action. It is chambered for the .257 Roberts, .270, and the .30-06 cartridges. It has a 22" barrel with open sights and a 5-round, integral magazine. The finish is blued, with a checkered walnut stock. There were approximately 2,500 manufactured in 1941.

| Exc. | V.G. | Good | Fair | Poor |
|------|------|------|------|------|
| 1250 | 1000 | 800 | 600 | 475 |

## Model 721

This is a bolt-action sporting rifle chambered for the .264 Magnum, .270, and the .30-06 cartridges. It has a 24" barrel with open sights and a 4-round magazine. The finish is blued, with a plain walnut stock. This model was also furnished in a number of other versions that varied as to the calibers chambered and options offered. These versions and their values are as follows. It was manufactured between 1948 and 1962.

**Standard Version**

| Exc. | V.G. | Good | Fair | Poor |
|------|------|------|------|------|
| 300 | 250 | 200 | 150 | 100 |

**Model 721 ADL**

| Exc. | V.G. | Good | Fair | Poor |
|------|------|------|------|------|
| 350 | 300 | 250 | 200 | 125 |

**Model 721 BDL--Select Stock**

| Exc. | V.G. | Good | Fair | Poor |
|------|------|------|------|------|
| 400 | 350 | 300 | 250 | 150 |

**Model 721A Magnum--.300 H&H**

| Exc. | V.G. | Good | Fair | Poor |
|------|------|------|------|------|
| 450 | 400 | 350 | 275 | 150 |

## Model 722

This version of the 721 features a shorter-length action. It is chambered for the .257 Roberts, .300 Savage, and the .308 cartridges. Its other specifications were similar. It was manufactured between 1948 and 1962.

| Exc. | V.G. | Good | Fair | Poor |
|------|------|------|------|------|
| 300 | 250 | 200 | 150 | 100 |

## Model 725 ADL

This is a bolt-action sporting rifle chambered for various popular calibers, with a 22" barrel and open sights. It has a 4-round magazine. The finish is blued with a checkered, walnut, Monte Carlo-type stock. It was manufactured between 1958 and 1961. The .222 caliber version is quite rare and should be individually appraised.

| Exc. | V.G. | Good | Fair | Poor |
|------|------|------|------|------|
| 375 | 325 | 275 | 225 | 150 |

## Model 725 Kodiak

This is a large, bolt-action sporting rifle chambered for the .375 H&H Mag. and the .458 Win. Mag. cartridges. It was offered with a 26" barrel with an integral muzzle break and open sights. It has a 3-round magazine. The finish is blued with a select, checkered walnut stock. It was manufactured in 1961.

| Exc. | V.G. | Good | Fair | Poor |
|------|------|------|------|------|
| 800 | 700 | 550 | 400 | 300 |

## Model 600

This is a compact, bolt-action sporting rifle chambered for various popular calibers. It has an 18.5" vent-rib barrel and features a unique bolt handle that is doglegged to the rear. The finish is blued, with a checkered walnut stock. It was manufactured between 1964 and 1967. The .222, .223, and the .35 Rem. chamberings are worth a sizeable premium and should be individually appraised. Values for the other calibers are as follows:

| Exc. | V.G. | Good | Fair | Poor |
|------|------|------|------|------|
| 400 | 325 | 250 | 175 | 125 |

## Model 600 Magnum

This version of the Model 600 is chambered for the 6.5mm Rem. Mag. and the .350 Rem. Mag. cartridges. It features a laminated walnut and beech stock and is furnished with a recoil pad. It was manufactured between 1965 and 1967. The .350 Rem. Mag. chambering is worth approximately 10 percent additional.

| Exc. | V.G. | Good | Fair | Poor |
|------|------|------|------|------|
| 575 | 500 | 425 | 350 | 275 |

## Model 660

This improved version of the Model 600 was manufactured between 1968 and 1971.

| Exc. | V.G. | Good | Fair | Poor |
|------|------|------|------|------|
| 500 | 425 | 350 | 250 | 200 |

## Model 660 Magnum

This is similar to the Model 660 except that it is chambered for the 6.5mm Rem Mag. and the .350 Rem. Mag. cartridges. It features a laminated stock and is furnished with a recoil pad. The .350 Mag. chambering is worth approximately 10 percent additional.

| Exc. | V.G. | Good | Fair | Poor |
|------|------|------|------|------|
| 600 | 500 | 450 | 350 | 275 |

## Model 78 Sportsman

This is a utility-grade, bolt-action sporting rifle chambered for various centerfire cartridges. It has a 22" barrel with open sights and a 4-round magazine. The finish is blued with a plain hardwood stock. It was introduced in 1985.

| NIB | Exc. | V.G. | Good | Fair | Poor |
|-----|------|------|------|------|------|
| 335 | 275 | 225 | 200 | 150 | 100 |

## Model 700 ADL

This is a bolt-action sporting rifle chambered for many popular cartridges from the .22-250 to the 7mm Rem. Mag. It features a 22" or 24" barrel and is furnished with open sights. It has a 4-round magazine. The finish is blued with a checkered, walnut, Monte Carlo-type stock. It was introduced in 1962.

| NIB | Exc. | V.G. | Good | Fair | Poor |
|-----|------|------|------|------|------|
| 450 | 375 | 300 | 250 | 200 | 125 |

## Model 700 BDL

This is the deluxe version of the 700 ADL. It features a hinged floorplate with handcut skipline checkering and a black forend tip and pistolgrip cap. It is available in a number of additional calibers between .17 Rem. and .338 Win. Mag.

| NIB | Exc. | V.G. | Good | Fair | Poor |
|-----|------|------|------|------|------|
| 465 | 400 | 325 | 275 | 225 | 150 |

## Model 700 Mountain Rifle

This is a lightweight version of the Model 700 chambered for various popular calibers. It has a 22", light, tapered barrel furnished without sights. The finish is blued with a satin-finished, checkered walnut stock. It was introduced in 1986.

| NIB | Exc. | V.G. | Good | Fair | Poor |
|-----|------|------|------|------|------|
| 470 | 425 | 350 | 300 | 250 | 175 |

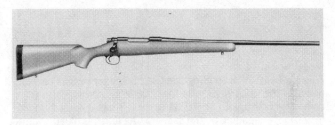

## Model 700KS Mountain Rifle

This version of the mountain rifle features a lightweight Kevlar stock. It was introduced in 1986.

| NIB | Exc. | V.G. | Good | Fair | Poor |
|-----|------|------|------|------|------|
| 875 | 750 | 600 | 500 | 400 | 300 |

## Model 700 Safari Grade

This is a larger, heavier-duty version of the Model 700BDL chambered for the .375 H&H, 8mm Rem. Mag., .416 Rem. Mag., and the .458 Win. Mag. cartridges. It has a 24" barrel with open sights and a 3-round magazine. The finish is blued with a select walnut stock. A Kevlar-stock version known as the KS Safari Grade is also available and would be worth approximately 20 percent additional. The Safari Grade was introduced in 1962.

| NIB | Exc. | V.G. | Good | Fair | Poor |
|-----|------|------|------|------|------|
| 875 | 750 | 600 | 500 | 400 | 300 |

## Model 700 RS

This is a bolt-action sporting rifle based on the Model 700, chambered for the .270 Win., .280 Rem., and the .30-06 cartridges. It has a 22" barrel with open sights and a 4-round magazine. The finish was blued, with a DuPont Rynite stock. It was manufactured in 1987 and 1988.

| Exc. | V.G. | Good | Fair | Poor |
|------|------|------|------|------|
| 500 | 425 | 350 | 250 | 150 |

## Model 700 FS

This version is similar to the Model RS, with a Kevlar fiberglass stock. It was manufactured in 1987 and 1988.

| Exc. | V.G. | Good | Fair | Poor |
|------|------|------|------|------|
| 550 | 475 | 400 | 300 | 200 |

## Model 788

This is a utility-grade, bolt-action sporting rifle chambered in various rifle calibers from .222 to the 7mm-08, as well as the .44 Magnum cartridge. It was offered with a 22" or 24" barrel with open sights. A carbine version with an 18" barrel was also available and would be worth approximately 10 percent additional. The finish is blued with a plain walnut stock. It was manufactured between 1967 and 1984.

| Exc. | V.G. | Good | Fair | Poor |
|------|------|------|------|------|
| 325 | 275 | 225 | 150 | 100 |

## Model Seven

This is a bolt-action sporting rifle chambered for various calibers between the .223 Rem. and the .308 Win. cartridges. It is a compact firearm with an 18.5" barrel. It has a 4- or 5-round magazine, depending on the caliber. The finish is blued, with a checkered walnut stock. This model was introduced in 1982.

| NIB | Exc. | V.G. | Good | Fair | Poor |
|-----|------|------|------|------|------|
| 450 | 400 | 325 | 275 | 200 | 100 |

## Model Seven FS

This version features a Kevlar fiberglas stock. It was introduced in 1987.

| NIB | Exc. | V.G. | Good | Fair | Poor |
|-----|------|------|------|------|------|
| 600 | 525 | 450 | 375 | 275 | 150 |

## Model 10A

This is a slide-action shotgun chambered for 12, 16, or 20 gauge. It was offered with 26" through 32" barrels with various chokes. It was a takedown gun with a blued finish and a plain walnut stock. It was manufactured between 1907 and 1929.

| Exc. | V.G. | Good | Fair | Poor |
|------|------|------|------|------|
| 375 | 300 | 250 | 200 | 125 |

## Model 11

This is a recoil-operated, semi-automatic shotgun produced under license agreements from Fabrique Nationale in Belgium. It is very similar to the Browning A-5. It is chambered for 12, 16, or 20 gauge and was offered with barrel lengths from 26" to 32" with various chokes. It is a takedown gun. The finish is blued, with a checkered walnut stock. There were approximately 300,000 manufactured between 1911 and 1948.
Solid Rib or Vent Rib--Add 30 Percent.

| Exc. | V.G. | Good | Fair | Poor |
|------|------|------|------|------|
| 350 | 300 | 225 | 175 | 100 |

### Model 11B Special--Engraved

| Exc. | V.G. | Good | Fair | Poor |
|------|------|------|------|------|
| 550 | 475 | 375 | 275 | 175 |

### Model 11D Tournament

| Exc. | V.G. | Good | Fair | Poor |
|------|------|------|------|------|
| 1000 | 800 | 650 | 450 | 300 |

### Model 11E Expert--Engraved

| Exc. | V.G. | Good | Fair | Poor |
|------|------|------|------|------|
| 1500 | 1250 | 1000 | 650 | 450 |

### Model 11F Premier--Heavily Engraved

| Exc. | V.G. | Good | Fair | Poor |
|------|------|------|------|------|
| 2750 | 2250 | 1850 | 1250 | 850 |

### Model 11R--20" Barrel Riot Gun

| Exc. | V.G. | Good | Fair | Poor |
|------|------|------|------|------|
| 350 | 300 | 250 | 175 | 100 |

## Model 17

This is a slide-action shotgun chambered for 20 gauge and offered with barrel lengths from 26" to 32" and various chokes. It is a takedown gun with a 4-round tubular magazine. The finish is blued, with a plain walnut stock. There were approximately 48,000 manufactured between 1917 and 1933.
Vent Rib--Add 25 Percent.

| Exc. | V.G. | Good | Fair | Poor |
|------|------|------|------|------|
| 350 | 300 | 250 | 175 | 100 |

## Model 29

This is a slide-action shotgun chambered for 12 gauge. It is similar to the Model 17 in all other respects. There were approximately 24,000 manufactured between 1929 and 1933.
Ventilated Rib--Add 25 Percent.

| Exc. | V.G. | Good | Fair | Poor |
|------|------|------|------|------|
| 300 | 250 | 200 | 125 | 75 |

## Model 31

This is a side-ejecting, slide-action shotgun chambered for 12, 16, or 20 gauge. It features barrel lengths of 26" to 32" with various chokes. It is a takedown gun with either a 2-round or 4-round tubular magazine. The finish is blued, with a walnut stock. There were approximately 160,000 manufactured between 1931 and 1949.
Solid Rib or Vent Rib--Add 25 Percent.

| Exc. | V.G. | Good | Fair | Poor |
|------|------|------|------|------|
| 400 | 325 | 275 | 200 | 125 |

## Model 870 Wingmaster

This is a slide-action shotgun chambered for 12, 16, and 20 gauge with a 26", 28", or 30" barrel with various chokes. It has a 5-round tubular magazine. The finish is blued, with a plain walnut stock. It was manufactured between 1950 and 1963.
Vent Rib--Add 10 Percent.

| Exc. | V.G. | Good | Fair | Poor |
|------|------|------|------|------|
| 250 | 225 | 200 | 150 | 100 |

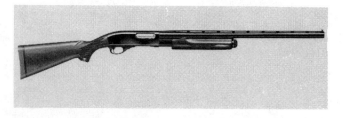

## Model 870 Field Wingmaster

This version of the 870 slide-action shotgun features twin slide rails and a checkered walnut stock. Otherwise, it is similar to its predecessor. It was introduced in 1964. Screw-in choke tubes are now standard, and the values given reflect this option. Without the tubes, subtract $50.

| NIB | Exc. | V.G. | Good | Fair | Poor |
|-----|------|------|------|------|------|
| 440 | 325 | 275 | 225 | 150 | 100 |

## Model 870 Magnum
This version of the Model 870 is chambered for 12 or 20 gauge with 3" Magnum chambers. It is offered standard with a recoil pad. It was introduced in 1964 and after 1987 became standard with choke tubes. The values reflect this. On models without the choke tubes, subtract $50.

| NIB | Exc. | V.G. | Good | Fair | Poor |
|-----|------|------|------|------|------|
| 440 | 325  | 275  | 225  | 150  | 100  |

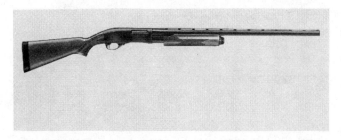

## Model 870 Express
This is a utility version of the Model 870 chambered for 12 gauge only, with 3" chambers. It is offered with a 28" vent-rib barrel with one choke tube. The metal is parkerized, and the hardwood stock is matte-finished. It was introduced in 1987.

| NIB | Exc. | V.G. | Good | Fair | Poor |
|-----|------|------|------|------|------|
| 235 | 200  | 175  | 150  | 100  | 75   |

## Model 870TA Trap
This is a trap-grade version chambered for 12 gauge only. It has a competition vent rib and a deluxe, checkered walnut stock. It was discontinued in 1986.

| Exc. | V.G. | Good | Fair | Poor |
|------|------|------|------|------|
| 375  | 300  | 250  | 175  | 125  |

## Model 870TB Trap
This version was offered with a 28" or 30", full-choke, vent-rib barrel and a select, trap-type, walnut stock. It was furnished with a recoil pad and was manufactured between 1950 and 1981.

| Exc. | V.G. | Good | Fair | Poor |
|------|------|------|------|------|
| 400  | 325  | 275  | 200  | 125  |

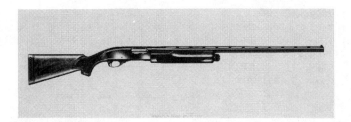

## Model 870TC Trap
This version is offered with a fancy-grade walnut stock and screw-in chokes.

| NIB | Exc. | V.G. | Good | Fair | Poor |
|-----|------|------|------|------|------|
| 575 | 475  | 400  | 350  | 250  | 150  |

## Model 48 Sportsman
This is a semi-automatic shotgun chambered for 12, 16, or 20 gauge and offered with a 26", 28", or 32" barrel with various chokes. It has a 3-round tubular magazine. The finish is blued, with a checkered walnut stock. There were approximately 275,000 manufactured between 1949 and 1959.
Vent Rib--Add 20 Percent.

| Exc. | V.G. | Good | Fair | Poor |
|------|------|------|------|------|
| 325  | 300  | 250  | 175  | 100  |

## Model 11-48
This is a recoil-operated, semi-automatic shotgun chambered for 12, 16, 20, and 28 gauge, as well as .410. It was offered with 26" through 32" barrels with various chokes. The finish is blued, with a walnut stock. There were approximately 425,000 manufactured between 1949 and 1968.

| Exc. | V.G. | Good | Fair | Poor |
|------|------|------|------|------|
| 300  | 250  | 200  | 150  | 75   |

## Model 58 Sportsman
This is a gas-operated, semi-automatic shotgun chambered for 12, 16, or 20 gauge with a 26", 28", or 30" barrel with various chokes. It has a 3-round tubular magazine. The finish is blued, with scroll engraving and a walnut stock. There were approximately 270,000 manufactured between 1956 and 1963.

| Exc. | V.G. | Good | Fair | Poor |
|------|------|------|------|------|
| 300  | 250  | 200  | 150  | 75   |

## Model 878 Automaster
This is a gas-operated, semi-automatic shotgun that is similar to the Model 58. It was chambered for 12 gauge only and was offered with a 26", 28", or 30" barrel with various chokes. The finish is blued, with a walnut stock. There were approximately 60,000 manufactured between 1959 and 1962.

| Exc. | V.G. | Good | Fair | Poor |
|------|------|------|------|------|
| 275  | 225  | 175  | 125  | 75   |

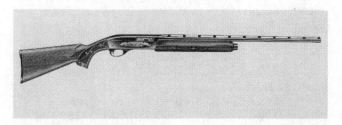

## Model 1100
This is a gas-operated, semi-automatic shotgun chambered for 12, 16, 20, or 28 gauge, as well as .410. The 28 gauge and .410 version would be worth approximately 20 percent additional. It was offered with barrel lengths from 26" to 30" with various chokes. Screw-in choke tubes were added in 1987, and the values given reflect them. If they are not present, subtract $50. The finish is blued, with a checkered walnut stock. This version was manufactured between 1963 and 1988.

| Exc. | V.G. | Good | Fair | Poor |
|------|------|------|------|------|
| 400  | 325  | 275  | 200  | 100  |

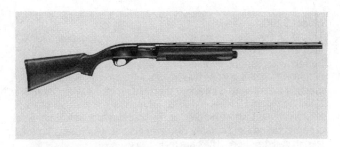

## Model 11-87 Premier
This is Remington's latest semi-automatic shotgun. It features a self-compensating, gas-operated action that will accept interchangeable power loads. It is chambered for 12 gauge with a 3" chamber and is offered with 26" through 32" vent-rib barrels with screw-in chokes. It has a tubular magazine and a polished blue finish with a checkered walnut stock. It was introduced in 1987.

| NIB | Exc. | V.G. | Good | Fair | Poor |
|-----|------|------|------|------|------|
| 560 | 475  | 425  | 350  | 275  | 175  |

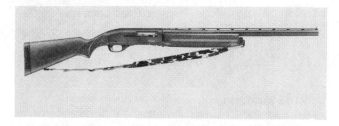

## Model SP-10

This is a gas-operated, semi-automatic, 10-gauge shotgun. It has 3.5" chambers and features a special, recoil-reducing action. It is offered with a 26" or 30" barrel with a ventilated rib and screw-in chokes. The finish is matte-blued with a satin-finished, checkered walnut stock.

| NIB | Exc. | V.G. | Good | Fair | Poor |
|---|---|---|---|---|---|
| 1275 | 1000 | 800 | 650 | 550 | 400 |

## Model 32

This is an Over/Under double-barrel shotgun chambered for 12 gauge. It has 26", 28", or 30" separated barrels. It features a boxlock action with a single-selective trigger and ejectors. There were approximately 15,000 manufactured between 1932 and 1942. There were several grades available that differed in the amount of ornamentation and the quality of materials and workmanship utilized in their construction. They are as follows:

### Standard Grade
Solid or Vent Rib--Add 10 Percent.

| Exc. | V.G. | Good | Fair | Poor |
|---|---|---|---|---|
| 2400 | 1900 | 1600 | 1250 | 1000 |

### Model 32 Skeet

| Exc. | V.G. | Good | Fair | Poor |
|---|---|---|---|---|
| 2750 | 2250 | 1950 | 1500 | 1250 |

### Model 32 TC

| Exc. | V.G. | Good | Fair | Poor |
|---|---|---|---|---|
| 3000 | 2500 | 2250 | 1750 | 1450 |

### Model 32D

| Exc. | V.G. | Good | Fair | Poor |
|---|---|---|---|---|
| 3500 | 3000 | 2500 | 2000 | 1650 |

### Model 32E Expert

| Exc. | V.G. | Good | Fair | Poor |
|---|---|---|---|---|
| 4500 | 3500 | 3000 | 2500 | 2000 |

### Model 32F Premier

| Exc. | V.G. | Good | Fair | Poor |
|---|---|---|---|---|
| 7000 | 5500 | 4000 | 3250 | 2500 |

## Model 3200

This is an Over/Under, double-barrel shotgun chambered for 12 gauge. It was offered with 26", 28", or 30", vent-rib, separated barrels with various choke combinations. It features a boxlock action with a single-selective trigger and automatic ejector. The finish is blued, with a checkered walnut stock. It was manufactured between 1973 and 1980. There were a number of variations available that differed in the options offered, degree of ornamentation, and quality of materials and workmanship utilized in construction. They are as follows:

### Field Grade

| Exc. | V.G. | Good | Fair | Poor |
|---|---|---|---|---|
| 800 | 725 | 600 | 450 | 300 |

### Model 3200 Magnum--3" Chambers

| Exc. | V.G. | Good | Fair | Poor |
|---|---|---|---|---|
| 1000 | 850 | 750 | 550 | 450 |

### Model 3200 Skeet

| Exc. | V.G. | Good | Fair | Poor |
|---|---|---|---|---|
| 800 | 725 | 600 | 450 | 300 |

### Model 3200 4-Gauge Set

| Exc. | V.G. | Good | Fair | Poor |
|---|---|---|---|---|
| 4500 | 3750 | 3000 | 2250 | 1500 |

### Model 3200 Trap

| Exc. | V.G. | Good | Fair | Poor |
|---|---|---|---|---|
| 850 | 775 | 650 | 500 | 350 |

### Model 3200 Special Trap--Deluxe Wood

| Exc. | V.G. | Good | Fair | Poor |
|---|---|---|---|---|
| 1000 | 850 | 750 | 550 | 450 |

### Model 3200 Competition Trap--Engraved

| Exc. | V.G. | Good | Fair | Poor |
|---|---|---|---|---|
| 1250 | 1000 | 850 | 650 | 550 |

### Model 3200 Premier--Heavily Engraved

| Exc. | V.G. | Good | Fair | Poor |
|---|---|---|---|---|
| 2250 | 2000 | 1750 | 1500 | 1000 |

### Model 3200 "One of One Thousand"--1,000 Produced

| Exc. | V.G. | Good | Fair | Poor |
|---|---|---|---|---|
| 2000 | 1750 | 1500 | 1100 | 800 |

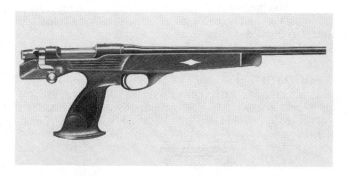

## Model XP-100

This is a bolt-action pistol designed for varmint shooting. It is chambered for the .221 Rem. Fireball and the .223 Rem. cartridges. It features a 14.5" barrel with a vent rib and adjustable sights. The finish is blued with a one-piece, contoured nylon stock. It was introduced in 1963.

| NIB | Exc. | V.G. | Good | Fair | Poor |
|---|---|---|---|---|---|
| 375 | 325 | 275 | 225 | 175 | 100 |

## Model XP-Silhouette

This version is similar to the XP-100 except that it is chambered for the .35 Rem. and the 7mm Rem. benchrest cartridges. It has a 15" barrel furnished without sights but drilled and tapped for a scope.

| NIB | Exc. | V.G. | Good | Fair | Poor |
|---|---|---|---|---|---|
| 380 | 325 | 275 | 225 | 175 | 100 |

### Model XP-100 Custom

This is a high-grade version available only through Remington's Custom Gunshop. It is chambered for the .223 Rem., .250 Savage, 6mm Benchrest, 7mm Benchrest, 7mm-08, and the .35 Rem. cartridges. It is offered with a standard-weight or heavy-weight 15" barrel and either a contoured walnut or nylon stock. It was introduced in 1986.

| NIB | Exc. | V.G. | Good | Fair | Poor |
|-----|------|------|------|------|------|
| 900 | 800  | 650  | 550  | 425  | 300  |

Remington "XP-100" Custom HB heavy barrel long range single shot pistol; Calibers: .223 Rem., .250 Sav., 6mm BR Rem., 7mm Br Rem. and 7mm-08 Rem. (In right and left-hand versions)

Remington XP-100R custom pistol bolt action centerfire repeater (with synthetic stock of "Kevlar" ®); Calibers: .223 Rem. (without sights), 7mm-08 Rem. & .35 Rem. (as shown).

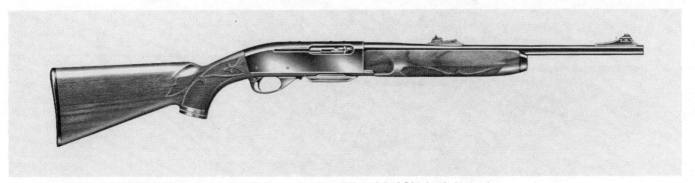

Remington Model 7400 Carbine autoloading centerfire rifle with 18½-inch barrel.

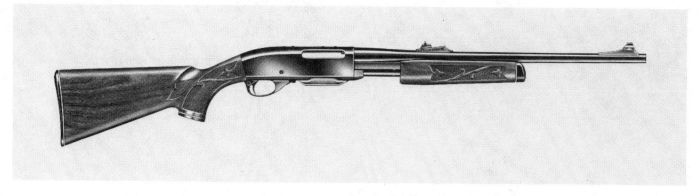

Remington Model 7600 Carbine centerfire pump action rifle with 18½-inch barrel.

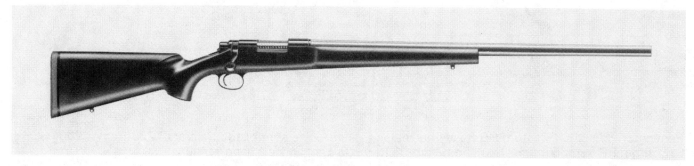

Remington Model 40-XB "Varmint Special" bolt action centerfire rifle with synthetic stock of "Kevlar." ®

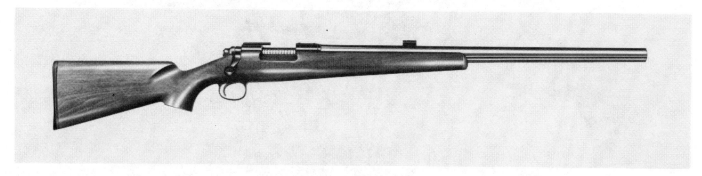

Remington Model 40-XBBR bench rest bolt action center fire rifle.

Remington Model 40-XB "Rangemaster" bolt action center fire target rifle.

Remington Model Seven custom ''KS'' lighweight centerfire rifle, synthetic stock of ''Kevlar'' ® aramid fiber; calibers: .223 Rem., 7mm BR Rem., 7mm-08 Rem., .35 Rem. and .350 Rem. Mag.

Remington Model 700 ''AS'' bolt action centerfire rifle with synthetic stock.

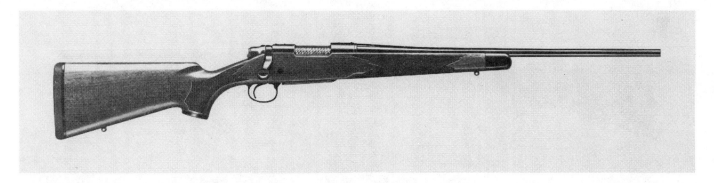

Remington Model 700 mountain rifle, short action version; Calibers: 243 win., 7mm-08 Rem., & 308 Win.

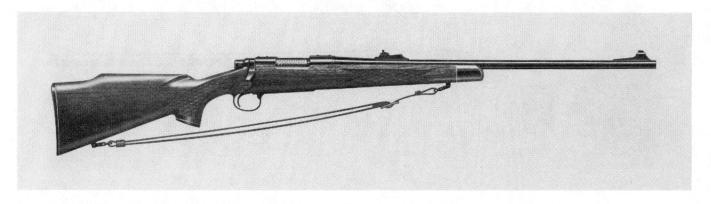

Remington Model 700 BDL, bolt action centerfire rifle (short action with 24-inch barrel).

Remington Model 700 BDL Magnum; calibers: 7mm Rem. Mag., .300 Win. Mag., .338 Win. Mag. & .35 Whelen.

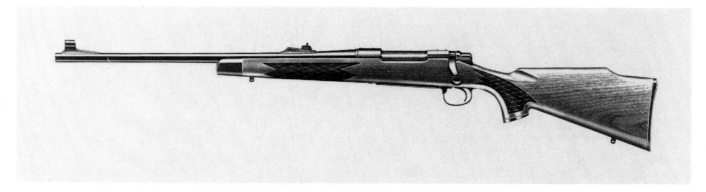

Remington Model 700 BDL left-hand bolt action centerfire rifle.

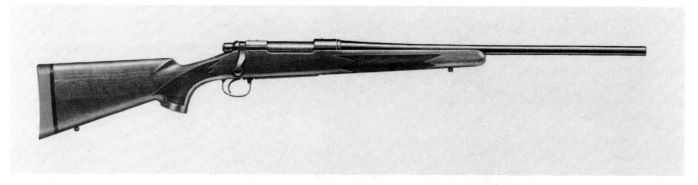

Remington Model 700 Classic bolt action centerfire rifle, Magnum caliber version.

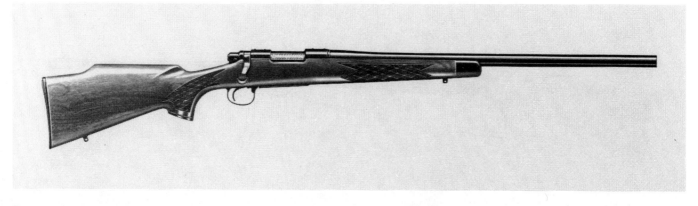

Remington Model 700 BDL "Varmint Special" bolt action centerfire rifle.

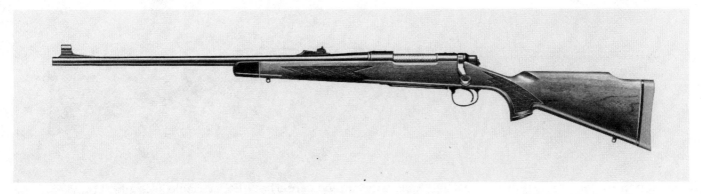

Remington Model 700 BDL magnum, left-hand action; calibers: 7mm Rem. Mag. & .338 Win. Mag.

Remington Model 700 BDL left-hand bolt action (short) centerfire rifle; calibers: .22-250 Rem., .243 Win. & .308 Win.

Remington Model 700 Custom bolt action centerfire rifle, Grade IV.

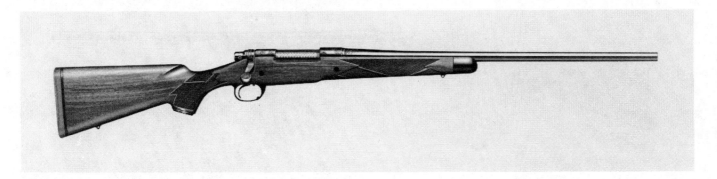

Remington Model 700 Custom bolt action centerfire rifle, Grade III.

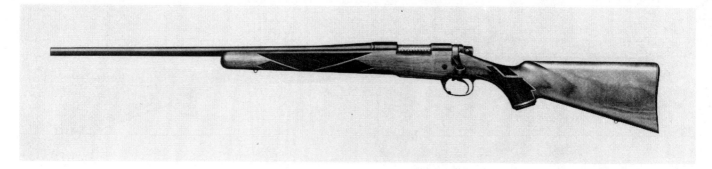

Remington Model 700 Custom Grade II, left hand short action centerfire rifle, available in Grades I to IV.

Remington Model 700 Custom bolt action centerfire rifle, Grade II.

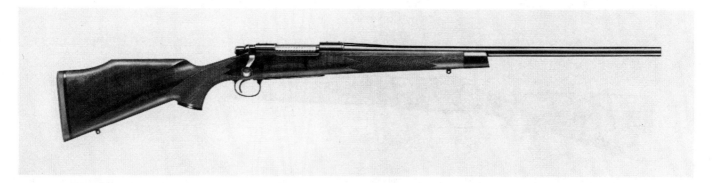

Remington Model 700 Custom bolt action centerfire rifle, Grade I.

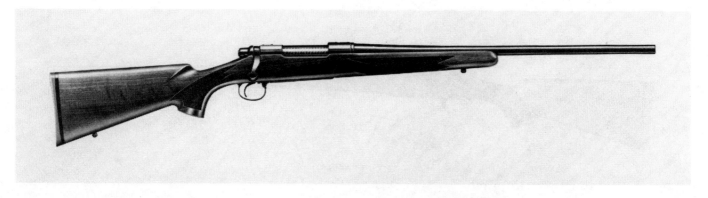

Remington Model 700 "Classic" bolt action centerfire rifle, limited edition - .25-06 Rem.

Remington Model 700 Safari Classic without sights: 8mm Rem. Mag. and .375 H&H Mag.; With sights:
.416 Rem. Mag.* and .458 Win Mag.
   ** Heavy barrel.

Remington Model 700 Safari KS, Synthetic stock of "Kevlar" aramid fiber; Calibers: 8mm Rem. Mag.,
.375 H&H Mag. 416 Rem. mag & .458 Win. Mag.

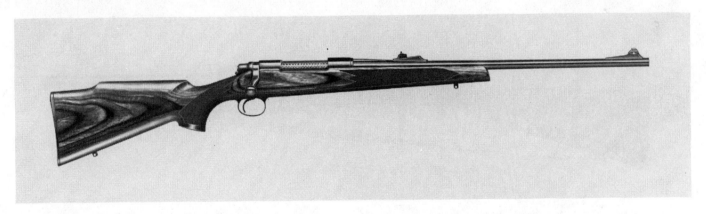

Remington Model 700 ADL "LS" bolt action centerfire rifle with laminated stock; Calibers: .243 Win.,
.270 Win., 30-06 & 7mm Rem. Magnum.

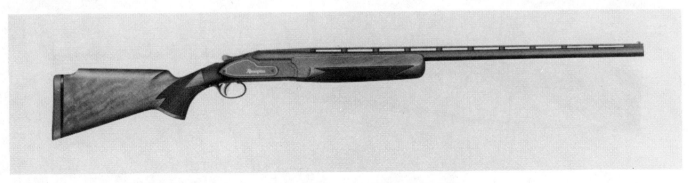

Remington Model 90-T super single trap gun, barrel lengths: 30", 32" & 34".

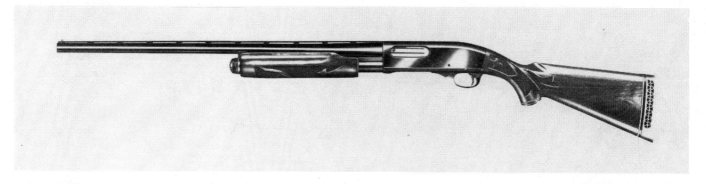

Remington Model 870 "Wingmaster" left-hand field grade pump action shotgun; 12- and 20-gauges (shown with ventilated rib).

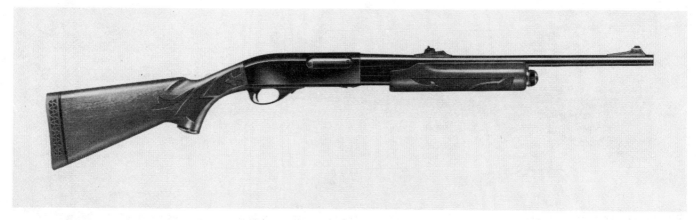

Remington Model 870 pump action 20 gauge "lightweight" deer gun.

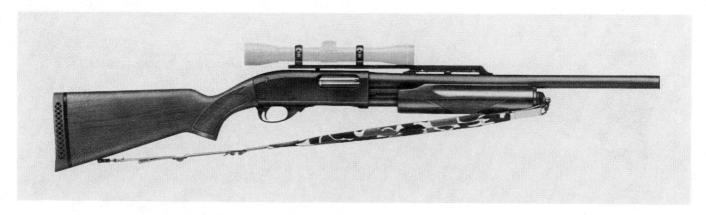

Remington Model 870 SP deer gun, pump action shotgun with 3" chamber, cantilever scope mount and interchangeable rifled and improved cylinder "REM" chokes.

Remington Model 870 SP Magnum pump action shotgun, 3 inch chamber (shown with 26-inch barrel).

Remington Model 870 youth gun, 20-gauge lightweight pump action shotgun with interchangeable "REM" chokes. Stock: shortened 1½ inches. Barrel: 21 inches.

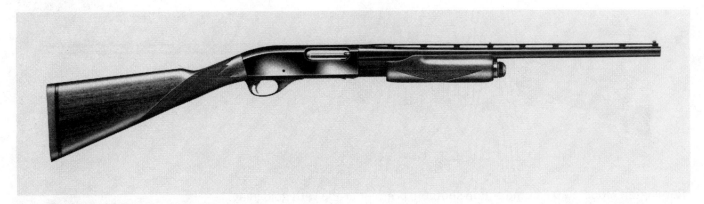

Remington Model 870 "Special Field" pump action shotgun with 21-inch vent rib barrel (20 gauge lightweight version).

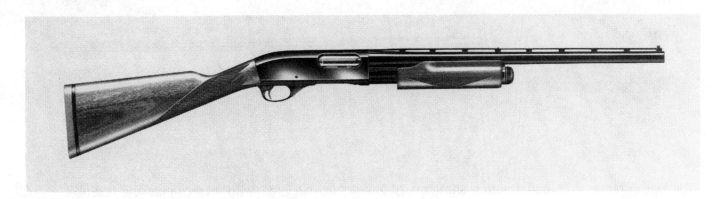

Remington Model 870 "Special Field" pump action shotgun with 21-inch vent rib barrel.

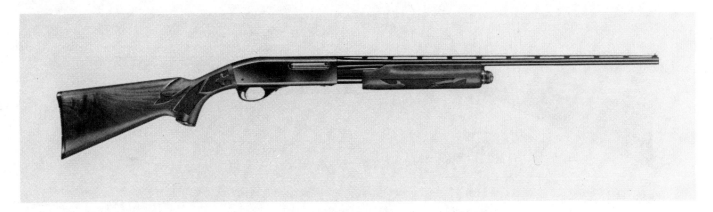

Remington Model 870 pump action shotgun, field grade small bore: 28-gauge & .410.

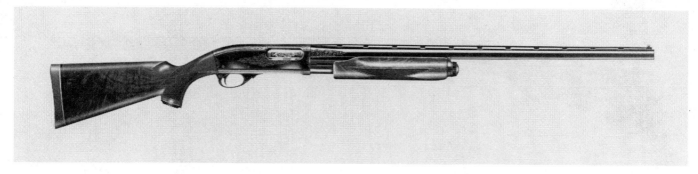

Remington Model 870 D tournament grade pump action shotgun.

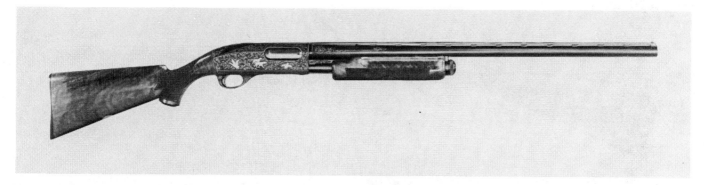

Remington Model 870 F pump action shotgun, premier grade with gold inlay.

Remington Model 870 pump action shotgun, 20-gauge "lightweight" with interchangeable "REM" chokes.

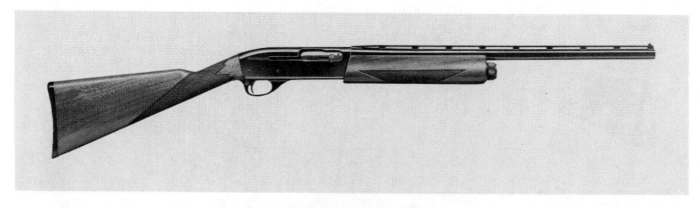

Remington Model 110 LT-20 "Special Field" 20-gauge autoloading shotgun with 21-inch vent rib barrel.

Remington Model 110 LT-20 autoloader, 20-gauge lightweight shotgun with interchangeable "REM" chokes.

Remington Model 110 LT-20 youth gun, 20-gauge lightweight autoloading shotgun with interchangeable "REM" chokes. Stock: shortened 1½ inches. Barrel: 21 inches.

Remington Model 1100 LT-20 magnum 20-gauge lightweight autoloader with interchangeable "REM" chokes.

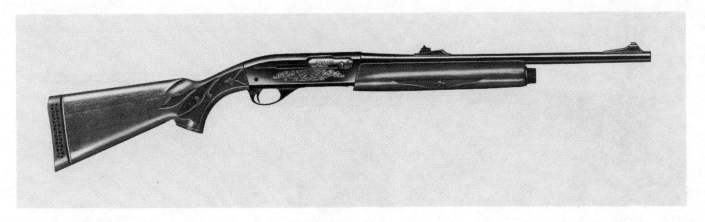

Remington Model 1100 LT-20 20-gauge lightweight autoloading deer gun.

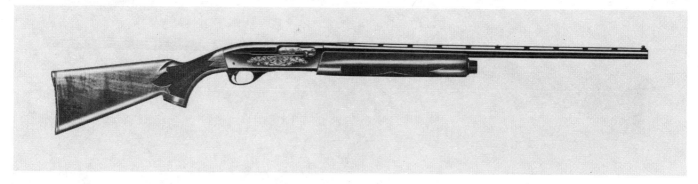

Remington Model 1100 LT-20 tournament skeet 20-gauge autoloading shotgun.

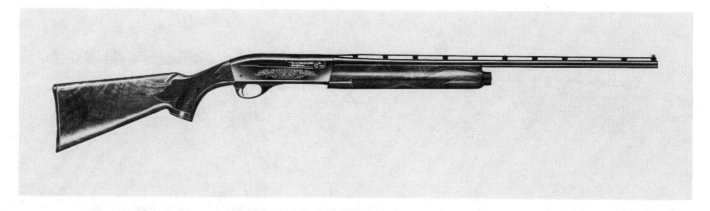

Remington Model 1100 tournament skeet autoloading shotgun, small bore version: 410 & 28 gauges.

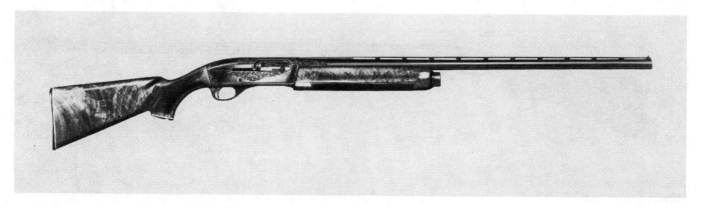

Remington Model 1100D tournament grade 12-gauge, 5 shot.

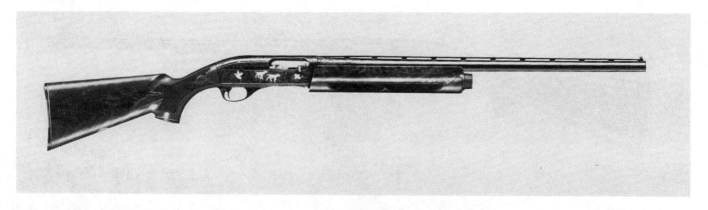

Remington Model 1100 F autoloading shotgun, premier grade with gold inlay.

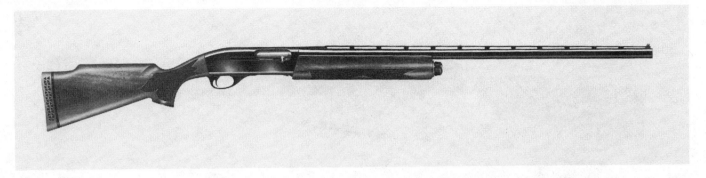

Remington Model 11-87 "Premier" autoloading trap gun with 3 interchangeable "REM" chokes (shown with Monte Carlo stock).

Remington Model 11-87 "Premier" 12-gauge autoloading shotgun with interchangeable "REM" chokes (handles all 2¾" & 3" magnum shells).

Remington Model 11-87 SP Magnum autoloading shotgun with interchangeable "REM" chokes (handles all 2¾" & 3" magnum shells).

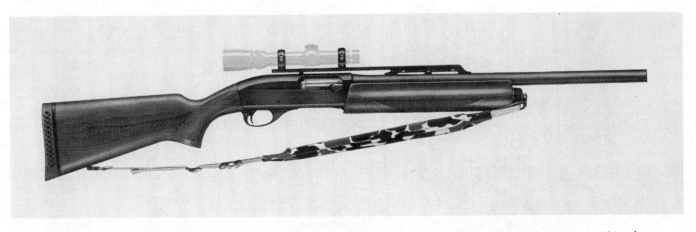

Remington Model 11-87 SP deer gun autoloading shotgun with 3" chamber, cantilever scope mount and interchangeable rifled and improved cylinder "REM" chokes.

Remington Model 11-87 SP deer gun autoloading action with 3" chamber (21" barrel with rifle sights).

Remington Model 11-87 Police 12-gauge autoloading shotgun (21" barrel with 3" chamber & rifle sights).

## RENETTE, GASTINE
### Paris, France

### Model 105
This is a side-by-side double-barrel shotgun chambered for 12 and 20 gauge. It has an Anson & Deeley boxlock action and various barrel lengths and choke combinations. Double triggers are standard, as well as automatic ejectors. The frame is case-colored, with blued barrels and a hand-checkered French walnut stock.

| Exc. | V.G. | Good | Fair | Poor |
|------|------|------|------|------|
| 1750 | 1600 | 1250 | 900 | 750 |

### Model 98
This is a more deluxe version of the Model 105.

| Exc. | V.G. | Good | Fair | Poor |
|------|------|------|------|------|
| 2500 | 2250 | 1750 | 1400 | 1100 |

### Model 202
This is a full sidelock-action, side-by-side shotgun chambered for 12 or 20 gauge. It has a Purdey-type locking system and was available on a made-to-order basis as far as barrel length and chokes were concerned. The receiver is scroll-engraved and coin-finished.

| Exc. | V.G. | Good | Fair | Poor |
|------|------|------|------|------|
| 3500 | 3000 | 2500 | 1750 | 1250 |

### Model 353
This is the top-of-the-line SxS with hand-detachable sidelocks and a deluxe engraved finish.

| Exc. | V.G. | Good | Fair | Poor |
|------|------|------|------|------|
| 9000 | 7500 | 5000 | 4250 | 3000 |

### Type G Rifle
This is a SxS double rifle chambered for the .30-06, 9.3x74R, and .375 H&H cartridges. It has 24" barrels with express sights, double triggers, automatic ejectors, and floral engraving. The finish is blued, with a select walnut stock.

| Exc. | V.G. | Good | Fair | Poor |
|------|------|------|------|------|
| 2250 | 1850 | 1500 | 1150 | 950 |

### Type R Deluxe
This is a more deluxe version of the Type G with gamescene engraving and higher-grade French walnut in the stock and forend.

| Exc. | V.G. | Good | Fair | Poor |
|------|------|------|------|------|
| 2500 | 2250 | 1750 | 1450 | 1150 |

### Type PT President
This is the best grade with the finest wood and gold inlays.

| Exc. | V.G. | Good | Fair | Poor |
|------|------|------|------|------|
| 3200 | 2750 | 2000 | 1750 | 1250 |

## RENWICK ARMS CO.
### SEE--Perry & Goddard

## RETOLAZA HERMANOS
### Eibar, Spain

This company was formed in 1890, producing a "Velo-Dog"-type revolver. They were one of the pioneers in the Eibar-type semi-automatic business and remained operative until the Spanish Civil War.

### Brompetier
This Velo-Dog-type revolver is chambered for the 6.35mm and the 7.65mm cartridges. It is a solid-framed hammerless with an integral ejector rod. It has a 2.5" barrel and a folding trigger. There is a safety catch on the left side of the frame. It was manufactured until 1915.

| Exc. | V.G. | Good | Fair | Poor |
|------|------|------|------|------|
| 135 | 110 | 90 | 70 | 45 |

### Gallus or Titan
This is a blowback-operated semi-automatic that is chambered for the 6.35mm cartridge. It is the usual Eibar 1906 Browning copy without a grip safety. It is marked either "Gallus" or "Titan" and is blued, with molded plastic grips with a circle that shows the caliber.

| Exc. | V.G. | Good | Fair | Poor |
|------|------|------|------|------|
| 150 | 125 | 100 | 75 | 50 |

### Liberty, Military, Retolaza or Paramount
These three models are identical blowback-operated semi-automatics chambered for the 6.35mm or 7.65mm cartridges. They have 3" barrels and 8-shot magazines. They are typical Eibar-type pistols and were made during WWI.

| Exc. | V.G. | Good | Fair | Poor |
|------|------|------|------|------|
| 150 | 125 | 100 | 75 | 50 |

### Puppy
This is a solid-frame hammerless revolver chambered for the .22 Short cartridge. It has a folding trigger and a 5-shot cylinder, with the name "Puppy" stamped on the barrel.

| Exc. | V.G. | Good | Fair | Poor |
|------|------|------|------|------|
| 125 | 100 | 75 | 50 | 25 |

### Stosel
This blowback-operated semi-automatic is chambered for the 6.35mm cartridge. It is a 1906 Browning copy that is blued, with plastic grips. The slide is marked "Automatic Pistol Stosel No. 1 Patent." It was manufactured prior to WWI.

| Exc. | V.G. | Good | Fair | Poor |
|------|------|------|------|------|
| 150 | 125 | 100 | 75 | 50 |

### Titanic
This model was named after the ship that sunk in 1912. It is a blowback-operated semi-automatic that is chambered for the 6.35mm cartridge. It is a 1906 Browning copy that has a partial rib on the top of the slide. It has a 2.5" barrel, and the slide is marked "1913 Model Automatic Pistol Titanic Eibar." It is blued, with plastic grips.

| Exc. | V.G. | Good | Fair | Poor |
|------|------|------|------|------|
| 150 | 125 | 100 | 75 | 50 |

## REUNIES
### Liege, Belgium

This company was founded in 1909 to produce a semi-automatic pistol. After WWI the company was reorganized under the name of Fabrique d'Armes Unies and manufactured a single-action pistol that was patterned after the Colt Single Action Army. They ceased production in 1931.

### Dictator

This is a blowback-operated semi-automatic pistol chambered for the 6.35mm cartridge. This unique design consists of a one-piece frame and tubular receiver. The bolt is one piece and tubular in design. The rear of the bolt is solid and forms the breech block, while the front end is hollow and encloses the barrel. The barrel is 1.5" in length; and the finish is blued, with plastic grips. It has a 5-shot magazine; and the name "Dictator," along with the company name, is marked on the receiver. This was the first of the wrap-around bolt designs and, as such, is credited with being a great step forward in firearms design. Submachine guns of WWII owe their success to this design breakthrough.

| Exc. | V.G. | Good | Fair | Poor |
|------|------|------|------|------|
| 175 | 150 | 125 | 100 | 75 |

### Texas Ranger or Cowboy Ranger

This is a single-action Colt copy, that is chambered for the .38 Special cartridge. It has a 5.5" barrel and is gate-loaded, with an integral ejector rod and housing. It is marked "Texas Ranger" or "Cowboy Ranger," along with the caliber and the company name. The finish is blued, and the quality is only fair. It was manufactured between 1922 and 1931.

| Exc. | V.G. | Good | Fair | Poor |
|------|------|------|------|------|
| 150 | 125 | 100 | 75 | 50 |

# REUTH, F.
## Hartford, Connecticut

### Animal Trap Gun

This is a unique firearm constructed of cast iron. It is chambered from .28 to .50 caliber percussion. It has either a single barrel 3.5" in length or 5" double barrels. This weapon fires long, barbed arrows and has a triggering device that is attached by a cord to a bait and which is fired when the quarry pulls at the bait. It is marked "F. Reuth's Patent, May 12, 1857." There were a few hundred manufactured between 1858 and 1862. The double-barrel model is more common than the single barrel and is worth approximately 20 percent less.

| Exc. | V.G. | Good | Fair | Poor |
|------|------|------|------|------|
| 450 | 400 | 350 | 250 | 200 |

# RHEINMETALL
## Sommerda, Germany

### Dreyse 6.35mm

This is a blowback-operated, semi-automatic pocket pistol chambered for the 6.35mm cartridge. This model has a 2" barrel and is striker fired. It has a manual safety catch and a 6-round magazine. The finish is blued, with plastic grips with "RFM" molded into them. The slide is marked "Dreyse." This pistol was manufactured to a patent taken out in 1909 by Louis Scmeisser.

| Exc. | V.G. | Good | Fair | Poor |
|------|------|------|------|------|
| 300 | 250 | 200 | 150 | 100 |

### Dreyse 7.65mm

This is a larger, blowback-operated, semi-automatic pistol chambered for the 7.65mm cartridge. It is striker fired and is quite unusual in its design. The cocking serrations are found on the front of the slide, which pivots forward. This is a rather complex pistol to dismantle and is best left to the experienced. The barrel is 3.6" in length, and the magazine holds 7 rounds. This pistol was manufactured commercially before WWI and at the start of the war was adopted as a secondary weapon for staff officers. It is marked "Dreyse Rheinmetall Abt. Sommerda." The finish is blued, with plastic grips.

| Exc. | V.G. | Good | Fair | Poor |
|------|------|------|------|------|
| 275 | 225 | 175 | 125 | 90 |

### Dreyse 9mm

This is a still larger, blowback-operated, semi-automatic pistol. It is chambered for the 9mm Parabellum cartridge. This cartridge is very powerful for a blowback action, and it is necessary to have a very heavy recoil spring to handle the recoiling mass. This makes cocking difficult, so the Dreyse has a cocking lever that disconnects the recoil spring and aids in the cocking of the weapon. The barrel is 5" in length, and the magazine holds 8 rounds. The slide is marked "Rheinische Mettellwaaren Und Maschinenfabrik, Sommerda." The finish is blued, and the grips are plastic. This was not a successful design as when the pistol begins to show wear, it becomes hazardous due to the tremendous recoil of the 9mm cartridge in a worn blowback action. There were few manufactured during WWI, and it was not produced after the war.

| Exc. | V.G. | Good | Fair | Poor |
|------|------|------|------|------|
| 750 | 650 | 500 | 400 | 300 |

### Rheinmetall

This is a more conventional pistol than the Dreyse designs, and it is chambered for the 7.65mm cartridge. It is patterned after the 1912 Browning design and has a 3.65" barrel. It is a blowback action, and the magazine holds 8 rounds. The slide is marked "Rheinmetell ABT. Sommerda." This finish is blued, and the grips are smooth walnut. It was manufactured after WWI.

| Exc. | V.G. | Good | Fair | Poor |
|------|------|------|------|------|
| 275 | 225 | 175 | 125 | 90 |

# RHODE ISLAND ARMS CO.
## Hope Valley, Rhode Island

### Morrone
This is an Over/Under boxlock that is chambered for 12 or 20 guage. The barrels are plain and are offered in 26" or 28" lengths with various choke combinations. The gun has extractors and a single trigger. The finish is blued, with either a straight or pistol grip checkered walnut stock. There were only 450 produced in 12 gauge and 50 in 20 gauge. They were manufactured between 1949 and 1953.

| Exc. | V.G. | Good | Fair | Poor |
|------|------|------|------|------|
| 1250 | 1000 | 750 | 600 | 450 |

# RICHLAND ARMS CO.
## Blissfield, Michigan

Richland Arms was an importer of reasonably good quality Spanish Over/Unders, Side-by-Sides, and single-shot shotguns. They ceased operations in 1986.

### Model 41 Ultra O/U
This model is chambered for 20 and 28 gauge, as well as .410. It has 26" or 28" vent-rib barrels and various chokes. It has a single non selective trigger, extractors, and a silver-finished receiver with engraving. The stock is checkered walnut. It was imported until 1986.

| Exc. | V.G. | Good | Fair | Poor |
|------|------|------|------|------|
| 275 | 250 | 200 | 150 | 100 |

### Model 747 O/U
This model is similar to the Model 41 except that it is chambered for 20 gauge only. It has a single-selective trigger.

| Exc. | V.G. | Good | Fair | Poor |
|------|------|------|------|------|
| 425 | 350 | 300 | 250 | 175 |

### Model 757 O/U
This is a 12 gauge that has a Greener boxlock action and double triggers. The barrels are the same as the Model 747, and the stock is checkered walnut. This model was imported in 1986 only.

| Exc. | V.G. | Good | Fair | Poor |
|------|------|------|------|------|
| 300 | 250 | 200 | 175 | 125 |

### Model 787 O/U
This was a 12-gauge Over/Under that is similar to the Model 757 but is furnished with screw-in choke tubes. It was imported in 1986 only.

| Exc. | V.G. | Good | Fair | Poor |
|------|------|------|------|------|
| 450 | 375 | 325 | 275 | 200 |

### Model 808 O/U
This is an early model that is chambered for 12 gauge and has 26", 28", or 30" vent-rib barrels with various choke combinations. It has a single trigger, extractors, and a boxlock action. The checkered stock is walnut. This model was manufactured in Italy between 1963 and 1968.

| Exc. | V.G. | Good | Fair | Poor |
|------|------|------|------|------|
| 425 | 350 | 300 | 250 | 175 |

### Model 80 LS
This is a break open single-barrel, single shot that is chambered for 12 or 20 gauge and .410. The barrel is 26" or 28" with various chokes. It has a blued finish and a walnut stock. It was imported in 1986 only.

| Exc. | V.G. | Good | Fair | Poor |
|------|------|------|------|------|
| 150 | 125 | 100 | 80 | 60 |

### Model 200
This is a side-by-side double that is chambered for 12, 16, 20, and 28 gauge, as well as .410. The barrels are 22", 26", or 38" in length, with various choke combinations. It has an Anson & Deeley boxlock action, double triggers, and extractors. The finish is blued, and the stock is checkered walnut.

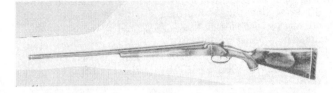

| Exc. | V.G. | Good | Fair | Poor |
|------|------|------|------|------|
| 325 | 300 | 250 | 200 | 125 |

### Model 202
This is similar to the Model 200, with two sets of interchangeable barrels. This model, as well as the Model 200, was imported between 1963 and 1985.

| Exc. | V.G. | Good | Fair | Poor |
|------|------|------|------|------|
| 300 | 275 | 225 | 175 | 100 |

### Model 711 Magnum
This model is a side-by-side that is chambered for 10, 12, 20, or 28 gauge, as well as .410. It has magnum-length chambers in all respective gauges and barrel lengths of 30" and 32" with full chokes. The action is a boxlock with extractors and double triggers. The finish is blued, and the checkered walnut stock is furnished with a recoil pad. This model was imported between 1963 and 1985.

| Exc. | V.G. | Good | Fair | Poor |
|------|------|------|------|------|
| 350 | 300 | 250 | 200 | 150 |

### Model 707 Deluxe
This is a side-by-side double that is chambered for 12 or 20 gauge. It has 3" chambers and 26", 28", or 30" barrels with various choke combinations. It has double triggers, extractors, and a boxlock action. The finish is blued, and the checkered stock is walnut.

| Exc. | V.G. | Good | Fair | Poor |
|------|------|------|------|------|
| 350 | 300 | 250 | 200 | 150 |

# RICHMOND ARMORY
## Richmond, Virginia

### Carbine
This weapon was manufactured for use by the Confederate States of America and is extremely collectible. We recommend qualified individual appraisal if a transaction is contemplated. This muzzle-loading carbine is chambered for .58 caliber percussion and has a 25" round barrel and a full-length stock that is held on by two barrel bands. It was manufactured from parts that were captured at the Harper's Ferry Armory in 1861. The locks are marked "Richmond, VA" and dated from 1861 to 1865. There are sling swivels in front of the triggerguard and on the front barrel band; a third swivel is on the underside of the

buttstock. The quantity manufactured is not known. They were made between 1861 and 1865.

| Exc. | V.G. | Good | Fair | Poor |
|------|------|------|------|------|
| 5000 | 4000 | 2500 | 1750 | 1000 |

## Musketoon

This weapon is very similar to the carbine except that the barrel is 30" in length and the front sight is also the bayonet lug. There is no sling swivel on the buttstock. This weapon was also manufactured between 1861 and 1865.

| Exc. | V.G. | Good | Fair | Poor |
|------|------|------|------|------|
| 6000 | 5000 | 3250 | 2250 | 1500 |

## Rifled Musket

This model is also similar to the Carbine, with a 40" barrel and a full-length stock held on by three barrel bands. The front sling swivel is on the middle barrel band instead of on the front band. The Rifled Musket was also manufactured between 1861 and 1865.

| Exc. | V.G. | Good | Fair | Poor |
|------|------|------|------|------|
| 4000 | 3000 | 2000 | 1500 | 900 |

# RIEDL RIFLE CO.
### Westminster, California

## Single Shot Rifle

This is a falling-block single shot that is chambered for all calibers. The barrel lengths offered are from 22" to 30". The action is operated by a rack and pinion, and the trigger is fully adjustable. There were no sights furnished, but a scope mount or target sight bases were standard. The rifle was basically a made-to-order proposition and was available in chrome moly or stainless steel. It is blued, with a checkered walnut stock.

| Exc. | V.G. | Good | Fair | Poor |
|------|------|------|------|------|
| 500 | 450 | 400 | 300 | 225 |

# RIGBY, JOHN & CO., LTD.
### London, England

The firm of Rigby is regarded as one of the top gunmaking firms in the world and has been so regarded for many, many years. They predominantly produce custom-built firearms and pioneered the large-caliber express rifles that have been used for dangerous game. It is impossible to accurately price weapons of this quality, and we furnish estimated values for reference only. We strongly urge that anyone contemplating the sale or purchase of one of these fine weapons secure competent individual appraisal.

## Boxlock Shotgun

This side-by-side double-barrel shotgun is produced in any gauge, with barrel lengths and choke combinations to the customer's specifications. They are furnished standard with double triggers and automatic ejectors. The high-grade, hand-checkered walnut stock is also produced to the customer's specification. There are three grades that differ by the degree of ornamentation and general quality of materials and workmanship.
20 Gauge--Add 25 Percent.
28 Gauge--Add 45 Percent.
.410--Add 70 Percent.

### Chatsworth Grade

| Exc. | V.G. | Good | Fair | Poor |
|------|------|------|------|------|
| 4000 | 3000 | 2500 | 1750 | 1250 |

### Sackville Grade

| Exc. | V.G. | Good | Fair | Poor |
|------|------|------|------|------|
| 5500 | 4500 | 3750 | 2750 | 2000 |

## Boxlock Game Gun

This gun is chambered for 12, 20, or 28 gauge, is manufactured to order, and features deep-relief engraving. It is similar to the Sackville and is currently manufactured.

| NIB | Exc. | V.G. | Good | Fair | Poor |
|-----|------|------|------|------|------|
| 7500 | 6000 | 5000 | 4500 | 3000 | 2500 |

## Sidelock Shotgun

This gun is similar in features and quality to the Boxlock except that it has a full, hand-detachable sidelock action.
20 Gauge--Add 25 Percent.
28 Gauge--Add 45 Percent.
.410--Add 70 Percent.

### Sandringham Grade

| Exc. | V.G. | Good | Fair | Poor |
|------|------|------|------|------|
| 9000 | 8000 | 6500 | 4000 | 2750 |

### Regal Grade

| Exc. | V.G. | Good | Fair | Poor |
|------|------|------|------|------|
| 12500 | 10000 | 7500 | 6500 | 5000 |

## Sidelock Game Gun

This model is chambered for 12 or 20 gauge and is considered to be Rigby's best quality side-by-side shotgun. It is ornately engraved and features the highest quality hand-checkered walnut. All options are to the customer's specifications. This model is currently being manufactured.

| NIB | Exc. | V.G. | Good | Fair | Poor |
|-----|------|------|------|------|------|
| 20000 | 17000 | 13500 | 10000 | 8000 | 6500 |

## Magazine Rifle

This bolt-action rifle is based on a Mauser action and is chambered for many standard calibers. It has barrel lengths of 21" through 24" and either a 3- or 5-shot magazine, depending on the caliber chambered. It features folding express sights and a hand-checkered walnut semi-pistol grip stock. The finish is blued. This model was introduced prior to WWII and is still in production on a custom-order basis.

| NIB | Exc. | V.G. | Good | Fair | Poor |
|-----|------|------|------|------|------|
| 4500 | 3750 | 2750 | 2250 | 1750 | 1200 |

## Large Bore Magazine Rifle

This model is similar to the standard Magazine Rifle but is chambered for the .375 Holland & Holland, .404, .416 Rigby, .458 Winchester Magnum, and .505 cartridges. It features a Brno square-bridge Magnum action, has a barrel length between 21" and 24", and has a four-shot box magazine.

| NIB | Exc. | V.G. | Good | Fair | Poor |
|-----|------|------|------|------|------|
| 4750 | 4000 | 3000 | 2500 | 2000 | 1500 |

## Single Shot Rifle

This model is based on a Farquharson falling block action. It is activated by a triggerguard lever. It is chambered for many English and European calibers and has a 24" barrel and an automatic ejector. This model is finely engraved and blued, with a deluxe, hand-checkered walnut pistol-grip stock. It is no longer manufactured.

| Exc. | V.G. | Good | Fair | Poor |
|------|------|------|------|------|
| 4000 | 3500 | 2750 | 2000 | 1500 |

### Third Quality Boxlock Double Rifle

This model is chambered for cartridges from 275 Magnum up to and including the 577 Nitro Express. It has barrels from 24" through 28" in length, folding express sights, double triggers, and automatic ejectors. It has a hand-checkered walnut stock. The finish is blued, with some engraving.

| Exc. | V.G. | Good | Fair | Poor |
|------|------|------|------|------|
| 12500 | 10500 | 8500 | 7000 | 5000 |

### Second Quality Boxlock Double Rifle

This is a high-grade model that was actually considered the best quality boxlock gun. It was made to order and features the highest grade of materials and workmanship.

| Exc. | V.G. | Good | Fair | Poor |
|------|------|------|------|------|
| 16000 | 14000 | 10500 | 8000 | 6000 |

### Best Quality Sidelock Double Rifle

Many of the features found on this model, such as caliber and barrel lengths, are similar to those of the Boxlock guns. This is Rigby's finest quality firearm. It is profusely engraved and features the highest quality materials and workmanship found in the firearms industry. This rifle is currently manufactured.

| NIB | Exc. | V.G. | Good | Fair | Poor |
|-----|------|------|------|------|------|
| 35000 | 30000 | 25000 | 20000 | 15000 | 12000 |

## RIGDON, ANSLEY & CO.
### Augusta, Georgia

### 1851 Colt Navy Type

This revolver was manufactured for use by the troops of the Confederate States of America and was based on the 1851 Colt Navy Revolver. It is chambered for .36 caliber percussion and has a part-round/part-octagonal 7.5" barrel with an integral loading lever. The unfluted cylinder holds 6 shots. The finish is blued, with brass gripstraps and one-piece walnut grips. The early production model is marked "Augusta, GA. C.S.A." The standard model is simply marked "C.S.A." There were approximately 1,000 manufactured in 1864 and 1865. This Company was put out of business by General Sherman's march to the sea.

**Early Production Model**

| Exc. | V.G. | Good | Fair | Poor |
|------|------|------|------|------|
| 7500 | 6500 | 5000 | 3500 | 2000 |

**Standard Production Model**

| Exc. | V.G. | Good | Fair | Poor |
|------|------|------|------|------|
| 6500 | 5500 | 4000 | 2750 | 1750 |

## RIPOMANTI, GUY
### St. Etienne, France
### Importer--Wes Gilpin
### Dallas, Texas

### Morton's Ltd.
### Lexington, Kentucky

### Side x Side Shotgun

This is a very high-grade shotgun offered on a strictly made-to-order basis. There is a boxlock model that begins at $8,500 and a sidelock that is priced from $22,500. These prices rise depending on the options and embellishments desired. These guns are rarely seen on the used-gun market; but if a transaction is contemplated, we strongly urge competent individual appraisal. The shotguns are imported by Gilpin's.

### Side x Side Double Rifles

These guns are extremely high-grade and basically made to order. They are very rarely encountered on today's market. They have been imported since 1988. They range in price from $11,000 up. If a transaction is contemplated, we strongly urge competent individual appraisal. These guns are imported by Morton's.

### Over/Under Double Rifle

This is a boxlock action Over/Under chambered for the 9.3x74R cartridge. The barrels are 23.5" in length and have express sights. There are double triggers and automatic ejectors. This model is highly engraved and features a high-grade, hand-checkered walnut stock. It was introduced in 1989 and is imported by Morton's.

| NIB | Exc. | V.G. | Good | Fair | Poor |
|-----|------|------|------|------|------|
| 7000 | 5750 | 4750 | 4000 | 3000 | 2250 |

## RIZZINI
### Brescia, Italy
### Importer--W.L. Moore & Co.
### West Lake Village, California

This company manufactures approximately 25 very high-grade shotguns per year. These guns are produced strictly on a custom-order basis and are very rarely found on the market. There are basically two models--a boxlock and a sidelock--and their prices start at approximately $14,000 for the boxlock and $22,000 for the sidelock. We strongly suggest that a qualified individual appraisal be secured if a transaction is contemplated.

## ROBAR ET CIE
### Liege, Belgium

This company began producing firearms in 1910 and continued in the business until 1958. They produced reasonable quality handguns that were widely exported and are definitely not considered rare on today's market.

### Jieffeco

This is a blowback-operated semi-automatic pistol designed by Rosier in 1907. It was the first pistol this company made. It is chambered for the 6.35mm or 7.65mm cartridges and has a 3" barrel. The design was obviously patterned after the 1900 Browning. It is blued, with plastic grips; and it is marked "Pistolet Automatique Jieffeco Depose Brevete SGDG." This model was manufactured until 1914.

| Exc. | V.G. | Good | Fair | Poor |
|------|------|------|------|------|
| 175 | 150 | 125 | 100 | 75 |

## Melior

This is a blowback-operated semi-automatic that is chambered for the 6.35mm or 7.65mm cartridges. It has a 2.5" barrel and is similar to the Jieffeco design. The slide is marked "Melior Brevete SGDG." It was blued, with plastic grips; and it was manufactured before WWI.

| Exc. | V.G. | Good | Fair | Poor |
|------|------|------|------|------|
| 175 | 150 | 125 | 100 | 75 |

## New Model Melior

This blowback-operated semi-automatic is patterned after the 1910 Model Browning design and is chambered for the 6.35mm, 7.65mm, 9mm Short, and the .22 l.r. cartridges. The barrel is 2" in length, and the slide is marked "Melior Brevets-Liege, Belgium." The finish is blued, with plastic grips. This model was produced until the company ceased operations in 1958.

| Exc. | V.G. | Good | Fair | Poor |
|------|------|------|------|------|
| 175 | 150 | 125 | 100 | 75 |

## Mercury

This is simply a trade name for the New Melior pistol chambered for the .22 l.r. cartridge and destined for import to the U.S.A. via Tradewinds of Tacoma, Washington. They are marked "Mercury Made in Belgium." They are finished in blue or nickel-plated and were manufactured between 1946 and 1958.

| Exc. | V.G. | Good | Fair | Poor |
|------|------|------|------|------|
| 175 | 150 | 125 | 100 | 75 |

## ROBBINS & LAWRENCE
### Windsor, Vermont

### Pepperbox

This revolving pepperbox-type pistol is chambered for .28 and .31 caliber percussion. The five-barrel clusters are either 3.5" or 4.5" in length. It is necessary to unscrew the barrels to load the hinged breech section that pivots downwards for capping. It has a ring-type trigger for cocking and an additional trigger for firing. It has an iron frame with scroll engraving. The frame is blued; the barrels, browned; and the grips are of walnut. The barrels are marked "Robbins & Lawrence Co. Windsor, VT. Patent. 1849." There are two types--one with fluted barrels chambered for both calibers, and a ribbed type chambered for .31 caliber only. There were approximately 7,000 manufactured between 1851 and 1854.

| Exc. | V.G. | Good | Fair | Poor |
|------|------|------|------|------|
| 750 | 650 | 600 | 450 | 300 |

## ROBERTSON
### Philadelphia, Pennsylvania

### Pocket Pistol

This pocket pistol is patterned after the Henry Deringer Philadelphia-type pistol. It is chambered for .41-caliber percussion, with barrel lengths between 3" and 4.5". The barrel is marked "Robertson, Phila." It has a wooden ramrod, iron locks, and a walnut stock.

| Exc. | V.G. | Good | Fair | Poor |
|------|------|------|------|------|
| 750 | 650 | 500 | 400 | 300 |

## ROBINSON, ORVIL
### SEE--Adirondack Arms Company

## ROGERS & SPENCER
### Willowvale, New York

### Army Revolver

This solid-framed revolver is chambered for .44-caliber percussion and has a 7.5" octagonal barrel with an integral loading lever. It has single-action lockwork and a blued finish, with a case-colored hammer and loading lever and two-piece walnut grips. The barrel is marked "Rogers & Spencer/Utica, N.Y." There are government inspector's marks "RPB" stamped on the grips and on some of the other parts. There were approximately 5,800 manufactured between 1863 and 1865. The contract was not completed in time for use in the Civil War.

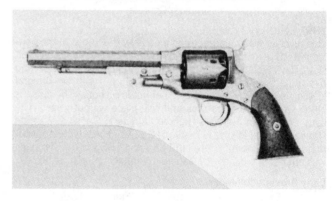

| Exc. | V.G. | Good | Fair | Poor |
|------|------|------|------|------|
| 975 | 850 | 750 | 600 | 450 |

## ROHM GMBH
### Sonthein/Brenz, Germany

This company manufactured cheap handguns under a long list of trade names. These pistols were nearly all meant for import to the pre-GCA 1968 U.S.A. The passage of this law virtually eliminated the import of the Rohm firearms, and they are not often encountered on today's market. There are basically three types of Rohm revolver: 1) the cheap, solid-frame, gate-loading models; 2) the cheap, solid-frame swingout-cylinder revolvers; and 3) the better quality, solid-frame, swingout-cylinder revolvers. The model designation of these pistols consists of the initials RG followed by a number. This designation is found on a disk inletted in the grips. The serial number and the caliber are usually all that would be found on the pistol itself. These pistols have no collector value; and, quite frankly, most knowledgeable shooters would question their utility value as well. They are all worth under $75 in the best of condition regardless of the model designation.

## ROMERWERKE
### Suhl, Germany

### Romer

This is a blowback-operated semi-automatic pistol chambered for the .22 l.r. cartridge. It is offered with a 2.5" or 6.5" barrel and has a 7-round magazine and fixed sights. The barrels are interchangeable on this pistol, and this is accomplished simply by depressing a catch in the triggerguard. It is striker fired and marked "Kal. .22 Long Rifle" on the barrel, with "Romerwerke Suhl" stamped on the slide. The finish is blued, and the grips are plastic. This pistol was manufactured between 1924 and 1926.

| Exc. | V.G. | Good | Fair | Poor |
|------|------|------|------|------|
| 500 | 450 | 400 | 300 | 225 |

## RONGE, J. B.
### Liege, Belgium

### Bulldog

This is a cheap "Bulldog"-type revolver chambered for the .32, .380, and the .45 caliber cartridges. The barrel is 3" in length, and there are no markings save for the grips, which feature an embossed "RF" inside a medallion. This company supplied revolvers to other outlets, who marked their own names prior to sale. The company manufactured revolvers between 1880 and 1910.

| Exc. | V.G. | Good | Fair | Poor |
|------|------|------|------|------|
| 150 | 125 | 100 | 75 | 50 |

## ROSS RIFLE CO.
### Quebec, Canada

This rifle was designed in 1896 by Sir Charles Ross. There were several sporting versions produced, and in 1902 the rifle was adopted by the Royal Canadian Mounted Police as a service rifle. This rifle has a straight-pull bolt action, with a locking system that was based on the Mannlicher rifle. The Ross was tested by the British as a possible service rifle on two occasions, and twice it was rejected as being not robust enough for battlefield conditions. In 1915 the Canadian Army took the Ross to war and found it wanting. The Lee-Enfield was found to be a much superior design. As the Ross bolt became worn, it became difficult to close the bolt. It was also possible to incorrectly assemble the bolt and to fire it in this condition with potentially disastrous results. There were approximately 420,000 Ross military rifles manufactured between 1903 and 1915.

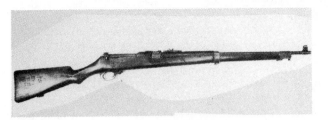

### Mark I

This rifle is chambered for the .303 cartridge, and the barrel is 28" in length. This model has the "Harris Controlled Platform Magazine" that allows the spring to be depressed by an external lever to ease and speed loading.

| Exc. | V.G. | Good | Fair | Poor |
|------|------|------|------|------|
| 300 | 250 | 200 | 150 | 100 |

### Mark I Carbine

This is similar to the Mark I Rifle, with a 22" barrel that would not accept a bayonet.

| Exc. | V.G. | Good | Fair | Poor |
|------|------|------|------|------|
| 350 | 300 | 250 | 200 | 150 |

### Mark 2

This is a modified version chambered for the standard .303 British cartridge. It also has a more serviceable tangent rear sight.

| Exc. | V.G. | Good | Fair | Poor |
|------|------|------|------|------|
| 300 | 250 | 200 | 150 | 100 |

### Mark 3

This model was introduced in 1910 and was supposed to feature improved internal lockwork. It also was changed to accept the standard British stripper clip.

| Exc. | V.G. | Good | Fair | Poor |
|------|------|------|------|------|
| 325 | 275 | 225 | 175 | 125 |

### Mark 3B

This was the final Ross rifle and the only one to be used by the British. It has a magazine cutoff similar to that of the Lee-Enfield. This model was declared obsolete in 1921.

| Exc. | V.G. | Good | Fair | Poor |
|------|------|------|------|------|
| 350 | 300 | 250 | 200 | 150 |

### Sporting Rifle

This is a commercial version of the Ross rifle. It is chambered for the .280 Ross or the .303 British cartridges and is based on the military action. The barrel is 24", and there are open sights. The finish is blued, with a checkered walnut stock. The sporting rifles were manufactured until 1910.

| Exc. | V.G. | Good | Fair | Poor |
|------|------|------|------|------|
| 275 | 225 | 200 | 150 | 125 |

### Caution!

There are many knowledgeable people who deem the Ross rifle unsafe to fire. This situation should definitely be considered before attempting to shoot one.

## ROSSI, AMADEO
### Leopoldo, Brazil
### Importer--Interarms
### Alexandria, Virginia

### Overland Shotgun

This is a side-by-side double-barrel shotgun chambered for 12 or 20 gauge, as well as .410. It has barrel lengths of 26" or 28", exposed hammers, and double triggers. This model has manual extractors. The finish is blued, with a hardwood stock. It was discontinued in 1988.

| Exc. | V.G. | Good | Fair | Poor |
|------|------|------|------|------|
| 250 | 225 | 200 | 150 | 100 |

## Squire Shotgun

This is a side-by-side double-barrel shotgun chambered for 12 or 20 gauge, as well as .410. It has a matte ribbed barrel that is 20", 26", or 28" in length with various choke combinations. It has double triggers and manual ejectors. The finish is blued, with a hardwood stock. It is chambered for 3" Magnum shells.

| NIB | Exc. | V.G. | Good | Fair | Poor |
|-----|------|------|------|------|------|
| 350 | 300  | 250  | 200  | 150  | 100  |

## Model 92

This is a lever-action, saddle-ring carbine that is chambered for .357 Magnum, .44 Magnum, and the .44-40 cartridges. It is patterned after the original Winchester Model 92 and has either a 16" or a 20" round barrel. The finish is blued, with a hardwood stock. There is an engraved version that features etched engraving and better-grade wood, that is worth 20 percent additional.

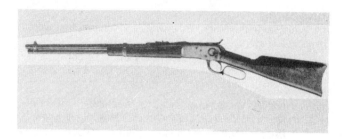

| NIB | Exc. | V.G. | Good | Fair | Poor |
|-----|------|------|------|------|------|
| 285 | 225  | 175  | 150  | 100  | 75   |

## Model 62

This is a slide-action rifle that was copied from the Winchester 1890 Gallery Gun. It is chambered for the .22 l.r. cartridge and has either a 16.5" or a 23" round or octagonal barrel. This is a takedown-type rifle, with a 13-shot tubular magazine under the barrel. The finish is blued, with a hardwood stock. A stainless-steel version is also available.

| NIB | Exc. | V.G. | Good | Fair | Poor |
|-----|------|------|------|------|------|
| 200 | 175  | 150  | 125  | 100  | 75   |

## Model 59

This model is similar to the Model 62 except that it is chambered for the .22 Magnum cartridge and has a 10-shot tubular magazine.

| NIB | Exc. | V.G. | Good | Fair | Poor |
|-----|------|------|------|------|------|
| 250 | 225  | 175  | 150  | 125  | 100  |

## Model 65

This model is a lever-action, saddle-ring carbine chambered for the .44 Special/.44 Magnum cartridge. It has a 20" barrel with open sights and a full-length tubular magazine that holds 10 rounds. The finish is blued, with a hardwood stock. This model was introduced in 1989.

| NIB | Exc. | V.G. | Good | Fair | Poor |
|-----|------|------|------|------|------|
| 300 | 250  | 200  | 175  | 150  | 125  |

## Model 31

This model is a double-action revolver chambered for the .38 Special cartridge. It has a 4" barrel and a 5-shot cylinder. It is finished in blue or nickel-plated, with hardwood grips. This model was not imported after 1985.

| Exc. | V.G. | Good | Fair | Poor |
|------|------|------|------|------|
| 125  | 100  | 75   | 50   | 40   |

## Model 51

This is a double-action revolver chambered for the .22 l.r. It has a 6" barrel with adjustable sights and a 6-shot cylinder. This model is blued, with walnut grips. It was not imported after 1985.

| Exc. | V.G. | Good | Fair | Poor |
|------|------|------|------|------|
| 125  | 100  | 75   | 50   | 40   |

## Model 511 Sportsman

This double-action revolver is chambered for the .22 l.r. cartridge and has a matte-ribbed 4" barrel with adjustable sights. It is constructed of stainless steel with hardwood grips and was introduced in 1986.

| NIB | Exc. | V.G. | Good | Fair | Poor |
|-----|------|------|------|------|------|
| 225 | 200  | 150  | 125  | 100  | 75   |

## Model 68

This is a double-action revolver chambered for the .38 Special cartridge, with a 2" or 3" barrel and a 5-shot cylinder. It is available either blued or nickel-plated, with hardwood grips.

| NIB | Exc. | V.G. | Good | Fair | Poor |
|-----|------|------|------|------|------|
| 185 | 150  | 125  | 100  | 75   | 50   |

## Model 69

This Model is similar to the Model 68 except that it is chambered for the .32 Smith & Wesson cartridge and has a 3" barrel, 6-round cylinder, and walnut grips. It is available either blued or nickel-plated and was not imported after 1985.

| Exc. | V.G. | Good | Fair | Poor |
|------|------|------|------|------|
| 125  | 100  | 75   | 50   | 40   |

## Model 70

This double-action revolver is chambered for the .22 l.r. cartridge and has a 3" barrel and a 6-shot cylinder. It is available either blued or nickel-plated, with hardwood grips. It was not imported after 1985.

| Exc. | V.G. | Good | Fair | Poor |
|------|------|------|------|------|
| 125 | 100 | 75 | 50 | 40 |

## Model 84

This is a stainless-steel double-action revolver chambered for the .38 Special cartridge. It has a ribbed 3" or 4" barrel with fixed sights. It is blued, with checkered hardwood grips. It was imported in 1985 and 1986 only.

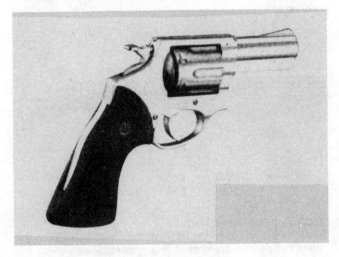

| Exc. | V.G. | Good | Fair | Poor |
|------|------|------|------|------|
| 200 | 175 | 150 | 125 | 100 |

## Model 851

This model is similar to the Model 84, with a 3" or 4" vent-rib barrel. It has adjustable sights and a 6-shot cylinder and is constructed of stainless steel with walnut grips. It was introduced in 1985.

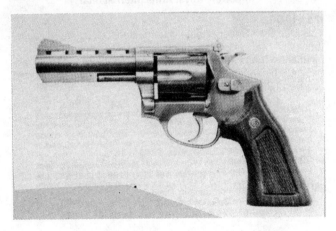

| NIB | Exc. | V.G. | Good | Fair | Poor |
|-----|------|------|------|------|------|
| 250 | 225 | 200 | 150 | 125 | 100 |

## Model 89

This stainless-steel double-action revolver is similar to the Model 84 except that it is chambered for the .32 Smith & Wesson cartridge. It has a 3" barrel and a 6-shot cylinder. It was imported in 1985 and 1986 and is being imported once again.

| NIB | Exc. | V.G. | Good | Fair | Poor |
|-----|------|------|------|------|------|
| 225 | 200 | 175 | 150 | 125 | 100 |

## Model 951

This model is a double-action revolver chambered for the .38 Special cartridge. It has a 3" or 4" vent-rib barrel and a 6-shot cylinder. It is available with a blued finish and hardwood grips. It was introduced in 1985.

| NIB | Exc. | V.G. | Good | Fair | Poor |
|-----|------|------|------|------|------|
| 225 | 200 | 175 | 150 | 125 | 100 |

## Model 971

This model is similar to the Model 951 except that it is chambered for the .357 Magnum cartridge and has a solid-ribbed 4" barrel with a shrouded ejector rod. It has adjustable sights and a 6-shot cylinder. The finish is blued, with hardwood grips. It was introduced in 1988.

| NIB | Exc. | V.G. | Good | Fair | Poor |
|-----|------|------|------|------|------|
| 250 | 225 | 200 | 175 | 150 | 125 |

## Model 971 Stainless

This model is similar to the Model 971 except that it is constructed of stainless steel and has checkered black rubber grips. It was introduced in 1989.

| NIB | Exc. | V.G. | Good | Fair | Poor |
|-----|------|------|------|------|------|
| 250 | 225 | 200 | 175 | 150 | 125 |

# ROTH-SAUER
### SEE--J. P. Sauer & Son

# ROTH-STEYR
### Austria-Hungary

## Model 1907

This unique self-loading pistol was the first semi-automatic pistol adopted as a service arm for a major power. It is chambered for the 8mm cartridge and has a 5" barrel. It fires from an unusual locked breech. It has a very long bolt that is solid at the rear, with a sleeve for the striker. The front part of the bolt is hollow and fits closely over the end of the barrel. Upon firing, the recoiling barrel turns 90 degrees, releasing the bolt for its rearward travel. This pistol was used predominantly as a cavalry sidearm by the Austro-Hungarian army. It is blued, with grooved wooden grips.

| Exc. | V.G. | Good | Fair | Poor |
|------|------|------|------|------|
| 400 | 350 | 300 | 200 | 125 |

# ROTTWIEL
### Rotwiel, West Germany
### Importer--Dynamit Nobel of America Northvale, New Jersey

## Model 650
This model is a field-grade Over/Under shotgun chambered for 12 gauge only. It has 28" vent-rib barrels with six screw-in choke tubes. It has a single-selective trigger and automatic ejectors. The receiver is modestly engraved and coin-finished. It is furnished with a hand-checkered, select walnut stock. This model was not imported after 1986.

| Exc. | V.G. | Good | Fair | Poor |
|------|------|------|------|------|
| 700 | 600 | 500 | 400 | 375 |

## Model 72
This model is a field-grade Over/Under shotgun chambered for 12 gauge only. It has 28" vent-rib barrels with screw-in choke tubes. It features a matte-blued receiver, single-selective trigger, and automatic ejectors. It has a hand-checkered, select walnut stock. This model was not imported after 1987.

| Exc. | V.G. | Good | Fair | Poor |
|------|------|------|------|------|
| 1750 | 1650 | 1500 | 1000 | 750 |

## Model 72 American Skeet
This model is a skeet-grade Over/Under shotgun that is chambered for 12 gauge only. It has a 26.75" vent-rib barrel with a single-selective trigger and automatic ejectors. It features screw-in choke tubes. The matte-finished receiver is slightly engraved and blued, with a hand-checkered French walnut stock. This model was not imported after 1987.

| Exc. | V.G. | Good | Fair | Poor |
|------|------|------|------|------|
| 1750 | 1650 | 1500 | 1000 | 750 |

## Model 72 Ajustable American Trap
This model is a trap-grade Over/Under shotgun chambered for 12 gauge only, with a 34" vent-rib barrel that features an adjustable point of impact. The finish is similar to the American Skeet Model. This model was not imported after 1986.

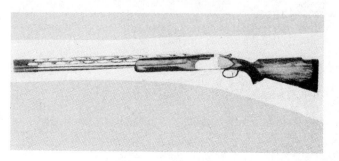

| Exc. | V.G. | Good | Fair | Poor |
|------|------|------|------|------|
| 1500 | 1400 | 1200 | 900 | 650 |

## Model 72 American Trap
This model is a trap-grade Over/Under shotgun similar to the Model 72 AAT, without the adjustable point of impact. It was not imported after 1987.

| Exc. | V.G. | Good | Fair | Poor |
|------|------|------|------|------|
| 1750 | 1650 | 1500 | 1000 | 950 |

## Model 72 International Skeet
This model is a skeet-grade Over/Under shotgun chambered for 12 gauge, with 26.75" vent-rib barrels choked skeet-and-skeet. Its other features are similar to the Model 72AT. It was not imported after 1987.

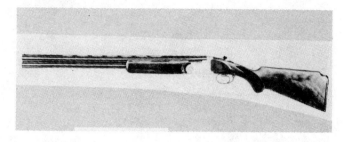

| Exc. | V.G. | Good | Fair | Poor |
|------|------|------|------|------|
| 1750 | 1650 | 1500 | 1000 | 950 |

## Model 72 International Trap
This model is similar to the International Skeet, with 30" high-ribbed barrels that are choked improved-modified-and-full. It was not imported after 1987.

| Exc. | V.G. | Good | Fair | Poor |
|------|------|------|------|------|
| 1750 | 1650 | 1500 | 1000 | 950 |

# ROYAL AMERICAN SHOTGUNS
### Woodland Hills, California
### Importer--Royal Arms International

## Model 100
This is an Over/Under shotgun chambered for 12 and 20 gauge. It has 26", 28", or 30" vent-rib barrels with various choke combinations. It has a boxlock action, double triggers, and extractors. It is blued, with a checkered walnut stock. It was imported between 1985 and 1987.

| Exc. | V.G. | Good | Fair | Poor |
|------|------|------|------|------|
| 350 | 300 | 250 | 175 | 150 |

## Model 100AE
This model is similar to the Model 100 except that it has a single trigger and automatic ejectors.

| Exc. | V.G. | Good | Fair | Poor |
|------|------|------|------|------|
| 375 | 325 | 275 | 200 | 175 |

## Model 600
This is a side-by-side double barrel chambered for 12, 20, and 28 gauge, as well as .410. It has 25", 26", 28", and 30" vent-rib barrels with various choke combinations. The action is a boxlock, and it has double triggers and extractors. It also features chrome-lined bores and an automatic safety. It is blued, with a checkered walnut stock. This model was imported between 1985 and 1987. It was manufactured in Spain.

| Exc. | V.G. | Good | Fair | Poor |
|------|------|------|------|------|
| 375 | 325 | 275 | 200 | 175 |

## Model 800
This side-by-side is chambered for 12, 20, and 28 gauge, as well as .410. It is a true quick detachable sidelock gun. The barrels are 24", 26", and 28" in length with various choke combinations. It is fully scroll-engraved and features double triggers and automatic ejectors. It has cocking indicators, vented firing pins, and a Churchill-type rib. The receiver is coin-finished, and the stock is checkered select walnut with a straight English-style grip. This model was imported between 1985 and 1987.

| Exc. | V.G. | Good | Fair | Poor |
|------|------|------|------|------|
| 750 | 650 | 600 | 475 | 400 |

# RUBY ARMS COMPANY
**Guernica, Spain**

## Ruby
This is a blowback-operated semi-automatic pistol chambered for the 6.35mm or 7.35mm cartridges. It has a 3.5" barrel with fixed sights and a 6-shot detachable magazine. This pistol is of the typical poor-quality "Eibar" type with a blued finish and plastic grips. It is suspected that these pistols were actually manufactured by Gabilondo and marked "Ruby" for marking purposes only. They were manufactured prior to the Spanish Civil War.

| Exc. | V.G. | Good | Fair | Poor |
|------|------|------|------|------|
| 175 | 150 | 100 | 75 | 50 |

# RUPERTUS, JACOB
**Philadelphia, Pennsylvania**

## Army Revolver
This is an extremely rare revolver chambered for .44 caliber percussion. It has a 7.25" octagon barrel with an integral loading lever that pivots to the side instead of downward. The hammer is mounted on the side, and there is a pellet priming device located on the backstrap. There is only one nipple on the breach that lines up with the top of the cylinder. The cylinder is unfluted and holds 6 shots. The finish is blued, with walnut grips; and the frame is marked "Patented April 19, 1859." There were less than 12 manufactured in 1859. It would behoove one to secure a qualified independent appraisal if a transaction were contemplated.

| Exc. | V.G. | Good | Fair | Poor |
|------|------|------|------|------|
| 6000 | 5000 | 3750 | 2750 | 2000 |

## Navy Revolver
This model is equally as rare as the Army model. It is chambered for .36-caliber percussion. Otherwise it is quite similar in appearance to the Army model. There were approximately 12 manufactured in 1859. Both of these Revolvers were manufactured for test purposes and were not well-received by the military, so further production was not accomplished.

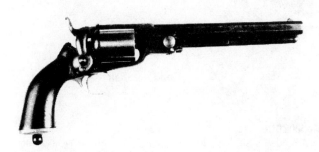

| Exc. | V.G. | Good | Fair | Poor |
|------|------|------|------|------|
| 6000 | 5000 | 3750 | 2750 | 2000 |

## Pocket Model Revolver
This is a smaller version of the Army and Navy model, chambered for .25 caliber percussion. It has no loading lever and has a 3-1/8" octagonal barrel. There were approximately 12 manufactured in 1859.

| Exc. | V.G. | Good | Fair | Poor |
|------|------|------|------|------|
| 4000 | 3250 | 2500 | 1850 | 1500 |

## Single Shot Pocket Pistol
This is a single-shot pocket pistol chambered for .22 r.f., .32 r.f., .38 r.f., and .41 r.f. It will be found with barrel lengths from 3" through 5" that are part-round and part-octagonal in configuration. The barrel rotates to the side for loading. The frame is iron; the finish, blued. The grips are walnut. The barrel is marked "Rupertus Pat'd. Pistol Mfg. Co. Philadelphia." There were approximately 3,000 manufactured between 1870 and 1885. The .41-caliber version would be worth approximately 25 percent additional.

| Exc. | V.G. | Good | Fair | Poor |
|------|------|------|------|------|
| 300 | 250 | 225 | 175 | 125 |

## Double Barrel Pocket Pistol
This rather unique pocket pistol is chambered for the .22-caliber rimfire cartridge and has side-by-side, round 3" barrels that are fired by a single hammer with a selective sliding firing pin that is either mounted in the frame or on the hammer. The frame is iron with a spur trigger and a squared butt. The finish is blued, with walnut grips. The barrel is marked the same as on the Single Shot Pocket Pistol. It is a very rare pistol that was manufactured in the 1870's and 1880's.

| Exc. | V.G. | Good | Fair | Poor |
|------|------|------|------|------|
| 750 | 650 | 500 | 400 | 300 |

## Spur Trigger Revolver
This is a single-action revolver chambered for either .22-caliber rimfire with a 2.75" round barrel and an unfluted cylinder, or .41 caliber rimfire with a 2-7/8" round barrel and a 5-shot semi-fluted cylinder. Both models have iron frames and are either blued or nickel-plated, with walnut birdshead grips. The .41-caliber version is marked "Empire 41" and also "J. Rupertus Phila. Pa." and would be worth an approximate 40 percent premium over the .22-caliber version, which is marked "Empire Pat. Nov. 21, 71." This version also bears the Rupertus name. There were approximately 1,000 manufactured in .22 caliber and considerably less in the .41 caliber. They were produced in the 1870's and 1880's.

| Exc. | V.G. | Good | Fair | Poor |
|------|------|------|------|------|
| 300 | 250 | 225 | 175 | 125 |

# S.A.C.M.
**SEE--French State**

# S.A.E.
**Eibar, Spain**
**Importer--Spain America Enterprises, Inc. Miami, Florida**

## Model 210S
This model is a side-by-side double-barrel shotgun chambered for 12 or 20 gauge, as well as .410. It has 26" or 28" barrels with 3" chambers and a boxlock action. It features double triggers and manual extractors and has a moderately engraved silver-finish receiver, blued barrels, and a checkered walnut stock. This model was imported in 1988 only.

| Exc. | V.G. | Good | Fair | Poor |
|------|------|------|------|------|
| 425 | 375 | 300 | 225 | 175 |

## Model 340X

This model is a side-by-side double-barrel shotgun chambered for 10 or 20 gauge. It has 26" barrels and features a Holland & Holland-type sidelock action. It has double triggers and automatic ejectors. The receiver is moderately engraved and case-colored, with blued barrels and an English-style, straight-grip, checkered walnut stock. It was imported in 1988 only.

| Exc. | V.G. | Good | Fair | Poor |
|------|------|------|------|------|
| 700 | 600 | 500 | 400 | 300 |

## Model 209E

This model is similar to the Model 340X except that it is offered in .410 and features more profuse engraving and a better-grade walnut stock. It was also imported in 1988 only.

| Exc. | V.G. | Good | Fair | Poor |
|------|------|------|------|------|
| 900 | 800 | 700 | 550 | 400 |

## Model 70

This is an Over/Under double-barrel shotgun chambered for 12 or 20 gauge with 3" chambers. It has 26" vent-rib barrels with screw-in chokes. It features a boxlock action, single trigger, and automatic ejectors. It is available with a moderately engraved blue- or silver-finished receiver, blued barrels, and a matte-finished checkered walnut stock. This Model was imported in 1988 only.

| Exc. | V.G. | Good | Fair | Poor |
|------|------|------|------|------|
| 400 | 300 | 250 | 200 | 150 |

## Model 66C

This model is a skeet- or trap-grade Over/Under shotgun chambered for 12 gauge only. It has 26" or 30" vent-rib barrels that are choked for skeet or trap. It is a boxlock action that features false sideplates that are fully engraved with 24-kt. gold inlays. It has a single trigger and automatic ejectors. The finish is blued, with a checkered walnut Monte Carlo stock and beavertail forearm. It was imported in 1988 only.

| Exc. | V.G. | Good | Fair | Poor |
|------|------|------|------|------|
| 900 | 800 | 700 | 575 | 450 |

# S.E.A.M.
## Eibar, Spain

This company was actually a marketing organization and engaged in very little manufacturing. Many of its products were produced by the firm of Urizar and appeared to be identical to pistols sold by Grand Precision, which was another marketing organization. Due to the confusing nature of gunmaking firms in Spain at this time, these unclear circumstances will never be rectified.

## Praga

This is a blowback-operated pocket pistol chambered for 7.65mm. It is of typical low "Eibar" quality. It is marked "Praga Cal 7.65" on the side of the slide. The finish is blued, with black plastic grips that bear the S.E.A.M. trademark, a floral band with a crown in the center.

| Exc. | V.G. | Good | Fair | Poor |
|------|------|------|------|------|
| 175 | 150 | 125 | 90 | 65 |

## S.E.A.M.

This is a diminutive, blowback-operated semi-automatic pistol that features an open-top slide. It is chambered for 6.35mm and has a 2" barrel. The finish is blued, and the slide is marked "Fabrica de Armas SEAM." The grips are black plastic, with the initials "SEAM" molded into the top. There is also another 6.35mm model bearing the same name that was a direct copy of the Walther Model 9. The values of both of these models are similar.

| Exc. | V.G. | Good | Fair | Poor |
|------|------|------|------|------|
| 175 | 150 | 125 | 90 | 65 |

## Silesia

This is a blowback-operated semi-automatic pistol chambered for 7.65mm. It has a 3" barrel and is of the typical low-quality "Eibar" construction. The name "Silesia" is marked on the slide. The finish is blued, and the black plastic grips bear a "SEAM" medallion.

| Exc. | V.G. | Good | Fair | Poor |
|------|------|------|------|------|
| 175 | 150 | 125 | 90 | 65 |

# SKB ARMS COMPANY
## Tokyo, Japan
## Importer--SKB Company USA
## Manhein, Pennsylvania

This is an old-line Japanese gun company that has been in business for over 100 years. They have manufactured firearms for a number of different companies, most notably Ithaca.

## Model 100

This is a side-by-side double-barrel shotgun chambered for 12 or 20 gauge. The barrel lengths are from 25" to 30" with various choke combinations. It has a boxlock action with a single-selective trigger and automatic ejectors. The finish is blued, with a hand-checkered walnut stock. This Model was not imported after 1980.

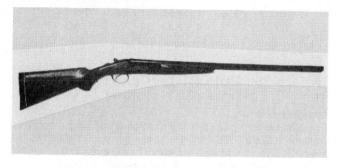

| Exc. | V.G. | Good | Fair | Poor |
|------|------|------|------|------|
| 475 | 425 | 375 | 300 | 250 |

## Model 150

This model is similar to the Model 100, with a moderately scroll-engraved receiver, a beavertail forearm, and a select grade of walnut. It was imported between 1972 and 1974.

| Exc. | V.G. | Good | Fair | Poor |
|------|------|------|------|------|
| 525 | 475 | 425 | 350 | 300 |

## Model 200

This model is also similar to the Model 100, with a scalloped receiver that was moderately engraved and coin- finished.

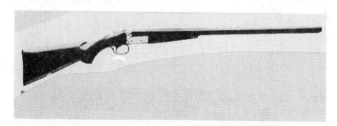

| Exc. | V.G. | Good | Fair | Poor |
|------|------|------|------|------|
| 550 | 500 | 450 | 375 | 325 |

## Model 200E

This model is similar to the Model 200, with an English-style straight-grip stock. It was imported until 1988.

| Exc. | V.G. | Good | Fair | Poor |
|------|------|------|------|------|
| 750 | 675 | 600 | 475 | 375 |

## Model 300
This model is similar to the Model 200, with a greater amount of engraving and a better-grade walnut stock.

| Exc. | V.G. | Good | Fair | Poor |
|------|------|------|------|------|
| 750 | 675 | 600 | 475 | 375 |

## Model 400E
This model is similar to the Model 400, with engraved false sideplates and an English-style straight-grip stock. It was imported until 1989.

| Exc. | V.G. | Good | Fair | Poor |
|------|------|------|------|------|
| 975 | 875 | 750 | 600 | 500 |

## Model 480E
This model is similar to the Model 400E, with more engraving, a coin-finished receiver, and a better-grade walnut stock.

| Exc. | V.G. | Good | Fair | Poor |
|------|------|------|------|------|
| 1200 | 1000 | 850 | 650 | 550 |

## Model 500
This is an Over/Under, field-grade, double-barrel shotgun chambered for 12, 20, or 28 gauge, as well as .410. It has 26", 28", or 30" vent-rib barrels with various choke combinations. The finish is blued, with a checkered walnut stock. This model was imported between 1966 and 1979.

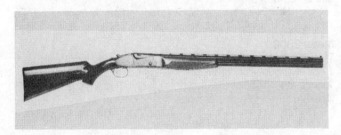

| Exc. | V.G. | Good | Fair | Poor |
|------|------|------|------|------|
| 500 | 450 | 375 | 300 | 250 |

## Model 600
This model is similar to the Model 500, with a silver-plated receiver and a better-grade walnut stock.

| Exc. | V.G. | Good | Fair | Poor |
|------|------|------|------|------|
| 700 | 625 | 550 | 450 | 325 |

## Model 600 Magnum
This is the Model 600 with 3" Magnum chambers in 12 gauge only. It was imported between 1969 and 1972.

| Exc. | V.G. | Good | Fair | Poor |
|------|------|------|------|------|
| 725 | 650 | 575 | 475 | 350 |

## Model 600 Trap Gun
This model is similar to the Model 600, with a high comb trap stock and a recoil pad. The barrels are 30" or 32" in length, choked for trap shooting.

| Exc. | V.G. | Good | Fair | Poor |
|------|------|------|------|------|
| 675 | 600 | 525 | 425 | 300 |

## Model 600 Skeet Gun
This model is similar to the Model 600 Trap except that it is chambered for 12, 20, or 28 gauge, as well as .410, and has 26" or 28" barrels that are choked skeet-and-skeet.

| Exc. | V.G. | Good | Fair | Poor |
|------|------|------|------|------|
| 700 | 625 | 550 | 450 | 325 |

## Model 600 Skeet Combo Set
This model is the Model 600 Skeet with a matched set of barrels in all gauges. It is furnished in a fitted case.

| Exc. | V.G. | Good | Fair | Poor |
|------|------|------|------|------|
| 700 | 625 | 550 | 450 | 325 |

## Model 680E
This model is similar to the Model 600 with scroll engraving and a select, English-style straight-grip stock. It was imported between 1973 and 1976.

| Exc. | V.G. | Good | Fair | Poor |
|------|------|------|------|------|
| 725 | 650 | 575 | 475 | 350 |

## Model 700 Trap Gun
This model is similar to the Model 600 Trap, with a wide competition rib, a greater amount of engraving, and better-grade walnut. It was imported between 1969 and 1975.

| Exc. | V.G. | Good | Fair | Poor |
|------|------|------|------|------|
| 825 | 750 | 675 | 575 | 450 |

## Model 700 Skeet Gun
This model is similar to the Model 700 Trap Gun except that it is barrelled and choked skeet-and-skeet. It is also available in 20 gauge.

| Exc. | V.G. | Good | Fair | Poor |
|------|------|------|------|------|
| 850 | 775 | 700 | 600 | 475 |

## Model 800 Trap Gun
This model is similar to the Model 700 Trap, with a greater degree of engraving and higher-grade walnut. It was imported between 1969 and 1975.

| Exc. | V.G. | Good | Fair | Poor |
|------|------|------|------|------|
| 1200 | 1000 | 850 | 650 | 550 |

## Model 800 Skeet Gun
This model is similar to the Model 800 Trap except that it is chambered for 12 or 20 gauge and has either 26" or 28" skeet-choked barrels. It was imported between 1969 and 1975.

| Exc. | V.G. | Good | Fair | Poor |
|------|------|------|------|------|
| 1200 | 1000 | 850 | 650 | 550 |

## Model 880 Crown Grade
This model is chambered for 12, 20, or 28 gauge, as well as .410. It is offered with various barrel lengths and choke combinations. It is a boxlock with ornately engraved false sideplates. The receiver is coin-finished, and it has a single-selective trigger and automatic ejectors. It utilizes select walnut for the stock, which is checkered in a fleur-de-lis pattern. This model was not imported after 1980.

| Exc. | V.G. | Good | Fair | Poor |
|------|------|------|------|------|
| 1700 | 1500 | 1250 | 1100 | 900 |

## Model 505
This is a field-grade, Over/Under double-barrel shotgun chambered for 12 or 20 gauge, with screw-in choke tubes. It has 3" Magnum chambers, a single-selective trigger, and automatic ejectors. The finish is blued, with a hand-checkered walnut stock and recoil pad. It is a current production model.

| NIB | Exc. | V.G. | Good | Fair | Poor |
|-----|------|------|------|------|------|
| 750 | 675 | 600 | 500 | 450 | 375 |

The 505 Series is also produced in trap and skeet configurations, which are valued at approximately 5 percent additional.

## Model 505 Three-Gauge Skeet Set
This model is chambered for 20 and 28 gauge, as well as .410. It is furnished with three extra sets of skeet barrels in a fitted aluminum case.

| NIB | Exc. | V.G. | Good | Fair | Poor |
|-----|------|------|------|------|------|
| 1850 | 1650 | 1400 | 1100 | 900 | 750 |

## Model 605
This model is similar to the Model 505, with a moderately engraved silver-finished receiver and a higher-grade walnut stock.

| NIB | Exc. | V.G. | Good | Fair | Poor |
|-----|------|------|------|------|------|
| 900 | 750 | 650 | 550 | 400 | 350 |

The 605 Series is also available in trap or skeet configurations. The values are similar.

### Model 605 Three-Gauge Skeet Set
This model is similar to the Model 605, chambered for 20 or 28 gauge, as well as .410, with the extra barrels furnished in a fitted aluminum case.

| NIB | Exc. | V.G. | Good | Fair | Poor |
|------|------|------|------|------|------|
| 2000 | 1800 | 1550 | 1250 | 1000 | 850 |

### Model 885
This model is similar to the older Model 800, available in skeet or trap models. It has a scroll-engraved, coin-finished receiver with game scenes engraved on the boxlock action, with false sideplates. It has a high-grade, hand-checkered walnut stock and was imported in 1988 only.

| Exc. | V.G. | Good | Fair | Poor |
|------|------|------|------|------|
| 1250 | 1050 | 900 | 700 | 600 |

### Model 7300
This is a slide-action shotgun chambered in 12 and 20 gauge. It features twin action bars and is blued, with a hand-checkered walnut stock. This model was not imported after 1980.

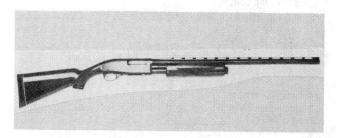

| Exc. | V.G. | Good | Fair | Poor |
|------|------|------|------|------|
| 300 | 250 | 200 | 150 | 100 |

### Model 7900
This model is similar to the Model 7300 except that it is either a trap or skeet gun and is manufactured in those respective configurations.

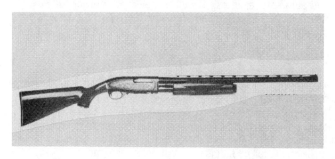

| Exc. | V.G. | Good | Fair | Poor |
|------|------|------|------|------|
| 350 | 300 | 250 | 200 | 150 |

### Model 300
This is a recoil-operated auto-loading shotgun chambered for 12 or 20 gauge. It is offered with 26", 28", or 30" barrels with various chokes. The finish is blued, with a checkered walnut stock. It was imported between 1968 and 1972.
Vent-Rib Barrel--Add 20 Percent.

| Exc. | V.G. | Good | Fair | Poor |
|------|------|------|------|------|
| 300 | 250 | 200 | 150 | 100 |

### Model 1300
This model is simply the latest designation for the Model 300. It features a standard vent-rib barrel with screw-in chokes and has been imported since 1988.

| NIB | Exc. | V.G. | Good | Fair | Poor |
|------|------|------|------|------|------|
| 450 | 400 | 350 | 300 | 200 | 150 |

### Model XL 900 MR
This is a gas-operated semi-automatic shotgun chambered for 12 gauge, with 26" through 30" vent-rib barrels. It has an alloy receiver with an etched gamescene. The finish is blued, with a checkered walnut stock. It was not imported after 1980.

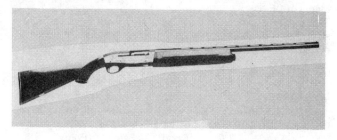

| Exc. | V.G. | Good | Fair | Poor |
|------|------|------|------|------|
| 325 | 275 | 225 | 175 | 125 |

### Model 1900
This is the current designation for the Model 900. It is chambered in 12 or 20 gauge and is offered with 22", 26", or 28" vent-rib barrels with screw-in chokes. It has 3" Magnum chambers and an etched receiver. It is blued, with a gold trigger and a checkered walnut stock.

| NIB | Exc. | V.G. | Good | Fair | Poor |
|------|------|------|------|------|------|
| 500 | 425 | 375 | 300 | 250 | 175 |

### Model 3000
This is a gas-operated semi-automatic shotgun chambered for 12 or 20 gauge. It features a 3" Magnum chamber and would shoot 2-3/4" or 3" shells interchangeably. It has a squareback-styled receiver with gamescenes etched on both sides. The finish is blued, and it has a high-grade, hand-checkered walnut stock. It was not imported after 1989.

| Exc. | V.G. | Good | Fair | Poor |
|------|------|------|------|------|
| 475 | 400 | 350 | 250 | 150 |

## SKS
### Communist Bloc

### SKS
This is a gas-operated semi-automatic rifle with a 20.5" barrel. It is chambered for the 7.62mm cartridge. It has a 10-round, fixed box magazine. It features a tangent rear sight and an attached folding bayonet. The finish is blued, with a wood stock and handguard. It was developed by the Soviet Union and was the first of their rifles to use this intermediate round. It is a simple, strong weapon that was used in nearly every Communist country on earth. It was manufactured in the Soviet Union, as well as in Yugoslavia, and in China--where it was known as the Type 56. This weapon is militarily obsolete and has been imported in vast quantities into the United States.

| Exc. | V.G. | Good | Fair | Poor |
|------|------|------|------|------|
| 250 | 200 | 150 | 100 | 75 |

## SSK INDUSTRIES
### Bloomingdale, Ohio

This company utilizes modified Thompson Center receivers to produce their specialized single-shot pistols. They manufacture perhaps the most powerful handguns in the world and have also produced various limited-edition guns for handgun hunters over the years.

### SSK-Contender
This is a fully customized Thompson Center receiver with an SSK barrel that is available chambered for 74 different cartridges. It is available chambered from .17Bee up to and including the .588 JDJ, a monstrous cartridge capable of dropping any

animal on the planet with a well-placed shot. It is a custom-made gun made basically to customer's specifications. It has a hard chrome finish and is available with optional iron sights or scope rings.

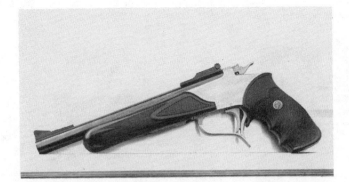

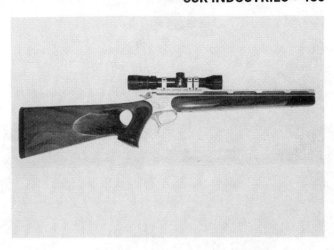

| NIB | Exc. | V.G. | Good | Fair | Poor |
|-----|------|------|------|------|------|
| 575 | 500 | 475 | 425 | 350 | 275 |

### SSK-XP100

This is a fully customized version of the bolt-action Remington XP100 pistol. It is chambered for many various calibers and is furnished with scope mounts and rings.

| NIB | Exc. | V.G. | Good | Fair | Poor |
|-----|------|------|------|------|------|
| 650 | 600 | 550 | 500 | 400 | 300 |

### .50 Caliber XP100

This is a specialized, big game hunting version of the Standard SSK XP100 pistol. It is furnished with a special muzzle break and a reinforced fiberglas stock.

| NIB | Exc. | V.G. | Good | Fair | Poor |
|-----|------|------|------|------|------|
| 1750 | 1500 | 1250 | 1000 | 750 | 500 |

SSK Ruger Redhawk conversions.

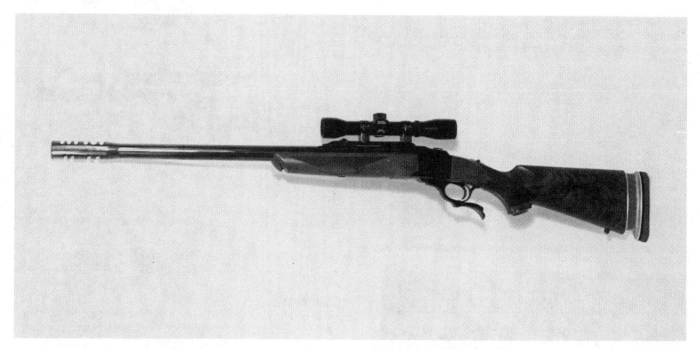

SSK Custom Ruger #1 .577 Nitro Express.

SSK Custom Ruger Redhawk "Beast."

SSK Custom TCR Rifle available from .17 Rem.

J.D. Jones with wildebeast .411 JDJ Custom.

J.D. Jones with elephant — Zimbabwe, 1984 .375 JDJ.

Mark Hampton with Cape buffalo .375 JDJ.

## S.W.D., INC.
### Atlanta, Georgia

**Cobray M-11**
This is a semi-automatic, assault-type pistol that is chambered for the 9mm Parabellum cartridge. It is manufactured from steel stampings, fires from a closed-bolt position, and has a 32-round magazine. The finish is parkerized.

| Exc. | V.G. | Good | Fair | Poor |
|---|---|---|---|---|
| 225 | 200 | 175 | 125 | 100 |

**M-11 Carbine**
This version is similar to the standard M-11 except that it has a 16.25" barrel with a full-length shroud and a telescoping steel-wire stock.

| Exc. | V.G. | Good | Fair | Poor |
|---|---|---|---|---|
| 250 | 225 | 200 | 150 | 125 |

**Terminator**
This is a single-shot, assault-type shotgun that is chambered for 12 or 20 gauge. It has an 18" cylinder bore barrel and fires from an open-bolt position. The finish is parkerized.

| Exc. | V.G. | Good | Fair | Poor |
|---|---|---|---|---|
| 100 | 80 | 70 | 60 | 50 |

## SACKET, D. D.
### Westfield, Massachusetts

**Underhammer Pistol**
This bootleg-type pistol is chambered for .34 or .36 caliber percussion and has a part-octagonal/part-round barrel 3" or 4" in length. It is marked, "D. D. Sacket/ Westfield/Cast Steel." There were two models produced--one with a round walnut butt and the other with a pointed butt. The number manufactured is unknown. This firearm was produced in the 1850's.

| Exc. | V.G. | Good | Fair | Poor |
|---|---|---|---|---|
| 500 | 400 | 350 | 250 | 175 |

## SAFARI ARMS
### Phoenix, Arizona

This company was in business between 1978 and 1987. In 1987 Olympic Arms of Olympia, Washington, purchased Safari Arms and is currently manufacturing these pistols under their own trademark.

**Enforcer**
This semi-automatic pistol is based on the Browning 1911 design. It is chambered for .45 ACP. It has a 3.9" barrel and a 6-shot detachable magazine. This is a compact pistol that is furnished with either the flat or arched mainspring housings. It has adjustable sights and is furnished in either blue, Armaloy, electroless nickel-plate, or a parkerized finish. The grips are either checkered walnut or neoprene. There is also an anodized aluminum lightweight version. Manufacture of this pistol was discontinued in 1987.

| Exc. | V.G. | Good | Fair | Poor |
|---|---|---|---|---|
| 700 | 600 | 500 | 400 | 350 |

**Match Master**
This model is similar to the Enforcer except that it is a full-sized version with a 5" barrel.

| Exc. | V.G. | Good | Fair | Poor |
|---|---|---|---|---|
| 700 | 600 | 500 | 400 | 350 |

**Black Widow**
This model is similar to the Enforcer, with a contoured gripstrap and ivory Micarta grips with a scrimshawed Black Widow. It was discontinued in 1987.

| Exc. | V.G. | Good | Fair | Poor |
|---|---|---|---|---|
| 700 | 600 | 500 | 400 | 350 |

**Model 81**
This model is similar to the Black Widow without the scrimshawed grips. It is also offered chambered for the .38 Special cartridge. This model was discontinued in 1987.

| Exc. | V.G. | Good | Fair | Poor |
|---|---|---|---|---|
| 800 | 700 | 600 | 500 | 400 |

**Model 81L**
This model is similar to the Model 81 except that it has a 6" barrel.

| Exc. | V.G. | Good | Fair | Poor |
|---|---|---|---|---|
| 850 | 750 | 650 | 550 | 450 |

**Ultimate Unlimited**
This is a bolt-action, single-shot, target pistol chambered for various calibers. It has a 15" barrel and a laminated stock. The finish is blued. It was discontinued in 1987.

| Exc. | V.G. | Good | Fair | Poor |
|---|---|---|---|---|
| 850 | 750 | 650 | 550 | 450 |

**Survivor I Conversion Unit**
This unit is used to convert a Model 1911 frame into a bolt-action carbine that is chambered for the .223 cartridge. It features a 16.25" barrel and a folding stock.

| Exc. | V.G. | Good | Fair | Poor |
|---|---|---|---|---|
| 300 | 275 | 250 | 200 | 150 |

**Counter Sniper Rifle**
This is a target-grade bolt-action rifle chambered for the .308 cartridge. It has a 26" heavy barrel and utilizes 20-round detachable M-14 magazines. It is matte-blued, with a camouflaged composite stock. This model was discontinued in 1987.

| Exc. | V.G. | Good | Fair | Poor |
|---|---|---|---|---|
| 1200 | 1050 | 850 | 650 | 450 |

# SAKO
### Riihimaki, Finland

This is one of the finest bolt-action rifles manufactured. They are extremely high quality and enjoy a reputation for fine accuracy. Earlier models manufactured before 1972, when they began being imported by Garcia, are considered collectible and will bring an approximate 25 percent premium. This in no way reflects on the quality of the current manufactured firearms.

### Standard Sporter
This is a bolt-action rifle that is chambered for various popular cartridges. It is produced with short, medium, or long actions to handle different-sized cartridges. It has a high quality barrel in various lengths. The finish is blued, with a hand-checkered walnut stock.

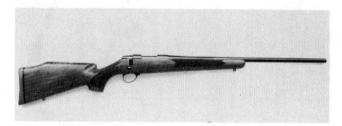

| Exc. | V.G. | Good | Fair | Poor |
|------|------|------|------|------|
| 600  | 550  | 450  | 350  | 250  |

### Deluxe Model
This model is similar to the Standard Sporter, with an engraved floorplate and a skipline-checkered Monte Carlo stock with a rosewood pistolgrip cap and forearm tip.

SAKO DELUXE LIGHTWEIGHT

| Exc. | V.G. | Good | Fair | Poor |
|------|------|------|------|------|
| 800  | 700  | 600  | 450  | 350  |

### Finnbear
This model is produced with the long action in various larger calibers up to .375 Holland & Holland. It is available with a 20" carbine barrel and a full-length Mannlicher-type stock or a 23.5" barrel. The finish is blued, with a checkered walnut stock.
.458 Winchester Magnum, 20 Produced, Values Doubled.

| Exc. | V.G. | Good | Fair | Poor |
|------|------|------|------|------|
| 800  | 700  | 600  | 450  | 350  |

### Forester
This model is similar to the Finnbear except that it is made with a medium action chambered for intermediate cartridges.

| Exc. | V.G. | Good | Fair | Poor |
|------|------|------|------|------|
| 800  | 700  | 600  | 450  | 350  |

### Vixen
This is the short-action model of this series.

| Exc. | V.G. | Good | Fair | Poor |
|------|------|------|------|------|
| 800  | 700  | 600  | 450  | 350  |

### FN Action
This model is chambered for .270 Winchester and .30- 06. It has a long Mauser action that was produced by Fabrique Nationale. It was manufactured between 1950 and 1957.

| Exc. | V.G. | Good | Fair | Poor |
|------|------|------|------|------|
| 600  | 550  | 450  | 350  | 250  |

### FN Magnum Action
This model was produced on a Fabrique Nationale Magnum action and is chambered for .300 Holland & Holland and .375 Holland & Holland. It was manufactured between 1950 and 1957.

| Exc. | V.G. | Good | Fair | Poor |
|------|------|------|------|------|
| 700  | 650  | 550  | 450  | 350  |

### Finnwolf
This is a lever-action rifle chambered for various popular cartridges. It has a 4-shot detachable magazine. The finish is blued, with a checkered walnut stock. This model was manufactured between 1962 and 1974.

| Exc. | V.G. | Good | Fair | Poor |
|------|------|------|------|------|
| 600  | 550  | 450  | 350  | 250  |

### Anniversary Model
This bolt-action rifle that has a 24" barrel and is chambered for 7mm Remington Magnum only. The finish is blued, and it has a select, hand-checkered walnut stock. There were only 1,000 manufactured. This, as well as any commemorative, should be NIB to realize its full resale potential.

| NIB  | Exc. | V.G. | Good | Fair | Poor |
|------|------|------|------|------|------|
| 1200 | 1050 | 850  | 750  | 550  | 450  |

### Hunter
This is a current production bolt-action rifle available with either the short, medium, or long action. It is chambered for various cartridges from .17 Remington up to .375 Holland & Holland. It is offered with a 21.25" or 22" barrel and has a blued finish with a hand-checkered French walnut stock.

| NIB | Exc. | V.G. | Good | Fair | Poor |
|-----|------|------|------|------|------|
| 875 | 750  | 650  | 500  | 400  | 350  |

### Carbine
This model is similar to the Hunter. It is available in the medium or long action only. It has an 18.5" barrel with open sights and was introduced in 1986.

| NIB | Exc. | V.G. | Good | Fair | Poor |
|-----|------|------|------|------|------|
| 875 | 750  | 650  | 500  | 400  | 350  |

### FiberClass
This model is similar to the Hunter, chambered for cartridges from .25-06 through .375 Holland & Holland, with a black fiberglas stock.

SAKO FIBERCLASS

| NIB  | Exc. | V.G. | Good | Fair | Poor |
|------|------|------|------|------|------|
| 1200 | 1000 | 850  | 700  | 600  | 500  |

### FiberClass Carbine
This model is similar to the standard Carbine, with a black fiberglas stock. It was introduced in 1986.

| NIB  | Exc. | V.G. | Good | Fair | Poor |
|------|------|------|------|------|------|
| 1200 | 1000 | 850  | 700  | 600  | 500  |

### Mannlicher Carbine
This model is chambered for the .222 Remington through .375 Holland & Holland. It is available in all three action lengths with an 18.5" barrel, open sights, and a full-length, Mannlicher-type stock.

SAKO CARBINE (FULL STOCK)

| NIB | Exc. | V.G. | Good | Fair | Poor |
|-----|------|------|------|------|------|
| 950 | 850 | 750 | 650 | 500 | 400 |

## Sako PPC

This is a target-grade bolt action that is chambered for the .22 PPC or 6mm PPC cartridges. It is available with a 21.75" barrel and a 4-shot magazine in the Hunter model or with a 23.75" barrel in single-shot configuration in the Benchrest model. The finish is blued, with a deluxe, oil-finished, checkered walnut stock. It has been imported since 1989.
Deluxe Model--Add $275.

| NIB | Exc. | V.G. | Good | Fair | Poor |
|-----|------|------|------|------|------|
| 1100 | 900 | 750 | 600 | 500 | 400 |

## Varmint

This model is available in the short and medium action and is chambered for .222 Remington through .308 Winchester. It has a 22.75" heavy barrel and is furnished without sights. The finish is blued; and the stock is select, checkered walnut.

SAKO VARMINT (HEAVY BARREL)

| NIB | Exc. | V.G. | Good | Fair | Poor |
|-----|------|------|------|------|------|
| 975 | 875 | 775 | 675 | 525 | 425 |

## Classic Grade

This model is available in all three action lengths and is chambered from .17 Remington through 7mm Remington Magnum. It has a blued finish and a classic, European-styled stock made of hand-checkered French walnut. This model was discontinued in 1985.

| Exc. | V.G. | Good | Fair | Poor |
|------|------|------|------|------|
| 850 | 750 | 650 | 550 | 400 |

## Deluxe Grade

This model is available with all three action lengths and is chambered from .223 Remington through .375 Holland & Holland. It has a 21" or 22" barrel. The finish is blued, with a high-grade, skipline-checkered walnut stock with a rosewood forend tip and pistolgrip cap.

| NIB | Exc. | V.G. | Good | Fair | Poor |
|-----|------|------|------|------|------|
| 1150 | 950 | 800 | 650 | 550 | 450 |

## Super Deluxe

This is a special-order, limited-edition rifle available in all three action lengths. It features a presentation-grade, carved and checkered walnut stock with a rosewood forend tip and pistolgrip cap.

| NIB | Exc. | V.G. | Good | Fair | Poor |
|-----|------|------|------|------|------|
| 2250 | 1850 | 1600 | 1250 | 950 | 750 |

## Safari Grade

This is a classic-style, high-grade rifle available in the long action and chambered for .300 Winchester Magnum, .338 Winchester Magnum, and the .375 Holland & Holland cartridges. It has a 22" barrel with open sights and a four-shot magazine. The finish is blued, with a presentation-grade, hand-checkered walnut stock.

| NIB | Exc. | V.G. | Good | Fair | Poor |
|-----|------|------|------|------|------|
| 2250 | 1850 | 1600 | 1250 | 950 | 750 |

## Model 78

This Model is built on a short action and is chambered for .22 l.r. or .22 Hornet. It has a 22" barrel, a blued finish, and a checkered walnut stock. It was discontinued in 1986.

| Exc. | V.G. | Good | Fair | Poor |
|------|------|------|------|------|
| 500 | 450 | 400 | 300 | 250 |

## Model 2700

This is a long-action rifle chambered from .270 through .300 Winchester Magnum. It has a 22" barrel, blued finish, and a select, hand-checkered walnut stock. This Model was discontinued in 1985.

| Exc. | V.G. | Good | Fair | Poor |
|------|------|------|------|------|
| 800 | 700 | 600 | 450 | 350 |

# SALVATOR DORMAS
## Vienna, Austria

This firm was founded by Archduke Karl Von Salvator and Lieutenant Ritter Von Dormas in 1886. This partnership was responsible for designing the Skoda machine gun, as well as various Austrian rifle designs. In 1892 Von Salvator died; but Dormas insisted that his name remain part of the company, as much of their development work was his. In 1894 their semi-automatic pistol appeared.

## Model 1894

This is a blowback-operated semi-automatic pistol that is chambered for an 8mm rimmed cartridge designed especially for this firearm. It has a 5" barrel that is fixed and surrounded by a recoil spring and jacket. The cocking spur is located underneath the barrel. The rear end of it passes into the receiver and is connected to the breechblock. The pistol is fired by an external hammer and has a detachable 5-round magazine that is loaded into the butt through the top when the action is opened. There were very few manufactured, either by the firms of Steyr or Skoda. The finish is blued, with black plastic grips. Although the design was sound and should have been successful, the pistol simply could not compete with the heavy-caliber, locked-breech pistols that were popular during this era.

| Exc. | V.G. | Good | Fair | Poor |
|------|------|------|------|------|
| 850 | 650 | 550 | 450 | 350 |

# SAM, INC.
### Reston, Virginia
### Special Service Arms Mfg., Inc.

## Model 88 Crossfire
This is an assault-type weapon that is quite unique. It features a combination of a 12 gauge shotgun and a .308 Winchester rifle in an Over/Under configuration. The unique aspect is that they are both semi-automatic weapons. The first shot is activated by a slide, and then the weapon functions in a semi-automatic mode. There are dual gas pistons and rotating bolts and a three-position selector switch that designates either the rifle, shotgun, or safety. There are two box magazines, a 20-round rifle and 7-shot shotgun. The barrels are 20" in length. It has a matte black finish and a composition stock. This model was introduced in 1989. Due to the current mass hysteria in our country regarding assault-type weapons, it is impossible to accurately evaluate weapons of this nature; and we strongly urge a competent local individual appraisal if a transaction is contemplated.

# SAMCO GLOBAL ARMS, INC.
### Miami, Florida

This company is an importer of surplus military firearms. They currently import the products of Mauser, Lee Enfield, Styr, Hakim, etc. The products will be found under their own headings in this text.

# SARASQUETA, FELIX
### Eibar, Spain
### Importer--SAE, Inc. Miami, Florida

## Merke
This is an Over/Under double-barrel shotgun chambered for 12 gauge only. It has 22" or 27" ribbed and separated barrels with various choke combinations. It has a single non-selective trigger and manual extractors. The finish is blued, with a checkered hardwood stock and recoil pad. This model was imported in 1986 only.

| Exc. | V.G. | Good | Fair | Poor |
|------|------|------|------|------|
| 275 | 250 | 225 | 150 | 100 |

# SARASQUETA, J. J.
### Eibar, Spain
### Importer--American Arms, Inc. Overland Park, Kansas

## Model 107E
This Is a side-by-side double-barrel shotgun chambered for 12, 16, or 20 gauge. It has various length barrels and choke combinations. It has double triggers and automatic ejectors. The finish is blued, with a checkered walnut stock. This Model was discontinued in 1984.

| Exc. | V.G. | Good | Fair | Poor |
|------|------|------|------|------|
| 375 | 300 | 275 | 225 | 175 |

## Model 119E
This Model is similar to the 107E, with better-grade materials and workmanship.

| Exc. | V.G. | Good | Fair | Poor |
|------|------|------|------|------|
| 475 | 400 | 375 | 325 | 275 |

## Model 130E
This is a still more deluxe version that features engraving.

| Exc. | V.G. | Good | Fair | Poor |
|------|------|------|------|------|
| 800 | 700 | 600 | 450 | 350 |

## Model 131E
This Model is similar to the 107E, with a heavily engraved receiver.

| Exc. | V.G. | Good | Fair | Poor |
|------|------|------|------|------|
| 1100 | 900 | 800 | 650 | 500 |

## Model 1882 E LUXE
This Model has a single-selective trigger and is ornately engraved with gold inlays. A silver-inlaid model is available for 10 percent less.

| Exc. | V.G. | Good | Fair | Poor |
|------|------|------|------|------|
| 800 | 700 | 600 | 450 | 350 |

# SARASQUETA, VICTOR
### Eibar, Spain

This Spanish company manufactured reasonably high-grade side-by-side double-barrelled shotguns. They produced a number of different models that varied basically by the amount of engraving, the grade of walnut, and the overall quality that was utilized. There is a boxlock version as well as a sidelock version. They are listed as follows:

## Model 3
This is the basic Sarasqueta model designation. It is a side-by-side double-barrelled shotgun chambered for 12, 16, or 20 gauge. It is available in various barrel lengths and choke combinations. It has double triggers, automatic ejectors, and a checkered, English-style straight stock. It is available in either a boxlock or a full sidelock action. The sidelock is worth approximately 20 percent more than the boxlock version.

| Exc. | V.G. | Good | Fair | Poor |
|------|------|------|------|------|
| 600 | 500 | 450 | 350 | 300 |

The following model designations are available as either boxlocks or sidelocks, and the sidelock versions are worth approximately 25 percent more than the boxlock. The difference between these grades, as was stated earlier, is the degree of ornamentation and the quality of materials and workmanship.

## Model 4
| Exc. | V.G. | Good | Fair | Poor |
|------|------|------|------|------|
| 600 | 550 | 475 | 400 | 300 |

## Model 4E (Auto-ejectors)
| Exc. | V.G. | Good | Fair | Poor |
|------|------|------|------|------|
| 675 | 625 | 550 | 450 | 350 |

## Model 203
| Exc. | V.G. | Good | Fair | Poor |
|------|------|------|------|------|
| 650 | 600 | 525 | 425 | 325 |

## Model 203E
| Exc. | V.G. | Good | Fair | Poor |
|------|------|------|------|------|
| 700 | 650 | 575 | 475 | 375 |

## Model 6E
| Exc. | V.G. | Good | Fair | Poor |
|------|------|------|------|------|
| 800 | 750 | 625 | 525 | 425 |

## Model 7E
| Exc. | V.G. | Good | Fair | Poor |
|------|------|------|------|------|
| 850 | 800 | 675 | 575 | 475 |

## Model 10E
| Exc. | V.G. | Good | Fair | Poor |
|------|------|------|------|------|
| 1750 | 1500 | 1250 | 950 | 750 |

## Model 11E
| Exc. | V.G. | Good | Fair | Poor |
|------|------|------|------|------|
| 1850 | 1600 | 1350 | 1150 | 850 |

## Model 12E
| Exc. | V.G. | Good | Fair | Poor |
|------|------|------|------|------|
| 2200 | 1850 | 1500 | 1300 | 1000 |

# SARDIUS
**Israel**
**Importer--Armscorp of America, Inc.**

### SD-9
This is a double-action semi-automatic pistol chambered for the 9mm Parabellum cartridge. It has a 3" barrel and a 6-shot detachable magazine. This is a compact pistol with a matte black finish and composition grips. It features a 3-dot sight system and has been imported since 1988.

| NIB | Exc. | V.G. | Good | Fair | Poor |
|-----|------|------|------|------|------|
| 350 | 300  | 250  | 200  | 150  | 100  |

# SAUER, J. P. & SON
**Suhl, Germany**
**Importer--Sigarms, Inc.**
**Tysons Corner, Virginia**

### Bolt Action Rifle
This is a Mauser-actioned rifle chambered for .30-06 and most popular European cartridges. It has either a 22" or 24" barrel, with a raised solid rib. It has a three-leaf folding express sight as well as double-set triggers. It is constructed of Krupp steel. The finish is blued, with a classic-style checkered walnut stock. This model was manufactured prior to WWII.

| Ex. | V.G. | Good | Fair | Poor |
|-----|------|------|------|------|
| 700 | 600  | 500  | 400  | 300  |

### Model 200
This is a bolt-action rifle chambered for various popular calibers from .243 Winchester up to 9.3x62. It was made with short- and medium-length actions and has a 24" interchangeable barrel. It features a set trigger and a 4-round detachable magazine. The finish is blued, and the stock is checkered walnut. This model was discontinued in 1987.
Extra barrels--Add $235.

| Exc. | V.G. | Good | Fair | Poor |
|------|------|------|------|------|
| 650  | 550  | 500  | 425  | 350  |

### Model 200 Lightweight
This is similar to the Model 200, with a lightweight, alloy receiver. It was discontinued in 1987.

| Exc. | V.G. | Good | Fair | Poor |
|------|------|------|------|------|
| 600  | 500  | 400  | 325  | 250  |

### Model 200 Lux
This is similar to the Model 200, with a high-grade walnut stock, rosewood forend tip, and pistolgrip cap. It features a jeweled bolt and gold-plated trigger. It was not imported after 1987.

| Exc. | V.G. | Good | Fair | Poor |
|------|------|------|------|------|
| 700  | 600  | 550  | 475  | 400  |

### Model 200 Carbon Fiber
This is similar to the Model 200, with a synthetic carbon fiber stock. It was imported in 1987 and 1988.

| Exc. | V.G. | Good | Fair | Poor |
|------|------|------|------|------|
| 800  | 750  | 650  | 500  | 400  |

### Model 90
This is a bolt-action rifle chambered for many various calibers between .222 Remington and .458 Winchester Magnum. It is available with either a short, medium, or long action and features either a 23" or 26" barrel. The detachable magazine holds either 3 or 4 shots, depending on the caliber. The finish is blued, and the stock is checkered select walnut. This Model was discontinued in 1989.

| Exc. | V.G. | Good | Fair | Poor |
|------|------|------|------|------|
| 800  | 700  | 600  | 450  | 400  |

### Model 90 Stutzen
This is similar to the Model 90, with a full-length Mannlicher-style stock. It was not imported after 1989.

| Exc. | V.G. | Good | Fair | Poor |
|------|------|------|------|------|
| 825  | 725  | 625  | 475  | 425  |

### Model 90 Safari
This version is chambered for the .458 Winchester Magnum cartridge and has a 24" barrel. It was imported between 1986 and 1988.

| Exc. | V.G. | Good | Fair | Poor |
|------|------|------|------|------|
| 1250 | 1100 | 950  | 750  | 600  |

The Model 90 series of bolt-action rifles was available in a deluxe version that differed with the grade of workmanship and materials utilized. This deluxe series would be worth approximately 60 percent additional. There were optional engraved models; these should be individually appraised.

### Model 90 Supreme
This is similar to the Model 90 Deluxe, with a jeweled bolt, gold-plated trigger, and a high gloss, deluxe walnut stock. It was introduced in 1987.

| NIB  | Exc. | V.G. | Good | Fair | Poor |
|------|------|------|------|------|------|
| 1500 | 1250 | 1100 | 950  | 750  | 650  |

### Luftwaffe Survival Drilling
This 3-barrelled gun consists of a side-by-side 12 gauge over a 9.3x74R barrel. The barrels are 28" in length. This model was manufactured as a survival weapon for Luftwaffe pilots to utilize during WWII. The finish is blued, with a walnut stock. There is an eagle over swastika marked on the stock and the breech end of the right barrel. This drilling was furnished with an aluminum case and accessories.

| Exc. | V.G. | Good | Fair | Poor |
|------|------|------|------|------|
| 5000 | 4000 | 3500 | 2500 | 2000 |

### Model 3000 Drilling
The side-by-side shotgun barrels of this model are chambered for either 12 or 16 gauge. The rifle barrel is chambered in various metric and American calibers. It has a boxlock action with a Greener crossbolt and a double-barrel locking lug. It features cocking indicators and an automatic sight. There are double triggers, and the receiver is lightly scroll-engraved. The finish is blued, with a select checkered walnut stock.

| NIB  | Exc. | V.G. | Good | Fair | Poor |
|------|------|------|------|------|------|
| 3400 | 2900 | 2500 | 2000 | 1500 | 1250 |

### Model 54 Combo
This is an Over/Under combination gun chambered for 16 gauge over various metric and American calibers. The barrels are 24" in length with double triggers, automatic ejector, and a Greener crossbolt boxlock action. The coin finished receiver is lightly engraved, and the stock is checkered select walnut. It was discontinued in 1986.

| Exc. | V.G. | Good | Fair | Poor |
|------|------|------|------|------|
| 2200 | 2000 | 1750 | 1400 | 1200 |

### Model 60
This is a side-by-side double-barrel shotgun chambered for 12, 16, or 20 gauge. It has various length barrels and choke combinations and features a boxlock action with manual extractors and double triggers. The finish is blued, with a checkered walnut stock. This Model was manufactured prior to WWII.

| Exc. | V.G. | Good | Fair | Poor |
|------|------|------|------|------|
| 700  | 625  | 550  | 400  | 300  |

### Royal Model
This is a side-by-side double-barrel shotgun chambered for 12 or 20 gauge. It features 26", 28", or 30" barrels with various choke combinations. It features a boxlock action with an engraved, scalloped frame. There are cocking indicators, a single selective trigger, and automatic ejectors. The finish is blued, with a checkered walnut stock. It was manufactured between 1955 and 1977.

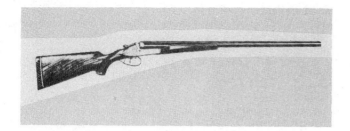

| Exc. | V.G. | Good | Fair | Poor |
|------|------|------|------|------|
| 1500 | 1250 | 1000 | 750 | 500 |

### Grade I Artemis

This side-by-side double-barrel shotgun is chambered for 12 gauge only. It features 28" modified-and-full choke barrels. It has a full Holland & Holland-type detachable sidelock, single-selective trigger, automatic ejector, and fine scroll engraving. The finish is blued, with a deluxe checkered walnut stock. It was manufactured between 1966 and 1977.

| Exc. | V.G. | Good | Fair | Poor |
|------|------|------|------|------|
| 5000 | 4250 | 3500 | 2500 | 2000 |

### Grade II Artemis

This is similar to the Grade I except that it is profusely engraved.

| Exc. | V.G. | Good | Fair | Poor |
|------|------|------|------|------|
| 6500 | 5750 | 4750 | 3500 | 3000 |

### Model 66

The Model 66 is available in three different grades that vary only in the quality of materials and workmanship and the degree and grade of engraving. There is a field-grade gun, as well as a skeet and trap model. All are available in the three grades. They are chambered for 12 gauge only and have either a 28", 26", or 30" barrel, depending on their configuration. They have Krupp steel barrels, Holland & Holland-type sidelocks, a single-selective trigger, and automatic ejectors. The finish is blued, with a checkered walnut stock. They were manufactured between 1966 and 1975.

### Grade I

| Exc. | V.G. | Good | Fair | Poor |
|------|------|------|------|------|
| 2000 | 1800 | 1500 | 1150 | 800 |

### Grade II

| Exc. | V.G. | Good | Fair | Poor |
|------|------|------|------|------|
| 3000 | 2800 | 2500 | 2150 | 1800 |

### Grade III

| Exc. | V.G. | Good | Fair | Poor |
|------|------|------|------|------|
| 3750 | 3500 | 2850 | 2500 | 2000 |

### Roth-Sauer

This model was built on a patent held by Georg Roth but actually designed by Krnka, a fine Czechoslovakian gun designer of the time. It is an unnecessarily complicated pistol that utilizes the long recoil system. The barrel and breechblock recoil together while the bolt is rotated 20 degrees to unlock it. As the barrel returns, the bolt comes into battery. During this procedure, the spent case is ejected, a fresh cartridge is chambered, and the striker is cocked. It is chambered for a 7.65mm cartridge that is smaller and less powerful than the standard 7.65mm cartridge. It has a 4.5" barrel. The finish is blued, with "Patent Roth" marked on top of the frame. The serial num-

ber is found on the bottom of the butt, and the black plastic grips have an ornate oval that frames a bearded human figure. This was Sauer's trademark of the time.

| Exc. | V.G. | Good | Fair | Poor |
|------|------|------|------|------|
| 950 | 800 | 650 | 450 | 300 |

### Model 1913

This is a blowback-operated, semi-automatic pocket pistol that was chambered originally in 7.65mm. After WWI a 6.35mm version was introduced. The barrel length is either 2.5" or 3", with fixed sights. It has a fixed barrel with a light tubular slide that retains a separate breech block by the use of a knurled screwcap at its rear. A spring catch that is part of the rear sight locks this cap into position. It features a 7-shot detachable box magazine and is striker-fired. There is a safety catch on the left that disengages the trigger and locks the sear. The company name is marked on the top of the slide. The finish is blued, with black plastic grips that carry the word "Sauer" across the top and the caliber across the bottom. This model was manufactured between 1913 and 1930.

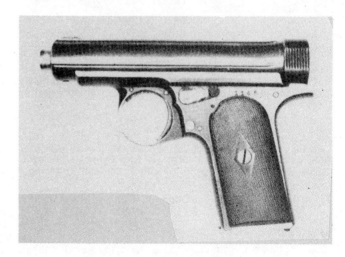

| Exc. | V.G. | Good | Fair | Poor |
|------|------|------|------|------|
| 300 | 250 | 200 | 150 | 100 |

### .25 WTM

This is a simplified, blowback-operated, semi-automatic pocket pistol. It is chambered for 6.35mm and has a 2.5" barrel. It has a fixed barrel with a large ejection port on the slide. It features a separate breechblock that is held in place by a spring catch that protrudes from the rear of the slide. It is striker-fired with a cocking indicator. "WTM" is marked on the left of the slide. "JP Sauer & Sohn Suhl" is marked on the right of the slide along with the caliber designation. The finish is blued, with black plastic grips bearing the company name and the caliber designation. This model was introduced in 1924.

| Exc. | V.G. | Good | Fair | Poor |
|------|------|------|------|------|
| 300 | 250 | 200 | 150 | 100 |

### Model 28
This is a modified version of the Model WTM that has an altered slide contour with an integral breechblock. The lower edge of the grip is marked "Cal.6.35 28." This version was manufactured from 1928 until 1939.

| Exc. | V.G. | Good | Fair | Poor |
|------|------|------|------|------|
| 275 | 225 | 175 | 125 | 90 |

### Behorden Model
This is a blowback-operated, semi-automatic pocket piston chambered for 7.65mm. It is basically an improved Model 1913 and follows the same general design. It has a 3" barrel and a tubular slide and breechblock that is removed much like the Model 1913. This model features a loaded chamber indicator, and the trigger has a security lock that has to be depressed as the trigger is squeezed. It was called the Behorden Model, which means authority's or official model, in order to make it more desirable for police and military use inside Germany. It was used by several police forces and as a secondary staff officers' pistol by the army. It was manufactured between 1930 and 1937.

| Exc. | V.G. | Good | Fair | Poor |
|------|------|------|------|------|
| 300 | 250 | 200 | 150 | 100 |

### Model 38H
This is a blowback-operated, double-action, semi-automatic pistol that was a completely new and unique design for its time. It was rated as one of the best pocket pistols ever produced and, if it wasn't for WWII, undoubtedly would have been a commercial success. The Model 38H is chambered for 7.65mm. It has a fixed 3.25" barrel. The slide has a separate breechblock pinned into it. It is fired by an internal hammer and features a de-cocking lever on the left side of the frame. The lockwork is double-action, making this a very versatile pistol. There is a

safety catch at the rear of the slide that locks the hammer and a loaded chamber indicator. On later-production guns (1944-45), the safety catch was omitted. The slide is marked, "JP Sauer & Sohn Cal.7.65." The finish is blued, with black plastic grips carrying the monogram "SuS." This was an extremely well-made firearm, and nearly 100 percent of its production was taken by the Nazis and used in WWII. It is a mystery as to why the company did not revive this fine pistol after the war was over. It was manufactured from 1939 to 1945.

| Exc. | V.G. | Good | Fair | Poor |
|------|------|------|------|------|
| 350 | 300 | 275 | 200 | 150 |

## SAVAGE INDUSTRIES
### Utica, New York

This company was founded by Arthur W. Savage in 1894. He was an interesting man, to say the least. He was born in Jamaica, where he managed a coffee plantation. He worked in Australia for a time and designed a torpedo that was used by the Brazilian navy. He worked as a superintendent on a railroad before he began designing firearms. After a stint with the Savage Arms Corporation, he sold out in 1904, began a tire company, grew citrus fruit, drilled for oil, and prospected for gold. He died at the age of 84 in 1941. The company eventually moved to Chicopee Falls, Massachusetts, and since 1959 is located in Westfield, Massachusetts.

### Model 1895
This is a lever-action sporting rifle chambered for the .303 Savage cartridge. It is offered with either a 22", 26", or 30" barrel. It features a solid, closed-top receiver that ejects from the side. It utilizes a 5-shot rotating magazine that indicates how many rounds remain. The finish is blued, with a walnut stock. It is marked "Savage Repeating Arms Co. Utica, N.Y. U.S.A. Pat. Feb. 7, 1893." There were approximately 6,000 manufactured between 1895 and 1899.
22" or 30" Barrel--Add 10 Percent.

| Exc. | V.G. | Good | Fair | Poor |
|------|------|------|------|------|
| 1500 | 1250 | 1000 | 750 | 500 |

## Model 1899

This is an improved version of the Model 1895 chambered for .25-35, .30-30, .303 Savage, .32-40, and the .38-55 cartridges. It is offered with a 20" round barrel and 22" round barrel, as well as a 26" round or octagonal barrel. It is marked "Savage Arms Company, Utica, N.Y. Pat. Feb. 7, 1893." There were approximately 75,000 manufactured between 1899 and 1917. A take-down model is available and would be worth approximately 25 percent additional. There are a number of minor variations available within this model that have become quite collectible. We recommend seeking a qualified appraisal if in doubt.

| Exc. | V.G. | Good | Fair | Poor |
|------|------|------|------|------|
| 650 | 600 | 500 | 400 | 275 |

## Model 99A

This was an improvement on the Model 1899, that is chambered for the .30-30, .250-3000, .300 Savage, and the .303 Savage cartridges. It has a 24" round barrel. The finish is blued, with a straight-grip stock and crescent buttplate. It was manufactured between 1920 and 1936.

| Exc. | V.G. | Good | Fair | Poor |
|------|------|------|------|------|
| 550 | 500 | 400 | 300 | 200 |

## Model 99B

This is a take-down version of the Model 99A. It was manufactured between 1920 and 1936.

| Exc. | V.G. | Good | Fair | Poor |
|------|------|------|------|------|
| 900 | 750 | 500 | 400 | 250 |

## Model 99E

This version is chambered for the .22 Hi Power cartridge in addition to the other chamberings offered in the Model 99A. It has a 22" barrel and was manufactured between 1920 and 1936.

| Exc. | V.G. | Good | Fair | Poor |
|------|------|------|------|------|
| 900 | 750 | 500 | 400 | 250 |

## Model 99F

This is a lightweight take-down version of the Model 99E. It was manufactured between 1920 and 1942.

| Exc. | V.G. | Good | Fair | Poor |
|------|------|------|------|------|
| 500 | 400 | 300 | 200 | 150 |

## Model 99G

This is a take-down version that features a checkered stock. It was manufactured between 1920 and 1942.

| Exc. | V.G. | Good | Fair | Poor |
|------|------|------|------|------|
| 650 | 500 | 400 | 300 | 250 |

## Model 99R

This version features a pistol-grip stock and semi-beavertail forearm. It was manufactured between 1936 and 1942.

| Exc. | V.G. | Good | Fair | Poor |
|------|------|------|------|------|
| 500 | 400 | 300 | 200 | 150 |

## Model 99RS

This version is similar to the Model 99R, with a Lyman aperture sight. It was manufactured between 1936 and 1942.

| Exc. | V.G. | Good | Fair | Poor |
|------|------|------|------|------|
| 600 | 500 | 400 | 300 | 200 |

## Model 99T

This is a lightweight version with a solid frame and checkered pistol-grip stock. It was manufactured between 1936 and 1942.

| Exc. | V.G. | Good | Fair | Poor |
|------|------|------|------|------|
| 450 | 350 | 300 | 200 | 150 |

## Model 99K

This version features an engraved receiver with a high-grade walnut stock. It has the Lyman aperture sight and was manufactured between 1931 and 1942.

| Exc. | V.G. | Good | Fair | Poor |
|------|------|------|------|------|
| 2000 | 1750 | 1500 | 1200 | 850 |

## Model 99EG

This was a post-war version that added the .243, .308, and the .358 cartridges. It was manufactured between 1946 and 1960.

| Exc. | V.G. | Good | Fair | Poor |
|------|------|------|------|------|
| 350 | 300 | 250 | 200 | 175 |

## Model 99R

This is another post-war model that added three additional calibers, has a 24" barrel, and is furnished with sling-swivel studs. It was manufactured between 1946 and 1960.

| Exc. | V.G. | Good | Fair | Poor |
|------|------|------|------|------|
| 350 | 300 | 250 | 200 | 175 |

## Model 99RS

This post-war model was offered with a Redfield receiver sight. It was manufactured between 1946 and 1958.

| Exc. | V.G. | Good | Fair | Poor |
|------|------|------|------|------|
| 350 | 300 | 250 | 200 | 175 |

## Model 99A

This is a post-war version of the original 99A with a 20" or 22" barrel and a standard rifle buttplate. It was manufactured between 1971 and 1981.

| Exc. | V.G. | Good | Fair | Poor |
|------|------|------|------|------|
| 350 | 300 | 250 | 200 | 175 |

## Model 99DL

This version is chambered for the .243 and the .308 cartridges. It features a Monte Carlo-type walnut stock. It was manufactured between 1960 and 1973.

| Exc. | V.G. | Good | Fair | Poor |
|------|------|------|------|------|
| 350 | 300 | 250 | 200 | 175 |

## Model 99DE Citation

This model features an engraved receiver and pressed checkering. It was manufactured between 1968 and 1970.

| Exc. | V.G. | Good | Fair | Poor |
|------|------|------|------|------|
| 850 | 750 | 500 | 400 | 300 |

## Model 99PE

This version is heavily engraved and has a gold-plated receiver and lever. It utilizes high-grade walnut with hand-cut checkering. It was manufactured between 1966 and 1970.

| Exc. | V.G. | Good | Fair | Poor |
|------|------|------|------|------|
| 1250 | 1000 | 750 | 500 | 300 |

## Model 99C

This is the current version of the lever-action Model 99 series. It is chambered for the .243, .284 Winchester, 7mm-08, or the .308 cartridges. It has a 22" barrel with open sights. The action features a cocking indicator and a sliding tang safety. It has a detachable 4-round magazine. The finish is blued, with a checkered walnut stock with recoil pad. It was introduced in 1965.

| NIB | Exc. | V.G. | Good | Fair | Poor |
|-----|------|------|------|------|------|
| 525 | 450 | 375 | 300 | 225 | 175 |

## Model 1895 Anniversary Edition

This is a replica of the original Model 1895, that commemorated Savage's 75th year in business. It is chambered for the .308 cartridge and has a 24" octagonal barrel. The receiver is engraved. It has a straight walnut stock with a Schnabel forend. There is a medallion inlaid in the stock and a brass crescent buttplate. There were 9,999 manufactured in 1970. As with all commemoratives, it must be NIB with all supplied materials to command collector interest.

| NIB | Exc. | V.G. | Good | Fair | Poor |
|-----|------|------|------|------|------|
| 400 | 350 | 300 | 250 | 200 | 150 |

## Model 1903

This is a slide-action rifle chambered for the .22 rimfire cartridge. It has a 24" barrel with open sights. The finish is blued, with a walnut pistolgrip stock. It was manufactured between 1903 and 1921.

| Exc. | V.G. | Good | Fair | Poor |
|------|------|------|------|------|
| 250 | 200 | 150 | 100 | 75 |

## Model 1909

This version has a 20" round barrel. It was manufactured between 1909 and 1915.

| Exc. | V.G. | Good | Fair | Poor |
|------|------|------|------|------|
| 250 | 200 | 150 | 100 | 75 |

## Model 1914

This version features a 24" octagonal barrel. It is blued, with a walnut stock. It was manufactured between 1914 and 1924.

| Exc. | V.G. | Good | Fair | Poor |
|------|------|------|------|------|
| 275 | 225 | 175 | 125 | 100 |

## Model 25

This is a slide-action, take-down rifle with a hammerless receiver and a tubular magazine. It is chambered for the .22 rimfire cartridges and has a 24" octagonal barrel with open sights. The finish is blued, with a plain walnut stock. It was manufactured between 1925 and 1929.

| Exc. | V.G. | Good | Fair | Poor |
|------|------|------|------|------|
| 350 | 300 | 250 | 200 | 150 |

## Model 29

This version had a 22" octagonal barrel, which was switched to a round barrel on models manufactured after WWII. It has open sights. The early models have a checkered walnut stock; later models are plain. It was manufactured between 1929 and 1967.

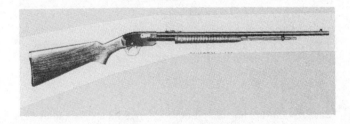

| Exc. | V.G. | Good | Fair | Poor |
|------|------|------|------|------|
| 275 | 225 | 175 | 125 | 100 |

## Model 170

This is a slide-action, centerfire rifle chambered for the .30-30 and the .35 Remington cartridges. It has a 22" barrel with folding sight and a 3-round tubular magazine. The finish is blued, with a checkered walnut stock. It was manufactured between 1970 and 1981.

| Exc. | V.G. | Good | Fair | Poor |
|------|------|------|------|------|
| 200 | 175 | 125 | 100 | 75 |

## Model 1904

This is a bolt-action, single-shot rifle chambered for the .22 rimfire cartridges. It has an 18" barrel and is blued, with a straight walnut stock. It was manufactured between 1904 and 1917.

| Exc. | V.G. | Good | Fair | Poor |
|------|------|------|------|------|
| 150 | 125 | 100 | 75 | 50 |

## Model 1905

This version is similar to the Model 1904 but has a 24" barrel and a take-down feature. It was manufactured between 1905 and 1919.

| Exc. | V.G. | Good | Fair | Poor |
|------|------|------|------|------|
| 150 | 125 | 100 | 75 | 50 |

## Model 19 NRA

This is a bolt-action repeating rifle chambered for the .22 l.r. cartridge. It has a 25" barrel with an adjustable aperture sight. The finish is blued, with a military-type stock. During WWII approximately 6,000 of these rifles were produced as military training models and are so marked. They would be worth an additional 15 percent. There were approximately 50,000 manufactured total between 1919 and 1937.

| Exc. | V.G. | Good | Fair | Poor |
|------|------|------|------|------|
| 225 | 175 | 150 | 100 | 75 |

## Model 19L

This version has a Lyman receiver sight. It was manufactured between 1933 and 1942.

| Exc. | V.G. | Good | Fair | Poor |
|------|------|------|------|------|
| 350 | 300 | 250 | 200 | 150 |

## Model 19M

This version features a 28" heavy target barrel with scope bases instead of sights. It was manufactured between 1933 and 1942.

| Exc. | V.G. | Good | Fair | Poor |
|------|------|------|------|------|
| 350 | 300 | 250 | 200 | 150 |

## Model 19H

This version is chambered for the .22 Hornet cartridge. It was manufactured between 1933 and 1942.

| Exc. | V.G. | Good | Fair | Poor |
|------|------|------|------|------|
| 500 | 450 | 350 | 300 | 200 |

## Model 10 Target

This is a bolt-action target rifle chambered for the .22 l.r. cartridge. It has a 25" barrel with an adjustable aperture sight. It features a speed-lock action. The finish is blued, with a walnut target-type stock. It was manufactured between 1933 and 1946.

| Exc. | V.G. | Good | Fair | Poor |
|------|------|------|------|------|
| 250 | 200 | 150 | 100 | 75 |

## Model 3

This is a single-shot, bolt-action rifle chambered for the .22 rimfire cartridges. It has a 24" barrel with open sights. The finish is blued, with a plain walnut stock. It was manufactured between 1933 and 1952.

| Exc. | V.G. | Good | Fair | Poor |
|------|------|------|------|------|
| 100 | 80 | 60 | 50 | 35 |

## Model 4

This is a bolt-action repeating rifle chambered for the .22 rimfire cartridges. It has a 24" take-down barrel with open sights. It features a 5-round magazine and is blued, with either a checkered or plain walnut stock.

| Exc. | V.G. | Good | Fair | Poor |
|------|------|------|------|------|
| 125 | 100 | 80 | 60 | 50 |

### Model 4M

This version is chambered for the .22 rimfire Magnum cartridge.

| Exc. | V.G. | Good | Fair | Poor |
|------|------|------|------|------|
| 125  | 100  | 80   | 60   | 50   |

### Model 5

This version is similar to the Model 4 except that it features a tubular magazine. It was manufactured between 1936 and 1961.

| Exc. | V.G. | Good | Fair | Poor |
|------|------|------|------|------|
| 125  | 100  | 80   | 60   | 50   |

### Model 1920

This is a bolt-action sporting rifle with a Mauser-type action. It is chambered for the .250-3000 and the .300 Savage cartridges. It features a 22" or 24" barrel with open sights and has a 5-shot magazine. The finish is blued, with a checkered walnut stock with a Schnabel forend. It was manufactured between 1920 and 1926.

| Exc. | V.G. | Good | Fair | Poor |
|------|------|------|------|------|
| 350  | 300  | 250  | 175  | 125  |

### Model 40

This is a bolt-action sporting rifle chambered for the .250-3000, .300 Savage, .30-30, and the .30-06 cartridges. It is offered with a 22" or 24" barrel with open sights. It has a 4-round magazine. The finish is blued, with a plain walnut stock. It was manufactured between 1928 and 1940.

| Exc. | V.G. | Good | Fair | Poor |
|------|------|------|------|------|
| 350  | 300  | 250  | 175  | 125  |

### Model 45 Super

This version of the Model 40 has a Lyman receiver sight and a checkered walnut stock. It was manufactured between 1928 and 1940.

| Exc. | V.G. | Good | Fair | Poor |
|------|------|------|------|------|
| 400  | 350  | 300  | 200  | 150  |

### Model 35

This is a bolt-action repeating rifle chambered for the .22 l.r. cartridge. It has a 22" barrel with open sights and a 5-round detachable magazine. The finish is blued, with a hardwood Monte Carlo stock.

| Exc. | V.G. | Good | Fair | Poor |
|------|------|------|------|------|
| 100  | 80   | 70   | 50   | 35   |

### Model 46

This version is similar to the Model 35, with a tubular magazine. It was manufactured between 1969 and 1973.

| Exc. | V.G. | Good | Fair | Poor |
|------|------|------|------|------|
| 100  | 80   | 70   | 50   | 35   |

### Model 340

This is a bolt-action sporting rifle chambered for the .22 Hornet, .222 Remington, .223, and the .30-30 cartridges. It is offered with a 22" or 24" barrel with open sights. It has a 4- or 5-round magazine, depending on the caliber. The finish is blued, with a plain walnut stock. It was manufactured between 1950 and 1985.

| Exc. | V.G. | Good | Fair | Poor |
|------|------|------|------|------|
| 250  | 200  | 175  | 125  | 90   |

### Model 342

This version is similar to the Model 340 except that it is chambered for the .22 Hornet cartridge. It was manufactured between 1950 and 1955.

| Exc. | V.G. | Good | Fair | Poor |
|------|------|------|------|------|
| 250  | 200  | 175  | 125  | 90   |

### Model 110 Sporter

This is a bolt-action sporting rifle chambered for various popular cartridges. It has a 22" barrel with open sights and a 4-round magazine. The finish is blued, with a checkered walnut stock. It was manufactured between 1958 and 1963.

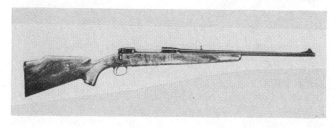

| Exc. | V.G. | Good | Fair | Poor |
|------|------|------|------|------|
| 200  | 150  | 125  | 100  | 75   |

### Model 110-M

This is a long-action version chambered for Magnum calibers between 7mm Magnum and the .338 Winchester Magnum cartridges. The stock features a recoil pad. It was manufactured between 1963 and 1969.

| Exc. | V.G. | Good | Fair | Poor |
|------|------|------|------|------|
| 275  | 225  | 200  | 150  | 100  |

### Model 110-D

This version is chambered for popular calibers between .22-250 and the .338 Winchester Magnum cartridges. It is similar to the Model 110 but features a detachable box magazine, an adjustable rear sight, and a checkered walnut stock. It was manufactured between 1966 and 1988.

| Exc. | V.G. | Good | Fair | Poor |
|------|------|------|------|------|
| 350  | 300  | 250  | 200  | 150  |

### Model 110-P Premier Grade

This version is similar to the Model 110 except that it has a high-grade, French walnut stock that is skipline checkered with a rosewood forend tip and pistolgrip cap. The Magnum model is furnished with a recoil pad and is worth approximately 5 percent additional. It was manufactured between 1964 and 1970.

| Exc. | V.G. | Good | Fair | Poor |
|------|------|------|------|------|
| 450  | 375  | 325  | 250  | 200  |

### Model 110-PE

This version is similar to the Model 110-P, with an engraved receiver, floorplate, and triggerguard. It was manufactured between 1968 and 1970.

| Exc. | V.G. | Good | Fair | Poor |
|------|------|------|------|------|
| 650  | 575  | 500  | 400  | 300  |

Savage's current line of bolt-action, centerfire sporting rifles begins with the Model 110-F and consists of a number of subvariations. They differ basically in the options offered and, in some cases, ornamentation, as well as quality of materials utilized in their construction. They are as follows:

### Model 110-F--DuPont Rynite Stock and Sights

| NIB | Exc. | V.G. | Good | Fair | Poor |
|-----|------|------|------|------|------|
| 450 | 400  | 350  | 300  | 250  | 200  |

### Model 110-FX--Without Sights

| NIB | Exc. | V.G. | Good | Fair | Poor |
|-----|------|------|------|------|------|
| 400 | 350  | 300  | 250  | 200  | 150  |

### Model 110-G--Checkered Hardwood Stock and Sights

| NIB | Exc. | V.G. | Good | Fair | Poor |
|-----|------|------|------|------|------|
| 375 | 325  | 275  | 225  | 175  | 125  |

### Model 110-GX--Without Sights

| NIB | Exc. | V.G. | Good | Fair | Poor |
|-----|------|------|------|------|------|
| 350 | 300  | 250  | 200  | 150  | 100  |

## Model 1912

This is a blowback-operated semi-automatic rifle chambered for the .22 l.r. cartridge. It features a 20" take-down barrel with open sights. The finish is blued, with a walnut stock. It was manufactured between 1912 and 1916.

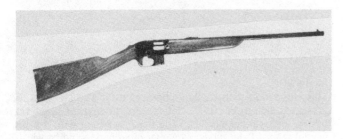

| Exc. | V.G. | Good | Fair | Poor |
|------|------|------|------|------|
| 350 | 300 | 200 | 125 | 90 |

## Model 6

This is a blowback-operated semi-automatic rifle chambered for the .22 rimfire cartridges. It has a 24" take-down barrel with a tubular magazine. The pre-WWII version has a checkered stock; the post-war version is plain. It was manufactured between 1938 and 1968. The pre-war version would be worth approximately 10 percent additional.

| Exc. | V.G. | Good | Fair | Poor |
|------|------|------|------|------|
| 150 | 125 | 100 | 75 | 50 |

## Model 7

This version is similar to the Model 6 but utilizes a detachable box magazine. The pre-WWII version is worth approximately 10 percent additional. It was manufactured between 1939 and 1951.

| Exc. | V.G. | Good | Fair | Poor |
|------|------|------|------|------|
| 150 | 125 | 100 | 75 | 50 |

## Model 60

This is a semi-automatic rifle chambered for the .22 l.r. cartridge. It has a 20" barrel with an open sight and a tubular magazine. The finish is blued, with a checkered walnut Monte Carlo-type stock. It was manufactured between 1969 and 1972.

| Exc. | V.G. | Good | Fair | Poor |
|------|------|------|------|------|
| 100 | 80 | 70 | 50 | 35 |

## Model 88

This is an economy version of the Model 60, that features a hardwood stock. It was manufactured between 1969 and 1972.

| Exc. | V.G. | Good | Fair | Poor |
|------|------|------|------|------|
| 100 | 80 | 70 | 50 | 35 |

## Model 90 Carbine

This version of the Model 60 has a 16.5" barrel and a carbine-type stock and forearm held on by a barrel band.

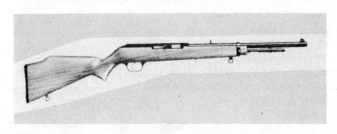

| Exc. | V.G. | Good | Fair | Poor |
|------|------|------|------|------|
| 100 | 80 | 70 | 50 | 35 |

## Model 24

This is an Over/Under combination gun chambered for .22 over .410. It has 24" separated barrels with an open sight. It is a break-open action with an external hammer. The finish is blued, with a plain walnut stock. It was manufactured between 1950 and 1965. There is an entire series of subvariations of the Model 24. They differ basically in the calibers chambered, materials used in construction, and general configuration.

| Exc. | V.G. | Good | Fair | Poor |
|------|------|------|------|------|
| 150 | 125 | 100 | 75 | 50 |

### Model 24S--20 Gauge

| Exc. | V.G. | Good | Fair | Poor |
|------|------|------|------|------|
| 160 | 140 | 125 | 100 | 75 |

### Model 24MS--22 Rimfire Magnum

| Exc. | V.G. | Good | Fair | Poor |
|------|------|------|------|------|
| 150 | 125 | 100 | 75 | 50 |

### Model 24DL--Satin Chrome With Checkered Stock

| Exc. | V.G. | Good | Fair | Poor |
|------|------|------|------|------|
| 150 | 125 | 100 | 75 | 50 |

### Model 24 Field--Lightweight Version

| Exc. | V.G. | Good | Fair | Poor |
|------|------|------|------|------|
| 175 | 150 | 125 | 100 | 75 |

### Model 24C--Nickel Finish

| Exc. | V.G. | Good | Fair | Poor |
|------|------|------|------|------|
| 200 | 175 | 150 | 125 | 100 |

### Model 24VS--.357 Magnum/20 Gauge, Nickel Finish

| Exc. | V.G. | Good | Fair | Poor |
|------|------|------|------|------|
| 250 | 200 | 175 | 150 | 125 |

### Model 24F--DuPont Rynite Stock

| NIB | Exc. | V.G. | Good | Fair | Poor |
|-----|------|------|------|------|------|
| 350 | 300 | 250 | 200 | 150 | 100 |

## Model 420

This is a field-grade Over/Under shotgun chambered for 12, 16, or 20 gauge. It has a 26", 28", or 30" barrel with various chokes. It features a boxlock action with double triggers and extractors. A single-trigger version is available and would be worth approximately 15 percent additional. The finish is blued, with a walnut stock. It was manufactured between 1938 and 1942.

| Exc. | V.G. | Good | Fair | Poor |
|------|------|------|------|------|
| 400 | 325 | 275 | 200 | 150 |

## Model 430

This version is similar to the Model 420 but features a solid rib and a checkered walnut stock with recoil pad. The single-trigger version would be worth approximately 15 percent additional.

| Exc. | V.G. | Good | Fair | Poor |
|------|------|------|------|------|
| 450  | 375  | 325  | 225  | 175  |

## Model 220

This is a single-barrel, break-open, hammerless shotgun chambered for 12, 26, and 20 gauge, as well as .410. It is offered with a 26" through 32" barrel with various chokes. The finish is blued, with a plain walnut stock. It was manufactured between 1938 and 1965.

| Exc. | V.G. | Good | Fair | Poor |
|------|------|------|------|------|
| 100  | 80   | 70   | 50   | 35   |

## Model 720

This is a recoil-operated semi-automatic shotgun based on the Browning A-5 action. It is chambered for 12 or 16 gauge and is offered with 26" through 32" barrels with various chokes. The finish is blued, with a checkered walnut stock. It was manufactured between 1930 and 1949.

| Exc. | V.G. | Good | Fair | Poor |
|------|------|------|------|------|
| 300  | 250  | 200  | 150  | 100  |

## Model 726 Upland Sporter

This version features a 2-round magazine and was manufactured between 1931 and 1949.

| Exc. | V.G. | Good | Fair | Poor |
|------|------|------|------|------|
| 300  | 250  | 200  | 150  | 100  |

## Model 740C Skeet

This is similar to the Model 726 but features a 24.5" barrel with a Cutts Compensator and a skeet-type stock. It was manufactured between 1936 and 1949.

| Exc. | V.G. | Good | Fair | Poor |
|------|------|------|------|------|
| 300  | 250  | 200  | 150  | 100  |

## Model 745

This version of the Model 720 is chambered for 12 gauge only, with a 28" barrel and a lightweight alloy receiver. It was manufactured between 1940 and 1949.

| Exc. | V.G. | Good | Fair | Poor |
|------|------|------|------|------|
| 275  | 225  | 175  | 125  | 75   |

## Model 755

This is a semi-automatic shotgun chambered for 12 and 16 gauge. It has 26" through 30" barrels with various chokes. The finish is blued, with a checkered walnut stock. The SC designation is equipped with a Savage Super Choke and would be worth approximately $10 additional. It was manufactured between 1949 and 1958.

| Exc. | V.G. | Good | Fair | Poor |
|------|------|------|------|------|
| 275  | 225  | 175  | 125  | 75   |

## Model 775

This version of the Model 755 features a lightweight alloy receiver. The 775SC has the Savage Super Choke and would be worth approximately $10 additional. It was manufactured between 1950 and 1966.

| Exc. | V.G. | Good | Fair | Poor |
|------|------|------|------|------|
| 275  | 225  | 175  | 125  | 75   |

## Model 750

This is a recoil-operated semi-automatic shotgun patterned after the Browning A-5. It is chambered for 12 gauge and has a 26" or 28" barrel with various chokes. The finish is blued, with a checkered walnut stock. The Model 750SC has the Savage Super Choke. The Model 750AC has a poly choke. Either would be worth approximately $10 additional. It was manufactured between 1960 and 1967.

| Exc. | V.G. | Good | Fair | Poor |
|------|------|------|------|------|
| 275  | 225  | 175  | 125  | 75   |

## Model 30

This is a slide-action shotgun chambered for 12, 16, and 20 gauge, as well as .410. It features 26" through 30" vent-rib barrels with various chokes. The finish is blued, with a plain walnut stock. Later models are checkered and would be worth approximately $10 additional. It was manufactured between 1958 and 1970.

| Exc. | V.G. | Good | Fair | Poor |
|------|------|------|------|------|
| 225  | 175  | 150  | 100  | 75   |

## Model 242

This is a side-by-side double-barrel shotgun chambered for .410. It has 26" full-choke barrels and exposed hammers. It features a single trigger and extractors. The finish is blued, with a hardwood stock. It was manufactured between 1977 and 1981.

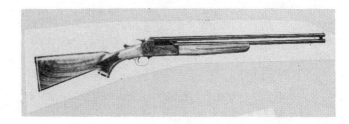

| Exc. | V.G. | Good | Fair | Poor |
|------|------|------|------|------|
| 150  | 125  | 100  | 75   | 50   |

## Model 550

This is a side-by-side double-barrel shotgun chambered for 12 or 20 gauge. It features 26", 28", or 30" barrels with various choke combinations. It has a boxlock action with a single trigger and automatic ejectors. The finish is blued, with a checkered hardwood stock. It was manufactured between 1971 and 1973.

| Exc. | V.G. | Good | Fair | Poor |
|------|------|------|------|------|
| 275  | 225  | 175  | 125  | 75   |

## Model 440

This is an Over/Under shotgun chambered for 12 or 20 gauge with 26", 28", or 30" vent-rib barrels with various choke combinations. It features a boxlock action with a single-selective trigger and extractors. The finish is blued, with a checkered walnut stock. This model was imported from Italy by Savage between 1968 and 1972.

| Exc. | V.G. | Good | Fair | Poor |
|------|------|------|------|------|
| 500  | 425  | 350  | 250  | 175  |

## Model 444 Deluxe

This version features automatic ejectors and a higher-grade walnut stock. It was imported between 1969 and 1972.

| Exc. | V.G. | Good | Fair | Poor |
|------|------|------|------|------|
| 550 | 475 | 400 | 300 | 225 |

## Model 440T

This is the competition trap version of the Model 440 chambered for 12 gauge only with 30" full-and-improved-modified chokes. It features a wide, competition-style rib and a trap-type stock with recoil pad. It was imported between 1969 and 1972.

| Exc. | V.G. | Good | Fair | Poor |
|------|------|------|------|------|
| 550 | 475 | 400 | 300 | 225 |

## Model 330

This is an Over/Under shotgun chambered for 12 or 20 gauge with 26", 28", or 30" barrels with various choke combinations. It features a boxlock action with single-selective triggers and extractors. The finish is blued, with a checkered walnut stock. It was manufactured in Finland by Valmet and was imported between 1969 and 1980.

| Exc. | V.G. | Good | Fair | Poor |
|------|------|------|------|------|
| 500 | 425 | 350 | 250 | 175 |

## Model 333

This version features a ventilated rib and automatic ejectors. It was imported between 1973 and 1980.

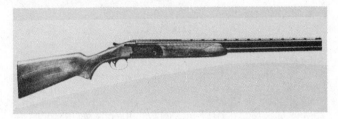

| Exc. | V.G. | Good | Fair | Poor |
|------|------|------|------|------|
| 550 | 475 | 400 | 300 | 225 |

## Model 333T

This is the trap version with a 30" vent-rib barrel and a trap-type stock with recoil pad. It was imported between 1972 and 1980.

| Exc. | V.G. | Good | Fair | Poor |
|------|------|------|------|------|
| 550 | 475 | 400 | 300 | 225 |

## Model 2400

This was an Over/Under combination gun chambered for 12 gauge over a .222 or .308 rifle barrel. It has 23.5" barrels with a solid rib and folding sight. It is blued, with a checkered Monte Carlo stock. This gun was made in Finland by Valmet and was imported between 1975 and 1980.

| Exc. | V.G. | Good | Fair | Poor |
|------|------|------|------|------|
| 600 | 525 | 450 | 350 | 275 |

Although it is plain to see that the Savage company was known primarily for rifles and shotguns, in the early part of this century they produced a very collectible semi-automatic pistol that was produced between 1907 and 1928. It is not entirely certain who invented the Savage pistol, and there are a number of theories on the matter. The company also produced a large .45-caliber version that was entered in the U.S. Army test trials. The Savage pistol survived the rigorous test, and there were approximately 300 manufactured. Eventually, this pistol was withdrawn; and the Colt 1911 became our standard service pistol. The Savage pistols were somewhat commercially successful and were of the highest quality in materials and fit-and-finish. Subsequently, they were expensive to produce and eventually were withdrawn because they could not compete against other pistols that were less expensive to produce. By 1928 semi-automatic pistol production was, for the most part, over.

## Model 1907

This is a single-action semi-automatic pistol chambered for the .32 ACP or the .380 ACP cartridges. It has a 4.25" barrel in .380 and a 3.75" barrel in .32. It features either a 9-round or 10-round detachable magazine, depending on the caliber. It features fixed sights and an external hammer. It is blued with checkered, hard rubber grips. The .380 version is worth approximately 10 percent additional. The Model 1907 is easily distinguished from the later models as it has 28 narrow cocking grooves on the slide. This model was manufactured between 1907 and 1916. A factory nickel version was produced but is extremely rare and would be worth approximately 75 percent additional. Be extremely cautious of re-nickeled guns; there are talented refinishers out there.

| Exc. | V.G. | Good | Fair | Poor |
|------|------|------|------|------|
| 300 | 250 | 200 | 125 | 75 |

## Model 1915

This version is similar in appearance to the Model 1907 except that it features a grip safety and an internal hammer. It has nine wide cocking grooves on the slide and was not particularly well-received. It was offered in the same chamberings as the Model 1907, and the .380 ACP version would be worth approximately 10 percent additional. This model was manufactured between 1915 and 1917.

| Exc. | V.G. | Good | Fair | Poor |
|------|------|------|------|------|
| 350 | 300 | 250 | 150 | 100 |

## Model 1917

The model 1917 features a spurred external hammer, and the grip safety was removed. The cocking grooves are similar to the Model 1907. The butt is flared and larger, and it features wedge-shaped grips. It filled the hand better than previous models. It was chambered the same as its predecessors, and the .380 ACP version would be worth approximately 10 percent additional. It was manufactured between 1917 and 1928.

| Exc. | V.G. | Good | Fair | Poor |
|------|------|------|------|------|
| 275 | 225 | 175 | 100 | 75 |

## U.S. Army Test Trial

This is a large single-action semi-automatic pistol chambered for the .45 ACP cartridge. It was submitted for the Army test trials and survived. It was chosen along with the Colt for further testing. After two years they were withdrawn from contention, and the remaining pistols were sold in 1912 at auction. There were approximately 300 manufactured that eventually wound up in the commercial marketplace. After the Army lost interest, the Savage company ceased production of this pistol.

| Exc. | V.G. | Good | Fair | Poor |
|------|------|------|------|------|
| 5000 | 4000 | 3000 | 2250 | 1750 |

## Model 101

This is a single-shot pistol that appears to be a single-action, frontier-type revolver. It is chambered for the .22 l.r. cartridge and has a 5.5" barrel with adjustable sights. The barrel and cylinder are one piece and swing out of the frame to the side to eject the spent cartridge and load. The finish is blued, with wood grips; and it was manufactured between 1960 and 1968. This represented the first pistol that Savage produced after nearly 40 years.

| Exc. | V.G. | Good | Fair | Poor |
|------|------|------|------|------|
| 175  | 150  | 125  | 90   | 75   |

# SAVAGE & NORTH
## Middletown, Connecticut

### Figure 8 Revolver

This somewhat unique revolver is chambered for .36-caliber percussion. It has a 7" octagonal barrel and a 6-shot unfluted cylinder. There is an integral loading lever mounted under the barrel. The barrel is marked "E. Savage, Middletown. CT./H.S. North. Patented June 17, 1856." There are four basic versions of this revolver. The first model has a rounded brass frame, and the mouths of the chamber fit into the end of the breech. There were only 10 of these manufactured. The second model has a rounded iron frame and a different-type loading lever that is marked "H.S. North, Patented April 6, 1858." There were approximately 100 manufactured. The third model has a flat-sided brass frame with round recoil shields. The pistol grip has been modified, and the loading lever is of the more modern type. There were approximately 400 manufactured. The fourth model is quite similar to the third model, with an iron frame. There were approximately 50 manufactured. All of the models are blued with two-piece, hump-backed walnut grips. They were manufactured between 1856 and 1859.

**First Model**

| Exc. | V.G. | Good | Fair | Poor |
|------|------|------|------|------|
| 5000 | 4000 | 3500 | 2500 | 2000 |

**Second Model**

| Exc. | V.G. | Good | Fair | Poor |
|------|------|------|------|------|
| 3500 | 3000 | 2500 | 1800 | 1500 |

**Third Model**

| Exc. | V.G. | Good | Fair | Poor |
|------|------|------|------|------|
| 3750 | 3250 | 2750 | 2000 | 1750 |

**Fourth Model**

| Exc. | V.G. | Good | Fair | Poor |
|------|------|------|------|------|
| 4000 | 3500 | 3000 | 2250 | 1800 |

# SAVAGE REVOLVING FIREARMS CO.
## Middletown, Connecticut

### Navy Revolver

This is a 36-caliber percussion revolver with a 7" octagonal barrel and a hinged integral loading-lever assembly. It has a 6-shot unfluted cylinder and an iron flatsided frame. The triggerguard is heart-shaped. The frame is marked "Savage R.F.A. Co./H.S. North Patented June 17, 1856/Jan. 18, 1859, May 15, 1860." This was a military revolver, and approximately 12,000 were purchased by the government and have military inspector's markings. There were approximately 20,000 manufactured between 1861 and 1865. This revolver was used by Union forces during the Civil War; and we recommend qualified, independent appraisals.

| Exc. | V.G. | Good | Fair | Poor |
|------|------|------|------|------|
| 1750 | 1500 | 1250 | 850  | 500  |

# SCHALK, G. S.
## Pottsville, Pennsylvania

### Rifle Musket

This is a single-shot muzzleloader chambered for .58-caliber percussion. It has a 40" round barrel and a full-length walnut stock held on by three barrel bands. The lock plate was from a surplus U.S. Model 1917 musket with the original markings removed. The barrel is marked "G. Schalk Pottsville 1861." It has iron mountings, and the metal parts are in the white. It has a steel ramrod mounted on the left of the barrel. There is a bayonet lug under the muzzle. There were approximately 100 manufactured and sold to the Pennsylvania Militia in 1861.

| Exc. | V.G. | Good | Fair | Poor |
|------|------|------|------|------|
| 2000 | 1750 | 1500 | 1200 | 750  |

# SCHALL
## Hartford, Connecticut

### Target Pistol

This is a unique and rare firearm chambered for .22 l.r. It has a 5" barrel and features a 10-round magazine which feeds a manual repeating action. The finish is blued, with walnut grips.

| Exc. | V.G. | Good | Fair | Poor |
|------|------|------|------|------|
| 450  | 400  | 350  | 250  | 175  |

# SCHMIDT, HERBERT
## Ostheim, West Germany

This company went into business in the early 1950's and marketed a number of inexpensive .22-caliber revolvers. They were sold under a number of different names, depending on the country to which they were being exported.

### Model 11, Liberty 11, and Eig Model E-8

The above names all applied to a double-action revolver chambered for .22 rimfire. It has a 2.5" barrel and a solid frame with a 6-shot cylinder that swings out for loading. The finish is blued, with plastic grips. The maker's name is not visible unless the grips are removed. This model was manufactured in the 1950's and 1960's.

| Exc. | V.G. | Good | Fair | Poor |
|---|---|---|---|---|
| 75 | 65 | 50 | 40 | 25 |

### Model 11 Target
This model has a 5.5" barrel and adjustable sights; otherwise, it is similar to the standard Model 11. It will be found under all the different trade names listed above. It also was manufactured in the 1950's and 1960's.

| Exc. | V.G. | Good | Fair | Poor |
|---|---|---|---|---|
| 80 | 70 | 55 | 45 | 30 |

### Frontier Model or Texas Scout
This model is a single-action revolver that is chambered for .22 l.r. It has a 5" barrel with an ejector rod housing underneath it. The sights are fixed; the finish, blued with plastic grips.

| Exc. | V.G. | Good | Fair | Poor |
|---|---|---|---|---|
| 75 | 65 | 50 | 40 | 25 |

## SCHMIDT, E. & COMPANY
### Houston, Texas

### Pocket Pistol
This pistol was patterned after the Henry Deringer Philadelphia-style pistol. It is chambered for .45-caliber percussion and has a 2.5" round barrel with a single gold band at the muzzle and double gold bands at the breech. It features German silver mountings, a blued finish, and a checkered walnut stock. The barrel is marked "E. Schmidt & Co. Houston." It is a fairly rare pistol and was manufactured in the 1850's.

| Exc. | V.G. | Good | Fair | Poor |
|---|---|---|---|---|
| 2500 | 2250 | 1750 | 1250 | 1000 |

## SCHMIDT-RUBIN
### Neuhausen, Switzerland

### Model 1889
This was one of the few successful straight-pull bolt-action rifles ever designed. It is chambered for 7.5mm Swiss and has a barrel length of 30.75". It has a 12-round, detachable box magazine. The finish is blued, with a full-length walnut stock held on by two barrel bands. The adjustable open sights are of military configuration, and there is a bayonet lug at the muzzle. Although this was considered to be a successful design, this point is arguable as the rifle was never tested under true service conditions. The Swiss are not known for fighting wars. There were approximately 212,000 rifles manufactured.

| Exc. | V.G. | Good | Fair | Poor |
|---|---|---|---|---|
| 250 | 200 | 175 | 125 | 90 |

### Model 1896
This is similar to the Model 1889, with a slightly shortened action to increase the weapon's efficiency. There were 137,000 Model 1896 rifles manufactured.

| Exc. | V.G. | Good | Fair | Poor |
|---|---|---|---|---|
| 275 | 225 | 200 | 150 | 125 |

### Model 1897 Cadet Rifle
This is a lightened version intended to be used by younger cadets of smaller stature. It was produced with a spiked bayonet. There were 7,000 manufactured.

| Exc. | V.G. | Good | Fair | Poor |
|---|---|---|---|---|
| 300 | 250 | 200 | 150 | 100 |

### Model 1900
This is a shortened version that was issued to bicyclists. It has a 6-round magazine. There were 18,750 manufactured between 1900 and 1904.

| Exc. | V.G. | Good | Fair | Poor |
|---|---|---|---|---|
| 400 | 350 | 300 | 200 | 150 |

### Model 1905 Carbine
This is a short-barrelled, full-stock carbine with a 6-round magazine. It used the same action as the Model 1900 and had no provision for attaching a bayonet. There were 7,900 manufactured.

| Exc. | V.G. | Good | Fair | Poor |
|---|---|---|---|---|
| 350 | 300 | 250 | 200 | 150 |

### Model 1911
This model was identical to its predecessors except that it was designed to utilize a longer, more powerful cartridge that fired a pointed bullet. The action was internally redesigned with stronger bolt lugs. The magazine capacity was reduced to six rounds, and a pistol grip was added to the stock. There were 133,000 manufactured.

| Exc. | V.G. | Good | Fair | Poor |
|---|---|---|---|---|
| 150 | 125 | 100 | 80 | 60 |

### Model 1911 Carbine
This version is similar to the 1911 rifle except that the barrel is 23.30" in length. There were 185,000 manufactured.

| Exc. | V.G. | Good | Fair | Poor |
|---|---|---|---|---|
| 175 | 150 | 125 | 100 | 75 |

### Model 1931
This was the first radical modification to the Schmidt-Rubin action. The 1931 Model required only half the length of operation as the former designs. It still functioned in the same manner. This model replaced all previous rifles and carbines and remained in service until 1957. It was undoubtedly the best of the Schmidt-Rubin designs. The barrel length is 25.7", and it has a 6-round, detachable box magazine. There were 528,180 manufactured.

| Exc. | V.G. | Good | Fair | Poor |
|---|---|---|---|---|
| 175 | 150 | 125 | 100 | 75 |

## SCHNEIDER & CO.
### Memphis, Tennessee

### Pocket Pistol
This pistol was manufactured by F. J. Bitterlich of Nashville, Tennessee, and marketed by Schneider. It is chambered for .41 caliber percussion and has a 3.5" octagonal barrel. The barrel is marked "Schneider & Co./Memphis, Tenn." The finish is blued with two types of walnut stock, either a square butt or birdshead design. This pistol was manufactured between 1850 and 1859.

| Exc. | V.G. | Good | Fair | Poor |
|---|---|---|---|---|
| 1500 | 1250 | 1000 | 800 | 650 |

## SCHNEIDER & GLASSICK
### Memphis, Tennessee

### Pocket Pistol
This is a .41-caliber percussion derringer with a 2.5" barrel, German silver mountings, and a walnut stock. The barrel is marked "Schneider & Glassick, Memphis, Tenn." This gun was made by F. J. Bitterlich of Nashville, Tennessee, between 1859 and 1862 to be sold by the firm of Schneider & Glassick.

| Exc. | V.G. | Good | Fair | Poor |
|---|---|---|---|---|
| 1750 | 1500 | 1250 | 1000 | 800 |

## SCHULER, AUGUST
### Suhl, Germany

**Reform**

This is an unusual repeating pistol chambered for 6.35mm. It has four barrels arranged vertically, that are 2.5" in length. Each barrel has a separate chamber; and when the trigger is pulled, a barrel is fired and the next barrel raised into position. Each pull on the trigger repeats the process, eventually firing all the barrels. The barrel block can then be removed, reloaded, and replaced. The finish is blued, with walnut grips. This is a very lightweight, thin weapon and is easily concealed. As the semi-automatic became more popular, production of this weapon ceased. It was manufactured between 1907 and 1914.

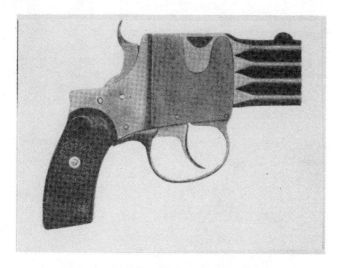

| Exc. | V.G. | Good | Fair | Poor |
|------|------|------|------|------|
| 850  | 750  | 650  | 450  | 300  |

## SCHULTZ & LARSEN
### Otterup, Denmark

**Model 47 Match Rifle**

This is a single-shot, bolt-action target rifle chambered for the .22 long rifle cartridge. It has a 28" heavy barrel with micrometer-adjustable target sights and a fully adjustable set trigger. The finish is blued, with a heavy walnut free-rifle-type stock.

| Exc. | V.G. | Good | Fair | Poor |
|------|------|------|------|------|
| 700  | 650  | 550  | 400  | 350  |

**Model 61 Match Rifle**

This is similar to the Model 47 except that the forearm has an adjustable palm rest and the overall quality is somewhat higher.

| Exc. | V.G. | Good | Fair | Poor |
|------|------|------|------|------|
| 900  | 850  | 750  | 600  | 500  |

**Model 62 Match Rifle**

This is a single-shot, center-fire, bolt-action rifle chambered for various popular calibers. It also features a 28" heavy barrel with adjustable target sights and a set trigger. It is blued, with a free rifle stock and palm rest.

| Exc. | V.G. | Good | Fair | Poor |
|------|------|------|------|------|
| 1000 | 900  | 750  | 650  | 550  |

**Model 54 Free Rifle**

This model is chambered for American centerfire cartridges only with the exception of the 6.5x55mm. It has a 27" heavy barrel with target sights and a free-rifle-type stock.

| Exc. | V.G. | Good | Fair | Poor |
|------|------|------|------|------|
| 850  | 800  | 700  | 550  | 450  |

**Model 68 DL**

This was a sporting-type bolt-action rifle chambered for various calibers from .22-250 through .458 Winchester Magnum. It has a 24" Bofors steel barrel and receiver. The finish is blued, with a select checkered French walnut stock. There is a fully adjustable trigger. Only the .458 model has open sights.

| Exc. | V.G. | Good | Fair | Poor |
|------|------|------|------|------|
| 750  | 700  | 600  | 450  | 400  |

## SCHWARZLOSE, ANDREAS
### W.Berlin, Germany

**Military Model 96**

This is a recoil-operated, locked-breach, semi-automatic pistol chambered for 7.63mm Mauser. It has a 6.5" barrel and is striker-fired with a locking rotary bolt. The detachable box magazine holds seven rounds. It features adjustable sights. The finish is blued, with checkered walnut grips. This was a well-designed pistol; but it was released just as the Mauser and Mannlicher pistols hit the market, and their designs were superior. Therefore, the Schwarzlose was not a commercial success.

| Exc. | V.G. | Good | Fair | Poor |
|------|------|------|------|------|
| 3000 | 2750 | 2250 | 1750 | 1000 |

**Model 08**

This is a blow-forward semi-automatic pistol chambered for the 7.65mm cartridge. It has a 4" barrel and a detachable 7-round box magazine. There is a grip safety located on the front edge of the grip strap underneath the triggerguard. The finish is blued, with checkered black plastic grips. The right rear of the frame is marked "Schwarzlose" over an engraving of a machine gun.

| Exc. | V.G. | Good | Fair | Poor |
|------|------|------|------|------|
| 475  | 400  | 350  | 300  | 200  |

## SCOTT, W. C., LTD.
### Birmingham, England

This is an old-line English gun company that produces very high quality firearms. Currently, their operations are being run through the firm of Holland & Holland of London, England. Those interested in their products should contact Holland & Holland. We strongly recommend that these guns be independently appraised if a transaction is contemplated.

**Kinmount**

This is a side-by-side double-barrel shotgun chambered for 12, 16, 20, and 28 gauge. It is offered with various length barrels and choke combinations. It features a boxlock action and automatic ejectors and is available with a single non-selective trigger. It is scroll-engraved and blued, with a deluxe, hand-checkered walnut stock.

| NIB | Exc. | V.G. | Good | Fair | Poor |
|-----|------|------|------|------|------|
| 5700 | 5000 | 4000 | 3000 | 2500 | 2000 |

### Bowood

This is similar to the Kinmount, with more extensive engraving and slightly higher quality materials.

| NIB | Exc. | V.G. | Good | Fair | Poor |
|-----|------|------|------|------|------|
| 6500 | 5750 | 4750 | 3500 | 2750 | 2250 |

### Chatsworth

This model is similar to the Bowood except that it is considered to be the best-grade boxlock-action gun. It is heavily scroll-engraved and features a high-grade, hand-checkered walnut stock.

| NIB | Exc. | V.G. | Good | Fair | Poor |
|-----|------|------|------|------|------|
| 8500 | 7500 | 6000 | 5000 | 3750 | 2750 |

## SEAVER, E. R.
### New York, New York

### Pocket Pistol

This is a single-shot pocket pistol chambered for .41 caliber percussion. It has a 2.5" round barrel and was patterned after the Henry Deringer Philadelphia-type pistol. The finish is blued, with German silver mountings and a walnut stock. It was manufactured in the late 1850's.

| Exc. | V.G. | Good | Fair | Poor |
|------|------|------|------|------|
| 750 | 650 | 550 | 400 | 300 |

## SECURITY INDUSTRIES
### Little Ferry, New Jersey

### Model PSS

This is a stainless-steel double-action revolver chambered for the .38 Special cartridge. It has a 2" barrel with a 5-shot cylinder, fixed sights, and walnut grips. It was manufactured between 1973 and 1978.

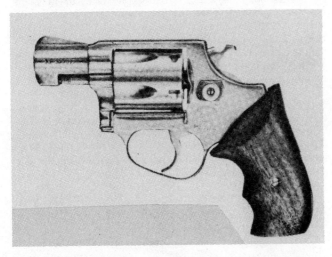

| Exc. | V.G. | Good | Fair | Poor |
|------|------|------|------|------|
| 200 | 150 | 125 | 100 | 75 |

### Model PM357

This is similar to the PSS .38 except that it has a 2.5" barrel and is chambered for the .357 Magnum cartridge. It was manufactured between 1975 and 1978.

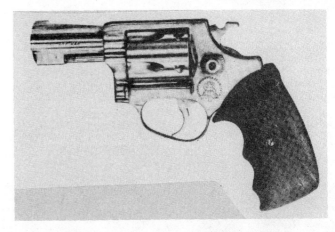

| Exc. | V.G. | Good | Fair | Poor |
|------|------|------|------|------|
| 250 | 200 | 175 | 150 | 100 |

### Model PPM357

This model is similar to the PM357 except that it has a 2" barrel and a spurless hammer. It was manufactured between 1975 and 1978.

| Exc. | V.G. | Good | Fair | Poor |
|------|------|------|------|------|
| 250 | 200 | 175 | 150 | 100 |

## SEDCO INDUSTRIES, INC.
### Lake Elsinore, California

### Model SP22

This is a single-action, blowback-operated, semi-automatic pocket pistol chambered for the .22 l.r. cartridge. It has a 2.5" barrel and is finished either in black or nickel-plated with plastic pearl grips. It was introduced in 1989.

| NIB | Exc. | V.G. | Good | Fair | Poor |
|-----|------|------|------|------|------|
| 75 | 65 | 55 | 50 | 35 | 25 |

## SEDGELY, R. F., INC.
### Philadelphia, Pennsylvania

### Springfield Sporting Rifle

This model was based on a 1903 Springfield bolt action. It is chambered for various calibers that were popular at the time. It has a 24" barrel with a Lyman receiver sight. The finish is blued with a checkered walnut stock. This model was manufactured before WWII.

| Exc. | V.G. | Good | Fair | Poor |
|------|------|------|------|------|
| 600 | 550 | 475 | 350 | 250 |

### Springfield Carbine

This model is similar to the Sporting Rifle, with a 20" barrel and a full-length Mannlicher-style stock.

| Exc. | V.G. | Good | Fair | Poor |
|------|------|------|------|------|
| 650 | 600 | 500 | 400 | 300 |

## SEECAMP, L. W. CO., INC.
### Milford, Connecticut

### LWS .25 ACP Model

This is a blowback-operated, double-action, semi-automatic pocket pistol chambered for the .25 ACP cartridge. It has a 2" barrel and fixed sights. It is constructed of matte-finished stainless steel, has a 7-round detachable magazine, and exhibits very high quality. There were approximately 5,000 manufactured between 1982 and 1985.

| Exc. | V.G. | Good | Fair | Poor |
|------|------|------|------|------|
| 350 | 300 | 250 | 200 | 150 |

## LWS .32 ACP Model

This is a blowback-operated, double-action, semi-automatic pocket pistol chambered for the .32 ACP cartridge. It has a 2" barrel and is constructed of either matte or polished stainless steel. The detachable magazine holds six rounds. There are approximately 100 pistols per month currently being manufactured.

| NIB | Exc. | V.G. | Good | Fair | Poor |
|-----|------|------|------|------|------|
| 350 | 300 | 250 | 200 | 150 | 125 |

## Matched Pair

This set consists of a matte-finished Model LWS .25 ACP and a polished Model LWS .32 cased with the same serial number. There were 200 sets produced before the BATF prohibited serial number duplication.

| Exc. | V.G. | Good | Fair | Poor |
|------|------|------|------|------|
| 900 | 800 | 700 | 500 | 350 |

# SEMMERLING
### Waco, Texas
### SEE--American Derringer Corporation

# SHARPS RIFLE MANUFACTURING COMPANY
### Hartford, Connecticut

Christian Sharps, the founder of this company, was born in 1811. He learned his trade working for John Hall at the Harper's Ferry Arsenal. In 1848 he patented his first breechloader design and had it manufactured by the firm of A. S. Nippes in Mill Creek, Pennsylvania. This firm produced the first two Sharps rifles before he moved on to the firm of Robbins & Lawrence in Windsor, Vermont, who manufactured a number of variations until 1855, when Sharps set up his own manufacturing facility in Hartford, Connecticut. In 1874 when Christian Sharps died, the company was reorganized as the Sharps Rifle Company. They remained at Hartford until 1876, when the plant was moved to Bridgeport, Connecticut. They remained in Bridgeport until 1881, when the company ceased operations.

Christian Sharps never really got along well with the other principals involved in the Sharps Rifle Manufacturing Company, and in 1853 he totally removed himself from the operations of that firm. In 1854 he formed C. Sharps & Company and began manufacturing a percussion, breechloading single-shot pistol and rifle. In 1859 he produced a 4-shot pepperbox and later in 1862 went into partnership with W. Hankins to form a company called Sharps & Hankins. They produced breechloading pistols and 4-barrel pepperboxes until 1866, when Hankins left the firm. The company was again called C. Sharps & Company until it ceased to exist after Sharps's death in 1874.

Sharps rifles are extremely collectible and very valuable on today's market. It would behoove anyone interested in them to avail oneself of the fine literature written on the subject. We also strongly recommend securing qualified, individual appraisals if transactions are contemplated.

## Model 1849

This is a breechloading rifle chambered for .44 caliber percussion. It has a 30" barrel with a wooden cleaning rod mounted beneath it. The breech is activated by the triggerguard lever, and there is an automatic disk-type capping device on the right side of the receiver. The finish is blued and case-colored. The stock is walnut with a brass patchbox, buttplate, and forend cap. It is marked "Sharps Patent 1848." There were approximately 200 manufactured in 1849 and 1850 by the A. S. Nippes Company. This model is also known as the 1st Model Sharps.

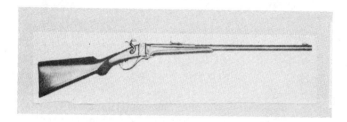

| Exc. | V.G. | Good | Fair | Poor |
|------|------|------|------|------|
| 6000 | 4500 | 4000 | 3000 | 2500 |

## Model 1850

This model is quite similar to the Model 1849, with its most notable difference being the Maynard priming mechanism mounted on the breech. It is marked "Sharps Patent 1848" on the breech. The barrel is marked "Manufactured by A. S. Nippes Mill Creek, Pa." The priming device is marked "Maynard Patent 1845." There were approximately 200 manufactured in 1850. This model is also known as the 2nd Model Sharps.

| Exc. | V.G. | Good | Fair | Poor |
|------|------|------|------|------|
| 5000 | 4000 | 3500 | 2500 | 2000 |

## Model 1851 Carbine

This is a single-shot breechloading rifle chambered for .52 caliber percussion. It has a 21.75" barrel and utilizes the Maynard tape priming device. The finish is blued and case-colored, with a walnut stock and forearm held on by a single barrel band. The buttplate and barrel band are brass, and the military versions feature a brass patchbox. The tang is marked "C. Sharps Patent 1848." The barrel is marked "Robbins & Lawrence," and the priming device is marked "Edward Maynard Patentee 1845." There were approximately 1,650 total manufactured by Robbins & Lawrence in Windsor, Vermont, in 1851. A number of them were purchased by the U.S. Government and bear U.S. inspectors' markings. They are worth approximately 75 percent more than the standard sporting rifle. The sporting rifle is similar to the military carbine except that it has no barrel band and is also offered in .36 and .44 percussion caliber.

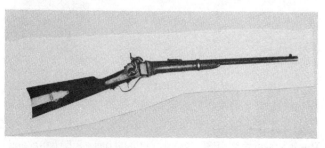

| Exc. | V.G. | Good | Fair | Poor |
|------|------|------|------|------|
| 5000 | 4000 | 3500 | 2500 | 2000 |

## Model 1852

This model is also known as the Slant Breech Carbine and is a single-shot breechloading carbine chambered for .36, .44, and .52 caliber percussion. The standard barrel length is 21.5" in the carbine configuration and 27" for the rifle. It is similar in appearance to the 1851 version but is equipped with the Sharps patent pellet-priming device instead of the Maynard device. The finish is blued, with a case-colored frame, breechblock, lever, and triggerplate. The stock is walnut with a brass patchbox in the butt. The barrel is marked "Sharps Rifle Manufg. Co. Hartford, Conn." Military models bear U.S. inspectors' stamps. The tang is marked "Sharps Patent 1848." In addition to the carbine, there is also a military rifle, sporting rifle, and a smooth-bore shotgun. There were approximately 4,500 total manufactured by Robbins & Lawrence between 1853 and 1855. The values are as follows:

### Military Carbine

| Exc. | V.G. | Good | Fair | Poor |
|------|------|------|------|------|
| 1500 | 1250 | 1000 | 800 | 500 |

### Military Rifle--27" Barrel, Bayonet Lug

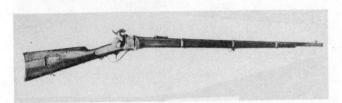

| Exc. | V.G. | Good | Fair | Poor |
|------|------|------|------|------|
| 4000 | 3000 | 2500 | 1750 | 1200 |

### Sporting Rifle

| Exc. | V.G. | Good | Fair | Poor |
|------|------|------|------|------|
| 1250 | 1000 | 850 | 650 | 400 |

### Shotgun

| Exc. | V.G. | Good | Fair | Poor |
|------|------|------|------|------|
| 1000 | 850 | 650 | 500 | 400 |

## Model 1853

This version is quite similar to the Model 1852 and differs by the addition of a spring retainer on the right side of the frame, that holds the lever hinge pin in place. The company itself regarded them as the same models. They were available in the same basic variations, and a total of 10,300 were manufactured between 1854 and 1858. It is interesting to note that the abolitionist John Brown ordered 200 of these carbines, and 102 of them were captured from him in his failed Harper's Ferry raid in 1858. This model was also manufactured by Robbins & Lawrence.

### Military Carbine

| Exc. | V.G. | Good | Fair | Poor |
|------|------|------|------|------|
| 1500 | 1000 | 850 | 650 | 400 |

### Military Rifle

| Exc. | V.G. | Good | Fair | Poor |
|------|------|------|------|------|
| 2000 | 1500 | 1250 | 1000 | 800 |

### Sporting Rifle

| Exc. | V.G. | Good | Fair | Poor |
|------|------|------|------|------|
| 1250 | 850 | 650 | 500 | 350 |

### Shotgun

| Exc. | V.G. | Good | Fair | Poor |
|------|------|------|------|------|
| 900 | 750 | 550 | 400 | 300 |

## Model 1855

This is a single-shot breechloading rifle chambered for .52-caliber percussion. It features the Maynard tape priming device with a hinged, downward-opening trapdoor. It has a 21.75" barrel and was the last of the slant-breech models. The finish is blued and case-colored, and the stock is walnut. The forearm is held on by a barrel band. There is a sling ring mounted on the left side of the weapon. The barrel is marked "Sharps Rifle Manufg. Co. Hartford Conn." The military versions have U.S. inspectors' marks. The tang is marked "Sharps Patent 1848"; and the priming device, "Edward Maynard Patentee 1845." This rifle was in production when Robbins & Lawrence ceased operations, and the greater share were produced by Sharps at their Hartford manufacturing facility. There were approximately 700 manufactured total between 1855 and 1856.

| Exc. | V.G. | Good | Fair | Poor |
|------|------|------|------|------|
| 2500 | 2000 | 1750 | 1250 | 850 |

## Model 1855 U.S. Navy Rifle

This variation of the Model 1855 carbine has a 28" barrel with a bayonet lug near the muzzle. There is a Navy anchor stamped at the breech. There were approximately 260 manufactured in 1855.

| Exc. | V.G. | Good | Fair | Poor |
|------|------|------|------|------|
| 3500 | 2750 | 2000 | 1500 | 1000 |

## Model 1855 British Carbine

This version is similar to the standard 1855 carbine but has British proofs. There were approximately 6,000 manufactured between 1855 and 1877. It is a scarce variation as most were shipped overseas. Beware of fraudulent examples.

| Exc. | V.G. | Good | Fair | Poor |
|------|------|------|------|------|
| 1500 | 1250 | 1000 | 750 | 600 |

## Sharps Straight Breech Models

This series consists of a group of breechloading single-shot rifles whose actions are activated by the triggerguard lever. They are chambered for .52-caliber percussion and feature the Sharps pellet priming system. There were approximately 115,000 total manufactured in this series at Sharps manufacturing facility in Hartford between 1859 and 1866. They are all blued and case-colored and have oil-finished walnut stocks with inspector's markings on the left side. They feature iron mountings on most examples. The variations and values are as follows:

### Model 1859 Carbine--22" Barrel, Brass Mountings

| Exc. | V.G. | Good | Fair | Poor |
|------|------|------|------|------|
| 2250 | 1750 | 1250 | 1000 | 750 |

### Model 1859 Carbine--Iron Mountings

| Exc. | V.G. | Good | Fair | Poor |
|------|------|------|------|------|
| 1500 | 1250 | 850 | 600 | 400 |

### Model 1863 Carbine

| Exc. | V.G. | Good | Fair | Poor |
|------|------|------|------|------|
| 1500 | 1250 | 850 | 600 | 400 |

### Model 1865 Carbine

| Exc. | V.G. | Good | Fair | Poor |
|------|------|------|------|------|
| 1750 | 1500 | 1250 | 900 | 700 |

### Model 1859 Rifle--30" Barrel

| Exc. | V.G. | Good | Fair | Poor |
|------|------|------|------|------|
| 1750 | 1500 | 1250 | 900 | 700 |

### Model 1859 Rifle--36" Barrel

| Exc. | V.G. | Good | Fair | Poor |
|------|------|------|------|------|
| 2500 | 2000 | 1750 | 1250 | 1000 |

### Model 1863 Rifle--Without Bayonet Lug

| Exc. | V.G. | Good | Fair | Poor |
|------|------|------|------|------|
| 1500 | 1250 | 1000 | 800 | 500 |

### Model 1865 Rifle--Without Bayonet Lug

| Exc. | V.G. | Good | Fair | Poor |
|------|------|------|------|------|
| 2250 | 1800 | 1500 | 1200 | 950 |

### Sporting Rifle

This version features an octagonal barrel and was manufactured from actions that were rejected by the government. They usually feature high-grade walnut stocks and double-set triggers. There were only about 100 manufactured.

| Exc. | V.G. | Good | Fair | Poor |
|------|------|------|------|------|
| 3000 | 2500 | 2000 | 1500 | 1000 |

### Coffee-Mill Model

This is a highly collectible variation that features a coffee-mill grinding device built into the buttstock. It has a removable handle. It was designed to allow the cavalry troopers to grind coffee beans in the field. This device was attached to carbines by the firm of McMurphy of New Jersey. It was used for government test purposes, and a very small number of condemned rifles were used for this purpose. There was a very limited quantity produced, and one must exercise a great deal of caution as they would not be difficult for a talented individual to fake. We strongly recommend securing a qualified, individual appraisal on this model.

| Exc. | V.G. | Good | Fair | Poor |
|-------|-------|------|------|------|
| 12500 | 10000 | 8500 | 6000 | 4000 |

### Metallic Cartridge Conversions

In 1867, after the conclusion of the Civil War, the government made a decision to convert the percussion military arms they had in storage to fire metallic cartridges. The Sharps Models 1859, 1863, and 1865 were chosen for this purpose. They were converted to both .52-70 rimfire and centerfire cartridges. There is some discrepancy that arises from this caliber designation since the bore diameter is actually .50 caliber. When the conversion process took place, bores that measured under .5225 were left unlined. Models with larger bores were sleeved to .50 caliber. Both of these variations used the same ammunition, and one can only wonder about the accuracy of the oversized-bore models. There were approximately 32,000 rifles and carbines converted.

| Exc. | V.G. | Good | Fair | Poor |
|------|------|------|------|------|
| 1000 | 850 | 700 | 500 | 400 |

### Model 1869

This is a breechloading single-shot rifle chambered for the .44-77 and the .50-70 cartridges. It was made with barrel lengths of 26", 28", and 30". The military rifle has a 30" barrel; and the military carbine, either a 21" or a 24" barrel. It is blued and case-colored, with an oil-finished or varnished walnut stock. The sporting rifle has a pewter forend tip, and the forearms of the military models are held on by a barrel band. The barrel is marked "Sharps Rifle Manufg. Co. Hartford Connecticut." The frame is marked "C. Sharps Patent Sept. 12th 1848." There were approximately 1,000 total manufactured between 1869 and 1871. The variations in values are as follows:

#### Carbine--.50-70, Saddle Ring on Frame

| Exc. | V.G. | Good | Fair | Poor |
|------|------|------|------|------|
| 1500 | 1250 | 950 | 600 | 500 |

#### Military Rifle--.50-70, 30" Barrel With Three Barrel Bands

| Exc. | V.G. | Good | Fair | Poor |
|------|------|------|------|------|
| 3000 | 2500 | 2000 | 1500 | 1000 |

#### Sporting Rifle--26" Barrel, .44-77 and .50-70

| Exc. | V.G. | Good | Fair | Poor |
|------|------|------|------|------|
| 2500 | 2000 | 1500 | 1000 | 750 |

### Model 1874

This was perhaps the rifle that earned Sharps its greatest reputation. It became known as the "Buffalo Rifle." There are a number of variations, calibers, and barrel lengths. It is essentially a single-shot breech-loading rifle whose action is activated by the triggerguard lever. The finish is blued and case-colored, and the stock is either oil-finished or varnished walnut. There are three distinct types of barrel markings: the first, "Sharps Rifle Manufg. Co. Hartford, Conn."; the second, "Sharps Rifle Co. Hartford, Conn."; and the third and last marking was "Sharps Rifle Co. Bridgeport, Conn." In 1876 the famous trademark "Old Reliable" was marked on the barrels. This marking is usually found on Bridgeport-marked rifles only. If it is found on an earlier gun, it means that manufacture was accomplished with use of left-over parts. The calibers are marked at the barrel top near the breech. The Hartford-manufactured barrels have a collar around them where they fit into the frame. The variations and their values are as follows:

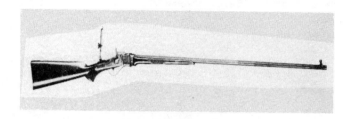

#### Military Carbine--.50-70, 21" Barrel

| Exc. | V.G. | Good | Fair | Poor |
|------|------|------|------|------|
| 2500 | 2250 | 1850 | 1250 | 950 |

### Military Rifle

This version is chambered for the .45-70 and the .50-70 centerfire cartridges. It features a 30" barrel with a full-length forearm held on by three barrel bands. There were approximately 1,750 made.

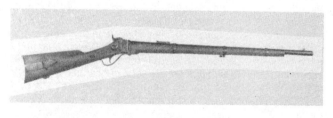

| Exc. | V.G. | Good | Fair | Poor |
|------|------|------|------|------|
| 2000 | 1750 | 1500 | 1000 | 800 |

### Hunter's Rifle

This version is chambered for the .40, .44, .45- 70, and .50-70 cartridges. It features 26", 28", or 30" round barrels with open sights that are mounted on the barrel. There were approximately 600 manufactured.

| Exc. | V.G. | Good | Fair | Poor |
|------|------|------|------|------|
| 3000 | 2500 | 2000 | 1500 | 1000 |

### Business Rifle

This is a utility version chambered for .40-70 and the .45-75 cartridges. It is offered with a 26", 28", or 30" round barrel with adjustable sights. It features double-set triggers and weighs 10.5 lbs. There were approximately 1,600 manufactured.

| Exc. | V.G. | Good | Fair | Poor |
|------|------|------|------|------|
| 2250 | 1750 | 1500 | 1200 | 1000 |

## Sporting Rifle

This very popular version is chambered for various large calibers of the era. It is offered with either octagonal or half-octagonal barrels from 22" to 36" in length. The barrel weights offered are from 7.5 lbs. to 25 lbs. The heavier barrels are worth a premium. It would be difficult to generalize this value, and we recommend an appraisal on these extremely heavy-barrelled buffalo rifles. This variation is offered with either single- or double-set triggers and open sights, as well as Bernier tang sights. There were approximately 6,500 manufactured.

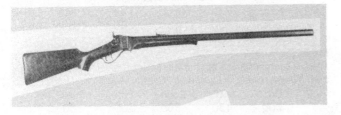

| Exc. | V.G. | Good | Fair | Poor |
|------|------|------|------|------|
| 3000 | 2500 | 2000 | 1750 | 1250 |

## Creedmoor Rifle

This version was produced for competition shooting. The restrictions at the Creedmoor matches allowed a maximum weight of 10 lbs. with a single trigger. Most are chambered for the .44-90 cartridge and have a 32" octagonal barrel. The walnut stock features a checkered pistol grip and forend. The Vernier sight was calibrated to 1,300 yards. There were only 134 manufactured.

| Exc. | V.G. | Good | Fair | Poor |
|------|------|------|------|------|
| 6500 | 5500 | 4000 | 2750 | 2000 |

## Mid-Range Rifle

This version is chambered predominantly for the .40-70 caliber. It has a 30" octagonal or half-octagonal barrel and a single trigger. It weighs approximately 9 lbs. and has a Vernier tang sight calibrated to 600 yards. The front sight features a wind gauge and spirit level. There were approximately 100 manufactured.

| Exc. | V.G. | Good | Fair | Poor |
|------|------|------|------|------|
| 5000 | 4000 | 3000 | 2000 | 1500 |

## Long-Range Rifle

This version is chambered for the .44-90 and the .45-100 cartridges. It features a 34" octagonal barrel and has a checkered pistolgrip stock and forend. The Vernier tang sight was calibrated to 1,300 yards, and the globe front sight features a wind gauge and spirit level. There were approximately 85 manufactured.

| Exc. | V.G. | Good | Fair | Poor |
|------|------|------|------|------|
| 6500 | 5500 | 4000 | 2750 | 2000 |

## Schuetzen Rifle

This version was most-often chambered in .40-50 with a 30" octagonal barrel. It has a checkered pistolgrip stock and forend and features a large Schuetzen-type buttplate. It has double-set triggers and a Vernier tang sight. There were approximately 70 manufactured. All have the Bridgeport barrel address, and most were purchased by members of a single New York shooting club.

| Exc. | V.G. | Good | Fair | Poor |
|------|------|------|------|------|
| 6500 | 5500 | 4000 | 2750 | 2000 |

## Model 1877

This version is also known as the English Model. It is similar in configuration to the Model 1874 and is chambered for the .45-70 cartridge. It features 34" or 36" barrels and is blued and case-colored, with a checkered, varnished walnut stock and forend. The barrel is marked "Sharps Rifle Co. Bridgeport, Conn. Old Reliable." This version was produced for long-range, Creedmoor target shooters. It weighs under 10 lbs. and has a single trigger. It has a lightweight, narrow lock so that most of

its weight would be located forward in the barrel. There were approximately 100 manufactured in 1877 and 1878.

| Exc. | V.G. | Good | Fair | Poor |
|-------|------|------|------|------|
| 10000 | 8500 | 6000 | 4500 | 2750 |

## Model 1878 Sharps-Borchardt

This Model was developed by Hugo Borchardt when he was associated with the Sharps Company. In later years he became famous for the automatic pistol that bore his name, as well as his association with the development of the Luger pistol. This rifle was made in a number of variations, calibers, and barrel lengths and had a distinctive, internal-hammer, flat-sided action that was decidedly ahead of its time in appearance. Their finish is blued and case-colored, with either oil-finished or varnished walnut stocks. The barrels are marked "Sharps Rifle Co. Bridgeport Conn. U.S.A. Old Reliable." The frame is marked "Borchardt Patent Sharps Rifle Co. Bridgeport Conn. U.S.A." The variations and their values are as follows:

## Carbine

This version is chambered for the .45-70 cartridge and has a 24" barrel. The forearm is held on by one barrel band, and the sights are of military configuration. There were approximately 385 manufactured.

| Exc. | V.G. | Good | Fair | Poor |
|------|------|------|------|------|
| 1700 | 1500 | 1250 | 1000 | 750 |

## Military Rifle

This version is chambered for the .45-70 cartridge and has a 32.25" barrel with a cleaning rod mounted underneath it. It features military-type sights and a full-length forearm held on by two barrel bands. There were approximately 7,000 produced.

| Exc. | V.G. | Good | Fair | Poor |
|------|------|------|------|------|
| 1250 | 1000 | 800 | 600 | 500 |

## Sporting Rifle

This version is chambered for the .45-70 cartridge and has a 30" round or octagonal barrel of various weights. There were approximately 600 manufactured.

| Exc. | V.G. | Good | Fair | Poor |
|------|------|------|------|------|
| 1500 | 1250 | 1000 | 800 | 650 |

## Hunter's Rifle

This version is chambered for .40 caliber and has a 26" barrel. It features a plain uncheckered stock. There were approximately 60 manufactured.

| Exc. | V.G. | Good | Fair | Poor |
|------|------|------|------|------|
| 1350 | 1150 | 900 | 700 | 550 |

## Business Rifle

This is a utility version chambered for .40 caliber with a 28" octagonal barrel and a plain stock. There were approximately 90 manufactured.

| Exc. | V.G. | Good | Fair | Poor |
|------|------|------|------|------|
| 1350 | 1150 | 900 | 700 | 550 |

## Officer's Rifle

This version is chambered for the .45-70 cartridge and has a 32" barrel. It features a better-grade, checkered walnut stock. There were approximately 50 manufactured.

| Exc. | V.G. | Good | Fair | Poor |
|------|------|------|------|------|
| 1800 | 1650 | 1400 | 1250 | 900 |

## Express Rifle

This version is chambered for the .45-caliber cartridge and has a 26" octagonal barrel. It has a high-grade, checkered walnut stock with a hard rubber buttplate. It is available with double-set triggers. There were approximately 30 manufactured.

| Exc. | V.G. | Good | Fair | Poor |
|------|------|------|------|------|
| 4500 | 3500 | 2500 | 1750 | 1250 |

### Short-Range Rifle

This version is chambered for .40 caliber and has a 26" round barrel. It has a checkered pistol-grip stock with a hard rubber buttplate. It features a short-range, Vernier rear sight with a wind-gauge front sight. There were approximately 150 manufactured.

| Exc. | V.G. | Good | Fair | Poor |
|------|------|------|------|------|
| 3000 | 2250 | 1500 | 1350 | 1000 |

### Mid-Range Rifle

This version is similar to the Short-Range model, with a 30" barrel and a rear sight calibrated to 600 yards. There were approximately 200 manufactured.

| Exc. | V.G. | Good | Fair | Poor |
|------|------|------|------|------|
| 3000 | 2250 | 1750 | 1500 | 1250 |

### Long-Range Rifle

This version is similar to the Mid-Range Rifle, with a rear sight calibrated out to 1,200 yards and an interchangeable front sight that features a wind gauge and spirit level. There were approximately 230 manufactured.

| Exc. | V.G. | Good | Fair | Poor |
|------|------|------|------|------|
| 5000 | 4000 | 3000 | 2000 | 1500 |

The following models were manufactured by C. Sharps & Company as well as the Sharps & Hankins Company. They were manufactured in Philadelphia, Pennsylvania, between 1864 and Christian Sharps's death in 1874.

### Breech-Loading, Single-Shot Pistol

This is a rather unusual falling-block pistol whose action is activated by a combination lever/triggerguard. It is chambered for .31 or .34 percussion. A larger version was also manufactured, chambered for .36 caliber percussion. This larger version would be worth approximately 10 percent additional. The barrel length is either 5" or 6.5" and round in configuration. The finish is blued and case-colored. The grips are walnut. It features a pellet priming device mounted on the frame. The barrel is marked "Sharps Patent Arms Mf Fairmount Phila., Pa." There were approximately 900 manufactured of both types between 1854 and 1877.

| Exc. | V.G. | Good | Fair | Poor |
|------|------|------|------|------|
| 2500 | 2000 | 1500 | 1000 | 750 |

### Pistol-Grip Rifle

This is a breechloading, single-shot percussion arm chambered for .31 or .38 caliber percussion. It has a falling-block action operated by the triggerguard lever. They are encountered with various-length barrels; most are 28". It was produced with the same action as the Breech-Loading Pistol. The finish is blued and case-colored, with a walnut stock and forend and German silver mountings. There is a ramrod mounted underneath the barrel. There were very few manufactured in the 1850's.

| Exc. | V.G. | Good | Fair | Poor |
|------|------|------|------|------|
| 2500 | 2000 | 1500 | 1000 | 750 |

### Percussion Revolver

This is a single-action pocket revolver chambered for .25-caliber percussion. It has a 3" ribbed octagonal barrel that is hinged and pivots upward for loading. It features a 6-shot unfluted cylinder. It seemed to be patterned after the early Smith & Wesson revolvers. The finish is blued, with two-piece walnut grips. It features a scroll-engraved frame. The barrel is marked "C. Sharps & Co., Phila., Pa." There were approximately 2,000 manufactured between 1857 and 1858.

| Exc. | V.G. | Good | Fair | Poor |
|------|------|------|------|------|
| 1250 | 1000 | 750 | 500 | 400 |

### 4-Shot Pepperbox Pistols

In the years 1859 to 1874, a number of these distinctive pocket pistols were produced both by the Sharps Company and the firm of Sharps & Hankins. They are breech-loading pistols chambered for the .22, .30, or the .32 rimfire cartridges. The barrel lengths vary from 2.5" to 3.5". The 4-barrel clusters slide forward on the frame for loading. There is a barrel latch located at the front of the frame. They are single-action and feature spur triggers. They were offered with various finishes, but most have blued barrels and silver-plated brass frames or case-colored iron frames. The grips are either walnut or gutta-percha. There were many thousand manufactured. There are a number of different variations. They are as follows:

### Model 1

This version was produced by C. Sharps & Co. and is so marked. It is chambered for the .22 rimfire cartridge.

| Exc. | V.G. | Good | Fair | Poor |
|------|------|------|------|------|
| 500 | 450 | 350 | 200 | 150 |

### Model 2

This is a larger variation chambered for the .30-caliber rimfire, with a brass frame. It is marked "C. Sharps & Co."

| Exc. | V.G. | Good | Fair | Poor |
|------|------|------|------|------|
| 500 | 450 | 350 | 200 | 150 |

### Model 3

This version is chambered for the .32 short rimfire cartridge and is marked "Address Sharps & Hankins Philadelphia Penn."

| Exc. | V.G. | Good | Fair | Poor |
|------|------|------|------|------|
| 450 | 375 | 300 | 175 | 100 |

### Model 4

This version is chambered for the .32 long rimfire cartridge and has a rounded birdshead grip. It is marked "C. Sharps Patent Jan. 25, 1859." There is a rare variation with a 3.5" barrel that is not serial-numbered that is worth an approximate 100 percent premium. It is rarely encountered.

| Exc. | V.G. | Good | Fair | Poor |
|------|------|------|------|------|
| 500 | 450 | 350 | 200 | 150 |

### Model 1862 Carbine

This is a single-shot breechloading carbine that is chambered for the .52 rimfire cartridge. It was manufactured by Sharps & Hankins. The barrel slides forward on the frame when it is released by the triggerguard action lever. There are three variations offered with either a 19" or 24" barrel. The finish is blued and case-colored, with a walnut buttstock. The frame is marked "Sharps & Hankins Philada." There were approximately 13,000 manufactured between 1862 and 1877. The variations and their respective values are as follows:

### Navy Model

This version has a leather-covered 24" barrel, that was supposed to protect it against rusting. This leather covering was retained by two screws at the breech and a steel band at the muzzle. Examples with the leather missing will be identifiable by the screw holes. The Navy purchased approximately 6,700 of these.

| Exc. | V.G. | Good | Fair | Poor |
|------|------|------|------|------|
| 1100 | 900 | 750 | 500 | 400 |

### Army Model

This version has a 24" barrel and does not have the leather covering or the screw holes used to retain it. There were approximately 1,500 purchased by the Army and used in the Civil War.

| Exc. | V.G. | Good | Fair | Poor |
|------|------|------|------|------|
| 1250 | 1000 | 800 | 600 | 450 |

### Short Cavalry Carbine

This version has a 19" blued barrel and a saddle ring mounted on the left of the frame. There were approximately 1,000 manufactured.

| Exc. | V.G. | Good | Fair | Poor |
|------|------|------|------|------|
| 1400 | 1100 | 900 | 700 | 500 |

## Model 1861 Navy Rifle

This Model was manufactured by Sharps & Hankins and is so marked. It is chambered for the .52-caliber rimfire cartridge. It is a single-shot breechloader, and the barrels slide forward on the frame when the triggerguard lever is activated. The barrel is 32.75" in length. The finish is blued and case-colored. The stock is of walnut with a full-length forend held on by three barrel bands. There is a bayonet lug at the muzzle end of the barrel. There were approximately 700 manufactured in 1861 and 1862.

| Exc. | V.G. | Good | Fair | Poor |
|------|------|------|------|------|
| 1300 | 1100 | 950 | 700 | 500 |

# SHATTUCK, C. S.
### Hatfield, Massachusetts

## Boom

This was an inexpensive, spur-trigger, single-action pocket revolver chambered for .22-caliber rimfire. It has a 2" octagonal barrel and a 6-round fluted cylinder that swings out for loading. It has an iron frame and is nickel-plated, with a rosewood birds-head butt. The barrel is marked "Boom" and also "Pat. Nov. 4, 1879." A pistol of this nature was normally referred to as a "suicide special." The swing-out cylinder makes this model somewhat unique. It was manufactured in the 1880's.

| Exc. | V.G. | Good | Fair | Poor |
|------|------|------|------|------|
| 250 | 200 | 150 | 100 | 75 |

## Pocket Revolver

This is a spur-trigger single-action revolver chambered for .32-caliber rimfire. It has a 3.5" octagonal barrel and a 5-shot fluted cylinder that swings out for loading. The barrel is marked "C. S. Shattuck Hatfield, Mass. Pat. Nov. 4, 1879." The finish is nickel-plated, with checkered black rubber grips. This pistol is also unique in having the swing-out cylinder. There have been specimens noted with portraits of Abraham Lincoln and James Garfield molded into the butt. Models with these grips would be worth approximately 25 percent additional. There were several thousand manufactured in the 1880's.

| Exc. | V.G. | Good | Fair | Poor |
|------|------|------|------|------|
| 300 | 250 | 200 | 150 | 100 |

# SHAW & LEDOYT
### Stafford, Connecticut

## Underhammer Pistol

This is a bootleg-type single shot that is chambered for .31-caliber percussion. It has 2.5" to 3.5" part-round/part-octagonal length barrel. The frame is marked "Shaw & LeDoyt/Stafford. Conn." The finish is blued, with a pointed, brass-trimmed walnut handle. This pistol was manufactured in the 1850's.

| Exc. | V.G. | Good | Fair | Poor |
|------|------|------|------|------|
| 500 | 400 | 300 | 200 | 150 |

# SHAWK & MCLANAHAN
### St. Louis, Missouri

## Navy Revolver

This is a single-action revolver with a conventional-type trigger and triggerguard that is chambered for .36 caliber percussion. It has an 8" round barrel and a 6-shot unfluted cylinder. There is an integral loading lever under the barrel. The backstrap is marked "Shawk & McLanahan, St. Louis, Carondelet, Mo." The finish is blued, with a brass frame and two-piece walnut grips. There were approximately 100 manufactured in 1858. They

were most possibly used by Union forces during the Civil War; and competent, individual appraisals should be secured if a transaction is contemplated.

| Exc. | V.G. | Good | Fair | Poor |
|------|------|------|------|------|
| 5500 | 4500 | 4000 | 3000 | 2000 |

# SHERIDEN PRODUCTS., INC.
### Racine, Wisconsin

## Knockabout

This is a single-shot pistol chambered for the .22 rimfire. It has a 5" barrel with fixed sights. The finish is blued, with checkered plastic grips. This model was manufactured between 1953 and 1960.

| Exc. | V.G. | Good | Fair | Poor |
|------|------|------|------|------|
| 125 | 100 | 90 | 75 | 50 |

# SHILEN RIFLES, INC.
### Ennis, Texas

## Model DGA Sporter

This is a high quality bolt-action rifle that is chambered for various popular American calibers from .17 Remington up to .358 Winchester. It has a 24" barrel that is furnished without sights. The box magazine holds three rounds. The finish is blued with a select claro walnut stock.

| Exc. | V.G. | Good | Fair | Poor |
|------|------|------|------|------|
| 600 | 550 | 450 | 400 | 350 |

## Model DGA Varminter

This Model is similar to the Sporter except that it is chambered for the smaller, high-velocity cartridges only and has a 25" medium heavyweight barrel.

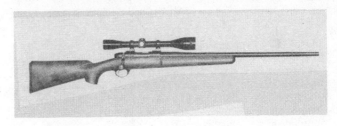

| Exc. | V.G. | Good | Fair | Poor |
|------|------|------|------|------|
| 600 | 550 | 450 | 400 | 350 |

## Model DGA Silhouette Rifle

This Model is similar to the Varminter, chambered in .308 Winchester only.

| Exc. | V.G. | Good | Fair | Poor |
|------|------|------|------|------|
| 600 | 550 | 450 | 400 | 350 |

## Model DGA Benchrest Rifle

This is a bolt-action single shot chambered for various calibers. It is offered with a 26" medium-weight or heavy barrel. It has no sights. The finish is blued, with a choice of standard or thumbhole stock in either fiberglas or walnut.

| Exc. | V.G. | Good | Fair | Poor |
|------|------|------|------|------|
| 700 | 650 | 550 | 500 | 450 |

# SHILOH RIFLE MFG. CO., INC.
### Big Timber, Montana

This company is dedicated to producing a modern version of the Sharps rifle that is as good or better than the original models. The company was founded in 1976 in Farmingdale, New York, as a division of Drovel Tool Company. Models bearing this address will bring a premium. In 1983 Shiloh moved to Big Timber, Montana, and concentrated on rifle manufacturing only. In 1985 the company began marketing their products on a factory-to-FFL dealer direct basis and are still doing this today. Their products are of the highest quality and, much like the originals, are available with various custom-order options. The values we supply are for the basic models; and we recommend qualified, individual appraisal on models that feature custom options, as these options can have a drastic effect on value.

## Model 1863 Military Rifle

This model is chambered for .54-caliber percussion. It is a breechloader with a 30" round barrel with open sights. It comes standard with a single trigger, but a double-set trigger is available upon request. The finish is blued, with a case-colored receiver. The stock is select walnut with a full-length forearm held on by three barrel bands.

| NIB | Exc. | V.G. | Good | Fair | Poor |
|-----|------|------|------|------|------|
| 850 | 800  | 700  | 600  | 500  | 400  |

## Model 1863 Sporting Rifle

This model is similar to the Military Rifle, with a 30" tapered octagonal barrel, sporting-type sights, and a half-length Schnabel forearm.

| NIB | Exc. | V.G. | Good | Fair | Poor |
|-----|------|------|------|------|------|
| 750 | 700  | 600  | 500  | 400  | 350  |

## Model 1863 Military Carbine

This model is similar to the Military Rifle, with a 22" round barrel and a half stock held on by one barrel band. It has a saddle bar and ring.

| NIB | Exc. | V.G. | Good | Fair | Poor |
|-----|------|------|------|------|------|
| 750 | 700  | 600  | 500  | 400  | 350  |

## Model 1862 Confederate Robinson

This model is similar to the 1863 Carbine, with a 21.5" barrel and a brass buttplate and barrel band. It features a swing swivel on the butt.

| NIB | Exc. | V.G. | Good | Fair | Poor |
|-----|------|------|------|------|------|
| 800 | 750  | 650  | 550  | 450  | 400  |

## Model 1874 Express Rifle

This model is chambered for various early-American black powder cartridges. It has a 34" tapered octagon barrel with a sporting tang and globe front sight. It features double-set triggers; and the finish is blued, with a case-colored receiver. The pistolgrip stock is select-grade walnut with a shotgun-type buttplate and a Schnabel forearm.

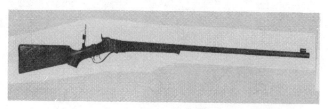

| NIB | Exc. | V.G. | Good | Fair | Poor |
|-----|------|------|------|------|------|
| 850 | 800  | 700  | 600  | 500  | 400  |

## Montana Roughrider Rifle

This model is similar to the Express Rifle with a choice of either tapered octagonal or half-round/half-octagonal barrels in lengths from 24" to 34" in 2" increments.

| NIB | Exc. | V.G. | Good | Fair | Poor |
|-----|------|------|------|------|------|
| 750 | 700  | 600  | 500  | 400  | 350  |

## No. 1 Deluxe Rifle

This model is similar to the Montana Roughrider, available with a 30" tapered octagonal barrel.

| NIB | Exc. | V.G. | Good | Fair | Poor |
|-----|------|------|------|------|------|
| 800 | 750  | 650  | 550  | 450  | 400  |

## No. 3 Standard Sporter

This model is similar to the No. 1 Deluxe, with a military-style, straight-grip buttstock and a steel buttplate.

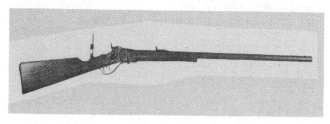

| NIB | Exc. | V.G. | Good | Fair | Poor |
|-----|------|------|------|------|------|
| 750 | 700  | 600  | 500  | 400  | 350  |

## The Business Rifle

This model has a 28" heavy tapered round barrel and is furnished standard with a military-style buttstock and steel buttplate.

| NIB | Exc. | V.G. | Good | Fair | Poor |
|-----|------|------|------|------|------|
| 750 | 700  | 600  | 500  | 400  | 350  |

## The Saddle Rifle

This model has a 26" tapered octagonal barrel and a shotgun buttstock with a straight grip and cheekrest.

| NIB | Exc. | V.G. | Good | Fair | Poor |
|-----|------|------|------|------|------|
| 800 | 750  | 650  | 550  | 450  | 400  |

## Model 1874 Military Rifle

This model features a 30" round barrel with military-type sights, a military-style buttstock, and a full-length forearm held on by three barrel bands. It has a single trigger, and a patch box is optional.

| NIB | Exc. | V.G. | Good | Fair | Poor |
|-----|------|------|------|------|------|
| 850 | 800  | 700  | 600  | 500  | 400  |

## Model 1874 Carbine

This model has a 24" round barrel with buckhorn-type sights and a single trigger assembly standard. It has the straight-grip, military-type buttstock with steel buttplate.

| NIB | Exc. | V.G. | Good | Fair | Poor |
|-----|------|------|------|------|------|
| 750 | 700  | 600  | 500  | 400  | 350  |

## The Jaeger

This model was designed for the modern hunter. It is available with a half-octagonal 26" barrel, buckhorn sights, and a shotgun-style pistolgrip buttstock.

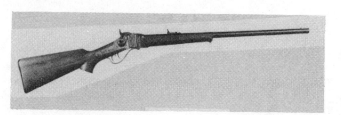

| NIB | Exc. | V.G. | Good | Fair | Poor |
|-----|------|------|------|------|------|
| 800 | 750  | 650  | 550  | 450  | 400  |

## Hartford Model

This model is similar to the No. 3 Standard Sporter, with the Hartford collar around the barrel where it meets the receiver. It features a pewter forend tip.

| NIB | Exc. | V.G. | Good | Fair | Poor |
|-----|------|------|------|------|------|
| 1400 | 1250 | 1000 | 850 | 650 | 500 |

## Model 1874 Military Carbine

This Model is similar to the Military Rifle, with a 22" round barrel and buckhorn sights. It has a military-style buttstock with a barrel band on the forearm. It features a steel buttplate and a saddle bar and ring. It is available chambered for .40-70, .45-70, and .50-70 only.

| NIB | Exc. | V.G. | Good | Fair | Poor |
|-----|------|------|------|------|------|
| 750 | 700 | 600 | 500 | 400 | 350 |

There are at least seven custom rifles available from Shiloh, and it is suggested that anyone interested in their acquisition contact the Company for an informative brochure.

# SIG
### Neuhausen, Switzerland
### Importer--Mandall Shooting Supplies
### Scottsdale, Arizona

## P 210

This is a single-action, locked-breech semi-automatic pistol chambered for 7.65mm or 9mm Parabellum. It has a 4.75" barrel and an 8-round detachable magazine. It is rated by many as the finest semi-automatic pistol ever manufactured; and when designated, the SP 47/8 was the standard service pistol of the Swiss Army after 1949. The finish is blued, with ribbed plastic grips. It has been in production for over 40 years.

| Exc. | V.G. | Good | Fair | Poor |
|------|------|------|------|------|
| 1500 | 1300 | 1100 | 800 | 700 |

## P 210-1

This model is similar to the P 210, with a high-polished finish, wood grips, and micrometer-adjustable sights. It was not imported after 1986.

| Exc. | V.G. | Good | Fair | Poor |
|------|------|------|------|------|
| 1700 | 1500 | 1250 | 1000 | 750 |

## P 210-2

This model has a sand-blasted and blued finish, plastic grips, and fixed sights. It was not imported after 1987.

| Exc. | V.G. | Good | Fair | Poor |
|------|------|------|------|------|
| 1300 | 1200 | 1000 | 750 | 600 |

## P 210-5

This is the target model, with a matte finish, micrometer-adjustable sights, walnut grips, and an extended barrel. This was a limited-production item and is rarely encountered on today's market. It was discontinued in 1987.

| Exc. | V.G. | Good | Fair | Poor |
|------|------|------|------|------|
| 1850 | 1650 | 1450 | 1100 | 900 |

## P 210-6

This model is similar to the P 210-5, with a standard-length barrel. It was not imported after 1987.

| Exc. | V.G. | Good | Fair | Poor |
|------|------|------|------|------|
| 1500 | 1350 | 1150 | 900 | 700 |

This company also manufactures three very high quality assault-type rifles. They are the PE-57, the SIG-AMT, and the SG 550/551. They are extremely expensive; and due to the mass hysteria regarding weapons of this type that currently grips our country, we feel that competent, individual appraisals should be secured if a transaction is contemplated.

# SIG-HAMMERLI
### Lenzburg, Switzerland

This high-grade target pistol was manufactured through a collaboration of Sig and the firm of Hammerli.

## Model P240 Target Pistol

This is a single-action, semi-automatic target pistol chambered for either .32 Smith & Wesson Long Wadcutter or .38 Midrange. It has a 5.9" barrel and a 5-shot detachable magazine. It features adjustable target sights and a fully adjustable trigger. The finish is blued, with adjustable thumbrest walnut grips. This model was not imported after 1986.

| Exc. | V.G. | Good | Fair | Poor |
|------|------|------|------|------|
| 1300 | 1150 | 950 | 750 | 600 |

## .22 Conversion Unit

This unit consists of a barrel, slide, and magazine that would convert the P240 to fire the .22 l.r. cartridge.

| Exc. | V.G. | Good | Fair | Poor |
|------|------|------|------|------|
| 500 | 450 | 400 | 300 | 200 |

# SIG-SAUER
### Eckernforde, West Germany
### Importer--Sigarms
### Herndon, Virginia

## P 220

This is a high-quality, double-action semi-automatic pistol chambered for .22 l.r., .38 Super, 7.65mm, and 9mm Parabellum, and is currently chambered in .45ACP. It has a 4.4" barrel and fixed sights and features the de-cocking lever that was found originally on the Sauer Model 38H. There are two versions of this pistol--one with a bottom magazine release and the other with the release on the side as on the Model 1911 Colt. The frame is a lightweight alloy that is matte-finished and anodized blue with black plastic grips. This model was manufactured from 1976.

| NIB | Exc. | V.G. | Good | Fair | Poor |
|-----|------|------|------|------|------|
| 750 | 700 | 600 | 500 | 350 | 275 |

**P 225**

This is similar to the Model P 220 except that it is chambered for 9mm. It is a more compact pistol, with a 3.85" barrel. It has an 8-shot detachable magazine and adjustable sights. The finish is matte blued or electroless nickel plate with black plastic grips.

| NIB | Exc. | V.G. | Good | Fair | Poor |
|-----|------|------|------|------|------|
| 775 | 725 | 625 | 500 | 350 | 275 |

**P 226**

This model is a compact, high-capacity pistol with a 4.4" barrel. It is available with a 15- or 20-round detachable magazine and high-contrast sights. It is either blued, electroless nickel plated, or, on special order, has a polymer finish known as K-Kote. This model was introduced in 1983.

| NIB | Exc. | V.G. | Good | Fair | Poor |
|-----|------|------|------|------|------|
| 800 | 750 | 650 | 550 | 400 | 300 |

**P 230**

This is a semi-automatic, compact, pocket-type pistol chambered for .22 l.r., .32 ACP, .380 ACP, and 9mm Ultra. It has a 3.6" barrel and either a 10-, 8-, or 7-round magazine, depending on the caliber chambered. The finish is blued, with wood grips; and it was manufactured from 1976. The .32 ACP and the .380 ACP versions are the only ones currently available.

| NIB | Exc. | V.G. | Good | Fair | Poor |
|-----|------|------|------|------|------|
| 500 | 400 | 350 | 300 | 250 | 200 |

**SSG 2000**

This is a high-grade, bolt-action, sniping-type rifle chambered for .223, 7.5mm Swiss, .300 Weatherby Magnum, and .308 Winchester. It has a 24" barrel and was furnished without sights. It has a 4-round box magazine. The finish is matte blued with a thumbhole-style stippled walnut stock with an adjustable cheekpiece. This model was discontinued in 1986.

| Exc. | V.G. | Good | Fair | Poor |
|------|------|------|------|------|
| 2500 | 2250 | 2000 | 1500 | 1000 |

# SIMPLEX
### Liege, Belgium

**Simplex**

This is a blowback-operated semi-automatic pistol chambered for the 8mm Simplex cartridge. It was patented in 1901 by Bergmann and outwardly resembles the larger military Bermann-Bayard pistol. It is actually much simpler in design. The barrel is 2.75" and is round, with a rib. The weapon is hammer-fired and marked "Pat. Brevete DRGM." It is blued, with black plastic grips on which the word "Simplex" has been molded. The magazine capacity is eight rounds. The magazine is a detachable box located in front of the triggerguard. It was manufactured between 1904 and 1914 and was not commercially successful, probably because it required a special cartridge that would not fit other weapons.

| Exc. | V.G. | Good | Fair | Poor |
|------|------|------|------|------|
| 750 | 650 | 500 | 400 | 300 |

# SIMPSON, R. J.
### New York, New York

**Pocket Pistol**

This is a single-shot pocket pistol chambered for .41 percussion and patterned after the Henry Deringer Philadelphia-type pistol. It has a 2.5" round barrel with German silver mountings and a walnut stock. It was made between 1855 and 1865.

| Exc. | V.G. | Good | Fair | Poor |
|------|------|------|------|------|
| 750 | 650 | 500 | 400 | 300 |

# SIMSON & COMPANY
### Suhl, Germany
### SEE--Luger

This was a long-established German sporting firm that received a military contract in 1922 to supply the German military with Parabellum pistols. The Simson pistols were assembled from existing stocks of parts that were built up during WWI. The contract lasted until 1932. These pistols will be found in the Luger section of this book.

**Model 1922**

This is a blowback-operated, semi-automatic pocket pistol chambered for 6.35mm. It has a 2" barrel and is striker-fired. It has a 6-shot detachable magazine and is marked "Selbstlade Pistole Simson DRP." It is also marked "Waffenfabrik Simson & Co Suhl." It is blued, with black plastic grips with the word "Simson" molded diagonally across them.

| Exc. | V.G. | Good | Fair | Poor |
|------|------|------|------|------|
| 500  | 450  | 400  | 300  | 200  |

## Model 1927

This model is similar to the Model 1922 except that the frame is slightly flatter and the Simson trademark (three overlapping triangles with the letter "S" inside) is marked on the left of the frame. Simson ceased manufacture of both of these handguns in the early 1930's.

| Exc. | V.G. | Good | Fair | Poor |
|------|------|------|------|------|
| 500  | 450  | 400  | 300  | 200  |

## SIRKIS INDUSTRIES, LTD.
### Ramat-Gan, Israel
### Importer--Armscorp of America
### Baltimore, Maryland

### SD 9

This is a double-action semi-automatic chambered for the 9mm Parabellum cartridge. It has a 3" barrel with a loaded-chamber indicator and fixed sights. It has a 7-shot detachable magazine and is constructed, for the most part, of metal stampings. The finish is blued, with plastic grips. It was imported between 1986 and 1988. This pistol is currently known as the Sardius.

| Exc. | V.G. | Good | Fair | Poor |
|------|------|------|------|------|
| 325  | 275  | 225  | 175  | 125  |

## Model 35 Match Rifle

This was a single-shot, bolt-action target rifle chambered for the .22 l.r. cartridge. It has a 26" full-floating heavy barrel with micrometer adjustable target sights and a fully adjustable trigger. The finish is blued, with a select walnut stock. This Model was not imported after 1985.

| Exc. | V.G. | Good | Fair | Poor |
|------|------|------|------|------|
| 600  | 550  | 500  | 400  | 300  |

## Model 36 Sniper's Rifle

This is a gas-operated semi-automatic rifle chambered for .308. It has a 22" barrel with a flash suppressor and adjustable sights. The finish is matte blued, with a synthetic carbon fiber stock. This model was discontinued in 1985.

| Exc. | V.G. | Good | Fair | Poor |
|------|------|------|------|------|
| 675  | 600  | 550  | 450  | 350  |

## SLOTTER & CO.
### Philadelphia, Pennsylvania

### Pocket Pistol

This is a single-shot pocket pistol chambered for .41 percussion. The barrel lengths are from 2.5" to 3.5", and it was patterned after the Henry Deringer Philadelphia-type pistol. The mountings are engraved German silver, and the stocks are varnished walnut with checkered handles. They are often marked either "J. P. Lower" or "Slotter/& Co. Phila." They were manufactured between 1860 and 1869.

| Exc. | V.G. | Good | Fair | Poor |
|------|------|------|------|------|
| 950  | 850  | 750  | 600  | 450  |

## SMITH
## AMERICAN MACHINE WORKS
### Springfield, Massachusetts

### Smith Carbine

This is a single-shot breechloading carbine that is chambered for .50-caliber percussion. It has a 21.75" round barrel with an octagonal breech. The action is opened by depressing a latch in front of the triggerguard, allowing the barrel to break similarly to a modern single-barrel shotgun. The barrel is marked "Address/Poultney & Trimble/Baltimore, USA" and "Smith's Patent/June 23 1857." Some have been noted marked "American Arms Co./Chicopee Falls." The finish is blued, with a case-colored breech. The stock is walnut with a sling ring mounted at the breech. There were approximately 30,000 manufactured and purchased by the United States military. The sales agents were Poultney & Trimble of Baltimore, Maryland.

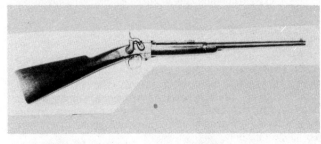

| Exc. | V.G. | Good | Fair | Poor |
|------|------|------|------|------|
| 1500 | 1250 | 1000 | 750  | 500  |

## SMITH, OTIS
### Rockfall, Connecticut

This company manufactured a line of single-action, spur-trigger revolvers that are chambered for .22, .32, .38, and .41 rimfire cartridges. The pistols have varying barrel lengths. The cylinder access pin is retained by a button on the left side of the frame. The cylinder usually holds five shots. The finishes are either blued or nickel-plated, with birdshead grips. The quality was considered to be mediocre.

## Model 1883 Shell-Ejector
This is a single-action, break-open, self-ejecting revolver with a ribbed 3.5" barrel chambered for .32 centerfire. It has a 5-shot fluted cylinder and a spur trigger. It was quite well-made. The finish is nickel-plated, with black plastic grips.

| Exc. | V.G. | Good | Fair | Poor |
|---|---|---|---|---|
| 250 | 200 | 150 | 100 | 75 |

## Model 1892
This is a double-action, concealed-hammer revolver chambered for the .38 centerfire cartridge. It has a 4" barrel and, for the first time, a conventional trigger and triggerguard. It is gate-loaded and has a solid frame. It is nickel-plated with black plastic grips and also appeared under the Maltby, Henley & Company banner marked "Spencer Safety Hammerless" or "Parker Safety Hammerless." The Otis Smith Company ceased operations in 1898.

| Exc. | V.G. | Good | Fair | Poor |
|---|---|---|---|---|
| 250 | 200 | 150 | 100 | 75 |

# SMITH, L. C.
### Syracuse, New York
### Hunter Arms Company
### Fulton, New York

The L. C. Smith is one of the finest American-made double-barrel shotguns and is very collectible in today's market. It was manufactured between 1880 and 1888 in Syracuse, New York; and between 1890 and 1945, in Fulton, New York, by the Hunter Arms Company. In 1945 Marlin Firearms Company acquired Hunter Arms, and the L. C. Smith was made until 1951. In 1968 the L. C. Smith was resurrected for five years, and production ceased totally in 1973. The values given are approximate for standard production models; and we strongly feel that competent, individual appraisals should be secured, especially on the rarer and higher-grade models, if a transaction is contemplated.

The values given are for fluid steel, hammerless guns only. Damascus-barrelled guns have become very collectible if they are in very good or better condition, and values are approximately the same as for the fluid steel models. Damascus guns in less than good condition are worth considerably less.

## Early Hammerless Shotguns
The following models were manufactured between 1890 and 1913. They are chambered for 10, 12, 16, and 20 gauge and were produced with various barrel lengths and choke combinations. They feature full sidelock actions. The difference in the models and their values is based on the degree of ornamentation and the quality of materials and workmanship utilized in their construction. The general values furnished are for 10-, 12-, or 16-gauge guns only.
20 Gauge--Add 50 Percent
Single-Selective Trigger--Add $250
Automatic Ejectors--Add 30 Percent

### 00 Grade--60,000 Manufactured
| Exc. | V.G. | Good | Fair | Poor |
|---|---|---|---|---|
| 1500 | 1250 | 1000 | 650 | 400 |

### 0 Grade--30,000 Manufactured
| Exc. | V.G. | Good | Fair | Poor |
|---|---|---|---|---|
| 1600 | 1350 | 1050 | 700 | 450 |

### No. 1 Grade--10,000 Manufactured
| Exc. | V.G. | Good | Fair | Poor |
|---|---|---|---|---|
| 2500 | 2000 | 1500 | 800 | 550 |

### No. 2 Grade--13,000 Manufactured
| Exc. | V.G. | Good | Fair | Poor |
|---|---|---|---|---|
| 3000 | 2250 | 1750 | 900 | 700 |

### No. 3 Grade--4,000 Manufactured
| Exc. | V.G. | Good | Fair | Poor |
|---|---|---|---|---|
| 3500 | 2750 | 1800 | 1000 | 750 |

### Pigeon Grade--1,200 Manufactured
| Exc. | V.G. | Good | Fair | Poor |
|---|---|---|---|---|
| 3500 | 2750 | 1800 | 1000 | 750 |

### No. 4 Grade--500 Manufactured
| Exc. | V.G. | Good | Fair | Poor |
|---|---|---|---|---|
| 10000 | 7500 | 5000 | 3000 | 2000 |

### A-1 Grade--700 Manufactured, All Damascus, No 20-Gauge
| Exc. | V.G. | Good | Fair | Poor |
|---|---|---|---|---|
| 5000 | 3500 | 2500 | 1750 | 1000 |

### No. 5 Grade--500 Manufactured
| Exc. | V.G. | Good | Fair | Poor |
|---|---|---|---|---|
| 8500 | 7000 | 5000 | 2750 | 2000 |

### Monogram Grade--100 Manufactured
| Exc. | V.G. | Good | Fair | Poor |
|---|---|---|---|---|
| 11000 | 8500 | 6000 | 3750 | 2500 |

### A-2 Grade--200 Manufactured
| Exc. | V.G. | Good | Fair | Poor |
|---|---|---|---|---|
| 15000 | 10000 | 7500 | 4500 | 3750 |

### A-3 Grade--20 Manufactured
This version is too rare to generalize a value.

## Later Production Hammerless Shotguns
These variations were manufactured at Fulton, New York, between 1914 and 1951. They are side-by-side double-barrel shotguns chambered for 12, 16, and 20 gauge, as well as the .410. They are offered with various barrel lengths and choke combinations. They feature a full sidelock action and are available with double or single triggers, extractors, and automatic ejectors. The finishes are blued and case-colored, with checkered walnut stocks that are of either straight, semi-pistolgrip, or pistolgrip configurations. The various models differ as to the degree of ornamentation and the quality of materials and workmanship utilized in their construction. These are very collectible American shotguns, and we strongly recommend securing a qualified, individual appraisal if a transaction is contemplated. The values supplied are for 12- and 16-gauge models only.
20 Gauge--Add 35 Percent
.410--Add 500 Percent
Single-Selective Trigger--Add $250
Automatic Ejectors--Add 30 Percent

### Field Grade
| Exc. | V.G. | Good | Fair | Poor |
|---|---|---|---|---|
| 1250 | 1000 | 750 | 500 | 350 |

### Ideal Grade
| Exc. | V.G. | Good | Fair | Poor |
|---|---|---|---|---|
| 1500 | 1200 | 900 | 600 | 450 |

### Trap Grade
| Exc. | V.G. | Good | Fair | Poor |
|---|---|---|---|---|
| 1600 | 1300 | 1000 | 700 | 500 |

### Specialty Grade
| Exc. | V.G. | Good | Fair | Poor |
|---|---|---|---|---|
| 3000 | 2500 | 1750 | 1000 | 600 |

### Eagle Grade
| Exc. | V.G. | Good | Fair | Poor |
|---|---|---|---|---|
| 5000 | 4000 | 3000 | 1750 | 1250 |

### Skeet Special Grade
| Exc. | V.G. | Good | Fair | Poor |
|---|---|---|---|---|
| 3000 | 2500 | 1750 | 1000 | 600 |

## Premier Skeet Grade

| Exc. | V.G. | Good | Fair | Poor |
|------|------|------|------|------|
| 3000 | 2500 | 1750 | 1000 | 600 |

## Crown Grade

With this grade, automatic ejectors became standard equipment. The .410 is extremely rare in this model and non-existent in higher grades; there were only six manufactured, and they cannot be generally evaluated.

| Exc. | V.G. | Good | Fair | Poor |
|------|------|------|------|------|
| 6000 | 4500 | 3750 | 2750 | 2000 |

## Monogram Grade

This version is offered standard with automatic ejectors and a single-selective trigger.

| Exc. | V.G. | Good | Fair | Poor |
|-------|-------|------|------|------|
| 12500 | 10000 | 7500 | 5000 | 3750 |

There were two higher grades offered--the Premier Grade and the Deluxe Grade. They are extremely rare, and there have not been enough transactions to generally evaluate them.

## Fulton Model

This is a utility, side-by-side double-barrel shotgun chambered for 12, 16, or 20 gauge. It is offered with various barrel lengths and choke combinations. It has double triggers and extractors. Although this is technically not an L. C. Smith, it was manufactured by Hunter Arms Company.

| Exc. | V.G. | Good | Fair | Poor |
|------|------|------|------|------|
| 650 | 550 | 450 | 300 | 200 |

## Fulton Special

This was a slightly higher-grade version of the utility Fulton gun.

| Exc. | V.G. | Good | Fair | Poor |
|------|------|------|------|------|
| 750 | 650 | 500 | 350 | 250 |

## Hunter Special

This is a similar utility-grade gun that features the rotary locking-bolt system found on the L. C. Smith shotguns.

| Exc. | V.G. | Good | Fair | Poor |
|------|------|------|------|------|
| 600 | 500 | 400 | 250 | 175 |

## Single Barrel Trap Guns

These are high-grade, break-open, single-shot trap guns chambered for 12 gauge only. They features 32" or 34" vent-rib barrels that are full-choked. They have boxlock actions and are standard with automatic ejectors. The finish is blued and case-colored, and they have a checkered walnut stock with a recoil pad. The various models differ in the amount of ornamentation and the quality of the materials and workmanship utilized in their construction. There was a total of approximately 2,650 manufactured between 1917 and 1951. Although these firearms are actually rarer and just as high a quality as their side-by-side counterparts, they are simply not as collectible as the side-by-side variations. It would still behoove the astute firearms investor to secure a qualified, individual appraisal if a transaction is contemplated.

## Olympic Grade

| Exc. | V.G. | Good | Fair | Poor |
|------|------|------|------|------|
| 1500 | 1250 | 950 | 700 | 600 |

## Specialty Grade

| Exc. | V.G. | Good | Fair | Poor |
|------|------|------|------|------|
| 2000 | 1750 | 1300 | 1000 | 800 |

## Crown Grade

| Exc. | V.G. | Good | Fair | Poor |
|------|------|------|------|------|
| 3500 | 3000 | 2250 | 1500 | 1250 |

## Monogram Grade

| Exc. | V.G. | Good | Fair | Poor |
|------|------|------|------|------|
| 6000 | 5000 | 3500 | 2500 | 1750 |

## Premier Grade

| Exc. | V.G. | Good | Fair | Poor |
|-------|------|------|------|------|
| 10000 | 8500 | 5500 | 4000 | 2750 |

## Deluxe Grade

| Exc. | V.G. | Good | Fair | Poor |
|-------|-------|------|------|------|
| 14000 | 12500 | 9500 | 7500 | 4500 |

## 1968 Model

This is a side-by-side double-barrel shotgun chambered for 12 gauge with a 28" vent-rib barrel, choked full-and-modified. It features a sidelock action with double triggers and extractors. The finish is blued and case-colored, with a checkered walnut stock. This shotgun was manufactured by Marlin between 1968 and 1973.

| Exc. | V.G. | Good | Fair | Poor |
|------|------|------|------|------|
| 700 | 600 | 550 | 450 | 300 |

## 1968 Deluxe Model

This is similar to the 1968 Model but features a Simmons floating rib and a beavertail-type forearm. It was manufactured by Marlin between 1971 and 1973.

| Exc. | V.G. | Good | Fair | Poor |
|------|------|------|------|------|
| 1000 | 850 | 750 | 600 | 400 |

# SMITH & WESSON
## Springfield, Massachusetts

The gun manufacturing company known as Smith & Wesson became reality in 1852 with the team of Horace Smith and Daniel B. Wesson entering into a partnership. They were both experienced in the field of firearms design, and the initial venture of the newly chartered firm was to be a novel lever-action repeating handgun that was based on an improvement of an existing patent. This handgun was to be known as the iron-frame Volcanic, and there were 1,000 produced before 1855, when Smith & Wesson sold their rights to the recently formed Volcanic Repeating Arms Company. The Volcanic Company did not last long before it was absorbed by the forerunner to the Winchester Company, the New Haven Arms Co. Meanwhile, Smith & Wesson had left Volcanic and headed for Springfield, Massachusetts, where they formed a second partnership and began the manufacture and development of revolving handguns. This time the partners entered into an exclusive agreement with Rollin White, the patent holder for the bored-through cylinder. For the sum of 25 cents per unit, Smith & Wesson would have sole rights to manufacture metallic cartridge arms. They were astute enough to put in a clause making White responsible for legal costs incurred in stopping infringements. The history of the Smith & Wesson Company is closely tied to the development of our young country, and--like Colt, Winchester and other arms companies--a great deal of historic significance is attributed to the earlier models. The collection of Smith & Wesson handguns has always been extremely popular. They manufactured over 100 different models--most in significant quantities to provide incentive for acquisition. The literature available on the company and its products is quite informative; and while it is not as well documented as Colt, education on the subject is available. The company's records are fairly complete for most models, and they will provide authentication if requested. The recent history of the company has been somewhat complex, as it has been bought and sold a number of times by holding companies who weren't remotely connected to the firearms business. In 1957 they were purchased and became a wholly owned subsidiary of the Bangor Punta Corporation. In 1983 the company was purchased by Lear Sigler Corp. This company retained ownership only four years; and in May of 1987, S&W was sold to R.L. Tompkins, a plumbing company from Great Britain.

Smith & Wesson, for the most part, identified their different models by numerical designation. This led to the adoption of nicknames which sometimes became more widely used than the proper nomenclature. We list the models in order of their numerical progression--supplying the nicknames as well, if they are applicable.

It is important to bear in mind, with the Smith & Wesson line as well as with Colt, that there are a great number of variances that can affect the values. The embellishments, engraving, precious grip materials, casing, as well as provenance, can affect value. Many famous, as well as infamous, personages used the products of this company to establish their place in history. All this considered, it surely would behoove the interested individual to avail oneself of the information available on the subject before embarking on a journey of acquisition.

## SMITH & WESSON ANTIQUE HANDGUNS

### Model 1, 1st Issue Revolver

This was the first metallic cartridge arm produced by S&W. It is a small revolver that weighs approximately 10 ounces and is chambered for the .22 short rimfire cartridge. The octagonal barrel is 3.25" long. It holds 7 shots. The barrel and non-fluted cylinder pivot upward upon release of the protruding bayonet-type catch under the frame. This model has a square butt with rosewood grips. The frame is made of brass and is silver-plated. The barrel and cylinder are blued. The barrel is stamped with the company name and address; the patent dates also appear. The edges of the frame are rounded on the 1st Issue, and the sideplate is round. Smith & Wesson manufactured approximately 11,670 of these revolvers between 1857 and 1860. Since this was the first of its kind, it is not difficult to understand the need for the number of variations within this model designation. Many small improvements were made on the way to the next model. These variations are as follows:

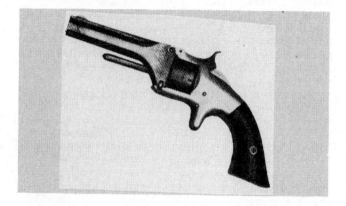

### 1st Type
Serial range 1 to low 200's, revolving recoil shield, bayonet type catch on frame.

| Exc. | V.G. | Good | Fair | Poor |
|------|------|------|------|------|
| 5000 | 4000 | 3000 | 2000 | 1000 |

### 2nd Type
Serial range low 200's to 1,130, improved recoil plate.

| Exc. | V.G. | Good | Fair | Poor |
|------|------|------|------|------|
| 3000 | 2250 | 1750 | 900 | 500 |

### 3rd Type
Serial range 1,130 to low 3,000's, bayonet catch dropped for spring-loaded side catch.

| Exc. | V.G. | Good | Fair | Poor |
|------|------|------|------|------|
| 2250 | 1750 | 1400 | 850 | 450 |

### 4th Type
Serial range low 3,000's to low 4,200's, recoil shield made much smaller.

| Exc. | V.G. | Good | Fair | Poor |
|------|------|------|------|------|
| 2250 | 1750 | 1400 | 850 | 450 |

### 5th Type
Serial range low 4,200's to low 5,500's, has 5-groove rifling instead of 3.

| Exc. | V.G. | Good | Fair | Poor |
|------|------|------|------|------|
| 2250 | 1750 | 1400 | 850 | 450 |

### 6th Type
Serial range low 5,500's to end of production 11,670. A cylinder ratchet replaced the revolving recoil shield.

| Exc. | V.G. | Good | Fair | Poor |
|------|------|------|------|------|
| 2000 | 1500 | 1250 | 750 | 400 |

### Model 1 2nd Issue
This model is physically very similar in appearance to the 1st Issue. There are several notable differences that make identification rather simple. The sides of the frame on the 2nd Issue are flat--not rounded as on the 1st Issue. The sideplate is irregular in shape--not round like on the 1st Issue. There have been 2nd Issues noted with full silver or nickel plating. Smith & Wesson manufactured approximately 117,000 of these revolvers between 1860 and 1868. The serial numbers started at 11,671 where the 1st Issue left off.

There were approximately 4,400 revolvers marked "2D Qual'ty" on the barrels. These revolvers were slightly defective and were sold at a lesser price. They will bring an approximate 100% premium on today's market.

| Exc. | V.G. | Good | Fair | Poor |
|------|------|------|------|------|
| 450 | 400 | 350 | 275 | 125 |

### Model 1 3rd Issue
This is an improved version of its forerunners. Another .22 short rimfire, 7-shot revolver, this Model has a fluted cylinder and a round barrel with a raised rib. It features birdshead type grips of rosewood and is either fully blued, nickel-plated, or two-toned with the frame nickel and the barrel and cylinder blued. There are two barrel lengths offered--3.25" and 2- 11/16" eleven sixteenths inches. Serial numbering began with #1 and continued to 131,163. They were manufactured between 1868 and 1881.

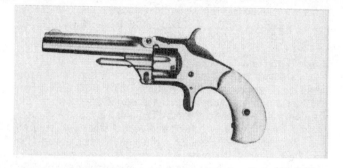

### Shorter Barrelled Version

| Exc. | V.G. | Good | Fair | Poor |
|------|------|------|------|------|
| 400 | 350 | 300 | 250 | 100 |

### Longer Barrelled Version

| Exc. | V.G. | Good | Fair | Poor |
|------|------|------|------|------|
| 450 | 400 | 350 | 275 | 125 |

### Model 1-1/2 1st Issue
This model was the first of the .32-caliber rimfire revolvers that S&W produced. It is a larger version of the Model 1 but is physically similar in appearance. The Model 1-1/2 was offered with a 3.5" or 4" octagonal barrel and has a 5-shot non-fluted cylinder and a square butt with rosewood grips. The finish is blued or nickel-plated. The serial numbering on this model ran from #1-26,300; and, interestingly to note, S&W had most of the parts for this revolver manufactured on contract by King & Smith of Middletown, Connecticut. Smith & Wesson merely assembled and finished them. They were produced between 1865 and 1868.

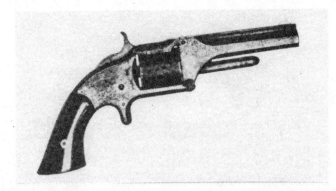

| Exc. | V.G. | Good | Fair | Poor |
|------|------|------|------|------|
| 450 | 400 | 350 | 275 | 125 |

### Model 1-1/2 2nd Issue

This model is an improved version of the 1st Issue. It is somewhat similar in appearance with a few notable exceptions. The barrel is 2.5" or 3.5" in length, round with a raised rib. The grip is of the birdshead configuration, and the 5-shot cylinder is fluted and chambered for the .32 rimfire long cartridge. The cylinder stop is located in the top frame instead of the bottom. The finish and grip material are the same as the 1st Issue. There were approximately 100,700 manufactured between 1868 and 1875.

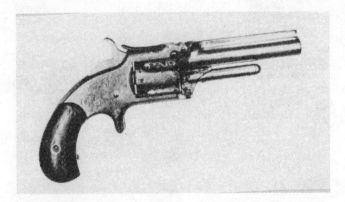

### Transitional Model

Approximately 1,000-1,200 of these were produced by fitting 1st Issue cylinders and barrels to 2nd Issue frames. These revolvers fall into the serial number range 27,200-28,800.

| Exc. | V.G. | Good | Fair | Poor |
|------|------|------|------|------|
| 1250 | 1000 | 800 | 650 | 400 |

**3.5" Barrel**

| Exc. | V.G. | Good | Fair | Poor |
|------|------|------|------|------|
| 400 | 350 | 300 | 250 | 100 |

**2.5" Barrel**

| Exc. | V.G. | Good | Fair | Poor |
|------|------|------|------|------|
| 500 | 400 | 350 | 300 | 150 |

### Model 1 1/2 Single Action

This model represented the first .32 S&W caliber topbreak revolver which automatically ejected the spent cartridges upon opening. This model has a 5-shot fluted cylinder and a birdshead grip of wood or checkered hard rubber and was offered with barrel lengths of 3", 3.5", 6", 8", and 10". This model pivots downward on opening and features a rebounding hammer which made the weapon much safer to fully load. There were approximately 97,574 manufactured between 1878 and 1892.

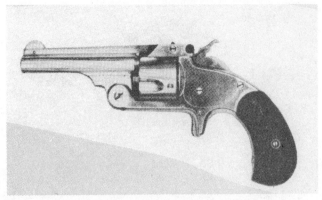

**Early Model Without Strain Screw--Under #6,500**

| Exc. | V.G. | Good | Fair | Poor |
|------|------|------|------|------|
| 450 | 400 | 350 | 200 | 125 |

**Later Model With Strain Screw**

| Exc. | V.G. | Good | Fair | Poor |
|------|------|------|------|------|
| 450 | 400 | 350 | 200 | 125 |

**8" or 10" Barrel Model**

| Exc. | V.G. | Good | Fair | Poor |
|------|------|------|------|------|
| 800 | 700 | 500 | 400 | 250 |

### Model 2 Army or Old Model

This revolver was extremely successful from a commercial standpoint. It was released just in time for the commencement of hostilities in the Civil War. Smith & Wesson had, in this revolver, the only weapon able to fire self-contained cartridges and be easily carried as a backup by soldiers going off to war. This resulted in a backlog of more than three years before the company finally stopped taking orders. This model is chambered for .32 rimfire long and has a 6-shot non-fluted cylinder and 4", 5", or 6" barrel lengths. It has a square butt with rosewood grips and is either blued or nickel-plated. There were approximately 77,155 manufactured between 1861 and 1874.

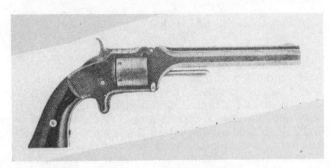

**5" or 6" Barrel**

| Exc. | V.G. | Good | Fair | Poor |
|------|------|------|------|------|
| 550 | 500 | 450 | 300 | 200 |

**4" Barrel--Rare! Fakes Noted**

| Exc. | V.G. | Good | Fair | Poor |
|------|------|------|------|------|
| 1000 | 850 | 700 | 500 | 300 |

### .38 1st Model Single Action

This model is sometimes called the "Baby Russian." It is a topbreak, automatic-ejecting revolver chambered for the .38 S&W cartridge. It is offered with either a 3.25" or 4" round barrel with a raised rib, has a 5-shot fluted cylinder, and is finished in blue or nickel plating. The butt is rounded, with wood or checkered hard rubber grips inlaid with the S&W medallion. It has a spur trigger. There were approximately 25,548 manufactured in 1876 and 1877.

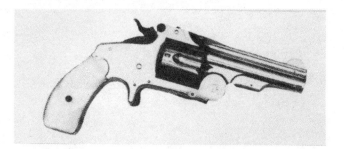

| Exc. | V.G. | Good | Fair | Poor |
|------|------|------|------|------|
| 400  | 350  | 300  | 200  | 150  |

### .38 2nd Model Single Action

With the exception of an improved and shortened ejector assembly and the availability of additional barrel lengths of 3.25", 4", 5", 6", 8", and 10", this model is quite similar in appearance to the 1st Model. There were approximately 108,255 manufactured between 1877 and 1891.

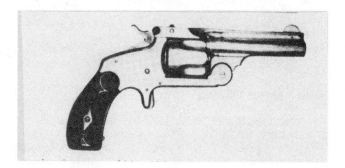

**8" and 10" Barrel**

| Exc. | V.G. | Good | Fair | Poor |
|------|------|------|------|------|
| 750  | 675  | 550  | 400  | 300  |

**Shorter Barrels**

| Exc. | V.G. | Good | Fair | Poor |
|------|------|------|------|------|
| 350  | 300  | 250  | 125  | 100  |

### .38 3rd Model Single Action

This model differs from the ones previously discussed chiefly in that it has a triggerguard. It is chambered for the .38 S&W cartridge, has a 5-shot fluted cylinder, and is a topbreak design with automatic ejection upon opening. The barrel lengths are 3.25", 4", 5", and 6". The finish is blued or nickel-plated. The butt is rounded, with checkered hard rubber grips featuring S&W medallions. There were approximately 26,850 manufactured between 1891 and 1911.

| Exc. | V.G. | Good | Fair | Poor |
|------|------|------|------|------|
| 600  | 550  | 450  | 300  | 175  |

### .38 Mexican Model Single Action

This extremely rare model is quite similar in appearance to the 3rd Model Single Action. The notable differences are the flat hammer sides with no outward flaring of the spur. The spur trigger assembly was not made integrally with the frame but is a separate part added to it. One must excercise extreme caution as S&W offered a kit that would convert the triggerguard assembly of the Third Model to the spur trigger of the Mexican Model. This, coupled with the fact that both models fall within the same serial range, can present a real identification problem. Another feature of the Mexican Model is the absence of a half cock. There were only 2,000 Mexican Models manufactured between 1891 and 1911.

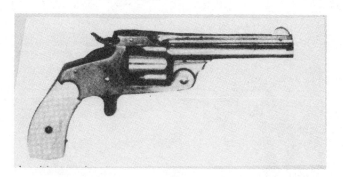

| Exc.  | V.G.  | Good | Fair | Poor |
|-------|-------|------|------|------|
| 1500  | 1250  | 900  | 650  | 450  |

### Model .320 Revolving Rifle

This model is very rare and unique--a prize to a S&W collector. The Revolving Rifle is chambered for the .320 S&W Rifle cartridge, has a 6-shot fluted cylinder and is offered with a 16", 18", and 20" barrel. Only 76 of the rifles are nickel-plated, and the remainder of the production is blued. The butt is rounded, with reddish-colored checkered hard rubber grips and a forearm of the same material. There is a detachable shoulder stock with a black hard rubber buttplate featuring the S&W logo. The rifle was furnished in a leather carrying case with accessories. As fine a firearm as this was, it was a commercial failure for S&W; and they finally came to the realization that the public did not want a revolving rifle. They manufactured only 977 of them between 1879 and 1887.

Values Are for Complete Unit.
Deduct 40 Percent Without Stock.

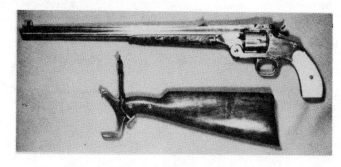

| Exc.  | V.G.  | Good  | Fair  | Poor  |
|-------|-------|-------|-------|-------|
| 8000  | 6500  | 4500  | 2500  | 1700  |

### .32 1st Model Double Action

This is one of the rarest of all S&W revolvers. There were only 30 manufactured. It also has a straight-sided sideplate which weakens a revolver frame. Perhaps this was the reason that so few were made. This model was the first break-open, double-action, automatic-ejecting .32 that S&W produced. It features a 3" round barrel with raised rib, a 5-shot fluted cylinder, and round butt with plain, uncheckered, black hard rubber grips. The finish is blued or nickel-plated. All 30 of these revolvers were manufactured in 1880.

| Exc.  | V.G.  | Good  | Fair  | Poor  |
|-------|-------|-------|-------|-------|
| 3500  | 2800  | 2000  | 1500  | 950   |

## .38 1st Model Double Action

This model is similar in appearance to the .32 1st Model but is chambered for the .38 S&W cartridge. The grips are checkered, and there were 4,000 manufactured in 1880.

| Exc. | V.G. | Good | Fair | Poor |
|------|------|------|------|------|
| 2500 | 2250 | 1750 | 1250 | 950 |

## .32 2nd Model Double Action

This revolver is chambered for the .32 S&W cartridge and has a 3" round barrel with a raised rib. The 5-shot cylinder is fluted, and the finish is blued or nickel-plated. It is a topbreak design with a round butt. The grips are either checkered or floral- embossed hard rubber with the S&W monogram. This model has an oval sideplate, eliminating the weakness of the 1st Model. There were approximately 22,142 manufactured between 1880 and 1882.

| Exc. | V.G. | Good | Fair | Poor |
|------|------|------|------|------|
| 300 | 250 | 200 | 125 | 100 |

## .38 2nd Model Double Action

This is similar in appearance to the .32 2nd Model but is chambered for the .38 S&W cartridge. There were approximately 115,000 manufactured between 1880 and 1884.

| Exc. | V.G. | Good | Fair | Poor |
|------|------|------|------|------|
| 300 | 250 | 200 | 125 | 100 |

## .32 3rd Model Double Action

This Model incorporates internal improvements that are not evident in appearance. The most notable identifiable difference between this Model and its predecessors is in the surface of the cylinder. The flutes are longer; there is only one set of stops instead of two; and the free groove is no longer present. There were approximately 21,232 manufactured in 1882 and 1883.

| Exc. | V.G. | Good | Fair | Poor |
|------|------|------|------|------|
| 300 | 250 | 200 | 125 | 100 |

## .38 3rd Model Double Action

Essentially the same in appearance as the .32 Model but chambered for the .38 S&W cartridge, it is also offered with a 3.25", 4", 5", 6", 8", and 10" barrel. There were approximately 203,700 manufactured between 1884 and 1895.

### 8" and 10" Barrel

| Exc. | V.G. | Good | Fair | Poor |
|------|------|------|------|------|
| 1000 | 900 | 700 | 500 | 400 |

### Standard Barrel

| Exc. | V.G. | Good | Fair | Poor |
|------|------|------|------|------|
| 300 | 250 | 200 | 125 | 100 |

## .32 4th Model Double Action

This model is quite similar in appearance to the 3rd Model except that the triggerguard is oval in shape instead of the squared back of the previous models. There were also internal improvements. There were approximately 239,600 manufactured between 1883 and 1909.

| Exc. | V.G. | Good | Fair | Poor |
|------|------|------|------|------|
| 325 | 275 | 225 | 150 | 100 |

## .38 4th Model Double Action

This is the .38 S&W version of the 4th Model. There were approximately 216,300 manufactured between 1895 and 1909.

| Exc. | V.G. | Good | Fair | Poor |
|------|------|------|------|------|
| 300 | 250 | 200 | 125 | 100 |

## .32 5th Model Double Action

The only difference between this model and its predecessors is that this model has the front sight machined as an integral part of the barrel rib. On the other models, the sight was pinned in place. There were approximately 91,417 manufactured between 1909 and 1919.

| Exc. | V.G. | Good | Fair | Poor |
|------|------|------|------|------|
| 300 | 250 | 200 | 125 | 100 |

## .38 5th Model Double Action

This model is the same as the .32 except that it is chambered for the .38 S&W cartridge. There were approximately 15,000 manufactured between 1909 and 1911.

| Exc. | V.G. | Good | Fair | Poor |
|------|------|------|------|------|
| 350 | 300 | 250 | 150 | 125 |

## Model No.3 1st Model Single Action

This model represented a number of firsts for the Smith & Wesson Company. It was the first of the top-break, automatic ejection revolvers. It was also the first Smith & Wesson in a large caliber (it is chambered for the .44 S&W American cartridge as well as the .44 rimfire Henry on rare occasions). It was also known as the 1st Model American. This large revolver is offered with an 8" round barrel with a raised rib. It has a 6-shot fluted cylinder and a square butt with walnut grips. It is blued or nickel-plated. It is interesting to note that this model appeared three years before Colt's Single Action Army and perhaps, more than any other model, was associated with the historic American West. There were only 8,000 manufactured between 1870 and 1872.

### Standard Production Model

| Exc. | V.G. | Good | Fair | Poor |
|------|------|------|------|------|
| 2500 | 2250 | 1850 | 950 | 650 |

**Transition Model—Serial Range #6466-6744**
Shorter cylinder (1.423"), improved barrel catch.

| Exc. | V.G. | Good | Fair | Poor |
|------|------|------|------|------|
| 3000 | 2500 | 2000 | 1150 | 700 |

**U.S. Army Order--Serial Range #125-2199**
1000 produced with "U.S." stamped on top of barrel; "OWA," on left grip.

| Exc. | V.G. | Good | Fair | Poor |
|------|------|------|------|------|
| 3500 | 3000 | 2500 | 1500 | 800 |

**.44 Rimfire Henry Model**
Only 100 produced throughout serial range.

| Exc. | V.G. | Good | Fair | Poor |
|------|------|------|------|------|
| 4000 | 3500 | 3000 | 1750 | 1200 |

**Model No.3 2nd Model Single Action**
This is basically an improved version of the 1st Model. The most notable difference is the larger diameter trigger pivot pin and the frame protrusions above the trigger to accommodate it. The front sight blade on this model is made of steel instead of nickel silver. This model is commonly known as the 2nd Model American. There have been 5.5", 6", 6.5", and 7" barrels noted; but they are extremely scarce and would bring a 40 percent premium over the standard 8" model --so one should be quite wary of shortened fraudulent specimens. There were approximately 20,735 manufactured, including 3,014 chambered for .44 rimfire Henry, between 1872 and 1874.

**.44 Rimfire Henry**

| Exc. | V.G. | Good | Fair | Poor |
|------|------|------|------|------|
| 3250 | 2750 | 2000 | 1250 | 750 |

**Standard 8" Model**

| Exc. | V.G. | Good | Fair | Poor |
|------|------|------|------|------|
| 2500 | 2000 | 1500 | 950 | 550 |

**Model 3 Russian 1st Model**
This model is quite similar in appearance to the 1st and 2nd Model American revolvers. The markings on this revolver are different; and the caliber for which it is chambered, .44 S&W Russian, is different. There were approximately 20,000 Russian-Contract revolvers. The serial range is #1-20,000. They are marked in Russian Cyrillic letters. The Russian double-headed eagle is stamped on the rear portion of the barrel with inspector's marks underneath it. All of the Contract guns have 8" barrels and lanyard swivels on the butt. These are rarely encountered, as most were shipped to Russia. The commercial run of this model numbered approximately 4,655. The barrels are stamped in English and include the words "Russian Model." Some are found with 6" and 7" barrels, as well as the standard 8". There were also 500 revolvers that were rejected from the Russian Contract series and sold on the commercial market. Some of these are marked in English; some, Cyrillic. Some have the Cyrillic markings ground off and the English restamped. This model was manufactured from 1871 to 1874.

**Russian Contract Model**

| Exc. | V.G. | Good | Fair | Poor |
|------|------|------|------|------|
| 3000 | 2500 | 1750 | 850 | 550 |

**Commercial Model**

| Exc. | V.G. | Good | Fair | Poor |
|------|------|------|------|------|
| 2000 | 1500 | 1250 | 750 | 450 |

**Rejected Russian Contract Model**

| Exc. | V.G. | Good | Fair | Poor |
|------|------|------|------|------|
| 2000 | 1500 | 1250 | 750 | 450 |

**Model 3 Russian 2nd Model**
This revolver was known as the "Old Model Russian." This is a complicated model to understand as there are many variations within the model designation. The serial numbering is quite complex as well, and values vary greatly due to relatively minor model differences. Before purchasing this model, it would be advisable to secure competent appraisal as well as to read refer-

ence materials solely devoted to this firearm. This model is chambered for the .44 S&W Russian, as well as the .44 rimfire Henry cartridge. It has a 7" barrel and a round butt featuring a projection on the frame that fits into the thumb web. The grips are walnut, and the finish is blue or nickel-plated. The triggerguard has a reverse curved spur on the bottom. There were approximately 85,200 manufactured between 1873 and 1878.

**Commercial Model**
6,200 made, .44 S&W Russian, English markings.

| Exc. | V.G. | Good | Fair | Poor |
|------|------|------|------|------|
| 1500 | 1250 | 950 | 600 | 400 |

**.44 Rimfire Henry Model**
500 made.

| Exc. | V.G. | Good | Fair | Poor |
|------|------|------|------|------|
| 2200 | 1750 | 1300 | 850 | 600 |

**Russian Contract Model**
70,000 made; rare, as most were shipped to Russia. Cyrillic markings; lanyard swivel on butt.

| Exc. | V.G. | Good | Fair | Poor |
|------|------|------|------|------|
| 1750 | 1500 | 1250 | 800 | 550 |

**1st Model Turkish Contract**
.44 rimfire Henry, special rimfire frames, serial numbered in own range #1-1,000.

| Exc. | V.G. | Good | Fair | Poor |
|------|------|------|------|------|
| 3000 | 2500 | 1750 | 850 | 550 |

**2nd Model Turkish Contract**
Made from altered centerfire frames from the regular commercial serial range. 1,000 made. Watch for fakes.

| Exc. | V.G. | Good | Fair | Poor |
|------|------|------|------|------|
| 2750 | 2250 | 1500 | 750 | 500 |

**Japanese Govt. Contract**
5,000 made between the #1-9,000 serial range. The Japanese naval insignia, an anchor over two wavy lines, found on the butt. The barrel is Japanese proofed, and the words "Jan.19, 75 REISSUE July 25, 1871" are stamped on the barrel, as well.

| Exc. | V.G. | Good | Fair | Poor |
|------|------|------|------|------|
| 1500 | 1250 | 950 | 600 | 400 |

**Model 3 Russian 3rd Model**
This revolver is also known as the "New Model Russian". It is chambered for the .44 S&W Russian and the .44 rimfire Henry cartridge. The barrel is 6.5", and the round butt is the same humped-back affair as the 2nd Model. The grips are walnut; and the finish, blue or nickel-plated. The most notable differences in appearance between this model and the 2nd Model are the shorter extractor housing under the barrel and the integral front sight blade instead of the pinned-on one found on the previous models. This is another model that bears careful research before attempting to evaluate. Minor variances can greatly affect values. Secure detailed reference materials and qualified appraisal. There were approximately 60,638 manufactured between 1874 and 1878.

## Commercial Model
.44 S&W Russian, marked "Russian Model" in English, 13,500 made.

| Exc. | V.G. | Good | Fair | Poor |
|------|------|------|------|------|
| 1250 | 1000 | 800 | 500 | 300 |

## .44 Rimfire Henry Model

| Exc. | V.G. | Good | Fair | Poor |
|------|------|------|------|------|
| 2000 | 1750 | 1250 | 750 | 550 |

## Turkish Model
5,000 made of altered centerfire frames, made to fire .44 rimfire Henry. "W" inspector's mark on butt. Fakes have been noted; be aware.

| Exc. | V.G. | Good | Fair | Poor |
|------|------|------|------|------|
| 1750 | 1500 | 1250 | 800 | 550 |

## Japanese Contract Model
1,000 made; has the Japanese naval insignia, an anchor over two wavy lines, stamped on the butt.

| Exc. | V.G. | Good | Fair | Poor |
|------|------|------|------|------|
| 1250 | 1000 | 800 | 500 | 300 |

## Model 3 Russian 3rd Model
The German firm of Ludwig Loewe produced a copy of this model that is nearly identical to the S&W. This German revolver was made under Russian contract, as well as for commercial sales. The contract model has different Cyrillic markings than the S&W and the letters "HK" as inspector's marks. The commercial model has the markings in English. The Russian arsenal at Tula also produced a copy of this revolver with a different Cyrillic dated stamping on the barrel.

## German and Russian copies

| Exc. | V.G. | Good | Fair | Poor |
|------|------|------|------|------|
| 1500 | 1250 | 950 | 600 | 400 |

## Model No. 3 Schofield
In 1870 Major George W. Schofield heard about the new S&W Model 3 revolver and wrote to the company expressing a desire to be an exclusive sales representative for them. At that time S&W was earnestly attempting to interest the government in this revolver and obviously felt that the Major could be of help in this endeavor, perhaps because his brother General John Schofield was president of the Small Arms Board. Major Schofield was sent one Model 3 revolver and 500 rounds of ammunition free of charge. After testing the revolver, Schofield felt that it needed a few changes to make it the ideal cavalry sidearm. With the company's approval, Schofield made these changes, secured patents, and proceeded to sell them. The company eventually began production of what became known as the Model 3 Schofield 1st Model. The Major was paid a 50-cent royalty per revolver. The eventual production of this model ran to a total of 8,969, with the last one sold in 1878. What was hoped to be the adopted government-issue sidearm never materialized--for a number of reasons. First, the Colt Single Action Army being used by the cavalry had a longer chamber than the S&W and could fire the Schofield ammunition. The Schofield could not fire the longer Colt .45 cartridges. This resulted in disastrous mixups on more than one occasion, when Colt ammunition was issued to troops armed with the Schofields. It was eventually decided to drop the S&W as an issue weapon. At this time the company was not happy about paying the 50-cent royalty to Major Schofield. Sales of their other models were high; and they simply did not care about this model, so they eventually ceased its production. It was a very popular model on the American Frontier and is quite historically significant.

## Model 3 Schofield 1st Model
The modifications that made this model differ from the other Model 3 revolvers were quite extensive. The Schofield is chambered for the .45 S&W Schofield cartridge. The topbreak latch was moved from the barrel assembly to the frame. It was modified so that the action could be opened by simply pulling back on the latch with the thumb. This made it much easier to reload on horseback, as the reins would not have to be released. A groove was milled in the top of the raised barrel rib to improve the sighting plain. The extractor was changed to a cam-operated rather than rack-and-gear system. The removal of the cylinder was simplified. There were 3,000 contract Schofields and 35 commercial models. The contract revolvers were delivered to the Springfield Armory in July of 1875. These guns are stamped "US" on the butt and have the initials "L," "P," or "W" marking various other parts. The grips have an inspector's cartouche with the initials "CW," "JRJr," or "JFEC." There were 35 1st Models made for and sold to the civilian market; these revolvers do not have the "US" markings. The Schofield has a 7" barrel, 6-shot fluted cylinder, and walnut grips. The 1st Model is blued, with a nickel-plated original finish gun being extremely rare.

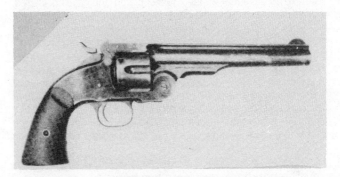

## "US" Contract-- 3,000 Issued

| Exc. | V.G. | Good | Fair | Poor |
|------|------|------|------|------|
| 2500 | 2000 | 1500 | 950 | 650 |

### Civilian Model--35 Made

| Exc. | V.G. | Good | Fair | Poor |
|------|------|------|------|------|
| 3500 | 3000 | 2250 | 1250 | 800 |

## Model 3 Schofield 2nd Model
The difference between the 1st and 2nd Model Schofield revolvers is in the barrel latch system. The 2nd Model latch is rounded and knurled to afford an easier and more positive grip when opening the revolver. A group of 3,000 of these revolvers was delivered to the Springfield Armory in October of 1876, and another 1,000 were delivered in April of 1877. These 2nd Model contract revolvers were all blued. There were an additional 649 civilian guns sold, as well. The civilian models were not "US" marked and were offered either blued or nickel-plated.

## "US" Contract--4,000 Issued

| Exc. | V.G. | Good | Fair | Poor |
|------|------|------|------|------|
| 2800 | 2250 | 1750 | 1100 | 750 |

### Civilian Model--646 Made

| Exc. | V.G. | Good | Fair | Poor |
|------|------|------|------|------|
| 2250 | 1800 | 1500 | 850 | 600 |

## Model 3 Schofield
After the government dropped the Schofield as an issue cavalry sidearm, the remaining U.S. inventory of these revolvers was sold off as military surplus. Many were sold to National Guard units; and the remainder were sold either to Bannerman's or to Schuyler, Hartley & Graham, two large gun dealers who then resold the guns to supply the growing need for guns on the Western frontier. Schuyler, Hartley & Graham sold a number of guns to the Wells Fargo Express Co. These weapons were

nickel-plated and had the barrels shortened to 5", as were many others sold during this period. Beware of fakes when contemplating purchase of the Wells Fargo revolvers.

### Wells Fargo & Co. Model

| Exc. | V.G. | Good | Fair | Poor |
|------|------|------|------|------|
| 2250 | 1800 | 1500 | 850 | 600 |

### New Model No. 3 Single Action

The S&W company, at this time, was quite interested in perfecting the Model 3 revolver. The Russian contracts were almost filled; and time was on their side, so they decided to spend the time necessary to improve on this design. In 1877 this project was undertaken. The extractor housing was shortened; the cylinder retention system was improved; and the shape of the grip was changed to a more streamlined and attractive configuration. This New Model has a 3.5", 4", 5", 6", 6.5", 7", 7.5", or 8" barrel length with a 6-shot fluted cylinder. The 6.5" barrel and .44 S&W Russian chambering is the most often encountered variation of this model, but it is also chambered for .32 S&W, .32-44 S&W, .320 S&W Rev. Rifle, .38 S&W, .38-40, .38-44 S&W, .41 S&W, .44 rimfire Henry, .44 S&W American, .44-40, .45 S&W Schofield, .450 Rev., .45 Webley, .455 MkI and .455 MkII. They are either blued or nickel-plated and have checkered hard rubber grips with the S&W logo molded into them or walnut grips. There are many sub-variations within this model designation, and the potential collector should secure detailed reference material that deals with this model. There were approximately 35,796 of these revolvers manufactured between 1878 and 1912. Nearly 40 percent were exported to fill contracts with Japan, Australia, Argentina, England, Spain, and Cuba. There were some sent to Asia, as well. The proofmarks of these countries will establish their provenance but will not add appreciably to standard values.

### Standard Model

6.5" barrel, .44-S&W Russian.

| Exc. | V.G. | Good | Fair | Poor |
|------|------|------|------|------|
| 1250 | 1000 | 750 | 600 | 450 |

Calibers other than .44 S&W Russian and barrel lengths other than 6.5" will bring premiums depending on rarity of the combination. It is necessary to secure individual appraisal, as the number of variations places the pricing of these revolvers outside the purview of this book.

### Japanese Naval Contract

This was the largest foreign purchaser of this model. There were over 1,500 produced with the anchor insignia stamped on the frame.

| Exc. | V.G. | Good | Fair | Poor |
|------|------|------|------|------|
| 1300 | 1100 | 800 | 650 | 500 |

### Japanese Artillery Contract

This variation is numbered in the 25,000 serial range. They are blued, with a 7" barrel and a lanyard swivel on the butt. Japanese characters are stamped on the extractor housing.

| Exc. | V.G. | Good | Fair | Poor |
|------|------|------|------|------|
| 1750 | 1500 | 1000 | 800 | 600 |

### Maryland Militia Model

This variation is nickel-plated, has a 6.5" barrel, and is chambered for the .44 S&W Russian cartridge. The butt is stamped "U.S.," and the inspector's marks "HN" and "DAL" under the date 1878 appear on the revolver. There were 280 manufactured between serial numbers 7126 and 7405.

| Exc. | V.G. | Good | Fair | Poor |
|------|------|------|------|------|
| 3500 | 3000 | 2250 | 1500 | 1000 |

### Australian Contract

This variation is nickel-plated, is chambered for the .44 S&W Russian cartridge, and is marked with the Australian Colonial Police Broad Arrow on the butt. There were 250 manufactured with 7" barrels and detachable shoulder stocks. The stock has the Broad Arrow stamped on the lower tang. There were also 30 manufactured with 6.5" barrels without the stocks. They all are numbered in the 12,000-13,000 serial range.

### Revolver Only

| Exc. | V.G. | Good | Fair | Poor |
|------|------|------|------|------|
| 1750 | 1500 | 1000 | 800 | 600 |

### Stock Only

| Exc. | V.G. | Good | Fair | Poor |
|------|------|------|------|------|
| 500 | 400 | 350 | 250 | 200 |

### Argentine Model

This was essentially not a factory contract but a sale through Schuyler, Hartley and Graham. They are stamped "Ejercito/Argentino" in front of the triggerguard. The order amounted to some 2,000 revolvers between the serial numbers 50 and 3400.

| Exc. | V.G. | Good | Fair | Poor |
|------|------|------|------|------|
| 1500 | 1250 | 950 | 700 | 500 |

### Turkish Model

This is essentially the New Model No. 3 chambered for the .44 rimfire Henry cartridge. It is stamped with the letters "P", "U" and "AFC" on various parts of the revolver. The barrels are all 6.5"; the finish, blued with walnut grips. Lanyard swivels are found on the butt. There were 5,461 manufactured and serial numbered in their own range, starting at #1 through #5,461 between 1879 and 1883.

| Exc. | V.G. | Good | Fair | Poor |
|------|------|------|------|------|
| 2000 | 1750 | 1450 | 850 | 600 |

### New Model No. 3 Target Single Action

This revolver is very similar in appearance to the standard New Model No. 3. It has a 6.5" round barrel with a raised rib and 6-shot fluted cylinder and is finished in blue or nickel plated. The grips are either walnut or checkered hard rubber with the S&W logo molded into them. This model is chambered in either .32-44 S&W Target or .38-44 S&W Target. This model was offered with a detachable shoulder stock as an option. These stocks are extremely scarce on today's market. There were approximately 4,333 manufactured between 1887 and 1910. Shoulder Stock--Add 40 Percent.

| Exc. | V.G. | Good | Fair | Poor |
|------|------|------|------|------|
| 1250 | 1000 | 850 | 600 | 400 |

### New Model No. 3 Frontier Single Action

This is another model very similar in appearance to the standard New Model No. 3. It has a 4", 5", or 6.5" barrel and is chambered for the .44-40 Winchester cartridge. Later the company converted 786 revolvers to .44 S&W Russian and sold them to Japan. This model is either blued or nickel-plated and has checkered grips of walnut or hard rubber. They are serial numbered in their own range from #1 through #2,072 and were manufactured from 1885 until 1908. This model was designed to compete with the Colt Single Action Army but was not successful.

### .44-40 Commercial Model

| Exc. | V.G. | Good | Fair | Poor |
|------|------|------|------|------|
| 2000 | 1750 | 1500 | 1000 | 750 |

### Japanese Purchase Converted to .44 S&W Russian

| Exc. | V.G. | Good | Fair | Poor |
|------|------|------|------|------|
| 2000 | 1750 | 1500 | 1000 | 750 |

### New Model No. 3 .38 Winchester

This variation was the last of the No.3's to be introduced. It was offered in .38-40 Winchester as a separate model from 1900 until 1907. The finish is blue or nickel plate, and the grips are checkered hard rubber or walnut. 4" or 6.5" barrels were offered. This model was not at all popular, as only 74 were manufactured in their own serial range #1 through #74. Today collectors seek this model most avidly, as it is extremely rare.

| Exc. | V.G. | Good | Fair | Poor |
|------|------|------|------|------|
| 2000 | 1750 | 1500 | 1000 | 750 |

### .44 Double Action 1st Model

This model is a topbreak revolver that automatically ejects the spent cartridge cases upon opening. The barrel latch is located at the top and rear of the cylinder; the pivot, in front and at the bottom. This model was also known as "The D.A. Frontier" or "The New Model Navy." The revolver is chambered for the .44S&W Russian. It is also found on rare occasions chambered for the .38-40 and the .44-40 Winchester. The barrel lengths are 4", 5", 6", and 6.5", round with a raised rib. The cylinder holds 6 shots and is fluted. It has double sets of stop notches and long free grooves between the stops. It is serial numbered in its own range, beginning at #1. There were approximately 54,000 manufactured between 1881 and 1913.

### Standard .44 S&W Russian

| Exc. | V.G. | Good | Fair | Poor |
|------|------|------|------|------|
| 1000 | 800 | 600 | 400 | 250 |

### .44-40 Serial Range #1-15,340

Barrel marked ".44 Winchester cartridge"; 15,340 made.

| Exc. | V.G. | Good | Fair | Poor |
|------|------|------|------|------|
| 1250 | 1000 | 800 | 600 | 400 |

### .38-40 Serial Range #1-276

Very rare; 276 made; ".38 Winchester cartridge" on barrel.

| Exc. | V.G. | Good | Fair | Poor |
|------|------|------|------|------|
| 2200 | 1800 | 1400 | 950 | 600 |

### Model 44 Double Action Wesson Favorite

The Favorite is basically a lightened version of the 1st Model D.A. .44. The barrel is thinner and is offered in 5" length only. There are lightening cuts in the frame between the triggerguard and the cylinder; the cylinder diameter was smaller, and there is a groove milled along the barrel rib. The Favorite is chambered for the .44 S&W Russian cartridge and has a 6-shot fluted cylinder with the same double-cylinder stop notches and free grooves as the 1st Model Double Action .44. The company name and address, as well as the patent dates, are stamped into the edge of the cylinder instead of on the barrel rib. It is serial numbered in the same range, between #8,900 and 10,100. The revolver

was most often nickel-plated but was also offered blued. The grips are walnut or checkered hard rubber with the S&W logo molded in. There were approximately 1,000 manufactured in 1882 and 1883.

Blued Model--Add 25 Percent. Watch for Fakes!

**Nickel Plated**

| Exc. | V.G. | Good | Fair | Poor |
|------|------|------|------|------|
| 3000 | 2500 | 2000 | 1250 | 800 |

### Safety Hammerless 1st Model Double Action

This model was a departure from what was commonly being produced at this time. Some attribute the Safety Hammerless design to D. B. Wesson's hearing that a child had been injured by cocking and firing one of the company's pistols. This story has never been proven. Nevertheless, the concealed hammer and grip safety make this an ideal pocket pistol for those needing concealability in a handgun. This is a small revolver chambered for .32 S&W and .38 S&W cartridges. It has a 5-shot fluted cylinder and is offered with a 2", 3", and 3.5" round barrel with a raised rib. The butt is rounded and has checkered hard rubber grips with the S&W logo. The finish is blue or nickel-plated. The revolver is a topbreak, automatic-ejecting design; and the 1st Model has the latch for opening located in the rear center of the topstrap instead of at the sides. The latch is checkered for a positive grip. This model is commonly referred to as the "Lemon Squeezer" because the grip safety must be squeezed as it is fired. There were approximately 5,125 manufactured in .38 S&W in 1887 and 91,417 in .32 between 1888 and 1902.

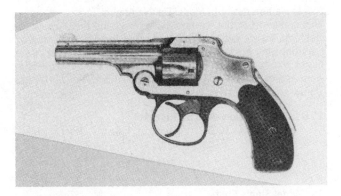

### .38 S&W Model

Also offered with a 6" barrel. RARE! Add 50 Percent.

| Exc. | V.G. | Good | Fair | Poor |
|------|------|------|------|------|
| 550 | 450 | 400 | 250 | 150 |

### .32 S&W Model

| Exc. | V.G. | Good | Fair | Poor |
|------|------|------|------|------|
| 400 | 350 | 300 | 200 | 100 |

### Safety Hammerless 2nd Model Double Action

This model is quite similar in appearance to the 1st Model. The only major difference is in the latch. This model, also called "The Lemon Squeezer," has a catch made up of two checkered buttons on the sides of the frame. A 6"-barrelled version was also offered in the .32 S&W version. There were 37,350 manufactured in .38 S&W between 1887 and 1890. 78,500 were made in .32 S&W between 1902 and 1909.

**.38 S&W**

| Exc. | V.G. | Good | Fair | Poor |
|------|------|------|------|------|
| 400 | 350 | 300 | 200 | 100 |

**.32 S&W**

2" Barrel "Bicycle Revolver"--Add 50 Percent.

| Exc. | V.G. | Good | Fair | Poor |
|------|------|------|------|------|
| 400 | 350 | 300 | 200 | 100 |

### Safety Hammerless 3rd Model Double Action

With the exception of minor internal changes, there are virtually no differences in this and the 2nd Model "Lemon Squeezer." There were 73,500 made in .38 S&W between 1890 and 1898. There were approximately 73,000 in .32 S&W manufactured between 1909 and 1937.

**.38 S&W**

| Exc. | V.G. | Good | Fair | Poor |
|------|------|------|------|------|
| 375 | 325 | 275 | 175 | 100 |

**.32 S&W**

2" Barrel--Add 50 Percent.

| Exc. | V.G. | Good | Fair | Poor |
|------|------|------|------|------|
| 300 | 275 | 200 | 150 | 100 |

### Safety Hammerless 4th Model Double Action

This model was produced in .38 S&W only, and the only difference in the 4th Model and the 3rd Model is the adoption of the standard two-button type of barrel latch as found on most of the top-break revolvers. ".38S&W Cartridge" was also added to the left side of the barrel. There were approximately 104,000 manufactured between 1898 and 1907.

| Exc. | V.G. | Good | Fair | Poor |
|------|------|------|------|------|
| 300 | 275 | 200 | 150 | 100 |

### Safety Hammerless 5th Model Double Action

This is the last of the "Lemon Squeezers," and the only appreciable difference between this model and the 4th Model is that the front sight blade on the 5th Model is an integral part of the barrel and not a separate blade pinned onto the barrel. There were approximately 41,500 manufactured between 1907 and 1940.

2" Barrelled Version--Add 50 Percent.

| Exc. | V.G. | Good | Fair | Poor |
|------|------|------|------|------|
| 300 | 275 | 200 | 150 | 100 |

### 1st Model Single Shot

This unusual pistol combines the frame of the .38 Single Action 3rd Model with a single shot barrel. This is a top-break and functions exactly as the revolver models do. The barrel length is 6", 8", or 10"; and the pistol is chambered for .22 l.r., .32 S&W, and .38 S&W. The finish is blue or nickel-plated, with a square butt. The grips are checkered hard rubber extension types for a proper target hold. This pistol is considered quite rare on today's market, as only 1,251 were manufactured between 1893 and 1905.

**.22 L.R.**

| Exc. | V.G. | Good | Fair | Poor |
|------|------|------|------|------|
| 700 | 650 | 450 | 250 | 150 |

**.32 S&W**

| Exc. | V.G. | Good | Fair | Poor |
|------|------|------|------|------|
| 750 | 700 | 500 | 300 | 200 |

**.38 S&W**

| Exc. | V.G. | Good | Fair | Poor |
|------|------|------|------|------|
| 900 | 800 | 600 | 400 | 300 |

### 2nd Model Single Shot

The 2nd Model Single Shot has a frame with the recoil shield removed, is chambered for the .22 l.r. only, and is offered with the 10" barrel. The finish is blue or nickel-plated, and the grips are checkered hard rubber extension types. There were approximately 4,617 manufactured between 1905 and 1909.

| Exc. | V.G. | Good | Fair | Poor |
|------|------|------|------|------|
| 600 | 500 | 350 | 200 | 150 |

### 3rd Model Single Shot

The basic difference between this model and the 2nd Model is that this pistol could be fired double-action as well as single-action, and the frame came from the double-action perfected model. There were 6,949 manufactured between 1909 and 1923.

| Exc. | V.G. | Good | Fair | Poor |
|------|------|------|------|------|
| 600 | 500 | 350 | 200 | 150 |

## SMITH & WESSON HANDGUNS

### Straight Line Single Shot

This is a unique pistol that very much resembles a semiautomatic. The barrel is 10" in length and pivots to the left for loading. It is chambered for .22 l.r. and is finished in blue, with walnut grips inlaid with the S&W medallions. The hammer is straight-line in function and does not pivot. There were 1,870 manufactured between 1925 and 1936.

| Exc. | V.G. | Good | Fair | Poor |
|------|------|------|------|------|
| 1250 | 1000 | 750 | 500 | 400 |

### Hand Ejector 1st Model Double Action

This model was the first time S&W made a revolver with a swing-out cylinder. Interestingly, there is no cylinder latch; but the action opens by pulling forward on the exposed portion of the cylinder pin. This frees the spring tension and allows the cylinder to swing free. Another novel feature of this model is the cylinder stop location. It is located in the top of the frame over the cylinder. This model is chambered for the .32 S&W Long cartridge, has a 6-shot fluted cylinder, and is offered with 3.25", 4.25", and 6" long barrels. It is available with either a round or square butt, has checkered hard rubber grips, and is blued or nickel-plated. The company name, address, and patent dates are stamped on the cylinder instead of on the barrel. There were approximately 19,712 manufactured between 1896 and 1903.

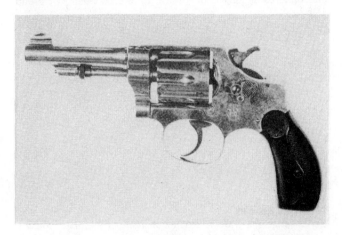

| Exc. | V.G. | Good | Fair | Poor |
|------|------|------|------|------|
| 450 | 400 | 350 | 250 | 175 |

### Hand Ejector Model of 1903
This model is quite different from its predecessor. The cylinder locks front and back; the cylinder stop is located in the bottom of the frame, and the familiar sliding cylinder latch is found on the left side of the frame. The barrel lengths are 3.25", 4.25", and 6". The 6-shot cylinder is fluted, and the revolver is chambered for .32 S&W Long. It is offered either blued or nickel-plated, and the round butt grips are checkered hard rubber. There were approximately 19,425 manufactured in 1903 and 1904.

| Exc. | V.G. | Good | Fair | Poor |
|------|------|------|------|------|
| 300 | 250 | 200 | 150 | 100 |

### Hand Ejector 3rd Model
This model differs from the Model of 1903 internally, and the serial range #263,001-534,532 is really the only way to differentiate the two. There were approximately 271,531 manufactured between 1911 and 1942.

| Exc. | V.G. | Good | Fair | Poor |
|------|------|------|------|------|
| 300 | 250 | 200 | 150 | 100 |

### 1st Model Ladysmith
This model was designed primarily as a defensive weapon for women. Its small size and caliber made it ideal for that purpose. The 1st Model Ladysmith is chambered for .22 l.r. and has a 7-shot fluted cylinder and 2.25", 3", and 3.5" barrel lengths. It is either blued or nickel-plated and has a round butt with checkered hard rubber grips. The 1st Model has a checkered cylinder-latch button on the left side of the frame. There were approximately 4,575 manufactured between 1902 and 1906.

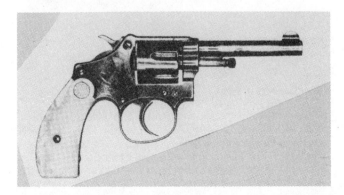

| Exc. | V.G. | Good | Fair | Poor |
|------|------|------|------|------|
| 1250 | 1000 | 850 | 650 | 450 |

### 2nd Model Ladysmith
This is essentially quite similar in appearance to the 1st Model, the difference being in the pull-forward cylinder latch located under the barrel, replacing the button on the left side of the frame. The new method allowed lockup front and back for greater action strength. The 2.25" barrel length was dropped; caliber and finishes are the same. There were approximately 9,400 manufactured between 1906 and 1910.

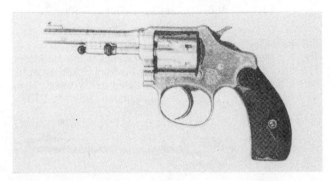

| Exc. | V.G. | Good | Fair | Poor |
|------|------|------|------|------|
| 1150 | 900 | 800 | 600 | 400 |

### 3rd Model Ladysmith
This model is quite different in appearance to the 2nd Model, as it features a square butt and smooth walnut grips with inlaid S&W medallions. The barrel lengths remained the same, with the addition of a 2.5" variation. The underbarrel cylinder lockup was not changed, nor were the caliber and finishes. There were approximately 12,200 manufactured between 1910 and 1921.

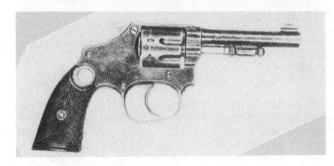

| Exc. | V.G. | Good | Fair | Poor |
|------|------|------|------|------|
| 1150 | 900 | 800 | 600 | 400 |

### .38 Hand Ejector 1st Model M&P
This was an early swing-out cylinder revolver, and it has no front lockup for the action. The release is on the left side of the frame. This model is chambered for .38 Long Colt and .38 S&W Special calibers, has a 6-shot fluted cylinder, and is offered with a 4", 5", 6", or 6.5" barrel. The finish is blued or nickel-plated; the grips, checkered walnut or hard rubber. There were approximately 20,975 manufactured between 1899 and 1902.

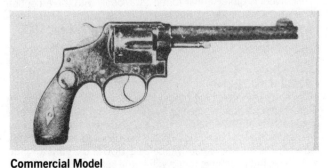

### Commercial Model
| Exc. | V.G. | Good | Fair | Poor |
|------|------|------|------|------|
| 750 | 650 | 600 | 450 | 350 |

### U.S. Navy Model
1,000 produced in 1900, .38 Long Colt, 6" barrel, blued with checkered walnut grips, "U.S.N." stamped on butt, serial range #5,001-6,000.

| Exc. | V.G. | Good | Fair | Poor |
|------|------|------|------|------|
| 700 | 600 | 550 | 400 | 300 |

### U.S. Army Model
1,000 produced in 1901, same as Navy Model except that it is marked "U.S.Army/Model 1899" on butt, "K.S.M." and "J.T.T." on grips, serial range #13,001- 14,000.

| Exc. | V.G. | Good | Fair | Poor |
|------|------|------|------|------|
| 700 | 600 | 550 | 400 | 300 |

### .38 Hand Ejector 2nd Model M&P
The 2nd Model is very similar in appearance to the 1st Model. The major difference is the addition of the front lockup under the barrel, and the ejector rod was increased in diameter. There were approximately 12,827 manufactured in 1902 and 1903.

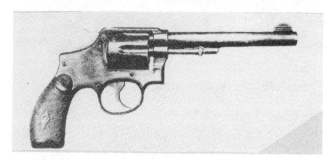

### Commercial Model .38 S&W Special

| Exc. | V.G. | Good | Fair | Poor |
|------|------|------|------|------|
| 400 | 350 | 300 | 250 | 200 |

### U.S. Navy Model
1,000 produced in 1902, .38 Long Colt caliber, "U.S.N." and anchor stamped on butt, 6" barrel, blued, serial range #25,001-26,000.

| Exc. | V.G. | Good | Fair | Poor |
|------|------|------|------|------|
| 550 | 500 | 400 | 300 | 250 |

### .32-20 Hand Ejector 1st Model
This model was one of S&W's early swing-out cylinder models. It had a surprisingly modern appearance, even to the cylinder release latch on the left side of the frame. The ejector rod, however, does not lock in the front as do modern designs. This model is chambered for the .32-20 Winchester cartridge, has a 6-shot fluted cylinder, and is offered with a 4", 5", 6", and 6.5" barrel. The finish is blued or nickel-plated, with case-colored hammer and trigger. The butt is round; and the grips, either of walnut or checkered hard rubber. There were approximately 5,311 manufactured between 1899 and 1902.

| Exc. | V.G. | Good | Fair | Poor |
|------|------|------|------|------|
| 450 | 400 | 350 | 250 | 150 |

### .32-20 Hand Ejector 2nd Model
This model is quite similar to the 1st Model, with the exception of a front lockup lug on the bottom of the barrel. There were approximately 4,499 manufactured between 1902 and 1905.

| Exc. | V.G. | Good | Fair | Poor |
|------|------|------|------|------|
| 450 | 400 | 350 | 250 | 150 |

### .22/32 Hand Ejector
This is a very interesting model from a collector standpoint. A San Francisco firearms dealer by the name of Phillip B. Bekeart requested that S&W manufacture a .22- caliber target-grade revolver on the heavier .32 frame. He believed in his idea so strongly that he immediately ordered 1,000 of the guns for himself. This initial order is found within the serial range #1-3,000 and are known to collectors as true Bekearts. The remainder of the extensive production run are simply .22/.32 Hand Ejectors.

This model is chambered for .22 l.r, and has a 6-shot fluted cylinder and 6" barrel. The finish is blue, with square butt and checkered extension-type walnut grips. There were only 292 revolvers of his initial order delivered to Mr. Bekeart, but the first 1,000 pistols are considered to be True Bekearts. The production number of each respective pistol is stamped into the base of the extended wooden grips. S&W went on to manufacture several hundred thousand of these revolvers between 1911 and 1953.

### "The True Bekeart"
Serial range #1-3,000, production number stamped on butt. Professional appraisal should be secured.

| Exc. | V.G. | Good | Fair | Poor |
|------|------|------|------|------|
| 550 | 500 | 400 | 300 | 250 |

### Standard Model

| Exc. | V.G. | Good | Fair | Poor |
|------|------|------|------|------|
| 350 | 300 | 250 | 200 | 125 |

### .44 Hand Ejector 1st Model
This model is also known by collectors as the ".44 Triple lock" or "The New Century." The triple lock nickname came from a separate locking device located on the extractor rod shroud that is used in addition to the usual two locks. This model is chambered for the .44 S&W Special cartridge. On a limited basis, it is also chambered for .44 S&W Russian, .44-40, .45 Colt, .45 S&W Special, .450 Eley, and .455 Mark II. The fluted cylinder holds 6 shots, and the barrel is offered in lengths of 4", 5", 6.5", and 7.5". The finish is blued or nickel-plated; and the grips are checkered walnut, with the gold S&W medallion on later models. There were approximately 15,375 manufactured between 1908 and 1915.

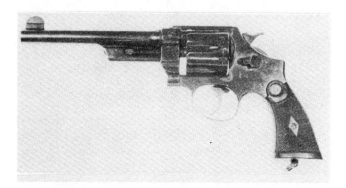

### .44 S&W Special and .455 Mark II

| Exc. | V.G. | Good | Fair | Poor |
|------|------|------|------|------|
| 650 | 600 | 500 | 350 | 200 |

### Other Calibers (Rare)

| Exc. | V.G. | Good | Fair | Poor |
|------|------|------|------|------|
| 850 | 750 | 600 | 450 | 300 |

### .44 Hand Ejector 2nd Model
This model is quite similar in appearance to the 1st Model. The major difference is the elimination of the third or triple lock device and the heavy ejector rod shroud. Other changes are inter-

nal and not readily apparent. This model is also standard in .44 S&W Special chambering but is offered rarely in .44-40 and .45 Colt. Specimens have been noted with adjustable sights. There were approximately 34,624 manufactured between 1915 and 1937.

**.44 S&W Special**

| Exc. | V.G. | Good | Fair | Poor |
|------|------|------|------|------|
| 650 | 600 | 500 | 350 | 200 |

**.44-40 or .45 Colt**

| Exc. | V.G. | Good | Fair | Poor |
|------|------|------|------|------|
| 750 | 650 | 550 | 400 | 250 |

### .44 Hand Ejector 3rd Model or Model of 1926

This model is similar in appearance to the 2nd Model but brought back the heavy ejector rod shroud of the 1st Model without the triple lock device. There were approximately 33,054 manufactured between 1926 and 1950.

**.44 S&W Special**

| Exc. | V.G. | Good | Fair | Poor |
|------|------|------|------|------|
| 500 | 450 | 350 | 275 | 200 |

**.44-40 or .45 Colt**

| Exc. | V.G. | Good | Fair | Poor |
|------|------|------|------|------|
| 600 | 500 | 400 | 300 | 250 |

**Target Model**

| Exc. | V.G. | Good | Fair | Poor |
|------|------|------|------|------|
| 1500 | 1250 | 900 | 750 | 500 |

### S & W 35 Automatic Pistol 1st Model

Production of the 35 Automatic was S&W's first attempt at an auto-loading pistol. As was always the case, the company strived for maximum safety and dependability. This model has a 3.5" barrel and a 7-shot detachable magazine and is chambered in .35 S&W Automatic, a one-time-only cartridge that eventually proved to be the major downfall of this pistol from a commercial standpoint. There were two separate safety devices--a revolving cam on the backstrap and a grip safety on the front strap that had to be fully depressed simultaneously while squeezing the trigger. The finish is blue or nickel-plated; and the grips are walnut, with the S&W inlaid medallions. The magazine release on the 1st Model slides from side to side and

is checkered, very expensive to manufacture, and destined to be modified. There were approximately 3,000 1st Models manufactured in 1913 and 1914.

| Exc. | V.G. | Good | Fair | Poor |
|------|------|------|------|------|
| 650 | 500 | 400 | 300 | 200 |

### S&W 35 Automatic Pistol 2nd Model

The only notable difference between the 1st and 2nd Models is the magazine release catch. On the 2nd Model the catch slides front and back and is serrated. This change seems irrelevant but resulted in a considerable savings in machining costs. Production of this model started and stopped a number of times for revolver production for England and then again in 1918 for WWI. Production was ceased finally in 1921 after a total of 8,350 1st and 2nd Models were manufactured.

| Exc. | V.G. | Good | Fair | Poor |
|------|------|------|------|------|
| 600 | 450 | 350 | 250 | 150 |

### S&W 32 Automatic Pistol

In 1921 it became apparent to the powers that controlled S&W that the .35-caliber automatic was never going to be a commercial success. Harold Wesson, the new president, began to redesign the pistol to accept the .32 ACP, a commercially accepted cartridge, and to streamline the appearance to be more competitive with the other pistols on the market, notably Colt's. This new pistol used as many parts from the older model as possible for economy's sake. The pivoting barrel was discontinued, as was the cam-type safety in the rear grip strap. A magazine disconnector and a reduced-strength recoil spring to ease cocking were employed. The barrel length was kept at 3.5", and the 7-shot magazine was retained. The finish is blued only, and the grips are smooth walnut. There were only 957 of these manufactured between 1924 and 1936. They are eagerly sought by collectors.

| Exc. | V.G. | Good | Fair | Poor |
|------|------|------|------|------|
| 1250 | 950 | 750 | 600 | 450 |

### U.S. Service Model of 1917

WWI was on the horizon, and it seemed certain that the U.S. would become involved. The S&W people began to work with the Springfield Armory to develop a hand-ejector model that would fire the .45-caliber government cartridge. This was accomplished in 1916 by the use of half-moon clips. The new revolver is quite similar to the .44 Hand Ejector in appearance. It has a 5.5" barrel, blued finish with smooth walnut grips, and a lanyard ring on the butt. The designation "U.S. Army Model 1917" is stamped on the butt. After the War broke out, the government was not satisfied with S&W's production and actually took control of the company for the duration of the War. This was the very first time that the company was not controlled by a Wesson. The factory records indicate that there were 163,476 Model 1917's manufactured between 1917 and 1919, the WWI years. After the war, the sale of these revolvers continued on a commercial and contract basis until 1949, when this model was finally dropped from the S&W product line.

**Military Model**

| Exc. | V.G. | Good | Fair | Poor |
|------|------|------|------|------|
| 400 | 350 | 300 | 200 | 150 |

**Brazilian Contract**

25,000 produced for the Brazilian government in 1938. The Brazilian crest is stamped on the sideplate.

| Exc. | V.G. | Good | Fair | Poor |
|------|------|------|------|------|
| 300 | 250 | 200 | 150 | 100 |

**Commercial Model**

High gloss blue and checkered walnut grips.

| Exc. | V.G. | Good | Fair | Poor |
|------|------|------|------|------|
| 450 | 400 | 350 | 275 | 200 |

## SMITH & WESSON MODERN HANDGUNS

With the development of the Hand Ejector Models and the swingout cylinders, Smith & Wesson opened the door to a number of new advancements in the revolver field. This new system allowed for a solid frame, making the weapon much stronger than the old top-break design. Smith & Wesson also developed the different basic frame sizes and designated them with letters. The I frame, which later developed into the J frame, was used for the .22/.32 and the small, concealable .38 revolvers. The medium K frame was used for .38 duty- and target-type weapons. The N frame was the heavy-duty frame used for the larger .357 and .44 and .45 caliber revolvers. The hand ejector went through many evolutionary changes over the years, and it would be beyond the purview of a book of this nature to detail all of these changes. We strongly recommend that one secure a detailed volume that deals exclusively with Smith & Wesson (see the bibliography), and learn all that is available on this fascinating firearm. For our purposes, we catalog the models by their numerical designations, describe them briefly, and offer current values. It is important to note that the S&W revolver that we see marketed by the company today has undergone many changes in reaching its present configuration. The early models featured five screws in their construction, not counting the grip screw. There were four screws fastening the sideplate and another through the front of the triggerguard that retained the cylinder stop plunger. The first step saw the elimination of the top sideplate screw, and the five-screw Smith & Wesson became the four-screw. Later the frame was changed to eliminate the cylinder stop plunger screw, and the three-screw was born. Some models were offered with a flat cylinder latch that was serrated instead of the familiar checkering. Recently in 1978, the method of attaching the barrel to the frame was changed; and the familiar pin was eliminated. At the same time, the recessed cylinder commonly found on magnum models was also eliminated. All of these factors have a definite effect on the value and collectible desirability of a particular S&W. Again, let me emphasize that there are some excellent works dealing exclusively with the Smith & Wesson; and one should learn all that is possible before investing.

As a General Rule, Additional Percent Values as Follows:
Five-Screw Model—Add 40 Percent.
Four-Screw Model—Add 20 Percent.
Flat Latch—Add 25 Percent.
Not Pinned or Recessed—Deduct 10 Percent.

## Model 10

This model has been in production in one configuration or another since 1904. It was always the mainstay of the S&W line. The Model 10 is built on the K, or medium frame, and was always meant as a duty gun. It was offered with a 2", 3", 4", 5", or 6" barrel. Currently only the 4" and 6" are available. A round or square butt is offered. It is chambered for the .38 Special and is offered in blue or nickel plate, with checkered walnut grips. The model designation is stamped on the yoke after 1957 on all S&W revolvers.

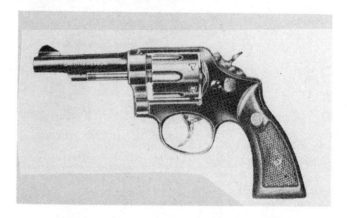

| NIB | Exc. | V.G. | Good | Fair | Poor |
|-----|------|------|------|------|------|
| 325 | 250 | 200 | 150 | 125 | 90 |

## Victory Model

Manufactured during WWII, this is a Model 10 with a sandblasted and parkerized finish, a lanyard swivel, and smooth walnut grips. The serial number has a V prefix.

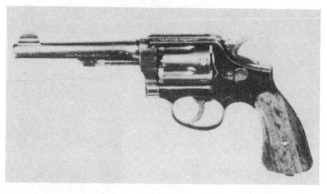

| Exc. | V.G. | Good | Fair | Poor |
|------|------|------|------|------|
| 275 | 225 | 175 | 100 | 75 |

## Model 11

This is the "Victory Model" produced for the British. It is chambered for the .38 S&W Cartridge. Nicknamed the .38/200 British Service Revolver, there were 568,204 manufactured between 1940 and 1945.

| Exc. | V.G. | Good | Fair | Poor |
|------|------|------|------|------|
| 250 | 200 | 150 | 100 | 75 |

## Model 12

The Model 12 was introduced in 1952 and is merely a Model 10 with a lightweight alloy frame and cylinder. In 1954 the alloy cylinder was replaced with one of steel.
Alloy Cylinder Model--Add 40 Percent.

| Exc. | V.G. | Good | Fair | Poor |
|------|------|------|------|------|
| 275 | 225 | 150 | 125 | 100 |

### Model 13 "Air Force"
In 1953 the Air Force purchased a large quantity of Model 12's with alloy frames and cylinders. They were intended for use by flight crews as survival weapons in emergencies. This model was not officially designated "13" by S&W, but the Air Force stamped "M13" on the top strap. This model was rejected by the Air Force in 1954 because of trouble with the alloy cylinder.

| Exc. | V.G. | Good | Fair | Poor |
|------|------|------|------|------|
| 800 | 750 | 600 | 450 | 250 |

### Model 13 M&P
This is simply the Model 10 M&P chambered for the .357 Magnum. It was introduced in 1974.

| Exc. | V.G. | Good | Fair | Poor |
|------|------|------|------|------|
| 300 | 250 | 200 | 175 | 125 |

### Model 14
This model is also known as the "K-38." In 1957 "Model 14" was stamped on the yoke. This model is offered in a 6" barrel with adjustable sights. In 1961 a single-action version with faster lock time was offered. This would be worth a small premium. This model was discontinued in 1981.
Single Action Model--Add 10 Percent.

| Exc. | V.G. | Good | Fair | Poor |
|------|------|------|------|------|
| 300 | 250 | 200 | 175 | 125 |

### Model 15
Also known as the "Combat Masterpiece," this model was produced on the urging of law enforcement officers who requested the "K-38" with a 4" barrel. The model went into production in 1950 and was discontinued in 1987.

| Exc. | V.G. | Good | Fair | Poor |
|------|------|------|------|------|
| 300 | 250 | 200 | 175 | 125 |

### Model 16
Also known as the "K-32," this model is identical in appearance to the Model 14 except that it is chambered for .32 S&W. The Model 16 did not enjoy the commercial popularity of the Model 14 and was dropped from the line in 1973.

| Exc. | V.G. | Good | Fair | Poor |
|------|------|------|------|------|
| 650 | 550 | 450 | 300 | 250 |

### K-32 Combat Masterpiece
S&W produced a limited number of 4" barrelled K-32 revolvers. They were never given a number designation, as they were discontinued before 1957 when the numbering system began.

| Exc. | V.G. | Good | Fair | Poor |
|------|------|------|------|------|
| 700 | 650 | 500 | 350 | 300 |

### Model 17
This is the numerical designation that S&W placed on the "K-22" in 1957. This target model .22 rimfire revolver has always been very popular. It is offered in 6" and 8" barrel lengths, with all target options. The finish is blued, and it has checkered walnut grips.

| NIB | Exc. | V.G. | Good | Fair | Poor |
|-----|------|------|------|------|------|
| 375 | 300 | 250 | 200 | 150 | 100 |

### Model 18
This is the model designation for the 4"-barrelled "Combat Masterpiece" chambered for the .22 rimfire.

| Exc. | V.G. | Good | Fair | Poor |
|------|------|------|------|------|
| 350 | 300 | 250 | 200 | 125 |

**NOTE:** On "K-Frame" Target Models
The factory eliminated the upper corner screw from the side plate in 1955. The 5-screw became a 4-screw.
Model number designations were stamped on the yoke in 1957.
Cylinder stop changed eliminating screw in front of triggerguard in 1961.

### Model 19
This model was introduced in 1954 at the urging of Bill Jordan, a competition shooter with the U.S. Border Patrol, who went on to become one of our most respected gun writers. It was built on the "K-Frame" and was the first medium frame revolver chambered for the powerful .357 Magnum cartridge. Since its inception the Model 19 has been one of S&W's most popular revolvers. It was the first revolver to be introduced as a three-screw model. Originally it was offered with a 4" barrel; the 6" became available in 1963. The finish is blued or nickel-plated, and the grips are checkered walnut. 1959 saw the Goncalo Alves target stocks appear. In 1968 a 2.5" round-butt version was introduced. The Model 19 has been the basis for two commemoratives--the Texas Ranger/with Bowie Knife and the Oregon State Police/ with Belt Buckle.

| NIB | Exc. | V.G. | Good | Fair | Poor |
|-----|------|------|------|------|------|
| 350 | 300 | 250 | 200 | 150 | 100 |

### Texas Ranger Cased with Knife
NIB
750

### Oregon State Police Cased with Buckle
NIB
900

### Model 20
This model was known as the "38/44 Heavy Duty" before the change to numerical designations. It was brought out in response to requests from law enforcement personnel in the 20's for a stronger, more powerful sidearm. This model, along with the .38/44 S&W Special cartridge, was the company's answer. The revolver was manufactured with a standard 5" long barrel but has been noted rarely as short as 3.5" and as long as 8-3/8". It was built on the large N frame and is blued or nickel-plated, with checkered walnut grips. Eventually the popularity of the .357 Magnum made the Model 20 superfluous, and it was discontinued in 1966.
Pre-War .44 Special--Add 50 Percent.

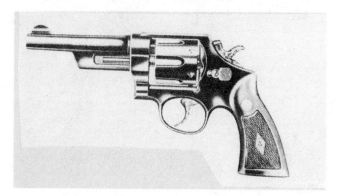

| Exc. | V.G. | Good | Fair | Poor |
| --- | --- | --- | --- | --- |
| 375 | 325 | 250 | 200 | 150 |

### Model 21
This model was known as the "1950 Military" and the "4th Model .44 Hand Ejector" before the Model 21 designation was applied in 1957. The Model 21 was built on the N frame and is quite rare, as only 1,200 were manufactured in 16 years of production.

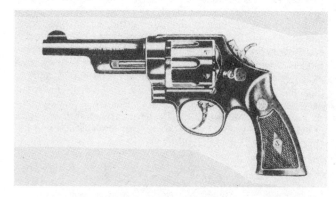

| Exc. | V.G. | Good | Fair | Poor |
| --- | --- | --- | --- | --- |
| 1500 | 1200 | 950 | 650 | 500 |

### Model 22
This model was known as the "1950 .45 Military" before 1957. It is very similar in appearance to the Model 21 except that it is chambered for the .45 Auto Rim or .45 ACP cartridge. Half-moon clips are used with the latter. There were 3,976 manufactured between 1950 and 1966.

| Exc. | V.G. | Good | Fair | Poor |
| --- | --- | --- | --- | --- |
| 750 | 650 | 550 | 300 | 200 |

### Model 23
The .38/44 Outdoorsman was the model name of this N frame revolver before the 1957 designation change. This is simply the Model 20 with adjustable sights. It was introduced in 1931 as a heavy-duty sporting handgun with hunters in mind. It features a 6.5" barrel and blued finish and was the first S&W to have the new checkered walnut "Magna" grips. After 1950 this revolver was thoroughly modernized and had the later ribbed barrel. There were a total of 8,365 manufactured before the model was discontinued in 1966. 6,039 were of the modernized configuration.

| Exc. | V.G. | Good | Fair | Poor |
| --- | --- | --- | --- | --- |
| 500 | 400 | 300 | 200 | 125 |

### Model 24
This model was introduced as the .44 Target Model of 1950. It is simply the N-Frame Model 21 with adjustable target sights. This revolver was quite popular with the long-range handgunning devotees and their guru, Elmer Keith. The introduction of the .44 Magnum in 1956 began the siren song of the Model 24, and it was finally discontinued in 1966. It was re-introduced in 1983 and 1984--and then was dropped again.

| Exc. | V.G. | Good | Fair | Poor |
| --- | --- | --- | --- | --- |
| 750 | 650 | 500 | 400 | 250 |

### Model 25
Also known as the .45 Target Model of 1955, this was an improved version of the 1950 Target .45 which became the Model 26 in 1957. The Model 25 features a heavier barrel 4", 6.5" or 8" in length with blued or nickel-plated finish. All target options were offered. The Model 25 is chambered for the .45 ACP or .45 Auto-rim cartridges. This model is still available chambered for .45 Colt as the Model 25-5.

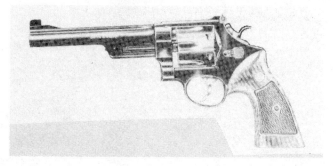

| Exc. | V.G. | Good | Fair | Poor |
| --- | --- | --- | --- | --- |
| 650 | 550 | 400 | 300 | 200 |

### Model 25-5 125th Anniversary with Case
NIB
450

### Model 25-2
This is the discontinued modern version of the Model 25 chambered in .45 ACP. The 6.5" barrel is shortened to 6" and is available in a presentation case.

| Exc. | V.G. | Good | Fair | Poor |
| --- | --- | --- | --- | --- |
| 350 | 300 | 225 | 200 | 150 |

### Model 26
This is the numerical designation of the 1950 .45 Target Model. This large N frame revolver is basically the same as the Model 25 but has a lighter, thinner barrel. This caused its unpopularity among competitive shooters who wanted a heavier revolver. This brought about the Model 25 and the demise of the Model 26 in 1961 after only 2,768 were manufactured.

| Exc. | V.G. | Good | Fair | Poor |
| --- | --- | --- | --- | --- |
| 750 | 650 | 500 | 400 | 250 |

### Factory Registered .357 Magnum

In the early 1930's, a gun writer named Phillip B. Sharpe became interested in the development of high performance loads to be used in the then popular .38/44 S&W revolvers. He repeatedly urged the company to produce a revolver especially made to handle these high pressure loads. In 1934 S&W asked Winchester to produce a new cartridge that would create the ballistics that Sharpe was seeking. This new cartridge was made longer than the standard .38 Special case so that it could not inadvertently be fired in an older gun. The company never felt that this would be a commercially popular venture and from the onset visualized the ".357 Magnum" as a strictly deluxe handbuilt item. They were to be individually numbered, in addition to the serial number, and registered to the new owner. The new Magnum was to be the most expensive revolver in the line. The gun went on the market in 1935, and the first one was presented to J. Edgar Hoover. The gun, however, was to become a tremendous success. S&W could only produce 120 per month, and this did not come close to filling orders. In 1938 the practice of numbering and registering each revolver was discontinued after 5,500 were produced. The ".357 Magnum," as it was designated, continued as one of the company's most popular items.

The factory registered model was built on the N frame. It could be custom ordered with any barrel length from 3.5" up to 8-3/8". The finish is blue, and the grips are checkered walnut. This model was virtually hand built and test targeted. A certificate of registration was furnished with each revolver. The registration number was stamped on the yoke of the revolver with the prefix "Reg." This practice ceased in 1938 after 5,500 were produced.

| Exc. | V.G. | Good | Fair | Poor |
|------|------|------|------|------|
| 1250 | 1000 | 800 | 550 | 400 |

### Pre-War .357 Magnum

This is the same as the factory registered model without the certificate and the individual numbering. Approximately 1,150 were manufactured between 1938 and 1941. Production ceased for WWII weapons production.

| Exc. | V.G. | Good | Fair | Poor |
|------|------|------|------|------|
| 650 | 550 | 450 | 300 | 250 |

### .357 Magnum - Model 27

In 1948 after the end of WWII, production of this revolver commenced. The new hammer block and short fall hammer were utilized, and the barrel lengths offered were 3.5", 5", 6", 6.5", and 8-3/8". In 1957 the model designation was changed to Model 27; and in 1975 the target trigger, hammer and Goncalo Alves target grips were made standard. This revolver is still available from S&W and has been in production longer than any other N frame.

| NIB | Exc. | V.G. | Good | Fair | Poor |
|-----|------|------|------|------|------|
| 425 | 375 | 300 | 250 | 200 | 150 |

### Model 28

The Model 27 revolver was extremely popular among law enforcement officers, and many police agencies were interested in purchasing such a weapon--except for the cost. In 1954 S&W produced a new model called, at the time, the "Highway Patrolman." This model had all the desirable performance features of the deluxe Model 27 but lacked the cosmetic features that drove up the price. The finish is a matte blue; the rib is sandblasted instead of checkered or serrated, and the grips are the standard checkered walnut. Barrel lengths are 4" and 6.5". On late models the 6.5" barrel was reduced to 6", as on all S&W's. The model designation was changed to Model 28 in 1957, and this model remained quite popular up to the advent of the "Wonder 9's" for police use. S&W discontinued the Model 28 in 1986.

| Exc. | V.G. | Good | Fair | Poor |
|------|------|------|------|------|
| 275 | 250 | 200 | 150 | 100 |

### Model 29

In the early 1950's, handgun writers, under the leadership of Elmer Keith, were in the habit of loading the .44 Special cartridge to high performance levels and firing them in the existing .44 Hand Ejectors. They urged S&W to produce a revolver strong enough to consistently fire these heavy loads. In 1954 Remington, at the request of S&W produced the .44 Magnum cartridge. As was the case with the .357 Magnum, the cases were longer so that they would not fit in the chambers of the older guns. The first .44 Magnum became available for sale in early 1956. The first 500 were made with the 6.5" barrel; the 4" became available later that year. In 1957 the model designation was changed to 29, and the 8-3/8" barrel was introduced. The Model 29 is available in blue or nickel plate. It came standard with all target options and was offered in a fitted wood case. The Model 29 is considered by many knowledgeable people to be the finest revolver S&W has ever produced. The older Model 29 revolvers are in a different collector category than most modern S&W revolvers. The early five-screw models can be worth a 50 percent premium in excellent condition. One must regard these revolvers on a separate basis and have individually appraised for proper valuation.

| NIB | Exc. | V.G. | Good | Fair | Poor |
|-----|------|------|------|------|------|
| 475 | 425 | 350 | 300 | 275 | 225 |

### 5" Barrel Model 29

This is the rarest of the Model 29's. 500 were manufactured in 1958. Watch for fakes!

| NIB | Exc. | V.G. | Good | Fair | Poor |
|-----|------|------|------|------|------|
| 1250 | 1000 | 750 | 650 | 450 | 300 |

### Note on N Frame Revolvers

N frame models were changed from 5-screw to 4-screw between 1956 and 1958. Serial number S175,000.

Triggerguard screw was eliminated in 1961.

The pinned barrel and recessed cylinder were discontinued in 1978.

## Model 629

This revolver is simply a stainless-steel version of the late Model 29.

| NIB | Exc. | V.G. | Good | Fair | Poor |
|-----|------|------|------|------|------|
| 500 | 450 | 400 | 350 | 300 | 250 |

## Model 30

This model was built on the small I frame. In 1960 this frame size was dropped, and the J frame became standard for all small revolvers that S&W produced. The Model 30 is chambered for the .32 S&W long cartridge. It has a 6-shot cylinder and 2", 3", 4", and 6" barrel lengths. It has fixed sights and is either blued or nickel-plated. The butt is round, with checkered walnut grips. It was discontinued in 1977.

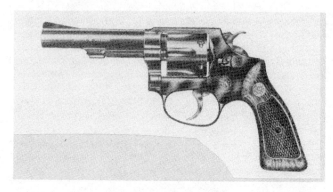

| Exc. | V.G. | Good | Fair | Poor |
|------|------|------|------|------|
| 300 | 250 | 200 | 150 | 100 |

## Model 31

This model is the same as the Model 30 with a square butt. It was known as the Regulation Police before 1957. It is now discontinued.

| Exc. | V.G. | Good | Fair | Poor |
|------|------|------|------|------|
| 275 | 250 | 200 | 150 | 100 |

## .32 Regulation Police Target

Discontinued in 1957, the Target model of the Regulation Police is quite rare. All specifications are the same except for the addition of adjustable sights.

| Exc. | V.G. | Good | Fair | Poor |
|------|------|------|------|------|
| 325 | 300 | 250 | 200 | 150 |

## Model 32

This model, known as the Terrier prior to 1957, was introduced in 1936. It is essentially a Regulation Police chambered for .38 Special and having a 2" barrel and round butt. It is offered in blue or nickel plate and has a 5-shot cylinder, fixed sights, and checkered walnut grips. This model was discontinued in 1974.

| Exc. | V.G. | Good | Fair | Poor |
|------|------|------|------|------|
| 350 | 300 | 250 | 200 | 150 |

## Model 33

This model is simply the Regulation Police with a square butt and 4" barrel chambered for the .38 Special.

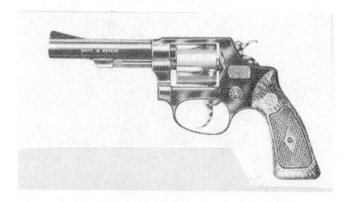

| Exc. | V.G. | Good | Fair | Poor |
|------|------|------|------|------|
| 325 | 275 | 225 | 175 | 125 |

## Model 34

Introduced in 1936 as the .22/32 Kit Gun, it has a 2" or 4" barrel, either round or square butt, and adjustable sights. The revolver is a .32 Hand Ejector chambered for the .22 rimfire. It is built on the J frame and is offered blued or nickel-plated. The Model 34 is currently in production.

| NIB | Exc. | V.G. | Good | Fair | Poor |
|-----|------|------|------|------|------|
| 350 | 300 | 250 | 225 | 175 | 125 |

## Model 35

This is a square-butt, 6"-barrelled version of the Kit Gun. It was known prior to 1957 as the .22/32 Target. This model was discontinued in 1973.

| Exc. | V.G. | Good | Fair | Poor |
|------|------|------|------|------|
| 400 | 350 | 300 | 250 | 200 |

### Model 36

This model, known as the Chief's Special, was introduced in 1950. It was built on the J frame and is chambered for the .38 Special cartridge. It holds 5 shots, has a 2" or 3" barrel, and was initially offered in a round butt. In 1952 a square-butt version was released. It is finished in blue or nickel plate and has checkered walnut grips.

| NIB | Exc. | V.G. | Good | Fair | Poor |
|-----|------|------|------|------|------|
| 325 | 300 | 250 | 200 | 150 | 100 |

### Chief's Special Target - Model 50

Since 1955 a very limited number of Chief's Specials with adjustable sights have been manufactured. They have been offered with 2" or 3" barrels, round or square butts, and either blue or nickel-plated. Between 1957 and 1965, these target models were stamped Model 36 on the yoke. The revolvers manufactured between 1965 and the model discontinuance in 1975 were marked Model 50. This is a very collectible revolver.

| Exc. | V.G. | Good | Fair | Poor |
|------|------|------|------|------|
| 400 | 350 | 300 | 250 | 200 |

### Model 37

Introduced in 1952 as the Chief's Special Airweight, this revolver initially had an alloy frame and cylinder. In 1954, following many complaints regarding damaged revolvers, the cylinders were made of steel. Barrel lengths, finishes, and grip options on the Airweight are the same as on the standard Chief Special. In 1957 the Model 37 designation was adopted.

| NIB | Exc. | V.G. | Good | Fair | Poor |
|-----|------|------|------|------|------|
| 350 | 300 | 275 | 225 | 175 | 125 |

### Model 38 - Airweight Bodyguard

This model was introduced in 1955 as the Airweight Bodyguard. This was a departure from S&W's usual procedure in that the alloy-framed version came first. The Model 38 is chambered for .38 Special and is available with a 2" barrel standard. Although a 3" barrel was offered, it is rarely encountered. The frame of the Bodyguard is extended to conceal and shroud the hammer. This makes this model a pocket revolver, as it can be drawn without snagging. It is available either blue or nickel-plated, with checkered walnut grips.

| NIB | Exc. | V.G. | Good | Fair | Poor |
|-----|------|------|------|------|------|
| 375 | 325 | 300 | 250 | 200 | 150 |

### Bodyguard - Model 49

This model was introduced in 1959 and is identical in configuration to the Model 38 except that the frame is made of steel.

| NIB | Exc. | V.G. | Good | Fair | Poor |
|-----|------|------|------|------|------|
| 350 | 300 | 250 | 200 | 150 | 100 |

### Model 649

This stainless-steel version of the Model 49 was introduced in 1986.

| NIB | Exc. | V.G. | Good | Fair | Poor |
|-----|------|------|------|------|------|
| 375 | 325 | 275 | 225 | 175 | 125 |

### Model 40 Centennial

This model was introduced in 1952, Smith & Wesson's 100th anniversary. This explains the "Centennial Model" designation. They are of the Safety Hammerless design. This model was built on the J frame and features a fully concealed hammer and a grip safety. The Model 40 is chambered for the .38 Special cartridge. It is offered with a 2" barrel in either blue or nickel plate. The grips are checkered walnut. The Centenial was discontinued in 1974.

| Exc. | V.G. | Good | Fair | Poor |
|------|------|------|------|------|
| 400 | 350 | 300 | 250 | 200 |

### Model 42 - Airweight Centennial

This model is identical in configuration to the Model 40 with an aluminum alloy frame. It was also discontinued in 1974.

| Exc. | V.G. | Good | Fair | Poor |
|------|------|------|------|------|
| 450 | 400 | 350 | 250 | 125 |

## Model 43

This model was built on the J frame, is chambered for .22 rimfire, has a 4" barrel, and is offered in a round or square butt, with checkered walnut grips. It has adjustable sights and is either blued or nickel-plated. The frame is made of aluminum alloy. Except for this, it is identical to the Model 34 Kit Gun. The Model 43 was introduced in 1958 and was discontinued in 1974.

| Exc. | V.G. | Good | Fair | Poor |
|------|------|------|------|------|
| 450  | 400  | 350  | 250  | 125  |

## Model 51

This model is simply the Model 34 Kit Gun chambered for the .22 Winchester Magnum rimfire.

| Exc. | V.G. | Good | Fair | Poor |
|------|------|------|------|------|
| 300  | 250  | 200  | 150  | 100  |

## Model 651

This stainless-steel version of the Model 51 .22 Magnum Kit Gun was manufactured between 1983 and 1987.

| Exc. | V.G. | Good | Fair | Poor |
|------|------|------|------|------|
| 325  | 275  | 225  | 175  | 125  |

**Note on J Frame Revolvers;**

In 1953 the cylinder stop plunger screw was eliminated.

In 1955 the top corner sideplate screw was eliminated.

In 1957 the numerical model designation was stamped on the yoke.

In 1966 the flat latch was changed to the present contoured cylinder release.

## Model 45

This model is a special purpose K-Frame M&P chambered for the .22 rimfire. It was designed as a training revolver for police departments and the U.S. Postal Service. This model was manufactured in limited quantities between 1948 and 1957. In 1963 production abruptly began and ended again. There were 500 of these revolvers released on a commercial basis, but they are rarely encountered.

| NIB | V.G. | Good | Fair | Poor |
|-----|------|------|------|------|
| 750 | 650  | 550  | 350  | 250  |

## Model 48

This model is identical to the Model 17, K-22, except that it is chambered for the .22 Winchester Magnum rimfire. It was available with the same options as the Model 17 and was built on the K frame. It was introduced in 1959 and was discontinued in 1986.

| Exc. | V.G. | Good | Fair | Poor |
|------|------|------|------|------|
| 325  | 300  | 250  | 200  | 150  |

## Model 53

Introduced in 1961, the Model 53 was chambered for a totally new cartridge developed by Remington Arms Co. called the .22 Jet. The cartridge was based on the .357 Magnum necked down to .22 caliber, firing a 60-grain projectile at approximately 2,200 ft/sec. from the 8" barrel. This cartridge was brought out in response to the "Wildcatters" who were converting their Model 17's. The revolver that S&W brought out to chamber this new true .22 Magnum was based on the Model 19 K frame. It was offered with a 4", 6", and 8-3/8" barrel. The finish is blue,

with checkered walnut grips. The sights are adjustable, and the revolver is furnished with cylinder inserts that would convert the Model 53 to fire .22 rimfire cartridges. The frame has two firing pins--one for centerfire and the other for rimfire. The hammer has a selective striker. The new high velocity cartridge created functioning problems, and the model was discontinued in 1974 after approximately 15,000 were manufactured.

| Exc. | V.G. | Good | Fair | Poor |
|------|------|------|------|------|
| 750  | 650  | 500  | 350  | 300  |

## Model 56

In 1962, in response to an order from the Air Force for a 2" heavy-barrelled K frame with adjustable sights, S&W brought out the Model 56. This revolver has a slightly heavier frame to accommodate the barrel and a longer rear sight that overlaps the barrel and is chambered for .38 Special. It was produced until 1964, and there were approximately 15,200 manufactured. The model was replaced by the Model 15 that was now offered with a 2" barrel.

| Exc. | V.G. | Good | Fair | Poor |
|------|------|------|------|------|
| 550  | 450  | 375  | 300  | 200  |

## Model 57

This model was introduced in 1963. It is, for all intents and purposes, identical to the Model 29, chambered for the .41 Magnum cartridge. It was intended to fill a gap and to be the ultimate law enforcement cartridge. The Model 57 has not realized that potential.

| NIB | Exc. | V.G. | Good | Fair | Poor |
|-----|------|------|------|------|------|
| 425 | 375  | 300  | 275  | 200  | 150  |

## Model 657

This is the stainless steel version of the Model 57.

| NIB | Exc. | V.G. | Good | Fair | Poor |
|-----|------|------|------|------|------|
| 450 | 400  | 325  | 300  | 250  | 175  |

## Model 58

This is a fixed sight, 4" barrel M&P, chambered for the .41 Magnum cartridge. It is available blued or nickel-plated, with the checkered walnut Magna grips. It was manufactured between 1964 and 1968.

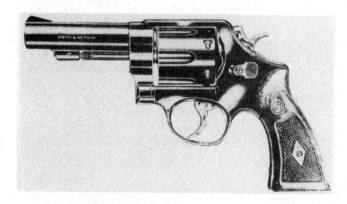

| Exc. | V.G. | Good | Fair | Poor |
|------|------|------|------|------|
| 375  | 325  | 275  | 225  | 175  |

## Model 60

This was the pioneer effort in the stainless-steel handgun. S&W released it in 1965. This revolver is essentially a Model 36 Chief's Special in stainless steel. A J frame .38 Special, it has checkered walnut grips. This was a commercial success and is still very popular.

| NIB | Exc. | V.G. | Good | Fair | Poor |
|-----|------|------|------|------|------|
| 375 | 325 | 300 | 250 | 200 | 150 |

## Model 63
This model is simply the Model 34 .22/32 Kit Gun made of stainless steel.

| NIB | Exc. | V.G. | Good | Fair | Poor |
|-----|------|------|------|------|------|
| 375 | 325 | 300 | 250 | 200 | 150 |

## Model 64
This model is the stainless-steel version of the Model 10 M&P. It was introduced in 1970.

| NIB | Exc. | V.G. | Good | Fair | Poor |
|-----|------|------|------|------|------|
| 350 | 300 | 275 | 225 | 175 | 125 |

## Model 65
This is the stainless-steel version of the Model 13 M&P .357 Magnum. It was introduced in 1974.

| NIB | Exc. | V.G. | Good | Fair | Poor |
|-----|------|------|------|------|------|
| 350 | 300 | 275 | 225 | 175 | 125 |

## Model 66
Released in 1971, this is the stainless-steel version of the Model 19 or Combat Magnum. It is chambered for the .357 Magnum, has adjustable sights, a square butt with checkered walnut grips, and was initially offered with a 4" barrel. In 1974 a 2.5"-barrel, round-butt version was made available. It is currently available in a 6" barrel, as well as with all target options.

| NIB | Exc. | V.G. | Good | Fair | Poor |
|-----|------|------|------|------|------|
| 375 | 300 | 250 | 200 | 150 | 125 |

## Model 67
This is the 4"-barrelled stainless-steel version of the Model 15 Combat Masterpiece. In appearance it is similar to the Model 66 except that it is chambered for the .38 Special. This model was discontinued in 1988.

| Exc. | V.G. | Good | Fair | Poor |
|------|------|------|------|------|
| 300 | 250 | 200 | 150 | 125 |

## Model 650
This model is the J frame, stainless-steel version of the .22 Winchester Magnum rimfire Kit Gun, with a 3" heavy barrel, round butt, and fixed sights. This model was manufactured between 1983 and 1987.

| Exc. | V.G. | Good | Fair | Poor |
|------|------|------|------|------|
| 250 | 200 | 175 | 125 | 100 |

## Model 651
This is the Model 51 .22 Winchester Magnum rimfire revolver, with 4" barrel and adjustable sights made of stainless steel. It was manufactured between 1983 and 1987.

| Exc. | V.G. | Good | Fair | Poor |
|------|------|------|------|------|
| 275 | 225 | 200 | 150 | 125 |

## Model 520
This revolver was built on the N frame, is chambered for the .357 Magnum cartridge, and has a 4" barrel. It is an M&P model with fixed sights, blued finish, and checkered walnut Magna grips. There were 1,000 manufactured to fill an order by the New York State Police. "N.Y.S.P." is stamped on the frame. The state of New York never completed the purchase, and the revolvers were sold through commercial outlets.

| Exc. | V.G. | Good | Fair | Poor |
|------|------|------|------|------|
| 325 | 275 | 225 | 175 | 125 |

## Model 581
The Model 581 represented the first total redesign on a revolver for S&W in many years. It is built on the L frame, a new frame that is between the smaller K frame and the larger N frame. The reasoning behind this change is that the larger frame would stand up better to a steady diet of Magnum loads. This new design also incorporates a full-length barrel underlug, similar to that found on the Colt Python. This heavier barrel adds weight and a better balance to the revolver. The 581 version is the M&P fixed sight-type. Chambered for the .357 Magnum, it is offered with a 4" barrel in blue or nickel finish with checkered walnut grips. It is also known as the "Distinguished Service Magnum." It was introduced in 1985.

| NIB | Exc. | V.G. | Good | Fair | Poor |
|-----|------|------|------|------|------|
| 350 | 300 | 275 | 225 | 175 | 125 |

## Model 681
Identical in configuration to the 581, this model is made of stainless steel.

| NIB | Exc. | V.G. | Good | Fair | Poor |
|-----|------|------|------|------|------|
| 375 | 325 | 300 | 250 | 200 | 150 |

## Model 586
This revolver is the target version of S&W's new L frame series. The 586 is available with a 4", 6", or 8" barrel and has adjustable sights, target stocks, and all target options. It is offered either blued or nickel-plated. The 586 was introduced in 1986.

| NIB | Exc. | V.G. | Good | Fair | Poor |
|-----|------|------|------|------|------|
| 375 | 325 | 300 | 250 | 200 | 150 |

## Model 686
Known as "The Distinguished Combat Magnum", this is the stainless-steel version of the 586. It was introduced in 1986.

| NIB | Exc. | V.G. | Good | Fair | Poor |
|-----|------|------|------|------|------|
| 425 | 375 | 325 | 275 | 225 | 175 |

## Model 39
This was the first double action semi-automatic pistol produced in the U.S. It was released for sale in 1955. The Model 39 came standard with a lightweight alloy frame. It is chambered for the 9mm Parabellum cartridge. The barrel is 4" in length; and the finish, blued or nickel-plated with checkered walnut grips. The sights are adjustable for windage only, and the detachable magazine holds 8 shots. The Model 39 was discontinued in 1982.

| Exc. | V.G. | Good | Fair | Poor |
|------|------|------|------|------|
| 350 | 300 | 275 | 200 | 150 |

### Model 39 Steel Frame
S&W forged 1,000 Model 39 frames of steel early in the production run. These frames were not used except for some military test guns. Eventually the company decided to use these frames and produced 927 steel-framed pistols before 1966. These pistols were sold through normal distribution channels and today represent a find for the S&W collector.

| Exc. | V.G. | Good | Fair | Poor |
|------|------|------|------|------|
| 1000 | 800 | 650 | 500 | 400 |

### Model 59
This model is quite similar to the Model 39. The exception is the large grip that is needed to house the double-column 14-shot detachable magazine. This pistol came about in 1971 in response to a military order and was produced with black checkered plastic grips. It has the same specifications as the Model 39 with these two exceptions. The model was discontinued in 1981.

| Exc. | V.G. | Good | Fair | Poor |
|------|------|------|------|------|
| 375 | 325 | 300 | 225 | 175 |

### Model 439
This is simply an improved version of the Model 39. It has fully adjustable sights. It offers all the same features and finishes as the Model 39 and was discontinued in 1988.

| Exc. | V.G. | Good | Fair | Poor |
|------|------|------|------|------|
| 400 | 350 | 325 | 250 | 200 |

### Model 639
This is the stainless-steel version of the 439 9mm pistol. It features an ambidextrous safety and all other options of the Model 439.

| Exc. | V.G. | Good | Fair | Poor |
|------|------|------|------|------|
| 425 | 375 | 350 | 275 | 225 |

### Model 459
This improved-sight version of the 15 shot Model 59 9mm pistol was discontinued in 1988.

| Exc. | V.G. | Good | Fair | Poor |
|------|------|------|------|------|
| 400 | 350 | 300 | 250 | 200 |

### Model 659
This stainless-steel version of the Model 459 9mm pistol features an ambidextrous safety and all other options of the Model 459.

| Exc. | V.G. | Good | Fair | Poor |
|------|------|------|------|------|
| 450 | 400 | 350 | 300 | 250 |

### Model 539
This is yet another version of the Model 439 9mm pistol. It incorporates all the features of the Model 439 with a steel frame instead of aluminum alloy. This model was discontinued in 1983.

| Exc. | V.G. | Good | Fair | Poor |
|------|------|------|------|------|
| 400 | 350 | 300 | 250 | 200 |

### Model 559
This variation of the Model 459 9mm pistol has a steel frame instead of aluminum alloy. It is identical in all other respects.

| Exc. | V.G. | Good | Fair | Poor |
|------|------|------|------|------|
| 450 | 400 | 350 | 300 | 250 |

### Model 469
The Model 469 was brought out in answer to the need for a more concealable high-capacity pistol. It is essentially a "Mini" version of the Model 459. It is chambered for the 9mm Parabellum and has a 12-round detachable magazine with a finger-grip extension and a shortened frame. The barrel is 3.5" long; the hammer is bobbed and does not protrude; the safety is ambidextrous. The finish is matte blue, with black plastic grips. The Model 469 was discontinued in 1988.

| Exc. | V.G. | Good | Fair | Poor |
|------|------|------|------|------|
| 375 | 325 | 275 | 200 | 150 |

### Model 669
This is a stainless steel version of the Model 469 9mm pistol. All of the features of the 469 are incorporated. The Model 669 was manufactured from 1986 to 1988.

| Exc. | V.G. | Good | Fair | Poor |
|------|------|------|------|------|
| 425 | 350 | 300 | 250 | 200 |

## Model 645

The Model 645 is a large-framed, stainless-steel double-action pistol chambered for the .45 ACP cartridge. It has a 5" barrel, adjustable sights, and a detachable 8-shot magazine. It is offered with fixed or adjustable sights and an ambidextrous safety. The grips are molded black nylon. S&W manufactured this pistol between 1986 and 1988.

| Exc. | V.G. | Good | Fair | Poor |
|------|------|------|------|------|
| 450 | 400 | 350 | 300 | 250 |

## Model 745 - IPSC

This model is similar in outward appearance to the Model 645 but is quite a different pistol. The Model 745 is a single-action semi-auto chambered for the .45 ACP cartridge. The frame is made of stainless steel; and the slide, of blued carbon steel. The barrel is 5", and the detachable magazine holds 8 rounds. The sights are fully adjustable target types. The grips are checkered walnut.

| Exc. | V.G. | Good | Fair | Poor |
|------|------|------|------|------|
| 650 | 600 | 500 | 450 | 350 |

## Model 41

The Model 41 was introduced to the shooting public in 1957. It is a very high quality .22-rimfire target pistol. It has an alloy frame, steel slide, and either a 5.5" or 7- 3/8" barrel. It has a detachable 10-shot magazine, adjustable target sights, and checkered walnut target grips. The finish is blue.
Discontinued Barrels:
5" With Extended Sight--Add $50.
5.5" Heavy With Extended Sight--Add $60.
7.5" With Muzzle Brake--Add $40.

| NIB | Exc. | V.G. | Good | Fair | Poor |
|-----|------|------|------|------|------|
| 550 | 450 | 350 | 300 | 225 | 150 |

## Model 41-1

This model was introduced in 1960 and is chambered for the .22 short rimfire only. It was developed for the International Rapid Fire competition. In appearance it is quite similar to the Model 41 except that the slide is made of aluminum alloy, as well as the frame, in order to lighten it to function with the .22 short cartridge. This model was not a commercial success like the Model 41, so it was discontinued after fewer than 1,000 were manufactured.

| Exc. | V.G. | Good | Fair | Poor |
|------|------|------|------|------|
| 750 | 650 | 500 | 375 | 225 |

## Model 46

This was a lower-cost version of the Model 41. It was developed for the Air Force in 1959. Its appearance was essentially the same as the Model 41 with a 7" barrel. Later a 5" barrel was introduced, and finally in 1964 a heavy 5.5" barrel was produced. This economy target pistol never had the popularity that the more expensive Model 41 had, and it was discontinued in 1968 after approximately 4,000 pistols were manufactured.

| Exc. | V.G. | Good | Fair | Poor |
|------|------|------|------|------|
| 500 | 450 | 375 | 300 | 200 |

## Model 61 Escort

In 1970 the Model 61 was offered for sale. It was actually the only true pocket automatic that S&W produced. This pistol is chambered for the .22 long rifle cartridge, and has a 5 shot detachable magazine and 2.5" barrel. It is finished in blue or nickel-plated, with checkered plastic grips. The quality of this pistol never measured up to S&W's standards, and it was dropped in 1974.

| Exc. | V.G. | Good | Fair | Poor |
|------|------|------|------|------|
| 300 | 250 | 200 | 150 | 100 |

## Model 52

This model was introduced in 1961 as a high quality big-bore target pistol. It is chambered for the .38 Special Mid-Range cartridge and functions only with wadcutter bullets. In appearance it resembles the Model 39; and its action is quite similar, though locked to function as a single-action only. It has a 5" barrel and a 5-shot detachable magazine and is finished in blue with checkered walnut grips. There were approximately 3,500 manufactured before the original Model 52 was discontinued in 1963.

| Exc. | V.G. | Good | Fair | Poor |
|------|------|------|------|------|
| 650 | 550 | 450 | 350 | 250 |

## Model 52-1

In 1963 the action was changed from a locked-out double action to a true single action. The new model designation was adopted, and they were produced in this configuration until 1971. This model is similar to the original Model 52 in all other aspects.

| Exc. | V.G. | Good | Fair | Poor |
|------|------|------|------|------|
| 550 | 450 | 350 | 300 | 225 |

### Model 52-2

In 1971 a new, more efficient extractor was added to the Model 52 design; and the designation was again changed. It has remained in this configuration since and is still offered by S&W.

| NIB | Exc. | V.G. | Good | Fair | Poor |
|-----|------|------|------|------|------|
| 700 | 650  | 550  | 450  | 350  | 300  |

### Model 52-A

In 1961 S&W produced 87 special pistols for the Army Marksmanship Training Unit. They are chambered for the .38 AMU cartridge, an experimental semi-rimless .38 Special round. The Army, after testing a few of these pistols, decided that they were not interested in them. In 1964 S&W, after stamping the letter A after the 52 designation, released the 87 pistols through normal distribution channels. They represent one of the ultimate finds for a S&W collector today.

| Exc. | V.G. | Good | Fair | Poor |
|------|------|------|------|------|
| 2500 | 2000 | 1500 | 1000 | 750  |

### Model 422 Field

This .22-rimfire pistol was introduced in 1987. It has a 4.5" or 6" barrel, an alloy frame and steel slide, and a 10-shot detachable magazine. The Field Model has fixed sights and black plastic grips and is matte blued.

| NIB | Exc. | V.G. | Good | Fair | Poor |
|-----|------|------|------|------|------|
| 200 | 175  | 150  | 125  | 100  | 75   |

### Model 422 Target

This is similar to the Field Model, with adjustable sights and checkered walnut grips.

| NIB | Exc. | V.G. | Good | Fair | Poor |
|-----|------|------|------|------|------|
| 250 | 200  | 175  | 150  | 125  | 100  |

### Model 622 Field

This is a stainless-steel version of the Model 422 Field.

| NIB | Exc. | V.G. | Good | Fair | Poor |
|-----|------|------|------|------|------|
| 225 | 200  | 175  | 150  | 125  | 100  |

### Model 622 Target

This is the stainless-steel version of the Model 422 Target.

| NIB | Exc. | V.G. | Good | Fair | Poor |
|-----|------|------|------|------|------|
| 275 | 225  | 200  | 175  | 150  | 125  |

### Model 3904

In 1989 S&W redesigned the entire line of 9mm semi-automatic handguns. The 3904 is chambered for the 9mm Parabellum and has an 8-shot detachable magazine and 4" barrel with a fixed bushing. The frame is alloy, and the triggerguard is squared for two-hand hold. The magazine well is beveled, and the grips are one-piece wrap-around made of delrin. The three-dot sighting system is employed.

| NIB | Exc. | V.G. | Good | Fair | Poor |
|-----|------|------|------|------|------|
| 500 | 450  | 400  | 350  | 300  | 250  |

### Model 3906

This is the stainless-steel version of the Model 3904. The features are the same. It was introduced in 1989.

| NIB | Exc. | V.G. | Good | Fair | Poor |
|-----|------|------|------|------|------|
| 550 | 500  | 450  | 400  | 350  | 275  |

### Model 5904

This high-capacity, 15-shot version of the Model 3904 was introduced in 1989.

| NIB | Exc. | V.G. | Good | Fair | Poor |
|-----|------|------|------|------|------|
| 525 | 475  | 425  | 375  | 325  | 250  |

### Model 5906

This is the stainless-steel version of the Model 5904.

| NIB | Exc. | V.G. | Good | Fair | Poor |
|-----|------|------|------|------|------|
| 575 | 525  | 475  | 425  | 375  | 300  |

### Model 6904

This is the concealable, shortened version of the Model 5904. It has a 12-shot magazine, fixed sights, bobbed hammer, and a 3.5" barrel.

| NIB | Exc. | V.G. | Good | Fair | Poor |
|-----|------|------|------|------|------|
| 500 | 450  | 400  | 350  | 300  | 250  |

### Model 6906

This is the stainless-steel version of the compact Model 6904.

| NIB | Exc. | V.G. | Good | Fair | Poor |
|-----|------|------|------|------|------|
| 550 | 500  | 450  | 400  | 350  | 275  |

## Model 4506
This is the newly designed double action .45 ACP pistol. It is all stainless-steel and has a 5" barrel, 8-shot detachable magazine, and wrap-around black delrin grips.

| NIB | Exc. | V.G. | Good | Fair | Poor |
|-----|------|------|------|------|------|
| 650 | 600  | 550  | 500  | 400  | 300  |

## SMITH & WESSON LONG ARMS

### Model A Rifle
This is a bolt-action with 23.75" barrel, chambered for .22-250, .243, .270, .308, .30-06, 7mm Magnum, and .300 Winchester Magnum. It has a folding rear sight and a checkered Monte Carlo stock with contrasting rosewood forend tip and pistolgrip cap. It was manufactured for S&W by Husqvarna of Sweden.

| Exc. | V.G. | Good | Fair | Poor |
|------|------|------|------|------|
| 375  | 325  | 275  | 200  | 150  |

### Model B
This is the same as the Model A with a Schnabel forend and 20.75" barrel.

| Exc. | V.G. | Good | Fair | Poor |
|------|------|------|------|------|
| 400  | 350  | 300  | 250  | 200  |

### Model C
This is the same as the Model B with a cheekpiece.

| Exc. | V.G. | Good | Fair | Poor |
|------|------|------|------|------|
| 425  | 375  | 325  | 275  | 225  |

### Model D
This is the Mannlicher-stocked version.

| Exc. | V.G. | Good | Fair | Poor |
|------|------|------|------|------|
| 550  | 500  | 400  | 350  | 250  |

### Model E
This is the Model D without a cheekpiece.

| Exc. | V.G. | Good | Fair | Poor |
|------|------|------|------|------|
| 500  | 450  | 400  | 350  | 250  |

### Model 1500 Deluxe
This rifle was made for S&W by Howa Machine in Japan. It is chambered for .222 through .300 Winchester Magnum. It has a 22" barrel and a walnut Monte Carlo stock with skipline checkering.

| Exc. | V.G. | Good | Fair | Poor |
|------|------|------|------|------|
| 350  | 300  | 250  | 200  | 150  |

### Model 1500 Deluxe Varmint
This is similar to the 1500 Deluxe, with a 24" heavy barrel. It is chambered for the varmint calibers.

| Exc. | V.G. | Good | Fair | Poor |
|------|------|------|------|------|
| 350  | 300  | 250  | 200  | 150  |

### Model 1500 Mountaineer
This is similar to the rest of the series but lighter in weight.

| Exc. | V.G. | Good | Fair | Poor |
|------|------|------|------|------|
| 325  | 275  | 225  | 175  | 125  |

### Model 1700 Classic Hunter
This is a bolt-action rifle with 22" barrel, no sights, and a removable 5-round magazine. It has a nicely checkered walnut stock with Schnabel forend. It was imported from Howa of Japan.

| Exc. | V.G. | Good | Fair | Poor |
|------|------|------|------|------|
| 400  | 350  | 300  | 250  | 200  |

S&W discontinued the importation of the Howa line in 1984.

### Model 916 Slide Action Shotgun
This is offered in 12, 16, and 20 gauge and has barrel lengths of 20"-30" with various chokes. It has a plain stock and barrel. It was imported from Howa of Japan.

| Exc. | V.G. | Good | Fair | Poor |
|------|------|------|------|------|
| 175  | 150  | 125  | 100  | 75   |

### Model 916T
This is the same as the Model 916 with interchangeable barrel capability.

| Exc. | V.G. | Good | Fair | Poor |
|------|------|------|------|------|
| 200  | 175  | 150  | 125  | 100  |

### Model 3000 Slide Action
This is offered in 12 and 20 gauge. It has 3" chambers and 22"-30" barrel lengths and features a checkered walnut stock and forend.

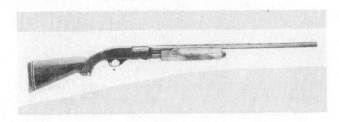

| Exc. | V.G. | Good | Fair | Poor |
|------|------|------|------|------|
| 300  | 275  | 200  | 150  | 125  |

### Model 3000 Police
This paramilitary-style riot gun has an 18" or 20" barrel, a matte blue or parkerized finish, and a combat-style finish on the stock.

| Exc. | V.G. | Good | Fair | Poor |
|------|------|------|------|------|
| 325  | 300  | 250  | 200  | 150  |

### Model 1000 Autoloader
Made by Howa Machine, this gas-operated shotgun has an alloy receiver with engraving. It was offered in 12 or 20 gauge with barrel lengths from 22"-30" and various chokes. The walnut stock is checkered, and the barrel features a vent rib.

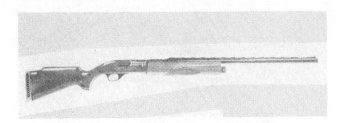

| Exc. | V.G. | Good | Fair | Poor |
|------|------|------|------|------|
| 375  | 325  | 275  | 225  | 150  |

### Model 1000 Super 12
This version could handle all pressure loads from Trap to Magnum interchangeably.

| Exc. | V.G. | Good | Fair | Poor |
|------|------|------|------|------|
| 500  | 400  | 300  | 250  | 175  |

# SNAKE CHARMER
### Little Field, Texas
### Sporting Arms Manufacturing, Inc.

**Snake Charmer**

This is a single-shot, break-open shotgun chambered for .410. It has an 18.5" barrel and is constructed of stainless steel. It has a molded plastic, modified pistolgrip stock and forend with a built-in shell holder in the stock. This model is currently manufactured.

| NIB | Exc. | V.G. | Good | Fair | Poor |
|-----|------|------|------|------|------|
| 150 | 125 | 100 | 75 | 50 | 25 |

# SNEIDER, CHARLES E.
### Baltimore, Maryland

**2-Cylinder Revolver**

This unique, single-action, spur-trigger revolver is chambered for .22 caliber rimfire. It has a 2.75" ribbed octagonal barrel. This revolver has two separate 7-shot unfluted cylinders mounted--one facing the muzzle and the other facing the shooter. The barrel pivots forward to remove the cylinders for loading. When the first cylinder is emptied, the cylinder pin rotates to allow the second cylinder to be placed in the firing position. They have a spur trigger and either a brass or iron frame. The finish is blued, with square-butt walnut grips. The barrel is marked "E. Sneider Pat. March 1862." The quantity produced is not known, but they are considered to be quite rare and were manufactured between 1865 and 1869.

| Exc. | V.G. | Good | Fair | Poor |
|------|------|------|------|------|
| 5000 | 4000 | 3000 | 2500 | 2000 |

# SODIA, FRANZ
### Ferlach, Austria

The arms of Franz Sodia are considered to be among the finest quality to come out of Europe. He manufactured double barrelled shotguns as well as drillings and combination guns. His weapons are profusely ornamented with precious metal inlays and should definitely be appraised by competent individuals before any transaction is attempted. We feel that the variations in values that are encountered make it impossible to evaluate weapons of this type in a book of this nature.

# SOKOLOVSKY CORP. SPORT ARMS
### Sunnyvale, California

**.45 Automaster**

This is a single-action semi-automatic pistol chambered for .45 ACP. It has a 6" barrel with Millet adjustable sights. It has a 6-shot detachable magazine and is totally free of external appendages. The construction is of stainless steel with checkered grips. There have only been 50 of these unique pistols manufactured since 1984.

| NIB | Exc. | V.G. | Good | Fair | Poor |
|-----|------|------|------|------|------|
| 3250 | 2750 | 2250 | 1750 | 1250 | 800 |

# SPALDING & FISHER
### Worchester, Massachusetts

**Double Barrelled Pistol**

This is a side-by-side pistol chambered for .36-caliber percussion. The standard barrel length is 5.5". There are double hammers that are operated by a single trigger. The top of the barrel is marked "Spalding & Fisher." The frame is iron and is blued, with rounded-type walnut grips. This company was a marketing agent and probably did not ever manufacture guns. This pistol was manufactured in the 1850's.

| Exc. | V.G. | Good | Fair | Poor |
|------|------|------|------|------|
| 500 | 400 | 350 | 250 | 175 |

# SPANG & WALLACE
### Philadelphia, Pennsylvania

**Pocket Pistol**

This model is chambered for .36-caliber percussion and was patterned after the Henry Deringer-type pistol. The barrel is round and varies in lengths from 2.5" to 6". The mountings are German silver, and the stock is walnut. The barrel is marked "Spang & Wallace/Phila." There is scroll engraving on the lock and the hammer. This firearm was manufactured between 1855 and 1863.

| Exc. | V.G. | Good | Fair | Poor |
|------|------|------|------|------|
| 750 | 650 | 550 | 400 | 300 |

# SPENCER
### Boston, Massachusetts

**Spencer Carbine**

This was one of the most popular firearms used by Union forces during the Civil War. It is chambered for a metallic rimfire cartridge known as the "No. 56." It is actually a .52 caliber and was made with a copper case. The barrel is 22" in length. The finish is blued, with a carbine-length walnut stock held on by one barrel band. There is a swing swivel at the butt. There were approximately 50,000 manufactured between 1863 and 1865.

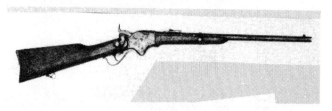

| Exc. | V.G. | Good | Fair | Poor |
|------|------|------|------|------|
| 1500 | 1250 | 950 | 750 | 450 |

**Military Rifle--Navy Model**

This model is similar to the carbine, with a 30" round barrel and a full-length walnut stock held on by three barrel bands. It features an iron forend tip and swing swivels. The Civil War production consisted of two models. A Navy Model was manufactured between 1862 and 1864 (there were approximately 1,000 of these so marked).

| Exc. | V.G. | Good | Fair | Poor |
|------|------|------|------|------|
| 1750 | 1500 | 1250 | 900 | 600 |

**Military Rifle--Army Model**

There were approximately 11,450 produced for the Army during the Civil War. They are similar to the Navy Model except that the front sight doubles as a bayonet lug. They were manufactured in 1863 and 1864.

| Exc. | V.G. | Good | Fair | Poor |
|------|------|------|------|------|
| 1650 | 1400 | 1100 | 800 | 500 |

## Springfield Armory Post-War Alteration

After the conclusion of the Civil War, approximately 11,000 carbines were refurbished and rechambered for .50- caliber rimfire. The barrels were sleeved, and a device known as the "Stabler Cut-off" was added to convert the arm to single-shot function. Often they were refinished and restocked. The inspector's marks "ESA" will be found in an oval cartouche on the left side of the stock. These alterations took place in 1867 and 1868.

| Exc. | V.G. | Good | Fair | Poor |
|------|------|------|------|------|
| 1250 | 1000 | 800  | 650  | 400  |

## Model 1865 Contract

This model was manufactured by the Burnside Rifle Company in 1865. They are similar to the Civil War-type carbine and are marked "By Burnside Rifle Co./Model 1865." There were approximately 34,000 manufactured. Old records show that 30,500 were purchased by the United States Government, and 19,000 of these had the Stabler Cut-off device.

| Exc. | V.G. | Good | Fair | Poor |
|------|------|------|------|------|
| 1200 | 950  | 750  | 600  | 350  |

There were a number of other variations in the Spencer line. It would behoove anyone interested in collecting this fine Civil War firearm to educate oneself on these variances and to secure individual appraisal if transactions are contemplated. A book of this nature cannot possibly get into the idiosyncrasies and complicated model variations of every manufacturer. Space will simply not permit it.

## SPENCER REVOLVER
### Maltby, Henley & Company
### New York, New York

### Safety Hammerless Revolver

This is a .32-caliber centerfire revolver with a 3" ribbed round barrel. It is double-action only and has no exposed hammer. The distinctive feature is that it was completely constructed of brass with the exception of the cylinder that was made of steel. The barrel is marked "Spencer Safety Hammerless Pat. Jan. 24, 1888 & Oct. 29, 1889." This revolver was manufactured in the 1890's.

| Exc. | V.G. | Good | Fair | Poor |
|------|------|------|------|------|
| 300  | 250  | 200  | 150  | 100  |

## SPIES, A. W.
### New York, New York

### Pocket Pistol

This is a .41-caliber percussion pistol that was patterned after the Henry Deringer-type pistol. It has a 2.5" barrel, German silver mountings, and a walnut stock. It was manufactured in the late 1850's.

| Exc. | V.G. | Good | Fair | Poor |
|------|------|------|------|------|
| 750  | 650  | 500  | 400  | 300  |

## SPILLER & BURR
### Atlanta, Georgia

### Navy Revolver

This single-action revolver was manufactured for use by the Confederate States of America during the Civil War. It was patterned after the Whitney-type Navy revolver. It is chambered for .36 caliber percussion and has either a 6" or 6.5" octagonal barrel. The unfluted cylinder holds six shots. The frame is brass; the remainder is blued, with two-piece walnut grips. Some barrels are marked "Spiller & Burr"; some models are not marked. The frame is usually marked "C.S." There were approximately 1,450 manufactured between 1862 and 1865.

The earlier models were manufactured at Atlanta, Georgia, with later productions at the Macon Armory in Macon, Georgia. This model, as with all Confederate Civil War weapons, is extremely collectible. One must be wary of fakes, and we strongly recommend competent, individual appraisal if a transaction is contemplated.

| Exc. | V.G. | Good | Fair | Poor |
|------|------|------|------|------|
| 5000 | 4250 | 3500 | 2750 | 1750 |

## SPIRLET, A.
### Liege, Belgium

Spirlet was erroneously credited with inventing the top-hinged tip-up revolver. This weapon was around well before Spirlet's time. Actually, the patent that he held covers lockwork and an ejection system that was used on tip-up revolvers. Although he manufactured some of these tip-up revolvers himself, there were never enough of them to establish him as little more than a small custom gunmaker. Revolvers that he manufactured bear his name and address on the breech end of the barrel. Many other makers utilized his developments.

## SPRINGFIELD ARMORY (MODERN)
### Geneseo, Illinois

### M1 Garand Rifle

This is a modern reproduction of the WWII service rifle. It is chambered for .270 (discontinued), .308 Winchester, and .30-06. It is a gas-operated semi-automatic with a 24" barrel and a walnut stock. It has adjustable sights and an 8-shot, clip-fed internal magazine.

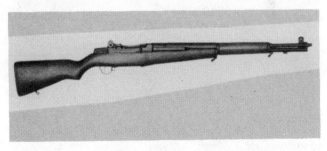

| Exc. | V.G. | Good | Fair | Poor |
|------|------|------|------|------|
| 775  | 650  | 550  | 400  | 300  |

### M1 National Match

This is similar to the standard M1, with a National Match barrel and sights.

| Exc. | V.G. | Good | Fair | Poor |
|------|------|------|------|------|
| 900  | 800  | 650  | 500  | 400  |

### MI Ultra Match

This model is similar to the National Match, with a glass-bedded walnut stock.

| Exc. | V.G. | Good | Fair | Poor |
|------|------|------|------|------|
| 1000 | 900  | 750  | 600  | 500  |

### M1-D Sniper Rifle

This model is basically a National Match version with an original M84 telescopic sight, flash suppressor, leather cheek pad and sling. It is chambered for .30-06 only.

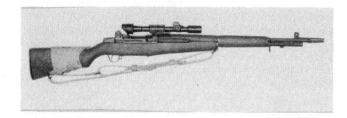

| Exc. | V.G. | Good | Fair | Poor |
|------|------|------|------|------|
| 1000 | 900 | 750 | 600 | 500 |

## M1 Tanker Rifle

This is a reproduction of the 18.25" barrelled T-26 Model that was authorized but never actually used in WWII. It is chambered for either .30-06 or .308 Winchester.

| Exc. | V.G. | Good | Fair | Poor |
|------|------|------|------|------|
| 800 | 700 | 550 | 400 | 300 |

Springfield Armory also imported the Italian BM59 Rifle. This was originally a Beretta conversion of our M1 Service Rifle that incorporated a 19.5" barrel and a 20-round detachable box magazine. Due to the current hysteria we are experiencing over assault-type weapons, it is impossible to accurately evaluate weapons of this nature. We strongly advise securing competent, local, individual appraisal if a transaction is contemplated. We list the different models for reference purposes only.

## Standard Rifle

This model has the 19.5" barrel and 20-round magazine and is chambered for 7.62mm. It was furnished with a grenade launcher and compensator. A winter trigger and bipod were also included.

## Alpine Rifle

This model was furnished with a pistolgrip-type stock and also was available as a paratrooper model, with a folding stock. Otherwise, it was similar to the Standard Rifle.

## Nigerian Rifle

This is similar to the Standard Model, with a pistolgrip-type stock.

## BM59 M1 Grand

There were only 200 of these rifles imported into the U.S.A. They have the original Beretta M1 receiver and are not Springfield Armory replicas.

The following rifles are replicas manufactured by Springfield Armory and are of the highest quality. They are, for the most part, semi-automatic versions of service weapons that were used by the United States, as well as foreign countries. As with the BM59, they fall into the same category; and evaluation in a publication of this nature is, in our opinion, inadvisable. We

strongly recommend competent, individual appraisal if a transaction is contemplated. We list the individual models for reference purposes only.

## M1A Rifle

This is a civilian semi-automatic version of the M14 Service Rifle. It is chambered for .243 (discontinued) and 7.62mm (NATO). It has a 22" barrel, a matte finish, and either a wood or fiberglass stock.

## M1A E-2

This is similar to the standard M1A Rifle, with the E-2-type target stock.

## M1A National Match

This model is similar to the standard M1A Rifle, with precision National Match barrel, sights, and various essential parts. It has a glass-bedded Match stock and a tuned action.

## Super Match

This is similar to the National Match, with an air-gauged, Douglas or Hart heavy barrel.

## M1A-A1 Bush Rifle

This model is similar to the standard M1A Rifle, with an 18.25" barrel. It is available with a folding stock.

## M14 Vietnam Commemorative

This model is similar to a standard M1A Rifle, with a high-polished and blued finish and many gold-plated small parts. It was produced with a select walnut stock that has a commemorative medallion inlaid in the butt. There were two versions--one for the Army and one for the Marine Corps. There were 1,500 of each manufactured in 1987 only. This rifle was marketed by the American Historical Foundation of Richmond, Virginia.

## SAR-48

This is a faithful copy of the Fabrique Nationale FN-LAR Rifle. It is chambered for .308 Winchester, has a 21" barrel, and is operated by a fully adjustable gas system. It has a 20-round detachable magazine and adjustable sights. The finish is black, with a black composition stock. The rifle is furnished with two magazines, bayonet, cleaning kit, magazine loader, and sling.

## SAR-48 Bush Rifle

This model is similar to the standard SAR-48 rifle, with an 18" barrel. A folding-stock paratrooper's model is also available.

## SAR-48 .22 Caliber

This is a .22-caliber rimfire version of the standard SAR-48 rifle.

## M6 Scout

This is a break-open, Over/Under survival gun chambered for .22 l.r., .22 Magnum, or .22 Hornet over .410. The barrels are 18" in length. The finish is black, with a black composition stock that houses extra cartridges.

| Exc. | V.G. | Good | Fair | Poor |
|------|------|------|------|------|
| 125 | 100 | 80 | 60 | 40 |

## Model 1911-A1

This is a Springfield-manufactured copy of the Colt 1911-A1 military semi-automatic pistol. It is chambered for 9mm, .38 Super, or .45 ACP. It is offered with either a blued or parkerized finish. This model was introduced in 1985.

| NIB | Exc. | V.G. | Good | Fair | Poor |
|-----|------|------|------|------|------|
| 425 | 375 | 350 | 300 | 250 | 200 |

## Combat Commander

This is a copy of the Colt Model 1911 A1 Combat Commander chambered for .45 ACP only. It was introduced in 1988.

| NIB | Exc. | V.G. | Good | Fair | Poor |
|-----|------|------|------|------|------|
| 475 | 425 | 400 | 350 | 300 | 250 |

## Custom Carry Gun

This is a combat version of the standard Model 1911 A1. It has high visibility sights, a tuned action, and an extended safety. It was introduced in 1988.

| NIB | Exc. | V.G. | Good | Fair | Poor |
|-----|------|------|------|------|------|
| 750 | 675 | 550 | 450 | 400 | 300 |

## National Match Model

This version features a National Match barrel and bushing that is custom-fitted to the frame and slide. It has adjustable target sights and checkered walnut grips. It was introduced in 1988.

| NIB | Exc. | V.G. | Good | Fair | Poor |
|-----|------|------|------|------|------|
| 850 | 750 | 650 | 550 | 450 | 350 |

## Competition Grade

This model is hand-tuned with a match grade trigger, low-profile combat sights, an ambidextrous safety, and a Commander-type hammer. It is furnished with Pachmayr grips. It was introduced in 1988.

| NIB | Exc. | V.G. | Good | Fair | Poor |
|------|------|------|------|------|------|
| 1050 | 950 | 850 | 700 | 600 | 500 |

## A Model Master Grade Competition Pistol

This model is similar to the custom carry gun, with a National Match barrel and bushing. It was introduced in 1988.

| NIB | Exc. | V.G. | Good | Fair | Poor |
|------|------|------|------|------|------|
| 1700 | 1500 | 1250 | 950 | 800 | 700 |

## Model B-1 Master Grade Competition Pistol

This version is a full-blown, compensated pin gun. It is specially built for USPSA/IPSC competition. It was introduced in 1988.

| NIB | Exc. | V.G. | Good | Fair | Poor |
|------|------|------|------|------|------|
| 2000 | 1750 | 1250 | 950 | 850 | 750 |

## Omega

This is a unique 1911-type pistol that is chambered for .38 Super, 10mm Norma, or .45 ACP. It is available with either a 5" or 6" polygon-rifled barrel. The barrel and slide are offered either ported or plain. The sights are adjustable, and the gun is capable of competition accuracy. It is furnished with Pachmayr grips and was introduced in 1987.
Caliber Conversion Units--Add $675.

| NIB | Exc. | V.G. | Good | Fair | Poor |
|-----|------|------|------|------|------|
| 850 | 750 | 650 | 500 | 400 | 300 |

# SPRINGFIELD ARMORY
### Springfield, Massachusetts

This was America's first federal armory. They began producing military weapons in 1795. They have supplied military weapons to the United States throughout its glorious history.

## Model 1841 Cadet Musket

This is a single-shot, muzzle-loading rifle chambered for .57-caliber percussion. It has a 40" round barrel with a full-length stock held on by three barrel bands. This rifle features no rear sight. It is browned and case-colored, with iron mountings. There is a steel ramrod mounted under the barrel. The lockplate is marked "Springfield" with the date of manufacture and "US" over an eagle motif. There were approximately 450 produced between 1844 and 1845.

| Exc. | V.G. | Good | Fair | Poor |
|------|------|------|------|------|
| 5000 | 4000 | 3000 | 2500 | 1850 |

## Model 1842 Musket

This is a single-shot muzzleloader chambered for .69-caliber percussion. It has a 42" round barrel and a full-length stock held on by three barrel bands. The finish is white with iron mountings and a steel ramrod mounted beneath the barrel. There were a total of approximately 275,000 manufactured between 1844 and 1855 by both the Springfield Armory and the Harper's Ferry Armory. They are so marked.

| Exc. | V.G. | Good | Fair | Poor |
|------|------|------|------|------|
| 1250 | 1000 | 750 | 450 | 350 |

### Model 1847 Musketoon

This is a single-shot muzzleloader chambered for .69-caliber percussion. It has a 26" round smooth-bore barrel. The finish is white, with a full-length walnut stock held on by two barrel bands. The lock is marked "Springfield." There were approximately 3,350 manufactured between 1848 and 1859.

| Exc. | V.G. | Good | Fair | Poor |
|------|------|------|------|------|
| 1750 | 1500 | 1000 | 850 | 600 |

### Model 1855 Musket

This is a single-shot muzzleloader chambered for .58-caliber percussion. It has a 40" round barrel with a full- length stock held on by three barrel bands. It has iron mountings and a ramrod mounted under the barrel. The front sight acts as a bayonet lug. The finish is white with a walnut stock. The lock is marked "U.S. Springfield." There was also a Harper's Ferry-manufactured version that is so marked. There were approximately 59,000 manufactured between 1857 and 1861.

| Exc. | V.G. | Good | Fair | Poor |
|------|------|------|------|------|
| 1500 | 1250 | 1000 | 750 | 550 |

### Model 1855 Rifled Carbine

This is a single-shot muzzleloader chambered for .54 caliber percussion. It has a 22" round barrel with a 3/4-length stock held on by one barrel band. The finish is white with iron mountings and a ramrod mounted under the barrel. The lock is marked "Springfield" and dated. There were approximately 1,000 manufactured between 1855 and 1856.

| Exc. | V.G. | Good | Fair | Poor |
|------|------|------|------|------|
| 3500 | 3000 | 2500 | 1750 | 1250 |

### Model 1863 Rifled Musket

This is a single-shot muzzleloader chambered for .58-caliber percussion. It has a 40" round barrel and a full-length stock held on by three barrel bands. The finish is white with iron mountings, and the lock is marked "U.S. Springfield" and dated 1863. There were approximately 275,000 manufactured in 1863.

| Exc. | V.G. | Good | Fair | Poor |
|------|------|------|------|------|
| 1250 | 1000 | 750 | 600 | 400 |

### Model 1868 Rifle

This is a single-shot "Trapdoor" rifle chambered for the .50-caliber centerfire cartridge. It features a breech-block that pivots forward when a thumblatch at its rear is depressed. It has a 32.5" barrel and a full-length stock held on by two barrel bands. It has iron mountings and a cleaning rod mounted under the barrel. It features an oil-finished walnut stock. The lock is marked "US Springfield." It is dated either 1863 or 1864. The breechblock features either the date 1869 or 1870. There were approximately 51,000 manufactured between 1868 and 1872.

| Exc. | V.G. | Good | Fair | Poor |
|------|------|------|------|------|
| 800 | 675 | 500 | 400 | 250 |

### Model 1869 Cadet Rifle

This is a single-shot "Trapdoor" rifle chambered for .50-caliber centerfire. It is similar to the Model 1868 with a 29.5" barrel. There were approximately 3,500 manufactured between 1869 and 1876.

| Exc. | V.G. | Good | Fair | Poor |
|------|------|------|------|------|
| 1000 | 850 | 650 | 500 | 450 |

### Model 1870

There are two versions of this "Trapdoor" breechloader --a rifle with a 32.5" barrel and a carbine that features a 22" barrel and a half-stock held on by one barrel band. They are both chambered for .50-caliber centerfire and feature the standard Springfield lock markings and a breechblock marked 1870" or "Model 1870." There were a total of 11,500 manufactured between 1870 and 1873. Only 340 are carbines; they are extremely rare.

**Rifle**

| Exc. | V.G. | Good | Fair | Poor |
|------|------|------|------|------|
| 1250 | 1000 | 750 | 600 | 500 |

**Carbine**

| Exc. | V.G. | Good | Fair | Poor |
|------|------|------|------|------|
| 3250 | 2750 | 2000 | 1500 | 1000 |

### Model 1873

This is a "Trapdoor" breechloading rifle chambered for the .45-70 cartridge. The rifle version has a 32.5" barrel with a full-length stock held on by two barrel bands. The carbine features a 22" barrel with a half-stock held on by a single barrel band, and the cadet rifle features a 29.5" barrel with a full-length stock and two barrel bands. The finish of all three variations is blued and case-colored, with a walnut stock. The lock is marked "US Springfield 1873." The breechblock is either marked "Model 1873" or "US Model 1873." There were approximately 73,000 total manufactured between 1873 and 1877.

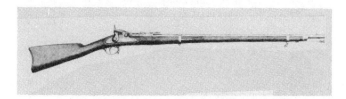

**Rifle--50,000 Manufactured**

| Exc. | V.G. | Good | Fair | Poor |
|------|------|------|------|------|
| 1250 | 1000 | 750 | 600 | 500 |

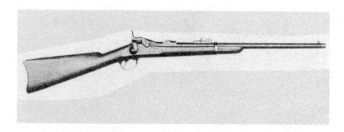

**Carbine--20,000 Manufactured**

| Exc. | V.G. | Good | Fair | Poor |
|------|------|------|------|------|
| 2500 | 2000 | 1500 | 1000 | 750 |

**Cadet Rifle--3,000 Manufactured**

| Exc. | V.G. | Good | Fair | Poor |
|------|------|------|------|------|
| 1250 | 1000 | 750 | 600 | 500 |

### Model 1875 Officer's Rifle

This is a high-grade "Trapdoor" breechloader chambered for the .45-70 cartridge. It has a 26" barrel and a half-stock fastened by one barrel band. It is blued and case-colored, with a scroll-engraved lock. It has a checkered walnut pistolgrip stock with a pewter forend tip. There is a cleaning rod mounted beneath the barrel. This rifle was not issued but was sold to army officers for personal sporting purposes. There were only 477 manufactured between 1875 and 1885.

| Exc. | V.G. | Good | Fair | Poor |
|------|------|------|------|------|
| 7500 | 6500 | 5000 | 3500 | 3000 |

### Model 1877

This is a "Trapdoor" breechloading rifle chambered for the .45-70 cartridge. It was issued as a rifle with a 32" barrel and a full-length stock held on by two barrel bands, a cadet rifle with a 29.5" barrel, and a carbine with a 22" barrel, half-stock, and single barrel band. This version is similar to the Model 1873. In fact, the breechblock retained the Model 1873 marking. The basic differences are that the stock is thicker at the wrist and the breechblock was thickened and lowered. This is basically a mechanically improved version. There were approximately 12,000 manufactured in 1877 and 1878.

**Rifle--3,900 Manufactured**

| Exc. | V.G. | Good | Fair | Poor |
|------|------|------|------|------|
| 1400 | 1200 | 850 | 700 | 550 |

### Cadet Rifle--1,000 Manufactured

| Exc. | V.G. | Good | Fair | Poor |
|------|------|------|------|------|
| 1500 | 1300 | 1000 | 850 | 650 |

### Carbine--2,950 Manufactured

| Exc. | V.G. | Good | Fair | Poor |
|------|------|------|------|------|
| 3000 | 2500 | 1800 | 1250 | 850 |

## Model 1880

This version features a sliding combination cleaning rod/bayonet that is fitted in the forearm under the barrel. It retained the 1873 Breechblock markings. There were approximately 1,000 manufactured for trial purposes in 1880.

| Exc. | V.G. | Good | Fair | Poor |
|------|------|------|------|------|
| 1500 | 1300 | 1000 | 850 | 650 |

## Model 1881 Marksman Rifle

This is an extremely high-grade Trapdoor breech-loading rifle chambered for the .45-70 cartridge. It has a 28" round barrel and is similar to the Model 1875 Officer's Rifle in appearance. It features a full-length, high-grade, checkered walnut stock held on by one barrel band. It has a horn Schnabel forend tip. The metal parts are engraved, blued, and case-colored. It has a Vernier aperture sight as well as a buckhorn rear sight on the barrel and a globe front sight with a spirit level. There were only 11 manufactured to be awarded as prizes at shooting matches. This is perhaps the supreme rarity among the Trapdoor Springfields, and one should be extremely cognizant of fakes.

| Exc. | V.G. | Good | Fair | Poor |
|-------|-------|-------|-------|-------|
| 35000 | 27500 | 22500 | 15000 | 10000 |

## Model 1881 Shotgun

This version has a 26" round smooth-bore barrel that is chambered for 20 gauge. It was used by hunters and scouts at western forts. There were approximately 1,376 manufactured between 1881 and 1885. This version is particularly susceptible to fakery. We advise a qualified appraisal.

| Exc. | V.G. | Good | Fair | Poor |
|------|------|------|------|------|
| 1750 | 1500 | 1200 | 850 | 700 |

## Model 1884

This is also a breechloading trapdoor single-shot rifle chambered for the .45-70 cartridge. It was issued as a standard rifle with a 32.75" barrel, a cadet rifle with a 29.5" barrel, and a military carbine with a 22" barrel. The finish is blued and case-colored. This model features the improved Buffington rear sight. It features the socket bayonet and a walnut stock. There were approximately 232,000 manufactured between 1885 and 1890.

### Rifle--200,000

| Exc. | V.G. | Good | Fair | Poor |
|------|------|------|------|------|
| 750 | 650 | 500 | 350 | 250 |

### Cadet Rifle--12,000

| Exc. | V.G. | Good | Fair | Poor |
|------|------|------|------|------|
| 850 | 750 | 600 | 400 | 300 |

### Carbine--20,000

| Exc. | V.G. | Good | Fair | Poor |
|------|------|------|------|------|
| 1000 | 850 | 700 | 500 | 400 |

## Model 1888

This version is similar to its predecessors except that it features a sliding, ramrod-type bayonet that was improved so that it stays securely locked when in its extended position. The breechblock was still marked "Model 1884." This was the last Springfield Trapdoor rifle produced. There were approximately 65,000 manufactured between 1889 and 1893.

| Exc. | V.G. | Good | Fair | Poor |
|------|------|------|------|------|
| 750 | 650 | 500 | 350 | 250 |

## Trapdoor Fencing Musket

This is a non-gun that was used by the Army in teaching bayonet drills. They had no desire to damage serviceable rifles during practice, so they produced this version to fill the bill. There were basically four types produced.

### Type I

This version is similar to the Model 1873 rifle without a breech or lock. The finish is rough, and it is unmarked. It was designed to accept a socket bayonet. One should secure a qualified appraisal if a transaction is contemplated. There were 170 manufactured in 1876 and 1877.

| Exc. | V.G. | Good | Fair | Poor |
|------|------|------|------|------|
| 800 | 650 | 500 | 400 | 300 |

### Type II

This version is basically a Model 1884 with the hammer removed and the front sight blade ground off. It accepted a socket bayonet that was covered with leather and had a pad on its point.

| Exc. | V.G. | Good | Fair | Poor |
|------|------|------|------|------|
| 500 | 400 | 300 | 250 | 200 |

### Type III

This version is similar to the Type II except that it is shortened to 43.5" in length. There were approximately 1,500 manufactured between 1905 and 1906.

| Exc. | V.G. | Good | Fair | Poor |
|------|------|------|------|------|
| 750 | 650 | 450 | 350 | 300 |

### Type IV

This version is similar to the Type III except that the barrel was filled with lead. There were approximatley 11,000 manufactured between 1907 and 1916.

| Exc. | V.G. | Good | Fair | Poor |
|------|------|------|------|------|
| 500 | 400 | 300 | 250 | 200 |

## Model 1870 Rolling Block

This is a single-shot breechloading rifle with a rolling-block action. It is chambered for .50-caliber centerfire and has a 32.75" barrel. It has a full-length forend held on by two barrel bands. The finish is blued and case-colored, with a cleaning rod mounted under the barrel. The stock and forend are walnut. The frame is marked "USN Springfield 1870." There is an anchor motif marked on the top of the barrel. It also features government inspector's marks on the frame. This rifle was manufactured by Springfield Armory under license from Remington Arms Company for the United States Navy. The first 10,000 produced were rejected by our navy and were sent to France and used in the Franco-Prussian War. For that reason, this variation is quite scarce and would bring a 20 percent premium. There was also a group of approximately 100 rifles that were converted to the .22 rimfire cartridge and used for target practice aboard ships. This version is extremely rare. There were approximately 22,000 manufactured in 1870 and 1871.

### Standard Navy Rifle

| Exc. | V.G. | Good | Fair | Poor |
|------|------|------|------|------|
| 800 | 700 | 600 | 400 | 300 |

### Rejected Navy Rifle

| Exc. | V.G. | Good | Fair | Poor |
|------|------|------|------|------|
| 700 | 600 | 500 | 350 | 250 |

### .22 Caliber

| Exc. | V.G. | Good | Fair | Poor |
|------|------|------|------|------|
| 2000 | 1750 | 1250 | 900 | 750 |

## U.S. Krag Jorgensen Rifle

This firearm will be found listed in its own section of this text.

## Model 1903

This rifle was a successor to the Krag Jorgensen and was also produced by the Rock Island Arsenal. It was initially chambered for the .30-03 cartridge and very shortly changed to the .30-06 cartridge. Its original chambering consisted of a 220-grain, round-nosed bullet. The German army introduced its spitzer bullet so our Government quickly followed suit with a 150-grain, pointed bullet designated the .30-06. This model has a 24" barrel and was built on what was basically a modified Mauser action. It features a 5-round integral box magazine. The finish is blued, with a full-length, straight-grip walnut stock with full handguards held on by two barrel bands. The initial version was issued with a rod-type bayonet that was quickly discontinued when President Theodore Roosevelt personally disapproved it. There were approximately 74,000 produced with this rod-bayonet; and if in an unaltered condition, these would be worth a great deal more than the standard variation. It is important to note that the early models with serial numbers under 800,000 were not heat-treated sufficiently to be safe to fire with modern ammunition. There were a great many produced between 1903 and 1930. The values represented reflect original specimens; WWII alterations would be worth approximately 15 percent less.

### Rod Bayonet Version (Unaltered)

| Exc. | V.G. | Good | Fair | Poor |
|------|------|------|------|------|
| 4500 | 3750 | 3250 | 2500 | 2000 |

### Standard Model 1903

| Exc. | V.G. | Good | Fair | Poor |
|------|------|------|------|------|
| 350  | 300  | 250  | 200  | 150  |

### Model 1903 Mark I

This version is similar to the original except that it was cut to accept the Pedersen device. This device allows the use of a semi-auto bolt insert that utilizes pistol cartridges. The rifle has a slot milled into the receiver that acts as an ejection port. The device was not successful and was scrapped. There were approximately 102,000 rifles that were produced with this mill-cut between 1918 and 1920. The values given are for the rifle alone--not for the device.

| Exc. | V.G. | Good | Fair | Poor |
|------|------|------|------|------|
| 350  | 300  | 250  | 200  | 150  |

### Model 1903 A1

This version is a standard Model 1903 rifle that was fitted with a Type C, semi-pistolgrip stock. All other specifications were the same.

| Exc. | V.G. | Good | Fair | Poor |
|------|------|------|------|------|
| 400  | 350  | 300  | 250  | 200  |

### Model 1903 A3

This version was introduced in May of 1942 for use in WWII. It basically consisted of improvements to simplify mass production. It features an aperture sight and various small parts that were fabricated from stampings; this includes the triggerguard, floor plate, and barrel band. The finish is parkerized. This model was manufactured by Remington and Smith Corona.

| Exc. | V.G. | Good | Fair | Poor |
|------|------|------|------|------|
| 300  | 250  | 200  | 150  | 100  |

### Model 1903 A4

This is a sniper-rifle version of the Model 1903. It is fitted with permanently mounted scope locks and furnished with a telescopic sight known as the M73B1. This scope was manufactured by Weaver in El Paso, Texas, and was commercially known as the Model 330C. The rifle has no conventional iron sights mounted.

| Exc. | V.G. | Good | Fair | Poor |
|------|------|------|------|------|
| 750  | 650  | 500  | 400  | 300  |

### Model 1903 NRA National Match

This version was based on a standard 1903 service rifle that was selected for having excellent shooting qualities. The parts were then hand-fit, and a special rifled barrel was added which was checked for tolerance with a star gauge. The muzzle of this barrel was marked with a special star with six or eight rays radiating from it. These NRA rifles were drilled and tapped to accept a Lyman No. 48 rear sight. They are marked with the letters "NRA" and have a flaming-bomb proofmark on the triggerguard. There were approximately 18,000 manufactured between 1921 and 1928.

| Exc. | V.G. | Good | Fair | Poor |
|------|------|------|------|------|
| 600  | 550  | 450  | 350  | 250  |

### Model 1903 NRA Sporter

This version is similar to the National Match rifle but features a half-length, sporter-type stock with one barrel band. It also features the Lyman No. 48 receiver sight. This version was produced for commercial sales. There were approximately 6,500 manufactured between 1924 and 1933.

| Exc. | V.G. | Good | Fair | Poor |
|------|------|------|------|------|
| 650  | 600  | 500  | 400  | 300  |

### Model 1917

In 1917 when the United States entered WWI, there was a distinct rifle shortage. There were production facilities set up for the British-pattern 1914 rifle. This "Enfield" rifle was redesigned to accept the .30-06 cartridge and was pressed into service as the U.S. rifle Model 1917. This rifle appears similar to the British-pattern 1914 rifle. In fact, they are so similar that in WWII, when over a million were sold to Britain for use by their home guard, it was necessary to paint a 2" stripe around the butt so that the caliber was immediately known. The barrel length is 26", and it has a 5-round integral box magazine. The finish is matte-blued, with a walnut stock. The breech is marked "U.S. Model 1917." This was a very robust and heavy-duty rifle, and many are used in the manufacture of large-bore custom rifles to this day. There were approximately 2,200,000 manufactured by Remington and Winchester between 1917 and 1918. The majority were produced at Eddystone, Pennsylvania.

| Exc. | V.G. | Good | Fair | Poor |
|------|------|------|------|------|
| 350  | 300  | 250  | 200  | 150  |

### Model 1922

This is a bolt-action training rifle chambered for the .22 rimfire cartridge. It appears similar to the Model 1903 but has a 24.5" barrel and a half-length stock without hand guards, held on by a single barrel band. It has a 5-round detachable box magazine. The finish is blued, with a walnut stock. The receiver is marked "U.S. Springfield Armory Model of 1922 Cal. 22." It also has the flaming-bomb ordnance mark. There were three basic types of the Model 1922: the standard issue type, the NRA commercial type, and the models that were altered to M1 or M2. There were a total of approximately 2,000 manufactured between 1922 and 1924. The survival rate of the original-issue types is not very large as most were converted.

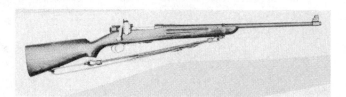

### Issue Type

| Exc. | V.G. | Good | Fair | Poor |
|------|------|------|------|------|
| 1000 | 850  | 650  | 450  | 400  |

### Altered Type

| Exc. | V.G. | Good | Fair | Poor |
|------|------|------|------|------|
| 650  | 550  | 450  | 300  | 250  |

**NRA Type--Drilled and Tapped for Scope**

| Exc. | V.G. | Good | Fair | Poor |
|---|---|---|---|---|
| 900 | 750 | 600 | 400 | 300 |

**Model 1922 M1**

This version is quite similar to the Model 1922, with a single firing pin that hits the top of the cartridge and a detachable box magazine that does not protrude from the bottom of the stock. The finish is parkerized; and the stock, of walnut. There were approximately 20,000 manufactured between 1924 and 1933.

**Unaltered Type**

| Exc. | V.G. | Good | Fair | Poor |
|---|---|---|---|---|
| 850 | 750 | 650 | 400 | 350 |

**Altered to M2**

| Exc. | V.G. | Good | Fair | Poor |
|---|---|---|---|---|
| 550 | 500 | 400 | 300 | 250 |

**Unaltered NRA Type**

| Exc. | V.G. | Good | Fair | Poor |
|---|---|---|---|---|
| 650 | 550 | 450 | 300 | 250 |

**NRA Type Altered to M2**

| Exc. | V.G. | Good | Fair | Poor |
|---|---|---|---|---|
| 550 | 500 | 400 | 300 | 250 |

**Model M2**

This is an improved version of the Model 1922 M1 that features an altered firing mechanism with a faster lock time. It has a knurled cocking knob added to the bolt and a flush-fitting detachable magazine with improved feeding. There were approximately 12,000 manufactured.

| Exc. | V.G. | Good | Fair | Poor |
|---|---|---|---|---|
| 600 | 500 | 400 | 300 | 200 |

**U.S. Rifle M1 (Garand)**

Springfield Armory was one of the manufacturers of this WWII service rifle. It is listed in the Garand section of this text.

## SPRINGFIELD ARMS COMPANY
### Springfield, Massachusetts

**Dragoon**

This is an unconventional-appearing, single-action revolver chambered for .40-caliber percussion. It has either a 6" or 7.5" round barrel. Some models have an integral loading lever mounted under the barrel; others did not. The unfluted cylinder holds six shots. The finish is blued, with rounded walnut grips. The topstrap is marked "Springfield Arms Company." There are four basic variations that comprised a total production of approximately 110 pistols manufactured in 1851. The values for the four variations are quite similar.

| Exc. | V.G. | Good | Fair | Poor |
|---|---|---|---|---|
| 4500 | 4000 | 3000 | 2000 | 1500 |

**Navy Model**

This is another unconventional-appearing, single-action revolver chambered for .36-caliber percussion. It has a 6" round barrel with the hammer mounted in the center of the frame. It has a 6-shot unfluted cylinder that features etched decorations. The finish is blued, with a case-colored frame and two-piece walnut grips. The topstrap is marked "Springfield Arms Company." There were actually two models--one features a single trigger; and the other, a double trigger in which the front trigger is utilized to revolve the cylinder. Both models feature integral loading levers mounted under the barrels. The total production was approximately 250 revolvers made in 1851.

| Exc. | V.G. | Good | Fair | Poor |
|---|---|---|---|---|
| 1500 | 1250 | 1000 | 800 | 600 |

**Belt Model**

This single-action revolver is chambered for .31- caliber percussion and is offered with either a 4", 5", or 6" round barrel. The hammer is mounted in the center of the frame, and the unfluted cylinder holds six shots and has etched decorations. Some versions feature an integral loading lever loaded on the cylinder pin. The finish is blued, with case-colored frame and two-piece walnut grips. There are several models. The first is marked "Jaquith's Patent 1838" on the frame, and the topstrap was marked "Springfield Arms." It has no loading lever, and there were approximately 150 manufactured.

| Exc. | V.G. | Good | Fair | Poor |
|---|---|---|---|---|
| 850 | 750 | 650 | 450 | 375 |

**Warner Model**

This is similar to the Jaquith model but is marked "Warner's Patent/Jan. 1851." There were approximately 150 of these.

| Exc. | V.G. | Good | Fair | Poor |
|---|---|---|---|---|
| 1250 | 1000 | 800 | 600 | 450 |

**Double Trigger Model**

This model is similar to the others but has two triggers--the front one is utilized to revolve the cylinder. This variation has an integral loading lever. There were approximately 100 produced in 1851.

| Exc. | V.G. | Good | Fair | Poor |
|---|---|---|---|---|
| 850 | 750 | 650 | 450 | 375 |

**Pocket Model Revolver**

This model is a single-action revolver chambered for .28-caliber percussion. It has a 2.5" round barrel, and the hammer is mounted in the center of the frame. There is no loading lever on this model. The etched cylinder is unfluted and holds six shots. The finish is blued, with a case-colored frame and rounded, two-piece walnut grips. It is marked "Warner's Patent Jan. 1851," as well as "Springfield Arms Company." There are several variations. The earliest model has no groove on the cylinder and has a rounded frame. There were approximately 525 manufactured in 1851.

| Exc. | V.G. | Good | Fair | Poor |
|---|---|---|---|---|
| 550 | 475 | 400 | 300 | 200 |

**Ring Trigger Model**

This revolver was produced without a triggerguard and has a front ring-type trigger that is used to revolve the cylinder. The conventional rear trigger fires the weapon. There were approximately 150 manufactured in 1851.

| Exc. | V.G. | Good | Fair | Poor |
|---|---|---|---|---|
| 600 | 525 | 450 | 350 | 250 |

**Double Trigger Model**

This version has two triggers within a conventional-type trigger guard. The forward trigger rotates the cylinder. There were 350 manufactured in 1851.

| Exc. | V.G. | Good | Fair | Poor |
|---|---|---|---|---|
| 550 | 475 | 400 | 300 | 200 |

**Late Model Revolver**

On this model, cocking the hammer automatically revolves the cylinder. There is a deep groove at the rear of the cylinder, and the markings are "Warner's Patent/James Warner, Springfield, Mass." There were approximately 500 manufactured in 1851.

| Exc. | V.G. | Good | Fair | Poor |
|---|---|---|---|---|
| 500 | 425 | 350 | 250 | 175 |

## SQUIBBMAN
### SEE--Squires, Bingham Mfg. Co., Inc.
### Rizal, Philippine Islands

## SQUIRES BINGHAM MFG. CO., INC.
### Rizal, Philippine Islands

This manufacturer produced inexpensive weapons under the trademark Squibman. They were of reasonable quality with good workmanship and materials.

### Model 100D
This is a double-action, swing-out cylinder revolver chambered for the .38 Special cartridge. It has a vent- ribbed 3", 4", or 6" barrel. It features adjustable sights and a matte black finish with wooden grips.

| Exc. | V.G. | Good | Fair | Poor |
|------|------|------|------|------|
| 125 | 100 | 80 | 60 | 40 |

### Model 100DC
This model is similar to the 100D, without the ventilated rib.

| Exc. | V.G. | Good | Fair | Poor |
|------|------|------|------|------|
| 125 | 100 | 80 | 60 | 40 |

### Model 100
This is a simpler version with a tapered barrel and plain, uncheckered wooden grips. Otherwise, it is similar to the Model 100D.

| Exc. | V.G. | Good | Fair | Poor |
|------|------|------|------|------|
| 125 | 100 | 80 | 60 | 40 |

### Thunder Chief
This model is similar to the 100D but is also offered chambered for the .22 l.r. and the .22 rimfire Magnum cartridges. It has a heavier barrel with a ventilated rib and a full-length, shrouded ejector rod. The grips are Philippine ebony.

| Exc. | V.G. | Good | Fair | Poor |
|------|------|------|------|------|
| 150 | 125 | 100 | 80 | 60 |

## STAFFORD, T. J.
### New Haven, Connecticut

### Pocket Pistol
This is a spur-trigger, single-shot pocket pistol chambered for .22-caliber rimfire. It has a 3.5" octagonal barrel that tips downward for loading. The barrel is marked "T. J. Stafford New Haven Ct." The frame is silver-plated brass. The barrel is either blued or silver-plated, and the grips are rosewood or walnut in a square butt configuration. There were a few hundred manufactured in the early 1860's.

| Exc. | V.G. | Good | Fair | Poor |
|------|------|------|------|------|
| 300 | 250 | 200 | 150 | 100 |

### Large Frame Model
Stafford also manufactured a large-frame version of their single-shot pistol chambered for the .38 rimfire cartridge. It has a 6" octagonal barrel, and the other specifications are similar to the .22-caliber version. This .38-caliber pistol is quite rarely encountered on today's market. It was also manufactured in the early 1860's.

| Exc. | V.G. | Good | Fair | Poor |
|------|------|------|------|------|
| 400 | 350 | 300 | 250 | 200 |

## STANDARD ARMS CO.
### Wilmington, Delaware

### Model G
This was the first successful gas-operated auto-loading rifle in the United States. It is chambered for .25-35, .30-30, .25 Remington, .30 Remington, and .35 Remington. The barrel is 22" in length, with open sights. It has a box magazine that loads from the bottom and features a gas port that could be closed, allowing the rifle to operate as a slide-action. The finish is blued, with a walnut straight-grip stock. It was manufactured circa 1910.

| Exc. | V.G. | Good | Fair | Poor |
|------|------|------|------|------|
| 450 | 400 | 350 | 250 | 150 |

## STAR, BONIFACIO ECHEVERRIA
### Eibar, Spain
### SEE--Echeverria

## STARR, EBAN T.
### New York, New York

### Single Shot Deringer
This single-shot pocket pistol is chambered for the .41 rimfire cartridge. It has a 2.75" round barrel that pivots downward for loading. It has a manual extractor. The hammer is mounted on the right side, and the trigger is a button on the front of the frame. The frame is silver-plated brass; the barrel, either blued or silver-plated. The grips are checkered walnut. The left side of the frame is marked "Starr's Pat's May 10, 1864." There were a few hundred manufactured between 1864 and 1869.

| Exc. | V.G. | Good | Fair | Poor |
|------|------|------|------|------|
| 500 | 400 | 300 | 200 | 100 |

### Four Barreled Pepperbox
This pocket-type pistol is chambered for the .32-caliber rimfire cartridge. It has a four-barrelled cluster that is 2.75" to 3.25" in length. The barrels tip forward for loading. The hammer is located on the right side of the frame, and the trigger is of the button type. It has a silver-plated brass frame with blued barrels and walnut grips. The frame is marked "Starr's Pat's May 10, 1864." There are six basic variations of this model as follows:

### First Model
This model has a fluted breech and a barrel release mounted on the right side of the frame.

| Exc. | V.G. | Good | Fair | Poor |
|------|------|------|------|------|
| 750 | 650 | 550 | 400 | 300 |

### Second Model
This model has a flat breech.

| Exc. | V.G. | Good | Fair | Poor |
|------|------|------|------|------|
| 650 | 550 | 450 | 300 | 200 |

### Third Model
This model has a rounded breech with a visible firing-pin retaining spring.

| Exc. | V.G. | Good | Fair | Poor |
|------|------|------|------|------|
| 450 | 350 | 250 | 200 | 150 |

### Fourth Model
This version has a rounded breech with no visible springs.

| Exc. | V.G. | Good | Fair | Poor |
|------|------|------|------|------|
| 450 | 350 | 250 | 200 | 150 |

### Fifth Model
This model has a larger, less rounded handle with thinner grips.

| Exc. | V.G. | Good | Fair | Poor |
|------|------|------|------|------|
| 400 | 300 | 200 | 150 | 100 |

### Sixth Model
The Sixth Model is similar to the Fifth Model, with a longer frame.

| Exc. | V.G. | Good | Fair | Poor |
|------|------|------|------|------|
| 700 | 600 | 500 | 350 | 300 |

## STARR ARMS COMPANY
### New York, New York

### 1858 Navy Revolver
This is a large, double-action revolver chambered for .36-caliber percussion. It has a 6" round barrel with an integral loading lever mounted beneath it and a 6-shot unfluted cylinder. The finish is blued, with a case-colored hammer, trigger, and loading lever. The two-piece grips are walnut. The frame is marked "Starr Arms Co. New York." There were approximately 3,000 manufactured between 1858 and 1860.

## Standard Model

| Exc. | V.G. | Good | Fair | Poor |
|------|------|------|------|------|
| 750 | 675 | 550 | 400 | 300 |

## Martially Marked (JT)

| Exc. | V.G. | Good | Fair | Poor |
|------|------|------|------|------|
| 1000 | 850 | 750 | 550 | 400 |

## 1858 Army Revolver

This is a large, double-action revolver chambered for .44-caliber percussion. It has a 6" round barrel with an integral loading lever. The unfluted cylinder holds six shots. The finish is blued, with a case-colored hammer, trigger, and loading lever, and two-piece walnut grips. The frame is marked "Starr Arms Co. New York." There were approximately 23,000 manufactured in the late 1850's to the early 1860's. Most found will be martially marked, and no premium exists for this feature.

| Exc. | V.G. | Good | Fair | Poor |
|------|------|------|------|------|
| 650 | 575 | 500 | 350 | 250 |

## 1863 Army Revolver

This is a single-action revolver chambered for .44-caliber percussion. It has an 8" round barrel with an integral loading lever mounted beneath it. It has a 6-shot unfluted cylinder. The finish is blued, with a case-colored hammer and loading lever. The grips are walnut. The frame is marked "Starr Arms Co., New York." This model was designed to be stronger and simpler to manufacture than the early double-action Starrs and except for the Colt and Remington was the most used revolving handgun by Union forces in the Civil War. Most will be found with martial markings. There were approximately 32,000 manufactured between 1863 and 1865.

| Exc. | V.G. | Good | Fair | Poor |
|------|------|------|------|------|
| 650 | 575 | 500 | 350 | 250 |

## Percussion Carbine

This is a single-shot breechloader that is activated by downward pressure on the triggerguard, allowing the breechblock to lower and tip backwards. It is chambered for .54-caliber percussion and has a 21" round barrel and a walnut half-stock fastened by one barrel band. The mountings are iron; the finish, blued with a case-colored lock and frame. The lock is marked "Starr Arms Co./Yonkers, N.Y."

| Exc. | V.G. | Good | Fair | Poor |
|------|------|------|------|------|
| 900 | 800 | 700 | 500 | 400 |

## Cartridge Carbine

This single-shot falling-block breechloader is chambered for the .52-caliber rimfire cartridge. It has a 21" round barrel and a walnut stock held on by one barrel band. The finish is blued, with a case-colored lock and frame. The mountings are iron, and the stock is walnut. It is marked "Starr Arms Co./Yonkers, N.Y." There were approximately 5,000 manufactured before the company went out of business in 1867.

| Exc. | V.G. | Good | Fair | Poor |
|------|------|------|------|------|
| 1000 | 900 | 800 | 600 | 500 |

## STEEL CITY ARMS, INC.
### Pittsburgh, Pennsylvania

### Double Deuce

This is a blowback-operated, semi-automatic, double-action pocket pistol. It is chambered for .22 l.r., has a 2.5" barrel, and is constructed of matte finish stainless steel with plain rosewood grips. It has a 7-round detachable box magazine and was introduced in 1984.

| Exc. | V.G. | Good | Fair | Poor |
|------|------|------|------|------|
| 300 | 250 | 200 | 150 | 100 |

## STENDA WAFFENFABRIK
### Suhl, Germany

### Pocket Pistol

This is a blowback-operated semi-automatic pistol chambered for the 7.65mm cartridge. This pistol is extremely similar to the "Beholla," the "Leonhardt," and the "Menta." Stenda took over the production of the Beholla pistol design at the close of WWI. The only major difference in the Stenda design was the elimination of the Beholla's worst feature, the pin that went through the slide and retained the barrel. It was replaced by a sliding catch that anchored it in place and unlocked the slide so that the barrel could be removed without the need of a vise and drift pin. The fastest way to identify the Stenda pistol is that there are no holes through the slide and there is a catch on the frame above the trigger. The finish is blued, with plastic grips; and the slide is marked "Waffenfabrik Stendawerke Suhl." There were approximately 25,000 manufactured before production ceased in 1926.

| Exc. | V.G. | Good | Fair | Poor |
|------|------|------|------|------|
| 250 | 225 | 200 | 150 | 100 |

## STERLING ARMAMENT LTD.
### London, England
### Importer--Cassi, Inc.
### Colorado Springs, Colorado

This is an old-line company that engages in the manufacture of paramilitary- and military-type weapons. Their current production is affected by the mass hysteria gripping our Country regarding assault-type weapons, making it extremely difficult to accurately evaluate them at this time. We list their current production for reference purposes only.

### Parapistol MK 7 C4

This is a semi-automatic, assault-type pistol chambered for 9mm Parabellum. It features a blowback action with a floating firing pin, has a 4" barrel, and fires from the closed-bolt position. It is available with detachable box magazines, with capacities of 10, 15, 20, 30, 34, or 68 rounds. The finish is black wrinkle paint.

### Parapistol MK 7 C8
This version is similar to the Model C4, with a 7.8" barrel.

### Sterling MK 6
This is a semi-automatic version of the Sterling Submachine Gun. It is chambered for 9mm Parabellum and has a shrouded 16.1" barrel with a folding metal stock and a side-mounted magazine. It is also painted with black wrinkle paint.

# STEVENS, J. ARMS CO.
## Chicopee Falls, Massachusetts

In 1864 this firm began doing business as J. Stevens & Company. In 1888 it was incorporated as the J. Stevens Arms & Tool Company. It operated as such until 1920, when it was taken over by the Savage Arms Company. It has operated as an independent division in this organization since. This Company produced a great many firearms--most that were of an affordable nature. They are widely collected, and one interested in them should take advantage of the literature available on the subject.

### Vest Pocket Pistol
This is a single-shot pocket pistol chambered for the .22 and the .30 rimfire cartridges. The .22-caliber version is rarely encountered and would be worth approximately 10 percent more than the values illustrated. It has a 2.75" part-octagonal barrel that pivots upward for loading. It has an external hammer and a spur-type trigger. The frame is nickel-plated or blued, with a blued barrel. The odd-shape flared grips are made of rosewood. The first models were marked "Vest Pocket Pistol" only. Later models have the barrels marked "J. Stevens & Co. Chicopee Falls, Mass." There were approximately 1,000 manufactured between 1864 and 1876.

| Exc. | V.G. | Good | Fair | Poor |
|------|------|------|------|------|
| 800 | 700 | 600 | 500 | 375 |

### Pocket Pistol
This is a more conventional-appearing, single-shot pocket pistol chambered for either the .22 or the .30 rimfire cartridges. It has a 3.5" part-octagonal barrel that pivots upward for loading. It features a plated brass frame with either a blued or nickel-plated barrel and rosewood, two-piece grips. The barrel is marked "J. Stevens & Co. Chicopee Falls, Mass." There were approximately 15,000 manufactured between 1864 and 1886.

| Exc. | V.G. | Good | Fair | Poor |
|------|------|------|------|------|
| 350 | 300 | 250 | 150 | 100 |

### Gem Pocket Pistol
This is a single-shot, derringer-type pocket pistol chambered for either the .22 or .30 rimfire cartridges. It has a 3" part-octagonal barrel that pivots to the side for loading. It has a nickel-plated brass frame with either a blued or plated barrel. It has birdshead grips made of walnut or rosewood. The barrel is marked "Gem," and the Stevens name or address does not appear on this firearm. There were approximately 4,000 manufactured between 1872 and 1890.

| Exc. | V.G. | Good | Fair | Poor |
|------|------|------|------|------|
| 400 | 350 | 300 | 200 | 150 |

### .41 Caliber Derringer
This is a single-shot pocket pistol chambered for the .41 rimfire cartridge. It has a 4" part-octagonal barrel that pivots upward for loading. It has a spur trigger and an external hammer. The frame is plated brass with a blued barrel. It has walnut birdshead grips. This firearm is completely unmarked except for a serial number. There were approximately 100 manufactured in 1875.

| Exc. | V.G. | Good | Fair | Poor |
|------|------|------|------|------|
| 750 | 700 | 600 | 500 | 400 |

### Single Shot Pistol
This is a single-shot pistol chambered for the .22 or .30 rimfire cartridges. It has a 3.5" part-octagonal barrel that pivots upward for loading. It is quite similar in appearance to the original pocket pistol. It has a plated brass frame and either a blued or nickel-plated barrel with walnut, square-butt grips. The barrel is marked "J. Stevens A&T Co." There were approximately 10,000 manufactured between 1886 and 1896.

| Exc. | V.G. | Good | Fair | Poor |
|------|------|------|------|------|
| 300 | 250 | 200 | 150 | 100 |

### No. 41 Pistol
This is a single-shot pocket pistol chambered for the .22 and .30 short cartridges. It has a 3.5" part-octagonal barrel that pivots upward for loading. It features an external hammer and a spur-type trigger. It has an iron frame with the firing pin mounted in the recoil shield. It is either blued or nickel-plated, with square-butt walnut grips. There were approximately 90,000 manufactured between 1896 and 1916.

| Exc. | V.G. | Good | Fair | Poor |
|------|------|------|------|------|
| 300 | 250 | 200 | 150 | 100 |

### Stevens Tip Up Rifles
This series of rifles was produced by Stevens beginning in the 1870's through 1895. There are a number of variations, but they are all quite similar in appearance. They feature a distinctive sloped frame made of iron and nickel-plated. Most frames are similar in size, but there is a slightly lighter frame used on the "Ladies Model" rifles. These Tip Up Rifles are chambered for various calibers from the .22 rimfire to the .44 centerfire cartridges. They are offered with barrel lengths of 24", 26", 28", or 30". The actions are nickel-plated, as well as the triggerguards and the buttplates. The barrels are blued, and the two-piece stocks are of walnut. They are offered with various buttplates and sights. A shotgun version is also offered. There are a number of variations that differ only slightly, and the model numbers are not marked on the rifles. We suggest securing a qualified appraisal if in doubt. The major variations and their values are as follows:

### Ladies Model--.22 or .25 Rimfire Only, 24" or 26" Barrel
| Exc. | V.G. | Good | Fair | Poor |
|------|------|------|------|------|
| 800 | 750 | 650 | 550 | 450 |

### Tip Up Rifle--Without Forend
| Exc. | V.G. | Good | Fair | Poor |
|------|------|------|------|------|
| 500 | 400 | 300 | 200 | 150 |

### Tip Up Rifle--With Forend, Swiss-Type Buttplate
| Exc. | V.G. | Good | Fair | Poor |
|------|------|------|------|------|
| 550 | 450 | 350 | 250 | 175 |

### Tip Up Shotgun--All Gauges, 30" or 32" Barrel
| Exc. | V.G. | Good | Fair | Poor |
|------|------|------|------|------|
| 350 | 300 | 200 | 150 | 100 |

### Ideal Single Shot Rifle
This excellent rifle was manufactured by Stevens between 1896 and 1933. It is a single-shot, falling-block-type action that is activated by a triggerguard-action lever. It was produced in many popular calibers from .22 rimfire up to .30-40. It was also manufactured in a number of special Stevens calibers. It was offered with various-length barrels in many different grades, from plain Spartan starter rifles up to some extremely high-grade Schuetzen-type target rifles with all available options. In 1901 Harry Pope of Hartford, Connecticut, went to work for Stevens and brought his highly respected barrel to the Stevens Company. He remained an employee for only two years, and the firearms produced during this period have the name "Stevens-Pope" stamped on the top of the barrel in addition to the other factory markings. Rifles marked in this manner and authenticated would be worth an approximate 50 percent premium if they are in very good to excellent condition. Due to numerous variations and options offered, we strongly recommend securing a qualified appraisal, especially on the higher-grade Ideal series rifles, if a transaction is contemplated.

## No. 44

This version is chambered for various calibers and is offered with a 24" or 26" barrel. It has an open rear sight with a Rocky Mountain-type front sight. The finish is blued and case-colored, with a walnut stock. There were approximately 100,000 manufactured between 1896 and 1933.

| Exc. | V.G. | Good | Fair | Poor |
|------|------|------|------|------|
| 450 | 400 | 350 | 250 | 150 |

## No. 44-1/2

This rifle is similar in appearance to the No. 44 but features an improved action. It has barrel lengths up to 34" and will be found with the Stevens-Pope barrel. It was manufactured between 1903 and 1916.

| Exc. | V.G. | Good | Fair | Poor |
|------|------|------|------|------|
| 500 | 450 | 400 | 300 | 200 |

## No. 044-1/2

This version is also known as the English Model rifle and is similar to the No. 44-1/2 except that it has a shotgun butt and a tapered barrel. There were a number of options offered which would affect the value. It was manufactured between 1903 and 1916.

| Exc. | V.G. | Good | Fair | Poor |
|------|------|------|------|------|
| 600 | 550 | 500 | 400 | 300 |

## No. 45

This version is also known as the range rifle. It is chambered for various calibers from the .22 rimfire to .44-40. Its identifying features are the Beach sights with an additional Vernier tang sight and a Swiss-type buttstock. It is offered with a 26" or 28" part-octagonal barrel. It was manufactured between 1896 and 1916. Values for a standard version are as follows:

| Exc. | V.G. | Good | Fair | Poor |
|------|------|------|------|------|
| 650 | 600 | 550 | 450 | 350 |

## No. 47

This version is similar to the No. 45, with a pistolgrip buttstock.

| Exc. | V.G. | Good | Fair | Poor |
|------|------|------|------|------|
| 750 | 700 | 650 | 550 | 450 |

## No. 49

This model is also known as the "Walnut Hill Rifle." It is a high-grade target rifle chambered for many calibers between the .22 rimfire and the .44-40. It is offered with a 28" or 30" part-octagonal barrel that is medium- or heavy-weight. It was furnished with a globe front sight and a Vernier tang sight. It is blued with a case-colored frame and has a high-grade, checkered, varnished walnut stock that has a high comb and features a pistol grip, cheekpiece, Swiss-type buttplate, and a loop-type triggerguard lever that resembles that of a lever-action rifle. The receiver is engraved, and there were a number of options available that would increase the value when present. We recommend an appraisal when in doubt. This rifle was manufactured between 1896 and 1932.

| Exc. | V.G. | Good | Fair | Poor |
|------|------|------|------|------|
| 1450 | 1250 | 1000 | 800 | 550 |

## Model 50

This version is identical to the Model 49 but was offered with a higher-grade walnut stock.

| Exc. | V.G. | Good | Fair | Poor |
|------|------|------|------|------|
| 1650 | 1450 | 1250 | 1000 | 700 |

## Model 51

This version is known as the "Schuetzen Rifle" and is quite similar to the No. 49 except that it features double-set triggers, a higher-grade walnut stock, a wooden insert in the triggerguard action lever, and a heavy, Schuetzen-type buttplate. There were many options available on this model, and we recommend securing an appraisal when in doubt. It was manufactured between 1896 and 1916.

| Exc. | V.G. | Good | Fair | Poor |
|------|------|------|------|------|
| 2000 | 1800 | 1500 | 1000 | 800 |

## No. 52

This version is also known as the "Schuetzen Junior." It is similar to the No. 51 except that it features more engraving and a higher-grade walnut stock. It was manufactured between 1897 and 1916.

| Exc. | V.G. | Good | Fair | Poor |
|------|------|------|------|------|
| 2100 | 1900 | 1600 | 1100 | 900 |

## No. 54

This is similar to the No. 52 except that it has double-set triggers and a palmrest, as well as a very heavy, Swiss-style buttplate. It is offered with a 30" or 32" part-octagonal heavy barrel. This was Stevens' top-of-the-line rifle. It was offered with many options, and an appraisal should be secured if in doubt. It was manufactured between 1897 and 1916.

| Exc. | V.G. | Good | Fair | Poor |
|------|------|------|------|------|
| 2500 | 2200 | 1800 | 1400 | 1000 |

## No. 55

This version is one of the Stevens' Ideal Ladies Models. It is chambered for the smaller rimfire calibers between .22 short and .32 long rimfire. It features a 24" or 26" part-octagonal barrel with a Vernier tang sight. The finish is blued and case-colored, with a checkered pistolgrip walnut stock that features a Swiss-type buttplate. This is a lighter-weight rifle that was manufactured between 1897 and 1916.

| Exc. | V.G. | Good | Fair | Poor |
|------|------|------|------|------|
| 1250 | 1000 | 800 | 600 | 400 |

## No. 56

This Ladies Model rifle is similar to the No. 55 except that it is chambered for centerfire cartridges and has a higher-grade walnut stock. It was made on the improved No. 44-1/2 action. It was manufactured between 1906 and 1916.

| Exc. | V.G. | Good | Fair | Poor |
|------|------|------|------|------|
| 1250 | 1000 | 800 | 600 | 400 |

## No. 404

This version is chambered for the .22 rimfire cartridge only. It features a 28" round barrel with a globe front sight and a Lyman No. 42 receiver sight. The finish is blued and case-colored. It has a walnut straight-grip stock with a semi-beavertail forend. It features a shotgun-type buttplate. It was manufactured between 1910 and 1916.

| Exc. | V.G. | Good | Fair | Poor |
|------|------|------|------|------|
| 750 | 650 | 550 | 400 | 300 |

## No. 414

This version is also known as the Armory Model and is chambered for the .22 l.r. cartridge only. It was built on a No. 44 action and features a 26" round barrel. It has a Rocky Mountain front sight with a Lyman receiver sight at the rear. The finish is blued and case-colored, with a straight-grip walnut stock and forend held on by a single barrel band. It was manufactured between 1912 and 1932.

| Exc. | V.G. | Good | Fair | Poor |
|------|------|------|------|------|
| 600 | 500 | 450 | 300 | 250 |

## Boys Rifles

The Stevens Company produced an extensive line of smaller, single-shot rifles chambered for small calibers and intended primarily for use by young shooters. These firearms have become quite collectible and are considered a field of speciality by many modern collectors. There are many variations that were available with a number of options that would affect their value. We supply information and values for the major variations but would recommend securing a qualified appraisal if in doubt.

### "Favorite" Rifles

This series of rifles is chambered for the .22, .25, and .32 rimfire. It has a 22" part-octagonal barrel and is blued, with a case-colored frame. It has a takedown-type action with an interchangeable barrel feature. It was available with optional sights, as well as buttplates. There were approximately 1,000,000 manufactured between 1893 and 1939. The variations are as follows:

### 1st Model Favorite

This version is chambered for the .22 or .25 rimfire cartridge. It has a removable sideplate on the right side of the receiver not found on any other variation. There were approximately 1,000 manufactured between 1893 and 1894.

| Exc. | V.G. | Good | Fair | Poor |
|------|------|------|------|------|
| 850 | 750 | 650 | 500 | 350 |

### No. 17

This is the standard, plain version with open sights.

| Exc. | V.G. | Good | Fair | Poor |
|------|------|------|------|------|
| 350 | 300 | 250 | 175 | 125 |

### No. 20

This version is chambered for the .22 or .32 rimfire shot cartridges and has a smooth-bore barrel and no rear sight.

| Exc. | V.G. | Good | Fair | Poor |
|------|------|------|------|------|
| 350 | 300 | 250 | 175 | 125 |

### No. 21

This version is known as the Bicycle Rifle and features a 20" barrel with open sights standard. It was furnished with a canvas carrying case that would be worth approximately a 10 percent premium. It was manufactured between 1898 and 1903.

| Exc. | V.G. | Good | Fair | Poor |
|------|------|------|------|------|
| 300 | 250 | 200 | 150 | 100 |

### No. 21 Ladies Model

This version bears the same model number as the Bicycle Rifle but has a 24" barrel and a high-grade, checkered walnut stock with a Swiss buttplate. It features a Vernier tang sight. It was manufactured between 1910 and 1916.

| Exc. | V.G. | Good | Fair | Poor |
|------|------|------|------|------|
| 600 | 500 | 400 | 300 | 250 |

### No. 16

This version is known as the "Crack Shot." It is chambered for .22 or .32 rimfire cartridges with a 20" round barrel. It has a rolling-block-type action with a thumb lever on the side. It is a utility-type rifle with open sights, a blued and case-colored finish, and a plain two-piece walnut stock with a rubber buttplate. The barrel is marked "Crack Shot" along with the standard Stevens' barrel address markings. It was manufactured between 1900 and 1913.

| Exc. | V.G. | Good | Fair | Poor |
|------|------|------|------|------|
| 300 | 250 | 200 | 150 | 100 |

### No. 16-1/2

This version is similar to the No. 16 except that it is chambered for the .32 rimfire shot cartridge with a smooth-bore barrel. It was manufactured between 1900 and 1913.

| Exc. | V.G. | Good | Fair | Poor |
|------|------|------|------|------|
| 325 | 275 | 225 | 175 | 125 |

### No. 23

This version is chambered for the .22 rimfire cartridge. It has a 20" round barrel that pivots to the right for loading. There is a barrel release on the frame. This version is blued and case-colored, with a plain walnut buttstock and no forend. It was manufactured between 1894 and 1897.

| Exc. | V.G. | Good | Fair | Poor |
|------|------|------|------|------|
| 350 | 300 | 250 | 200 | 150 |

### No. 15

This version is also known as the "Maynard Junior." It is chambered for the .22 rimfire cartridge and has an 18" part-octagonal barrel. The action is similar to the Civil War Maynard rifle with a triggerguard-activating lever. The finish is all blued, with a bored-type buttstock and no forearm. The barrel is marked "Stevens-Maynard, J. R." in addition to the standard Stevens' barrel address. It was manufactured between 1902 and 1912.

| Exc. | V.G. | Good | Fair | Poor |
|------|------|------|------|------|
| 250 | 225 | 200 | 150 | 100 |

### No. 15-1/2

This is a smooth-bore version of the No. 15.

| Exc. | V.G. | Good | Fair | Poor |
|------|------|------|------|------|
| 275 | 250 | 225 | 175 | 125 |

### No. 14

This version is also known as the Little Scout. It is a utility, take-down rifle that is blued, with a one-piece bored-type stock. It features a rolling-block-type action and was manufactured between 1906 and 1910.

| Exc. | V.G. | Good | Fair | Poor |
|------|------|------|------|------|
| 300 | 250 | 200 | 150 | 125 |

### No. 14-1/2

This version is similar to the No. 14 except that it has a two-piece stock. It is also marked "Little Scout." It was manufactured between 1911 and 1941.

| Exc. | V.G. | Good | Fair | Poor |
|------|------|------|------|------|
| 275 | 250 | 225 | 175 | 125 |

### No. 65

This version is known as the "Little Krag." It is a single-shot bolt-action rifle chambered for the .22 rimfire cartridge. It has a one-piece stock and a 20" round barrel that was marked "Little Krag." This version is quite scarce. It was manufactured between 1903 and 1910.

| Exc. | V.G. | Good | Fair | Poor |
|------|------|------|------|------|
| 275 | 250 | 225 | 175 | 125 |

### No. 12

This version is also known as the "Marksman." It is chambered for the .22, .25, and the .32 rimfire cartridges. It has a 22" barrel that pivots upward for loading. It is activated by an S-shaped triggerguard lever. It was manufactured between 1911 and 1930.

| Exc. | V.G. | Good | Fair | Poor |
|------|------|------|------|------|
| 275 | 250 | 225 | 175 | 125 |

### No. 26

This version is also known as the "Crack Shot." It has a rolling-block-type action and is chambered for .22 or the .32 rimfire cartridges. It is offered with an 18" or 20" round barrel. It is blued and has a two-piece stock. It was manufactured between 1912 and 1939.

| Exc. | V.G. | Good | Fair | Poor |
|------|------|------|------|------|
| 275 | 250 | 225 | 175 | 125 |

### No. 26-1/2

This is the smooth-bore version of the No. 26.

| Exc. | V.G. | Good | Fair | Poor |
|------|------|------|------|------|
| 300 | 250 | 200 | 150 | 125 |

### No. 11

This is a single-shot, rolling-block rifle chambered for the .22 rimfire cartridge. It has a 20" barrel, is blued, and has a bore-type stock without a buttplate. This was the last model offered in the Boys Rifle series. It was manufactured between 1924 and 1931.

| Exc. | V.G. | Good | Fair | Poor |
|------|------|------|------|------|
| 200 | 175 | 150 | 100 | 75 |

## Model 71

This was a re-introduced version of the "Stevens Favorite." It is chambered for the .22 l.r. cartridge and has a 22" octagonal barrel. The finish is blued and case-colored, with a plain walnut stock that has an inlaid medallion and a crescent buttplate. There were 10,000 manufactured in 1971.

| Exc. | V.G. | Good | Fair | Poor |
|------|------|------|------|------|
| 200  | 175  | 150  | 100  | 75   |

## Model 72

This is a re-introduced version of the Crack Shot that features a single-shot, falling-block action. It is chambered for the .22 rimfire cartridge and has a 22" octagon barrel with open sights. It is blued and case-colored, with a straight walnut stock. It was introduced in 1972.

| Exc. | V.G. | Good | Fair | Poor |
|------|------|------|------|------|
| 175  | 150  | 125  | 100  | 75   |

## Model 70

This is a slide-action rifle chambered for the .22 rimfire cartridge. It is also known as the "Visible Loading Rifle." It features a 20" round barrel with a 3/4-length, tubular magazine. The finish is blued and case-colored, and it has a walnut stock. It features open sights but was available with other options. It was offered as the No. 701/2, 71, 71-1/2, 72, and 72-1/2. These different model numbers denote various sight combinations. Otherwise, they are identical. They were manufactured between 1907 and 1932.

| Exc. | V.G. | Good | Fair | Poor |
|------|------|------|------|------|
| 275  | 250  | 200  | 150  | 100  |

## No. 80

This is a slide-action repeating rifle chambered for the .22 rimfire cartridge. It has a 24" round barrel with a tubular magazine. It features open sights and is blued, with a walnut stock. It was manufactured between 1906 and 1910.

| Exc. | V.G. | Good | Fair | Poor |
|------|------|------|------|------|
| 300  | 275  | 225  | 175  | 125  |

## High Power Rifle

This is a series of lever-action hunting rifles chambered for the .25, .30-30, .32, and the .35 centerfire cartridges. It features a 22" round barrel with a tubular magazine. The finish is blued, with a walnut stock. It is available in four variations--the No. 425, No. 430, No. 435, and the No. 440. These designations denote increased ornamentation and high quality materials and workmanship used in construction. There were approximately 26,000 manufactured between 1910 and 1917.

### No. 425

| Exc. | V.G. | Good | Fair | Poor |
|------|------|------|------|------|
| 500  | 450  | 400  | 300  | 200  |

### No. 430

| Exc. | V.G. | Good | Fair | Poor |
|------|------|------|------|------|
| 650  | 600  | 500  | 400  | 300  |

### No. 435

| Exc. | V.G. | Good | Fair | Poor |
|------|------|------|------|------|
| 1000 | 800  | 700  | 600  | 400  |

### No. 440

| Exc. | V.G. | Good | Fair | Poor |
|------|------|------|------|------|
| 2250 | 2000 | 1750 | 1250 | 850  |

## Model 89

This is a single-shot, Martini-type, falling-block rifle chambered for the .22 l.r. cartridge. It has an 18.5" barrel and a triggerguard loop-lever activator. The finish is blued, with a straight walnut stock. It was introduced in 1976 and is no longer manufactured.

| Exc. | V.G. | Good | Fair | Poor |
|------|------|------|------|------|
| 100  | 80   | 70   | 60   | 40   |

## Model 987

This is a blowback-operated semi-automatic rifle chambered for the .22 l.r. cartridge. It has a 20" barrel with a 15-round tubular magazine. The finish is blued, with a hardwood stock.

| Exc. | V.G. | Good | Fair | Poor |
|------|------|------|------|------|
| 120  | 100  | 90   | 80   | 60   |

Beginning in 1869 the Stevens Company produced a series of single-shot, break-open target and sporting pistols that pivot upward for loading. They are chambered for the .22 and the .25 rimfire cartridges, as well as various centerfire cartridges from the .32 short Colt to the .44 Russian. These pistols were made with various barrel lengths and have either a spur trigger or conventional trigger with a guard. They are all single-actions with exposed hammers. The finishes are nickel-plated frames with blued barrels and walnut grips. These variations and their values are as follows:

## Six-Inch Pocket Rifle

This version is chambered for the .22 rimfire cartridge and has a 6" part-octagonal barrel with open sights. The barrel is marked "J. Stevens & Co. Chicopee Falls, Mass." There were approximately 1,000 manufactured between 1869 and 1886.

| Exc. | V.G. | Good | Fair | Poor |
|------|------|------|------|------|
| 400  | 350  | 300  | 200  | 125  |

## No. 36

This version is known as the Stevens-Lord Pistol. It is chambered for various rimfire and centerfire calibers up to .44 Russian. It is offered with a 10" or 12" part- octagonal barrel and features a firing pin in the frame with a bushing. It has a conventional trigger with a spurred triggerguard. It features the standard Stevens' barrel address. It was named after Frank Lord, a target shooter well-known at this time. There were approximately 3,500 manufactured from 1880 to 1911.

| Exc. | V.G. | Good | Fair | Poor |
|------|------|------|------|------|
| 550  | 500  | 400  | 300  | 200  |

## First Issue Stevens-Conlin

This version is chambered for the .22 or .32 rimfire cartridges. It has a 10" or 12" part-octagonal barrel. It features a plated brass frame with a blued barrel and checkered walnut grips with a weighted butt cap. This version has a spur trigger either with or without a triggerguard. It was named after James Conlin, the owner of a shooting gallery located in New York City. There were approximately 500 manufactured between 1880 and 1884.

| Exc. | V.G. | Good | Fair | Poor |
|------|------|------|------|------|
| 850  | 750  | 650  | 450  | 350  |

## Second Issue Stevens-Conlin No. 38

This version is similar to the First Issue, with a conventional trigger and spurred triggerguard, as well as a fully adjustable rear sight. There were approximately 6,000 manufactured between 1884 and 1903.

| Exc. | V.G. | Good | Fair | Poor |
|------|------|------|------|------|
| 650  | 550  | 450  | 350  | 250  |

## No. 37

This version is also known as the Stevens-Gould and was named after a nineteenth century firearms writer. It resembles the No. 38 without the spur on the triggerguard. There were approximately 1,000 manufactured between 1889 and 1903.

| Exc. | V.G. | Good | Fair | Poor |
|------|------|------|------|------|
| 850  | 750  | 650  | 450  | 350  |

## No. 35

This version is chambered for the .22 rimfire, the .22 Stevens-Pope, and the .25 Stevens cartridges. It is offered with a 6", 8", or 10" part-octagonal barrel. The firing pin has no bushing. It features an iron frame that is either blued or plated with a blued barrel. It has plain walnut grips with a weighted buttcap. It featured open sights. There were approximately 43,000 manufactured between 1923 and 1942.

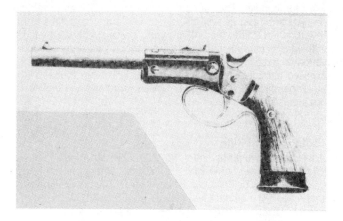

| Exc. | V.G. | Good | Fair | Poor |
|------|------|------|------|------|
| 350 | 300 | 250 | 150 | 100 |

## No. 35 Target

This version is similar to the No. 35 but has a better quality triggerguard and sights. There were approximately 35,000 manufactured between 1907 and 1916.

| Exc. | V.G. | Good | Fair | Poor |
|------|------|------|------|------|
| 375 | 325 | 275 | 175 | 125 |

## No. 43

This version is also called the Diamond and was produced in two distinct variations--called the First Issue and the Second Issue. The First Issue has a brass frame; and the Second Issue, an iron frame and no firing pin bushing. Otherwise they are quite similar and would be valued the same. They are chambered for the .22 rimfire cartridge and are offered with either a 6" or 10" part-octagonal barrel. The frames are either nickel-plated or blued with blued barrels and square-butt walnut grips. There were approximately 95,000 manufactured between 1886 and 1916.

| Exc. | V.G. | Good | Fair | Poor |
|------|------|------|------|------|
| 350 | 300 | 250 | 150 | 100 |

## No. 10 Target Pistol

This version was a departure from its predecessors. It very much resembles a semi-automatic pistol but is, in reality, a single-shot. It is chambered for the .22 rimfire cartridge and has an 8" round barrel that pivots upward for loading. It has a steel frame and is blued, with checkered rubber grips. Instead of the usual exposed hammer, this version has a knurled cocking piece that extends through the rear of the frame. There were approximately 7,000 manufactured between 1919 and 1933.

| Exc. | V.G. | Good | Fair | Poor |
|------|------|------|------|------|
| 450 | 400 | 350 | 250 | 150 |

## Pocket Rifles

This series of pistols is similar to the target and sporting pistols except that these were produced with detachable shoulder stocks that bear the same serial number as the pistol with which they were sold. They are sometimes referred to as Bicycle Rifles. The collector interest in these weapons is quite high; but it would behoove one to be familiar with the provisions of the Gun Control Act of 1968 when dealing in or collecting this variation-- as when the stock is attached, they can fall into the category of a short-barrelled rifle. Some are considered to be curios and relics, and others have been totally declassified; but some models may still be restricted. We strongly recommend securing a qualified, individual appraisal on these highly collectible firearms if a transaction is contemplated. The values we supply include the matching shoulder stock. If the stock number does not match the pistol, the values would be approximately 25 percent less; and with no stock at all, 50 percent should be deducted.

## Old Model Pocket Rifle

This version is chambered for the .22 rimfire cartridge and has an 8" or 10" part-octagonal barrel. It has a spur trigger and an external hammer on which the firing pin is mounted. The extractor is spring-loaded. It has a plated brass frame, blued barrel, and either walnut or rosewood grips. The shoulder stock is either nickel-plated or black. The barrel is marked "J. Stevens & Co. Chicopee Falls, Mass." There were approximately 4,000 manufactured between 1869 and 1886.

| Exc. | V.G. | Good | Fair | Poor |
|------|------|------|------|------|
| 650 | 575 | 475 | 350 | 250 |

## Reliable Pocket Rifle

This version is chambered for the .22 rimfire cartridge and in appearance is quite similar to the Old Model. The basic difference is that the extractor operates as a part of the pivoting barrel mechanism instead of being spring-loaded. The barrel is marked "J. Stevens A&T Co." There were approximately 4,000 manufactured between 1886 and 1896.

| Exc. | V.G. | Good | Fair | Poor |
|------|------|------|------|------|
| 650 | 575 | 475 | 350 | 250 |

## No. 42 Reliable Pocket Rifle

This version is similar to the first-issue Reliable except that it has an iron frame with the firing pin mounted in it without a bushing. The shoulder stock is shaped differently. There were approximately 8,000 manufactured between 1896 and 1916.

| Exc. | V.G. | Good | Fair | Poor |
|------|------|------|------|------|
| 650 | 575 | 475 | 350 | 250 |

## First Issue New Model Pocket Rifle

This version is the first of the medium-frame models with a frame width of 1". All of its predecessors have a 5/8"-wide frame. This model is chambered for the .22 and .32 rimfire cartridges and is offered with barrel lengths of 10", 12", 15", or 18" that are part-octagonal in configuration. The external hammer has the firing pin mounted on it. It has a plated brass frame, blued barrel, and either walnut or rosewood grips. The shoulder stock is nickel-plated and fitted differently than the small-frame models in that there is a dovetail in the butt and the top leg is secured by a knurled screw. The barrel is marked "J. Stevens & Co. Chicopee Falls, Mass." There were approximately 8,000 manufactured between 1872 and 1875.

| Exc. | V.G. | Good | Fair | Poor |
|------|------|------|------|------|
| 700 | 600 | 500 | 400 | 300 |

## Second Issue New Model Pocket Rifle

This version is similar to the First Issue except that the firing pin is mounted in the frame with a bushing. There were approximately 15,000 manufactured between 1875 and 1896.

| Exc. | V.G. | Good | Fair | Poor |
|------|------|------|------|------|
| 700 | 600 | 500 | 400 | 300 |

## Vernier Model

This version is similar to the Second Issue except that it features a Vernier tang sight located on the backstrap. There were approximately 1,500 manufactured between 1884 and 1896.

| Exc. | V.G. | Good | Fair | Poor |
|------|------|------|------|------|
| 750 | 650 | 550 | 450 | 350 |

## No. 40

This version is similar to its medium-frame predecessors except that it has a longer grip frame and a conventional trigger with triggerguard. There were approximately 15,000 manufactured between 1896 and 1916.

| Exc. | V.G. | Good | Fair | Poor |
|------|------|------|------|------|
| 500 | 450 | 375 | 300 | 200 |

## No. 40-1/2

This version is similar to the No. 40, with a Vernier tang sight mounted on the backstrap. There were approximately 2,500 manufactured between 1896 and 1915.

| Exc. | V.G. | Good | Fair | Poor |
|------|------|------|------|------|
| 750 | 650 | 550 | 450 | 350 |

## No. 34

This is the first of the heavy-frame pocket rifles that featured a 1.25"-wide frame. This version is also known as the Hunter's Pet. It is chambered for many popular cartridges from the .22 rimfire to the .44-40 centerfire. It is offered with a part-octagonal 18", 20", 22", or 24" barrel. It has a nickel-plated iron frame and blued barrel. The detachable stock is nickel-plated, and the grips are walnut. There were very few produced with a brass frame; and if located, these would be worth twice the value indicated. The firing pin is mounted in the frame with the bushing, and it features a spur trigger. There were approximately 4,000 manufactured between 1872 and 1900.

| Exc. | V.G. | Good | Fair | Poor |
|------|------|------|------|------|
| 650 | 575 | 475 | 350 | 250 |

## No. 34-1/2

This version is similar to the No. 34 except that it features a Vernier tang sight mounted on the backstrap. There were approximately 1,200 manufactured between 1884 and 1900.

| Exc. | V.G. | Good | Fair | Poor |
|------|------|------|------|------|
| 750 | 650 | 550 | 450 | 350 |

The Stevens Company produced a number of inexpensive, utilitarian, bolt-action rifles. These were both single-shot and repeaters. They have been very popular over the years as starter rifles for young shooters. Their values are quite similar, and we list them for reference purposes only.

**Model 053--Single Shot**
**Model 056--5-Shot Magazine**
**Model 066--Tube Magazine**
**Model 083--Single Shot**
**Model 084--5-Shot Magazine**
**Model 086--Tube Magazine**
**Model 15--Single Shot**
**Model 15Y--Single Shot**
**Model 419--Single Shot**
**Model 48--Single Shot**
**Model 49--Single Shot**
**Model 50--Single Shot**
**Model 51--Single Shot**
**Model 52--Single Shot**
**Model 53--Single Shot**
**Model 56--5-Shot Magazine**
**Model 66--Tube Magazine**

| Exc. | V.G. | Good | Fair | Poor |
|------|------|------|------|------|
| 90 | 80 | 70 | 50 | 25 |

## Model 416

This is a target rifle chambered for the .22 l.r. cartridge. It has a 24" heavy barrel with aperture sights. It features a 5-round detachable magazine and is blued, with a target-type walnut stock.

| Exc. | V.G. | Good | Fair | Poor |
|------|------|------|------|------|
| 200 | 175 | 150 | 100 | 75 |

## Model 322

This is a bolt-action sporting rifle chambered for the .22 Hornet cartridge. It has a 20" barrel with open sights and a detachable box magazine. The finish is blued, with a plain walnut stock.

| Exc. | V.G. | Good | Fair | Poor |
|------|------|------|------|------|
| 150 | 125 | 100 | 75 | 50 |

## Model 322-S

This version features an aperture rear sight.

| Exc. | V.G. | Good | Fair | Poor |
|------|------|------|------|------|
| 150 | 125 | 100 | 75 | 50 |

This company manufactured a number of single-barrel, break-open, single-shot shotguns. They were produced chambered for various gauges with various-length barrels and chokes. They are quite similar in appearance and were designed as inexpensive, utility-grade weapons. There is little or no collector interest in them at this time, and their values are similar. We list them for reference purposes only.

**Model 100**
**Model 102**
**Model 104**
**Model 105**
**Model 106**
**Model 107**
**Model 108**
**Model 110**
**Model 120**
**Model 125**
**Model 140**
**Model 160**
**Model 165**
**Model 170**
**Model 180**
**Model 89**
**Model 90**
**Model 93**
**Model 94**
**Model 944**
**Model 94A**
**Model 94C**
**Model 95**
**Model 958**
**Model 97**
**Model 970**

| Exc. | V.G. | Good | Fair | Poor |
|------|------|------|------|------|
| 90 | 80 | 75 | 50 | 25 |

## Model 182

This is a single-shot, break-open shotgun chambered for 12 gauge. It is offered with a 30" or 32" trap choked barrels and features a hammerless action with an automatic ejector and a lightly engraved receiver. The finish is blued, with a checkered trap-grade stock.

| Exc. | V.G. | Good | Fair | Poor |
|------|------|------|------|------|
| 125 | 100 | 75 | 50 | 25 |

## Model 185

This version features a half-octagonal barrel with an automatic ejector and a checkered walnut stock.
Damascus Barrel--Deduct 25 Percent.

| Exc. | V.G. | Good | Fair | Poor |
|------|------|------|------|------|
| 150 | 125 | 100 | 75 | 50 |

## Model 190

This is a 12-gauge hammerless gun with an automatic ejector. It is lightly engraved with a half-octagonal barrel.
Damascus Barrel--Deduct 25 Percent.

| Exc. | V.G. | Good | Fair | Poor |
|------|------|------|------|------|
| 150 | 125 | 100 | 75 | 50 |

## Model 195

This is another deluxe version that features engraving, a half-octagonal barrel, and a high-grade, checkered walnut stock.
Damascus Barrel--Deduct 25 Percent.

| Exc. | V.G. | Good | Fair | Poor |
|------|------|------|------|------|
| 275 | 250 | 200 | 150 | 100 |

The firm of J. Stevens produced a number of utility-grade, side-by-side double-barrel shotguns. These were excellent quality guns, with many of them still in use today. There is a modicum of collector interest, but values for most models are quite similar. They are chambered for 12, 16, or 20 gauge and have various length barrels and choke combinations. They feature double triggers except where noted and extractors. They are as follows:

**Model 315**
**Model 215--External Hammers**
**Model 235--External Hammers**
**Model 250--External Hammers**
**Model 255--External Hammers**
**Model 260--External Hammers, Damascus**
**Model 265--External Hammers**
**Model 270--External Hammers**
**Model 311--Hammerless**
**Model 3151--Hammerless**
**Model 330--Hammerless**
**Model 335--Hammerless**
**Model 345--Hammerless**
**Model 355--Hammerless**
**Model 365--Hammerless**
**Model 515--Hammerless**
**Model 5151--Hammerless**
**Model 530--Hammerless**
**Model 53M--Hammerless, Plastic Stock**

| Exc. | V.G. | Good | Fair | Poor |
|------|------|------|------|------|
| 200 | 175 | 150 | 100 | 75 |

**Model 311-R**
This version is chambered for 12 or 20 gauge and has 18.5" cylinder-bored barrels. It was designed as a riot gun to be used by prison guards.

| Exc. | V.G. | Good | Fair | Poor |
|------|------|------|------|------|
| 300 | 250 | 200 | 150 | 100 |

**Model 311-ST**
This version has a single-selective trigger.

| Exc. | V.G. | Good | Fair | Poor |
|------|------|------|------|------|
| 200 | 175 | 150 | 100 | 75 |

**Model 375**
This version is chambered for 12 or 16 gauge and features a lightly engraved boxlock receiver and a fancy, checkered walnut stock.

| Exc. | V.G. | Good | Fair | Poor |
|------|------|------|------|------|
| 200 | 175 | 150 | 100 | 75 |

**Model 385**
This is a more deluxe version that features a higher degree of engraving.

| Exc. | V.G. | Good | Fair | Poor |
|------|------|------|------|------|
| 250 | 200 | 175 | 150 | 100 |

The Stevens Company produced a number of bolt-action shotguns that are either single-shot or repeaters. They are chambered for the 20 gauge or .410 and are blued, with walnut stocks. The values for these utility-grade shotguns are similar.

**Model 237--Single Shot**
**Model 258--Clip Fed**
**Model 37--Single Shot**
**Model 38--Clip Fed**
**Model 39--Tube Magazine**
**Model 58--Clip Fed**
**Model 59--Tube Magazine**

| Exc. | V.G. | Good | Fair | Poor |
|------|------|------|------|------|
| 75 | 65 | 50 | 35 | 25 |

The J. Stevens Arms Company also produced a series of utility-grade slide-action shotguns. They are chambered for various gauges with various barrel lengths and chokes. The finishes are blued, with walnut stocks. The values are similar, and we list them for reference purposes as follows:

**Model 520**
**Model 522**
**Model 620**
**Model 621**
**Model 67**
**Model 67-VR**
**Model 77**
**Model 77S C**
**Model 77-AC**
**Model 77-M**
**Model 820**

| Exc. | V.G. | Good | Fair | Poor |
|------|------|------|------|------|
| 150 | 125 | 100 | 75 | 50 |

**Model 124**
This is a recoil-operated semi-automatic shotgun chambered for 12 gauge. It has a 28" barrel with various chokes, is blued, and has a brown plastic stock.

| Exc. | V.G. | Good | Fair | Poor |
|------|------|------|------|------|
| 125 | 100 | 75 | 65 | 50 |

**Model 67**
This is a slide-action shotgun chambered for 12 and 20 gauge, as well as .410. It has 3" chambers. It is offered with various-length barrels and choke tubes with a 5-shot tube magazine. It features a steel receiver and is blued, with a walnut stock. It was discontinued in 1989.

| Exc. | V.G. | Good | Fair | Poor |
|------|------|------|------|------|
| 200 | 175 | 150 | 100 | 75 |

**Model 675**
This is a slide-action shotgun chambered for 12 gauge with a 24" vent-rib barrel with iron sights. The finish is blued, with a hardwood stock and recoil pad. It was manufactured in 1987 and 1988.

| Exc. | V.G. | Good | Fair | Poor |
|------|------|------|------|------|
| 275 | 250 | 200 | 150 | 100 |

**Model 69-RXL**
This is a matte-finished riot version of the Model 67 series slide-action shotgun. It has an 18.25" cylinder-bore barrel and is furnished with a recoil pad. It was discontinued in 1989.

| Exc. | V.G. | Good | Fair | Poor |
|------|------|------|------|------|
| 200 | 175 | 150 | 100 | 75 |

**Stevens-Fox Model B**
This is a side-by-side double-barrel shotgun chambered for 12 or 20 gauge, as well as .410. It is offered with 26", 28", or 30" vent-rib barrels with double triggers and extractors. The BDE model features automatic ejectors and would be worth approximately 25 percent additional. The finish is blued, with a walnut stock.

| Exc. | V.G. | Good | Fair | Poor |
|------|------|------|------|------|
| 300 | 275 | 225 | 175 | 100 |

**Stevens-Fox Model B-SE**
This is a deluxe version with single trigger and automatic ejectors. It features a select walnut stock.

| NIB | Exc. | V.G. | Good | Fair | Poor |
|-----|------|------|------|------|------|
| 525 | 450 | 325 | 250 | 200 | 150 |

## Model 311

This is a side-by-side double-barrel shotgun chambered for 12 or 20 gauge, as well as .410. It has 3" chambers. It has 28" or 30" vent-rib barrels with various chokes, double triggers, and extractors. The finish is blued, with a walnut stock.

| Exc. | V.G. | Good | Fair | Poor |
|------|------|------|------|------|
| 300  | 275  | 225  | 175  | 125  |

## Model 311-R

This is an 18.25", cylinder-bore, law enforcement version of the Model 311.

| Exc. | V.G. | Good | Fair | Poor |
|------|------|------|------|------|
| 300  | 275  | 225  | 175  | 125  |

# STEYR
### Steyr, Austria

## Schonberger

This pistol is believed to be the first practical semi-automatic pistol ever commercially offered. Very few were manufactured. It is chambered for an 8mm bottle-neck cartridge that fires a 110-grain bullet at approximately 1,500 feet per second. The ammunition is peculiar to this weapon only and, at this time, is even rarer than the pistol. It has a 6" barrel and is loaded with the clip in front of the trigger. The finish is blued, with checkered walnut grips. There were approximately 36 manufactured in 1892 and 1893.

| Exc.  | V.G.  | Good  | Fair  | Poor  |
|-------|-------|-------|-------|-------|
| 2750  | 2500  | 2000  | 1500  | 1250  |

## Steyr Mannlicher Model 1894

This is a blow-forward semi-automatic pistol chambered for the 7.6mm Mannlicher cartridge. It is a hammer-fired weapon with a 5.5" barrel. It is marked "Model 1894" or "Model 1895," depending on which year it was made. The finish is blued, with checkered walnut grips. Production was quite limited, and it was manufactured in 1894 and 1895.

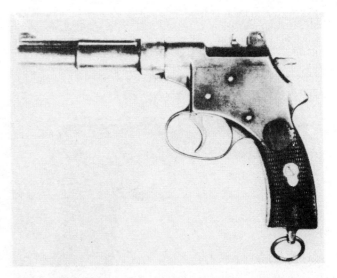

| Exc.  | V.G.  | Good  | Fair  | Poor  |
|-------|-------|-------|-------|-------|
| 2000  | 1750  | 1500  | 1000  | 800   |

## Model 1900/01

This is a blowback-operated semi-automatic pistol chambered for an 8mm cartridge that was designed specifically for this firearm. It was a rimless, straight-tapered design. Shortly afterwards it was redesigned to accept the 7.63mm cartridge, and no 8mm models were ever released. This model has a 6" barrel, is hammer-fired, and has a grip safety. It is generally regarded as one of the best-looking semi-automatic pistols ever produced. The finish is blued, with checkered walnut grips. This model was commercially successful in a moderate way and was carried, through private purchases, by many officers in the Austro-Hungarian army. Many were exported to South America, and it was officially adopted by the Argentine army in 1905. There were two Spanish copies of this weapon.

| Exc. | V.G. | Good | Fair | Poor |
|------|------|------|------|------|
| 750  | 700  | 600  | 500  | 400  |

## Roth-Steyr Model 1907

This is listed under its own section in this text.

## Model 1911 Steyr-Hahn

This is a conventional-type semi-automatic weapon whose design was influenced by the early Colt-Brownings. It is chambered for a powerful 9mm cartridge known as the 9mm Steyr. It uses a steel-jacketed bullet that is more pointed than most other 9mm's. It has a 5" barrel and is loaded from the top by means of a stripper clip. It has an external hammer. The finish is blued, with checkered walnut grips. This model was adopted by the Austro-Hungarian army as well as the armies of Romania and Chile. In 1938, when the Germans occupied Austria, many of these pistols were re-barreled to accept the 9mm Parabellum cartridge. The German version was marked "08." There is a commercial version of the Model 1911 available that was finished extremely well and marked "Osterreichische Waffenfabrik Steyr M1911 9mm." This model also has Austrian civilian proofs. The military versions are marked "Steyr" with the date of manufacture on the slide. The models sold to Romania and Chile bear these countries' respective crests. This pistol was manufactured until 1918 only.

| Exc. | V.G. | Good | Fair | Poor |
|------|------|------|------|------|
| 450 | 400 | 300 | 200 | 150 |

### Model 1909 Pocket Pistol
This pistol was sold under the Steyr name but was actually manufactured by Nicholas Piper of Liege, Belgium. It is a blowback-operated semi-automatic with a barrel that tips upwards. It is chambered for both the 6.35mm and 7.65mm cartridges. It has a 3" barrel and is fed by a detachable box magazine. The finish is blued, with black plastic grips that bear the Steyr logo. The receiver is marked "Oesterr Waffenfabrik Ges Steyr." This pistol was manufactured until 1914, when production ceased for WWI. Manufacture resumed in 1921 and continued until 1939.

| Exc. | V.G. | Good | Fair | Poor |
|------|------|------|------|------|
| 300 | 250 | 200 | 150 | 100 |

### Model P18
This is a delayed blowback semi-automatic pistol that utilizes gas pressure bled from the chamber during firing. It has a fixed 5" barrel and is chambered for the 9mm Parabellum cartridge. This is a large pistol with a double-stacked, 18-round box magazine. It was manufactured in 1974 under license from Steyr by L.E.S. of Morton Grove, Illinois. For a period of time this pistol was known as the Rogak.

| Exc. | V.G. | Good | Fair | Poor |
|------|------|------|------|------|
| 400 | 350 | 300 | 250 | 200 |

### Model GB

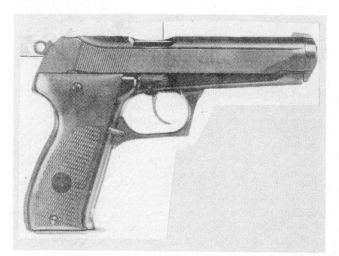

This is a double-action semi-automatic pistol with a gas-delayed blowback action. It is chambered for the 9mm Parabellum cartridge and has a 5.25" barrel with polygon rifling. It has an 18-shot, double-stacked magazine and is constructed of matte-finished blue steel with black plastic grips. It was not imported after 1988.

| Exc. | V.G. | Good | Fair | Poor |
|------|------|------|------|------|
| 450 | 400 | 350 | 275 | 200 |

### Steyr Mannlicher Model 1950
This is a high-quality, bolt-action sporting rifle chambered for .257 Roberts, .270 Winchester, and .30.06. It has a 24" barrel with a 5-shot rotary magazine. The finish was blued, with a checkered walnut stock and ebony forend tip and pistol grip cap. It was manufactured between 1950 and 1952.

| Exc. | V.G. | Good | Fair | Poor |
|------|------|------|------|------|
| 800 | 700 | 650 | 500 | 400 |

### Model 1950 Carbine
This is similar to the rifle model, with a 20" barrel and a full-length Mannlicher-type stock with a steel end cap. It was made between 1950 and 1952.

| Exc. | V.G. | Good | Fair | Poor |
|------|------|------|------|------|
| 1000 | 900 | 750 | 600 | 500 |

### Model 1952
This model is similar to the Model 1950, with a swept-back bolt handle that functions more efficiently when a scope is mounted. It was manufactured between 1952 and 1956.

| Exc. | V.G. | Good | Fair | Poor |
|------|------|------|------|------|
| 800 | 700 | 650 | 500 | 400 |

### Model 1952 Carbine
This model has a swept-back bolt handle and 20" barrel with the full-length stock.

| Exc. | V.G. | Good | Fair | Poor |
|------|------|------|------|------|
| 1000 | 900 | 750 | 600 | 500 |

### Model 1956 Rifle
This model is chambered for .243 and .30-06. It has a high comb stock and a 22" barrel. It was manufactured between 1956 and 1960.

| Exc. | V.G. | Good | Fair | Poor |
|------|------|------|------|------|
| 800 | 700 | 650 | 500 | 400 |

### Model 1956 Carbine
This is chambered for various additional calibers and has a 20" barrel and a full-length, Mannlicher-type stock. It was manufactured between 1956 and 1960.

| Exc. | V.G. | Good | Fair | Poor |
|------|------|------|------|------|
| 1000 | 900 | 750 | 600 | 500 |

### Model 1961 MCA Rifle
This version has a Monte Carlo stock.

| Exc. | V.G. | Good | Fair | Poor |
|------|------|------|------|------|
| 800 | 700 | 650 | 500 | 400 |

### Model 1961 MCA Carbine
This model is similar to the Rifle, with a 20" barrel and full-length stock.

| Exc. | V.G. | Good | Fair | Poor |
|------|------|------|------|------|
| 1000 | 900 | 750 | 600 | 500 |

### Model M72 L/M
This high quality bolt-action rifle is chambered for .243, .270, 7x57, 7x64, .308, and .30-06. It has a 23" fluted barrel and is available with either a single- or double-set trigger. The finish is blued, with a select checkered walnut stock. It was manufactured between 1972 and 1980.

| Exc. | V.G. | Good | Fair | Poor |
|------|------|------|------|------|
| 800 | 700 | 650 | 500 | 400 |

## Model SL

This is the current production bolt-action rifle chambered for various popular calibers. It has a 23.6" fluted barrel, double-set triggers, and a detachable rotary magazine.

| NIB | Exc. | V.G. | Good | Fair | Poor |
|-----|------|------|------|------|------|
| 1850 | 1650 | 1000 | 750 | 500 | 400 |

## Model SL Carbine

This model has a 20" fluted barrel with a full-length Mannlicher-style stock.

| NIB | Exc. | V.G. | Good | Fair | Poor |
|-----|------|------|------|------|------|
| 1950 | 1750 | 1050 | 800 | 550 | 450 |

## Model SL Varmint

This is a 26" heavy-barrelled version with a stippled pistol grip and ventilated forearm. It is chambered for .222, .22-250, .243, and .308. It is furnished without sights.

| NIB | Exc. | V.G. | Good | Fair | Poor |
|-----|------|------|------|------|------|
| 1950 | 1750 | 1050 | 800 | 550 | 450 |

## Model L

This model is similar to the Model SL except that it is chambered for 5.6x57, .22-250, 6mm Remington, .243, and .308. It is also available in the Carbine and Varmint configurations and valued the same as the Model SL.

## Model L Luxus

This is a deluxe version with higher quality materials and workmanship throughout.

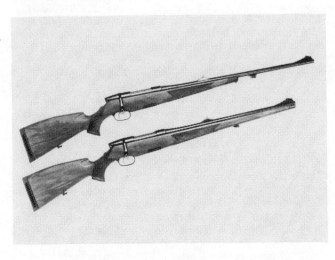

| NIB | Exc. | V.G. | Good | Fair | Poor |
|-----|------|------|------|------|------|
| 2400 | 2000 | 1100 | 800 | 600 | 550 |

## Model L. Luxus Carbine

This is similar to the Luxus Rifle, with a 20" barrel and a full-length Mannlicher-type stock.

| NIB | Exc. | V.G. | Good | Fair | Poor |
|-----|------|------|------|------|------|
| 2500 | 2100 | 1200 | 900 | 700 | 600 |

## Model M

The Model M bolt-action rifle is chambered in 6.5x57, 7x64, .270 Winchester, .30-06, and 9.3x62. It has a 23" fluted barrel and a detachable rotary magazine. It features double-set triggers. The finish is blued with a checkered walnut stock. A carbine version with a 20" barrel and full-length stock is also available and valued at approximately 10 percent additional.

| NIB | Exc. | V.G. | Good | Fair | Poor |
|-----|------|------|------|------|------|
| 1800 | 1600 | 950 | 700 | 500 | 400 |

## Professional Rifle

This model is similar to the Model M, with a 23.6" fluted barrel, matte finish, and a Cycolac stock.

| NIB | Exc. | V.G. | Good | Fair | Poor |
|-----|------|------|------|------|------|
| 1500 | 1400 | 950 | 700 | 600 | 500 |

## Model S

This model is chambered for 6.5x68, 8x68S, .300 Winchester Magnum, .338 Winchester Magnum, and the 7mm Remington Magnum. It is similar to the Model M except more heavy-duty, to handle the Magnum cartridges for which it is chambered. It has a 26" fluted barrel with a blued finish and a checkered walnut stock.

| NIB | Exc. | V.G. | Good | Fair | Poor |
|-----|------|------|------|------|------|
| 1950 | 1750 | 1150 | 900 | 700 | 600 |

## Tropical Rifle

This model is similar to the Model S except that it has a 26" heavy barrel and is chambered for .375 Holland & Holland and .458 Winchester Magnum. It was not imported after 1985.

| Exc. | V.G. | Good | Fair | Poor |
|------|------|------|------|------|
| 1200 | 1000 | 750 | 600 | 500 |

## Model SSG

This is an extremely precision, bolt-action rifle that was designed for serious competition or law enforcement anti-sniper work. It is chambered for the .243 Winchester or the .308 Winchester cartridges and has a 26" fluted barrel, a choice of single- or double-set triggers, and a 3- shot detachable magazine. The bolt is Teflon-coated. The finish is parkerized, and the standard stock is synthetic Cycolac in either a black or green finish. The basic difference in the four versions is in the sighting systems utilized.

### Marksman

| NIB | Exc. | V.G. | Good | Fair | Poor |
|-----|------|------|------|------|------|
| 1600 | 1250 | 800 | 600 | 500 | 400 |

**PII Sniper Rifle**

| NIB | Exc. | V.G. | Good | Fair | Poor |
|------|------|------|------|------|------|
| 1700 | 1350 | 900 | 700 | 600 | 500 |

**Match**

| NIB | Exc. | V.G. | Good | Fair | Poor |
|------|------|------|------|------|------|
| 1850 | 1500 | 1100 | 900 | 800 | 650 |

**Match UIT**

| NIB | Exc. | V.G. | Good | Fair | Poor |
|------|------|------|------|------|------|
| 2400 | 2000 | 1500 | 1150 | 1000 | 700 |

## Steyr AUG

This is a space-age, semi-automatic, assault-type rifle that incorporates the latest innovations in design and materials. It utilizes super-strength plastics throughout. It is chambered for the .223 Remington cartridge and has a 20" barrel. This rifle is built in the bullpup configuration and has an integral Swarovski scope built into the carrying handle. In its full automatic configuration, it is the service rifle of the Austrian army. Due to the mass hysteria surrounding weapons of this configuration, we do not supply a value and strongly recommend independent, local appraisals.

# STEYR HAHN
### SEE--Steyr

# STEYR MANNLICHER
### SEE--Steyr

# STOCK, FRANZ
### Berlin, Germany

**Stock**

This is a blowback-operated semi-automatic pocket pistol chambered for the .22 l.r., 6.35mm, and 7.65mm cartridges. It is a fixed-barrel pistol with a coaxial recoil spring. The slide is open-topped and tubular in the front. This pistol was designed by Walter Decker and patented in 1915 and 1918. It was well-made, with a blued finish and black pistol grips with the name "Stock" at the top. The frame is marked "Franz Stock Berlin." It was manufactured into the early 1930's.

| Exc. | V.G. | Good | Fair | Poor |
|------|------|------|------|------|
| 300 | 275 | 250 | 150 | 100 |

# STOCKING & CO.
### Worchester, Massachusetts

**Pepperbox**

This is a single-action, pepperbox-type pistol chambered for either .28 or .31 caliber percussion. It has a six-barrel cluster from 4" to 6" in length. The hammer has an extremely long cocking spur, and the triggerguard is sometimes found with a finger spur projecting from the rear. The frame is iron and scroll-engraved. The finish is blued, with rounded walnut grips. The barrel is marked "Stocking & Co., Worchester." This weapon was manufactured between 1846 and 1854.

| Exc. | V.G. | Good | Fair | Poor |
|------|------|------|------|------|
| 500 | 400 | 350 | 250 | 150 |

**Single Shot Pistol**

This is a single-action percussion pistol chambered for .36 caliber. It has a 4" part-round/part-octagonal barrel and the same long hammer spur as the Pepperbox. The barrel is marked similarly to the Pepperbox. It was manufactured between 1849 and 1852.

| Exc. | V.G. | Good | Fair | Poor |
|------|------|------|------|------|
| 375 | 325 | 250 | 175 | 125 |

# STOEGER, A. F.
### Hackensack, New Jersey

This was a sporting goods dealer that imported German Parabellum pistols into the United States after the close of WWI. Mr. Stoeger was the first to realize that although they were not technically known as such, they were commonly referred to as "Lugers." In 1923 he formally registered the name Luger as a trademark. Afterwards, he made arrangements with the firm of DWM to mark all of his pistols "A. F. Stoeger Inc. New York Luger Registered US Patent Office." DWM continued this practice until they ceased production of the Parabellum pistol. The

Stoeger Luger pistols comprise a distinct variation that is quite collectible and which is covered in the Luger section of this text.

### .22 Luger

In the early 1970's the Stoeger Arms Corporation, a derivative of the earlier A. F. Stoeger Corporation, introduced a simplified toggle-lock version of the Parabellum that was blowback-operated and chambered for the .22 l.r. cartridge. It has a forged aluminum frame with a steel barrel cross pinned into place. The barrel is either 4.5" or 5.5" in length, and the word "Luger" is prominently scroll-engraved on the right side of the frame. The finish is blued, with checkered plastic grips.

| Exc. | V.G. | Good | Fair | Poor |
|------|------|------|------|------|
| 300 | 250 | 200 | 150 | 100 |

### Target Luger

This is similar to the standard model, with an extension at the rear of the frame on which an adjustable target sight was mounted.

| Exc. | V.G. | Good | Fair | Poor |
|------|------|------|------|------|
| 325 | 275 | 225 | 175 | 125 |

### Luger Carbine

This was a limited-production, deluxe version that features an 11" barrel and is chambered for .22 l.r. The finish is blued; and there is a walnut forearm, as well as checkered walnut grips. This model was furnished in a red velvet-lined, black leatherette case. There were only several hundred manufactured in the 1970's.

| Exc. | V.G. | Good | Fair | Poor |
|------|------|------|------|------|
| 450 | 400 | 350 | 250 | 175 |

# STREET SWEEPER
### Atlanta, Georgia

### Street Sweeper

This is a semi-automatic 12-gauge shotgun manufactured in an assault-type configuration. It has an 18" barrel and fires in the double-action mode. It features a 12-round, rotary, drum-type magazine. The finish is matte black. It was introduced in 1989.

| NIB | Exc. | V.G. | Good | Fair | Poor |
|-----|------|------|------|------|------|
| 600 | 500 | 400 | 350 | 250 | 200 |

# RUGER, STURM & CO.
### Southport, Connecticut

In 1946 W. B. Ruger applied for his first patent on a blowback-operated, semi-automatic, .22-caliber pistol. In 1949 Mr. Ruger and Alexander Sturm released this pistol for sale, and the Ruger dynasty began. This pistol was as perfect for the American marketplace as could be. It was accurate, reliable, and inexpensive and insured the new company's success. In 1951 Alexander Sturm passed away, but Mr. Ruger continued forward. At this time the fledgling television industry was popularizing the early American West, and Colt had not re-introduced the Single Action Army after WWII. Ruger decided that a Western-style six shooter would be a successful venture, and the Single Six was born. This was not a Colt copy but a new design based on the western look.

Again Ruger scored in the marketplace, and this has been pretty much the rule ever since. With few exceptions this company has shown itself to be very accurate in gauging what the gun-buying public wants. They have expanded their line to include double-action revolvers, single shots, semi-auto and bolt-action rifles, percussion revolvers, and even a semi-auto wonder nine. They have stayed ahead of the legal profession as much as possible by introducing safety devices and comprehensive instruction manuals and generally insured their future success. For such a relatively new company, collector interest in certain models is quite keen. There are a number of factors that govern Ruger collector values.

All models made in 1976 were designated "200th Year of Liberty" models and if in NIB condition will bring up to a $100 premium if a market is found. The newer models that have a safety warning stamped on the barrel are generally purchased only by shooters and have no collector appeal whatsoever. The astute individual must be aware of these nuances when dealing in Rugers. There are some excellent works written on the Ruger (not as many as there are on the Colt or the Smith & Wesson), but the new collector can educate himself if he so desires. We list this company's models in chronolgical order.

### Standard Model "Red Eagle Grips"

This is a blowback semi-automatic with a fixed, exposed, 4.75" or 6" barrel. The receiver is tubular, with a round bolt. There is a 9-shot detachable magazine, and the sights are fixed. The finish is blued, and the black plastic grips on this first model has the trademark Ruger Eagle inlaid in red. There were approximately 25,600 manufactured before Alexander Sturm's death in 1951. They fall in the 12000-34000 serial number range.

| Exc. | V.G. | Good | Fair | Poor |
|------|------|------|------|------|
| 600 | 500 | 425 | 300 | 225 |

### Standard Model

This model is identical to the Red Eagle except that after Sturm's death the Eagles were black and have remained so ever since. This pistol was produced from 1952--1982. There are a great many variations of this pistol, but a book dealing with this pistol alone should be consulted as the differences in variations are very subtle and valuation of these variations is definitely a matter for individual appraisal.

| Exc. | V.G. | Good | Fair | Poor |
|------|------|------|------|------|
| 150 | 125 | 100 | 80 | 65 |

### Mark I Target Model

The success of the Ruger Standard Model led quite naturally to a demand for a more accurate target model. In 1951 a pistol that utilized the same frame and receiver with a 5.25", heavy target-type barrel and adjustable sights was introduced. This was followed shortly by a 6.75" tapered barrel. This model enjoyed well-deserved success and was manufactured from 1951--1982.

Factory Installed Muzzle Brake--Add $100; Watch for Fakes!

| Exc. | V.G. | Good | Fair | Poor |
|------|------|------|------|------|
| 200 | 175 | 150 | 125 | 90 |

### Single Six Revolver

This is a .22 rimfire, 6-shot, single-action revolver. It was offered with 4.5", 5.5", 6.5", and 9.5" barrel lengths and a fixed sight. It is based in appearance on the Colt Single Action Army, but internally it is a new design that features coil springs instead of the old-style, flat leaf springs. It also features a floating firing pin and is generally a stronger action than what was previously available. The early model had a flat loading gate and was made this way from 1953--1956, when the contoured gate became standard. Early models had checkered hard rubber grips--changed to smooth walnut on later models. Both had inlaid black eagles. This model was manufactured from 1953 --1972.

Flat Gate--Add $50.

| Exc. | V.G. | Good | Fair | Poor |
|------|------|------|------|------|
| 250 | 200 | 150 | 125 | 100 |

### Single Six .22 Magnum Model

This model is similar to the Single Six except that it is chambered for the .22 rimfire Magnum and the frame was so marked. It was offered in the 6.5" barrel length only and was manufactured for three years. The serial numbers are in the 300000--340000 range.

| Exc. | V.G. | Good | Fair | Poor |
|------|------|------|------|------|
| 275 | 225 | 175 | 150 | 125 |

### Lightweight Single Six

This model is similar to the Single Six, with an alloy frame and 4-5/8" barrel. This variation was produced between 1956 and 1958 and was in the 200000-210000 serial range. Examples have been noted with alloy cylinders.

| Exc. | V.G. | Good | Fair | Poor |
|------|------|------|------|------|
| 300 | 250 | 200 | 150 | 110 |

### Single Six Convertible

This model is similar to the Single Six but is furnished with an extra .22 rimfire Magnum cylinder.

| Exc. | V.G. | Good | Fair | Poor |
|------|------|------|------|------|
| 275 | 225 | 175 | 125 | 100 |

### Super Single Six

Introduced in 1964, this is the Single Six with adjustable sights.

| Exc. | V.G. | Good | Fair | Poor |
|------|------|------|------|------|
| 275 | 225 | 175 | 125 | 100 |

### Bearcat

This is a scaled-down version of the single action. It is chambered for .22 rimfire and has a 4" barrel and an unfluted, roll-engraved cylinder. The frame is alloy, and it has a brass grip frame and triggerguard. The finish is blue, and the grips are walnut with eagle inlays. This model was manufactured from 1958--1973.

| Exc. | V.G. | Good | Fair | Poor |
|------|------|------|------|------|
| 250 | 225 | 200 | 150 | 110 |

### Super Bearcat

This model is similar to the Bearcat, with a steel frame and, on later models, a blued steel triggerguard and grip frame. The early examples still used brass.

| Exc. | V.G. | Good | Fair | Poor |
|------|------|------|------|------|
| 300 | 250 | 225 | 175 | 125 |

### Blackhawk Flattop

The success of the Single Six led to the production of a larger version chambered for the .357 Magnum cartridge. This model is a single action, with a 6-shot fluted cylinder and a flat top strap with adjustable "Micro sight." The barrel length is 4-5/8", 6.5", and 10". The finish is blue with checkered hard rubber grips on the early examples and smooth walnut on later ones. There were approximately 45,000 manufactured between 1955 and 1962.

7.5" Barrel--Add 20 Percent.
10" Barrel-- Add 50 Percent.

| Exc. | V.G. | Good | Fair | Poor |
|------|------|------|------|------|
| 400 | 350 | 300 | 225 | 150 |

### Blackhawk Flattop .44 Magnum

In 1956 the .44 Magnum was introduced, and Ruger jumped on the bandwagon. This is very similar in appearance to the .357 but has a slightly heavier frame and a larger cylinder. It was available in a 6.5", 7.5", and 10" barrel. It was manufactured from 1956--1963.

7.5" Barrel--Add 20 Percent.
10" Barrel-- Add 50 Percent.

| Exc. | V.G. | Good | Fair | Poor |
|------|------|------|------|------|
| 600 | 550 | 475 | 350 | 225 |

### Blackhawk

This model is similar to the "Flattop," but the rear sight is protected by two raised protrusions--one on each side. It was available chambered for the .357 Magnum, .41 Magnum, or the .45 Colt cartridge. Barrel lengths are 4- 5/8" or 6.5". The finish is blue, and the grips are walnut with Ruger medallions.

| Exc. | V.G. | Good | Fair | Poor |
|------|------|------|------|------|
| 350 | 300 | 250 | 175 | 125 |

### Blackhawk Convertible

This model is the same as the Blackhawk with an extra cylinder to change or convert calibers. The .357 Magnum has a 9mm conversion, and the .45 Colt has a .45 ACP cylinder.

**.357/9mm**

| Exc. | V.G. | Good | Fair | Poor |
|------|------|------|------|------|
| 325 | 275 | 225 | 150 | 100 |

**.45 L.C./.45ACP**

| Exc. | V.G. | Good | Fair | Poor |
|------|------|------|------|------|
| 375 | 325 | 275 | 175 | 125 |

### Super Blackhawk

The formidable recoil of the .44 Magnum cartridge was difficult to handle in a revolver with a small grip such as found on the Blackhawk, so it was decided to produce a larger-framed revolver with increased size in the grip. The rear of the trigger guard was squared off, and the cylinder was left unfluted to increase mass. This model was offered with a 7.5" barrel; 6.5" examples have been noted and are worth approximately 50 percent more. This model is blued and has smooth walnut grips with medallions. The very first of these revolvers were offered in a fitted wood case and are very rare today. The Super Blackhawk was made from 1959-1972.

| Exc. | V.G. | Good | Fair | Poor |
|------|------|------|------|------|
| 350 | 300 | 250 | 200 | 125 |

### Early Model in Wood Presentation Case

| Exc. | V.G. | Good | Fair | Poor |
|------|------|------|------|------|
| 1000 | 850 | 650 | 475 | 350 |

### Hawkeye Single Shot

The shooting public wanted a small-caliber, high-velocity handgun. The Smith & Wesson Model 53, chambered for the .22 Jet, appeared in 1961; and the cartridge created extraction problems for a revolver. Ruger solved the problem with the introduction of the Hawkeye--a single shot that looked like a six shooter. In place of the cylinder was a breech block that cammed to the side for loading. This pistol was excellent from an engineering and performance standpoint but was not a commercial success. The Hawkeye is chambered for the .256 Magnum, a bottleneck cartridge, and has an 8.5" barrel and adjustable sights. The finish is blued with walnut, medallion grips. This pistol is quite rare as only 3,300 were produced in the early 1960's.

| Exc. | V.G. | Good | Fair | Poor |
|------|------|------|------|------|
| 1000 | 800 | 650 | 550 | 400 |

The Ruger firm has always demonstrated keen perception and in 1973 completely modified their single-action lockwork to accommodate a hammer block. This hammer block prevented accidental discharge should a revolver be dropped. In doing so, the company circumvented a great deal of potential legal problems and made collectibles out of the previous models. There are many individuals who simply do not care for the "New Models," as they are called, and will not purchase them; but judging from the continued success and growth of the Ruger company, those individuals must be the exception, not the rule.

**Super Single Six Convertible (New Model)**
This model is similar in appearance to the old model but has the new hammer block safety system. The frame has two pins instead of three screws, and opening the loading gate frees the cylinder stop for loading. Barrel lengths are 4-5/8", 5.5", 6.5", and 9.5". The sights are adjustable; the finish is blued. The grips are walnut with a medallion, and an interchangeable .22 Magnum cylinder is supplied. This model was introduced in 1973 and is currently in production.

| NIB | Exc. | V.G. | Good | Fair | Poor |
|---|---|---|---|---|---|
| 250 | 200 | 150 | 125 | 100 | 80 |

**Stainless Steel Single Six Convertible**
The same as the standard blued model but made from stainless steel. Offered with a 5.5" and 6.5" barrel only.

| NIB | Exc. | V.G. | Good | Fair | Poor |
|---|---|---|---|---|---|
| 325 | 250 | 200 | 175 | 125 | 100 |

**Colorado Centennial Single Six**
This model had a stainless steel grip frame, and the balance is blued. It has walnut grips with medallion insert. The barrel is 6.5", and the revolver is furnished with a walnut case with a centennial medal insert. There were 15,000 manufactured in 1975.

| NIB | Exc. | V.G. | Good | Fair | Poor |
|---|---|---|---|---|---|
| 300 | 250 | 200 | 175 | 125 | 100 |

**Model SSM Single Six**
This is the Single Six chambered for the .32 H&R Magnum cartridge.

| NIB | Exc. | V.G. | Good | Fair | Poor |
|---|---|---|---|---|---|
| 250 | 200 | 175 | 150 | 125 | 100 |

**Blackhawk (New Model)**
This model is similar in appearance to the old model Blackhawk, offered in the same calibers and barrel lengths. It has the hammer block safety device. It was introduced in 1973 and is currently in production.

| NIB | Exc. | V.G. | Good | Fair | Poor |
|---|---|---|---|---|---|
| 300 | 250 | 200 | 175 | 150 | 125 |

FULL RIGHT VIEW

**Stainless Steel Blackhawk (New Model)**
This is simply the New Model Blackhawk made from stainless steel.

| NIB | Exc. | V.G. | Good | Fair | Poor |
|---|---|---|---|---|---|
| 375 | 325 | 275 | 225 | 175 | 150 |

**Model SRM Blackhawk**
This is the New Model Blackhawk with a 7.5" or 10.5" barrel. It was chambered for the .357 Maximum and was intended for silhouette shooting. This model experienced problems with gas cutting on the top strap and was removed from production in 1984 after a very few were manufactured.

| Exc. | V.G. | Good | Fair | Poor |
|---|---|---|---|---|
| 350 | 300 | 250 | 200 | 125 |

**Blackhawk Convertible (New Model)**
This model is the same as the Blackhawk with interchangeable conversion cylinders--.357 Magnum/9mm and .45 Colt/.45 ACP. This model was discontinued in 1985.

| NIB | Exc. | V.G. | Good | Fair | Poor |
|---|---|---|---|---|---|
| 315 | 280 | 225 | 175 | 150 | 125 |

### Super Blackhawk (New Model)

This model is similar in appearance to the old model but has the hammer block safety device. It was manufactured from 1973 to the present and commenced at serial number 81-00001.

| NIB | Exc. | V.G. | Good | Fair | Poor |
|-----|------|------|------|------|------|
| 350 | 300  | 275  | 225  | 175  | 125  |

Catalog No. KS47N

### Super Blackhawk Stainless Steel

This model is the same as the blued version but is made of stainless steel.

| NIB | Exc. | V.G. | Good | Fair | Poor |
|-----|------|------|------|------|------|
| 375 | 325  | 300  | 250  | 200  | 150  |

### Bisley Model

This model has the modified features found on the famous old Colt Bisley Target model--the flattop frame, fixed or adjustable sights, and the longer grip frame that has become the Bisley trademark. The Bisley is available chambered for .22 LR, .32 H&R Magnum, .357 Magnum, .41 Magnum, .44 Magnum, and .45 Long Colt. The barrel lengths are 6.5" and 7.5"; cylinders are either fluted or unfluted and roll engraved. The finish is a satin blue, and the grips are smooth goncalo alves with medallions. The Bisley was introduced in 1986.

Smaller frame Ruger Bisley revolvers are chambered for .22 Long Rifle rimfire or .32 Magnum centerfire cartridges. The modified, longer grip, low hammer profile, and broad, curved trigger offer significant advantages when combined with the Ruger Single-Six design.

### .22 LR and .32 H&R Magnum

| NIB | Exc. | V.G. | Good | Fair | Poor |
|-----|------|------|------|------|------|
| 300 | 275  | 225  | 200  | 150  | 125  |

Large frame Ruger Bisley revolvers are chambered for the powerful .357 Magnum, .41 Magnum, .44 Magnum, and .45 Long Colt centerfire cartridges. Frame, cylinders and working components are the same as those found in the single-action Ruger Blackhawk design. Ruger Bisley models are available with fluted cylinders or with unfluted cylinders that are roll marked in a classic styling reminiscent of the turn of the century Bisley era. All models are satin polished and blued.

### .357 Magnum, .44 Magnum, and .45 Long Colt

| NIB | Exc. | V.G. | Good | Fair | Poor |
|-----|------|------|------|------|------|
| 350 | 325  | 275  | 250  | 200  | 175  |

### Old Army Percussion Revolver

This model is a .44 caliber percussion revolver with a 7.5" barrel. It has a 6-shot cylinder, with a blued finish and walnut grips.

| NIB | Exc. | V.G. | Good | Fair | Poor |
|-----|------|------|------|------|------|
| 300 | 275  | 225  | 175  | 125  | 100  |

### Old Army Stainless Steel

This model is the same as the blued version except that it is made of stainless steel.

| NIB | Exc. | V.G. | Good | Fair | Poor |
|-----|------|------|------|------|------|
| 375 | 300  | 250  | 200  | 150  | 125  |

## Double Action Revolvers
### Security Six

This revolver, also known as the Model 117, is chambered for the .357 Magnum cartridge and has a 2.75", 4", or 6" barrel. It features adjustable sights and a square butt, with checkered walnut grips. It was manufactured between 1970 and 1985.

| Exc. | V.G. | Good | Fair | Poor |
|------|------|------|------|------|
| 250 | 225 | 200 | 150 | 100 |

### Stainless Steel Model 717

This model is the Security Six made from stainless steel.

| Exc. | V.G. | Good | Fair | Poor |
|------|------|------|------|------|
| 275 | 250 | 225 | 175 | 125 |

### Speed Six

This model is known as the Model 207, chambered for .357 Magnum; Model 208, chambered for .38 Special; and Model 209, chambered for 9mm. It has a 2.75" or 4" barrel, fixed sights, and a round butt with checkered walnut grips and was blued. There are some with factory bobbed hammers. This model was introduced in 1973.

| Exc. | V.G. | Good | Fair | Poor |
|------|------|------|------|------|
| 250 | 225 | 200 | 150 | 100 |

### Models 737, 738, 739

These are the designations for the stainless-steel versions of the Speed Six. They are the same revolver except for the material used in the manufacture.

| Exc. | V.G. | Good | Fair | Poor |
|------|------|------|------|------|
| 275 | 250 | 225 | 175 | 125 |

### Police Service Six

This model is also known as the Model 107, chambered for .357 Magnum; the Model 108, chambered for the .38 Special; and the 109, chambered for the 9mm. The barrel is 2.75" or 4". It has fixed sights and a square butt, with checkered walnut grips. The finish is blued. The 9mm was discontinued in 1984; the other two calibers, in 1988.

| Exc. | V.G. | Good | Fair | Poor |
|------|------|------|------|------|
| 250 | 225 | 200 | 150 | 100 |

### Model 707 and 708

This is the designation for the stainless versions of the Police Service Six. It was not produced in 9mm, and only the 4" barrel was offered. This model was discontinued in 1988.

| Exc. | V.G. | Good | Fair | Poor |
|------|------|------|------|------|
| 275 | 250 | 225 | 175 | 125 |

*RUGER GP-100™*
*Double-Action Revolver*
*Cal. .357 Magnum*

**NEW**
The long ejector shroud on the Ruger GP-100 revolver helps to achieve the slight muzzle-heavy balance considered desireable for a steady hold and easy pointing. All GP-100 barrels are constructed with a wide top rib, longitudinally serrated to present a glare-free surface.
*Catalog Number GP-141*

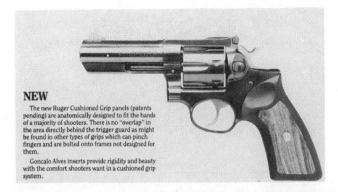

**NEW**
The new Ruger Cushioned Grip panels (patents pending) are anatomically designed to fit the hands of a majority of shooters. There is no "overlap" in the area directly behind the trigger guard as might be found in other types of grips which can pinch fingers and are bolted onto frames not designed for them.
Goncalo Alves inserts provide rigidity and beauty with the comfort shooters want in a cushioned grip system.

### GP-100

This model is chambered for the .357 Magnum/.38 Special. It has a 4" or 6" barrel and has a frame designed for constant use of heavy magnum loads. The rear sight has a white outline, and the front sight features interchangeable colored inserts. The finish is blued, and the grips are a new design made of rubber with smooth goncalo alves inserts. This model was introduced in 1986.

| NIB | Exc. | V.G. | Good | Fair | Poor |
|-----|------|------|------|------|------|
| 350 | 325 | 275 | 225 | 175 | 125 |

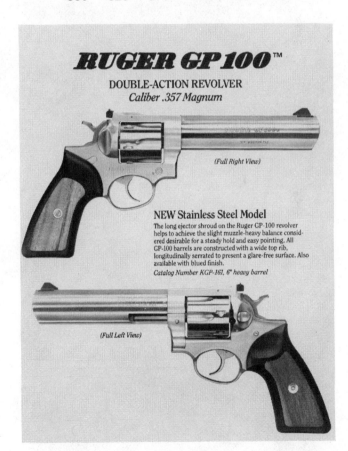

*RUGER GP 100™*
DOUBLE-ACTION REVOLVER
*Caliber .357 Magnum*

*(Full Right View)*

**NEW Stainless Steel Model**
The long ejector shroud on the Ruger GP-100 revolver helps to achieve the slight muzzle-heavy balance considered desirable for a steady hold and easy pointing. All GP-100 barrels are constructed with a wide top rib, longitudinally serrated to present a glare-free surface. Also available with blued finish.
*Catalog Number KGP-161, 6" heavy barrel*

*(Full Left View)*

### GP-100 Stainless

This model is the same as the GP-100 except that the material used is stainless steel.

| NIB | Exc. | V.G. | Good | Fair | Poor |
|-----|------|------|------|------|------|
| 375 | 350 | 300 | 250 | 200 | 150 |

### SP-101

This model is similar in appearance to the GP-100 but has a smaller frame and is chambered for the .22 l.r., 6- shot and for the .38 Special, 5-shot. The grips are all black synthetic, and the sights are adjustable for windage. Barrel lengths are 2" or 3", and construction is of stainless steel. This model was introduced in 1989.

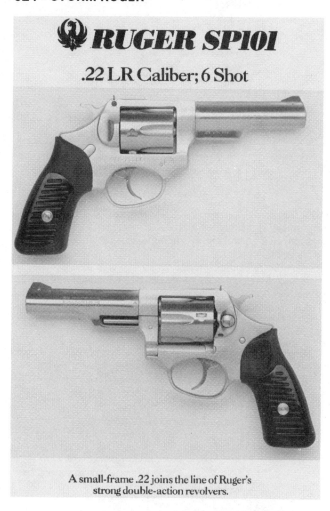

## RUGER SP101
### .22 LR Caliber; 6 Shot

A small-frame .22 joins the line of Ruger's
strong double-action revolvers.

| NIB | Exc. | V.G. | Good | Fair | Poor |
|-----|------|------|------|------|------|
| 375 | 350  | 300  | 250  | 200  | 150  |

RUGER Redhawk

NEW!
Alloy Steel Model with Blued Finish
in .41 Magnum and .44 Magnum Calibers

### Redhawk

This model is a large-frame, double-action revolver which was
chambered for the .357 Magnum until 1985 and which is still
chambered for the .41 Magnum and .44 Magnum cartridges.
The barrel lengths are 5.5" and 7.5". The finish is blue, and the
grips are smooth walnut. The Redhawk was introduced in
1979.

| NIB | Exc. | V.G. | Good | Fair | Poor |
|-----|------|------|------|------|------|
| 395 | 325  | 275  | 225  | 175  | 125  |

RUGER Redhawk
DOUBLE-ACTION REVOLVER

Catalog No. KRH-44-5"

### Redhawk Stainless Steel

The same as the blued version except constructed of stainless
steel.

| NIB | Exc. | V.G. | Good | Fair | Poor |
|-----|------|------|------|------|------|
| 375 | 350  | 300  | 250  | 200  | 150  |

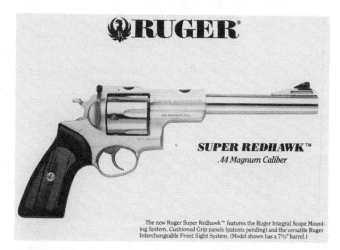

RUGER

SUPER REDHAWK™
.44 Magnum Caliber

The new Ruger Super Redhawk™ features the Ruger Integral Scope Mounting System, Cushioned Grip panels (patents pending) and the versatile Ruger
Interchangeable Front Sight System. (Model shown has a 7½" barrel.)

### Super Redhawk

This is a more massive version of the Redhawk. It weighs 53
ounces and is offered with a 7.5" or 9.5" barrel. It is made of
stainless steel, and the barrel rib is milled to accept the Ruger
scope-ring system. The grips are the combination rubber-and-
goncalo-alves type found on the GP-100. This revolver was introduced in 1987.

| NIB | Exc. | V.G. | Good | Fair | Poor |
|-----|------|------|------|------|------|
| 500 | 450  | 400  | 350  | 300  | 225  |

### Semi-Automatic Handguns (New Models)

## Mark II Standard Model

This is a generally improved version of the first Ruger pistol. There is a hold-open device, and the magazine holds 10 rounds. This model was introduced in 1982.

| NIB | Exc. | V.G. | Good | Fair | Poor |
|-----|------|------|------|------|------|
| 210 | 175  | 150  | 125  | 100  | 75   |

## Stainless Steel Mark II Standard Model

This model is the same as the Mark II Standard except that it is made of stainless steel.

| NIB | Exc. | V.G. | Good | Fair | Poor |
|-----|------|------|------|------|------|
| 275 | 250  | 200  | 150  | 125  | 100  |

## Mark II Target Model

This model incorporates the same improvements as the Mark II Standard but is offered with 5.5" bull, 6-7/8" tapered, and 10" heavy barrel. It has adjustable target sights and was introduced in 1982.

| NIB | Exc. | V.G. | Good | Fair | Poor |
|-----|------|------|------|------|------|
| 250 | 225  | 200  | 150  | 125  | 100  |

## Stainless Steel Mark II Target Model

This model is the same as the blued version but is made of stainless steel.

| NIB | Exc. | V.G. | Good | Fair | Poor |
|-----|------|------|------|------|------|
| 325 | 300  | 250  | 200  | 175  | 125  |

## Stainless Steel 1 of 5,000

This model is a special commemorative version of the first standard with the "Red Eagle" grips. It is made of stainless steel and had Bill Ruger's signature on it. The pistol is encased in a wood case.

| NIB | Exc. | V.G. | Good | Fair | Poor |
|-----|------|------|------|------|------|
| 500 | 450  | 400  | 325  | 250  | 175  |

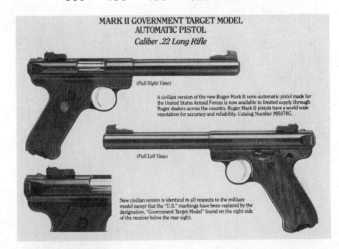

## Government Model

This model is similar to the blue Mark II Target, with a 6-7/8" bull barrel. It is the civilian version of a training pistol that the military is purchasing from Ruger. The only difference is that this model does not have the U.S. markings.

| NIB | Exc. | V.G. | Good | Fair | Poor |
|-----|------|------|------|------|------|
| 300 | 275  | 225  | 200  | 150  | 100  |

## P-85

This model represents Ruger's entry into the wonder nine market. The P-85 is a double-action, high-capacity (15-shot detachable magazine) semi-automatic, with an alloy frame and steel slide. It has a 4.5" barrel, ambidextrous safety, and three-dot sighting system. It has a matte black finish and black synthetic grips. The latest option for this model is a decocking device to replace the standard safety. There is also an optional molded locking case and extra magazine with loading tool available. It is more reasonably priced than many of its competitors. This pistol was introduced in 1987 and was sold at large premium for sometime due to limited supply and great demand. As of this writing, Ruger is producing this pistol in a new plant in Prescott, Arizona; and the premium situation no longer exists.

| NIB | Exc. | V.G. | Good | Fair | Poor |
|-----|------|------|------|------|------|
| 325 | 300  | 275  | 250  | 200  | 150  |

## P-85 Stainless Steel

This model is the same as the matte black version except that the slide is made of stainless steel.

| NIB | Exc. | V.G. | Good | Fair | Poor |
|-----|------|------|------|------|------|
| 355 | 335  | 300  | 275  | 225  | 175  |

## Semi-Automatic Rifles

## 10/22 Standard Carbine With Walnut Stock

This model has an 18.5" barrel and is chambered for the .22 l.r. It has a 10-shot, detachable rotary magazine and a folding rear sight. The stock is smooth walnut, with a barrel band and carbine-style buttplate. This rifle enjoys a fine reputation for accuracy and dependability and is considered an excellent value. It was introduced in 1984.

Birch Stock--Deduct $20.

| NIB | Exc. | V.G. | Good | Fair | Poor |
|-----|------|------|------|------|------|
| 185 | 165  | 125  | 100  | 75   | 50   |

## 10/22 Sporter

This model is similar to the Standard Carbine except that it has a Monte Carlo stock, beavertail forend, and no barrel band. It was manufactured between 1964 and 1971.

| Exc. | V.G. | Good | Fair | Poor |
|------|------|------|------|------|
| 165  | 125  | 100  | 75   | 50   |

## 10/22 Deluxe Sporter

The same as the Sporter with a checkered stock and better buttplate. This model was introduced in 1971.

| NIB | Exc. | V.G. | Good | Fair | Poor |
|-----|------|------|------|------|------|
| 200 | 165  | 125  | 100  | 75   | 50   |

## 10/22 International Carbine

This model is similar to the Standard Carbine, with a full-length, Mannlicher-style stock. It was manufactured between 1964 and 1971 and is fairly rare on today's market.

| Exc. | V.G. | Good | Fair | Poor |
|------|------|------|------|------|
| 450  | 400  | 350  | 275  | 200  |

## Model 44 Carbine

This model is a short, 18.5"-barrelled, gas-operated carbine chambered for the .44 Magnum cartridge. It has a 4-shot, non-detachable magazine, a folding rear sight, and a plain walnut stock. This is a very handy deer-hunting carbine manufactured between 1961 and 1985.

| Exc. | V.G. | Good | Fair | Poor |
|------|------|------|------|------|
| 350  | 300  | 250  | 200  | 150  |

## Deerstalker Model

The same as the Model 44 Carbine with "Deerstalker" stamped on it. This model was manufactured in 1961 and 1962 only.

| Exc. | V.G. | Good | Fair | Poor |
|------|------|------|------|------|
| 450  | 400  | 350  | 300  | 200  |

## Model 44RS

This is the Model 44 with sling swivels and an aperture sight.

| Exc. | V.G. | Good | Fair | Poor |
|------|------|------|------|------|
| 350  | 300  | 250  | 200  | 150  |

## Model 44 Deluxe Sporter

This version has a checkered sporter stock and was manufactured until 1971.

| Exc. | V.G. | Good | Fair | Poor |
|------|------|------|------|------|
| 400  | 350  | 300  | 250  | 200  |

## Model 44 International Carbine

This version features a full-length, Mannlicher-style stock. It was discontinued in 1971 and is quite collectible.

| Exc. | V.G. | Good | Fair | Poor |
|------|------|------|------|------|
| 700  | 600  | 525  | 400  | 275  |

## Model 44 25th Anniversary Model

This version is lightly engraved, has a medallion in the stock and was only made in 1985, the last year of production.

| NIB | Exc. | V.G. | Good | Fair | Poor |
|-----|------|------|------|------|------|
| 450 | 400  | 350  | 300  | 250  | 200  |

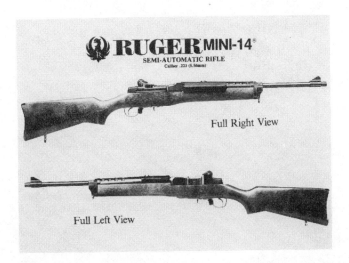

Full Right View

Full Left View

### Mini-14
This is a para-military style carbine chambered for the .223 Remington and on a limited basis for the .222 cartridge. It has an 18.5" barrel and is gas-operated. The detachable magazines originally offered held 5, 10, or 20 rounds. The high-capacity magazines are now discontinued, and prices of them are what the market will bear. The Mini-14 has a military-style stock and aperture sight. It was introduced in 1976.

| NIB | Exc. | V.G. | Good | Fair | Poor |
|-----|------|------|------|------|------|
| 425 | 375 | 325 | 275 | 225 | 150 |

Full Right View

Full Left View

Stainless Steel    Catalog No. K MINI-14/5

### Mini-14 Stainless Steel
The same as the Mini-14 except constructed of stainless steel.

| NIB | Exc. | V.G. | Good | Fair | Poor |
|-----|------|------|------|------|------|
| 450 | 400 | 350 | 300 | 250 | 175 |

### Mini-14 Ranch Rifle
This model is similar to the standard Mini-14, with a folding rear sight and the receiver milled to accept the Ruger scope-ring system. The rings are supplied with the rifle.

| NIB | Exc. | V.G. | Good | Fair | Poor |
|-----|------|------|------|------|------|
| 450 | 400 | 350 | 300 | 250 | 175 |

### Stainless Steel Mini-14 Ranch Rifle
This model is the same as the blued version except that it is made of stainless steel.

| NIB | Exc. | V.G. | Good | Fair | Poor |
|-----|------|------|------|------|------|
| 500 | 450 | 400 | 350 | 300 | 225 |

### GB Model
This model has a factory-installed folding stock, flash suppressor, and bayonet lug. It was designed and sold by Ruger to law enforcement agencies. A number have come on the civilian market through surplus sales and police trade-ins. With the assault-rifle hysteria, prices of this model have fluctuated wildly in some areas. Now that Ruger has discontinued the folding stock and the high capacity magazines, this could become even less predictable. It would behoove anyone contemplating purchase of this model to check their local ordinances and the current market in their area. Note that this is a semi-automatic and totally different than the full-auto version of this weapon available only through Class 3 dealers.

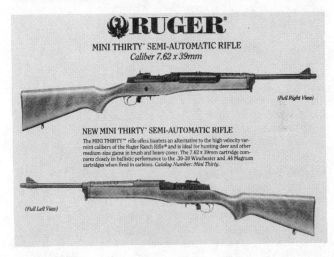

### Mini-30
This model was brought out by Ruger in 1987 in answer to the influx of weapons imported from China that were chambered for this cartridge--the 7.62mm x 39 Russian. This cartridge is touted as a fine hunting cartridge for deer-sized game; and by adding this chambering, the very handy Mini-14 becomes a legitimate hunting gun--and a new market opened. This model is similar in appearance to the standard Mini-14 and is supplied with Ruger scope rings.

| NIB | Exc. | V.G. | Good | Fair | Poor |
|-----|------|------|------|------|------|
| 450 | 425 | 375 | 300 | 250 | 175 |

### Single Shot Rifles
The late 1960's was a period of nostalgia in this country. The public longed for things gone by. This phenomena was perhaps caused by an overabundance of things made of plastic and aluminum. The gun-buying public wanted fine walnut and steel; the time of the single shot had arrived--and once more Ruger was quick to percieve and capitalize. The No. 1 was introduced in 1966 and has been successful ever since. This rifle combines high quality in materials and workmanship with the nostalgia of the single shot and has captured the American gun-buying public.

## Number 1-A

This fine rifle is a single-shot falling block that resembles the Farquharson but that is totally original in design. This variation is offered with a 22" or 26" lightweight barrel with a quarter rib and integral scope-mounting system. The rings are included. This rifle is chambered for the .243, .270, 7x57, and the .30-06. It is blued, with a nicely checkered walnut stock and Alexander Henry schnabel-style forearm. This model was introduced in 1966.

| NIB | Exc. | V.G. | Good | Fair | Poor |
|-----|------|------|------|------|------|
| 575 | 425  | 375  | 300  | 250  | 200  |

## Number 1-B

This model is similar to the 1-A but features a heavier sporter barrel and is chambered for nearly all popular calibers. It has a semi-beavertail forearm.

| NIB | Exc. | V.G. | Good | Fair | Poor |
|-----|------|------|------|------|------|
| 575 | 425  | 375  | 300  | 250  | 200  |

## Number 1-A Light Sporter

This variation is similar in appearance to the No. 1-A, with a folding rear sight mounted on the quarter rib and a ramp front sight. Scope rings are not supplied. The forearm is of the Alexander Henry design, and the front sling swivel is on a barrel band. It is offered in the same calibers.

| NIB | Exc. | V.G. | Good | Fair | Poor |
|-----|------|------|------|------|------|
| 575 | 425  | 375  | 300  | 250  | 200  |

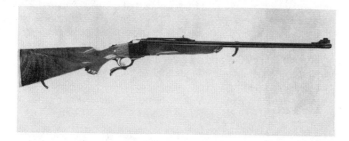

## Number 1-S Medium Sporter

This variation is similar to the Light Sporter, with a 26" medium-weight barrel. It is chambered for the 7mm Magnum, .300 Winchester Magnum, and the .338 Magnum. It is also chambered for the .45-70 with a 22" barrel.

| NIB | Exc. | V.G. | Good | Fair | Poor |
|-----|------|------|------|------|------|
| 575 | 425  | 375  | 300  | 250  | 200  |

## Number 1-H Tropical Rifle

This model is similar in appearance to the No. 1-S Medium Sporter but has a very heavy 24" barrel and is chambered for the .375 H&H Magnum and the .458 Winchester Magnum.

| NIB | Exc. | V.G. | Good | Fair | Poor |
|-----|------|------|------|------|------|
| 575 | 450  | 400  | 325  | 275  | 225  |

RUGER NO. 1 SPECIAL VARMINT
(Catalog No. 1-V)

## Number 1-V Varmint

This model is similar in appearance to the Number 1-B but features a 24" heavy barrel and is chambered for the .22-250, .220 Swift, .223, .243, .25-06, 6mm, and the .280. This model lacks the quarter rib and is fitted with target blocks to mount the larger high-power scopes.

| NIB | Exc. | V.G. | Good | Fair | Poor |
|-----|------|------|------|------|------|
| 575 | 425  | 375  | 300  | 250  | 200  |

## Number 1 International

This variation has a lightweight 20" barrel and the quarter rib with both sights and scope rings. It is chambered for the .243, .270, 7x57, and the .30-06 and features a full-length, Mannlicher-style forearm.

| Exc. | V.G. | Good | Fair | Poor |
|------|------|------|------|------|
| 425  | 375  | 300  | 250  | 200  |

## Number 3 Carbine

This model is a less-elaborate, inexpensive version of the Number 1. The action is the same except that the lever is less ornate in appearance and lacks the locking bar. The uncheckered stock is of a military carbine style with a barrel band. It is similar in appearance to the Model 44 and the 10/22. This serviceable rifle was chambered for the .22 Hornet, .30-40 Krag, and the .45-70 when it was released in 1972. Later chamberings added the .223, .44 Magnum, and the .375 Winchester. The barrel is 22" long, and there is a folding rear sight. This model was discontinued in 1987.

| Exc. | V.G. | Good | Fair | Poor |
|------|------|------|------|------|
| 275  | 225  | 175  | 150  | 125  |

## Bolt Action Rifles

Ruger introduced the Model 77R in 1968. It filled the need for a good quality, reasonably priced, bolt-action hunting rifle. It has been a commercial success. There are certain variations of this rifle that collectors actively seek. One should avail oneself of the specialized literature on this model and secure individual appraisals on the rare variations as the differences are slight and beyond the scope of this book.

## Model 77

This model was introduced in 1968. It is offered with a 22", 24", or 26" barrel. The Model 77 is chambered for most calibers from .22-250 through .338 Winchester Magnum. The action is of a modified Mauser type, finished in blue with a checkered walnut stock and red rubber buttplate. The rifle is available milled for Ruger scope rings or in the round-topstyle that allow the mounting of any popular scope ring system. This model is designated 77R when supplied with rings only; and 77RS, when supplied with rings and sights. This model is still manufactured.

| NIB | Exc. | V.G. | Good | Fair | Poor |
|-----|------|------|------|------|------|
| 475 | 425 | 350 | 300 | 250 | 200 |

## Model 77 Flat Bolt

This is an example of the slight variations that make this model collectible. This is essentially the same rifle with the knob on the bolt handle flattened. They were only produced in the configuration until 1972. Watch for fakes, and read specialized material.

| Exc. | V.G. | Good | Fair | Poor |
|------|------|------|------|------|
| 525 | 450 | 400 | 350 | 275 |

## Model 77 RL & RLS

This variation is similar to the standard model except that it features an ultra light 20" barrel and black forearm tip. This model is also available in an 18.5" carbine version with sights designated the RLS. They are chambered for the .257 Roberts, .270, and .30-06. Weight is only 6 pounds.

| NIB | Exc. | V.G. | Good | Fair | Poor |
|-----|------|------|------|------|------|
| 500 | 450 | 375 | 325 | 275 | 225 |

## Model 77 RSI

This version of the Model 77 has a full-length, Mannlicher-style stock and is chambered for the .270 and the .30-06.

| NIB | Exc. | V.G. | Good | Fair | Poor |
|-----|------|------|------|------|------|
| 550 | 475 | 400 | 350 | 300 | 250 |

## Model 77V Varmint

This variation is similar to the standard Model 77 except that it has a 24" heavy barrel that is drilled and tapped for target scope bases and has a wider beavertail forearm. It is chambered for the .22-250, .220 Swift, .243, 6mm,. 25-06, and .308.

| NIB | Exc. | V.G. | Good | Fair | Poor |
|-----|------|------|------|------|------|
| 475 | 425 | 350 | 300 | 250 | 200 |

## Model 77 RS African

This is a heavier-barrelled version, with a steel triggerguard and floorplate. Earlier versions were stocked with fine quality circassion walnut. This rifle is chambered for the .458 Winchester Magnum.

| NIB | Exc. | V.G. | Good | Fair | Poor |
|-----|------|------|------|------|------|
| 625 | 550 | 500 | 425 | 350 | 250 |

# RUGER MAGNUM RIFLE

### In .416 Rigby and .375 H & H calibers

## Model 77 Magnum
This new variation is deluxe in every way. It is stocked in fine quality circassion walnut, with black forearm tip and rifle pad. It features a new express rib with sights and a newly designed floor-plate latch that eliminates dumped cartridges under the heavy recoil of these magnum calibers. This model is chambered for the .375 H&H Magnum and the .416 Rigby. These are heavy rifles, at approximately 10 pounds. At this time, price has not been established. Estimated NIB $1,500.

## Model 77/22
This is a high quality, .22 rimfire rifle designed for the serious shooter. This model has a 20" barrel and a 10-shot, detachable rotary magazine. It is made of steel and stocked with checkered walnut. It is available with sights, scope rings, or both as an extra cost ($20) option. This model was introduced in 1984.

| NIB | Exc. | V.G. | Good | Fair | Poor |
|-----|------|------|------|------|------|
| 365 | 325  | 275  | 225  | 175  | 125  |

## Model 77/22 Synthetic Stock
This version is quite similar to the standard 77/22, with a black matte finished synthetic stock.

| NIB | Exc. | V.G. | Good | Fair | Poor |
|-----|------|------|------|------|------|
| 300 | 275  | 225  | 200  | 150  | 100  |

## Model 77/22 Stainless Steel/Synthetic Stock
This model is the same as the blued version except that it is made of stainless steel.

# RUGER M77 MARK II

### Stainless Steel Bolt-Action Rifle with All-Weather Stock

| NIB | Exc. | V.G. | Good | Fair | Poor |
|-----|------|------|------|------|------|
| 350 | 300  | 250  | 200  | 150  | 100  |

# RUGER 77/22 MAGNUM

### .22 Rimfire Bolt-Action Rifle; 9-Shot Rotary Clip

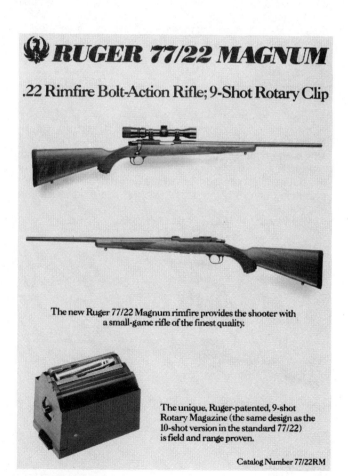

The new Ruger 77/22 Magnum rimfire provides the shooter with a small-game rifle of the finest quality.

The unique, Ruger-patented, 9-shot Rotary Magazine (the same design as the 10-shot version in the standard 77/22) is field and range proven.

Catalog Number 77/22RM

## Model 77/22M
This model is simply the 77/22 chambered for the .22 Magnum cartridge. The finish is blue, and the magazine capacity is 9 rounds.

| NIB | Exc. | V.G. | Good | Fair | Poor |
|-----|------|------|------|------|------|
| 370 | 325  | 275  | 225  | 175  | 125  |

### Model 77/22M Stainless Steel
This is the same as the blued 77/22M constructed of stainless steel.

| NIB | Exc. | V.G. | Good | Fair | Poor |
|-----|------|------|------|------|------|
| 350 | 300 | 250 | 200 | 150 | 100 |

### Shotguns

### Red Label Over/Under Early Production
Ruger introduced the Red Label in 20 gauge in 1977; the 12 gauge followed shortly afterwards. This high quality shotgun is offered with 3" chambers in 26" or 28" barrel lengths. Various chokes are available. They are boxlocks with automatic ejectors. The stock is of checkered walnut. The finish is blue on the earlier guns.

| NIB | Exc. | V.G. | Good | Fair | Poor |
|-----|------|------|------|------|------|
| 700 | 575 | 500 | 400 | 300 | 250 |

### Red Label Over/Under Current Production
The new 12 and 20 gauge Red Label shotgun has a stainless-steel receiver and blued barrels. They are offered with screw-in choke tubes. Otherwise they are similar to the earlier models.

| NIB | Exc. | V.G. | Good | Fair | Poor |
|-----|------|------|------|------|------|
| 900 | 800 | 600 | 475 | 400 | 300 |

Ruger's New model single-six revolver chambered for the new .32 magnum cartridge.

Ruger's New model single-six revolver.

Ruger's New model single-six revolver.

### NEW MODEL BLACKHAWK®
*.44 Magnum Caliber*

### NEW

The popular New Model Blackhawk single-action revolver is now offered in a 5½" barrel version that shoots .44 Magnum or .44 Special cartridges. This model has an all steel grip frame that accommodates walnut grip panels for comfortable and confident handling and a wide deeply serrated hammer spur that facilitates cocking. Its size, handling characteristics, and ballistic capabilities combine to make it the ideal camp and back-up gun on hunting trips.

Ruger New Model Blackhawk; .44 magnum caliber.

## RUGER®
## New Super Blackhawk

### .44 Magnum Stainless Steel
### Single Action Revolver
### Untapered Bull Barrel

Ruger New Super Blackhawk; .44 magnum, stainless steel, single action revolver; untapered bull barrel.

*New roll engraved cylinder.*

## NEW BISLEY

Large frame Ruger new model single-action Bisley revolvers are now
also available with fluted cylinders that are roll engraved in a motif
reminiscent of the turn-of-the century Bisley era. Earlier models
have fluted cylinders without roll engraving. All models are satin
polished and blued. Calibers: .357 Magnum, .41 Magnum,
.44 Magnum and .45 Long Colt.

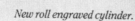

*New roll engraved cylinder.*

## NEW BISLEY

Small frame Ruger new model single-action Bisley revolvers are now
also available with fluted cylinders that are roll engraved in a classic
styling reminiscent of the turn-of-the century Bisley era. Earlier
models have fluted cylinders without roll engraving. All models are
satin polished and blued. Calibers: .22 Long Rifle and .32 H&R
Magnum.

# RUGER SP101

## .22 LR Caliber; 6 Shot

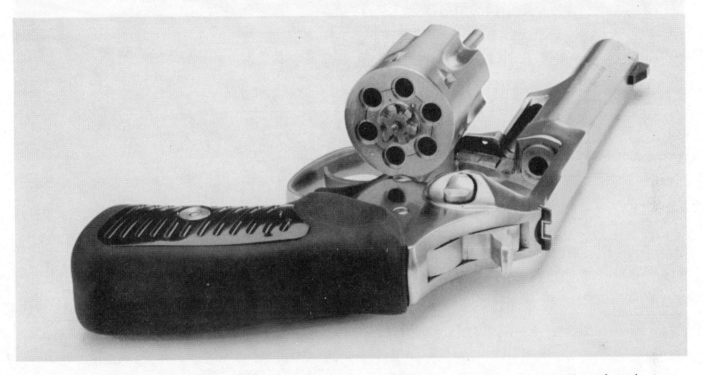

Ruger SP101 .22 LR caliber; 6 shot. The same attention to strength and secure cylinder lock-up found in the large-caliber Ruger double-action revolvers is evident in the SP101 .22 caliber.

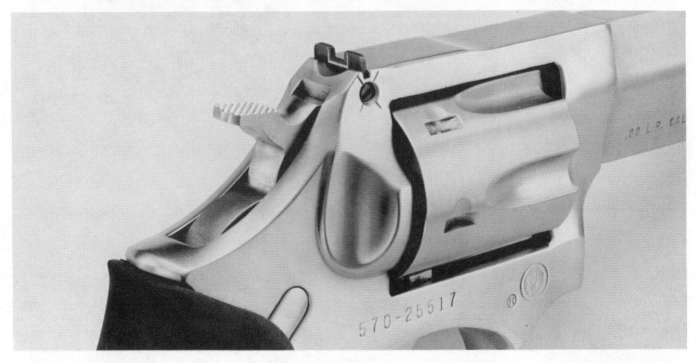

The white-outlined, square-notch rear sight on the .22 caliber SP101 is adjustable for windage.

# RUGER SP101

## .22 LR Caliber; 6 Shot

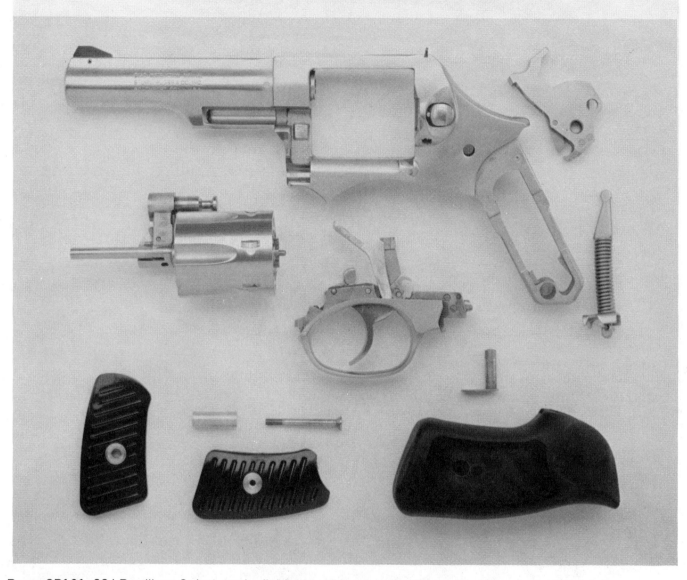

Ruger SP101 .22 LR caliber; 6 shot can be fieldstripped in a matter of seconds without special tools.

# RUGER GP100®

*.357 Magnum, Double Action Revolver*

## Ruger's GP100 Is Available in a Fixed Sight, Compact Grip Version

Ruger GP100 .357 magnum, double action revolver. Ruger's GP100 is available in a fixed sight, compact grip version, 3" barrel.

Ruger Redhawk double-action revolver.

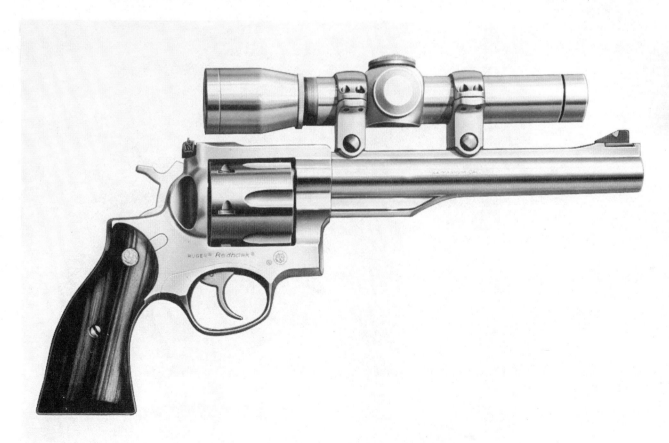

Redhawk revolver — KRH-44R with Ruger integral scope mounting system.

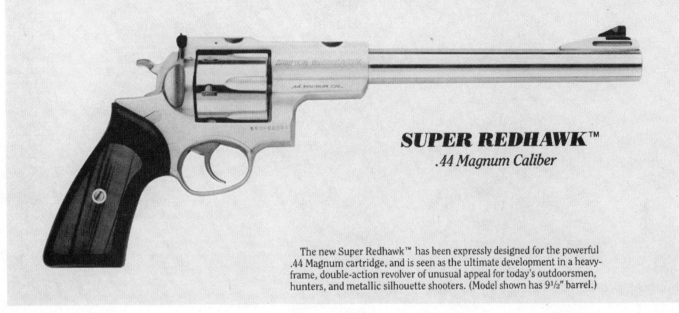

## SUPER REDHAWK™
### .44 Magnum Caliber

The new Super Redhawk™ has been expressly designed for the powerful .44 Magnum cartridge, and is seen as the ultimate development in a heavy-frame, double-action revolver of unusual appeal for today's outdoorsmen, hunters, and metallic silhouette shooters. (Model shown has 9½" barrel.)

## SUPER REDHAWK™
### .44 Magnum Caliber

The massive new Ruger Super Redhawk™ double-action revolver incorporates the exclusive Ruger Integral Scope Mounting System. The integral scope bases on the wide top strap offer a stronger mounting with no stress on the barrel. The Ruger Cushioned Grip System (patents pending) is another important feature of the Super Redhawk revolver. (Model shown has a 9½" barrel.)

Ruger Mark II standard model, full left view.

Ruger Mark II standard model, caliber .22 long rifle. Stainless steel.

# RUGER

## MARK II BULL BARREL MODEL PISTOL
### Caliber .22 Long Rifle

**NEW!**
**STAINLESS STEEL**

Ruger Mark II bull barrel model pistol, caliber .22 long rifle. Stainless steel.

Ruger Mark II target model pistol, full left view.

Ruger Decocker model P85, 9mm, parabellum, 15 shot. Ruger's new Decocker P85, preferred by many police departments, allows the shooter to decock the pistol without manipulating the trigger.

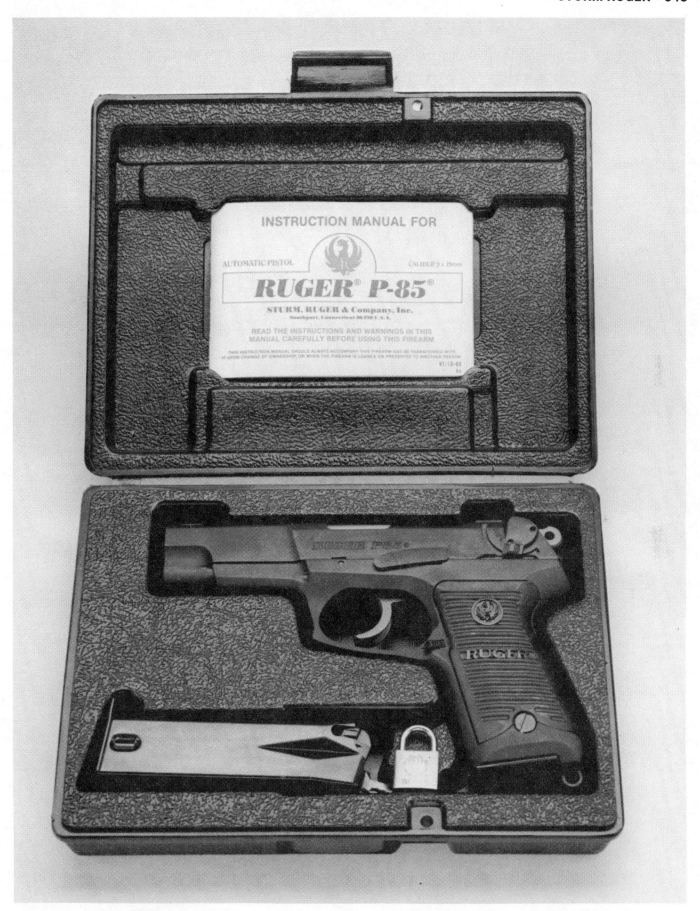

Ruger P85 9mm automatic pistol.

# RUGER P85®
## 9mm Automatic Pistol

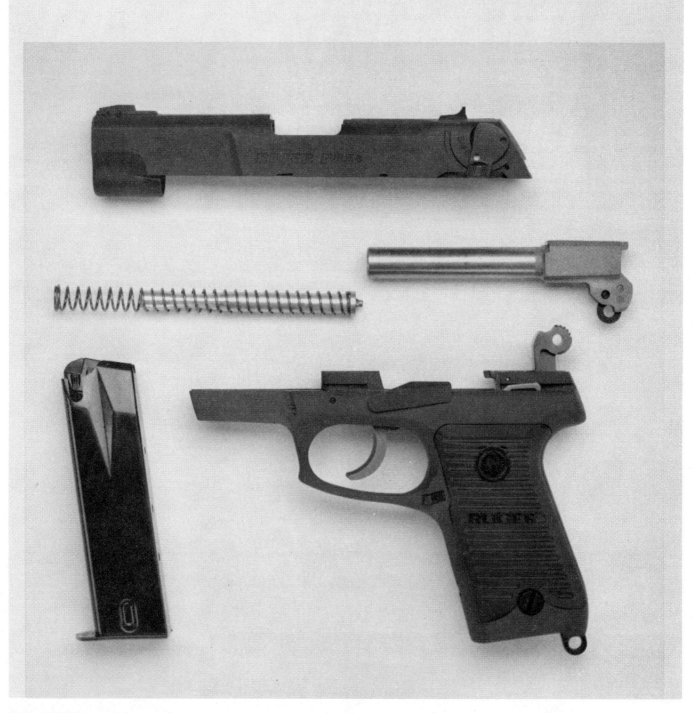

Ruger P85 9mm automoatic pistol.

# RUGER STAINLESS STEEL P85

## 9mm, 15 Shot

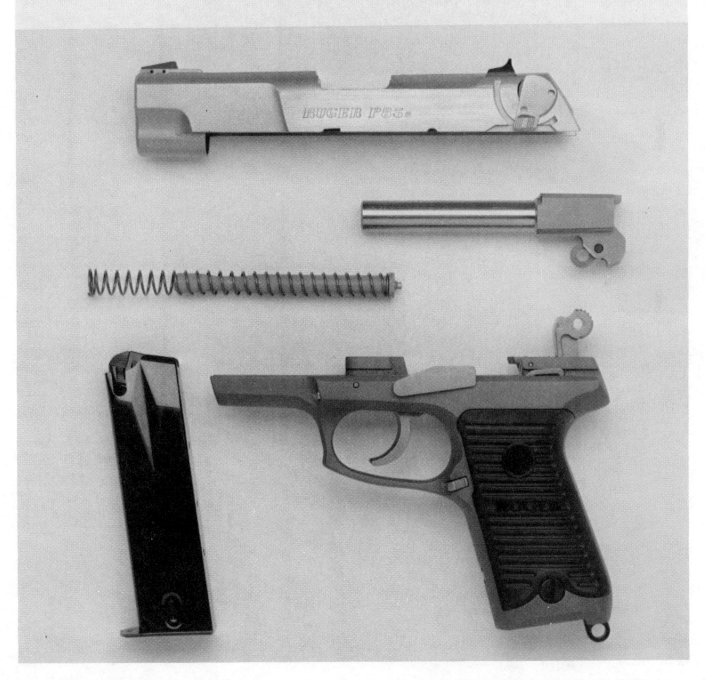

Ruger P85 9mm 15 shot. Basic fieldstripping of the stainless steel P85 is done quickly in the field without the use of tools.

Ruger .22 rimfire bolt-action rifle.

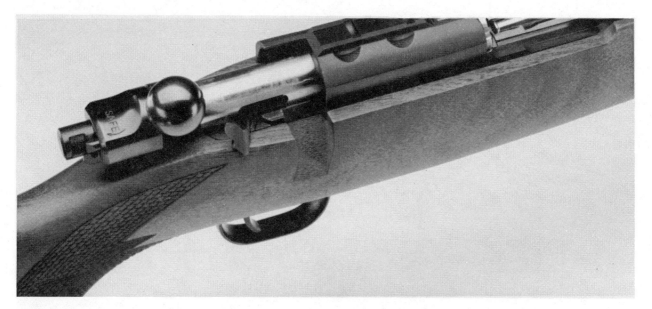

Bolt Open

Ruger 77.22 magnum .22 rimfire bolt-action rifle; 9-shot rotary clip.

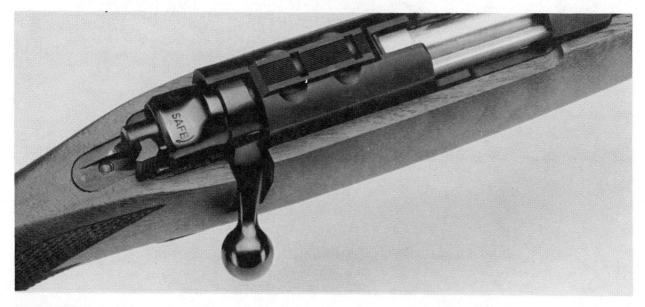

Bolt Closed

Ruger's magnum rimfire rifle is equipped with a readily accessible three-position safety that allows the shooter to unload the rifle with the safety on.

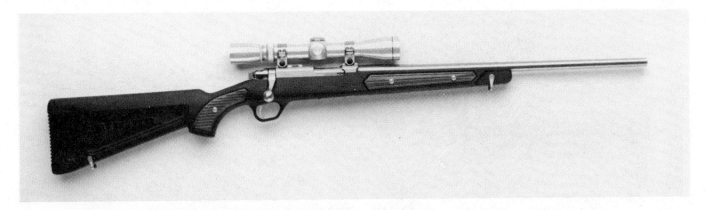

Ruger 77/22 .22 caliber rifle. The only all stainless steel, bolt-action rifle incorporating an impervious all-weather injection-moulded stock.

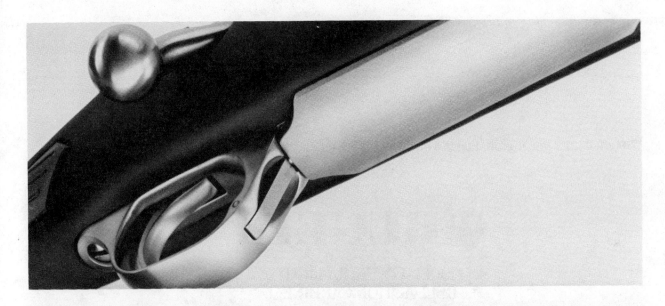

Ruger M77 Mark II stainless steel bolt-action rifle with all-weather stock. The redesigned, patented floor-plate latch (flush with the contours of the trigger guard) securely holds the floorplate and prevents accidental dumping of the cartridges. The readily accessible three-position safety allows the shooter to unload the rifle with safety on for optimum convenience and security.

Ruger M-77 Mark II .223 Remington. Ruger's new M-77 Mark II bolt action is the slender, ideal hunter.

Ruger Model-77 ultra light bolt-action carbine.

Ruger M-77RS bolt-action rifle.

Ruger magnum rifle. The Ruger magnum barrel and sighting rib, with cross serrations is machined from a single bar of steel. This feature has customarily been available only on the most expensive custom built big game rifles traditionally associated with the British, Bond Street African safari rifles.

## MINI THIRTY™ SEMI-AUTOMATIC RIFLE
### Caliber 7.62 x 39mm

*Scope not included*

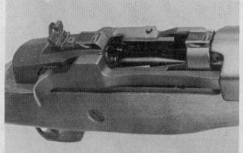

*While the MINI THIRTY™ is based on the Mini-14® Ranch Rifle, the barrel, receiver and bolt have been redesigned, to accommodate the larger 7.62 x 39mm cartridge. Details of the receiver, bolt face, rear sight, and Ruger Scope Mount bases are shown.*

*The new Ruger MINI THIRTY™ rifle is a modified version of the popular Ruger Mini-14® Ranch Rifle and is chambered for the 7.62 x 39mm cartridge to provide big bore performance in a compact, lightweight self-loading sporting rifle.*

*The 7.62 x 39mm bridges the gap between smallbore high-velocity varmint loads and big game calibers. Shown above are the .223 with Metal Case Boat-Tail Bullet and the 7.62 x 39mm with Full Metal Jacketed Bullet (center) and the Pointed Soft Point Bullet (right).*

Ruger Mini Thirty semi-automatic rifle. Caliber 7.62 x 39mm.

# RUGER®
## Screw-In Choke Inserts

### for the 12 Gauge "Red Label" Over & Under Shotgun with the Stainless Steel Receiver

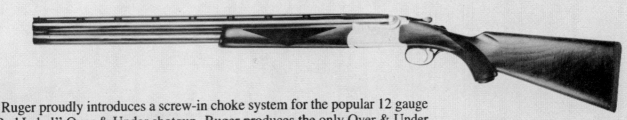

Ruger proudly introduces a screw-in choke system for the popular 12 gauge "Red Label" Over & Under shotgun. Ruger produces the only Over & Under shotgun that is made in America. Initial shipments are now being made. This new model will be offered with either 26″ or 28″ barrels and 3″ chambers.

This new system was designed for the upland game and waterfowl hunter as well as clay target shooters. Additionally, it is ideally suited for the game of sporting clays.

Ruger's screw-in chokes are easily installed with a key wrench packaged with each shotgun. The chokes fit flush to the muzzle with no visible distraction. Every shotgun is equipped with a Full, Modified, Improved Cylinder and two Skeet screw-in chokes. The muzzle edge of the chokes have been slotted for quick identification in or out of the barrels. The Full choke has 3 slots, Modified — 2 slots, Improved Cylinder — 1 slot, Skeet — no slots.

The Ruger Over & Under shotguns that are equipped with the screw-in chokes have a slightly different barrel configuration from the fixed choke models. Due to dimensional variations the screw-in chokes cannot be retrofitted into existing barrels.

Ruger screw-in choke inserts for the 12 gauge "Red Label" over and under shotgun with the stainless steel receiver.

# RUGER®
## Screw-In Choke Inserts

### for the 12 Gauge "Red Label" Over & Under Shotgun with the Stainless Steel Receiver

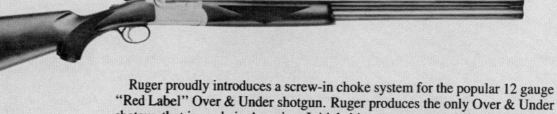

Ruger proudly introduces a screw-in choke system for the popular 12 gauge "Red Label" Over & Under shotgun. Ruger produces the only Over & Under shotgun that is made in America. Initial shipments are now being made. This new model will be offered with either 26" or 28" barrels and 3" chambers.

This new system was designed for the upland game and waterfowl hunter as well as clay target shooters. Additionally, it is ideally suited for the game of sporting clays.

The muzzle edge of the chokes have been slotted for quick and easy identification in or out of the barrels.

| CHOKE | NO. OF SLOTS |
|---|---|
| Full | 3 |
| Modified | 2 |
| Improved Cylinder | 1 |
| Skeet | None |

The Ruger Over & Under shotguns that are equipped with the screw-in chokes have a slightly different barrel configuration from the fixed choke models. Due to dimensional variations the screw-in chokes cannot be retrofitted into existing barrels.

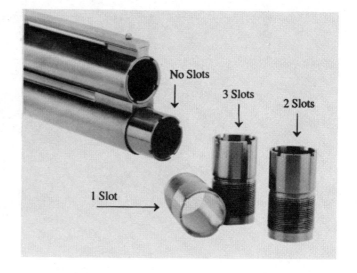

Ruger screw-in choke inserts for the 12 gauge "Red Label" over and under shotgun with the stainless steel receiver.

# SUNDANCE INDUSTRIES, INC.
## North Hollywood, California

### Model D-22M

This is a double-barrel, derringer-type pocket pistol chambered for .22 l.r. or .22 rimfire Magnum. It has 2.5" barrels and is a single-action design. It is constructed of steel and aluminum alloy and is finished in either black with simulated plastic pearl grips or polished chrome-plated with black grips. It was introduced in 1989.

| Exc. | V.G. | Good | Fair | Poor |
|------|------|------|------|------|
| 225  | 200  | 150  | 100  | 80   |

# SUTHERLAND, S.
## Richmond, Virginia

### Pocket Pistol

This is a single-shot pocket pistol chambered for .41-caliber percussion. It was patterned after the Henry Deringer pistol and has a round barrel from 2.5" to 4" in length. The fittings are German silver, and the stock is walnut. It was manufactured in the late 1850's.

| Exc. | V.G. | Good | Fair | Poor |
|------|------|------|------|------|
| 750  | 650  | 500  | 400  | 300  |

# SYMS, J. G.
## New York, New York

### Pocket Pistol

This is a single-shot pocket pistol chambered for .41-caliber percussion. It has barrel lengths from 1.5" to 3.5" and has German silver mountings and a walnut stock. It was manufactured in the 1850's.

| Exc. | V.G. | Good | Fair | Poor |
|------|------|------|------|------|
| 750  | 650  | 500  | 400  | 300  |

# TALLASSEE
## Tallassee, Alabama

### Carbine

This is a muzzle-loading, single-shot carbine chambered for .58-caliber percussion. It was patterned after the British Enfield carbine and was the only official Confederate calvary weapon. The round barrel is 25" in length, and the walnut full-length stock is held on by two barrel bands. It has a swivel-mounted, integral ramrod under the barrel and sling swivels on the front barrel band and the buttstock. The mountings are brass, and the lockplate is marked "C. S. Tallassee Ala." It is dated 1864. There were approximately 500 manufactured in 1864, and it is doubtful if they were finished in time to be issued before the cessation of hostilities. Due to the extreme rarity and collectibility of the Confederate Civil War weapons, we strongly recommend securing a qualified, independent appraisal.

| Exc. | V.G. | Good | Fair | Poor |
|------|------|------|------|------|
| 6500 | 5500 | 4500 | 3000 | 2000 |

# TANFOGLIO
## Valtrompia, Italy

This company went into the firearms business, manufacturing inexpensive pocket pistols in the late 1940's. They have been imported over the years into the United States by various different corporations, among them the Eig Corporation, as well as F.I.E. of Hialeah, Florida, and Excam, also of Florida. In 1968 the Gun Control Act made it extremely difficult for Tanfoglio to produce pistols that could be legally imported into this Country.

In recent years this shortcoming has been alleviated, and the current products sold by Excam and F.I.E. are not only legal but quite desirable to own.

### Sata

This is a blowback-operated pocket pistol chambered for 6.53mm or .22 rimfire. It has a fixed barrel that is 3" in length and is striker-fired. It has a top-mounted ejection port and a detachable box magazine. The pistol is marked "Pistola SATA Made in Italy" with the respective caliber also marked. The finish is blued, with checkered plastic grips with the word "SATA" molded into them.

| Exc. | V.G. | Good | Fair | Poor |
|------|------|------|------|------|
| 175  | 150  | 125  | 90   | 75   |

### Titan

This is a poor-quality, blowback-operated semi-automatic pistol that is chambered for 6.35mm. It has a fixed 2.5" barrel, open-topped slide, and an external hammer. It is marked "Titan 6.35." The finish is blued, with plastic grips. U.S. imported models are marked "Eig," and the caliber noted as .25 ACP.

| Exc. | V.G. | Good | Fair | Poor |
|------|------|------|------|------|
| 100  | 75   | 50   | 40   | 30   |

### TA 90 or TZ-75

This is a double-action semi-automatic pistol chambered for 9mm Parabellum. It is closely patterned after the Czechoslovakian CZ-75 pistol. It has a 4.75" barrel, all-steel construction, and a 15-round detachable double-stack magazine. The finish is either matte blue or satin chrome-plated. It has high-visibility fixed sights and either wood or rubber grips. When imported by Excam, it is known as the TA 90; F.I.E. calls it the TZ-75.

| NIB | Exc. | V.G. | Good | Fair | Poor |
|-----|------|------|------|------|------|
| 450 | 400  | 350  | 300  | 250  | 200  |

### TA 90B

This is a smaller, more compact version of the TA 90, with a 3.5" barrel, 12-round magazine, and Neoprene grips. It was introduced in 1986.

| NIB | Exc. | V.G. | Good | Fair | Poor |
|-----|------|------|------|------|------|
| 500 | 450  | 400  | 350  | 300  | 250  |

### TA 90 SS

This is a fully compensated version of the TA 90 with a ported 5" barrel, two-tone finish, and competition sights. It was introduced in 1989.

| NIB | Exc. | V.G. | Good | Fair | Poor |
|-----|------|------|------|------|------|
| 650 | 600  | 500  | 450  | 400  | 300  |

### TA 41

This is similar to the TA 90 except that it is chambered for the new .41 Action Express cartridge. It was introduced in 1989.

| NIB | Exc. | V.G. | Good | Fair | Poor |
|-----|------|------|------|------|------|
| 500 | 450  | 400  | 350  | 300  | 250  |

### TA 41 SS

This is similar to the TA 90 SS except that it is chambered for the .41 Action Express cartridge. It was introduced in 1989.

| NIB | Exc. | V.G. | Good | Fair | Poor |
|-----|------|------|------|------|------|
| 650 | 600  | 500  | 450  | 400  | 300  |

### TA 76

This is a Western-style single-action revolver chambered for the .22 l.r. cartridge. It has a 4.75" barrel and a 6-round, gate-loaded cylinder. It is offered either blued, chrome-plated, or with a brass backstrap and triggerguard. The grips are wood.

| NIB | Exc. | V.G. | Good | Fair | Poor |
|-----|------|------|------|------|------|
| 100 | 90   | 80   | 65   | 50   | 25   |

### TA 76M Combo

This model is similar to the TA 76 but also offered with a 6" or 9" barrel and an interchangeable .22 rimfire Magnum cylinder.

| NIB | Exc. | V.G. | Good | Fair | Poor |
|-----|------|------|------|------|------|
| 110 | 100  | 90   | 75   | 60   | 35   |

## TA 38SB

This is an Over/Under, 2-shot derringer that was patterned after the early Remington. It is chambered for .38 Special and has 3" barrels that tip up for loading. There is a hammerblock safety; and the finish is blued, with checkered nylon grips. This model was discontinued in 1985.

| Exc. | V.G. | Good | Fair | Poor |
|------|------|------|------|------|
| 100  | 90   | 80   | 60   | 40   |

# TANNER, ANDRE
### Switzerland

## Model 300 Free Rifle

This extremely accurate, single-shot target rifle is chambered for 7.5mm Swiss or .308. It was manufactured to precision specifications and features micrometer-adjustable aperture sights and a fully adjustable trigger. The finish is blued, with a deluxe walnut stock featuring a palm rest and adjustable cheekpiece. This model was not imported after 1988.

| Exc. | V.G. | Good | Fair | Poor |
|------|------|------|------|------|
| 3500 | 2750 | 2250 | 1750 | 1400 |

## Model 300S

This is similar to the Free Rifle without the palm rest. It is a repeating rifle with a 10-round magazine. It was discontinued in 1988.

| Exc. | V.G. | Good | Fair | Poor |
|------|------|------|------|------|
| 3000 | 2500 | 2000 | 1500 | 1300 |

## Model 50F

This version is chambered for the .22 l.r. cartridge. It features all the amenities of the Model 300 Free Rifle with a thumbhold stock. It was discontinued in 1988.

| Exc. | V.G. | Good | Fair | Poor |
|------|------|------|------|------|
| 2500 | 2000 | 1750 | 1400 | 1200 |

# TARPLEY
### Greensboro, North Carolina

## Carbine

This breechloading single-shot carbine was invented by Jere Tarpley and manufactured by the Garrett Company. It is chambered for .52-caliber percussion and designed to fire a paper cartridge. It has a 22" round barrel that is blued. The frame is brass and unfinished in appearance. The hammer is case-colored. The buttstock is walnut, and there is no forend at all. The mountings are iron, and it has a unique, two-leaf rear sight. The tang is marked, "J H Tarpley's Pat Feb 14, 1863." This was a Confederate weapon produced for use by the North Carolina Militia. There were only several hundred manufactured in 1863 and 1864. As with all Confederate Civil War weaponry, due to its extreme rarity and value, we urge securing competent, individual appraisal if a transaction is contemplated.

| Exc. | V.G. | Good | Fair | Poor |
|------|------|------|------|------|
| 9000 | 7500 | 6000 | 4000 | 3000 |

# TAURUS INTERNATIONAL MFG. CO.
### Porto Alegre, Brazil
### Importer--Taurus, Inc.
### Miami, Florida

## PT-92AF

This is a double-action semi-automatic pistol chambered for 9mm Parabellum. It has a 4.92" barrel with an exposed hammer and a 15-round detachable magazine. The finish is blued or satin-nickel plated, with smooth walnut grips and fixed sights. This model is very similar to the Beretta Model 92 SBF.

| NIB | Exc. | V.G. | Good | Fair | Poor |
|-----|------|------|------|------|------|
| 425 | 375  | 325  | 300  | 200  | 150  |

## PT-99AF

This model is similar to the PT-92AF, with adjustable sights.

| NIB | Exc. | V.G. | Good | Fair | Poor |
|-----|------|------|------|------|------|
| 460 | 400  | 350  | 325  | 225  | 175  |

## PT-58

This is a smaller version, chambered for .380 ACP. It has a 13-round detachable magazine. It was introduced in 1988.

| NIB | Exc. | V.G. | Good | Fair | Poor |
|-----|------|------|------|------|------|
| 400 | 350  | 300  | 250  | 200  | 150  |

## Model 65

This is a double-action, swing-out cylinder revolver chambered for .357 Magnum. It is offered with a 3" or 4" barrel and fixed sights and has a 6-round cylinder. The finish is either blued or satin-nickel plated, with walnut grips.

| NIB | Exc. | V.G. | Good | Fair | Poor |
|-----|------|------|------|------|------|
| 225 | 200  | 175  | 150  | 100  | 75   |

## Model 66

This is similar to the Model 65 but is also available with a 6" barrel. It has adjustable sights.

| NIB | Exc. | V.G. | Good | Fair | Poor |
|-----|------|------|------|------|------|
| 250 | 225  | 200  | 175  | 125  | 100  |

## Model 669

This version has a heavier, shrouded 4" or 6" barrel.

| NIB | Exc. | V.G. | Good | Fair | Poor |
|-----|------|------|------|------|------|
| 250 | 225 | 200 | 175 | 125 | 100 |

## Model 669 Stainless

This is a stainless steel version of the Model 669.

| NIB | Exc. | V.G. | Good | Fair | Poor |
|-----|------|------|------|------|------|
| 325 | 300 | 250 | 225 | 175 | 125 |

## Model 73

This is a swing-out cylinder, double-action revolver chambered for .32 Smith & Wesson long. It has a 3" heavy barrel and fixed sights and is either blued or satin-nickel plated, with walnut grips.

| NIB | Exc. | V.G. | Good | Fair | Poor |
|-----|------|------|------|------|------|
| 200 | 175 | 150 | 125 | 100 | 75 |

## Model 80

This is similar to the Model 73, with either a 3" or 4" standard-weight barrel chambered for .38 Special.

| NIB | Exc. | V.G. | Good | Fair | Poor |
|-----|------|------|------|------|------|
| 200 | 175 | 150 | 125 | 100 | 75 |

## Model 82

This is similar to the Model 80, with a heavy-weight barrel.

| NIB | Exc. | V.G. | Good | Fair | Poor |
|-----|------|------|------|------|------|
| 200 | 175 | 150 | 125 | 100 | 75 |

## Model 83

This version has a 4" heavy barrel and adjustable sights. Otherwise, it is similar to the Model 82.

| NIB | Exc. | V.G. | Good | Fair | Poor |
|-----|------|------|------|------|------|
| 200 | 175 | 150 | 125 | 100 | 75 |

## Model 85

This version was designed as a compact carry gun. It has a smaller frame and a 5-shot, swing-out cylinder. It is available with a 2" or 3" heavy barrel. It is either blued or satin-nickel plated, with checkered walnut grips.

| NIB | Exc. | V.G. | Good | Fair | Poor |
|-----|------|------|------|------|------|
| 220 | 190 | 175 | 150 | 125 | 100 |

## Model 85 Stainless

This is simply the Model 85 constructed of stainless steel.

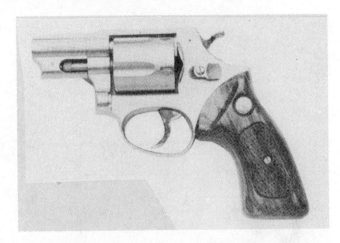

| NIB | Exc. | V.G. | Good | Fair | Poor |
|-----|------|------|------|------|------|
| 220 | 190 | 175 | 150 | 125 | 100 |

## Model 86 Target Master

This model has a 6" barrel with adjustable sights and is chambered for the .38 Special cartridge. It is blued, with checkered walnut grips.

| NIB | Exc. | V.G. | Good | Fair | Poor |
|-----|------|------|------|------|------|
| 275 | 225 | 200 | 175 | 125 | 100 |

## Model 94

This is a double-action, swing-out cylinder revolver chambered for .22 l.r. The cylinder holds nine shots, and it is offered with a 4" barrel with adjustable sights. The hammer and trigger are of target configuration. The finish is blued, with checkered walnut grips.

| NIB | Exc. | V.G. | Good | Fair | Poor |
|-----|------|------|------|------|------|
| 225 | 175 | 150 | 125 | 100 | 75 |

## Model 96 Target Scout

This version features a 6" barrel and the same target features as found on the Model 94. It is also chambered for .22 l.r.

| NIB | Exc. | V.G. | Good | Fair | Poor |
|-----|------|------|------|------|------|
| 275 | 250 | 200 | 175 | 150 | 100 |

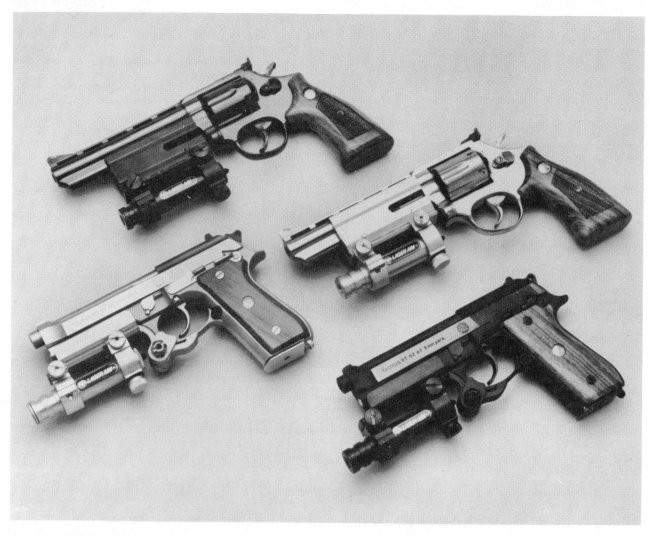

Laser sighted Taurus handguns.

Taurus - Model PT-92C Blue .9mm.

## TAYLOR, L. B.
### Chicopee, Massachusetts

**Pocket Pistol**
This is a single-shot, spur-trigger, derringer-type pistol chambered for the .32-caliber rimfire cartridge. It has a 3.5" octagonal barrel that pivots sideways for loading. It has a silver-plated brass frame with a blued barrel and walnut square-butt grips. The barrel is marked "L. B. Taylor & Co. Chicopee Mass." There were a few hundred manufactured in the late 1860's to early 1870's.

| Exc. | V.G. | Good | Fair | Poor |
|------|------|------|------|------|
| 300 | 250 | 200 | 150 | 100 |

## TERRIER ONE
### Importer--Southern Gun Distributors
### Miami, Florida

**Terrier One**
This is a double-action, solid-frame, swing-out cylinder revolver chambered for .32 Smith & Wesson. It has a 2.25" barrel with a 5-round cylinder. The finish is nickel-plated, with checkered walnut grips. It was manufactured between 1984 and 1987.

| Exc. | V.G. | Good | Fair | Poor |
|------|------|------|------|------|
| 75 | 65 | 50 | 30 | 25 |

## TERRY, J. C.
### Unknown

**Pocket Pistol**
This is a spur-trigger, single-shot, derringer-type pistol chambered for the .22-caliber rimfire cartridge. It has a 3.75" round barrel and a large rounded hammer that doubles as the breechblock. The frame is silver-plated brass with a blued barrel and either rosewood or walnut grips. The backstrap is marked "J. C. Terry/Patent Pending." There were several hundred manufactured during the late 1860's and early 1870's.

| Exc. | V.G. | Good | Fair | Poor |
|------|------|------|------|------|
| 450 | 400 | 350 | 250 | 200 |

## TEXAS GUNFIGHTERS
### Ponte Zanano, Italy
### Importer--Texas Gunfighters
### Irving, Texas

**Shootist Single Action**
This is a single-action, solid-frame revolver patterned after the Colt Single Action Army. It is chambered for .45 Long Colt and has a 4.75" barrel. The finish is nickel-plated, and it is built on the Colt Black Powder-style frame. It has one-piece walnut grips. This revolver is manufactured in Italy by the firm of Aldo Uberti. It was introduced in 1988.

| NIB | Exc. | V.G. | Good | Fair | Poor |
|-----|------|------|------|------|------|
| 650 | 550 | 500 | 400 | 350 | 250 |

**1 of 100 Edition**
This is a fully engraved version with genuine one-piece mother-of-pearl grips. It is furnished in a fitted case with an extra set of walnut grips. There were only 100 manufactured in 1988.

| NIB | Exc. | V.G. | Good | Fair | Poor |
|-----|------|------|------|------|------|
| 1400 | 1100 | 850 | 750 | 600 | 450 |

## TEXAS LONGHORN ARMS, INC.
### Richmond, Texas

**Jezebel**
This is a tip-up, single-shot pistol chambered for .22 l.r. or .22 rimfire Magnum. It has a 6" barrel and is constructed of stainless steel. It is available in a right- or left-hand version, with a walnut stock and forearm. It was introduced in 1987.

| NIB | Exc. | V.G. | Good | Fair | Poor |
|-----|------|------|------|------|------|
| 200 | 175 | 150 | 125 | 100 | 75 |

**Texas Border Special**
This company is manufacturing very high quality single-action pistols patterned after the Colt Single Action Army, with the loading gate on the left side of the frame to allow loading without shifting the gun in the hand. This version is chambered for .44 Special or .45 Colt. It has a 3.5" barrel with Pope-type rifling. The finish is blued, with a case-colored frame; and it has one-piece birdshead grips. One thousand of these pistols were handmade and offered with a lifetime warranty.

| NIB | Exc. | V.G. | Good | Fair | Poor |
|-----|------|------|------|------|------|
| 1500 | 1250 | 1000 | 800 | 600 | 500 |

**South Texas Army**
This model is similar to the Texas Border Special but is additionally available chambered for the .357 Magnum cartridge. It is offered with a 4.75" barrel and one-piece walnut conventional-type grips.

| NIB | Exc. | V.G. | Good | Fair | Poor |
|-----|------|------|------|------|------|
| 1500 | 1250 | 1000 | 800 | 600 | 500 |

**West Texas Target**
This version is available chambered for .32-20 and has a flat-top frame with a 7.5" barrel. Otherwise, it is similar to the South Texas Army model and is also offered in the same calibers.

| NIB | Exc. | V.G. | Good | Fair | Poor |
|-----|------|------|------|------|------|
| 1500 | 1250 | 1000 | 800 | 600 | 500 |

**Grover's Improved Number Five**
This model is chambered for .44 Magnum and has a 5.5" target-quality barrel. It features the design improvements that Elmer Keith espoused in 1926. There were 1,200 manufactured and serial-numbered K1-K1200. This model was introduced in 1988.

| NIB | Exc. | V.G. | Good | Fair | Poor |
|-----|------|------|------|------|------|
| 1000 | 850 | 750 | 650 | 500 | 400 |

**Mason Commemorative**
This model is chambered for .45 Colt and has a 4.75" barrel. It has the Mason's insignia engraved and inlaid in 18 kt. gold. The finish is blued, with presentation-grade walnut grips. This model was introduced in 1987. As with all commemoratives, premiums are only paid for models that are NIB with all supplied materials.

| NIB | Exc. | V.G. | Good | Fair | Poor |
|-----|------|------|------|------|------|
| 1500 | 1250 | 1000 | 800 | 600 | 500 |

**Texas Sesquicentennial Commemorative**
This is a deluxe version also chambered for .45 Colt, with a 4.75" barrel. It is heavily engraved in the older Nimschke style, features one-piece, genuine ivory grips, and is furnished in a fitted walnut presentation case. There were 150 of these Commemoratives manufactured in 1987. As with all commemoratives, this is desirable only when NIB with all supplied materials.

| NIB | Exc. | V.G. | Good | Fair | Poor |
|-----|------|------|------|------|------|
| 2500 | 2000 | 1750 | 1500 | 1000 | 750 |

## THAMES ARMS CO.
### Norwich, Connecticut

This was one of many small revolver manufacturers that operated in Norwich, Connecticut, during the latter part of the nineteenth century. Norwich is often known as the Eibar of the United States. The products of the Thames Company were of the usual double-action, break-open type with ribbed, round barrels chambered for the .32, .38, or .22 caliber cartridges. They are marked "Automatic Revolvers," referring to the fact that they feature the self-ejecting mechanism that functions as they are broken open. These revolvers were of mediocre quality and are not highly sought after by collectors in today's market. The values for all of their models are quite similar.

| Exc. | V.G. | Good | Fair | Poor |
|------|------|------|------|------|
| 150  | 125  | 100  | 75   | 50   |

## THIEME & EDELER
### Eibar, Spain

**Pocket Pistol**

This is a blowback-operated, semi-automatic, "Eibar"- type pistol chambered for the 7.65mm cartridge. It has a 3" barrel and a detachable box magazine. The finish is blued, with the letters "TE" stamped on the frame and also on the molded plastic grip. This company disappeared during the Spanish Civil War.

| Exc. | V.G. | Good | Fair | Poor |
|------|------|------|------|------|
| 175  | 150  | 100  | 75   | 50   |

## THOMPSON
### SEE--Auto Ordnance

## THOMPSON/CENTER ARMS
### Rochester, New Hampshire

**Contender**

This is a single-shot, break-open pistol that is interchangeably chambered for many popular calibers from .17 to the .35 Remington rifle cartridge. Included in this list are many specialized wildcat cartridges. This pistol is available with 10", 14", or 16" barrels and was formerly available with an 8.75" barrel. The break-open action is activated by a combination triggerguard action lever. The finish is either blued or Armour Alloy, which is a satin-chrome appearing finish. The latest grips are walnut with black rubber inserts. They formerly were all walnut. This pistol is designed primarily for long-range target shooting or hunting. There are a number of options available. It was introduced in 1967.

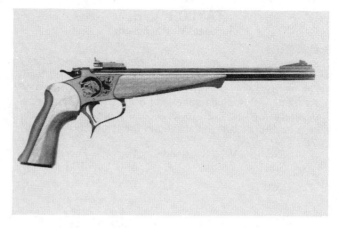

| NIB | Exc. | V.G. | Good | Fair | Poor |
|-----|------|------|------|------|------|
| 325 | 300  | 250  | 225  | 150  | 100  |

**Contender Carbine**

This model has an action that is similar to the Contender pistol and is interchangeably chambered for nine different calibers, including the .410 3" shot shell. It is offered with 21" interchangeable barrels with open sights. The finish is blued, and it has a full, walnut pistol-grip stock and forearm. It was introduced in 1986.

| NIB | Exc. | V.G. | Good | Fair | Poor |
|-----|------|------|------|------|------|
| 375 | 350  | 300  | 250  | 200  | 150  |

**Hunter**

This is a single-shot rifle with a break-open action that is activated by a top lever. It is interchangeably chambered for various popular calibers from the .22 Hornet to .308 Winchester. It has a 23" barrel in medium or light sporter weight. The finish is blued, with a checkered walnut stock. This model was introduced in 1983.

| NIB | Exc. | V.G. | Good | Fair | Poor |
|-----|------|------|------|------|------|
| 425 | 375 | 325 | 275 | 225 | 175 |

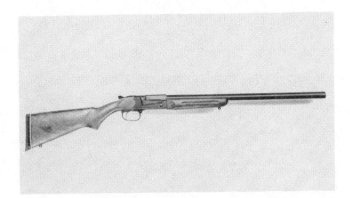

**Aristocrat**

This is similar to the Hunter model rifle except that the stock has a cheekpiece and there are double-set triggers. This model was discontinued in 1986.

| Exc. | V.G. | Good | Fair | Poor |
|------|------|------|------|------|
| 400 | 350 | 300 | 250 | 200 |

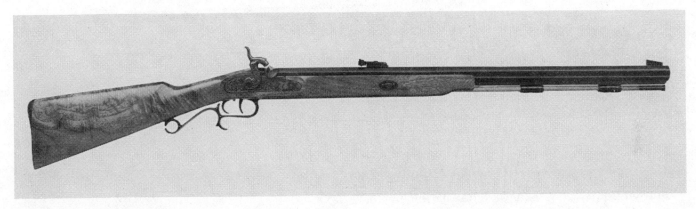

Thompson-Center Renegade Cap Lock Rifle.

Thompson-Center Renegade Cap Lock (lefthand).

Thompson-Center Renegade Hunter Model.

Thompson-Center Contender Carbine with Rynite stock.

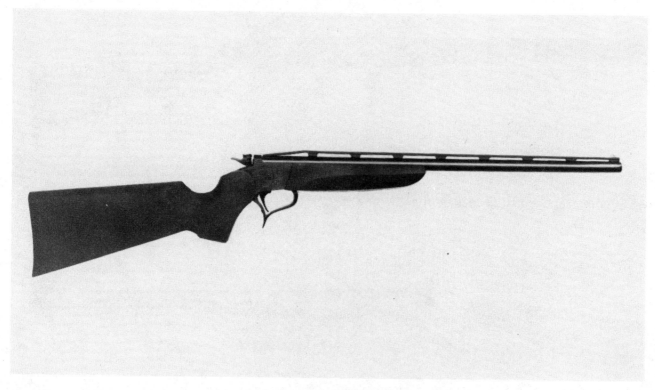

Thompson-Center Contender Carbine /410 GA smoothbore with Rynite stock.

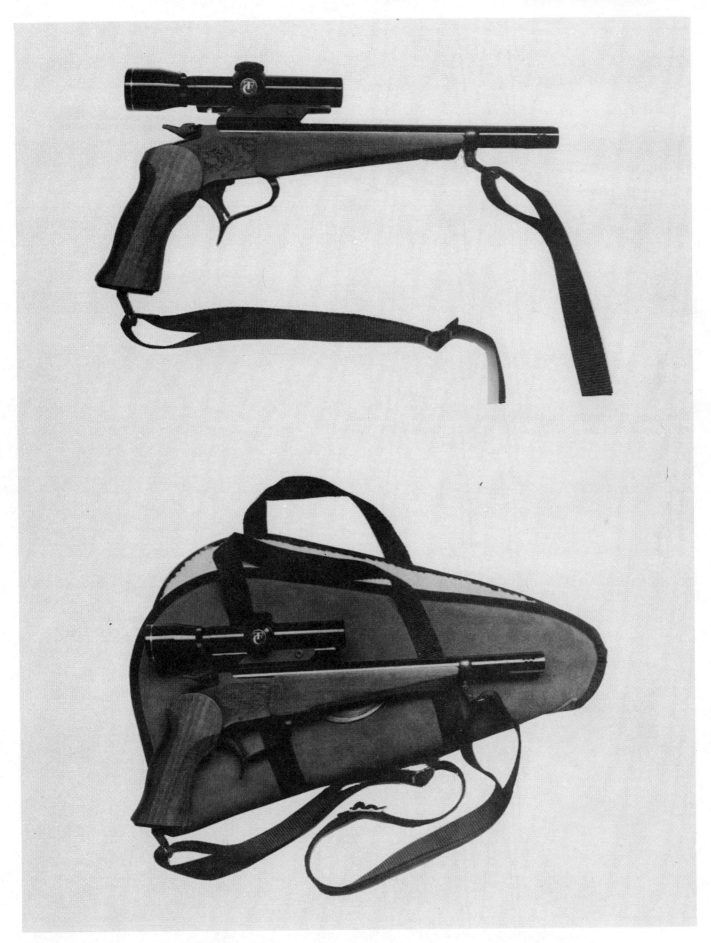

Thompson-Center Contender Hunter Package.

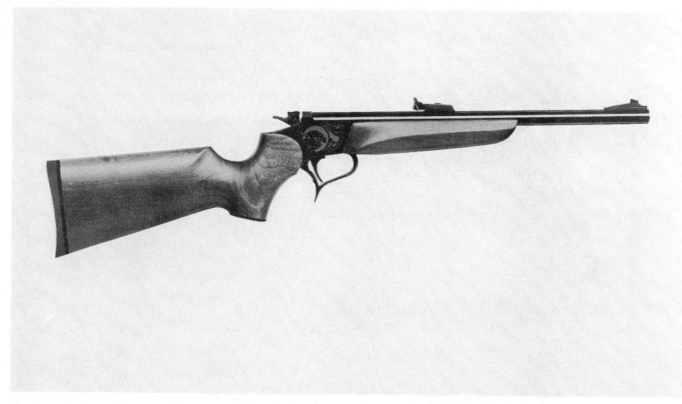

Thompson-Center Youth Model Carbine

Thompson-Center White Mountain Carbine .50 Cal. Cap Lock.

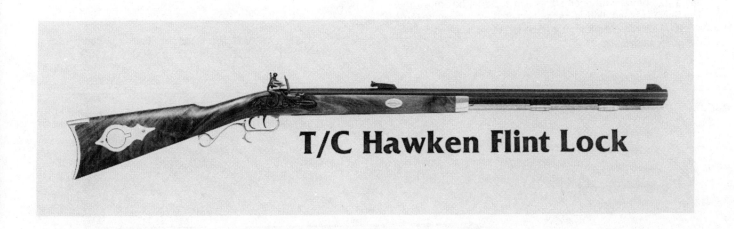

T/C Hawken Flint Lock

T/C Renegade Flint Lock

## TIKKA
**Tikkakoski, Finland**
**Importer--Stoeger Industries**
**South Hackensack, New Jersey**

### Bolt-Action Rifle

This rifle is built on a Mauser-type bolt action and is chambered for various calibers from .223 to .338 Winchester Magnum. It has a 22" barrel with open sights and a 3-shot box magazine. The finish is blued, with a hand-checkered walnut Monte Carlo stock. This rifle was formerly imported by Ithaca and sold as their LSA model.

TIKKA NEW GENERATION STANDARD GRADE

| Exc. | V.G. | Good | Fair | Poor |
|------|------|------|------|------|
| 650 | 575 | 500 | 400 | 300 |

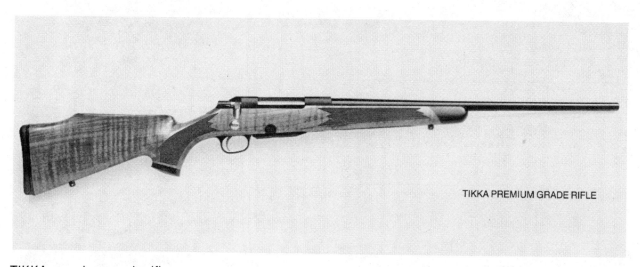

TIKKA PREMIUM GRADE RIFLE

TIKKA premium grade rifle

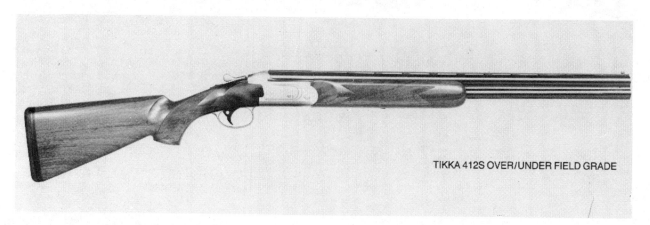

TIKKA 412S OVER/UNDER FIELD GRADE

TIKKA 412S over/under field grade

## TIPPING & LAWDEN
### Birmingham, England

**Thomas Revolver**
This is a solid-framed, 5-shot, double-action revolver chambered for the .32, .380, and .450 cartridges. It was designed and patented by J. Thomas of Birmingham. It has a 4.5" barrel and a very unusual method of cartridge extraction. There is a knob mounted under the barrel that is grasped and used to rotate the barrel in a counter-clockwise fashion. This rotation pulls the barrel and cylinder forward as a stationary extractor pulls the fired cases clear of the cylinder and allows them to fall free. The barrel and cylinder are then returned to battery in the same manner, and a loading gate is utilized to load the cylinder. The finish is blued, and the grips are checkered walnut. This model was manufactured between 1870 and 1877, when the Lawden brothers sold the business to Webley.

| Exc. | V.G. | Good | Fair | Poor |
|------|------|------|------|------|
| 550 | 450 | 400 | 300 | 175 |

## TIPPMAN ARMS
### Fort Wayne, Indiana

This company produced high quality working models of historically significant machine guns. They were manufactured to one-half scale and furnished with accessories and a case on an optional basis. They are as follows:

**Model 1917**
This is a one-half scale, faithful copy of the Browning M1917 belt-fed, water-cooled Machine Gun. It is chambered for .22 l.r. only. It functions in the semi-automatic mode and is fired from the closed-bolt position. The barrel is 10" in length. A tripod is included. It was manufactured in 1986 and 1987.

| Exc. | V.G. | Good | Fair | Poor |
|------|------|------|------|------|
| 1700 | 1500 | 1250 | 950 | 750 |

**Model 1919 A-4**
This was a one-half scale, faithful copy of the Browning 1919 A-4 Machine Gun. It is chambered for .22 l.r. and functions in the semi-automatic mode. The barrel was 11" in length. It is belt-fed and is fired from the closed-bolt position. It is furnished with a tripod and was manufactured in 1986 and 1987 only.

| Exc. | V.G. | Good | Fair | Poor |
|------|------|------|------|------|
| 1200 | 1000 | 750 | 600 | 500 |

**Model .50 HB**
This was a one-half scale copy of the famous "Ma Deuce" Browning .50-caliber Machine Gun. It is chambered for .22 rimfire Magnum and has an 18.25" barrel. It is belt-fed and is fired from the closed-bolt position. It is furnished with a tripod and was manufactured in 1986 and 1987 only.

| Exc. | V.G. | Good | Fair | Poor |
|------|------|------|------|------|
| 1800 | 1600 | 1350 | 1000 | 800 |

## TODD, GEORGE H.
### Montgomery, Alabama

**Rifled Musket**
This is a very rare Confederate firearm that is chambered for .58-caliber percussion. It is a single-shot muzzleloader that was patterned after the U.S. Model 1861 Musket. It has a 40" round barrel and a full-length stock that is held on by three barrel bands. It features brass mountings and a brass trigger, hammer, and lockplate. It has an iron ramrod with a bayonet lug. The lock is marked "George H. Todd/Montgomery, Ala." It is also dated. There were very few manufactured for use by the forces of the Confederate States of America. One should be very wary of fakes, as many have been noted. It would be quite advisable to secure qualified, individual appraisals on this, as well as on all other Confederate Civil War weapons.

| Exc. | V.G. | Good | Fair | Poor |
|------|------|------|------|------|
| 6000 | 5000 | 4000 | 2500 | 1750 |

## TOKAREV
### Soviet State Arsenals

**M 38 Rifle**
This is a gas-operated semi-automatic rifle chambered for the 7.62mm cartridge. It has a 24" barrel and a 10-round detachable box magazine. It has a two-piece wooden stock held on by two barrel bands. The upper handguard has rectangular cooling slots. There was a cleaning rod inserted along the right side of the stock. This model's construction proved to be fragile, and it was replaced in 1940. The finish is blued, with a hardwood stock.

| Exc. | V.G. | Good | Fair | Poor |
|------|------|------|------|------|
| 400 | 350 | 300 | 200 | 150 |

**M 40 Rifle**
This is an improved version of the M 38 that proved to be more robust. It is chambered for the 7.62mm cartridge and has the same external dimensions as its predecessor. There is only one barrel band, and the handguard is made of slotted sheet metal. This model features a muzzle break and was more successful in field operations. The finish is blued, with a hardwood stock.

| Exc. | V.G. | Good | Fair | Poor |
|------|------|------|------|------|
| 400 | 350 | 300 | 200 | 150 |

**TT30 & TT33**
This is a single-action semi-automatic pistol chambered for the 7.62mm cartridge. It owes much of its functional design to the Colt 1911 but features a unitized hammer-and-trigger assembly. It has a 4.5" barrel and an 8-round detachable box magazine. The finish is blued, with black plastic grips. This pistol was manufactured in several Eastern Bloc countries: Poland, Yugoslavia, Hungary, China, and North Korea. These pistols are virtually identical but bear different designations. The Chinese version is presently being imported in large numbers into the United States and is worth a good deal less than the highly collectible Soviet military model.
TT30--Add 25 Percent.

| Exc. | V.G. | Good | Fair | Poor |
|------|------|------|------|------|
| 450 | 400 | 300 | 250 | 175 |

## TOMISKA, ALOIS
### Pilsen, Czechoslovakia

Tomiska was born in Czechoslovakia in 1861. In 1890 he moved to Vienna, Austria, and became a gunsmith. In the early 1900's he worked on automatic pistol designs and secured several patents. He became involved with the firm of Ceska Zbrojovka, and worked there as a firearms designer until his death in 1946.

### Little Tom

This is a blowback-operated semi-automatic pistol chambered for the 6.35mm and 7.65mm cartridges. It has a fixed 2.5" barrel with a coaxial recoil spring. It features double-action lockwork and an external hammer. The slide is marked "Alois Tomiska Plzen Patent Little Tom." The finish is blued, with checkered wood grips with an inlaid medallion featuring the letters "AT." This pistol was manufactured between 1908 and 1918. After WWI, Tomiska sold the manufacturing rights to Wiener of Vienna, and manufacture of this pistol continued until 1925.

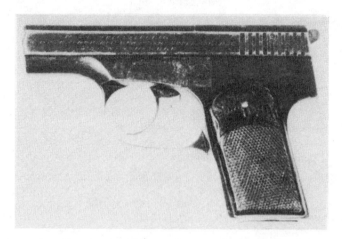

| Exc. | V.G. | Good | Fair | Poor |
|------|------|------|------|------|
| 475  | 425  | 350  | 250  | 175  |

## TRADEWINDS
### Tacoma, Washington

### Model H-170

This is a recoil-operated semi-automatic shotgun chambered for 12 gauge. It features a 26" or 28" vent-rib barrel with various chokes. It has a 5-round tubular magazine and an anodized alloy receiver. The finish is blued, with a checkered walnut stock.

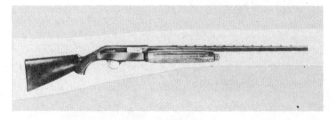

| Exc. | V.G. | Good | Fair | Poor |
|------|------|------|------|------|
| 300  | 250  | 225  | 150  | 100  |

### Model 260-A

This is a blowback-operated semi-automatic rifle chambered for the .22 l.r. cartridge. It has a 22.5" barrel with open sights and a 5-shot detachable magazine. The finish is blued, with a checkered walnut stock.

| Exc. | V.G. | Good | Fair | Poor |
|------|------|------|------|------|
| 200  | 175  | 125  | 100  | 75   |

### Model 311-A

This is a bolt-action repeating rifle chambered for the .22 l.r. cartridge. It has a 22.5" barrel with open sights and a 5-round detachable magazine. The finish is blued, with a checkered walnut stock.

| Exc. | V.G. | Good | Fair | Poor |
|------|------|------|------|------|
| 175  | 150  | 100  | 75   | 50   |

### Model 5000 "Husky"

This is a bolt-action rifle built on a Mauser-type action. It is chambered for five popular calibers from .22-250 to .30-06. It has a 24" barrel with adjustable sights and a 4-round detachable box magazine. The finish is blued, with a hand-checkered walnut stock.

| Exc. | V.G. | Good | Fair | Poor |
|------|------|------|------|------|
| 350  | 300  | 275  | 200  | 100  |

## TRANTER, WILLIAM
### Birmingham, England

### Model 1872

This is a large-framed, gate-loaded, double-action revolver. It is chambered for the .36 cartridge and has a 6" octagonal barrel and a 6-shot fluted cylinder. The finish is blued, with checkered walnut grips.

| Exc. | V.G. | Good | Fair | Poor |
|------|------|------|------|------|
| 750  | 650  | 500  | 300  | 200  |

### Model 1878

This was perhaps Tranter's best-known pistol. It was adopted by the British Army. It is chambered for the .45-caliber cartridge and has a 6" octagonal barrel and an integral ejector rod in a housing on the right side of the frame and barrel. This is a rather large pistol with a solid frame and double-action lockwork. It is gate-loaded, with a blued finish and checkered walnut grips with a lanyard ring at the butt. This pistol was manufactured between 1878 and 1887, when it was replaced by the Webley Mark I.

| Exc. | V.G. | Good | Fair | Poor |
|------|------|------|------|------|
| 650  | 550  | 450  | 275  | 175  |

It is important to note that William Tranter held a number of patents on the various revolver designs, and many of his designs were manufactured by other companies during this era. The words "Tranter's Patent" are found on the frames. He also manufactured revolvers for various marketing companies and allowed other companies to manufacture his designs under license. There were also a number of imitation-Tranter revolvers produced in Belgium. It would behoove one seriously interested in collecting the arms of this maker to educate oneself before purchases are contemplated.

## TRIPPLET & SCOTT
## MERIDAN MANUFACTURING COMPANY
### Meridan, Connecticut

**Repeating Carbine**

This is a 7-shot repeating carbine chambered for the .50 rimfire cartridge. It is offered with either a 22" or 30" round barrel. It has iron mountings and a walnut stock and forend held on by one barrel band. There is a sling swivel on the bottom and the top of the butt. It is loaded by a tubular magazine that is inserted in the buttstock, and the action functions by twisting the barrel in a circular motion until it is in line with the magazine that protrudes through the butt. There is a catch located behind the external hammer. The finish is blued, with a case-colored receiver. There were approximately 5,000 manufactured in 1864 and 1865.

| Exc. | V.G. | Good | Fair | Poor |
|------|------|------|------|------|
| 950 | 850 | 700 | 550 | 400 |

## TROCAOLA
### Eibar, Spain

This was another of the Eibar gunmakers who operated from the early 1900's and disappeared during the Spanish Civil War. They produced mediocre-quality copies of Smith & Wesson and Colt designs. The pistols they manufactured before 1914 were fairly well made and utilized good materials. They actually shared a British contract to supply revolvers in 1915. They produced revolvers chambered for the .32, .38, and .44 caliber cartridges. They are hinged, break-open designs with ribbed, round barrels and automatic ejection systems. They also produced swing-out cylinder, solid-frame, double-action revolvers such as their copy of the Smith & Wesson Triple Lock. Their products are identified by a circle with the letters "TAC" on the left side of the frame. This monogram resembles that of Smith & Wesson. The same monogram usually appears on the grips. The finishes are either blued or nickel. The pistols of this company are not eagerly sought after by collectors, and their values are quite similar.

| Exc. | V.G. | Good | Fair | Poor |
|------|------|------|------|------|
| 150 | 125 | 100 | 75 | 50 |

## TRYON, EDWARD K. & COMPANY
### Philadelphia, Pennsylvania

**Pocket Pistol**

This is a single-shot pocket pistol patterned very closely to the Henry Deringer-type pistol. It is chambered for .41-caliber percussion with a 2" or 4" barrel. It is marked "Tryon Philada." There were many produced between 1960 and 1975.

| Exc. | V.G. | Good | Fair | Poor |
|------|------|------|------|------|
| 650 | 600 | 500 | 375 | 275 |

## TUCKER SHERARD & COMPANY
### Lancaster, Texas

**Dragoon**

This is a .44-caliber percussion revolver patterned after the Colt Dragoon Revolver. It has a 7.75" round barrel with an integral loading lever mounted beneath it. The finish is blued, and the barrel is marked "Clark, Sherard & Co., Lancaster, Texas." The cylinder holds six shots, is unfluted, and has two acid-etched panels--one consisted of crossed cannons; the other, a large, five- pointed star and the words "Texas Arms." There were approximately 400 manufactured between 1862 and 1867. These revolvers were supposed to be used by the Texas Militia in the Civil War, but they were not delivered until after the hostilities had ceased and consequently were not used by Confederate troops. They are extremely rare and valuable; and a qualified, individual appraisal should definitely be secured if a transaction is contemplated.

| Exc. | V.G. | Good | Fair | Poor |
|------|------|------|------|------|
| 12500 | 10000 | 7500 | 5000 | 3000 |

## TUFTS & COLLEY
### New York, New York

**Pocket Pistol**

This is a very high quality, single-shot pocket pistol chambered in .44-caliber percussion. It has a 3.5" barrel and was patterned after the Henry Deringer-type Pistol. The hammer and lock are finely engraved, as are the German silver mountings. The stock is walnut, and the lock is marked "Tufts & Colley." The barrel is marked "Deringer/ Pattn." This pistol was manufactured in the 1850's.

| Exc. | V.G. | Good | Fair | Poor |
|------|------|------|------|------|
| 750 | 650 | 500 | 400 | 300 |

## TURBIAUX, JACQUES
### Paris, France
### SEE--Ames

## TURNER, THOMAS
### Redding, England

**Pepperbox**

This is a high quality, double-action, bar-hammer, pepperbox-type revolving pistol chambered for .476 caliber percussion. It has a fluted, smooth-bore, 6-barrel cluster. The iron frame is scroll-engraved, as is the hammer. The finish is blued, with a rounded checkered walnut grip. This weapon has a sliding safety catch behind the hammer. This pistol is quite large in size and was possibly used by the navy as a boarding pistol. It is marked "Thomas Turner, Redding" in an oval on the lefthand side.

| Exc. | V.G. | Good | Fair | Poor |
|------|------|------|------|------|
| 950 | 850 | 700 | 500 | 400 |

## TYLER ORDNANCE WORKS
### Tyler, Texas

**Tyler Texas Rifle**

This is an extremely rare Confederate firearm that is chambered for either .54 or .57 caliber percussion. The barrel lengths noted are from 28" to 38". Some have bayonet lugs; others did not. The walnut stocks are full-length and are held on by two barrel bands. They are marked either "Texas Rifle," "Hill Rifle," "Enfield Rifle," "Tyler Rifle," or "Austrian Rifle." They are extremely rare, and one should be very wary of fraudulent specimens. Qualified appraisal should be definitely secured if a transaction is contemplated.

| Exc. | V.G. | Good | Fair | Poor |
|------|------|------|------|------|
| 9500 | 8500 | 7000 | 5000 | 3000 |

# USAS 12
## DAEWOO PRECISION IND., LTD.
### South Korea
**Importer--Gilbert Equipment Company**
**Mobile, Alabama**

### USAS 12
This is a gas-operated, semi-automatic, assault-type shotgun chambered for 12 gauge. It has an 18.25" cylinder-bore barrel and is fed by either a 10-round detachable box magazine or a 20-round drum. The finish is parkerized, with a black synthetic stock and forearm. Due to the fact that this is an assault-type weapon and manufactured out of this country, at this time it is impossible to accurately evaluate it. If a transaction is contemplated, we would strongly advise securing qualified, local, individual appraisal.

### USAS 12
This is a gas-operated, semi-automatic, assault-type shotgun chambered for 12 gauge. It has an 18.25" cylinder-bore barrel and is fed by either a 10-round detachable box magazine or a 20-round drum. The finish is parkerized, with a black synthetic stock and forearm. Due to the fact that this is an assault-type weapon and manufactured out of this country, at this time it is impossible to accurately evaluate it. If a transaction is contemplated, we would strongly advise securing qualified, local, individual appraisal.

# U.S. ARMS CO.
### Riverhead, New York

### Abilene .357 Magnum
This is a single-action revolver patterned after the Colt Single-Action Army Revolver. It is chambered for the .357 Magnum cartridge and is offered with 4-5/8", 5-1/2", and 6-1/2" barrel. It features adjustable sights and a transfer-bar safety system. It has a 6-shot fluted cylinder; and the finish is blued, with smooth walnut grips. It was manufactured between 1976 and 1983. Stainless Steel Version--Add 30 Percent.

| Exc. | V.G. | Good | Fair | Poor |
|------|------|------|------|------|
| 250  | 225  | 200  | 150  | 100  |

### Abilene .44 Magnum
This model is similar to the .357 but is offered with a 7.5" and 8.5" barrel chambered for the .44 Magnum cartridge. It has a 6-shot unfluted cylinder.
Stainless Steel Version--Add 30 Percent.

| Exc. | V.G. | Good | Fair | Poor |
|------|------|------|------|------|
| 325  | 300  | 250  | 200  | 150  |

# UBERTI, ALDO
### Ponte Zanano, Italy
**Importer--Uberti USA, Inc.**
**New Milford, Connecticut**

This company manufactures high-grade reproductions of famous Western-style American firearms. Their products have been imported over the years by a number of different companies, and they currently have set up their own importation facility. They produce both black powder guns and the cartridge firearms that are included in this section.

### Henry Rifle
This is a brass-framed reproduction of the famous Winchester/Henry Rifle. It is chambered for the .44-40 cartridge, and this is basically the only departure from being a true and faithful copy. The octagonal barrel is 24.5" on the rifle model and 22.5" on the carbine model. This is a high quality rifle and amazingly close to the original in configuration. There are three grades of engraving also available.
Grade A--Add $235.
Grade B--Add $415.
Grade C--Add $625.

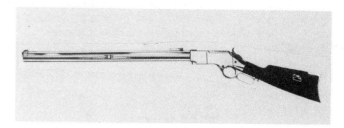

| NIB | Exc. | V.G. | Good | Fair | Poor |
|-----|------|------|------|------|------|
| 750 | 650  | 550  | 450  | 350  | 275  |

### 1866 Carbine
This is a faithful replica of the Winchester 1866. It is chambered for .22 l.r., .22 Magnum, .38 Special, and .44-40. It has a brass frame and a 19" round barrel. The finish is blued, with a walnut stock.

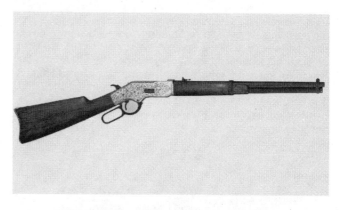

| NIB | Exc. | V.G. | Good | Fair | Poor |
|-----|------|------|------|------|------|
| 600 | 550  | 450  | 400  | 300  | 250  |

### 1866 Trapper Carbine
This model is similar to the standard carbine but is offered with a 16" or 18.5" barrel.

| NIB | Exc. | V.G. | Good | Fair | Poor |
|-----|------|------|------|------|------|
| 700 | 600  | 500  | 450  | 350  | 300  |

### 1866 Rifle
This model is similar to the Carbine, with a 24.25" octagonal barrel.

| NIB | Exc. | V.G. | Good | Fair | Poor |
|-----|------|------|------|------|------|
| 625 | 575  | 475  | 425  | 325  | 275  |

### 1873 Carbine
This is a reproduction of the Winchester 1873 chambered for .22 l.r., .22 Magnum, .357, and .44-40. It has a case-colored steel receiver and a 19" round barrel. It is also offered nickel-plated.

| NIB | Exc. | V.G. | Good | Fair | Poor |
|-----|------|------|------|------|------|
| 700 | 600  | 500  | 450  | 350  | 300  |

### 1873 Rifle
This model is similar to the Carbine, with a 24.25" octagonal barrel.

| NIB | Exc. | V.G. | Good | Fair | Poor |
|-----|------|------|------|------|------|
| 750 | 650 | 550 | 450 | 350 | 300 |

## Cattleman

This is a single-action revolver patterned very closely after the Colt Single-Action Army. It is chambered in various popular calibers from .22 l.r. to .45 Colt. It is offered with barrel lengths of 4.75", 5.5", and 7.5". It is offered with either a modern or black powder-type frame and brass or steel backstraps. The finish is blued, with walnut grips. A Sheriff's Model with a 3" barrel and no ejector rod chambered for .44-40 and .45 Colt is also available and is valued the same.

| NIB | Exc. | V.G. | Good | Fair | Poor |
|-----|------|------|------|------|------|
| 325 | 275 | 250 | 200 | 150 | 100 |

## Cattleman Target Model

This model is similar to the standard Cattleman, with an adjustable rear sight.

| NIB | Exc. | V.G. | Good | Fair | Poor |
|-----|------|------|------|------|------|
| 350 | 300 | 275 | 225 | 175 | 125 |

## Cattleman Buntline

This version is chambered for .357 Magnum or .45 Colt. It has an 18" round barrel, and it is cut for attaching a shoulder stock. Detachable Shoulder Stock--Add 25 Percent.

| NIB | Exc. | V.G. | Good | Fair | Poor |
|-----|------|------|------|------|------|
| 375 | 325 | 300 | 250 | 200 | 150 |

## Buntline Carbine

This version has the 18" barrel but is fitted with a permanently mounted shoulder stock with a brass buttplate and sling swivel.

| NIB | Exc. | V.G. | Good | Fair | Poor |
|-----|------|------|------|------|------|
| 450 | 400 | 350 | 300 | 250 | 200 |

## Buckhorn

This model is similar to the Cattleman and is available in similar barrel lengths, but it is chambered for the .44-40, .44 Special, and the .44 Magnum cartridge. It features a brass backstrap. The finish is blued, with smooth walnut grips.

| NIB | Exc. | V.G. | Good | Fair | Poor |
|-----|------|------|------|------|------|
| 350 | 300 | 275 | 225 | 175 | 125 |

## Buckhorn Carbine

This model is similar to the Cattleman Carbine except that it is chambered for the .44-40 or .44 Magnum cartridge.

| NIB | Exc. | V.G. | Good | Fair | Poor |
|-----|------|------|------|------|------|
| 450 | 400 | 350 | 300 | 250 | 200 |

## 1873 Stallion

This is a scaled-down version chambered for .22 l.r./.22 Magnum. It is blued with a case-colored frame and features one-piece walnut grips.

| NIB | Exc. | V.G. | Good | Fair | Poor |
|-----|------|------|------|------|------|
| 325 | 275 | 250 | 200 | 150 | 100 |

## 1875 Remington "Outlaw"

This is a replica of the original Remington cartridge pistol chambered for .357 Magnum, .44-40, and .45 Colt. It is offered with a 7.5" barrel and is either blued or nickel-plated, with walnut grips.

| NIB | Exc. | V.G. | Good | Fair | Poor |
|-----|------|------|------|------|------|
| 350 | 300 | 275 | 225 | 175 | 125 |

## 1890 Remington

This is a 5.5"-barrelled replica of the original Remington Pistol. It is chambered for .357 Magnum, .44-40, and .45 Colt. It was imported in 1986 and 1987 only. It was available in either blue or nickel-plate.

| Exc. | V.G. | Good | Fair | Poor |
|------|------|------|------|------|
| 350 | 300 | 275 | 225 | 175 |

## Model 1871 Rolling Block Pistol

This is a single-shot target pistol chambered for .22 l.r., .22 Magnum, .22 Hornet, or .357 Magnum. It has a 9.5" octagonal barrel and is blued, with a case-colored receiver and walnut grip and forearm.

| NIB | Exc. | V.G. | Good | Fair | Poor |
|-----|------|------|------|------|------|
| 300 | 250 | 225 | 200 | 150 | 100 |

## Model 1871 Rolling Block Carbine

This model is similar to the Pistol, with a 22.5" octagonal barrel and a full-length walnut stock.

| NIB | Exc. | V.G. | Good | Fair | Poor |
|-----|------|------|------|------|------|
| 350 | 300 | 275 | 225 | 175 | 125 |

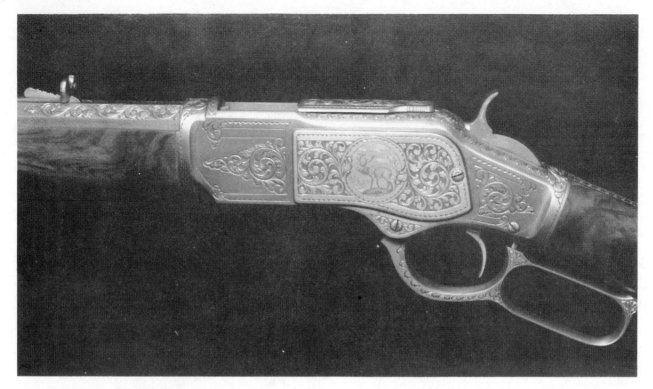

Uberti engraved 73 Winchester replica.

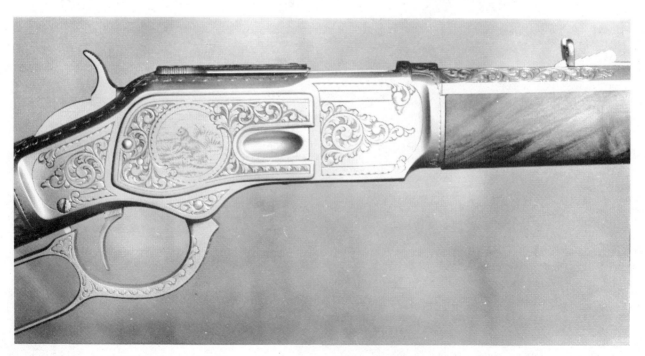

Uberti engraved 73 Winchester replica.

Uberti engraved 73 Winchester replica.

Uberti 1858 Remington replicas.

Uberti S.A.A. Colt replicas.

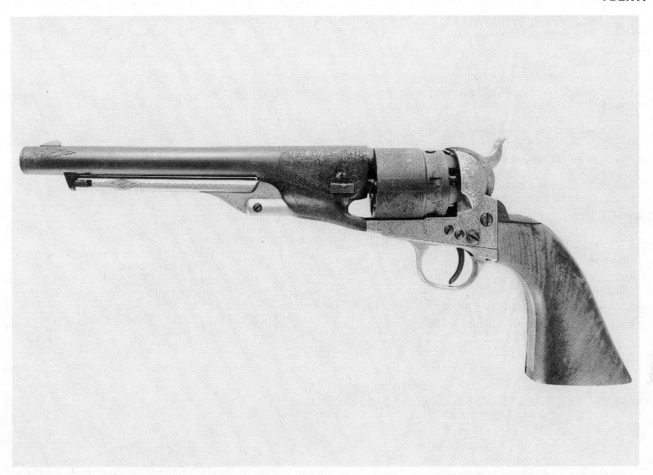

Uberti engraved 1860 Army Colt replica.

## UHLINGER, WILLIAM P.
### Philadelphia, Pennsylvania

**Pocket Revolver**

This was one of the many companies that produced revolvers that were definite infringements on the Rollin White patent that was owned by Smith & Wesson. In an attempt to hide their manufacture, they were produced under the following trade-names: D. D. Cone/Washington, D.C., W. L. Grant, J. P. Lower, and W. P. Uhlinger/Phila. Pa. There are three basic models of this revolver. They are all single-action spur triggers. The first two have octagonal barrels that are 2.75" or 3" in length. They have a blued finish and an iron frame, rosewood or walnut grips, and a square butt. The total production was approximately 10,000 pistols manufactured between 1861 and 1865.

**Long Cylinder (1-3/16")**

| Exc. | V.G. | Good | Fair | Poor |
|---|---|---|---|---|
| 350 | 300 | 275 | 200 | 150 |

**Short Cylinder (1")**

| Exc. | V.G. | Good | Fair | Poor |
|---|---|---|---|---|
| 250 | 225 | 200 | 150 | 100 |

**.32 Rimfire Model (5", 6", or 7" Barrel)**

| Exc. | V.G. | Good | Fair | Poor |
|---|---|---|---|---|
| 300 | 250 | 225 | 175 | 125 |

## ULTIMATE
### SEE--Camex-Blaser

## ULTRA LIGHT ARMS, INC.
### Granville, West Virginia

This company produces made-to-order, high-grade bolt-action rifles. They are built on different actions and use Douglas barrels in 22" or 24" lengths. They use custom triggers and feature reinforced graphite stocks with recoil pads included. These rifles are offered standard with matte finishes and many optional features. We supply the values for the standard models and suggest securing competent, individual appraisals if a transaction is contemplated.

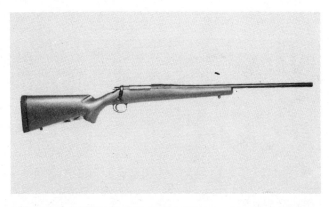

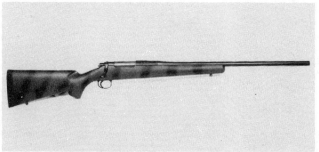

**Model 20 (Short Action)**

| NIB | Exc. | V.G. | Good | Fair | Poor |
|---|---|---|---|---|---|
| 2000 | 1750 | 1500 | 1250 | 900 | 700 |

**Model 24 (Long Action)**

| NIB | Exc. | V.G. | Good | Fair | Poor |
|---|---|---|---|---|---|
| 2100 | 1850 | 1600 | 1350 | 900 | 700 |

**Model 28 Magnum**

| NIB | Exc. | V.G. | Good | Fair | Poor |
|---|---|---|---|---|---|
| 2500 | 2250 | 1750 | 1500 | 1000 | 750 |

**Model 20 Hunter's Pistol**

This is a bolt-action repeating pistol designed with the serious hunter in mind. It is offered in various popular calibers with a 14", high quality, Douglas heavy barrel. It has a 5-shot magazine and is matte-blued, with a reinforced graphite Kevlar stock. It was introduced in 1987.

| NIB | Exc. | V.G. | Good | Fair | Poor |
|---|---|---|---|---|---|
| 1250 | 1000 | 850 | 750 | 600 | 500 |

## UNCETA
### Guernica, Spain

This company was established in Eibar, Spain, in 1908. They have produced consistently high quality products and were one of only three Spanish companies that were permitted to remain in operation after the Spanish Civil War. They are still in business to this day. They manufacture their products under the trademark "Astra" and, with the exception of some of their early "Eibar"-type pistols manufactured in the 1920's, have always been known for excellent quality products.

**Victoria**

This was the first pistol the company manufactured. It is a blowback-operated semi-automatic pistol chambered for the 6.35mm cartridge. It has a 2.5" barrel and a detachable box magazine. The finish is blued, with plastic grips. This model was manufactured in Eibar before 1913.

| Exc. | V.G. | Good | Fair | Poor |
|---|---|---|---|---|
| 300 | 250 | 200 | 150 | 100 |

### Campo Giro
This is found under its own section in this text.

### Astra 1911
This is simply the Victoria model redesignated in November of 1914. It is chambered for the 7.65mm cartridge.

| Exc. | V.G. | Good | Fair | Poor |
|------|------|------|------|------|
| 250  | 200  | 175  | 100  | 75   |

### Astra 1924
This is a blowback-operated, semi-automatic, "Eibar"-type pistol chambered for 6.35mm. It was patterned after the 1906 Browning without the grip safety. It has a 2.5" barrel and is blued, with plastic grips. The slide is marked "Esperanza y Unceta Guernica Spain Astra Cal 6.35 .25." The grips have the early sunburst Astra badge.

| Exc. | V.G. | Good | Fair | Poor |
|------|------|------|------|------|
| 225  | 175  | 125  | 100  | 75   |

### Astra 100
This is another tradename for the 7.65mm Victoria pistol.

| Exc. | V.G. | Good | Fair | Poor |
|------|------|------|------|------|
| 275  | 225  | 200  | 150  | 100  |

### Astra 200
This is a blowback-operated semi-automatic pistol chambered for the 6.35mm cartridge. It was patterned after the 1906 Browning with both a grip and magazine safety. It also features a manual safety catch on the frame. It has a 2.5" barrel and a 6-shot detachable magazine. It was available with various different finishes and grips. In the United States this model was designated the "Firecat." It was manufactured between 1920 and 1966.

| Exc. | V.G. | Good | Fair | Poor |
|------|------|------|------|------|
| 250  | 200  | 175  | 100  | 75   |

### Astra 400
This is a tubular-frame semi-automatic that was based on the Campo Giro design with considerable mechanical improvements. It was patterned after the Browning blowback design with a coaxial recoil spring surrounding the barrel and retained by a bushing. It is chambered for the 9mm Largo, the most powerful cartridge produced for a blowback-operated pistol. The reason that this is successful is the strength of the recoil and hammer springs. This pistol is very difficult to cock. It has a 6" barrel and a blued finish with checkered plastic grips. This pistol was introduced in 1921 and was adopted by the Spanish army. It was widely exported and also used by the French army in the 1920's. Production ceased in 1946 after approximately 106,000 had been manufactured.

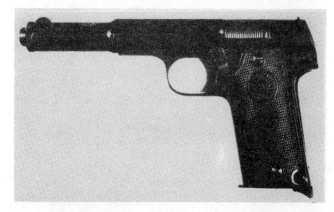

| Exc. | V.G. | Good | Fair | Poor |
|------|------|------|------|------|
| 350  | 300  | 250  | 200  | 125  |

### Astra 300
This is a smaller version of the Model 400 chambered for either 7.65mm or the 9mm short cartridge. It was adopted as a service pistol by the Spanish navy in 1928. During WWII approximately 85,000 of these pistols in both calibers were purchased by the Nazi government for use by the Luftwaffe and the German army. These pistols bear Waffenamt acceptance marks. There were approximately 171,000 manufactured before production ceased in 1947.
Nazi-Proofed--Add 25 Percent.

| Exc. | V.G. | Good | Fair | Poor |
|------|------|------|------|------|
| 325  | 275  | 225  | 175  | 100  |

### Astra 600
This slightly smaller version of the Model 400 is chambered for the 9mm Parabellum cartridge. It was manufactured to fill an order from the German government. There were approximately 10,500 manufactured in 1943 and 1944. A second batch of approximately 49,000 were manufactured for delivery in 1946; but since the War was over, they were sold commercially--many being used to arm post-war German police forces.

| Exc. | V.G. | Good | Fair | Poor |
|------|------|------|------|------|
| 300  | 250  | 200  | 150  | 100  |

### Astra 700

This is a version of the Model 400 chambered for the 7.65mm cartridge. There were approximately 4,000 manufactured in 1926.

| Exc. | V.G. | Good | Fair | Poor |
|------|------|------|------|------|
| 500  | 450  | 400  | 300  | 200  |

### Astra 800

This model is similar to the Astra 600, with the addition of an external hammer and a loaded-chamber indicator. It is chambered for the 9mm Parabellum cartridge and has an 8-shot detachable magazine. The safety catch was moved to the left rear of the frame, and the butt was curved at the bottom for an improved grip. The finish is blued, with plastic grips that have the word "Condor" molded into them. There were approximately 11,400 manufactured between 1958 and 1969.

| Exc. | V.G. | Good | Fair | Poor |
|------|------|------|------|------|
| 1000 | 850  | 750  | 500  | 400  |

### Astra 900

This was a faithful copy with some improvements of the C/96 "Broomhandle" Mauser Pistol. Its external configuration is quite similar to the original but is slightly heavier, due to the use of thicker metal in the upper receiver and barrel. There were approximately 34,500 manufactured between 1928 and 1937. Many were imported to China. Some were utilized by the Spanish security police. It is chambered for the 7.63mm Mauser cartridge. The finish is blued, with ribbed walnut grips. The Model 901, 902, and 903 are fully-automatic, select-fire versions of the Model 900.

| Exc. | V.G. | Good | Fair | Poor |
|------|------|------|------|------|
| 2000 | 1750 | 1250 | 750  | 500  |

### Astra 1000

This was the first post-war model and is a 7.65mm version of the Model 200 or "Firecat" pistol. It has a 12-round detachable magazine and a 4" barrel. It was manufactured in limited quantities in the late 1940's.

| Exc. | V.G. | Good | Fair | Poor |
|------|------|------|------|------|
| 500  | 450  | 400  | 300  | 200  |

### Astra 2000

This model is similar to the Model 200, with no grip safety and an external hammer. It is chambered for the .22 short or 6.35mm cartridge. It is blued, with plastic grips.

| Exc. | V.G. | Good | Fair | Poor |
|------|------|------|------|------|
| 300  | 250  | 200  | 150  | 100  |

### Astra 3000

This is an improved version of the Astra 300. It is chambered for 7.65mm or 9mm short. It has either a 6- or 7-round detachable magazine and features a loaded-chamber indicator on the slide. It was manufactured between 1948 and 1956.

| Exc. | V.G. | Good | Fair | Poor |
|------|------|------|------|------|
| 350  | 300  | 250  | 200  | 150  |

### Astra 4000

This is an external-hammer version of the Astra 3000. It is chambered for the .22 l.r., 7.65mm, or the 9mm short cartridges. It has a contoured butt and does not feature a grip safety. It is marked either "Mod 4000" or "Falcon" on import models. It was introduced in 1956.

| Exc. | V.G. | Good | Fair | Poor |
|------|------|------|------|------|
| 250  | 225  | 200  | 150  | 100  |

### Astra 5000

This model represents a major design change. It features a streamlined shape and bears a resemblance to the Walther PP Pistol. It features double-action lockwork and an external hammer. The safety catch locks the firing pin and drops the hammer. It is chambered for .22 l.r., 7.65mm, and the 9mm short cartridge. It is available either blued, chrome-plated, or in a stainless-steel version. It has a 3.5" barrel and a detachable box magazine. There is also a sport model available with a 6" barrel. This pistol was introduced in 1965 and is currently being manufactured.

| Exc. | V.G. | Good | Fair | Poor |
|------|------|------|------|------|
| 300  | 250  | 200  | 150  | 100  |

### Astra 7000

This is a larger version of the Model 2000 chambered for the .22 l.r. cartridge.

| Exc. | V.G. | Good | Fair | Poor |
|------|------|------|------|------|
| 275  | 250  | 225  | 150  | 100  |

## Constable A-60

This is a blowback-operated, double-action semi-automatic pistol chambered for the .380 ACP cartridge. It has a 3.5" barrel with adjustable sights and a 13-round double-stack magazine. It has an ambidextrous safety with a blued finish and plastic grips. It was introduced in 1986.

| NIB | Exc. | V.G. | Good | Fair | Poor |
|-----|------|------|------|------|------|
| 250 | 200 | 175 | 125 | 100 | 75 |

## Astra A-80

This is a semi-automatic double-action pistol chambered for either the 9mm, .38 Super, or the .45 ACP cartridges. It has a 15-shot magazine, 9 in .45. The barrel is 3.75" in length, and the finish is either blued or chrome-plated. It was introduced in 1982.

| NIB | Exc. | V.G. | Good | Fair | Poor |
|-----|------|------|------|------|------|
| 400 | 350 | 300 | 250 | 200 | 150 |

## Astra A-90

This model is similar to the A-80 and is chambered for 9mm or .45 ACP only, with a blued finish. It was introduced in 1986.

| NIB | Exc. | V.G. | Good | Fair | Poor |
|-----|------|------|------|------|------|
| 400 | 350 | 300 | 250 | 200 | 150 |

## Astra Cadix

This is a double-action, solid-frame revolver with a swing-out cylinder. It is chambered for .22 l.r. or the .38 Special cartridge. It has either a 9-shot or a 5-shot cylinder. The barrel is 4" or 6" in length. It has adjustable sights. The finish is blued, with plastic grips. It was manufactured between 1960 and 1968.

| Exc. | V.G. | Good | Fair | Poor |
|------|------|------|------|------|
| 175 | 150 | 125 | 90 | 70 |

## .357 D/A Revolver

This is a double-action, swing-out cylinder revolver chambered for the .357 Magnum cartridge. It is offered with a 3", 4", 6", or 8.5" barrel. It has a 6-shot cylinder and adjustable sights and is available either blued or in stainless steel, with checkered wood grips. It was manufactured between 1972 and 1988.
Stainless Steel--Add 10 Percent.

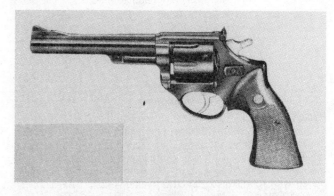

| Exc. | V.G. | Good | Fair | Poor |
|------|------|------|------|------|
| 250 | 225 | 200 | 150 | 100 |

## .44/.45 D/A Revolver

This is a large-frame, swing-out cylinder, double-action revolver chambered for the .41 Magnum, .44 Magnum, or the .45 ACP cartridge. It has a 6" or 8.5" barrel and a 6-shot cylinder. The finish is either blued or stainless steel, with checkered wood grips. It was manufactured between 1980 and 1987.
Stainless Steel--Add 25 Percent.

| Exc. | V.G. | Good | Fair | Poor |
|------|------|------|------|------|
| 350 | 300 | 250 | 200 | 150 |

## Terminator

This model is chambered for the .44 Special or .44 Magnum cartridge. It has a 2.75" shrouded barrel, adjustable sights, and a 6-shot cylinder. It is either blued or stainless steel and features rubber grips. This model was distributed by Sile in New York City.
Stainless Steel Version--Add 10 Percent.

| Exc. | V.G. | Good | Fair | Poor |
|------|------|------|------|------|
| 350 | 300 | 250 | 200 | 150 |

## Convertible Revolver

This model is chambered for the 9mm cartridge and is furnished with an extra .357 Magnum cylinder. It has a 3" barrel and holds six shots. It is blued, with checkered walnut grips. It was introduced in 1986.

| Exc. | V.G. | Good | Fair | Poor |
|------|------|------|------|------|
| 300 | 250 | 200 | 150 | 100 |

## UNION FIREARMS COMPANY
### Toledo, Ohio

### Reifgraber

This is a short recoil, gas-operated, single-action semi-automatic pistol. It is chambered for the .32 or .38 Smith & Wesson cartridge. It has a 3" barrel and a reciprocating bolt that is enclosed in a casing. The ported barrel directs gas into the casing, which boosts the short recoil operation. There is a rocker arm in the barrel extension that locks the bolt. The finish is blued, with checkered walnut grips. This pistol was designed between 1903 and 1907 by J. J. Reifgraber. There were approximately 100 manufactured.

| Exc. | V.G. | Good | Fair | Poor |
|------|------|------|------|------|
| 900 | 750 | 650 | 500 | 350 |

## Pocket Revolver

This is an automatic revolver similar in design to the Webley Fosbery. It is chambered for the .32 Smith & Wesson cartridge and has a 3" ribbed round barrel. It is double-action and features a cylinder that has helical slots that engage a pin in the frame. The cylinder recoils back and forth upon firing to bring the next loaded chamber into battery. The finish is blued, with plastic grips. There were very few manufactured.

| Exc. | V.G. | Good | Fair | Poor |
|------|------|------|------|------|
| 800 | 650 | 500 | 400 | 250 |

# UNION
## Unknown

### Pocket Pistol

This is a single-shot, Derringer-type pistol chambered for the .22 rimfire cartridge. It has a 2.75" round barrel that pivots to the side for loading. It has a spur trigger and an external hammer with a large cocking spur. The frame is iron. It is nickel-plated with rounded rosewood or walnut grips. The barrel is marked "Union."

| Exc. | V.G. | Good | Fair | Poor |
|------|------|------|------|------|
| 250 | 200 | 150 | 100 | 75 |

# UNIQUE
## Hendaye, France
## SEE--Pyrenees

# UNITED SPORTING ARMS, INC.
## Tucson, Arizona

### Seville

This is a single-action revolver patterned after the Colt Single Action Army. It is chambered for .357 Magnum, .41 Magnum, .44 Magnum, and .45 Colt. It is offered with a 4-58", 5-1/2", 6-1/2", and 7-1/2" barrel. It has adjustable target sights and is blued, with smooth walnut grips. This model was manufactured until 1986. A stainless-steel model is also available and is valued the same.

| Exc. | V.G. | Good | Fair | Poor |
|------|------|------|------|------|
| 375 | 350 | 300 | 250 | 200 |

### Seville .357 Maxi

This model is similar to the standard Seville but is offered in stainless steel with a 5.5" or 7.5" barrel. It is chambered for the .357 Maximum cartridge. It was discontinued in 1986.

| Exc. | V.G. | Good | Fair | Poor |
|------|------|------|------|------|
| 550 | 500 | 450 | 350 | 300 |

### Seville .375 USA

This version is offered with a 7.5" barrel in stainless steel and is chambered for the .375 USA cartridge. It was discontinued in 1986.

| Exc. | V.G. | Good | Fair | Poor |
|------|------|------|------|------|
| 600 | 550 | 500 | 400 | 350 |

### Seville .454 Magnum

This version is constructed of stainless steel, is offered with a 7.5" barrel only, and is chambered for the .454 Magnum cartridge. It has a 5-shot cylinder. It was discontinued in 1986.

| Exc. | V.G. | Good | Fair | Poor |
|------|------|------|------|------|
| 700 | 650 | 500 | 450 | 400 |

The Seville series was also available as a silhouette gun. This variation has a stainless steel grip frame and a blued barrel that is 10.5" in length. It is furnished with adjustable sights and Pachmayr grips. The caliber variations are the same as with the standard Seville, as are the values.

## Sheriff's Model

This is a single-action revolver patterned after the Colt Single Action Army, that was chambered for .357 Magnum/.38 Special, .44 Special, .44 Magnum, and the .45 Colt cartridge. It has a 3.5" barrel with adjustable sights and is either blued or stainless steel, with smooth walnut grips. This model was discontinued in 1986.

| Exc. | V.G. | Good | Fair | Poor |
|------|------|------|------|------|
| 400 | 350 | 325 | 250 | 200 |

# UNITED STATES ARMS
## Otis A. Smith Company
## Rockfall, Connecticut

### Single Action Revolver

This is a large single-action revolver that is chambered for the .44 rimfire or .44 centerfire cartridges interchangeably. The face of the hammer has two solidly mounted strikers--one that would ignite the rimfire; and the other, the centerfire primer. The round ribbed barrel is 7" in length, and there is an integral ejector rod mounted underneath the barrel. There is a unique, spring-operated loading gate. The finish is blued, with rosewood grips. The barrel is marked "United States Arms Company - New York." The top strap is marked "No. 44." This revolver was manufactured by the Otis A. Smith Company in the 1870's. It is quite rare on today's market.

| Exc. | V.G. | Good | Fair | Poor |
|------|------|------|------|------|
| 750 | 650 | 550 | 400 | 300 |

# UNITED STATES HISTORICAL SOCIETY
## Richmond, Virginia

This organization was established to market historical reproductions of famous American firearms. Their products are produced by the Williamsburg Firearms Manufactory and the Virginia Firearms Manufactory. They produce high quality replicas that are, for the most part, faithful to the originals.

### George Washington

This is a reproduction of a pistol said to be owned by the first president of the United States. It is a flintlock, and the number manufactured was restricted to 975. When it was issued, the initial price was $2,500. As with all commemoratives, this model is desirable when NIB and supplied with all furnished materials.

| NIB | Exc. | V.G. | Good | Fair | Poor |
|------|------|------|------|------|------|
| 4000 | 3000 | 2500 | 2000 | 1000 | 750 |

### Thomas Jefferson

This is a reproduction of Thomas Jefferson's pistol. It is a flintlock, and there were 1,000 manufactured. The price at issue was $1,900. It is desirable, for the most part, when NIB and including all originally supplied materials.

| NIB | Exc. | V.G. | Good | Fair | Poor |
|------|------|------|------|------|------|
| 3000 | 2000 | 1750 | 1500 | 750 | 500 |

### Hamilton-Burr Dueling Pistols

There were 1,200 matched sets produced. The initial issue price was $2,100.

| NIB | Exc. | V.G. | Good | Fair | Poor |
|------|------|------|------|------|------|
| 3000 | 2000 | 1750 | 1500 | 750 | 500 |

### Stonewall Jackson Pistol

This is an elaborately ornamented reproduction of a Colt Model 1851 Navy Pistol. It is chambered for .36 caliber and has a 7.5" barrel. It has walnut grips with a commemorative medallion and is cased with silver-plated accessories and a sterling silver medallion. There were 2,500 manufactured in 1988.

| NIB | Exc. | V.G. | Good | Fair | Poor |
|------|------|------|------|------|------|
| 2000 | 1500 | 1000 | 800 | 600 | 400 |

## Texas Paterson Edition
This is a faithful reproduction of the Colt Paterson Pistol. It is elaborately engraved and is furnished cased with accessories. There were 1,000 manufactured commencing in 1988.

| NIB | Exc. | V.G. | Good | Fair | Poor |
|---|---|---|---|---|---|
| 2500 | 2000 | 1500 | 1000 | 750 | 500 |

## Buffalo Bill Centennial
This is a reproduction of the Colt Model 1860 Army Pistol. It is chambered for .44 caliber percussion and has a 7.5" barrel. It has Wild West scenes etched and inlaid in gold. The finish is blued, with simulated ivory grips. It is furnished cased with accessories. There were 2,500 manufactured in 1983, and the initial issue price was $1,950.

| NIB | Exc. | V.G. | Good | Fair | Poor |
|---|---|---|---|---|---|
| 2000 | 1500 | 1000 | 800 | 600 | 400 |

## U.S. Calvary Model
This is a faithful reproduction of the Colt Model 1860 Army Revolver. It is chambered for .44-caliber percussion and has a 7.5" barrel. The finish is blued, with an etched cylinder scene that is gold-washed. It has stag grips. This model is furnished cased with an accompanying brass buckle. There were 975 manufactured, commencing in 1988.

| NIB | Exc. | V.G. | Good | Fair | Poor |
|---|---|---|---|---|---|
| 1500 | 1000 | 800 | 650 | 500 | 350 |

## Sam Houston Model
This is a faithful reproduction of the Walker Colt. It is chambered for .44-caliber percussion and has a 9" barrel. The finish is high polished and blued, with extensive etching and gold inlay. It has smooth walnut stocks inlaid with Sam Houston commemorative medallions. It is furnished cased with accessories. There were 2,500 manufactured.

| NIB | Exc. | V.G. | Good | Fair | Poor |
|---|---|---|---|---|---|
| 2250 | 1750 | 1500 | 1000 | 750 | 600 |

## Robert E. Lee Model
This is a faithful reproduction of the Colt 1851 Navy Pistol. It is chambered for .36-caliber percussion and has a 7.5" octagonal barrel. The finish is blued and gold-etched. The cylinder scene represents historical events from the Civil War. It has smooth walnut stocks inlaid with Robert E. Lee commemorative medallions. It is furnished cased with accessories. There were 2,500 manufactured.

| NIB | Exc. | V.G. | Good | Fair | Poor |
|---|---|---|---|---|---|
| 2500 | 2000 | 1500 | 1000 | 750 | 500 |

## H. Deringer Set
This is a cased pair of .41-caliber percussion pocket pistols that are faithful replicas of the Henry Deringer Philadelphia-type pistols. There are three versions available: one with sterling silver mountings, a second with 14 kt. gold mountings, and the third (of which there were only five pairs produced) 18 kt. gold with precious gemstone. The values are as follows:

### Silver Mounted
| NIB | Exc. | V.G. | Good | Fair | Poor |
|---|---|---|---|---|---|
| 2500 | 2000 | 1500 | 1000 | 750 | 500 |

### 14 Kt. Gold Mounted
| NIB | Exc. | V.G. | Good | Fair | Poor |
|---|---|---|---|---|---|
| 7500 | 5000 | 3500 | 2500 | 1750 | 1000 |

### 18 Kt. Mounted with Gemstone
Issue Price--$25,000

This company also offered a series of fully operational, non-firing miniatures. They were produced with the highest degree of workmanship and are quite sought after by collectors of miniature firearms. We recommend securing competent, individual appraisal on these collectibles, as we do not consider them to be within the purview of this publication.

# UNIVERSAL FIREARM
### Jacksonville, Arkansas

## Model 7312
This is an Over/Under double-barrel shotgun chambered for 12 gauge. It has 30" vent-ribbed barrels that are separated by a vented spacer. They are choked full-and-modified. The action is a boxlock with a single selective trigger and automatic ejectors. The barrels feature recoil-reducing ports. The action is engraved and case-colored, with a checkered, select walnut stock. It was discontinued in 1982.

| Exc. | V.G. | Good | Fair | Poor |
|---|---|---|---|---|
| 1700 | 1500 | 1250 | 900 | 650 |

## Model 7412
This version has extractors and a blued or coin-finished receiver. It was discontinued in 1982.

| Exc. | V.G. | Good | Fair | Poor |
|---|---|---|---|---|
| 1500 | 1250 | 1000 | 750 | 500 |

## Model 7712
This version is offered with 26" and 28" barrels with various choke combinations. It has a non-selective single trigger and extractors and is lightly engraved and blued, with a checkered walnut stock. It was discontinued in 1982.

| Exc. | V.G. | Good | Fair | Poor |
|---|---|---|---|---|
| 450 | 400 | 350 | 250 | 200 |

## Model 7812
This is similar to the Model 7712, with heavier engraving and automatic ejectors. It was discontinued in 1982.

| Exc. | V.G. | Good | Fair | Poor |
|---|---|---|---|---|
| 600 | 550 | 450 | 350 | 250 |

## Model 7912
This version is heavily engraved with a gold wash and has a single-selective trigger. Otherwise, it is similar to the Model 7812. It was discontinued in 1982.

| Exc. | V.G. | Good | Fair | Poor |
|---|---|---|---|---|
| 1200 | 1000 | 750 | 600 | 400 |

## Model 7112
This is a side-by-side double-barrel shotgun chambered for 12 gauge. It has 26" or 28" barrels with various choke combinations. It features an engraved, case-colored boxlock receiver, extractors, and double triggers. It has a checkered walnut stock. It was discontinued in 1982.

| Exc. | V.G. | Good | Fair | Poor |
|---|---|---|---|---|
| 350 | 300 | 250 | 200 | 100 |

## Double Wing
This was a side-by-side double-barrel shotgun chambered for 10, 12, and 20 gauge, as well as .410. It is offered with 26", 28", and 30" barrels with various choke combinations. It has a boxlock action, double triggers, and extractors. It has a checkered walnut stock. The 10-gauge version is worth approximately 20 percent additional. It was discontinued in 1982.

| Exc. | V.G. | Good | Fair | Poor |
|---|---|---|---|---|
| 350 | 300 | 250 | 200 | 100 |

## Model 7212
This is a single-barrel, break-open trap gun chambered for 12 gauge. It has a 30" competition-type, vent-rib barrel with a full choke. It features an engraved case-colored boxlock action, an automatic ejector, and a recoil-reducing ported barrel. It has a checkered walnut trap-type stock. It was discontinued in 1982.

| Exc. | V.G. | Good | Fair | Poor |
|---|---|---|---|---|
| 1000 | 850 | 650 | 450 | 300 |

## Model 1000 Military Carbine
This is a reproduction of the United States M1 Carbine. It is chambered for the .30 caliber cartridge, has an 18" barrel, and is satin blued, with a birch stock.

| Exc. | V.G. | Good | Fair | Poor |
|---|---|---|---|---|
| 250 | 225 | 200 | 100 | 75 |

### Model 1003

This is an M1 Carbine copy that is offered with a 16", 18", or 20" barrel.

| Exc. | V.G. | Good | Fair | Poor |
|------|------|------|------|------|
| 200  | 175  | 150  | 100  | 75   |

### Model 1010

This is similar to the Model 1003 but is offered with a nickel-plated finish.

| Exc. | V.G. | Good | Fair | Poor |
|------|------|------|------|------|
| 275  | 225  | 175  | 125  | 100  |

### Model 1015

This is a gold-plated version of the Model 1003.

| Exc. | V.G. | Good | Fair | Poor |
|------|------|------|------|------|
| 300  | 250  | 200  | 150  | 125  |

### Model 1005 Deluxe

This version features a high-polished and blued finish with a Monte Carlo-type, oil-finished walnut stock.

| Exc. | V.G. | Good | Fair | Poor |
|------|------|------|------|------|
| 250  | 225  | 150  | 100  | 75   |

### Model 1006 Stainless

This is similar to the Model 1000, constructed of stainless steel.

| Exc. | V.G. | Good | Fair | Poor |
|------|------|------|------|------|
| 275  | 225  | 175  | 125  | 100  |

### Model 1020 Teflon

This is similar to the Model 1005, with a Dupont Teflon-S finish, that is offered in either black or gray.

| Exc. | V.G. | Good | Fair | Poor |
|------|------|------|------|------|
| 275  | 225  | 175  | 125  | 100  |

### Model 1256 Ferret

This version is chambered for .256 Winchester Magnum. Otherwise, it is similar to the Model 1000.

| Exc. | V.G. | Good | Fair | Poor |
|------|------|------|------|------|
| 225  | 200  | 175  | 125  | 100  |

### Model 3000 Enforcer

This is a pistol version with an 11.25" barrel. It is furnished with either a 15- or 30-shot magazine and is available in all the finish options, as well as stainless steel.
Nickel Finish--Add 20 Percent.
Gold Plated--Add 40 Percent.
Stainless Steel--Add 30 Percent.
Teflon-S--Add 20 Percent.

**Blued**

| Exc. | V.G. | Good | Fair | Poor |
|------|------|------|------|------|
| 250  | 225  | 200  | 150  | 100  |

### Model 5000 Paratrooper

This is a folding-stock version with a 16" or 18" barrel. The finish is blued. A stainless-steel version known as the Model 5006 is also available and is worth approximately 20 percent additional.

| Exc. | V.G. | Good | Fair | Poor |
|------|------|------|------|------|
| 225  | 200  | 175  | 125  | 100  |

### 1981 Commemorative Carbine

This is a quality-finished version of the Model 1003 that was furnished cased with accessories. It was produced to commemorate the Fortieth Anniversary of WWII, 1941-1981. As with all commemoratives, it is desirable only when NIB with all furnished materials included.

| NIB | Exc. | V.G. | Good | Fair | Poor |
|-----|------|------|------|------|------|
| 500 | 350  | 300  | 250  | 200  | 150  |

### Model 2200 Leatherneck

This is a .22-caliber version of the M1 Carbine. It is blowback-operated and features an 18" barrel and a satin-blued finish. The stock is made of birch.

| Exc. | V.G. | Good | Fair | Poor |
|------|------|------|------|------|
| 250  | 225  | 200  | 150  | 100  |

## U.S. M1 CARBINE
### Various Manufacturers

The M1 Carbine is chambered for the .30 caliber cartridge. It was introduced in 1940 in answer to a request for a lightweight rifle suitable for arming machinegunners, artillery men, clerks, etc. The specifications for this light rifle were given to 25 manufacturing companies; and as soon as Winchester had developed the ammunition, production began. In May of 1941, eleven gun companies had submitted designs for testing. The version finally adopted was designed by Williams and was manufactured by Winchester. It was designated the Carbine M1. This is a gas-operated semi-automatic rifle with an 18" barrel fed by either a 15- or 30-round detachable box magazine. A selective-fire version known as the M2 is also available. The folding-stock paratrooper version is known as the M1A1. This was the most prolific American weapon used in WWII. The values are affected by the rarity of the manufacturer. We list them as follows:

**Inland**

| Exc. | V.G. | Good | Fair | Poor |
|------|------|------|------|------|
| 350  | 300  | 250  | 200  | 150  |

**Underwood**

| Exc. | V.G. | Good | Fair | Poor |
|------|------|------|------|------|
| 350  | 300  | 250  | 200  | 150  |

**S. G. Saginaw**

| Exc. | V.G. | Good | Fair | Poor |
|------|------|------|------|------|
| 350  | 300  | 250  | 200  | 150  |

**IBM**

| Exc. | V.G. | Good | Fair | Poor |
|------|------|------|------|------|
| 375  | 325  | 275  | 225  | 175  |

**Quality Hardware**

| Exc. | V.G. | Good | Fair | Poor |
|------|------|------|------|------|
| 375  | 325  | 275  | 225  | 175  |

**National Postal Meter**

| Exc. | V.G. | Good | Fair | Poor |
|------|------|------|------|------|
| 375  | 325  | 275  | 225  | 175  |

**Standard Products**

| Exc. | V.G. | Good | Fair | Poor |
|------|------|------|------|------|
| 350  | 300  | 250  | 200  | 150  |

**Rockola**

| Exc. | V.G. | Good | Fair | Poor |
|------|------|------|------|------|
| 375  | 325  | 275  | 225  | 175  |

**SG Grand Rapids**

| Exc. | V.G. | Good | Fair | Poor |
|------|------|------|------|------|
| 450  | 400  | 350  | 300  | 250  |

**Winchester**

| Exc. | V.G. | Good | Fair | Poor |
|------|------|------|------|------|
| 450  | 400  | 350  | 300  | 250  |

**Irwin Pedersen**

| Exc. | V.G. | Good | Fair | Poor |
|------|------|------|------|------|
| 950  | 750  | 550  | 450  | 350  |

### M1 A1 Paratrooper Model
This is a folding-stock version manufactured by Inland. It has crossed cannon proofs. There were approximately 110,000 manufactured between 1942 and 1945.

| Exc. | V.G. | Good | Fair | Poor |
|------|------|------|------|------|
| 400 | 350 | 300 | 250 | 200 |

# URIZAR, TOMAS
### Eibar, Spain

This company was founded in the early 1900's and produced inexpensive "Velo-dog" revolvers. In 1911 they began production of semi-automatic pistols and turned out many "Eibar"-type revolvers. They ceased operations in 1921.

### Celta, J. Cesar, Premier, Puma, and Union
The above model designations are tradenames for the same pistol and are marked accordingly. This is a blowback-operated semi-automatic pistol chambered for the 6.35mm cartridge. It has a 3" barrel and a detachable box magazine. It is of the usual "Eibar"-type construction and is a copy of the 1906 Browning without a grip safety. The finish is blued, with checkered plastic grips that carry a dragon motif. On the other side of the grip is a savage with a club. The barrel is stamped "TU."

| Exc. | V.G. | Good | Fair | Poor |
|------|------|------|------|------|
| 175 | 150 | 125 | 90 | 75 |

### Dek-Du
This is a poor-quality, 12-shot, Velo-dog, folding-trigger, hammerless revolver. It was chambered originally for the 5.5mm Velo-dog cartridge and later chambered for 6.35mm. It was manufactured between 1905 and 1912.

| Exc. | V.G. | Good | Fair | Poor |
|------|------|------|------|------|
| 125 | 100 | 75 | 50 | 25 |

### Express
This is a blowback-operated semi-automatic pistol chambered for the 6.35mm cartridge. It has a 2" ribbed barrel fixed to the frame. The finish is blued, with checkered wooden grips. The slide is marked "The Best Automatic Pistol Express." The caliber is also marked. There is also a 7.65mm version with a 4" ribbed barrel.

| Exc. | V.G. | Good | Fair | Poor |
|------|------|------|------|------|
| 150 | 125 | 100 | 75 | 50 |

### Imperial
This is a blowback-operated semi-automatic chambered for the 6.35mm cartridge. It has a 2.5" barrel and was manufactured for sale by the firm of Aldazabal, a practice not uncommon in Eibar during this period. It was manufactured circa 1914.

| Exc. | V.G. | Good | Fair | Poor |
|------|------|------|------|------|
| 150 | 125 | 100 | 75 | 50 |

### Le Secours or Phoenix
The above two designations apply to a blowback-operated, semi-automatic, "Eibar"-type pistol chambered for the 7.65mm cartridge. Either one or the other name is marked on the slide. The finish is blued, with plastic grips that carry the dragon motif.

| Exc. | V.G. | Good | Fair | Poor |
|------|------|------|------|------|
| 150 | 125 | 100 | 75 | 50 |

### Princeps
This is a blowback-operated, "Eibar"-type, semi-automatic pistol chambered for the 6.35mm or the 7.65mm cartridges. It is a copy of the Browning 1906, and the grip safety was usually left in place. This model is marked "Made in Spain Princeps Patent." It was also sold by the firm of Grand Precision.

| Exc. | V.G. | Good | Fair | Poor |
|------|------|------|------|------|
| 150 | 125 | 100 | 75 | 50 |

### Venus
This is a typical "Eibar"-type, blowback-operated semi-automatic pistol chambered for the 7.65mm cartridge. It is blued, with checkered plastic grips with the word "Venus" molded into them.

| Exc. | V.G. | Good | Fair | Poor |
|------|------|------|------|------|
| 150 | 125 | 100 | 75 | 50 |

# UZI ISRAELI MILITARY INDUSTRIES
### Importer--Action Arms, Ltd.
### Philadelphia, Pennsylvania

### Uzi Carbine Model B
This is a semi-automatic version of the famous Israeli Uzi Submachine Gun. It is chambered for 9mm, .41 Action Express,

and .45 ACP. It has a 16.1" barrel and is furnished with either 20-, 25-, or 32-round detachable box magazines. A 50-round snail drum is available in 9mm only. It has a folding metal stock and a black parkerized finish. It is furnished in a molded plastic case with accessories. Due to the current assault-weapon problem in our country, accurate evaluation of this weapon is impossible. We recommend securing qualified local appraisal if a transaction is contemplated. There is also an A Model Uzi, which is no longer produced and which brings quite a premium on the used-gun market.

## Uzi Mini-Carbine

This is a smaller version of the Model B Carbine chambered for 9 mm or .45 ACP only. It has a 19.75" barrel and was introduced in 1987. Again, we urge qualified appraisal.

## Uzi Pistol

This is a still smaller version with a 4.5" barrel and a pistol grip. It is furnished with a 20-round magazine in a molded carrying case.

# VALMET, INC.
### Jyvaskyla, Finland
### Importer--Stoeger, Inc.
### South Hackensack, New Jersey

This company is known for the production of extremely high quality sporting firearms. They have been in the business for many years. They have also produced several very high quality assault weapons that shared the same type action as the Soviet Kalashnikov weapon. We list their assault weapons as follows but strongly urge securing qualified appraisal if a transaction is contemplated.

## M-625

This is a semi-automatic version of the Finnish M-62. It is chambered for the 7.62x39 Russian cartridge. It has a 16.75" barrel. It features the Kalashnikov action that is gas piston-operated, with a rotary bolt. It has an adjustable rear sight and is furnished with either a 15- or 30-round detachable magazine. The buttstock is either tubular steel or hardwood. It was manufactured after 1962.

## M-715

This version is similar to the M-625 except that it is chambered for the .223 cartridge. It is also offered with a synthetic stock.

## Model 76

This is another Kalashnikov-actioned, assault-type rifle chambered for .223, 7.62x39mm, or the .308 cartridge. It has either a 16.75" or 20.5" barrel. Consult qualified appraisal on this model.

## Model 78

This version is chambered for the .308 cartridge and has a 24.5" barrel with a wood stock and integral tripod. It was introduced in 1987. Qualified appraisal should be consulted on this model.

## Lion

This is an Over/Under double-barrel shotgun chambered for 12 gauge. It is offered with a 26", 28", or 30" barrel with various choke combinations. It has a boxlock action with single-selective trigger and extractors. The finish is blued, with a checkered walnut stock. It was manufactured between 1947 and 1968.

| Exc. | V.G. | Good | Fair | Poor |
|------|------|------|------|------|
| 425  | 375  | 300  | 250  | 150  |

## Model 412 Shooting System

This Over/Under firearm features interchangeable barrels and can be found as an Over/Under shotgun, double-barrel rifle, or shotgun-rifle combination. These interchangeable barrels are simply installed and feature monobloc construction. It has a single-selective trigger and is available with automatic ejectors or extractors and cocking indicators. The finish is blued, with a checkered walnut stock.

## 412S Field Grade

This is a 12 gauge only, with screw-in choke tubes. It was introduced in 1986.

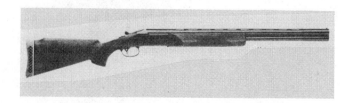

| NIB  | Exc. | V.G. | Good | Fair | Poor |
|------|------|------|------|------|------|
| 1000 | 850  | 750  | 600  | 500  | 400  |

## Model 412ST

This is a trap or skeet model with screw-in choke tubes.

| NIB  | Exc. | V.G. | Good | Fair | Poor |
|------|------|------|------|------|------|
| 1200 | 1000 | 900  | 750  | 600  | 500  |

## Model 412ST Premium Grade

This version features higher-grade walnut and finer checkering. It was introduced in 1987.

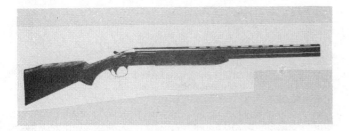

| NIB | Exc. | V.G. | Good | Fair | Poor |
|-----|------|------|------|------|------|
| 1500 | 1250 | 1100 | 950 | 750 | 600 |

## Model 412S Combination Gun

This version features a 12-gauge, 3" chambered barrel over a .222, .223, .243, .30-06, or .308 caliber barrel. It features a single-selective trigger and extractors.

| NIB | Exc. | V.G. | Good | Fair | Poor |
|-----|------|------|------|------|------|
| 1200 | 1000 | 900 | 750 | 600 | 500 |

## Model 412S Double Rifle

This model features Over/Under rifle barrels chambered for .243, .308, .30-06, .375 Holland & Holland, and the 9.3x73R cartridge. The barrels are 24" in length and feature extractors.

| NIB | Exc. | V.G. | Good | Fair | Poor |
|-----|------|------|------|------|------|
| 1250 | 1050 | 950 | 800 | 650 | 550 |

## Model 412K

This is an Over/Under double-barrelled rifle chambered for .308 or .30-06. It has 24" separated barrels, a single trigger, and extractors. It was not imported after 1986.

| Exc. | V.G. | Good | Fair | Poor |
|------|------|------|------|------|
| 750 | 650 | 550 | 400 | 350 |

## Hunter Model

This is a sporting version of the Kalashnikov-actioned assault rifle. It is chambered for the .223, .243, or .308 cartridges. It has a 20.5" barrel, is matte blued, and has a checkered select walnut stock. The magazines furnished are either 5, 9, or 20 rounds. It was introduced in 1986.

| NIB | V.G. | Good | Fair | Poor |
|-----|------|------|------|------|
| 800 | 750 | 650 | 450 | 350 |

# VALTION (LAHTI)
## SEE--Lahti

# VARNER SPORTING ARMS, INC.
## Marietta, Georgia

This is a high-grade modern rifle patterned after the Stevens Favorite Rifle. There are four basic models, and all are of excellent quality.

## Hunter

This version is chambered for the .22 l.r. cartridge. It has a 21.5" half-round/half-octagonal takedown barrel. It features an adjustable aperture sight and a blued finish with a select walnut stock and forearm. It was introduced in 1988.

| NIB | Exc. | V.G. | Good | Fair | Poor |
|-----|------|------|------|------|------|
| 375 | 325 | 275 | 225 | 150 | 100 |

## Hunter Deluxe

This version features a case-colored frame and action lever, with a better-grade walnut stock. It was introduced in 1988.

| NIB | Exc. | V.G. | Good | Fair | Poor |
|-----|------|------|------|------|------|
| 500 | 400 | 350 | 275 | 175 | 150 |

## Presentation Grade

This version features a target hammer and target trigger with better-grade, hand-checkered walnut stock and forearm. It is furnished with a takedown case and was introduced in 1988.

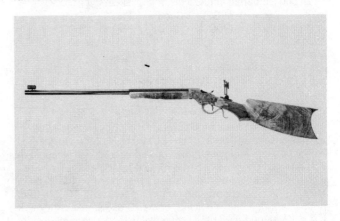

| NIB | Exc. | V.G. | Good | Fair | Poor |
|-----|------|------|------|------|------|
| 575 | 475 | 425 | 350 | 250 | 200 |

## Engraved Presentation Grade

### No. 1 Grade

| NIB | Exc. | V.G. | Good | Fair | Poor |
|-----|------|------|------|------|------|
| 650 | 550 | 500 | 450 | 350 | 250 |

### No. 2 Grade

| NIB | Exc. | V.G. | Good | Fair | Poor |
|-----|------|------|------|------|------|
| 775 | 650 | 600 | 550 | 450 | 300 |

### No. 3 Grade

| NIB | Exc. | V.G. | Good | Fair | Poor |
|-----|------|------|------|------|------|
| 1100 | 950 | 750 | 650 | 550 | 400 |

# VENUS WAFFENWERKE
## Zella Mehlis, Germany

### Venus

This is a rare, fixed-barrel, blowback-operated, semi-automatic pistol chambered for the 6.35mm, 7.65mm, and the 9mm short cartridges. It has a 3.5" barrel and was based on a Browning design. The recoil spring is mounted above the barrel, and it is fired by an internal hammer. It has a safety catch at the rear of the frame. The finish is blued, and the slide is marked "Original Venus Patent." The plastic grips have the monogram "OW." The man behind this pistol was Oskar Will, a noted gunsmith from Zella Mehlis. This pistol was manufactured from 1912 until the beginning of WWI. The business ceased operations during the War.

| Exc. | V.G. | Good | Fair | Poor |
|------|------|------|------|------|
| 600 | 500 | 400 | 250 | 175 |

## VERNEY-CARRON
### St. Etienne, France
### Importer--VenturaSeal Beach, California

**Concours**

This is an Over/Under double-barrel shotgun chambered for 12 gauge only. It features 26" or 28" vent-ribbed barrels with various choke combinations. It has a lightweight boxlock action with a self-opening feature. It has a single-selective trigger and automatic ejectors and is extensively engraved. The receiver is coin-finished, with blued barrels and a select French walnut, hand-checkered stock with either a straight, English-style or pistol grip. It was introduced in 1978 and is no longer imported.

| Exc. | V.G. | Good | Fair | Poor |
|------|------|------|------|------|
| 1000 | 850  | 750  | 600  | 450  |

**Skeet Model**

This model is similar to the field grade, with a 28" skeet-and-skeet choked barrel. It has a pistol-grip, skeet- type stock.

| Exc. | V.G. | Good | Fair | Poor |
|------|------|------|------|------|
| 1050 | 900  | 800  | 650  | 500  |

## VETTERLI
### Switzerland
### Various Manufacturers

This bolt-action repeating rifle was invented by Friderich Vetterli at Neuhausen, Switzerland, in 1867. The Vetterli was the first bolt-action repeating rifle to be adopted as a service weapon. It was adopted on January 8, 1869, and pre-dated the Fruwirth, which was adopted by the Austrian government on the 22nd of May, 1872. It is chambered for the copper-cased 10.2 Vetterli rimfire cartridge, the .41 Swiss, or the 10.4x38mm cartridge. It has a 12-round tubular magazine that is loaded through a side-gate similar to a Winchester lever action. The Vetterli has a swinging cover over the loading gate. The finish is blued, with a full-length walnut stock held on by one barrel band and an end-cap. There is a full-length cleaning rod located under the barrel. The receiver is tubular in configuration, and the triggerguard has a spur at the rear. It was manufactured between 1869 and 1881.

Carbine Model--Add 100 Percent.

| Exc. | V.G. | Good | Fair | Poor |
|------|------|------|------|------|
| 200  | 175  | 150  | 100  | 75   |

## VICKERS, LTD.
### Crayford/Kent, England

**Jubilee**

This is a single-shot, Martini-type, falling-block action rifle chambered for the .22 l.r. cartridge. It has a 28" heavy barrel with adjustable target sights. The finish is blued, and it has a pistolgrip target-type walnut stock. It was manufactured before WWII.

| Exc. | V.G. | Good | Fair | Poor |
|------|------|------|------|------|
| 450  | 400  | 350  | 275  | 200  |

**Empire**

This version is offered with a 27" or 30" medium-weight barrel, is also blued, and has a straight-grip walnut stock. Otherwise, it is similar to the Jubilee. It was also manufactured before WWII.

| Exc. | V.G. | Good | Fair | Poor |
|------|------|------|------|------|
| 400  | 350  | 300  | 225  | 150  |

## VICTORY ARMS CO., LTD.
### North Hampton, England
### Importer--Magnum Research, Inc.
### Minneapolis, Minnesota

**Model MC5**

This is a double-action semi-automatic pistol chambered for the 9mm Parabellum, .38 Super, .41 Action Express, 10mm, or the .45 ACP cartridges. It is offered with interchangeable 4.25", 5.75", or 7.5" barrels. It is featured with either a 10-, 12-, or 17-round magazine, depending on the caliber chambered. It has a de-cocking lever and a three-dot sight system. Millett sights are also available for an additional $60. The interchangeable barrels sell for an additional $100. The grips are stippled walnut. This Model was introduced in 1989.

| NIB | Exc. | V.G. | Good | Fair | Poor |
|-----|------|------|------|------|------|
| 500 | 450  | 400  | 300  | 250  | 200  |

## VIRGINIAN
### SEE--Interarms

## VOERE
### Kufstein, Austria

In 1987 this company was absorbed by the firm of Mauser-Werke. Rifles utilizing Voere actions are manufactured and marketed by KDF, Inc., of Seguin, Texas. Values for older-production rifles are as follows:

**Bolt Action Rifle**

This is a good quality bolt-action repeating rifle chambered for various popular calibers from .22-250 up to and including .458 Winchester Magnum. It has either 22" or 24" barrels with either a 3- or 4-round box magazine. The finish is blued, with a checkered, select walnut stock.

| Exc. | V.G. | Good | Fair | Poor |
|------|------|------|------|------|
| 350  | 300  | 250  | 200  | 100  |

**Semi-Auto Rifle**

This is a blowback-operated semi-automatic rifle chambered for the .22 l.r. cartridge. It is fired from the closed-bolt position, but an open-bolt model is also available, as is a full automatic version with an unbelievably rapid, cyclic rate of fire. It has a 20" barrel with adjustable sights and a detachable box magazine. The finish is blued, with a checkered hardwood stock.

| Exc. | V.G. | Good | Fair | Poor |
|------|------|------|------|------|
| 250  | 200  | 150  | 100  | 75   |

## VOLCANIC ARMS COMPANY
### New Haven, Connecticut

The Volcanic lever-action repeating pistol and rifle is an integral part in the history of the Winchester Arms Company. In 1855 what was then the Smith & Wesson Arms Company was changed to become the Volcanic Repeating Arms Company. It operated under this name for two years. In 1857 the company was renamed the New Haven Arms Company, and Oliver F. Winchester became more active in the operation of the company. Actually, he had invested money in 1855, when the company was known as Volcanic. The firearms produced by this company are as follows:

### Navy Pistol

This is a lever-action repeating pistol that is activated by a ring-shaped combination lever and triggerguard. It is chambered for the .38 rimfire cartridge and has a 6" barrel with a magazine tube running beneath it. The frame is brass; and the barrel, blued. The square butt grips are of varnished walnut. The barrel is marked "The Volcanic Repeating Arms Co. Patent New Haven Conn Feb 14, 1854." This model is also available with an 8" barrel and a 16" barrel. There was a detachable shoulder stock issued, but they are rarely encountered on today's market. Pistol With Shoulder Stock--Values Doubled.

#### 6" Barrel
| Exc. | V.G. | Good | Fair | Poor |
|------|------|------|------|------|
| 3500 | 3000 | 2500 | 1750 | 1250 |

#### 8" Barrel
| Exc. | V.G. | Good | Fair | Poor |
|------|------|------|------|------|
| 3000 | 2500 | 2000 | 1500 | 1000 |

#### 16" Barrel
| Exc. | V.G. | Good | Fair | Poor |
|------|------|------|------|------|
| 4000 | 3500 | 3000 | 2500 | 2000 |

### Lever-Action Carbine

This version is also chambered for the .38-caliber rimfire and is offered with barrel lengths of 16.5", 21", and 25". It features a straight-grip walnut stock with a brass crescent buttplate. The markings are the same as on the pistol.

#### 16.5" Barrel
| Exc. | V.G. | Good | Fair | Poor |
|------|------|------|------|------|
| 6000 | 5000 | 4000 | 3000 | 2500 |

#### 21" Barrel
| Exc. | V.G. | Good | Fair | Poor |
|------|------|------|------|------|
| 7000 | 6000 | 5000 | 4000 | 3500 |

#### 25" Barrel
| Exc. | V.G. | Good | Fair | Poor |
|------|------|------|------|------|
| 9500 | 8000 | 7000 | 6000 | 5500 |

## VOLUNTEER ENTERPRISES
### Knoxville, Tennessee
### SEE--Commando Arms

## VOLKSPISTOLE
### Various Makers
### Germany

### Volkspistole

This pistol is quite mysterious, as very few have ever been noted. It was designed as a cheaply manufactured, last-ditch weapon that was supposed to be used to flood the German countryside and cause casualties among the invaders at the close of WWII. It is chambered for the 9mm Parabellum cartridge and features a gas-operated, delayed blowback action. It has a 5.1" barrel with an 8-round, detachable box magazine. The construction is of steel stampings. It has no safety devices and no markings whatsoever. Examples noted are in the white, and there are no sights affixed to them. It appears that this weapon never actually went into production, and it would be impossible to estimate a value. Anyone encountering such a weapon would be wise to secure a qualified appraisal.

## VOUZLAUD
### Paris, France
### Importer--Waverly Arms Co.
### Suffolk, Virginia

### Model 315 E

This is a side-by-side double-barrel shotgun chambered for 12, 16, or 20 gauge. It has 20" barrels with various choke combinations. The boxlock action is lightly engraved and case-colored. It has double triggers and a select, straight-grip, French walnut stock. It was not imported after 1987.

| Exc. | V.G. | Good | Fair | Poor |
|------|------|------|------|------|
| 7500 | 6500 | 5500 | 4000 | 2500 |

### Model 315 EL

This model is similar to the 315 E, with more elaborate scroll engraving. It was discontinued in 1987. A 28-gauge or .410 version is available and would be worth an additional $1,000.

| Exc. | V.G. | Good | Fair | Poor |
|-------|------|------|------|------|
| 10000 | 8500 | 6500 | 5000 | 3000 |

### Model 315 EGL

This model is also similar to the 315 E, with extensive scroll engraving and a coin-finished receiver. The stock is of fancy-grade French walnut. It was discontinued in 1987.

| Exc. | V.G. | Good | Fair | Poor |
|-------|-------|-------|------|------|
| 15000 | 12500 | 10000 | 7500 | 5000 |

### Model 315 EGL-S

This model is similar to the 315 EGL, with ornate game-scene engraving and exhibition-grade French walnut. It features mon-obloc barrel construction. It was discontinued in 1987.

| Exc. | V.G. | Good | Fair | Poor |
|------|------|------|------|------|
| 5500 | 4500 | 3500 | 2500 | 1750 |

## WALCH, JOHN
### New York, New York

### Navy Revolver

This is a unique single-action revolver chambered for .36-caliber percussion. It has a 6" octagonal barrel and a 12-shot cylinder that has six chambers--each are doubly loaded with a total of 12 nipples. It has two hammers--one on the right and one on the left--and two corresponding triggers that release the hammers in turn to ignite the respective powder charges. The finish is blued, with two-piece walnut grips. The barrel is marked "Walch Firearms Co. NY." and "Patented Feb. 8, 1859." There were approximately 200 manufactured by the Union Knife Company in Naugatuck, Connecticut, for sale by John Walch in New York, who was also the patent holder.

| Exc. | V.G. | Good | Fair | Poor |
|------|------|------|------|------|
| 3500 | 3000 | 2750 | 2000 | 1500 |

## WALDMAN
### Germany

### Waldman

This is a blowback-operated semi-automatic pistol chambered for the 7.65mm cartridge. It has a 3.5" barrel and an 8-round detachable magazine. It is fired by an internal hammer and has a manual safety catch at the left rear of the frame. This pistol was of mediocre quality and is often confused with a number of its Spanish imitators using the same name or a derivative thereof. The finish is blued, with checkered walnut grips bearing the name Waldman. The slide is marked "1913 Model Automatic Pistol." Examples have been noted marked "American Automatic Pistol."

| Exc. | V.G. | Good | Fair | Poor |
|------|------|------|------|------|
| 250 | 225 | 200 | 150 | 100 |

## WALLIS & BIRCH
### Philadelphia, Pennsylvania

**Pocket Pistol**

This is a single-action pocket pistol chambered for .41-caliber percussion. It was patterned after the Henry Deringer-type pistol. It is offered with barrel lengths of 2.5" or 3". The markings are "Wallis & Birch Phila." The finish is blued, with a walnut stock and German silver mountings. It was made in the 1850's.

| Exc. | V.G. | Good | Fair | Poor |
|------|------|------|------|------|
| 650 | 600 | 500 | 400 | 300 |

## WALTHER, CARL
### Ulm, Germany

The firm of Carl Walther was founded in 1886 at Zella Mehlis. It flourished through the early years of the Twentieth Century. By 1908 it had become a large, established company and began producing a line of pocket automatic pistols that were a commercial success. By the 1930's Walther was one of the top pistol manufacturers in the world. Sporting and target rifles were still produced, but the firm was known primarily for their pistols. In 1938 the Heerespistole was chosen by the Third Reich as the new German service pistol to replace the Parabellum. During WWII the Walther factory produced military weapons under the code "480," "ac," or "qve."

At the end of the hostilities, this area of Germany was occupied by American forces; and the factory was destroyed by the liberated inmates of the Buchenwald Concentration Camp. The weapon collection located at the factory was looted and disappeared forever. This area became part of the Russian Occupation Zone, the factory was dismantled, and the machinery taken to Russia as war reparations. In the early 1950's the company was re-founded at Ulm and began producing calculators. By the 1960's they were again in the firearms business, producing as high a quality firearms as they did in their pre-War glory days.

**Model 1**

This was Walther's first semi-automatic pistol. It is chambered for 6.35mm. It has a 2" barrel that is fixed to the frame. It is blowback-operated and has fixed sights and a detachable magazine. The finish is blued, with checkered hard rubber grips.

| Exc. | V.G. | Good | Fair | Poor |
|------|------|------|------|------|
| 475 | 425 | 350 | 250 | 150 |

**Model 2**

This model is also chambered for the 6.35mm cartridge and has a coaxial recoil spring held in place by a knurled, screw-in muzzle bushing. It is fired by an internal hammer, and the rear sight acts as a loaded-chamber indicator. It is blued, with checkered rubber grips. This model was introduced in 1909.
Early Model with Pop-up Sight--Add 100 Percent.

| Exc. | V.G. | Good | Fair | Poor |
|------|------|------|------|------|
| 450 | 400 | 325 | 225 | 125 |

**Model 3**

This is basically a larger version of the Model 2 chambered for the 7.65mm cartridge. It was introduced in 1910. The ejection port is located on the left side of the slide.

| Exc. | V.G. | Good | Fair | Poor |
|------|------|------|------|------|
| 1500 | 1250 | 1000 | 750 | 500 |

**Model 4**

This is a still larger version of the Model 3 chambered for the 7.65mm cartridge. It was designed to be used as a police-type holster pistol rather than a pocket model. The butt was extended to accept an 8-shot magazine instead of the usual 6-shot. The barrel was lengthened to 3.5". This model was widely used by police forces and WWI military officers. In 1915 the German government gave Walther a contract for 250,000 of these pistols. It was introduced in 1910.

| Exc. | V.G. | Good | Fair | Poor |
|------|------|------|------|------|
| 375 | 300 | 250 | 150 | 100 |

**Model 5**

In appearance this is identical to the Model 2 but is built with better general quality. The only difference externally is the slide inscription on the Model 5, which reads "Walther's Patent Cal. 6.35." This model was introduced in 1913.

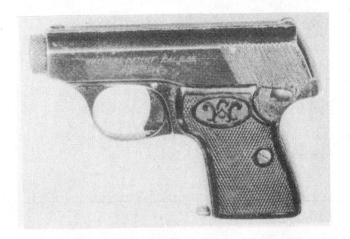

| Exc. | V.G. | Good | Fair | Poor |
|------|------|------|------|------|
| 400  | 350  | 300  | 200  | 150  |

## Model 6

This model is a larger version of the Model 4, and it is chambered for the 9mm Parabellum cartridge. It was designed as a secondary military pistol to satisfy the German army's need for 9mm service pistols. It is a blowback-operated pistol; and the army was not satisfied, as this powerful cartridge stressed this design to the very limit. It has a 3.5" barrel and an 8-shot detachable magazine. It is marked "Selbstlade Pistole Kal 9mm Walther's Patent." The ejection port was returned to the righthand side of the slide. There were only a few thousand of this model manufactured, of which very few have survived. This is the only Walther pistol that was never offered commercially. It was manufactured between 1915 and 1917.

| Exc. | V.G. | Good | Fair | Poor |
|------|------|------|------|------|
| 4000 | 3000 | 2500 | 1750 | 1000 |

## Model 7

The design of this model is quite similar to the Model 6, but it is considerably smaller and is chambered for the 6.35mm cartridge. It has a slide extension and a 3" barrel. It was manufactured between 1916 and 1918 and was used as a German staff officer's pistol. There were several thousand manufactured.

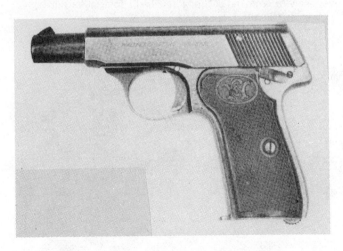

| Exc. | V.G. | Good | Fair | Poor |
|------|------|------|------|------|
| 600  | 500  | 400  | 300  | 250  |

## Model 8

This was Walther's post-WWI design. It is a blowback-operated semi-automatic chambered for the 6.35mm cartridge. It features a tapered full-length slide with a 2.75" barrel and an 8-shot detachable magazine. This was the first Walther that utilized the triggerguard as the stripping catch. It is blued, with plastic grips, and was manufactured between 1920 and 1945. This is considered to be one of the best 6.35mm pistols ever produced.

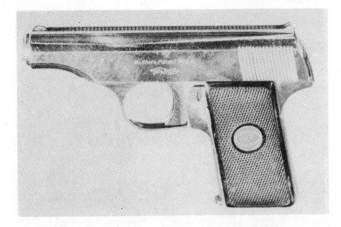

| Exc. | V.G. | Good | Fair | Poor |
|------|------|------|------|------|
| 400  | 350  | 300  | 200  | 150  |

## Model 9

This model is one of the smallest blowback-operated semi-automatic pistols ever produced. It is chambered for the 6.35mm cartridge and has a 2" barrel. The finish is blued, with plastic grips. It is striker-fired and was manufactured between 1921 and 1945.

| Exc. | V.G. | Good | Fair | Poor |
|------|------|------|------|------|
| 450  | 400  | 350  | 250  | 200  |

## Model PP

This is essentially an enlarged Model 8 with double-action lockwork and an external hammer. It is chambered for various cartridges and has a 3.75" barrel. The finish is blued or nickel-plated, with plastic grips. It has fixed sights and a detachable magazine. It has a loaded-chamber indicator and a magazine catch located behind the triggerguard. The safety catch blocks the firing pin and lowers the hammer. It was designed to be a police holster pistol. The initials PP stand for "Polizei Pistole." It made every other pocket pistol at the time obsolete and was used by police forces all over Europe in the 1930's. During WWII it was used by the German military, most notably the Luftwaffe. Wartime-finished pistols do not have the quality of finish as the commercial versions, and the loaded-chamber indicator was omitted on wartime-production guns.

It is unusual to note that the pre-War commercial markings were retained on wartime pistols, and the letter code "ac" was only used on late-production wartime pistols. There are many variations of the PP pistol, and the values fluctuate greatly from one to the other. We furnish a general listing but strongly recommend securing a qualified, individual appraisal for this highly collectible weapon.

Nickel-Plated--Add 20 Percent.
Alloy Frame--Add 20 Percent.

### .22 Caliber

| Exc. | V.G. | Good | Fair | Poor |
|---|---|---|---|---|
| 700 | 650 | 550 | 350 | 250 |

### .25 Caliber

| Exc. | V.G. | Good | Fair | Poor |
|---|---|---|---|---|
| 2500 | 2250 | 1750 | 1250 | 900 |

### .32 Caliber
Bottom Release Magazine--Add 60 Percent.

| Exc. | V.G. | Good | Fair | Poor |
|---|---|---|---|---|
| 450 | 400 | 350 | 275 | 175 |

### .380 Caliber

| Exc. | V.G. | Good | Fair | Poor |
|---|---|---|---|---|
| 850 | 750 | 650 | 500 | 400 |

### Wartime Production
There were various wartime-production versions that bear the Eagle N or Crown N proof marks, as well as other proofs and markings. These variations were produced between 1940 and 1945 and are listed as follows:

### Eagle N Proof
#### .22 Caliber

| Exc. | V.G. | Good | Fair | Poor |
|---|---|---|---|---|
| 700 | 650 | 550 | 350 | 250 |

#### .32 Caliber

| Exc. | V.G. | Good | Fair | Poor |
|---|---|---|---|---|
| 450 | 400 | 350 | 275 | 175 |

### Eagle C Marked (.32 Caliber) Nazi Police Units

| Exc. | V.G. | Good | Fair | Poor |
|---|---|---|---|---|
| 600 | 500 | 450 | 350 | 275 |

### Eagle F Marked (.32 Caliber) Forestry Police

| Exc. | V.G. | Good | Fair | Poor |
|---|---|---|---|---|
| 650 | 550 | 500 | 400 | 325 |

### NSKK Marked (.32 Caliber) Nazi Transport Corps

| Exc. | V.G. | Good | Fair | Poor |
|---|---|---|---|---|
| 1500 | 1250 | 1000 | 750 | 500 |

### SA Marked (.22 or .32 Caliber) SA Storm Troops

| Exc. | V.G. | Good | Fair | Poor |
|---|---|---|---|---|
| 1500 | 1250 | 1000 | 750 | 500 |

### PDM Marked (.32 Caliber) Postal Service

| Exc. | V.G. | Good | Fair | Poor |
|---|---|---|---|---|
| 800 | 750 | 650 | 450 | 350 |

### RJ Marked (.32 Caliber) Reich Justice Ministry

| Exc. | V.G. | Good | Fair | Poor |
|---|---|---|---|---|
| 800 | 750 | 650 | 450 | 350 |

### RFV Marked (.32 Caliber) Reich Finance Ministry

| Exc. | V.G. | Good | Fair | Poor |
|---|---|---|---|---|
| 700 | 650 | 550 | 350 | 250 |

### Czechoslovakian Contract With Rampant Lion

| Exc. | V.G. | Good | Fair | Poor |
|---|---|---|---|---|
| 800 | 750 | 650 | 450 | 350 |

### Panagraphed Slide

| Exc. | V.G. | Good | Fair | Poor |
|---|---|---|---|---|
| 800 | 750 | 650 | 450 | 350 |

### "ac" Code Late Wartime Production (1945)

| Exc. | V.G. | Good | Fair | Poor |
|---|---|---|---|---|
| 400 | 350 | 300 | 200 | 150 |

### Model PP Alloy Frame
Add 25 Percent.

### Model PPK
This version is very similar to the Model PP except that it is more compact and is designed for concealed- or pocket-carry. The butt was made without a steel backstrap, and it utilizes molded, one-piece plastic grips that form the side panels as well as the back strap. There are magazines that have a finger-spur addition mounted on the bottom plate. It is chambered for the same calibers as the Model PP and was introduced in 1930. The initials PPK stand for "Polizei Pistole Kriminal, "meaning that the pistol was designed for use by the Kripo (the detective branch of the German police force). The values are derived by the scarcity of the many variations. We list them as follows but strongly recommend securing qualified appraisal for this highly collectible firearm.

### Pre-War Production
#### .22 Caliber

| Exc. | V.G. | Good | Fair | Poor |
|---|---|---|---|---|
| 1000 | 800 | 650 | 500 | 400 |

#### .25 Caliber

| Exc. | V.G. | Good | Fair | Poor |
|---|---|---|---|---|
| 4000 | 3500 | 3000 | 2000 | 1000 |

### .32 Caliber
Bottom-Release Magazine--Add 50 Percent.

| Exc. | V.G. | Good | Fair | Poor |
|---|---|---|---|---|
| 500 | 450 | 400 | 300 | 200 |

### .380 Caliber

| Exc. | V.G. | Good | Fair | Poor |
|---|---|---|---|---|
| 1750 | 1500 | 1000 | 750 | 500 |

### Wartime Production
These pistols are either Eagle N proofed if manufactured after April of 1940 or Crown N proofed on pre-1940 specimens. The variations are as follows:

### Commercial Eagle N Proofed
This model has Waffenampt acceptance marks.

#### .22 Caliber

| Exc. | V.G. | Good | Fair | Poor |
|---|---|---|---|---|
| 800 | 750 | 650 | 450 | 350 |

#### .32 Caliber

| Exc. | V.G. | Good | Fair | Poor |
|---|---|---|---|---|
| 500 | 450 | 400 | 300 | 200 |

#### .380 Caliber

| Exc. | V.G. | Good | Fair | Poor |
|---|---|---|---|---|
| 1000 | 800 | 650 | 500 | 400 |

### Waffenampt High-Polished Finish

#### .22 Caliber

| Exc. | V.G. | Good | Fair | Poor |
|---|---|---|---|---|
| 1350 | 1100 | 950 | 750 | 600 |

#### .32 Caliber

| Exc. | V.G. | Good | Fair | Poor |
|---|---|---|---|---|
| 800 | 750 | 650 | 450 | 350 |

#### .380 Caliber

| Exc. | V.G. | Good | Fair | Poor |
|---|---|---|---|---|
| 1350 | 1100 | 950 | 750 | 600 |

### Eagle C Marked (.32 Caliber) Nazi Police
High-Polished Finish--Add 25 Percent.

| Exc. | V.G. | Good | Fair | Poor |
|---|---|---|---|---|
| 600 | 550 | 500 | 400 | 300 |

### Eagle F Marked (.32 Caliber) Forestry Police

| Exc. | V.G. | Good | Fair | Poor |
|---|---|---|---|---|
| 750 | 700 | 600 | 400 | 300 |

### Eagle L Marked (.32 Caliber) Provencial Police

| Exc. | V.G. | Good | Fair | Poor |
|---|---|---|---|---|
| 800 | 750 | 650 | 450 | 350 |

### RZM Marked (.32 Caliber) Nazi Party Purchasing Office For the SS and SA

| Exc. | V.G. | Good | Fair | Poor |
|---|---|---|---|---|
| 850 | 800 | 700 | 500 | 400 |

### PDM Marked (.32 Caliber) Postal Service

| Exc. | V.G. | Good | Fair | Poor |
|---|---|---|---|---|
| 1000 | 800 | 650 | 500 | 400 |

### RFV Marked (.32 Caliber) Reich Finance Ministry

| Exc. | V.G. | Good | Fair | Poor |
|---|---|---|---|---|
| 1000 | 800 | 650 | 500 | 400 |

### DRP Marked (.32 Caliber) Postal Service

| Exc. | V.G. | Good | Fair | Poor |
|---|---|---|---|---|
| 800 | 750 | 650 | 450 | 350 |

### Party Leader Model (.32 Cal.)
This pistol was an honor award for Third Reich political leaders. It has brown or black plastic grips that have the German eagle holding a swastika in its claws. This model has either the Crown N or the Eagle N proof marks. One must be very wary of fraudulent specimens. The grips have been known to be contemporarily manufactured. Secure a competent appraisal on this model.

| Exc. | V.G. | Good | Fair | Poor |
|---|---|---|---|---|
| 3000 | 2750 | 2250 | 1500 | 1000 |

### Panagraph Slide Model

| Exc. | V.G. | Good | Fair | Poor |
|---|---|---|---|---|
| 800 | 750 | 650 | 450 | 350 |

### W Suffix (.32 Caliber) W After Serial Number

| Exc. | V.G. | Good | Fair | Poor |
|---|---|---|---|---|
| 800 | 750 | 650 | 450 | 350 |

### K Suffix (.32 Caliber)

| Exc. | V.G. | Good | Fair | Poor |
|---|---|---|---|---|
| 600 | 550 | 450 | 350 | 250 |

### Czechoslovakian Contract with Rampant Lion

| Exc. | V.G. | Good | Fair | Poor |
|---|---|---|---|---|
| 1000 | 800 | 650 | 500 | 400 |

### Bottom Release Magazine

| Exc. | V.G. | Good | Fair | Poor |
|---|---|---|---|---|
| 1000 | 800 | 650 | 500 | 400 |

### 90 Degree Safety (.32 Caliber)

| Exc. | V.G. | Good | Fair | Poor |
|---|---|---|---|---|
| 700 | 650 | 550 | 450 | 350 |

### Stoeger Contract (Marked "AF Stoeger Inc. New York)

| Exc. | V.G. | Good | Fair | Poor |
|---|---|---|---|---|
| 800 | 750 | 650 | 450 | 350 |

### Heyer Contract (.32 Caliber) "Chas. A. Heyer & Co. Nairobi

| Exc. | V.G. | Good | Fair | Poor |
|---|---|---|---|---|
| 1250 | 1000 | 850 | 600 | 450 |

### Allemagne (.32 Commercial French)

| Exc. | V.G. | Good | Fair | Poor |
|---|---|---|---|---|
| 1000 | 800 | 650 | 500 | 400 |

### Model PPK Lightweight
This version was made of aluminum alloy.
Add 20 Percent to Standard Model Values.

### Presentation PPK
This model was constructed of soft aluminum and gold and was designed as a presentation model only and was never intended to be fired.

| Exc. | V.G. | Good | Fair | Poor |
|---|---|---|---|---|
| 2000 | 1750 | 1500 | 1000 | 750 |

The Heerespistole and the various P-38 models are listed under the German military section of this text.

### 1926 Sport Model
This is a blowback-operated semi-automatic pistol chambered for the .22 rimfire cartridge. It was a very accurate target pistol that was used to win the 1932 Olympics. It is blued, with checkered walnut grips.

| Exc. | V.G. | Good | Fair | Poor |
|---|---|---|---|---|
| 1000 | 800 | 650 | 500 | 400 |

## 1932 Target Model
This is a blowback-operated, semi-automatic target pistol chambered for .22 rimfire. It has either a 6" or 9" barrel with target sights. The finish is blued, with one-piece checkered walnut grips. It was introduced in 1928 and marketed by both Stoeger and Charles Heyer.

| Exc. | V.G. | Good | Fair | Poor |
|---|---|---|---|---|
| 1000 | 800 | 650 | 500 | 400 |

## Olympia Model
This is a blowback-operated, fixed-barrel, semi-automatic target pistol with an open-top slide and internal hammer. It has a 4", 6", 7.5", or 9" barrel. It features adjustable target sights and is blued, with checkered walnut grips. There are four barrel weights available, and their presence would add 25 percent to the listed values. It was manufactured between 1936 and 1940.

| Exc. | V.G. | Good | Fair | Poor |
|---|---|---|---|---|
| 850 | 750 | 650 | 500 | 400 |

## Olympic Jager Model
This is similar to the Olympia Model, with a 4" barrel and 10-round detachable magazine. It was manufactured between 1936 and 1940.

| Exc. | V.G. | Good | Fair | Poor |
|---|---|---|---|---|
| 800 | 750 | 650 | 450 | 350 |

## Olympia Rapid Fire Model
This version has an alloy slide and is chambered for the .22 short cartridge only. The barrel is 7.4" in length. It was manufactured between 1936 and 1940.

| Exc. | V.G. | Good | Fair | Poor |
|---|---|---|---|---|
| 800 | 750 | 650 | 450 | 350 |

## Olympia Funfkampf Model
This very high-grade, accurate target pistol is chambered for the .22 l.r. cartridge and has a 9.25" barrel, and a detachable 10-shot magazine. It has adjustable sights. The finish is blued, with checkered walnut grips. It was furnished with a set of barrel weights which, when present, would add 25 percent to the listed values. This model was manufactured in 1936.

| Exc. | V.G. | Good | Fair | Poor |
|---|---|---|---|---|
| 1000 | 800 | 650 | 500 | 400 |

## Post-War Semi-Automatic Pistols
## Model PP
This pistol is similar in configuration to the pre-War and wartime Model PP's with the same configuration and chambered for the same calibers. They were manufactured in West Germany between 1963 and 1987.

### .22 Caliber
| Exc. | V.G. | Good | Fair | Poor |
|---|---|---|---|---|
| 900 | 800 | 700 | 500 | 400 |

### .32 Caliber
| Exc. | V.G. | Good | Fair | Poor |
|---|---|---|---|---|
| 850 | 750 | 650 | 450 | 350 |

### .380 Caliber
| Exc. | V.G. | Good | Fair | Poor |
|---|---|---|---|---|
| 900 | 800 | 700 | 500 | 400 |

### French Manurhin Mfg. (All Calibers)
| Exc. | V.G. | Good | Fair | Poor |
|---|---|---|---|---|
| 400 | 350 | 300 | 250 | 200 |

The Model PP was available with factory engraving, either blued, chrome-plated, silver-plated, or gold-plated. These specimens should be individually appraised.

## 50th Anniversary Commemorative Model PP
This is a Model PP chambered for the .22 l.r. or .380 ACP cartridge. It features gold-plated parts with hand-carved walnut grips and was furnished in a presentation case with accessories. There were 500 imported into the United States in 1979.

| NIB | Exc. | V.G. | Good | Fair | Poor |
|---|---|---|---|---|---|
| 1750 | 1500 | 1200 | 950 | 750 | 500 |

## Model PP Sport
This model is similar to the PP, with a 5" barrel and adjustable sights. It features thumbrest grips.

### Walther Manufacture
| Exc. | V.G. | Good | Fair | Poor |
|---|---|---|---|---|
| 800 | 700 | 600 | 400 | 300 |

### Manurhin Manufacture
| Exc. | V.G. | Good | Fair | Poor |
|---|---|---|---|---|
| 700 | 600 | 500 | 300 | 200 |

## PP Sport Model C
This model is similar to the PP Sport but features single-action lockwork and a 7.75" barrel with a spur hammer. The finish is blued, with thumbrest grips.

| Exc. | V.G. | Good | Fair | Poor |
|---|---|---|---|---|
| 700 | 600 | 500 | 300 | 200 |

## Model PPK
The post-War PPK is similar in all respects to the pre-War and wartime-production guns. It is chambered for the same calibers. U.S. importation of this model was curtailed by passage of the Gun Control Act of 1968. The pistol was not large enough to meet our Government's criteria.

### .22 Caliber
| Exc. | V.G. | Good | Fair | Poor |
|---|---|---|---|---|
| 700 | 600 | 500 | 300 | 200 |

### .32 Caliber
| Exc. | V.G. | Good | Fair | Poor |
|---|---|---|---|---|
| 500 | 400 | 300 | 250 | 175 |

### .380 Caliber
| Exc. | V.G. | Good | Fair | Poor |
|---|---|---|---|---|
| 600 | 500 | 400 | 275 | 200 |

There were factory-engraved models that were either blued, silver-plated, or gold-plated. Qualified appraisals should be secured on these models.

## Model PPK Lightweight
This model is similar to the standard steel-framed version, with a dural alloy frame. It is chambered for .22 l.r. and the .32 ACP cartridge. The .22-rimfire version is worth a 25 percent premium.

| Exc. | V.G. | Good | Fair | Poor |
|------|------|------|------|------|
| 600 | 500 | 400 | 275 | 200 |

## U.S. Mfg. Model PPK
In 1986 the firm of Interarms began manufacturing this model under a licensing agreement with Walther of Germany. The specifications and quality of materials and workmanship are very similar to the original German-manufactured pistol. It is available both in a blued finish and in stainless steel.

| NIB | Exc. | V.G. | Good | Fair | Poor |
|-----|------|------|------|------|------|
| 550 | 500 | 400 | 350 | 275 | 200 |

## Model PPK/S
When the U.S. Gun Control Act of 1968 banned the import of the PPK, the Model PPK/S was introduced to meet the requirements of the import law. It is basically the PPK slide on the larger PP frame. It has a 3.25" barrel and is chambered for the same cartridges as the Model PPK.

**West German Mfg.**

| NIB | Exc. | V.G. | Good | Fair | Poor |
|-----|------|------|------|------|------|
| 600 | 500 | 400 | 275 | 200 | 175 |

**American Mfg. (Blue)**

| NIB | Exc. | V.G. | Good | Fair | Poor |
|-----|------|------|------|------|------|
| 550 | 450 | 375 | 225 | 175 | 150 |

**American Mfg. .380 Only (Stainless Steel)**

| NIB | Exc. | V.G. | Good | Fair | Poor |
|-----|------|------|------|------|------|
| 550 | 450 | 375 | 325 | 175 | 150 |

**Manurhin Mfg.**

| NIB | Exc. | V.G. | Good | Fair | Poor |
|-----|------|------|------|------|------|
| 400 | 350 | 275 | 225 | 150 | 100 |

## PPK/S Durgarde Manurhin
This model was manufactured in France and features a brushed-satin chrome finish. It is available in .22 l.r. or .380 ACP. It was manufactured under license from Walther.

| NIB | Exc. | V.G. | Good | Fair | Poor |
|-----|------|------|------|------|------|
| 400 | 350 | 275 | 225 | 150 | 100 |

There were various factory-engraved PPK/S pistols available either blued, chrome, or silver- or gold-plated. We recommend securing a qualified appraisal when contemplating purchase of these pistols.

## Model TP
This is a blowback-operated pocket pistol chambered for the .22 l.r. or .25 ACP cartridges. It is a modernized version of the original Model 9 and has a concealed hammer. The finish is blued, with checkered plastic grips. It was manufactured between 1962 and 1970. Its importation into the United States was stopped by the GCA-68.

**.22 Caliber**

| Exc. | V.G. | Good | Fair | Poor |
|------|------|------|------|------|
| 750 | 650 | 550 | 400 | 250 |

**.25 Caliber**

| Exc. | V.G. | Good | Fair | Poor |
|------|------|------|------|------|
| 500 | 400 | 350 | 300 | 200 |

## Model TPH
This is a blowback-operated, double-action, semi-automatic pocket pistol chambered for the .22 l.r. or .25 ACP cartridges. It has a 2.8" barrel with an aluminum-alloy frame. It features fixed sights; and the finish was blued, with plastic grips. It has been manufactured in West Germany from 1969. GCA-68 will not allow its import into the United States.

**.22 Caliber**

| NIB | Exc. | V.G. | Good | Fair | Poor |
|-----|------|------|------|------|------|
| 650 | 550 | 450 | 350 | 300 | 225 |

**.25 Caliber**

| NIB | Exc. | V.G. | Good | Fair | Poor |
|-----|------|------|------|------|------|
| 600 | 500 | 400 | 275 | 200 | 175 |

## Model TPH American
This version is constructed of stainless steel, is chambered for .22 l.r., has a 2.25" barrel, and is manufactured in America under license from Walther of Germany. It was introduced in 1987.

| NIB | Exc. | V.G. | Good | Fair | Poor |
|-----|------|------|------|------|------|
| 400 | 375 | 325 | 300 | 200 | 150 |

## Model PP Super
This is a police-type holster pistol that is a double-action, blowback-operated semi-automatic chambered for the 9x18mm or the .380 ACP cartridges. It has a 3.6" barrel with fixed sights. The finish is blued, with plastic grips. It was manufactured between 1975 and 1981.

| Exc. | V.G. | Good | Fair | Poor |
|------|------|------|------|------|
| 500 | 450 | 400 | 300 | 200 |

### Model P-38

This model was the standard service pistol in WWII Germany. The values and description of these military models will be found in the section dealing with German military weapons. There were a number of commercial models produced, and they are covered here. The post-War P-38 is chambered for .22 l.r., .30 Luger, or 9mm Parabellum. It has a 5" barrel with fixed sights and a matte black, anodized alloy frame. A steel-framed version is also available. The grips are molded plastic. Its form and function are similar to the wartime-production pistols. The finishes, of course, show a commercial polish.

**.22 Caliber**

| NIB | Exc. | V.G. | Good | Fair | Poor |
|-----|------|------|------|------|------|
| 1000 | 800 | 650 | 500 | 350 | 200 |

**Other Calibers**

| NIB | Exc. | V.G. | Good | Fair | Poor |
|-----|------|------|------|------|------|
| 600 | 500 | 450 | 400 | 300 | 200 |

**Steel-Framed (Introduced 1987)**

| NIB | Exc. | V.G. | Good | Fair | Poor |
|-----|------|------|------|------|------|
| 1400 | 1250 | 1000 | 750 | 500 | 400 |

There was also a factory-engraved version of the P-38 pistol that was either blued, chrome, or silver- or gold plated. We suggest that a qualified appraisal be secured when contemplating purchase.

### Model P-38K

This is a compact, concealable version of the P-38 with a 2.8" barrel. The front sight is mounted on the slide. It was imported between 1974 and 1980.

| Exc. | V.G. | Good | Fair | Poor |
|------|------|------|------|------|
| 600 | 500 | 450 | 400 | 300 |

### P-38 IV

This is an upgraded version of the P-38, chambered for 9mm Parabellum. It has a 4.5" barrel and an 8-shot, detachable box magazine. It has a steel slide and a lightweight alloy frame. It features a de-cocking lever and adjustable sights. The finish is blued, with plastic grips. It was not imported after 1982.

| Exc. | V.G. | Good | Fair | Poor |
|------|------|------|------|------|
| 600 | 500 | 450 | 400 | 300 |

### Model P-5

This is a double-action, semi-automatic pistol chambered for 9mm Parabellum. It has a 3.5" barrel with adjustable sights and a de-cocking lever. The finish is blued, with plastic grips.

| NIB | Exc. | V.G. | Good | Fair | Poor |
|-----|------|------|------|------|------|
| 800 | 750 | 650 | 500 | 400 | 300 |

### P-5 Compact

This is a smaller, more-concealable version of the P-5 pistol.

| NIB | V.G. | Good | Fair | Poor |
|-----|------|------|------|------|
| 1100 | 950 | 750 | 600 | 450 |

### 100th Year Commemorative P-5

This is a heavily engraved version of the P-5 pistol that was furnished in a walnut presentation case. It was introduced in 1987. As with all commemorative pistols, it must be NIB with all furnished materials to bring the top value.

| NIB | Exc. | V.G. | Good | Fair | Poor |
|-----|------|------|------|------|------|
| 2500 | 2000 | 1500 | 1200 | 800 | 600 |

### P-88

This is a double-action semi-automatic pistol chambered for the 9mm Parabellum cartridge. It has a 4" barrel with adjustable sights. It features a 15-shot double-stack magazine, a loaded-chamber indicator, and ambidextrous de-cocking lever. It has a lightweight alloy frame and is matte black finished, with black synthetic grips. It was introduced in 1987.

| NIB | Exc. | V.G. | Good | Fair | Poor |
|-----|------|------|------|------|------|
| 1200 | 1000 | 800 | 650 | 500 | 450 |

## Model GSP Target Pistol

This is a high-grade, extremely accurate, semi-automatic target pistol chambered for the .22 l.r. cartridge. It has a 4.5" barrel with adjustable sights. It has a 5-shot detachable magazine. The finish is blued, with walnut target grips. It is furnished with a fitted carrying case.

| NIB | Exc. | V.G. | Good | Fair | Poor |
|------|------|------|------|------|------|
| 1500 | 1250 | 1000 | 700 | 600 | 500 |

## Model GSP-C

This pistol is similar to the Model GSP except that it is chambered for the .32 Smith & Wesson Wadcutter cartridge.

| NIB | Exc. | V.G. | Good | Fair | Poor |
|------|------|------|------|------|------|
| 1650 | 1400 | 1100 | 800 | 700 | 600 |

## Model OSP Rapid Fire

This version is chambered for the .22 short cartridge only. It was introduced in 1968.

| NIB | Exc. | V.G. | Good | Fair | Poor |
|------|------|------|------|------|------|
| 1500 | 1250 | 1000 | 700 | 600 | 500 |

## Free Pistol

This is a highly sophisticated, single-shot target pistol. It is chambered for the .22 l.r. cartridge. It has an 11.7" heavy barrel with micrometer-adjustable target sights and fully adjustable grips. It features an advanced electronic trigger. The finish is blued.

| NIB | Exc. | V.G. | Good | Fair | Poor |
|------|------|------|------|------|------|
| 1800 | 1550 | 1200 | 900 | 700 | 550 |

## Model B

This is a bolt-action sporting rifle chambered for the .30-06 cartridge. It has a 22" barrel and a 4-round box magazine. It was offered with double-set triggers that would be worth a 20 percent premium. The finish is blued, with a checkered walnut stock.

| Exc. | V.G. | Good | Fair | Poor |
|------|------|------|------|------|
| 450 | 400 | 350 | 250 | 175 |

## Olympic Single Shot

This is a bolt-action target rifle chambered for the .22 l.r. cartridge. It has a 26" heavy barrel with adjustable target sights. The finish is blued, with a checkered walnut stock that features a palm rest and an adjustable buttplate. This model was discontinued before WWII.

| Exc. | V.G. | Good | Fair | Poor |
|------|------|------|------|------|
| 950 | 850 | 700 | 500 | 400 |

## Model V

This is a bolt-action single-shot rifle chambered for the .22 l.r. cartridge. It has a 26" barrel with adjustable sights and an unchecked walnut stock. It was manufactured before WWII.

| Exc. | V.G. | Good | Fair | Poor |
|------|------|------|------|------|
| 400 | 350 | 300 | 200 | 150 |

## Model V Champion

This is similar to the standard rifle, with a checkered walnut stock and adjustable target sights.

| Exc. | V.G. | Good | Fair | Poor |
|------|------|------|------|------|
| 450 | 400 | 350 | 250 | 200 |

## Model KKM International Match

This is a bolt-action, single-shot target rifle chambered for the .22 l.r. cartridge. It has a 28" heavy barrel with adjustable target sights. The finish is blued, with a walnut stock that features an accessory rail and an adjustable buttplate. It was manufactured after WWII.

| Exc. | V.G. | Good | Fair | Poor |
|------|------|------|------|------|
| 900 | 800 | 650 | 450 | 350 |

## Model KKM-S

This version is similar to the KKM, with an adjustable cheekpiece.

| Exc. | V.G. | Good | Fair | Poor |
|------|------|------|------|------|
| 950 | 850 | 700 | 500 | 400 |

## Model KKW

This version features a military-type stock.

| Exc. | V.G. | Good | Fair | Poor |
|------|------|------|------|------|
| 550 | 500 | 450 | 350 | 300 |

## Model KKJ Sporter

This is a bolt-action repeater that is chambered for the .22 l.r. cartridge. It has a 22.5" barrel with open sights and a 5-shot detachable magazine. The finish is blued, with a checkered walnut stock. Double-set triggers were available and would add 20 percent to the values given. This model was manufactured after WWII.

| Exc. | V.G. | Good | Fair | Poor |
|------|------|------|------|------|
| 550 | 500 | 450 | 350 | 300 |

## Model KKJ-MA

This version is chambered for the .22 rimfire Magnum cartridge.

| Exc. | V.G. | Good | Fair | Poor |
|------|------|------|------|------|
| 550 | 500 | 450 | 350 | 300 |

## Model KKJ-HO

This version is chambered for the centerfire .22 Hornet cartridge.

| Exc. | V.G. | Good | Fair | Poor |
|------|------|------|------|------|
| 750 | 700 | 600 | 450 | 350 |

## Model SSV Varmint

This is a single-shot bolt-action rifle chambered for the .22 l.r. cartridge. It has a 25.5" barrel with no sights furnished. The finish is blued, with a Monte Carlo-type walnut stock. This model was manufactured after WWII.

| Exc. | V.G. | Good | Fair | Poor |
|------|------|------|------|------|
| 600 | 550 | 475 | 375 | 300 |

## Model UIT BV Universal

This is a single-shot, bolt-action target rifle chambered for the .22 l.r. cartridge. It has a 25.5" heavy barrel with adjustable aperture sights. The finish is blued, with a walnut target-type stock with an adjustable buttplate and palmrest.

| NIB | Exc. | V.G. | Good | Fair | Poor |
|-----|------|------|------|------|------|
| 1750 | 1500 | 1250 | 900 | 650 | 500 |

## Model UIT Match

This version features a modified stock design with a stippled forearm and pistol grip. It is also available as the Model UIT-E with an electronic trigger that is worth approximately $50 additional.

| NIB | Exc. | V.G. | Good | Fair | Poor |
|-----|------|------|------|------|------|
| 1250 | 1000 | 750 | 600 | 450 | 400 |

## GX 1

This version is similar to the UIT Match, with an adjustable free-rifle type stock.

| NIB | Exc. | V.G. | Good | Fair | Poor |
|-----|------|------|------|------|------|
| 2250 | 2000 | 1750 | 1250 | 850 | 700 |

## Prone Model 400

This version is similar to the UIT Match, with a prone-type competition stock, and is furnished without sights.

| NIB | Exc. | V.G. | Good | Fair | Poor |
|-----|------|------|------|------|------|
| 750 | 700 | 600 | 450 | 350 | 300 |

## Model KK/MS Silhouette

This is a bolt-action target rifle chambered for the .22 l.r. cartridge. It is designed for silhouette shooting and has a 25.5" front-weighted barrel without sights. It features a thumbhole stock with an adjustable buttplate and stippled forend and pistolgrip. It was introduced in 1984.

| NIB | Exc. | V.G. | Good | Fair | Poor |
|-----|------|------|------|------|------|
| 1150 | 1000 | 850 | 700 | 550 | 400 |

## Running Boar Model 500

This model is similar to the Silhouette rifle, with a 23.5" barrel.

| NIB | Exc. | V.G. | Good | Fair | Poor |
|-----|------|------|------|------|------|
| 1350 | 1150 | 950 | 750 | 600 | 450 |

## Model WA-2000

This is a bolt-action repeating rifle chambered for the .308 or .300 Winchester Magnum cartridges. It was an extremely high-grade, custom-ordered rifle; and qualified appraisal is recommended as the options available have an effect on value. This model was not imported after 1988.

| Exc. | V.G. | Good | Fair | Poor |
|------|------|------|------|------|
| 6500 | 4750 | 3500 | 3000 | 2000 |

## Model SF

This is a side-by-side double-barreled shotgun chambered for 12 or 16 gauge with various choke combinations. It features a boxlock action with double triggers and extractors. The finish is blued, with a checkered, select walnut stock with sling swivels. This model is no longer imported.

| Exc. | V.G. | Good | Fair | Poor |
|------|------|------|------|------|
| 500 | 450 | 350 | 250 | 200 |

## Model SFD

This model is similar to the SF, with a cheekpiece on the walnut buttstock. It is also no longer imported.

| Exc. | V.G. | Good | Fair | Poor |
|------|------|------|------|------|
| 650 | 600 | 525 | 425 | 350 |

# WALTHER MANURHIN
## Mulhouse, France

The Manurhin-manufactured Walther pistols are listed in the Walther section of this text under their respective model headings.

# WARNANT, L. AND J.
## Ognee, Belgium

## Revolver

This company was established by the Warnant brothers in the late Nineteenth Century. Between 1870 and 1890 they manufactured hinged-frame, break-open pistols patterned after the Smith & Wesson designs. For the most part, they are chambered for .32, .38, and .45 caliber cartridges. They have round barrels of various lengths and automatic ejector systems. The quality is mediocre, and there is not a lot of collector interest in these pistols. They are valued in a similar manner.

| Exc. | V.G. | Good | Fair | Poor |
|------|------|------|------|------|
| 125 | 100 | 75 | 60 | 50 |

## Semi-Automatic Pistol

This is a blowback-operated, semi-automatic pocket pistol chambered for the 6.35mm cartridge. It features a steel receiver pinned to the frame. The barrel is fixed, and a separate bolt reciprocates within the receiver. It is actually an early example of an over-hung bolt design. The barrel is 2.5" in length, and it has a 5-shot detachable magazine. It is stamped "L&J Warnant Bte 6.35mm." The finish is blued, and the plastic grips have the monogram "L&JW." This pistol was introduced in 1908, and there were fewer than 2,000 manufactured.

| Exc. | V.G. | Good | Fair | Poor |
|------|------|------|------|------|
| 250 | 200 | 150 | 100 | 75 |

## 1912 Model
This is a blowback-operated semi-automatic pistol patterned after the 1903 Browning design. It is chambered for the 7.65mm cartridge and has a 3" barrel and a 7-shot detachable magazine. The slide is marked "L&J Warnant Brevetes Pist Auto 7.65mm." Before this pistol became established, WWI put a stop to its production.

| Exc. | V.G. | Good | Fair | Poor |
|------|------|------|------|------|
| 250 | 200 | 150 | 100 | 75 |

# WARNER ARMS CORPORATION
### Brooklyn, New York

The Warner Arms company was formed in 1912 and purchased the remaining inventory of the 1908 Schwarzlose pistols from Berlin, Germany. This pistol was marketed as the Warner in the United States sometimes with and sometimes without the Schwarzlose markings. This was not a successful enterprise, and in 1913 production ceased. At this time the rights to manufacture a semi-automatic pistol invented by Andrew Fyrberg was purchased. This pistol was marketed as the Infallible. At this time the company moved to Norwich, Connecticut, and began serious manufacture. In 1917 they merged with another company and became the Davis-Warner Arms Company and moved to Assonet, Massachusetts. They went out of business in 1919.

### Revolver
This is an unremarkable, double-action, break-open revolver chambered for the .32 centerfire cartridge. It has a 3.5" round ribbed barrel and a 5-shot cylinder. The quality is mediocre, and it is very similar to the scores of other like revolvers produced during this period.

| Exc. | V.G. | Good | Fair | Poor |
|------|------|------|------|------|
| 150 | 125 | 100 | 75 | 50 |

### Infallible
This is a blowback-operated, single-action, semi-automatic pocket pistol that utilizes a reciprocating bolt within a fixed receiver. It is striker-fired. It is chambered for the .32 ACP cartridge and has a 3" barrel with fixed sights. It has a 7-round detachable box magazine. The design was not very reliable, and the pistol was not a commercial success. The finish is blued, with checkered hard rubber grips. There were approximately 7,000 manufactured between 1913 and 1919.

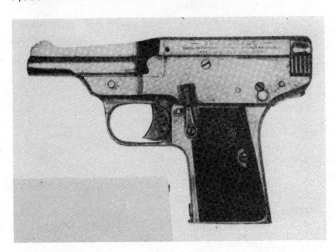

| Exc. | V.G. | Good | Fair | Poor |
|------|------|------|------|------|
| 350 | 300 | 250 | 150 | 100 |

# WARNER, CHAS.
### Windsor Locks, Connecticut
### Pocket Revolver
This is a single-action pocket revolver chambered for .31-caliber percussion. It has a 3" round barrel and a 6-shot unfluted cylinder. The cylinder is marked "Charles Warner. Windsor Locks, Conn." The finish is blued, with two-piece walnut grips. There were approximately 600 manufactured between 1857 and 1860.

| Exc. | V.G. | Good | Fair | Poor |
|------|------|------|------|------|
| 550 | 500 | 400 | 300 | 200 |

# WARNER, JAMES
### Springfield, Massachusetts
### Revolving Carbines
There are a number of different versions in the design of these revolving carbines. They are nearly all found in .40-caliber percussion with octagonal barrels between 20" and 24" in length. They all feature 6-shot cylinders. Most encountered are in quite well-used condition. These variations are as follows:

### Manually Revolved Grooved Cylinder
This version has a hook-type cylinder release located in front of the trigger. It appears to have two triggers. This release has to be depressed and the cylinder manually revolved for each successive shot. There is no loading lever. It is marked "James Walner/Springfield Mass." The finish is blued, with a walnut stock with patchbox. It has no forearm. There were approximately 75 manufactured in 1849.

| Exc. | V.G. | Good | Fair | Poor |
|------|------|------|------|------|
| 2000 | 1750 | 1500 | 1000 | 800 |

### Retractable Cylinder Model
This version has a cylinder that fits over the breech, and it must be retracted before it can be manually rotated. The cylinder release is a button located in front of the trigger. It is marked "James Warner/Springfield Mass" and with an eagle over the letters "U.S." The cylinder is etched, and there is no loading lever. It also has a walnut stock with patchbox and no forearm. There were approximately 25 manufactured in 1849.

| Exc. | V.G. | Good | Fair | Poor |
|------|------|------|------|------|
| 4500 | 3750 | 3000 | 2000 | 1500 |

### Automatic Revolving Cylinder
This version was manufactured by the Springfield Arms Company, which followed James Warner. It features an automatic revolving cylinder and an integral loading lever mounted under the barrel. It is marked "Warner's Patent/Jan. 1851" and "Springfield Arms Co." It has a walnut stock without the patchbox. There were approximately 200 manufactured in the 1850's.

| Exc. | V.G. | Good | Fair | Poor |
|------|------|------|------|------|
| 2000 | 1750 | 1500 | 1000 | 800 |

### Belt Revolver
This is a double-action, solid-frame revolver chambered for .31-caliber percussion. It is offered with a 4", 5", or 6" round barrel and an etched, 6-shot unfluted cylinder. The finish is blued, with two-piece walnut grips. There are no markings except the serial number. It was made in 1851.

| Exc. | V.G. | Good | Fair | Poor |
|------|------|------|------|------|
| 650 | 600 | 500 | 375 | 300 |

### Pocket Revolver
This single-action pocket revolver was produced in several different versions. The first model is chambered for .28-caliber percussion, has a 3" octagonal barrel, and is marked "James Warner Springfield Mass USA." It has a six-shot cylinder with the stop notches on the rear and is blued, with walnut grips. There were approximately 500 manufactured.

| Exc. | V.G. | Good | Fair | Poor |
|------|------|------|------|------|
| 600 | 550 | 450 | 400 | 350 |

### Second Model

This version is very similar to the first model, with the cylinder-stop notches on the side of the cylinder. The barrel lengths are either 3" or 4". Markings are "Warner's Patent 1857."

| Exc. | V.G. | Good | Fair | Poor |
|------|------|------|------|------|
| 500 | 450 | 400 | 300 | 250 |

### Third Model

This is similar to the Second Model except that it is chambered for .31-caliber percussion.

| Exc. | V.G. | Good | Fair | Poor |
|------|------|------|------|------|
| 450 | 400 | 350 | 250 | 200 |

### Single Shot Derringer

This is a single-shot pocket pistol chambered for the .41 rimfire cartridge. It has a 2.75" round barrel and a brass frame. It has a large breechblock that lifts upward and to the left for loading. The finish is blued, with walnut birdshead grips. This pistol is quite rare and was manufactured circa 1865. They are not marked.

| Exc. | V.G. | Good | Fair | Poor |
|------|------|------|------|------|
| 3500 | 2750 | 2250 | 1500 | 1250 |

### Pocket Revolver

This single-action revolver is chambered for the .30-caliber rimfire cartridge. It has a 3" round barrel and a 5-shot unfluted cylinder and utilizes the cylinder axis pin as an ejector. It is marked "Warner's Patent 1857." The finish is blued or nickel-plated, with two-piece walnut grips. There were approximately 1,000 manufactured in the late 1860's.

| Exc. | V.G. | Good | Fair | Poor |
|------|------|------|------|------|
| 450 | 400 | 350 | 250 | 150 |

# WEATHERBY
## South Gate, California

This corporation was founded in 1945 by Roy Weatherby. He pioneered the high-velocity hunting rifle. His rifles were designed to fire cartridges that he also produced. They are examples of fine craftsmanship and have been used to take some of the top trophy animals from all around the world. Formerly these rifles were manufactured in West Germany. They are currently produced in Japan. Although the Japanese rifles are, in my opinion, every bit as fine a weapon as the German versions, collectors have dictated an approximate 25 percent premium assessed to the German-manufactured versions. The values given are for the current-production Japanese weapons. Simply add the premium for a German-manufactured rifle.

### Mark V

This is a deluxe, bolt-action repeating rifle chambered for various popular standard calibers, as well as the full line of Weatherby cartridges from .240 Weatherby Magnum to .300 Weatherby Magnum. It is furnished with either a 24" or 26" barrel without sights. It has either a 3- or 5-round magazine, depending on the caliber. It has a deluxe, high-polish blued finish with a select, skip-line checkered walnut stock with a rosewood forearm tip and pistol-grip cap. This rifle is available with a lefthand action.

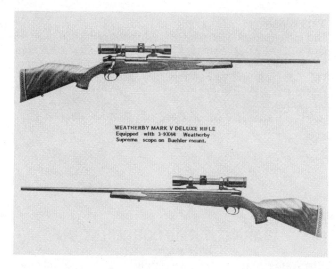

WEATHERBY MARK V DELUXE RIFLE
Equipped with 3-9X44 Weatherby
Supreme scope on Buehler mount.

| NIB | Exc. | V.G. | Good | Fair | Poor |
|-----|------|------|------|------|------|
| 1000 | 850 | 700 | 600 | 500 | 400 |

### Mark V .340 Weatherby Magnum

This version is chambered for a larger Magnum cartridge and is offered with the 26" barrel only.

| NIB | Exc. | V.G. | Good | Fair | Poor |
|-----|------|------|------|------|------|
| 1050 | 900 | 750 | 650 | 550 | 450 |

### Mark V .375 Weatherby Magnum

This version was manufactured in Germany only and is chambered for the currently obsolete .375 Weatherby Magnum cartridge. This version has become very collectible.

| Exc. | V.G. | Good | Fair | Poor |
|------|------|------|------|------|
| 1250 | 1150 | 900 | 750 | 600 |

### Mark V .378 Weatherby Magnum

This version is chambered for the .378 Weatherby Magnum cartridge and is considered to be one of the most powerful rifles currently available in the world. It is furnished with a 26" barrel only.

| NIB | Exc. | V.G. | Good | Fair | Poor |
|-----|------|------|------|------|------|
| 1200 | 1100 | 850 | 700 | 550 | 500 |

### Mark V .416 Weatherby Magnum

This is an extremely powerful rifle suitable for hunting the biggest game. It is the first new caliber to be released by Weatherby since 1965. It was introduced in 1989.

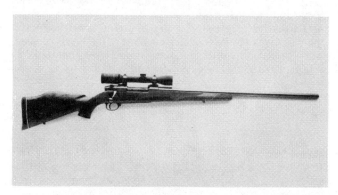

| NIB | Exc. | V.G. | Good | Fair | Poor |
|-----|------|------|------|------|------|
| 1250 | 1150 | 900 | 750 | 600 | 500 |

### Mark V .460 Weatherby Magnum

This is the most powerful commercial rifle available in the world. It is considered to be overkill for any game except the largest and most dangerous creatures that roam the African continent. It is available with a 24" or 26" heavy barrel with an integral, recoil-reducing muzzle brake. It has a custom reinforced stock.

| NIB | Exc. | V.G. | Good | Fair | Poor |
|-----|------|------|------|------|------|
| 1350 | 1200 | 1000 | 800 | 650 | 550 |

## Mark V Varmint

This version is chambered for the .22-250 and the .224 Weatherby cartridge. It is offered with a 24" or 26" heavy barrel.

| NIB | Exc. | V.G. | Good | Fair | Poor |
|-----|------|------|------|------|------|
| 975 | 800 | 750 | 550 | 450 | 400 |

## Mark V Euromark

This model features a hand-checkered, oil-finished, claro walnut stock with an ebony forend tip and pistol-grip cap. It has a satin blued finish. It was introduced in 1986.

| NIB | Exc. | V.G. | Good | Fair | Poor |
|-----|------|------|------|------|------|
| 1050 | 900 | 750 | 650 | 550 | 450 |

## Mark V Lazermark

This version had a laser-carved pattern on the stock and forearm in place of the usual checkering. It was introduced in 1985.

| NIB | Exc. | V.G. | Good | Fair | Poor |
|-----|------|------|------|------|------|
| 1100 | 1000 | 800 | 700 | 600 | 500 |

## Mark V Fibermark

This version has a matte blue finish and was furnished with a synthetic black, wrinkle-finished stock.

| NIB | Exc. | V.G. | Good | Fair | Poor |
|-----|------|------|------|------|------|
| 1150 | 1000 | 850 | 750 | 650 | 550 |

## Mark V Ultramark

This is a custom-finished version with a glass-bedded action and a special, high-polish blue. The action is hand-honed, and the walnut stock features basketweave checkering. It was introduced in 1989.

| NIB | Exc. | V.G. | Good | Fair | Poor |
|-----|------|------|------|------|------|
| 1250 | 1150 | 900 | 750 | 600 | 500 |

## 35th Anniversary Commemorative Mark V

This specially embellished rifle that commemorated the 35th anniversary of the company. There were 1,000 produced in 1980. As with all commemoratives, it must be NIB with all furnished materials to be worth top dollar.

| NIB | Exc. | V.G. | Good | Fair | Poor |
|-----|------|------|------|------|------|
| 1250 | 1150 | 900 | 750 | 600 | 500 |

## 1984 Olympic Commemorative Mark V

This is a specially embellished Mark V rifle that has gold-plated accents and an exhibition-grade walnut stock with a star inlay. There were 1,000 manufactured in 1984. This is a commemorative rifle and must be NIB to bring premium value.

| NIB | Exc. | V.G. | Good | Fair | Poor |
|-----|------|------|------|------|------|
| 2200 | 1800 | 1500 | 1000 | 800 | 650 |

## Safari Grade Mark V

This is a custom-order version that is available chambered from the .300 Weatherby Magnum through the .460 Weatherby Magnum. It is available with a number of custom options and can be ordered with an 8- to 10-month delivery delay.

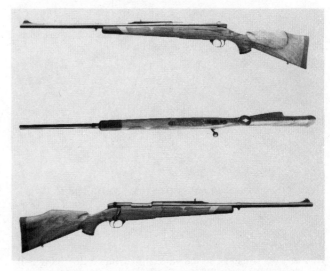

| NIB | Exc. | V.G. | Good | Fair | Poor |
|-----|------|------|------|------|------|
| 3000 | 2750 | 2000 | 1750 | 1400 | 1200 |

## Crown Grade Mark V

This is Weatherby's best-grade rifle and is available on a custom-order basis only. It features an engraved receiver and barrel with an exhibition-grade, hand-checkered walnut stock. It is also furnished with an engraved scope mount.

| NIB | Exc. | V.G. | Good | Fair | Poor |
|-----|------|------|------|------|------|
| 4500 | 3500 | 2750 | 2250 | 1750 | 1400 |

## Vanguard VGX

This is Weatherby's Japanese-manufactured economy rifle. It is chambered for various popular standard American cartridges from .22-50 to the .300 Winchester Magnum cartridge. It is a bolt-action repeater with a 24" barrel furnished without sights. It has either a 3-shot or 5-shot magazine; and the finish is polished blue, with a select, checkered walnut stock with a rosewood forend tip and pistol-grip cap. This model was discontinued in 1988.

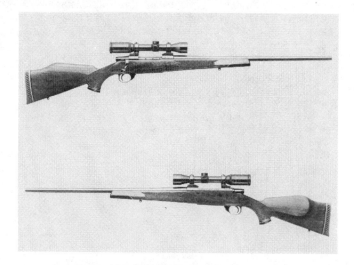

| Exc. | V.G. | Good | Fair | Poor |
|------|------|------|------|------|
| 500 | 400 | 350 | 300 | 250 |

## Vanguard VGS
This satin-finish version was also discontinued in 1988.

| Exc. | V.G. | Good | Fair | Poor |
|------|------|------|------|------|
| 450 | 350 | 300 | 250 | 200 |

## Vanguard VGL
This is a lightweight carbine version that has a 20" barrel. It was discontinued in 1988.

| Exc. | V.G. | Good | Fair | Poor |
|------|------|------|------|------|
| 450 | 350 | 300 | 250 | 200 |

## Fiberguard
This version has a matte-blued finish with a green fiberglas stock. It was discontinued in 1988.

| Exc. | V.G. | Good | Fair | Poor |
|------|------|------|------|------|
| 500 | 400 | 350 | 300 | 250 |

## Vanguard Classic I
This version is chambered for various popular standard calibers and has a 24" barrel and either a 3- or 5-shot magazine. It has a satin blue finish and a select checkered, oil-finished walnut stock. It was introduced in 1989.

| NIB | Exc. | V.G. | Good | Fair | Poor |
|-----|------|------|------|------|------|
| 475 | 400 | 375 | 300 | 250 | 200 |

## Vanguard Classic II
This is a more deluxe version with a higher-grade walnut stock.

| NIB | Exc. | V.G. | Good | Fair | Poor |
|-----|------|------|------|------|------|
| 600 | 550 | 475 | 400 | 300 | 250 |

## Vanguard VGX Deluxe
This version has a high gloss, Monte Carlo-type stock and a high polished blued finish. It was introduced in 1989.

| NIB | Exc. | V.G. | Good | Fair | Poor |
|-----|------|------|------|------|------|
| 600 | 550 | 475 | 400 | 300 | 250 |

## Vanguard Weatherguard
This version has a wrinkle-finished, black synthetic stock. It was introduced in 1989.

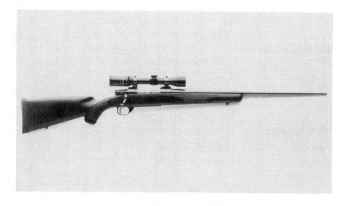

| NIB | Exc. | V.G. | Good | Fair | Poor |
|-----|------|------|------|------|------|
| 400 | 300 | 250 | 200 | 175 | 125 |

## Mark XXII
This is a semi-automatic rifle chambered for the .22 l.r. cartridge. There are two versions--one with a detachable magazine and the other with a tubular magazine. It has a 24" barrel with adjustable sights and a select checkered walnut stock with a rosewood forearm tip and pistol-grip cap. This model was originally produced in Italy and is currently manufactured in Japan.

| NIB | Exc. | V.G. | Good | Fair | Poor |
|-----|------|------|------|------|------|
| 450 | 350 | 300 | 250 | 200 | 150 |

## Centurion
This is a gas-operated semi-automatic shotgun chambered for 12 gauge. It is offered with various barrel lengths and chokes. It has a checkered walnut stock. It was manufactured between 1972 and 1981.

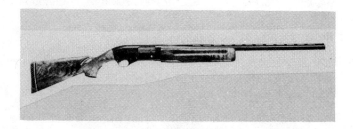

| Exc. | V.G. | Good | Fair | Poor |
|------|------|------|------|------|
| 350 | 300 | 250 | 200 | 150 |

## Centurion Deluxe
This version is slightly engraved and features a vent-ribbed barrel and higher-grade wood.

| Exc. | V.G. | Good | Fair | Poor |
|------|------|------|------|------|
| 375 | 325 | 275 | 225 | 175 |

## Model 82
This is a gas-operated semi-automatic shotgun chambered for 12 gauge with 2.75" or 3" chambers. It has various barrel lengths with vent ribs and screw-in choke tubes. It features an alloy receiver and a deluxe, checkered walnut stock. It is also available as the Buckmaster with a 22" open-choked barrel. This model was introduced in 1983.

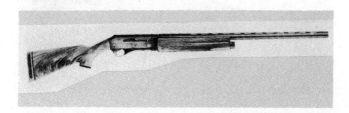

| NIB | Exc. | V.G. | Good | Fair | Poor |
|-----|------|------|------|------|------|
| 500 | 450 | 400 | 350 | 300 | 250 |

## Patrician
This is a slide-action shotgun chambered for 12 gauge. It is offered with various barrel lengths and choke combinations. It has a vent-rib barrel, a blued finish, and a checkered walnut stock. It was manufactured between 1972 and 1981.

| Exc. | V.G. | Good | Fair | Poor |
|------|------|------|------|------|
| 300 | 250 | 225 | 175 | 125 |

## Patrician Deluxe
This is a slightly engraved version with fancier-grade walnut.

| Exc. | V.G. | Good | Fair | Poor |
|------|------|------|------|------|
| 350 | 300 | 250 | 200 | 150 |

## Model 92
This is a slide-action shotgun chambered for 12 gauge with 2.75" or 3" chambers. It is offered with 26", 28", or 30" vent-rib barrels with screw-in choke tubes. It features a short, twin-rail slide action and an engraved alloy receiver. The finish is blued, with a deluxe checkered walnut stock. A Buckmaster model with a 22" open-choke barrel and rifle sights is also available.

| NIB | Exc. | V.G. | Good | Fair | Poor |
|-----|------|------|------|------|------|
| 350 | 300 | 250 | 200 | 175 | 125 |

## Regency Field Grade
This is an Over/Under double-barrelled shotgun chambered for 12 or 20 gauge. It has various length vent-ribbed barrels and a boxlock action with engraved false side plates. It features a single selective trigger and automatic ejectors. The finish is blued, with a checkered walnut stock. This model was imported from Italy between 1972 and 1980. It is also offered as a trap-grade with the same value.

| Exc. | V.G. | Good | Fair | Poor |
|------|------|------|------|------|
| 850 | 750 | 650 | 500 | 400 |

## Olympian
This model is similar to the Regency, with less engraving. It was not imported after 1980. A skeet and a trap model, as well as a field-grade model, were available. The values were similar.

| Exc. | V.G. | Good | Fair | Poor |
|------|------|------|------|------|
| 800 | 700 | 600 | 450 | 400 |

## Orion Grade I
This is an Over/Under double-barrel shotgun chambered for 12 or 20 gauge with 3" chambers. It is offered with 26" or 28" vent-rib barrels with screw-in chokes. It has a single-selective trigger and automatic ejectors. The boxlock action features no engraving. The finish is blued, with a checkered walnut stock. It was introduced in 1989.

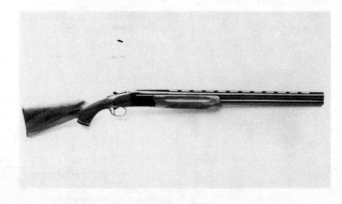

| NIB | Exc. | V.G. | Good | Fair | Poor |
|-----|------|------|------|------|------|
| 850 | 750 | 700 | 600 | 500 | 400 |

## Orion Grade II
This version is lightly engraved and has a high gloss finish. Otherwise, it is similar to the Grade I.

| NIB | Exc. | V.G. | Good | Fair | Poor |
|-----|------|------|------|------|------|
| 1000 | 900 | 800 | 650 | 550 | 450 |

## Orion Grade III
This version has a gamescene-engraved, coin-finished receiver and higher-grade walnut. It was introduced in 1989.

| NIB | Exc. | V.G. | Good | Fair | Poor |
|-----|------|------|------|------|------|
| 1100 | 1000 | 900 | 750 | 650 | 550 |

## Athena Grade IV
This is an Over/Under double-barrel shotgun chambered for 12, 20, and 28 gauge, as well as .410. It has 3" chambers. It is offered with various barrel lengths with vent ribs and screw-in choke tubes. It has a boxlock action with Greener crossbolt, single-selective trigger, and automatic ejectors. It has engraved false sideplates and a satin nickel-plated action. The barrels are blued, with a select checkered walnut stock. This model was introduced in 1989.

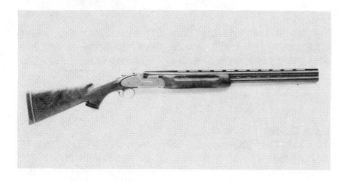

| NIB | Exc. | V.G. | Good | Fair | Poor |
|------|------|------|------|------|------|
| 2000 | 1750 | 1500 | 1200 | 950 | 750 |

**Competition Model Athena**

This is either a trap or skeet version with stock dimensions designed for either skeet or trap and competition-type ribs.

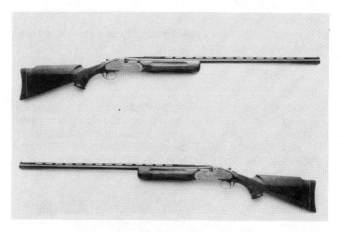

| NIB | Exc. | V.G. | Good | Fair | Poor |
|------|------|------|------|------|------|
| 1650 | 1400 | 1150 | 1000 | 750 | 600 |

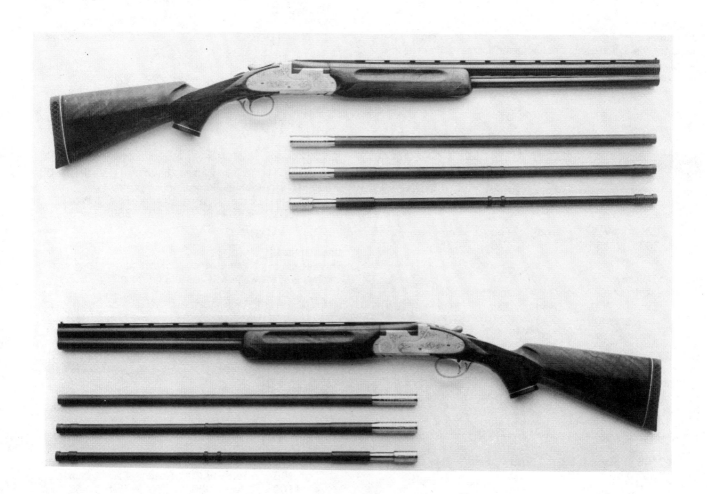

Weatherby Athena Master skeet tube set, 12 ga. 28'' skeet shotgun, plus two each 20, 28 and .410 ga. fitted, full length Briley tubes with integral extractors. Packed in custom fitted aluminum case (not shown).

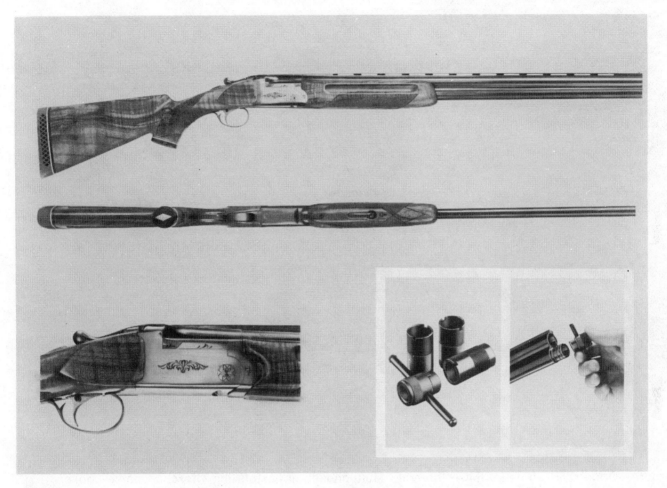

Weatherby Athena O/U Shotgun, IMC - Integral "Multi-choke" ⓣ flush-fitting interchangeable choke tubes.

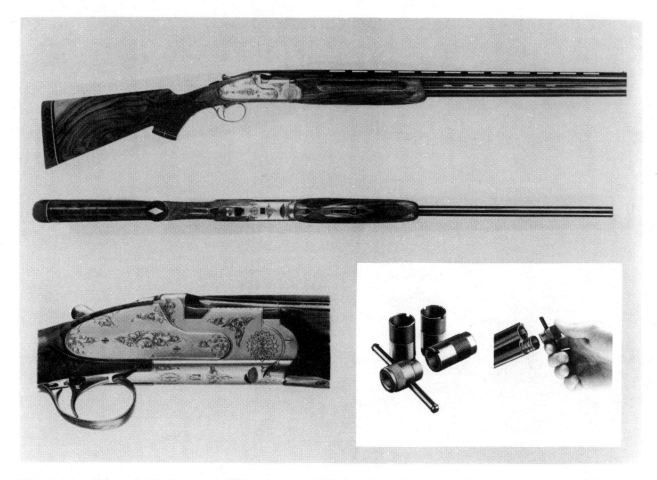

Weatherby Orion O/U Shotgun, IMC - Integral "Multi-choke" ⊤ flush-fitting interchangeable choke tubes.

## WEAVER ARMS
### Escondido, California

**Nighthawk Assault Pistol**
This is a semi-automatic, assault-type pistol that fires from the closed-bolt position. It is chambered for the 9mm Parabellum cartridge and has a 10" or 12" barrel. The upper receiver is made of lightweight alloy, and there is an ambidextrous safety. The finish is black with plastic grips. This model was introduced in 1987.

| Exc. | V.G. | Good | Fair | Poor |
|---|---|---|---|---|
| 450 | 400 | 350 | 300 | 250 |

**Nighthawk Carbine**
This version has a 16.1" barrel and a retractable shoulder stock. It is offered with a 25-, 32-, 40-, or 50- round detachable magazine. It utilizes the same magazines as the Uzi carbine. The finish is black with plastic grips. It has an ambidextrous safety. This model was introduced in 1984.

| Exc. | V.G. | Good | Fair | Poor |
|---|---|---|---|---|
| 550 | 500 | 450 | 400 | 350 |

## WEBLEY & SCOTT, LTD.
### Birmingham, England
### Importer--New England Arms Co.
### Kittery Point, Maine

This company currently manufactures high-grade double-barrel shotguns but has been in business since 1860, when it was founded as the firm of P. Webley & Son. In 1897 the company was changed to the Webley & Scott Revolver & Arms Company, Ltd. In 1906 it became Webley & Scott, Ltd. It is noted for manufacturing the Webley service pistols that were utilized by British armed forces and police units throughout the latter part of the 19th Century and the 20th Century. Webley firearms, especially their revolvers, are said to be among the best produced for the mass market. They are extremely reliable and robust and exhibit a good degree of accuracy.

**Model 1872 Royal Irish Constabulary**
This is a double-action revolver chambered for the .450 cartridge. The barrel is 3.25" in length, and it has fixed sights. It has a solid frame with a swivelling ejector rod housed in a hollow access pin. The cylinder holds five rounds and is gate loaded. The finish is blued, with checkered walnut grips. There is a lanyard ring on the butt. This model is also offered with a 2.5" barrel and a 3.5" barrel. The values would be similar.

| Exc. | V.G. | Good | Fair | Poor |
|---|---|---|---|---|
| 350 | 300 | 250 | 200 | 150 |

**Model 1880 Metropolitan Police**
This model is similar to the 1872 Royal Irish Constabulary but has a 6-shot cylinder and a 2.5" barrel. The caliber is .450.

| Exc. | V.G. | Good | Fair | Poor |
|---|---|---|---|---|
| 350 | 300 | 250 | 200 | 150 |

**Model 1880 James Hill Revolver**
This version is similar to the Metropolitan Police but is chambered for the .430 Eley cartridge. The initials "WJH" were stamped on the frame. This model was manufactured in the 1880's for James Hill, a London gunsmith.

| Exc. | V.G. | Good | Fair | Poor |
|---|---|---|---|---|
| 350 | 300 | 250 | 200 | 150 |

**New Model 1883 R.I.C.**
This version is similar to the Model 1880 but is chambered for the .455 cartridge. It has a 4.5" barrel and was able to fire at least seven different types of contemporary ammunition. It is also available with a 2.5" barrel designed for police use.

| Exc. | V.G. | Good | Fair | Poor |
|---|---|---|---|---|
| 250 | 200 | 175 | 125 | 100 |

**Model 1884 R.I.C. Naval**
This version has a brass frame and many brass external parts. The steel parts are black oxide to protect them from corrosion. The barrel length is 2.75" and octagonal in configuration. Octagonal barrels are rarely found on Webley revolvers. This pistol was manufactured for naval use and designed to be as corrosion-resistant as possible.

| Exc. | V.G. | Good | Fair | Poor |
|---|---|---|---|---|
| 300 | 250 | 225 | 175 | 125 |

**British Bulldog**
This is a double-action revolver chambered for the .455 cartridge. It features a short barrel and a 5-shot unfluted cylinder. It has a distinctive curved birdshead butt. The finish is blued, with checkered walnut grips. This is an extremely robust and durable pistol that was imported throughout the world. Many companies copied this model. It was manufactured from 1878 through 1914.

| Exc. | V.G. | Good | Fair | Poor |
|---|---|---|---|---|
| 350 | 300 | 250 | 200 | 150 |

### Model 1878 Army Express Revolver

This is a double-action revolver that is quite large and powerful. It was designed as a service pistol. It is chambered for the .455 cartridge and has a 6" barrel with an integral, spring-loaded ejector rod on the right side of the barrel. The finish is blued, with one-piece walnut grips and a lanyard ring on the butt. This model was introduced to compete with the Colt Single Action Army Revolver and was possibly influenced by the Colt design.

| Exc. | V.G. | Good | Fair | Poor |
|------|------|------|------|------|
| 375  | 325  | 275  | 225  | 175  |

### Webley Kaufmann Model 1880

This is a top-break, hinged-frame double-action revolver chambered for the .450 centerfire cartridge. It has a 5.75" barrel with a curved birdshead butt. The finish is blued, and the grips are walnut with a lanyard ring on the butt. This is a fairly rare model.

| Exc. | V.G. | Good | Fair | Poor |
|------|------|------|------|------|
| 475  | 425  | 350  | 275  | 200  |

### Webley-Green Model

This is a double-action, top-break revolver that is chambered for the .455 cartridge. It has a 6" ribbed barrel and a 6-shot cylinder. The cylinder flutes on this model are angular and not rounded in shape. The finish is blued, with checkered walnut, squared-butt grips. There is a lanyard ring on the butt. It was introduced in 1882 and manufactured until 1896.

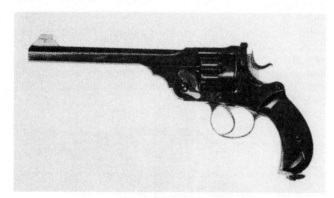

| Exc. | V.G. | Good | Fair | Poor |
|------|------|------|------|------|
| 475  | 425  | 350  | 275  | 200  |

### Mark I

This is a double-action, break-open revolver chambered for the .442 cartridge. It has a 4" ribbed barrel and a 6-shot fluted cylinder. The finish is blued, with checkered walnut birdshead grips and a lanyard ring on the butt. There have been examples noted chambered in the .455 and the .476 calibers. This was a very successful revolver from both a military and commercial standpoint. It was introduced in 1887 and manufactured until 1894.

| Exc. | V.G. | Good | Fair | Poor |
|------|------|------|------|------|
| 250  | 200  | 175  | 125  | 100  |

### Mark II

This is a modified and improved version of the Mark I, that features a larger hammer spur and an improved barrel catch. It was introduced in 1894 and manufactured until 1897.

| Exc. | V.G. | Good | Fair | Poor |
|------|------|------|------|------|
| 250  | 200  | 175  | 125  | 100  |

### Mark III

This model is externally similar to the Mark II but features changes in the cylinder and extractor mechanism. This produced a smoother-functioning pistol. It has a 4" barrel with a blued finish and checkered walnut birdshead grips. There is a lanyard swivel on the butt. This model was used throughout the Boer War. It was introduced in 1897.

| Exc. | V.G. | Good | Fair | Poor |
|------|------|------|------|------|
| 275  | 225  | 200  | 150  | 125  |

### Mark IV

This model is chambered for the .455 cartridge and has a 3", 4", 5", or 6" barrel. It is similar in appearance to the Mark III and became known as the "Boer War Model" because it was introduced at the start of that war. It was manufactured between 1899 and 1913.

| Exc. | V.G. | Good | Fair | Poor |
|------|------|------|------|------|
| 250  | 200  | 175  | 125  | 100  |

### Mark V

This model is extremely similar to the Mark IV, with a 4" barrel. It was manufactured between 1913 and 1915.

| Exc. | V.G. | Good | Fair | Poor |
|------|------|------|------|------|
| 275  | 225  | 200  | 150  | 125  |

## Mark VI

This model is similar to the Mark IV and Mark V, with a modified, flared-butt design. The barrel length is 6", but 4" versions have been noted. This version was offered with a detachable shoulder stock, which was rarely used and is rarely seen on today's market. This model was used in WWI and was manufactured between 1915 and 1921. At the close of the war, manufacture was moved to the Royal Small Arms Factory at Enfield, where small numbers were manufactured. The Enfield revolvers, except for the markings, are identical to those manufactured by Webley. In 1932 the Mark VI was replaced by the .38-caliber Enfield revolver, and the reign of the large-caliber service revolver was over.

| Exc. | V.G. | Good | Fair | Poor |
|------|------|------|------|------|
| 350  | 300  | 250  | 175  | 125  |

## Mark VI .22 Rimfire

This is a standard-size Mark V chambered for the .22 rimfire cartridge and used as a training pistol. It was manufactured in 1918 and is quite scarce.

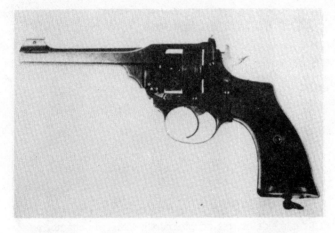

| Exc. | V.G. | Good | Fair | Poor |
|------|------|------|------|------|
| 475  | 425  | 350  | 250  | 200  |

## Webley-Fosbery Automatic Revolver

On this model the recoil automatically revolves the cylinder and cocks the hammer. It is chambered for either the .38 or the .455 Webley cartridge and has a 6" barrel. It is a hinged-frame, top-break revolver. The cylinder holds six shots. The finish is blued, with checkered walnut grips. There is an 8-shot version available that would bring a 100 percent premium as it is extremely rare. This revolver was manufactured between 1901 and 1939.

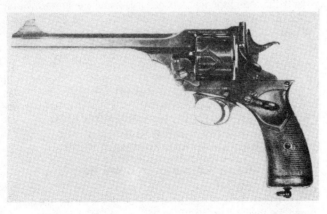

| Exc. | V.G. | Good | Fair | Poor |
|------|------|------|------|------|
| 700  | 550  | 500  | 350  | 275  |

## Model 1904

This is a large, single-action semi-automatic pistol that is chambered for the .455 Webley Auto cartridge. It has a 5" barrel and a 7-round detachable magazine. The sights are fixed, and the finish is blued. It has a grip safety and was manufactured between 1912 and 1945.

| Exc. | V.G. | Good | Fair | Poor |
|------|------|------|------|------|
| 750  | 650  | 500  | 400  | 300  |

## Model 1906

This is a blowback-operated semi-automatic pistol chambered for the .32 ACP or the .380 ACP cartridge. It has a 3.5" barrel and an 8-round detachable magazine. The triggerguard is made of spring steel and is used to lock the barrel to the frame. The finish is blued, with checkered plastic grips. This model was introduced in 1906 and was still on the market in 1940. It is also known as the Metropolitan Police Model.

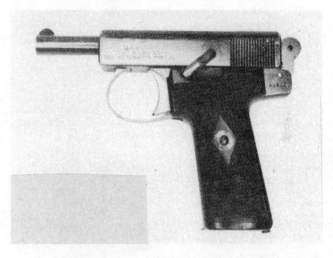

| Exc. | V.G. | Good | Fair | Poor |
|------|------|------|------|------|
| 250  | 225  | 200  | 150  | 100  |

## Model 1906 .25

This is a scaled-down version of the standard Model 1906 that is chambered for the .25 ACP cartridge and has an external hammer. It has a 2" barrel and a 6-shot detachable magazine. It was furnished with no sights at all and is considered to be an extremely unattractive pistol. It was also produced until 1940.

| Exc. | V.G. | Good | Fair | Poor |
|------|------|------|------|------|
| 200  | 175  | 150  | 100  | 75   |

## Model 1909

This is an improved version of the Model 1906 .25. It has a concealed hammer and actually operates very similarly to the 1906 .25 model. It was the smallest Webley handgun ever manufactured.

| Exc. | V.G. | Good | Fair | Poor |
|------|------|------|------|------|
| 250 | 225 | 200 | 150 | 100 |

### Model 1909 9mm

This is a single-action semi-automatic pistol chambered for the 9mm Browning long cartridge. It has a 5" barrel and an external hammer. The detachable magazine holds eight rounds, and there is a hold-open device activated by an empty magazine. It has a grip safety; and the finish is blued, with plastic grips. It was manufactured between 1909 and 1930. This version was adopted by the South African police in 1920.

| Exc. | V.G. | Good | Fair | Poor |
|------|------|------|------|------|
| 450 | 400 | 350 | 275 | 200 |

### Model 1912 Self-Loader

This is a large, heavy, single-action semi-automatic pistol that is chambered for the .455 cartridge. It is recoil-operated and has an external hammer. The round barrel is 5" in length, and there is a 7-shot detachable magazine. There is a grip safety; and the finish is blued, with either wood or rubber grips. There is a lanyard ring on the butt.

| Exc. | V.G. | Good | Fair | Poor |
|------|------|------|------|------|
| 450 | 400 | 350 | 275 | 200 |

### Model 1915 Self-Loader

This model was also known as the Mark I No. 2. It was issued to the Royal Flying Corps and was used to defend their airplanes. It is similar to the 1912 model, with a special rear sight designed to hit a moving target at ranges up to 200 yards. This version was only in production for two years because in 1916 the machine gun was introduced for use on aircraft.

| Exc. | V.G. | Good | Fair | Poor |
|------|------|------|------|------|
| 750 | 650 | 500 | 400 | 300 |

### Model 1911 Target Pistol

This is a single-shot pistol chambered for the .22 rimfire cartridge. It is similar in outward appearance to the Model 1906 Self-Loader but has no recoil system, and each shot has to be loaded singly by hand. The top of the slide is removed to allow this operation. It is offered with either a 4.5" or 9" barrel and was widely used as a training pistol.

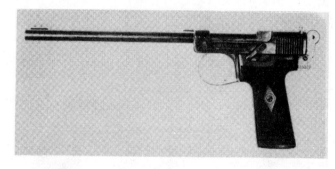

| Exc. | V.G. | Good | Fair | Poor |
|------|------|------|------|------|
| 400 | 350 | 300 | 200 | 150 |

### Model 700

This is a side-by-side double-barrelled shotgun chambered for 12 or 20 gauge. It has a boxlock action and double triggers. A single trigger is available and would bring an additional $50. The receiver is lightly engraved and case-colored. The remainder is blued, with a select, checkered walnut stock.

| Exc. | V.G. | Good | Fair | Poor |
|------|------|------|------|------|
| 1750 | 1500 | 1250 | 850 | 600 |

### Model 702

This is a more deluxe version of the Model 700.

| Exc. | V.G. | Good | Fair | Poor |
|------|------|------|------|------|
| 2750 | 2500 | 2000 | 1500 | 1000 |

### Model 701

This is the top-of-the-line model. It is heavily engraved with a hand-checkered, high-grade walnut stock. The single-trigger version would bring an additional $100.

| Exc. | V.G. | Good | Fair | Poor |
|------|------|------|------|------|
| 3200 | 2750 | 2250 | 1750 | 1250 |

# WEIHRAUCH, HANS HERMANN
### Melrichstadt, West Germany
### Importers--Beeman Precision Arms, Inc.
### Santa Rosa, California
### Helmut Hoffman Placitas, New Mexico

### Model HW 60M

This is a bolt-action, single-shot, match-grade target rifle chambered for the .22 l.r. cartridge. It has a 26.75" heavy barrel with adjustable target sights. The finish is blued, with a target-dimensioned walnut stock.

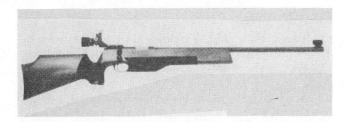

| NIB | Exc. | V.G. | Good | Fair | Poor |
|-----|------|------|------|------|------|
| 700 | 650 | 550 | 400 | 350 | 250 |

**Model HW 66**

This is a match-grade bolt-action rifle chambered for the .22 Hornet or the .222 Remington cartridges. It features a stainless-steel 26" barrel and is offered with double-set triggers. This model is imported exclusively by Hoffman. It has a blued finish and a match-grade walnut stock. It was introduced in 1989.

| NIB | Exc. | V.G. | Good | Fair | Poor |
|-----|------|------|------|------|------|
| 600 | 550 | 500 | 350 | 300 | 200 |

This company produced handguns in Germany before WWII. During the war they manufactured firearms using the code "eea." At the end of the war, their facility landed in Soviet hands; and they ceased to exist for a time. In 1950 the company was revived at Melrichstadt, West Germany. They apparently purchased the Arminius trademark from the firm of Friedrich Pickert. They produced four models under this trademark. They are as follows:

**Model HW-3**

This is a double-action, solid-frame, swing-out cylinder revolver chambered for the .22 l.r. or the .32 Smith & Wesson long cartridges. The barrel length is 2.75", and the cylinder holds either seven or eight shots. The finish is blued, with wood grips. In America this revolver was known as the Dickson Bulldog. In Europe it was known as the Gecado.

| Exc. | V.G. | Good | Fair | Poor |
|------|------|------|------|------|
| 75 | 50 | 40 | 35 | 25 |

**Model HW-5**

This is similar to the HW-3, with a 4" barrel. In America it was sold under the tradename "Omega."

| Exc. | V.G. | Good | Fair | Poor |
|------|------|------|------|------|
| 75 | 50 | 40 | 35 | 25 |

**Model HW-7**

This version is chambered for the .22 l.r. cartridge only. It has a 6" barrel with adjustable sights and an 8-shot cylinder. It was sold in the United States as the "Herter's Guide Model." A variation known as the HW-7S has target sights and thumbrest grips.

| Exc. | V.G. | Good | Fair | Poor |
|------|------|------|------|------|
| 75 | 50 | 40 | 35 | 25 |

**Model HW-9**

This model is similar to the HW-7, with a 6-shot cylinder and a 6" ventilated-rib barrel with target sights and target grips.

| Exc. | V.G. | Good | Fair | Poor |
|------|------|------|------|------|
| 75 | 50 | 40 | 35 | 25 |

These pistols all carry the Arminius trademark, a bearded head wearing a winged helmet. The model number will be found on the cylinder crane; the caliber, on the barrel; and the words "Made in Germany," on the frame.

## WEISBURGER, A.
### Memphis, Tennessee

**Pocket Pistol**

This is a single-shot pocket pistol patterned after the Henry Deringer type. It is chambered for .41-caliber percussion and has a 2.5" barrel, German silver mountings, and a walnut stock. It was made in the 1850's.

| Exc. | V.G. | Good | Fair | Poor |
|------|------|------|------|------|
| 750 | 650 | 500 | 400 | 300 |

## WESSON, DAN ARMS
### Monson, Massachusetts

**Model 11**

This is a double-action, solid-framed revolver with a swing-out cylinder. It is chambered for the .357 Magnum cartridge and holds six shots. It has an interchangeable 2.5", 4", or 6" barrel with fixed sights. The barrels are held in position with an external barrel nut. The finish is blued, with interchangeable walnut grips. This model was manufactured in 1970-71.
Extra Barrels-- Add 25 Percent.

| Exc. | V.G. | Good | Fair | Poor |
|------|------|------|------|------|
| 200 | 175 | 150 | 125 | 100 |

**Model 12**

This is similar to the Model 11, with adjustable target sights. It was manufactured in 1970-71.

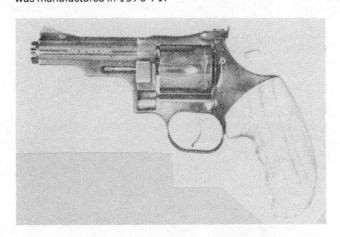

| Exc. | V.G. | Good | Fair | Poor |
|------|------|------|------|------|
| 250 | 225 | 200 | 175 | 125 |

**Model 14**

This is an improved version of the Model 11 that features a recessed barrel nut and is furnished with a spanner wrench that is used to change the barrels. It was manufactured between 1971 and 1975.

| Exc. | V.G. | Good | Fair | Poor |
|------|------|------|------|------|
| 225 | 200 | 175 | 150 | 100 |

## Model 15
This is similar to the Model 14, with adjustable target sights. It was manufactured between 1971 and 1975.

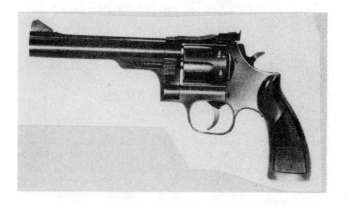

| Exc. | V.G. | Good | Fair | Poor |
|------|------|------|------|------|
| 250 | 225 | 200 | 175 | 125 |

## Model 8
This is similar to the Model 14 except that it is chambered for .38 Special only.

| Exc. | V.G. | Good | Fair | Poor |
|------|------|------|------|------|
| 200 | 175 | 150 | 125 | 100 |

## Model 9
This is similar to the Model 15, with adjustable sights. It is chambered for the .38 Special cartridge only. It was manufactured between 1971 and 1975.

| Exc. | V.G. | Good | Fair | Poor |
|------|------|------|------|------|
| 250 | 225 | 20Q | 175 | 125 |

## Model 22
This is the current-production model chambered for the .22 l.r. cartridge. It is a double-action, solid-frame, swing-out cylinder revolver with interchangeable solid-ribbed, vent-rib, or heavy vent-rib barrels in 2.5", 4", 6", or 8" lengths. The finish is blued, with interchangeable walnut grips.
Vent-Rib--Add $20.
Heavy Vent-Rib--Add $50.

| NIB | Exc. | V.G. | Good | Fair | Poor |
|-----|------|------|------|------|------|
| 350 | 300 | 250 | 200 | 175 | 150 |

## Model 22 Pistol Pac
This version includes a 2.5", 4", 6", or 8" barrel assembly with four interchangeable front sight blades and an extra set of grips furnished in an aluminum case.
Vent-Rib--Add $100.
Heavy Vent-Rib--Add $200.

| NIB | Exc. | V.G. | Good | Fair | Poor |
|-----|------|------|------|------|------|
| 625 | 525 | 425 | 325 | 250 | 200 |

## Model 722
This Model is identical to the Model 22 except that it is constructed of stainless steel. It is available in the same configurations, as well as the Pistol Pac, and would be valued at approximately 10 percent higher.

## Model 22M
This version is chambered for the .22 rimfire Magnum cartridge. Otherwise, it is identical to the Model 22 and is available in the same configurations, including the Pistol Pac. It is worth approximately 5 percent additional but can be more difficult to liquidate.

## Model 722M
This is the stainless-steel version of the Model 22M and is identical in all respects. It is available in the same configurations, including the Pistol Pac. It is valued approximately 15 percent higher than the blued version.

## Model 32
This version is similar to the Model 22 except that it is chambered for the .32 Harrington & Richardson Magnum cartridge. It is available in the same configurations, including the Pistol Pac, and would be valued the same.

## Model 14-2
This version is chambered for the .357 Magnum cartridge, is offered with a 4", 6", or 8" interchangeable barrel, and has fixed sights. It is also available in the Pistol Pac but includes only the three barrels and the extra grip, with no interchangeable fixed sights. This version is worth approximately 20 percent less than the Model 22.

## Model 8-2
This version is identical to the Model 14-2 except chambered for .38 Special only. It is also available as a Pistol Pac and is worth the same as the Model 14-2.

## Model 708
This is the stainless-steel version of the Model 8-2. It is worth approximately 15 percent more than the blued version.

## Model 15-2
This model is similar to the Model 15-2, with adjustable sights. It is available with a 2", 4", 6", 8", 10", 12", or 15" barrel. It is available in the same configurations, and there is a four-barrel Pistol Pac with an extra grip, four front sight blades, and an aluminum case available. It would be worth the same as the Model 22.

## Model 709
This is the stainless-steel version of the Model 15-2. It is available in the same configurations, including the Pistol Pac, and is worth approximately 10 percent additional.

## Model 714
This is the stainless-steel version of the Model 14-2. It is available in the same configurations, including the three-barrel Pistol Pac, and is worth approximately 20 percent additional.

## Model 15 Gold Series
This is a custom-worked revolver chambered for the .357 Magnum cartridge. It has a 6" or 8" heavy vent-ribbed barrel that is ported for recoil reduction. Dan Wesson's signature is stamped and gold-washed on the barrel shroud. The action is hand-honed, and it has an 18 kt. gold-plated trigger. It features custom, high-visibility sights. The finish is blued, with fancy hardwood grips. It was introduced in 1989.

| NIB | Exc. | V.G. | Good | Fair | Poor |
|-----|------|------|------|------|------|
| 550 | 450 | 400 | 350 | 250 | 200 |

## Model 375 V Supermag

This version is chambered for the .375 Supermag cartridge. It is offered with a 6", 8", or 10" vent-ribbed barrel. It has adjustable sights and a bright blue finish with smooth walnut grips. It was introduced in 1986.

| NIB | Exc. | V.G. | Good | Fair | Poor |
|-----|------|------|------|------|------|
| 500 | 400 | 350 | 300 | 250 | 200 |

## Model 740 V

This is the stainless-steel version of the Model 375 V. It is worth an additional 10 percent.

## Model 41 V

This version is similar to the Model 375 V but is chambered for the .41 Magnum cartridge.

| NIB | Exc. | V.G. | Good | Fair | Poor |
|-----|------|------|------|------|------|
| 425 | 375 | 325 | 275 | 225 | 175 |

## Model 41 V Pistol Pac

This version includes a 6" or 8" vent-ribbed barrel assembly with an extra grip and two front sight blades. It is furnished in an aluminum case.

| NIB | Exc. | V.G. | Good | Fair | Poor |
|-----|------|------|------|------|------|
| 625 | 525 | 425 | 325 | 250 | 200 |

## Model 741 V

This is similar to the Model 41 V except that it is constructed of stainless steel. It is also available as a Pistol Pac and is worth approximately 10 percent additional.

## Model 44 V

This version is similar to the Model 41 V except that it is chambered for the .44 Magnum cartridge. It is also available as a Pistol Pac and is worth approximately 10 percent additional.

## Model 744 V

This is the stainless-steel version of the Model 44 V. It is also available as a Pistol Pac and is worth approximately 20 percent additional.

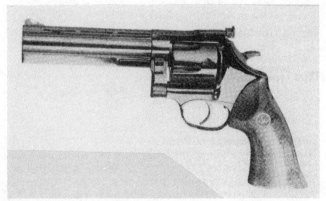

## Model 45 V

This model is chambered for the .45 Colt cartridge. Otherwise, it is similar to the Model 44 V. It is also available as a Pistol Pac and is valued the same as the Model 44 V.

## Model 745 V

This is the stainless-steel version of the Model 45 V and is worth approximately 20 percent additional.

# WESSON, EDWIN
### Hartford, Connecticut

## Dragoon

This is a large, military-type revolver chambered for .45-caliber percussion. It has a 7" round barrel and a 6-shot unfluted cylinder. The finish is blued and case-colored, with walnut grips that have a brass buttcap. This firearm is very rare and was manufactured in 1848 and 1849.

| Exc. | V.G. | Good | Fair | Poor |
|------|------|------|------|------|
| 6000 | 5000 | 4000 | 3250 | 2500 |

# WESSON, FRANK
### Worchester, Massachusetts
### Springfield, Massachusetts

This company manufactured firearms at Worchester, Massachusetts, from 1854 to 1865. They then relocated to Springfield, Massachusetts, where they operated between 1865 to 1875.

## Manual Extractor Model

This is a single-shot, spur-trigger, single-action pistol chambered for the .22 rimfire cartridge. It has a tip-up action and is offered with a 4" octagonal barrel. It has a thin brass frame and a squarebutt handle. The barrel catch is located in front of the trigger. This model has a manual extractor. There are no markings. There were approximately 200 manufactured in 1856 and 1857.

| Exc. | V.G. | Good | Fair | Poor |
|------|------|------|------|------|
| 750 | 650 | 500 | 400 | 250 |

## First Model Small Frame

This is a spur-trigger, single-shot pocket pistol chambered for the .22 rimfire cartridge. It pivots upward for loading and has a 3.5" part-round/part-octagonal barrel. Examples have been noted with barrel lengths from 3" to 6". It has a slim brass frame. The barrel is blued, with squarebutt walnut or rosewood grips. The barrel is pivoted by pulling on a long lever that protrudes from the bottom of the frame ahead of the trigger. This model is marked "Frank Wesson Worchester Mass/Pat'd Oct. 25, 1859 & Nov. 11, 1862." There are two variations. The first type has a rounded frame and an irregular-shaped sideplate. It is serial-numbered from #1-2500.

| Exc. | V.G. | Good | Fair | Poor |
|------|------|------|------|------|
| 650 | 550 | 450 | 300 | 150 |

## Second Type

The frame is flat-sided and has a circular sideplate. It is serial-numbered #1-1200. There were a total of approximately 15,000 of both versions manufactured between 1859 and 1882.

| Exc. | V.G. | Good | Fair | Poor |
|------|------|------|------|------|
| 550 | 450 | 350 | 250 | 125 |

## First Model Medium Frame

This is a larger version of the Small Frame, chambered for .30 rimfire or .32 rimfire. It has a 4" part-round/ part-octagonal barrel and features an iron frame. The frame is narrower at the barrel hinge point. There were approximately 1,000 manufactured between 1859 and 1862.

| Exc. | V.G. | Good | Fair | Poor |
|------|------|------|------|------|
| 500 | 400 | 300 | 200 | 100 |

## Medium Frame Second Model
This is similar to the First Model but has a longer spur trigger, and the frame is wider at the hinge point. There were approximately 1,000 manufactured between 1862 and 1870.

| Exc. | V.G. | Good | Fair | Poor |
|------|------|------|------|------|
| 500 | 400 | 300 | 200 | 100 |

## Small Frame Pocket Rifle
This is a spur-trigger, single-shot pistol chambered for the .22 rimfire cartridge. It has a 6" part-round/ part-octagonal barrel that pivots upward for loading, with a narrow brass frame. It is marked "Frank Wesson Worchester, Mass." The finish is blued, with squarebutt rosewood grips. It has no extractor. This model is found with a detachable skeleton shoulder stock. There are approximately 5,000 manufactured between 1865 and 1875.
Matching Shoulder Stock--Add 25 Percent.

**Pistol Only**

| Exc. | V.G. | Good | Fair | Poor |
|------|------|------|------|------|
| 600 | 500 | 400 | 300 | 200 |

## Medium Frame Pocket Rifle
This is a slightly larger version, chambered for .22, .30, and .32 rimfire cartridges. It has either a 10" or 12" part-octagonal barrel that pivots upward for loading. It is similar in other respects to the Small Frame. There were approximately 1,000 manufactured between 1862 and 1870.
Matching Shoulder Stock--Add 25 Percent.

**Pistol Only**

| Exc. | V.G. | Good | Fair | Poor |
|------|------|------|------|------|
| 600 | 500 | 400 | 300 | 200 |

## Model 1870 Small Frame Pocket Rifle
This is an improved version, chambered for the .22 rimfire cartridge. It has either a 10", 12", 15", 18", or 20" full octagonal barrel that rotates to the side for loading. It has a spur trigger and is found with either a brass or iron frame. This model features a half cock on the hammer and is blued, with squarebutt rosewood grips. It is marked "Frank Wesson Worchester Mass." There are three versions; values are similar.
Matching Shoulder Stock--Add 25 Percent.

**Pistol Only**

| Exc. | V.G. | Good | Fair | Poor |
|------|------|------|------|------|
| 500 | 400 | 300 | 200 | 150 |

## 1870 Medium Frame Pocket Rifle First Type
This version is slightly larger and is offered chambered for the .32-caliber rimfire cartridge. There were 5,000 manufactured between 1870 and 1893.
Matching Shoulder Stock--Add 25 Percent.

**Pistol Only**

| Exc. | V.G. | Good | Fair | Poor |
|------|------|------|------|------|
| 550 | 450 | 350 | 250 | 200 |

## 1870 Medium Frame Pocket Rifle Second Type
This version has an iron frame and a push-button, half-cock mechanism.
Match Shoulder Stock--Add 25 Percent.

**Pistol Only**

| Exc. | V.G. | Good | Fair | Poor |
|------|------|------|------|------|
| 450 | 400 | 300 | 200 | 150 |

## 1870 Medium Frame Pocket Rifle Third Type
This version has three screws in the left side of the frame. The frame is usually somewhat thicker.
Matching Shoulder Stock--Add 25 Percent.

**Pistol Only**

| Exc. | V.G. | Good | Fair | Poor |
|------|------|------|------|------|
| 450 | 400 | 300 | 200 | 150 |

## 1870 Large Frame Pocket Rifle First Type
This is a larger version of the Medium Frame. It is chambered for the .32, .38, .42, and .44 caliber rimfire cartridges. It has octagonal barrels from 15" to 24" in length. The frames are either brass or iron with a spur trigger and square butt. The finish is blued, with rosewood grips. It is marked "Frank Wesson Worchester, Mass Patented May 31, 1870." The action functions in the same manner as on the smaller versions but is longer and wider in size. The extractor on this model automatically lifts the cartridge from the breech when the action is opened. There were fewer than 250 of both variations manufactured between 1870 and 1880.
Matching Shoulder Stock--Add 25 Percent.

**Pistol Only**

| Exc. | V.G. | Good | Fair | Poor |
|------|------|------|------|------|
| 850 | 750 | 650 | 500 | 300 |

## 1870 Large Frame Pocket Rifle Second Type
This version is similar to the First Type but has the standard sliding Frank Wesson-type extractor.
Matching Shoulder Stock--Add 25 Percent.

**Pistol Only**

| Exc. | V.G. | Good | Fair | Poor |
|------|------|------|------|------|
| 850 | 750 | 650 | 500 | 300 |

## Small Frame Superposed Pistol
This is a very small, vest pocket-type derringer. It is chambered for the .22 short rimfire cartridge. It has either 2" or 2.5" octagonal superposed barrels that revolve to line up with the ring-type hammer. It has a spur trigger, brass frame, blued barrels, and rosewood birdshead grips. There is a front sight on each of the two barrels. There were approximately 3,500 manufactured between 1868 and 1880. This model is occasionally noted with a sliding, dagger-type bayonet located on the middle section between the barrels. This would add approximately 25 percent to its value. There were approximately 3,500 manufactured between 1868 and 1880.

| Exc. | V.G. | Good | Fair | Poor |
|------|------|------|------|------|
| 800 | 650 | 550 | 400 | 275 |

## Medium Frame Superposed Pistol
This model is similar to the Small Frame version except that it is chambered for the .32 short rimfire cartridge. The barrel lengths are between 2.5" and 3.5". It is also manually revolved. There are three versions, all of which may be found with the sliding bayonet-type dagger between the barrels that would add 25 percent to their values. There were approximately 3,000 manufactured between 1868 and 1880.

### First Type Marked "Patent Applied For"

| Exc. | V.G. | Good | Fair | Poor |
|------|------|------|------|------|
| 550 | 500 | 400 | 300 | 200 |

### Second Type Marked "Patent December 15, 1868"

| Exc. | V.G. | Good | Fair | Poor |
|------|------|------|------|------|
| 600 | 550 | 450 | 350 | 250 |

### Third Type Full-Length Fluted Barrels

| Exc. | V.G. | Good | Fair | Poor |
|------|------|------|------|------|
| 500 | 450 | 350 | 250 | 150 |

## Large Frame Superposed Pistol
This is a larger version chambered for the .41 short rimfire cartridge. It has manually rotated, 3" octagonal barrels that are full-length fluted and feature the sliding dagger-type bayonet standard on all specimens noted. Otherwise, it is similar to the Medium Frame version. There were approximately 2,000 manufactured between 1868 and 1880.

| Exc. | V.G. | Good | Fair | Poor |
|------|------|------|------|------|
| 850 | 750 | 650 | 500 | 300 |

## No. 1 Long Range Rifle

This is a falling-block, single-shot breechloader that is activated by a combination triggerguard lever. It has a back-action lock with the hammer mounted on the side. It is chambered for the .44-100 or the .45-100 cartridges. It has a 34" octagonal barrel with a tang-mounted sight. The finish is blued with a hand-checkered, walnut pistolgrip stock. It has a shotgun-type butt. It is marked "F. Wesson Mfr. Worchester, Mass. Long Range Rifle Creedmoor." There were very few manufactured in 1876.

| Exc. | V.G. | Good | Fair | Poor |
|------|------|------|------|------|
| 5000 | 4500 | 3500 | 2500 | 1750 |

## No. 2 Mid-Range or Hunting Rifle

This model is similar to the No. 1 except that the firing pin is located in a bolster on the right-hand side of the receiver. It features a rounded iron frame and a finger-loop action lever. It is offered with octagonal barrels between 28" and 34" in length. It is marked "F. Wesson, Maker Worchester, Mass." The 32" or 34" barrelled versions are also marked "Long Range Rifle Creedmoor" and would be worth an additional 20 percent. There were approximately 100 manufactured.

| Exc. | V.G. | Good | Fair | Poor |
|------|------|------|------|------|
| 4500 | 3750 | 3000 | 2000 | 1500 |

## No. 2 Sporting Rifle

This version has a center-mounted hammer. It is offered with part-octagonal barrels from 28" to 34" in length. It is chambered for the .38-100, .40-100, and .45-100 cartridges. There were fewer than 25 manufactured.

| Exc. | V.G. | Good | Fair | Poor |
|------|------|------|------|------|
| 4750 | 4000 | 3250 | 2250 | 1750 |

# WESSON & LEAVITT
# MASSACHUSETTS ARMS COMPANY
### Chicopee Falls, Massachusetts

## Revolving Rifle

This is a single-action revolving rifle chambered for .40-caliber percussion. It has a round stepped barrel from 16" to 24" in length. It has a six-shot, etched, unfluted cylinder. The finish is blued, with a round walnut grip with a buttstock permanently attached to it. There were approximately 25 manufactured in 1849.

| Exc. | V.G. | Good | Fair | Poor |
|------|------|------|------|------|
| 6000 | 5000 | 4000 | 3000 | 2000 |

## Dragoon

This model is basically a 7" round-barrelled pistol version of the Revolving Rifle. It is marked "Mass. Arms Co./Chicopee Falls." There are basically two versions. The first 30 produced were an early type that have a 6.25" barrel and would bring a premium of approximately 10 percent. The standard model that made up the remainder of the total production of 800 have the 7" barrel. These revolvers were manufactured in 1850 and 1851.

| Exc. | V.G. | Good | Fair | Poor |
|------|------|------|------|------|
| 2000 | 1750 | 1500 | 1000 | 750 |

# WESTERN ARMS
### SEE--Bacon

# WESTERN FIELD
### Montgomery Ward

Western Field is a trade name used by the firm of Montgomery Ward to sell rifles and shotguns through their retail outlets. They were manufactured by various domestic and foreign companies on a contract basis. They were usually the lower-end models offered by the particular company. Space in a publication of this nature precludes listing the myriad of models that

were available. Suffice it to say that there is very little, if any, collector base for Western Field firearms; and they would be valued by their worth as utility weapons only.

# WESTLEY RICHARDS & CO., LTD.
### Birmingham, England
### Importer--New England Arms Co.
### Kittery Point, Maine

The firearms manufactured by the firm of Westley Richards & Co., Ltd. are of the finest quality and are essentially produced on a made-to-order basis. They produce Over/Under sidelock and boxlock shotguns, as well as side-by-side doubles in the same configuration. They also manufacture a bolt-action magazine rifle, as well as a boxlock and detachable-sidelock double-barrel rifle. Prices for their firearms begin at $2,000 for the plainest functional model they offer and rapidly escalate to over $35,000. We feel that firearms of this quality and great value should be appraised on an individual basis and strongly urge this action if a transaction is contemplated.

# WHITE, ROLLIN
### Lowell, Massachusetts

## Pocket Pistol

This is a single-shot, spur-trigger pocket pistol chambered for either the .32 caliber rimfire with a 3" octagonal barrel or a rarer version chambered for the .38 rimfire cartridge with a larger frame and a 5" octagonal barrel. This version would be worth a 40 percent premium. Both of these versions have ribbed octagonal barrels and brass or iron frames that are either silver-plated or blued. It has a square butt with walnut grips and a breech that swivels to the right for loading. The extractor is manual. It is marked "Rollin White Arms Co. Lowell, Mass."

| Exc. | V.G. | Good | Fair | Poor |
|------|------|------|------|------|
| 650 | 550 | 450 | 300 | 200 |

## Pocket Revolver

This is a single-action, spur-trigger revolver chambered for the .22 rimfire cartridge. It has a 3.25" octagonal barrel and a 7-round unfluted cylinder. The frame is silver-plated brass with a blued barrel and cylinder. The squarebutt grips are of walnut. The barrel is marked "Made for Smith & Wesson by Rollin White Arms Co., Lowell, Mass." Some have been noted marked "Rollin White Arms Co. Lowell, Mass."; some have been noted marked "Lowell Arms Co., Lowell, Mass." The Smith & Wesson-marked versions are worth approximately 20 percent additional. There is a variation without an ejector and one with an ejector mounted on the right-hand side of the frame. The ejector model is worth approximately 25 percent additional. There were approximately 10,000 manufactured in the 1860's.

| Exc. | V.G. | Good | Fair | Poor |
|------|------|------|------|------|
| 500 | 450 | 400 | 300 | 200 |

# WHITNEY ARMS CO.
### New Haven, Connecticut

Whitney firearms are desirable from a collector's standpoint. Many are quite valuable. The number of different variations makes it advisable to secure a qualified appraisal if a transaction is contemplated.

## Model 1841 Rifle

This is a muzzle-loading single-shot rifle chambered for .54-caliber percussion. It has a 33" round barrel with a full-length walnut stock held on by two barrel bands. It has brass mountings and a patch box. The finish is brown with a blued trigger and barrel bands. The lock is case-colored. There is a steel ramrod mounted under the barrel. It is marked "E. Whitney" along with "U.S." military inspector's markings. There were approximately 22,500 manufactured between 1842 and 1854.

| Exc. | V.G. | Good | Fair | Poor |
|------|------|------|------|------|
| 1750 | 1500 | 1200 | 850 | 500 |

## Model 1855 Rifle

This model is similar to the Model 1841 Rifle except that it is chambered for .58-caliber percussion with a 40" round barrel and a full-length stock held on by three barrel bands. It features iron mountings with a pewter forend tip. The lock is fitted with the Maynard Tape Primer device. The finish is in the white with a walnut stock. There were approximately 2,000 manufactured between 1858 and 1863.

| Exc. | V.G. | Good | Fair | Poor |
|------|------|------|------|------|
| 1500 | 1250 | 1000 | 750 | 500 |

## Model 1861 Rifle

This is a single-shot muzzleloader chambered for the .69-percussion caliber. It has a 34" round barrel and a full-length stock held on by two barrel bands. It has iron mountings and is U.S. marked. The finish is in the white with an oil-finished walnut stock. It is marked "U.S./ Whitneyville." The lock is dated. There were approximately 10,000 manufactured between 1861 and 1864.

| Exc. | V.G. | Good | Fair | Poor |
|------|------|------|------|------|
| 1500 | 1250 | 1000 | 750 | 500 |

## Single Barrelled Percussion Shotgun

This firearm was manufactured by Whitney out of surplus .58-caliber rifle barrels that were opened up and converted to smooth-bore .60-caliber shotgun barrels. They are offered in lengths of 28" to 36" and are marked "Whitney Arms Co., Whitneyville, Conn. Homogeneous Wrought Steel." The finish is blued, with varnished walnut stocks that are crudely checkered. There were approximately 2,000 manufactured between 1866 and 1869. These guns are rarely encountered on today's market.

| Exc. | V.G. | Good | Fair | Poor |
|------|------|------|------|------|
| 850 | 750 | 600 | 450 | 250 |

## Double Barrelled Percussion Shotgun

The specifications for this version are similar to that of the single barrel except that there are two side-by-side barrels with double locks and hammers and double triggers. They are slightly more common than the Single Barrelled version.

| Exc. | V.G. | Good | Fair | Poor |
|------|------|------|------|------|
| 800 | 700 | 550 | 400 | 200 |

## Swing-Breech Carbine

This is a single-shot breechloading carbine chambered for the .46-caliber rimfire cartridge. It has a 22" round barrel with a button-released breechblock that swings to the side for loading. The finish is blued, with a walnut stock. There were fewer than 50 manufactured in 1866.

| Exc. | V.G. | Good | Fair | Poor |
|------|------|------|------|------|
| 3000 | 2750 | 2250 | 1500 | 1100 |

## Whitney-Cochran Carbine

This is a single-shot breechloading carbine chambered for the .44 rimfire cartridge. It has a 28" round barrel with a lever-activated breechblock that raises upward for loading. It was manufactured under license from J. W. Cochran. The finish is blued, with a walnut stock. There is a saddle ring on the left side of the frame. It is marked "Whitney Arms Co.-Whitneyville, Conn." This gun was produced for the 1867 Government Carbine Trials. There were fewer than 50 manufactured in 1866 and 1867.

| Exc. | V.G. | Good | Fair | Poor |
|------|------|------|------|------|
| 1750 | 1500 | 1200 | 850 | 600 |

## Excelsior

This is a single-shot rifle chambered for the .38, .44, or .50 rimfire cartridges. It is found with various-length octagonal or round barrels. The finish is blued, with a walnut stock and forearm held on by one barrel band. The breechblock pivots downward for loading. There is a center-mounted hammer. It is marked "Whitney Arms Co. Whitneyville Conn." The shorter-barrelled carbine versions have a saddle ring on the frame. There were approximately 200 manufactured between 1866 and 1870.

| Exc. | V.G. | Good | Fair | Poor |
|------|------|------|------|------|
| 1500 | 1250 | 1000 | 750 | 500 |

## Whitney-Howard Lever Action

This is a single-shot breechloader that is chambered for the .44 rimfire cartridge. It has also been noted as a shotgun chambered for 20-gauge smooth bore with barrels from 30" to 40" in length. The rifle version has barrel lengths from 22" to 28". The breechblock is opened by means of a combination lever and triggerguard. There is also a carbine version with barrel lengths of 18.5" or 19". There were approximately 2,000 manufactured totally between 1866 and 1870. Values are as follows:

**Shotgun**

| Exc. | V.G. | Good | Fair | Poor |
|------|------|------|------|------|
| 650 | 600 | 500 | 350 | 250 |

**Rifle**

| Exc. | V.G. | Good | Fair | Poor |
|------|------|------|------|------|
| 750 | 700 | 600 | 450 | 300 |

**Carbine**

| Exc. | V.G. | Good | Fair | Poor |
|------|------|------|------|------|
| 850 | 800 | 700 | 550 | 400 |

## Whitney Phoenix

There is very little known about the origin of this model. It is built on a patent issued to Whitney in 1874. There are a number of variations that are all marked "Phoenix, Patent May 24, 74." The Whitney name is not marked on any of the versions. They are all single-shot breechloaders with a breechblock that lifts to the right side and upward for loading. The barrels are all blued, with either case-colored or blued receivers and walnut stocks. There were approximately 25,000 total manufactured between 1867 and 1881. The models and values are as follows:

**Gallery Rifle**

This version is chambered for the .22 rimfire caliber and has a 24" half-octagonal barrel. Its production was quite limited.

| Exc. | V.G. | Good | Fair | Poor |
|------|------|------|------|------|
| 850 | 800 | 700 | 550 | 400 |

**Shotgun**

This is a smooth-bore version chambered for 10, 12, 14, 16, or 22 gauge. It has smooth-bore barrels between 26" and 32" in length. There were approximately 5,000 manufactured.

| Exc. | V.G. | Good | Fair | Poor |
|------|------|------|------|------|
| 600 | 550 | 450 | 300 | 200 |

**Military Rifle**

This version is chambered for the .433, .45 or .50 caliber centerfire cartridges. It has a 35" round barrel with a full-length, two-piece walnut stock held on by three barrel bands. There were approximately 15,000 manufactured. Many were sent to Central or South America.

| Exc. | V.G. | Good | Fair | Poor |
|------|------|------|------|------|
| 1250 | 1000 | 800 | 650 | 500 |

**Schuetzen Rifle**

This is a target-shooting version chambered for the .38, .40, or .44 centerfire cartridges. It has either a 30" or 32" octagonal barrel with a Schuetzen- type walnut stock and forearm that features hand-checkering. It has a nickel-plated, Swiss-style buttplate and adjustable sights with a spirit level. This model has been noted with double-set triggers. There were very few manufactured.

| Exc. | V.G. | Good | Fair | Poor |
|------|------|------|------|------|
| 2000 | 1750 | 1250 | 850 | 650 |

**Civilian Carbine**

This version is chambered for the .44-caliber centerfire and has a 24" round barrel. The finish is blued, with a case-colored frame and a walnut stock and forearm held on by one barrel band. It has military-type sights, buttplate, and a saddle ring mounted on the frame. There were approximately 500 manufactured.

| Exc. | V.G. | Good | Fair | Poor |
|------|------|------|------|------|
| 2000 | 1750 | 1250 | 850 | 650 |

**Military Carbine**

This version is chambered for the .433, .45, or .50 centerfire cartridges. It has a 20.5" round barrel and was manufactured for Central and South America. It is very rarely encountered on today's market.

| Exc. | V.G. | Good | Fair | Poor |
|------|------|------|------|------|
| 2000 | 1750 | 1250 | 850 | 650 |

**Whitney-Laidley Model 1 Rolling Block**

Whitney acquired manufacturing rights for this model from the inventors T. Laidley and C. A. Emery, who had received the patent in 1866. Whitney immediately started to modify the action to become competitive with the Remington Rolling Block. There were approximately 50,000 manufactured total between 1871 and 1881. There are a number of variations of this model as follows:

**Military Carbine**

There were approximately 5,000 manufactured chambered for the .433, .45, or .50 centerfire cartridges. It has a 20.5" round barrel with military-type sights and a saddle ring on the receiver. The finish is blued, with a case-colored frame and a walnut stock. Most of them were shipped to Central or South America.

| Exc. | V.G. | Good | Fair | Poor |
|------|------|------|------|------|
| 1250 | 1000 | 800 | 550 | 350 |

**Civilian Carbine**

This version is chambered for .44 rimfire or centerfire and .46 rimfire. It has either an 18.5" or 19.5" barrel. It is blued, with a case-colored frame. The stock is walnut. A nickel-plated version is also available. There were approximately 1,000 of this version manufactured.

| Exc. | V.G. | Good | Fair | Poor |
|------|------|------|------|------|
| 1250 | 1000 | 800 | 550 | 350 |

**Military Rifle**

This version is chambered the same as the Military Carbine but has either a 32.5" or 35" round barrel with a full-length two-piece stock held on by three barrel bands. The finish is blued, with a case-colored receiver and a walnut stock. There were approximately 30,000 manufactured. Most were shipped to Central or South America.

| Exc. | V.G. | Good | Fair | Poor |
|------|------|------|------|------|
| 1000 | 800 | 650 | 450 | 300 |

**Gallery Rifle**

This is a .22-caliber sporting-rifle version with a 24" octagonal barrel. The finish is similar to the Military Rifle. There were approximately 500 manufactured.

| Exc. | V.G. | Good | Fair | Poor |
|------|------|------|------|------|
| 900 | 800 | 600 | 400 | 300 |

**Sporting Rifle**

This version is chambered for .38, .40, .44, .45, or .50 centerfire, as well as .32, .38, or .44 rimfire. It features barrel lengths from 24" to 30" in either round or octagonal configurations. The finish is similar to the Military Rifle, and there were approximately 5,000 manufactured.

| Exc. | V.G. | Good | Fair | Poor |
|------|------|------|------|------|
| 1250 | 1000 | 800 | 550 | 350 |

**Creedmoor No. 1 Rifle**

This version is chambered for the .44-caliber cartridge and has a 32" or 34" barrel that is either round or octagonal in configuration. It has a blued finish with case-colored frame and a hand-checkered, select walnut stock and forearm. It features Vernier adjustable sights with a spirit level. It is marked "Whitney Creedmoor." There were fewer than 100 manufactured.

| Exc. | V.G. | Good | Fair | Poor |
|------|------|------|------|------|
| 3000 | 2500 | 2000 | 1250 | 750 |

**Creedmoor No. 2 Rifle**

This version is similar to the No. 1 Rifle except that it is chambered for the .40-caliber cartridge with either a 30" or 32" barrel.

| Exc. | V.G. | Good | Fair | Poor |
|------|------|------|------|------|
| 2750 | 2250 | 1750 | 1000 | 650 |

**Whitney-Remington Model 2 Rolling Block**

When Remington's patent for the Rolling Block action expired, Whitney was quick to reproduce the action, labeling it his "New Improved System." It is essentially quite similar to Remington's Rolling Block and is easily recognized when compared with the Model 1 because it has only two parts--the hammer and the breechblock. The frame is also rounded. The tang on this model is marked "Whitney Arms Company, New Haven, Ct USA." There were approximately 50,000 total manufactured between 1881 and 1888. There are a number of variations as follows:

**Shotgun**

This is a smooth-bore version chambered for 12, 14, 16, or 20 gauge. It is offered with barrel lengths between 26" and 30". Twenty-inch barrels have also been noted.

| Exc. | V.G. | Good | Fair | Poor |
|------|------|------|------|------|
| 650 | 550 | 450 | 300 | 200 |

**Military Carbine**

This version is chambered for the .433 and .45 centerfire cartridges. It has a 20.5" barrel and is blued, with a case-colored receiver and walnut stock. There were approximately 5,000 manufactured. Most were sent to South or Central America.

| Exc. | V.G. | Good | Fair | Poor |
|------|------|------|------|------|
| 1000 | 850 | 650 | 550 | 400 |

**Civilian Carbine**

This version is chambered for the .44 rimfire or centerfire cartridge with an 18.5" round barrel. The finish is similar to the Military Carbine. There were approximately 2,000 manufactured.

| Exc. | V.G. | Good | Fair | Poor |
|------|------|------|------|------|
| 1000 | 850 | 650 | 550 | 400 |

**Military Rifle**

This version is chambered for the .433, .45, or .50 centerfire cartridge. It has a 32.5" or 35" barrel. It is finished similarly to the Military Carbine. There were approximately 39,000 manufactured.

| Exc. | V.G. | Good | Fair | Poor |
|------|------|------|------|------|
| 1050 | 900 | 700 | 600 | 450 |

### No. 1 Sporting Rifle

This version is chambered for various popular sporting cartridges and is offered with barrel lengths from 26" to 30", either round or octagonal in configuration. The finish is blued, with a case-colored receiver and a varnished walnut stock. There were many options available that could radically affect the value, and a qualified appraisal would be advisable. There were approximately 3,000 manufactured.

| Exc. | V.G. | Good | Fair | Poor |
|------|------|------|------|------|
| 1100 | 950 | 750 | 650 | 500 |

### No. 2 Sporting Rifle

This is a smaller version of the No. 1 Rifle, chambered for the .22 rimfire, .32, .38, and .44-40 centerfire cartridges. Again, a qualified appraisal would be helpful, as many options can affect the value.

| Exc. | V.G. | Good | Fair | Poor |
|------|------|------|------|------|
| 950 | 850 | 650 | 550 | 400 |

### Whitney-Burgess-Morse Rifle

This is a lever-action repeating rifle chambered for the .45-70 Government cartridge. There are three variations. All have a magazine tube mounted beneath the barrel with blued finishes and walnut stocks. The barrels are marked "G. W. Morse Patented Oct. 28th, 1856." The tang is marked "A. Burgess Patented Jan 7th 1873, Patented Oct. 19th, 1873." There were approximately 3,000 total manufactured between 1878 and 1882. The variations are as follows:

### Sporting Rifle

This version has a 28" octagonal or round barrel. The magazine tube holds nine rounds. There are a number of options available that can increase the value drastically; and we recommend competent, individual appraisal. Value given is for a standard model.

| Exc. | V.G. | Good | Fair | Poor |
|------|------|------|------|------|
| 1250 | 1000 | 800 | 600 | 450 |

### Military Rifle

This version has a 33" round barrel with a full-length forearm held on by two barrel bands. It features military sights and has an 11-round tubular magazine. It has a bayonet lug and sling swivels. This variation is also found chambered for the .43 Spanish and .42 Russian cartridges. There were approximately 1,000 manufactured.

| Exc. | V.G. | Good | Fair | Poor |
|------|------|------|------|------|
| 1500 | 1250 | 1000 | 800 | 550 |

### Carbine

This version has a 22" round barrel with a full-length forearm held on by one barrel band. It has a 7-round tubular magazine and a saddle ring attached to the frame. There were approximately 500 manufactured.

| Exc. | V.G. | Good | Fair | Poor |
|------|------|------|------|------|
| 1750 | 1500 | 1250 | 1000 | 750 |

### Whitney-Kennedy Rifle

This is a lever-action repeating rifle that was manufactured in two sizes. It has a magazine tube mounted under the barrel and a blued finish with a case-colored lever. The stock is walnut. The barrel is marked "Whitney Arms Co New Haven, Conn. U.S.A." Occasionally, the word "Kennedy" is marked after the Whitney name. There are two major variations. One features a standard-type action lever; and the other, the same "S"-shaped lever that is found on the Burgess model. This version would be worth approximately 10 percent additional. As with many of the rifles of this era, there were many options available that will affect the values. We strongly recommend securing a qualified appraisal for all but the standard models if a transaction is contemplated. There were approximately 15,000 manufactured between 1879 and 1886. The variations of the Whitney-Kennedy and their values are as follows:

### Small Frame Sporting Rifle

This version is chambered for the .32-20, .38-40, and the .40-40 cartridges. It has a 24" barrel that is either round or octagonal in configuration. Examples will be noted with either a full-length or half-length tubular magazine.

| Exc. | V.G. | Good | Fair | Poor |
|------|------|------|------|------|
| 1500 | 1250 | 900 | 750 | 500 |

### Large Frame Sporting Rifle

This version is chambered for the .40-60, .45-60, .45-75, and the .50-90 cartridges. The .50-caliber version is uncommon and will bring a 20 percent premium. The barrel lengths offered are 26" or 28".

| Exc. | V.G. | Good | Fair | Poor |
|------|------|------|------|------|
| 1750 | 1500 | 1200 | 900 | 650 |

### Military Rifle

This is a large-frame model, chambered for the .40-60, .44-40, and the .45-60 cartridges. It has a 32.25" round barrel with either an 11- or 16-round tubular magazine. It has a full-length walnut forend held on by two barrel bands and features a bayonet lug and sling swivels. There were approximately 1,000 manufactured. Most were shipped to Central or South America.

| Exc. | V.G. | Good | Fair | Poor |
|------|------|------|------|------|
| 2250 | 1800 | 1500 | 1100 | 800 |

### Military Carbine

This is built on either the small-frame or large-frame action and is chambered for the .38-40, .44-40, .40-60, or .45-60 cartridges. It has either a 20" or 22" round barrel and a 9- or 12-round tubular magazine, depending on the caliber. It has a short forend held on by a single barrel band. There were approximately 1,000 manufactured. Most were sent to Central or South America.

| Exc. | V.G. | Good | Fair | Poor |
|------|------|------|------|------|
| 2250 | 1800 | 1500 | 1100 | 800 |

### Hooded Cylinder Pocket Revolver

This is an unusual revolver that is chambered for .28 caliber percussion. It has a manually rotated, 6-shot hooded cylinder that has etched decorations. The octagonal barrel is offered in lengths of 3" to 6". There is a button at the back of the frame that unlocks the cylinder so that it can be rotated. The finish is blued, with a brass frame and two-piece rounded walnut grips. It is marked "E. Whitney N. Haven, Ct." There were approximately 200 manufactured between 1850 and 1853.

| Exc. | V.G. | Good | Fair | Poor |
|------|------|------|------|------|
| 2500 | 2000 | 1750 | 1250 | 900 |

### Two Trigger Pocket Revolver

This is a conventional-appearing pocket revolver with a manually rotated cylinder. There is a second trigger located in front of the conventional triggerguard that releases the cylinder so that it can be turned. It is chambered for .32-caliber percussion and has an octagonal barrel from 3" to 6" in length. It has a 5-shot unfluted cylinder that is etched and a brass frame. The remainder is blued, with squared walnut two-piece grips. An iron-frame version is also available, but only 50 were produced. It would bring approximately 60 percent additional. There were approximately 650 total manufactured between 1852 and 1854.

| Exc. | V.G. | Good | Fair | Poor |
|------|------|------|------|------|
| 1500 | 1250 | 1000 | 750 | 550 |

### Whitney-Beals Patent Revolver

This was an unusual, ring-trigger pocket pistol that was made in three basic variations.

### First Model

This version is chambered for .31-caliber percussion and has barrels of octagonal configuration from 2" to 6" in length. It has a brass frame and a 6-shot cylinder. It is marked "F. Beals/New Haven, Ct." There were only 50 manufactured.

| Exc. | V.G. | Good | Fair | Poor |
|------|------|------|------|------|
| 2000 | 1750 | 1250 | 800 | 650 |

## .31 Caliber Model

This version has an iron frame and a 7-shot cylinder. The octagonal barrels are from 2" to 6" in length. It is marked "Address E. Whitney/Whitneyville, Ct." There were approximately 2,300 manufactured.

| Exc. | V.G. | Good | Fair | Poor |
|------|------|------|------|------|
| 1000 | 850 | 650 | 500 | 350 |

## .28 Caliber Model

Except for the caliber, this model is similar to the .31 Caliber Model. There were approximately 850 manufactured.

| Exc. | V.G. | Good | Fair | Poor |
|------|------|------|------|------|
| 1050 | 900 | 700 | 550 | 400 |

## Whitney 1851 Navy

This is a faithful copy of the 1851 Colt Revolver. It is virtually identical. There is a possibility that surplus Colt parts were utilized in the construction of this revolver. There were approximately 400 manufactured in 1857 and 1858.

| Exc. | V.G. | Good | Fair | Poor |
|------|------|------|------|------|
| 1800 | 1650 | 1250 | 800 | 550 |

## Whitney Navy Revolver

This is a single-action revolver chambered for .36-caliber percussion. It has a standard octagonal barrel length of 7.5". It has an iron frame and a 6-shot unfluted cylinder that is roll-engraved. The finish is blued, with a case-colored loading lever and two-piece walnut grips. The barrel is marked either "E. Whitney/N. Haven" or "Eagle Co." There are a number of minor variations on this revolver, and we strongly urge competent appraisal if contemplating a transaction. There were 33,000 total manufactured between 1858 and 1862.

### First Model

Nearly the entire production of the First Model is marked "Eagle Co." The reason for this marking is unknown. There are four distinct variations of this model. They are as follows:

### First Variation

This model has no integral loading-lever assembly and has a very thin top strap. There were only 100 manufactured.

| Exc. | V.G. | Good | Fair | Poor |
|------|------|------|------|------|
| 1750 | 1500 | 1250 | 850 | 550 |

### Second Variation

This version is similar to the First Variation, with an integral loading lever. There were approximately 200 manufactured.

| Exc. | V.G. | Good | Fair | Poor |
|------|------|------|------|------|
| 1250 | 1000 | 800 | 600 | 400 |

### Third Variation

This is similar to the Second, with a three-screw frame instead of four screws. The loading lever is also modified. There were approximately 500 manufactured.

| Exc. | V.G. | Good | Fair | Poor |
|------|------|------|------|------|
| 1250 | 1000 | 800 | 600 | 400 |

### Fourth Variation

This version has a rounded frame and a safety notch between the nipples on the rear of the cylinder. There have been examples noted marked "E. Whitney/N. Haven." There were approximately 700 manufactured.

| Exc. | V.G. | Good | Fair | Poor |
|------|------|------|------|------|
| 1250 | 1000 | 800 | 600 | 400 |

### Second Model

### First Variation

This version features a more robust frame with a brass triggerguard. The barrel is marked "E. Whitney/N. Haven." The cylinder pin is secured by a wing nut, and there is an integral loading lever. There were approximately 1,200 manufactured.

| Exc. | V.G. | Good | Fair | Poor |
|------|------|------|------|------|
| 800 | 650 | 500 | 400 | 300 |

### Second Variation

This version has six improved safety notches on the rear of the cylinder. There were approximately 10,000 manufactured.

| Exc. | V.G. | Good | Fair | Poor |
|------|------|------|------|------|
| 750 | 600 | 450 | 350 | 250 |

### Third Variation

This version has an improved, Colt-type loading-lever latch. There were approximately 2,000 manufactured.

| Exc. | V.G. | Good | Fair | Poor |
|------|------|------|------|------|
| 750 | 600 | 450 | 350 | 250 |

### Fourth Variation

This is similar to the Third except the cylinder is marked "Whitneyville." There were approximately 10,000 manufactured.

| Exc. | V.G. | Good | Fair | Poor |
|------|------|------|------|------|
| 750 | 600 | 450 | 350 | 250 |

### Fifth Variation

This version has a larger triggerguard. There were approximately 4,000 manufactured.

| Exc. | V.G. | Good | Fair | Poor |
|------|------|------|------|------|
| 750 | 600 | 450 | 350 | 250 |

### Sixth Variation

This version has the larger triggerguard and five-groove rifling instead of the usual seven-groove. There were approximately 2,500 manufactured.

| Exc. | V.G. | Good | Fair | Poor |
|------|------|------|------|------|
| 750 | 600 | 450 | 350 | 250 |

## Whitney Pocket Revolver

This is a single-action revolver chambered for .31-caliber percussion. It has octagonal barrels between 3" and 6" in length. It has a 5-shot unfluted cylinder that is roll-engraved and marked "Whitneyville." The frame is iron with a blued finish and a case-colored integral loading lever. The grips are two-piece walnut. The development of this model, as far as models and variations go, is identical to that which we described in the Navy Model designation. The values are different, and we list them for reference. Again, we recommend securing qualified appraisal if a transaction is contemplated. There were approximately 32,500 manufactured from 1858 to 1862.

### First Model
### First Variation

| Exc. | V.G. | Good | Fair | Poor |
|------|------|------|------|------|
| 950 | 850 | 700 | 550 | 400 |

### Second Variation

| Exc. | V.G. | Good | Fair | Poor |
|------|------|------|------|------|
| 850 | 750 | 600 | 450 | 300 |

### Third Variation

| Exc. | V.G. | Good | Fair | Poor |
|------|------|------|------|------|
| 750 | 650 | 500 | 350 | 250 |

### Fourth Variation

| Exc. | V.G. | Good | Fair | Poor |
|------|------|------|------|------|
| 750 | 650 | 500 | 350 | 250 |

### Fifth Variation

| Exc. | V.G. | Good | Fair | Poor |
|------|------|------|------|------|
| 750 | 650 | 500 | 350 | 250 |

### Second Model
### First Variation

| Exc. | V.G. | Good | Fair | Poor |
|------|------|------|------|------|
| 650 | 550 | 400 | 300 | 200 |

### Second Variation

| Exc. | V.G. | Good | Fair | Poor |
|------|------|------|------|------|
| 650 | 550 | 400 | 300 | 200 |

### Third Variation

| Exc. | V.G. | Good | Fair | Poor |
|------|------|------|------|------|
| 650 | 550 | 400 | 300 | 200 |

## Fourth Variation

| Exc. | V.G. | Good | Fair | Poor |
|------|------|------|------|------|
| 750 | 650 | 500 | 350 | 250 |

### New Model Pocket Revolver

This is a single-action, spur-triggered pocket revolver chambered for .28-caliber percussion. It has a 3.5" octagonal barrel and a 6-shot roll-engraved cylinder. It features an iron frame with a blued finish and two-piece walnut grips. The barrel is marked "E. Whitney/N. Haven." There were approximately 2,000 manufactured between 1860 and 1867.

| Exc. | V.G. | Good | Fair | Poor |
|------|------|------|------|------|
| 750 | 650 | 500 | 350 | 250 |

### Rimfire Pocket Revolver

This is a spur-trigger, single-action, solid-frame pocket revolver that was produced in three frame sizes, depending on the caliber. It is chambered for the .22, .32, and .38 rimfire cartridges. The frame is brass, and it is found in a variety of finishes--nickel-plated or blued, or a combination thereof. The birdshead grips are rosewood or hard rubber; ivory or pearl grips are sometimes encountered and will bring a slight premium in value. The barrels are octagonal and from 1.5" to 5" in length. The barrels are marked "Whitneyville Armory Ct. USA." They have also been noted with the trade names "Monitor," "Defender," or "Eagle." They were commonly referred to as the Model No. 1, No. 1.5, Model 2, or Model 2.5. The values for all are quite similar. There were approximately 30,000 manufactured of all types between 1871 and 1879.

| Exc. | V.G. | Good | Fair | Poor |
|------|------|------|------|------|
| 350 | 300 | 250 | 200 | 150 |

# WHITNEY FIREARMS COMPANY
## Hartford, Connecticut

### Wolverine

This is a blowback-operated, single-action, semi-automatic pistol chambered for the .22 l.r. cartridge. It has a 4.75" shrouded barrel and was styled in a very modern way that actually made this pistol years ahead of its time. It has an aluminum-alloy frame. The finish is either blued or nickel-plated, with plastic grips. There were approximately 13,000 blued models manufactured and 900 in nickel-plate. This pistol was manufactured between 1955 and 1962. Early models were designated the "Lightning." The slide is marked "Wolverine Whitney Firearms Inc., New Haven, Conn USA."

### Blue Finish

| Exc. | V.G. | Good | Fair | Poor |
|------|------|------|------|------|
| 450 | 400 | 350 | 250 | 200 |

### Nickel-Plated

| Exc. | V.G. | Good | Fair | Poor |
|------|------|------|------|------|
| 550 | 500 | 450 | 300 | 250 |

# WHITWORTH
## SEE--Interarms

# WICHITA ARMS, INC.
## Wichita, Kansas

### Classic Rifle

This is a very high quality single-shot bolt-action rifle chambered for various popular and wildcat cartridges up to the .308 Winchester. It has a 21" octagonal barrel and is furnished without sights. It is offered with a Canjar adjustable trigger and has a blued finish and a select checkered walnut stock.

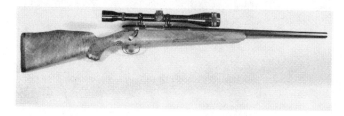

| NIB | Exc. | V.G. | Good | Fair | Poor |
|------|------|------|------|------|------|
| 3000 | 2500 | 2250 | 1850 | 1250 | 1000 |

### Varmint Rifle

This model is similar to the Classic Rifle except that it is chambered for the high-velocity, Varmint-type cartridges. It is featured with a round barrel instead of the octagonal one.

| NIB | Exc. | V.G. | Good | Fair | Poor |
|------|------|------|------|------|------|
| 2000 | 1750 | 1500 | 1250 | 1000 | 800 |

### Silhouette Rifle

This model is similar to the Classic Rifle, with a 24" heavy match barrel and a grey synthetic stock. It is furnished with a two-ounce Canjar trigger.

| NIB | Exc. | V.G. | Good | Fair | Poor |
|------|------|------|------|------|------|
| 2200 | 1900 | 1700 | 1000 | 850 | 650 |

### Wichita International Pistol

This is a single-shot, break-open target pistol chambered for various calibers from the .22 l.r. up to the .357 Magnum cartridge. It is constructed of stainless steel and is offered with a 10.5" or 14" barrel with either adjustable sights or scope mounts furnished. It has a walnut stock and forearm.

| NIB | Exc. | V.G. | Good | Fair | Poor |
|------|------|------|------|------|------|
| 500 | 450 | 400 | 350 | 300 | 200 |

### Wichita Classic Pistol

This model is chambered for various calibers up to the .308 Winchester. It is a bolt action with the bolt handle on the lefthand side so that a righthanded shooter does not have to change hands for loading. It is a single-shot with an 11.25" barrel. It is blued, with a select walnut stock.

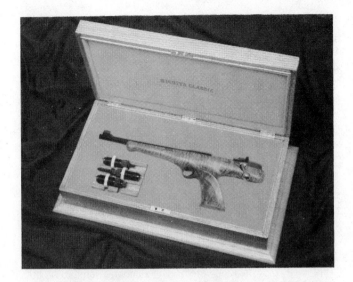

| NIB | Exc. | V.G. | Good | Fair | Poor |
|-----|------|------|------|------|------|
| 3000 | 2500 | 2250 | 1850 | 1250 | 1000 |

## Wichita Classic Engraved
This is a highly ornamented version of the Wichita Classic Pistol.

| NIB | Exc. | V.G. | Good | Fair | Poor |
|-----|------|------|------|------|------|
| 5000 | 4250 | 3500 | 2500 | 2000 | 1500 |

## Wichita Silhouette Pistol
This single-shot bolt-action pistol is chambered for the 7mm HMSA or the .308 Winchester cartridges. It has a 15" barrel with adjustable sights and a fully adjustable trigger. It features the lefthanded action for the righthanded shooter. The walnut stock has the pistol grip centrally located. The finish is blued.

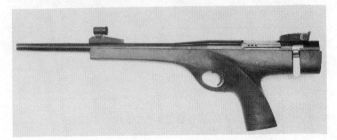

| NIB | Exc. | V.G. | Good | Fair | Poor |
|-----|------|------|------|------|------|
| 1100 | 950 | 750 | 600 | 500 | 400 |

## Wichita MK40
This model is similar to the Silhouette Pistol, with a 13" barrel and multi-range sights. It was originally furnished with a synthetic stock;, but as of 1988, walnut has been used. A stainless-steel version is available for approximately 20 percent additional.

| NIB | Exc. | V.G. | Good | Fair | Poor |
|-----|------|------|------|------|------|
| 1100 | 950 | 750 | 600 | 500 | 400 |

## WICKLIFFE RIFLES
## TRIPLE S DEVELOPMENT
### Wickliffe, Ohio

### Model 76
This is a single-shot, falling-block rifle chambered for various popular American cartridges from .22 Hornet up to the .45-70. It is furnished with either a 22" lightweight or a 26" heavy sporter-weight barrel. It is furnished without sights. It features a falling-block action activated by a combination triggerguard action lever. The finish is blued, with a select walnut stock. It was introduced in 1976.

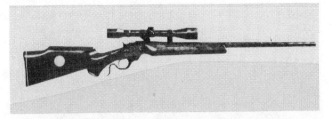

| Exc. | V.G. | Good | Fair | Poor |
|------|------|------|------|------|
| 400 | 350 | 300 | 250 | 175 |

### Model 76 Deluxe
This model is similar to the standard grade, with a nickel-silver pistolgrip cap and engine-turned breechblock, a higher polished finish, and better grade of wood. It was introduced in 1976.

| Exc. | V.G. | Good | Fair | Poor |
|------|------|------|------|------|
| 450 | 400 | 350 | 300 | 200 |

### Traditionalist
This version is similar to the Model 76, chambered for the .30-06 or .45-70 cartridge. It has a 24" barrel and is furnished with adjustable open sights and a hand-checkered, classic-style walnut buttstock. It was introduced in 1979.

| Exc. | V.G. | Good | Fair | Poor |
|------|------|------|------|------|
| 400 | 350 | 300 | 250 | 175 |

### Stinger
This version is similar to the Model 76 except that it is chambered for the .22 Hornet or the .223 Remington cartridges. It has a 22" barrel and a Monte Carlo-type stock. It is furnished with a Burris 6X scope and mounts. The receiver features an etched logo. It was introduced in 1979.

| Exc. | V.G. | Good | Fair | Poor |
|------|------|------|------|------|
| 400 | 350 | 300 | 250 | 175 |

### Stinger Deluxe
This version features a higher polished finish and better-grade walnut.

| Exc. | V.G. | Good | Fair | Poor |
|------|------|------|------|------|
| 475 | 400 | 350 | 300 | 200 |

## WIENER WAFFENFABRIK
### Vienna, Austria

### Little Tom
This is a double-action semi-automatic pistol designed by A. Tomiska. In 1919 he sold the manufacturing rights to Wiener of Austria. This pistol is chambered for either the 6.35mm or the 7.65mm cartridges. It has a 2.5" barrel and is blued, with either plain wood or plastic grips with the trademark on a medallion that was inlaid into them. The slide is marked "Wiener Waffenfabrik Patent Little Tom." The respective caliber is also

marked. The righthand side of the frame is marked "Made in Austria." There were approximately 10,000 manufactured between 1919 and 1925.

| Exc. | V.G. | Good | Fair | Poor |
|------|------|------|------|------|
| 500 | 450 | 400 | 250 | 175 |

# WILDEY FIREARMS CO., INC.
## Cheshire, Connecticut
## New Burg, New York
## Brookfield, Connecticut

### Wildey Auto Pistol
This is a unique, gas-operated, rotary-bolt, double-action semi-automatic pistol designed for use as a hunting or long-range target-silhouette gun. It is chambered for the .357 Peterbuilt, the .45 Winchester Magnum, or the .475 Wildey Magnum cartridges. It is offered with a 5", 6", 7", 8", or 10" ventilated-rib barrel. The gas-operated action is adjustable and features a single-shot cutoff. The rotary bolt has three heavy locking lugs. It is constructed of stainless steel and has adjustable sights with wood grips. The values of this rarely encountered pistol are based on not only the condition, but the caliber--as well as the serial number range, with earlier-numbered guns being worth a good deal more than the later or current-production models.

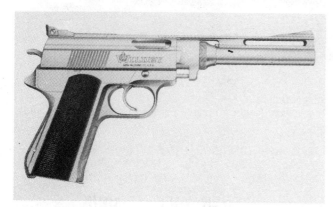

### Cheshire CT Address
This model was produced in .45 Winchester Magnum only and is serial-numbered from No. 1 through 2,489.

### Serial No. 1 through 200

| NIB | Exc. | V.G. | Good | Fair | Poor |
|-----|------|------|------|------|------|
| 2000 | 1750 | 1500 | 1250 | 900 | 600 |

### Serial Numbers Above 200 Would Be Worth Approximately $200 Less Respectively in Each Category of Condition.

### Survivor Model
This is the currently manufactured model produced in Brookfield, Connecticut.

| NIB | Exc. | V.G. | Good | Fair | Poor |
|-----|------|------|------|------|------|
| 1100 | 950 | 800 | 600 | 500 | 400 |

### Presentation Model
This is a factory-engraved version of the Survivor Model with hand-checkered grips. It is worth top dollar only in unfired condition with all furnished materials.

| NIB | Exc. | V.G. | Good | Fair | Poor |
|-----|------|------|------|------|------|
| 2500 | 2000 | 1500 | 1250 | 850 | 700 |

# WILKINSON ARMS CO.
## Covina, California

### Diane
This is a blowback-operated, single-action, semi-automatic pocket pistol chambered for the .25 ACP cartridge. It has a 2.25" barrel with fixed sights and a 6-shot detachable magazine. The finish is matte blued, with plastic grips.

| Exc. | V.G. | Good | Fair | Poor |
|------|------|------|------|------|
| 150 | 125 | 100 | 75 | 50 |

### Terry Carbine
This is a blowback-action semi-automatic carbine chambered for the 9mm Parabellum cartridge. It has a 16.25" barrel and is fired from the closed-breech position. It has adjustable sights and a 30-round detachable box magazine. The finish is matte blued, with either a black synthetic stock or a stock of maple.

| Exc. | V.G. | Good | Fair | Poor |
|------|------|------|------|------|
| 350 | 300 | 250 | 175 | 125 |

# WILLIAMSON
# MOORE FIREARMS COMPANY
## New York, New York

### Deringer
This is a single-shot derringer chambered for the .41-caliber rimfire cartridge. It also accepts a percussion chamber adapter. It has a 2.5" barrel that slides forward, exposing the breech for loading. The frame and the triggerguard are silver-plated brass with a blued barrel and a checkered walnut grip. The barrel is marked "Williamson's Pat. Oct. 2, 1866 New York." There were approximately 3,000 manufactured between 1866 and 1870.

| Exc. | V.G. | Good | Fair | Poor |
|------|------|------|------|------|
| 500 | 450 | 350 | 250 | 175 |

## WILSON, J. P.
### Ilion, New York

### Percussion Alarm Gun

This unusual little device is chambered for .22-caliber percussion. It consists of approximately a 1" rectangular brass block with a chamber bored into it that accepts a black-powder charge. There is no provision for a projectile. There is a spring-retained arm on top, that works as a hammer. As the device is activated by a door or a window, the hammer snaps closed, striking a percussion cap that causes the charge to fire, thereby creating an alarm notifying that the perimeter has been breached. It is marked "J. P. Wilson/Patented Feb. 8. 1859/Ilion., N.Y."

| Exc. | V.G. | Good | Fair | Poor |
|------|------|------|------|------|
| 250 | 200 | 175 | 100 | 50 |

## WINCHESTER REPEATING ARMS COMPANY
### New Haven, Connecticut

With the exception of Colt, no other firearm is as widely collected or respected for its part in the history and development of the United States of America as the Winchester Rifle. Indeed, one of its many models is actually known as "The Gun That Won the West." The history of the Winchester Company parallels the settlement of the American West, and many of its early lever-action and single-shot models have become widely sought after by collectors of Americana. It is important to note that the values of the early Winchester rifles have risen dramatically in recent years. They were available with many extra options that also have a radical effect on values. We strongly suggest that anyone contemplating investment in these firearms secure a qualified appraisal before acting.

One of the greatest advantages in collecting Winchester arms is that there are a number of quality informative publications available on the subject. One should avail oneself of this material and further a personal education before embarking on the collector's path. We supply information and values for the Winchester arms and their predecessors in a chronological order. It is fortunate that Winchester's factory records are nearly intact for many of their models. They offer an authentication service, and the astute collector will make use of this service.

### Hunt Repeating Rifle

In 1849 Walter Hunt developed what was technically the first Winchester rifle. This weapon fired a projectile that was hollow with the propellant packed within it. There was a cork disk with a hole through it on the back of this projectile that permitted the flash from the priming device to pass through it and ignite the powder. These cartridges were known as "Rocket Balls." Mr. Hunt fondly referred to his creation as the "Volition Repeater." It is believed that only the patent model was produced. It is located in the Winchester Museum. Of course, it is impossible to evaluate a weapon of this rarity.

### Jennings

This model is listed in its own section of this text.

### Smith & Wesson Lever Action Pistols

See Smith & Wesson section of this text.

### Volcanic Lever Action Firearms

This model is listed in its own section of this text.

The four preceding models were technically not Winchester firearms but contributed to the evolution of the final product. They are historically noteworthy as the immediate predecessors of the Winchester line and should be considered as such.

### Henry Rifle

At the time of the development of this Rifle, Oliver Winchester was the president of the New Haven Arms Company. The Henry Rifle was manufactured by the New Haven Arms Company. It was developed directly from the Volcanic and was chambered for the .44 rimfire cartridge. It has a 24" octagonal barrel with a tubular magazine machined integrally beneath it. This magazine holds 15 rounds. There is no forearm. The buttstock is made of walnut. There was a brass-frame version with a brass buttplate and a rarer iron-frame version as well. There were approximately 1,900 units that bore U.S. military markings "C.G.C." on the breech of the barrel and the stock. There was a total quantity of approximately 13,000 manufactured between 1860 and 1866. It was used on a very limited basis in the Civil War.

### Brass-Frame Model

| Exc. | V.G. | Good | Fair | Poor |
|------|------|------|------|------|
| 16500 | 12500 | 10000 | 6500 | 4000 |

### Iron-Frame Model--Several Hundred Manufactured

| Exc. | V.G. | Good | Fair | Poor |
|------|------|------|------|------|
| 25000 | 18500 | 13500 | 8500 | 6500 |

### Martially Marked

| Exc. | V.G. | Good | Fair | Poor |
|------|------|------|------|------|
| 2000 | 16500 | 11500 | 8000 | 6000 |

### Model 1866

In 1866 the company name was changed to "The Winchester Repeating Arms Company." Production facilities were moved to Bridgeport, Connecticut. The business offices remained in New Haven. In 1870 manufacturing operations moved back to New Haven. The Model 1866 was actually the first rifle to be produced under the Winchester name. It was chambered for the .44 rimfire cartridge and was made in three barrel lengths. The standard rifle has a 24" octagonal barrel; the carbine has a 20" round barrel; and the musket has a 27" round barrel. The carbine and the musket have one and two barrel bands, respectively, holding on the forearms. This model features a brass frame and a browned barrel with the remainder case-colored. It has a tubular magazine running beneath the barrel and a walnut stock.

The carbine features a saddle ring on the left side of the frame. The barrel is marked "Henry's Patent - Oct. 16, 1860 King's Patent - March 29, 1866" or "Winchester's - Repeating - Arms. New Haven., Ct. King's - Improvement - Patented March 29, 1866 Oct. 16, 1860." There were approximately 170,000 manufactured between 1866 and 1898. This is a very valuable and collectible model that consists of a great many minor variations which have drastic effects on values. We supply general values for the basic models but strongly recommend securing a competent appraisal if a transaction is contemplated.

### 1st Model

This version has the Henry & King's barrel marking, flat loading-gate cover, and two-screw upper tang. It was serial-numbered to approximately 15,500. No muskets were manufactured.

### Rifle

| Exc. | V.G. | Good | Fair | Poor |
|------|------|------|------|------|
| 16500 | 13000 | 8500 | 4750 | 3350 |

### Carbine

| Exc. | V.G. | Good | Fair | Poor |
|------|------|------|------|------|
| 11000 | 8000 | 5000 | 2500 | 1250 |

### 2nd Model

This version has a flared frame that meets the forearm and is serial-numbered between 15,500 and 25,000. No muskets were manufactured.

**Rifle**

| Exc. | V.G. | Good | Fair | Poor |
|------|------|------|------|------|
| 11000 | 8000 | 5000 | 2500 | 1250 |

**Carbine**

| Exc. | V.G. | Good | Fair | Poor |
|------|------|------|------|------|
| 9500 | 7000 | 4000 | 1250 | 650 |

### 3rd Model

This version has the Winchester New Haven barrel marking. The serial number was stamped behind the trigger and for the first time was visible without removing the stock. This version is serial-numbered between 25,000 to 149,000.

**Rifle**

| Exc. | V.G. | Good | Fair | Poor |
|------|------|------|------|------|
| 9500 | 7000 | 4000 | 1250 | 650 |

**Musket**

| Exc. | V.G. | Good | Fair | Poor |
|------|------|------|------|------|
| 8500 | 6500 | 2750 | 1000 | 500 |

**Carbine**

| Exc. | V.G. | Good | Fair | Poor |
|------|------|------|------|------|
| 8500 | 6500 | 2750 | 1000 | 500 |

### 4th Model

This version features the same barrel markings as the 3rd Model and has the serial number engraved in script on the lower tang. It was numbered between the 149,000 and 170,000 serial range. Late guns feature an iron buttplate.

**Rifle**

| Exc. | V.G. | Good | Fair | Poor |
|------|------|------|------|------|
| 8500 | 6500 | 2750 | 1000 | 500 |

**Musket**

| Exc. | V.G. | Good | Fair | Poor |
|------|------|------|------|------|
| 6000 | 4000 | 1750 | 650 | 400 |

**Carbine**

| Exc. | V.G. | Good | Fair | Poor |
|------|------|------|------|------|
| 7500 | 5500 | 2250 | 850 | 450 |

### Model 1873

This Model, perhaps more so than any other, could be termed "The Gun That Won the West." It is a lever-action repeating rifle chambered for the .32-20, .38-40, .44-40, and the .22 rimfire cartridge. It was offered as a standard rifle with a 24" round or octagonal barrel. This version has a crescent buttplate and a capped forend. The musket version has a 30", round barrel with a full-length forend held on by three barrel bands. It features a military carbine-type buttplate with adjustable sights. The carbine version has a 20" round barrel. The forend is held on by a barrel band, and it features a carbine-type buttplate. There is a saddle ring mounted on the left of the frame. The finish is blued and case-colored, with a walnut stock. The serial number is marked on the lower tang, and "Model 1873" and the Winchester name is stamped on the upper tang.

The barrel is marked with the Winchester address and the King's improvement patent date. There were approximately 700,000 centerfire versions and 19,500 chambered for the .22 rimfire cartridge manufactured between 1873 and 1919. There was a special group of high-grade rifles labeled the "1 of 1,000," of which 136 were produced. There were also eight "1 of 100" rifles. These markings are found on the breech. We strongly urge securing a qualified appraisal if contemplating a transaction on one of these models as there are undoubtedly a great many more fakes than authentic versions.
Deluxe Models--Add 50 Percent.

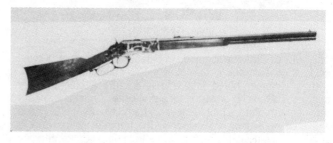

### 1st Model

This version is serial-numbered up to 31,000 and has a dust cover with guide grooves on the side.

**Rifle**

| Exc. | V.G. | Good | Fair | Poor |
|------|------|------|------|------|
| 6000 | 3750 | 1850 | 775 | 400 |

**Musket**

| Exc. | V.G. | Good | Fair | Poor |
|------|------|------|------|------|
| 6000 | 3750 | 1850 | 775 | 400 |

**Carbine**

| Exc. | V.G. | Good | Fair | Poor |
|------|------|------|------|------|
| 6750 | 4500 | 2400 | 1000 | 600 |

### 2nd Model

The dust cover slides on a central rail that is screwed onto the rear section of the frame. The serial number range is from 31,000 to 90,000.

**Rifle**

| Exc. | V.G. | Good | Fair | Poor |
|------|------|------|------|------|
| 5000 | 3000 | 1650 | 650 | 350 |

**Musket**

| Exc. | V.G. | Good | Fair | Poor |
|------|------|------|------|------|
| 3500 | 2450 | 1250 | 500 | 300 |

**Carbine**

| Exc. | V.G. | Good | Fair | Poor |
|------|------|------|------|------|
| 6000 | 3750 | 1850 | 775 | 400 |

### 3rd Model

This version features an integrally machined dustcover rail. The serial number range is from 90,000 to approximately 700,000.

**Rifle**

| Exc. | V.G. | Good | Fair | Poor |
|------|------|------|------|------|
| 4750 | 2750 | 1250 | 500 | 325 |

**Musket**

| Exc. | V.G. | Good | Fair | Poor |
|------|------|------|------|------|
| 4500 | 2500 | 1050 | 450 | 300 |

**Carbine**

| Exc. | V.G. | Good | Fair | Poor |
|------|------|------|------|------|
| 6000 | 3750 | 1850 | 775 | 400 |

### .22 Rimfire Rifle

This version features a 24" or 26" barrel and was manufactured between 1884 and 1904.

| Exc. | V.G. | Good | Fair | Poor |
|------|------|------|------|------|
| 5000 | 3000 | 1750 | 750 | 350 |

## Model 1876

This is a large caliber, lever-action rifle designed with the big game hunter in mind. It was chambered for the .40- 60, .45-60, .45-75, and the .50-95 cartridges. It was offered in a standard rifle with a 26" or 28" round or octagonal barrel with a forend that has a metal cap. It has a crescent buttplate. The musket version features a 32" round barrel and a full-length forend held on by one barrel band. It has a carbine-type buttplate and military sights. The carbine version has a 22" round barrel, with the forearm held on by one barrel band. There is a bayonet lug and a carbine-type buttplate. They all have tubular magazines mounted beneath the barrel. The finish is blued and case-colored, with walnut stocks. Serial numbers are stamped on the lower tang. The upper tang is marked "Model 1876."

The Winchester address and King's improvement patent dates are stamped on the barrel. The caliber marking is stamped on the bottom of the elevator block. This version is also known as the "Centennial Model" because it was introduced on the 100th anniversary of the U.S.A. There were approximately 64,000 manufactured between 1876 and 1897. A 1 of 1,000 and 1 of 100 versions were manufactured; as on the Model 1873, the same caution applies.

Deluxe Model--Add 50 Percent.

### 1st Model

This version has no dustcover and is serial-numbered from 1 to 3,000.

**Rifle**

| Exc. | V.G. | Good | Fair | Poor |
|------|------|------|------|------|
| 6000 | 3750 | 1850 | 775  | 400  |

**Musket**

| Exc. | V.G. | Good | Fair | Poor |
|------|------|------|------|------|
| 8500 | 5750 | 2750 | 2000 | 1500 |

**Carbine**

| Exc. | V.G. | Good | Fair | Poor |
|------|------|------|------|------|
| 6500 | 4250 | 2400 | 1300 | 750  |

### 2nd Model

This version features a dustcover and is serial-numbered from 3,000 to 30,000.

**Rifle**

| Exc. | V.G. | Good | Fair | Poor |
|------|------|------|------|------|
| 4750 | 2750 | 1250 | 500  | 350  |

**Musket**

| Exc. | V.G. | Good | Fair | Poor |
|------|------|------|------|------|
| 8000 | 5250 | 2250 | 1500 | 950  |

**Carbine**

| Exc. | V.G. | Good | Fair | Poor |
|------|------|------|------|------|
| 6500 | 4250 | 2400 | 1300 | 750  |

### 3rd Model

This version features an integrally machined dustcover guide rail. It is serial-numbered from 30,000 to 64,000.

**Rifle**

| Exc. | V.G. | Good | Fair | Poor |
|------|------|------|------|------|
| 5250 | 3250 | 1550 | 650  | 350  |

**Musket**

| Exc. | V.G. | Good | Fair | Poor |
|------|------|------|------|------|
| 7500 | 4750 | 1800 | 1100 | 700  |

**Carbine**

| Exc. | V.G. | Good | Fair | Poor |
|------|------|------|------|------|
| 6000 | 3750 | 1850 | 775  | 400  |

## Model 1885

This is a single-shot, falling-block breechloader chambered for many calibers from the .22 rimfire up to the large 50-caliber centerfire cartridges. It was offered with various-length barrels, either round or octagonal in configuration. There were a number of different versions of this high quality rifle. It was available as both a high-wall model (with an extremely strong action in which the breechblock was entirely covered on the sides by the action walls) and a low-wall version (in which the breechblock and the hammer spur is visible). The low-wall variation appeared after the serial number 5,000. There are two other basic variations that the collector considers. The thick-side frame has flat sides that do not flare to meet the stock. Most low-wall rifles feature the thick-side frame.

The thin-side frame features side walls that are milled out so that their sides flare to meet the stock. They are more common on the high-wall model. The finish of the single-shot rifles was blued and case-colored, with walnut stocks and forearms. Full-blue models appeared after serial number 90,000. The serial number is marked on the lower tang. The barrel has the Winchester address and patent dates. Later variations have the word "Winchester" stamped on the upper tang. This rifle was designed by John Browning and is highly sought after among both collectors and custom rifle builders. With this model, as well as with the other early Winchesters, we strongly recommend securing a qualified appraisal as many variations are present. There were approximately 140,000 manufactured between 1885 and 1920.

### Standard High-Wall Rifle

This version was chambered for a number of calibers and was offered with round or octagonal barrels between 24" and 30" in length. It has a straight-grip walnut stock with a crescent buttplate.

| Exc. | V.G. | Good | Fair | Poor |
|------|------|------|------|------|
| 3500 | 2450 | 1250 | 700  | 350  |

### Standard Low-Wall Rifle

This was similar to the configurations of the high-wall variations except that it featured the low-wall action.

| Exc. | V.G. | Good | Fair | Poor |
|------|------|------|------|------|
| 3250 | 2250 | 1050 | 600  | 300  |

### High-Wall Musket

This version was most-often chambered in .22 rimfire and has a 28" round barrel with a full-length forend held on by two barrel bands. It features military-type target sights and a shotgun-type buttplate. Many have martial markings and U.S. inspector's marks. Thick-side versions chambered for the .45-70 cartridge would be worth approximately 50 percent additional.

| Exc. | V.G. | Good | Fair | Poor |
|------|------|------|------|------|
| 4500 | 3250 | 2000 | 1400 | 750  |

### Low-Wall Musket (Winder Musket)

This version is similar in configuration to the high-wall musket, is chambered for the rimfire cartridge, and features the low-wall action. It was named after Colonel C. B. Winder, who was a prominent marksman of the day. It features a Lyman receiver sight with interchangeable disks.

| Exc. | V.G. | Good | Fair | Poor |
|------|------|------|------|------|
| 550  | 450  | 350  | 200  | 150  |

### High-Wall Schuetzen Rifle

This is a high-grade target version chambered for various center-fire calibers. It was offered with double-set triggers and a deluxe checkered stock with a Schuetzen-type buttplate, fancy scroll, triggerguard action lever, and a palmrest. It is usually found with a 30" octagonal barrel and was introduced in 1900.

| Exc. | V.G. | Good | Fair | Poor |
|------|------|------|------|------|
| 6000 | 4750 | 2800 | 1450 | 800  |

## Model 1886

This is a heavy-duty, lever-action repeating rifle chambered for various cartridges from the .33 W.C.F. to the .50-110 Express. The most desirable and popular chambering is the .45-70. This cartridge will bring a 15 percent premium in value. The Model 1886 rifle was designed for big game hunters and utilized the most powerful cartridges available in that era. It has various barrel lengths depending on the configuration. They are either round or octagonal. It utilizes a tubular magazine that is mounted beneath the barrel. The frame was stronger than any other previously offered, with vertical locking bolts that came through the action from top to bottom. There were many options available for this rifle.

It is essential that these weapons be individually appraised, as these options have a drastic effect on values. The Model 1886 was blued and case-colored; later models were all-blued. The stocks are walnut. It was offered with either a crescent, shotgun-type, or military carbine buttplate. The serial number is located on the lower tang. The upper tang features the "Model 1886" stamping. This rifle was designed by John Browning and was extremely popular in its day and remains so with Winchester collectors. There were approximately 160,000 total manufactured between 1886 and 1935. Antique variations produced before 1898 would be worth an approximate 20 percent premium.

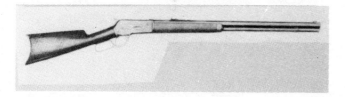

### Standard Rifle

This version has a 26" round or octagonal barrel with a steel forend cap. It was offered standard with an adjustable open sight, a straight-grip stock, and a crescent buttplate. All other versions would be considered options. Takedown rifles would be worth approximately 20 percent additional.

| Exc. | V.G. | Good | Fair | Poor |
|------|------|------|------|------|
| 5000 | 3500 | 1750 | 850 | 550 |

### Musket

This version has a 30" round barrel, with a full-length forearm held on by one barrel band. It features adjustable, military-type sights and is extremely rare. There were approximately 350 manufactured.

| Exc. | V.G. | Good | Fair | Poor |
|-------|-------|------|------|------|
| 17500 | 12500 | 8500 | 4750 | 2750 |

### Carbine

This version has a 22" round barrel, with a forend held on by one barrel band. It has a saddle ring mounted on the left of the frame and features a carbine-type buttplate.

| Exc. | V.G. | Good | Fair | Poor |
|-------|------|------|------|------|
| 14500 | 8000 | 5250 | 2800 | 1500 |

## Model 71

This version was introduced in 1935 and is the continuation of the Model 1886 line. The physical appearance is similar to that of the Model 1886. It was chambered for the .348 Winchester cartridge and was offered with either a 20" or 24" round barrel. It features a three-quarter length tubular magazine. The finish is blued, with a walnut stock. There were approximately 47,000 manufactured between 1935 and 1957. A deluxe model with checkered, select walnut stock was also available.

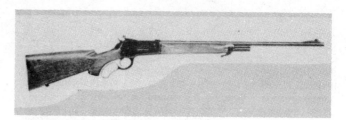

### Standard Model--24" Barrel

| Exc. | V.G. | Good | Fair | Poor |
|------|------|------|------|------|
| 850 | 650 | 500 | 400 | 300 |

### 20" Barrel Model

| Exc. | V.G. | Good | Fair | Poor |
|------|------|------|------|------|
| 3500 | 2500 | 1500 | 800 | 500 |

### Deluxe Model

| Exc. | V.G. | Good | Fair | Poor |
|------|------|------|------|------|
| 1500 | 950 | 750 | 500 | 400 |

## Model 1892

This rifle is a scaled-down version of the Model 1886 action. It was chambered for the .32-20, .38-40, and the .44-40 cartridges. The .25-20 and the .218 Bee cartridges were added at a later date and are somewhat rare. It was offered with various-length barrels depending on the configuration. It features a tubular magazine beneath the barrel. The finish was blued, with a walnut stock. Case colors were available as a special-order option. The upper tang is marked "Model 1892, Winchester." The barrel has the standard Winchester address. There were a number of options available for this rifle which would have a drastic effect on its value, and a qualified appraisal should be secured if one is in doubt. There were approximately 1,000,000 manufactured between 1892 and 1941. Antique versions manufactured before 1898 would be worth approximately a 25 percent premium.

### Standard Rifle

This version features a 24" round or octagonal barrel, a steel forend cap, and a crescent buttplate. Takedown versions would be worth approximately a 20 percent premium.

| Exc. | V.G. | Good | Fair | Poor |
|------|------|------|------|------|
| 2750 | 1850 | 850 | 475 | 275 |

### Musket

This version has a 30" round barrel, with a full-length forend held on by three barrel bands. It has a military-type buttplate and adjustable military sights. This version is very rare.

| Exc. | V.G. | Good | Fair | Poor |
|------|------|------|------|------|
| 5000 | 3500 | 2500 | 950 | 500 |

### Carbine

This variation has a 20" round barrel, with a forend held on by a barrel band. It has a saddle ring on the left side of the frame and a carbine-type buttplate.

| Exc. | V.G. | Good | Fair | Poor |
|------|------|------|------|------|
| 2650 | 1750 | 750 | 400 | 250 |

## Model 53

This version was a continuation of the Model 1892 design. It was chambered for the .25-20, .32-20, and the .44-40 cartridges. It was offered with a 22" round barrel and has a tubular, half-length magazine under the barrel. The finish is blued, with a walnut stock. The barrel is marked with the standard Winchester address and "Model 53." There were approximately 25,000 manufactured between 1924 and 1932. It was available either as a standard rifle or a takedown version. The values for both variations are the same.

| Exc. | V.G. | Good | Fair | Poor |
|------|------|------|------|------|
| 2250 | 1450 | 850 | 500 | 300 |

## Model 65

This version is very similar to the Model 1892. It is chambered for the .218 Bee, .25-20, and the .32-20 cartridges. It has a half-length tubular magazine and a 22" round barrel. The finish is blued with a walnut stock that had a checkered, steel, shotgun-type buttplate. There were approximately 5,700 manufactured between 1933 and 1947. The barrel is marked "Model 65."

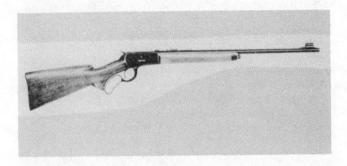

| Exc. | V.G. | Good | Fair | Poor |
|------|------|------|------|------|
| 3000 | 2200 | 1500 | 775 | 500 |

## Model 1894

This is Winchester's No. 1 production item. It was introduced in 1894 and has remained in production ever since. It had been chambered for the .25-35, .30-30, .32-40, .32 Winchester Special, and the .38-55 cartridges. Most have been produced in the .30-30 chambering. It is a lever-action repeating rifle with a tubular magazine under the barrel. It is similar in appearance to the Model 1892 but does not have the vertical locking bolts. It is available with various barrel lengths depending on the variation. The finish is blued and case-colored; later models are all-blued. The stock is walnut. The upper tang is marked "Model 1893 Winchester." The barrel bears the Winchester barrel address. This rifle was designed by John Browning. There have been millions produced during its long production run. Antique variations manufactured before 1898 would be worth an approximate 25 percent premium.

### Rifle

This version has a 26" octagonal barrel and a crescent-style buttplate. The forend has a steel cap. Takedown versions would add approximately 20 percent to the value.

| Exc. | V.G. | Good | Fair | Poor |
|------|------|------|------|------|
| 1750 | 1100 | 700 | 375 | 250 |

### Carbine

This version has a 20" round barrel with a saddle ring on the left side of the frame. Versions produced after 1925 did not feature the saddle ring and would be worth approximately 20 percent less. The values furnished here are for the pre-'64 Winchester carbines and should not be confused with the inexpensive later models that are still on the market today.

| Exc. | V.G. | Good | Fair | Poor |
|------|------|------|------|------|
| 800 | 600 | 450 | 325 | 250 |

## Model 55

This was a continuation of the Model 1894 design. It was chambered for the .25-35, .30-30, and the .32 Winchester Special cartridges. The round barrel is 24" in length, and it has a half-length tubular magazine. The finish is blued with a walnut stock with a checkered, shotgun-type buttplate. The barrel is marked "Model 55" in addition to the standard barrel address. There were approximately 20,000 manufactured between 1924 and 1932. The takedown version of this model is actually more commonly encountered than the solid-frame version and would be worth approximately 10 percent less.

| Exc. | V.G. | Good | Fair | Poor |
|------|------|------|------|------|
| 1500 | 950 | 600 | 375 | 275 |

## Model 64

This was also a continuation of the Model 1894 design. It is chambered for the .25-35, .30-30, .219 Zipper, and the .32 Winchester Special cartridges. It features barrel lengths from 20" to 26" that are round in configuration, and it has a three-quarter length tubular magazine. The finish is blued with a walnut stock, and "Model 64" appears on the barrel along with the standard Winchester barrel address. A takedown model was not offered. The .25-35 and the .219 Zipper chamberings would be worth approximately 50 percent additional.

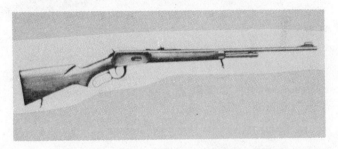

| Exc. | V.G. | Good | Fair | Poor |
|------|------|------|------|------|
| 1500 | 950 | 600 | 375 | 275 |

## Model 1895

The Model 1895 rifle was a milestone in the production of lever-action repeaters. It was the first version that used an integral box magazine located in front of the triggerguard instead of the usual tubular magazines that were utilized up to this time. This rifle was chambered for the .30-03, .30-06, .303 British, .30-40 Krag, .35 Winchester, .38-72, .40-72, .405 Winchester, and the 7.62mm Russian cartridges. This rifle was also designed by John Browning. It was also the first lever-action rifle that was chambered for the high-powered, smokeless cartridges that were currently becoming popular. One of its greatest claims to fame was that Teddy Roosevelt favored one chambered for the .405 Winchester cartridge as "Lion Medicine" on his African safaris. There were a number of variations and barrel lengths available. The finish was blued, with case colors available on a custom-order basis. The stock is walnut. The tang is marked "Winchester Model 1895." The Winchester name and address appear on the frame, and the caliber is marked on the breech of the barrel. There were approximately 426,000 manufactured between 1896 and 1931.

## Russian Model Musket

This version is chambered for the 7.62mm Russian cartridge. It has a 28" round barrel, with a full-length forearm held on by two barrel bands. This variation features Russian ordnance stamps, a stripper-clip guide on the top of the receiver, and a bayonet lug at the muzzle. There were 293,800 produced under a contract from the Imperial Russian government between 1915 and 1916.

| Exc. | V.G. | Good | Fair | Poor |
|------|------|------|------|------|
| 2750 | 1750 | 1200 | 750 | 350 |

### Standard Rifle

This version is chambered for the standard offered cartridges and has various-length round barrels. It has the contoured receiver sides and is serial-numbered between 5,000 and 425,000. A takedown model was available and would add approximately 20 percent to the value.

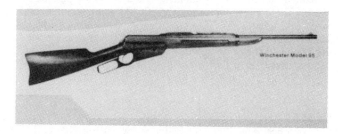

| Exc. | V.G. | Good | Fair | Poor |
|------|------|------|------|------|
| 2500 | 1500 | 1000 | 600 | 300 |

### Flatside Model

This version features a flat frame with no contours. It was offered in standard barrel lengths with a crescent-type buttplate. It has a one-piece lever and a two-piece magazine. It was serial-numbered under 5,000.

| Exc. | V.G. | Good | Fair | Poor |
|------|------|------|------|------|
| 3000 | 1850 | 1200 | 750 | 450 |

### Flatside Musket

This is a flatside version chambered for the .30-40 Krag cartridge. It has a 28" round barrel with a full-length stock but no hand guard. It is held on by two barrel bands. It features military-type sights and a shotgun-type buttplate. It was serial-numbered under 5,000.

| Exc. | V.G. | Good | Fair | Poor |
|------|------|------|------|------|
| 6000 | 4250 | 2750 | 1250 | 700 |

### Standard Musket

This version is similar to the Flatside Musket but has the contoured frame sides. It is chambered for .30-03 and .30-06, as well as the .30-40 Krag cartridges.

| Exc. | V.G. | Good | Fair | Poor |
|------|------|------|------|------|
| 3000 | 1850 | 1200 | 750 | 450 |

### Martially Marked Musket

This version was purchased by the U.S. Government and has the "US" inspector's marks on the frame. It is chambered for the .30-40 cartridge. This version should be authenticated. We recommend qualified appraisal.

| Exc. | V.G. | Good | Fair | Poor |
|------|------|------|------|------|
| 3450 | 2200 | 1500 | 1000 | 650 |

### Carbine

This version is chambered for the .30-03, .30-06, and the .303 British cartridges. It has the contoured frame sides and a 22" barrel. It has a half-length stock and a hand guard held on by one barrel band. It features a shotgun-type buttplate and adjustable, military-type sights. It is found with or without a saddle ring. U.S.-marked specimens would be worth approximately 80 percent additional if authenticated. We recommend appraisals.

| Exc. | V.G. | Good | Fair | Poor |
|------|------|------|------|------|
| 2750 | 1750 | 1200 | 750 | 350 |

### Double Barrel Shotgun

This is a side-by-side, double-barrel shotgun that was manufactured in England and was imported to be marketed by Winchester. They were sold at a company store that Winchester maintained in New York City. They are chambered for 10 or 12 gauge, with barrel lengths of 30" or 32". They have Damascus barrels with external hammers and double triggers. They were offered as either standard or engraved models. The center ribs are marked "Winchester Repeating Arms Co. New Haven, Con-

necticut U.S.A." The locks are marked "Class A, B, C, or D." They feature checkered, English walnut stocks. The utility gun is marked "Grade D," and the best-grade gun is marked "Match Gun." The shotguns were imported between 1879 and 1884.

### Class A, B, C, and D

| Exc. | V.G. | Good | Fair | Poor |
|------|------|------|------|------|
| 3500 | 2250 | 1400 | 750 | 350 |

### Match Gun

| Exc. | V.G. | Good | Fair | Poor |
|------|------|------|------|------|
| 4000 | 2500 | 1550 | 850 | 450 |

### Model 1887 Shotgun

This is a unique lever-action shotgun chambered for 10 or 12 gauge. It was offered with a 30" or 32" barrel and as a riot gun with a 20" barrel. It has a 5-round, tubular magazine and is blued and case-colored with a walnut pistolgrip stock. The lower tang has the standard Winchester address marking, and the left side of the frame has a stylized "WRA Co." marking. The gauge is marked on the breech end of the barrel on later models. The smooth-bore barrel features a brass-bead front sight, and the buttplate is either steel or hard rubber. This is a large shotgun designed for black powder loads by John Browning. There were approximately 65,000 manufactured between 1887 and 1901. The riot gun would be worth approximately 20 percent additional. Beware of fraudulent examples.

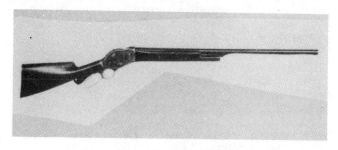

| Exc. | V.G. | Good | Fair | Poor |
|------|------|------|------|------|
| 1000 | 850 | 500 | 400 | 275 |

### Model 1901 Shotgun

This version is quite similar to the lever-action Model 1887 but is chambered for 10 gauge with a 32" barrel only. It also has a 5-round, tubular magazine and is marked "Model 1901" on the barrel breech. There were approximately 13,500 manufactured between 1901 and 1920.

| Exc. | V.G. | Good | Fair | Poor |
|------|------|------|------|------|
| 1500 | 1000 | 750 | 500 | 350 |

### Model 1893

This is a slide-action, exposed-hammer shotgun chambered for 12 gauge with either a 30" or 32" barrel. It has a 5-round, tubular magazine. The finish is blued, with a walnut pistol-grip stock. It features a hard rubber buttplate. This was Winchester's first slide-action shotgun, and it was designed by John Browning. There were approximately 34,000 manufactured between 1893 and 1897.

| Exc. | V.G. | Good | Fair | Poor |
|------|------|------|------|------|
| 1000 | 850 | 500 | 400 | 275 |

### Model 1897

This was a very popular slide-action, exposed-hammer shotgun chambered for 12 or 16 gauge. It was offered in a variety of barrel lengths and chokes. The standard lengths are 28" or 30". It has a 5-round, tubular magazine. The finish is blued, with a walnut stock that is either straight-gripped or has a pistolgrip. This was basically an improvement of the Model 1893. It was designed to fire smokeless powder loads. There were a number of variations offered, and a qualified appraisal is recommended if in doubt. This was a very commercially successful firearm for Winchester. There were over one million manufactured between 1897 and 1957.

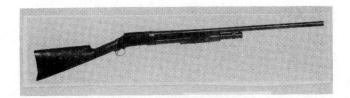

### Field Grade--Solid Frame or Takedown

| Exc. | V.G. | Good | Fair | Poor |
|------|------|------|------|------|
| 750  | 500  | 375  | 225  | 150  |

### Riot Gun--20" Barrel

| Exc. | V.G. | Good | Fair | Poor |
|------|------|------|------|------|
| 700  | 450  | 325  | 200  | 125  |

### Trench Gun

This version features a ventilated barrel shroud and hand guard, as well as a bayonet lug. It was used in WWI.

| Exc. | V.G. | Good | Fair | Poor |
|------|------|------|------|------|
| 800  | 550  | 425  | 275  | 200  |

### Winchester-Hotchkiss

This firearm is listed under the Hotchkiss section of this text.

### Winchester-Lee

This is a straight-pull, bolt-action rifle chambered for the 6mm Lee cartridge. It has a 24" round barrel in the sporting configuration and a 28" barrel on the military muskets. It has a detachable box magazine that holds five rounds. The finish is blued, with a walnut pistolgrip-type stock. There were a total of approximately 20,000 manufactured between 1895 and 1902. The variations and their values are as follows:

### Navy Issue Musket

This version has a 28" barrel and a full-length stock held on by two barrel bands. There is a hand guard over the breech end of the barrel, and it has military-type sights and a carbine-type buttplate. There is a bayonet lug at the muzzle. There are two basic versions. One is naval-issue and features U.S. inspector's marks as well as an anchor. There were approximately 15,000 of these. There is also a civilian version without the inspector's marking, anchor, or bayonet lug, of which approximately 3,300 were produced. The values for both versions are similar.

| Exc. | V.G. | Good | Fair | Poor |
|------|------|------|------|------|
| 1000 | 750  | 550  | 400  | 225  |

### Sporting Rifle

This version has a 24" tapered barrel. It has a half-length forearm and a shotgun-type, steel buttplate. It has sporting-type open sights. There were approximately 1,700 manufactured.

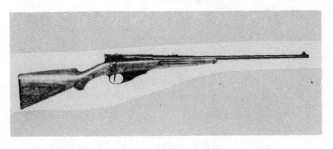

| Exc. | V.G. | Good | Fair | Poor |
|------|------|------|------|------|
| 1250 | 900  | 650  | 500  | 300  |

### Model 1890

This is a slide-action sporting rifle chambered for the .22 rimfire cartridge, as well as the .22 W.R.F. cartridge. It has a 24" octagon barrel with a three-quarter length tubular magazine. It was offered as both a solid frame and a takedown rifle. The finish is blued; early models have case-colored frames. The straight-grip buttstock and ribbed forearm are walnut. This rifle was designed by John and Matthew Browning and was Winchester's initial venture into the slide-action market. There were

approximately 850,000 total manufactured between 1890 and 1932. Deluxe versions bring sizeable premiums and should be individually appraised.

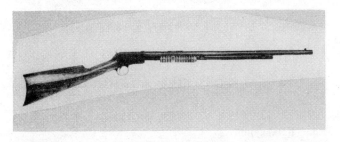

### 1st Model

This version has a solid frame and is serial number-numbered under 15,500.

| Exc. | V.G. | Good | Fair | Poor |
|------|------|------|------|------|
| 1500 | 1200 | 675  | 450  | 250  |

### 2nd Model

This is a takedown rifle serial-numbered under 326,600. The locking lugs are not visible.

| Exc. | V.G. | Good | Fair | Poor |
|------|------|------|------|------|
| 650  | 500  | 350  | 275  | 200  |

### 3rd Model

This is a takedown rifle that has notches milled in the sides of the frame that the locking lugs fit into. They are visible. This version includes the remainder of the production.

| Exc. | V.G. | Good | Fair | Poor |
|------|------|------|------|------|
| 650  | 500  | 350  | 275  | 200  |

### Model 1906

This was a slide-action rifle chambered for the .22 rimfire cartridge. It has an external hammer and is quite similar to the Model 1890 except that it was offered with a 20" round barrel. It also has a shotgun-type buttplate. It was designed to sell for a lower price than the Model 1890. It also would chamber the .22 short, long, or long-rifle cartridges. There were approximately 848,000 manufactured between 1906 and 1932.

| Exc. | V.G. | Good | Fair | Poor |
|------|------|------|------|------|
| 1050 | 750  | 500  | 350  | 175  |

### Model 62

This was an improved, modern version of the Model 1890. It retained the external hammer but would chamber the .22 short, long, or long-rifle cartridges interchangeably. It has a 23" tapered round barrel. There were approximately 409,000 manufactured between 1932 and 1958. Pre-war models feature a small forearm and would be worth approximately 25 percent additional. In 1940 the model was redesignated the 62A.

| Exc. | V.G. | Good | Fair | Poor |
|------|------|------|------|------|
| 500  | 400  | 300  | 225  | 150  |

### Model 61

This is a hammerless, slide-action sporting rifle chambered for the .22 rimfire cartridges. It was offered with a 24" round or octagonal barrel and has a tubular magazine. The finish is blued, with a plain walnut stock. There were approximately 340,000 manufactured between 1932 and 1963. Pre-war versions have a small forearm and would be worth approximately 20 percent additional. Pre-war versions with octagonal barrels would be worth approximately 100 percent additional.

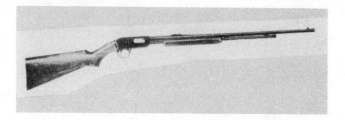

| Exc. | V.G. | Good | Fair | Poor |
|------|------|------|------|------|
| 650 | 500 | 375 | 275 | 200 |

### Model 61 Magnum
This version is similar to the Model 61 except that it is chambered for the .22 Win. Mag. cartridge. It was manufactured between 1960 and 1963.

| Exc. | V.G. | Good | Fair | Poor |
|------|------|------|------|------|
| 700 | 550 | 400 | 300 | 225 |

### Model 1903
This is a blowback-operated, semi-automatic rifle that was invented by Thomas Johnson. It is chambered for the .22 Winchester automatic rimfire cartridge. It has a 20" round barrel with open sights and a 10-round tubular magazine in the buttstock. The finish is blued with a walnut, straight-grip stock. There were approximately 126,000 manufactured between 1903 and 1932. Deluxe variations were available, and they should be individually appraised.

| Exc. | V.G. | Good | Fair | Poor |
|------|------|------|------|------|
| 750 | 600 | 400 | 300 | 175 |

### Model 1905
This is a semi-automatic sporting rifle chambered for the .32 Win. and the .35 Win. cartridges. It features a 22" round barrel with open sights and either a 5- or 10-round, detachable box magazine. It is cocked by depressing a rod that extends from the front of the forearm. The finish is blued with a plain walnut stock with a hard rubber, shotgun buttplate. There were approximately 29,000 manufactured between 1905 and 1920.

| Exc. | V.G. | Good | Fair | Poor |
|------|------|------|------|------|
| 800 | 700 | 475 | 350 | 225 |

### Model 1907
This was an improved version of the Model 1905 in response to a demand for a more powerful semi-automatic rifle. It is chambered for the .351 Win. cartridge. Otherwise, it is quite similar in appearance to the Model 1905. There is also a police version with an extended magazine that was quite popular among many city police departments and was used by the U.S. Ordnance Department in WWI. There were approximately 59,000 manufactured between 1907 and 1958.

#### Standard Model
| Exc. | V.G. | Good | Fair | Poor |
|------|------|------|------|------|
| 500 | 400 | 300 | 200 | 125 |

#### Police Model
| Exc. | V.G. | Good | Fair | Poor |
|------|------|------|------|------|
| 750 | 600 | 450 | 275 | 200 |

### Model 1910
This model is similar in appearance to the Model 1907 but is chambered for the .401 Winchester cartridge. It was offered with a 20" barrel and a 4-round box magazine. A number of these rifles were also purchased by the Ordnance Department to be used by guards in federal penitentiaries. There were approximately 21,000 manufactured between 1910 and 1936.

| Exc. | V.G. | Good | Fair | Poor |
|------|------|------|------|------|
| 700 | 550 | 400 | 225 | 150 |

### Model 55
This is a semi-automatic sporting rifle chambered for the .22 rimfire cartridge. It has a 22" round barrel with open sights. It features bottom ejection and was not serial-numbered. There were approximately 45,000 manufactured between 1958 and 1961.

| Exc. | V.G. | Good | Fair | Poor |
|------|------|------|------|------|
| 300 | 225 | 175 | 125 | 75 |

### Model 63
This is a semi-automatic sporting rifle chambered for the .22 l.r. cartridge. It is similar in appearance to the Model 1903. Initially, it was offered with a 20" barrel that was discontinued in 1936. It was then offered with a 23" round barrel with open sights. The finish is blued, with a plain walnut stock. It is cocked by depressing a rod that protrudes from the front of the forend. There were approximately 175,000 manufactured between 1933 and 1958.

20" Barrel Version--Add 100 Percent.
Grooved Receiver--Add 10 Percent.

| Exc. | V.G. | Good | Fair | Poor |
|------|------|------|------|------|
| 750 | 600 | 400 | 300 | 225 |

### Model 74
This is a blowback-operated, semi-automatic rifle chambered for the .22 rimfire cartridge. It has a 22" barrel with a removable bolt assembly and a tubular magazine in the buttstock. The rear of the receiver is square in configuration. The finish is blued, with a walnut stock. There were approximately 406,000 manufactured between 1939 and 1955.

| Exc. | V.G. | Good | Fair | Poor |
|------|------|------|------|------|
| 250 | 200 | 150 | 100 | 75 |

### Model 77
This is a blowback-operated, semi-automatic rifle chambered for the .22 l.r. cartridge. It has a 22" barrel and was offered with either a tubular magazine mounted beneath the barrel or a detachable box magazine. The finish is blued, with a walnut stock. There were approximately 215,000 manufactured between 1955 and 1962.

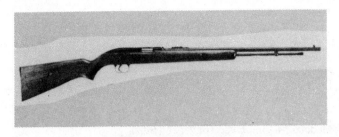

| Exc. | V.G. | Good | Fair | Poor |
|------|------|------|------|------|
| 200 | 150 | 125 | 90 | 75 |

### Model 88

This is a modern-styled, short-stroke, lever-action sporting rifle chambered for the .243, .284, .308, and the .358 cartridges. It was offered as either a rifle with a 22" barrel or a carbine with a 19" barrel and a one-piece stock held on by a barrel band. The finish is blued, with a walnut stock. The rifle version features basketweave checkering. There were approximately 285,000 manufactured between 1955 and 1973. Pre-'64 models would be worth approximately 20 percent additional. Values of this model are also affected by the calibers chambered due to rarity. The values given are for the .308 rifle.

.308 Carbine--Add 25 Percent.
.284 Carbine--Add 50 Percent.
.243 Rifle--Add 25 Percent.
.284 Rifle--Add 80 Percent.
.358 Rifle--Add 100 Percent.

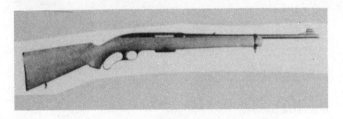

| Exc. | V.G. | Good | Fair | Poor |
|------|------|------|------|------|
| 550 | 425 | 300 | 225 | 150 |

### Model 100

This is a gas-operated, semi-automatic sporting rifle chambered for the .243, .284, and the .308 cartridges. It was offered as a carbine with a 19" barrel and a stock held on by one barrel band, as well as a 22"-barrelled rifle with a basketweave stock and no barrel band. It has open sights and a 4-round, detachable magazine. The finish is blued, with a walnut stock. Winchester has recently warned all consumers that this rifle is considered unsafe to fire due to a faulty firing pin system. They are currently attempting to find a method by which they can be modified to be fired safely. Until that point they should be simply regarded as the collectors' items that they are. Rifle prices are furnished. For carbines, add 20 percent.

Pre-'64 .243--Add 10 Percent.
Pre-'64 .284--Add 20 Percent.

| Exc. | V.G. | Good | Fair | Poor |
|------|------|------|------|------|
| 500 | 400 | 275 | 200 | 125 |

### Model 1900

This is a bolt-action, single-shot rifle chambered for the .22 rimfire cartridge. It is a takedown rifle with an 18" round barrel.

The finish is blued, with a one-piece walnut stock with no buttplate. There were approximately 105,000 manufactured between 1899 and 1902.

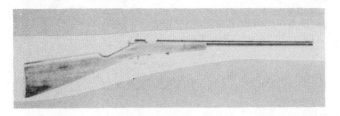

| Exc. | V.G. | Good | Fair | Poor |
|------|------|------|------|------|
| 450 | 375 | 300 | 200 | 125 |

### Model 1902

This is an improved version of the Model 1900. It has a fancier triggerguard, better steel in its construction, and a synthetic buttplate. There were approximately 650,000 manufactured betweeen 1902 and 1931.

| Exc. | V.G. | Good | Fair | Poor |
|------|------|------|------|------|
| 200 | 175 | 125 | 100 | 75 |

### Model 99

This version is similar to the Model 1902 except that it features a thumb-depressed trigger on the top of the wrist instead of the conventional trigger and guard located underneath the stock. There were approximately 75,000 manufactured between 1904 and 1923.

| Exc. | V.G. | Good | Fair | Poor |
|------|------|------|------|------|
| 750 | 600 | 400 | 250 | 125 |

### Model 1904

This version is similar to the Model 1902 except that it has a 21" round barrel and is chambered for the .22 extra long cartridge, as well as the standard chambering. There were approximately 302,000 manufactured between 1904 and 1931.

| Exc. | V.G. | Good | Fair | Poor |
|------|------|------|------|------|
| 200 | 175 | 125 | 100 | 75 |

During this period of time, Winchester produced approximately 243,000 British Enfield and 500,000 Model 1917 U.S. Enfield rifles for use in WWI. They are listed in their own section of this text.

### Model 36

This is a smooth-bore, 9mm, single-shot, bolt-action shotgun based on the Model 1902 rifle action. Most produced were exported to South America; and although there were approximately 26,000 manufactured before it was discontinued in 1927, they are relatively rare on today's market.

| Exc. | V.G. | Good | Fair | Poor |
|------|------|------|------|------|
| 400 | 300 | 250 | 150 | 100 |

### Model 41

This is an extremely well-made, single-shot, bolt-action shotgun chambered for the .410 shell. It has a 28" barrel and is blued, with a one-piece walnut stock. There were approximately 22,000 manufactured between 1920 and 1934.

| Exc. | V.G. | Good | Fair | Poor |
|------|------|------|------|------|
| 425 | 325 | 275 | 175 | 125 |

## Model 56

This is a bolt-action repeating rifle chambered for the .22 caliber rimfire cartridge. It is a medium-priced rifle that utilizes a detachable box magazine. The finish is blued with a plain, pistolgrip walnut stock. There were approximately 8,000 manufactured between 1926 and 1929.

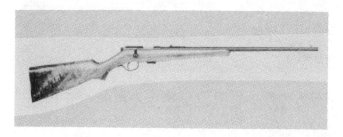

| Exc. | V.G. | Good | Fair | Poor |
|------|------|------|------|------|
| 550 | 450 | 350 | 250 | 175 |

## Model 57

This version is similar to the Model 56, with better sights and a forearm held on by a single barrel band. It was discontinued in 1936.

| Exc. | V.G. | Good | Fair | Poor |
|------|------|------|------|------|
| 500 | 400 | 300 | 200 | 125 |

## Model 58

This is another single-shot, bolt-action rifle chambered for the .22 rimfire cartridge. It was introduced in 1928 to offer a low-priced utility model to compete with the inexpensive foreign guns selling in America at that time. There were approximately 40,000 manufactured between 1928 and 1931.

| Exc. | V.G. | Good | Fair | Poor |
|------|------|------|------|------|
| 300 | 250 | 200 | 150 | 100 |

## Model 59

This is a pistolgrip-stock version of the Model 58. There were approximately 11,000 manufactured in 1930 only.

| Exc. | V.G. | Good | Fair | Poor |
|------|------|------|------|------|
| 500 | 400 | 300 | 250 | 175 |

## Model 60

The Model 60 is a more deluxe version of the Model 58. It has a longer barrel with better quality walnut and a nicer finish. A target version designated the Model 60A was also introduced, which had more deluxe sights. There were approximately 166,000 Model 60's produced before it was discontinued in 1932. There were only 6,000 target versions produced between 1933 and 1939; they would be worth approximately 50 percent additional.

| Exc. | V.G. | Good | Fair | Poor |
|------|------|------|------|------|
| 200 | 175 | 150 | 100 | 75 |

## Model 52 Target

This is a high-quality, bolt-action target rifle chambered for the .22 l.r. cartridge. It has a 28", standard-weight barrel with adjustable target sights and a 5-round, detachable magazine. There were a number of variations offered within this model designation. They were all finished in blue with a walnut, target-type stock. There were approximately 125,000 total manufactured between 1919 and 1979. The variations and their values are as follows:

Model 52 Target
Speedlock--Add 10 Percent.

| Exc. | V.G. | Good | Fair | Poor |
|------|------|------|------|------|
| 500 | 425 | 350 | 300 | 200 |

## Model 52--Heavy Barrel

| Exc. | V.G. | Good | Fair | Poor |
|------|------|------|------|------|
| 700 | 600 | 500 | 350 | 250 |

## Model 52-B--Improved Action

Heavy Barrel--Add 10 Percent.
Extra-heavy Barrel (Bull Gun)--Add 15 Percent.

| Exc. | V.G. | Good | Fair | Poor |
|------|------|------|------|------|
| 600 | 500 | 450 | 350 | 250 |

## Model 52-C--Improved Trigger and Stock

Heavy Barrel--Add 10 Percent.
Bull Gun--Add 15 Percent.

| Exc. | V.G. | Good | Fair | Poor |
|------|------|------|------|------|
| 750 | 650 | 600 | 450 | 275 |

## Model 52-D--Free-floating Barrel

| Exc. | V.G. | Good | Fair | Poor |
|------|------|------|------|------|
| 650 | 550 | 500 | 400 | 225 |

## Model 52 International Match

This version is similar to the Model 52-D, with a free-rifle-type stock featuring an accessory rail. It was manufactured between 1969 and 1979. A version with a prone-style stock was introduced in 1975 and would be worth a similar amount.

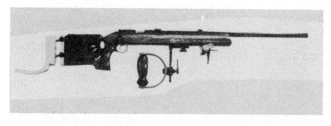

| Exc. | V.G. | Good | Fair | Poor |
|------|------|------|------|------|
| 800 | 700 | 650 | 550 | 250 |

## Model 52 Sporter

This is a sporting-rifle version of the Model 52 Target. It was offered with a 24", lightweight, round barrel with adjustable sights. The finish is blued with a select, checkered walnut stock with a cheekpiece. It is furnished with a black pistolgrip cap and forend tip and a checkered steel buttplate. There are four versions within this model designation.

## Model 52--Original Lock

| Exc. | V.G. | Good | Fair | Poor |
|------|------|------|------|------|
| 2500 | 1750 | 1400 | 950 | 750 |

## Model 52A--Improved Receiver

| Exc. | V.G. | Good | Fair | Poor |
|------|------|------|------|------|
| 2500 | 1750 | 1400 | 950 | 750 |

## Model 52B--Single-shot Adapter

| Exc. | V.G. | Good | Fair | Poor |
|------|------|------|------|------|
| 2500 | 1750 | 1400 | 950 | 750 |

## Model 52C--Adjustable Trigger

| Exc. | V.G. | Good | Fair | Poor |
|------|------|------|------|------|
| 2750 | 2000 | 1550 | 1000 | 800 |

## Model 54

This is a high-powered, bolt-action sporting rifle chambered for the .270, 7x57, .30-30, and the .30-06 cartridges. It has a 24" round barrel with open sights and a 5-round, integral box magazine. The finish is blued, with a checkered walnut stock. There were approximately 50,000 manufactured between 1925 and 1936. A carbine version with a 20" barrel and an uncheckered stock was introduced in 1927 and would be worth approximately 20 percent additional. It is advisable to have this model individually appraised as the rarer calibers, such as the 7x57 and the .30-30, can be worth a tremendous premium. It is also not difficult to produce fraudulent specimens.

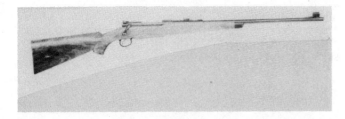

| Exc. | V.G. | Good | Fair | Poor |
|------|------|------|------|------|
| 650 | 550 | 400 | 300 | 225 |

## Model 54 Super Grade

This variation is similar to the Model 54 but is a more deluxe version. It features select walnut and has a black forend tip and pistolgrip cap. It was introduced in 1934. The same caution regarding appraisal should be followed with this example, as well as the standard model.

| Exc. | V.G. | Good | Fair | Poor |
|------|------|------|------|------|
| 750 | 650 | 500 | 400 | 300 |

## Model 54 National Match

This version is similar to the Model 54, except that it is furnished with Lyman receiver sights and a special target-type Marksman stock. It was introduced in 1935.

| Exc. | V.G. | Good | Fair | Poor |
|------|------|------|------|------|
| 800 | 700 | 550 | 450 | 350 |

## Model 67

This is a bolt-action sporting rifle chambered for .22 l.r. and the .22 W.R.F. cartridges. It was offered with a 20", 24", or 27" round barrel. The finish is blued, with a walnut stock. There were approximately 383,000 manufactured between 1934 and 1963.

| Exc. | V.G. | Good | Fair | Poor |
|------|------|------|------|------|
| 200 | 175 | 125 | 100 | 75 |

## Model 677

This version is similar to the Model 67 except that it is furnished without sights. There were approximately 2,200 manufactured between 1937 and 1939. The .22 W.R.F. chambering is extremely rare and should be worth approximately a 300 percent premium.

| Exc. | V.G. | Good | Fair | Poor |
|------|------|------|------|------|
| 450 | 350 | 300 | 225 | 125 |

## Model 68

This is a single-shot, bolt-action, .22 rifle that is similar to the Model 67. It is blued, with a walnut stock. There were approximatley 100,000 manufactured between 1934 and 1946.

| Exc. | V.G. | Good | Fair | Poor |
|------|------|------|------|------|
| 200 | 150 | 125 | 100 | 75 |

## Model 69

This is a bolt-action repeater chambered for the .22 rimfire cartridges. It has a 25" round barrel with either open sights or a peepsight. Later versions are designated the Model 69A and feature an improved lockwork. There were approximately 355,000 manufactured between 1935 and 1963.

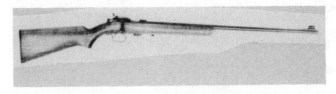

| Exc. | V.G. | Good | Fair | Poor |
|------|------|------|------|------|
| 225 | 175 | 150 | 125 | 100 |

## Model 697

This model is similar to the Model 69, with scope bases furnished in lieu of open sights. A .22 W.R.F. version was available and would be worth an approximate 100 percent premium.

| Exc. | V.G. | Good | Fair | Poor |
|------|------|------|------|------|
| 200 | 150 | 125 | 100 | 75 |

## Model 70

The "Pre-'64" Model 70 is regarded by some knowledgeable individuals as the finest bolt-action rifle ever commercially produced. Actions from this model are sought after by the finest custom craftsmen in the world to be used as the nucleus for their creations. It is basically an improved version of the Model 54 that was introduced in 1937. For 27 years it dominated the bolt-action rifle market and to this day is surrounded by a mystique that is virtually unequalled by any other sporting rifle. There were a number of styles and configurations offered within the model designation.

It was as close to a custom rifle as a major firearms manufacturer could offer. When evaluating this fine rifle, it is essential to realize the options that were offered, as well as the rarity of certain calibers in certain configurations. We offer an explanation and value for all of the basic types but strongly recommend that anyone interested in collecting this excellent rifle should first avail oneself of the excellent literature available on the subject and seek qualified, individual appraisal if a transaction is contemplated. The basic configurations and their subdivisions are as follows:

## Standard Model

The Standard Pre-'64 Model 70 was offered in the .22 Hornet*, .220 Swift*, .243, .250-3000*, .257 Roberts*, .264 Mag., .270, 7x57*, .300 Savage**, .30-06, .308, .300 Win. Mag.*, .338 Win. Mag.*, .35 Rem.**, .300 H&H, .375 H&H*, and 9mm**. This rifle was offered with a 24", 25", or 26" barrel with open sights. It has a 4- or 5-round magazine, depending on the caliber. The finish is blued, with a checkered walnut stock. It was manufactured between 1937 and 1963.

*-- Denotes rarer calibers; secure appraisal.

**--Extremely rare, almost never encountered; secure appraisal.

The Pre-'64 Model 70 Standard production can be divided into three basic types. The pre-war era between 1936 and early 1942 saw approximately 63,000 rifles manufactured. Most were chambered for the .30-06. These rifles can be readily identified by the clover leaf receiver tang. The second type was the transition model, during which approximately 160,000 rifles were produced between 1945 and 1951. During this period, increased labor costs resulted in a high quality rifle that was not quite the match of the pre-war examples. The third period saw approximately 360,000 rifles manufactured between 1952 and 1964. This version featured the straight-tang receiver and the introduction of the heavy Magnum cartridges.

The "Westerner" (.264 and .300 Win. Mag.), the "Alaskan" (.338 Win. Mag. and .375 H&H Mag.), and the "African" (.458 Win. Mag.) were introduced during this period. The "Varmint" rifle, chambered for .243 Win. and .220 Swift, was also introduced during this period. The basic values for a standard-grade Model 70 chambered for .243, .270, .30-06, or .308 are as follows:

.22 Hornet, .220 Swift, and .257 Robts.--Add 20 Percent.
.300 Win. Mag.--Add 30 Percent.
.338 Win. Mag.--Add 50 Percent.
.375 H&H--Add 80 Percent.
.250-3000--Add 125 Percent.
7x57--Add 400 Percent.

| Exc. | V.G. | Good | Fair | Poor |
|------|------|------|------|------|
| 850 | 750 | 600 | 450 | 300 |

## Featherweight Model 70

This version was offered with a 22" barrel and has an aluminum floorplate and triggerguard with either an aluminum or a plastic buttplate. It weighs 6.5 pounds. It is chambered for the .243, .264 Magnum, .270, .308, .30-06, and the .358. It was produced between 1952 and 1963, and all feature the straight-tang receiver.

.264 Mag.--Add 10 Percent.
.358 Mag.--Add 100 Percent.

| Exc. | V.G. | Good | Fair | Poor |
|------|------|------|------|------|
| 900 | 800 | 650 | 500 | 350 |

## Model 70 Super Grade

This is a more deluxe version of the Standard Model 70, that has slightly better-grade wood and features a black pistolgrip cap and forend tip. The Super Grade is worth approximately 75 percent more per caliber than a Standard Grade Model 70 rifle. In the "African" configuration, values are as follows:
.458 Win. Mag.--Add 20 Percent.

**.375 H&H**

| Exc. | V.G. | Good | Fair | Poor |
|------|------|------|------|------|
| 3500 | 2750 | 2000 | 1250 | 950 |

## Model 70 Westerner

This version is chambered for the .264 Win. Mag. and is offered with a 26" barrel.

| Exc. | V.G. | Good | Fair | Poor |
|------|------|------|------|------|
| 950 | 850 | 700 | 550 | 400 |

## Model 70 Alaskan

This version is chambered for the .338 Win. Mag. and the .375 H&H Mag. It is offered with a 25" barrel and is furnished with a recoil pad. It was produced between 1960 and 1963.

| Exc. | V.G. | Good | Fair | Poor |
|------|------|------|------|------|
| 1500 | 1250 | 950 | 600 | 400 |

## Model 70 Varmint

This version is chambered for the .243 and the .220 Swift cartridges. It is offered with a 26" heavy barrel with scope bases instead of sights. It has a heavier, Varmint-type stock. It was manufactured between 1956 and 1963.

| Exc. | V.G. | Good | Fair | Poor |
|------|------|------|------|------|
| 950 | 850 | 700 | 550 | 400 |

## Model 70 National Match

This is a target version chambered for the .30-06 cartridge. It was supplied with scope bases and a target-type stock. It was discontinued in 1960.

| Exc. | V.G. | Good | Fair | Poor |
|------|------|------|------|------|
| 1250 | 950 | 650 | 500 | 425 |

## Model 70 Target

This version is chambered for the .243 and the .30-06 cartridge. It was offered with a 24" medium-weight barrel and a target-type stock. It was discontinued in 1963.

| Exc. | V.G. | Good | Fair | Poor |
|------|------|------|------|------|
| 1250 | 950 | 650 | 500 | 425 |

## Model 70 Bull Gun

This version is chambered for the .30-06 and the .300 H&H cartridges. It features a 28" heavy barrel and a target-type stock.

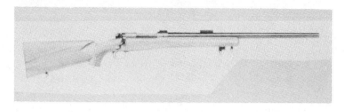

| Exc. | V.G. | Good | Fair | Poor |
|------|------|------|------|------|
| 2000 | 1750 | 1400 | 950 | 650 |

## Model 72

This is a bolt-action repeating rifle chambered for either the .22 l.r. or, in its gallery configuration, the .22 short cartridges. It has a tubular magazine and is offered with a 25", tapered, round barrel. The finish is blued, with a plain walnut stock. There were approximately 160,000 manufactured between 1938 and 1959.

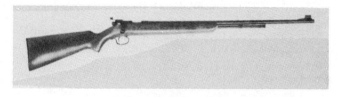

| Exc. | V.G. | Good | Fair | Poor |
|------|------|------|------|------|
| 250 | 200 | 150 | 100 | 75 |

## Model 75 Sporter

This is a bolt-action repeating rifle chambered for the .22 l.r. cartridge. It has a 24" barrel with open sights and uses a 5- or 10-round, detachable magazine. The finish is blued with a select, checkered walnut stock. There were approximately 89,000 manufactured between 1938 and 1958.

| Exc. | V.G. | Good | Fair | Poor |
|------|------|------|------|------|
| 700 | 550 | 400 | 300 | 200 |

## Model 75 Target

This version is similar to the Sporter except that it has a 28" heavy barrel with target sights. It was used by the U.S. Government as a training rifle in WWII.

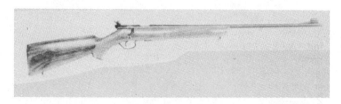

| Exc. | V.G. | Good | Fair | Poor |
|------|------|------|------|------|
| 550 | 400 | 300 | 175 | 100 |

## Model 1911

This is a recoil-operated, semi-automatic shotgun chambered for 12 gauge. It has a 26" or 28" barrel with various chokes. The finish is blued, with a laminated birch stock. There were approximately 83,000 manufactured between 1911 and 1925.

Winchester Model 1911

| Exc. | V.G. | Good | Fair | Poor |
|------|------|------|------|------|
| 600 | 450 | 350 | 250 | 150 |

## Model 36
This is a single-shot, bolt-action, smooth bore that is chambered for the 9mm shot cartridge. It has an 18" round barrel and is blued with a plain walnut stock. There were approximately 20,000 manufactured between 1920 and 1927.

| Exc. | V.G. | Good | Fair | Poor |
|---|---|---|---|---|
| 400 | 300 | 250 | 150 | 100 |

## Model 12
This is a slide-action, takedown shotgun chambered for 12, 16, 20, or 28 gauge. It is offered with 26", 28", 30", or 32" barrels with various chokes. It is a hammerless design. The finish is blued, with a plain walnut stock. There were over two million Model 12's produced in all grades between 1912 and 1976. This is a widely collected firearm. It was produced with a number of special-order options that would add drastically to the general values furnished here. We strongly recommend securing a competent, individual appraisal if a transaction is contemplated. The values given are for a 12-gauge, standard-grade gun. If in doubt as to the gauge, the buttstock can be removed and the correct gauge of the gun will be marked on the head of the stock screw.
16 Gauge--Subtract 5 Percent.
20 Gauge--Add 25 Percent.
28 Gauge--Add 600 Percent.
28 Gauge W/Cutts Compensator--Subtract 50 Percent from 28 Gauge Values.
Solid Rib--Add 20 Percent.
Vent Rib--Add 50 Percent.

| Exc. | V.G. | Good | Fair | Poor |
|---|---|---|---|---|
| 500 | 425 | 350 | 250 | 150 |

## Model 12 Duck Gun
This version is chambered for 12 gauge with a 3" chamber. It was offered with a 30" or 32", full-choke barrel and a solid rubber recoil pad. Otherwise, it is similar to the standard Model 12. It was manufactured between 1935 and 1963.
Solid Rib--Add 35 Percent.

| Exc. | V.G. | Good | Fair | Poor |
|---|---|---|---|---|
| 650 | 600 | 500 | 375 | 250 |

## Model 12 Featherweight
This version is similar to the standard Model, with a lightweight, alloy triggerguard. The serial number features the letter F suffix. It was manufactured between 1959 and 1962.

| Exc. | V.G. | Good | Fair | Poor |
|---|---|---|---|---|
| 400 | 325 | 250 | 175 | 125 |

## Model 12 Riot Gun
This version is chambered for 12 gauge and features a 20", cylinder-bore barrel. It is blued, with a plain walnut stock. It was manufactured between 1918 and 1963.

| Exc. | V.G. | Good | Fair | Poor |
|---|---|---|---|---|
| 400 | 325 | 250 | 175 | 125 |

## Model 12 Trench Gun
This version is chambered for 12 gauge and has a 20" barrel with a ventilated hand guard and bayonet lug. The finish is parkerized, with a walnut stock. It features U.S. Ordnance marks. It was used in WWII. Be wary of fakes.

| Exc. | V.G. | Good | Fair | Poor |
|---|---|---|---|---|
| 750 | 650 | 500 | 350 | 250 |

## Model 12 Skeet Gun
This version is chambered for 12, 16, 20, or 28 gauge and has a 26" barrel that is skeet-choked. The finish is blued, with a checkered pistolgrip stock. It was manufactured between 1933 and 1976. Values given are for a 12-gauge gun.
16 Gauge--Add 10 Percent.
20 Gauge--Add 20 Percent.
28 Gauge--Add 450 Percent.
Solid Rib--Add 20 Percent.
Vent Rib--Add 25 Percent.

| Exc. | V.G. | Good | Fair | Poor |
|---|---|---|---|---|
| 800 | 700 | 550 | 400 | 325 |

## Model 12 Trap Gun
This model is chambered for various gauges and features a 30" or 32", full-choked, ribbed barrel. It features a deluxe, checkered, trap-type stock furnished with a recoil pad. It was manufactured between 1938 and 1964.
Plastic Hydrocoil Stock--Add 10 Percent.

| Exc. | V.G. | Good | Fair | Poor |
|---|---|---|---|---|
| 850 | 750 | 600 | 450 | 350 |

## Model 12 Pigeon Grade
This is a deluxe, engraved version of the Model 12 Competition Gun. There were a number of grades of engraving offered, and this model should be individually appraised. It was manufactured from 1914 to 1964.
Vent Rib--Add 10 Percent.

| Exc. | V.G. | Good | Fair | Poor |
|---|---|---|---|---|
| 2250 | 1800 | 1250 | 750 | 475 |

## Model 25
This is a slide-action shotgun chambered for 12 gauge. It is basically a solid-frame version of the Model 12. It was offered with a 26" or 28" barrel with various chokes. There were approximately 88,000 manufactured between 1949 and 1954.

| Exc. | V.G. | Good | Fair | Poor |
|---|---|---|---|---|
| 400 | 350 | 275 | 175 | 100 |

## Model 37
This is a single-shot, break-open shotgun chambered for 12, 16, 20, and 28 gauge, as well as .410. It was offered with various barrel lengths and chokes. The finish is blued, with a plain walnut stock. One variation features a pistolgrip cap with the red letter W; this model is worth approximately 10 percent additional. There were approximately 1,000,000 manufactured between 1936 and 1963.
20 Gauge--Add 25 Percent.
.410--Add 30 Percent.
28 Gauge--Add 250 Percent.

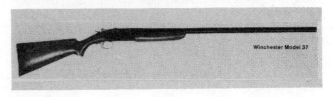

| Exc. | V.G. | Good | Fair | Poor |
|---|---|---|---|---|
| 150 | 125 | 100 | 75 | 50 |

## Model 42

This is a slide-action, takedown shotgun chambered for the .410. It was invented by William Roemer and patented in 1933. It was introduced the same year. It is similar in appearance but smaller than the Model 12. It was offered with a 26" or 28" barrel, either plain or ribbed. It features a hammerless action. The finish is blued, with a plain walnut pistolgrip stock. There were approximately 160,000 manufactured between 1933 and 1963. This is a very collectible firearm, and it would behoove anyone interested in acquiring it to educate oneself and to secure a competent appraisal if in doubt. Values for a standard-grade Model are as follows:
Solid Rib--Add 50 Percent.

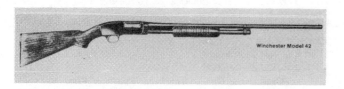

Winchester Model 42

| Exc. | V.G. | Good | Fair | Poor |
|------|------|------|------|------|
| 800 | 650 | 500 | 375 | 250 |

## Deluxe Model 42

This version features very high-grade walnut and is available with a number of degrees of ornamentation. It is difficult to generalize a value on this model; and we strongly recommend qualified, individual appraisal if a transaction is contemplated.

| Exc. | V.G. | Good | Fair | Poor |
|------|------|------|------|------|
| 2000 | 1750 | 1500 | 1000 | 750 |

## Competition Model 42

This version was offered in either a skeet or trap grade with corresponding barrel lengths and chokes. It was offered with a matted, solid-rib standard and checkered high-grade wood.

| Exc. | V.G. | Good | Fair | Poor |
|------|------|------|------|------|
| 1750 | 1450 | 1000 | 800 | 550 |

## Model 40

This is a long, recoil-operated, semi-automatic shotgun chambered for 12 gauge. It was offered with a 28" or 30" barrel with various chokes. The finish is blued, with a walnut stock. There were approximately 12,000 manufactured in 1940 and 1941. This was not a successful model due to poor design. Many were recalled by Winchester, and it is fairly rare on today's market.

| Exc. | V.G. | Good | Fair | Poor |
|------|------|------|------|------|
| 600 | 500 | 400 | 275 | 200 |

## Model 50

This is a recoil-operated, semi-automatic shotgun chambered for 12 or 20 gauge. It was offered with a 26" or 30", plain or vent-rib barrel. The finish is blued, with a walnut stock. There were approximately 195,000 manufactured between 1954 and 1961.
Competition Model--Add 10 Percent.
Deluxe Pigeon Grade Model--Add 300 Percent.
Simmons Vent Rib--Add 10 Percent.
20 Gauge--Add 10 Percent.

| Exc. | V.G. | Good | Fair | Poor |
|------|------|------|------|------|
| 450 | 375 | 300 | 200 | 125 |

## Model 59

This is a unique recoil-operated shotgun that is chambered for 12 gauge and has a 26", 28", or 30" plain barrel with various chokes. What was different about this model was that the barrel was fiberglas-wrapped and the receiver was constructed of a lightweight alloy. It also featured the first interchangeable screw-in choke tubes. This is a lightweight, 6.5-pound shotgun. There were approximately 82,000 manufactured between 1960 and 1965.

| Exc. | V.G. | Good | Fair | Poor |
|------|------|------|------|------|
| 600 | 500 | 400 | 275 | 200 |

## Model 24

This is a side-by-side, double-barrel shotgun chambered for 12, 16, or 20 gauge. It was offered with various-length barrels and choke combinations. It features a hammerless, boxlock action with double triggers and extractors. The finish is blued, with a walnut stock. There were approximately 115,000 manufactured between 1940 and 1957.

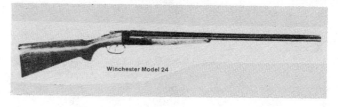

Winchester Model 24

| Exc. | V.G. | Good | Fair | Poor |
|------|------|------|------|------|
| 650 | 550 | 400 | 275 | 175 |

## Model 21

This is a very high-grade, side-by-side, double-barrel shotgun that is chambered for 12, 16, 20, or 28 gauge, as well as .410. This is basically a very deluxe shotgun that features many custom-order options. We furnish general values for standard field-grade guns but strongly recommend securing a competent, individual appraisal if a transaction is contemplated. The following values take into account automatic ejectors and a single-selective trigger on a 12-gauge gun.
Ventilated Rib--Add 15 Percent.
Double Triggers and Extractors--Subject 35 Percent.
16 Gauge--Add 40 Percent.
20 Gauge--Add 50 Percent.

Winchester Model 21 Grand American

| Exc. | V.G. | Good | Fair | Poor |
|------|------|------|------|------|
| 3000 | 2500 | 1850 | 1400 | 900 |

**NOTE:** Examples chambered for the 28 gauge and the .410 cannot be generally appraised in a publication of this nature. They are extremely rare and collectible and can easily be worth between $10,000 and $35,000. With firearms of this nature, competent appraisal is essential.

## Double Rifle

This is an Over/Under, double-barrel rifle chambered for the .257 Roberts, .270 Win., 7x65R, .30-06, and the 9.3x74R cartridges. It was offered with 23.5" barrels with express-type sights and claw-type scope mounts. It features a boxlock action with automatic ejectors. The receiver is heavily engraved and satin-finished. The barrels are blued, and the stock is hand-checkered select walnut. It was furnished with sling swivels. This model was discontinued in 1986.

| Exc. | V.G. | Good | Fair | Poor |
|------|------|------|------|------|
| 1800 | 1500 | 1100 | 800 | 700 |

## POST-1964 RIFLES AND SHOTGUNS

### Model 121

This is a single-shot, bolt-action rifle chambered for the .22 rimfire cartridge. It has a 20.75" barrel with open sights. The finish is blued, with a plain walnut stock. It was manufactured between 1967 and 1973. A youth model with a shorter stock was designated the 121Y and is valued the same.

| Exc. | V.G. | Good | Fair | Poor |
|------|------|------|------|------|
| 125 | 100 | 80 | 60 | 40 |

## Model 131

This is a bolt-action repeater chambered for the .22 rimfire cartridge. It has a 20.75" barrel with open sights and a 7-round, detachable magazine. The finish is blued, with a plain walnut stock. It was manufactured between 1967 and 1973. A tubular magazine version was designated the Model 141 and is valued the same.

| Exc. | V.G. | Good | Fair | Poor |
|------|------|------|------|------|
| 140 | 110 | 90 | 75 | 50 |

## Model 310

This is a single-shot, bolt-action rifle chambered for the .22 rimfire cartridge. It features a 22" barrel with open sights. The finish is blued, with a checkered walnut stock. It was manufactured between 1972 and 1975.

| Exc. | V.G. | Good | Fair | Poor |
|------|------|------|------|------|
| 200 | 150 | 125 | 100 | 75 |

## Model 320

This is a bolt-action repeating rifle that is similar in configuration to the Model 310 single shot. It has a 5-round, detachable box magazine. It was manufactured between 1972 and 1974.

| Exc. | V.G. | Good | Fair | Poor |
|------|------|------|------|------|
| 350 | 300 | 250 | 175 | 125 |

## Model 250

This is a lever-action repeating rifle with a hammerless action. It is chambered for the .22 rimfire cartridge and has a 20.5" barrel with open sights and a tubular magazine. The finish is blued, with a checkered pistolgrip stock. It was manufactured between 1963 and 1973.

| Exc. | V.G. | Good | Fair | Poor |
|------|------|------|------|------|
| 125 | 100 | 80 | 60 | 40 |

## Model 250 Deluxe

This version is similar to the Model 250 and is furnished with select walnut and sling swivels. It was manufactured between 1965 and 1971.

| Exc. | V.G. | Good | Fair | Poor |
|------|------|------|------|------|
| 150 | 125 | 100 | 75 | 50 |

## Model 255

This version is simply the Model 250 chambered for the .22 WMR cartridge. It was manufactured between 1964 and 1970.

| Exc. | V.G. | Good | Fair | Poor |
|------|------|------|------|------|
| 145 | 120 | 90 | 70 | 50 |

## Model 255 Deluxe

This version was offered with select walnut and sling swivels. It was manufactured between 1965 and 1973.

| Exc. | V.G. | Good | Fair | Poor |
|------|------|------|------|------|
| 175 | 150 | 125 | 100 | 75 |

## Model 270

This is a slide-action rifle chambered for the .22 rimfire cartridge. It has a 20.5" barrel and a tubular magazine. The finish is blued, with a checkered walnut stock. It was manufactured between 1963 and 1973.

| Exc. | V.G. | Good | Fair | Poor |
|------|------|------|------|------|
| 125 | 100 | 75 | 50 | 35 |

## Model 490

This is a blowback-operated, semi-automatic rifle chambered for the .22 l.r. cartridge. It has a 22" barrel with open sights and a 5-round, detachable magazine. The finish is blued, with a checkered stock. It was manufactured between 1975 and 1980.

| Exc. | V.G. | Good | Fair | Poor |
|------|------|------|------|------|
| 250 | 200 | 150 | 100 | 75 |

## Model 94

This is the post-'64 lever-action carbine chambered for the .30-30, 7-30 Waters, and the .44 Magnum cartridges. It is offered with a 20" or 24" barrel and has a 6- or 7-round, tubular magazine depending on barrel length. The round barrel is offered with open sights. The forearm is held on by a single barrel band. The finish is blued, with a straight-grip walnut stock. In 1982 it was modified to angle ejection to simplify scope mounting. It was introduced as a continuation of the Model 94 line in 1964.

| NIB | Exc. | V.G. | Good | Fair | Poor |
|-----|------|------|------|------|------|
| 285 | 225 | 175 | 125 | 100 | 75 |

**Model 94 Deluxe--Checkered Stock**

| NIB | Exc. | V.G. | Good | Fair | Poor |
|-----|------|------|------|------|------|
| 300 | 250 | 200 | 150 | 125 | 100 |

**Model 94 Win-Tuff--Laminated Stock**

| NIB | Exc. | V.G. | Good | Fair | Poor |
|-----|------|------|------|------|------|
| 300 | 250 | 200 | 150 | 125 | 100 |

**Model 94 XTR--Select, Checkered Walnut Stock--Disc. 1988**

| Exc. | V.G. | Good | Fair | Poor |
|------|------|------|------|------|
| 275 | 225 | 150 | 100 | 85 |

**Model 94 XTR Deluxe--Fancy Checkering**

| Exc. | V.G. | Good | Fair | Poor |
|------|------|------|------|------|
| 350 | 300 | 200 | 150 | 110 |

**Model 94 Trapper--16" Barrel**

| NIB | Exc. | V.G. | Good | Fair | Poor |
|-----|------|------|------|------|------|
| 285 | 225 | 175 | 125 | 100 | 75 |

**Model 94 Antique Carbine--Gold-plated Saddle Ring**

| Exc. | V.G. | Good | Fair | Poor |
|------|------|------|------|------|
| 250 | 200 | 175 | 125 | 90 |

**Model 94 Wrangler--.32 Win. Special**

| Exc. | V.G. | Good | Fair | Poor |
|------|------|------|------|------|
| 325 | 275 | 175 | 125 | 100 |

**Model 94 Wrangler II--Loop Lever**

| Exc. | V.G. | Good | Fair | Poor |
|------|------|------|------|------|
| 250 | 200 | 150 | 100 | 85 |

### Model 94 XTR Big Bore
This version is chambered for the .307, .356, or the .375 Win. cartridges. It features the angle-ejection and is blued with a walnut, Monte Carlo-type stock and recoil pad. The round barrel is 20" in length. It has a 6-round, tubular magazine. It was introduced in 1983.

| NIB | Exc. | V.G. | Good | Fair | Poor |
|-----|------|------|------|------|------|
| 300 | 250 | 200 | 150 | 125 | 100 |

### Model 9422 XTR
This is a deluxe lever-action rifle chambered for the .22 rimfire cartridges. It is a takedown rifle with a 20.5", round barrel and a tubular magazine. The finish is blued with a checkered, high-gloss, straight-grip walnut stock. It was introduced in 1922. A .22 Magnum version is also available and would be worth approximately $10 additional.

| NIB | Exc. | V.G. | Good | Fair | Poor |
|-----|------|------|------|------|------|
| 325 | 275 | 225 | 175 | 125 | 100 |

### Model 9422 XTR Classic
This version is similar to the standard Model 9422 XTR except that it features a 22.5" barrel and a satin-finished, plain, pistolgrip walnut stock. It was manufactured between 1985 and 1987.

| Exc. | V.G. | Good | Fair | Poor |
|------|------|------|------|------|
| 350 | 300 | 250 | 200 | 125 |

### Model 64
This is a post-1964 version of the lever-action Model 64. It is chambered for the .30-30 cartridge and has a 24", round barrel with open sights and a 5-round, two-thirds-length tubular magazine. The finish is blued with a plain walnut, pistolgrip stock. It was manufactured between 1972 and 1974.

| Exc. | V.G. | Good | Fair | Poor |
|------|------|------|------|------|
| 250 | 200 | 150 | 100 | 85 |

### Post-'64 Model 70
This is a bolt-action sporting rifle chambered for various popular calibers between .22-250 and .30-06. It features a 22" barrel with open sights and a 5-round, integral box magazine. The finish is blued with a Monte Carlo-type stock furnished with sling swivels. It was manufactured between 1964 and 1980.

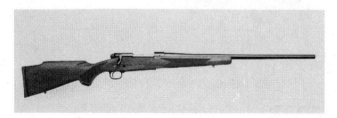

| Exc. | V.G. | Good | Fair | Poor |
|------|------|------|------|------|
| 375 | 325 | 250 | 200 | 125 |

### Model 70 Mannlicher
This is a full-length, Mannlicher-type stocked version of the Model 70 bolt-action rifle that is chambered for the .243, .270, .308, and the .306 cartridges. It features a 19" barrel with open sights. The finish is blued. It was discontinued in 1972.

| Exc. | V.G. | Good | Fair | Poor |
|------|------|------|------|------|
| 500 | 425 | 350 | 275 | 175 |

### Model 70 Target Rifle
This version is chambered for the .308 or the .30-06 cartridges. It was offered with a 24" heavy barrel without sights. It is furnished with bases for a target scope. The finish is blued with a heavy walnut target stock with a palmrest.

| Exc. | V.G. | Good | Fair | Poor |
|------|------|------|------|------|
| 650 | 550 | 450 | 350 | 250 |

### Model 70 International Match Army
This version is chambered for the .308 cartridge and has a 24" heavy barrel furnished without sights. It has an adjustable trigger and is blued, with a target-type heavy stock that had an accessory rail and an adjustable butt.

| Exc. | V.G. | Good | Fair | Poor |
|------|------|------|------|------|
| 750 | 650 | 500 | 400 | 300 |

### Model 70A
This is a utility version of the bolt-action Post-'64 Model 70. It was furnished without a hinged floorplate. The finish is blued, with a walnut stock. It was manufactured between 1972 and 1978.

| Exc. | V.G. | Good | Fair | Poor |
|------|------|------|------|------|
| 350 | 300 | 225 | 175 | 100 |

### Model 70 XTR Featherweight
This gun was built after the takeover by the U.S.R.A. Company. It is a bolt-action sporting rifle chambered for various calibers from .22-250 up to the .30-06 cartridges. It has a 22" barrel that is furnished without sights and features either a short- or medium-length action. It has a 5-round, integral magazine. The finish is blued, with a checkered walnut stock. It was introduced in 1981.

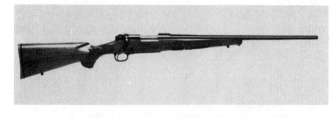

| NIB | Exc. | V.G. | Good | Fair | Poor |
|-----|------|------|------|------|------|
| 475 | 400 | 325 | 300 | 250 | 200 |

### Model 70 Fiftieth Anniversary Model
This is a commemorative version of the Post-'64 Model 70 bolt-action rifle. It is chambered for the .300 Win. Mag. and is offered with a 24" barrel. It is engraved and high-gloss blued with a deluxe, checkered walnut stock. There were 500 manufactured in 1987. In order to realize collector potential, it must be NIB with all supplied materials.

| NIB | Exc. | V.G. | Good | Fair | Poor |
|-----|------|------|------|------|------|
| 1000 | 800 | 600 | 450 | 350 | 250 |

### Model 70 XTR Super Express
This is a heavy-duty version of the Post-'64 Model 70 chambered for the .375 H&H and the .458 Win. Mag. cartridges. It is offered with a 22" or 24" heavy barrel and a 3-round, integral box magazine. This version has extra recoil lugs mounted in the stock and is blued with a select, straight-grain walnut stock and a recoil pad standard.

| NIB | Exc. | V.G. | Good | Fair | Poor |
|-----|------|------|------|------|------|
| 800 | 650 | 550 | 400 | 350 | 275 |

### Model 70 XTR Varmint
This version is chambered for .22-250, .223, and the .243 cartridges. It has a 24" heavy barrel and is furnished without sights. It has a 5-round magazine and is blued with a heavy walnut stock. It was introduced in 1972.

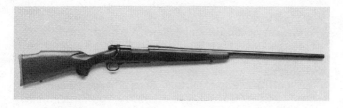

| NIB | Exc. | V.G. | Good | Fair | Poor |
|-----|------|------|------|------|------|
| 500 | 425 | 350 | 325 | 275 | 225 |

### Model 70 Winlight
This version is offered in various calibers between .270 and the .338 Win. Mag. It features a matte-blue finish and a fiberglas stock. It is offered with a 22" or a 24" barrel and a 3- or 4-round magazine. It was introduced in 1986.

| NIB | Exc. | V.G. | Good | Fair | Poor |
|-----|------|------|------|------|------|
| 650 | 600 | 500 | 400 | 300 | 250 |

### Ranger
This is a utility-grade, bolt-action rifle chambered for the .270 Win., .30-06, and the 7mm Rem. Mag. cartridges. It is offered with a 22" or a 24" barrel with open sights and has a 3- or 4-round box magazine. The finish is blued with a plain hardwood stock.

| NIB | Exc. | V.G. | Good | Fair | Poor |
|-----|------|------|------|------|------|
| 375 | 325 | 275 | 225 | 150 | 125 |

## POST-1964 SHOTGUNS
### Model 12 "Y" Series

### Model 12 Field Grade
This is a later version of the slide-action Model 12, chambered for 12 gauge only. It was offered with a 26", 28", or 30" vent-rib barrel with various chokes. The finish is blued with a jeweled bolt and a hand-checkered, select walnut stock. This version is easily recognizable as it has the letter Y serial number prefix. It was manufactured between 1972 and 1976.

| Exc. | V.G. | Good | Fair | Poor |
|------|------|------|------|------|
| 650 | 550 | 400 | 350 | 275 |

### Model 12 Super Pigeon Grade
This is a deluxe version that features extensive engraving and fancy checkering. It was offered with a tuned action and select, fancy-grade walnut. It was a limited-production item produced between 1964 and 1972. It was briefly re-introduced in 1984 and discontinued again in 1985.

| Exc. | V.G. | Good | Fair | Poor |
|------|------|------|------|------|
| 3000 | 2500 | 1850 | 1400 | 950 |

### Model 12 Skeet
This version is similar to the Field Grade but is offered with a 26", vent-rib, skeet-bored barrel. The finish is blued, with a skeet-type stock and recoil pad. It was manufactured between 1972 and 1975.

| Exc. | V.G. | Good | Fair | Poor |
|------|------|------|------|------|
| 700 | 650 | 550 | 350 | 300 |

### Model 12 Trap Grade
This version features a 30" vent-rib barrel with a full choke. It is blued with a trap-type, standard or Monte Carlo stock with a recoil pad. It was manufactured between 1972 and 1980.

| Exc. | V.G. | Good | Fair | Poor |
|------|------|------|------|------|
| 650 | 600 | 500 | 300 | 200 |

### Model 1200
This is a slide-action shotgun chambered for 12, 16, or 20 gauge. It was offered with a 26", 28", or 30", vent-rib barrel with various chokes. It has an alloy receiver and is blued, with a checkered walnut stock and recoil pad. It was manufactured between 1964 and 1981. This model was offered with the plastic Hydrocoil stock, and this would add approximately 35 percent to the values given.

| Exc. | V.G. | Good | Fair | Poor |
|------|------|------|------|------|
| 225 | 175 | 150 | 100 | 75 |

### Model 1300 XTR
This is the current slide-action shotgun offered by Winchester. It is chambered for 12 and 20 gauge with 3" chambers. It is a takedown gun that is offered with various-length vent-rib barrels with screw-in choke tubes. It has an alloy frame and is blued with a walnut stock. It was introduced in 1978.

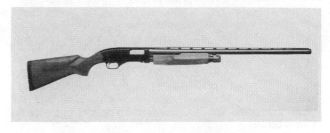

| Exc. | V.G. | Good | Fair | Poor |
|------|------|------|------|------|
| 300 | 250 | 200 | 150 | 100 |

### Model 1300 Waterfowl
This version is chambered for 12 gauge, 3" only. It has a 30" vent-rib barrel with screw-in choke tubes. It is matte-blued, with a satin-finished walnut stock and a recoil pad. It was introduced in 1984. A laminated Win-Tuff stock was made available in 1988 and would add $10 to the value.

| NIB | Exc. | V.G. | Good | Fair | Poor |
|-----|------|------|------|------|------|
| 350 | 300 | 250 | 200 | 150 | 100 |

### Model 1300 Turkey Gun

This version is similar to the Waterfowl, with a 22" barrel and screw-in chokes. It was manufactured between 1985 and 1988 only.

| Exc. | V.G. | Good | Fair | Poor |
|------|------|------|------|------|
| 300 | 250 | 200 | 150 | 100 |

### Model 1300 Win-Cam Turkey Gun

This version is similar to the Model 1300 Turkey Gun, with a green, laminated hardwood stock. It was introduced in 1987. A Win-Tuff version is also available and would add $20 to the values given.

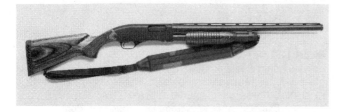

| NIB | Exc. | V.G. | Good | Fair | Poor |
|-----|------|------|------|------|------|
| 375 | 325 | 250 | 200 | 150 | 125 |

### Model 1300 Stainless Security

This version is chambered for 12 or 20 gauge and is constructed of stainless steel. It has an 18" cylinder-bore barrel and a 7- or 8-shot tubular magazine. It is available with a pistolgrip stock, which would add approximately 50 percent to the values given.

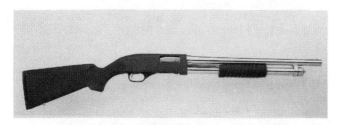

| NIB | Exc. | V.G. | Good | Fair | Poor |
|-----|------|------|------|------|------|
| 250 | 225 | 200 | 150 | 125 | 100 |

### Model 1400

This is a gas-operated, semi-automatic shotgun chambered for 12, 16, or 20 gauge. It was offered with a 26", 28", or 30" vent-rib barrel with various chokes. The finish is blued, with a checkered walnut stock. It was manufactured between 1964 and 1981. The Hydrocoil plastic stock was available on this model and would add approximately 35 percent to the values given.

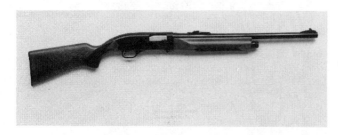

| Exc. | V.G. | Good | Fair | Poor |
|------|------|------|------|------|
| 250 | 225 | 200 | 150 | 100 |

### Model 1500 XTR

This is a gas-operated, semi-automatic shotgun chambered for 12 or 20 gauge, with a 28" vent-rib barrel with screw-in chokes. The finish is blued, with a walnut stock. It was manufactured between 1978 and 1982.

| Exc. | V.G. | Good | Fair | Poor |
|------|------|------|------|------|
| 300 | 250 | 225 | 175 | 125 |

### Super X Model 1

This is a self-compensating, gas-operated, semi-automatic shotgun chambered for 12 gauge. It was offered with a 26", 28", or 30" vent-rib barrel with various chokes. It features all-steel construction and is blued, with a checkered walnut stock. It was manufactured between 1974 and 1981.

| Exc. | V.G. | Good | Fair | Poor |
|------|------|------|------|------|
| 400 | 325 | 250 | 200 | 150 |

### Super X Model 1 Custom Competition

This is a custom-order trap or skeet gun that features the self-compensating, gas-operated action. It is available in 12 gauge only from the Custom Shop. It is offered with a heavy degree of engraving on the receiver and a fancy, checkered walnut stock. Gold inlays are available and would add approximately 50 percent to the values given. This model was introduced in 1987.

| NIB | Exc. | V.G. | Good | Fair | Poor |
|-----|------|------|------|------|------|
| 1300 | 1000 | 850 | 700 | 600 | 450 |

### New Model 1400

This is a gas-operated, semi-automatic shotgun chambered for 12 or 20 gauge. It is offered with a 22" or 28" vent-rib barrel with screw-in chokes. The finish is blued, with a checkered walnut stock. It was introduced in 1989.

| NIB | Exc. | V.G. | Good | Fair | Poor |
|-----|------|------|------|------|------|
| 400 | 350 | 300 | 250 | 200 | 125 |

### Model 1400 Ranger

This is a utility-grade, gas-operated, semi-automatic shotgun chambered for 12 or 20 gauge. It is offered with a 28" vent-rib barrel with screw-in chokes, as well as a 24" slug barrel with rifle sights. The finish is blued, with a checkered stock. A combination two-barrel set that includes the deer barrel would be worth approximately 20 percent additional. This model was introduced in 1983 and is currently produced.

| NIB | Exc. | V.G. | Good | Fair | Poor |
|-----|------|------|------|------|------|
| 340 | 300 | 250 | 200 | 150 | 100 |

### Model 23 XTR

This is a side-by-side, double-barrel shotgun chambered for 12 or 20 gauge. It is offered with 25.5", 26", 28", or 30" vent-rib barrels with 3" chambers and various choke combinations. It is a boxlock gun that features a single trigger and automatic ejectors. It is scroll-engraved with a coin-finished receiver, blued barrels, and a checkered, select walnut stock. It was introduced in 1978. This model is available in a number of configurations that differ in the amount of ornamentation and the quality of materials and workmanship utilized in their construction. These models and their values are as follows:

**Grade I--Discontinued**

| Exc. | V.G. | Good | Fair | Poor |
|------|------|------|------|------|
| 900 | 750 | 650 | 500 | 400 |

**Pigeon Grade--With Winchokes**

| Exc. | V.G. | Good | Fair | Poor |
|------|------|------|------|------|
| 1000 | 850 | 750 | 600 | 500 |

**Pigeon Grade Lightweight--Straight Stock**

| Exc. | V.G. | Good | Fair | Poor |
|------|------|------|------|------|
| 1300 | 1000 | 900 | 750 | 600 |

### Golden Quail

This series was available in 28 gauge and .410, as well as 12 or 20 gauge. It features 25.5" barrels that are choked improved cylinder/modified. It features a straight-grip, English-style stock with a recoil pad. The .410 version would be worth approximately 10 percent more than the values given. This series was discontinued in 1987.

| Exc. | V.G. | Good | Fair | Poor |
|------|------|------|------|------|
| 1500 | 1250 | 1100 | 850 | 750 |

## Model 23

### Model 23 Light Duck

This version is chambered for 20 gauge and was offered with a 28" full and full-choked barrel. There were 500 manufactured in 1985.

| Exc. | V.G. | Good | Fair | Poor |
|------|------|------|------|------|
| 1500 | 1250 | 1100 | 850 | 750 |

### Model 23 Heavy Duck

This version is chambered for 12 gauge with 30" full and full-choked barrels. There were 500 manufactured in 1984.

| Exc. | V.G. | Good | Fair | Poor |
|------|------|------|------|------|
| 1500 | 1250 | 1100 | 850 | 750 |

## Model 21

This is a very high-quality, side-by-side, double-barrel shotgun that features a boxlock action and is chambered for 12, 16, 20, and 28 gauges, as well as .410. It is featured with various barrel lengths and choke combinations. Since 1960 the Model 21 has been available on a custom-order basis only. It is available in five basic configurations that differ in the options offered, the amount of ornamentation, and the quality of materials and workmanship utilized in their construction. We supply general values for this model but strongly urge securing a qualified appraisal if a transaction is contemplated. The earlier Model 21 shotguns were listed previously in this text.

### Standard Grade--No Engraving

| NIB | Exc. | V.G. | Good | Fair | Poor |
|-----|------|------|------|------|------|
| 8000 | 6000 | 4500 | 3750 | 2500 | 1750 |

### Custom Grade--Engraved

| NIB | Exc. | V.G. | Good | Fair | Poor |
|-----|------|------|------|------|------|
| 11500 | 8000 | 6500 | 5500 | 4250 | 2750 |

### Grand American Grade--Gold Inlaid, Two Sets of Barrels

| NIB | Exc. | V.G. | Good | Fair | Poor |
|-----|------|------|------|------|------|
| 22500 | 17500 | 14000 | 10000 | 7000 | 5000 |

### Grand American Small Gauge

| NIB | Exc. | V.G. | Good | Fair | Poor |
|-----|------|------|------|------|------|
| 35000 | 27500 | 22500 | 15000 | 11000 | 7500 |

## Model 101 Field Grade

This is an Over/Under, double-barrel shotgun chambered for 12, 20, and 28 gauge, as well as .410. It was offered with 26", 28", or 30" vent-rib barrels with various choke combinations. As of 1983 screw-in chokes have been standard, and models so furnished would be worth approximately $50 additional. This is a boxlock gun with a single-selective trigger and automatic ejectors. The receiver is engraved; the finish, blued with a checkered walnut stock. It was manufactured between 1963 and 1987.

28 Gauge--Add 40 Percent.
.410--Add 50 Percent.

| Exc. | V.G. | Good | Fair | Poor |
|------|------|------|------|------|
| 750 | 650 | 500 | 375 | 300 |

### Waterfowl Model

This version of the Model 101 is chambered for 12 gauge with 3" chambers. It has 30" or 32" vent-rib barrels and a matte finish.

| Exc. | V.G. | Good | Fair | Poor |
|------|------|------|------|------|
| 1250 | 1000 | 850 | 650 | 500 |

### Model 101 Magnum

This version is similar to the Field Grade, chambered for 12 or 20 gauge with 3" Magnum chambers. It was offered with 30" barrels with various chokes. The stock is furnished with a recoil pad. It was manufactured between 1966 and 1981.

| Exc. | V.G. | Good | Fair | Poor |
|------|------|------|------|------|
| 775 | 675 | 525 | 400 | 325 |

### Model 101 Skeet Grade

This version was offered with 26" skeet-bored barrels with a competition rib and a skeet-type walnut stock. It was manufactured between 1966 and 1984.

| Exc. | V.G. | Good | Fair | Poor |
|------|------|------|------|------|
| 950 | 850 | 750 | 500 | 400 |

### Model 101 Three-Gauge Skeet Set

This combination set was offered with three barrels, chambered for 20 and 28 gauge, as well as .410. It was furnished with a fitted case and manufactured between 1974 and 1984.

| Exc. | V.G. | Good | Fair | Poor |
|------|------|------|------|------|
| 1850 | 1450 | 1000 | 750 | 650 |

### Model 101 Trap Grade

This version is chambered for 12 gauge only and was offered with 30" or 32" competition ribbed barrels, choked for trap shooting. It is furnished with a competition-type stock. It was manufactured between 1966 and 1984.

| Exc. | V.G. | Good | Fair | Poor |
|------|------|------|------|------|
| 1250 | 1000 | 850 | 650 | 500 |

### Model 101 Pigeon Grade

This is a more deluxe engraved version of the Model 101, chambered for 12, 20, or 28 gauge, as well as .410. It features a coin-finished receiver with a fancy checkered walnut stock. It was introduced in 1974.

| Exc. | V.G. | Good | Fair | Poor |
|------|------|------|------|------|
| 1500 | 1250 | 1000 | 800 | 700 |

### Super Pigeon Grade

This is a very deluxe version of the Model 101, chambered for 12 gauge. It is heavily engraved with several gold inlays. The receiver is blued, and it features a high-grade walnut stock with fleur-de-lis checkering. It was imported between 1985 and 1987.

| Exc. | V.G. | Good | Fair | Poor |
|------|------|------|------|------|
| 4000 | 3500 | 2750 | 2000 | 1650 |

### Model 101 Diamond Grade

This is a competition model, chambered for all four gauges. It was offered in either a trap or skeet configuration with screw-in chokes, an engraved matte-finished receiver, and a select checkered walnut stock. The skeet model features recoil-reducing muzzle vents.

| Exc. | V.G. | Good | Fair | Poor |
|------|------|------|------|------|
| 1600 | 1250 | 1000 | 750 | 600 |

### Model 501 Grand European

This is an Over/Under, double-barrel shotgun chambered for 12 or 20 gauge. It was available in trap or skeet configurations and was offered with a 27", 30", or 32" vent-rib barrel. It is heavily engraved and matte-finished, with a select checkered walnut stock. It was manufactured between 1981 and 1986.

| Exc. | V.G. | Good | Fair | Poor |
|------|------|------|------|------|
| 1500 | 1150 | 950 | 700 | 550 |

### Model 501 Presentation Grade

This is a deluxe version chambered in 12 gauge only. It is ornately engraved and gold-inlaid. The stock is made out of presentation-grade walnut. It was furnished with a fitted case. It was manufactured between 1984 and 1987.

| Exc. | V.G. | Good | Fair | Poor |
|------|------|------|------|------|
| 3000 | 2500 | 2000 | 1500 | 1250 |

### Combination Gun

This is an Over/Under rifle/shotgun combination chambered for 12 gauge over .222, .223, .30-06, and the 9.3x74R cartridges. It features 25" barrels. The shotgun tube has a screw-in choke. It is engraved in the fashion of the Model 501 Grand European and features a select checkered walnut stock. It was manufactured between 1983 and 1985.

| Exc. | V.G. | Good | Fair | Poor |
|------|------|------|------|------|
| 2250 | 2000 | 1750 | 1250 | 1000 |

## Express Rifle

This is an Over/Under, double-barrelled rifle chambered for the .257 Roberts, .270, 7.7x65R, .30-06, and the 9.3x74R cartridges. It features 23.5" barrels with a solid rib and express sights. It is engraved with gamescenes and has a satin-finished receiver. The stock is checkered select walnut. It was manufactured in 1984 and 1985.

| Exc. | V.G. | Good | Fair | Poor |
|------|------|------|------|------|
| 1750 | 1500 | 1250 | 1000 | 750 |

## Model 96 Xpert

This is a utility-grade, Over/Under, double-barrel shotgun that is mechanically similar to the Model 101. It is chambered for 12 or 20 gauge and was offered with various barrel lengths and choke combinations. It has a boxlock action with single-selective trigger and automatic ejectors. The plain receiver is blued, with a checkered walnut stock. It was manufactured between 1976 and 1982. A competition-grade model for trap or skeet was also available and would be worth approximately the same amount.

| Exc. | V.G. | Good | Fair | Poor |
|------|------|------|------|------|
| 650 | 550 | 450 | 350 | 275 |

## WINCHESTER COMMEMORATIVE RIFLES

Since the early 1960's, Winchester has produced a number of special Model 1894 rifles and carbines that commemorated certain historic events, places, or individuals. In some cases they are slightly embellished and in others are quite ornate. The general liquidity of these commemoratives has not been as good as would be expected. In some cases they were produced in excessive amounts and could not, in all honesty, be considered limited-production items. In any case, in our opinion one should purchase weapons of this nature for their enjoyment factor as the investment potential is not sufficient reason for their purchase. As with all commemoratives, in order to realize the collector potential they must be NIB with all supplied materials including, in the case of Winchester, the colorful outer sleeve that encased the factory carton. If a Winchester commemorative rifle has been cocked leaving a line on the hammer or the lever, many collectors will show little or no interest in its acquisition. If they have been fired, they will realize little premium over a standard, post-'64 Model '94. A number of commemoratives have been ordered by outside concerns and are technically not factory issues. Most have less collectibility than the factory-issued models. There are a number of concerns that specialize in marketing the total range of Winchester commmemorative rifles. We list the factory-issue commemoratives with their current value, their issue price, and the number manufactured.

### 1964 Wyoming Diamond Jubilee--Carbine

| NIB | Issue | Amt. Mfg. |
|-----|-------|-----------|
| 1750 | 100 | 1,500 |

### 1966 Centennial--Rifle

| NIB | Issue | Amt. Mfg. |
|-----|-------|-----------|
| 425 | 125 | — |

### 1966 Centennial--Carbine

| NIB | Issue | Amt. Mfg. |
|-----|-------|-----------|
| 425 | 125 | 102,309 |

### 1966 Nebraska Centennial--Rifle

| NIB | Issue | Amt. Mfg. |
|-----|-------|-----------|
| 1000 | 100 | 2,500 |

### 1967 Canadian Centennial--Rifle

| NIB | Issue | Amt. Mfg. |
|-----|-------|-----------|
| 275 | 125 | — |

### 1967 Canadian Centennial--Carbine

| NIB | Issue | Amt. Mfg. |
|-----|-------|-----------|
| 275 | 125 | 90,301 |

### 1967 Alaskan Purchase Centennial--Carbine

| NIB | Issue | Amt. Mfg. |
|-----|-------|-----------|
| 1250 | 125 | 1,500 |

### 1968 Illinois Sesquicentennial--Carbine

| NIB | Issue | Amt. Mfg. |
|-----|-------|-----------|
| 275 | 110 | 37,648 |

### 1968 Illinois Sesquicentennial--Rifle

| NIB | Issue | Amt. Mfg. |
|-----|-------|-----------|
| 275 | 110 | 37,648 |

### 1968 Buffalo Bill--Carbine

| NIB | Issue | Amt. Mfg. |
|-----|-------|-----------|
| 275 | 130 | 112,923 |

### 1968 Buffalo Bill--Rifle

| NIB | Issue | Amt. Mfg. |
|-----|-------|-----------|
| 275 | 130 | — |

### 1968 Buffalo Bill "1 or 300"--Rifle

| NIB | Issue | Amt. Mfg. |
|-----|-------|-----------|
| 2500 | 1000 | 300 |

### 1969 Theodore Roosevelt--Rifle

| NIB | Issue | Amt. Mfg. |
|-----|-------|-----------|
| 350 | 135 | — |

### 1969 Theodore Roosevelt--Carbine

| NIB | Issue | Amt. Mfg. |
|-----|-------|-----------|
| 350 | 135 | 52,386 |

### 1969 Golden Spike Carbine

| NIB | Issue | Amt. Mfg. |
|-----|-------|-----------|
| 300 | 120 | 69,996 |

### 1970 Cowboy Commemorative Carbine

| NIB | Issue | Amt. Mfg. |
|-----|-------|-----------|
| 400 | 125 | 27,549 |

### 1970 Cowboy Carbine "1 of 300"

| NIB | Issue | Amt. Mfg. |
|-----|-------|-----------|
| 3000 | 1000 | 300 |

### 1970 Northwest Territories (Canadian)

| NIB | Issue | Amt. Mfg. |
|-----|-------|-----------|
| 800 | 150 | 2,500 |

### 1970 Northwest Territories Deluxe (Canadian)

| NIB | Issue | Amt. Mfg. |
|-----|-------|-----------|
| 1400 | 250 | 500 |

### 1970 Lone Star--Rifle

| NIB | Issue | Amt. Mfg. |
|-----|-------|-----------|
| 350 | 140 | — |

### 1970 Lone Star--Carbine

| NIB | Issue | Amt. Mfg. |
|-----|-------|-----------|
| 350 | 140 | 38,385 |

### 1971 NRA Centennial--Rifle

| NIB | Issue | Amt. Mfg. |
|-----|-------|-----------|
| 275 | 150 | 21,000 |

### 1971 NRA Centennial--Musket

| NIB | Issue | Amt. Mfg. |
|-----|-------|-----------|
| 275 | 150 | 23,400 |

### 1972 Yellow Boy (European)

| NIB | Issue | Amt. Mfg. |
|-----|-------|-----------|
| 1400 | 250 | 500 |

### 1973 Royal Canadian Mounted Police (Canadian)

| NIB | Issue | Amt. Mfg. |
|-----|-------|-----------|
| 600 | 190 | 9,500 |

### 1973 Mounted Police (Canadian)

| NIB | Issue | Amt. Mfg. |
|-----|-------|-----------|
| 1200 | 190 | 5,100 |

### 1974 Texas Ranger--Carbine

| NIB | Issue | Amt. Mfg. |
|-----|-------|-----------|
| 550 | 135 | 4,850 |

### 1974 Texas Ranger Presentation Model

| NIB | Issue | Amt. Mfg. |
|-----|-------|-----------|
| 3000 | 1000 | 150 |

**1974 Apache (Canadian)**

| NIB | Issue | Amt. Mfg. |
|---|---|---|
| 600 | 150 | 8,600 |

**1975 Commanche (Canadian)**

| NIB | Issue | Amt. Mfg. |
|---|---|---|
| 600 | 230 | 11,500 |

**1975 Klondike Gold Rush (Canadian)**

| NIB | Issue | Amt. Mfg. |
|---|---|---|
| 600 | 240 | 10,500 |

**1975 Klondike Gold Rush--Dawson City Issue (Canadian)**

| NIB | Issue | Amt. Mfg. |
|---|---|---|
| 8000 | — | 25 |

**1976 Sioux (Canadian)**

| NIB | Issue | Amt. Mfg. |
|---|---|---|
| 600 | 280 | 10,000 |

**1976 Little Bighorn (Canadian)**

| NIB | Issue | Amt. Mfg. |
|---|---|---|
| 600 | 300 | 11,000 |

**1976 U.S. Bicentennial Carbine**

| NIB | Issue | Amt. Mfg. |
|---|---|---|
| 500 | 325 | 19,999 |

**1977 Wells Fargo**

| NIB | Issue | Amt. Mfg. |
|---|---|---|
| 350 | 350 | 19,999 |

**1977 Legendary Lawman**

| NIB | Issue | Amt. Mfg. |
|---|---|---|
| 400 | 375 | 19,999 |

**1977 Limited Edition I**

| NIB | Issue | Amt. Mfg. |
|---|---|---|
| 1100 | 1500 | 1,500 |

**1977 Cheyenne--.22 Cal. (Canadian)**

| NIB | Issue | Amt. Mfg. |
|---|---|---|
| 650 | 320 | 5,000 |

**1977 Cheyenne--.44-40 Cal. (Canadian)**

| NIB | Issue | Amt. Mfg. |
|---|---|---|
| 600 | 300 | 11,225 |

**1978 Cherokee--.22 Cal. (Canadian)**

| NIB | Issue | Amt. Mfg. |
|---|---|---|
| 650 | 385 | 3,950 |

**1978 Cherokee--.30-30 Cal. (Canadian)**

| NIB | Issue | Amt. Mfg. |
|---|---|---|
| 600 | 385 | 9,000 |

**1978 "One of One Thousand" (European)**

| NIB | Issue | Amt. Mfg. |
|---|---|---|
| 7500 | 5000 | 250 |

**1978 Antler Game Carbine**

| NIB | Issue | Amt. Mfg. |
|---|---|---|
| 350 | 375 | 19,999 |

**1979 Limited Edition II**

| NIB | Issue | Amt. Mfg. |
|---|---|---|
| 1100 | 1500 | 1,500 |

**1979 Legendary Frontiersman Rifle**

| NIB | Issue | Amt. Mfg. |
|---|---|---|
| 350 | 425 | 19,999 |

**1979 Matched Set of 1,000**

| NIB | Issue | Amt. Mfg. |
|---|---|---|
| 2500 | 3000 | 1,000 |

**1979 Bat Masterson (Canadian)**

| NIB | Issue | Amt. Mfg. |
|---|---|---|
| 600 | 650 | 8,000 |

**1980 Alberta Diamond Jubilee (Canadian)**

| NIB | Issue | Amt. Mfg. |
|---|---|---|
| 800 | 650 | 2,700 |

**1980 Alberta Diamond Jubilee Presentation (Canadian)**

| NIB | Issue | Amt. Mfg. |
|---|---|---|
| 2250 | 1900 | 300 |

**1980 Saskatchewan Diamond Jubilee (Canadian)**

| NIB | Issue | Amt. Mfg. |
|---|---|---|
| 600 | 695 | 2,700 |

**1980 Saskatchewan Diamond Jubilee Presentation (Canadian)**

| NIB | Issue | Amt. Mfg. |
|---|---|---|
| 2000 | 1995 | 300 |

**1980 Oliver Winchester**

| NIB | Issue | Amt. Mfg. |
|---|---|---|
| 450 | 375 | 19,999 |

**1981 U.S. Border Patrol**

| NIB | Issue | Amt. Mfg. |
|---|---|---|
| 580 | 1195 | 1,000 |

**1981 U.S. Border Patrol--Member's Model**

| NIB | Issue | Amt. Mfg. |
|---|---|---|
| 1000 | 695 | 800 |

**1981 Calgary Stampede (Canadian)**

| NIB | Issue | Amt. Mfg. |
|---|---|---|
| 2000 | 2200 | 1,000 |

**1981 Canadian Pacific Centennial (Canadian)**

| NIB | Issue | Amt. Mfg. |
|---|---|---|
| 425 | 800 | 2,000 |

**1981 Canadian Pacific Centennial Presentation (Canadian)**

| NIB | Issue | Amt. Mfg. |
|---|---|---|
| 2000 | 2200 | 300 |

**1981 Canadian Pacific Employee's Model (Canadian)**

| NIB | Issue | Amt. Mfg. |
|---|---|---|
| 650 | 800 | 2,000 |

**1981 John Wayne (Canadian)**

| NIB | Issue | Amt. Mfg. |
|---|---|---|
| 900 | 995 | 1,000 |

**1982 John Wayne**

| NIB | Issue | Amt. Mfg. |
|---|---|---|
| 725 | 600 | 49,000 |

**1982 Duke**

| NIB | Issue | Amt. Mfg. |
|---|---|---|
| 2950 | 2250 | 1,000 |

**1982 John Wayne "1 of 300" Set**

| NIB | Issue | Amt. Mfg. |
|---|---|---|
| 7500 | 10000 | 300 |

**1982 Great Western Artist I**

| NIB | Issue | Amt. Mfg. |
|---|---|---|
| 1250 | 2200 | 999 |

**1982 Great Western Artist II**

| NIB | Issue | Amt. Mfg. |
|---|---|---|
| 1250 | 2200 | 999 |

**1982 Annie Oakley**

| NIB | Issue | Amt. Mfg. |
|---|---|---|
| 500 | 699 | 6,000 |

**1983 Chief Crazy Horse**

| NIB | Issue | Amt. Mfg. |
|---|---|---|
| 450 | 600 | 19,999 |

**1983 American Bald Eagle**

| NIB | Issue | Amt. Mfg. |
|---|---|---|
| 850 | 895 | 2,800 |

**1983 American Bald Eagle--Deluxe**

| NIB | Issue | Amt. Mfg. |
|---|---|---|
| 2750 | 2995 | 200 |

**1983 Oklahoma Diamond Jubilee**

| NIB | Issue | Amt. Mfg. |
|---|---|---|
| 1400 | 2250 | 1,001 |

**1984 Winchester-Colt Commemorative Set**

| NIB | Issue | Amt. Mfg. |
| --- | --- | --- |
| 2000 | 3995 | 2,300 |

**1985 Boy Scout 75th Anniversary--.22 Cal.**

| NIB | Issue | Amt. Mfg. |
| --- | --- | --- |
| 400 | 615 | 15,000 |

**1985 Boy Scout 75th Anniversary--Eagle Scout**

| NIB | Issue | Amt. Mfg. |
| --- | --- | --- |
| 1900 | 2140 | 1,000 |

**Texas Sesquicentennial Model--Rifle--.38-55 Cal.**

| NIB | Issue | Amt. Mfg. |
| --- | --- | --- |
| 2500 | 2995 | 1,500 |

**Texas Sesquicentennial Model--Carbine--.38-55 Cal.**

| NIB | Issue | Amt. Mfg. |
| --- | --- | --- |
| 650 | 695 | 15,000 |

**Texas Sesquicentennial Model Set with Bowie Knife**

| NIB | Issue | Amt. Mfg. |
| --- | --- | --- |
| 5500 | 7995 | 150 |

**1986 Model 94 Ducks Unlimited**

| NIB | Issue | Amt. Mfg. |
| --- | --- | --- |
| 650 | — | 2,800 |

**1986 Statue of Liberty**

| NIB | Issue | Amt. Mfg. |
| --- | --- | --- |
| 7000 | 6500 | 100 |

**1986 120th Anniversary Model--Carbine--.44-40 Cal.**

| NIB | Issue | Amt. Mfg. |
| --- | --- | --- |
| 850 | 995 | 1,000 |

**1986 European 1 of 1,000 Second Series (European)**

| NIB | Issue | Amt. Mfg. |
| --- | --- | --- |
| 6000 | 6000 | 150 |

Winchester Model 9422 Wintuff.

Winchester Ranger lever action rifle.

Winchester Model 9422 walnut.

Winchester Model 94 Ranger with Bushnell Sportview 4 power scope and see-through mounts.

Winchester Model 70 lightweight Win-Tuff, laminated stock.

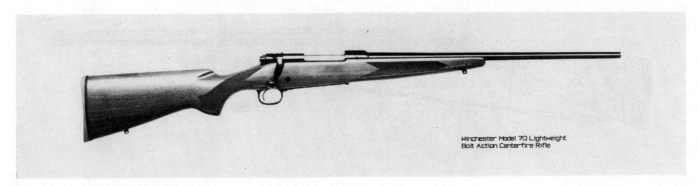

Winchester Model 70 lightweight bolt action centerfire rifle.

Winchester Model 70 lightweight Win-Cam, laminated stock.

Winchester Model 70 Super Grade bolt action rifle.

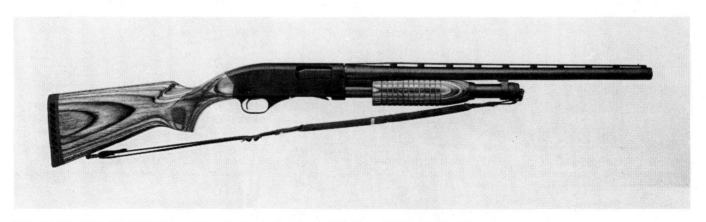

Winchester Model 1300 Wintuff waterfowl shotgun with sling, 28'' barrel - 12-gauge.

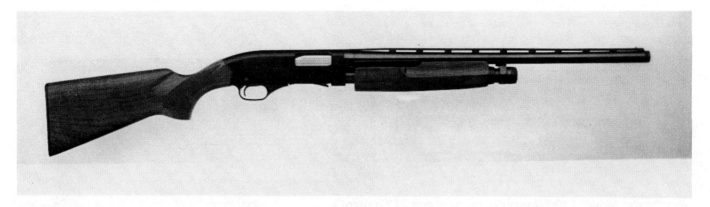

Winchester Model 1300 walnut pump shotgun - beavertail forend, 22" barrel - 12 or 20-gauge.

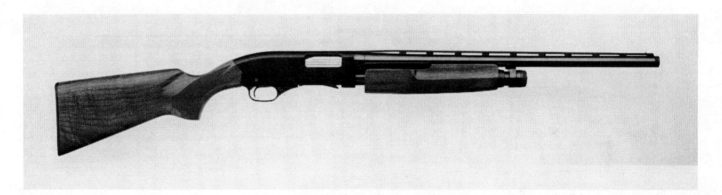

Winchester Model 1300 walnut pump shotgun - beavertail forend, 22" barrel - 20-gauge.

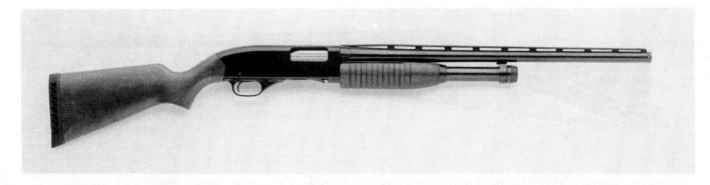

Winchester M1300 walnut, ladies/youth pump shotgun - 20-gauge.

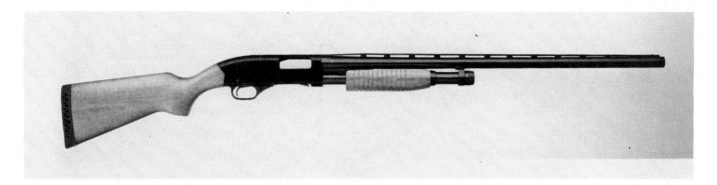

Winchester Model 1300 Ranger pump shotgun - 12-gauge.

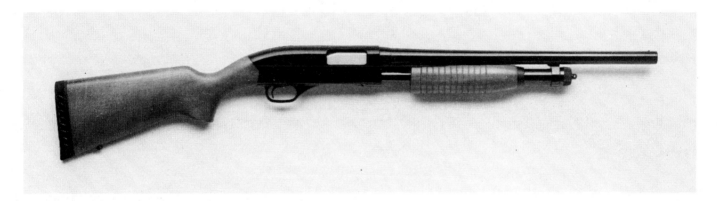

Winchester Model 1300 Defender pump action combination shotgun.

Winchester Model 1300 "Slug Hunter" pump shotgun fully rifled 22" barrel, sights drilled and tapped, laminated Wintuff stock - scope not included.

Winchester Model 1300 walnut "Slug Hunter" pump shotgun fully rifled 22" barrel, sights drilled and tapped - scope not included.

Winchester Model 1400 walnut "Slug Hunter" with Sabot tube - rifle sights, semi-auto - 22" barrel - 12-gauge, drilled & tapped - scope not included.

# WINDSOR
### Windsor, Vermont
### Robbins & Lawrence
### Hartford, Connecticut

## Windsor Rifle

This is a single-shot muzzleloader chambered for .577 percussion. It has a 39" round barrel with a full-length walnut stock held on by three barrel bands. The lock is marked "Windsor," and the weapon was patterned after the British Enfield rifle. In fact, the British government contracted Robbins & Lawrence to produce a number of these weapons to be used in the Crimean War. The quick finish to this War caused the company to go bankrupt, as their products were no longer needed. The finish is white with brass mountings, and a steel ramrod is mounted beneath the barrel. The front sight acts as a bayonet lug. There were approximately 16,000 manufactured between 1855 and 1858.

| Exc. | V.G. | Good | Fair | Poor |
|------|------|------|------|------|
| 1500 | 1250 | 1000 | 750 | 500 |

# WINSLOW ARMS CO.
### Camden, South Carolina

## Bolt Action Rifle

This is a high-grade, semi-custom sporting rifle built around a number of quality actions. It is offered in all popular calibers from .17 Remington to the .458 Winchester Magnum. It has a 24" barrel and a 3-shot magazine. The larger Magnum models have a 26" barrel and a 2-shot magazine. There are two basic stocks offered--the Conventional Bushmaster that features a standard pistolgrip and a beavertail forearm; also the Plainsmaster that has a full-curled, hooked pistol grip and a wide, flat beavertail forearm. They both feature Monte Carlo designs and come standard with recoil pads and sling swivels. They are offered in a choice of popular woods with rosewood forend tips and pistolgrip caps. This rifle is offered in eight grades that differ with the ornamentation and features offered. The values reflected here are for the standard models, and they can be affected by options. If in doubt, secure a qualified appraisal.

### Commander Grade
| Exc. | V.G. | Good | Fair | Poor |
|------|------|------|------|------|
| 500 | 450 | 400 | 350 | 300 |

### Regal Grade
| Exc. | V.G. | Good | Fair | Poor |
|------|------|------|------|------|
| 600 | 550 | 450 | 375 | 325 |

### Regent Grade
| Exc. | V.G. | Good | Fair | Poor |
|------|------|------|------|------|
| 750 | 700 | 500 | 450 | 350 |

### Regimental Grade
| Exc. | V.G. | Good | Fair | Poor |
|------|------|------|------|------|
| 950 | 850 | 650 | 550 | 450 |

### Crown Grade
| Exc. | V.G. | Good | Fair | Poor |
|------|------|------|------|------|
| 1400 | 1250 | 1000 | 750 | 600 |

### Royal Grade
| Exc. | V.G. | Good | Fair | Poor |
|------|------|------|------|------|
| 1550 | 1400 | 1150 | 850 | 700 |

### Imperial Grade
| Exc. | V.G. | Good | Fair | Poor |
|------|------|------|------|------|
| 3500 | 3000 | 2500 | 2000 | 1450 |

### Emperor Grade
| Exc. | V.G. | Good | Fair | Poor |
|------|------|------|------|------|
| 6000 | 5000 | 4000 | 3000 | 2000 |

# WISEMAN, BILL & CO.
### Bryan, Texas

## Rifle

This is a high quality, basically made-to-order rifle built on the fine Sako action. It utilizes a McMillan stainless-steel barrel and has a laminated stock with Teflon-finished metal parts. The action is glass-bedded, and it is offered standard with a Pachmayr decelerator recoil pad and sling swivels. There are four basic models--the Hunter, Hunter Deluxe, Maverick, and the Varminter. Values vary according to the options desired, and the Company or a qualified appraiser should be contacted if a transaction is contemplated. The values offered here are for the basic, standard model only.

| Exc. | V.G. | Good | Fair | Poor |
|------|------|------|------|------|
| 1500 | 1250 | 1000 | 750 | 600 |

## Silhouette Pistol

This version is similar to the rifle, chambered in various popular calibers, with a 14" fluted stainless-steel barrel. It has a laminated pistolgrip stock and is furnished without sights. It was introduced in 1989.

| Exc. | V.G. | Good | Fair | Poor |
|------|------|------|------|------|
| 1300 | 1000 | 800 | 600 | 500 |

# WOODWARD, JAMES & SONS
### London, England

This company has produced some of the highest-grade shotguns the world has ever known. They are an old-line, London gunmaking company. Prior to WWII they were purchased by the firm of Purdey & Sons, another of the most respected firearms companies in the world. The firearms manufactured by Woodward are known as not only the finest, but among the most expensive. Values start in the $16,000 range and escalate upward. It would be irresponsible to attempt to evaluate weapons of this nature in this type of publication. We strongly urge that anyone interested in acquiring such a firearm seek the most competent, individual appraisal possible.

# WURFFLEIN, ANDREW
### Philadelphia, Pennsylvania

## Pocket Pistol

This is a .41-caliber percussion pistol patterned after the Henry Deringer-type. It has barrel lengths of 2.5" to 3", engraved German silver mountings, and a walnut stock. It is marked "A. Wurfflein/Phila." It was manufactured in the 1850's and 1860's.

| Exc. | V.G. | Good | Fair | Poor |
|------|------|------|------|------|
| 750 | 650 | 500 | 400 | 300 |

## Single Shot Target Pistol

This pistol is chambered for the .22-caliber rimfire cartridge. It has a part-octagonal barrel that is between 8" and 16" in length. It pivots downward for loading. The finish is blued, with walnut grips. It is marked "W. Wurfflein Philad'a Pa. U.S.A. Patented June 24th, 1884." There is a detachable shoulder stock offered which would be worth an additional 35 percent. There were a few hundred manufactured between 1884 and 1890.

| Exc. | V.G. | Good | Fair | Poor |
|------|------|------|------|------|
| 550 | 450 | 400 | 300 | 200 |

## Single Shot Rifle

This is a single-shot sporting or target rifle chambered for various calibers from .22 rimfire to .44 centerfire. It has barrel lengths from 24" to 28" in length of octagonal configuration. There were approximately 2,000 manufactured between 1880 and 1890. There were a number of variations and options available which would have a great effect on the values. We recommend acquiring a qualified appraisal if a transaction is contemplated. The standard sporting rifle would be valued as follows.

| Exc. | V.G. | Good | Fair | Poor |
|------|------|------|------|------|
| 600  | 500  | 450  | 350  | 250  |

## Mid-range Model

This version has a 28" or 30" part-octagonal barrel and was available with many options. Values for a standard model are as follows.

| Exc. | V.G. | Good | Fair | Poor |
|------|------|------|------|------|
| 850  | 800  | 700  | 500  | 400  |

## Model No. 2

This was the best-grade rifle that Wurfflein offered. In its standard configuration, it would be worth as follows.

| Exc. | V.G. | Good | Fair | Poor |
|------|------|------|------|------|
| 1000 | 900  | 800  | 600  | 500  |

# XL
# HOPKINS & ALLEN
## Norwich, Connecticut

## Derringer

This is a single-shot, derringer-type pocket pistol chambered for the .41-caliber rimfire cartridge. It has a 2.75" octagonal barrel and is found with either an iron or a brass frame. The barrel pivots to the side for loading. The finish is usually two-toned with a nickel-plated frame and blued barrel. It has rosewood birdshead grips. It has a spur trigger and is marked "XL Derringer." It was manufactured by Hopkins & Allen but does not bear their markings. There were several thousand manufactured in the 1870's.

| Exc. | V.G. | Good | Fair | Poor |
|------|------|------|------|------|
| 400  | 350  | 300  | 250  | 150  |

## Vest Pocket Derringer

This is a diminutive pistol chambered for the .22-caliber rimfire cartridge. It has a 2.25" stepped round barrel that pivots to the side for loading. It has a spur trigger with an iron frame. The finish is plated, with walnut birdshead grips. The barrel is marked "XL Vest Pocket." This firearm was also manufactured by Hopkins & Allen but does not bear their markings. It was manufactured from 1870 through the 1890's.

| Exc. | V.G. | Good | Fair | Poor |
|------|------|------|------|------|
| 350  | 300  | 250  | 200  | 100  |

# XPERT
# HOPKINS & ALLEN
## Norwich, Connecticut

## Xpert Derringer

This is a single-shot pocket pistol chambered for the .22- or .30-caliber rimfire cartridges. It has barrel lengths from 2.25" to 6", round in configuration. This model has a thin breechblock that pivots outward to the lefthand side for loading. The finish is nickel-plated, with rosewood birdshead grips. It is marked "Xpert-Pat. Sep. 23. 1878." This firearm was manufactured by Hopkins & Allen but does not bear their markings. There were fewer than 2,000 produced in the 1870's.

| Exc. | V.G. | Good | Fair | Poor |
|------|------|------|------|------|
| 300  | 250  | 200  | 150  | 100  |

# Z-B RIFLE CO.
## Brno, Czechoslovakia

## Varmint Rifle

This is a Mauser bolt-action rifle chambered for the .22 Hornet cartridge. It has a 23" barrel with a three-leaf, folding rear sight. It is offered standard with double-set triggers. The finish is blued, with a select walnut checkered stock.

| Exc. | V.G. | Good | Fair | Poor |
|------|------|------|------|------|
| 850  | 750  | 650  | 500  | 400  |

# ZANOTTI, FABIO
## Brescia, Italy
## Importer--New England Arms Co.
## Kittery Point, Maine

This is an old-line manufacturer of quality sporting shotguns. They are available on a custom-order basis through New England Arms Co.

## Model 625

This is a side-by-side double-barrel shotgun chambered for 12 gauge through .410. It has a boxlock action with automatic ejectors and a single-selective trigger. The finish is blued, with a hand-checkered, select walnut stock.

| Exc. | V.G. | Good | Fair | Poor |
|------|------|------|------|------|
| 3000 | 2500 | 2000 | 1500 | 1000 |

## Model 626

This version is either scroll- or gamescene-engraved. Otherwise, it is similar to the Model 625.

| Exc. | V.G. | Good | Fair | Poor |
|------|------|------|------|------|
| 3700 | 3200 | 2500 | 1550 | 1100 |

## Giacinto

This is a high quality boxlock gun with external hammers and double triggers.

| Exc. | V.G. | Good | Fair | Poor |
|------|------|------|------|------|
| 5000 | 4500 | 3750 | 2500 | 1500 |

## Maxim

This is a high quality, side-by-side double-barrel shotgun that has all the features of the Model 625 with a fully detachable sidelock action.

| Exc. | V.G. | Good | Fair | Poor |
|------|------|------|------|------|
| 7500 | 6500 | 5000 | 3500 | 2250 |

## Edward

This is a more ornately engraved version of the Maxim sidelock gun.

| Exc.  | V.G. | Good | Fair | Poor |
|-------|------|------|------|------|
| 10000 | 8000 | 6500 | 5000 | 3500 |

## Cassiano I

This is an extremely high quality sidelock gun that is very heavily engraved with exhibition-grade walnut in the stock.

| Exc.  | V.G. | Good | Fair | Poor |
|-------|------|------|------|------|
| 11000 | 9000 | 7000 | 6000 | 4000 |

## Cassiano II

This is a heavily engraved, inlaid version of the Cassiano I sidelock gun.

| Exc.  | V.G.  | Good | Fair | Poor |
|-------|-------|------|------|------|
| 12500 | 10000 | 8500 | 7000 | 5000 |

## Cassiano Executive

This is Zanotti's best-grade firearm. It is available on a custom-order basis only. All options drastically raise the values, and it is essential that this model be individually appraised.

| Exc.  | V.G.  | Good  | Fair | Poor |
|-------|-------|-------|------|------|
| 15000 | 12500 | 10000 | 8500 | 6500 |

## ZEHNER, E. WAFFENFABRIK
### Suhl, Germany

### Zehna
This is a blowback-operated semi-automatic pistol chambered for the 6.35mm cartridge. It was invented by Emil Zehner. It has a 2.5" barrel and a 5-round detachable magazine. The finish is blued, with checkered black plastic grips with the monogram "EZ" at their top. The slide is marked "Zehna DRPa." Later models have the caliber marking on the slide. There were approximately 20,000 manufactured between 1921 and 1927.

| Exc. | V.G. | Good | Fair | Poor |
|------|------|------|------|------|
| 350  | 300  | 250  | 175  | 100  |

## ZEPHYR
### Eibar, Spain
### Importer--Stoegers

### Woodlander II
This is a double-barrel shotgun chambered for 12 or 20 gauge. It has various length barrels and choke combinations. It features a lightly engraved boxlock action with double triggers and extractors. The finish is blued, with a checkered walnut stock.

| Exc. | V.G. | Good | Fair | Poor |
|------|------|------|------|------|
| 500  | 450  | 400  | 300  | 200  |

### Uplander
This side-by-side double-barrel shotgun is chambered for 12, 16, 20, and 28 gauge, as well as the .410. It has various barrel lengths and choke combinations. It features a sidelock action that is lightly engraved, double triggers, and automatic ejectors. The finish is blued, with a checkered walnut stock.

| Exc. | V.G. | Good | Fair | Poor |
|------|------|------|------|------|
| 600  | 550  | 500  | 400  | 300  |

### Upland King
This is a more deluxe version of the Uplander, chambered for 12 and 16 gauge only. It has ventilated ribbed barrels and is fully engraved.

| Exc. | V.G. | Good | Fair | Poor |
|------|------|------|------|------|
| 800  | 700  | 600  | 500  | 400  |

### Vandalia
This was a single-barrel trap gun chambered for 12 gauge. It has a 32" full-choke barrel and is engraved. The finish is blued, with a checkered walnut stock.

| Exc. | V.G. | Good | Fair | Poor |
|------|------|------|------|------|
| 700  | 600  | 550  | 450  | 350  |

### Sterlingworth II
This model is similar to the Woodlander, except that it features a sidelock action.

| Exc. | V.G. | Good | Fair | Poor |
|------|------|------|------|------|
| 700  | 600  | 550  | 450  | 350  |

### Victor Special
This is a side-by-side double-barrel shotgun chambered for 12 gauge only. It has a 25", 28", or 30" barrel with various choke combinations. It features double triggers, extractors, and a blued finish with a checkered walnut stock.

| Exc. | V.G. | Good | Fair | Poor |
|------|------|------|------|------|
| 450  | 400  | 300  | 250  | 175  |

### Thunderbird
This is a side-by-side double-barrel shotgun chambered for the 10-gauge Magnum shell. It has 32" full-choke barrels with double triggers and automatic ejectors. The finish is blued and moderately engraved. The stock is of checkered French walnut.

| Exc. | V.G. | Good | Fair | Poor |
|------|------|------|------|------|
| 800  | 700  | 600  | 500  | 400  |

### Honker
This is a single-barrel, break-open shotgun chambered for 10 gauge. It has a 36" full-choke vent-rib barrel. It is lightly engraved, with a blued finish and checkered walnut stock.

| Exc. | V.G. | Good | Fair | Poor |
|------|------|------|------|------|
| 500  | 450  | 400  | 300  | 200  |

## ZOLI USA, ANGELO
### Brescia, Italy
### Importer--Same
### Addison, Illinois

### Slide Action Shotgun
This model is chambered for 12 gauge and is available in various barrel lengths with screw-in choke tubes. It is chambered for the 3" Magnum shell. The finish is blued, with a checkered walnut stock.

| NIB | Exc. | V.G. | Good | Fair | Poor |
|-----|------|------|------|------|------|
| 325 | 300  | 250  | 200  | 150  | 100  |

### Diano I
This is a folding, single-shot, break-open shotgun chambered for 12 or 20 gauge, as well as .410. It has various barrel lengths and chokes, with a vent-rib. The finish is blued, with a walnut stock.

| NIB | Exc. | V.G. | Good | Fair | Poor |
|-----|------|------|------|------|------|
| 125 | 100  | 90   | 80   | 60   | 40   |

### Diano II
This model is opened with a bottom lever instead of the top lever found on the Diano I.

| NIB | Exc. | V.G. | Good | Fair | Poor |
|-----|------|------|------|------|------|
| 125 | 100  | 90   | 80   | 60   | 40   |

### Apache
This is a lever-action shotgun chambered for the 3" 12-gauge shell. It has a 20" barrel and is available with screw-in chokes. The finish is blued, with a walnut stock.

| NIB | Exc. | V.G. | Good | Fair | Poor |
|-----|------|------|------|------|------|
| 475 | 425  | 350  | 300  | 250  | 150  |

### Quail Special
This is a side-by-side double-barrel shotgun chambered for the 3" .410. It has 28" barrels with a single trigger. The finish is blued, with a walnut stock.

| NIB | Exc. | V.G. | Good | Fair | Poor |
|-----|------|------|------|------|------|
| 250 | 225  | 200  | 175  | 125  | 100  |

### Falcon II
This model is similar to the Quail Special but is offered with 26" or 28" barrels and double triggers.

| NIB | Exc. | V.G. | Good | Fair | Poor |
|-----|------|------|------|------|------|
| 250 | 225  | 200  | 175  | 125  | 100  |

### Pheasant
This is a side-by-side double-barrel shotgun chambered for the 3" 12-gauge shell. It has 28" barrels with a single trigger and automatic ejectors. The finish is blued, with a checkered walnut stock.

| NIB | Exc. | V.G. | Good | Fair | Poor |
|-----|------|------|------|------|------|
| 425 | 375  | 325  | 300  | 250  | 200  |

### Classic
This model is a side-by-side double-barrel shotgun chambered for the 3" 12-gauge shell. It is offered with 26" through 30" barrels with screw-in choke tubes. It has a single-selective trigger and automatic ejectors. The finish is blued, with a checkered walnut stock.

| NIB | Exc. | V.G. | Good | Fair | Poor |
|-----|------|------|------|------|------|
| 700 | 650  | 600  | 500  | 350  | 250  |

### Snipe

This is an Over/Under shotgun chambered for .410. It is offered with 26" or 28" barrels and a single trigger.

| NIB | Exc. | V.G. | Good | Fair | Poor |
|-----|------|------|------|------|------|
| 275 | 250 | 225 | 175 | 150 | 100 |

### Dove

This model is similar to the Snipe.

| NIB | Exc. | V.G. | Good | Fair | Poor |
|-----|------|------|------|------|------|
| 300 | 275 | 250 | 200 | 175 | 125 |

### Texas

This is a folding Over/Under shotgun chambered for 12 and 20 gauge, as well as .410. It is offered with 26" or 28" barrels with double triggers. It opens by means of a bottom lever.

| NIB | Exc. | V.G. | Good | Fair | Poor |
|-----|------|------|------|------|------|
| 300 | 275 | 250 | 200 | 175 | 125 |

### Field Special

This version is chambered for 12 or 20 gauge with 3" chambers and is offered with various barrel lengths and choke combinations, with a single trigger and extractors. The finish is blued, with a walnut stock.

| NIB | Exc. | V.G. | Good | Fair | Poor |
|-----|------|------|------|------|------|
| 325 | 300 | 275 | 225 | 200 | 150 |

### Pigeon Model

This is a slightly more deluxe version of the Field Special.

| NIB | Exc. | V.G. | Good | Fair | Poor |
|-----|------|------|------|------|------|
| 400 | 350 | 300 | 250 | 225 | 175 |

### Standard Model

This version is similar to the Pigeon Model.

| NIB | Exc. | V.G. | Good | Fair | Poor |
|-----|------|------|------|------|------|
| 450 | 400 | 350 | 300 | 275 | 200 |

### Special Model

This version has screw-in chokes and a single-selective trigger.

| NIB | Exc. | V.G. | Good | Fair | Poor |
|-----|------|------|------|------|------|
| 525 | 475 | 400 | 350 | 325 | 250 |

### Deluxe Model

This version has an engraved receiver and better-grade walnut.

| NIB | Exc. | V.G. | Good | Fair | Poor |
|-----|------|------|------|------|------|
| 750 | 675 | 575 | 500 | 400 | 300 |

### Presentation Model

This version features engraved false sideplates and higher-grade walnut.

| NIB | Exc. | V.G. | Good | Fair | Poor |
|-----|------|------|------|------|------|
| 850 | 750 | 650 | 575 | 450 | 350 |

### St. George's Target

This is a 12-gauge, Over/Under, competition-grade trap or skeet gun. It has various barrel lengths and competition choke combinations. It features a single-selective trigger and automatic ejectors. The finish is blued, with a checkered select walnut stock.

| NIB | Exc. | V.G. | Good | Fair | Poor |
|-----|------|------|------|------|------|
| 1050 | 900 | 700 | 600 | 550 | 450 |

### Patricia Model

This is a high-grade Over/Under shotgun chambered for the 3" .410 only. It has 28" vent-rib barrels with various choke combinations, a single-selective trigger, and automatic ejectors. It is engraved and blued, with a high-grade, checkered walnut stock.

| NIB | Exc. | V.G. | Good | Fair | Poor |
|-----|------|------|------|------|------|
| 1350 | 1100 | 950 | 750 | 650 | 550 |

### Condor

This is an Over/Under combination gun chambered for 12 gauge over .308 or .30-06. It has a boxlock action with double triggers and extractors. The finish is blued, with a checkered walnut stock. It features sling swivels.

| NIB | Exc. | V.G. | Good | Fair | Poor |
|-----|------|------|------|------|------|
| 750 | 700 | 650 | 550 | 450 | 400 |

### Airone

This model is similar to the Condor, with false sideplates.

| NIB | Exc. | V.G. | Good | Fair | Poor |
|-----|------|------|------|------|------|
| 800 | 750 | 700 | 600 | 500 | 450 |

### Leopard Express

This is an Over/Under, double-barrelled express rifle chambered for the .308, .30-06, 7x65R, and the .375 Holland & Holland cartridges. It features a boxlock action with 24" barrels with folding express sights. It has double triggers and extractors. The finish is blued, with a checkered walnut stock.

| NIB | Exc. | V.G. | Good | Fair | Poor |
|-----|------|------|------|------|------|
| 1500 | 1250 | 950 | 750 | 600 | 500 |

## ZOLI, ANTONIO
### Brescia, Italy
### Importer--Antonio Zoli USA, Inc.
### Fort Wayne, Indiana

### Silver Hawk

This is a side-by-side double-barrel shotgun chambered for 12 or 20 gauge. It has various barrel lengths and choke combinations. It has a double trigger with a lightly engraved receiver. It is blued, with a checkered walnut stock.

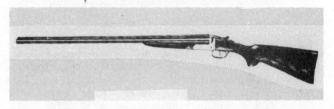

| Exc. | V.G. | Good | Fair | Poor |
|------|------|------|------|------|
| 450 | 400 | 350 | 300 | 250 |

### Ariete M3

This is a side-by-side double-barrel shotgun chambered for 12 gauge only. It is offered with 26" or 28" matte rib barrels. It has a non-selective single trigger and automatic ejectors. It features scroll engraving and a blued finish with a checkered walnut stock. It is furnished with a fitted case.

| NIB | Exc. | V.G. | Good | Fair | Poor |
|-----|------|------|------|------|------|
| 600 | 500 | 450 | 400 | 350 | 300 |

### Empire

This version is chambered for 12 or 20 gauge with 27" or 28" barrels with various choke combinations. The boxlock action is engraved and coin-finished. It features a high-grade, checkered walnut stock.

| NIB | Exc. | V.G. | Good | Fair | Poor |
|-----|------|------|------|------|------|
| 1650 | 1450 | 1200 | 1000 | 750 | 600 |

### Volcano Record

This is a high-grade, side-by-side shotgun chambered for 12 gauge. It has 28" barrels with various choke combinations. It features a H&H-type sidelock action with Purdey triple locks. It has a single-selective trigger and automatic ejectors. It has a heavily engraved receiver that is silver-finished and a high-grade, checkered walnut stock.

| NIB | Exc. | V.G. | Good | Fair | Poor |
|-----|------|------|------|------|------|
| 6000 | 5250 | 4000 | 3000 | 2500 | 2000 |

### Volcano Record ELM

This is the top-of-the-line Zoli gun that is custom-built to the customer's specifications. We recommend securing an appraisal as options have a drastic effect on values.

| NIB | Exc. | V.G. | Good | Fair | Poor |
|-----|------|------|------|------|------|
| 14500 | 12500 | 10000 | 8500 | 7000 | 5500 |

### Silver Snipe

This is an Over/Under shotgun chambered for 12 or 20 gauge. It features various length, vent-rib barrels with a single trigger and extractors. It is lightly engraved and blued, with a walnut stock.

| Exc. | V.G. | Good | Fair | Poor |
|------|------|------|------|------|
| 500 | 450 | 400 | 325 | 275 |

### Golden Snipe

This is a slightly more deluxe version with automatic ejectors.

| Exc. | V.G. | Good | Fair | Poor |
|------|------|------|------|------|
| 550 | 500 | 450 | 375 | 300 |

### Delfino

This version is chambered for 12 or 20 gauge with 3" chambers. It features 26" or 28" vent-rib barrels, has a non-selective single trigger and automatic ejectors, and is blued, with light engraving and a select checkered walnut stock.

| NIB | Exc. | V.G. | Good | Fair | Poor |
|-----|------|------|------|------|------|
| 425 | 375 | 325 | 275 | 250 | 200 |

### Ritmo Hunting Gun

This version is chambered for the 3" 12-gauge shell and has 26" or 28" vent-rib barrels that are separated. It features a single-selective trigger and automatic ejectors. It is lightly engraved and blued, with a checkered walnut stock.

| NIB | Exc. | V.G. | Good | Fair | Poor |
|-----|------|------|------|------|------|
| 600 | 550 | 500 | 400 | 350 | 275 |

### Condor Model

This is a 12-gauge skeet gun with 28" barrels, choked skeet-and-skeet. It has a wide competition rib, single-selective trigger, and automatic ejectors. The silver-finished receiver is engraved, and it has a checkered walnut stock.

| NIB | Exc. | V.G. | Good | Fair | Poor |
|-----|------|------|------|------|------|
| 900 | 800 | 650 | 550 | 400 | 300 |

### Angel Model

This is the field-grade version of the Condor Model.

| NIB | Exc. | V.G. | Good | Fair | Poor |
|-----|------|------|------|------|------|
| 900 | 800 | 650 | 550 | 400 | 300 |

### Ritmo Pigeon Grade IV

This is a live-pigeon competition gun chambered for 12 gauge. It has 28" separated vent-rib barrels, a single-selective trigger, and automatic ejectors. It has a heavily engraved, silver-finished receiver with a high-grade, checkered walnut stock. It is furnished with a fitted case.

| NIB | Exc. | V.G. | Good | Fair | Poor |
|-----|------|------|------|------|------|
| 1800 | 1600 | 1250 | 900 | 750 | 650 |

### Model 208 Target

This is a competition 12 gauge in either trap or skeet configuration. It features 28" or 30" barrels with a wide vent rib, single-selective trigger, and automatic ejectors. The finish is blued, with a checkered walnut stock.

| NIB | Exc. | V.G. | Good | Fair | Poor |
|-----|------|------|------|------|------|
| 1000 | 850 | 700 | 600 | 500 | 400 |

### Model 308 Target

This is a more deluxe version of the Model 208.

| NIB | Exc. | V.G. | Good | Fair | Poor |
|-----|------|------|------|------|------|
| 1600 | 1400 | 1050 | 750 | 550 | 450 |

### Combinato

This is an Over/Under combination gun chambered for 12 or 20 gauge over .222 or .243. It features a gamescene-engraved boxlock action. It has double triggers with a folding rear sight. It has a silver-finished receiver with a checkered walnut stock.

| NIB | Exc. | V.G. | Good | Fair | Poor |
|-----|------|------|------|------|------|
| 700 | 625 | 550 | 450 | 375 | 300 |

### Safari Deluxe

This version has false sideplates and is elaborately engraved. Otherwise, it is similar to the Combinato.

| NIB | Exc. | V.G. | Good | Fair | Poor |
|-----|------|------|------|------|------|
| 2800 | 2250 | 1850 | 1500 | 1200 | 950 |

### Express Rifle

This is an Over/Under express rifle chambered for the .30-06, 7x65R, and 9.3x74R. It has single triggers and automatic ejectors. It is blued, with a checkered walnut stock.

| NIB | Exc. | V.G. | Good | Fair | Poor |
|-----|------|------|------|------|------|
| 4000 | 3500 | 3000 | 2500 | 1850 | 1450 |

### Express EM

This is a more highly ornamented deluxe version of the Express Rifle.

| NIB | Exc. | V.G. | Good | Fair | Poor |
|-----|------|------|------|------|------|
| 4500 | 4000 | 3500 | 3000 | 2250 | 1750 |

### Savana E

This is a side-by-side express rifle chambered for the .30-06, 7x65R, and the 9.3x74R cartridges. It features a boxlock action, double triggers, and automatic ejectors. It is lightly engraved and blued, with a checkered walnut stock.

| NIB | Exc. | V.G. | Good | Fair | Poor |
|-----|------|------|------|------|------|
| 6000 | 5250 | 4500 | 3500 | 2750 | 2000 |

### Savana Deluxe

This version is a more deluxe, gamescene-engraved version of the Savana E.

| NIB | Exc. | V.G. | Good | Fair | Poor |
|-----|------|------|------|------|------|
| 8000 | 7000 | 6000 | 4750 | 3500 | 3000 |

### AZ 1900

This is a bolt-action hunting rifle chambered for the .243 Winchester, .270 Winchester, 6.5x55, .380 Winchester, and the .30-06 cartridges. It has a 24" barrel and features open sights. It is blued, with a checkered walnut stock.

| NIB | Exc. | V.G. | Good | Fair | Poor |
|-----|------|------|------|------|------|
| 500 | 450 | 400 | 350 | 250 | 200 |

### AZ 1900 Deluxe

This version has a higher-grade, checkered walnut stock.

| NIB | Exc. | V.G. | Good | Fair | Poor |
|-----|------|------|------|------|------|
| 550 | 500 | 450 | 400 | 300 | 250 |

### AZ 1900 Super Deluxe

This version is lightly engraved and has a high-grade, checkered walnut stock.

| NIB | Exc. | V.G. | Good | Fair | Poor |
|-----|------|------|------|------|------|
| 800 | 700 | 600 | 500 | 400 | 300 |

# ZULAICA, M.
### Eibar, Spain

This company was founded in the early 1900's and manufactured "Velo-dog"-pattern pocket revolvers. In 1905 they produced an unusual revolver that is rarely seen today. After this they began producing the usual "Eibar"-type automatics. They went out of business in 1930.

### Zulaica

This is a solid-frame revolver chambered for the .22 l.r. cartridge. It has a 6-shot cylinder that has zigzag grooves on its exterior surface. It has a straight-sided butt and a rather deep frame. It is fired by an external hammer. The frame is hollow and has a rod inside of it that connects to the breechblock. There is a serrated cocking piece connected to this rod that is found at the top rear of the frame. When fired, the cartridge case blows from the cylinder and activates the breechblock similar to a semi-automatic pistol. Although this revolver is ingenious and a totally original design, it is rather complicated; and it is not surprising that it was not a commercial success.

| Exc. | V.G. | Good | Fair | Poor |
|------|------|------|------|------|
| 750 | 600 | 500 | 350 | 250 |

## Royal

This model designation was given to a number of different semi-automatic pistols manufactured by this company. The first two are blowback-operated semi-automatics chambered for the 6.35mm and the 7.65mm cartridges. They were basically patterned after the 1903 Browning with some features that could be deemed original. The location of the safety catch is different from that of the Browning. Both of these pistols have a shield with the letter Z inside, marked on the slide and the grips. The finish is blued, with black plastic grips.

| Exc. | V.G. | Good | Fair | Poor |
|------|------|------|------|------|
| 175 | 150 | 125 | 100 | 75 |

## Royal

This model is simply a mediocre, "Eibar"-type, blowback-operated semi-automatic pistol. It is chambered for the 7.65mm cartridge and is marked "Automatic Pistol 7.65 Royal." The finish is blued, with plastic grips.

| Exc. | V.G. | Good | Fair | Poor |
|------|------|------|------|------|
| 150 | 125 | 100 | 75 | 50 |

## Royal

This is a large version but nevertheless the usual "Eibar"-type, blowback-operated semi-automatic pistol. It is chambered for the 7.65mm cartridge but has a 5.5" barrel and a long butt that houses a 12-shot detachable magazine. This was a post-war model that is marked exactly the same as the previous Royal. It is blued, with plastic grips.

| Exc. | V.G. | Good | Fair | Poor |
|------|------|------|------|------|
| 175 | 150 | 125 | 100 | 75 |

## Royal

This was the last of the Zulaica Royal models and differed from all the others. This was an external copy of the C/96 "Broomhandle" Mauser pistol. The internal lockwork was simplified and pinned permanently to the frame. Repair or maintenance of this model is nearly impossible. This firearm was poorly finished and manufactured of even poorer material. It was discontinued within three years. There is a select-fire, fully automatic version available. This pistol is blued, with wooden grips.

| Exc. | V.G. | Good | Fair | Poor |
|------|------|------|------|------|
| 750 | 650 | 600 | 400 | 250 |

## Vincitor

This is a blowback-operated semi-automatic pistol, of which two versions are available. The first, based on the 1906 Browning, is chambered for the 6.35mm cartridge. The second model was based on the 1903 Browning and is chambered for the 7.65mm cartridge. They are both blowback-operated semi-automatic pistols that were put on the market in 1914. They are blued, with plastic grips, and are marked "SA Royal Vincitor." They did not remain in production for a very long time.

| Exc. | V.G. | Good | Fair | Poor |
|------|------|------|------|------|
| 175 | 150 | 125 | 100 | 75 |

# FIREARMS MANUFACTURERS AND IMPORTERS

Action Arms, Ltd.
P.O.Box 9573
Philadelphia, PA 19124

AMAC, Inc.
2202 Redmond Road
Jacksonville, AR 72076

American Arms, Inc.
715 E. Armour Road
N. Kansas City, MO 64116

American Derringer Corp.
127 N. Lacy Drive
Waco, TX 76705

Armes De Chasse
P.O. Box 827
Chadds Ford, PA 19317

Arminex Ltd.
7127 E. Sahuaro Drive
#107A
Scottsdale, AZ 85254

Armscorp of America
4424 John Avenue
Baltimore, MA 21227

Auto-Ordnance Corp.
Williams Lane
West Hurley, NY 12491

Bailons Gunmakers, Ltd.
94-95 Bath Street
Birmingham, England B4 6HG

Barrett Firearms Mfg.
8211 Manchester Highway
P.O.Box 1077
Murfreesboro, TN 37130

Beretta USA Corp.
17601 Beretta Drive
Accokeek, MD 20607

Charles Boswell Gunmakers
212 East Morehead Street
Charlotte, NC 28202

Browning
Route 1
Morgan, UT 84050

Calico
405 East 19th Street
Bakersfield, CA 93305

Caspian Arms, Ltd.
14 North Main Street
Hardwick, VT 05843

Champlin Firearms
P.O. Box 3191/Woodring Airport
Enid, OK 73702

Charter Arms Corp.
430 Sniffens Lane
Stratford, CT 06497

Chipmunk Mfg., Inc.
114 East Jackson
Medford, OR 97501

E. J. Churchill, Ltd.
Ockley Road, Dorking
Surrey, England RH5 4PU

Colt Firearms
P.O. Box 1868
Hartford, CT 06101

Coonan Arms
830 Hampden Avenue
St. Paul, MN 55114

Dakota Arms, Inc.
HC55, Box 326
Sturgis, SD 57785

Davis Industries
15150 Sierra Bonita Lane
Chino, CA 91710

New Detonics Mfg. Corp.
21438 N. 7th Avenue
Suite F
Phoenix, AZ 85027

DuBiel Arms Co.
1800 West Washington Avenue
#205
Sherman, TX 75090-5359

EMF Co., Inc.
1900 E. Warner Avenue
1-D
Santa Ana, CA 92705

Excam, Inc.
4480 East 11th Avenue
Hialeah, FL 33013

F.N. Manufacturing, Inc.
P.O. Box 104
Columbia, SC 29202

Falcon Firearms Mfg. Corporation
P.O. Box 3748
Granada Hills, CA 91344

Feather Industries
2300 Central Avenue
Boulder, CO 80301

Federal Ordnance, Inc.
1443 Potrero Avenue
S. El Monte, CA 91733

F.I.E. Corporation
4530 N.W. 135th Street
Opa-Locka, FL 33054

Freedom Arms
P.O. Box 1776
Freedom, WY 83120

Renato Gamba
Via Michelangelo, 64
Gardone, Italy 1-25063

Gibbs Guns, Inc.
Route 2, 411 Highway
Greenback, TN 37742

Glock, Inc.
6000 Highlands Parkway
Smyrna, GA 30082

Goncz Company
11526 Burbank
#18
N. Hollywood, CA 91601

Grendel, Inc.
P.O. Box 560908
Rockledge, FL 32956

Griffin & Howe
36 West 44th Street
#1011
New York, NY 10036

Griffin & Howe, Inc.
33 Claremont Road
Bernardsville, NJ 07924

Hatfield International
224 North 4th
St. Joseph, MO 64501

Heckler & Koch, Inc.
21480 Pacific Boulevard
Sterling, VA 22170

Heym America Inc.
1426 East Tillman Road
Fort Wayne, IN 46816

Holmes Firearms
Route 6, Box 242
Fayetteville, AR 72703

Hyper Single, Inc.
520 East Beaver
Jenks, OK 74037

Illinois Arms
2300 Central Avenue, Suite K
Boulder, CO 80301

Interarms
10 Prince Street
Alexandria, VA 22313

Intratec
12405 SW 130th Street
Miami, FL 33186

Ithaca Gun/Ithaca Acq. Corp.
891 Route 34 B
King Ferry, NY 13081

Jennings Firearms
3680 Research Way
Carson City, NV 89706

K.B.I. Inc.
P.O. Box 11933
Harrisburg, PA 17108

KDF
2485 Highway 46 North
Seguin, TX 78155

Kimber of Oregon, Inc.
9039 SE Jannsen Road
Clackamas, OR 97015

Krieghoff International
P.O. Box 549
Ottsville, PA 18942

L.A.R. Manufacturing
4133 West Farm Road
West Jordan, UT 84084

Law Enforcement Ordnance Corp.
P.O. Box 336
Ridgeway, PA 15853

Ljutic Industries
732 North 16th Avenue
Suite 22
P.O. Box 2117
Yakima, WA 98907

Lorcin Engineering Co., Inc.
6471 Mission Boulevard
Riverside, CA 92509

Magnum Research, Inc.
7110 University Avenue N.E.
Minneapolis, MN 55432

Marlin Firearms
100 Kenna Drive
North Haven, CT 06473

Maverick Arms Inc.
P.O. Box 586
Industrial Boulevard
Eagle Pass, TX 78853

G. McMillan & Co.
21438 North 7th Avenue
Phoenix, AZ 85027

Military Armament Corp.
P.O. Box 1156
Stephenville, TX 76401

M.O.A. Corp.
175 Carr
Brookville, OH 45309

O. F. Mossberg & Sons, Inc.
Seven Grasso Avenue
North Haven, CT 06473

North American Arms
1800 N 300 W
Spanish Fork, UT 84660

Parker Reproductions
124 River Road
Middlesex, NJ 08846

Perazzi USA Inc.
1207 South Shamrock Avenue
Monrovia, CA 91016

P.S.M.G. Gun Co.
10 Park Avenue
Arlington, MA 02174

Raven Arms
1300 Bixby Drive
City of Industry, CA 91745

Remington Arms Co., Inc.
1007 Market Street
Wilmington, DE 19898

Seecamp, L.W.C.
301 Brewster Road
Milford, CT 06460

Shiloh Rifle Mfg. Co., Inc.
P.O. Box 279
Ind. Park
Big Timber, MT 59011

Smith & Wesson
2100 Roosevelt Road
Springfield, MA 01102

Sokolovsky Inc.
P.O. Box 70113
Sunnyvale, CA 94086

Springfield Armory, Inc.
420 West Main Street
Geneseo, IL 61254

SSK Industries
721 Woodvue Lane
Wintersville, OH 43952

Steyr-Mannlicher GmbH
108 Morrow Avenue
Trussville, AL 35173

Stoeger Industries
55 Ruta Court
South Hackensack, NJ 07606

Sturm, Ruger & Co., Inc.
10 Lacey Place
Southport, CT 06490

Taurus International
4563 SW 71st Avenue
Miami, FL 33155

Texas Longhorn Arms
P.O. Box 703
Richmond, TX 77469

Thompson/Center Arms Co.
Farmington Road
Rochester, NH 03867

Uberti USA, Inc.
P.O. Box 469
Lakeville, CT 06039

Ultra Light Arms, Inc.
P.O. Box 1270
Granville, WV 26534

Varner Sporting Arms Inc.
1004-F Cobb Parkway North
Marietta, GA 30062

Weatherby, Inc.
2781 Firestone Boulevard
South Gate, CA 90280

Westley Richards & Co., Ltd.
40 Grange Road, Bournbrook
Birmingham, England B29 6A

Dan Wesson Arms
293 Main Street
Monson, MA 01057

Wichita Arms
444 Ellis
Wichita, KS 67211

Wildey, Inc.
P.O. Box 475
Brookfield, CT 06804

Wilkinson Arms
26884 Pearl Road
Parma, ID 83660

Winchester/U.S. Repeating Arms Co. Inc.
275 Winchester Avenue
New Haven, CT 06511

Winslow Arms
P.O. Box 783
Camden, SC 29020

Antonio Zoli USA Inc.
P.O. Box 6190
Fort Wayne, IN 46896

# GUN COLLECTORS ASSOCIATIONS

Alaska Gun Collectors Association
P.O. Box 101522
Anchorage, Alaska 99510

Ark-La-Tex Gun Collectors Association
919 Hamilton Road
Bossier City, LA 71111

Bay Colony Weapons Collectors, Inc.
47 Homer Road
Belmont, MA 02178

Boardman Valley Collectors Guild
County Road 600
Manton, MI 49663

Browning Collectors Association
1306 Walcott Drive
Ogden, UT 84402

Collectors Arms Dealers Association
P.O. Box 427
Thomson, IL 61285

California Rifle & Pistol Association, Inc.
12062 Valley View Street
Garden Grove, CA 92645

Central Illinois Gun Collectors Assn., Inc.
Box 875
Jacksonville, IL 62651-0875

Central Penn Antique Arms Association
978 Thistle Road
Elizabethtown, PA 17022

Chisholm Trail Antique Gun Association
1906 Richmond
Wichita, KS 67203

Colt Collectors Association
17694 Isleton Court
Lakeville, MN 55044

The Corpus Christi Antique Gun Collectors
   Association
P.O. Box 9392
Corpus Christi, TX 78410

Dallas Arms Collectors Association, Inc.
Rt. 1, Box 282-B
DeSoto, TX 75115

Fort Lee Arms Collectors
P.O. Box 1716
South Hackensack, NJ 07606

Hawaii Historic Arms Association
Box 1733
Honolulu, HI 96806

Houston Gun Collectors Association
P.O. Box 53435
Houston, TX 77052

Indianhead Firearms Association
Route 9, Box 186
Chippewa Falls, WI 54729

Indian Territory Gun Collectors Association
Box 4491
Tulsa, OK 74159

Iroquois Arms Collectors Association
214 70th Street
Niagara Falls, NY 14304

Jefferson State Arms Collectors
521 South Grape
Medford, OR 97501

Jersey Shore Antique Arms Collectors
P.O. Box 100
Bayville, NJ 08721

Kentuckiana Arms Collectors Association
P.O. Box 1776
Louisville, KY 40201

Kentucky Gun Collectors Association
P.O. Box 64
Owensboro, KY 42376

Lehigh Valley Military Collectors Association
P.O. Box 72
Whitehall, PA 18052

Long Island Antique Gun Collectors
   Association
35 Beach Street
Farmingdale, L.I., NY 11735

Maryland Arms Collectors Association
P.O. Box 20388
Baltimore, MD 21284-0388

Memphis Antique Weapons Association
4672 Barfield Road
Memphis, TN 38117

Minnesota Weapons Collectors Association
P.O. Box 662
Hopkins, MN 55343

Missouri Valley Arms Collectors Association
P.O. Box 33033
Kansas City, MO 64114

Montana Arms Collectors Association
308 Riverview Drive
East Great Falls, MT 59404

National Automatic Pistol Collectors
Association
Box 15738-TOGS
St. Louis, MO 63163

National Rifle Association
1600 Rhode Island Avenue N.W.
Washington, D.C. 20036

New Hampshire Arms Collectors, Inc.
P.O. Box 6
Harrisville, NH 03450

Northeastern Arms Collectors
Association, Inc.
P.O. Box 185
Amityville, NY 11701

Ohio Gun Collectors Association
P.O. Box 24F
Cincinnati, OH 45224

Oregon Arms Collectors
P.O. Box 25103
Portland, OR 97225

Pelican Arms Collectors Association
P.O. Box 747
Clinton, LA 70722

Pennsylvania Antique Gun Collectors
Association
28 Fulmer Avenue
Havertown, PA 19083

Pikes Peak Gun Collectors Guild
406 E. Uintah
Colorado Springs, CO 80903

Potomac Arms Collectors Association
P.O. Box 2676
Laurel, MD 20811

Remington Society of America
380 South Tustin Avenue
Orange, CA 92666

Ruger Collectors Association, Inc.
P.O. Box 1778
Chino Valley, AZ 86323

Sako Collectors Association, Inc.
1725 Woodhill Lane
Bedford, TX 76021

Santa Barbara Antique Arms Collectors
Association
P.O. Box 6291
Santa Barbara, CA 93160-6291

San Bernardino Valley Arms Collectors
1970 Mesa Street
San Bernardino, CA 92405

Santa Fe Gun Collectors Association
1085 Nugget
Los Alamos, NM 87544

San Fernando Valley Arms Collectors
Association
P.O. Box 65
North Hollywood, CA 91603

Shasta Arms Collectors Association
P.O. Box 3292
Redding, CA 96049

Smith & Wesson Collectors Association
P.O. Box 321
Bellevue, WA 98009

Tampa Bay Arms Collectors Association
2461 67th Avenue South
St. Petersburg, FL 33712

Washington Arms Collectors, Inc.
P.O. Box 7335
Tacoma, WA 98407

Weapons Collectors Society of Montana
3100 Bancroft
Missoula, MT 59801

Weatherby Collectors Association, Inc.
P.O. Box 128
Moira, NY 12957

Willamette Valley Arms Collectors
Association, Inc.
P.O. Box 5191
Eugene, OR 97405

Winchester Arms Collectors Association
308 Riverview Drive East
Great Falls, MT 59404

Ye Connecticut Gun Guild
U.S. Route 7
Kent Road
Cornwall Bridge, CT 06754

Zumbro Valley Arms Collectors, Inc.
Box 6621
Rochester, MN 55901

# BIBLIOGRAPHY

Bady, Donald  Colt Automatic Pistols. Alhambra, California: Borden Publishing Company, 1973.

Baer, Larry L.  The Parker Gun.  Los Angeles, California: Beinfeld Publications, 1980.

Belford, James, & Dunlap, Jack  The Mauser Self-Loading Pistol.  Alhambra, California: Borden Publishing, 1969.

Bishop, Chris, and Drury, Ian  Combat Guns.  Secaucus, New Jersey: Chartwell Books, 1987.

Bogdanovic & Valencak,  The Great Century of Guns.  New York, New York: Gallery Books, 1986.

Breathed, John, Jr. & Schroeder, Joseph, Jr.  System Mauser.  Chicago, Illinois: Handgun Press, 1967.

Brophy, Lt. Col. William S., USAR, Ret.  The Krag Rifle.  Los Angeles, California: Beinfeld Publications, 1980.

Brophy, Lt. Col. William S., USAR, Ret.  L.C. Smith Shotguns.  Los Angeles, California: Beinfeld Publications, 1977.

Brophy, Lt. Col. William S., USAR, Ret.  Marlin Firearms.  Harrisburg, Pennsylvania: Stackpole Books, 1989.

Butler, David F.  The American Shotgun.  New York, New York: Winchester Press, 1973.

Buxton, Warren  The P 38 Pistol.  Dallas, Texas: Taylor Publishing Company, 1978.

Carr, James  Savage Automatic Pistols.  Carr.

Chant, Christopher  The New Encyclopedia of Handguns.  New York, New York: Gallery Books.

Cormack, A. J. R.  Small Arms, a Concise History of Their Development.  Profile Publications, Ltd.

Cormack, A. J. R.  Small Arms in Profile.  Volume I, Garden City, New York: Doubleday & Company, Inc., 1973.

de Haas, Frank  Bolt Action Rifles.  Northfield, Illinois: Digest Books, Inc., 1971.

de Haas, Frank  Single Shot Rifles and Actions.  Northfield, Illinois: Digest Books, Inc., 1969.

Ezell, Edward C.  Small Arms Today.  Harrisburg, Pennsylvania: Stackpole Books.

Flayderman, Norm  Flayderman's Guide to Antique American Firearms.  Second Edition.  Northfield, Illinois: DBI Books, 1980.

Frasca & Hill  The .45-70 Springfield.  Northridge, California: Springfield Publishing Company, 1980.

Graham, Copec & Moore  A Study of the Colt Single Action Army Revolver.  Dallas Texas: Taylor Publishing Company, 1976.

Gun Digest.  1967 through 1989 Editions.  Northfield, Illinois: DBI Books.

Guns of the World. Los Angeles, California: Petersen Publishing Company, 1972.

Hoffschmidt, E. J.  Know Your .45 Auto Pistols Models 1911 & A1.  Southport, Connecticut: Blacksmith Corporation, 1974.

Hoffschmidt, E. J.  Know Your Walther PP & PPK Pistols.  Southport, Connecticut: Blacksmith Corporation, 1975.

Hogg, Ian V. German Pistols and Revolvers 1871-1945. Harrisburg, Pennsylvania: Stackpole Books, 1971.

Hogg, Ian V., and Weeks, John. Military Small Arms of the 20th Century. Fifth Edition. Northfield, Illinois: DBI Books, 1985.

Hogg, Ian v., and Weeks, John. Pistols of the World. Revised Edition. Northfield, Illinois: DBI Books, 1982.

Honeycutt, Fred L., Jr. Military Pistols of Japan. Lake Park, Florida: Julin Books, 1982.

Jinks, Roy The History of Smith & Wesson. North Hollywood, California: Beinfield Publications, 1977.

Kenyon, Charles, Jr. Lugers at Random. Chicago, Illinois: Handgun Press, 1969.

Leithe, Frederick E. Japanese Handguns. Alhambra, California: Borden Publishing Company, 1968.

Madis, George The Winchester Book. Brownsboro, Texas: Art & Reference House, 1971.

Madis, George The Winchester Model 12. Brownsboro, Texas: Art & Reference House, 1982.

Markham, George Japanese Infantry Weapons of World War Two. New York, New York: Hippocrene Books, Inc., 1976.

Murray, Douglas P. The 99 A History of the Savage Model 99 Rifle. Murray, 1976.

Myatt, Major Frederick, M.C. Pistols and Revolvers. New York, New York: Crescent Books, 1980.

Olson, Ludwig Mauser Bolt Rifles. Third Edition. Montezuma, Iowa: Brownell & Sons, 1976.

Pender, Roy G., III Mauser Pocket Pistols 1910-1946. Houston, Texas: Collectors Press, 1971.

Rankin, James Walther Models PP & PPK. Rankin, 1980.

Reese, Michael II Luger Tips. Union City, Tennessee: Pioneer Press, 1976.

Schroeder, Joseph J. Gun Collector's Digest, Volume II. Northfield, Illinois: Digest Books, Inc., 1977.

Schwing, Ned The Winchester Model 42. Iola, Wisconsin: Krause Publications, 1990.

Sellers, Frank Sharps Firearms. Second Printing. North Hollywood, California: Beinfield Publications, 1982.

Serven, James E. 200 Years of American Firearms. Chicago, Illinois: Follett Publishing Company, 1975.

Sheldon, Douglas G. A Collector's Guide to Colt's .38 Automatic Pistols. Sheldon, 1987.

Stadt, Ronald W. Winchester Shotguns & Shotshells. Tacoma, Washington: Armory Publications, 1984.

Stevens, R. Blake The Browning High Power Automatic Pistol. Toronto, Canada: Collector Grade Publications, 1984.

Stoeger's Catalog & Handbook. 1939 Issue. Hackensack, New Jersey: Stoeger Arms Corporation.

Sutherland & Wilson The Book of Colt Firearms. Kansas City, Missouri: Sutherland, 1971.

Wahl, Paul Paul Wahl's Big Gun Catalog/1. Cut And Shoot, Texas: Paul Wahl Corporation, 1988.

Walter, John The German Rifle. Ontario, Canada: Fortress Publishing, Inc., 1979.

Whitaker, Dean H. The Winchester Model 70 1937-1964. Dallas, Texas: Taylor Publishing Company, 1978.

Wilkerson, Don The Post War Colt Single Action Army Revolver. Dallas, Texas: Taylor Publishing Company, 1978.

Wilson, R. L. Colt An American Legend. New York, New York: Abbeville Press, 1985.

Wilson, R. L. The Colt Heritage. New York, New York: Simon & Schuster.

# INDEX

# Gun List provides a service and stands beside it.

It starts with our 26 issues per year. This keeps you up on the ever changing firearms market. A revolving selection of thousands of guns and related products keeps you exposed to competitive pricing. You'll deal with individual gun buffs offering single firearms and dealers that have extensive selections to sample.

It continues with a one-year subscription price that brings your per issue cost to only 96¢. And there's even greater savings with the two and three year terms.

The index is a very important feature. We don't throw a hodgepodge of gun ads at you. Simply find your area of interest, in the wide variety of firearms listed and then go directly to it.

The accessories, services and miscellaneous products are kept in order too. Shop and compare prices quickly and easily here.

It's clean and easy-to-read. Whether you want to spend 5 or 50 minutes browsing through the pages you'll not experience eye fatigue. We keep it clean and neat for your reading pleasure.

You'll return again and again to these helpful pages to find special buys and to see what's happening in the gun buying, selling and trading world.

# GUN LIST - the indexed firearms paper

*It's your best source for quality and service.*
*Get thousands of firearms bargains every two weeks.*

**Gun List**
**700 E. State St.**
**Iola, WI 54990-0001**
**Business Phone 1-715-445-2214**

VISA and MASTERCARD users:
1-800-258-0929. Hours: 6:30 a.m.
to 8 p.m. CST Monday-Friday;
8 a.m. to 2 p.m. Saturday

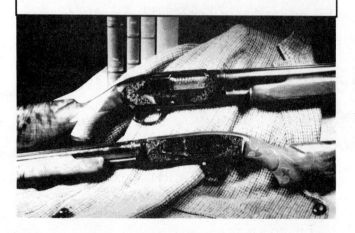

# WISCONSIN
## OUTDOOR JOURNAL

### The "Home State Authority" for all Wisconsin sportsmen.

## Six Times Per Year You Get Complete Coverage On Wisconsin's...

...seasonal hunting and fishing activities
...interviews with local sportsmen
...interesting historical events
...unique local sporting celebrations and contests
...important conservation topics
...regional field reports

In short, **WISCONSIN OUTDOOR JOURNAL** has everything you want to know to make your leisure time sporting activities the best they can be.

### If you love Wisconsin's outdoor sporting scene - 👉 we'll keep you in-touch! 👈

### Subscribe Today!

Contact: **Wisconsin Outdoor Journal**
**Circulation Dept. ABI**
**700 E. State St.**
**Iola, WI 54990-0001**

**Phone: Business 715-445-2214**
M-F 8:00 am to 5:00 pm CST
**Order 1-800-258-0929**
M-F 6:30 am - 8:00 pm CST, Sat. 8:00 am - 2:00 pm CST

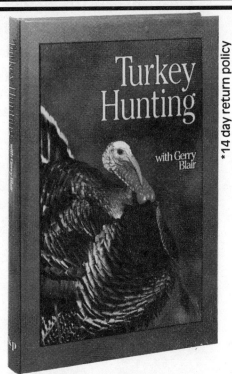